Health and Healing
in Comparative Perspective

Health and Healing in Comparative Perspective

Elizabeth D. Whitaker
California Polytechnic State University
at San Luis Obispo

PEARSON
Prentice
Hall

Upper Saddle River, New Jersey 07458

Library of Congress Cataloging-in-Publication Data

Health and healing in comparative perspective / [edited by] Elizabeth
    D. Whitaker.
       p. cm.
Includes bibliographical references
ISBN 0-13-127383-3
1. Medical anthropology.   2. Healing.   3. Diseases.   4. Public health.
5. Racism.   I. Whitaker, Elizabeth Dixon, 1962
    [DNLM: 1. Anthropology.   2. Medicine.   3. Health.   4. Disease
—ethnology.   5. Complementary Therapies.   6. Cross-Cultural Comparison.
GN 296 H434 2006]
GN296.H413 2006
320.4'61—dc22   2005016534

Editorial Director: Leah Jewell
AVP, Publisher: Nancy Roberts
Senior Marketing Manager: Marissa Feliberty
Editorial Assistant: Lee Peterson
Marketing Assistant: Anthony DeCosta
Full-Service Project Management: Jan Pushard, Pine Tree Composition, Inc.
Production Liaison: Cheryl Keenan
Prepress and Manufacturing Buyer: Ben Smith
Interior Design and Illustrations: Pine Tree Composition, Inc.
Cover Art Director: Jayne Conte
Cover Designer: Jayne Kelly

This book was set in 10.5/12 Horley Old Style by Pine Tree Composition, Inc., and was printed
and bound by Courier/Westford. The cover was printed by Phoenix Color Corp.

Credits and acknowledgments from other sources gratefully used with permission appear on the
appropriate pages in the textbook.

Pearson Education LTD.
Pearson Education Singapore, Pte. Ltd
Pearson Education, Canada, Ltd
Pearson Education—Japan
Pearson Education Australia PTY, Limited

Pearson Education North Asia Ltd
Pearson Educación de Mexico, S.A. de C.V.
Pearson Education Malaysia, Pte. Ltd
Pearson Education, Upper Saddle River, New Jersey

10 9 8 7 6 5 4 3 2 1
ISBN 0-13-127383-3

Contents

PART TWO: BIOCULTURAL APPROACHES   **133**

PART THREE: CULTURE-ORIENTED APPROACHES 271

PART FOUR: SPECIAL TOPICS AND CASE STUDIES

445

Biotechnology and Bioethics

Preface

SCOPE

While working with students in medical anthropology, I have noticed that discussions and written work turn frequently to comparisons and contrasts across places, peoples, and time periods. At the same time, my colleagues in public health, medicine, and health and fitness have shown me that practitioners in other fields share a lively interest in anthropological perspectives, methods, and data. This reader answers the need for a book that provides both fascinating comparative ethnographic detail and a theoretical framework for organizing and interpreting information about health.

While there are many health-related fields represented in this book, its core discipline is medical anthropology and its main focus is the comparative approach. Cross-cultural comparison gives anthropological analysis breadth while the evolutionary time scale gives it depth. These two features have always been fundamental to anthropology and continue to distinguish it among the social sciences. A third feature is the in-depth knowledge of culture produced by anthropological methods such as participant-observation, involving long-term presence in and research among a study population.

Medical anthropology is the part of anthropology that focuses upon the human experience of health and disease. Evolutionary and comparative approaches are particularly relevant given that the health of the mind/body is an inescapably biocultural phenomenon, standing at the intersection of history, biology, and culture. In addition, many health-related topics such as illness, healing, and death are human universals, but they by no means take a uniform shape everywhere. Accordingly, the readings that follow emphasize comparisons and contrasts, whether across healing traditions, population groups, or time periods. By weaving biological and cultural approaches throughout the text, the book builds a model of the relationship between humans and diseases over historical and evolutionary time scales. There are practical implications both for understanding disease processes and cultural coping mechanisms, and for making the most of historical lessons to manage current health concerns.

Anthropological studies of health help to illustrate the point that the concept of culture is better understood as an adjective than a noun. That is, cultures are not coterminous with particular groups of people, nor static features that pertain to individuals and directly explain their actions, as is often assumed in health research and medical care. Rather, the concept of culture describes fluid, permeable, changeable sets of collective beliefs, values, and behaviors that inform, shape, and constrain the worldviews and personal choices of individuals, but not always in the same manner or to the same degree. The articles in this collection illuminate some of the subtle and yet not unknowable workings of culture across a variety of case examples.

The selections range from small-scale, detailed analyses to large-scale comparisons across world regions. In this way, the book benefits from both the attention to context that is possible in localized analyses, and the explanatory power of broad-based, carefully executed comparisons across a larger number of units of analysis. Both the minutely reductionist and the majestically expansionist frames of vision have their place in the pursuit of knowledge. Likewise, both quantitative and qualitative approaches are appropriate tools of anthropological analysis and appear throughout the text. Some studies are highly data-driven; others depend upon close analysis of interview and other ethnographic material. The inclusion of studies using such a variety of approaches allows for the development of a global perspective on health and healing that is grounded in concrete, local contexts.

SELECTION OF ARTICLES

Medical anthropology and related disciplines concern themselves with a wide field of analysis, making it impossible to provide a set of selections that covers all relevant topics and theoretical concerns. While it has been a pleasure to select writings for this volume, it has been distressing to decide against huge numbers of excellent works. My choices were guided by the following considerations:

- Authorship representing an international community of scholars and a range of disciplines including anthropology, epidemiology, medicine, and nursing.
- Recent publication. More than half of the selections have been published within the last five years, and all but three within the past ten.
- Broad geographical coverage, with preference for selections that make direct comparisons.
- Clear, readable writing style.
- Variable degree of difficulty, theoretical sophistication, and gravity of topics.
- Coverage of themes that intersect with those raised in other selections.

Some of the selections may be very troubling, others amusing. They may evoke surprise, curiosity, dismay, or even frustration and anger, but one quality they all share is that they are highly engaging. Many of the selections are challenging, for they have been written for a professional audience, but course instructors will be able to guide readers through difficult passages, theoretical discussions, or technical material.

ORGANIZATION

The book is divided into four parts. Part I concerns healing traditions and patient-healer interactions. It begins with an overview of the field of medical anthropology and its history, followed by a comparative case study of the cultural construction of illness concepts. A second group of articles includes studies of biomedicine, humoral medicine, homeopathy, and nonwestern medical systems, and introduces topics such as explanatory models and medical pluralism. This is complemented by an essay on the nature of knowledge and the experience of conducting ethnographic research among healers, and a set of selections on patients and healers in shamanism, biomedicine, and nursing.

Part II focuses upon biocultural approaches in medical anthropology. It begins with the topic of cultural and biological adaptation, variation, and plasticity. These concepts are illustrated through the examples of adjustments to high altitude and the interlocking genetic, cultural, and environmental factors associated with lactose tolerance and adaptation to malaria. This is followed by readings on evolution and health that explore the interaction between microbes and humans, and the emergence of chronic diseases as major threads to human health. A related topic is human health and demography in history and prehistory, which is covered by a group of selections that includes ones connecting historical processes to current health issues. Part II concludes with readings on the effects of economic and ecological changes on disease distributions, and the interplay between indigenous medicine and environmental crisis.

Part III is composed of selections with a culture-oriented emphasis. It begins with two theoretical works, one on comparative frameworks for analyzing health beliefs, the other a classic on the anthropological study of the body. The next reading explores the culture of risk, individual responsibility, and blame. The topic of screening and genetic testing raised in the selection connects to the following set of readings on the mind-body interface in placebo and nocebo effects. The concept of explanatory models is then introduced and complemented by analysis of social and politico-economic contexts including critical perspectives on compliance, individual agency, and socioeconomic inequality. The final readings in this part of the book focus upon stigma and race and racism, topics which intersect with those raised in the earlier readings on risk, nocebo effects, explanatory models, and agency.

Part IV is devoted to special topics and case studies, in which the models introduced earlier in the text are applied to specific health-related concerns. This final section of the book begins with two selections presenting divergent perspectives on obesity/overweight and non-insulin-dependent diabetes mellitus. These selections are interesting both for their substantive contributions and because they promote discussion of the influence of theoretical perspectives on interpretations of health issues. They prepare readers to analyze critically the selections that follow. These are organized in sections on food and food use, infant and child health, sex and gender, and biotechnology and bioethics. The selections build upon the preceding three parts of the book, and strengthen the global perspective on health that is developed throughout the text.

I have chosen not to organize Part IV in terms of specific diseases or the infectious-chronic disease divide, so as not to reify or privilege the categories of Western biomedicine at the expense of others and to reflect the reality that many afflictions do not respect these divisions. Meanwhile, I have decided to incorporate some topics into other parts of the book rather than setting them apart in this one. For example, there is no special section on mental health, in an effort to avoid the separation between mind and body that is such a prominent topic in Part III. Likewise, articles about ethnopharmacology are interspersed throughout the book, since this area of medical anthropology touches upon many others.

USING THIS BOOK

The best way to use this book is to read the articles in order, given that they build upon each other. The selections work together within their groupings as outlined in the Table of Contents, and there is a stream of ideas that flows from one set of selections to the next. In addition, there are overarching themes and theoretical points interwoven throughout the four parts of the book, as noted in the section overviews and chapter introductions. The theoretical and substantive arguments presented in the progression of fifty-six selections grant a measure of clarity to the complex story of human health.

The overviews at the beginning of each of the four parts of the book highlight some of the more important points in the selections and draw connections between them. The overviews end with a small number of suggested films, placed in this way to allow enough time for them to be seen over an interval of a few weeks even if they would best be seen alongside specific readings. The selections begin with a short discussion and a list of questions to keep in mind while reading. Readers may find it helpful to return to these questions after finishing the selections.

Most selections include bibliographies that may be helpful for further study. In addition, the overviews and selection introductions include additional references, with an emphasis on recent, comparative works. Full publication information for these citations has been placed in the Reference section at the end of the book.

Due to space constraints, I reluctantly have omitted portions of text in some selections, as indicated by a series of dots. Original publication information has been placed at the beginning of each selection. The original publications should be consulted by readers interested in acknowledgments and sources of financial support for each selection.

As a final note, the fact that I chose each of the selections in the book should not be taken to mean that I endorse everything stated in them, and I would like to emphasize that I do not expect readers to approve of or agree with everything they read here. Readers should analyze the selections with a critical eye, paying attention to the construction of the arguments presented and to the interpretation of data. On the other hand, I believe that the selections provide many useful tools that can be applied to a range of material, and that by the time the book is finished, the reader will be equipped with a unique and useful framework for understanding human health and health care.

ACKNOWLEDGMENTS

I would like to thank the editor of this book, Nancy Roberts, for welcoming my proposal, arranging for the book's publication, and seeing it through the production process with energy, efficiency, and grace. I appreciate her expertise as well as her patience and kindness. I thank her colleagues at Prentice Hall and the production team led by Jan Pushard at Pine Tree Composition for skillfully transforming the manuscript into a polished volume.

To the authors of the selected articles I would like to express my admiration and gratitude. I am indebted to the many permissions editors who responded to my requests with great promptness and courtesy. I heartily thank the following reviewers who enthusiastically endorsed my idea for the book and who provided constructive and concrete suggestions about its organization and content: Robert McCarl, Boise State University; Michael J. Simonton, Northern Kentucky University; Sarah Strauss, University of Wyoming; and Jean M. Wynn, Manchester Community College.

I would like to thank the students, colleagues, and friends who have contributed directly and indirectly to the creation of this book, including those with whom I have worked at American University, California Polytechnic State University, and the University of Bologna. I would like to give special thanks to Federico Bianchi, Barbara Blazek, Peter Brown, Rita Cantagalli, Franco Capirossi, Massimo Capirossi, Barbara Cook, Carole Counihan, Susan Currier, Joe Dent, Adriana Destro, Luther Gerlach, Joan Gero, Bill Leap, Patrick McKim, Don Giancarlo Menetti, Luca Montefiori, Julie Owolabi, Mauro Pesce, Ivo Quaranta, Elizabeth Radel, Siddiqur Rahman, Jana Rehak, Heather Schacht Reisenger, Tiziana Sagrini, Gregorio and Siony Sayat, and Brett Williams.

My husband, Stephen Whitaker, and our daughters Ernestine, Emma, and Sarah contributed directly to the book by reviewing drafts and physically preparing manuscript pages. I am indebted to my parents, sisters, in-laws, and other relatives for showing an unflagging curiosity about the topics that fascinate me. I thank them for giving me proof that the material I have gathered in this volume will be interesting and valuable to fellow students of human health.

Health and Healing
in Comparative Perspective

Part I

Healers and Healing Traditions

All societies have healing systems for dealing with illness and injury, but they do so in many different ways. The selections in this part of the book compare medical traditions and patient–healer relationships across cultures. The purpose is to develop a decentered perspective on world health and healing. To this end, the selections include analyses of not just non-Western medical systems but also the kind of medicine that is dominant in the United States and Europe, known as biomedicine or scientific medicine. Like other healing systems, biomedicine developed in a specific cultural and historical context. It is embedded in current social and politico-economic structures and varies across cultures (see Good 1995; Payer 1996).

In North America and Europe, there is a growing interest in alternative medicine and the medical systems of other cultures among students and professors, health professionals, and the public. There also has been increased scrutiny of biomedicine and structural factors that affect the fair delivery of health services (see Baer 2001; Inhorn and Brown 1997; Lindenbaum and Lock 1993; Nichter and Nichter 1996; Romanucci-Ross et al. 1997; Whiteford and Manderson 2000). Both intellectual curiosity and dissatisfaction with some aspects of biomedicine fuel these pursuits. Some patients and health professionals decry the depersonalized, hurried relationship between patient and healer that is often a feature of biomedical care. There are inequalities in access to both private and public health services. Meanwhile, the chronic diseases that have become the major public health problems of industrialized societies are complex, long-term conditions whose multiple causes are difficult to identify and separate using traditional reductionistic approaches. Unlike many acute infectious diseases, chronic diseases defy the "magic bullet" solutions that have brought spectacular successes in the struggle between humans and pathogens.

The worldwide vision and evolutionary time frame of medical anthropology provide both tools and substantive data for the study of disease patterns and cultural responses across time and space (on comparative methods, see Ember and Ember 2001). In selection 1, Charles Leslie reviews the history of medical anthropology and the kinds of research questions it has pursued. The second selection, by Margaret Lock, raises questions about the meaning of terms such as health, disease, illness, and specific disease entities and categories. This is important because it is humans who give meaning to illness and injury. In the United States, industrial metaphors about pumps, computers, and electrical systems and military metaphors such as "battalions" of "killer" (cytotoxic) T cells and other specialized components of the immune system are common in scientific and popular discussions of bodily processes (see Martin 1994). These metaphors grow out of particular sociohistorical contexts. There is no objective, culture-neutral way to think about health and disease.

Not all cultures agree about what constitutes disease, or how to classify diseases. Disease labels come and go, as the history of "diseases" such as homosexuality makes clear (see Terry 1999). Even the broad categories of infectious and chronic diseases are permeable. Infectious disease exposure and outcome depend on environmental and constitutional factors such as nutrition, hygienic conditions, immune function, and concurrent disease, whereas infectious agents play a role in a number of chronic diseases, such as cancer and coronary artery disease. Finally, as Lock shows through cross-cultural comparison of menopausal symptoms, seemingly "natural" or "normal" life stages and bodily processes are culturally constructed. What is considered pathological in one culture may be considered unremarkable in another. The image of typical menopause in the United States is based not on the general population but on a small sample of women who visit their physicians, indicating that standards of normality itself are cultural constructions.

To scientific medicine, disease is an observable physical phenomenon that expresses damage brought on by a pathogen or an internal functional abnormality. Particular disease agents are thought to bring predictable sequences of events, such that diseases may be categorized by their causes. This perspective is very useful for the control of many infectious diseases. It is less adapted to capturing the complex forces and multiple causes of disease in different individuals or groups of individuals (what Lock calls "local biologies"). In addition, the biomedical approach tends to individualize disease and obscure other relevant factors such as family context, socioeconomic status, or environmental quality. The shift toward an emphasis on individual pathology was part of an overall transformation of Western medicine in which treatment moved from the home to the clinic, and patients came to be seen as instances of a disease rather than persons embedded in a broader epidemiological picture (see selections 3, 11; Foucault 1973).

Medical anthropologists contrast "disease" as a process involving the interaction between a host organism and an environmental insult, such as a pathogen, toxin, or metabolic abnormality, against "illness" as the overall experience of disease (see Hahn 1995). The purpose is to draw attention to social and psychological dimensions of being ill. However, the categories of disease and illness do not always go hand in hand; there can be disease without illness and illness without disease. In addition, separating the two may play into the biomedical distinction between objective signs and subjective symptoms that may contribute to a devaluing of the patient's point of view. That is, disease is considered real but illness is not. Sickness is a term that is sometimes used to express both of the others simultaneously.

If cultural definitions of disease vary, we can expect that cultural beliefs about health also vary. The World Health Organization defines health as not a simple absence of disease, but a state of complete physical and psychosocial well-being. The General Assembly of the United Nations takes this a step further, arguing for the universal right to a quality of life sufficient to ensure the health and well-being of not just individuals but also their families. Although these definitions may be difficult to implement, the selections in this book show that they are in keeping with nonbiomedical healing traditions in which health is a dynamic process involving the entire environmental and social situation of individuals, rather than a static state of nondisease.

Various systems of classification have been proposed for comparing diverse healing traditions (see Fábrega 1997; selection 26). All healing systems have a set of components on which such contrasts may be based. These components include theories of disease causation, models for diagnosing disease, relevant treatment procedures, behavioral standards for regulating patient–healer interactions, and social systems for passing on medical knowledge to new healers.

For example, all healing systems use symbolic healing processes, from praying to saints or gods to wearing white coats and adorning oneself with medical equipment. Healing systems are sometimes classified according to the degree to which they emphasize spiritual or religious causes and treatments of disease and other forms of misfortune (see Foster 1976). Some healing systems such as shamanism openly emphasize spiritual forces, whereas others such as biomedicine or humoral medicine downplay them in favor of naturalistic factors (although there is recognition within biomedicine that religious adherence is related to preventive health-care utilization and health outcomes; see Benjamins and Brown 2004). Nevertheless, these systems overlap. Selection 9 describes a Peruvian shamanic healer who also prescribes antibiotics, while selection 8 describes the role of spiritual healing practices in amplifying the effectiveness of biomedical treatment in a New York hospital.

Healing systems may also be classified in terms of social organization. In small foraging and agricultural societies, healing roles tend to be diffuse, and healers, including those who distinguish themselves as especially capable, work at other economic tasks contemporaneously. In contrast, in larger-scale, more complex societies, healing roles may be full-time professions, and medical care tends to be more institutionalized. Another way to compare healing activities is to divide them into those that occur at the popular or household level, where most illness episodes are managed (see Kitson 2003; Wayland 2001); those that are managed by folk healers operating without a formal organization to oversee training and maintain standards; and those that fall within the purview of professional medical systems, such as biomedicine or Ayurveda. As the selections in Part I show, these sectors may coexist and merge in particular cultural settings.

The authority of healers depends in part on treatment outcome, but how this is defined varies widely. For example, in healing systems that emphasize spiritual or social forces, treatment is not limited to the individual patient but may require the reconciliation of social groups or the performance of collective rituals to rectify a religious transgression. Some treatments or remedies may be evaluated in the short term, others over the span of many years.

The authority of healers and healing professions has two components. Social authority refers to one's ability to bring about desired behavior in another person, or to achieve compliance in the other person. Cultural authority refers to the domain of knowledge and values and resides not just in people but also in objects such as medical treatises. The two forms do not necessary appear together or to the same degree (see selections 5, 6, 8–11). Where social and cultural authority are both strong, a healing profession may be able to organize and institutionalize to the point of eliminating competing medical systems. This was the case for scientific medicine in Europe and the United States during the last century, in contrast to previous times when medical professionals enjoyed relatively little public esteem or governmental support (see selection 3; Foucault 1973; Starr 1982). The past few decades have seen a questioning of biomedicine's social and cultural authority as a result of growing awareness of health disparities, treatment failures and medical errors, allocation of resources away from primary health care, and unsatisfactory relationships with health professionals.

Part I contains a group of four selections that focuses on the characteristics of diverse healing traditions, from localized ethnomedical systems to the "great traditions" of classical Hippocratic medicine, Ayurveda and Unani, traditional Chinese medicine, and biomedicine (see Foster 1994; Hsu 1999; Leslie 1997; Lloyd and Silvin 2002). Selection 3, by Don G. Bates, begins the set with an analysis of biomedicine as an anomalous system compared to those that preceded it and those that are now considered "alternative" to it. This is followed by Judy F. Pugh's selection on the Indian medical traditions Ayurveda and Unani, which provides substantive detail to fill in the framework developed by Bates concerning classical medicine. Homeopathic medicine is the focus of Michael B. Whiteford's selection on medical pluralism or the coexistence of many thriving medical traditions in Mexico. Selection 6, by Russel Barsh, discusses medicinal plant use in indigenous medical systems, raising issues about how cultures assess the efficacy of medical treatments and how healing knowledge is transmitted across generations.

The following five selections are dedicated to patient–healer relationships. They consider patient and healer understandings or explanatory models, through a focus on clinical narrative or the interactive construction of stories by health professionals and patients and their relatives. Healers are the readers simultaneously of individual patients' stories and of an overarching narrative text of medical research, technological development, and professional standards. Through explanations and predictions, healers give shape to patients' experiences of illness and engage patients in a treatment program. Socioeconomic, political, and cultural contexts play a large role in the formation of these narrative strategies (see Part III; Good 1995; Kleinman 1980, 1988; Mattingly 1998; Mattingly and Garro 2001).

Selection 7, by Joan Cassell, concerns the practice of anthropological research among healers and invites reflection on the nature of knowledge and the process by which it is developed. This is followed by Linda Miller Van Blerkom's comparison of shamanic healing across cultural contexts, including U.S.

hospital wards, which shows how elements of this type of healing may be found in unexpected places. The selection by Michael Fobes Brown about a healing session involving a Peruvian shaman provides both support of Van Blerkom's explanation of shamanic healing and a counterpoint in its illumination of the negative sides of shamanism. Brown emphasizes the political content of the healing relationship for both healers and patients, and both selections highlight the performance aspects of healing.

Returning to biomedical healers, selection 10, by Ruth E. Malone, focuses on space, touch, and non-verbal communication in nurse–patient relationships and the effects of institutional changes on both the quality of care and the job satisfaction of health workers. Part I closes with Beverly Ann Davenport's analysis of a type of medical training that calls into question some common assumptions about the uniformity and inevitability of the process by which physicians distance themselves from patients and from the social forces that impinge on health. These final two selections of Part I both reaffirm and challenge ideas presented in previous selections about the hegemonic social organization, unequal power relationships, and depersonalizing tendencies of biomedicine. They reinforce the point that healing systems are flexible and responsive to the social, economic, and cultural systems in which they are embedded.

Suggested films

Bridge: How Islam Saved Western Medicine. 1998. Hermann Jamek, producer. 50 min.

Doctors of Two Worlds. 1989. Richard Solomons, producer. 54 min.

Healers of Ghana. 1996[1993]. David D. Ohl, producer. 58 min.

The Knowledge of Healing (Tibetan Medicine). 1997. Franz Reichle, producer. 89 min.

Survivor MD. 2001. Julie Crawford, producer (Nova). 168 min.

1   BACKING INTO THE FUTURE

Charles Leslie

All academic fields have a history on which new concepts and knowledge are built. In this selection, Charles Leslie roots the discipline of medical anthropology in the intellectual currents and sociocultural contexts of anthropology as it evolved over the first half of the twentieth century. The essay emphasizes the continuing importance of evolutionary and cross-cultural perspectives in medical anthropology and provides a rich bibliography of important books and articles.

In the 1940s and 1950s, especially through assistance in postwar "modernization" efforts, the first generation of medical anthropologists contrasted health beliefs and healing systems from around the world to Western ones. The intellectual developments of the 1960s and 1970s generated a rethinking among medical anthropologists of accepted categories such as tradition and modernity, or scientific versus folk medicine. This brought greater recognition of the fact that non-Western medical systems are pluralistic (with a number of healing traditions in various competing, overlapping, and cross-referring relationships), alive to international ideas and practices, and grounded in shifting historical and sociocultural contexts. There was also a new scrutiny of Western biomedicine and its own social and historical roots. Since then, medical anthropologists have explored other levels of analysis, including the relationship between humans and their diseases over evolutionary time and the impact of inequality, poverty, racism, and gender on illness experiences and disease distributions and outcomes.

A more open recognition of the fact that anthropologists are instruments of research has meant that they and their social relationships are no longer banished from academic writing. Advocacy is promoted as anthropologists engage more directly with the social and political problems they encounter. Anthropologists now tend to be careful to avoid typifying or generalizing about the people they study and ground their accounts in specific historical contexts. All these elements make for a stronger discipline capable of linking substantive data to a species-wide, long-term theoretical framework.

Questions to keep in mind

What makes medical anthropology different from other disciplines concerned with health?

How have the main emphases of anthropology and medical anthropology changed over time, and how have these changes been related to broader social forces?

How does anthropological research manage to combine natural science and humanistic elements?

What are some of the lessons anthropologists have learned over the past century about how to conduct research and communicate results?

We back into the future when we call ourselves anthropologists and undertake new research that will be recognizably anthropological. The tradition we identify with is multistranded rather than a single line of descent.

We have traditions and must pick and choose between them. Furthermore, creative work in any tradition changes it. We traditionalists are on a moving train, whether or not we like to think so.

I will refer to the academic traditions of North American anthropology since they are the ones I know best, but I also have in mind Britain, France, and other European countries. In America during the first quarter of the 20th century the Boasians thought of themselves as radicals who were creating a new science by professionalizing the heritage of amateur observations by missionaries, traders, and government agents and by exposing the

Source: Leslie, C. 2001. "Backing into the Future." © The American Anthropological Association. Reprinted from *Medical Anthropology Quarterly.* Vol. 15 No. 4 pp. 428–439, by permission.

pseudoscientific character of social Darwinism and various speculative constructions of cultural history. They felt that they were at the beginning of a new discipline and that they had ahead of them an enormous amount of work to establish archaeological chronologies, to analyze evidence that would establish a genuine record of human evolution, to record and classify languages, folklore, kinship terms, and so on. In every direction there was a great deal to be done, but there were very few of them to do it.

Today there are thousands of anthropologists divided into numerous subdisciplines, and in the case of medical anthropology, redivided by topical and geographic specialties. Although our subdiscipline is relatively new, we are, with other anthropologists, uncomfortable heirs to colonial traditions that began in the 19th century and continued through the first half of the 20th century as British, French, and other European anthropologists worked primarily in colonies of their home countries, while American anthropologists studied American Indian cultures. After the Second World War the rapid expansion of money for training and research through the National Science Foundation, the National Institutes of Health, the Wenner-Gren Foundation, and other nongovernmental organizations funded the expansion of fieldwork by American anthropologists throughout the world. Finally, in the 1960s and 1970s, the struggles of decolonization that culminated in Vietnam and Algeria and the increasing demand for racial justice in the United States and South Africa caused us to acknowledge that some of the most influential research in 20th-century anthropology was permeated by the assumptions and overt prejudices of colonialism. I refer, for example, to the Orientalism in Kroeber's widely used textbook, to racism in Malinowski's diary, to Evans-Pritchard's imperialist perspective, analyzed by Clifford Geertz, to Margaret Mead's ahistorical conception of autonomous local cultures in Samoa and New Guinea, and, indeed, to the whole tradition that anthropologists studied peoples without histories, which Eric Wolf took apart.

Yet, after a century in which anthropology was transformed into a major academic discipline, we can look back on having made genuine scientific progress in our understanding of human evolution and of cultural changes recorded in archaeological research. Similar progress has occurred in our understanding of contemporary languages and cultures throughout the world. I don't want to debate the concept of scientific progress and will be satisfied if those who question it will at least allow that students today have better methods of research and vastly more empirical knowledge available to them in all these fields of scholarship than existed in 1900. Creative new work throughout the century modified the discipline, but it remains recognizable because, as Kroeber pointed out, it never was defined by a particular methodology or subject matter. In the middle of the century I was taught, and still believe, that anthropology is marked by a natural science and humanistic outlook that (1) considers humanity from a species-wide and long-time perspective, (2) while observing and interpreting local variations as far as possible in the context of their occurrence (e.g., anthropology is a science grounded in field research).

If a primary task of the Boasians in the first half of the 20th century was to refute pseudoscientific concepts of human biology and cultural history, in the second half of the century reforming leaders among cultural anthropologists repudiated the claims of scientific objectivity and theory building, which they attributed to philosophical positivism. One objection was that positivist conceptions of science are based largely on the experimental laboratory sciences and are thus historically misleading and a poor guide for research in a discipline grounded in descriptive fieldwork. There were other objections, but the point I want to make is that anthropologists have debated issues of spurious and genuine science from the beginning of the discipline. If current disputes about positivism, humanism, modernism, and postmodernism seem particularly intense, it is only because we experience them close-up. Some disaffected anthropologists assert that the discipline is shipwrecked by our differences, yet over the past 50 years a few exemplary scholars have maintained traditions that brought various fields of research together in the first place. Recall W. W. Howells and Eric Wolf, and think today of Jack Goody, or, among physical anthropologists, Matt Cartmill, or the archaeologist Ian Hodder.

Medical anthropology emerged as a special field of research and training following World

War II. It had roots in our long-standing interest in shamanism and other forms of ritual curing and in studies of culture-bound syndromes, personality variation, and mental illness in the psychological anthropology of the 1940s and 1950s. However, the main stimulus came from applied anthropology, as senior scholars were brought in to act as consultants on health care projects in Latin America, Asia, and Africa, or in Native American and Hispanic communities in the United States.

In the Cold War rhetoric of the time, aid to friendly "third world countries" would strengthen their governments and forestall revolutionary discontent. In stark contrast to all but the poorest communities in North America and Europe, infectious diseases were the main cause of morbidity and mortality, and in some decolonizing countries 50 percent or more of the infants born each year died before their fifth birthday. In this situation, antibiotics, called "miracle drugs," added a demonstration effect comparable to that of surgery to validate neocolonial claims of Western superiority in medicine, science, and culture. Their use, combined with programs to improve sanitation and nutrition, was a prominent component of large-scale foreign aid programs.

The physicians and public health experts who directed international projects were soon confronted with noncompliance on the part of those they sought to help. Clinics were underutilized, instructions to boil water were ignored, and in other ways "target populations" failed to comply with professional advice. Project workers were usually convinced that local traditions were riddled with superstition that subverted their efforts to introduce rational behavior based on scientific medical knowledge. The problem, as they saw it, was a conflict between modernity and tradition, rational and irrational cultures. On the whole, their anthropological consultants accepted this formulation of the problem. They were as awed as other members of their own culture were by the professional authority of physicians trained in medical science. However, in their role as ethnological experts, they encouraged a degree of cultural relativism by suggesting ways that programs could acknowledge the validity of a few local customs and perhaps use traditional concepts to explain desirable new practices. Benjamin D. Paul's *Health, Culture, and Community* (1955) was a col-

lection of case studies of this kind, and it served as a basic text for the next 15 years as the term *medical anthropology* gained currency.

Among health professionals in this period, George Foster was the most visible and influential anthropologist. He worked tirelessly as a conference participant and consultant to enhance the reputation of anthropology in the field of international health. Foster, Benjamin Paul, and others organized training programs in the 1960s and 1970s, encouraging students to undertake the first independently formulated and sustained field research that made medical anthropology a scholarly specialization.

The climate of cultural and political turmoil in the 1960s politicized the romantic self-image anthropologists cultivated as skeptical critics of ethnocentrism. Thus, much work by second-generation medical anthropologists has been informed by left-wing sentiments, sometimes Marxist, but more often in the liberal tradition that came to be disparagingly labeled "politically correct." We had to rethink the dichotomy between tradition and modernity that had dominated the social sciences and the neocolonial developmental projects in the 1950s and 1960s. We immediately realized that it had little analytic value for understanding Ayurvedic revivalism in South Asia, the Maoist advocacy of Chinese medicine, or the action of folk practitioners throughout Latin America, Asia, and Africa, who were adding antibiotic injections to their repertoires of ritual curing and herbal remedies.

In our own society at the same time, critics were challenging the rationality of biomedical knowledge, along with the organization and conduct of practice. In particular, reformers within medicine as well as outsiders faulted an epistemology that encouraged a dehumanizing focus on body parts, malfunctions, and lesions, that separated mind and body, that treated homosexuality as a pathology, and that medicalized alcoholism, pregnancy, and birthing. I will not pursue the demystification of biomedicine, although it has been a prominent topic in medical sociology and anthropology and overlaps science and technology studies, a field ripe with possibilities for new research. But I must at least pause in this paragraph to note that Margaret Lock and Deborah Gordon's *Biomedicine Examined* (1988) is one signpost on this path of enquiry. So is Robbie Davis-Floyd and Carolyn Sargent's *Childbirth and Authoritative Knowledge: Cross-Cultural Perspectives* (1997). Also, there are mountains in this landscape. I refer, for example, to major studies of the medicalization of pregnancy and birthing by Robbie Davis-Floyd (1992), Gertrude Jacinta Fraser (1998), and Rayna Rapp (1999). These books set standards for those entering this area of research.

The second-generation medical anthropologists participated in the creation of an "interpretive anthropology" while rejecting the dismal science aspects of ethnological functionalism and the conventional model of medical knowledge and practice that their predecessors had borrowed from physicians. The term *interpretive anthropology* refers loosely to the reorientation of cultural anthropology led by Leach, Geertz, and Victor Turner, to name a few. Scholars with a positivist viewpoint have criticized this orientation as insufficiently scientific, an issue I will return to in brief discussions of two postmodernist studies. Other scholars have criticized interpretive anthropology for neglecting issues of political economy, yet these approaches complement each other in major works of medical anthropology. I want to make a different point in this article: that if we back into the future by building on what we have accomplished so far, the new work will be humanistic at the same time that it continues our natural science tradition of field research conducted with a species-wide and long-time perspective.

Second-generation medical anthropologists began publishing in the 1970s and the third generation in the 1990s. Together they are now training a fourth generation. The body of work they have created can be compared to a landscape with hills and valleys of cultivated fields, pastures, roads, and footpaths. The anthropological mountains are highly accomplished books recording sustained ethnological research. They are frequently important contributions to African, Latin American, and other regional studies, and to research in adjacent and overlapping disciplines such as social medicine, clinical psychology, and the history and sociology of science and medicine. They are often prize-winning works. We recommend them to colleagues as classics in our field. There were no mountains when the Society for Medical Anthropology was founded 30 years ago. The first moun-

tains that appeared in our landscape were Gilbert Lewis's *Knowledge of Illness in Sepik Society* (1975) and John Janzen's *The Quest for Therapy in Lower Zaire* (1978). Arthur Kleinman's *Patients and Healers in the Context of Culture* (1980) soon followed. Nancy Scheper-Hughes's *Death without Weeping* (1992), Allan Young's *The Harmony of Illusions* (1995), and numerous other works now compose an Alpine landscape. They represent the best that we have accomplished. I use the plural because we are a community of scholars from which gifted individuals draw their sustenance.

Signposts mark the roads and paths that traverse our landscape. These are programmatic works, usually edited volumes or special issues of journals based on conferences organized to encourage a particular direction for new research. An example would be Benjamin Paul's volume, the signpost in applied anthropology that directed us toward creating a distinctive field of research. A recent example would be *The Performance of Healing* (1996), edited by Carol Laderman and Marina Roseman to draw attention to the poetics of ritual curing with the hope of stimulating new work using performance theory and concepts in aesthetic philosophy.

Maps are occasionally posted at rest stops on the main road through the landscape. These are textbooks and supplementary readers for college courses. Although they are important for the development of medical anthropology, I will put them aside.

I use this landscape metaphor to illustrate traditions I hope we will continue to build on. Others may have as much promise for future work (I have touched on feminist studies of biomedicine), but I am loath to predict the future.

HISTORY, EVOLUTION, AND INFECTIOUS DISEASES

A species-wide, long-time perspective informs a great deal of medical anthropology, although it is usually assumed or otherwise implicit. Most of us do not directly pursue the notion that we have evolved and continue to evolve in contexts of reciprocal biological and cultural change. Still, in contrast to other social scientists, this is a major subject within our discipline and thus an element of our awareness. In the 1950s and 1960s the first generation of medical anthropologists read and cited historians like Erwin Ackerknecht and Henry Sigerist, who were familiar with anthropological literature and wrote social histories of medicine encompassing centuries or even millennia. Even so, their work had little influence on the theoretical development of the discipline compared to the influence among second- and third-generation medical anthropologists of Michel Foucault's historical perspective. I want to set aside consideration of Foucault's influence to consider instead evolutionary conceptions of health systems and medical care.

Alexander Alland's *Adaptation in Cultural Evolution: An Approach to Medical Anthropology* (1970) was a signpost proposing research on the cultural ecology of infectious diseases. Alland argued from Darwinian theory and the cultural ecology of the period that in traditional non-Western communities natural selection favored practices that became standard in the culture because they had the consequence of helping to avoid infections. As a guide for new research, however, Alland's book was not persuasive. It appeared at a time when Marxist theories enjoyed renewed influence in the social sciences, and, in another vein, Clifford Geertz was advocating "thick description." Alland, on the other hand, ignored the maladaptive health care effects of colonial conquest and rule, poverty, gender discrimination, and religious and ethnic conflicts in the African communities he described. Furthermore, his ethnographic descriptions were thin and unsupported by epidemiological evidence.

In contrast, the large-scale patterns of exploitation, conflict, and change that William H. McNeill analyzed in the rise and spread of urban civilizations made his book, *Plagues and Peoples* (1976, revised edition 1999), a mountain in the landscape of medical anthropology. McNeill drew extensively in several chapters on research by anthropologists, but, more importantly, he displayed an anthropological perspective by using a general theory of biological adaptations between microorganisms and their hosts in constructing narratives of the social effects of infectious epidemic diseases on human communities from Paleolithic times to the present day.

A second mountain appeared 21 years after McNeill's book, Horacio Fabrega's *Evolution of Sickness and Healing* (1997). This is a programmatic work and thus a signpost giving directions for future research, but its ambitious scale and detailed argument make it a mountain. Observing that in human and other species "appetitive, physiological, and immunological systems are designed to react adaptively . . . when they are disturbed or injured" (1997:32), Fabrega argues that this is "linked to a biology of sickness, altruism, and healing . . . arising from . . . genetic variation and selection . . . during social and cultural evolution" (1997:74). He calls such linkages SH (sickness-healing) adaptations, asserting that "medical genes" program both biological responses to illness and "medical memes" that produce healing "behavior, knowledge, and technology" (1997:184, 214). He devotes chapters to stages in the evolution of SH adaptations, discusses other evolutionary issues at length, summarizes his ideas in tables, and includes an extensive "Outline of the Evolution of Sickness and Healing" in an appendix. Fabrega's book appears to me to be an isolated peak in the landscape of medical anthropology. If other scholars take up his ideas in their own research, the results should be interesting and controversial (which is a compliment).

In a programmatic book, *The Anthropology of Infectious Disease,* Marcia C. Inhorn and Peter J. Brown "bemoan the relative abandonment" of this field and the fragmentary character of the existing literature (1997:14). They write that while the WHO Tropical Disease Research Program, along with the Primary Health Care and the Child Survival movements, have recruited a few anthropologists to work on various aspects of infectious diseases, the only topic that has occupied a number of anthropologists is the AIDS pandemic (1997:15). Inhorn and Brown's summary of work that has been accomplished and their identification of research needs constitute a useful signpost for future work. In this respect I want to call attention to two of the anthropological mountains in AIDS research, Paul Farmer's *AIDS and Accusation: Haiti and the Geography of Blame* (1992), and its twin peak, *Infections and Inequalities: The Modern Plagues* (1999). The later book says much about tuberculosis as well. Farmer combines interpretive and political economy approaches to the social aspects of infectious diseases, arguing throughout these works that we should cultivate a "critical epistemology" (1999:40). He does this by identifying misleading units of analysis in epidemiological research, such as the practice of using the borders of a nation to delimit the unit of analysis when microorganisms ignore such borders and human communities exist in a globalizing world. Another example is the conceptualization of risk groups through the lens of social stereotypes and race prejudice. In this manner, too, Farmer analyzes a common practice among anthropologists of confusing cultural differences with the structural injustices of inequality and poverty.

The heterogeneity of discourse in anthropology is a good thing, as Marcus and Fischer (1986) observed, and some of it may indeed signal what they called a "crisis of representation." I disagree, however, when this idea is used to oppose the scientists among us to the humanists. A central concern of my account of our anthropology traditions can be seen by comparing Paul Farmer's books to Stephanie Kane's *Aids Alibis; Sex, Drugs and Crime in the Americas* (1998) and by comparing the studies of Asian medicine by Hsu and Cohen.

Farmer develops arguments and records empirical evidence in a linear manner that readers will readily identify as scientific. In contrast, Kane's book is a pastiche that Merrill Singer identifies in a favorable review with postmodernism. Singer writes that while some anthropologists will find Kane's method interesting, others "worry sincerely that our discipline's obituary will be written in this artistically compelling but ultimately nonanthropological approach to conveying research insights" (2000:663). *Aids Alibis* is a journalistic effort to examine the alibis of those who may know better but neglect to protect themselves from infection or from infecting others, the alibis of officials who use AIDS as a reason for the "war on drugs," and the alibis of those who use the war on drugs as an excuse for racism and for building more prisons. The stories in this collage were collected during field research and from acquaintances, newspapers, and other media. A work of this kind depends for its effectiveness on the narrative thrust of the writing. It is a kind of anthropological literature, but is it science? It belongs to a genre that addresses a large public rather than an audience limited to members of the author's academic discipline. We conventionally agree that works by Margaret Mead, Ashley-Montague, Melvin Konner, and others contribute to our discipline. Some authors, Loren Eisley, for example, are more literary than others. With respect to Kane's book, we should note that popular science literature often involves social advocacy, but so does scholarly research. What we call significance and relevance in paradigmatically scientific works of medical anthropology clearly imply some degree of advocacy. A humanistic perspective and passionate social commitments fuel Paul Farmer's science. I am confident that numerous medical anthropologists will carry this tradition into the 21st century.

HEALTH CARE AND MEDICAL PRACTICES IN ASIAN SOCIETIES

After the Second World War cultural anthropologists shifted away from describing communities as primitive isolates and began to orient their research by sharing concepts of historical transformation with other social scientists: modernization, Westernization, professionalization, medicalization, globalization, and so on. These processes occur in time frames that differ from those of evolutionary adaptation. They vary in length and scope according to the issue being addressed. For example, the medicalization of birthing began at different times in different social classes and in different urban and rural communities in the United States from the 18th century on. It affected the whole society only in the second half of the 20th century. One may trace other medicalization processes back to Renaissance efforts to control plague epidemics or to Quaker reform movements to build asylums for the insane. David Arnold's *Colonizing the Body: State Medicine and Epidemic Disease in Nineteenth-Century India* (1993) is an important recent book in Asian studies that analyzes the development of colonial and medical hegemony by describing responses to smallpox, cholera, and plague epidemics. Arnold shows the ways that issues of health care, including indigenous and English medical knowledge and practices, were involved in forming British conceptions of India, colonial institutions, and Indian resistance to those institutions. This kind of research overlaps our discipline, and I, for one, consider it anthropological.

In the early 1960s I became interested in the ways that learned practitioners of traditional humoral medicine in South Asia responded during the 19th and 20th centuries to the developments in the world system of biomedicine. In the very different circumstances of South Asia, China, and Japan, these physicians challenged the world system, asserting the value of their ancient science and striving to professionalize their practices by founding colleges, hospitals, professional societies, and companies to produce traditional medicines. This in turn influenced the ways that lay people understood and used the plural systems of therapy available to them. To encourage new research on this subject, I did what scholars usually do and organized a conference. The plan was to cultivate a long-term historical perspective (I called it "civilizational") by starting with papers on ancient and medieval texts. An evolutionary perspective would be introduced in papers about whether or not practices in these traditions and in the world system have affected Darwinian adaptations. A comparative perspective was introduced by inviting sociological papers on biomedical institutions in the Soviet Union and in capitalist countries, alternative political models at that time for third world countries. The ethnological papers would be the core of the conference, and they would describe medical pluralism in local settings, setting aside ritual curing because this had preoccupied earlier work, with the idea that this conference was to focus on coexisting humoral and biomedical institutions. Finally, papers would describe the different cultural and political histories of medical revivalism in China, Japan, and India. The signpost erected by that conference was *Asian Medical Systems: A Comparative Study* (Leslie 1976). A great deal of new work was accomplished between that conference and a second one to encourage epistemological analyses (Bates 1995).

Medical pluralism and epistemology are prominent aspects of two studies by third-generation medical anthropologists working in Asia: Elisabeth Hsu's *The Transmission of Chinese Medicine* (1999) and Lawrence Cohen's *No Aging in India: Alzheimer's, the Bad Family, and Other Modern Things* (1998). Although the term *medical plural-*

ism may suggest analyses of the ways laypeople negotiate resort to different kinds of therapy, this is not a topic for either author. Hsu is the first scholar to publish a sustained ethnographic description of a college of traditional medicine. She enrolled as a student, as numerous foreigners, including anthropologists, have done in these Chinese institutions. Since schools of traditional medicine exist in Korea, India, Pakistan, and other Asian countries as well as in China, her book opens a major topic for comparative research. The pluralistic character of Chinese medicine is a central topic in her book, as she analyzes medical concepts, styles of knowing, and modes of teaching in the government college, comparing them to the very different versions of traditional learning and practice she experienced as the private student of a high-status senior physician and as an apprentice with a *qigong* master. This puts the analysis of epistemological variation at the center of her description of medical pluralism.

The composition of Hsu's book is less literary than Cohen's book, but both works have a conventional structure that begins with an outline of what is to follow, develops chapter by chapter a complex set of arguments, and concludes with a full summary of those arguments. I think that this structure and other ways in which these books are alike will be carried forward in the 21st century. I will list several ways in which they resemble each other:

They are first-person accounts. In contrast to relegating information about the social relationships involved in fieldwork to a brief description in a preface or appendix, the anthropologists appear throughout these books as particular kinds of people interacting with others in the communities under study. An anonymous reviewer of this article commented that anthropology is "unique in its acceptance of personal experience (the experiential knowledge of the fieldworker) as a legitimate means of knowledge production (although of course we have also done a lot of soul-searching about this issue as well)."

Typifications of people, events, and cultures are avoided or, where they occur, are subordinate to description that focuses on particularities of the subject. Thus, customs are described by recounting the actions of individual people in specific times and places. This, along with a dominant use of the past tense, historicizes the ethnology, locating it in the real time of the fieldwork.

Ethnological narratives are located in larger curves of history, to borrow a phrase from A. N. Whitehead (1925). In Hsu's book this is the period of standardization and professionalization of traditional medicine, processes subject to the hegemony of biomedicine but that have incorporated cultural nationalism and a Maoist metaphysics. Cohen's ethnology explores conceptions of senility in urban India, located historically by reference to the colonial past, by the history of dementia diagnoses in modern medicine, and by the symbolism of Alzheimer's in American and Indian popular cultures.

In closing, I want to observe a major difference between these seminal works, somewhat comparable to the difference between the books by Stephanie Kane and Paul Farmer. Hsu's book is a straightforward account of research that raises no problems about the author's gift for ethnographic observation, her scientific intentions, and analytic skills. Literary devices, on the other hand, frame Cohen's work, and he uses an unsettling "juxtapositional ethnography" of "multiple sites . . . unlike the conventional sociology and anthropology of India" (1998:8). His work is scientific because it is grounded in excellent ethnographic observation and in extensive knowledge and critical analyses of research on aging. His descriptions are responsible to the facts as, with skeptical intelligence and insight, he describes himself figuring them out. Yet he prefaces his book with a poem by James Merrill and a quotation from Kipling. As an ethnologist, he indicates that he assumes the role of a contemporary Candide, who innocently (read: objectively, without preconceptions) observes the Human Comedy (foolish, contradictory, ambiguous, earnestly self-deceived). As in Voltaire's book, or *Tom Jones*, his chapters have headings indicating the narrative: Chapter One, "in which anthropologists construe, and neurons and nations conjoin," Chapter Two, "in which Alzheimer's is revealed as a metaphor for old age, senility has a history, and the relation between witches and kings offers a subaltern physiology," and so on. But this Candide has Kierkegaard rather than Dr. Pangloss as a master. The world he sees has a tragic edge to it. At the end of his book, he repeats something his immigrant grandmother said to him, "It will break your heart." Cohen's book is

as scientific as Hsu's, and hers is as humanistic as his. His is postmodern, hers is not.

CONCLUSION

I have tried to describe the humanistic interdisciplinary natural science tradition that I believe we have on the whole cultivated. The literary turn in cultural anthropology has provoked accusations of antiscience, and for a few scholars this may be so, but in the research with which I am familiar the accusations are false. Those who worry about the effect of this development on the discipline are foolish because it is a self-limiting practice that requires writing skills few academics possess. Medical anthropology can claim a few gifted writers, but most of our prose can be fairly and unflatteringly called "academic." We put up signposts and hope that others will follow their directions, but this, of course, is a vanity. Innovative work cannot be predicted; if it could be, it would not be innovative.

From the beginning, I think, most anthropologists have considered the discipline, and our recent subdisciplinary part of it, to be more than a science. It has been a world view, an occupation, a way of life, an entertainment, and, obviously, in Cohen's case, for he wears his heart on his sleeve, an existential search for meaning. Most of us who attempt innovative work earn our bread as college teachers. We are happy when a student discovers anthropology and wants to make it her or his life work. We will back into the future carrying the tradition forward. For a while it will be, in part, postmodern, but then?

REFERENCES

Alland, Alexander. 1970. *Adaptation in Cultural Evolution: An Approach to Medical Anthropology.* New York: Columbia University Press.

Arnold, David. 1993. *Colonizing the Body: State Medicine and Epidemic Disease in Nineteenth Century India.* Berkeley: University of California Press.

Bates, Don. 1995. *Knowledge and the Scholarly Medical Traditions.* Cambridge: Cambridge University Press.

Cohen, Lawrence. 1998. *No Aging in India: Alzheimer's, the Bad Family, and Other Modern Things.* Berkeley: University of California Press.

Davis-Floyd, Robbie E. 1992. *Birth as an American Rite of Passage.* Berkeley: University of California Press.

Davis-Floyd, Robbie E., and Carolyn F. Sargent, eds. 1997. *Childbirth and Authoritative Knowledge: Cross-Cultural Perspectives.* Berkeley: University of California Press.

Fabrega, Horacio. 1997. *Evolution of Sickness and Healing.* Berkeley: University of California Press.

Farmer, Paul. 1992. *AIDS and Accusation: Haiti and the Geography of Blame.* Berkeley: University of California Press.

———. 1999. *Infections and Inequalities: The Modern Plagues.* Berkeley: University of California Press.

Fraser, Gertrude Jacinta. 1998. *African American Midwifery in the South: Dialogues of Birth, Race, and Memory.* Cambridge, MA: Harvard University Press.

Hsu, Elisabeth. 1999. *The Transmission of Chinese Medicine.* Cambridge: Cambridge University Press.

Inhorn, Marcia C., and Peter J. Brown, eds. 1997. *The Anthropology of Infectious Disease: International Health Perspectives.* Amsterdam: Gordon and Breach.

Janzen, John M. 1978. *The Quest for Therapy in Lower Zaire.* Berkeley: University of California Press.

Kane, Stephanie. 1998. *AIDS Alibis: Sex, Drugs, and Crime in the Americas.* Philadelphia: Temple University Press.

Kleinman, Arthur. 1980. *Patients and Healers in the Context of Culture: An Exploration of the Borderland between Anthropology, Medicine, and Psychiatry.* Berkeley: University of California Press.

Laderman, Carol, and Marina Roseman, eds. 1996. *The Performance of Healing.* New York: Routledge.

Leslie, Charles, ed. 1976. *Asian Medical Systems: A Comparative Approach.* Berkeley: University of California Press.

Lewis, Gilbert. 1975. *Knowledge of Illness in a Sepik Society: A Study of the Gnau, New Guinea.* London: The Athlone Press, University of London.

Lock, Margaret, and Deborah Gordon, eds. 1988. *Biomedicine Examined.* Dordrecht: Kluwer Academic.

Marcus, George E., and Michael M. J. Fischer. 1986. *Anthropology as Cultural Critique: An Experimental Moment in the Human Sciences.* Chicago: University of Chicago Press.

McNeill, William H. 1999 [1976]. *Plagues and Peoples.* Garden City, NY: Anchor Press/Doubleday.

Paul, Benjamin D., ed. 1955. *Health, Culture and Community: Case Studies of Public Reactions to Programs.* New York: Russell Sage Foundation.

Rapp, Rayna. 1999. *Testing Women, Testing the Fetus: The Social Impact of Amniocentesis in America.* New York: Routledge.

Scheper-Hughes, Nancy. 1992. *Death without Weeping: The Violence of Everyday Life in Brazil.* Berkeley: University of California Press.

Singer, Merrill. 2000. Review of *AIDS Alibis. American Anthropologist* 102:663.

Whitehead, Alfred North. 1925. *Science and the Modern World.* New York: Macmillan.

Young, Allan. 1995. *The Harmony of Illusions: Inventing Post-Traumatic Stress Disorder.* Princeton, NJ: Princeton University Press.

■ ■ ■ ■ ■ ■ ■ ■ ■

2   MENOPAUSE: LESSONS FROM ANTHROPOLOGY

Margaret Lock

This case study illustrates the humanistic and natural science approach advocated by Leslie in the previous selection. Through comparative analysis, this selection shows that concepts about the body, health, and gender are culturally constructed, even with respect to "natural" bodily functions like menopause. Lock argues that biology and culture exist in a continuous interactive relationship subject to variation on both sides. Not all women everywhere report the same symptoms associated with menopause, while the rate of heart attacks, strokes, osteoporosis, and other health problems in older women varies considerably

Source: Lock, M. 1998. "Menopause: Lessons from Anthropology." *Psychosomatic Medicine* 60(4):410–419. Used by permission from the publisher.

across populations. The experience of reproductive senescence depends on "local biologies" shaped by individual and population-level factors including reproductive patterns, diet (especially phytoestrogen intake), cultural expectations, and behaviors such as exercise, smoking, and the use of medications.

The way in which culture assigns meaning to biological processes may seem obvious in unfamiliar medical systems, but it is no less evident in the history of Western medicine. Well into the twentieth century, medical textbooks covered diseases such as hysterism, onamism (masturbation), homosexuality, and nervous exhaustion. Today, there are new conditions such as premenopausal syndrome, chronic fatigue syndrome, and Gulf War syndrome. Likewise, menopause and andropause (the gradual decline in testosterone levels in some men that may contribute to frailty and reduced sexual desire and function) are concepts with a specific history and sociocultural roots. They have come to be seen as diseaselike conditions—requiring hormone replacement therapy with estrogen and testosterone, respectively—only in the past century and especially the last few decades.

The persistence of significant scientific doubts about the effectiveness and harmful side effects of such treatments (see Couzin 2003) makes it clear that cultural concepts about femininity, masculinity, and aging are at work in contributing to the widespread use of hormone replacement therapies. Over the past century, cultural changes associated with industrialization have given rise to a negative paradigm of old age presupposing disability and decline (Featherstone and Hepworth 2001), often ascribed to reductions in hormone levels. Such a negative notion is not necessarily shared by other populations, in which older age may be a time of increased activity, creativity, and social position (see Amoss and Harrell 1981; Lamb 2000).

Lock shows that, contrary to a common misperception about demographics, there have always been people who lived into old age, but the way they have been perceived and treated depends as much on cultural beliefs as possible physiological decline.

Questions to keep in mind

What cultural beliefs about aging and menopause do you take for granted because of your own cultural background?

How do these beliefs vary from those surrounding konenki in Japan as described by Lock?

In what ways are beliefs about menopause related to cultural and socioeconomic conditions in different historical periods?

What are some examples of cultural expectations and individual behaviors that influence "local biologies"?

INTRODUCTION

It is widely acknowledged that the end of menstruation is a complex biosocial and biocultural process. Nevertheless, researchers often assume that biological changes associated with this stage of the life cycle are essentially universal, and that differences in the subjective experience of individual women can be accounted for by variation among psychological, social, and cultural factors.

Although, of course, reproductive senescence among women is universal, recent anthropological research suggests that menopause should not be conceptualized as an invariant biological transformation, and that it is more appropriate to think of biology and culture as being a continuous feedback relationship of ongoing exchange, in which both are subject to variation. For example, cross-cultural studies indicate that the incidence of symptoms taken as characteristic of menopause in North America and Europe, especially hot flashes and night sweats, cannot be assumed to be distributed equally among populations of perimenopausal and postmenopausal women. Data from Japan, Taiwan, China, Indonesia, India, the Yucatan and other sites reveal that women in these locations report relatively few vasomotor symptoms (see below).

Nor should populations of postmenopausal women be considered equally at increased risk for heart disease, osteoporosis, or other late onset chronic problems. It is well established that there is considerable cross-cultural variation in the incidence of these diseases. Taken together, these results suggest that additional nuanced comparative research is in order, in which biological, nutritional, life-style, psychological, and social variables are all taken into consideration.

In this study, I will first outline an anthropological approach to the study of menopause, in which it is argued that all knowledge about what constitutes this life cycle transition, including contemporary medical knowledge, is culturally produced. The main portion of this study is devoted to a presentation of survey findings from Japan in connection with the menopausal transition. These data are comparable with results obtained when the same questionnaire was used in Canada and the United States. Significant differences in symptom reporting at menopause are evident, notably that Japanese reporting is lower than in North America. The Japanese findings are culturally contextualized through the use of open-ended interviews and textual analysis.

Current professional and popular knowledge about menopause in North America is dominated by an assumption that menopause heralds the beginning of a decline in health, a decline precipitated by lowered estrogen levels. This assumption is often justified by means of an erroneous claim: that because mean female life expectancy until the turn of the century in North America and Northern Europe was less than 50 years, virtually no women lived much past that age until the recent past[1]. Such statements are misleading, especially when linked with a second claim, namely that a postreproductive phase in humans goes against nature because virtually no mammals, primates included, have a life span that extends much beyond reproductive senescence[2]. These arguments assume that postmenopausal life is a recent phenomenon, the result of technological and cultural interventions that have influenced longevity, and that women past reproductive age are, in effect, biological anomalies.

The final portions of this study use data from biological anthropology and from demography to counter these assumptions. When combined with the empirical findings from Japan, these data strongly suggest that a decline in health is not in-herently associated with postreproductive female life. The evidence indicates that research that proposes to establish what protects the majority of women from a difficult time at menopause can be of great value, together with investigations into the living conditions and life styles that contribute to a healthy old age. Research of this kind would provide a balance to certain pessimistic and overgeneralized views currently in circulation in connection with postmenopausal women and their health.

MENOPAUSE AS CULTURAL CONSTRUCT

Recent anthropological research into menopause begins with a set of assumptions different from those of most clinicians. Historical and cross-cultural research suggests that menopause is best understood, not as a fact, but as a construct. The current dominant understanding of menopause, both medical and among women in Europe and North America, is that it is equivalent to the end of menstruation. However, such an understanding is recent in origin, and in other cultural contexts does not "fit" with local accounts of female middle age.

For example, in 1813 Henry Halford made the following observation: "I should observe, that though this climacteric disease is sometimes equally remarkable in women as in men, yet most certainly I have not noticed it so frequently, nor so well characterized in females." Halford was writing about that "period of life at which the vital forces begin to decline, commencing from about 45 until 60 years of age." He described a general decay of strength, tiredness, loss of weight, and appetite, and added: "The patient sometimes suspects he has a fever and might also experience head and chest pains, vertigo, rheumatic pains, swollen legs and sluggish bowels. . ." but ". . . above all, anxiety of mind and sorrow have laid the surest foundation for the malady." Halford concluded by wondering whether it was the prospect of death that ". . . inflicted the wound in the patient's peace of mind"[3].

The term menopause was invented in 1821 by the French physician Gardanne. From the middle of the 19th century onward, it gradually came into wide circulation in medical circles in Europe to describe what was known in English in daily parlance as the "dodging time," that is, the years before and after the last menstruation. The concept usually used in educated circles from medieval times onward to express the idea of a transition at midlife, the climacteric, made no distinction between men and women, although this changed at the end of the 19th century. Thus Gardanne, in creating the idea of menopause, deliberately sought to single out the aging of women as worthy of medical attention.

It was more than a century, however, before more than a few physicians paid serious attention to menopause. Edward Tilt in England was a well known exception for his work, clinical and theoretical, in the latter half of the last century, as was his colleague, Andrew Currier, in the United States. Robert Barnes, another physician interested in menopause, in 1973 wrote: "[p]hysicians do, indeed, talk of the climacteric in man; but the analogy is more fanciful than real"[4]. He went on:

> There is nothing to compare with the almost sudden decay of the organs of reproduction which marks the middle age of woman. While those organs are in vigor, the whole economy of woman is subject to them. Ovulation and menstruation, gestation and lactation by turns absorb and govern almost all the energies of her system. The loss of these functions entails a complete revolution.—Barnes, 1873, pp. 263, 264.

The assumption that menopause is a "revolutionary" transition seems to be shared by a many physicians today. There are exceptions, of course, including the Novaks, father and son, at Johns Hopkins University, and the influential physicians associated with them who have argued for many years in gynecological textbooks that menopause should be regarded as a physiological phenomenon that is protective in nature[5]. The 1990 statement of Margery Gass and Robert Rebar is also noteworthy: "Many women pass through menopause with no problems and no complaints. They should be encouraged to pursue healthy life-styles"[6].

Knowledge about what constitutes normal and abnormal, and what is defined as disease, together with the way in which individuals subjectively experience and report symptoms, varies through time and space. Life cycle transitions, in particular those of women, have increasingly become sub-

jected to medical management throughout this century. This process of medicalization, although it has often served to markedly increase the health and well being of women, has inevitably focused attention on pathology. In the case of menopause, until recently research was usually performed on small samples in clinical settings, and extrapolations were made from these findings to the population at large[7]. It has been only over the past 15 years that reliable data about the normal menopausal transition has gradually become available[8,9,10]. Such data, both from North America and other locations, indicates that a revolutionary transition may not be the most appropriate way of thinking about menopause.

CROSS-CULTURAL RESEARCH ON MENOPAUSE

Anthropological research performed by Flint[11] among an East Indian population, Flint and Samil[12] in Indonesia, Walfish et al.[13] among Africans living in Israel, and Yeh[14] working in Taiwan revealed low symptom reporting at menopause among these groups of women. Beyene[15] found that a sample of Mayan women reported no hot flashes or cold sweats, in contrast to the Greek peasant women whom she also studied, whose experience of symptoms was similar to those reported in northern Europe. Beyene argues on the basis of her findings that menopause should be interpreted as a biocultural event. She suggests that diet and reproductive history (which in the Mayan case consists of many pregnancies and extended cycles of amenorrhea associated with prolonged lactation and malnutrition), as well as other variables, influence the time of onset and the subjective experience of menopause.

Using a life span approach to menopause, Leidy[16] has argued recently that the range of variation in age at menopause and in symptom reporting is influenced, among other things, by family history. She points out that, "Genetically, parents pass to their daughters the parameters for number of oocytes and/or rate of atresia. Behaviorally, a mother's activity while pregnant affects the ovarian store her daughter possesses at birth. From birth until menopause the environment and behavior of the individual affects her own ovarian stores"[16]. When diet, reproductive history, use of the Pill, smoking, medication use—to name just the most obvious variables—are included in the behavioral repertoire, the argument against a uniform biological profile at the end of menstruation is overwhelming. To these behaviors additional cultural influences must be added, including the impact of language, symbolic meanings attributed to this stage of the life cycle, cultural stereotypes, and expectations about menopause, all of which are in a reciprocal relationship with the neuroendocrine system, creating what I term "local biologies,"[17] an idea to which I will return below.

JAPAN, CANADA, AND THE UNITED STATES: A COMPARATIVE STUDY

Results of a three-nation comparative study conducted in the 1980s highlight the complexity of the problems that we are addressing in this study. Analysis of data sets composed of 7802 Massachusetts women[10], 1307 Manitoban women[18], and 1225 Japanese women, all aged between 45 and 55 years, revealed some remarkable differences in symptom reporting (Table 2.1). The focus of my analysis in this study is on the Japanese findings. (See Avis et al.[19] for additional details on the comparative project, and Lock[17] for a book-length report on the Japanese findings.)

The Japanese data were collected from three parts of Japan—southern Nagano, a rural area, where most of the women either manage or work on farms; the southern part of the city of Kyoto, where the women are employed in factories and in other blue-collar jobs; and in a suburb of Kobe, where most of the women are, as the Japanese say, "professional housewives." There was a 76% response rate to a questionnaire designed to be directly comparable with the Massachussetts and Manitoba studies. At all three sites, the samples were selected from a general and not a clinical population of women. We treated women who had undergone gynecological surgery as a separate category in our analyses. Our primary objective was to obtain comparative data on the normal menopausal transition. To contextualize the Japanese data appropriately, in addition to the questionnaire, I conducted many open-ended interviews in Japanese with women, physicians, and Japanese feminists, among others; I also read widely in Japanese professional and popular literature.

Considerable caution is necessary when working in cross-cultural settings on issues related to health and illness. It is imperative that instruments and scales developed in Europe and North America not be applied without appropriate culturally relevant modifications. Given that language and culture significantly shape the experience and subjective reporting of symptoms, translation of concepts and terms across cultures

Table 2.1 Percentage Distribution of Menopause Status in Each Study

	Study		
Menopausal Status	*Japan*	*Canada*	*United States*
Surgical menopause	9.9	10.5	28.6
Total (100%)[a]	1225.0	1307.0	7802.0
Natural menopause	35.7	35.5	43.9
Perimenopause	31.5	26.2	38.2
Premenopause	32.8	38.3	17.9
Surgical menopause	9.9	20.5	28.6
Total (100%)[b]	1225.0	1307.0	7802.0

[a] Totals exclude subjects with missing data.
[b] Totals exclude subjects with surgical menopause.

becomes a demanding task and presents a limitation on data collection that can never be entirely overcome. Before having the Manitoba questionnaire translated for use in Japan, I conducted interviews with 25 middle-aged women to establish their understanding about menopause, and I also interviewed five Japanese gynecologists. It was immediately evident that the Japanese word konenki, usually translated into English as menopause, does not convey the same meaning as does menopause. At the time I did the research, neither Japanese women nor Japanese doctors considered the end of menstruation to be a significant marker of female middle age; in part, I came to realize this after completing the research, because very few women associated that event with distressing symptoms. The term konenki is similar to the idea of the climacteric, that is, it is understood as a long, gradual process to which the end of menstruation is just one contributing factor. Most Japanese respondents placed its timing at age 45 or even earlier, lasting until nearly 60. Before creating the questionnaire, it was important, therefore, to establish just what is in the minds of people when the term konenki is used; otherwise, considerable miscommunication would have been a likely outcome.

A second difficulty arose because there is no word in Japanese to clearly designate the hot flash, even though Japanese is a language in which very fine discriminations can be made in connection with bodily states. One can simply say, "to suddenly become hot," which conveys too broad a meaning. It is also possible to use nobose, which means a sudden rush of blood to the head or a "hot fit," a term usually used in connection with feelings of vertigo or dizziness, or when talking about someone who is "hot-headed." A second term, hoteri, translates simply as feeling hot or flushed, and is most often used when someone becomes flushed after drinking alcohol, as do many Japanese because of an absence of the enzyme aldehyde dehydrogenase. It was decided to use both hoteri and nobose together with a third term, kyu na nekkan, meaning to have a sudden feverish feeling, a term that had already been used in a small survey conducted by a Japanese gynecologist. This finding about terminology suggests more than that one must be cautious about translation of terms; it indicates that the experience of a hot flash is either

not noticed, noticed but not named, or not experienced very often in Japan. Research in China, Indonesia, and the Yucatan, among other places, also found no local term for the hot flash. It is interesting to note that historically in England, at least, there was such a term, namely "hot blooms," suggesting that hot flashes were marked among English women, whereas they apparently pass unnoticed in many other parts of the world.

Care also had to be taken when selecting the term to be used in the questionnaire for depression, because the description of this state cannot be glossed easily into an equivalent Japanese term. Furthermore, I found that many symptoms that do not appear on a standardized list of menopausal symptoms, such as the Blatt Menopausal Index [20], had to be included; in particular, shoulder stiffness, ringing in the ears, a heavy feeling in the head, and others. These are symptoms that Japanese women and their doctors commonly associate with konenki. Symptoms were also included in the questionnaire that had been used by Japanese doctors in small questionnaires conducted with patient samples. Many of these symptoms had originally been taken from German lists of menopausal symptoms created earlier in the century; included were such sensations as "a feeling of ants crawling on one's skin," which had been given the technical term of "formication." Only one Japanese woman reported this symptom.

The final symptom list in Japanese was composed of 51 items as opposed to the original 26 used in North America. The check list was not described to informants as a list of menopausal symptoms. General symptoms, including the common cold and constipation, were included, to avoid responses based on stereotypical ideas about menopause. The symptom list was one part of a questionnaire designed to elicit a range of information about reproductive health and use of health care services in general. Women at all three sites were asked to respond "yes" or "no" to the question: "thinking back over the past 2 weeks, have you experienced any of the following?" Similarly, women were asked to recall medication use over the past 2 weeks. This period of recall was selected to minimize bias [21].

A list of core symptoms was created that revealed significant differences in the rates of reporting across the three subject groups. The results

Table 2.2 A Comparison of the Rates of Core Symptoms, Reported by Study

	Study			
Symptom	*Japan*	*Canada*	*United States*	χ^2 *(2 df)*
Diarrhea/constipation	24.3	12.8	21.4	62.8[*]
Persistent cough	4.2	9.2	10.3	68.4[*]
Upset stomach	6.3	12.9	16.1	85.1[*]
Shortness of breath	3.1	5.2	13.6	177.6[*]
Sore throat	10.5	9.1	10.7	2.9
Backaches	24.2	26.8	29.6	17.7[*]
Headaches	27.5	33.8	37.2	45.2[*]
Aches/stiffness in joints	14.3	31.4	38.6	279.1[*]
Dizzy spells	7.1	12.3	11.1	21.4[*]
Lack of energy	6.0	39.8	38.1	503.3[*]
Irritability	11.5	17.1	29.9	246.6[*]
Feeling blue/depressed	10.3	23.4	35.9	365.1[*]
Trouble sleeping	11.7	30.4	30.6	189.8[*]
Lack of appetite	4.6	4.0	3.4	5.8
Hot flashes	12.3	33.9	34.8	226.6[*]
Cold or night sweats	3.8	19.8	11.4	158.2[*]
Hot flashes/sweats (combined)	14.7	36.1	38.0	252.5[*]
Total (100%)	1225.0	1307.0	7802.0	

[*]$p < .01$.

show that the Japanese responses are consistently different from those in both the United States and Canada. For 13 of the 16 core symptoms, both the Canadian and United States women reported (sometimes markedly) higher rates than did the Japanese women (Table 2.2). For only one symptom (combined for purposes of the analysis as diarrhea/constipation) was Japanese reporting somewhat higher, and this comes as no surprise, given the consumption of white rice.

In addition, the rates of multiple symptom reporting by Japanese women were consistently low (Table 2.3). No association was evident between menopausal status and general symptom reporting among the Japanese respondents, although among both Canadian and American women there was an increase of general symptom reporting during the perimenopause and early postmenopause. Japanese reporting of hot flashes was low, 13.5% and 15.2% for perimenopausal and postmenopausal women, respectively, in the previous 2 weeks; hot flashes, although at a low incidence, was associated with menopausal status. Reporting of night sweats was extremely low and not associated with menopausal status (Table 2.4). Only 19% of Japanese women in this study had experienced a hot flash at some time in the past, and reporting of both frequency and intensity was much lower than among United States and Canadian respondents. Table 2.2 also showed that reporting of sleep disturbance by Japanese respondents, at 11.5%, was low, corroborating their reports about lack of severity of hot flashes. I have gone to great lengths to establish that these results are not simply due to under-reporting on the part of Japanese women[22],

Table 2.3 A Comparison of the Number of Core Symptoms, Reported by Study

	Study		
No. of Symptoms Reported	*Japan*	*Canada*	*United States*
0	26.7	13.8	15.4
1–4	63.4	60.0	50.3
5+	9.7	26.2	34.1
Total (100%)	1225.0	1307.0	7305.0

Table 2.4 Vasomotor Symptoms, Reported by Menopausal Status

Menopausal Status	Japan[*]	Manitoba[†]	Massachusetts[†]
Hot Flashes			
Premenopause	6.4	13.8	17.9
Perimenopause	13.5	39.7	38.1
Postmenopause	15.2	41.5	43.9
Total (100%)	1104.0	1039.0	5505.0
	$\chi^2 = 15.77$	$\chi^2 = 84.17$	$\chi^2 = 269.510$
Night Sweats			
Premenopause	4.1	10.6	5.5
Perimenopause	4.0	27.6	11.7
Postmenopause	3.0	22.2	11.3
Total (100%)	1104.0	1039.0	5484.0
	$\chi^2 = 0.772$	$\chi^2 = 33.71$	$\chi^2 = 31.335$

[a] Massachusetts *N* differs because of missing data. Cases of surgical menopause have been removed.

[*] *p* = .00 and .68.

[†] *p* = .00.

and they are corroborated by two small studies conducted by Japanese researchers[23]. Although North American reporting of hot flashes was higher (more than 40% for postmenopausal women), hot flashes are not the most frequently reported symptom in the core symptom list.

The majority of Japanese women, when asked in interviews to describe their experience of konenki, responded along the following lines:

> I've had no problems at all, no headaches or anything like that. . . I've heard from other women that their heads felt so heavy that they couldn't get up.
>
> The most common problems I've heard about are stiff shoulders, headaches, and aching joints.
>
> I get tired easily, that's konenki for sure, and I get stiff shoulders.
>
> My eyesight became worse, and sometimes I get ringing in the ears. I hear that some housewives get so depressed that they can't go out of the house.

A few women, 12 of 105 interviewed, made statements that sound more familiar to North American ears:

> The most noticeable thing was that I would suddenly feel hot; it happened every day, three times or so. I didn't go to the doctor or take any medication, I wasn't embarrassed and I didn't feel strange. I just thought it was my age.

When interviewed, Japanese gynecologists indicated that shoulder stiffness is the most common symptom reported by Japanese patients; some physicians did not list hot flashes when asked to describe menopausal symptoms. Over the past few years, however, a few Japanese gynecologists have become increasingly involved in international meetings on the subject of menopause; they have now published widely in women's magazines in Japan where they describe hot flashes as the "typical" symptom of menopause. It will be interesting to see to what extent symptom reporting by women changes in the future, if at all, as a result of these publications.

Similar to vasomotor symptoms, Japanese reporting in connection with feeling "blue" or depressed was low, and not associated with menopausal status, inasmuch as it is highest among premenopausal women (Table 2.5). Canadian reporting, although higher than the Japanese, also shows little change across menopausal status. These different patterns of reporting argue strongly against any simple causal link between declining endogenous estrogen levels and reporting of depression, or even hot flashes (see also Avis and McKinlay[24]).

It is well known that Japanese women currently enjoy the longest life expectancy in the world. The incidence of breast cancer and of heart disease in men and women is about one third of that in North America. The figures for osteoporosis are not well established, but the ongoing work of Ross

**Table 2.5 The Percentage Feeling Blue/
Depressed, Reported
by Menopausal Status**

Menopausal Status	Feeling Blue/Depressed		
	Japan	Canada	United States
Premenopause	12.7	24.1	29.1
Perimenopause	9.5	23.2	38.1
Postmenopause	8.9	23.0	33.8

et al.[25] shows that the incidence for both Chinese and Japanese women is less than half that of Caucasian women in North America, even though bone density is often less among Asian women. The present study showed that only 28% of Japanese respondents suffer from a chronic health problem (diabetes, allergies, asthma, arthritis, high blood pressure), as opposed to 45% of Manitoban women and 53% of Massachusetts women. Taken together, these figures suggest that middle-aged Japanese women enjoy good health in comparison with women in North America.

Japanese women who are, at present, around 50 years of age were born at the end of the war, and most experienced nutritional deprivation as very small children; however, virtually none of them have smoked, alcohol and coffee consumption is low, and the usual diet is low in fat and rich in soy beans and vegetables. Research indicates that soy beans are a source of natural estrogens and, therefore, diet may be one part of the cultural repertoire that contributes to the lower symptom reporting of hot flashes on the part of Japanese women[26]. In this cohort of women, considerable exercise and weight bearing has always been part of their daily lives. Obviously this picture will change as succeeding generations of Japanese women become middle aged in their turn. However, the population as a whole is highly educated and, because women are socialized to be concerned about health, many will undoubtedly continue to follow a traditional diet and undertake regular exercise. Japanese women also make extensive use of herbal medicines and teas, some of which have a high phytoestrogen content[17].

The longitudinal research of both McKinlay and Kaufert[9,24], reveals that menopause is not a difficult time for the majority of North American women. Together with the Japanese findings and other cross-cultural work, their research suggests that we would do well to ask what protects the majority of women from experiencing discomfort at menopause. Moreover, the longevity and overall good health status of Japanese women invites additional systematic investigation. Together with the epidemiologists Marmot and Davey Smith[27], I conclude that these factors can probably be attributed, in large part, to the even distribution of wealth in Japanese society, little poverty, and equal access to good health care and social benefits, to which is added universal public education of a high quality and a long tradition of both public and familial investment in preventive medicine. In addition, it seems most likely that the traditional Japanese diet—low in fat, high in protein and natural estrogens—plays an important role.

THE CULTURAL CONSTRUCTION OF KONENKI

Changing demography and the burgeoning number of aging women who may become a burden to the health care system have stimulated the medicalization of menopause in North America. The "graying" of society also raises many concerns in Japan, especially because demographic changes that occurred over the course of about 100 years in Europe and North America have taken just 25 years in Japan. Thus far, however, attention has been focused, not so much on the health of middle-aged women, but rather on their role as caregivers of elderly relatives.

The three-generation household, the ie, was for three quarters of a century—from the Meiji Restoration (1867) until the end of the Second World War—recognized as the official family unit in Japan. In this household are enshrined the ancestors, representatives of moral and spiritual values. Modeled on the samurai system of feudal times, and laced with a little late 19th century European sentiment, the "good wife and wise mother" was expected to discipline herself for service to the household, in particular for the nurturance and well-being, physical and spiritual, of all other family members[28]. Whereas feudal Japan exhibited an acute sensitivity to class and occupational differences, with the creation of the early modern state, difference, in theory, was obliterated. For the first time, Japanese women were appealed to as a unified body in terms of gendered social roles to be performed within the confines of the ie[29].

As part of such a family, a woman reaches the prime of life in her fifties, and at that time enjoys the acme of her responsibility, which, although it gradually wanes, is never extinguished unless she succumbs to severe senility or some other catastrophe. Many Japanese women still live in these circumstances, and their days are filled with monitoring the household economy, care and education of children and grandchildren, and care of dependent in-laws, to which is often added piece work done at home or participation in the household enterprise, usually farming or a small business. Although in feudal Japan, upper class women were sometimes described as a "borrowed womb," from the end of the 19th century, all women came to be thought of not so much as vehicles for reproduction, but primarily as family nurturers in addition to economically productive members of society. They retained these tasks throughout the life cycle, although their specific duties changed through time. Reproduction was obviously important, and the bearing of a son particularly so, but through the years the Japanese have been remarkably flexible about the formal adoption into their families of not only children, but also adults, should the need arise. Hence, the dominant image of a woman in Japan in recent times has been that of a nurturer, a quality with which all women are assumed to be "biologically" endowed[28].

The nuclear household, in which approximately 60 per cent of Japanese currently live, lacking both enshrined ancestors and the elders, is thought by many commentators to be a fragile "pathological" conglomeration[30,31]. Members of the nuclear family—men, women, and children—are thought to be particularly vulnerable to what has been termed "diseases of civilization," including a range of neuroses, behavioral disorders, and deviant behavior. These diseases are made factual by catchy diagnostic labels such as "school refusal syndrome," "high-rise apartment neurosis," "moving day depression," "death from overwork" and so on[32]. One of them is "menopausal syndrome," a problem believed to have surfaced only in postwar years, and which is particularly associated with middle class "professional housewives" who live in urban environments. When asked whether he thought that all women experience trouble at konenki, a Kobe gynecologist answered:

> No, I don't think so. Women who have no purpose in life (ikigai) have the most trouble. Housewives who are relatively well off, who have only one or two children and lots of free time come to see me most often. Menopausal syndrome is a sort of "luxury disease" (zeitakubyo), I'm sure women never used to come running to a doctor before the war with this kind of problem.

A physician who works in the countryside stated emphatically that rural women are much too busy to experience distress at konenki, the implication clearly being that any discomfort they may feel is of minor importance, something that an active and busy woman will "ride over" (norikoeru) with ease[17].

The irony of this rhetoric does not pass unnoticed by feminist commentators in Japan[33]. Women have been excluded systematically from the official full time work force in postwar years, despite the fact that many of them put in a full day's work on a regular basis (it is estimated that less than 30% of Japanese women are in fact "professional housewives"). The majority of women who work outside the home in Japan are classified as part-time employees; they work long hours with no benefits and are subject to hiring and firing as the national economy waxes and wanes.

Nevertheless, the "homebody" is idealized. She is the standard by which all women are measured. However, it is often argued that once she becomes middle aged the house-wife residing in a nuclear family has time on her hands, in contrast to women who live in extended families. This stereotype is deceptive because a high proportion of women become, often for many years, the principal care givers for their parents-in-law who choose to reside with the younger generation when they become frail and sick[17]. Increasingly, one reads stories in Japanese newspapers where 70-year-old women are caring for 95-year-old dependent relatives. The government, wishing to avoid increasing health care costs for elderly citizens, actively encourages a return to extended family living and provides, among other things, tax reduction incentives, claiming that elders have a right to be cared for by their daughters-in-law.

Not surprisingly, it is the issue of home nursing and the new extended family that takes up the energy of activist women in Japan today. Against the urgency of this situation, the end of menstruation fades into the background, particularly so because of the moralistic rhetoric associated with it. In a country driven overwhelmingly by the work ethic, few people relish being accused, even indirectly, of succumbing to an illness associated with luxury and indolence. My survey research revealed that housewives do not report any more symptoms than do other Japanese women at menopause; low symptom reporting was distributed rather evenly across the farming, factory employed, and housewife samples. However, there is a small but significant increase of reporting of back pain, shoulder stiffness, tiredness, and irritability among a large proportion of women taking care of elderly relatives[17].

MATURATION FOR SOCIETY

Despite a concern about the "graying" of the nation, aging itself is not thought of as an anomaly. On the contrary, Japan is a society exquisitely sensitive to the passing of time, and positively wallows, on occasion, in the ephemeral nature of human life. Life cycle transitions of both men and women formerly were marked and celebrated as social events; continuity with past generations and the presence of the ancestors reinforce the notion that each individual is part of a larger cosmically ordained order[34]. Women who are at present middle aged were immersed in this ideology as children and the majority still embrace it[17,35]. Movement through the life cycle, in theory, is experienced subjectively in terms of how one's relationships with other people shift through time, and for women particularly, life is expected to become meaningful according to their accomplishments for others rather than for themselves[36]. Under these circumstances, the end of menstruation is not a very potent symbol, and 24% of the sample who had ceased menstruating for more than 1 year reported that they had no sign of konenki. Although there is some mourning for the loss of youth and sexual attractiveness on the part of a few women, emphasis is given by most to what is described as the inevitable process of aging itself: to graying hair, changing eyesight, faulty short-term memory, and so on[37]. There is, therefore, no marked gender distinction in the aging process in Japan. Furthermore, these signs of aging, although they obviously represent irretrievable youth, are primarily signifiers for the future—for what may be in store in terms of an enfeebled body (but not necessarily a sick body), and hence an inability to work and to contribute to society.

CREATING THE DISCOURSE OF KONENKI

The end of menstruation has been recognized for many hundreds of years in Sino/Japanese medicine as an occurrence that can leave "stale blood" in the body, the cause in some women of many nonspecific symptoms that often last a few years, including dizziness, palpitations, headaches, chilliness, stiff shoulders, and a dry mouth[38]. It was believed that many other events also produce stale blood and associated nonspecific symptoms, and no specific term was created to gloss any discomfort associated with the end of menstruation. Toward the end of the 19th century, Japanese medicine, under the influence of German medicine, created the term konenki to convey the European concept of the climacterium. Nishimura[39] has suggested that konenki could, until recently, be used to refer to all life cycle transitions, both male and female, regardless of age. This interpretation is very close to the meaning given to the term climacterium as it was used until the latter half of the 19th century in Europe. Contemporary Japanese has no term that expresses in everyday language the event of the end of menstruation, although there is, of course, a technical term, much as menopause was a technical term in English and little used in daily conversation until as recently as 50 years ago.

One part of German discourse about the climacterium that made good intuitive sense to the Japanese medical world was the concept of the "autonomic nervous system." This idea, when it was first clearly articulated in 1898, caused a stir in medical circles everywhere[40], particularly so in Japan where it "fitted" with the holistic physiological approach characteristic of Sino/Japanese medicine. Later, in the 1930s, when a close association was postulated between the endocrine system and the autonomic nervous system[40], Japanese physicians comfortably adopted this idea, and postulated a connection between disturbances in the autonomic nervous system and konenki, an association that the majority of Japanese physicians and women continue to make today[17,41,42]. The dominant discourse in Japan is one in which most symptoms are not linked directly to a decline in estrogen levels, but rather are thought to be caused by a destabilization of the autonomic nervous system.

Another factor that no doubt worked in Japan against the construction of a narrowly focused discourse on the aging ovary and declining estrogen levels, was that Japanese doctors, unlike their Western counterparts, had practiced little surgery before the 20th century. Surgery was a specialty that was disparaged by the powerful, physiologically oriented herbalists of the traditional medical system. Furthermore, anatomy as it was conceived in Enlightenment medical discourse in Europe had relatively little impact in Japan until the 20th century, and autopsies and dissection were not practiced widely. Japanese gynecologists did not, therefore, have first-hand experience of removing and dissecting many hundreds of ovaries, as was the case for many late 19th century European and North American gynecologists[43]. In Japan, physicians remained predominantly physiologically rather than anatomically oriented until the postwar years.

One other result of the emphasis given in Japan to physiological changes associated with konenki has been that, until recently, the majority of Japanese women, those few who consult with a doctor at this stage of the life cycle, usually go to see an internist and not a gynecologist, because gynecology is primarily a surgical specialty. In all, these differences have ensured that the discourse on konenki is markedly different from that for menopause in North America. Stiff shoulders, headaches, ringing in the ears, tingling sensations, and dizziness are the symptoms that form the core of the konenki experience, an experience that is, in part, contingent upon "local" biology, inasmuch as hot flashes and other vasomotor symptoms occur rather infrequently.

It is evident to most Japanese gynecologists that konenki is not the same thing, either conceptually or experientially, as menopause. The more than 30 physicians I interviewed in Japan are of the opinion that hot flashes are infrequently experienced by Japanese women, and, in any case, cause little distress. More than one gynecologist inquired as to why "Western" women are so disturbed by hot flashes. That the hot flash is not the key signifier of distress at konenki has meant that there has been relatively little incentive over the years for Japanese doctors to prescribe hormone therapy for relief of this symptom. Furthermore, the Pill remains unavailable in Japan for contraceptive purposes. Both doctors and women regularly report in survey research that they are concerned about possible iatrogenesis caused by long-term use of the Pill[44], and this fear extends to the use of HRT.

In Japan, until recently, most obstetrics and gynecology have been delivered by individual physicians who own small hospitals where their income is derived largely from deliveries, abortions, and minor surgery. Recently, however, gynecologists find their medical practice less lucrative than was formally the case because women now choose to be delivered in tertiary care facilities, and also because the abortion rate is going down, due to a more sophisticated use of contraception (despite the unavailability of the Pill). Until 5 years ago, konenki had not been medicalized to any great extent by either internists or gynecologists, but this situation is changing, in part, due to the economic pressures under which many gynecologists in private practice now find themselves (the Japanese gynecologists I interviewed suggested this interpretation[17]). Some doctors have established counseling services for middle-aged patients, whereas others are busy writing books and articles on the subject of konenki for popular consumption. However, despite these changing practices and the presence of an aggressive pharmaceutical industry, relatively little use has been made thus far of HRT, which is prescribed less frequently than are herbal medications[45]. Whether this situation will change radically over the next few years should be carefully observed.

In summary, the construction of knowledge and associated medical practices in Japan about the end of menstruation, both professional and popular, is remarkably different from that in North America. This situation is due, in part, to the subjective experience of Japanese women. This difference is influenced, I argue, by "local biologies," a concept that demands systematic investigation in the future. Dietary practices may well be implicated, but it is possible that genetics are also involved. Local biologies do not, of course, determine subjective experience, but rather work together with culturally infused knowledge to pattern it. Because a negative stereotype about laziness has been associated with the experience of menopausal symptoms in Japan, women who experience difficulties usually have not sought medical assistance. Certain physicians now seek to resolve this impasse by taking a more rigorous, scientific approach to konenki, but, to date, herbal medication remains the medicine of choice of the relatively few women who resort to medication.

One or two gynecologists writing for women's magazines warn readers that lowered estrogen levels have been associated with an increased risk for stroke and Alzheimer's disease. These warnings may encourage certain women to take HRT on a life-long basis, but this tendency will be countered by widespread fears about iatrogenesis, fears that have been documented in connection with the Pill, in addition to many other medications. It is of note that, compared with North America, rather little is written by medical experts in Japan about a possible association between lowered estrogen levels and heart disease. It is stroke and senility, and not heart disease, that are iconic in Japan of a miserable old age, one that causes trouble for other family members. A few Japanese women are actively seeking better medical care for konenki, and their efforts may well work toward eradicating the stigmatizing stereotypes associated in Japan with this life cycle transition.

MENOPAUSE AS BIOLOGICAL ADAPTATION

I turn now to an entirely different kind of data. Providing an explanation for the evolution of menopause among human females continues to present a fascinating challenge to biologists, primatologists, and anthropologists. Although disputes remain among researchers as to the function of menopause, there is no argument that menopause evolved very early in the evolutionary history of human females.

Among monkeys, it is well established that rhesus macaques experience menopause when approximately two thirds of their life cycle is completed, the profile of which is hormonally similar to that of human females, although the ovaries do not show such marked changes as in humans. One study showed temperature changes suggestive of hot flashes in monkeys[46]. Based on years of systematic primate observation, Blaffer-Hrdy found that many individual female macaques and langurs survive to old age and that, in contrast to elderly males, they play an important protective role against predation in the life of the troupe. Chimpanzee work by Jane Goodall demonstrated, as did that of Blaffer-Hrdy, that the matriline is important, and that elderly females protect not only their own daughters but also their grandchildren and, at times, more distantly related youngsters[47]. These researchers conclude that the presence of postreproductive females in primate groups is biologically adaptive.

Very recent findings of early hominids in East Africa suggest that the first major adaptation from apes to humans was that of upright posture. These "walking chimps" had a short life expectancy and lived, as far as we can tell, rather noncooperative lives. It was not until the emergence of homo erectus, 1,700,000 years ago, that shorter arms and a larger brain clearly had evolved. It is not yet established when estrus ceased. Between 1,500,000 and 1,200,000 years ago, early hominids started to live in cooperative groups, share food, and develop technologically assisted hunting. These changes indicate very strongly that language was also evolving during this time. With an increased brain size came a dramatically lengthened time of dependency of human infants and juveniles before maturation, requiring prolonged adult attention not found among apes. Peccei[48] has argued, on the basis of mathematical modeling, that reproductive senescence permitting extended investment in dependent children from early pregnancies is biologically advantageous. Lifelong reproduction would probably have exposed older children to neglect, whereas attention was focused on newborns, thus making the survival of older siblings problematic.

Peccei[48] argues that menopause evolved around 1.5 million years ago, the result of selective pressures in favor of females who became prematurely infertile, and that it probably occurred somewhat earlier than 50 years of age.

In contrast to Peccei's argument, the "grandmother hypothesis" posits that postreproductive life in human females was advantageous because, similar to ape communities, older members of society, unhampered by dependent infants, provided group protection. Such protection would have resulted in improved inclusive fitness of the group. On the basis of data obtained from the Ache, a hunting and gathering society in Paraguay, Hill and Hurtado[49] argue that the grandmother hypothesis, although not proven, makes good intuitive sense. Furthermore, evidence from a range of contemporary hunting and gathering societies shows that women can collect more food if they leave infants in the care of older women while foraging and, moreover, that freedom from dependent infants leads to better cooperation in communal endeavors other than the basic procurement of food. These hypotheses, the one in favor of direct maternal investment in living offspring, and the second, arguing that the presence of postreproductive females in groups leads to greater inclusive fitness, are not mutually exclusive. Together they suggest strongly that women of postreproductive age have had a major contributory role in society that was probably biologically adaptive since the evolution of contemporary humankind. These advantages clearly remain of relatively little importance in contemporary society, but, on the other hand, menopause cannot be disposed of as a biological anomaly.

POSTMENOPAUSAL LIFE AS CULTURAL ARTIFACT

In closing, I turn to the often repeated idea that a post-menopausal life span is a recent cultural artifact, the result of technological interventions into the process of human aging. A recent article by Gail Sheehy[50] stated, for example, "At the turn of the century, a woman could expect to live to the age of forty-seven or eight," a sentiment expressed widely not only in popular literature but also in scientific articles. Gosden[1], writing a text for biol-

ogists, is explicit that the very existence of postmenopausal women is something of an artifact, the result of our ". . . recent mastery of the environment." Another frequently expressed opinion, which appears in a gynecological textbook[51], is that the human female is the only member of the class Mammalia to live beyond menopause, is an anomaly, and thus vulnerable to ill health. In countering these assertions, it may be helpful to pose some questions: If the human life span has increased only very recently, why do virtually all bodily functions senesce as though humans were adapted to live well into their seventies and beyond? Why is the human life span potential estimated at somewhere between 95 and more than 100 years of age? This potential is associated, as with other mammals, with brain size, and is evident from the early days of *Homo sapiens*, 100,000 years ago. A related question is that, if the human life span has been no more than 50 years until recently, then why does male reproductive function not senesce markedly by what is described today as middle age?

Cross-cultural data once again proves useful in reconstructing what the human life span may have been like in times past. Data from hunter gatherer societies show that 20% of all individuals survive to age 60, and about 10% survive to age 70[52,53]. The most important figures to consider, however, are not life expectancy at birth, because until recently infant mortality accounted for most deaths, and maternal mortality was also frequently high. Once these "artifacts" are removed, it is clear that old women have always been present and, moreover, as Kertzer and Laslett[54] have pointed out, remaining life expectancy of mature adults has changed remarkably little throughout human history. In Scotland, for example, between 1871 and 1977 the remaining life expectancy at age 50 has increased by only 7 years, and in Japan between 1891 and 1989 the remaining life expectancy for 50-year-old women increased by 12 years from 70 to 82[1,55]. It is true, of course, that more women live to old age than was formerly the case, but this should not necessarily incite the idea that we are in a era where the female life cycle is artificially extended through technological interventions beyond its "natural" span.

We are witnessing now in Russia, a decline in life expectancy of more than 3 years over a very short time, which clearly suggests that longevity is dependent on social conditions and, moreover, that changes in population longevity are manifested quite rapidly as a result of altered social circumstances[56]. Infant and maternal mortality, incidence of disease, and longevity are all inextricably associated with the distribution of wealth and resources in any given society.

The greater longevity of women than men noted in all technologically advanced societies remains unaccounted for. It has been postulated that this difference is due to life style and not genetics[57]. Clearly, menopause does not pose any obvious disadvantage to women when gender difference in longevity is at issue. Postmenopausal life is a complex biosocial process, one in which declining estrogen levels are but one factor among many others. To separate the postulated effects of menopause from aging processes in general and to target declining estrogen levels for medicalization is to inappropriately transform an as yet poorly understood biosocial process into one of simple cause and effect relationships. This is not to suggest that certain women do not benefit greatly from medical care and medication, but we have paid scant attention to the millions of women around the world who live in good health to an advanced old age without medical intervention.

Menopause is frequently described today as a deficiency disease or as ovarian failure[58–60]. Using this model, the functioning of bodies of younger women is set up implicitly as the standard for all women, and any possible advantages to the biological changes associated with aging, especially to lowered estrogen levels, are ignored. So, too, are the marked differences, biological and social, among populations of middle-aged and older women. There can be no argument that poverty plays a greater role in determining health in later life than does estrogen levels. The data presented in this study strongly suggest that culturally mediated life styles also make a major contribution to the health of women as they age, which we would do well to investigate additionally.

NOTES

1. Gosden R: *The Biology of Menopause: The Causes and Consequences of Ovarian Aging.* London, Academic Press, 1985

2. Dewhurst J: *Integrated Obstetrics and Gynecology for Postgraduates.* Oxford, Blackwell, 1981

3. Halford H: On the climacteric disease. In *College of Physicians in London, Medical Transitions,* Vol. 4. London, Longman 1913

4. Barnes R: *A Clinical History of the Medical and Surgical Diseases of Women.* London, J and A. Churchill, 1873

5. Novak ER, Seegar Jones G, Jones HW: *Novak's Textbook of Gynecology.* Baltimore, Williams & Wilkins, 1975

6. Gass M, Rebar R: Management of problems during menopause. *Compr Ther* 16:3–10, 1990

7. McKinlay S, McKinlay J: Selected studies on the menopause. *J Biosoc Sci* 5:533–555, 1973

8. Holte A, Mikkelsen A: The menopausal syndrome: A factor analytic replication. *Maturitas* 13:193–203, 1991

9. Kaufert P, Gilbert P, Tate R: The Manitoba Project: A reexamination of the link between menopause and depression. *Maturitas* 14:143–155, 1992

10. McKinlay S, Brambilla D, Posner J: The normal menopausal transition. *Hum Biol* 4:37–46, 1992

11. Flint M: *Menarche and Menopause of Rajput Women.* Unpublished PhD dissertation. New York, City University of New York, 1974

12. Flint M, Suprapti Samil R: Cultural and subcultural meanings of the menopause. In Flint M, Kronenberg F, Utian W (eds), *Multidisciplinary Perspectives on Menopause.* Ann N Y Acad Sci 592:134–148, 1990

13. Walfish S, Antonovsky A, Maoz B: Relationship between biological changes and symptoms and health behavior during the climacteric. *Maturitas* 6:9–17, 1984

14. Yeh A: *The Experience of Menopause Among Taiwanese Women.* Honors Thesis, Department of East Asian Languages and Civilizations, Harvard University, Boston, 1989

15. Beyene Y: Cultural significance and physiological manifestations of menopause: A biocultural analysis. *Cult Med Psychiatry* 10:47–71, 1986

16. Leidy LE: Biological aspects of menopause: Across the lifespan. *Annu Rev Anthropol* 23:231–253, 1994

17. Lock M: *Encounters with Aging: Mythologies of Menopause in Japan and North America.* Berkeley, University of California Press, 1993

18. Kaufert P, Gilbert P, Hassard T: Researching the symptoms of menopause: An exercise in methodology. *Maturitas* 10:117–131, 1988

19. Avis NE, Kaufert PA, Lock M, et al: The evolution of menopausal symptoms. In Burger H (ed), *Balliere's Clinical Endocrinology and Metabolism,* Vol 7. London, Harcourt, Brace Jovanovich, 1993

20. Blatt MG, Weisbader H, Kupperman HS: Vitamin E and the climacteric syndrome. *Arch Intern Med* 91:792–799, 1953

21. Lock M: "Menopause in cultural context." *Exp Gerontol* 29:307–317, 1994

22. Lock M: Hot flushes in cultural context: The Japanese case as a cautionary tale for the west. In *Progress in Basic and Clinical Pharmacology*, Vol 6. The Climacteric Hot Flush. Basel: Karger, 1991, 40–60

23. Mori Ichiro: Konenki shogai. *Sanfujinka MOOK* No. 3:243–253, 1978, an unpublished study

24. Avis NE, McKinlay SM: A longitudinal analysis of women's attitudes toward the menopause: Results from the Massachusetts Women's Health Study. *Maturitas* 13:65–79, 1991

25. Ross PD, Norimatsu H, Davis JW, et al: A comparison of hip fracture incidence among native Japanese, Japanese Americans, and American Caucasians. *Am J Epidemiol* 133:801–809, 1991

26. Adlercreutz H, Hamalainen E, Gorbach S, et al: Dietary phytooestrogens and the menopause in Japan. *Lancet* 339:1233, 1992

27. Marmot MG, Davey Smith G: Why are the Japanese living longer? *Br Med J* 299:1547–1551, 1989

28. Mitsuda K: Kindaiteki boseikan no juyo to kenkei: kyoiku suru hahaoya kara ryosai kenbo e [The importance and transformation of the condition of modern motherhood: From education mother to good wife and wise mother]. In Wakita H (ed), *Bosei o tou [What is motherhood?]*. Kyoto, Jinbunshoin, 1985, 100–129

29. Nolte S, Hastings SA: The Meiji state's policy. In Bernstein GL (ed), *Recreating Japanese Women, 1600–1945*. 1991, Berkeley: University of California Press, 151–174

30. Mochida T: Editorial Comment, "Focus on the Family." *Japan Echo* 3:75–76, 1980

31. Eto J: The breakdown of motherhood is wrecking our children. *Japan Echo* 6:102–109, 1979

32. Lock M: New Japanese mythologies: Faltering discipline and the ailing housewife in Japan. *Am Ethnologist* 15:43–61, 1988

33. Higuchi K: Women at home. *Japan Echo* 12:51–57, 1985

34. Smith R: *Ancester Worship in Contemporary Japan*. Palo Alto, Stanford University Press, 1974

35. Lebra T: *Japanese Women: Constraint and Fulfillment*. Honolulu, University of Hawaii Press, 1984

36. Plath D: *Long Engagements*. Palo Alto, Stanford University Press, 1980, 139

37. Lock M: Ambiguities of aging: Japanese experience and perceptions of menopause. *Cult Med Psychiatry* 10:23–46, 1986

38. Yasui H, Hirauma N: Kanpo de kangaeru konenki shogai to wa donna mono deshoka [When using the thinking associated with herbal medicine, what are menopausal disorders?] *Fujin Gaho* September, 370–379, 1991

39. Nishimura H: *Josei to kanpo*. Osaka, Sogensha, 1981

40. Sheehan D: Discovery of the autonomic nervous system. *AMA Arch Neurol Psychiatry* 35:1081–1115, 1936

41. Lock M, Kaufert P, Gilbert P: Cultural construction of the menopausal syndrome: The Japanese case. *Maturitas* 10:317–332, 1988

42. Rosenberger N: The process of discourse: Usages of a Japanese medical term. *Soc Sci Med* 34:237–247, 1992

43. Laqueur T: *Making Sex: Body and Gender from the Greeks to Freud*. Cambridge, MA, Harvard University Press, 1990

44. Mainichi Daily News: Interview with Takuro Kobayashi, "Pill Researcher." February 23, 1987

45. Japan Pharmaceutical Manufacturer's Association: *Data Book, 1989*. Tokyo, 1990

46. Dierschke DJ: Temperature changes suggestive of hot flushes in rhesus monkeys: Preliminary observations. *J Med Primatol* 14:271–280, 1985

47. Blaffer-Hrdy S: "Nepotists" and "altruists": The behavior of old females among macaques and langur monkeys. In Amoss P, Harrell S (eds), *Other Ways of Growing Old*. Stanford, Stanford University Press, 1981, 59–76

48. Peccei JS: A hypothesis for the origin and evolution of menopause. *Maturitas* 21:83–89, 1995

49. Hill J, Magdalena Hurtado A: The evolution of premature reproductive senescense and menopause in human females: An evaluation of the grandmother hypothesis. *Hum Nature* 2:313–350, 1991

50. Sheehy G: *The Silent Passage: Menopause*. New York, Random House, 1992 (Portion first published in Vanity Fair, October 1991, 227)

51. Dewhurst J: *Integrated Obstetrics and Gynecology for Postgraduates*. Oxford, Blackwell, 1981

52. Howell N: *Demography of the Dobe! Kung*. New York, Academic Press, 1979

53. Weiss KM: Evolutionary perspective on human aging. In Amoss P, Harrell S (eds), *Other Ways of Growing Old*. Palo Alto, Stanford University Press, 1989, 25–58

54. Kertzer D, Laslett P: *Aging in the Past: Demography, Society and Old Age*. Berkeley, University of California Press, 1995

55. Koseisho Jinko Mondai KenkyUsho: *1989 Jinko no doko-Nihon to sekai [Where are the 1989 population trends going? Japan and the World]*. Tokyo, Kosei Tokei Kyokai, 1989

56. UNICEF: Central and Eastern Europe in Transition. Public Policy and Social Conditions. Crisis in Mortality, Health and Nutrition. Economies in Transition Studies. *Regional Monitoring Report*, No. 2. Florence, Italy, UNICEF, August 1994, 36

57. Zhang XH, Sasaki S, Kesteloot H: The sex ratio of mortality and its secular trends. *Int J Epidemiol* 24:720–729, 1995

58. Shorr E: The menopause. *Bull N Y Acad Sci* 16:453–474, 1940

59. Notelovitz M: Estrogen replacement-therapy: Indications, contra-indications agent selection. *Am J Obstet Gynecol* 161:1832–1841, 1989

60. Whitehead M: Longterm usage of hormones: Is it beneficial in preventing post-menopausal osteoporosis? *Midlife Wellness* 1:2–8, 1993

■ ■ ■ ■ ■ ■ ■ ■ ■

3   WHY NOT CALL MODERN MEDICINE "ALTERNATIVE"?

Don G. Bates

We begin this section on comparative medical systems with a selection that challenges the status of scientific medicine as the norm and standard in medical care and argues that modern medicine is instead an anomalous system of theory and practice when compared to all others across time and geography. These other medical systems share more features with each other than any one does with scientific medicine. They include the classical medical paradigm formed during Greek and Roman times and dominant until the nineteenth century, other forms of medicine such as homeopathy and hydrotherapy that emerged as alternatives to the heroic or allopathic medicine of nineteenth-century Europe and North America, and medical traditions elsewhere in the world, including Chinese, Unani, Ayurveda, and indigenous healing systems. In a seminal article in medical anthropology, George Foster (1976) classified the non-Western systems among these as naturalistic healing systems, as opposed to personalistic systems emphasizing sorcery and spiritual forces as causes of disease and other misfortunes (see selections 8, 9, 26; Finkler 1994).

The hegemony and uniformity of scientific medicine during the first three quarters of the twentieth century, especially in North America, were unusual compared to previous and subsequent medical pluralism there and in most societies (see the following selections, as well as Kaptchuk and Eisenberg 2001a; Kunitz 2002). The preeminence of scientific medicine was the result of vast successes in taming many infectious diseases made possible through the germ theory of disease. It was also related to the institutionalization of the profession, to the exclusion of other healers, through collaboration between the medical sector and the governments of many industrializing countries (see Starr 1982; Foucault 1973).

The features of scientific medicine that distinguish it from other systems are embedded in particular cultural, socioeconomic, and technological conditions. These features explain both the strengths of scientific medicine and the deficiencies that induce discontented patients to seek treatment from alternative systems they feel are more attentive to the humanistic elements of healing (see Kaptchuk and Eisenberg 2001b; Reilly 2001). In this selection, Bates argues that, paradoxically, as modern medicine recognizes these deficiencies and moves toward patients, it may do so at a cost to its effectiveness and lead patients to new sources of dissatisfaction.

Questions to keep in mind

What makes modern scientific medicine alternative, relative to the classical paradigm and other medical systems?

Source: Bates, Don G. "Why Not Call Modern Medicine 'Alternative'?" *Perspectives in Biology and Medicine* 43:4 (2000), 502–518. © The Johns Hopkins University Press. Reprinted with permission of The Johns Hopkins University Press.

How have changes in the relationship between expert and popular knowledge affected medical theory and practice?

In what ways has modern medicine retained or revived elements of the classical paradigm?

What are some of the features of scientific medicine about which people are dissatisfied?

Which of these features are central to the strength and success of scientific medicine?

What are some reasons for caution about promoting the public's recourse to alternative medicine?

What shape do you think scientific and alternative medical systems will take in the future?

We call it "modern" medicine, "scientific" medicine, and "biomedicine," but if the term weren't already in use, we could just as reasonably call it "alternative" medicine. That only becomes obvious, though, if we look at the orthodox medicine of the 20th century in a broader historical and cultural context. That is what I am going to do in this article, as a way of thinking about where modern medicine is going, and whether it has anything to learn from alternative medicine. To do this, however, I am not going to compare alternative medicine with modern medicine directly. Instead, I will contrast what I call the "classical" with the "20th-century" paradigm [1, 2]. But first I need to explain what I mean by *classical, 20th-century,* and *paradigm,* and how each of these relate to the practices we conventionally call "alternative."

As is well known, the history of medicine in the West has its roots in fifth-century BCE classical Greece, a tradition which was still responsible for the dominant orthodoxy in Europe and North America just two centuries ago [3]. Although it varied over the centuries, it is still reasonable to call all of it Hippocratic or Galenic medicine, based as it was on the texts and traditions surrounding the Hippocratic corpus of writings from around 400 BCE, and those of his devoted follower, Galen, 600 years later. Admittedly, the so-called scientific revolution of the 17th century had a big impact on the understanding of how the healthy body works, but it had very little effect on the way that medicine was practiced [4].

In fact, a distant descendent of that Hippo-Galenic tradition—sometimes called "heroic" medicine[1]—was the orthodoxy of the day, when, in the late 18th, but particularly early 19th centuries, some other forms of medicine began to appear: homeopathy, Thomsonianism, magnetic therapy, hydropathy, and later osteopathy, naturopathy, chiropractic, Christian Science, and the like—all in conscious opposition to that orthodoxy [5]. And it was this that gave rise to the label *alternative,* but alternative not so much to the new *scientific* medicine, which was only just developing, as to that earlier, *heroic* medicine, itself a version of the classical tradition. Moreover, that classical tradition became known as *allopathy,* initially to contrast it with homeopathy, but later, to distinguish heroic medicine from these various alternatives, in general.

So, first of all, it is this ancient Hippo-Galenic tradition, represented in the early 19th century by heroic medicine or allopathy that I am calling the *classical* paradigm. Nevertheless, I am going to argue that, despite their label, the alternative medicines maintained many similarities to the classical paradigm from which they were claiming to be different, while both alternatives and heroic medicine were radically different from the new medicine of the 20th century. Thus, I wish to claim, what we today call alternative medicines are really *remnants of* that classical paradigm, even though they started out claiming to be *alternatives to* it (and even if, since then, some of those so-called alternatives have evolved a bit from their 19th-century roots).

As for the *20th-century* paradigm, what I mean is the medical model that began to evolve over the course of the 19th century, and that came to dominate all medical practice to an extraordinary degree in the first two-thirds to three-quarters of the century just finished. Thus, on the one hand, I am using *20th-century* to cover *modern, scientific,* and *bio-,* but, on the other hand, I do not want the label to obscure the fact that public perceptions of that model have begun to change over the last two or three decades. For while the 20th-century model still overwhelmingly applies in practice, the public's attitude towards it does seem to be changing. More and more, the focus seems to be at least as much on the ways in which it falls short of our ideal as on its remarkable successes. And the renewed interest in alternatives seems to be an important symptom of that unease.

Moreover, on a more personal level, by *20th-century*, I also mean that model of medicine which I was taught in the 1950s and which had two particularly striking features: the remarkable domination of the germ theory as the chief model of a disease and its treatment; and the equally remarkable hegemony of scientific medicine, and corresponding lack of medical diversity, especially in North America. At best, some marginal alternatives were still lingering, and there was the odd movement like neo-holism among the scientifically trained [6]. But none of this in any way diminished the perceptual or institutional predominance of scientific medicine.

In general, then, these are what I mean by *classical* and *20th-century*. As for *paradigm*, I am of course thinking of Kuhnian paradigms, and I admit that that concept has been widely criticized (even by Kuhn, himself) for being too vague. Nevertheless, it continues to be a popular synonym for *model*, probably just because both terms *are* vague. And it is that vague feeling of meaningfulness that I want to capture here, rather than any precise, detailed claim about some rigorously coherent entity that "really" exists out there in the world or that is literally and faithfully subscribed to within some culture or era. Moreover, I am talking about these two paradigms predominantly as they are perceived by people in North America and Western Europe, where both the classical and the 20th-century paradigms have their historical and cultural roots. The sketches of these paradigms do not necessarily apply to the perceptions of people in other cultures, where other systems of traditional or indigenous medicine either have predominated or still do.

For that reason, I regard the following lists of characteristics of the two paradigms as largely stereotypes, caricatures, or superficial depictions of thinking and talking about health and disease over time. Indeed, given the remarkable complexities of the therapeutic act, such superficiality could

hardly be avoided. Even worse, I have deliberately biased them in favor of the classical paradigm, in order to capture what I sense to be the sources of public unhappiness with present-day scientific medicine, as manifest in the expanding popularity of alternatives. Nor do I want it to be thought that the sometimes radical contrasts that are offered here mean that I believe these paradigms to be polar opposites. Rather, I am only trying to capture the *relative* tendencies, emphases, and priorities that are commonly perceived to be characteristic of each.

But if these two paradigms are so obviously artifactual, why bother? Well, despite their limitations, I believe that each of them *does* capture important features of their actual practices. Moreover, because of that, and also because the comparison itself helps to focus attention on some of the implicit assumptions built into them, I believe that each model puts its finger on an internal coherence that each paradigm actually has and that most people intuit, a rough sense of rational cohesion that is reflected in the attitudes and conversations we have about them.

In other words, I think these paradigmatic sketches can be used *heuristically*, as credible tools which capture our thinking and discourse about the ways in which modern and alternative medical systems differ from each other. But I must emphasize that no one system of medical practice is going to fit neatly or exclusively into one paradigm or the other. I only want to claim that, if any particular system of medicine were to be measured against *all* of the features being listed here for each paradigm, the *cumulative* effect would be that it would much more clearly belong to the one than to the other.[2]

I shall therefore proceed as follows. First, a list of generally well-known characteristics of each paradigm will be sketched out under a series of headings: "health," "sickness," "diagnosis," "therapy," "theory" and "doctor/patient relationship." (Since surgery is not a consistent feature of the classical paradigm, its existence and significance will be noted only later.) Under each heading, these characteristics will be listed in brief, followed by some elaboration of those points which need a bit of further explanation. Even so, such comments will be kept to a minimum. Finally, after all the comparisons are finished, I will return to some broader comments concerning the two paradigms, including a few brief remarks about where we are now and where we might be going in the century ahead, so as to suggest a tentative answer to the question raised in the title.

Health

Classical Paradigm	20th-Century Paradigm
individual person	universal body
body and soul	materialistic body reducible (at least in principle) to physics and chemistry
body a container of humors and energies	highly complex machinery of minute, interacting parts and chemicals
ecological physiology	physiology focused on the interior of a universal body
dynamic equilibrium that is "natural," harmonious	"normal" structures, functions, and chemistry

---

COMMENTS

In the Western medical tradition, the relationship between body and soul is a long, complicated, and variable story. Suffice it to say that the word *soul* had a medical, physiological, or biological (itself a 19th-century term) meaning that preceded, and never exactly coincided with, any religious sense of that word [7]. Moreover, there was a complex and varying sense in which soul embraced mind, and it was not until Descartes, in the 17th century, that soul came more to be equated solely with the notion of mind, at least in medical discourse. Even after Descartes, and up into the 19th century, what had been explained by the medical concept of "soul" was still partly covered by the concept of vital forces, which either continued to possess mind-like capabilities, or, at the very least, were principled exceptions to the physical world [8].

Which brings me to one more comment having to do with mind. Throughout this scheme, it will be noticed that present-day psychiatry, psychotherapy, and psychoanalysis do not fit neatly into either paradigm, but seem to have a foot in both camps, and, in addition, tend to vary over time, and with respect to different kinds of illness [9,10, esp. pp. xxiff].

By ecological physiology, I mean a physiology that does not stop at the skin, but which is closely interactive, to varying degrees, with anything from the immediately surrounding environment to the distant planets and stars. Similarly, there is not only a language of equilibrium within the body, but harmony with the surrounding world to which the body is related—not just by causes, but, as a microcosm to the macrocosm, by virtue of correspondences.

And, finally, the concept of "normal," in the sense in which we use that term today—a statistical average with reference to a defined population—was only introduced into clinical medicine in the 19th century, in contrast to the ancient Greek tradition of "natural," a state perceived to be as nature intended it, based on our knowledge of what nature is like.

Sickness

Classical Paradigm	20th-Century Paradigm
illness (particular event)	disease (generic entity)
holistic	localistic
multiple, interacting causes, conditions, correspondences	"the" cause
imbalance	pathology, deviation from the norm

COMMENTS

Although, since the time of Aristotle, in the fourth century BCE, anatomy has been a part of the Western tradition, *anatomical* pathology only began to develop in the late 18th century. In other words, prior to that time, morphology—knowledge of the body's structure—had very little to do with concepts of how the person was sick, beyond the idea that the body is a container with an internal, dynamic landscape where disturbances occur. Granted, there were parts that could be broken or wounded (in which case they would sometimes be dealt with by the very limited capabilities of the largely separate practice of surgery), individual organs that could malfunction, or a set of regions whose interrelations could be disturbed. Or one particular area could be the initial site or final resting place of some process (such as rotting). Nevertheless, the focus for understanding and explaining most malevolent processes, and particularly those that would be the target of any therapy, was overwhelmingly on the humors, energies and psychic faculties that had no anatomy but instead perfused the body as a whole.

To say that 20th-century medicine is only interested in "the" cause is a good example of the stereotyping and oversimplification I warned about at the outset. Yet, under the influence of the germ theory, this notion of a discrete disease with a specific cause that could be targeted with a magic bullet has been the transcendent metaphor of medical thinking through most of the century. To see this kind of imaging at work, one only needs to think of talk (not now so common as it was) about "the" cause of cancer, as if cancer were a single disease with a single cause. Furthermore, insofar as our medicine has talked this way, it has reflected a way of thinking that, while not unique in the Western tradition, was nevertheless uncommon before the time of Pasteur. Even in the case of epidemic diseases, and even when contagion was accepted as part of the causal understanding (which, in traditional learned medicine, it rarely was), such "a" cause was almost always only one part of a much more complex story.

Diagnosis

Classical Paradigm	*20th-Century Paradigm*
know the person	know the disease
look at person/bodily discharges	hands-on, even invasive examination
symptoms	signs
describe the event	identify the cause
prognosis more important	prognosis less important

COMMENTS

Before the 19th century, when the findings of clinical examination (resulting from such things as the invention of percussion and mediate auscultation) were linked with those of the newly developed anatomical pathology found at autopsy, symptoms largely *were* the disease. That is to say, the explanatory distance between the observed phenomena and the underlying pathological condition was not nearly so great as the notion "sign" implies. The classic example, of course, was fevers: a fever was a kind of illness, not a symptom of it. In a few instances, though, such as the feel of the pulse or appearance of the urine, the classical tradition more closely approximated the present-day notion of signs. Hence, there were times when a diagnosis was made, just by looking at the urine, without the patient even being present.

But even pulse lore and uroscopy were not sources of signs in quite the same way, because the concept of illness, and therefore what it was that was being uncovered by these signs, was not that of a disease to be identified, not a thing to which the pulse or urine was pointing a finger. Rather, the diagnosis was the determining of a *condition*, an ongoing event, specific to the particular circumstances of the particular patient. Thus, diagnosis was very closely related to, and really just a part of prognosis which, in turn, did not merely mean a prediction as to the future course of the illness, but, often more importantly, a retrodiction of what had already taken place, and a recognition of the current phase of the ongoing process. In other words, in the classical paradigm, the crucial question is not what is "the" disease, but what is the particular process, and just where in that process was the healer entering into the picture?

Therapy

Classical Paradigm	*20th-Century Paradigm*
personal hygiene/prevention	treat the disease
manage, care for	eliminate the cause, cure
assist healing power of nature	often actively oppose nature
gentle, often herbal, dietary, "natural" (do no harm)	often aggressive, chemical, "artificial"
efficacy of *treatment* perceived by patient and doctor alike	efficacy of *outcome* measured and decreed by doctor

---

COMMENTS

Until the 17th century, the first priority of the professional, learned physician was to advise his (and it was "his" almost exclusively by this time) client on how to maintain health through the proper regimen which focussed on things like the six "nonnaturals": sleep and wakefulness, motion and rest, food and drink, air, evacuation and repletion, and the passions or emotions. Only after 1600 did the treatment of the ill begin to replace regimen for the healthy as the learned physician's first priority [11]. In many other medical traditions, too, prevention is more emphasized than cure. The primary goal of Ayurvedic medicine, for instance, is to lengthen life. Indeed, claims to cure with some particular herb or drug were often seen as quackery or charlatanism by the scholarly traditions of medicine.

Thus, in the late 17th century, the use of cinchona, or Peruvian bark, in the treatment of intermittent fevers was problematic because, rather than letting nature take her course, whereby the morbific matter would be discharged through sweats, the use of this new herb merely stopped up that natural process, a claim that was supported by and "explained" the fact that patients often suffered relapses. And even when the curing effects of quinine (the bark's "active" ingredient, we would say) could no longer be disputed, its effectiveness was still thought to arise from its "tonic" effect.

Moreover, in the classical paradigm, efficacy was demonstrated by the remedy's capacity to affect the body as it was intended to do—to purge, cause vomiting, let blood, heat, cool, etc. For example, when at the end of the 18th century, William Withering showed the value of foxglove (digitalis) in reducing "dropsy" (diuresis being clear evidence that the herb was "effective"), it was also noted that it slowed the pulse. Hence, around 1800, it became almost a panacea, especially for the tachycardia which was an essential feature (not merely a sign) of fevers, and it is not likely that the patient needed any reassurance from the doctor that it "worked"—i.e., slowed the pulse—especially when you consider the large doses that were often used [12, esp. pp. 400–412].

Theory

Classical Paradigm	*20th-Century Paradigm*
models of explanation largely based on world of patient's everyday experience	models of explanation largely based on a world not accessible to, nor understood by, the patient
exoteric or exotic	esoteric
richly imbued with psychic explanations	psychic explanations avoided as much as possible
theory driven by practice as much as the reverse	practice more driven by science than reverse

COMMENTS

Since any healing art has to do with the human body, and since, in any culture, that body's relationship to the outer world is central to any understanding of it, medicine and the ways of understanding the world are always closely associated [13, pp. 2–7]. So, even if the 20th-century body is ultimately made up of atoms and molecules, so too the Galenic body was made up of the four elements—earth, air, fire, water—and therefore that is not what really distinguishes the theoretical framework of the one from the other. Rather, what makes the difference are the entities and events out there in the world that are used to understand the body.

In the classical paradigm, the thoughts, ideas, images, reasons, analogies, and metaphors which were enlisted in order to understand and talk about the body in health and illness typically came out of such things as the common, everyday experiences of the kitchen and the rural countryside [14]. Cooking, fermenting, growing, rotting: these were the sorts of processes that furnished some of the most fundamental explanatory resources, along with winds, forces, energies, volitional or psychic faculties or agents. Then, of course, there were the larger models of society, such as hierarchy, governance, administration, and also features of the cosmos, such as astrology, that were used to explain the body, in health and disease, as, indeed to explain nature and the world itself. But whatever models of explanation were used, they had in common the fact that, quite apart from medicine or anyone's education, they were all part of a reality, or at least an easily provoked conceptual space, which the patient and healer were likely to share.

This is not to deny that, in any system where healing practices are left to a special group of people, those healers lay claim to special skills, knowledge, or techniques which are not accessible to their patients. Otherwise, they would have no reason to claim any special role as healers. But the realm from which any such special knowledge or techniques comes, in the classical paradigm, is still one that the layperson can easily imagine and, in some sense, lives in. Thus, even if an appeal is made to some drug or technique that is exotic (a characteristic that could enhance its potency or credibility), for the patient that is all that it is—novel, strange, or paradoxical—but it still exists within some familiar realm of folk physics and folk psychology [15]. Thus, putting cow dung on a wound might seem exotic, but, especially in a rural society that revered cows, using such material would be neither unfamiliar nor seem entirely unreasonable.

In the 20th-century paradigm, though, the conceptual space within which the body is understood, investigated, and manipulated is esoteric rather than exotic, being only comprehensible and accessible to a limited number of people with an adequate amount and type of (formal or informal) education, and with access (at least conceptually) to that exclusive world of the laboratory within which instrumental technology has helped both to create a radically different and uncommon conceptual space, and to apply its findings to medical care. Thus, not only is the subvisible world of molecular structures, chemical reactions, and physical forces inaccessible to common human experience, but even the *ways* by which that world is made accessible and understood are as esoteric as the phenomena themselves.

The computer offers a contemporary analogy. What is on the screen, or can be accomplished with the keyboard or a mouse, is now widely familiar, while what goes on behind the screen is not only unknown but unknowable—even unimaginable (apart from a few invisible "organs," like the memory or hard drive, which are understood at about the same crude level as most people understand, say, the liver). But whereas the computer is radically an example of the other, one's mind and body are the ultimate example of the self (and, in some ways, only "knowable" to the self), so that it is difficult to accept that our health problems can only be understood and managed by the medical equivalent of a computing engineer.

Moreover, it is not just a remote theoretical space that modern medicine occupies; it is also a realm within which the domain of common experience is often rejected *in principle*. Popularity and tradition, for example, have virtually no value as scientific evidence. The fact that acupuncture has been used for 2,000 years counts as zero evidence that it is effective. After all, bloodletting enjoyed an equally long tradition before it was dropped in the late 19th century. Moreover, such things as anecdotal accounts are dismissed *because* they are based on the testimony of personal experience. As a result, health, illness, and the outcomes of treat-ment are not so much experienced *by* as detected and reported *to* the patient.

Doctor–Patient Relationship

Classical Paradigm	*20th-Century Paradigm*
in home or office	in office, clinic, or hospital
doctor often dependent on patient	patient usually dependent on doctor

---

COMMENTS

In the 20th century, in order to be looked after by the doctor, the patient must not only enter a foreign conceptual landscape, as mentioned above, but she or he must usually meet the doctor in the doctor's own physical location. For these reasons alone, it is not surprising if the patient feels more passive and dependent. However, in most places where this kind of medicine is practiced, there is an added loss of leverage owing to the state's monopoly on the doctor's accreditation and third-party payment for her or his services. Ironically, therefore, where the term *patient* originally referred to someone to whom things happen (and as a result of which they fell ill), in the 20th century it has come more to imply someone who must passively accept what happens to her or him in the doctor's office.

This, then, completes our brief survey of these two paradigms. In depicting and commenting on the classical paradigm, I have depended largely on the Hippo-Galenic tradition, partly because it is the tradition of which I have been a student for many years, partly because it is, after all, the antecedent to 20th-century medicine. And I have also pointed out that the birth of alternative medicine was more in reaction to the early 19th-century heroic medicine version of that classical tradition, than it was to the newly developing 20th-century paradigm. In fact, in the later 19th century, many of the alternatives were competing with that traditional orthodoxy, and with each other, for the right to be seen *as*—or at least to be a *part of*—the new scientific medicine.

This brings me back to my earlier question about how alternative medicine belongs in the classical paradigm. A major problem, of course, is that *alternative* is a generic term which, even in the 19th century, covered a wide range of sectarian healing practices that were as likely to be in competition with each other as with allopathic medicine. But dealing with this issue in any detail is not really necessary, because at the superficial level at which this analysis is being done, all of them—homeopathy, Thomsonianism, naturopathy, osteopathy, and chiropractic, to name only the most prominent ones—were obviously far closer to the classical paradigm than to that of the 20th century. And, whatever changes they may have since gone through, they remain so. In other words, I offer the spelled-out lists of features of the classical paradigm as my argument for including various alternative medicines within it.

In fact, I would even go so far as to suggest that if compared under these lists of characteristics, all other major medical traditions—for instance, various Chinese, Unani, or Ayurvedic traditions, or other indigenous practices which have at least some theoretical component to "explain" and justify their practices—are sufficiently more like each other than any one of them is like modern medicine that they could all be comprehended under the rubric "classical paradigm."

This, then, is the reason why it seems to me that it would be quite reasonable to characterize this newest, 20th-century paradigm as the truly "alternative" medicine, in the sense that in any broad historical and cultural context, it is unique and exceptional. More than that, I would offer the very fact of the similarities among various members of the classical paradigm, over time and coming from very different cultures, as evidence that modern medicine is, by comparison, quite counter-intuitive. In this sense, it might even be called "alien" medicine.

Certainly it is hard to escape the feeling that scientific medicine represents a profound shift in every category of the therapeutic act. Had he wished to, Kuhn might well have used this revolution from the classical to the 20th-century paradigm as yet another illustration of his claim that a succeeding paradigm is "incommensurable" with that which preceded it at least in the sense that the meaning of pretty well every major term—*health, sickness, diagnosis,* and *therapy*—has to be revised before the shift can be clearly grasped. The two models do seem to be cognitive worlds apart.

On the other hand, if he were still with us, Kuhn might reasonably complain that modern medicine should not be characterized as a scientific paradigm in the first place. For, despite much rhetoric to the contrary, we all recognize that even scientific medicine is not and cannot be simply a branch of science, any more than business can be a branch of economics. At the very best, it is an applied science. Indeed, given the unique realm in which it functions—where science and the human being (and not just body) meet—it could never more than modestly reduce the contingencies of a particular human life to the universals upon which so much scientific knowledge depends. As was astutely noted many centuries ago, "There is no science of the individual" [16, p. 446].

Recently, and for slightly different reasons, this unusual modern, scientific form of medicine has also given rise to another term: *biomedicine* [17]. The *bio-*, of course, is meant to point to its strong biological, and therefore material and scientific, orientation, but the term is frequently used in a critical, even mildly pejorative sense, in order to emphasize (1) the ways in which this caricature fails to make adequate provision for the social and cultural complexities that form a part of any medical practice, complexities which not even modern scientific medicine can escape; and (2) the ways in which biomedicine itself fails to deal adequately with many of the things we find attractive about the classical paradigm, particularly its more humanistic, patient-oriented approach [18].

However, no claim is being made here that what we are calling the 20th-century paradigm is anything more than a caricature of modern medicine. Unquestionably, an adequate account would need to be infinitely more detailed and substantially modified, but I am more concerned here to capture common perceptions, and, even more, common *attitudes* towards it (especially among those who are unhappy with it) than I am to give a fully accurate or complete description of it. Second, the

way I have characterized it is consistent precisely with the views of those who use the term *biomedicine* in a pejorative way.

But having said that, I think it is only fair to pay a bit of attention to the positive side of the ledger. For instance, at least some notice should be taken of another major shift that has come about in the 20th century, a shift reflected in the fact that the term *medicine* has come to refer to much more than just the treatment of the individual patient depicted in the paradigms above. Public health largely came into being in the 19th century, and its powerful tools for preventing illness owe much to medicine in the sense of "medical science." As such, it has more than a little to do with the level of health attained today, a level which, at least in developed countries, has no equal in history.

Sadly, the value to health of such matters as clean water, pasteurized milk, vaccinations, etc., is all too visible when we look at those populations that do not have adequate supplies of them. On the other hand, those same measures tend to be quite invisible in our own surroundings. Just because they are so effective, we commonly assume that health is our default position, and prevention is unnoticed because, whenever it succeeds, it produces nonevents. And even when, at the individual level, we consciously pursue health—pay attention to vitamins, get some exercise, stop smoking—we are still inclined to overlook the fact that the knowledge upon which we base these practices also came from 20th-century medicine. In other words, some of the virtues of the classical paradigm—the emphasis on diet, healthy living, regimen, etc.—certainly have their equivalents in modern medicine but, in a world of mass media and general education, there isn't the same need for these issues to be addressed by the individual doctor dealing with an individual patient. In other words, they are neither contrary to, nor omitted from, the 20th-century paradigm: they are just handled by other means.

Now let's look a little more closely at the relationship between alternative and scientific medicine per se. In the 19th century, the word *alternative* was fostered by some of its own devotees (especially chiropractors) to suggest that the traditional, orthodox medicine of the day, and their own practices or theories, were mutually exclusive. Nor is that sense of *alternative* all that uncommon, today. Indeed, a potential patient may well think of *alternative* not only as meaning "mutually exclusive," but, what is more, rejoice in that "fact." For one thing, it provides a satisfying option for someone who feels skeptical or even antagonistic towards established medical practices, just because they *are* established. In addition, for patients who have conditions which established medicine has been unable to resolve, different, even contradictory, therapeutic practices may appeal, just because they are alternative. After all, patients are notoriously pragmatic—they value effects more than explanations—and the wider the choice on the smorgasbord of health care, the happier they are likely to be.

On the other hand, even among caregivers, a feeling that different medical systems are mutually exclusive has never been universal. Later in the 19th century, for instance, many physicians who subscribed either to the old traditional orthodoxy, or, more commonly, to the evolving but not yet very effective new scientific orthodoxy, combined either one or both of these with homeopathy in a combination they called "eclectic" medicine. Even today, combinations of alternative and orthodox practices are becoming more and more common in North America. And at all times, as the use of the term "complementary" in place of "alternative" suggests, there have been advocates of harmony, or at least mutual tolerance in an atmosphere of medical pluralism.

Indeed, in most societies and throughout history, the usual pattern has been one of medical pluralism, in which a diversity of medical practices—some more, others less compatible—have coexisted. Therefore, the previously mentioned hegemony of scientific medicine through the first three-quarters of the 20th century, especially in North America, has been somewhat atypical [e.g.,19]. And its unusualness is even more striking, given that things were largely in the reverse in the 19th century, when, given the political climate of the new republic, medical pluralism was probably more widespread in America than it was in Britain and Europe. So if, in the years to come, alternative medicine becomes more common and more accepted once again, that should perhaps be seen more as a return to the way things have historically been, rather than as some disturbing fragmentation of, or departure from, the scientific ideal.

That having been said, it must still be conceded that some people, particularly those closely connected with science in general and scientific medicine in particular, will remain uneasy about the presence of alternative practices, to the extent that they have no basis in science. Even if the 20th-century paradigm lacks or actively ignores certain features of the classical paradigm—such as being more patient-oriented; being more open to a role for the mind, soul, or whatever; applying to a wider range of conditions for which people feel they need help; and so on—still, there is the worry that (1) people with serious conditions may be diverted towards treatment that is not effective in cases where modern medicine could have helped; (2) without scientific scrutiny, some alternative treatments might prove to be harmful; and (3) also because of the lack of scientific regulation, patients risk being exploited by fraud.

But again something needs to be said about the other side of the coin. Stimulated to some extent by this new enthusiasm for alternatives, modern medicine has recently been taking more notice of its own shortcomings with respect to patient satisfaction, and this has led to greater attention to things like the "patient-centered approach" to practice, a more patient-oriented "outcomes research," and a more positive interest in the possible virtues of the placebo effect [20,21]. Thus, in the years ahead, the 20th-century paradigm may well shift somewhat more towards the classical paradigm, at least with respect to patient-centeredness.

But just how far *can* scientific medicine go in that direction? There are at least two problems. The first has to do with the fact that the therapeutic act is notoriously complex. Who—the doctor or the patient—is to say that a person is ill? That she or he has been "cured" or helped in some way? That the healer's practices are responsible for that improvement? Within what time frame and social context are those effects to be measured? And according to what and—just as importantly—whose criteria?

It is with respect to questions like these that the difference in orientation of the two paradigms matters most to people. After all, patients are the ones who are suffering and who are receiving the care, so shouldn't they be the ones to decide the answers to these questions? Certainly, from a marketing point of view they should, and, in the more consumer-oriented classical paradigm, they do. Yet it has been a fundamental strength of the 20th-century paradigm, and a coherent part of its very nature, that it tends to downplay or even to disregard the kinds of criteria upon which patients would like to provide *their* answers to these questions, particularly when they conflict with, or at least distort those that are scientifically and technologically based. Thus, it seems that by its very nature, a biologically and scientifically oriented medicine *cannot avoid* falling short of full patient satisfaction, however much it may try to do otherwise.

The other problem is that not only does the very nature of scientific medicine make it hard for it to be as patient-oriented as its customers would like, that same nature is in some ways driving it in the opposite direction. First, there is its continuing (because very successful and scientifically necessary) focus on a materialistic, or at least non-psychical, concept of the body, i.e., its strongly "biological" rather than "psychological" orientation (even with regard to the study of the mind, itself); second, there is a concomitant trend towards an ever-greater reliance on instruments and technology as resources for studying health and disease, as well as for examining and treating the patient; and third, the increasing use of artificial substances, of natural substances in artificial ways, of genetic engineering, of organ transplants, and even of artificial replacements for or additions to body parts. All of these developments have a great potential for adding to the effectiveness of scientific medicine, while simultaneously aggravating our doubts about its humanistic qualities. Moreover, as that last mentioned feature begins to shift biomedical science more and more from just *discovering* our nature towards also *creating* it, it will also increasingly challenge the traditional, almost sacred, boundary lines that have so far defined what it is that makes a human, human. A brave new world could still be on the way.

While there is obviously much that can and should be done to improve modern medicine's patient friendliness, there ultimately may be an inherent limit to what it can do in this regard, a limit that will force modern medicine to choose, on occasion, between being more humanitarian and being more effective. If that is so, it truly is an alien medicine.

In the long run, though, it could be that future generations of humans will be much more comfort-able with a strongly biological understanding of their bodies and with the technological means of caring for it. They may, from our perspective today, become more like aliens themselves. In fact, in the era of the Internet, when vastly increased numbers of people will have ever-increasing opportunities to learn about their biological selves and the sciences of life, perhaps the attitude of the patient will migrate more towards scientific medicine than that of medicine towards the patient. Certainly it is already the case that, despite a certain amount of displeasure with biomedicine, there is a vast if often silent support for it, evident in the fact that people are much more unhappy when that medicine is not fully available to them than when it fails to live up to their expectations. Conversely, almost all support for alternative medicine is based not on any wish for it to replace scientific medicine, but rather for it to become an increasingly complementary or additional medicine. In other words, maybe we are living in an era of paradigm shift.

Why not call modern medicine "alternative"? Because we can't. It has already become the name for the other side of the coin. Besides, in the institutional sense, homeopathy, naturopathy, acupuncture, and all the rest certainly are "alternatives" to the established version of medical care. But none of this should prevent us from noticing that in a broader historical and cultural context, using *alternative* to describe the 20th-century paradigm is warranted, at least in the deeper sense of its being so unlike all the other forms of medicine that have ever existed. In some sense, it is incommensurable, not just with the classical paradigm, but more fundamentally with our most basic intuitions about who we are, intuitions which are more clearly reflected in all those other healing traditions across many centuries and cultures.

What can we learn from alternative medicine? We already know that its patient-centeredness accounts for much of its popularity, and we are also aware that, paradoxically, that same patient-centeredness is not always in the best interests of the patient's health, whatever its impact on the patient's attitude. But what I have been trying to point out is that that paradox also works in the other direction. Part of what makes modern medicine so effective unavoidably includes precisely those elements that sometimes make it patient-unfriendly. In other words, at least in our present world, effectiveness and patient-friendliness may, at certain points, be mutually exclusive. To the extent that this is so, merely recognizing the gap between patient and doctor will not necessarily lead to its being closed.

On the other hand, perhaps in the new millennium there will be a greater convergence between our intuitions about ourselves and how science has come to know us, a convergence that might result, for instance, from such things as the greater materialization of the mind, combined with a scientific psychology based on some sophisticated version of the theories of emergence, complexity, or maybe even chaos. Truly an alien medicine for an alien people!

NOTES

1. "Heroic" medicine did not involve any basic change in theory or practice, but rather the vigorously increased application of such things as purging and bloodletting, as advocated, for example, by Benjamin Rush.

2. It is true, for example, that the Paracelsianism of the late 16th and 17th centuries has several characteristics that are more akin to their counterparts in the 20th-century model—the conception of diseases as entities, the use of metallic therapies, the prominence of cure over care, etc.—than to the classical paradigm to which, by implication, it is being assigned here. And, undoubtedly, of all the variations to the Hippo-Galenic tradition, Paracelsianism is probably the farthest from the classical and the closest to the 20th-century paradigm. But if *all* of its features are compared, I think it will still be found to be closer to the former than to the latter.

REFERENCES

1. Rosenberg, C. E. The therapeutic revolution: Medicine, meaning, and social change in 19th-century America. *Persp. Biol. Med.* 20:485–506, 1977.

2. Warner, J. H. *The Therapeutic Perspective: Medical Practice, Knowledge, and Identity in America, 1820–1885.* Cambridge: Harvard Univ. Press, 1986.

3. Conrad, L., et al. *The Western Medical Tradition.* Cambridge: Cambridge Univ. Press, 1995.

4. Wear, A. Medical practice in late 17th- and early 18th-century England: Continuity and union. In *The Medical Revolution of the 17th Century,* edited by R. French and A. Wear. Cambridge: Cambridge Univ. Press, 1989.

5. Gevitz, N. Unorthodox medical theories. In *Companion Encyclopedia of the History of Medicine,* edited by W. F. Bynum and R. Porter. London: Routledge, 1993. 603–33.

6. Lawrence, C., and G. Weisz, eds. *Greater Than the Parts: Holism in Biomedicine, 1920–1950,* edited by C. Lawrence and G. Weisz. New York: Oxford Univ. Press, 1998.

7. Walker, D. P. Medical *spirits* and God and the soul. In *Spiritus,* edited by M. Fattori and M. Bianchi. Rome: Ateneo, 1984.

8. Hall, T. S. *History of General Physiology.* Vol. 2. Chicago: Univ. of Chicago Press, 1975.

9. Engel, G. L. The need for a new medical model: A challenge for biomedicine. *Science* 196:129–36, 1977.

10. American Psychiatric Assn. *Diagnostic and Statistical Manual of Mental Disorders.* 4th ed. Washington, DC: American Psychiatric Assn., 1994.

11. Cook, H. J. The new philosophy and medicine in seventeenth-century England. In *Reappraisals of the Scientific Revolution,* edited by D. Lindberg and R. S. Westman. Cambridge: Cambridge Univ. Press, 1990.

12. Ackerknecht, E. Aspects of the history of therapeutics. *Bull. Hist. Med.* 36:389–419, 1962.

13. Bates, D. Scholarly ways of knowing: An introduction. In *Knowledge and the Scholarly Medical Traditions,* edited by D. Bates. Cambridge: Cambridge Univ. Press, 1995.

14. Trawick, M. Writing the body and ruling the land: Western reflections on Chinese and Indian medicine. In *Knowledge and the Scholarly Medical Traditions,* edited by D. Bates. Cambridge: Cambridge Univ. Press, 1995.

15. Bates, D. Closing the circle: How Harvey and his contemporaries played the game of truth, part I. *Hist. Sci.* 36:213–32, 1998.

16. Temkin, O. *The Double Face of Janus.* Baltimore: Johns Hopkins Univ. Press, 1977.

17. Fabrega, H. J. *Disease and Social Behavior: An Interdisciplinary Perspective.* Cambridge: MIT Press, 1974.

18. Lock, M., and D. Gordon, eds. *Biomedicine Examined.* Dordrecht: Kluwer Academic Press, 1988.

19. Maretzki, T. W., and E. Seidler. Biomedicine and naturopathic healing in West Germany: A historical and ethnomedical view of a stormy relationship. *Culture Med. Psychiat.* 9:383–421, 1985.

20. Clancy, C. M., and J. M. Eisenberg. Outcomes research: Measuring the end result of health care. *Science* 282:245–46, 1998.

21. Kaptchuk, T. J. Powerful placebo: The dark side of the randomised clinical trial. *Lancet* 351:1722–25, 1998.

■ ■ ■ ▨ ▨ ▨ ■ ■ ■

4 CONCEPTS OF ARTHRITIS IN INDIA'S MEDICAL TRADITIONS: AYURVEDIC AND UNANI PERSPECTIVES

Judy F. Pugh

The Indian medical traditions Ayurveda and Unani are examples of the classical or naturalistic medical systems described by Bates in selection 3. This selection compares and contrasts these two healing traditions as a demonstration of the resilience of ancient medical systems and their adaptability to today's conditions of medical pluralism. Through an analysis of explanatory models of both patients and healers, the selection shows how the experience and interpretation of a given disorder may vary significantly across cultures and medical traditions. It also provides detailed descriptions of two humoral medical systems, which have many connections to humoral beliefs and practices elsewhere in Asia, South and Central America, the Middle East, and the folk traditions of Europe and North America (see Foster 1994; selection 33).

Humoral medical systems, including Ayurveda and Unani, tend to consider rheumatic disorders to be cold and windy diseases calling for treatment with hot remedies. This seemingly simple model is part of a complex field of ideas in India about the body and its internal architecture and flows, the individual constitution, the effects of atmospheric and climatic conditions, and the impact of immoderate behaviors. Such ideas originate in ancient medical knowledge and explain current ailments such as pinching pain from excessive wind, swollen joints from a combination of heat and wind, or stiffness in joints rooted in the same forces that cause excessive phlegm in wintertime and sicknesses such as coughs and colds.

Bates notes that those who use classical medical systems are concerned primarily with prevention and care of the whole body/mind and therefore are loath to make claims about curing. Pugh shows that healers who practice Ayurveda and Unani talk with arthritis patients not just about their health problems but also about their digestion, constitution, and personal habits. Treatment emphasizes the stimulation of digestion, the avoidance of wind and cold sources, and the production of heat through medicated oils, diet, and oral medications. Diagnosis and treatment are based on the same humoral model: the care of rheumatic disorders or any other health condition requires substances and behaviors that are opposite to the causes. In contrast, although biomedicine offers treatments and is concerned predominantly with their effectiveness, at present it lacks a comprehensive model that can explain the causes of rheumatism and arthritis.

Questions to keep in mind

In what ways do the models described by Pugh intersect with classical medical systems outlined by Bates?

How do the beliefs and practices of Ayurveda and Unani relative to joint disorders relate to humoral ideas about the body and about behavioral, constitutional, and environmental causes of arthritis and rheumatism?

Are you familiar with any humoral beliefs in North America or Europe?

Source: Reprinted from *Social Science and Medicine,* Vol. 56, Pugh, J. F., "Concepts of Arthritis in India's Medical Traditions: Ayurvedic and Unani Perspectives," Pages 415–424, Copyright (2003), with permission from Elsevier.

What are some differences between Ayurveda and Unani, in general and in relation to joint disorders? How do beliefs about joint disorders in Ayurveda and Unani conflict or converge with those of bio-medicine?

INTRODUCTION

Arthritis and rheumatism form a complex array of disorders. They are significant sources of suffering and disability, and their prevalence and impact are increasing all around the globe as people are living longer lives. These ailments, inscribed in the firm terrain of joints, muscles, and connective tissues, made visible through X-rays and measured bio-chemically through quantifiable traces in the blood, might seem to correspond to the category of "naturally given" disorders, but in fact, they may have quite different conceptualizations in different socio-cultural settings and health-care traditions. The cultural and therapeutic constructions of these widespread and often puzzling afflictions remain to be fully explored by anthropologists and social scientists.

The social sciences have largely neglected the cultural construction of arthritis and its place in plural medical environments. The anthropological literature contains brief references to concepts and treatments of arthritis, rheumatism, and joint disorders in many different societies, from hunter-gatherers to peasant farmers to modern urbanites, but these descriptions are usually embedded in studies devoted to other aspects of health and ill-ness or to social life more generally.[1] Some medical anthropological and sociological work on chronic pain in the US contains interpretations of arthritis patients' suffering and its personal meanings (Good, 1992) and short discussions of patients' body images and metaphors related to back and joint pain (Zborowski, 1969). Sociological, psy-chological, and health services studies of arthritis in the US tend to concentrate on the disorder's dis-ability-related effects on people's social relation-ships and self-esteem (see, for example, Goodenow, Reisine, & Grady, 1990), and they oc-casionally include reports on arthritis in ethnic communities (see Husaini & Moore, 1990). They have not, however, widely examined cultural con-structions of arthritis or patient illness models. Anthropological studies of culture and disability in various third-world settings might offer valu-able insight into local understandings of joint dis-orders but these have mostly bypassed arthritis in favor of such pressing problems as blindness, deaf-ness, leprosy, and extreme physical deformities (see, for instance, Ingstad & Whyte, 1995). Several biomedically and biologically oriented anthropol-ogy projects have examined various joint-related topics, including orthopedic problems in Nepal (Anderson, 1984), Mexican bone-setters' treat-ments of musculoskeletal disorders (Anderson, 1987), and the efficacy of Tibetan arthritis reme-dies in north India (Ryan, 1997), but local cate-gories, symptoms, and meanings of arthritis and joint disorders have not been explored.

An anthropological approach to these under-studied aspects of arthritis begins with some basic questions. How do various cultural traditions and therapeutic systems conceptualize rheumatic problems and their treatments? What types of arthritic and joint conditions do they identify, and what range of symptoms and causes do they em-phasize? What sorts of principles shape their ther-apeutic concepts and their treatment practices? Focusing on these kinds of topics takes us into local health-care settings as well as offering an opportunity to think cross-culturally and cross-medically about rheumatic disorders.

Among major therapeutic systems, biomedi-cine stands out for its clinically detailed model of rheumatic disease.[2] Its researchers have developed a fine-grained knowledge of joint structure and a sophisticated diagnostic technology to identify more than one hundred rheumatic disorders. Its disease domain includes osteoarthritis, rheuma-toid arthritis, gout, and fibromyalgia, which may variously underlie such common conditions as lower-back pain, a frozen shoulder, neck pain, sci-atica, hand and knee pain, along with an array of muscle aches and joint pains popularly known as rheumatism. Rheumatologists regard genetics, aging, injury, and abnormal use as basic causes of rheumatism,[3] and they usually minimize or discount the etiological effects of climate and food, although they acknowledge that cold or damp conditions and some foods may exacerbate patients' discomfort.[4] Treatments focus heavily on pain control, primarily through oral analgesics and secondarily through various physical therapies; joint replacement surgery is now offered as another treatment option.

Humoral medical systems, which operate alongside biomedicine in many parts of the world, present a very different perspective on arthritis and rheumatism.[5] These traditions, which were developed in Ancient Greece, the Islamic Near East, India, and China, have spread across continents and oceans through trade, migration, and conquest. Widely considered natural and holistic, they connect illness to people's daily habits and activities, their diet, their bodily constitution, the weather and the environment. Today humoral ideas and practices are found in various forms all across Asia, the Middle East, and South and Central America, as well as in folk practices and immigrant communities in Europe and North America, and in the burgeoning field of a complementary medicine in the West.

Humoral traditions typically characterize rheumatic disorders as "cold", sometimes "windy"—conditions best remedied with "hot" medicines and external applications of heat. Medical anthropologists have reported these kinds of humoral concepts in a range of societies. For example, in Tzintzuntzan, Mexico, "cold" is considered the cause of rheumatism and calls for "hot" substances such as rosemary in alcohol to be rubbed onto the joints (Foster, 1988, p. 125). In Morocco, the "coldness" of wind and water may penetrate the body and enter the bones and organs, giving rise to arthritis, rheumatism, neuralgia, sciatica, migraine, paralysis, and other chronic degenerative illnesses (Greenwood, 1992, pp. 294, 299). And in Taiwan, many postpartum women, who are already in a "cold" condition, will avoid contact with cold wind and water for a month, since these elements can enter the body and later contribute to arthritis and rheumatism, literally "wind-and-moisture disease," as well as other chronic aches and pains (Pillsbury, 1978, pp.

13–14). These widely held humoral concepts hold valuable keys to the cross-cultural study of rheumatic disorders and warrant closer anthropological inquiry.

India (and South Asia more generally) is an important region in which to pursue humoral constructions of arthritis and joint disorders. Many Indians suffer from joint pain and rheumatic problems; osteoarthritis is widespread and rheumatoid arthritis, the far less prevalent but more incapacitating form of the disease, affects an estimated ten million Indians, 80% of which are women (Times of India, 1999). Arthritis and rheumatism sufferers seek treatment from the country's diverse health-care specialists: biomedical physicians, humoral practitioners, homeopaths, and various types of folk healers. Humoral concepts of illness are widespred in the region, and Ayurveda, the classical Hindu tradition, and Unani, the Greco-Arab healing tradition, form a significant component of the health care system. Their classic texts describe various types of rheumatic problems, and their pharmacopoeias often contain more remedies for rheumatism and arthritis than for any other ailment except stomach and intestinal problems (see, for example, Nadkarni, 1976).

Here, as elsewhere, however, the anthropological literature lacks full-fledged descriptions of these humoral concepts. Brief comments in numerous ethnographie and medical anthropological studies mention Indians' ideas of rheumatic afflictions as "cold, windy" ailments caused by cold, windy foods, cooling activities, or environmental cold to be treated with heating medicaments and external applications of heat (see, for instance, Lewis, 1965; Carstairs, 1967; Henry, 1977; Pool, 1987; Nichter, 1987). Tabor's (1981) work on Ayurvedic practitioners in Gujarat contains a valuable description of their approaches to hospitalized arthritis patients; Ramesh and Hyma (1981, p. 76) mention that some Ayurvedic practitioners in the city of Madras (Chennai) specialize in rheumatism; Wolffers (1988, p. 54) reports on Sri Lankan rheumatism sufferers' strategies of using home remedies first, and then, if necessary, of consulting biomedical doctors and Ayurvedic physicians in roughly equal numbers. The present paper aims to add to this anthropological literature with a detailed descriptive account of arthritis in India's Ayurvedic and Unani medical traditions.

METHODS: A POLYSYNTHETIC APPROACH

Together Unani and Ayurveda constitute the heart of India's humoral medical heritage. However, scholars have tended to examine them separately and to focus primarily on Ayurveda.[6] The present account covers both of these traditions and their interconnections, suggesting that this broader unit of study more fully represents the region's humoral constructions of arthritis (and other illnesses). The paper conceptualizes Ayurveda and Unani as a polysynthetic field of ideas and practices: it argues that their perspectives show numerous parallels and convergences and blend into a common humoral currency that circulates between humoral practitioners and their ethnically diverse patient-clienteles.

This polysynthetic approach emphasizes the complex concepts of illness and healing that inform Ayurvedic and Unani constructions of rheumatic disorders. Hot/cold *are* important features here, but concentrating on these qualities and their classificational polarities does not adequately reveal the more complex nature of these traditions' illness constructions. Works by Zimmermann (1979, 1987) and Tabor (1981) on Ayurveda and by Good (1994) on Greco-Islamic medicine have demonstrated the importance of the somatic frameworks and physiological models that inform these humoral traditions and their hot/cold features. Following these perspectives, this discussion will describe constructions of arthritis by tracing a conceptual network in which humors and hot/cold qualities intergrade with somatic and physiological models, etiological ideas, and therapeutic principles. The convergence of Ayurveda and Unani is manifested throughout.

Research data derive primarily from anthropological fieldwork on Unani and Ayurveda in the New Delhi/Old Delhi metropolitan area, from humoral medical texts, and from various secondary sources on health and illness. Classical Ayurvedic and Unani works by Caraka (1976), Susruta (1980), and Ibn Sina (1930) and writings by leading contemporary practitioners provide foundational concepts of rheumatic disorders. Data on individual humoral practitioners and their approaches to arthritis and joint-pain patients come from field studies of two *hakims* and one *vaid*

in the New Delhi/Old Delhi area. These practitioners include: (1) Nur Mohammad, an elderly, informally trained Muslim *hakim* associated with the shrine of a Muslim saint and serving a clientele of Muslims, Hindus, and Sikhs; (2) Abdur Rahim, a middle-aged, formally trained Muslim *hakim* with a clinic in Old Delhi and a clientele of Muslims, Hindus, and Sikhs; (3) Om Prakash, a middle-aged Hindu *vaid* with a pharmacy and clinic in New Delhi and primarily Hindu and Sikh patients. Research activities involved discussions with these practitioners, observations of their clinical practices, and informal interactions with some of their patients. Participation in Muslim family life and everyday activities in a mixed Muslim/ Sikh/Hindu area of Old Delhi provide additional insight into lay concepts of rheumatic illness. The South Asian anthropological literature and several short field projects on Ayurvedic arthritis medicines in the US contribute supporting materials.

THE DOMAIN OF "ARTHRITIC DISORDERS" IN AYURVEDA AND UNANI

Rheumatic disorders have an ancient presence in the subcontinent's medical traditions. Zysk (1991, pp. 92–96) has found that "wind diseases" were well known in the time of early Buddhist monastic medicine and other heterodox therapeutic traditions around 400 B.C. These "wind afflictions" included "wind in the limbs" and "wind in the joints" (Zysk, 1991, pp. 92–96). Zysk offers that "the emphasis placed on wind (*vata*) points to the significant place it held in the early formulations of an etiology based on 'peccant,' or faulty, humors" (1991, p. 96). Treatments such as bloodletting, administration of decocted oil, and sweating were intended to remove noxious wind and other harmful substances.

Some two thousand years ago, the Ayurvedic physicians Caraka and Susruta elaborated the category of "wind diseases." These numerous disorders typically involve various forms of pain, stiffness, and blockage, including joint, bone, and muscle problems, paralysis, deafness, lockjaw, and spasmodic disorders, as well as certain types of stomach and intestinal disturbances, chest pains, and headaches (see Caraka, 1976, pp. 363–367). The category known as "wind in the joints" constitutes Ayurveda's primary analogue to biomedicine's categories of "rheumatism" and "arthritis." Caraka's list of these ailments includes pain and stiffness in the hands, neck, back, waist, calf, ankle, and foot, along with two types of sciatica and two types of gout (Caraka, 1976, pp. 272, 353). Susruta identifies rheumatic conditions of neck stiffness, sciatica, swelling of the knee joints, loss of movement in the shoulder joints, contraction of arm and leg muscles, various conditions of numbness and paralysis, lameness, deafness, and spinal deformities (Susruta, 1980, p. 53).[7]

Nearly one thousand years ago, the preeminent Greco-Islamic physician Ibn Sina, or Avicenna, built on the legacy of Galen and Hippocrates and their concepts of humoral disorders. He discusses causes and cures for rheumatism, joint pain, limb pain, back pain, sciatica, gout, neuralgia, and ostalgia (Ibn Sina, 1930, pp. 191, 193, 422), and he identifies arthritis, sciatica, and gout as chronic (Ibn Sina, 1930, pp. 472, 493).[8]

Present-day terms for arthritis, rheumatism, and joint disorders reflect the contemporary mix of humoral and biomedical influence in the region. Many north Indians use various Hindi and Urdu terms that translate as "joint disorder" (*gathiya*, from *ganth*, "joint"), "pain in the joints" (*joron men dard*), "wind disease" (*vata rog, badi*), or simply "wind" (*vata, vayu, bai, bad*). These terms recur in Hakim Nur Mohammad's often lively discussions with Muslim, Hindu, and Sikh patients as he reclines on an old rope-strung bed in the shady portico of the saint's shrine; in Vaid Om Prakash's quiet interactions with the Hindu and Sikh customers who come to consult him about their ailments and buy medicines and household sundries; and in Hakim Abdur Rahim's cut-and-dried interactions with the steady flow of Hindu, Muslim, and Sikh patients in his Old Delhi clinic. Leading *vaids* and *hakims* and ordinary practitioners may also use technical humoral terms, such as "wind in the joints" (*sandhivat*), "wind of internal wastes" (*amavat*), and "pain in the joints" (*waja'-e-mafasil*), in more formal explanations of illness categories. English speakers refer to "rheumatism" and "arthritis" and sometimes mention specific problems such as "lumbago," "gout," "sciatica," and "spondylosis." Under the influence of bio-

medicine, humoral practitioners and laypersons alike may also refer to "osteoarthritis" and "rheumatoid arthritis."

"Wind" is obviously a key concept in these humoral perspectives. Both Unani and Ayurvedic practitioners and many laypersons regard wind as a natural component of the body. The Ayurvedic system involves the humors wind, bile, and phlegm, as well as blood and other substances, and the Unani system works with the humors yellow bile, black bile, phlegm, and blood, along with wind and other fluids. Wind circulates through organs, tissues, joints, and muscles, and it is considered essential to bodily health and normal physiological processes. It can be pathogenic, however, when it becomes excessive or disturbed ("deranged," in local parlance), or when it settles in various organs and joints. In the three Delhi clinics under study, wind is one of the most frequent illness references and the one most often cited in discussions of joint pain and other arthritic conditions. These health-related concepts of wind extend to rural areas of north India as well. Villagers in Uttar Pradesh, for instance, "consider 'wind' to be a more potent cause of illness than either phlegm or bile" (Opler, 1963, p. 35), and Rajasthani villagers have a notion of wind as "a sort of gas, trapped within the bodily tissues, which moves from place to place, giving rise to swellings, aches and pains" (Carstairs, 1967, p. 82).

Arthritis and rheumatism are generally considered "cold" disorders. The idea of coldness reflects symptomatically in joint stiffness and etiologically in the association of rheumatic disorders with cold influences. Cold chills the joints and the body itself and promotes the production of excess internal wind. Other cold humors—phlegm in Ayurveda and Unani, and black bile in Unani—may also contribute to these disorders. For example, Caraka links sciatica to disturbances of phlegm and wind (Caraka, 1976, p. 353); Ibn Sina associates sciatica with black bile (Ibn Sina, 1930, p. 171); and present-day practitioners also regard these humors as possible causes.

While "cold" predominates in most rheumatic conditions, "hot" humors and substances may also be involved. These hot fluids include blood and bile in Ayurveda, and blood and yellow bile in Unani, and in each case, they can combine with wind to produce warm, swollen, painful joints.

These symptoms are typical of gout (known as "wind-blood" or "wind-bile" in Ayurveda) and other types of rheumatic swellings, including those now associated with rheumatoid arthritis. *Hakim* Abdur Rahim, who is familiar with many biomedical concepts, understands rheumatoid arthritis as an inflammatory joint condition that is typically associated with internal derangements, and Unani researchers Mohiuddin, Sultana, and Khadri (1977, p. 10) mention types of arthritis, including rheumatoid arthritis, that are accompanied by fever and marked by warm skin in the affected areas. These perspectives concur with Tabor's findings that Gujarati *vaids* distinguish rheumatic conditions with fever, and that some *vaids* include rheumatoid arthritis in this category (Tabor, 1981, p. 446). I would note, too, that wind's traditional etiological linkage to deformity and paralysis enhances its conceptual fit with the symptoms of rheumatoid arthritis.

In Unani and Ayurvedic clinics in the Delhi area and in people's everyday experiences, common symptoms of rheumatic disorders include pain, stiffness, restricted movement, and sometimes swelling, frequently affecting the hands and fingers, shoulders, neck, low back (or "waist"), buttocks, knees, legs, and feet. Sufferers may report one or more affected areas and regard them as variously involving joints, muscles, bones, nerves, or tendons.

Symptoms of joint stiffness may be expressed as problems of restricted movement and limited mobility. People may complain of difficulties in sitting down, bending, standing up, and lifting and grasping objects, as well as limitations in walking, traveling, and working. People may also describe the joints themselves, for example, referring to joints and muscles as "stiff." Pool (1987) reports Gujarati tribal villagers' references to the "frozen" or "congested joints" associated with rheumatism, and he notes the parallels between these problems and the "congestion" typical of colds and coughs.

Rheumatic pains have their own local expressions. Patients may complain of a single localized pain, multiple pains, and sometimes a more diffuse ache described as "body pain." "Pinching pains" literally "pinch" joints and muscles, and "piercing pains" involve "sharp," "pricking" sensations within joints or in the surrounding skin. Early Buddhist healers' disease-category "wind in the joints" literally meant "wind piercing every joint" (Zysk, 1991, p. 95), and present-day Ayurvedic physicians regard pain that "pierces like needles" as characteristic of rheumatic disorders and other "wind diseases."[9] Some rheumatic problems have their own distinctive aches, such as "stitch pain" in the side or back, and "gripping pain" in the buttock and leg in sciatic conditions. Like other forms of pain, these joint aches range from "light" or "mild" to "severe" and "terrible." When pain and disability become chronic or severe, sufferers experience their ailments as conditions marked by "heaviness," "weakness," and "fatigue." These feelings resonate with broad cultural notions of suffering as a "weight" or "burden" (see Pugh, 1991).

SOMATIC HOLISM AND RHEUMATIC DISORDERS

These humoral constructions of rheumatic disorders are rooted in a holistic concept of the body and its systemic organization. Ayurvedic and Unani texts describe various bones, joints, muscles, ligaments, tendons, muscles, and nerves. Their writings consider this supportive frame of bones and muscles to be influenced by environmental factors and personal activities, *and* to be integrated into the body's interior space of organs, channels, and circulating fluids and gases. This somatic model, which operates across Ayurveda and Unani and at both professional and popular levels, comprehends arthritis within a more general concept of illness, rather than through a specialized theory of joint disorders.[10]

The body's physiological system, with its networks of organs and its channels of moving humors and other substances, plays an important role in rheumatic disorders. Digestion, centered in the stomach, liver, and intestines, sustains basic life-activities: its "heat" transforms, or "cooks," food into humors, nutrients, and other substances.[11] Nourishment is carried to other organs, joints, and tissues, and waste products are separated out and eliminated. Digestive impairments can generate degraded humors, excessive or noxious wind, and other harmful substances, which can travel to various organs, joints, and muscles. Constipation produces a buildup of wind and deleterious substances that may recirculate throughout the body, and when these wastes settle in joints and muscles, they can give rise to chronic and sometimes disabling arthritic conditions.[12]

This complex of ideas informs leading scholar–physicians' and ordinary *vaids'* and *hakims'* understandings of arthritic conditions. *Hakim* Abdul Hameed, a central figure in Unani medicine, discusses the role of bad digestion in producing "poisons" that contribute to arthritis (Hameed, 1981, p. 75). Vaidya Bhagwan Dash, a prominent Ayurvedic physician, stresses the role of indigestion and constipation in producing the noxious "wastes" that settle in the joints of arthritis sufferers (Dash, 1981, p. 34).

The three practitioners in the present study also hold these ideas about joint disorders and their underlying physiology. *Vaid* Om Prakash believes that many illnesses, including joint problems, are closely related to digestion and elimination, and especially to wind or "gas," which he usually refers to as "stomach wind." Echoing both Caraka and Ibn Sina, he states that "wind is the root cause of so many diseases." Speaking about indigestion, hyperacidity, and constipation, he states that the resulting "gas" can cause rheumatism and numerous other problems as well. For instance, "gas" can circulate to the brain, where it produces all sorts of derangements, including paralysis, stroke, even insanity. *Hakim* Nur Mohammad in the saint's shrine and *Hakim* Abdur Rahim in his Old Delhi clinic also see these systemic imbalances as primary contributors to many types of illness, and they link common joint pain and stiffness to poor digestion, constipation, and gas.

These ideas about the pathogenic effects of internal disturbances extend to ordinary people as well. North Indians widely believe, for example, that bad digestion and constipation are major contributors to rheumatism and many other illnesses. Residents in my Old Delhi neighborhood may attribute various illnesses, including rheumatism, to digestive disturbances, and they sometimes use "digestive powders" to maintain proper systemic functioning. Villagers in north India often "regard indigestion or cold as the cause of general illness or malaise lasting for three or four days" (Khare, 1963, p. 37). They usually attend closely to digestion and elimination (Minturn & Hitchcock, 1966, p. 73), and other South Asians, Sri Lankans, for

example, express these same kinds of concerns (Nichter, 1987, pp. 378–379).

ETIOLOGICAL PROCESSES IN RHEUMATIC DISORDERS

Classic Ayurvedic and Unani texts, contemporary practitioners, and laypeople widely share a loose set of ideas about the causes of rheumatic disorders. Humoral understandings of the body and the interconnections between internal processes and external influences form the backdrop for these etiological concepts.

Weather and Temperature

The most encompassing influence on arthritic disorders is the weather and the seasonal cycle, which generates an annual round of physiological changes and disease susceptibilities.[13] These seasonal models describe the pathogenic effects of heat, cold, daily temperature variations, wind, water quality, and other factors. Caraka uses the classical Sanskrit six-season calendar (rainy season, autumn, winter, frosty season, spring, and summer), and Ibn Sina follows the four-season Greek and Middle Eastern calendar (autumn, winter, spring, and summer). Although the two calendars count the seasons somewhat differently, they both identify essentially the same climatic and meteorological influences on rheumatism and arthritis and mark the six- to seven-month period spanning the rains, the autumn, and the winter as the prime time for rheumatic problems in north India.

Caraka describes how the rainy season, with its damp, chilly weather, its storms, and its polluted water supply produces derangements of wind, a basic cause of joint pain and other rheumatic problems (Caraka, 1976, pp. 140–141). Following the rainy season, the autumn ushers in a period when diurnal swings between warm, sunny days and cool nights can give rise to various ailments, including disorders of bile and blood and their accompanying digestive and rheumatic difficulties (Caraka, 1976, pp. 142–143). Winter's cold days and sharp winds chill the joints and dampen digestive "fire," resulting in internal disruptions and deranged wind; in addition, the body's wintertime production of excess phlegm can exacerbate arthritic complaints (Caraka, 1976, pp. 135–137). Following the winter, rheumatic complaints show a decline through the frosty season, spring, and summer.

Ibn Sina provides a strikingly similar account. He describes autumn as a time of potentially serious disorders: its disjunctive mix of hot sun by day and cool air by night unbalances the body, and its stagnating sediments of yellow bile and black bile produce pains in the joints, back, and hips (Ibn Sina, 1930, pp. 190–91). Winter's damp, cold, windy weather and the body's overabundant phlegm make colds common and cause pain in the chest, side, back, and loins (Ibn Sina, 1930, p. 192). By contrast, spring and summer are far less conducive to rheumatic complaints.

Today people widely link flare-ups in rheumatic pain and stiffness to damp or cold weather. North Indians regard the rainy season as having "chilly" effects, and even when the daily temperatures are quite high, they may still wear extra clothing in order to ward off damp and cold. Rheumatism sufferers try to minimize exposure to atmospheric cold and wind during autumn and winter and to avoid overexposure to the wind all year around. Some annual almanacs provide useful predictions of the particular periods within the rainy season, autumn, and winter when wind disorders are likely to be more common or more severe than usual.

Everyday Activity and Thermal Conditions

People's ideas about the effects of cold conditions and sharp temperature swings often influence their everyday activities. Many people routinely try to avoid excessively cooling activities, such as eating too many cold foods in one meal, sitting in a draft, sitting too long under a fan, or bathing at night, especially in winter, all of which may contribute to colds and coughs as well as joint and muscle pains. People also believe in the rheumatism-inducing effects of activities that heat and then rapidly cool the body. North Indian villagers, for instance, say that joint problems may develop "if a man works strenuously and becomes overheated, and then suddenly goes into a cool place" (Lewis, 1965, p. 292). Similar ideas crop up in

Delhi residents' comments on the potentially harmful effects of air conditioning.

Diet

Food has figured as a major contributor to rheumatic disorders from ancient medical texts to contemporary humoral ideas and practices. People in the Delhi area and across north India widely regard cold, windy foods as primary causes of rheumatic disorders. Cold foods chill the body and dampen "digestive fire," thus promoting the production of gas and other toxic matters, and windy foods generate "gas" in the stomach and intestines. Foods that are sour, hard-to-digest, and constipating may also contribute to these internal disturbances. People try to make seasonal dietary adjustments, however, such as favoring wintertime consumption of heavy, oily foods in order to warm the body, stimulate the digestive fire, maintain health, and prevent ailments like colds and rheumatism.

Personal Constitution and Temperament

Individual constitution is considered a basic factor in people's susceptibilities to illness, including arthritis. Both humoral practitioners and laypeople widely regard "cold natured" or "windy natured" people as more prone to rheumatic disorders, and Sri Lankans similarly characterize people with arthritic or rheumatic complaints as "windy natured" (Nichter, 1987, p. 379). People with phlegmatic or bilious constitutions may also be susceptible, depending on seasonal influences and their own personal habits. Ibn Sina warns, for instance, that phlegmatic-type people may suffer rheumatic flare-ups in the spring when the winter's accumulated phlegm begins to loosen and circulate throughout the body (Ibn Sina, 1930, p. 188).

Age

Classic Unani and Ayurvedic theory indicates that the body cools and dries with advancing age and becomes more vulnerable to cold, windy disorders. Wind contributes to numerous health problems for older people, including arthritis, constipation, tremors, and memory loss (Ibn Sina, 1930, pp.

432–436; Lad, 1998, p. 35), and Ibn Sina, for example, recommends special regimens to the elderly to avert conditions such as joint troubles. These humoral concepts inform local understandings of the prevalence of arthritic disorders in older people, and these ideas about body and aging remain salient in urban and rural areas (see Lamb, 2000).

Use and Injury

Humoral medicine recognizes the impact of wear and tear on joints and muscles. Caraka advises protecting the body against the effects of strenuous labor, overexertion, and fatigue (Caraka, 1976, pp. 124–125), and contemporary Ayurvedic physicians point to the effects of sprains, trauma, and posture on low back pain (lumbago), neck problems (cervical spondylosis), and sciatica (see Dash, 1981, pp. 98, 125, 131). Injuries and overuse can cause structural damage, which in turn creates spaces that trap noxious wind and other harmful substances around the joints and muscles.

Heredity

Classic Ayurvedic and Unani texts do not include rheumatism and arthritis in their lists of hereditary conditions. Today, however, some practitioners do mention heredity, particularly in relation to rheumatoid arthritis. *Hakim* Abdur Rahim holds this idea, and the writings of the well-known *Hakim* Abdul Hameed also comment on hereditary factors (Hameed, 1981, p. 75).

THE LOGIC OF TREATMENT

The logic of humoral etiology and physiology shapes the diagnosis and treatment of arthritis. *Vaid* Om Prakash and *Hakims* Nur Mohammad and Abdur Rahim use similar diagnostic procedures: they check patients' pulse at the wrist to detect internal imbalances, and they discuss the particulars of the patients' complaints. Interactions typically cover symptoms and their onset and duration, as well as personal habits, diet, and problems related to digestion, constipation, and urination. What circulates between these practitioners and their patients is a polysynthetic blend of ideas and understandings about wind, gas, cold-

ness, pain, and various bodily conditions and processes. *Vaids* and *hakims* may tell patients that wind or stomach or intestinal disturbance has caused their joint problems, or they may simply discuss symptoms and provide a treatment without directly identifying a cause.

Vaids and *hakims* typically recommend dietary adjustments, topical oils, and oral medications. They may select specific foods and medications that will best match a patient's particular set of symptoms, such as the intensity of pain or the presence or absence of constipation or indigestion. A brief look at these Ayurvedic and Unani remedies will bring out their convergences and their conceptual fit with humoral constructions of rheumatism and the body.

Diet

Practitioners often list prohibited and recommended dietary items for their patients. Commonly prohibited items are cold, windy, sour, hard-to-digest, constipating foods. All three practitioners, for instance, tell patients with joint problems (and other wind ailments) to avoid rice and lentils, the rice because it produces constipation, and the lentils because they generate wind. *Vaid* Om Prakash may also prohibit battered/fried vegetables, yogurt, alcohol, tea, and coffee. *Hakim* Nur Mohammad usually tells patients to consume wheat instead of rice and to avoid bananas and potatoes, which are considered hard to digest, and yogurt, which is cold and sour. *Hakim* Abdur Rahim also proscribes "heavy" foods and cold, sour foods like yogurt. The well-known *Vaid* Bhagwan Dash recommends wheat, garlic, onion, ginger, bitter gourd, papaya, and green bananas, and he may allow "old rice," which is less likely to cause constipation than newly harvested rice (see Dash, 1981, pp. 130, 136).

Medicated Oils

Vaids and *hakims* usually advise rheumatism patients to massage affected areas with medicated oil. *Hakim* Nur Mohammad and *Hakim* Abdur Rahim may recommend one of several Unani antirheumatic oils, and *Vaid* Om Prakash prescribes Ayurvedic and also Unani rheumatism liniments, as well as new Ayurvedic pharmaceutical balms.

These various preparations contain common household oils (such as mustard seed oil or sesame oil) medicated with herbs selected to warm joints and muscles, disperse trapped wind, and relieve pain and stiffness. Practitioners may also recommend that patients wrap painful areas in a warm cloth and/or apply external heat.

Oral Medications

Pills and confections are designed to initiate symptom relief and to correct underlying physiological disturbances. *Hakims* Nur Mohammad and Abdur Rahim recommend standard Unani rheumatism medications, and *Vaid* Om Prakash recommends common Ayurvedic formulas and an occasional Unani formula. These various medicines draw their ingredients from a pool of antirheumatic plants, hot spices, and other substances. Compounds may contain: digestives to stimulate "digestive fire"; carminatives to relieve gas; purifiers to cleanse the blood; and diaphoretics and laxatives to flush accumulated wastes from the system. The logic of these oral medications directly reflects humoral understandings of the physiology of arthritic disorders.

These therapeutic regimens of diet, oil massage, and oral medication represent a wide-spectrum approach that works externally and internally to manage both the symptoms and the causes of rheumatic disorders.

CONCLUSION

Exploring Ayurveda and Unani together brings out their polysynthetic perspective on arthritic disorders. Their categories of joint disorders, their etiologies, and their physiological concepts form broadly shared concepts of arthritis, and their practitioners employ identical diagnostic and therapeutic procedures. What stands out across these two traditions is the polysynthetic network of concepts and images that resonates between humoral practitioners and their diverse clienteles and constitutes a South Asian humoral model of arthritic disorders.

This humoral model provides a useful framework for the comparative study of cultural constructions of arthritis. It suggests that anthro-

pologists explore more fully the underpinnings of the widespread notion of rheumatism as a cold, windy ailment treated with hot medicine, an understanding that has been reported across many different societies. These inquiries might examine hot/cold qualities and their entailments, the natural environment and the seasons, the health-related aspects of individual constitution and personal activity, the body's systemic organization, the role of diet, digestion, and elimination, and the logic of various forms of treatment. Other humoral traditions may share numerous features with Ayurveda and Unani but they may also involve important concepts not found in the Indian setting and will all have their own local contexts and interpretations. These kinds of studies will contribute to the development of a comparative perspective on rheumatic disorders and their diverse cultural and therapeutic constructions.

NOTES

1. For short references to rheumatic problems in various types of societies and geographical locales, see: Ohnuki-Tierney (1981) on the Sakhalin Ainu; Book, Dixon, and Kirchner (1983) on native Alaskans; Janzen (1978) on the BaKongo of Zaire; Lewis (1965) on peasant villagers in north India; Anderson (1987) on a Mexican peasant healer; Herzfeld (1991) on city-dwellers on Crete; and Lock (1980) on urban Japanese. Usage of the terms "arthritis" and "rheumatism" may vary by country and within and among biomedical, traditional medical, and popular discourses. See Wood (1979) for details on arthritis in early human populations.

2. This overview of the biomedical perspective on rheumatic disorders draws from informational literature distributed by the Arthritis Foundation (for example, Arthritis Foundation, 1998) and from medical handbooks (Currey & Hull, 1987; Grelsamer & Loebl, 1996; Khan, 1992).

3. While researchers identify genetics, aging, injury, and overuse as contributors to rheumatic problems, they admit that they do not understand their exact causal mechanisms. The Arthritis Foundation (1998, p. 3) says simply that "what causes most types of arthritis is unknown."

4. Some rheumatologists state quite unequivocally that "neither climate nor diet play a vital role" in rheumatic disorders (see Grelsamer & Loebt, 1996, p. 39).

5. See Helman (2000) for an overview of humoral medicine.

6. For detailed anthropological studies of these traditions, see, among others, Zimmermann (1987), Kakar

(1982, pp. 219–251), Nichter (1987), and Nordstrom (1988) on Ayurveda, and Pugh (1991) on Unani. Khare (1996) describes various cultural understandings that form a backdrop for practiced medicine in biomedicine, Ayurveda, Unani, and other health-systems in India. See Kutumbiah (1962) and Khan (1986) on the classical Ayurvedic and Unani traditions, respectively.

7. Ayurvedic terms for specific types of rheumatic disorders include: gout: *vata-pitta* (wind-bile), *vata-rakta* (wind-blood); lumbago: *kati-vat* (wind in the low back/waist); sciatica: *kativat, gridhrasi* (grip, catch); cervical spondylosis: *grioa sandhigata vat* (wind in the neck joint). Susruta (*Susruta samhita*, p. 53) gives Ayurvedic terms for other rheumatic conditions.

8. Unani terms include: gout: *niqris;* lumbago: *dard kamer* (waist pain); sciatica: *'asab nisai ka dard* (pain in the feminine nerve, i.e., in the nerve in the buttocks).

9. Shastri (1971) contains several Ayurvedic descriptions of pain, including the pain of "wind diseases."

10. This discussion presents a model of the body broadly shared by Ayurveda and Unani. Classic texts by Caraka and Ibn Sina contain more detailed accounts. Zimmermann (1979) stresses classical Ayurveda's fluid body concept and contrasts it with the more schematic anatomy delineated in classical Greek medicine.

11. For discussions of digestion and related processes, see Caraka (*Caraka samhita*, pp. 566–569), Ibn Sina (*The canon of medicine*, pp. 88–92). Good (1994) describes digestion and physiology in Greek and Islamic medicine.

12. These "wastes" are referred to as *ama* in Ayurveda and *fazla* in Unani.

13. Zimmermann (1980) discusses the classical Sanskrit calendar and its model of seasonal changes in the body.

REFERENCES

Anderson, R. T. (1984). An orthopedic ethnography in rural Nepal. *Medical Anthropology, 8*(1), 46–59.

Anderson, R. T. (1987). The treatment of musculoskeletal disorders by a Mexican bonesetter (*sobador*). *Social Science & Medicine, 24*(1), 43–46.

Arthritis Foundation (1998). *Arthritis answers.* Atlanta: Arthritis Foundation.

Book, P. A., Dixon, M., & Kirchner, S. (1983). Native healing in Alaska: Report from serpentine hot springs. *The Western Journal of Medicine, 139*(6), 119–123.

Caraka (1976). *Caraka samhita.* Vol. 1: *Sutra sthana.* R. K. Sharma, & B. Dash (Eds.), Varanasi: Chowkhamba.

Carstairs, G. M. (1967). *The twice-born: A study of a community of high-caste Hindus.* Bloomington: Indiana University Press.

Currey, H. L. F., & Hull, S. (1987). *Rheumatology for general practitioners.* Oxford: Oxford University Press.

Dash, B. (1981). *Ayurvedic cures for common diseases.* Delhi: Hind Pocket Books.

Foster, G. M. (1988). The validating role of humoral therapy in traditional Spanish-American therapeutics. *American Ethnologist, 15*(1), 120–135.

Good, B. (1994). *Medicine, rationality, and experience: An anthropological perspective.* Cambridge: Cambridge University Press.

Good, M. J. D. (1992). Work as a haven from pain. In M. J. D. Good, P. Brodwin, B. J. Good, & A. Kleinman (Eds.), *Pain as human experience: an anthropological perspective* (pp. 49–76). Berkeley: University of Californis Press.

Goodenow, C., Reisine, S. T., & Grady, K. E. (1990). Quality of social support and associated social and psychological functioning in women with rheumatoid arthritis. *Health Psychology, 9*(3), 266–284.

Greenwood, B. (1992). Cold or spirits? ambiguity and syncretism in Moroccan therapeutics. In S. Feierman, & J. Janzes (Eds.), *The social basis of health and healing in Africa* (pp. 285–314). Berkeley: University of California Press.

Grelsamer, R. P., & Loebl, S. (1996). *The Columbia Presbyterian osteoarthritis handbook.* New York: Macmillan.

Hameed, A. (1981). *Hamdard matab.* Delhi: Hamdard Dawakhana.

Helman, C. (2000). *Culture, health and illness* (4th ed.). Oxford: Butterworth-Heinemann.

Henry, E. O. (1977). A north Indian healer and the sources of his power. *Social Science & Medicine, 11,* 309–317.

Herzfeld, M. (1991). *A place in history: Social and monumental time in a Cretan town.* Princeton: Princeton University Press.

Husaini, B. A., & Moore, S. T. (1990). Arthritis disability, depression, and life satisfaction among Black elderly people. *Health and Social Work, 15*(4), 253–260.

Ibn Sina (1930). The canon of medicine. In: O. C. Gruner, (Ed.), *A treatise on the canon of medicine of Avicenna.* London: Luzac and Company.

Ingstad, B., & Whyte, S. R. (Eds.). (1995). *Disability & culture.* Berkeley: University of California Press.

Janzen, J. M. (1978). *The quest for therapy: Medical pluralism in lower Zaire.* Berkeley: University of California Press.

Kakar, S. (1982). *Shamans, mystics, and doctors.* New York: Alfred Knopf.

Khan, A. P. (1992). *Arthritis: Causes, prevention & treatment.* Delhi: Orient Paperbacks.

Khan, M. S. (1986). *Islamic medicine.* London: Routledge & Kegan Paul.

Khare, R. S. (1963). Folk medicine in a north Indian village. *Human Organization, 22*(1), 36–40.

Khare, R. S. (1996). Dava, daktar, and dua: An anthropology of practiced medicine in India. *Social Science & Medicine, 43*(3), 837–848.

Kutumbiah, P. (1962). *Ancient Indian medicine.* Bombay: Orient Longman.

Lad, V. D. (1998). *The complete book of Ayurvedic home remedies.* New York: Harmony Books.

Lamb, S. (2000). *White saris & sweet mangoes: Aging, gender, & body in north India.* Berkeley: University of California Press.

Lewis, O. (1965). *Village life in northern India.* New York: Vintage Books.

Lock, M. (1980). *East Asian medicine in urban Japan: Varieties of medical experience.* Berkeley: University of California Press.

Minturn, L., & Hitchcock, J. T. (1966). *The Rajputs of Khalapur, India.* New York: Wiley.

Mohiuddin, S. G., Sultana, G., & Khadri, S. K. (1977). *Clinical study of waja'-ul-mafasil.* New Delhi: Central Council for Research in Unani Medicine.

Nadkarni, A. K. (1976). *Indian materia medica.* Bombay: Popular Prakashan.

Nichter, M. (1987). Cultural dimensions of hot, cold and sema in Sinhalese health culture. *Social Science & Medicine, 25*(4), 377–387.

Nordstrom, C. (1988). Exploring pluralism: The many faces of Ayurveda. *Social Science & Medicine, 27*(5), 479–489.

Ohnuki-Tierney, E. (1981). *Illness and healing among the Sakhalin Ainu: A symbolic interpretation.* Berkeley: University of California Press.

Opler, M. E. (1963). The cultural definition of illness in village India. *Human Organization, 22*(1), 32–35.

Pillsbury, B. L. K. (1978). 'Doing the month': Confinement and convalescence of chinese women after childbirth. *Social Science & Medicine, 12,* 11–22.

Pool, R. (1987). Hot and cold as an explanatory model: The example of Bharuch district in Gujarat, India. *Social Science & Medicine, 25*(4), 389–399.

Pugh, J. F. (1991). The semantics of pain in Indian culture and medicine. *Culture, Medicine and Psychiatry, 15,* 19–43.

Ramesh, A., & Hyma, B. (1981). Traditional Indian medicine in practice in an Indian metropolitan city. *Social Science & Medicine, 15D,* 69–81.

Ryan, M. (1997). Efficacy of the Tibetan treatment for arthritis. *Social Science & Medicine, 44*(4), 535–539.

Shastri, V. K. (1971). *Rog wigyan.* Patiala: Lalit Prakashan.

Susruta (1980). In: P. Ray, H. Gupta, & M. Roy (Eds.). *Susruta samhita.* New Delhi: Indian National Science Academy.

Tabor, D. C. (1981). Ripe and unripe: Concepts of health and sickness in Ayurvedic medicine. *Social Science & Medicine, 15B,* 439–455.

Times of India, 2 December 1999.

Wolffers, I. (1988). Illness behavior in Sri Lanka: results of a survey in two Sinhalese communities. *Social Science & Medicine, 27*(5), 545–552. (Special issue, B. Pfleiderer (Ed.), *Permanence and change in Asian health traditions.*

Wood, C. S. (1979). *Human sickness and health: A biocultural view.* Palo Alto: Mayfield.

Zborowski, M. (1969). *People in pain.* San Francisco: Jossey-Bass.

Zimmermann, F. (1979). Remarks on the conception of the body in Ayurvedic medicine. Manuscript.

Zimmermann, F. (1980). Rtu-satmya: The seasonal cycle and the principle of appropriateness. *Social Science & Medicine, 14B,* 99–106.

Zimmermann, F. (1987). *The jungle and the aroma of meats: As ecological theme in Hindu medicine.* Berkeley: University of California Press.

Zysk, K. G. (1991). *Asceticism and healing in ancient India; Medicine in the Buddhist monastery.* Oxford: Oxford University Press.

■ ■ ■ ■ ■ ■ ■ ■ ■

5   HOMEOPATHIC MEDICINE IN THE CITY OF OAXACA, MEXICO: PATIENTS' PERSPECTIVES AND OBSERVATIONS

Michael B. Whiteford

As we saw in selection 3, the predominance of scientific medicine in the United States and other industrialized countries over the first-three quarters of the twentieth century is an historical anomaly, given that a multiplicity of healing traditions is the norm in most places and times. This selection about recourse to homeopathic and other healers in a Mexican city also addresses the alternative–mainstream medicine dichotomy. Whiteford shows that patients seek different healers for different ailments. For some ailments, homeopathic medicine seems to be the mainstream choice. In addition, homeopathic healers are often trained biomedical physicians, blurring the boundaries between the two. This is similar to the practice of traditional Chinese medicine by a majority of Chinese biomedical physicians (see Harmsworth and Lewith 2001) and the use of alternative therapies along with biomedical ones by some physicians in Europe and the United States (see Baer 2001; Kaptchuk and Eisenberg 2001b; Reilly 2001).

Like the naturalistic healing systems discussed in previous selections, homeopathy includes the premise that equilibrium in internal vital forces or energy flows is central to good health, while imbalances cause sickness. There is an emphasis on diet and lifestyle in the prevention and treatment of disease, in addition to the use of homeopathic medicines that promote the same natural responses provoked by the disease itself (see also Jonas, Kaptchuk, and Linde 2003). As a result of these beliefs about balance and equilibrium, and in contrast to biomedical treatment, the same set of symptoms in two people is likely to be treated in two different ways. This is a common feature of traditional medical systems (see selection 6).

Social contexts of medical pluralism invite attention to the concept of medical decision making, or what is known as the "hierarchy of resort." In Oaxaca, patients are served by a number of thriving, coexisting medical traditions. Whiteford argues that no one tradition has a monopoly on the public's imagination regarding the causes, treatment, and prevention of ill health. International biomedical knowledge and practice is just one complementary system that may be absorbed, transformed, or altered in local contexts, in what has been called "glocalization" (see Høg and Hsu 2002; Rekdal 1999).

Questions to keep in mind

What kinds of healers are there in Oaxaca, and to what extent do the patients in the study seek treatment from them?

For what kinds of ailments do homeopathic physicians claim to have an especially useful form of treatment, and how well do they match the set of ailments commonly reported by the patients in the study?

Source: Whiteford, M. B. 1999. "Homeopathic Medicine in the City of Oaxaca, Mexico: Patients' Perspectives and Observations." © 1999 by the American Anthropological Association. Reprinted from *Medical Anthropology Quarterly* Vol. 13 No. 1 pp. 69–78, by permission.

Is homeopathic medicine an alternative medical system in Oaxaca, or is it a mainstream one (with respect to institutional structure, professional training, patient population, and practitioner characteristics)?

What are some gender differences and similarities in Oaxaca regarding health and homeopathic and other kinds of medical care?

The interest in medical pluralism and "complementary" medicine is a rapidly growing phenomenon in the United States.[1] In part, this is a reaction to dissatisfaction with various aspects of the general approach and outcome of the prevailing conventional "scientific" (e.g., allopathic) medical models. At the same time, there is an increasingly strong conviction that "alternative" approaches (e.g., naturalistic medicine, including acupuncture, chiropractic, *ayurveda,* homeopathy, and psychic healing) can be highly effective (cf. Berman 1992; Finkler 1991; Furnham and Bhagrath 1993; Furnham and Smith 1988; Patel 1987; Salmon 1984).

For a variety of historical and cultural reasons, the tensions between allopathic (or biomedical) and alternative medical models found in the United States have not been so widely adhered to in much of the rest of the world, including most of Latin America. This does not mean that there have not been many of the same strains between 20th-century Western-based medical paradigms and other models for diagnosing illness and proposing methods of treatment. But for many of the affected populations, particularly those living in rural areas, no single medical worldview necessarily has been regarded as superior to others in all circumstances.

Over the years a considerable amount of important data have been gathered that examine certain types of nontraditional medical options. The literature is replete with books and articles that describe a variety of traditional healers and patterns of medical resort. Much has been written not only on how these approaches address individual needs, but also on how they fit into the broader matrix of health care delivery. In contrast, very little has been written specifically on the role of homeopathic care.

An earlier study on medical choice and decision making done in the city of Oaxaca, Mexico, suggested that homeopathic treatment occupies an important and often overlooked niche in the discussion and investigation of approaches to health care (Whiteford 1995). This study, designed in part to fill this void in the well-studied field of patterns of medical resort in Latin America, reports the findings on the medical worldview of patients seeking homeopathic care.

Previous research conducted on medical decision making in a working-class neighborhood in Oaxaca resulted in several findings relevant to the current study: First, residents routinely rely upon or have easy access to an impressively wide range of sources of advice for practically any health-related issue. Second, while many individuals believe in the standard Western medical paradigm of disease causation, it appears to be only one of their complementary explanations about why people get sick and what they need to do to get well and stay healthy. In subscribing to a more eclectic medical worldview than is probably the case for many in the United States, individuals are able to draw upon the expertise of a number of different kinds of medical personnel that might appear to an outsider to represent very divergent, if not conflicting, perspectives.

Homeopathic physicians and care fit nicely into this panorama of curing alternatives. Many people feel that illnesses that are not responsive to Western medicine are often effectively treated by homeopaths. Because of their naturalistic approach, including the use of herbs and other botanical remedies in treatment, homeopaths occupy a special niche, and are nationally recognized as professional practitioners of medicine (Finkler 1991:71). Most homeopathic physicians in Mexico are graduates of allopathic medical schools; just as one might study endocrinology or otorhinolaryngology, many of these doctors have studied homeopathy as a postgraduate specialization. Thus, people feel that homeopathic physicians can be consulted for practically any type of illness.

Nevertheless, when discussing treatment and curers, individuals in the previous study were very clear about distinguishing types of physicians, using the terms *alópata* (allopath) and *homeópata* (homeopath) with the same clarity as most U.S. patients would discuss medical doctors and doctors of chiropractic.

This study reports findings on the medical worldview of patients seeking homeopathic care in Oaxaca. Data were collected through interviews with 174 patients in the waiting rooms of homeopathic physicians. Interviews with some of these physicians were also conducted to obtain their perspectives on the efficacy of homeopathic medicine. In an attempt to contribute to the discussion of medical pluralism, the objectives of this study are (1) to describe and discuss homeopathic practices, asking why homeopathy is consulted and by whom; and (2) to examine some of the differences between males' and females' perceptions of health care.

BACKGROUND

Residents of Oaxaca have access to an impressively wide range of sources of advice for practically any health-related issue. The major metropolitan center for the region, Oaxaca, with approximately 300,000 inhabitants, is the hub of the formally organized medical facilities and activities in the area. The roster of specialists is impressive and probably commensurate with other bustling urban centers of this size. In the city of Oaxaca alone, there are more than two dozen sanatoria, clinics, and hospitals. The yellow pages of the most recent telephone book include a list of physicians whose specialties range from acupuncture to urology. Among these specialists are approximately 50 physicians who, according to its most recent directory, are members of the Colegio de Médicos Homeópatas (the association of homeopathic physicians in Oaxaca); slightly more than 30 of them currently practice homeopathic medicine in the city.

In addition, Oaxaqueños patronize a wide range of alternative health care specialists, many of whom fall under the generic category of *curandero* (healer). Specifically, these include *espiritistas* (spiritists), some of whom are renowned for their curative powers in far corners of the country, *hueseros* (bonesetters), *sobadoras* (masseurs), and *parteras* (midwives). As Press (1971, 1978) wrote two decades ago, urban areas are magnets for all kinds of alternative healers, and Oaxaca is no exception.

Developed by the German physician Samuel Hahnemann (1755–1843) in the early 19th century, homeopathic treatment is based on the notion that the natural defenses of the body can be stimulated by treatments that produce the same symptoms as the malady itself (Patel 1987). This idea of *similia similibus curentur,* or "let like be treated by like," one of the basic principles of homeopathic medicine, is called the "Law of Similars" (Vithoulkas 1983). In other words, as part of the diagnosis and treatment, the practitioner uses a substance that, if ingested in large quantities, would cause symptoms similar to those the complainant is experiencing. In order to reduce the severity of reaction, homeopathic healers reduce the doses of the substance given (Ullman 1988b:6). Ullman notes, "Homeopathic medicine is a natural pharmaceutical system that utilizes microdoses of substances from the plant, mineral, and animal kingdoms to arouse a person's natural healing response" (Ullman 1988a:43).

There are three important aspects of homeopathic medicine worth mentioning here. First, one of the principal tenets of homeopathy is the belief that an individual's health is regulated by a "vital force" or energy flow. In a healthy individual, this vital force exists in a state of dynamic equilibrium. When this balance is upset, the individual becomes sick.

Second, the process of diagnosis and treatment is thorough and time consuming. Homeopathy emphasizes the uniqueness of the patient's condition (cf. Cant and Sharma 1996; Lecomte 1983) and the importance of matching the "idiosyncratic characteristics" of each individual (cf. Ullman 1988b:11) with the remedies prescribed.[2]

Third, while homeopathic physicians generally feel the efficacy of their medicine is useful in almost any situation, they also claim that their approach is particularly useful in cases of chronic conditions. To a certain extent they have no difficulties blending certain aspects of their earlier training in allopathy with homeopathy. As one physician told me, "When someone comes to you with a broken bone, you set it using the techniques you learned in medical school. Similarly, if someone has a cut that requires stitching, you rely on skills you learned studying allopathy. What you do after that involves homeopathic knowledge and treatment." One homeopathic physician was working on an advanced degree in psychology. He felt that his expertise in this field would help him be a better overall practitioner.

Homeopathic medicine has been practiced in Mexico for almost a century and a half (Finkler 1991:50). At the end of the last century the National School of Homeopathy was created, an entity that is today supported by the Mexican Ministry of Health. Its current curriculum is quite similar to that found in biomedical schools. While homeopathy enjoys a wide following in Mexico, it is not without some very vocal critics, who occasionally argue that it is not a science (Finkler 1991:54). In spite of this, Finkler found a number of allopathic physicians in Mexico City who routinely employed alternative curing techniques, including homeopathy, in their healing repertoire (1991:92, 94).

For several decades, homeopathic medicine has been practiced in Oaxaca. The profession experienced considerable growth in the late 1970s with the arrival of Dr. Proceso Sánchez, one of the country's most famous homeopaths. Dr. Proceso, as he is affectionately known, was instrumental in the establishment of the College of Homeopathic Medicine, which is now recognized by the educational accrediting body for the state of Oaxaca. The College licenses homeopaths and serves as a watchdog to make sure the profession maintains a reasonable level of orthodoxy in therapy and theory. Its members teach the homeopathy curriculum during evenings and weekends to physicians wishing to specialize in this branch of medicine; they also work to promote and improve homeopathy's public image. By the middle of the 1990s, there were approximately 50 members of the College of Homeopathic Medicine.

METHODOLOGY

Data for this study came from two primary sources. Almost 200 patients from 20 different clinics were interviewed using a structured interview schedule. Additional data came from interviews conducted with homeopathic physicians. These interviews looked at health care providers' perceptions of the efficacy of naturalistic medicines, and focused especially on the place that homeopathic medicines occupy in offering alternatives to allopathic treatments.

The sample of patients interviewed was gathered in a three-step process. First, from the most recent directory of members of the Colegio de Médicos Homeópatas, a potential sampling universe of 34 homeopathic physicians, about two-thirds of whom were male and one-third of whom were female, was identified. Second, a gender-proportional random sample of 20 physicians—in whose clinics the interviews took place—was drawn (with an additional six replacements). Third, interviewers in each clinic were free to interview any consenting adult patient. Patients from slightly more than half ($N = 20$, or nearly 59 percent) of the private practices in the city were interviewed. A total of 174 interviews were completed (an average of nine per practice).

The sample of patients was composed of 55 men (32 percent) and 119 women (68 percent), whose ages ranged from 16 to 98 years (with a mean age of 39 years). In comparison to the Mexican population as a whole, participants in this study were quite well educated, with an average of 12 years of classroom work (the range was no formal schooling to 21 years of education). Patients represented varied occupations. Among those interviewed were college professors, schoolteachers, an oral surgeon, a priest, two nuns, several accountants, an architect, a number of businesspeople, government functionaries, housewives, and students. Most of those employed were white-collar professionals; there were only a couple of individuals who listed their occupation as peasant farmer or construction worker.

The "typical" patient appeared to be a Roman Catholic, 38-year-old female, who was just shy of having completed a high school education.[3] She lived in a household with three other individuals, and the chances were about fifty-fifty that she worked outside of the home.

DISCUSSION OF THE FINDINGS

One of the first observations that emerges from this study is that the following and popularity of homeopathic medicine is growing in Oaxaca. Although 20 percent of the sample had received homeopathic care for at least five years, slightly more than one-third of the patients interviewed had seen homeopaths for less than a year. This finding was corroborated by homeopathic physicians, who mentioned that the number of patients they saw was continually increasing. An allopathic neurosurgeon supported this finding, reiterating that he was somewhat baffled by, and in awe of, the growth of homeopathic medicine. In addition to having a private practice, this individual also worked at the local medical school and commented—again with some amazement—that he had noticed for the past several years that some of the brightest young graduates were going into homeopathic medical training.

Patients were asked to assess their own state of health and to comment on how their physical and emotional health status affected them. Almost two-thirds of the respondents said their health was acceptable, and one-half of the interviewees indicated that their health probably had improved over the past year. Males' and females' perceptions of their own health differed significantly. In general, women saw their health as more improved than did men. The respondents were asked whether their health caused them to alter their daily activities within the past month. Approximately one-half of the group responded affirmatively.

Physical problems ranged from an inability to perform strenuous activities, like running or lifting heavy objects, to the inability to carry groceries or to kneel down or walk long distances. Emotional difficulties included being nervous or agitated, feeling "so down in the dumps that nothing would cheer you up," or being "downhearted and blue."

Patients were asked to compare their perceptions of their own health status with their perceptions of others' health. While they clearly recognized that they would not seek medical relief without good reason[4] less than one-fifth of the sample believed that they got sick anymore easily than others. About one-third of those interviewed believed they were as healthy as anyone. Men consistently thought that they were as healthy as anyone else, and thought so to a significantly greater extent (F ratio 4.37, $p \leq .05$) than women.[5] They were also more confident than women that they would stay healthy.

Individuals who consulted with homeopathic physicians experimented with a variety of forms of medical resort, and enumerated 19 types of alternative medical practitioners. Two-thirds of the patients had used massage therapy, almost one-third had visited herbalists, one-quarter had used the services of a bonesetter, and around one-fifth had consulted with acupuncturists and injectionists.[6] These individuals were not timid about seeking out and trying new techniques, and reported a willingness to try hypnotherapy, music therapy, yoga, and color therapy. Nor were they reluctant to consult an allopathic physician when they believed that such an approach would be more effective. They also used home remedies and over-the-counter drugs without hesitation.

A series of questions focused on the extent to which clients took charge of maintaining their health. We asked patients about the importance of regular check-ups, about maintaining their health, and whether treatments should concentrate on "symptoms" or on the "whole" person. On two of the three issues, there was a clear consensus. Almost everyone (96 percent) felt that a regular visit to an attending physician was an essential factor in staying healthy. There was almost an equally strong feeling (90 percent) that an individual had to "put some special effort" into maintaining her or his health. The sample was almost equally divided on the question of treating symptoms (50 percent) or the whole individual (45 percent). Men more than women (F ratio 3.71, $p \leq .05$) agreed that treatment should focus more on the totality of the individual than on specific symptoms. The study group was almost evenly divided on the use or avoidance of food additives or preservatives, although fully one-third tried daily to avoid both. However, women made a significantly greater effort than men (F ratio 3.68, $p \leq .05$) to exclude these foreign substances from their diets.

How effective is homeopathy as a panacea for all ailments? Interviewees were read a list of maladies and were asked which type of physician (allopath or homeopath) they would choose in each case. A number of individuals simply said, "I go to a homeopath for everything." In the cases of certain types of chronic or persistent illnesses, such as allergies or asthma, homeopaths were chosen overwhelmingly. For acute or particularly pernicious maladies, such as cancers, pneumonia, or cholera, even patients who would go to a homeopath for practically everything else said they would seek care from an allopathic practitioner.[7]

Some important differences emerged between men and women in their opinions about certain illnesses and their choice of healers. Males consistently opted to see allopaths, whereas females were unfailingly loyal to homeopathic practitioners. Generally speaking, where these differences in perception emerged, they focused on particularly virulent illnesses (e.g., cancers, cholera, and pneumonia).

Further corroboration of people's faith in the efficacy of homeopathic treatment emerged from a series of questions that addressed the degree or level of satisfaction that patients had with their physician and course of treatment. Several things warrant brief discussion. First, there was incredibly strong agreement that homeopaths are regarded as highly personable and effective health care providers. Second, almost 90 percent of the group felt that homeopaths could almost always cure patients. Further examination of women's attitudes about the efficacy of their primary care physicians suggests that they had greater faith than men in exactly how far-reaching and effective homeopathic treatment can be. In responses that were significantly different from those of men, women stated, for example, that while homeopathic physicians might not be able to prevent illnesses (F ratio 3.91, $p \leq .05$), they were very effective in curing maladies once they occurred (F ratio 13.42, $p \leq .001$).

Patients were asked to identify their most common medical complaints during the preceding six months. Mood swings headed the list, followed by back pains and persistent colds. At least one-third of the sample listed such things as back problems, stiff necks, or headaches as being very important. In addition, problems with bowel movements (either constipation or diarrhea) were health concerns. Significant differences between males and females centered on three problems. Men complained more often than women about having insomnia (F ratio 5.03, $p \leq .01$), and women had more problems with persistent colds (F ratio 4.72, $p \leq .05$) and chronic headaches (F ratio 6.66, $p \leq .01$).

SUMMARY AND CONCLUSIONS

That interest in homeopathic medicine is growing is corroborated by data from more than half of the private practices in the city of Oaxaca. We found that the average interviewee had become a new homeopathic patient in the past year. Moreover, patients were uniformly positive about the type of care received and about their prospects for getting better as a result of that care. They had great faith and confidence in their practitioners and the courses of treatment they offered. While both men and women expressed confidence that homeopathic treatment is effective for a wide range of ailments, they differed in their commitment to homeopathic treatment for afflictions like cancer, cholera, and malaria. Women more than men were committed to homeopathic therapy, and men more than women preferred the care of an allopathic physician.

The growth of interest in homeopathy does not mean patients are reluctant to explore other curing alternatives. Individuals feel quite comfortable drawing upon the expertise of a number of different kinds of medical personnel who might appear to an outsider to represent very divergent, if not conflicting, perspectives.

Some of the important discoveries to emerge from this work focus on the differences in perceptions and attitudes among male and female patients in a number of areas. In some areas, women appear to anticipate and take action to monitor and improve their health more readily than men. They report more often than men that their health is better than a year ago and are optimistic that it will continue to improve. Further, they are more likely to take steps to make sure their overall health improves by doing such things as excluding from their diet items they regard as harmful (additives and preservatives) and buying foodstuffs carefully to make sure they are safe and fresh. People are attracted to the homeopathic approach in part because of its emphasis on natural products, including the use of herbs and other botanical remedies in treatment.

That men and women have different perspectives regarding health and health care activities is not a new discovery. However, the direction of the difference is interesting. The women in the study, in contrast to poorer women in Mexico (cf. Finkler

1991), have a sense of their own abilities to help themselves. In contrast to poor women so often described in the literature, these women have an essentially positive attitude about their abilities to control their health. The question then becomes, what does homeopathy specifically offer to women (and men) in their quest for control over health?

Focusing on the whole person with special and particular needs is an important concept in homeopathic health care. Homeopathic physicians would state that two people who present essentially the same symptoms in all likelihood would be treated very differently. They state that one of the reasons office visits are often lengthy is the time required to understand how a particular problem relates to the whole person. In fact, Reed and colleagues, in citing the work of Jacobs, report that "homeopathic physicians spend twice as much time with their patients," but order half as many laboratory tests as do allopathic physicians (1993:85). Homeopaths in Oaxaca would probably concur with this observation. Several homeopathic physicians commented on the lengthy reviews of patient medical histories that were common among their colleagues and observed that this was the primary reason homeopaths could not (or did not) practice in the government-run hospitals and clinics.

Patients find the appeals of homeopathic medicine to be many and tantalizing. Both practitioners and patients emphasize that homeopathic medicine is holistic medicine, an approach that underscores understanding how the entire human organism works—it does not just try to "fix" one part that does not seem to be working well. As one physician told me, to be a good homeopath, one needs to be a physician, a psychologist, a sociologist, and (he noted with a twinkle in his eye) a good anthropologist. One of the appeals of homeopathic medicine turns on the remedies themselves. They are inexpensive and are all supposed to be made in laboratories (mainly in Europe) that ensure that all of the ingredients are "natural."

When I first arrived in Oaxaca to begin this research, a colleague asked what I planned to study. "Alternative medical practices," I responded. "What?" he asked. "Homeopathic medicine," I replied. "Oh," he quickly countered, "that's not alternative medicine." Findings from this study suggest that his observation is solidly on the mark.

NOTES

1. The terms *alternative* and *complementary* medicine here are juxtaposed with the numerically more dominant and politically more powerful biomedical, or allopathic, medicine systems.

2. These conclusions do not evoke controversy from any quarter and contain features commonly found in a number of medical systems. In order to arrive at the proper dosage, a process called "potentization" takes place. This process involves diluting the medicinal substance one part by volume with 99 parts of distilled water or ethyl alcohol, followed by vigorous shakings ("succusions") (cf. Ullman 1988b:11–12; Vithoulkas 1983:100–101). The process of successive dilutions on a decimal scale (1:10) or a centismal scale (1:100) depends on the illness and the original potency (toxicity) of the medicinal substance. Homeopaths believe that serial dilutions can be made to a dilution of $1:10^{24}$ without losing the original substance altogether. The feeling is that beyond this level of dilution the preparation no longer contains any molecules of the original substance. Nevertheless, while recognizing the absence of scientific explanation or proof to support their contention, homeopaths argue that further dilutions, up to a dilution of $1:10^{200,000}$ can take place with extremely beneficial results. Practitioners postulate "that some new form of energy is released by this technique of dilution and succusions. The energy that is contained in a restrained form in the original substance is somehow released and transmitted to the molecules of the solvent, in which it can be enhanced *ad infinitum*" (Vithoulkas 1983:101). Reed and colleagues note that Davenas and collaborators have written about the "memory of water" theory, again suggesting that the water-alcohol combination becomes altered by the medicine during the process of dilution and succusion and that this structure is retained well after the actual substances have dissipated (Reed et al. 1992:83).

3. Winter and colleagues, in their 1987 study of the city of Oaxaca, conducted a systematic sample of approximately 3,600 households drawn from a random selection of blocks within each of the city's 54 fiscal sectors in order to interview 630 female household heads. They observed that the average woman was 39.53 years and had 5.48 years of education (1993:1353). While the average age of women in their study was approximately the same as that in the current investigation, the women who visited homeopathic physicians were considerably better educated than the average female head of household in the Winter et al. study.

4. Homeopathic consultations, by local standards, are not inexpensive. While the price of a visit varied, charges tended to be in the $15–25 (U.S.) range.

5. The comparative figures used in the following discussion represent the differences between the means and F level from the ANOVA between males and females.

6. Injectionists are individuals whose services are varied. Sometimes they simply inject medicines prescribed by allopathic physicians or recommended by a pharmacist or a neighbor. On other occasions they diagnose and prescribe medicines themselves.

7. Homeopathic physicians agree with a perception of treatment modalities that distinguishes between chronic versus acute illnesses.

REFERENCES

Berman, Brian M., ed. 1992. *Alternative Medicine: Expanding Medical Horizons*. Report to the National Institutes of Health on Alternative Medical Systems and Practices in the United States, prepared under the auspices of the Workshop on Alternative Medicine, Chantilly, VA, September 14–16.

Cant, Sarah, and Ursula Sharma. 1996. Demarcation and Transformation within Homoeopathic Knowledge: A Strategy of Professionalization. *Social Science and Medicine 42*(4):579–588.

Finkler, Kaja. 1991. *Physicians at Work, Patients in Pain: Biomedical Practice and Patient Response in Mexico*. Boulder, CO: Westview Press.

Furnham, Adrian, and Ravi Bhagrath. 1993. A Comparison of Health Beliefs and Behaviours of Clients of Orthodox and Complementary Medicine. *British Journal of Clinical Psychology 32*:237–246.

Furnham, Adrian, and Chris Smith. 1988. Choosing Alternative Medicine. A Comparison of the Beliefs of Patients Visiting a General Practitioner and a Homeopath. *Social Science and Medicine 26*(7):685–689.

Lecomte J. 1983. Homeopathy and the Law. *World Health Forum 4*(2):111–113.

Patel, Mahesh S. 1987. Problems in the Evaluation of Alternative Medicine. *Social Science and Medicine 25*(6):669–678.

Press, Irwin. 1971. The Urban Curandero. *American Anthropologist 73*:741–756.

———. 1978. Urban Folk Medicine: A Functional Overview. *American Anthropologist 80*:71–84.

Reed, John C., et al. 1992. Alternative Systems of Medical Practice. In *Alternative Medicine: Expanding Medical Horizons*. Brian Berman, ed. Pp. 67–111. Report to the National Institutes of Health on Alternative Medical Systems and Practices in the United States, prepared under the auspices of the Workshop on Alternative Medicine, Chantilly, VA, September 14–16.

Salmon, J. Warren, ed. 1984. *Alternative Medicines: Popular and Policy Perspectives*. London: Tavistock Publications.

Ullman, Dana. 1988a. Homeopathy: Medicine for the 21st Century. *The Futurist 22*(4):43–47.

———. 1988b. *Homeopathy: Medicine for the 21st Century*. Berkeley, CA: North Atlantic Books.

Vithoulkas, George. 1983. Homeopathy: A Therapy for the Future? *World Health Forum 4*(2):99–101.

Whiteford, Michael B. 1995. Como Se Cura: Patterns of Medical Choice among Working Class Families in the City of Oaxaca, Mexico. In *The Cultural Dimension of Development*. D. M. Warren, L. J. Slikkerveer, and D. Brokensha, eds. Pp. 218–230. London: Intermediate Technology Publications.

Winter, Mary, Earl Morris, and Arthur Murphy. 1993. The Health Status of Women in Oaxaca: Determinants and Consequences. *Social Science and Medicine 37*(11):1351–1358.

■ ■ ■ ■ ▨ ▨ ■ ■ ■ ■

6   THE EPISTEMOLOGY OF TRADITIONAL HEALING SYSTEMS

Russel Barsh

Medicines are important tools of many healing systems, particularly naturalistic systems such as Ayurveda, Unani, traditional Chinese medicine, homeopathy, and indigenous medical traditions throughout the world. The study of these medicines is called ethnopharmacology (see selections 13, 25, 31, 44; Prendergrast et al. 1998). This selection compares biomedical studies of traditional remedies, undertaken as a result of rising awareness that most of these remedies are effective and might be adopted into the Western pharmacopoeia.

Barsh argues that it is much more productive to ask traditional healers for direction than to select plants for testing based on their taxonomic relationship to other plants with desirable pharmacological properties. It is likely that laboratory studies underestimate the effectiveness of traditional remedies, due to problems related to procuring information, obtaining samples, and processing plants. Some plants have multiple uses, whereas others are more effective in combination. Healers take account of the patient's history, constitution, and behavior when prescribing remedies, so that different medicines may be used for the same symptoms in different people, as seen in the previous selection.

In addition, there are issues concerning the nature of knowledge that make the entire enterprise of testing efficacy by Western scientific methods problematic (see Fábrega 2002; Hassel et al. 2002). Different medical traditions have different standards of evidence and ideas about the purpose, outcome, and timing of treatment by methods that may not involve pharmaceuticals, such as acupuncture or chiropractic. Moreover, healers teach and learn through complex processes beyond simple verbal or digital transmission methods, just as Western medical education includes long periods of learning by imitation and observation. Barsh argues that in traditional medical systems, this kind of guided learning is even more important, given the relative absence of a distinction between theory and practice. Theory is continually tested and refined through everyday practice and empirical observation. The cumulative result may be just as scientific since theory is revised if it fails to predict future events accurately.

Barsh suggests that outside observers may not ever have the privilege of learning from traditional healers unless they show sufficient commitment to using the knowledge properly and responsibly. Knowledge imposes duties of respect to the natural world, to the people who might benefit from it, and to future generations to whom it will be transmitted. A purely textual approach therefore represents an obstruction in research on indigenous medicines. The researcher's approach to involvement in the field of study raises important issues taken up again in the next selection.

Questions to keep in mind

Why is it important to be precise and accurate in spreading knowledge of how to use traditional plant medicines?

What factors may explain why some studies fail to find evidence of plant remedy effectiveness?

What are empathic and analog forms of learning, and what do they tell us about the amount and kind of information that can be gained verbally?

As a sub-discipline of anthropology, ethnobotany is a century old, with roots in the early work of the Bureau of American Ethnology; the clinical study of aboriginal Americans' medicinal uses of plants is at least two centuries older (Vogel 1970). Since the 1970s, however, the publication of ethno-botanical and ethnomedical surveys has accelerated markedly, accompanied by more exhaustive laboratory testing of herbal remedies' biological activity (Sofowara 1993). According to a recent United Nations report (Daes 1993:23), U.S. government health agencies alone have spent more than $8 million since 1986 to collect thousands of medicinal plant species in more than 22 countries. The commercial stakes are high; world sales of the cancer-fighting drugs *vincristine* and *vinblastine*, derived from a single traditional medicinal plant in Madagascar, have already exceeded $100 million.

Traditional pharmacopoeia have not only yielded a large number of drugs effective against cancer, but also against heart disease, parasites, and neural dysfunction (Phillipson 1994; Marston *et al.* 1993; Amato 1992; Huxtable 1992). Researchers have recently recognized the validity of ethnoveterinary traditions (*e.g.,* Hadani and Shimshony 1994; Sugimoto *et al.* 1992a, 1992b). Novel bioactive molecules have been identified from the "indigenous" or "folk" traditions of all regions including Europe, as well as the literate *ayurvedic* (India), *kampo* (Japan), and Chinese medical traditions. Several journals are devoted largely, or entirely to this line of study (e.g., *Journal of Ethnopharmacology, Journal of Natural Products, Planta Medica, American Journal of Chinese Medicine*) although clinical and laboratory findings are also reported in dozens of more general medical and biochemical journals.

Selection of plant species for biochemical screening based on the known properties of related species is reportedly about one-fourth as efficient as a selection guided by traditional healers (Balick 1990). This suggests that traditional medical knowledge can be objective, or empirical, perhaps to the extent as Western experimental sciences. It has indeed been argued that the best places to look for new drugs are societies that have not only lived a long time in the same ecosystem, but which have a "conservative" medical tradition with accurate means of transmitting knowledge (Cox 1990). Are all medical systems equally "conservative," or are there significant variations in their empirical rigor?

Empiricism is easy to confirm in literate traditions such as that of pre-colonial Vietnam (Loi and Dung 1991), since they left exhaustive written records of the historical search for safer and more effective remedies. Empiricism can nonetheless also be *implied* from the content of traditional "folk" pharmacopoeia if: (1) most remedies do contain bioactive compounds that have at least some of the medical properties claimed for them; (2) the proportion of bioactive compounds found in the pharmacopoeia is significantly greater than in nature; (3) "folk" healers prepare traditional remedies in ways which isolate their most bioactive compounds or remove toxic ones; (4) healers combine plants in ways that create medically significant synergistic effects. To the extent that a traditional pharmacopoeia shares these characteristics, it would appear to build upon clinical trials and observations rather than language, symbolism, structural logic, or unchallenged tradition.

DATA

Remedy Effectiveness

A high proportion of plant extracts used by traditional healers have been shown to be effective, *in vitro* and in clinical trials, for the specific applica-

tions claimed. Table 6.1 summarizes the findings of 100 research reports published during the five-year period, 1990–1994. Articles were selected from the *MedLine* CD-ROM database which includes medical and biochemistry journals from all countries in all languages, and is comparable in its coverage to the *Index Medicus*. Articles were only included in Table 6.1 if they reported original laboratory tests or clinical data; multiple reports from the same experiment were counted as one, and review articles were excluded. Also excluded were a large number of articles listing the traditional medical uses of plants, the chemical constituents of medicinal plants, or the molecular structures of these constituents, without testing their efficacy. A small number of reports concerned remedies derived from animal material rather than plants: earthworms, insects, and vertebrate bones.

. . .

Two points must be stressed in interpreting these data. First, it must be presumed that positive results are more likely to be reported, hence the ratio of positive to negative laboratory findings shown here may well overestimate the total efficacy of traditional pharmacopoeia. I have sampled a relatively small time period, moreover, and this kind of research is still clearly in its infancy. Empty cells in the table should not be taken as evidence that regional medical traditions *lack* effective remedies for those particular applications.

Bearing these cautions in mind, traditional pharmacopoeia do seem to address a very broad and comparable spectrum of medical concerns in all regions.

The extent to which laboratory studies did *not* confirm the claims of traditional healers may simply reflect failure to prepare extracts properly. On the whole, biochemists are working from lists of species with limited information on their specific preparation and uses (*e.g.,* Bohlin 1993; Marston *et al.* 1993). They may be testing the wrong part of the plant, or collecting the plant under the wrong conditions. The crude extract may contain both useful drugs and antagonists, which the traditional preparation method separates. Or, the drug is only given in combination with other plant extracts which modify its chemistry *in vivo* or act as catalysts (e.g. Kroes *et al.* 1993; Johri and Zutshi 1992).

Table 6.1 Published Reports on the Efficacy of Traditional Remedies (1990–1994) by Biochemical Applications and Regional Sources

Effective Use	Literate Traditions			Indigenous/Folk Traditions				
	Ayurvedic	Chinese	Japanese	Europe	Mid-East	Africa	Americas	SE Asia
Abortifactant	1	—	—	—	—	1	—	—
Analgesic/sedative	—	—	—	—	1	—	3	—
Antibacterial	2	—	1	1	1	4	6	—
Antifilarial	—	—	—	—	1	—	—	—
Antifungal	—	—	—	—	1	1	2	—
Anti-molluscoidal	—	—	—	—	—	—	—	1
Anti-protozoan	—	—	—	—	—	4	4	1
Anticlotting	—	3	—	—	—	—	—	—
Antihistamine	1	—	1	—	—	—	1	—
Antipyretic	1	1	—	1	2	2	2	—
Anti-sickling	—	—	—	—	—	1	—	—
Antivenom	—	—	—	—	—	—	1	—
Cancer suppression	—	2	—	—	1	—	—	—
Cholesterol reduction	1	—	—	—	—	—	—	—
Diabetes/metabolism	2	1	3	1	3	—	—	—
Drug facilitator	2	—	—	—	—	—	—	—
Hepatoprotection[1]	1	1	3	—	—	—	2	—
Immune system disorders	1	2	2	—	—	—	—	—
Muscle/vascular relaxant	1	2	1	1	2	3	2	—
Neurotransmission	1	—	1	—	—	—	—	—
Thyroid disorders	—	—	—	1	—	—	—	—
Ulcer prevention[2]	1	1	1	1	2	—	1	—
Urinary stones	1	—	—	—	—	—	—	—
Ineffective	—	—	—	—	1	—	1	—
Toxic/mutagenic	—	1	—	—	1	1	2	—
Total Publications (#)	16	15	12	5	11	16	23	2

[1]Lipid peroxidation antagonists and free-radical scavengers.
[2]Gastric and/or nephritic lesions.

Aggregate Effectiveness

The most persuasive evidence of empiricism in traditional systems of phytotherapy comes from evaluations of entire pharmacopoeia, rather than selected individual herbal remedies. A large number of extracts can be screened simultaneously by testing their effect on a strain of *Staphylococcus aureus* or some other human pathogen, grown in standard laboratory cultures. Naturally, this method *underestimates* the total effectiveness of a society's traditional pharmacopoeia, since it does not test each individual remedy for its own specific traditional use. A particular remedy could be useless in combating the test pathogen, yet highly effective against other microbes, or in stimulating natural human immune-system responses. Large-scale screening studies indicate very high levels of effectiveness, nonetheless.

Large-scale standard bioassays confirmed that 82 out of 96 plants used by British Columbia Indians have significant antibiotic activity, for example (McCutcheon *et al.* 1992). Similarly, 86 percent of plants in the traditional Samoan pharmacopoeia display some bioactivity (Cox 1993). Seven out of eight medicinal plants used to combat infections in Mexico were effective against a broad spectrum of gram-positive and gram-negative bacteria, and contained at least 23 different effective compounds (Rojas *et al.* 1992). In more restrictive tests, 17 out of 30 plants in the traditional Rwandan pharmacopoeia were effective against the protozoan pathogen *Trichomonas vaginalis* (Hakizamungu *et al.* 1992): 11 out of 50 plants in the Cuban folk pharmacopoeia displayed at least some cardiotonic, hypotensive, or brochodilator effects (Carbajal *et al.* 1991), and 28 out of 68 plants used in Guatemala to combat respiratory disease were effective against either *Staphylococcus* or *Streptococcus* (Caceres *et al.* 1991). One-third of the plants utilized by traditional Tanzanian healers to alleviate malaria are effective *in vitro* against *Plasmodium falciparum* (Gessler *et al.* 1994).

In his exhaustive study of 16th century Aztec medicine, Ortiz de Montellano (1990:191) concluded that 60 percent of the remedies in use could have cured the ailments for which they were generally prescribed (*etic* validity), and 85 percent could have produced the physiological effects that Aztec physicians associated with the healing process such as sweating (*emic* validity). He did not conduct experiments, but made inferences from the presence of tannins, saponins, alkaloids, and other compounds with well-known physiological effects in plants found in the Aztec pharmacopoeia. Some of these plants may contain novel compounds which have not yet been assayed for bioactivity, thus further research could lead to an even more favorable assessment of Aztec pharmacy.

These results are not merely artifacts of the natural abundance of bioactive compounds in the ecosystem. Experimentally, for example, the species selected by an East African phytotherapist identified more bioactive compounds, than a random selection of plant species from the same ecosystem (Taniguchi and Kubo 1993).

It is also significant that hardly any herbals have been found to be useful in ways which had *not* already been recognized by traditional phytotherapists. The one notable exception is *Catharanthus roseus*, or Madagascar rosy periwinkle. Traditionally utilized to treat diabetes, it also contains a group of novel alkaloids that are effective against certain cancers (Noble 1990). No further ethnography has been carried out to confirm that this property of *C. roseus* was previously unknown, however, among Malagasy healers. Similarly, the discovery of taxol, a cancer-suppressing compound from Pacific Northwest yew bark, was first reported by American biochemists as serendipitous, but yew is utilized in Chinese medicine to combat cancers (Han 1994), and my own work

has confirmed that it was long known in Salish phytotherapy.

A recent survey of traditional phytotherapy in Sumatra's Seberida District concluded that half the pharmacopoeia was merely of "magical" value, although the same plant species were also used by other peoples in southeast Asia (Mahyar *et al.* 1991). This was based on ethnography, rather than clinical studies, and it is possible that researchers were simply misinterpreting folk explanations of the underlying nature and treatment of some illnesses. An herbal decoction may have a "magical" power, as explained to patients by shamanic healers, and still possess clinical bioactivity—if only as a sedative or analgesic.

At the same time, researchers may be given incomplete data on the preparation and uses of plants deliberately, particularly if they are not fully trusted by traditional healers, or are regarded as unable to use this knowledge safely. Significantly, many ethnobotanical surveys are still conducted by interviewing ordinary people, rather than well-respected healers. This shortcut saves time, but tends to reduce the accuracy and adequacy of data greatly. Surveys of everyday knowledge have generally identified fewer effective remedies and more toxic ones (e.g. Weigel *et al.* 1994). This should not be surprising. Comparisons of medical professionals with everyday medical beliefs on the streets of New York or Toronto would yield similar results.

Preparation Methods

The chemical complexity of plants means that many different drugs can be produced from each species. The Warao of Venezuela's Amazonia, for example, prepare 259 drugs from 100 plant species (Wilbert and Haiek 1991). In Samoa, Dittmar (1991) found a very high degree of agreement between phytotherapists' choice of different parts of *Hernandia* spp to treat specific complaints, and the distribution of different bioactive compounds in different organs of this plant. Unfortunately, there is little ethnographic data on the preparation of specific extracts. The use of solvents such as animal or vegetable fat, water temperature and standing time (for fermentation or precipitation) could significantly affect the chemistry of the prepared drug.

Plants are structurally differentiated, and the mix of compounds produced by each specialized organ of a plant fluctuate markedly with the seasons, the plant's reproductive cycle, its health, intensity of herbivory, parasite loads, and soil chemistry. A phytotherapist must not only know which species to select and where to best find it, but the extent to which the location, season, and condition of individual plants affect the presence and concentration of its useful properties. A phytotherapist must understand the localization of those properties (e.g., in the buds, fruits, bark, leaves, or roots), and how to extract them (e.g., whether they are water-soluble or fat-soluble) in a manner that minimizes contamination with other toxic or antagonistic chemical compounds found in the same plant organs.

This is one important reason why superficial knowledge of herbals can be very dangerous: errors of selection or preparation can produce a useless or even fatal product. Many common medicinal plants can be toxic or mutagenic at levels greater than the medically-effective dose (e.g., Malone and Rother 1994; Abena *et al.* 1994; Hoyos *et al.* 1992; Hong *et al.* 1992; Nath *et al.* 1992; Mossa *et al.* 1991). Others contain toxic components that must be removed or neutralized (e.g., Ng *et al.* 1991).

There are a growing number of clinical reports of *adverse* effects from traditional remedies, including toxicity from lead salts in some Chinese, ayurvedic, Arab, and Mexican folk preparations (Markowitz *et al.* 1994; Keen *et al.* 1994; Yanez *et al.* 1994; Dunbabin *et al.* 1992; Woolf 1990); toxic organic molecules in plant extracts used in traditional African, Mexican, and Chinese remedies (Bah *et al.* 1994; Kadiri et al 1992; Ojogwu 1992; McVann *et al.* 1992; Dunn *et al.* 1991; Ng *et al.* 1991); and infection from bacterial contamination of Mexican remedies prepared from desiccated rattlesnakes (Kraus *et al.* 1991).

It should be stressed that nearly all reports of toxicity involve individual diagnostic cases, rather than laboratory or clinical trials under controlled conditions. In other words, physicians have reported symptoms which they attribute to the toxicity of traditional remedies, ingested before the patient sought allopathic treatment. Often little data is available on the identity or composition of the herbal remedy, the conditions under which it was prescribed, or indeed whether it was prescribed by a traditional healer at all. The consequences of taking "home remedies" without expert advice, or of using traditional herbals improperly, are thus confounded with instances where traditional drugs have had toxic effects even when properly used.

An example of toxicity from the improper use of an effective drug is the oral administration of margosa oil, a potent topical antiseptic (Lai *et al.* 1990; *cf.* Bye and Dutton 1991). In Mexico, many popular "home remedies" for *empacho* are either useless (*e.g.*, cooking oil), or dangerous lead and bismuth salts which may offer temporary relief from discomfort, but are eventually toxic (Cortes Gallo *et al.* 1993). These adverse effects are no more attributable to "professional" practice of medicine, than overdoses, misuse of drugs, or home remedies in Western industrialized countries. Another possible reason for toxicity may be poor quality control in compounding remedies, *e.g.*, the high levels of bufadienolides found in commercial samples of the traditional Chinese medicine *liu-shen-wan* (Hong and Yeung 1992). Still another possibility is interaction between traditional and allopathic remedies in the same patient. *Mouboumou,* a traditional remedy for diarrhea in Zaire, seems to be safe and effective if taken alone, but neutralizes chloroquinine when the two are taken together (Tsakala *et al.* 1990).

In one of the rare reports of toxicity in the laboratory study of a traditional herbal, three African plants traditionally used against malaria were found to be potently bioactive, but lethal to rats (Agomo *et al.* 1992). Since crude extracts were employed, it is quite possible that the extracts were incompletely refined, the dose was too high, or the remedies required compounding with other herbal products to offset toxic components. These possibilities were not explored in subsequent research.

Compound Prescriptions

The adverse effects of some of the components of a plant extract can be managed by combining it with an extract containing *antagonists.* The chemistry of a compound drug containing several different extracts can be extremely complex. Some constituents neutralize each other, or facilitate one another's biological effects. Some react to create new molecular structures. These reactions may take place *in vitro*, or may require the presence of organic chemicals found in the patient such as gastric enzymes.

An illustration of the importance of herbal compounding is *Heimia salicifolia,* widely used in Latin American folk remedies. It contains several bioactive alkaloids, which affect different metabolic pathways (Malone and Rother 1994). Most therapeutic uses of *Heimia* would require the addition of other herbs to "turn off" some of these alkaloids, and this may explain why phytotherapists identify *Heimia* as effective for an extraordinary range of applications including inflammation, fever, bladder control, constipation, and syphilis. This suggests the reason why so many medicinal plants identified by ethnobotanists are reported to have multiple, and seemingly inconsistent uses. They may contain a variety of active constituents, which must be selected either through the process of preparation, or by the addition of other plant extracts which "turn on" or "turn off" particular chemical compounds.

Similarly, the Mexican folk remedy *azarcon,* while composed mainly of toxic lead tetroxide, contains small quantities of other minerals which alter the metabolism and toxicity of the lead in animal models (Yanez *et al.* 1994). Neither the components of *azarcon* nor the theory behind their combination have been unreported, but the *in vivo* results suggest a conscious effort to control the undesirable effects of lead, an element which was very widely used in allopathic medicine until the discovery of less toxic alternatives in the 1920s.

Compound drug formulae may have completely different effects than their herbal constituents. An elegant example is the compound *trikatu* in ayurvedic medicine (Johri and Zutshi 1992). One of its components is rich in piperine, an alkaloid which facilitates the bioavailability of other drugs consumed with it, exactly as ayurvedic healers claim. The ayurvedic compound *Nimba arishta* also contains a biological catalyst, *Woodfordia fruticosa* flowers, the effects of which have been confirmed *in vitro* although the biochemical mechanism remains obscure (Kroes *et al.* 1993). The effect of drugs may also be influenced greatly by diet, and there has been inadequate attention to the dietary recommendations made by traditional healers (Etkin and Ross 1991).

Several different drugs are used, either in a balanced compound, or as alternatives selected according to individual patients, to treat a single syndrome. Among the Warao, for example, 259 drugs were used by phytotherapists to treat just 52 syndromes (Wilbert and Haiek 1991). In the Pacific Northwest, likewise, Salish healers utilize drugs from an array of different tree barks to treat the same syndromes (Turner and Hebda 1990). Researchers rarely study an indigenous pharmacopoeia as an integrated system of diagnosis and prescription, however, in which different individuals may be given different remedies according to an empirical protocol (*cf.* Bourdy and Walter 1992; Wilbert and Haiek 1991). While there have been meticulous studies of some folk theories of disease, moreover, they have not been followed by tests of external or objective validity (e.g., Maskarinec 1992; Lambert 1992).

The pharmacological properties of different plants may be encoded explicitly in the folk system of botanical or medical taxonomy (e.g., Messer 1991), but this may be insufficient for clinical purposes, like the classification of drugs as "calcium-blockers" or "glycosides" in Western allopathic medicine. Knowledge of the individual drug and the individual patient are still required before the efficacy, or even the safety of a prescription can be forecast, either in the traditional or allopathic systems. Indeed, one of the complaints frequently leveled at contemporary allopathic physicians by patients is their inattention to the individual, e.g., selecting drugs by sequential trial-and-error ("take this and call me if there are side-effects") rather than taking adequate time for medical histories and physical examination.

I suspect that a better understanding of the logic of compounding is crucial, because it is the stage at which the healer *individualizes* the remedy. Failure to explore this level of traditional practice may deprive us of important insights about variability in human physiology as well as the interactions of drugs *in vivo.*

DISCUSSION

Extant laboratory and clinical studies suggest that a *majority* of the remedies used in traditional pharmacopoeia are not only effective, but require careful preparation, including compounding, to ensure that they have strong, selective, and non-toxic effects. What may we infer from the fact that a *minority* of traditional remedies seem ineffective or even toxic? Does this prove that healers continue to utilize these remedies, despite their evident uselessness, because they accord them "magical" properties? That healers are slaves to tradition? Or, that many of the researchers testing these remedies lack adequate knowledge of their proper preparation and clinical use? Three lines of analysis may shed light on these questions.

Serendipity

Could a clinically-valid pharmacopoeia develop simply from a long accumulation of fortunate, serendipitous discoveries? Given adequate time, it may be argued, nature creates all of the "experiments" needed to learn the useful properties of plants, even in complex combination. If this were true, however, societies that have experienced relatively recent ecological changes or migration should have much less extensive and less reliable knowledge of phytotherapy (Cox 1990). Migrations in the South Pacific, and significant human modification of the Amazonian forest ecosystems, probably occurred within the past millennium or two, but these societies are not especially deficient in medical knowledge. Similarly, European settlers quickly learned and modified the medical systems of indigenous Americans, just as I find indigenous healers in North America using many introduced European plant species.

On the other hand, there is field evidence of a "learning curve" for recent immigrants. In Bolivia, three-fourths of the remedies used by Chimane Indians against protozoan parasites were effective *in vitro* compared with one-fifth of the remedies popular among Latino settlers (Fournet *et al.* 1994). This may suggest, in the terms proposed by Cox, that the settlers have a less conservative, or less rigorous system of medicine, but a simpler explanation would be that they are still in a stage of exploration, experimentation, and imitation of the practices of their indigenous neighbors. It would be interesting to examine the settlers' pharmacopoeia to compare the remedies they brought with them from their former homes, with those learned from the Chimane, or found in the new environment by experimentation.

Unfortunately, there is little comparable data on the quantity or quality of pharmacological knowledge from different "folk" societies. There is also little data on variability in clinical practices *within* particular societies. In Western psychiatry, for example, differences in individual experiences, theories and practices are considerable and play an important role in maintaining a critical scientific discourse (Gaines 1983). Similarly, a recent survey of 292 traditional healers in Uganda found that they used different herbs, and different doses in treating diarrhea (Anokbonggo *et al.* 1990), suggesting an experimental and competitive medical community. In Fiji (Viti Levu) 25 years ago, I recorded instances in which traditional psychotherapists competed to cure problem patients, and later met to compare notes. More attention should be paid to this kind of direct evidence of scientific processes in traditional medicine.

Multifariousness

Not only are folk pharmacopoeiae largely valid in clinical terms, but each one seems to possess remedies for a broad range of infections and metabolic disorders, uniquely chosen from local plant communities. Remedies for macrofiliarial parasites are used worldwide, for example, utilizing at least 90 plant species (Comley 1990). Effective remedies against the protozoan pathogen *Plasmodium,* which causes malaria, have been found throughout the tropics (Presber *et al.* 1991). Drugs capable of managing the symptoms of diabetes have been identified in all major Aslan medical traditions, as well as Middle Eastern and European folk traditions, though not in the Americas (Table 6.1). Diabetes appears to be correlated with a shift from hunting, foraging or horticulture to a diet dominated by grains, however (O'Den 1991; Barsh 1994a, 21), and nearly all ethnomedical research in the Americas has focused on horticultural and hunting peoples. I am aware of at least one herbal remedy for diabetes that is widely prescribed by Blackfoot and Cree healers today, and which, interestingly, was not reported in the past to have this application. Contemporary healers, confronting new health problems, are apparently discovering new uses for familiar *materia medica.*

Bioactive molecules occur naturally in plants chiefly as defense mechanisms, or as secondary metabolites (Cox 1990). That is, they do not generally play a direct role in plants' own metabolism, and often do not have any known function. Many of the bioactive constituents in plants are "trivial," in the sense that they are widespread throughout the plant kingdom (Pereira *et al.* 1994), while others are exceptionally complex and unique to individual species. Paraguayan phytotherapists compound closely-related species (Schmeda Hirschmann and Bordas 1990), suggesting that they are conscious of differences in their chemical composition.

Various species of the genus *Strychnos* (Loganiaceae) are employed in traditional pharmacopoeiae from Africa, Asia and Latin America, for example, but their chemical constituents and medical applications vary considerably, and some species are extremely toxic (Quetin LeClercq *et al.* 1990). Hence traditional healers could not have discovered useful medicines in new environments simply by searching for familiar genera. They would have had to experiment with each novel species to determine its specific properties, which could differ markedly.

I have heard indigenous people from different regions explain, in strikingly similar terms, that "everything you need" for health can be found in each ecosystem—if you know where to look. Consider the case of oral contraceptives, prepared by societies worldwide from more than 50 different plants which, although botanically unrelated, all contain estrogen or closely analogous steroids (Barsh 1994b). Useful compounds may be widely dispersed in nature, but they are not always located in predictable places. The multifarious character of naturally-occurring drugs means that each society's knowledge is localized, is not readily transferable to other ecosystems, and therefore probably results from independent investigations and experiments.

This raises interesting questions about the evolutionary aspects of the distribution of medicinal compounds in plant communities. The search for food and medicine involve essentially the same processes of adaptation. An organism which selectively ingests plants that improve its fitness, and transmits this selection grid to its offspring either genetically or through imitative learning, has an adaptive advantage. The "discovery" and transmission of preferences for medicinal plants, is no more mysterious than the adaptation of food preferences to new environments. Self-medication by gorillas with wild ginger, a species rich in terpenes and effective against intestinal worms, has recently been documented (Tutin *et al.* 1991), and further research with gorillas and other primates is underway. Food preferences can lead in turn to co-adaptation or co-evolution, if the consumer helps disseminate seeds or spores of the food species (Tomback 1983). Likewise, the selection and cultivation of foods may be influenced by their medicinal as well as nutritive properties (Etkin 1988).

It is not inconceivable that the earliest hominids began choosing medicinal plants from the ecological inventories available to them, as they migrated into different environments, and indirectly promoted the increase and wider distribution of some of these species by scattering their spores or seeds. Deliberate transplantation of medicinal plants may have come later, although the published evidence for this practice in contemporary Amazonia has been disputed (Parker 1992). This could explain why some of the medicinal characteristics of plants have been maintained, genetically, despite these molecules' apparent lack of any direct function in the plants in which they are found.

Traditional Pedagogy

There is an implicit assumption, in the research methodology used to elicit traditional pharmacological knowledge, that this information is ordinarily recorded and transmitted verbally, or *digitally* (numbers and/or words). To the extent that this assumption is valid, a visitor can obtain complete, reliable maps of the traditional knowledge-system by asking questions, and recording the answers. This is, plainly, the principal pedagogy of academic medicine and science, which worship the word, in particular the printed word. What if substantial portions of traditional knowledge are transmitted and learned non-verbally? After all, a university-trained allopathic physician must endure a residency during which s/he is chiefly engaged in *guided and imitative practice:* following an experienced physician on rounds, being shown how to touch and smell patients, imitating a mentor's reactions to situations. Why would we assume that traditional healers' skills are *more* verbal-based than this?

Tribal and industrial societies share two other forms of learning and knowing which are not verbal or digital, but figure prominently in the maintenance of practical skills. For convenience, we may refer to these pedagogies as *analog* and *empathic*. In cybernetics, *analog* describes an information system which converts one quantity or process into another, without using digits as an intermediary. A phonograph—almost obsolete, now is an analog system that converts vibrations directly into physical grooves on wax or plastic, and then back again. The advantage of inserting a digital-conversion step in the technology is to facilitate screening the signal, to delete unwanted information, or "noise." Digitization necessarily involves *simplifying* the signal, separating useful from useless information at the cost of reducing the complexity of the useful information, which is converted into averaged units (smooth curve to step-curve).

Most North American children learn to pitch a baseball. There is a relatively straightforward method of representing the trajectory of a pitched ball digitally using parabolic geometry; using calculus and vector mathematics the instantaneous effects of wind currents and spin can be forecast with some accuracy, assuming that they can be measured reliably. Children learn this in school, but it does not make any of them better pitchers. Skill at pitching is acquired through practice, imitation, and the "unconscious" acquisition of ability to anticipate the interactions of mass, momentum, spin, windspeed and direction, and other factors. The measurement of these factors and their combination is never consciously digitized; indeed, professional coaches usually warn players to *avoid* thinking about what they are doing.

. . .

Returning to the example of medical residency, much of the daily *practice* of allopathic medicine is empathic, which is why it can only be learned by observation, imitation, and experience. Any attempt to digitize the interactions of actual human bodies with microbes becomes so complex, and at the same time so over-simplified, that it no longer provides adequate practical guidance. If the learning of traditional medicine is also largely em-

pathic, then verbal research loses most of the practical details, and it is illusory to suppose that we have any accurate idea of the prescription of traditional remedies. Driven, in haste, by the commercial search for novel medicinal molecules, studies of traditional medicine have indeed barely "scratched the surface" of other knowledge systems—as if a Warao healer were to spend a month at the Harvard Medical School, *asking questions* through a Harvard student who possessed some nontechnical knowledge of English and Warao. This method would yield a vast amount of verbal information, perhaps a list of commonly-used antibiotics, but the Warao would gain little working knowledge of Western medicine, and would utilize those antibiotics at their peril.

Verbal assessments of traditional medical systems are inadequate. Until outside observers take the time to learn healing skills in their own, nonverbal idiom, any test of the clinical claims of traditional remedies is likely to underestimate their efficacy considerably.

There are other obstacles to the validity of ethnopharmacological research arising from traditional pedagogy. Traditional epistemology, I believe, stresses the *process* of learning as opposed to the Western preoccupation with the *content* of what is taught. In those indigenous North American systems with which I am most familiar, the prospective student must establish a direct personal *relationship* with the teacher through gifting, ceremony, and sometimes adoption as kin, before being given knowledge of any sensitivity or power. Once established, such a relationship involves life-long responsibilities to practice and teach knowledge properly, and (frequently) to provide services freely or for a token payment. The teacher assumes personal lifetime responsibility for the pupil's conduct and expertise. As my own traditional teachers warned me whenever I asked a technical question, "heavy, heavy," which is to say that getting my wish would be a burden to be borne forever.

Traditional pre-occupations with process reflect ethical concerns. Useful knowledge is not a commodity, but a part of a relationship with other humans, animals and plants. Possessing knowledge imposes duties on the possessor which, if neglected, may render the knowledge useless or even dangerous. Asking about the proper use of an herb is inviting perpetual duties to the teacher, the animals that eat the herb as part of their diet, people in need of healing, and to the plant itself. If the use of the herb is conceived as a legacy from remote ancestors who made a compact with the plant world, the terms of the bargain must be kept faithfully. In functional terms, the prospective healer is bound by ideas and rituals that efface any selfish conceit.

Without re-opening at length the ethical debates which have raged in anthropology for decades, I question what proportion of researchers in ethnomedicine or ethnopharmacology have committed to *practice* those arts they have been taught. This is not an matter of confidentiality, privacy, or intellectual property rights, but of the validity of data. If traditional healers refrain from teaching essential details, except to pupils they know will practice the art, what they teach to the non-practitioner may fall short of a workable system. A Western physicist asked to explain the mechanism of a nuclear bomb would probably behave similarly, omitting key operating details unless there is a very sound reason to entrust the listener with the building of a working device.

CONCLUSION

It may be asked whether traditional healing is truly "scientific" or merely "empirical." A body of knowledge based on observations does not meet the Western philosophical criteria for "science" unless it is *organized* in accordance with *theories* (O'Hear 1989:55). Theories are simply assertions about the interrelationships among observable events which are consistent with previous observations, and appear capable of predicting future events to an arbitrary level of reliability (Fetzer 1993:44). In complex systems—to a mathematician, systems affected by "strange" or "chaotic" attractors (Kauffman 1993:178)—the theory that produces the *best* predictions may still be relatively unreliable, like theories of meteorology or theories of human behavior.

The diversity and relative unpredictability of human behavior and physiology at the *individual* level does not prevent us from conceiving and testing theories, but weakens the usefulness of theories as guides to practical action. Contrariwise, practitioners such as engineers or physicians may be the beneficiaries of theoretical developments, while

rarely paying conscious attention to theory in their work. To a great extent, the course of Western science has been marked by a divergence, institutionally, between practitioners and the creators of theory. As a result, Western scholars may be more conscious of "theory," and of a dialectic between theory and praxis, than scholars in other traditions of inquiry. Traditional healing, I would argue, makes no distinctions of this kind but tests theory at an individual practice level in each generation.

· · ·

A theory is no less of a theory when it is expressed in the form of a *model*, furthermore. Models are actual or imaginary systems that mimic the operation of theories (Kaplan 1964:263). We routinely use "solar systems" as models of atomic structure and electrical switching systems as models of brain function. Since the use of models is a way of talking about theories, a body of empirical knowledge is scientific if it uses models to systematize observations. Models refer to shared experiences within a culture, and they need not themselves be "true." A model of disease based on the vagaries of spirits, rather than the vagaries of microbes is nonetheless evidence of science, if it can be used to systematize past observations and predict future events.

Perhaps we must attend more carefully to the process of discovery and validation of models in traditional healing systems. In a life of practice, healers explore the limits of what they have been taught and discover errors or contradictions. To what extent do they revise the supporting models—for example, stories, rituals and taxonomies—when teaching the next generation? The answer to this question would lead us closer to evidence of a unifying scientific paradigm in traditional and contemporary literate societies, and is a challenge to researchers prepared to undertake the social obligations of becoming adepts rather than bystanders of traditional healing systems.

REFERENCES

Abena, A. A., G. S. Kintsangoula-Mbava, J. Diantama, and D. Bioka. 1993. Effects analgesiques d' un extrait brut d' Argeratum Conyzoides chez le rat. *Encephale* 19:329–332.

Agomo, P. U., J. C. Idigo, and B. M. Afolabi. 1992. Antimalarial Medicinal Plants and their Impact on

Cell Populations in Various Organs of Mice. *African Journal of Medicine and Medical Sciences* 21:39–46.

Amato, Ivan. 1992. From 'Hunter Magic,' A Pharmacopoeia? *Science* 258:1306.

Anokbonggo, W. W., R. Odoi-Admone, and P. M. Oluju. 1990. Traditional Methods in Management of Diarrhoeal Diseases in Uganda. *Bulletin of The World Health Organization* 68:359–363.

Bah, Moustapha, Robert Bye, and Rogelio Pereda-Miranda. 1994. Hepatotoxic Pyrrolizidine Alkaloids in the Mexican Medicinal Plant Packera Candidissima (Asteraceae: Senecioneae). *Journal of Ethnopharmacology* 43:19–30.

Balick, Michael J. 1990. Ethnobotany and the Identification of Therapeutic Agents from the Rainforest. In *Bioactive Compounds from Plants*. Derek J. Chadwick and Joan Marsh, eds. Pp. 22–31. New York: John Wiley and Sons.

Barsh, Russel L. 1994a. Canada's Aboriginal Peoples: Social Integration or Disintegration? *Canadian Journal of Native Studies* 14:1–46.

———. 1994b. Indigenous Peoples' Perspectives on Population and Development. *Boston College Environmental Affairs Law Review* 21:271–276.

Bohlin, Lars. 1993. Research on Pharmacologically Active Natural Products at the Department of Pharmacognosy, Uppsala University. *Journal of Ethnopharmacology* 28:225–231.

Bourdy, G., and A. Walter. 1992. Maternity and Medicinal Plants in Vanuatu; 1. The Cycle of Reproduction. *Journal of Ethnopharmacology* 37:179–196.

Bye, S. N., and M. F. Dutton. 1991. The Inappropriate Use of Traditional Medicines in South Africa. *Journal of Ethnopharmacology* 34:253–259.

Caceres, A., A. V. Alvarez, A. E. Ovando, and B. E. Samayoa. 1991. Plants Used in Guatemala for the Treatment of Respiratory Diseases; 1. Screening of 68 Plants against Gram-Positive Bacteria. *Journal of Ethnopharmacology* 31:193–208.

Carbajal, Daisy, Angel Casaco, Lourdes Arruzazabala, Ricardo Gonzalez, and Victor Fuentes. 1991. Pharmacological Screening of Plant Decoctions Commonly used in Cuban Folk Medicine. *Journal of Ethnopharmacology* 33:21–24.

Comley, J. C. W. 1990. New Macrofilaricidal Leads from Plants? *Tropical Medicine and Parasitology* 41:1–9.

Cortes Gallo, G., M. A. Hernandez Gonzalez, M. A. Ayala Garcia, A. Rocha Moreles, F. Aguinaga Jasso, J. J. Morales Aguirre, and J. A. Bribiesca Lopez. 1993. La Cura del Empacho: Una Practica Comun y Peligrosa. *Boletin Medico del Hospital Infantil de Mexico* 50:44–47.

Cox, Paul A. 1990. Ethnopharmacology and the Search for New Drugs. In *Bioactive Compounds from Plants*.

Pp. 40–47. Derek J. Chadwick and Joan Marsh, eds. New York: John Wiley and Sons.

———. 1993. Saving the Ethnopharmacological Heritage of Samoa. *Journal of Ethnopharmacology* 28:181–188.

Daes, Erica-Irene. 1993. Study on the Protection of the Cultural and Intellectual Property of Indigenous peoples. UNDOC E/CN.4/Sub.2/1993/28.

Dittmar, Alexandra. 1991. The Effectiveness of Hernandia spp. (Hernandiaceae) in Traditional Samoan Medicine and According to Scientific Analyses. *Journal of Ethnopharmacology* 33:243–251.

Dunbabin, David W., George A. Tallis, Phillip Y. Popplewell, and Raymond A. Lee. 1992. Lead poisoning from Indian Herbal Medicine (Ayurveda). *Medical Journal of Australia* 157:835–836.

Dunn, J. P., J. E. Krige, R. Wood, O. C. Bornman, and J. Terblanche. 1991. Colonic Complications After Toxic Tribal Enemas. *British Journal of Surgery* 78: 545–548.

Etkin, Nina L. 1988. Ethnopharmacology: Biobehavioral Approaches in the Anthropological Study of Indigenous Medicines. *Annual Review of Anthropology* 17:23–42.

Etkin, Nina L., and Paul J. Ross. 1991. Should We Set a Place for Diet in Ethnopharmacology? *Journal of Ethnopharmacology* 32:91–101.

Fetzer, James H. 1993. *Philosophy of Science*. New York: Paragon House.

Fournet, Alain, Alcira A. Barrios, and Victoria Munoz. 1994. Leishmanicidal and Trypanocidal Activities of Bolivian Medicinal Plants. *Journal of Ethnopharmacology* 41:19–37.

Gaines, Atwood D. 1982. Cultural Definitions, Behavior and the Person in American Psychiatry. In *Cultural Conceptions of Mental Health and Therapy*. Anthony J. Marsella and Geoffrey M. White, eds. Pp. 167–192. Dordrecht: D. Reidel.

Gessler, M. C., M. H. H. Nkunya, L. B. Mwasumbi, M. Heinrich, and M. Tanner. 1994. Screening Tanzanian Medicinal Plants for Antimalarial Activity. *Acta Tropica* 56:65–77.

Hadani, A., and A. Shimshony. 1994. Traditional Veterinary Medicine in the Near East: Jews, Arab Bedouins and Fellahs. *Revue Scientifique et Technique* 13:581–597.

Hakizamungu, Etienne, Luc Van Puyvelde, and Marc Wery. 1992. Screening of Rwandese Medicinal Plants for Anti-Trichomonas Activity. *Journal of Ethnopharmacology* 36:143–146.

Han, Rui. 1994. Highlight on the Studies of Anti-Cancer Drugs Derived from Plants in China. *Stem Cells* 12:53–63.

Hong, Z., K. Chan, and H. W. Yeung. 1992. Simultaneous Determination of Bufadienolides in the Traditional Chinese Medicine Preparation,

Liu-shen-wan, by Liquid Chromatography. *Journal of Pharmacy and Pharmacology* 44:1023–1026.

Hoyos, Luz Stella, William W. Au, Moon Y. Heo, Debra L. Morris, and Marvin S. Legator. 1992. Evaluation of the Genotoxic Effects of a Folk Medicine, Petiveria Alliacea (Anamu). *Mutation Research* 280:29–34.

Huxtable, Ryan J. 1992. The Pharmacology of Extinction. *Journal of Ethnopharmacology* 37:1–11.

Johri, R. K., and U. Zutshi. 1992. An Ayurvedic Formulation 'Trikatu' and its Constituents. *Journal of Ethnopharmacology* 37:85–91.

Kadiri, S., A. Ogunlesi, K. Osinfade, and O. O. Akinkugbe. 1992. The Causes and Course of Acute Tubular Necrosis in Nigerians. *African Journal of Medicine and Medical Sciences* 21:91–96.

Kaplan, Abraham. 1964. *The Conduct of Inquiry; Methodology for Behavioral Science.* San Francisco: Chandler.

Kauffman, Stuart A. 1993. *The Origins of Order; Self-Organization and Selection in Evolution.* New York: Oxford University Press.

Keen, R. W., A. C. Deacon, H. T. Delves, J. A. Moreton, and P. G. Frost. 1994. Indian Herbal Remedies for Diabetes as a Cause of Lead Poisoning. *Postgraduate Medical Journal* 70:113–114.

Kraus, Arnoldo, Generoso Guerra-Bautista, and Donato Alarcon-Segovia. 1991. Salmonella Arizona Arthritis and Septicemia Associated with Rattlesnake Ingestion by Patients with Connective Tissue Diseases; a Dangerous Complication of Folk Medicine. *Journal of Rheumatology* 18:1328–1331.

Kroes, B. H., A. J. J. van den Berg, A. M. Abeysekera, K. T. de Silva, and K. P. Labadie. 1993. Fermentation in Traditional Medicine: the Impact of Woodfordia Fruticosa Flowers on the Immunomodulatory Activity, and the Alcohol and Sugar Contents of Nimba Arishta. *Journal of Ethnopharmacology* 40:117–125.

Lai, S. M., K. W. Lim, and H. K. Cheng. 1990. Margosa Oil Poisoning as a Cause of Toxic Encephalopathy. *Singapore Medical Journal* 31:463–465.

Lambert, Helen. 1992. The Cultural Logic of Indian Medicine: Prognosis and Etiology in Rajasthani Popular Therapeutics. *Social Science and Medicine* 34: 1069–1076.

Lo, Yu-Chiang, Che-Ming Teng, Chieh-Fu Chen, Chien-Chih Chen, and Chuang-Ye Hong. 1994. Magnolol and Honokiol Isolated from Magnotia Officinalis Protect Rat Heart Mitochondria Against Lipid Peroxidation. *Biochemical Pharmacology* 47:549–553.

Loi, Do Tat, and Nguyen Xuan Dung. 1991. Native Drugs of Vietnam: Which Traditional and Scientific Approaches? *Journal of Ethnopharmacology* 32:51–56.

Mahyar, Uway W., John S. Burley, C. Gyllenhaal, and D. D. Soejarto. 1991. Medicinal Plants of Seberida (Riau Province, Sumatra, Indonesia). *Journal of Ethnopharmacology* 31:217–237.

Malone, M. H., and A. Rother. 1994. Heimia Salicifolia: A Phytochemical and Phytopharmacologic Review. *Journal of Ethnopharmacology* 42:135–159.

Markowitz, Steven B., Carol M. Nunez, Susan Klitzman, Abdulrehman A. Munshi, Woo Sup Kim, Josef Eisinger, and Philip J. Landrigan. 1994. Lead Poisoning Due to Hai Ge Fen; the Porphyrin Content of Individual Erythrocytes. *Journal of the American Medical Association* 271:932–934.

Marston, A., M. Maillard, and K. Hostettmann. 1993. Search for Anti-Fungal, Molluscoidal and Larvicidal Compounds from African Medicinal Plants. *Journal of Ethnopharmacology* 28:215–223.

Maskarinec, Gregory G. 1992. A Shamanic Etiology of Affliction from Western Nepal. *Social Science and Medicine* 35:723–734.

McCutcheon, A. R., S. M. Ellis, R. E. W. Hancock, and G. H. Towers. 1992. Antibiotic Screening of Medicinal Plants of the British Columbian Native Peoples. *Journal of Ethnopharmacology* 37:213–223.

McVann, A., T. Havlik, P. H. Joubert, and F. S. E. Monteagudo. 1992. Cardiac Glycoside Poisoning Involved in Deaths from Traditional Medicines. *South African Medical Journal* 81:139–141.

Messer, Ellen. 1991. Systematic and Medicinal Reasoning in Mitla Folk Botany. *Journal of Ethnopharmacology* 33:107–128.

Mossa, S., M. Tariq, A. Mohsin, A. M. Ageel, M. A. al-Yahya, M. S. al-Said, and S. Rafatullah. 1991. Pharmacological Studies on Aerial Parts of *Calatropis Procera.* *American Journal of Chinese Medicine* 19: 223–231

Nath, D., N. Sethi, R. K. Singh, and A.K. Jain. 1994. Commonly used Indian Abortifacient Plants with Special Reference to their Teratologic Effect in Rats. *Journal of Ethnopharmacology* 36:147–154.

Ng, T. H. K., T. W. Chan, Y. L. Yu, C. M. Chang, H. C. Ho, S. Y. Leung, and P. P. H. But. 1991. Encephalography and Neuropathy Following Ingestion of a Chinese Herbal Broth Containing Podophyllin. *Journal of the Neurological Sciences* 101: 107–113.

Noble, Robert L. 1990. The Discovery of the Vinca Alkaloids—Chemotherapeutic Agents Against Cancer. *Biochemistry and Cell Biology* 68:1344–1351.

O'Dea, Kerin. 1991. Traditional Diet and Food Preferences of Australian Aboriginal Hunter-Gatherers. *Philosophical Transactions of the Royal Society of London B 334:* 233–241.

O'Hear, Anthony. 1989. *Introduction to the Philosophy of Science.* Oxford: Clarendon Press.

Ojogwu, E. I. 1992. Drug Induced Acute Renal Failure—A Study of 35 Cases. *West African Journal of Medicine* 11:185–189.

Ortiz de Montellano, Bernard R. 1990. *Aztec Medicine, Health, and Nutrition.* New Brunswick, NJ and London: Rutgers University Press.

Parker, Eugene. 1992. Forest Islands and Kayapo Resource Management in Amazonia: A Reappraisal of the *Apete. American Anthropologist* 93:406–443.

Pereira, N. A., B. M. Pereira, M. C. do Nascimento, J. P. Parente, and W. B. Mores. 1994. Pharmacological Screening of Plants Recommended by Folk Medicine as Snake Venom Antidotes. IV. Protection Against Jararaca Venom by Isolated Constituents. *Planta Medica* 60:99–100.

Phillipson, J. David. 1994. Natural Products as Drugs. *Transactions of the Royal Society of Tropical Medicine and Hygiene 88* (Supplement 1):17–19.

Presber, W., D. K. Hermann, and B. Hegenscheid. 1991. Wirkung Eines Extraktes aus Cochospermum Anolense ("Burututu") auf Plasmodium Berghei im Mausemalaria-Suppressionstest. *Angewandte Parasitologie 32*:7–9.

Quetin-Leclercq, Joelle, Luc Angenot, and Norman G. Bisset. 1990. South American Strychnos Species; Ethnobotany (except curare) and Aalkaloid Screening. *Journal of Ethnopharmacology* 28:1–52.

Rojas, Alejandra, Lourdes Hernandez, Rogello Pereda Miranda, and Rachel Mata. 1992. Screening for Antimicrobial Activity of Crude Drug Extracts and Pure Natural Products from Mexican Medicinal Plants. *Journal of Ethnopharmacology* 35:275–283.

Schmeda Hirschmann, Guillermo and Eugenia Bordas. 1990. Paraguayan Medicinal Compositae. *Journal of Ethnopharmacology* 28:163–171.

Sofowara, Abayomi. 1993. Recent Trends in Research into African Medicinal Plants. *Journal of Ethnopharmacology* 28:209–214.

Sugimoto, Koji, Nobuo Sakurai, Haruyuki Shirasawa, Yutaka Fujises, Kiyoshi Shibata, Kanzo Shimoda, and Jun Sakata. 1992*a*. Bovine Cases of Urolithiasis Treated with Traditional Herbal Medicine, P-3. *Journal of Veterinary Medical Science* 54:579–582.

Sugimoto, Koji, Nobuo Sakurai, Yutaka Fujise, Haruyuki Shirasawa, Kiyoshi Shibata, Masako Matsuo, Toshie Takahashi, Yumiko Komori, Toshiaki Nikai, and Hisayoshi Sugihara, and Yohichi Fukuda. 1992*b*. Identification of Effective Component from a Traditional Herbal Medicine and the Inhibitory Effects on Experimental Glomerular Lesion in Mice. *Journal of Veterinary Medical Science* 54:111–118.

Taniguchi, Makoto, and Isao Kubo. 1993. Ethnobotanical Drug Discovery Based on Medicine Men's Trials in the African Savanna: Screening of East African Plants for Anti-Microbial Activity II. *Journal of Natural Products* 56:1539–1546.

Tsakala, M., L. Tona, V. Tamba, N. Mawanda, L. Vielvoye, J. Dufey. and J. Gillard. 1990. Etude In Vitro de L'absorption de la Chloroquinine par un Remede Antidiarraheique Employe Traditionellement en Afrique. *Journal de Pharmacie de Belgique* 45:268–273.

Tomback, Diana F. 1983. Nutcrackers and Pines: Coevolution or Coadaptation? *In. Coevolution* Pp. 179–223. Matthew H. Nitecki ed. Chicago: University of Chicago Press.

Turner, Nancy J., and Richard J. Hebda. 1990. Contemporary Use of Bark for Medicine by Two Salishan Native Elders of Southeast Vancouver Island, Canada. *Journal of Ethnopharmacology* 29:59–72.

Tutin, Caroline E.G., et al. 1991. Foraging Profiles of Sympatric Lowland Gorillas and Chimpanzees in the Lope Reserve, Gabon. *Philosophical Transactions of the Royal Society of London Series B (Biological Sciences) 334*:179–186.

Vogel, Virgil J. 1970. *American Indian Medicine.* Norman, OK: University of Oklahoma Press.

Weigel, M. M., R. X. Armijos, R. J. Racines, C. Zurita, R. Izurieta, E. Herrera, and E. Hinosja. 1994. Cutaneous Leishmniasis in Subtropical Ecuador: Popular Perceptions, Knowledge, and Treatment. *Bulletin of the Pan American Health Organization* 28: 142–155.

Wilbert, Werner, and Gerard Haiek. 1991. Phytochemical Screening of a Warao Pharmacopoeia Employed to Treat Gastrointestinal Disorders. *Journal of Ethnopharmacology* 34:7–11.

Woolf, David A. 1990. Aetiology of Acute Lead Encephalopathy in Omani Infants. *Journal of Tropical Pediatrics* 36:328–330.

Yanez, Leticia, Lilia Batres, Leticia Carrizales, Martha Santoyo, Virgilio Escalante, and Fernando Diaz-Barriga. 1994. Toxicological Assessment of Azarcon, a Lead Salt Used as a Folk Remedy in Mexico. I. Oral Toxicity in Rats. *Journal of Ethnopharmacology 41:* 91–97.

■ ■ ■ ■ ■ ■ ■ ■ ■ ■

7   PERTURBING THE SYSTEM: "HARD SCIENCE," "SOFT SCIENCE," AND SOCIAL SCIENCE, THE ANXIETY AND MADNESS OF METHOD

Joan Cassell

To introduce the final set of readings of Part I, this selection explores the researcher's role in developing hypotheses, studying, and writing about the dynamics between patients and healers. Cassell challenges the idea that the researcher should or is able to avoid interfering with and thereby modifying the field of study. Given that even sciences such as physics recognize the impossibility of noninterference, she asks why we should expect social science researchers to be any less intrusive. Like Barsh in the previous selection, Cassell argues for active involvement in research, in the full spirit of anthropological participant-observation.

A hierarchy persists across social and behavioral sciences and within anthropology itself, placing academic traditions that claim the most objectivity and methodological rigor above those that are considered subjective, personal, and less constrained by method. Cassell suggests that these constructions fit within a series of cultural oppositions aligned into female and male groups, such that the highly regarded "hard" sciences are associated with masculinity and the "soft" ones with femininity. Yet, in her research on end-of-life issues in intensive care units, Cassell finds that there is an inverse relationship between the precision of the methodology and the degree to which the research is able to capture the complexity of human interactions and experiences. The tighter the methodology, the less likely it is that the research can discover anything not anticipated in the study design. Thus, valuing "hard" over "soft" science approaches may limit the production of knowledge.

Cassell explains that bringing children to the field inevitably "perturbs the system" and yields information that may not be accessible otherwise, for children cannot be taught to remove themselves from their immediate surroundings and their interactions with other people. Researchers also can do this on their own if they are genuinely involved and not overly restrained in their research. In this way they may gain an insider's perspective, while their analytical activities allow them to tack back and forth between intimate, everyday knowledge and a larger theoretical framework. Cassell does this by taking notes during participant observation and later transcribing and supplementing them, coding the material, analyzing coded elements to discover patterns and create new codes, and writing up results. Through these activities, she distances herself from the field of study and is able to develop and refine her theoretical insights.

Questions to keep in mind

If social and cultural norms affect all phases and aspects of scholarly research, interpretation, and communication, to what degree can we understand the phenomena under consideration?

What are the Heisenberg principle and the Hawthorne and Rashomon effects, and how do they relate to scientific knowledge?

Is it ethical to refrain from acting when one observes unethical or dangerous behavior during field research?

Is it wrong for anthropologists to allow themselves to be co-opted by the people they study? If they do so, does this mean that they are no longer effective as anthropologists?

THE ANXIETY OF METHOD

[I]f there is one point of consensus among sociologists concerning field methods, it is this: the sociologist is there to study a social scene and not to change it, so whenever possible, do not interfere (Anspach 1993:211).

Sociologists tend to be much concerned with methods. Anthropologists have written about methods (e.g., Narroll and Cohen 1970; Pelto and Pelto 1978; Weller and Romney 1990; Bernard 1994), but as a group they are generally more relaxed than sociologists and less impressed by what is frequently presented as *the scientific paradigm*: do not interfere with, and thus alter, the social scene under observation.

The history of the two disciplines may affect the level of methodological anxiety. Sociologists traditionally studied their own societies, where their activity could be observed by others. In addition, sociology has as ancestors Comte (1974), the father of positivism, who portrayed the natural sciences as branches with sociology at the summit, having the capacity to explain the phenomena uncovered by the lower branches, and Durkheim (1938, 1951), who advocated conceptualizing social facts as "things" to be objectively studied, classified, and measured apart from their individual occurrences.

The anthropological ancestors, on the other hand, were less concerned about the methodological purity of their data. Consider the Victorian anthropologist, J. G. Frazer, about whom the story is told that, when asked about natives he had known, responded, "But heaven forbid!" (Evans-Pritchard 1951:72): a British gentleman might write about "savages" but he did not associate with them. Then, think of Malinowski (1955:99), whose idyllic picture of being set down by himself on a tropical isle "paddling on the lagoon, watching the natives under the blazing sun at their garden work, following them through the patches of jungle and

on the winding beaches and reefs" was challenged by the posthumous publication of his diaries (1967; Geertz 1967; Wax 1972). Finally, contemplate Evans-Pritchard, who wrote an anthropological classic, *The Nuer* (1940), based on intermittent, somewhat limited, visits to a group being "pacified" by military means during his study (Rosaldo 1986).[1] Few readers were in a position to check the methods or findings of the early anthropological studies of exotic peoples.

A PERSONAL NOTE ON METHODOLOGY[2]

As a graduate student in psychology in the mid-1960s, I was disturbed by my course in experimental psychology. The young professor kept teaching the class *how*—how to identify and construct a "parsimonious" "elegant" "scientific" experiment—while I kept trying to inquire *why*—why take all the trouble to do this? At the time, I lacked the language and knowledge to formulate my gut reaction to her teachings, and she was too newly hatched from graduate school to understand my objections. It seemed to me, had I but words to express it, that the more elegant and well-designed an experiment, the less it had to do with actual human beings relating to one another in the "booming buzzing confusion" of real life. After obtaining a master's degree in psychology, I switched with relief to a graduate program in anthropology, which promised to deal with human interaction in real life and real time.

As an anthropology graduate student, however, I encountered an interesting phenomenon. Those professors, and authorities assigned as course reading, who advocated "rigorous" "formal" "scientific" methods disdained their colleagues who conducted "sloppy" "unscientific" research, whose writings were dismissed as a species of literature. The mantle of Science seemed to confer an unquestioned intellectual—and moral—superiority upon those who assumed it.

After graduating in 1975, it took me a long time to find my "voice." Eventually, I rejected my advisor's advice to write in the passive voice; it surely *sounded* more scientific, but was far duller. I also jettisoned the fly-on-the-wall fantasy of the social scientist as a transparent unseen observer, who did her best not to influence the actions she was observing. Of course my presence influenced what went on. How could it not? Attempting not to influence what went on, whether in a rural Jamaican village or a feminist consciousness-raising group, pretending not to influence it, writing as though what occurred was not affected, began to seem rather like Winnie the Pooh, rising skyward holding a balloon, hoping he looked like a black cloud rather than a bear with a balloon seeking honey. If this were "science," I wanted none of it.

The attitude of "scientific" superiority still flourishes in the "behavioral" sciences. Recently, I was treated with undisguised disdain by a senior researcher who conducts "unbiased" "rigorous" studies of linguistic phenomena that are so meticulously "scientific" that his data are apparently untouched by human hands: they are analyzed by a computer. Not only was I a woman, which was bad enough, I was an uppity woman who was unimpressed by the contributions his efforts might make to our study. This distinguished man made it clear that as a researcher I was almost below contempt.

This encounter, plus others that occurred while conducting research in a biomedical milieu, made me wonder about the hierarchy of impersonality that endows some researchers with the moral and intellectual hauteur to look down on others.

WHAT MAKES AN INQUIRY SCIENTIFIC?

Is science a search for knowledge or understanding? Or is it defined by methodology or methodologies—the more "objective," "value-free," "impersonal," the more "scientific"? Is science defined by how you seek? What you find? Who you are?[3]

I do not pretend or aspire to be a scientist. (Surely not, if being a scientist condemns me to produce soporific graph-ridden reports in the passive voice or be constrained by a rigid, impersonal methodology.) If not exactly a tabula rasa, I am comparatively ignorant of current scientific knowledge and epistemology. What I begin with is a simple question: if the great physicist, Heisenberg, determined that, even in physics, observing something alters whatever is being observed, why all the fuss about "objectivity" and hands-off observation? And, if facts and values cannot, in truth, be disentangled (MacIntyre 1981; Putnam 2002), what does "value-free" research consist of?

Philosophers, historians, and sociologists of science have critiqued allegedly value-neutral scientific research, showing how cultural factors influence findings and formulations in the natural, medical, and social sciences (Pickering 1984; Harding 1987; Galison 1987; Smith and Wise 1989; Haraway 1991; Keller 1985, 1992). Some, but not all, of these critics are feminists. Evelyn Fox Keller (1992:26), who began as a physicist, observes:

> Careful attention to what questions get asked, of how research programs come to be legitimated and supported, of how theoretical disputes are resolved, of "how experiments end" reveals the working of cultural and social norms at every stage.

Keller indicates how the conventional accounts scientists offer of their successes, as well as their descriptions of the "laws of nature," are rooted in metaphor, which is by no means culture- or value-free (see Hrdy 1999 and Martin 1997a, 1997b).

If such post Kuhnian inquiry is convincing—and I, for one, find it so—then why does the objectivity-impersonality-value-free hierarchy still exist? Why is "hard" science considered superior to "soft"?

Keller argues that the language, tacit presuppositions, expectations, and assumptions shared by natural (or "hard") scientific researchers—which include the assumption that scientific language is transparent and neutral and, therefore, does not require examination—encourages the reliance upon shared conventions and metaphors, which are inevitably culture-based. (Thus, Emily Martin [1997a: 85–93] points out that the metaphor of the powerful free-ranging sperm finding, penetrating, and fertilizing the passive egg, hence producing the embryo, is more closely related to traditional gender ideology than to what actually occurs when sperm and egg meet.)

Something else is going on, as a number of feminist scholars have indicated. Popular beliefs, or "myths," about male and female nature influence the hierarchy of "scientific" value. In a series of cultural dichotomies, objectivity, reason, and mind are cast as male, while subjectivity, feeling, and nature are perceived as female (Keller 1985:7). In this tacit division, between public and private, impersonal and personal, masculine and feminine, the masculine polarity is valorized. Consequently, in a barely disguised (tautological) phallic metaphor, "hard" science is more scientific than "soft."

This anxiety of method—who wants to be defined as soft?—extends beyond the social sciences. In medicine, surgery is more valorized, more masculine, more "scientific"—even when conducted by women—than psychiatry (Cassell 1998), while biologically based psychiatrists disdain their "softer" colleagues, who converse with patients rather than treating them with drugs (Luhrmann 2000). Academic surgeons, who conduct scientific research (preferably "hard" research), look down upon those in private practice. And in critical care medicine, until recently, the investigation of compassionate end-of-life care was slighted by those interested in "harder" more "scientific" issues. Even when the topic became intellectually acceptable, researchers attempted to apply "rigorous" "objective" "value-free" methods, as though these would help erase the stigma of subjectivity.

APPLYING "OBJECTIVE" METHODS TO A SUBJECTIVE ISSUE: THE MADNESS OF METHOD

Many biomedically based research articles on end-of-life issues in the intensive care unit (ICU) miss the mark. Some are hortatory, admonishing doctors what should and should not be done. Others parrot basic principles, such as "benevolence" or "autonomy," with little guidance in applying these principles in the day-by-day, hour-by-hour care of gravely ill patients, who are often so sick (in addition to being intubated and highly sedated) that a term such as "autonomy" has little relevance to their situation. Other research programs make such drastic errors in understanding the social structure of medicine, in taking into account the on-the-ground dynamics of doctor-nurse interaction, that they make egregious social mistakes (e.g., in who should tell what to whom); thereby, nullifying their expensive efforts at improving practice. "Validated instruments" are apparently more highly regarded than perceptive researchers; the medium, the "objective" "value-free" qualities of the methodology, becomes more important than those who utilize it. There seems to be an almost automatic assumption that if the tools are sufficiently "scientific," almost anyone can brandish them and get good results. This, as any surgeon will tell you, is nonsense.

Another problem undermines some research efforts. As Mularski and colleagues (2001:N21) note:

> the physician is accustomed to a leadership role, regardless of knowledge base. Physicians tend to take it for granted that they know more than anyone else about subjects related to medicine; the more senior the physician, the more confident he or she is, of his or her knowledge base.

When this certitude is linked to a difficulty many physicians exhibit in *listening* rather than holding forth (e.g., Curtis et al. 2001; Tulsky et al. 1995), we find studies where the senior physician-researchers are unable to attend to, and consequently learn from, nonmedical colleagues and, more importantly, from the people they are purportedly studying. The ability to listen is as crucial in studying human interaction as it is in conducting effective end-of-life discussions (Field and Cassel 1997:61-64; Fins and Solomon 2001). One must be able listen to *silences* as well as words, to attend to what people are not saying as well as what they say (E. J. Cassell 1985). This overconfidence and underreceptiveness, added to an excessive reliance upon method rather than theoretical insight and creative imagination, can lead to self-fulfilling prophecies, or a kind of routine journeyman application of instruments to groups, as though such mechanical procedures will inevitably produce significant results.

Let me emphasize that I am *not* condemning all biomedical writings on end-of-life issues. Some are outstanding (e.g., Cook et al. 1999; Fins and Solomon 2001; Breen et al. 2001). But a number of research reports seem, somehow, off-kilter: one knows no more after reading them than before.

PERTURBING THE SYSTEM

Some years ago, I was on a panel where a medical anthropologist, prominent in a program on medical ethics, described how, when conducting research in a hospital, she kept silent when observing unethical and, on occasion, dangerous behavior by medical personnel. She said she did not want to ruin her "rapport" with the staff. I was appalled: not only was her stance profoundly unethical, I was not at all sure it was methodologically sound. Is it truly necessary or scientific to conceal who you are, what you feel, your own values and reactions, while trying to elicit those of the people you are studying? Is it really more scientific to try to avoid influencing what goes on, pretending that your presence has little or no effect on those you study?

Sociologist Renée Ansbach (1993:211), in her superb study of a neonatal ICU describes, with a twinge of what almost sounds like regret, how once she did intervene: she deliberately asked a question that led a resident to formulate a treatment plan for a neonate with a dismal prognosis, in a situation where the doctors had been postponing making a difficult decision. Nevertheless, in another section of her methodological appendix, Ansbach wonders "why a detached stance toward research subjects should necessarily be considered 'objective' or 'free of bias'" (ibid.:205). (One gets the impression that Ansbach is, at best, somewhat ambivalent about the detached stance her mentors may well have recommended.) In similar fashion, Robert Zussman (1992:235), also a sociologist, in a methodological appendix to his study of two intensive care units, tells how he did not wear a white coat, because it would "seem a type of deception entirely out of the spirit of notions of informed consent and patient's rights."

Ansbach (1993:206–208) explains why and how she did not get co-opted when she adopted a more participatory style in her second research site, mentioning her attempt to avoid the "Hawthorne effect." Zussman is anxious about pretending to be a doctor, as though wearing a white coat would deceive any of the residents, nurses, and attendings with whom he interacted. But why work so hard to avoid the Hawthorne effect if the Heisenberg effect still holds?[4]

I do not expect to sway those investigators who suffer from what has been characterized as "physics envy" (incorrectly, considering Heisenberg's indeterminacy principle). But other ways to conduct social research do exist.[5]

Rather than pretending to herself and her audience that she is utterly neutral, objective, and value-free—a state that is, in point of fact, almost impossible to achieve—the researcher can join in. The anthropological method, par excellence, is participant observation—and the observing social scientist can *participate* in whatever is going on as much as possible.[6] This does refer to what has been belittled as "going native"—whatever the fantasies of social researchers, rarely do the people studied mistake the investigator for one of their own. White coat or not, they know who you are. But if you are there for some time, as a living, reacting fellow human being, rather than a human pretending to be a disembodied fly-on-the-wall, the people you are studying will create a space, a role, for you.

As a researcher, I no longer even attempt to be "objective" or invisible. I react to what goes on: I agree with some statements, disagree with others, am upset by some actions, delighted by others, disapprove of some people, admire others. This does not mean I cast myself as a central figure in what goes on in the surgical intensive care unit I am presently studying. I am an observer, very much on the sidelines. But I am by no means neutral or value-free. I say what I think: I do not proclaim it, nor do I interrupt the flow of activities. But I have, on occasion, interjected a comment during patient rounds, pointing out, for example, that behavior by a family characterized as "difficult," might be related to social class, and that attempting to gain the family's trust by listening to its concerns could save time and trouble in caring for that patient. Other times, I've quietly complimented someone for defending a course of action or viewpoint I supported.

Such highly participatory research has pitfalls. The researcher can become what some sociologists would disapprovingly describe as "co-opted" (Freidson 1970; Millman 1976). Let me note that sociologists, such as Freidson and Millman, who accuse colleagues who express favorable sentiments toward doctors of being co-opted, do not necessarily conduct "objective" research, themselves. Their supposedly "value-free" investigations depict physicians as venal, collusive in hiding misbehavior, contemptuous of patients, and falsely omniscient.[7]

In polarized field situations, and most situations contain contending factions and viewpoints, the anthropologist tends to view happenings through the lens of those individuals she finds most sympathetic. But if she can manage to spend time with people belonging to more than one group or faction, she may experience the "Rashomon effect" of the same occurrences viewed from such differing perspectives that "reality" becomes fractured, the issue then becoming *whose* reality.[8] For example, when I spend time with surgeons who send patients to the surgical intensive care unit I am presently studying, I am immersed in an utterly different set of concerns, viewpoints, and ethical relationships than when I am with the critical care doctors. When the two groups disagree about patient management, it is no longer a question of which is the "real" reality, of who has right on his or her side, so much as a demonstration of utterly divergent epistemological "standpoints" or "moral economies" (Daston 1995; Lock 2001:487–489).[9] Thus, I have come to believe that operating surgeons and intensivists are guided by two different ethics: a "covenantal" ethic, emphasizing fidelity and trust as well as prudence and public-spiritedness (May 1996) as opposed to one of limited good.[10] Rather than there being a "right" and a "wrong" way of relating to patients, there are two "right" and completely defensible ways: a situation which is ethically and theoretically far more interesting. (This, however, is another issue, to be explored in a subsequent essay.)

Participation, while conducting participant observation, comes in many varieties and degrees. Anthropologists have married into the study group (Mageo 1996; Qureshi 2000); apprenticed themselves to a local sorcerer (Stoller and Olkes 1987);[11] at times gone so far as to enter the occult system, taking an active part in magical healing sessions (Turner 1987, 1996) or fighting off attacks from other sorcerers (Favret-Saada 1977/1980; Stoller and Olkes 1987). Are these researchers co-opted? Surely, if this refers to having such intense sympathy for the host people that the researcher becomes their spokesperson, fighting their battles and explaining their viewpoint to the wider world. This is a traditional role for anthropologists who study peoples whose customs and beliefs have been outlawed and whose land has been seized by members of a more powerful society. In such a situation, these researchers would perceive "value-free objectivity" as copping out.

A more relevant question is: when studying a powerful profession such as medicine, am I co-opted? Probably, on occasion. I surely sympathize with many of the people I study, and I tend, while studying them, to perceive reality through their eyes. In this respect, my data-collection and processing techniques are helpful. Conducting research, I participate, as much as a researcher, who knows a good bit about doctors but little about medicine, can. I take brief fieldnotes while observing, more or less as mnemonics. That afternoon or evening, I type up my notes, using the scribbled fieldnotes to reconstruct not only what occurred but how I felt about it. Subsequently, I code my notes, using categories I have generated (e.g., "end-of-life," "teaching," "Dr. X"), utilizing a computer program designed for qualitative research. The coding places a distance between me, the occurrences, and my feelings about what occurred. When comparing various instances of a code (e.g., all the instances of "teaching"), I perceive differences and similarities; this comparison generates insight about occurrences, leading to additional categories, or several categories being combined as a larger class. Coding adds a second degree of distance from my emotional identification. Writing up my findings creates the third degree of distancing. No longer involved with the individuals and activities in the "field," I can reinterpret occurrences, placing something in a more inclusive category, or entirely altering my interpretation of what went on. Co-optation attenuates as, drawing back to view a larger picture, I perceive how I may have been manipulated, or have manipulated myself, into a sympathy or position I no longer hold.

INSTRUMENTS VERSUS IMMERSION

Hypothetico-deductive research on social issues involving human interaction, employing rigorous validated instruments, can support or refute the initial hypothesis. By ignoring context and "irrelevant" variables, such research focuses narrowly on the phenomena being examined. Of course, values can creep in—in the unspoken assumptions that guide the ordering and phrasing of questions and the choice of "subjects" to whom the instrument will be presented. Values may also enter, as many researchers realize, in the difference between those who choose to respond to a questionnaire and those who refuse to do so.

But in the end, however well-designed, such research cannot surprise the investigator. The hypothesis is supported or disconfirmed: the fact that the truly interesting, influential phenomena were not addressed by the instrument—if this is indeed so—is not indicated. These phenomena remain undiscovered. Context and complex, ambiguous interactions are just "noise" interfering with the inquiry. The more "rigorous" the investigation, the less the complexity of human motives and interaction are taken into account.

This is an effective type of research, when using mice in the laboratory to study sepsis or manipulating rats to discover the most effective way to preserve the liver. The intentions of the animals, their social interactions, if any, are utterly irrelevant. These must be filtered out behaviorally or, if necessary, through research design.

Such methodology has distinct limitations, however, when dealing with human interaction. The investigator can find out nothing that was not covered by the original hypothesis.

So-called value-free observation by sociologists who attempt to avoid perturbing the system may also have problems. (Note, I say "may" have problems; I am not claiming that such research is *invariably* problematic.) The "rigorous" "value free" quality of the research may be demonstrated more in the objective, Olympian tone taken by the investigator when describing findings (e.g., Freidson 1970, 1975) than in the initial prejudices or presuppositions that guided the study.

One of the reasons anthropologists are less apprehensive about freely interacting with the host people is that, when conducting research in distant sites, we often bring our families with us. A young child cannot be taught to be reticent, objective, or value-free in the field. Children interact and, as a parent, you too interact, frequently with quite a bit of emotion. One of the things you learn, with children in the field, is that such open and unguarded interaction brings rich rewards in the form of data (Cassell 1987). When you and your children perturb the system, you learn things you would discover no other way.

You do not need children to perturb the system. The researcher's words, actions, and interactions can elicit actions and reactions from the people studied. Neutrally inquiring "Why did you (he, or they) do that?" does not necessarily bring more or better data than asking "Why in the world did you (he, or they) ever do *that!*" Thus, when I told the women surgeons I was studying that they needed the kind of doctor's wife I had been for almost 30 years, several then discussed the difficulties of not having someone to assume the emotional, social, and, on occasion, physical responsibilities of daily life (Cassell 1998).

Another example of emotionally entering the system is found in Meyerhoff's study of elderly Jews, ignored by their successful children, who frequented a senior citizen's center:

> One day, she lunched with the old people who, contentious at best, were particularly difficult: they fought about the food, argued about the silverware, battled about every detail. When bowls of apples and oranges were passed out for dessert, the fruit at her table was snatched up, leaving only three bruised apples; two women seized the best, leaving her with an apple that turned out to be completely rotten inside. Myerhoff wondered how she could have ever found these selfish, petulant, aggressive people interesting. That night she dreamed about the apple, which had a message written on its skin. A few days later, she remembered the dream and understood the message: the "selfish" people at her table for lunch were, themselves, too bruised to accept a damaged piece of fruit; they felt too much like rotten, unwanted fruit, and their struggle for the better apples was a way of repudiating their own condition (1978:188–189).

There is no way "rigorous" "objective" "value-free" research could arrive at such a stunning insight (also see Rosaldo 1984).

Margaret Mead used to say that the fieldworker was her own measuring instrument, and, as instrument, you engage all your conscious and unconscious endowments (see Devereux 1967). Immersing yourself in the system, having strong feelings about places, people, behavior can help give you an insider's knowledge of that system. No, you're not a native, a true insider, but to the extent you engage with those studied and enter the system to the best of your ability, you learn about that system, the way it works and does not work, what affects it, which individuals facilitate its workings and which ones, in contrast, gum up the works.

DESCRIBING THE SYSTEM: THE ETHNOGRAPHIC MONOGRAPH

When a researcher enters the system, the first thing to consider is the degree of participation. The second is the subsequent description of that participation. In recent years, anthropologists, who have rejected the disembodied fly-on-the-wall fantasy, have turned to embodied descriptions of their research (see Stoller 1989).[12]

It is a matter of taste and temperament. Some will denigrate such unabashedly subjective, highly participatory accounts as mere "literature," "memoir," or postmodern pretentiousness. Others will find such "narrative ethnography" (Tedlock 1991, 1992) more interesting, involving, and communicative of what actually occurs in an alien social setting than the "flat, neutral, and 'sludgy'" writing frequently presented as objective value-free social scientific discourse (Stoller 1989:137).

It is obvious that I am one of those who writes herself into what occurred. I was there. I reacted. I do not pretend otherwise. Whenever possible, I try to bring the reader to the research site with me, perhaps to see what I saw, to feel what I felt, or, if I've given enough detail, perhaps to take strong exception to my position and conclusions.

CARING AND MEDICAL CARE

An intensive care unit is an exhausting site to study. It is suffused with agonizing human experiences and emotions: death, tragedy, loss, sorrow, fear, pain. I've observed some doctors hide behind technology, shielding themselves from the emotional fallout by concentrating on high-tech "solutions" to the terrible (in every sense of the word) problems afflicting patients.

Dying, however, is not amenable to altering a drug dose or devising a new technical "fix."

Perhaps a researcher can also shield herself from sorrow by attempting to conduct objective value-free research on subjective emotion-drenched issues. I value compassion and empathy, in doctors, nurses, and researchers, too highly to take what I perceive as an easy, and eventually unproductive, way out.

I have observed medical personnel *practicing* care (Benner and Gordon 1996; Kohn and McKechnie 1998). Caring-in-practice involves a profound sensitivity to everyone with whom the practitioner comes in contact, and what can only be described as a kind of "love" for others and for one's work (Murray 2000). The Greeks called this virtue *agape*. It is not quantifiable, but it *is* recognizable.

As a social researcher I try to practice such caring. To do so, one must be committed to one's work and to the truth: to discovering, understanding, and then communicating just what is going on amidst the confusion and "noise" of human motives, behavior, and emotions.

Caring-in-practice, or *agape*, is displayed in varied ways by various researchers in varied situations (e.g., Waterston 1999; Singer et al. 2000). No fixed ground rules exist. What is central, indeed crucial, is the investigator's intense involvement with and commitment to those who are studied, the subject of study, and the moral principles underlying research.

Caring-in-practice may also translate in the ICU setting into bearing witness: observing and describing the tragedy of illness and loss; the difficulties and on occasion discord of families; the concern and on occasion callousness of medical personnel; and the frustration of expressions of caring by the larger medical system.

This is how I now see my role. (Naturally, this view may alter.) Is this science? Well, to tell the truth, I don't care: I prize insight and understanding more than the benison of science. But then again, I might be more of a scientist than I realize.

NOTES

1. Rosaldo critiques Evans-Pritchard for ignoring the relationship of "imperial domination" between himself and the Nuer.

2. In thinking about these issues, I have found Sandra Harding's (1987: 2–3) distinctions between "method," "methodology," and "epistemology" helpful: a research *method* is a technique for (or way of proceeding in) gathering evidence; a *methodology* is a theory and analysis of how research does or should proceed; an *epistemology* is a theory of knowledge.

3. For an informed and provocative view of what science is, and is not, see Bauer 1992, who contends that scientists in practice do not actually use what is commonly presented as "the scientific method," and that dispassionate, objective, systematic pursuit of knowledge is more a scientific ideal than actuality. He also argues that those who are most faithful to "the myth" of the scientific method are social scientists, who, he believes, are not scientists at all.

4. The *Hawthorne effect* refers to a famous series of studies on the productivity of workers where various conditions were manipulated, each change increasing productivity, at least for a time (Mayo 1933); Mayo's conclusions were that *being studied* increased productivity. These experiments have subsequently been challenged on various methodological grounds (Kolata 1998). The *Heisenberg effect,* also called the uncertainty or indeterminancy principle, specifies that observing something (notably, subatomic particles) alters that which is observed.

5. Let me emphasize that, despite my embattled tone, I am not criticizing scientific research, not even "scientific" social science research. It is not the only game in town, however, and for certain subjects—those that are emotion-drenched, such as death, and loss, and sorrow—I have doubts that this is the most effective way to proceed. For those who prefer to conduct "objective" "value-free" research, that's fine. Different folks, different strokes. What exasperates me is the tone of superiority so many of these researchers take toward colleagues who seek alternate routes toward understanding. Among the points I'm trying to make is that the definition of "science" (as many feminist critics and philosophers of science have pointed out) is contestable, and that "rigor" is not inevitably yoked to value-free—or soporific—social science.

6. The level of participation does not necessarily divide neatly down disciplinary boundaries: highly participative sociologist and positivist anthropologists exist. To give one example of participation: when sociologist Charles Bosk (1979) was conducting research for his outstanding study on surgical training, his interest and enthusiasm so impressed attending surgeons that several offered to sponsor his entry into medical school. Bosk's book, however, was criticized by some colleagues for its sympathetic portrayal of physicians (personal communication).

7. Medical sociologist Marianne Paget's (1998:58–69) description of Friedson's writings on medical mistakes as employing "the language of blame and culpability" also applies to Millman's work (1976; also see Cassell, n.d.).

8. In *Rashomon,* a Japanese film produced in 1950, the same event is viewed through the eyes of the three characters who participated; each view is utterly incompatible with the others; the film makes no judgment as to what is the "real" truth. The "truth" for each character conflicts with the others' realities.

9. See Harding (1987:181–189) for a feminist "take" on standpoints.

10. See Zussman's (1992:186–218) discussion of "the last bed" for somewhat different view of the same phenomena.

11. When local sorcerers were reticent with Evans-Pritchard (1937), who was studying witchcraft and magic in Africa, he sent his "personal servant" to be initiated (being quite open about the information being passed on to the researcher); he then used the material thus gained to draw out rival practioners.

12. Jean Briggs' classic dissertation on her life among the Eskimo was one of the earliest of such accounts; it has remained in print since its publication in 1970. I remember hearing a sociologist, who had been an editor at Harvard University Press when the book was accepted for publication, describe the pitched battles as to whether Harvard should publish such a personal, "unscientific" account.

REFERENCES

Ansbach, Renée R. 1993. *Deciding Who Lives: Fateful Choices in the Intensive-Care Nursery.* Berkeley: University of California Press.

Bauer, Henry H. 1992. *Scientific Literacy and the Myth of the Scientific Method.* Urbana: University of Illinois Press.

Benner, Patricia, and Suzanne Gordon. 1996. Caring Practice. In *Caregiving: Readings in Knowledge, Practice, Ethics, and Politics.* Suzanne Gordon, Patricia Benner, and Nel Noddings, eds. Pp. 40–55. Philadelphia: University of Pennsylvania Press.

Bernard, H. Russell. 1994. *Research Methods in Anthropology: Qualitative and Quantitative Approaches.* Thousand Oaks, Calif.: Sage.

Bosk, Charles. 1979. *Forgive and Remember: Managing Medical Failure.* Chicago: University of Chicago Press.

Breen, Catherine M., Amy Abernethy, Katherine Abbot, and James A. Tulsky. 2001. Conflict Associated with Decisions to Limit Life-Sustaining Treatment in Intensive Care Units. *Journal of General Internal Medicine* 16:283–289.

Briggs, Jean. 1970. *Never in Anger.* Cambridge, Mass.: Harvard University Press.

Cassell, Eric, J. 1985. *Talking with Patients: The Theory of Doctor-Patient Communication*, Vol. 1. Cambridge, Mass.: MIT Press.

Cassell, Joan. 1991. *Expected Miracles: Surgeons at Work.* Philadelphia: Temple University Press.

———. 1998. *The Woman in the Surgeon's Body.* Cambridge, Mass.: Harvard University Press.

———. n.d. Social Scientists Studying Doctors: 1951 to 2001. *Annual Review of Anthropology.* In press.

Cassell, Joan, ed. 1987. *Children in the Field: Anthropological Experiences.* Philadelphia: Temple University Press.

Comte, August. 1974. *Cours de philosophie positive* (The Positive Philosophy: with a new introduction by Abraham S. Blumberg). Six volumes. New York: AMS Press. (Originally published 1855.)

Cook, Deborah J., Mita Giacomini, Nancy Johnson, and Dennis Willms. 1999. Life Support in the Intensive Care Unit: A Qualitative Investigation of Technological Purposes. *Canadian Medical Association Journal* 161:1109–1113.

Curtis, J. Randall, Donald L. Patrick, Sarah E. Shannon, Patsy D. Treece, Ruth A. Engleberg, and Gordon D. Rubenfeld. 2001. The Family Conference as a Focus to Improve Communication About End-of-Life Care in the Intensive Care Unit: Opportunities for Improvement. *Critical Care Medicine* (Supplement) 29:N26–N33.

Daston, Lorraine. 1995. The Moral Economy of Science. *Osiris* 10:3–24.

Devereux, George. 1967. *From Anxiety to Method in the Behavioral Sciences.* New York: Humanities Press.

Durkheim, Emile. 1938. *The Rules of Sociological Method.* Sarah A. Solovay and John H. Mueller, trs. George E. G. Catlin, ed. New York: Free Press. (First Published in 1894.)

———. 1951. *Suicide: A Study in Sociology.* John A. Spaulding and George Simpson, trs. George Simpson, ed. New York: Free Press. (First Published in 1897.)

Evans-Pritchard, E. Evans. 1937. *Witchcraft, Oracles and Magic among the Azande.* Oxford: Clarendon Press.

———. 1940. *The Nuer, a Description of the Modes of Livelihood and Political Institutions of a Nilotic People.* Oxford: Oxford University Press.

———. 1951. *Social Anthropology.* London: Cohen & West. Reprinted with additional essays as *Social Anthropology and Other Essays.* New York: Free Press.

Favret-Saada, Jeanne. 1977/1980. *Deadly Words: Witchcraft in the Bocage.* London: Cambridge University Press.

Field, Marilyn J., and Christine K. Cassel. eds. 1997. *Approaching Death: Improving Care at the End of Life.* Washington, D.C.: National Academy Press.

Fins, Joseph J., and Mildred Z. Solomon. 2001. Communication in Intensive Care Settings: The Challenge of Futility Disputes. *Critical Care Medicine* (Supplement) 29:N10–N15.

Freidson, Eliot. 1970. *Profession of Medicine: A Study of the Sociology of Applied Knowledge.* 2nd ed. New York: Dodd. Mead.

———. 1975 *Doctoring Together: A Study of Professional Social Control.* New York: Elsevier.

Galison, Peter Louis. 1987. *How Experiments End.* Chicago: University of Chicago Press.

Geertz, Clifford. 1967. Under the Mosquito Net. *New York Review of Books* 9(4):12–13.

Haraway, Donna J. 1991. *Simians, Cyborgs, and Women: The Reinvention of Nature.* New York: Routledge.

Harding, Sandra. 1987. Introduction: Is there a Feminist Method? and Conclusion: Epistemological Questions. In *Feminism and Methodology.* Sandra Harding, ed. Pp. 1–14, pp. 181–189. Bloomington: University of Indiana Press.

Hrdy, Sarah Blaffer. 1999. *Mother Nature: A History of Mothers, Infants, and Natural Selection.* New York: Pantheon Books.

Keller, Evelyn Fox. 1985. *Reflections on Gender and Science.* New Haven: Yale University Press.

———. 1992. *Secrets of Life, Secrets of Death: Essays on Language, Gender and Science.* New York: Routledge.

Kohn, Tamara, and Rosemary McKechnie, eds. 1998. *Extending the Boundaries of Care: Medical Ethics and Caring Practices.* New York: Oxford (Berg).

Kolata, Gina. 1998. Scientific Myths that Are Too Good to Die. *New York Times*, December 6.

Lock, Margaret. 2001. The Tempering of Medical Anthropology: Troubling Natural Categories. *Medical Anthropology Quarterly* 15:478–492.

Luhrman, T. M. 2000. *Of Two Minds: The Growing Disorder in American Psychiatry.* New York: Alfred A. Knopf.

MacIntyre, Alasdair. 1981. *After Virtue: A Study in Moral Theory.* Notre Dame, Ind.: University of Notre Dame Press.

Mageo, Jeanette Marie. 1996. Spirit Girls and Marines: Possession and Ethnopsychiatry as Historical Discourse in Samoa. *American Ethnologist* 23:61–82.

Malinowski, Bronislaw. 1955. Myth in Primitive Psychology. In *Magic, Science and Religion and Other Essays.* Pp 93–148. New York: Doubleday Anchor. (First published in 1926.)

———. 1967. *A Diary in the Strict Sense of the Term.* Norbert Guterman, tr. New York: Harcourt, Brace & World.

Martin, Emily. 1997a. How Science Has Constructed a Romance Based on Stereotypical Male–Female Roles. In *Situated Lives: Gender and Culture in Everyday Life*. Louise Lamphere, Helena Ragoné, and Patricia Zavella, eds. Pp. 85–98. New York: Routledge.

——. 1997b. Medical Metaphors of Women's Bodies: Menstruation and Menopause. In *Writing on the Body: Female Embodiment and Feminist Theory*. Katie Conboy, Nadia Medina, and Sarah Stanbury, eds. Pp. 15–41. New York: Columbia University Press.

May, William E. 1996. *Testing the Medical Covenant: Active Euthanasia and Health Care Reform*. Grand Rapids, Mich.: William B. Eerdmans Publishing.

Mayo, Elton. 1933. *Human Problems of an Industrial Civilization*. New York: MacMillan.

Millman, Marcia. 1976. *The Unkindest Cut: Life in the Backrooms of Medicine*. New York: Morrow.

Mularski, Richard, Paul Bascom, and Molly L. Osborn. 2001. Educational Agendas for Interdisciplinary End-of-Life Curricula. *Critical Care Medicine* (Supplement) 29:N16–N23.

Murray, John F. 2000. *Intensive Care: A Doctor's Journal*. Berkeley: University of California Press.

Myerhoff, Barbara. 1978. *Number Our Days*. New York: E. P. Dutton.

Naroll, Raoul, and Ronald Cohen, eds. 1970. *A Handbook of Method in Cultural Anthropology*. Garden City, N.Y.: Natural History Press.

Paget, Miranne A. 1988. *The Unity of Mistakes: A Phenomenological Interpretation of Medical Work*. Philadelphia: Temple University Press.

Pelto, Pertti J., and Gretel H. Pelto. 1978. *Anthropological Research: The Structure of Inquiry*, 2nd ed. Cambridge: Cambridge University Press.

Pickering, Andrew. 1984. *Constructing Quarks: A Sociological History of Particle Physics*. Chicago: University of Chicago Press.

Putnam, Hilary. 2002. *The Collapse of the Fact/Value Dichotomy and other Essays*. Cambridge, Mass.: Harvard University Press. In press.

Qureshi, Regula. 2000. How Does Music Mean? *American Ethnologist* 27:805–838.

Rosaldo, Renato. 1984. Grief and a Headhunter's Rage: On the Cultural Force of Emotions. In *Text, Play and Story: The Construction and Reconstruction of Self and Society*. Edward M. Bruner, ed. Pp. 178–195. Washington, D.C.: American Ethnological Society.

——. 1986. From the Door of His Tent: The Fieldworker and the Inquisitor. In *Writing Culture: The Poetics and Politics of Ethnography*. James Clifford and George E. Marcus, eds. Pp. 77–97. Berkeley: University of California Press.

Singer, Merrill, Elsa Huertas, and Glenn Scott. 2000. Am I My Brother's Keeper?: A Case Study of the Responsibilities of Research. *Human Organization* 59: 389–400.

Smith, Crosbie, and M. Norton Wise. 1989. *Energy and Empire: A Biographical Study of Lord Kelvin*. Cambridge: Cambridge University Press.

Stoller, Paul. 1989. *The Taste of Ethnographic Things: The Senses in Anthropology*. Philadelphia: University of Pennsylvania Press.

Stoller, Paul, and Cheryl Olkas. 1987. *In Sorcery's Shadow: A Memoir of Apprenticeship Among the Songhay of Niger*. Chicago: University of Chicago Press.

Tedlock, Barbara. 1991. From Participant Observation to the Observation of Participation: The Emergence of Narrative Ethnography. *Journal of Anthropological Research* 47:69–94.

——. 1992. *The Beautiful and the Dangerous: Encounters with Zuni Indians*. New York: Penguin.

Turner, Edith L. B. 1987. *The Spirit of the Drum: A Memoir of Africa*. Tucson: University of Arizona Press.

——. 1996. *The Hands Feel It: Healing and Spirit Presence among a Northern Alaskan People*. DeKalb: Northern Illinois University Press.

Tulsky, James. A., Margaret A. Chesney, and Bernard Lo. 1995. How Do Medical Residents Discuss Resuscitation with Patients? *Journal of General Internal Medicine* 10:436–442.

Waterston, Alisse. 1999. *Love, Sorrow and Rage: Destitute Women in a Manhattan Residence*. Philadelphia: Temple University Press.

Wax, Murray L. 1972. Tenting with Malinowski. *American Sociological Review* 37:1–13.

Weller, Susan, and A. Kimball Romney. 1990. *Metric Scaling: Correspondence Analysis*. Newbury Park, Calif.: Sage.

Zussman, Robert. 1992. *Intensive Care: Medical Ethics and the Medical Profession*. Chicago: University of Chicago Press.

8 CLOWN DOCTORS: SHAMAN HEALERS OF WESTERN MEDICINE

Linda Miller Van Blerkom

Spiritual treatment, understood broadly, is an important part of healing in many non-Western societies and a central if not always openly recognized aspect of healing in biomedical care as well (see Part III; Connor and Samuel 2001; Csordas 1999). Van Blerkom explains that spiritual treatment refers to the type of healing that attends to the patient as a social being and psychophysical entity and gives meaning to the illness experience. The need for more of this in biomedical care has been recognized by some hospitals, which have begun to provide clowns on pediatric hospital wards. This selection shows that clown doctors in New York may actually increase the effectiveness of biomedical care through the use of techniques similar to those recorded for clown healers and shamans in other cultures. The enhancement of treatment occurs through a number of mechanisms, from provoking emotional responses that trigger the psychosocial pathways in the placebo effect, to improving the social support of patients by diverting relatives from the worries and fears they unwittingly communicate to child patients.

Comparison of the clown doctors with similar figures in other cultures, especially Native American cultures, yields a shared set of activities, qualities, and appearances. These include "contrary" behaviors in which the normal order of things is reversed, theatrics that extricate disease, object removal, song and dance, and storytelling. The wacky and in many ways inverted appearance of clowns can evoke strong feelings of amusement and fear at the same time. This ambiguity is a central characteristic of shamans, as Van Blerkom explains.

Clowns in New York hospitals and clown healers and shamans around the world commonly manipulate culturally specific symbols and thereby invoke and strengthen the power of suggestion. Through their unusual appearance and activities, these healers engage people on a psychophysical level that straddles common distinctions separating mind and body, disease and illness, and scientific and alternative medicine. Van Blerkom suggests that additive medicine is a better term than alternative, because the healing effects are joint rather than separate. The question becomes not whether spiritual or symbolic methods are effective but whether they enhance other kinds of healing.

Questions to keep in mind

What are some specific ways in which the New York clowns mimic the appearance and activities of clown healers and shamans in other societies?

What are the stated purposes of bringing clowns into the hospital? What are some other purposes suggested through the comparison with shamans?

How do parents, patients, and health professionals feel about the clowns, and what positive effects do they think they bring about?

How might the presence of clowns improve the effectiveness of biomedical care?

Source: Van Blerkom, L. M. 1995. "Clown Doctors: Shaman Healers of Western Medicine." © 1995 by the American Anthropological Association. Reprinted from *Medical Anthropology Quarterly* Vol. 9 No. 4 pp. 462–475, by permission.

On Monday, Wednesday, and Friday mornings, Dr. Winona Do-More prepares for her rounds in the pediatric cardiology unit of a large New York City hospital. She checks her hospital badge, white coat (with red heart on the sleeve), glasses, makeup (including red nose), oxygen tubing (worn twisted around her head), and bag of medical instruments (kazoo, bells, whistles, and other noisemakers). Satisfied that all is ready, she leaves the changing room for another day of funny-bone removals, squeakectomies, and bed-pandemonium. Dr. Winona Do-More is not a medical doctor; she is a clown doctor with the Big Apple Circus Clown Care Unit.[1]

The Clown Care Unit (CCU) is a group of professional clowns who work in the pediatric wards of New York City hospitals. Created in 1986 by Michael Christensen ("Dr. Stubs"), cofounder and creative director of the Big Apple Circus, the CCU began with two clowns in one hospital and has since grown to 35 clowns serving seven medical centers throughout New York City plus a summer program at Paul Newman's Hole-in-the-Wall Gang Camp for children with cancer and chronic blood diseases. Clowns typically work in groups of two or three, three days a week, and spend these days cheering patients, their families, and hospital staff.

Their activities include entertaining bored children and mothers in crowded outpatient clinic waiting rooms, distracting anxious families in inner-city emergency rooms, comforting parents of children in intensive care units, and distracting small AIDS or cancer patients during painful and frightening procedures. They spread joy and mayhem wherever children might be found in what is otherwise an environment not designed with children in mind. In many ways, CCU clowns resemble shamans and traditional healers of non-Western societies. The inclusion of clowns in pediatric hospitals reflects growing interest in and respect for alternative, or, more correctly, complementary styles of healing. Western medicine is oriented toward allopathic treatment of clinical symptoms, while traditional non-Western healing more frequently addresses a patient's social condition and construction of the illness experience. One cannot deny the efficacy of physicians compared to shamans, but integrating doctors with complementary practitioners such

as clown doctors may render Western medicine even more effective.

CLOWNS AND SHAMANS

A review of the literature shows that comparing clowns and shamans is not new. Clowning and other popular entertainment (magic tricks, sword swallowing, juggling, acrobatics, etc.) originated with shamanistic performances (Kirby 1974). Some trace the derivation of all performing arts to shamanism (Flaherty 1988; LaBarre 1979). Turner (1985:235–236) includes clowns and fools with shamans, tricksters, healers, and other characters in a list of liminal figures found in rites of passage dealing with social crisis and affliction. Both clowns and shamans mediate between order and chaos, sacred and profane, real and supernatural, culture and anticulture, or nature (Charles 1945:32–33; Willeford 1969: 100–150). This mediation of culture and nature is central to the healing arts and sciences (Moerman 1979:59). In the language of semiotics, clown performances are metacultural texts, acts of communication about culture, that invert cultural rules, thereby provoking emotional responses (Bouissac 1985:151–175). Whether the antics of clowns produce mirth or agitation in the observer, such folly has long been associated with psychological healing (Willeford 1969:29).

Clown figures with healing functions occur in other societies, particularly in Native American cultures. Institutionalized clowning is best developed among the Pueblos. Charles ranks Pueblo clowns with the Commedia dell'Arte as among the "four major groups of clown societies . . . known to exist or to have existed" (1945:30). Not all Pueblo clown societies function as healers, but some do. For example, the Zuni Ne'wekwe is a highly regarded medicine society, some of whose members are clowns who improvise farces and burlesques during curing ceremonies (Bunzell 1932:498). The Laguna Koshare and Santa Clara Kossa are sometimes called on for curing, although most Koshares do not heal (Parsons and Beals 1934:495). Other clown societies for which curing is a primary function occur among the Yaqui and Mayo Indians of Sonora (Parsons and Beals

1934:506). Iroquois False Faces use clown-like theatrics to exorcise disease (Towson 1976:13).

Plains Indian clowning takes the form of "contrary" behavior, such as talking or performing actions backward and in other ways violating natural and social conventions (Steward 1931:198). Modern Plains Indians consider circus clowns similar to contraries (Towson 1976:13). Some of these contraries function as healers, but only if they are of the comic type or "buffoon"; "serious" contraries, such as the Oglala Heyoka, never cure (Ray 1945:91). Healing buffoons include the Plains Ojibway Windigokan and Plains Cree Wetigokan, who use contrary behavior and ragged costumes, as well as dancing, singing, whistling, and shaking rattles in their curing (Ray 1945:84–87; Steward 1931:203). The Canadian Dakota (Wahpeton) consider clowns to be the most powerful shamans (Ray 1945:86).

CLOWNS, SHAMANS, AND COMPLEMENTARY MEDICINE

Medical anthropologists have frequently contrasted Western and non-Western medical systems. Foster (1976) classified non-Western medical systems into personalistic and naturalistic, depending upon whether illness-causation beliefs involved supernatural entities or natural processes. He placed Western, presumably scientific, medicine in a different category altogether. Kleinman (1973:206) pointed out that medicine deals with two kinds of reality, "scientific" and "ordinary," that is, with biophysical and human dimensions. Western physicians concentrate on the biophysical dimension and treat the symptoms of disease. In contrast, indigenous healers address the human dimension, the illness, by providing and manipulating the personal, social, and cultural meanings of the illness experience (Kleinman and Sung 1979:7–8). This distinction between "disease," a biological reality, and "illness," an experience and social role (Eisenberg 1977), has become common usage in medical anthropology, especially in studies of non-Western and alternative medical systems (Leslie 1980:195). Moerman (1979) also wrote of this dichotomy between biomedicine's allopathic treatment of physical symptoms and the shaman's concern with the whole patient and the

mental predicates of disease. He called the former "specific therapy" and referred to the shaman's more holistic approach as "general therapy" and "symbolic healing," whereby the healer manipulates symbols within a cultural system of meaning so as to promote psychosomatic transformation. Symbols central to a society's medical system are particularly important (Finkler 1980:271, 300; Kleinman 1973).

These comparisons of Western and non-Western medical systems echo distinctions made between the biomedical establishment and holistic medicine. Proponents of holism accuse physicians of bioreductionism and of focusing more on the disease entity than on the individual's illness experience (McKee 1988). According to some, it is this illness experience, and the feeling that biomedicine does not pay adequate attention to the whole person, that induces people to seek alternative therapies (Furnham and Forey 1994:467–468; Leslie 1980:193). And many people are turning to alternative medicine. A recent survey showed that Americans make more visits annually to alternative providers than to primary-care physicians, and they spend more on these unconventional therapies than on hospitalizations (Eisenberg et al. 1993). A community survey in London also found substantial use of alternative therapies (Murray and Shepherd 1993). Both studies found that most of these people also sought treatment from physicians (in fact, the London study showed *more* frequent visits to general practitioners by users of alternative medicine). For this reason *complementary* or *additive* medicine better describes this practice than does *alternative*.

Western medical practitioners increasingly recognize the need to escape the limitations of a bioreductionist view of health and disease. This can be seen in the integrational model of medicine—espoused by the mental health movement, family practice, psychosomatic medicine, and public health—that views a person as more than a collection of cells and symptoms (Aakster 1986:269). Biomedicine increasingly accepts a health care role for some kinds of complementary practitioners. The U.S. National Institutes of Health now include an Office of Alternative Medicine to screen and evaluate alternative therapies. A recent British Medical Association report concedes that some unorthodox therapies, such as acupuncture and homeopathy, are useful, and urges physicians to become better informed so they can refer patients to other practitioners (Gould 1993:44). In Denmark, centers for integrated medicine have been established, where conventional and alternative practitioners cooperate (Launs 1989). Physicians in some non-Western societies, for example China and India, work alongside practitioners of traditional medical systems (Jingfeng 1987; Last 1990:359–360), and the World Health Organization has established a new department, the Traditional Medicine Program, that urges member states to integrate indigenous healers into the general health system (Jingfeng 1987:659).

Complementary or additive medicine is attractive in theory, but questions remain about the efficacy of non-Western and unorthodox medical systems. While some complementary therapies such as chiropractic and homeopathy have yielded evidence of efficacy in clinical trials (Gibson et al. 1980; Kirkaldy-Willis and Cassidy 1985), attempts to gauge that of shamans and most forms of complementary medicine are plagued with problems such as lack of proper controls, subjectivity of patient self-reporting, and incongruence between emic illness categories and etic, or biomedical, disease definitions. This article does not address this question, but suggests instead that the question is wrongly focused. Rather than asking whether clowns, shamans, or unorthodox healers have efficacy by themselves, patterns of usage suggest one should ask whether they enhance the efficacy of biomedicine when used as a complementary or additive system.

METHODS

This article is based on participant-observation of the CCU and its activities. Five groups of clown doctors were observed for one workday each, in five New York City hospitals. A written record was kept of time, context, actors, clowns' actions, and patient/parent/nurse reactions. The clowns' behavior was the main observational focus. Their activities were recorded in as much detail as possible, especially during interaction with patients, parents, and nurses. The behavior of the "audi-

ence" was also noted, and any obvious effects of clown visits on mood or behavior.

This was supplemented by many hours of interviews with CCU clowns. Other sources of data were two hospital staff evaluation meetings and a monthly CCU staff meeting. The former provided information concerning medical personnel's attitudes toward and relationships with the clowns. The latter combined CCU business (hospital assignments, scheduling, relations with hospital directors and staff), rehearsal, and "emotional hygiene"—a ritual activity during which clowns shared their affective reactions to distressing hospital experiences and received emotional support from the group, a healing ritual in itself. Brief interviews with parents and hospital staff were supplemented by their written evaluations of the CCU, which allowed me to gain some idea of attitudes toward and subjective effects of the clowns.

A DAY IN THE LIFE OF DR. DO-MORE

A CCU clown's typical day begins in a hospital changing room, where he or she dons makeup and costume, assuming a clown doctor character in the process. The clowns work in groups of two or three, with one clown (generally the most experienced) designated the supervisor. At New York Hospital, this is Dr. Do-More, who was trained in mime and physical comedy and has been with the CCU for six years. Her associates are Dr. Bobo, a graduate of the Moscow Circus School with many years of work on the stage in Russia as well as a university degree in directing, and Dr. Fidget, experienced in mime, physical movement, magic, music, and children's theater. Both Dr. Bobo and Dr. Fidget have been CCU clowns for four years. They all wear outlandish costumes topped off by a doctor's white coat with "Big Apple Circus" on the back. They carry doctor's bags filled with magic tricks, puppets, musical instruments, bubble solution, juggling balls, and other props.

At 10:00 A.M. they leave the changing area, exchanging gags with anyone they meet in the halls, elevators, or waiting rooms on their way to the pediatric cardiology outpatient clinic. After entering the clinic playing music and blowing bubbles, they look to see which rooms contain waiting patients. They stay out of rooms with doctors' examinations or treatments in progress, but one doctor leaves when the clowns arrive, explaining to the patient, "We have a specialist to see you now." In come the clowns, with Dr. Fidget blowing soap bubbles, Dr. Bobo playing a balalaika, and Dr. Do-More popping red foam-rubber clown noses out of the respirator tubing wrapped around her head. In other rooms, babies get soft lullabies and bubbles, and teenagers get slapstick sketches with ribald humor.

Puppets are popular. Dr. Fidget has a pesky blue jay who gobbles up all the bubbles, then begins nipping the other clowns' ears, noses, necks, and pockets. She hides a lifelike furry puppet under her coat, in her hat, in a child's bed, and even under a nurse's sweater, while the nurse plays along: "Doctor, is there an animal in here? You know we don't allow animals in the hospital!"

A little girl in the waiting room is frightened of clowns and hides behind her mother. The clowns act terrified of her and attempt to hide behind each other, the chairs, and even another mother. Soon the little girl is giggling and chasing them.

After a half hour in cardiology, the clowns go upstairs to pediatric hematology and oncology. They perform magic tricks and gags for parents in the waiting room, then stop at the nurses' station to find out whether any patients are off-limits. "We could definitely use a clown in here," one nurse says, pointing to a nearby treatment room where a frightened child is connected to an intravenous unit. While Dr. Fidget distracts her with bubbles, magic tricks, and a funny dance, Dr. Do-More squirts other children and parents with a tiny squirt gun, and Dr. Bobo dances and plays the harmonica. They pull clown noses, tiny toy animals, and even an entire litter of sponge-rubber baby rabbits from children's ears and noses. One child becomes overly excited, punching and grabbing at the clowns and their props, so Dr. Do-More signals that it's time to move on.

At 11:10, in pediatric intensive care, after checking with the nurses' station about any restrictions and washing their hands and toys, the clowns console and distract the tearful parents of a young girl in a coma. The girl's breathing quickens noticeably as the clowns sing to her and stroke her, and her eyelids briefly flutter (the clowns relate that two children came out of coma while they were visiting). For other children and parents in the intensive care unit, the clowns sing, dance, play instruments, put on a puppet show, and hand out autographed pictures.

Next stop is the Children's Clinical Research Center, where nurses greet the clowns warmly and participate in a few gags. The blue jay puppet is nipping their behinds, picking pockets, and stealing scarves. Dr. Bobo sneezes marbles out of his nose. Several children in this section are in isolation with chicken pox, but this doesn't deter the clowns, who make faces and puppet antics outside the windows.

At noon they break for lunch in the hospital cafeteria. They're out of character now, as physicians have requested no clowning in the lunch room. Anywhere else in the hospital, however, doctors are fair game.

After lunch they return to pediatric cardiology, to amuse the afternoon patients and their parents by making funny paper hats the children may keep and by performing squeak removals, or "squeakectomies." After half an hour they move to a general pediatrics ward, where they stop to sing to a long-term patient. They proceed down the hall with a brief visit to every room. Dr. Do-More distracts a burned child from her pain with bubbles and magic tricks while Dr. Bobo tries to fool some older children in the solarium. They figure out all his tricks, but this is intentional, for the clowns are rehearsed to make themselves appear silly and the children feel in charge. Dr. Fidget has lost her furry animal puppet (which is under her coat, bushy tail sticking out of the back of her collar) and is frantically, and unsuccessfully, looking for it. A physician arrives to see a patient. Dr. Bobo pulls a scarf out of the doctor's tie.

Around 2:15 the clowns leave the ward, exchanging bad jokes with nurses on the way out. In the crowded hallway of the outpatient burn clinic they discover an old friend, a girl who had spent six months in the burn unit recovering from a plane crash. She pokes all their squeaky places and asks if they have any new tricks. While she and Dr. Do-More toss scarves around people's heads, Dr. Bobo goes up and down the hall with a metal cup, kerplunking quarters into it from out of doorknobs, fathers' noses, and other unusual places. He plays a racy Russian song on his balalaika, and

Drs. Do-More and Fidget do a hula. After several more tricks and gags, they go to the inpatient burn unit.

The intensive burn unit is a serious place. Here each clown puts on a fresh sterile gown and cap before entering each room, and these patients can't touch any of the toys and props. This is also the unit the clowns find most difficult emotionally. The injuries they see here are often serious and disfiguring.

The workday ends at 3:00 p.m., when the clowns head back to the changing room, remove their makeup and costumes, and assume their "normal" identities. The work appears to take a great deal out of them, and they head home on the subway, tired and emotionally drained.

RESEMBLANCE TO SHAMANS

Like traditional healers in many societies, clowns wear unusual costumes. The clothes of a clown violate cultural conventions—jarring colors; plaids, stripes, and polka dots all together; a brassiere worn as a hat. Clown makeup further effects the transformation from cultural person to anticultural other, and is similar to the face paint and masks of non-Western ritual healers. Like the shaman role, the clown figure transcends culture and is nearly universal (Willeford 1969).

Both types of actors are viewed with some ambivalence. Much of the respect given the indigenous healer results from fear of sorcery (Kleinman and Sung 1979:9). In addition, the ethnographic literature abounds with descriptions of the strange appearance, personality, and actions of the shaman (for many examples, see Eliade 1964). Thus, fear of this individual is easy to explain. Similarly, small children are frequently afraid of clowns, whose bizarre appearance suggests the dangers of the unknown and uncanny, and whose performances dramatize common childhood fears.

The use of puppets by CCU clowns is reminiscent of shaman helper spirits. Indeed, some shamans use puppets to represent these spirits in their rituals (Kirby 1974:10). Most clowns have two or three well-developed puppet characters, each with its own strange voice. Both clowns and shamans use ventriloquism.

Music, rhythmic drumming, singing, and chanting are found in both non-Western curing and CCU clown performances. Shamans use drumming and chanting to enter altered states of consciousness. Several clowns reported being in "another space" or "a different consciousness" while performing; all assume clown characters when they put on their makeup and costumes. Kirby (1974:14) suggests that popular entertainments that summon a different reality from the ordinary (e.g., magic tricks, escape acts, absurd skits) originated in shaman trances. Furthermore, both clowns and shamans use rituals, that is, repetitive, stylized, exaggerated actions in a predetermined order, with an evocative style and a collective dimension. When done by clowns, we call them performances.

Sleight of hand is important in both types of performance. Many shamans can seemingly cut off and reattach a body part, effect Houdini-like escapes from binding ropes, or produce the appearance or sound of spirits (Kirby 1974). Extremely common is the sucking shaman, whose apparent removal of the cause of illness, in the form of a bloody worm or tiny dart point, is echoed in the clowns' pulling of red noses, scarves, and other items out of children's ears, noses, and so on. They frequently do this in the context of removing a squeak or extracting a pain (after asking a child where it hurts, the clown will remove something from that body part). Legerdemain is an important part of many healing rituals, as it enhances belief in the healer's efficacy. The power of suggestion is important for all styles of curing. Considering the near universality of object removal, it must be a powerful healing metaphor.

This reliance on magic tricks illustrates how in their respective societies, both clowns and shamans are viewed as acting in some other, abnormal context. Shamans are believed to travel and function in supernatural realms. In trance, they communicate with spirit helpers, retrieve lost souls, and find solutions to the problem of illness. Clowns also operate outside of and, in this case, contrary to the usual cultural rules and norms. Like Native American contraries, circus clowns invert the cultural order by breaking cultural (and natural) rules in their performances (Bouissac 1985:164 ff.; Kerman 1992:15). They violate conventional rules of dress and behavior; their props fall up instead of down. CCU clowns bend many hospital rules, or appear to; the "animal in the room" sketch illustrates this. One is supposed to be quiet and reserved in the hospital setting. The clowns are noisy and boisterous.

Shamans and other healers manipulate symbols of their societies' medical systems in ways that may enlist the power of suggestion or placebo effect (Finkler 1980:300–301; Kleinman 1973). For example, patients of a Mexican spiritualist believe that illness results from imbalance in the body's "hot" and "cold" humors, and that "cleaning" has beneficial effects. In this system, healers who treat illness with herbs, foods, or therapies that have the appropriate "heat" or "coldness," and/or prescribe "cleaning," are able to effect cures (Finkler 1980). While the physiological basis remains to be delineated, it is clear that dualist philosophies of the mind-body relationship are inadequate to explain this phenomenon, and it probably involves the mediation of language and other cultural symbols (Byerly 1976; Moerman 1979). Suggestion is not the power of mind over body; rather it is the functioning of the entire physical system, which includes the brain/mind. Cultural symbolism, linguistic or otherwise, sets this process in motion (Lévi-Strauss 1967). The power of placebos lies in the power of symbols.

Clown doctors also use medical symbolism. CCU performances play with the physician character and poke fun at hospital procedures. Clown dress suggests that of a doctor (white coat, reflecting mirror on a hat, stethoscope around the neck), but with absurd additions (the coat is painted in wild colors, the mirror bounces about on a foot-long spring, and the stethoscope is used to blow bubbles). Medical paraphernalia is used in unusual ways, such as making music with oxygen tubing and hypodermic syringes. Clowns address each other as "Doctor" but act quite unlike real ones. For example, "Dr. Meatloaf," as his alter ego "Igor," shuffles into a pediatric emergency room in Harlem wearing black buck teeth, grunting, and acting like a hunchbacked imbecile, while his associate, "Dr. Gizmo," introduces him as the hospital's chief of pediatric medicine. At this point, Igor emerges from the restroom trailing a 15-foot piece of toilet paper and begins climbing over chairs (including those with people sitting in them) and trying to sit on women's laps. This sketch is reminiscent of Pueblo clown performances that burlesque powerful people, illness, and scatological functions (Steward 1931:189–191).

The clowns say they parody doctors and play with hospital equipment to lighten up the atmosphere and make children less afraid of doctors and their instruments, but one can also recognize another shamanistic function: psychosocial support (Foster and Anderson 1978:128; Kleinman and Sung 1979:24). By involving the social group, illness and curing are given public recognition and the patient receives group support (Murphy 1964:80). Shamanistic rituals reinforce social roles and can be therapeutic for families struggling to cope with illness and disorder. Social workers dealing with families in crisis have adopted similar practices (Laird 1984).

The social environment of a hospitalized child consists largely of family members and hospital staff. CCU clowns entertain all these individuals, reducing family tension created by the illness and making the hospital atmosphere happier. Parents' written evaluations of the clowns include comments such as "They make us both very happy," "It works for both child and parent," and "Clowns boost the morale of the parents as well as the kids." When asked to rate on a scale of 1 (disliked a lot) to 5 (liked a lot) how *they* (not the child) felt about the clowns, all except two of forty parents chose 5; the other two chose 4. One clown told me of a routine he uses in which a hospitalized child turns a squirt gun on her siblings. He believes this reduces patient resentment towards healthy siblings. As another example, the CCU makes a point of interacting with parents of ailing babies who are not old enough to respond to clowns, for when parents' spirits are lifted, less stress is communicated to their infants.

Another clown organization that engages in social healing is the clown ministry, a new movement in American Protestantism (Kerman 1992; Litherland 1982). These practitioners are professionally trained in both ministry and clowning, which they use for both liturgy and pastoral ministry. According to Kerman, the clown ministry has two purposes: renewal of liturgy and social healing. For the latter purpose, it focuses on nursing homes and hospitals, attempting to "lift up" their audience. Like the CCU, it has an explicit ethic of letting the clowns be the subjects of jokes and not making fun of other people.

Lifting the spirits of hospital staff improves the institutional atmosphere and the morale of professionals who are overworked, or who must deal with terminal patients or the effects of child abuse. They believe this improves the quality of their caregiving. Evaluations of the CCU by hospital staff unanimously praise the clowns' work. Doctors and nurses who administer traumatic procedures such as surgery, blood drawing, or radiation therapy report that having clowns distract the children makes their jobs easier. The medical director of one pediatric inpatient unit reported that clowns improve the care of children because staff members feel better about their work and can respond more positively to their patients. Caregivers feel more relaxed when the clowns are there. The mood is more upbeat, they say: "The whole unit is brighter," "The atmosphere always changes for the better," "It makes our job easier," and there are "more positive interactions between parents, staff, and patients." One overworked nurse in an understaffed unit wrote that clowns relieve her stress and even help her answer patients' calls for assistance.

Another way clowns act upon hospitalized children's social relations is by empowering patients. "Power to the children" is an expressed philosophy of the CCU. Pediatric patients are perhaps the most powerless of all hospitalized people. Poked and prodded, examined and ordered about, subjected to painful procedures they don't understand, children frequently react with fear, noncompliance, tantrums, and withdrawal. Noncompliance can be an expression of a patient's rejection of the power structure of a situation and an attempt to regain some control. The effects of treatment are improved if the power differential can be equalized (Elsass 1992:335–336).

This goal of patient empowerment can be seen in the structure of clown routines. Built into the CCU's standard performances are situations that make clown doctors (and frequently a real doctor or nurse as well) appear silly and inept, while the children are smart and capable. A clown might pretend to be afraid of the child and attempt to hide in obvious places. Or a magic trick keeps backfiring until the child shows the clown how to do it right. An animal puppet is hidden from the doctor, but the child always knows, and controls, where it is. These interactive performances are carefully rehearsed, as witnessed at a monthly clown meeting, in which CCU director Michael Christensen had two clowns practice one routine over and over again until he was satisfied that the patient's reaction would be one of empowerment rather than frustration.

Shaman performances may lead to patient psychological reactions such as transference and catharsis, which may relieve anxiety (Foster and Anderson 1978:128; Murphy 1964:78, 81). Catharsis is frequently associated with shamanistic curing (Kirby 1974:9), and it can be produced by clowns as well. Parsons and Beals (1934:499–500) describe the emotional release afforded by Native American clown performances that satirize anxiety-producing aspects of human experience (including illness). Indigenous clowns universally address, through humor, issues of greatest emotional interest to their observers (Charles 1945:32; Steward 1931:198).

Humor itself is cathartic (Holland 1982:88–103). Laughter not only makes one feel better, but it can also be a powerful distraction. One CCU clown tells of his experience with an 11-year-old boy who had been doused with gasoline and set on fire by an older boy:

> He was conscious but in terrible pain with major burns over more than half his body. I went right into emergency with him. When the surgeons began cutting away dead flesh, I began telling funny stories and promising circus tickets and making scarves appear and disappear—anything to keep his mind off the agony. Pretty soon he was rolling his eyes in amazement and finally I actually got him laughing behind his medical mask. It was incredible. He was staring death in the face—and he was having fun! [Darrach 1990:82]

DISCUSSION

CCU clowns don't claim to cure anything. They assert that what they do is make the hospital environment more child-friendly. In the absence of biomedical treatment, it's unlikely that they would effect any cures, except possibly for psychosomatic and anxiety-derived illnesses. However, they do have a beneficial role to play in Western medicine today, in collaboration with those of physicians, nurses, and other mainstream health care providers. For the clown, like the shaman, addresses that aspect of healing that is not as well developed in modern Western medicine, the treatment of the whole person, the social milieu, and the mental predicates of illness. The clown helps the patient and family provide meaning to the illness experience and resolve personal and social problems that result from it. This in turn increases patient satisfaction, compliance, and perhaps outcome. The medical establishment increasingly recognizes the need for providing this level of care, but physicians are not always in a position to give it. The inclusion of clowns among pediatric hospital personnel is a practical strategy for resolving this problem. Collaborative efforts between physicians and traditional or unorthodox healers have been advocated (for example, see Bastien 1987) or even implemented (Jingfeng 1987; Launs 1989; Leslie 1980), but this approach is rare in the United States, where folk medicine is less accepted. The clown, on the other hand, is a symbolic type familiar to and appreciated by most American children, so the potential for its use is greater than that of other unorthodox practitioners.

Another reason why clown doctors can assist in the treatment of young patients is that children, while somewhat enculturated into their society's medical system and beliefs about illness causation and treatment, are not as fully "vaccinated" against belief in magic and alternate realities as their parents. That is, from a child's point of view, magical effects just might be possible. This enhances their suggestibility with regard to the clowns' tricks. Some children may believe the CCU *are* doctors, but doctors with special powers. Furthermore, clowns, and circus in general, represent "humanity freed from the constraints of culture," and this appeals to children more than to adults (Bouissac 1985:8).

Clown therapy is also important for terminal patients, such as children suffering from cancer or AIDS. There are few family crises more serious than the death of a child. The individual, too, faces a profound need to cope with the expectation of mortality. Pain and suffering must be dealt with. Kleinman and Sung (1979:16) observed Taiwanese patients with terminal diseases who had been discharged from hospitals as untreatable but who were receiving treatment from shamans. These patients and their families reported feeling psychologically better and had a more satisfying social life as a result.

CONCLUSIONS

Clowns are like shamans in several ways. Both use weird costumes, props, and behaviors. Common to both kinds of performance are sleight of hand, ventriloquism, music, and feats of skill that seem to break natural and cultural laws. Both shamans and clown doctors employ social healing, suggestion, and manipulation of cultural symbols drawn from the society's medical system. Both pay more attention to the patient's illness experience and social milieu than physicians frequently do.

Integrating clown doctors into the medical care of hospitalized children is particularly appropriate for the obvious reason that clowns and children are a natural combination. Children are more receptive to the clowns' uncanny antics. Children are less enculturated into the orthodox medical belief system that values pharmaceutical and surgical intervention over "magic." Incapacitated children are vulnerable to the communication of their parents' and caregivers' anxiety, so any relief the clowns provide these individuals should improve the child's social and medical environment. Use of clowns in conjunction with other health care personnel can promote patient satisfaction and compliance, especially in children, which may contribute to more positive clinical outcomes.

NOTE

1. Big Apple Circus Clown Care Unit® and Clown Care Unit® are registered trademarks.

REFERENCES

Aakster, C. W. 1986. Concepts in Alternative Medicine. *Social Science and Medicine* 22:265–273.

Bastien, Joseph W. 1987. *Healers of the Andes: Kallawaya Herbalists and their Medicinal Plants.* Salt Lake City: University of Utah Press.

Bouissac, Paul. 1985. *Circus and Culture: A Semiotic Approach.* Lanham, MD: University Press of America.

Bunzell, R. L. 1932. *Introduction to Zuni Ceremonialism.* Washington, DC: Bureau of American Ethnology, 47th Annual Report.

Byerly, Henry. 1976. Explaining and Exploiting Placebo Effects. *Perspectives in Biology and Medicine* 19:423–436.

Charles, Lucile Hoerr. 1945. The Clown's Function. *Journal of American Folklore* 58:25–34.

Darrach, Brad. 1990. Send in the Clowns. *Life Magazine* 13(10):76–85.

Eisenberg, David M., Ronald C. Kessler, Cindy Foster, Frances E. Norlock, David R. Calkins, and Thomas L. Delbanco. 1993. Unconventional Medicine in the United States: Prevalence, Costs, and Patterns of Use. *New England Journal of Medicine* 328:246–252.

Eisenberg, Leon. 1977. Disease and Illness: Distinctions between Professional and Popular Ideas of Sickness. *Culture, Medicine, and Psychiatry* 1:9–23.

Eliade, Mircea. 1964. *Shamanism: Archaic Techniques of Ecstasy.* Princeton: Princeton University Press.

Elsass, Peter. 1992. The Healing Space in Psychotherapy and Theatre. *New Theatre Quarterly* 8:333–342.

Finkler, Kaja. 1980. Non-Medical Treatments and Their Outcomes. *Culture, Medicine and Psychiatry* 4: 271–310.

Flaherty, Gloria. 1988. The Performing Artist as the Shaman of Higher Civilization. *MLN* 103:519–539.

Foster, George M. 1976. Disease Etiologies in Non-Western Medical Systems. *American Anthropologist* 78:773–782.

Foster, George M., and Barbara Anderson. 1978. *Medical Anthropology.* New York: John Wiley and Sons.

Fumham, Adrian, and Julie Forey. 1994. The Attitudes, Behaviors, and Beliefs of Patients of Conventional vs. Complementary (Alternative) Medicine. *Journal of Clinical Psychology* 50:458–469.

Gibson, S. L. M., A. D. McNeill, and W. W. Buchanan. 1980. Homeopathic Therapy in Rheumatoid Arthritis: Evaluation by Double-Blind Clinical Therapeutic Trial. *British Journal of Clinical Pharmacology* 9: 453–459.

Gould, Donald. 1993. Beyond the Old Fashioned Fringe. *New Scientist* 139(July 31):44–45.

Holland, Norman N. 1982. *Laughing: A Psychology of Humor.* Ithaca, NY: Cornell University Press.

Jingfeng, Cai. 1987. Toward a Comprehensive Evaluation of Alternative Medicine. *Social Science and Medicine* 25:659–667.

Kerman, Judith B. 1992. The Clown as Social Healer: A Study of the Clown Ministry Movement. *Journal of American Culture* 15:9–16.

Kirby, E. T. 1974. The Shamanistic Origins of Popular Entertainments. *Drama Review* 18(1):5–15.

Kirkaldy-Willis, W. H., and J. D. Cassidy. 1985. Spinal Manipulation in the Treatment of Low-Back Pain. *Canadian Family Physician* 31:535–540.

Kleinman, Arthur M. 1973. Medicine's Symbolic Reality: On a Central Problem in the Philosophy of Medicine. *Inquiry* 16:206–213.

Kleinman, Arthur, and Lilian H. Sung. 1979. Why Do Indigenous Practitioners Successfully Heal? *Social Science and Medicine* 13B:7–26.

LaBarre, Weston. 1979. Shamanic Origins of Religion and Medicine. *Journal of Psychedelic Drugs* 11:7–11.

Laird, Joan. 1984. Sorcerers, Shamans, and Social Workers: The Use of Ritual in Social Work Practice. *Social Work* 29:123–129.

Last, Murray. 1990. Professionalization of Indigenous Healers. In *Medical Anthropology: Contemporary Theory and Method.* T. M. Johnson and C. F. Sargent, eds. Pp. 349–366. New York: Praeger.

Launs, Laila. 1989. Integrated Medicine—A Challenge to the Health-Care System. *Acta Sociologica* 32:237–251.

Leslie, Charles. 1980. Medical Pluralism in World Perspective. *Social Science and Medicine* 14B:191–195.

Lévi-Strauss, Claude. 1967. The Effectiveness of Symbols. In *Structural Anthropology.* Pp. 181–201. Garden City, NJ: Anchor Books.

Litherland, Janet. 1982. *The Clown Ministry Handbook.* Colorado Springs: Meriwether.

McKee, Janet. 1988. Holistic Health and the Critique of Western Medicine. *Social Science and Medicine* 26:776–784.

Moerman, Daniel E. 1979. Anthropology of Symbolic Healing. *Current Anthropology* 20:59–80.

Murphy, Jane M. 1964. Psychotherapeutic Aspects of Shamanism on St. Lawrence Island, Alaska. In *Magic, Faith, and Healing.* A. Kiev, ed. Pp. 53–83. New York: Macmillan.

Murray, Joanna, and Simon Shepherd. 1993. Alternative or Additional Medicine? An Exploratory Study in General Practice. *Social Science and Medicine* 37:983–988.

Parsons, Elsie Clews, and Ralph L. Beals. 1934. The Sacred Clowns of the Pueblo and Mayo-Yaqui Indians. *American Anthropologist* 36:491–514.

Ray, Verne F. 1945. The Contrary Behavior Pattern in American Indian Ceremonialism. *Southwestern Journal of Anthropology* 1:75–113.

Steward, Julian H. 1931. The Ceremonial Buffoon of the American Indian. Ann Arbor (University of Michigan): *Papers of the Michigan Academy of Science, Arts, and Letters* 14:187–207.

Towson, John H. 1976. *Clowns.* New York: Hawthorn Books.

Tumer, Victor. 1985. *On the Edge of the Bush.* Tucson: University of Arizona Press.

Willeford, William. 1969. *The Fool and His Scepter.* Evanston, IL: Northwestern University Press.

9   SHAMANISM AND ITS DISCONTENTS

Michael Fobes Brown

The previous selection focused on the sunny side of shamanic healing, showing how the appearance and performance of spiritual healers, including clowns, play upon the mechanisms involved in the placebo effect and positively influence the treatment process. In this selection, Brown emphasizes the political context of shamanic healing in indigenous societies, where the power of shamans comes from the same source as that of sorcerers and therefore brings an uncomfortable, unstable mixture of distrust and esteem to those who take on the burden of helping others. The benefits of shamanism in terms of individual well-being and social solidarity come at the cost of uncertainty and ambiguity projected far into the future, for each healing ritual reinforces the need for other shamanic treatments.

While most studies focus on the shaman's manipulation of symbols and other aspects of the healing performance, Brown pays attention to the understandings and reactions of patients and their relatives. He provides a transcript and visual description of a healing session, opening a window on a complex and lengthy interaction. Both shamans and patients and families make references during healing sessions to violence and their own intentions with respect to protecting against or avenging sorcery. This illustrates the point that the healing ritual is at once a private and public or political event. Through his remarks the shaman reaffirms his power and his utility in the future, while the families force him to demonstrate his commitment to neutralizing rather than causing harm.

Many of the shaman's activities resonate with those outlined in the previous selection, such as object removal (sucking out invisible poison darts), communication with an unseen spirit world, manipulation of culturally specific symbols such as local animals and their behaviors and qualities, and transfer of the patient's pain and suffering to the healer (see Van Blerkom's description of the clowns' emotional and physical exhaustion). In addition, shamans in the area studied by Brown use trance-inducing hallucinogenic drugs that cause intermittent stomach pain, retching, and vomiting for several hours. The unpleasantness of the healing session combined with his ambiguous status as healer and possible sorcerer makes the shaman's profession a painful, difficult, and possibly very dangerous one.

Questions to keep in mind

What are some ways in which Aguaruna shamanic healers are responsive to sociocultural and economic circumstances?

Is Yankush a faithful protector of traditional values and ways of healing? Which of his practices are idiosyncratic or innovative?

What purposes do the darkness, unusual sounds, and shifting speech registers serve during the healing session?

In what ways does Brown's involvement in this research and analysis converge with the arguments of Cassell (selection 7) and Barsh (selection 6)?

Source: Brown, M. F. 1988. "Shamanism and Its Discontents." © 1988 by the American Anthropological Association. Reprinted from *Medical Anthropology Quarterly* Vol. 2 No. 2 pp. 102–120, by permission.

Like depictions of the Roman god Janus, the anthropological image of shamanism has two opposed faces. The first portrays shamans as charismatic protectors of traditional values, helping their clients to maintain structures of meaning or to construct new ones appropriate to changing circumstances. The second face, more rarely documented, is admirably captured in Christopher Crocker's characterization of Bororo shamans as "ambiguous, suspicious personages . . . socially approved if fundamentally distrusted" (Crocker 1985:237).

Perhaps the most influential investigation of shamanism's heroic face is Lévi-Strauss's analysis of a Cuna Indian chant performed for women experiencing protracted labor (1963). Through a series of comparisons with contemporary psychoanalysis, Lévi-Strauss shows how symbols, skillfully manipulated by the shaman, effect important changes in the patient—changes that, he concludes, are ultimately experienced at the somatic level. The shaman mobilizes a profound but largely tacit knowledge of the society's collective representations to craft the appropriate "myth" that will rebuild the shattered experience of the patient into a sheltering architecture of significance.

Yet the shamanism of Lévi-Strauss's analysis is curiously asocial. The patients themselves appear only as passive participants, the shaman's assessment as unquestioned orthodoxy. When the analytical perspective situates shamanism in its social and political space, a more troubled image tends to emerge (e.g., Atkinson 1987; Steedly 1988; Taussig 1987). One sees that the stories shamans weave exert only a provisional, contested control over their patients' understanding. The shaman's power is granted grudgingly by society; shamanic revelation may be subject to challenge by those who both need and fear it.

Through a textual analysis of rhetoric and counter-rhetoric in an Aguaruna Indian healing session, this article assesses shamanism's second face in an Amazonian setting. My general goal is to lift the veil of romanticism from the session so that it can be seen in a way that more closely resembles the participants' view of it: as a highly charged event involving elements of struggle, uncertainty, ambivalence, and partial revelation. If there is a "social myth" enacted in the ritual, it is a

collective and interactive one, not simply the invention of an autonomous ritual specialist (cf. Joralemon 1986). And that "myth" may only replace one type of chaos with another. At its heart, the Aguaruna healing session is the kind of encounter that Foucault calls an "agonism," that is, "a relationship which is at the same time reciprocal incitation and struggle; less of a face-to-face confrontation which paralyzes both sides than a permanent provocation" (1982:222).

AGUARUNA SHAMANISM IN THE ALTO RÍO MAYO, PERU

Like most Amazonian natives of the late 20th century, the Aguaruna of Peru are part of a local cultural mosaic that includes other tribal groups, recently arrived peasant farmers, and the usual host of entrepreneurs and swindlers drawn to regions on the margins of civil control. The Aguaruna negotiate a place for themselves in this social arena by defending their land rights and by responding cannily to sudden shifts in economic conditions. In the Alto Mayo valley, Aguaruna communities are now integrated into the local system of cash-crop agriculture. Yet despite economic transformation, the proselytizing efforts of Protestant missionaries, and the impact of primary education, the Aguaruna maintain a strong cultural identity—an identity reflected, among other ways, in the continued vitality of shamanic practice and its dark alter ego, sorcery beliefs.[1]

The key features of Aguaruna shamanism are typical of the native societies of Western Amazonia. Shamans (*iwishín*) are men who have acquired the ability to communicate directly with powerful beings during visions induced by psychoactive plants.[2] When serious illness strikes, people suspect that sorcery is behind it. Sorcerers (*túnchi* or *wáwek*) may secretly introduce tiny darts into the bodies of their victims, darts that fester and produce illness. By drinking an infusion of the hallucinogens *datém (Banisteriopsis caapi)* and *yáji (B. cabrerana)* (referred to as *yáji* when mixed together), a shaman enters a trance that he uses to search the patient's body for such darts, which can sometimes be removed by fanning and sucking. While in this altered state, the shaman may also bear witness to distant events and combat the community's hidden adversaries. Ordinarily, the patients themselves do not take hallucinogens during healing sessions, though many have had experience with psychoactive plants in other contexts.

The sociological implications of shamanism are, of course, much more tangled than this simple good-against-evil description would suggest. For a number of reasons, it is dangerous to be an *iwishín*. First, shamanic practice necessitates regular use of hallucinogens. In the throes of a healing vision, the shaman is vulnerable to attack by sorcerers and their spirit familiars. But the immediate threats to the shaman's life are more prosaic. Because the shaman can identify sorcerers—people who may be marked for death because of this accusation—he inevitably has enemies. More important, because all shamans are themselves potential sorcerers, possessing the ability to kill if they so desire, they are prime suspects when there are deaths suggestive of sorcery. Indeed, the good name of a shaman is always contextual: his skills are extolled by close kinsmen but cited as evidence of his homicidal propensities by non-kin.

It is a commonplace to note the equivocal political status of shamans in Amazonian systems of social control, especially among Jivaroan peoples, and I have little to add to existing accounts (e.g., Colajanni 1984; Descola and Lory 1982; Harner 1972; Seymour-Smith 1982). What has not been explored in detail, however, is the extent to which even a shaman's close kinsmen and allies are uncomfortable in the presence of his powers. In the Alto Río Mayo, if one poses the question, "Do you have an *iwishín* in your community?" the reply is likely to be: "No, we get along well here. We have no problems." The most recent expression of local attitudes toward shamans was an attempt by an inter-village organization, the Organización Aguaruna del Alto Mayo (OAAM), to establish an official list of fees for the services of "traditional doctors" and to require all *iwishín* to seek formal recognition from the organization (OAAM 1984). An informant close to OAAM leaders reported that there was also some discussion about the advisability of imposing a tax on practicing *iwishín*, though as of 1986 such a policy had not yet been implemented. The intent of the proposal, according to the people I spoke with, was to force all shamans to identify themselves, thereby bringing their power into the public eye so that it could be

more easily observed and controlled. All the evidence at my disposal suggests that this ambivalence toward *iwishín* has been part of Aguaruna social reality for decades and cannot be attributed to rapid culture change.

In view of the dangers of the role and its dubious social status, why would anyone become a shaman? The shamans to whom I spoke emphasized their desire to assist afflicted kinsmen. It bears mentioning, however, that the rapid settlement of the Alto Mayo has opened new economic opportunities for enterprising healers. Local peasant farmers, who associate the Aguaruna with the powerful and shadowy spirits of the forest, are willing to pay substantial fees for the ministrations of a sympathetic *iwishín*. Factors of individual temperament—including curiosity about the spirit world, a desire for influence in one's community, and an ability to endure or even enjoy the perils of frequent intoxication by powerful hallucinogens—also undoubtedly attract certain people to the shaman's role.

Late in 1977, I took up residence in the community where the most active shaman in the Alto Mayo resided. The local preeminence of this *iwishín*, whom I shall call Yankush, rested in part on the belief that he had acquired some of his shamanic powers among Spanish-speaking mestizos of the Peruvian coast. Far from being an assiduous guardian of cultural tradition, he had introduced a number of idiosyncratic methods into his practice, including the abbreviation of the traditional healing session[3] and the occasional use of alcohol to help him arrive at a trance state. He had also integrated the prescription of pharmaceutical products into his healing performances. Highly regarded by mestizo colonists, he was sometimes referred to as "Professor Yankush." His fame among colonists seemed to raise rather than lower his standing among the Aguaruna. It is Yankush who presides over the session that is the focus of this article.

HEALING SESSION, 18 JANUARY 1978

The session begins after sunset, for the *iwishín* needs absolute darkness to be able to find the sorcerer's darts in his patients. As night falls and the patients and other interested parties assemble in his house, Yankush drinks the hallucinogenic preparation, *yáji*. After a time, he begins to yawn in a curious, exaggerated fashion. This signals that the hallucinogen has taken effect: powerful beings called *pásuk* are entering the shaman's chest to assist him in his curing acts. Yankush's utterances encompass several distinctive styles or, as I shall call them, "registers": (1) a normal discursive register consisting of simple declarative statements; (2) a normal shamanic register, performed as song, which includes divinatory and metaphorical statements presented in a compressed style still intelligible to other participants; and (3) a cryptic shamanic register, also sung, employing an esoteric lexicon.[4] The cryptic register resembles Cuna healing chants (Sherzer 1983:134) in that its specific meaning is opaque to laymen, though they do have a general notion of the register's content. In the following text, both shamanic registers are marked in bold type.[5]

The performance also includes the energetic participation of the patients' kinsmen, who shout words of encouragement to Yankush, move his divinatory pronouncements in certain directions with their questions, and make their own strong declarations when their fears of sorcery are confirmed. So polyphonic is the texture of the session that I was unable to transcribe all of the comments, questions, jokes, and cries of dismay uttered during the two-hour event. There was simply too much going on. The following text focuses principally on the utterances of Yankush and his two main interlocutors, the husbands of the patients.

Participants

A group of people have arrived from another village in the Alto Mayo valley that is approximately a day's travel away. The group includes two couples: Chapaik and her husband Katan, and Yamanuanch and her husband Shimpu (all pseudonyms). They have prevailed upon Yankush to take *yáji* in order to diagnose the illnesses that have afflicted both Chapaik and Yamanuanch. Neither woman is seriously ill, but both complain of chronic pains of various sorts. Yankush's wife, Tumus, is also slightly unwell, and she receives treatment at the end of the session as the patients and their families file out of the house. Because no one is danger-

ously ill, the overall atmosphere of the healing session is intense but genial. Several other residents of Yankush's community are also present, including two anthropologists, Margaret Van Bolt and the author. With the exception of the anthropologists, all of those who participate consider themselves to be kin, though the two patients and their husbands are only distant relatives of Yankush (see Figure 9.1).[6]

The Event

At about 7:00 P.M., the anthropologists arrive at Yankush's house with Utijat and Chimi, close kinsmen of Yankush who reside in the community. Yankush has taken the *yáji* and is resting in the bedroom. He gets up and ambles out to chat. Katan, Chapaik, Shimpu, and Yamanuanch arrive. At about 7:30, Yankush goes out, saying he will defecate. People chat informally. He returns and sits on a stool with his back to the room. He whistles, holding a fan of *sámpi* leaves. He sings softly, then talks informally with people, still facing the wall. He yawns in a drawn-out fashion, indicating that *pásuk* are entering his body. He begins to shake the fan. He takes off his sweater, then combs his hair, still facing away from the participants.

> YANKUSH **"I, I, I, I, I. With Tsunki** [spirit being of aquatic realm and ultimate source of shamanistic power] **I am seated."** He falls silent. He spits, then shakes his fan while breaking into wordless song. He stands up, still facing the wall.
>
> KATAN, *shouting:* "Let's listen! He's intoxicated now, so let's listen!" Yankush sits down again, still singing. His daughter brings him a small bottle of an unidentified liquid. He rubs this liquid on his
> 10 neck.
>
> KATAN: "Sing to your own body so that others won't bewitch you."
>
> UTIJAT: "Others know you are curing. They can hurt you. Be careful!"
> 15 Yankush faces participants. Katan brings in two large banana leaves. Shimpu moves the lantern to put Yankush in shadow.
>
> YANKUSH *(to Katan):* "Mother's brother, bring your wife." Both patients come forward and
> 20 sit in front of Yankush. They take off their dresses but remain covered with blankets below the waist. One woman turns over to lie on her stomach.

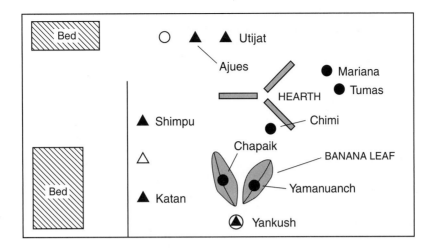

Figure 9.1   Adults present at shamanic healing session, 18 January 1978.

KATAN: "Take the darts out. See where the sickness is!"

SHIMPU (indicating Yamanuanch): "She can't eat. Her throat hurts."

UTIJAT: "Think powerfully!" Yankush looks at Chapaik, sucks on her back, and spits. He drinks from a bottle (later identified as *kistián ámpi,* "mestizo medicine"), faces toward wall, and vomits.

KATAN: "If you can't cure her, tell me the truth. Throw it [the sorcery substance] out! . . . Look, stand up to the intoxication. If you cure her, I'll always receive you well in my house. Throw it [sorcery substance] away!" Yankush turns to face Yamanuanch. Shimpu and others begin to shout.

VARIOUS: "Show him where it hurts!" Yankush appears to suck on chest of Yamanuanch.

YAMANUANCH: "My throat hurts too."

YANKUSH: "You'll get well." Yankush takes off his shirt, facing the wall again. He turns to look at Yamanuanch.

KATAN: "Sit well, think well!"

YANKUSH (shaking fan in direction of Yamanuanch): "Her chest is bad [i.e., diseased]." He sucks the afflicted spot and spits noisily. He turns quickly to Chapaik.

VARIOUS MEN: "Tell him where it hurts!"

YANKUSH: "You can give her an injection."

KATAN: "Nephew, look at all the places that hurt!"

YANKUSH: "Give her an injection. She will recover. She is not sick with sorcery, but a cold in her throat." He looks at Chapaik while singing, touching her with his left hand. He sucks on Chapaik's back, spits, then sings above Chapaik. He yawns noisily, then kneels to suck on her back. He hawks noisily and spits.

YANKUSH: "You can give her an injection of *wíchu* [unidentified; probably a corruption of the name of a pharmaceutical product]. You can give her three injections. She will get well."

KATAN: "Tomorrow I'll get the medicine."

YANKUSH: **"With various injections she'll get better."** Turns to Yamanuanch. "She has sickness in her stomach."

SHIMPU: "Is she going to die? If so, tell me!" Yankush leans over Yamanuanch, sucks, and spits.

KATAN: "Why would they want to bewitch me? I always give people food when they come to visit. Why bewitch my wife? I'm angry." Yankush stands singing over Yamanuanch. He drinks from the bottle of "mestizo medicine." He sings over Yamanuanch for several minutes: **"If my enemies want to bewitch me, here I am. They can't hurt me. I see everything. She had darts in her stomach, and I took them out."**

UTIJAT: "See well in order to cure!"

YANKUSH: **"Your throat is sore from vomiting. I will heal you. Your stomach hurts right there. I'll heal it. When I first began curing, few people came. Now many come because I can cure. If they are weak, I can heal them. If they have rheumatism, I can cure them. You will return to your house. I see your soul dancing there, getting drunk at parties. Perhaps you've been given an injection. This makes your stomach hurt. There are a few darts there."**

CHIMI: "If there are any darts there when she gets back home, they may say that Yankush put them there. So take them all out!"

KATAN: "There are no sorcerers there [in the patient's community]. Who will have done this bewitching? If my wife dies, I could kill any man out of anger. Little nephew, cure my wife well. I don't want to be bothering you here. I live far away."

AJUES: "Why hasn't Uyum [a kinsman in a distant community] come? Is he making war?" (Here Ajues is calling on the shaman's visionary powers to see events in a distant location.)

YANKUSH: "Did your wife ever have colic [*kúliku*] before?"

SHIMPU: "No, never."

YANKUSH: "Now colic wants to grab her. You can give her ten drops of a medicine for colic . . . [still singing over Yamanuanch]. **Colic wants to grab her. Her body is weak, sick.**" He sucks noisily, spits. "**Colic does not heal quickly. It gets better, then comes again. I will cure it completely. In this part [indicating throat?] there is no sickness. You vomited so much** that a piece of a sorcery dart is stuck in your throat. I'll remove it." He sucks on her throat and spits. **"How have you been bewitched? Sometimes it is done so that a person will be sick for years but not die. I can cure this. If you have a piece of dart in your throat, the vomiting has made it more painful. I can take it out."** (Speaking now) "Before you had much sorcery inside you. Now I'm taking it all out. You are better. Receive an injection, and you'll get better." He sucks and spits.

UTIJAT: "Make her well! You are a good curer."

YANKUSH: "I'll see everything. Nothing will remain."

KATAN: "If she has a lot of illness and you can't take all of it out, take out half so that I can cure her easily with medicine. You are a curer, you can do this for me." Yankush sucks on Chapaik and spits. He yawns loudly, and looks at Chapaik.

YANKUSH: **"In Achu they killed a person. A sorcerer was killed."**

OTHERS: "Who could it be?" Yankush drinks from the bottle of "mestizo medicine," then puts it down on the floor. He looks at Chapaik, touching her with his left hand. He sucks, spits, then vomits.

KATAN: "Cure well! You are a shaman!"

YANKUSH: "When I'm intoxicated, I cure well. Don't say that I wasn't intoxicated enough."

KATAN: "There are others who are not as brave as I" (alluding to his anger if his wife dies of sorcery).

YANKUSH: **"On a piece of iron I walk on tiptoes . . ."** (rest of segment of curing song is inaudible).

KATAN: "Cure well! Don't let her be sick!" Yankush stands over Chapaik, fanning her with his leaf-fan. He touches her back with his left hand. He sucks and spits noisily, then begins to sing. (Segment is indecipherable on tape.)

KATAN: "Blow the sickness away!" (To Chapaik) "You said that your head and neck hurt. Tell him where so that he will cure you."

YANKUSH (turning to Yamanuanch, shaking his leaf-fan): **"If she has illness, I will see it and take it out."** He sucks on Yamanuanch's stomach and spits. "She can't die. I will heal her."

KATAN: "She can't die, because I have few fam-
170 ily left. We will be few if she dies."

YANKUSH: "Tumus [Yankush's wife] is sick
[with natural illness], not bewitched."

UTIJAT: "Once I was sick like that, but after
taking medicine I got well. I almost died."

175 *UTIJAT and KATAN:* "Fan her! Blow the sickness away!"

YANKUSH: "Her stomach is stuck together inside. I'm going to loosen it. **I'll take out the sickness.**" Sucks, spits. **"Sickness has hit several**
180 **times, but I've removed it so that it will heal."**
He begins to sing, facing the wall behind his stool.

KATAN: "You all, don't talk so much! If you
speak, the healer won't be able to see. Be quiet, or
he'll make a mistake!"

185 *YANKUSH:* "There is a war in another place
and they've killed someone. His kinsmen return
crying." He faces Yamanuanch and begins to sing.
**"This person is weak inside. I'll make her well
and strong. The earth never dies. When I**
190 **heal her, she will be the same, never dying.**
You are well. You lack only a little treatment to be
completely healed. I'm taking out the darts. Afterwards you should have an injection, but you
195 will recover slowly. Take off your blanket so that I
can see your chest. Stains or wounds come out on
your breast. Have you had this before?"

YAMANUANCH: "Yes."

YANKUSH: "Can you give her an injection?"

200 *SHIMPU:* "Yes, I can."

UTIJAT: "See how the birth of the woman's
child will be."

YANKUSH: "I can't see that." To the patient:
"I'll return to you again." (Turns to Chapaik.)

205 *UTIJAT:* "Look at me to see if I should take
the name 'Tobacco'." (People laugh because Utijat is known in the village by several humorous
nicknames, some of which he invented for himself.)

210 *KATAN:* "Look there! She says that her liver
hurts. Show him where it hurts. In her stomach it
is hard. There's a line of pain there. Look there
first, look where the *yáji* tells you. Her chest is
215 tight. It won't let her breathe." Yankush sucks on
Chapaik's stomach, then spits. Those present remark that there is much *kaag* (the sorcerer's special saliva) in the saliva that Yankush spits out.

KATAN: "It's understandable that a stranger
220 might want to fight with me, but why bewitch my

wife? Yankush says that there is something in her
body. Since he has strength, he should look carefully and blow away the sickness." To Yankush:
"If there's only a little, take it out. If there is sick-
225 ness, see it. Look to see what will cure her as fast
as possible. Cure it! Cure it! See what will happen
next! This woman came far to be cured. Some
women don't want to live, and they take their own
230 lives with poison. She doesn't want to die. Who
can cure her? Look at them [i.e., the patients].
Many come here and leave recovered. Sometimes
shamans can't see. But look carefully anyway!
Look!"

235 *UTIJAT:* "Look to see if my soul is married to a
mestizo woman!" (laughter)

KATAN: "Show him where it hurts in your
liver."

240 *YANKUSH:* "She could get well fast, but the
'tobacco' [i.e., curer] hasn't discovered the sickness yet. Her body is weak."

KATAN: "Now that you are with *yáji*, look well!
Throw out the sickness!"

245 *UNIDENTIFIED WOMAN:* "She says she
has *tsúak* [a powerful hallucinogen, *Brugmansia*
sp., sometimes used for self-cures]. Can she take
it?"

YANKUSH: "You can take two injections, then
250 you can take *tsúak*."

KATAN: "After looking into her, you should tell
us what medicine to buy."

YANKUSH (indicating Chapaik): "She doesn't
have much, just a little sickness."

255 *KATAN:* "Can I give her injections for her
liver?"

YANKUSH: "Yes, that's all right." To Chapaik:
"Mother, I'll fan you. **I'm concentrating to
throw out sickness, like a tireless jaguar. My**
260 **song continues, continues. With my help she
will become like the tapir, which doesn't
know how to refuse any kind of food."**

KATAN: "It's true that tapirs never reject food.
265 When I eat tapir it tastes good. Delicious!" (Tapir
is traditionally a prohibited food item for the
Aguaruna, though it is now increasingly eaten in
the Alto Mayo because game is scarce.)

270 *YANKUSH:* "When she gets well she can eat the
monkey *wájiam*. The pains in your stomach have
made you weak. But with this fanning you will get
better. We'll see how it will turn out. **I speak to
you like the *mankúp*** [species of bear], **which**

275 never gets sick."

KATAN: "Tell him if you don't have pains in
your head. Little nephew, she says that her head
seems to swell, then her ears close up tight."

YANKUSH: "From here in her head I took out
280 darts and threw them away. Tomorrow I will see
all, and then we can leave this curing."

CHAPAIK *(getting up):* "I want you to see into
me again on Saturday, and when I come again."

285 YANKUSH: "When you come again, bring me a
gift of cloth. With another healing session you will
recover."

YAMANUANCH: "What kind of injection
should I get?"

290 YANKUSH: "An injection for colic. You can
take drops of Diafa [apparently a commercial
medicine] in water several times. You can take
drops of Diafa without an injection. This is the
295 only sickness that is hurting you." To Shimpu:
"There was something sticky in her body, but I
took it all out. Only a little colic remains there.
She'll get well soon. This colic made her body
weak."

SHIMPU: "Can she eat *wájiam* [a species of
300 monkey]?"

YANKUSH: "She can eat it when she's better,
after a week. **Through her body I say the sickness will not continue. The agile dog never
tires, hopping about. She should be this way. I
305 say that her stomach should never reject food,
as the tapir never rejects food.** It's all right. She
won't die. It's nothing."

KATAN: "How are the grandchildren I left behind in Shimpiyacu?"

310 YANKUSH: "All right. They're fine."

KATAN: "Will I arrive home safely?"

YANKUSH: "Yes. Don't worry any more."
Mariana helps Tumus lie down in front of
Yankush. Others are saying goodbye and leaving.

315 MARIANA: "Tell him to fan your head. Lie
down. Show him where your liver hurts most."

YANKUSH: "**She has *súgku*.** [In this context,
súgku means "natural" or "epidemic" illness as
opposed to sorcery-induced illness.] **After much
320 suffering, she'll get better.**"

OTHERS: "Surely she will die of suffering!"

YANKUSH: "Her other sickness is gone. Now
another illness has grabbed her, the same that infected the others. **The offspring of the tapir
325 never becomes ill. Be like this.**" Chimi and Uti-

jat take their leave. All the others have left except
Yankush, his wife Tumus, and Tumus's mother
Mariana. The anthropologists leave. It is 9:05 P.M.

FIRST READING: SHAMANIC CLARIFICATION AND TRANSFERENCE

To gain some analytical purchase on an event of
this complexity, we must identify the central features of the session and follow the developing roles
of the protagonists. In doing so, I shall first offer a
conventional interpretation of Yankush's therapeutic efforts, one that stresses his attempts to grapple
with the chaotic effects of illness and wrest from
them some meaning so as to assure the patients
that their sufferings will soon come to an end. I
shall then advance a second reading of this event
that challenges the first by questioning the alleged
order created through healing discourse.

The central acts pondered by the participants in
this encounter have to do with "seeing" as it is effected through the powerful agency of the
shaman's gaze. The participants repeatedly urge
Yankush to "see where the sickness is" (line 24). In
response, Yankush reassures them that he can "see
everything" (line 80). Later he describes Yamanuanch's illness as resembling "wounds or stains" on
her chest (line 196). Yankush's gaze encompasses
not only the ability to see the hidden danger in his
patients but also to observe events distant in space
and time, including violent acts in other communities (lines 140 and 186). Though not realized in
this session, the ultimate achievement of the
shamanic gaze is the identification of the sorcerer
who sends the illness. Thus Yankush's power lies
in his ability to search the darkness for the glim-
mer of hidden forces and veiled motives. His manifest ability to see the illness inside his patients is
enhanced by the darkness; paradoxically, the
shaman's penetrating gaze is most effective when
others cannot see at all.

According to the ideology of Aguaruna
shamanic practice, the acuity of the shaman's gaze
is based on two factors: (1) the quantity and
strength of the *yáji* that he has consumed before
the session, and (2) the presence in his body of the
very *tséntsak* (spirit-darts) that he seeks within his
patients. Throughout the session, Yankush em-

phasizes the intensity of his hallucinogen-induced vision. He declares, for instance, "Don't say that I wasn't intoxicated enough," which is presaged by Katan's imperative "Stand up to the intoxication" earlier in the event. The bitter *yáji* enables him to do his dangerous work, but his willingness to submit to its rigors is also keenly noted evidence of his commitment as a healer. Ultimately, however, even the power of *yáji* as the catalyst of the shamanic gaze depends upon the strength of the shaman's own spirit-darts: the Alto Mayo Aguaruna assert that *yáji* will not intoxicate someone who lacks them. In other words, the shaman's spirit-darts give the vision form and meaning, permitting him to neutralize the venomous *tséntsak* lodged in his patient's body.[7]

Although the central discursive focus of the healing session concerns sight, the principal channels of communication are almost exclusively auditory because of the enfolding darkness. There is, of course, a tactile dimension while Yankush works on the bodies of the patients, but in essence he translates a visual experience into an acoustic one. He employs the three speech registers mentioned earlier; he also whistles, hums, shakes his fan of *sámpi* leaves, yawns extravagantly, noisily sucks on the patients, and is periodically convulsed by paroxysms of hawking, spitting, and vomiting.

As a speech event, the ritual can be roughly divided into four parts.

1. The session opens with Yankush and the participants talking informally in the ordinary discursive register. As the hallucinogen begins to take effect, however, the shaman's messages change registers and expand into other communicative "channels" and "codes" (Fitzgerald 1975:208–209): his explosive yawns herald the arrival of the *pásuk* spirits; he shakes the leaf-fan; conspicuous spitting commences; he begins to sing rather than speak. Katan and other men shout words of encouragement.

2. By the time curing begins in earnest (beginning approximately at line 28), Yankush's actions shift to sucking, utterances in the shamanic register, and retching.

3. Beginning at line 140, the exchanges of Yankush and the other participants jump from the particulars of the cases at hand to events in distant places: the murder of a sorcerer in Achu and a violent encounter in an unidentified community.

4. As the session enters its final exchanges (from line 235), Yankush moves gradually back to ordinary speech as he and the patients' families work out a schedule for additional sessions and plan the dietary and medicinal regime that will hasten recovery.

What does this nervous movement between registers mean, and why should Yankush's communications expand into other channels during the session? At the most superficial level, the unusual sounds and shifting registers mark the event's "otherness" for the participants, for they are indices of Yankush's entry into an altered state of consciousness and his struggle against the evil work of sorcerers. The various forms of communication also show considerable redundancy of coding (Fitzgerald 1975:228) that serves to emphasize the event's key symbols. The noise of fanning or energetic sucking, for example, reinforces the repeated references to the extraction of spirit-darts.

Yankush's utterances mark the transference held to be central to all symbolic healing (Dow 1986). The patient's struggle is taken on by the healer, who attempts to define and resolve the issues at hand and to restore the patient to some form of wholeness. In the case before us, the shaman removes the sources of pain, neutralizes their harmful power, and assimilates them into his own shamanic substance. As Lévi-Strauss notes, in the therapeutic transference sought by the shaman "the manipulation must be carried out through symbols, that is, through meaningful equivalents of things meant which belong to another order of reality" (1963:196). Here the patient's experience of suffering constitutes a disordered whole involving different aspects of bodily function. During the ritual, a complex bodily experience is transformed into an intricate auditory experience which, through the extraction of spirit-darts, eventually becomes focused and simplified. Healing symbols, like religious metaphors, "recast the inchoate (and ineffable) whole of primary experience into various manageable domains" (Fernandez 1977:126).

Although the level of mythic detail elucidated by Lévi-Strauss in his analysis of a Cuna ritual is not to be found in the Aguaruna rite, Yankush does employ figurative language to suggest to his patients that he has removed the source of their illness and put them on the path to recovery. "You will return to your house. I see your soul dancing there, getting drunk at parties . . .", he sings (lines 91–92). And later Yankush makes ample use of tropes to weave his fabric of healing images: "The earth never dies. When I heal her, she will be the same, never dying [lines 189–190]. . . . The agile dog never tires, hopping about. She should be this way. I say that her stomach should never reject food, as the tapir never rejects food" (lines 303–306).

Beginning with line 258, Yankush employs a series of animal similes, some of which are picked up for discussion by Katan. Yankush claims to concentrate "like a tireless jaguar" to make Chapaik "become like a tapir, which doesn't know how to refuse any kind of food." Presently there is a discussion of permitted food items for the patient—specifically, whether Chapaik can safely eat the flesh of *wájiam*, a species of monkey. This exchange is representative of a broader pattern of interest in the links between humans and animals prominent in Aguaruna health care practices. The treatment of most identifiable illness includes a set of appropriate food avoidances or prohibitions, called *wakemtái*, that are linked to the illness symptoms by analogical reasoning. People suffering from skin lesions, for instance, should avoid eating armadillo "because the lesions will then dig into the flesh as the armadillo claws into the ground." Analogies to the animal world can be used therapeutically as well. In a special healing chant for infants, the sick child may be likened to the offspring of vultures, "which can eat rotten things without harm." The goal is to transfer the resistance of the vulture's chicks to the suffering child.[8] Yankush's statements, then, draw on a shared etiological and therapeutic framework that extends beyond the special case of sorcery.

The drama of Yankush's multi-channel communication is intensified by the contribution of Katan and Shimpu, who shout words of encouragement, urge the healer to protect himself against the dangers he willingly incurs on their behalf, emphatically declare their concern for their wives, and direct his visionary powers in ways that are of interest to the gathered participants. The weighty exchanges between Yankush and these men are leavened on two occasions by the humor of Utijat (lines 205 and 235), who is known in the community for his idiosyncratic wit.

Although the patients themselves are passive throughout most of the session, one can reasonably suppose the event helps them to redefine themselves as "healed" or at least moving toward recovery. Yankush repeatedly says that he has taken much of the sickness from their bodies and that they will soon feel better. Besides providing them with provisional explanations for their ailments, Yankush also suggests specific therapeutic measures that include recommendations for diet and commercial pharmaceuticals, as well as the use of the hallucinogen *tsúak* to obtain healing visions (cf. Brown 1978). Moreover, the patients have been the objects of intense expressions of concern by the session's participants. Chapaik's brisk remarks near the end of the ritual ("I want you to see into me again on Saturday") imply that she is satisfied with his efforts, though hardly in awe of his powers.

SECOND READING: DISSIDENT SUBTEXTS

Having developed a rather orthodox symbolic interpretation of the healing session, I wish to advance another interpretation of the session's exchanges, one that illuminates the subtle negotiations between Yankush and his clients, especially Katan, who plays a prominent part in the proceedings. Katan's initial contributions to the ritual take the form of shouts of encouragement (e.g., line 47, "Sit well, think well!") and blandishments (lines 35–36, "If you cure her, I'll always receive you well in my house"). His mood changes to indignation, however, as he contemplates the possibility that his wife is the victim of sorcery: "Why would they want to bewitch me? I always give people food when they come to visit. Why bewitch my wife? I'm angry" (lines 73–75). But it is Chimi's subsequent remark that offers a clue to the subversive undercurrents. "If there are any darts there when she gets home," she shouts (lines 95–96), "they may say that Yankush put them there. So take them all out!"

Chimi's remark is an unusually frank rendering of a threat implicit in all Aguaruna healing sessions. The nature of shamanic power is believed to invite malfeasance on the part of the healer. People see that he can heal; they suspect that he can also kill. A demonstration of a shaman's commitment to healing (as opposed to killing) is his willingness to take on patients, the intensity with which he works on them during the healing session, and their subsequent recovery. If he declines to treat people, if he proves reluctant to work hard at healing, if too many patients die, troubling questions may arise. Is the shaman really a sorcerer? Is he taking advantage of his credulous clients to pursue sorcery under the guise of healing?[9]

So Yankush is under pressure to demonstrate his efficacy and good will by a thorough treatment of the two patients. On the heels of Chimi's comment, Katan interjects: "Who will have done this bewitching? If my wife dies, I could kill any man out of anger" (lines 101–102). This is echoed later by his comment, "There are others who are not as brave as I" (line 150). Katan's boastful declarations are rhetoric with a purpose. Aguaruna men argue that the best means of protecting one's family from sorcery is to make direct threats to suspected sorcerers. Katan uses this healing session as a social stage on which he can publicly emphasize his determination to repay sorcery with violence. Although an event such as this is not public in a strict sense, it will be widely discussed throughout the Alto Mayo in the days to follow. Katan hopes that his show of strength will deter sorcerers from continuing their secret assaults. The declarations are also for Yankush's benefit, should he be tempted to pursue sorcery himself.

Soon after these veiled threats, Yankush divines the killing of a shaman in a neighboring valley, reporting it first in the shamanic register, then discursively (line 140). He immediately refocuses on a patient, entering into a period of noisy sucking and violent retching, after which he comments, "Don't say that I wasn't intoxicated enough" (lines 148–149). These rapid moves between distant political events and the specifics of healing, repeated several times during the session, mark Yankush's trance as significantly different from the classic form of spirit mediumship in which the medium is totally separated from his or her ordinary self, with no subsequent recollection of trance utterances (Lambek 1981:73). The discreteness of the latter form of trance gives the medium the license to

speak of forbidden subjects and even to elaborate an "antistructural world" that "challenges the larger society through its creation of new norms that upend conventional morality" (DeBernardi 1987:330).[10]

But the antistructural world of the Aguaruna shaman cannot be a desired social norm; it can only be invoked to defend against the antistructural antagonism of one's enemies. Nor can Yankush deny the authorship of his shamanic powers, despite the assistance of his *pásuk* spirit-helpers. He must therefore tread carefully, stressing his own willingness to heal while distancing himself from the work of sorcerers. In the sequence under scrutiny (lines 140–149), he declares that a sorcerer has been assassinated, thereby validating belief in the existence of sorcerers and in the power of his shamanic gaze. The revelation also implicitly reaffirms the notion that sorcerers can and should be killed. Finally, he emphasizes his own strenuous efforts at curing, which are public signs of his good intentions. These quick rhetorical shifts are representative of his approach to the entire session, which consists of abrupt movements between the shamanic antistructure (constituted by his song) and the demands of his clients, who advance their own agendas whenever they can.

Yankush and his clients thus find themselves caught in a labyrinth of contradiction. By calling on the services of a shaman, the patients and their kinsmen implicitly validate the very system of shamanic power that threatens them. They take some comfort in the fact that Yankush, as the most public of practitioners, pursues his activities in the front regions of society, where he is subject to intense scrutiny. Yet they also use the healing session to make their statement to Yankush and all shamans, in effect saying, "We are strong. We will give no quarter to hidden sorcerers."

For his part, Yankush uses the persuasive power of metaphor and the broad communicative powers of ritual in an attempt to imbue the patients' suffering with a sense of meaning. But to support his precarious status as a shamanic practitioner in the front regions of social life, he must arouse the participants' moral outrage at the work of unknown shamans who work their evil craft in the back regions. This inevitably suggests the possibility that the healing effected through the ceremony is provisional or, worse still, a deadly form of hypocrisy.

Aguaruna shamans and their clients are thus locked into an uneasy "dialectic of control" (Giddens 1979:93) in which they constantly renegotiate the terms of their relative autonomy and dependence, even as they reproduce the shamanic system itself.

CONCLUSIONS

My intent has been to lay bare the powerful fusion of psychological and political elements taking place within the crucible of Aguaruna shamanic practice. Much of the discussion during the healing session has an explicit political quality: even when communicating in the shamanic register, Yankush alludes to conflicts and killings, public acts and private motives. The emotional intensity of the event is engendered by the shaman in concert with the other participants, whose outbursts are often quite self-consciously directed to a wider audience. This intricately textured social experience is brought to bear on the physical condition of specific patients but may come to affect the political condition of larger social units in the region.

Both the shaman and his interlocutors make effective use of rhetoric in an attempt to assert their control over the session. Yankush avails himself of an Aristotelian rhetorical form called the *enthymeme*, the manipulation of reasoning based on public opinion (Burke 1950:56), the purpose of which is to persuade the patients of his healing skills and his good intentions. Against the enthymemic rhetoric of Yankush is pitted the more oblique counter-rhetoric of Katan and Chimi, which stresses the power of the community over the sinister schemes of sorcerer–shamans. This exchange elevates the emotional intensity of the encounter, contributing to an atmosphere that the Aguaruna regard as both dangerous and therapeutic.

But does this ritual serve to create, in the words of Fitzgerald (1975:232), "an island of structure in an otherwise rather disorderly social world"? This question can be answered affirmatively only from a synchronic perspective—that is, by ignoring the session's place in the ongoing history of Yankush, the patients and their kinsmen, and the Alto Río Mayo as a whole. Looked at diachronically, each

shamanic performance has an element of incompleteness, for the shaman's motives and behavior are always subject to public scrutiny. Closure is achieved only at the shaman's death, if even then. Although the session may help the patients understand the source of their physical discomfort, it also raises and leaves unresolved alarming possibilities. The suspicion that Chapaik and Yamanuanch are troubled by sorcery is now confirmed. But who are the sorcerers? When will they strike again and will it be in a more lethal way? Could Yankush be using his cover as a healing shaman to do them secret harm, perhaps even during the curing session itself? Does a recurrence of illness signify a new episode of sorcery, or does it mean that the shaman's claims of efficacy are exaggerated? These questions will echo through local politics long after the healing session witnessed here. Although there is a provisional order forged in the ritual, it can never be definitive—for if it were, all sorcerers would be identified and eliminated, all mysterious illnesses banished from the Aguaruna world. The vexing questions raised in the shamanic encounter and the contested nature of shamanic knowledge itself guarantee the social reproduction of the shaman–sorcerer complex.

Yankush's reputation is built in part on his appropriation of symbols of non-Indian culture, most notably "mestizo medicine" and pharmaceuticals. This intense interest in alien shamanic practices, which has a long-established tradition in Jivaroan societies (Harner 1972:119–125), is usually interpreted as being founded on the belief that the foreign is more powerful than the local. One wonders, though, whether the search for knowledge in distant places represents instead an unconscious impulse to acquire forms of power free of the constraints and counterclaims of local political life—in other words, a wish to escape from the dialectic of control that troubles both the shaman and his clients. In his use of pharmaceuticals Yankush searches for a form of domination that is uncontestable. Aguaruna laity express a similar wish when they speak of "eliminating *iwishín* once and for all," thus ridding society of the threat of sorcery. In both responses we see the implicit acknowledgment that shamanism is more than the ritual enactment of cosmological principles, more than spiritual ideology. It is also a robust instrument of social control, which like all forms of power generates its measure of opposition and discontent.

An analysis that directs itself to the fissures in the social edifice runs the risk of overlooking the ways in which practices contribute to social solidarity (Ortner 1984:157). It cannot be denied that Aguaruna healing rituals provide a focus for kingroup unity and the expression of key cultural values. The cathartic exposure of the hidden sources of illness, accompanied by dramatic demonstrations of concern, puts healing sessions among the strongest expressions of the cohesiveness of the group (however defined) available in Aguaruna society. What I have tried to show here is that this solidarity is achieved at substantial cost—for the participants vanquish illness from the physical body only by shifting the locus of uncertainty to the body politic.

Author's Postscript—2004. L. Shane Greene, an anthropologist who began fieldwork among the Aguaruna of the Alto Río Mayo in 1998, reports that the shaman identified by the pseudonym "Yankush" in my article was assassinated in the late 1990s by kinsmen from another Aguaruna village who became convinced that Yankush was the sorcerer responsible for recent deaths in their community. His death illustrates the highly politicized nature of shamanic healing among the Aguaruna and many other indigenous groups of the Amazon.

NOTES

1. The particulars of my field research among the Aguaruna of the Alto Río Mayo are described in Brown (1984, 1986). Although my most extensive research was conducted in 1976–78, some of the material presented here was collected during brief visits in 1984, 1985, and 1986. Brown (1984:227–232) includes a complete transcript of another healing session over which Yankush presided.

2. I recorded one instance of a woman who practiced as an *iwishín*, but her case was considered highly unusual by people in the Alto Mayo. Nor have I found any references to women serving as healing shamans among neighboring Jivaroan societies. Women may, however, be identified as sorcerers, though sorcery accusations against women are infrequent and, to the best of my knowledge, rarely lead to homicide.

3. I know of no sources that provide transcripts of healing sessions from other Jivaroan populations. Such descriptions as are available, however, do suggest that *iwishín* traditionally worked well into the

night when they treated their patients. None of the sessions I witnessed in Yankush's house lasted more than three hours, and several were substantially shorter.

4. In their detailed analysis of psychotherapeutic interviews, Labov and Fanshel (1977:35) distinguish among several "fields of discourse" that bear some resemblance to what I have called registers because they demonstrate marked differences in content. Nevertheless, the term "register" (Halliday 1978:35) better expresses the lexical differences between ordinary speech and shamanic utterance, as well as the shift from speech to song.

5. To obtain the text presented here, I reviewed a tape recording of the healing session with an Aguaruna informant, who helped me transcribe and interpret Yankush's songs and the statements of other participants. Although my relations with Yankush were generally cordial, he declined to assist me in the transcription of his songs, on the grounds that the words were a professional secret. Several passages in the cryptic shamanic register are marked as "untranslatable" or "indecipherable" because lay informants could not understand them. Although I regretted not being able to obtain a complete transcript, these difficulties made me aware that the specific content of much of the shaman's song is unknown to other participants and therefore peripheral to the session as they experience it. Readers interested in complete translations of Jivaroan shamanic chants should consult Pellizzaro (1978).

6. I have not elaborated on the specific genealogical links among the participants, because they do not seem especially germane to an understanding of the events that follow. The fluid kindred-based groups found among the Aguaruna and other Jivaroans have a developmental cycle that can exert a profound influence on local politics (see Colajanni 1984), but such factors shed little light on the events of this particular ritual.

7. Pellizzaro (1978) states that for the Shuar, Jivaroan neighbors of the Aguaruna, a curing shaman must have spirit-darts of the same category as the darts he removes from patients. If he attempts to extract a dart of a category previously unknown to him, he can be overpowered and killed.

8. Details of Aguaruna food prohibitions, healing chants, and the perceived links between humans and animals in Aguaruna ethnomedicine can be found in Brown (1984:174–200, 243–258).

9. This occupational hazard of shamans is outlined in Colajanni's detailed account of the murder of an Achuar shaman in Ecuador (1984). His informants report that good shamans never refuse to undertake a healing session, nor do they consider bewitching people. Said one man, "I always advised a shaman that he should never bewitch anyone, that he should cure well, that he ought to suck deeply [at curing sessions], and that if he were murdered I would avenge him"

(1984:239, my translation). Later in the same essay, Colajanni mentions that suspicions about a specific shaman intensified when he was perceived to have begun to treat his kin negligently with regard to their need for shamanic healing (1984:243).

10. Lewis (1981) argues persuasively that the distinction between spirit mediumship and shamanism is largely terminological. Because of space limitations I have not undertaken a detailed comparison of the literature on shamans and mediums, but it bears noting that studies of the latter have traditionally been more alert to issues of social power than have works on New World shamanism.

REFERENCES

Atkinson, Jane Monnig. 1987. The Effectiveness of Shamans in an Indonesian Ritual. *American Anthropologist* 89:342–355.

Brown, Michael Fobes. 1978. From the Hero's Bones: Three Aguaruna Hallucinogens and Their Uses. In *The Nature and Status of Ethnobotany*. Richard I. Ford, ed. Pp. 118–136. University of Michigan Museum of Anthropology, Anthropological Papers No. 67.

———. 1984. *Una paz incierta: historia y cultura de las comunidades aguarunas frente al impacto de la carretera marginal*. Lima: Centro Amazónico de Antropología y Aplicación Práctica.

———. 1986. *Tsewa's Gift: Magic and Meaning in an Amazonian Society*. Washington: Smithsonian Institution Press.

Burke, Kenneth. 1950. *A Rhetoric of Motives*. Berkeley: University of California Press.

Colajanni, Antonio. 1984. Prácticas chamanicas y cambio social. La muerte de un hechicero achuar: hechos y interpretaciones. In *Relaciones interétnicas y adaptación cultural*. Pp. 227–252. Sucua, Ecuador: Colección Mundo Shuar.

Crocker, Jon Christopher. 1985. *Vital Souls: Bororo Cosmology, Natural Symbolism, and Shamanism*. Tucson: University of Arizona Press.

DeBernardi, Jean. 1987. The God of War and the Vagabond Buddha. *Modern China* 13:310–332.

Descola, Philippe, and Jean-Luc Lory. 1982. Les guerriers de l'invisible: sociologie comparative de l'agression chamanique en Papouasie Nouvelle-Guinée (Baruya) et en Haute-Amazonie (Achuar). *L'ethnographie* 87–88:85–109.

Dow, James. 1986. Universal Aspects of Symbolic Healing: A Theoretical Synthesis. *American Anthropologist* 88:56–69.

Fernandez, James W. 1977. The Performance of Ritual Metaphors. In *The Social Use of Metaphor: Essays on the Anthropology of Rhetoric*. David J. Sapir and Jon Christopher Crocker, eds. Pp. 100–131. Philadelphia: University of Pennsylvania Press.

Fitzgerald, Dale K. 1975. The Language of Ritual Events among the Ga of Southern Ghana. In *Sociocultural Dimensions of Language Use*. Mary Sanches and Ben G. Blount, eds. Pp. 205–234. New York: Academic Press.

Foucault, Michel. 1982. The Subject and Power. In *Michel Foucault: Beyond Structuralism and Hermeneutics*, 2nd ed. Hubert L. Dreyfus and Paul Rabinow, authors. Pp. 208–226. Chicago: University of Chicago Press.

Giddens, Anthony. 1979. *Central Problems in Social Theory*. Berkeley: University of California Press.

Halliday, M. A. K. 1978. *Language as Social Semiotic: The Social Interpretation of Language and Meaning*. London: Edward Arnold.

Harner, Michael J. 1972. *The Jívaro: People of the Sacred Waterfalls*. Berkeley: University of California Press.

Joralemon, Donald. 1986. The Performing Patient in Ritual Healing. *Social Science and Medicine* 23(9):841–845.

Labov, William, and David Fanshel. 1977. *Therapeutic Discourse: Psychotherapy as Conversation*. New York: Academic Press.

Lambek, Michael. 1981. *Human Spirits: A Cultural Account of Trance in Mayotte*. New York: Cambridge University Press.

Lévi-Strauss, Claude. 1963. The Effectiveness of Symbols. In *Structural Anthropology*. Claire Jacobson and Brooke Grundfest Schoepf, transls. Pp. 181–201. New York: Anchor.

Lewis, I. M. 1981. What is a Shaman? *Folk* 23:25–35.

OAAM (Organización Aguaruna del Alto Mayo) 1984 *Reglamiento de la Organización Aguaruna del Alto Mayo*. (Document in files of the author.)

Ortner, Sherry. 1984. Theory in Anthropology Since the Sixties. *Comparative Studies in Society and History* 26:126–166.

Pellizzaro, Siro. 1978. *El uwishín*. Mundo Shuar, Serie F, No. 3. Sucúa, Ecuador.

Seymour-Smith, Charlotte. 1982. Shamanism Among the Peruvian Jívaro. Paper read at the 44th International Congress of Americanists, Manchester, England.

Sherzer, Joel. 1983. *Kuna Ways of Speaking: An Ethnographic Perspective*. Austin: University of Texas Press.

Steedly, Mary Margaret. 1988. Severing the Bonds of Love: A Case Study in Soul Loss. *Social Science and Medicine*. (In press.)

Taussig, Michael. 1987. *Shamanism, Colonialism, and the Wild Man: A Study in Terror and Healing*. Chicago: University of Chicago Press.

10   DISTAL NURSING

Ruth E. Malone

Nurses are healers whose activities involve both curing and caring functions, although it is not always easy to separate the two because to care often *is* to cure (see Part III). This selection argues that cost-cutting changes to hospital practices, which distance nurses from patients, compromise the effectiveness of nursing care. Malone explains that where nurses come to be seen as technical workers or managers of lower-skilled, often temporary staff who perform discrete, disconnected functions, it becomes more difficult to know what matters in any individual patient's case. In contrast, where healing practices are built on proximity, and caring is undertaken as a matter of course rather than seen as a waste of time or a distraction from technical tasks, the healing relationship is more human and satisfying to both patients and healers.

This selection shows how organizational changes affecting the structuring of place and space experienced by nurses and patients have a direct impact on nurses' ability to provide meaning to patient suffering; to elicit, understand, and communicate patient narratives; and to advocate on behalf of individual patients. For example, structured "S.O.A.P." notes ("Subjective, Objective, Assessment, Plan"; see also selection 11), as opposed to free-form charting, force nurses to eliminate social contextual detail in favor of technical information provided in a predetermined order and thereby impoverish communication between health professionals. Transformations such as these come at a considerable price in terms of the quality of nursing care and overall relationships between patients and healers. They undermine the ability of hospital staff to appreciate the individuality of patients as people embedded in social relationships and consequently to make moral decisions in their interest.

This selection adds additional elements and insights to our understanding of patient–healer relationships through its analysis of physical space and bodily perception and its description of actual nursing practices and their importance to both patients and healers. Malone also explicates the lines of communication and interaction among nurses that shape what is known about patients and the kind of care they receive. The analysis shows how larger institutional features and power relationships affect healing practices, and how healing systems are responsive to social-structural changes.

Questions to keep in mind

What are the changes occurring within the health care sector in the United States (and increasingly in Canada and Western Europe also) that affect nurse–patient proximity?

Compare Table 10.1 with the schematics in selection 3. In what ways do the institutional changes favoring distal nursing take scientific medicine a step further from the kind of patient care characteristic of nonbiomedical healing systems?

Compare the story about George with the one about the unnamed elderly woman later in the article. What differences between proximal and distal approaches to nursing care do these stories illustrate?

Source: Reprinted from *Social Science and Medicine,* Vol. 56, Malone, R. E., "Distal Nursing," Pages 2317–2326, Copyright (2003), with permission from Elsevier.

The only space where the moral act can be performed is the social space of "being with," continually buffeted by the criss-crossing pressures of cognitive, aesthetic, and moral spacings. In this space, the possibility to act on the promptings of moral responsibility must be *salvaged,* or *recovered,* or *made anew;* against odds—sometimes overwhelming odds—the responsibility must exchange its now invalidated or forgotten priority for the superiority over technical–instrumental calculations . . . If it happens, it will happen only as an accomplishment. There is not and there will never be any guarantee that it will indeed happen. But it does happen, daily and repeatedly—each time that people care, love, and bring succour to those who need it (Bauman, 1993, p. 185).

No practices can survive for any length of time unsustained by institutions (MacIntyre, 1984, p. 194).

All human relationships have spatial aspects. This is true not only because we are material beings with bodies that move and have volume, but because our proximity to or distance from others and from places have meaning for us. When we are sick, these often taken-for-granted proximities and distances become revealed to us in our experience of displacement—from familiar routines and places, but also often from our own bodies, which we may experience as having betrayed or even abandoned us (van Manen, 1998). Leaving behind the place of *home* and entering into the unfamiliar institutional spaces of the hospital, our understandings of intimacy and distance are challenged by intrusive examinations, loss of private space, the threatened foreshortening of our life horizons, and the need to depend upon the kindness of strangers as we seek not only wellness, but re-emplacement in our bodies and our lives. In hospitals, nurses are among the strangers to whom we turn.

Nursing as a human practice also has spatial aspects. Since relationship with the patient is considered central to nursing practice, nursing depends at least in part upon sustaining some meaningful *proximity* to patients. This paper considers the spatial–structural dynamics of nurse–patient relationships within hospitals under conditions of organizational restructuring. Hospital nursing, I argue in this paper, is increasingly constrained by spatial–structural practices that disrupt nursing's relations with patients by reducing or eliminating heretofore taken-for-granted proximity. Three "nested" kinds of proximity are threatened: physical, narrative, and moral. Examining these proximities through a place–space lens suggests that structurally, nursing is becoming increasingly "distal" to patient care.

The plan of the paper is as follows: First, I situate the paper within several perspectives on space and place; next, I discuss three types of "nested" proximity that characterize nurse–patient relationships; third, I describe spatial–structural changes under conditions of hospital restructuring within the United States and show how these reduce proximity and constrain nurse–patient (as well as nurse–nurse) relationships. I conclude with a discussion of the potential implications of this loss of proximity for nursing and, drawing on social theories of spatial production, the power relations "distal nursing" conceals and reinforces.

THEORETICAL PERSPECTIVES: SPACE AND PLACE

At least two broad strands of discourse are relevant to this discussion: phenomenological perspectives on space and place in philosophy, which suggest that place grounds our subjective, embodied experience and can only be understood through experience (Casey, 1993; Malpas, 1999), and critical geographical and historical perspectives which draw attention to the power relationships instantiated in places and spaces (Foucault, 1963/1975, 1979; Lefebvre, 1992/1974; Massey, 1994, 1995). Very roughly, the former focuses more closely on the "micro" level of experience and subjectivity as shaped by place and space and the latter on "macro" structures that shape the possibilities for spatial relationships between groups. Each of these perspectives can be useful in considering the spatial dynamics of hospital nursing.

For some phenomenologists, place has a special ontological primacy. Malpas (1999) argues that understanding of place is grasped through narrative, while Casey suggests it is grasped more directly through bodily experience as "persons-in-places" (Casey, 1993, p. 30). For both, *place* is experience-near, characterized by a sense of unity and coherence, while *space* is more abstract, a conceptualization we are even able to develop only because we first understand ourselves *as* emplaced.

In this perspective, it is because we are *not* disembodied subjects set over against a separate background or environment, but persons-in-place, that proximity and distance have relevance in our relations with others.

Another strand of space/place theory concerns itself with power relationships and how they shape and are shaped by spatial relationships. This perspective emphasizes that space is neither neutral nor passive (Lefebvre, 1992/1974). Rather, it is shaped by human social activities. The social construction of "space" and "place" is characterized by tension and conflicts between the "global" and the "local," the material and the metaphorical; the boundaries between these are fluid, and the very identity of places as such is constantly at issue (Massey, 1994, 1995). Material changes shaped by power inequities may reconfigure places and spaces and with them, the power relations they instantiate. Foucauldian perspectives on power are also relevant to this discussion. Power, as Foucault shows us, not only conceals itself, but conceals through spatial forms that reinforce power relations (Foucault, 1963/1975, 1979; Rabinow, 1984).

NESTED PROXIMITIES IN NURSING

Within nursing, Liaschenko (1994, 1997) was perhaps the first to suggest that geographical concepts are relevant to understanding the nurse–patient relationship at all levels. Liaschenko argued that although ethical concerns are commonly considered to arise out of the local, intimate aspect of nurse–patient relationship, they often originate at a larger structural scale. Liaschenko suggested that patients, by virtue of their social positions, have different spatial vulnerabilities, and that this was at least partially due to nursing's "gendered" spatiality. In this paper, I seek to extend this work by proposing that hospital nursing is itself spatially vulnerable insofar as it depends upon a taken-for-granted proximity to patients that is acutely threatened by the localized spatial and power dynamics of macro-originated economic and ideological pressures.

At least three types of proximity are at issue: *physical proximity,* which I define as a nearness within which nurses physically touch and care for patients' bodies; *narrative proximity,* in which nurses come to "know the patient" (Tanner, Benner, Chesla, & Gordon, 1993) by hearing and trying to understand (and, in turn, transmit to one another) the patient's "story" (of the illness for him/her, of his/her particular life); and *moral proximity,* in which nurses encounter the patient as other, recognize that a moral concern to "be for" exists, and are solicited to act on a patient's behalf. These proximities are nested: physical proximity sets up the possibility for dialogue with the patient and family through which aspects of the patient's narrative may be grasped, and it is through understanding the patient as a person with a life (Liaschenko, 1995) that nurses are able to begin to appreciate the moral significance of issues for him/her and to act accordingly on his behalf when he/she is unable to do so.

Physical proximity between nurses and patients is so taken-for-granted that nurses' subordinate social status has been attributed to the physical nature of nurses' contact with the diseased body and its effluvia. Learning how to wash the body, how to assist with toileting, and how to prevent skin breakdown during long illnesses are part of every nurse's basic educational preparation, and clinical knowledge includes learning how to provide physical comfort through positioning the body. In addition, assessment of patient condition through direct physical contact, such as touching the patient to assess the warmth, moisture, and texture of the skin, is basic to hospital nursing. However, the relationship of physical proximity is not merely one of application of technique, as van Manen has pointed out. Physical contact, such as washing, may also be part of inviting a "reuniting" or "re-emplacing" of the patient in a "livable relation with his or her body" (van Manen, 1998, p. 9).

Narrative proximity in nursing has two aspects: coming to "know the patient" (Tanner et al., 1993) through hearing directly or piecing together from family and other sources a story of what the illness means in his or her life, and respectfully transmitting this knowledge in narrative form to others who care for the patient. The latter aspect has implications for both the care of this particular patient and for the transmission within nursing of socially embedded knowledge, as Benner's work on nursing practice has shown (Benner, Hooper-Kyriakidis, & Stannard, 1999; Benner, Tanner, & Chesla, 1992; Benner et al., 1992; Benner & Wrubel, 1989). In using the word narrative, I mean "a more or less coherent written, spoken, or (by extension) enacted account of occurrences" (Hunter, 1996, p. 306) rather than narrative in any formal linguistic or literary sense. Through listening to patients and telling each other stories about *particular* patients within the context of the local situation, nurses impart informal but important knowledge of how to make qualitative distinctions between particular patients and their experiences (Rubin, 1996), a point to which I will return.

Nursing, as the profession most charged with bearing witness to the patient's distress or healing on a day to day, hour by hour basis, also involves a kind of moral proximity. It is in our direct, face to face encounter with the Other, as Levinas has noted (Levinas, 1981), that we are solicited to act, that recognition arises that there are both mutual vulnerabilities (Malone, 2000) and power inequities in the caregiving relationship. Gadow (1980) has asserted that nursing's heart is "existential advocacy," a being-for patients. One cannot "be for" an abstract class of patients in this way; one is called upon to be for *this* patient, at this moment, in all his or her complexity.

That moral proximity is nested within physical and narrative proximity is illustrated through drawing on an example from Benner's work. Benner cites the narrative of a nurse who cared for a 60-year-old African American man who was quadriplegic from a previous accident, disfigured by radical neck surgery for cancer, admitted to the hospital from a long term care facility with severe respiratory problems and put on ventilator support. The physicians' rather bleak assessment of the patient's quality of life, based on their more experience–distant perceptions of the clinical features of the patient's condition, led them to discuss withdrawing ventilator support and letting the patient die. The nurse, however, argued strenuously against this:

> I think we could have made a decision on not treating [George] fully, based upon what he looked like and what we thought he was. And I really stood up for him. I don't think some people ever got beyond just looking at him and saying, 'This man is disfigured and not able to take care of himself . . .' . . . He was an incredible fighter . . . even withdrawn, he was actively withdrawn . . . I don't think they [the physicians who wanted to withdraw ventilator support] stood with him and looked at him or gave him a Pepsi, or saw him watch the ball game [on televi-

sion]. He really derived a lot of pleasure from living . . . I think it was more a case of their perception of quality of life versus our perceptions of George's quality of life as we got to know him more, and what he was like at the skilled nursing facility . . . He was a spokesperson for the patients, he helped people who had alcohol and drug problems. He had a girlfriend there who was also wheelchair-bound and they used public transportation together. They were the Valentine King and Queen. I think the doctors just looked at him and saw "This is as good as it gets, and this is really depressing, and he is really depressed, so why continue?" (Benner et al., 1996, p. 21).

What is important to notice in this narrative is its focus on situating the patient in his particularity and how this is accomplished by means of proximity. The nurse contrasts the doctors' "just looking at him" (in an objectifying, biomedically focused way) with "standing with him" or "seeing him watch the ball game" in day by day interactions. Learning more about the patient's situatedness in his everyday life—establishing a narrative proximity that was possible only due to their ongoing physical proximity—the nurses were able to see past his dismaying functional impairment to his personhood, his emplacement in a life. Through narrative proximity, nurses gain moral proximity, as they stake out the particular and the local as essential to decision making and transmit the message that it is insufficient to consider only general clinical features in an abstract sense; in a sense, the patient must be *emplaced* (as a person-in-place) in a life context in order to interpret what is a moral course of action.

Another important element to notice in this narrative is the interrelationship between proximity and *time*. This nurse was able to make her case not merely because she had been physically near to the patient, which of course the physicians also had been, but because she had been near long enough to "get to know him." Proximity is thus not merely spatial, but temporal as well.

Certainly, nurses do not sustain all three types of proximity in their relationships with every patient. When circumstances are unambiguous and routine, or hospitalizations are brief and uncomplicated, the nurse–patient relationship may likewise appropriately be brief and routine, requiring minimal proximity. But, increasingly, as will be discussed below, only patients with the most complex and potentially complicated conditions qualify for admission to hospitals, suggesting a need for more nurse–patient proximity rather than less. I shift now to considering some of the recent macro-level changes that have altered nurse–patient proximities.

STRUCTURAL–SPATIAL CHANGES AFFECTING PROXIMITIES

During the past decade, an unprecedented cluster of structural changes has occurred within the health care sector in general; the effects of these changes have been especially pronounced within United States hospitals (although similar scenarios are unfolding across Canada and Western Europe as cost-cutting pressures increase) and upon nurses specifically (Norrish & Rundall, 2001; Sochalski, Aiken, & Fagin, 1997). Discussion of the larger, interrelated economic and social factors that have shaped these extensive changes is beyond the scope of this paper; the aim here is to call attention to their local spatial–structural effects on nurse–patient relationships within hospitals, which are considerable. The changes to which I refer include but are not limited to: shifts toward treatment of patients in outpatient and home settings, reduced length of stay for hospitalized patients; work redesign strategies aimed at reducing costs; use of so-called "flexible" staffing, which involves using more part-time and temporary staff; certain efficiency measures, including changes in charting and reporting practices; and an emphasis on abstract classification systems and "standardization" of care.

Collectively, these changes reduce nurse–patient proximity in several ways. First and most obviously, they reduce time available for direct physical contact between nurses and patients. As noted above, proximity involves not only spatial but temporal nearness. As patients leave hospitals more quickly and work redesign strategies redistribute nurses' work to lower-paid, lower-skilled workers, nurses become "care managers," positioned distally as overseers rather than proximally as direct care providers. Nurses thus have less time to spend with any particular patient as they spend more time on administrative and general clinical oversight and/or are replaced by nonnurse administrative staff (Aiken & Fagin, 1997; Wiener, 2000). Instead of nurses, patients may have "care partners" or "service partners" who may have as little as two weeks of orientation for their new roles (Wiener, 2000). The increased reliance on "flexible" staffing likewise means that a patient may have a different nurse each day as hospitals turn to registries for temporary staff. This minimizes possibilities for the sustained engagement with patients that is required to develop narrative proximity, or knowledge of the patient's story. The changes also reduce proximity among nurses themselves, as fewer nurses are spread more thinly as supervisors of lower-cost workers.

Certain traditional practices requiring physical proximity and long regarded as basic to good nursing care have also been jettisoned in "redesigning" nursing work. For example, the back rub, a way to assess patients' hydration, nutritional and circulatory status as well as a comforting tactile practice that allowed patients access to a nurse's uninterrupted attention, is no longer a part of routine nursing care in most institutions (Connelly, 1999; Meintz, 1995). The back rub, usually provided as part of evening or bedtime routine, was a few moments of comforting physical contact that was often accompanied by dialogue between nurse and patient. As with the bed bath (van Manen, 1998), the backrub opens a space within which a healing relationship may take form. Backrub conversation thus often consisted of more than mere small talk: it provided an opportunity for coaching, nonthreatening teaching, and development of a more fine-grained, situated understanding of this particular patient—an important part of understanding the patient in the "place" of his life outside. As nurse staffing decreased, such practices were identified as nonessential functions and eliminated in many facilities (Meintz, 1995).

Because, as discussed above, physical proximity is necessary for development of narrative proximity in the nurse–patient relationship, these changes also have implications for nurses' role as hearers and bearers of the patient's story. However, it is not only the loss of physical proximity that is involved (and with it the opportunities for hearing the patient's story), but also the loss of organizationally supported modes of communication through which such stories might be transmitted among nurses.

For example, 25 years ago, nursing notes in patient charts actually took the form of short narratives, written by the nurse caring for the patient on each shift. While some institutions structured these according to various parameters, such as using different colored inks to denote the different shifts of work, they were, for the most part, relatively free-form written accounts of the patient's day that included whatever the nurse felt might be relevant to those who would be caring for the patient in the following hours or days. These notes might, for example, include notations about who visited the patient, situating the patient in a context of relationships; about how the patient was coping with the demands of treatment; about complaints of and treatment for pain; or about specific questions or fears voiced by the patient. Sometimes the notes offered synopses of discussions or direct quotations from patients or family members.

During the late 1970s and 1980s, many institutions began requiring more highly structured forms of nurses' notes, such as subjective, objective, assessment, plan (SOAP) charting. Though their purpose was to provide an organizing framework, minimize redundancy and make the notes more efficiently usable, such schemes also had the consequence of restricting individual nurses' prerogative to choose the way in which the patient/nurse relational narrative would be conveyed. Today, in order to minimize the time the preparation of nursing notes requires, many institutions structure nurses' notes in the form of care plan check-off boxes or computer-assisted algorithms, which use a standardized format.

While such "charting by exception" (that is, only noting that which does not appear to follow a standard expected course) can be helpful in some respects, it also systematically truncates and structures the communication about patients that is shared in written form between nurses. Check-off boxes simply cannot accommodate narrative forms of communication. The selection of what it is important to note and how to note it are no longer the purview of the individual nurses caring for the patient, but are now prescribed in advance as a standard classification scheme in which individual nurses' interpretations may be viewed as usually unwelcome or technically aberrant deviations. The structuring of nurses' written communications into such distally determined forms reinforces the perception that nursing itself is an activity that can be reduced to a series of discrete tasks or points on such a prespecified "clinical pathway" (which is in turn congruent with the spatially redesigned role of nurse as distally located "manager" of others who carry out such tasks).

Finally, the above-mentioned cluster of interrelated changes in hospital settings disrupt moral proximity in nurse–patient relationships, by constituting patients in terms of their classification within abstract systems and constituting care as consisting of the above-mentioned distally directed, standardized tasks rather than direct human engagement. Here I include the well-intentioned movements within nursing management toward defining and implementing abstract classification systems that could be used for "outcomes research," as well as the interconnected emphasis on standardized care plans or standardized "pathways" for biomedically defined conditions. Bowker and Star (1999) make the point that such abstract systems can never entirely capture what is important to know and do in a particular patient's case. Some specifications remain irretrievably implicit, and, as they observe, "what is left implicit becomes doubly invisible: it is the residue left over when other sorts of invisible work have been made visible" (p. 247).

Benner, who has perhaps developed the strongest critique of such abstracting strategies to describe nursing practice, cautions that "once nursing practice [is] defined as isolated units of behavior, diagnoses, and interventions without the significance of those actions (the in-order-to's, and for-the-sake-of's, for-that-purpose, to-that-end), there is no way to get back to everyday integrative clinical knowledge that always entails engaged reasoning in particular clinical situations. Thus, articulating nursing knowledge into the available economic and scientific language creates conflict and incongruities with the knowledge and ethos embedded in the actual caring practices of nurses" (Benner, 2000, p. 296). The effort to become increasingly explicit in defining discrete interventions based on abstractions from aggregated data paradoxically fuels a flight from the particularity and complexity of actual patient situations. The problem for nurse–patient moral proximity is that such distally directed, abstracting approaches either trivialize or ignore the profound contingency within any human interaction, contingency that permits the other to emerge in all his or her particularity, soliciting our moral responsibility.

DISTAL NURSING: DANGERS

There are potential dangers in making nursing distal, not the least of which is that as nurses lose their proximities with patients and with one another, and see their work in terms of fulfilling extralocal demands for categorical and procedural efficiency and uniformity, they will likewise lose their sustaining narrative and moral traditions and will take up their work as mere technicians. This may reshape nursing as a "we're just running the trains" occupation (Lifton, 1986, p. 400). Under such circumstances, caring begins to stand out as something unusual and ultimately deviant. In a study of emergency room nurses and patients (Malone, 1995, 1998, 2000), I talked with an emergency nurse who had counseled a sobbing, drug addicted woman about a treatment program. "I took about 15, 20 minutes *out*—and I really talked with her," she said. It is significant (and not, in my experience, atypical in contemporary hospitals) that the nurse understood herself to be taking time "out" to provide this kind of support for a patient, even though it was an entirely appropriate and needed intervention. Such humane support is implicitly seen as *external* to the "real" nursing work of managing the technical tasks necessary for discharge production. Caring practices may be reduced to such snatched moments of near-covert connection, morally satisfying but risking possible sanction and carried out in the absence of institutional recognition and support.

Frank argues, drawing on the work of Dorothy Smith, that the move to the generalizing extralocal perspective means that patients are regarded as instances of a category and that, in the process, there is an "erasure" of suffering from the illness experience that can increase suffering (Frank, 2001). Earlier research on nursing practice seems to bear out this idea. Rubin (1996) studied nurses who appeared clinically "disengaged," identified by their head nurses as experienced but not expert, and found that a striking feature of these nurses' practice was their inability to remember particular details about their patients. That is, these nurses did not have at their disposal the narratives about patients that other nurses did.

"Not only could they not describe a critical incident that had made a difference in their practice; most could not even remember the specifics of a particular case, even the most recent," observed Rubin (1996, p. 172). For example, Rubin discusses a nurse who told a story about ending a patient's life through her own administration of an injection that slowed and eventually stopped the patient's breathing.

> I'll tell you one that I'm sure you've heard before about someone who . . . was admitted on a Saturday and had a chronic illness and was elderly and had lost her home and was being asked to move into a nursing home and she had to give up her pets and so on. And by Sunday, she . . . had changed her mind, was ready to die and was dying and there wasn't a lot that could be done to prevent it anyway unless she wanted to be intubated and have a long course and probably die anyway, and opted not to be intubated and to take— what did she take?—some minor Valium or something. I've forgotten what, and stopped breathing, basically (Rubin, 1996, p. 172).

The nurse, Rubin notes, seemed not to recognize the enormity of the life changes thrust upon this woman except in terms of an abbreviated list of nonspecific, categorical conditions: "elderly," "chronic illness," "give up pets," "and so on." The rapidity with which the decision to die was made is not questioned, and as Rubin discusses, the nurse does not describe engaging in any serious discussion or deliberation about other measures or alternative scenarios—in fact, these are quickly dismissed ("probably die anyway"). The nurse's description (which Rubin describes more fully and contrasts with the highly detailed, situated narratives of nurses in the same study who were identified as clinical experts), does not include acknowledgment of the patient's suffering; it characterizes the situation in terms of a choice made independently and autonomously by the patient, wherein the nurse's role is merely one of instrumentality, of providing the technical means.

These nurses, Rubin argues, "assume that the objective features of the situation . . . have only one meaning and that that meaning is the same for everyone" (p. 176). They are unable to make the kinds of qualitative distinctions among patients that narrative and moral proximities encourage. They are, it could be argued, perfect "distal nurses"—disengaged from patients as persons, regarding the work of patient care as technical management and efficient production, unlikely to perceive or raise difficult issues based on the particularity of any individual patient.

Table 10.1 contrasts this "distal" view of nursing with the "proximal" perspective that is associated with nursing's particularistic narrative traditions. Distal nursing is a highly rationalized, abstract representation of what nurses do that makes perfect sense within a perspective distant from actual care situations. From this even-more-distal perspective, patients are meaningful only in the aggregate, the hospital is itself understood only as institutional space, and the knowledge that counts is generated based on abstractions from the aggregate. In contrast, proximal nursing understands patients as particular persons situated within social worlds, works to shape the hospital as a place of healing, and privileges knowledge derived from the patient's life and the experience of providing care.

SPATIAL–STRUCTURAL POWER DYNAMICS

Distal nurses fit perfectly within a spatial–structural ordering for health care that preserves and reinforces existing economic and power relations.

Scholars from Heidegger (Heidegger, 1977) to Foucault (Foucault, 1963/1975, 1979; Rabinow, 1984) and others have called attention to the technologically totalizing and rationalizing character of modernity, which emphasizes an instrumental "ordering for ordering's sake." Malpas (2000) describes how this technological understanding tends toward revealing or presenting to us things and relations in terms of objectified commodities or available resources. The spatial–structural power dynamics at work in US healthcare increasingly favor construction of all aspects of healthcare in terms of commodity exchange (Malone, 1999). Nursing becomes a technical means for transforming illness and injury into consumption of services. Switching bedside nurses to distal managers serves the commodification process by constituting nursing care as a cheaper product that, in turn, frees up funds for consumptive acquisition of technological equipment and administrative and information systems, both of which reinforce commodification—the equipment as commodity and the systems as ways to efficiently manage commodity acquisition and distribution.

Human practices such as proximal nursing that undermine classification and commodification (through insistence on narrative, particularity and subjective experience, for example) constitute sources of resistance and thus must be tightly controlled. Foucault's notion of "dividing practices" comes to mind. These are "modes of manipulation that combine the mediation of a science (or pseudo-science) and the practice of exclusion"

Table 10.1   Distal and Proximal Perspectives on Nursing

Distal	Proximal
Hospital as institutional space	Hospital as healing place
Hospital as place of business	Hospital as place of care
Concern with abstract and general	Concern with particular
Illnesses as diagnoses	Illnesses as narratively understood
Practice as technical management	Practice as human engagement
Diagnoses as objective	Diagnoses as socially negotiated
Subjectivity as interior, suspect	Subjectivity tied to particular places
Knowledge as objective	Knowledge as situated
Meaning as irrelevant and personal	Meaning as shared and essential to healing
Values as outside scope	Values as reflected in practices
Nurses as managers	Nurses as healers

(Rabinow, 1984, p. 8). The spatial–structural separation of nurses from patients, the truncation of nurses' traditional narrative modes of communication in favor of institutionally sanctioned fragments, and the bureaucratic emphasis on classification and standardization may be considered dividing practices, the aim of which is to order, objectify and control.

It is also useful to consider Lefebvre's (1992/1974) distinction between *representational spaces,* or space as directly *lived* by its inhabitants, which I equate with nurses' proximal, narratively structured "re-emplacing" relations with patients, and *representations of space,* or abstract *space* as conceived by healthcare managers, policymakers and planners, which I equate with the rationalizing character of modernity. "In spatial practice," argues Lefebvre, "the reproduction of social relations is predominant. The representation of space, in thrall to both knowledge and power, leaves only the narrowest leeway to representational spaces, which are limited to works, images, and memories whose content . . . is so far displaced that it barely achieves symbolic force . . . Within this space . . . lived experience is crushed, vanquished by what is 'conceived of'" (Lefebvre, 1992/1974, pp. 50–51).

However, Lefebvre argues that there are inherent contradictions in such abstracting spatial–structural power relations. Because one of the characteristics of this rationalizing power is the elimination of differences, practices that demand consideration of particularity set up a tension that highlights the failure of abstract spatial structures to honor human experience. This creates the possibility for more holistic spatial relations. Such a new or reformed space, according to Lefebvre, "will put an end to those localizations which shatter the integrity of the individual body, the social body, the corpus of human needs, and the corpus of knowledge" (Lefebvre, 1992/1974, p. 52).

Proximal nursing thus emerges as a powerful form of spatial resistance that reveals, sustains, and creates alternative ways of constructing illness, care, and relationship. Proximal nursing is a practice of resistance precisely because it resists abstraction and commodification and because its commitment to the face to face care of persons reemphasizes particularities that create contradictions and difficulties within dominant representations of space. It is, therefore, no surprise that the discourses of embodiment, narrative, and situational ethics have recently become so urgent within nursing and other healthcare disciplines. These are discursive efforts to sustain corresponding dimensions of physical, narrative, and moral proximity in relations between patients and healers.

CONCLUSION

This paper has argued that spatial–structural ordering procedures at work in US hospitals increasingly reshape nursing as a "distal" practice, disrupting nurses' physical, narrative, and moral proximity to patients. Loss of proximity threatens nursing's traditional appreciation for the particular in clinical and moral decision making and may create a distanced, "we're just running the trains" mentality. Nursing's power lies in its honoring of the particular and relational; it is thus important to understand that "proximal" nursing is a source of human resistance to modernity's tendency toward abstract, commodified ordering and a challenge to existing power relations.

A major shortage of hospital nurses now exists, most acutely in states such as California where these changes in healthcare were first widely adopted. While the demographics of an aging nursing workforce, wider career opportunities for the young women who still make up the majority of nurses, and other factors play a role, I would argue that the departure of experienced nurses from hospitals may also have to do with their discomfort in the role of "distal nurse" and the tensions involved in resisting it or reconciling it with their narratively developed understandings of practice. If we want educated practitioners who engage with us on a human level, as opposed to merely processing our bodies, we must consider how spatial–structural power relations further or obstruct relationships between patients and healers.

REFERENCES

Aiken, L. H., & Fagin, C. M. (1997). Evaluating the consequences of hospital restructuring. *Medical Care,* (35), 10.

Bauman, Z. (1993). Social spaces: Cognitive, aesthetic, moral. In Z. Baumann (Ed.), *Postmodern ethics* (pp. 145–185). Oxford, UK: Blackwell.

Benner, P. (2000). The quest for control and the possibilities of care. In M. A. Wrathall, & J. Malpas (Eds.), *Heidegger, coping, and cognitive science,* Vol. 2 (pp. 293–309). Cambridge: MIT Press.

Benner, P., Hooper-Kyriakidis, P., & Stannard, D. (1999). *Clinical wisdom and interventions in critical care: A thinking-in-action approach.* Philadelphia: Saunders.

Benner, P., Tanner, C., & Chesla, C. (1992). From beginner to expert: gaining a differentiated clinical world in critical care nursing practice. *Advances in Nursing Science, 14*(3), 13–28.

Benner, P., Tanner, C., & Chesla, C. (1996). *Expertise in nursing practice: Caring, clinical judgment, and ethics.* New York: Springer.

Benner, P., & Wrubel, J. (1989). *The primacy of caring: Stress and coping in health and illness.* Menlo Park, CA: Addison-Wesley.

Bowker, G. C., & Star, S. L. (1999). *Sorting things out: Classification and its consequences.* Cambridge, MA: MIT Press.

Casey, E. S. (1993). *Getting back into place: Toward a renewed understanding of the place-world.* Bloomington: Indiana University Press.

Connelly, J. (1999). 'Back rub!': Reflections on touch. *Lancet, 354*(Suppl. 3), SIII2–4.

Foucault, M. (1963/1975). *The birth of the clinic.* New York: Random House.

Foucault, M. (1979). *Discipline and punish.* New York: Vintage Books (A. Sheridan, Trans.).

Frank, A. W. (2001). Can we research suffering? *Qualitative Health Research, 11*(3), 353–362.

Gadow, S. (1980). Existential advocacy: Philosophical foundation of nursing. In S. F. Spicker, & S. Gadow (Eds.), *Nursing: Images and ideals/opening dialogue with the humanities.* New York: Springer.

Heidegger, M. (1977). *The question concerning technology.* New York: Harper and Row (W. Lovitt, Trans.).

Hunter, K. M. (1996). Narrative, literature, and the clinical exercise of practical reason. *Journal of Medicine and Philosophy, 21,* 303–320.

Lefebvre, H. (1992/1974). *The production of space.* Oxford, UK: Blackwell.

Levinas, E. (1981). *Otherwise than being or beyond essence.* The Hague: Martinus Nijhoff.

Liaschenko, J. (1994). The moral geography of home care. *Advances in Nursing Science, 17*(2), 16–26.

Liaschenko, J. (1995). Ethics in the work of acting for patients. *Advances in Nursing Science, 18*(2), 1–12.

Liaschenko, J. (1997). Ethics and the geography of the nurse–patient relationship: Spatial vulnerabilities and gendered space. *Scholarly Inquiry for Nursing Practice: An International Journal, 11*(1), 45–59.

Lifton, R. (1986). *The Nazi doctors: Medical killing and the politics of genocide.* New York: Basic Books.

MacIntyre, A. (1984). *After virtue* (2nd ed.). Notre Dame, IN: University of Notre Dame Press.

Malone, R. E. (1995). Heavy users of emergency services: Social construction of a policy problem. *Social Science & Medicine, 40*(4), 469–477.

Malone, R. E. (1998). Whither the almshouse? Overutilization and the role of the emergency department. *Journal of Health Politics, Policy and Law, 23*(5), 795–832.

Malone, R. E. (1999). Policy as product: Morality and metaphor in health policy discourse. *Hastings Center Report, 29*(3), 16–22.

Malone, R. E. (2000). Dimensions of vulnerability in emergency nurses' narratives. *Advances in Nursing Science, 23*(1), 1–11.

Malpas, J. E. (1999). *Place and experience: a philosophical topography.* Cambridge, UK: Cambridge University Press.

Malpas, J. (2000). Urbanity, modernity and the technological. In H. Bott, C. Hubig, F. Pesch, & G. Schroeder (Eds.), *Stadt and kommunikation im digitalen zeitalter* (pp. 211–226). Frankfurt: Campus Verlag.

Massey, D. (1994). A global sense of place. In: *Space, place, and gender* (pp. 146–156). Oxford, UK: Polity Press.

Massey, D. (1995). The conceptualization of place. In D. Massey, & P. Jess (Eds.), *A place in the world? Places, cultures, and globalization* (pp. 46–85). Oxford, UK: Oxford University/The Open University.

Meintz, S. (1995). Whatever became of the back rub? *RN, 58*(4), 49–50, 53, 56.

Norrish, B. R., & Rundall, T. G. (2001). Hospital restructuring and the work of registered nurses. *Milbank Quarterly, 79*(1), 55–79.

Rabinow, P. (Ed.), (1984). *The Foucault Reader.* New York: Pantheon Books.

Rubin, J. (1996). Impediments to the development of clinical knowledge and ethical judgment in critical care nursing. In P. Benner, C. A. Tanner, & C. A. Chesla (Eds.), *Expertise in nursing practice: Caring, clinical judgment, and ethics.* New York: Springer Publishing Company.

Sochalski, J., Aiken, L. H., & Fagin, C. M. (1997). Hospital restructuring in the United States, Canada, and Western Europe: An outcomes research agenda. *Medical Care, 35*(10) (Supplement), OS13–OS25.

Tanner, C. A., Benner, P., Chesla, C., & Gordon, D. R. (1993). The phenomenology of knowing the patient. *Image: Journal of Nursing Scholarship, 25*(4), 273–280.

van Manen, M. (1998). Modalities of body experience in illness and health. *Qualitative Health Research,* 8(1), 7–24.

Wiener, C. L. (2000). *The elusive quest: Accountability in hospitals.* New York: Aldine De Gruyter.

■ ■ ■ ■ ■ ■ ■ ■ ■ ■

11   WITNESSING AND THE MEDICAL GAZE: HOW MEDICAL STUDENTS LEARN TO SEE AT A FREE CLINIC FOR THE HOMELESS

Beverly Ann Davenport

The previous selection introduced the concept of witnessing on the part of nurses, the biomedical healers most involved in attending to the patient's life situation on an ongoing basis. The current selection focuses on physicians-in-training in a nontraditional learning environment where witnessing is an explicit ideology expressed in self-conscious opposition to the objectifying tendencies of biomedicine (see selection 7). As the previous selections have shown, these tendencies, symbolized in the concept of the powerful medical gaze, are a main focus of scholarly and popular criticisms of biomedicine.

This selection reveals biomedical practitioners to be more reflexive and sensitive to human concerns than such critiques often assume. The students and faculty Davenport studies make continuous efforts to balance their learned tendency to focus on technical aspects of the patient's condition with an approach that foregrounds and respects the individuality and suffering of each person. In short, these health workers experience a struggle, or tension, between gazing and witnessing.

The tension is inherent also in mainstream medical practice, where physician–patient relationships may seem to rest on the physical level but also inevitably include a moral or salvational plane. Davenport explains that formal medical education tends to suppress or override the desire to alleviate suffering that inspires students to take up their profession in the first place. This is a predictable result of the nature of biomedical knowledge and the structure of biomedicine as an institution. The gaze expresses an understanding of patients as objects, separate from their diseases, whose suffering and distress are dismissed as so much noise.

Davenport shows how the clinic staff attempts to resist this construction of patients while simultaneously utilizing valuable knowledge associated with the objectifying gaze. Students and instructors engage in a continual process of reflexive analysis and assessment of their own and others' behavior, and patients also insert themselves into the process as active participants rather than passive objects. In this way, the training process does not simply reproduce the structure of biomedicine but instead may end up transforming it.

Questions to keep in mind

How does the clinic's philosophy and operation alter the usual power relationship between doctors and patients?

Source: Davenport, B. A. 2000. "Witnessing and the Medical Gaze: How Medical Students Learn to See at a Free Clinic for the Homeless." © 2000 by the American Anthropological Association. Reprinted from *Medical Anthropology Quarterly* Vol. 14 No. 3 pp. 310–327, by permission.

How do they affect physical, narrative, and moral proximity, as described by Malone in the previous selection?

In what ways is witnessing a moral act? In what ways is it a political one?

Do medical students in the clinic take on the suffering of their patients in similar ways or to the same degree as described for clown doctors, shamans, and nurses in the previous three selections?

How does student training in the clinic resemble the imitative and observational ways of learning described in selection 6?

I went to the clinic for the first time some time, like, about a year ago . . . towards the end of the first quarter . . . and um, it was a really intense experience. . . . It was actually a very big day 'cause it was also the first day of my preceptorship . . . and so I was just around the corner from [the site of the Wednesday night clinic], and that raised all sorts of things in my mind. I came to really, really, really enjoy it [the required preceptorship] but . . . it paled in comparison to the clinic.

I was paired with a second-year student . . . and we saw . . . this one woman, I remember her name, I remember everything about her. . . . She was about 19 years old. She had been a runaway at about 15 or so. She was using a lotta speed, and she was suicidal and really depressed and um, she came in . . . why did she come in? I think she had a cold. She was also working as a sex worker, kind of. She had this really fucked up relationship with this older man who was basically her pimp and also her drug supplier. . . .

I hardly said a thing. I just mostly witnessed the interaction between the second-year student and her, and it was really sensitive, like a really good encounter that uncovered all of this unhappiness and . . . it really blew me away. I guess how I described it to myself at the time was that up until that moment in my life I had considered myself to be somewhat experienced in the world . . . um, but I felt like there was nothing in my life that had at all prepared myself for that moment, and I really didn't know what to think or say. . . . And I remember the post-clinic meeting, you know, I just remember thinking, "I don't know what I'm thinking" (*laughs*). I was so transformed and moved and just blown away. . . .

And then I guess I volunteered a couple of other times that I don't remember really in any way, but at some point I was realizing that I was learning so much more in these encounters than I was in my classes. And I was becoming increasingly unhappy and marginally functional as a traditional medical student. . . . I mean other circumstances in my life were contributing to this, but I was feeling increasingly severed from whatever had initially motivated me to go through the awful nonsense of medical school. And also feeling overwhelmed by just all this universe of facts and figures that I'm supposed to be competent in but have no way of organizing . . . and yet, you know, I'd go to clinic and I would feel a sense of learning that was more real and memorable and concrete to me and a sense of, I dunno, it wasn't always like I'd learn something, but that I would at least feel alive about this process that I was going through. [Extract from an interview with Ivan, a second-year medical student, fall 1997]

How and what do medical students learn to see in encounters with patients? It is commonplace to read in the theoretical and popular literature how the process of medical education teaches students to "objectify" their patients, that is, transform them into problematic body parts rather than view them as whole human beings in fully contextualized psychological and social environments.[1] This article addresses this question in a unique context, clinics for homeless people run by medical students attending a university in a city in the United States, which I will refer to as Angel Bay. What happens when clinical teaching and learning take place in a site away from the formal center of medical education, and which has an ideology that is explicit in its oppositional stance to the prevailing practices of the patient-provider relationship?

Michel Foucault addressed the historical and epistemological roots of objectification in *The Birth of the Clinic* (1994). He described how the emerging medical discourse led to a way of viewing patients that he called the "medical gaze." The change Foucault described was fundamental. Over the course of the 18th century, the question the doctor asked the patient was transformed from "What is the matter with you?" to "Where does it hurt?" (Foucault 1994:xviii). This notion of the gaze, of seeing a "case" or a "condition" rather than a human being, has become a dominant paradigm in critiques of modern medicine.

This article examines aspects of the medical gaze that I observed while conducting ethnographic fieldwork with the medical students' Campaign on Homelessness. I found that among this group of students and their supervising faculty, there was a struggle to maintain a balance between *gazing,* as Foucault might term it, and *witnessing,* their indigenous term for acknowledging the whole lives of the population they served. My research was driven by questions situated at the intersection of the anthropology of medical education, professional socialization, and the doctor–patient relationship. Although Foucauldian theory informed my fieldwork and my initial inquiry, it was necessary to move beyond Foucault in order to truly understand the processes I witnessed. Specifically, Byron Good's discussion of the mediation between the soteriological and the physiological practices of medicine and Anthony Giddens's concept of "social reflexivity" significantly enriched my analysis.

The aim of this selection is to demonstrate how a synthesis of the theoretical positions of Foucault, Good, and Glides can illuminate the practice of medical education in the micro-settings of clinical encounters. I use extensive field data to demonstrate this and to ground the theoretical discussion.

BEYOND THE MEDICAL GAZE

The Birth of the Clinic describes the discursive transformation that allowed late 18th-century French physicians to justify their "educational" display of the poor patients who came to the hospitals of Paris for treatment and help. The unwritten and unspoken contract between the doctor and the impoverished patient was that by presenting one's self for help, one was obliged to let one's body become an object for presentation. Foucault argued that through the practice of autopsy, medical scientists learned to understand and treat disease better, as they saw it mapped on to the dead bodies of their patients: "It is when death became the concrete a priori of medical experience that death could detach itself from counter-nature and become *embodied* in the *living bodies* of individuals"

(Foucault 1994:196, emphasis in original). The changing discursive practices within the field of medicine reflected a changed relationship of man to himself—man allowed himself, for the first time, to be constituted as an object of science (Foucault 1994:197).

Led by medicine, the "human sciences," through their production of knowledge, developed increasingly refined "technologies of power." This interrelation is what Foucault refers to as "power/knowledge":

> First the hospital, then the school, then, later, the workshop were not simply "reordered" by the disciplines; they became, thanks to them, apparatuses such that any mechanism of objectification could be used in them as an instrument of subjection, and any growth of power could give rise in them to possible branches of knowledge; it was this link, proper to the technological systems, that made possible within the disciplinary element the formation of clinical medicine, psychiatry, child psychology, educational psychology and the rationalization of labour. It is a double process, then: an epistemological "thaw" through a refinement of power relations; *a multiplication of the effects of power through the formation and accumulation of new forms of knowledge.* [1995:224, emphasis added]

The very language that is used in knowledge production is fraught with relations of power. However, because this language is cast as "objective," the fact of that power is hidden from its users. This is the nature of discourse. It is this fact that is so frightful in the vision of the modern world that Foucault presents in *Discipline and Punish:* we are all caught in the social webs created by the interplay of knowledge and power. Even those who are aware of the objectifying aspects of the power-knowledge relation are unable to develop effective ways of breaking free of its sticky strands.

Though this vision has been criticized because it leaves so little room for agency or resistance (see, for example, Turner 1994), many analyses of medical practice appear to support it. For example, Mizrahi notes:

> Treating patients as absent when they are physically present denies the existence of the human subject. By treating most patients as subjectless objects, the house staff eliminated them as active participants in patient care. . . . Techniques of objectification were

applied in collegial and patient interaction and appeared to be grounded in the basic process and structure of graduate medical training, such as doctors' behavior on rounds. They also seem basic to the professional orientation of medicine, for they help doctors to separate the patient from the disease; to deny pain and suffering, especially if it is not in their estimate organically based; and to discredit or dismiss commonplace or uncomplicated illness. [1986:99]

Similarly, Waitzkin (1979) points out that the macro power relations in capitalist U.S. society are reproduced in miniature in doctors' examination rooms. His analysis of taped conversations between doctors and patients reveals the multiple ways physicians act as agents of social control. Even mainstream medical educators have recognized the problem of objectification. One can pick up almost at random any copy of *Academic Medicine* published over the past five years and find at least one study measuring the effectiveness of educational interventions designed to improve communications skills and/or editorial or philosophical essays calling for renewed efforts to ensure that physicians-in-training receive sufficient training in the arts of compassion (see Coles 1998; Hafferty 1998; Hafferty and Franks 1994; Regan-Smith 1998). These articles demonstrate the concern and awareness medical educators have regarding the widespread perception of physicians as lacking in the ability to treat their patients as whole persons.

But these examples ignore alternative evidence suggesting that the picture is not so stark. Even in the examples cited above, the reader can see that some practitioners (at least some of those who publish in *Academic Medicine*) want to do more than simply teach their students to objectify their patients. Byron Good's suggestion (1994:65–87) that medicine be seen as a symbolic form (a term he borrows from the philosopher Cassirer) offers a more nuanced analytical approach. For Good, one of the core activities of medicine as a symbolic form is the process of mediation between its technical and *soteriological* aspects, that is, between human physiology and human salvation with all the moral connotations implied in the latter term.

Good acknowledges the medical gaze, and he sees it as a given of the scientific epistemology that informs medical practice. But he insists that notions of the salvational aspects of medical practice

are never far away. Objectification is thus mitigated because the medical culture is both shaped by and shapes the social world of which it is a part (this is the central purpose of symbolic forms). Students enter medicine with a passion to alleviate suffering, a motivation not sufficiently measured in terms of scientific curiosity. In his fieldwork Good shows that the discourse between faculty and students "tacks back and forth between engagement in clinical practices and moral reflection" (1994:87).

It is this aspect of Good's argument that is compelling in the present context. Good's analysis is important because as he looks at the processes of medical education, he reinserts the agency of individual students and professors. Also, he reminds us that the desire to save people from suffering has been compelling would-be healers for a long time (compare Balint 1957, who uses the term *apostolic function* to express the same thing).

When Good mentions Foucault in this discussion, he points out that Foucauldian analysis is limited because it "excludes the centrality of experience and in large measure, the dialogical qualities of discourse" (1994:69). However, Good's work seems less in opposition to Foucault than an enrichment of his framework. Many of the examples Good cites could easily be read as cases of how medical discourse, rather than changing them, shapes the object of practice and reproduces power relations. What Good emphasizes are the experiential/phenomenological aspects of individuals becoming doctors. Though the structure of medicine influences these actors, it does not simply reproduce itself through them. Their actions can also transform it.

Anthony Giddens's notion of social reflexivity supplies a conceptual tool for understanding how this process works. Williams and Calnan define *social reflexivity* as "the susceptibility of most aspects of social activity, and material relations with nature, to chronic revision in the light of new information and knowledge" (1996:1612). Social reflexivity is a condition of "later modernity" and leads to an almost continual examination, scrutiny, reappraisal, and revision of social beliefs and practices. In their article on how the lay and medical worlds interact, Williams and Calnan argue that the objectified docile bodies found in current social science critiques of medicine are not as passive as they are made out to be. They point to a variety of ways that practices are shaped by social reflexivity; the power flows are not unidirectional. I believe this concept, which is compatible with both Foucauldian power/knowledge and the tension between physiology and soteriology examined by Good, is useful in understanding the world of learning embodied in the Campaign on Homelessness. I turn now to the field data to elucidate these connections.

SETTING THE SCENE AND METHODOLOGY

Angel Bay is a large city on the western coast of the United States. Lack of affordable housing, the increasing economic divide between the urban poor and the technocrat classes, a labor market with few opportunities for the unskilled and undereducated, and radically limited facilities to care for those with severe, chronic mental illness have all contributed to a substantial homeless problem there (Susser 1996; Walker et al. 1990). In 1990, medical students at the local state university initiated the Campaign on Homelessness (the "Campaign"), which now operates clinics four days a week at various sites throughout the city and which also has a mission to educate the university community about the causes and conditions of homelessne. One way the Campaign meets this objective is through an elective course offered each fall that attempts to describe the historical, socialstructural, and phenomenological worlds of homelessness. Participation in this elective is required before any medical student is permitted to volunteer at the Clinic; thus, the elective is heavily subscribed by first-year students.

In the summer of 1997, I began participant–observation research with the students and faculty preceptors who comprise the Campaign. The data presented here are drawn primarily from my field notes of their interactions in the clinical milieu but are also informed by my observations in other settings. . . . I observed at the Clinic on all four days of operation: Tuesday, Wednesday, Thursday, and Saturday. Clinics are held in two different locations and draw on different elements of the homeless population of Angel Bay, depending on the day

of the week. On Tuesdays and Thursdays, the site is a large city-operated men's shelter near the freeway in the warehouse district. . . . On Wednesdays, the Clinic is located in a community organization storefront located in the skid row section of downtown, an area known for its concentration of single-room-occupancy (SRO) hotels and an extremely active drug trade.

In the 17 times I went to the Clinic, I participated in seven student-preceptor-patient interactions from beginning to end, that is, from the moment the student(s) and a patient walked into the examination room for the initial history and physical, through the presentation of the patient's history to the preceptor, to the preceptor's follow-up examination of the patient in the presence of the student. By hanging out at the work table where the clinic coordinator (generally, a more experienced second-year student) directed the activities of the Clinic, and around which students and preceptors gathered during slow times or while writing up their S.O.A.P. notes, I was able to observe dozens of other formal and informal teaching moments, from which I built this analysis.

GAZING AND WITNESSING: PRACTICES OF SOCIAL REFLEXIVITY

It is by entering the asylums where poverty and sickness languish together that he [the medical student] will feel those painful emotions, that active commiseration, that burning desire to bring comfort and consolation. . . . It is there that he will learn to be religious, humane, compassionate. [Menuret, *Essai sur les moyens de former de bons medecins,* Paris, 1791; quoted in Foucault 1994:84]

The Ideology of Witnessing

Witnessing is the indigenous term Clinic volunteers use to describe the action of attentive listening to the people who go there for help. It entails respectful focus on the entirety of a person's life situation, not merely on their ailment. It implies treating each person who walks into the clinic as an individual, not a representative of a class. *Witnessing* expresses the central value of the Clinic's ideology. In the settings where discourse dominates—the annual Fall Retreat, the monthly Soma meetings, and the Homeless elective lectures—witnessing is advocated in direct opposition to the values that prevail in other medical education settings.

First-year students who took the fall Homeless elective heard this ideology expressed early on. The very first lecturer, a specialist in health care for homeless people, spoke of the importance of "meeting people where they are," of withholding judgment and focusing on the quality of the attention students provided to the patients. She used a vivid image to remind the class of the need to see beyond appearances: "Can you see the spark in the eyes of the homeless person covered with lice?" That same day, the next lecturer, himself a frequent clinic preceptor, picked up the refrain. Referring to the failing social system that contributes to clinic patients' miseries, he exclaimed, "We're not gonna fix it, but we're gonna bear witnesss."

The notion of witnessing resonates at multiple levels. Notice Ivan's language in the extended quote that begins this article: "I hardly said a thing. I just mostly *witnessed* the interaction between the second-year student and her" (referring to the patient whose life story affected him so profoundly). Here, *witnessing* means to quietly observe. But, as used by the volunteers at the Clinic, *witness* implies an engagement with the event that *observe* lacks. *Witness* also means to testify, to speak out on someone's behalf. This is implicit in the language of the second lecturer quoted above, who spoke of "a clinic that you run that bears witness to these stories." Here, *bearing witness* has a very clear moral/religious connotation, exactly as Good (1994) has suggested. One bears witness for one's convictions, even when they may be unpopular or when the act of witnessing may be personally dangerous. Discipleship is also implicit in the notions of witnessing—a powerful metaphor for the relationship between preceptors and students (as well as between more and less experienced students) at the Clinic. Within the local world of the Campaign on Homelessness, *witnessing* encompassed all of these meanings.[2]

Ann Swidler argues that ideology plays a crucial role in periods of social transformation. She writes, "when people are learning new ways of organizing individual and collective action, practicing unfa-

miliar habits until they become familiar, then doctrine, symbol and ritual directly shape action" (1986:278). The witnessing ideology is the Campaign's conscious attempt to change the way medicine constructs its objects. The activities of the Clinic are structured along the lines of classic clinical training—learning how to get a history and conduct a physical exam under the supervision of an experienced senior physician—but the forms belie the Campaign's challenge to medical education as usual.

This opposition was explicit in the discussions at the Fall Retreat. For example, one faculty preceptor responded to a second-year student who expressed his concern that he didn't know enough medicine to really help the Clinic's patients by saying, "At your level you're more in touch with the whole person. Focus on organs later. Tap into what it means to be a healer and hold on; many of us feel like it was squished out of us during our education." Another second-year student reflected on how different the experience of working at the Clinic was from what he thought would be his likely experience as a third year on the wards. A preceptor introduced himself to a large group of first-year students assembled for a lecture in the Homeless elective class as a "recovering family practice resident." The comments of these students and teachers demonstrate a stance toward their own medical education and residency training that is consistent with Giddens's concept of social reflexivity.

Witnessing is also seen as a way to counter the symbolic violence of the medical gaze (Bourdieu 1991). At the retreat and in interviews, medical students expressed their fear of exploiting the Clinic's patient population, given its vulnerability and their own lack of clinical expertise. At the retreat, Jean, a second year, described her intense feelings on this point, particularly in her early days of volunteering. She wondered if there were a way to ease such feelings for the incoming first years. Dr. Rudnytsky asked her why she felt such feelings needed fixing. He insisted that they were a screening test: the fact that one had such concerns about exploitation and abuse was evidence of suitability for working with this population.

The value of witnessing was sometimes applied as a salve for the helplessness that volunteers felt in the face of the overwhelming social problems the clinic's patients forced them to confront; other times, it eased the feelings of inadequacy that students expressed over their lack of knowledge. But it was more than that—it was an ideological attempt to alter the balance of power between patients and practitioners in favor of patients. How this played out in the actual activities of the Clinic demonstrates the tensions between witnessing and gazing, as well as between the poles of physiology and soteriology that are the motive forces behind the Clinic's existence. Though preceptors consciously questioned and offered resistance to the kind of training they knew the students were getting in their required classes, they also knew that their students needed to be able to function effectively in that other environment; they themselves had come through the same system. At the retreat, the preceptor did not say, "Forget about organs"; he said, "Focus on organs later." In the ideology of the Clinic, the emphasis was on witnessing. In the micro-practices of teaching and learning in the actual clinical encounters, the actors' actions alternated: now gazing, now witnessing, now gazing again.

Ideology in Action: Quality, Not Quantity

The students and preceptors hold staff meetings at the beginning and end of each clinic session. In the pre-clinic meeting the more experienced students and preceptors inculcate the practice of witnessing into their less experienced peers. One way this is expressed is through the repetition of the phrase "quality, not quantity," which I heard at almost every pre-clinic meeting I attended. In the context of the Clinic, "quality, not quantity" means taking time to gather a full history on each patient, not simply the medical aspects of the patient's complaint, but also his or her social and psychological environment. The Women's Clinic coordinator's checklist exhorts the coordinator to "remind everyone of the philosophy of the clinic: we emphasize quality interactions, providing this population with a sensitive entry into the health care system and a setting where women can feel safe, as well as a non-judgmental learning environment for students." Similar language can be found in the Men's Clinic and Wednesday Night coordinators' checklists. When the pre-clinic meeting must be

brief because of the number of patients waiting to be seen, the mantra of "quality, not quantity" becomes shorthand for witnessing.

Micro-Practices 1: History Taking.   The practice of witnessing is evident in the way patient histories are taken. In six of the seven student–patient interactions I observed, this meant a gentle, thorough probing of the patient's history, beginning with what brought him or her to the clinic that day, but encompassing a far broader domain. The following vignette is typical:

> Adam began the history taking, eliciting immediately a story about Mr. Williams's problems with getting on SSI, losing his job of 37 years working at a printing press/publishing house—initially, a really depressing presentation. Jean jumped in. She was masterful. She kept saying "sounds like" and either summarizing or rephrasing things that he [Mr. Williams] had said or made reference to in a way that would bring out more information. For example, she said, "Sounds like you had a different kind of life up until about a year ago. What changed?". . . thereby bringing out this work history, plus the fact that he had severe vision problems that needed to be addressed (that's why he's seeking SSI). She was sensitive and gentle both with him and with Adam, the first-year medical student (this being his first time at the clinic). I kept wondering how she had learned this. [Field notes, fall 1997]

This selection also demonstrates how, in general, a more experienced and a less experienced student pair up to work together at the Clinic. They usually negotiate how tasks will be accomplished, with the less experienced student expressing trepidation about his or her ability to do what is required. The second-year student's encouragement and modeling of appropriate behavior are important elements in the teaching practices of the Campaign. Jean's questioning brought out a fascinating life story and gave all of us who witnessed the exchange a richer understanding of Mr. Williams than would have been possible had she (and Adam) focused solely on the medical issue that brought him to the Men's Clinic—blisters on his feet. Jean's commentary on this exchange afterward was revealing:

> Jean and Adam discussed the way the interview went immediately after Mr. Williams left. Adam was concerned about how long he should let Mr. Williams

"ramble on" about his life and social history before he jumped "to the important medical stuff." . . . Jean pointed out that the real medical problem is sometimes/often revealed in the stories—she brought up the guy with the severe inguinal hernia who showed up complaining of a cough, but who, upon feeling more comfortable with her, let his real concern come out. She said, "Patients never tell us their history in the order specified in our H&PE [history and physical examination] handbook." She said this in a joking way—making the important point that the history-taker needs to attend to what the patient is saying, even if it isn't the first thing that the history-taker needs in order to be able to write up the history in the proper, medically approved order. [Field notes, fall 1997]

In this exchange, Jean told Adam that allowing a patient to "ramble on" was a powerful interview technique, not evidence of inefficiency or inexperience. But she couched this message in terms of "gazing"—Patients never tell us their history in the order specified in our H&PE handbook—that is, she was asserting that what is "medically important" would be revealed in the "witnessing" process.[3] History taking then, is an important context for students to put the witnessing ideology of the Campaign on Homelessness into practice. But as this example illustrates, history taking is also a locus of struggle between gazing and witnessing.

Micro-Practices 2: Patient Presentations. A conflict exists between the goal of understanding a fully rendered human being and the need to accomplish a "medical" task. Students at the Clinic know that they must be able to shape the long and complex stories their patients tell them into a (re)presentation for their preceptors. The Clinic policy is for this presentation to take place in the examination room, with the patient present, active as a witness while his or her story is being told. This practice differs dramatically from what occurs more typically in clinical training, where the student and supervisor confer out of earshot of the patient or, if in front of her, speak as though she were not there (Anspach 1997). For example, in a Wednesday Night pre-clinic meeting, Dr. Stanley, one of the preceptors who has been with the clinic since its founding and who is viewed by students and preceptors alike as an "elder statesman" of the Campaign, underlined the clinic coordinator's "quality, not quantity" remarks by emphasizing

the importance of presenting in front of patients and by explicitly contrasting this to the bad experiences the patients have had in other health care settings. Often in these presentations, however, students receive more messages about gazing than they do about witnessing, as the following example illustrates:

Tina [Dr. Swenson, the preceptor] emerged from the other examination room and came in. Jordan [first-year medical student] presented to her. Again, Peaches [the patient] was sitting on the examination table. Jordan and I were together on the left, Tina on the right. The discussion was between Tina and Jordan. Peaches attempted to engage, include herself in the discussion of symptoms. She was interested, asking her own questions, interrupting the flow of highly technical language, looking for the reasons why heroin use might cause irregular periods. More history came out, including the fact that she now remembered that sometimes she was regular when she was using, sometimes she was irregular when she was using. . . . She also remembered that she had been on the pill between her first and second child (a period of about six years), and that might explain her regularity. Tina decided that BC pills would be the solution for her irregularity and offered her a three-month supply. She wanted to do a pregnancy test first, because of the danger of giving the pill to someone who is pregnant. She asked Peaches about her history of high blood pressure; Peaches stated that there was no problem there. The pregnancy test came out negative, as expected; Tina gathered three packs of BC pills, opened one to show Peaches how to use them and after the explanation was complete, noticed the pack of Newport cigarettes near her (Peaches's girlfriend had given them to her when she left for work) and asked about her smoking. Peaches said she didn't smoke that much, about one pack per day, but Tina became reluctant to give her the pills because of the danger of a thromboembolism, which can come on suddenly and without warning. She apologized, urged her to quit smoking, supported her decision to check in with [a local heroin-kicking program] to see about getting clean again, and wished her well. [Field notes, winter 1998]

Here, the patient is mostly "talked over," despite her attempts to participate in Jordan's presentation of what is, after all, her story. The issues of her drug use, her decision to move to Angel Bay City from the East Coast, all become secondary to the stated objective of her visit to the Women's Clinic, her irregular periods. The ultimate irony, of course, is that a heroin-user is advised to quit smoking in order to take birth control pills to relieve the symptom of irregular periods, which is caused by her heroin addiction in the first place. I do not use this example to belittle the good intentions of the preceptor, nor to question her medical judgment but, rather, to show how easily witnessing turns into gazing.

Micro-Practices 3: The Physical Exam.   The Clinic is a teaching environment, and technical communication between the student and preceptor that sometimes excludes the patient is to be expected. The following excerpt from an interview with a preceptor reveals how he believed he managed to balance the teaching of the technical and pathophysiologic aspects of medicine with the interpersonal:

> . . . and so sometimes with really fascinating stuff, that's why we spend a little more time on just the physiology, like that guy with liver failure. . . . But . . . while you're teaching the technical you're also teaching the interpersonal. . . . [For example, I might say to a student] "This is how you examine a thyroid gland," and then I'll demonstrate here as I'm talking to patients (*miming an examination technique*)— "OK, ma'am this is blah-de-blah. My name is Dr. Rittenhouse, this is how I'm gonna do it, please sit here, now let me feel on your neck here, let me know if I'm choking you too much," and I'm demonstrating interpersonal skills while I'm showing the technical skills and at the same time I'm saying now [to the student], "Sometimes this lobe of the thyroid may be a little hyperactive, so you'll notice it down here." . . . We're doing ALL this stuff. [Interview excerpt, fall 1997]

In the interactions I observed, preceptors varied in the extent to which this ideal typical behavior was practiced. In one case, for example, a preceptor skillfully conducted a history and physical exam on a woman who was complaining of shoulder pain that she attributed to an abscess. He moved very close into her physical space, smoothly bantering with her about her heroin addiction and her attempt to get into a buprenorphine study. All the while, he was instructing the second-year medical student who had initially examined her, both explaining and modeling techniques for conducting a physical and eliciting more aspects of a patient's history simultaneously.

When he left the room briefly, Ellie, the patient, exclaimed, "He's good, he knows what he's talking about."

At almost the opposite extreme, a preceptor at the Men's Clinic made almost no attempt to engage his male patient as he conducted a neurological exam on him, despite the patient's passing remark that he had spent time in San Quentin prison, "where the doctors are like vets [i.e., veterinarians]." Despite the stylistic range, however, what was consistent in these encounters was the simplification of a complicated set of physical, psychological, and social problems uncovered by the student into something you could *see*, and therefore address medically.

Micro-Practices 4: Charting.   Another context where "the gaze" predominated in teaching messages was in filling out patient charts, commonly referred to as "S.O.A.P. notes." Making choices about what got written on the form and what was excluded occupied an extraordinary amount of clinic time. I estimated that students spent at least as much time composing S.O.A.P. notes as they did examining and treating patients. Three central observations are important here. First, students were repeatedly told to put the definite and specific on these forms, that which they felt confident about, that which was treatable. This often meant that they were compelled to reduce the social histories they had gathered into at most a sentence or two, focusing the bulk of their time, energy, and writing on their patients' most concrete and immediate physical problems. Second, students received explicit instructions from preceptors with regard to the medico-legal aspects of record keeping, as the following example demonstrates:

> When I got back to the clinic, Jordan [first-year medical student], Fifi [first-year, advanced-practice nursing student], and Tina [MD preceptor] were charting. There was back and forth about what should be put on a chart. . . . Jordan was concerned because she didn't know all the proper abbreviations. Tina pointed out that it was more important that she get the general idea of organizing information in a S.O.A.P. format, that she would learn the abbreviations during her third year. During the charting, Tina wrote little addenda or urged that the students write addenda to various elements of the chart to make sure that the records were complete from a legal standpoint. For example, Adelaide's . . .

complaint of chest pain generated a teaching point about writing "atypical, not consistent with heart disease" in the medical records. Similarly, Ginger's frequent sweats generated the phrase "afebrile" to be added to the record. Again, Adelaide's depression (which was defined as "life-threatening") required careful charting to make sure it was appropriately dealt with. [Field notes, winter 1998]

This type of instruction was very common across all of the clinics.

A third important aspect of S.O.A.P. note writing is that it was an occasion where a lot of student-to-student teaching took place. I frequently heard more experienced students give less experienced students advice on terminology and phrasing in S.O.A.P. notes, usually introduced by the expression, "I would say . . ." Occasionally, I saw some critical examination of the process. For example, when Jean and Adam began writing up the record on Mr. Williams, Jean prefaced her remarks by observing "how snotty" she thought it was that in common medical practice what the patients report is "subjective" and what the doctor sees is "objective." Her remarks revealed a critical awareness of the power dynamic at play in medical practice, and one that, at least in this arena, she thought it important to resist.

Though S.O.A.P. note writing tended to be an occasion where "gazing" prevailed, sometimes a preceptor's comments about the note revealed a shift back to witnessing. The form used by the Clinic required that one primary diagnosis be checked off from a list of ICD-9 codes grouped mostly by organ system. Providers could also check off as many secondary diagnoses as they wished. In one case, a student seeking guidance from a preceptor asked, "Secondary diagnosis of chemical dependence?" The preceptor responded, "Yeah, that and loneliness." She went on, "Loss of housing is on the form as a secondary diagnosis, too."

Micro-Practices 5: Post-Clinic Meetings. The post-clinic meetings were also arenas of "gazing" discourse. These meetings were similar to rounds, where each patient seen during the session was presented to the group by the student or students who had treated him or her. Again, the nature of the Clinic as a site for learning medicine meant that discussions of pathophysiology in the day's

most "interesting" case often predominated. Even the most fervent advocates of witnessing could switch easily into an objectified analysis of a patient. For example, at the end of a clinic one rainy February night, Rich (the preceptor) asked Wilson (a first-year medical student) to discuss the patient he'd seen who had come in complaining of scabies. Wilson began by referring to "the patient" and was immediately stopped by Rich, who insisted that he use the patient's name, George. He asked Wilson to tell the group as much as he could about George's life and what he knew about how he lived from day to day:

> Rich emphasized the importance of knowing what people do all day long, saying, "You need to know this." They then returned to the medical presentation. Rich pointed out that the patient's skin was a mess. Wilson began describing the skin, Rich corrected his word choice, substituting *excoriations.* Rich also pointed out that he had gynecomastia from liver disease, palmar erythema, and capet medusa (i.e., a spidery pattern of veins around the belly button). He also had ascites (fluid in the belly). Rich described these patients as "Seagram's Coolers" (they're wet and they're dry—i.e., ascites plus dry skin). Rich also said he looked cirrhotic and pointed out that a symptom of liver failure is "itchiness." [Field notes, February 1998]

Notice how easily Rich slipped back into the language of his city hospital residency: George became a "Seagram's Cooler," that is, a case, a disease merely mapped on to this particular human body. And then, a few turns later in the conversation, Rich returned to witnessing by reminding the students sitting around the table that social issues below the surface (of the presenting medical problem) are so rich and so important to explore. I followed up on this point with him in an interview a week later, asking him to reflect on his interaction with Wilson that night, and specifically asking about his insistence on Wilson referring to his patient by his given name:

> . . . though there isn't any set curriculum I've set aside for homeless that I want the students to get when they're there, one thing I want them to get is that their sense of humanity and caring for others is as developed in their first and second years as it ever will be. And perhaps may get eroded as time goes on. So that's their greatest strength, and I want them to

feel confident and good about their experience. . . . The other thing that happens in medicine is we deeply depersonalize our patients extensively over time, and that gets more and more specialized until you're a specialist in the second and fourth cranial nerves, that's all you do is look at those nerves, and nothing else matters and this, you know, you forget the part that's the human around it. And a homeless person, it's much more important to recognize that those cranial nerves don't have a lot to do with the person's day-to-day existence and it's important to recognize the whole person. So I try to go against the trend of depersonalizing patients by using third person singular: "This is a 46-year-old white man who comes in with a history of blah blah blah." I want them to make it more, I guess this is still the same, grammatical form, but make it more of a person. And I want them to interject their own selves, make it more of a first-person dialog: "So I met Bill. And Bill was disheveled. . . ." It's very different than "This is a 46-year-old disheveled man." And the differences between those two sentences to me are huge. They're both describing the same person and both using the same words, but you say, "I met Bill and he looked disheveled to me" gives, enters into a subjectivity and questioning as opposed to *this is what he is*, this is his label. [Interview excerpt, February 1998]

Rich wanted his students at the Clinic to think of their patients as *subjects;* this is the essence of witnessing. His dialogue with Wilson demonstrated one of the central theoretical arguments of this article: "the irruption of the fundamentally moral dimension of illness into this rational-technical sphere" (Good 1994:85). His insistence on the ideology of witnessing altered his practice, even though it was filtered through the forms of gazing discourse. That rainy night, Rich taught Wilson a lesson on how to see *both* the disease and the man who was suffering from it.

CONCLUSION

In this article, I have argued that Foucauldian theory provides only partial insight into the processes taking place in the clinics of the Campaign on Homelessness. I have asked the reader to consider both Byron Good's analysis of how medicine constructs its objects and Calnan and Williams's use of Giddens's term *social reflexivity*

in order to better understand these activities. I have shown how in the micro-settings of the Clinic, the physical–technical and the soteriological sides of medicine were in constant and necessary tension with each other.

The preceptors and the students manifested social reflexivity—scrutiny and revision of social beliefs and practices—in their efforts to teach and learn techniques of medicine by caring for the Clinic's patients. Espousing the ideology of witnessing was a way to alter the substance of clinical practice, even as the practice itself retained many aspects of its classic form.

Within the setting of this clinic for the homeless we have seen how discourse affected actual practices within medical culture, even if only at the outskirts. But the Campaign on Homelessness in Angel Bay is not isolated. There is a widespread interest in service and student-run clinics in U.S. medical schools (Cohen 1995; Collins 1995; Evered et al. 1996; Fiore 1995; Pi 1995; Poulsen 1995; Ratner 1995; Sanderson 1996; Seifer 1998; Yap and Thornton 1995), and there is evidence that these activities feed back into the formal educational arenas as well (Eckenfels 1997). Foucault's analysis helps us to penetrate the micro-physics of power/knowledge as a feature within medical education, but the practices of social reflexivity demonstrated by the Campaign's use of the witnessing ideology serve as demonstrations of resistance within the structure that can transform it, even as the agents are transformed by it.

Within the Clinic's setting, students learned an alternative behavioral vocabulary for interacting with patients. Preceptors were well aware that their teaching was going against the grain of convention, and they made every effort to bolster their students' beliefs in the importance of the practice of witnessing—considering the whole person when looking at a patient—because it was not likely to be a message they heard anywhere else. This is the meaning in Rich's remarks: "One thing I want them to get is that their sense of humanity and caring for others is as developed in their first and second years as it will ever be. *And perhaps may get eroded as time goes on*" (emphasis added). For the volunteers of the Clinic, having an alternative vocabulary to take with them into their formal clinical training may serve as a defense against such erosion.

In *Historical Metaphors and Mythical Realities*, Marshall Sahlins charged that structuralism operated from the premise of the old French saying, "The more things change, the more they remain the same" (1981:6–7). In the Clinic, many things "remain the same": many of the practices are not all that different from what happens in more conventional contexts. But the witnessing ideology evinces a cultural transformation that inverts that famous saying. The preceptors and students are not "technicians of the micro-physics of power" (Foucault 1995); they are active agents, pushing back against and transforming the structure, even as they operate within its constraints.

NOTES

1. See, for example, three excellent memoirs of medical school—Melvin Konner's *Becoming A Doctor* (1987), Toni Martin's *How To Survive Medical School* (1983), and Perry Klass's *A Not Entirely Benign Procedure* (1987) — for first-hand accounts of the educational process. Frederic Hafferty (1991), Terry Mizrahi (1986), Daniel Segal (1984), and Howard Waitzkin (1979) describe this process from the perspective of academic social science.

2. In the 1960s, members of the Religious Society of Friends, colloquially known as Quakers, "witnessed for peace" in protest against the Vietnam War. *Witnessing* can thus also be defined as a *political* activity, a point made by one of the clinic preceptors who read an earlier draft of this article.

3. This exchange contrasts with an example in Scheper-Hughes and Lock's seminal essay, "The Mindful Body" (1987:8). In that example, medical students failed to make the connection between the distressing social context of a woman's life and her debilitating headaches.

REFERENCES

Anspach, Renee. 1997. The Language of Case Presentation. In *The Sociology of Health and Illness: Critical Perspectives*. 5th edition. Peter Conrad, ed. Pp. 320–338. New York: St. Martin's Press.

Balint, Michael. 1957. *The Doctor, His Patient and the Illness*. London: Pitman Medical.

Bourdieu, Pierre. 1991. *Language and Symbolic Power*. Gino Raymond and Matthew Adamson, trans. Cambridge, MA: Harvard University Press.

Cohen, Jerry. 1995. Eight Steps for Starting a Student-Run Clinic. *Journal of the American Medical Association* 273:434–435.

Coles, Robert. 1998. The Moral Education of Medical Students. *Academic Medicine* 73:55–58.

Collins, Ann C. 1995. The Hahnemann Homeless Clinics Project: Taking Health Care to the Streets and Shelters. *Journal of the American Medical Association* 273:433.

Eckenfels, Edward J. 1997. Contemporary Medical Students' Quest for Self-Fulfillment through Community Service. *Academic Medicine* 72:1043–1050.

Evered, John O., Krista L. Burris, and William C. Steinmann. 1996. The Ozanam Inn Clinic in New Orleans. *Academic Medicine* 71:935.

Fiore, David C. 1995. A Homeless Shelter Medical Clinic Organized and Staffed by Family Practice Residents. *Western Journal of Medicine* 163:537–540.

Foucault, Michel. 1994. *The Birth of the Clinic: An Archaeology of Medical Perception*. New York: Vintage Books.

———. 1995. *Discipline and Punish: The Birth of the Prison*. New York: Vintage Books.

Good, Byron. 1994. *Medicine, Rationality and Experience: An Anthropological Perspective*. Cambridge: Cambridge University Press.

Hafferty, Frederic. 1991. *Into the Valley: Death and the Socialization of Medical Students*. New Haven, CT: Yale University Press.

———. 1998. Beyond Curriculum Reform: Confronting Medicine's Hidden Curriculum. *Academic Medicine* 73:403–407.

Hafferty, Frederic, and Ronald Franks. 1994. The Hidden Curriculum, Ethics, Teaching and the Structure of Medical Education. *Academic Medicine* 69:861–871.

Klass, Perri. 1987. *A Not Entirely Benign Procedure: Four Years as a Medical Student*. New York: Putnam.

Konner, Melvin. 1987. *Becoming A Doctor: A Journey of Initiation in Medical School*. New York: Viking.

Martin, Toni. 1983. *How To Survive Medical School*. New York: Holt, Rinehart, and Winston.

Mizrahi, Terry. 1986. *Getting Rid of Patients: Contradictions in the Socialization of Physicians*. New Brunswick, NJ: Rutgers University Press.

Pi, Randy. 1995. The Asian Clinic at UC Davis: Serving a Minority Population for Two Decades. *Journal of the American Medical Association* 273:432.

Poulsen, Eric J. 1995. Student-Run Clinics: A Double Opportunity. *Journal of the American Medical Association* 273:430.

Ratner, Adam J. 1995. Hector. *Journal of the American Medical Association* 273:436.

Regan-Smith, Martha. 1998. "Reform without Change": Update 1998. *Academic Medicine* 73:505–507.

Sahlins, Marshall. 1981. *Historical Metaphors and Mythical Realities*. Ann Arbor: University of Michigan Press.

Sanderson, Susan. 1996. Medical Students Find Learning is Enriched by Community Service Experiences. *Association of American Medical Colleges Reporter* 6(1):1–4.

Scheper-Hughes, Nancy, and Margaret Lock. 1987. The Mindful Body: A Prolegomenon to Future Work in Medical Anthropology. *Medical Anthropology Quarterly* 1:6–41.

Segal, Daniel. 1984. Playing Doctor, Seriously: Graduation Follies at an American Medical School. *International Journal of Health Services* 14:379–396.

Seifer, Sarena D. 1998. Service-Learning: Community-Campus Partnerships for Health Professions Education. *Academic Medicine* 73:273–277.

Susser, Ida. 1996. The Construction of Poverty and Homelessness in U.S. Cities. *Annual Review of Anthropology* 25:411–435.

Swidler, Ann. 1986. Culture in Action: Symbols and Strategies. *American Sociological Review* 51: 273–286.

Turner, Terence. 1994. Bodies and Anti-bodies: Flesh and Fetish in Contemporary Social Theory. In *Embodiment and Experience.* Thomas Csordas, ed. Pp. 27–47. Cambridge: Cambridge University Press.

Waitzkin, Howard. 1979. Medicine, Superstructure and Micropolitics. *Social Science and Medicine* 13A: 601–609.

Walker, Dick, and the Bay Area Study Group. 1990. The Playground of U.S. Capitalism? The Political Economy of the San Francisco Bay Area in the 1980s. In *Fire in the Hearth: The Radical Politics of Place in America.* Mike Davis, Steven Hiatt, Marie Kennedy, Susan Ruddick, and Michael Sprinker, eds. Pp. 3–81. London: Verso.

Williams, Simon J., and Michael Calnan. 1996. The "Limits" of Medicalization?: Modern Medicine and the Lay Populace in "Late" Modernity. *Social Science and Medicine* 42:1609–1620.

Yap, O. W. Stephanie, and David J. Thornton. 1995. The Arbor Free Clinic at Stanford: A Multidisciplinary Effort. *Journal of the American Medical Association* 273:431.

Part II

Biocultural Approaches

Health and sickness are inescapably biocultural phenomena. Human biology does not operate in isolation, for cultural processes affect biological ones and vice versa. Indeed, the capacity for culture is a product of human biological evolution. The human brain allows for the use of language and other forms of symbolic communication that are the basis of culture. The brain's flexible as opposed to preprogrammed behavioral responses are what allow humans to learn and absorb culture. Social life seems to have been a major force in the development of these capacities, and healing may be as old as humanity itself. There is evidence that throughout hominid evolution there has been caregiving within foraging bands, although this is controversial (see DeGusta 2003; Lebel and Trinkaus 2002).

Culture, in turn, shapes human biology. Socioeconomic conditions directly affect growth and development in infants and children. The same pathogen can produce vastly different epidemics in different historical and geographical settings, with different attack rates, sickness profiles, and mortality rates. By the same token, different social and politico-economic conditions favor different pathogens: "tropical" diseases such as malaria or yellow fever are linked to poverty as much as geography. Politico-economic forces meanwhile may limit people's choices and force them to behave in ways that are unfavorable to their health. Lifestyle factors can lead to high rates of chronic diseases such as heart disease and cancer in some populations, whereas different patterns of diet and physical activity are associated with low rates of these same diseases in other populations. There are significant variations in disease patterns within populations, and this has been the case since the emergence of the earliest stratified societies. These factors are recognized in the biocultural approach to the study of human biology that informs the selections in this part of the book (see also Ehrlich 2000; Goodman and Leatherman 1998; Stinson et al. 2000).

Part II begins with selections on human plasticity, variation, and adaptation, especially in relation to stressors such as diseases (see Dressler 1999; Panter-Brick and Worthman 1999; Weiss 1998). Plasticity refers to the universal human capacity to deal with a large range of environmental conditions that is a product of our common genetic endowment. Variation refers to the phenomenon of inherited biological differences among individuals and groups. Both concepts are related to the concept of adaptation. Adaptation refers to the process by which genetic mutations may benefit their bearers through either traits or physiological processes that allow individuals to achieve increased rates of survival and reproduction in a given environment. Cultural adaptations have the same impact. Maladaptation refers to the opposite outcome.

It is important to keep in mind that cultural evolution does not operate at the same pace or under the same constraints as biological evolution. In addition, although a quantitative measure (survival, reproduction, growth) may be used to assess adaptation or maladaptation, it is not always possible to evaluate causes and consequences without falling into circular logic. Also, whereas biological evolution occurs at the level of individual organisms (or rather, genes), cultural evolution involves both the individual and group levels.

Examples that illustrate human plasticity include immediate and prolonged immune response to infection, growth stunting in starvation conditions, and increased numbers of red blood cells with higher levels of hemoglobin in high-altitude environments, as described by Christopher Wills in selection 12. Wills also suggests that some population differences in responses to extreme environments are due to genetic variation.

Using the example of sickle-cell anemia in populations exposed to malaria, in selection 14, Nina L. Etkin explains how changes in gene frequencies as a result of natural selection may increase the chances of survival and reproduction of the bearers of beneficial mutations, but at a cost. A mutation leads to a distortion in the hemoglobin molecule and reduces the life span of the red blood cells. The mutation benefits carriers (with one copy of the defective gene) through red blood cells that make poor hosts for the malaria parasite, but has great costs for those with sickle cell disease (with both copies) due to potentially fatal anemia.

The variation in skin color among human beings is the outcome of a long process of genetic adaptation to different levels of exposure to sunlight, as discussed by Bruce A. Cohn in selection 14. Cohn describes a classic illustration of coevolution that is linked to skin color variation: the ability to digest lactose beyond weaning age is a genetic adaptation that occurred in conjunction with the cultural innovation of the domestication of animals useful for dairying.

Cultural adaptations may be very swift, or develop over many centuries or longer. Cultural adaptations to high altitude and low humidity include special clothing, coming down to a lower altitude for childbirth, and periodically drinking tea (selection 12). Antibiotics, oral rehydration therapy, quarantine, and protective foods are cultural adaptations to infectious diseases (selection 13). Sunscreen use in light-skinned people is a cultural adaptation to ultraviolet radiation (selection 14).

To assess genetic variation between groups, the frequencies of specific alleles of individual genes are compared. As Alan H. Goodman explains in selection 15, in the vast majority of cases these genes are inherited independently of one another, such that traits tend not to be inherited in clusters. That is, variability on one point is not usually matched by variability on another. This is a main reason why the concept of race is not useful in analyzing population differences in disease. On the other hand, human populations have specific evolved immune defenses that reflect their unique history of infectious disease (see Cooke and Hill 2001; Frank 2002; Wills 1996).

The concepts of plasticity and variation highlight the need for a comparative approach to the study of human biology. Growth and development, disease, and aging are very different processes in different environments (see Ellison 2001). This point was made in Part I with reference to intercultural variation in the menopause experience. Another example is puberty. Girls begin to menstruate at an average age of 12.5 years in industrialized societies today, and this is widely assumed to represent a biological standard. However, the age was higher in Western countries in past decades, and in preindustrial societies today it is around 16 (see selection 17). These differences indicate how important it is not to make assumptions about what is "normal" based on a limited sample of the world's population.

The diachronic, comparative approach to biology is fundamental to "Darwinian" or "evolutionary" medicine (see Trevathan et al. 1999). Two main emphases of this field are host–pathogen interactions and evolutionary explanations for disease patterns in particular historical periods. The first takes as a starting point the ongoing embrace or "dance" ("battle" according to prevailing military metaphors) between humans and pathogens (see Wakeford 2001; Wills 1996). In selection 16, Randolph M. Nesse and George C. Williams argue that common responses to infection such as fever or iron deficiency are often beneficial. They are the outcome of humanity's shared evolutionary history of infection and defense against infection.

Selection 16 also considers the strategies pathogens use to spread among hosts, including insect and other kinds of vectors. Changes in the availability of vectors and the quality of the environment—from the quantity of minerals in the human gastrointestinal tract to the level of organic matter in a river—can favor or disfavor the reproduction and spread of pathogens and can affect their virulence. Occasionally, human actions succeed in completely halting transmission of a pathogen (see Koplow 2003), although experience has shown that this is extremely uncommon and usually unfeasible (see Aylward et al. 2000).

Human activities play a significant role in shaping the environmental conditions facing pathogens. For example, the misuse and overuse of antibiotics in medicines and cleaning agents have given resistant bacterial strains the opportunity to outlast and outproduce susceptible strains. Antibiotic resistance is a major concern in hospitals, but seems to be occurring at the household level as well. Antibiotic soaps and nonprescription medicines allow people to create hospital-like environments where resistant variants thrive (see Levy 2001).

Selections 17 and 18 by S. Boyd Eaton et al. consider the impact of major changes in lifestyle on human disease patterns. They show that the low physical activity and high energy and high fat diet of most modern humans are recent inventions, in conflict with a human metabolic and cardiovascular system adapted for a very different way of life. The discordance accounts for the rise in the chronic diseases and health conditions that are now the major health concerns of the industrialized countries, including obesity, non-insulin-dependent diabetes, hypertension, cancer, and heart disease. Others include hearing loss, dental caries, acne, myopia, and possibly some forms of mental illness (see Cordain et al. 2002a, 2002b; McGuire and Troisi 1998). The chronic diseases are increasingly common in developing countries as well, which face a double burden because infectious diseases continue to thrive where nutritional and sanitary conditions are poor. Stress related to social inequality, Westernization, migration, and political instability is a factor beyond diet and exercise that affects the health of disadvantaged populations and subpopulations through its impact on neuroendocrine, immune, and cardiovascular functioning (see Daniel et al. 1999; Dressler 1999; Dressler and Bindon 2000).

Selections 19 through 23 consider disease distributions in particular historical periods to paint a picture of human health over time and illuminate the factors that affect the kinds of diseases that prevail in certain contexts (see Crosby 2004; McNeill 1999; Watts 1998). Selection 19, by Ronald Barrett et al., explains that "the" epidemiologic transition to low mortality rates and from infectious to chronic diseases as the major killers in Western Europe and other industrialized societies is but one of several major transitions and one that did not affect the entire population at the same rate. A previous transition associated with the adoption of an agricultural way of life had increased mortality and fertility rates for several thousand years before they fell over the past two centuries. The more recent shift was due largely to social and ecological changes leading to reduced poverty and improved nutrition, hygiene, and sanitation (see McKeown 1979, 1988; Pelto and Pelto 1983).

Most studies of early transitions from foraging to agriculture demonstrate an overall decline in health and average life expectancy, as Debra L. Martin and Alan H. Goodman document in selection 20 (see Swedlund and Armelagos 1990). These findings go against the prevailing wisdom that agriculture and settlement automatically improve health due to increased material well-being and access to medical care. Similar negative effects occur today when foragers or nomadic pastoralists take on a settled way of life, as shown by Nanette L. Barkey et al. in selection 21. In both cases the effects are not uniform but impact disproportionately on disadvantaged social classes.

Selections 22 and 23 compare a single disease across different time periods. Although biological, ecological, and socioeconomic conditions have changed, there are lessons from history about the potential effectiveness of political interventions and the role of local to global economic forces in shaping epidemic and endemic diseases. Matthew Gandy and Alimudden Zumla focus on tuberculosis and highlight the importance of sociopolitical failures in treatment delivery and provision of adequate living conditions as opposed to individual failures in compliance with medical directions. Monica Schoch-Spana examines the 1918 influenza pandemic and raises questions about not only how agricultural practices and human movements provide easier routes of viral transmission but also how a bioterrorist attack or large-scale epidemic would affect political and social systems in the United States today.

The last set of readings in Part II concerns the ecology and geography of disease (see Haggett 2000). Peter J. Brown and Elizabeth D. Whitaker compare the history of malaria and pellagra in two parts of

Italy to show that agricultural transformations can have not only negative impacts but also positive ones, although the benefits may accrue unevenly across social classes. However, continued agricultural intensification and industrialism have brought changes to the environment of a greater magnitude in terms of ecological change and potential health impacts than any previous human activities (see Patz et al. 1996). The resulting changes in temperature and rainfall affect ecosystem dynamics and consequently the distribution and life cycle of pathogens, insect vectors, and animal reservoirs of disease, with possible impacts on disease virulence (see selection 16). These changes are contributing to a third epidemiologic transition unfolding today (see selection 19), which involves the emergence or re-emergence of a number of infectious diseases. In addition, human-induced climate change may reduce the productivity of agriculture, leading to reduced nutrition and increased disease in contrast to the positive outcomes described in selection 24.

Climate change and more direct human modifications of the environment are the subject of Charles Anyinam's discussion of indigenous medicines in selection 25. While the environment sets the parameters for indigenous medicine use, the gathering of medicines from animals, plants, and soil can affect ecosystems in turn. Anyinam leads us into Part III by suggesting that the way people think about nature and religion may be the most dangerous factor causing environmental degradation. Indigenous healing systems tend to be relatively careful custodians of ecological systems, given a worldview in which the natural and spirit worlds coincide (see also selections 26, 27, 29, 32). With shifts toward the secular outlook common in Western societies, this protection may be compromised and with it humanity's resources for caring for the sick.

Suggested films

Influenza 1918. 1998. Robert Kenner Films (PBS). 60 min.

Plagued. 1992. Janet Bell, producer (NY: Filmmakers Library). [Part I, The Origins of Disease, 52 min.; Part II, Epidemics, Products of Progress, 52 min.; Part III, Invisible Armies, 52 min.].

Plague War. 1998. Jim Gilmore and Peter Malloy, producers (Frontline). 60 min.

Who Are You? 1993. David Sington, producer (WGBH/Boston and BBC-TV). 60 min.

World in the Balance. 2004. Sarah Holt and David Carnochan, producers (Nova). 120 min.

12 LIVING AT THE EDGE OF SPACE

Christopher Wills

Human beings have colonized a wide range of environments across the planet, adapting in both biological and cultural ways. As a result, the allelic frequency of particular genes varies between groups that have been living for long periods of time in particular geographical areas. However, this kind of variation does not tend to follow culturally constructed racial lines (see selections 13, 14, 15, 40, 42). At the same time, growth and development depend on interlocking social, economic, cultural, and biological influences such that vast differences in morphology can arise between individuals with a shared genetic constitution. For example, body proportions and height can change dramatically in a single generation due to altered living conditions affecting factors such as nutrition, infectious disease, and psychophysical stress (see selection 48; Mascie-Taylor and Bogin 1995; Ruff 2002). The following selections focus on the remarkable variability and plasticity of human beings.

To illustrate, this selection considers biological responses to low oxygen concentration in the two highest inhabited places on Earth, the Tibetan plateau and the high Andes (see also Beall 2000). In both places, local people have particular physical characteristics that make them better able to withstand the relative lack of oxygen and the cold dry air than people who come from lower altitudes and become acclimatized, including those who remain many years. There are differences in the type and degree of these characteristics between the two populations, making the Tibetans better adapted than the Andean populations. The former do not suffer from mountain sickness, and their babies are born at normal weight, just as if they lived at sea level.

To tease apart facultative adaptations that are within the repertoire of all human beings exposed to high altitudes—increased red blood cell count and eventually increased lung capacity—from genetic adaptations, Wills compares Andean people, Tibetans, and Chinese people living near the Tibetan plateau who visit periodically. He argues that although no specific genetic adaptations have yet been found, the very long time over which the Tibetan plateau has been settled, and the character of the adaptations themselves, lend support to the idea that such changes are likely to have occurred. Even the yaks that share the same environment have their own, similar adaptations.

Questions to keep in mind

What are the biological and cultural responses to high altitude described in the article, and how do they differ among the different groups studied?

What characteristics of Tibetan people's arteries make them able to maintain high rates of blood flow, even where oxygen is scarce, and for women to maintain adequate blood flow during pregnancy?

In what ways are yaks adapted to living at high altitude? How are they similar to human adaptations?

What information is needed to demonstrate genetic as opposed to physiological adaptation to harsh conditions?

Source: From *Children of Prometheus* by Christopher Wills. Copyright (c) 1998 by Christopher Wills. Reprinted by permission of Perseus Books PLC, a member of Perseus Books, L.L.C.

Those who sweat get frostbite easily, but I never sweat when I am climbing. . . . Sometimes it has been suggested that I have "three lungs" because I have so little trouble at great heights. At this I laugh with my two mouths. But I think it is perhaps true that I am more adapted to heights than most men; that I was born not only in, but for the mountains. I climb with rhythm, and it is a natural thing for me. My hands, even in warm weather; are usually cold, and doctors have told me that my heartbeat is quite slow. . . . On a recent tour of India, with the heat and the crowds, I became more sick than I have ever been in my life on a mountain.

Tenzing Norgay,
Tiger of the Snows (1955)

Even though we have yet to visit other planets, some of us have spread into environments that are almost as alien, with profound evolutionary consequences. Think of these migrations as a kind of practice run for our future attempts to colonize Mars or the planets of a nearby star.

The world has four roofs. One is in East Africa and encompasses the highlands of Ethiopia; our ancestors have lived there for millions of years. A second, which was colonized by humans only in recent historical times, is the Colorado Plateau. A third—far higher than either of these and inhabited for perhaps ten thousand years—is the high Andes, extending along much of the western rim of South America.

But the roof of the world that everybody thinks of first is the Tibetan plateau. This region encompasses some 800,000 square miles, an area more than twice as large as the high Andes. The plateau has been pushed up by a slow, grinding, but irresistible collision between two great pieces of the Earth's crust: the tectonic plate that carries the Indian subcontinent, and the immense mainland of Asia itself.

As India has plowed into Asia's southern rim during the course of the last fifty million years, the most obvious result of this collision has been the Himalayas. These mountains, however, form only the southernmost part of a massive pile of ancient seabed material that has been shoved ahead of the Indian plate, like snow in front of some vast snowplow. Squeezed into accordion pleats by the force of the collision, this material has been formed into range after range of peaks. Each spring fierce rivers wear away the rocks of the high-altitude valleys between the peaks, where in spite of everything a little life manages to cling.

The nearest I have come to this roof of the world was a visit to the desert town of Dunhuang in Gansu Province of western China. Dunhuang is located one hundred kilometers from the Tibetan Plateau's northern edge, squarely at a junction of the Great Silk Road. People have lived there for a long time. The famous Buddhist caves at nearby Mogao have yielded, among other treasures, the earliest known printed book, the famous *Diamond Sutra*, which can be dated from clues in the text to A.D. 868.[1] But these are by no means the first traces of human occupation. In the nearby Taklimakan Desert, Chinese and European archaeologists have found more than a hundred well-preserved mummies of a Caucasian people who lived in the area four thousand years ago. The origin and fate of these people, so different in appearance and culture from the present-day inhabitants, is a complete mystery.

The immediate countryside around Dunhuang is relatively flat, invaded in places by rolling sand dunes from the desert to the south. Beyond the desert is a range of six-thousand-meter peaks known as the Denghe Nanshan, which stand out vividly whenever the air is clear. Even from so far away, these immense mountains dominate the landscape. The sky to the south of them is pale with reflected snow from range after range of still mightier mountains. And it is there that some members of our species who have migrated to the edge of space can be found.

A MYSTERIOUS HISTORY

We know little about the history of human penetration of the Tibetan plateau. Perhaps a Shangri-La or two is still hidden somewhere among those remote peaks and valleys. Whether there is or not, people have dwelt in this most extreme of lands since long before written records. The severity of their lives has, until recently, been counterbalanced by their remoteness, which has made them relatively safe from invaders.

Among the diverse inhabitants of the plateau, the Sherpas of Nepal are the people who have interacted the most with the outside world. They are not native to Nepal, but migrated there during the seventeenth century from southern Tibet. Sherpas are brilliant mountaineers and make up an essential part of any climbing expedition in the Himalayas. Their mountaineering skills and ability to carry heavy loads at high altitudes have made such expeditions possible and have enabled numerous well-heeled Manhattanites to stagger to the tops of the world's highest mountains. The Sherpa Tenzing Norgay was the second person to stand on the top of Everest, courteously dropping a few feet behind Edmund Hillary during the final scramble to the summit.

The Sherpas and other indigenous peoples of the plateau have adapted remarkably to the need to live their entire lives at around four thousand meters, where each lungful of air has only a third as many molecules of oxygen as at sea level. But has this adaptation been a truly evolutionary one? Do the Sherpas actually carry genes, or combinations of genes, that are different from those carried by people who live at sea level? If so, then in the course of acquiring these genes, they have undergone a true evolutionary change.

This question is difficult to answer because it is hard to distinguish between genetic adaptations and those that are merely physiological. Any human body has the capacity to adapt fairly rapidly to extreme conditions. At high altitudes the number of red blood corpuscles in our blood can rise substantially, and over time even our lung capacity can increase somewhat. Further, any of us can soften the impact of the cold simply by bundling up warmly, by not exposing our extremities more than necessary, and so on. Are the Sherpas really different genetically from the rest of us? Or do they have these physiological adaptations simply because they have lived their entire lives, beginning at the moment of conception, at high altitudes?

The theory of evolution predicts that any population that lives under such extreme conditions for many generations should become better and better adapted; the poorly adapted members of the population will die or fail to reproduce. In order to see whether natural selection has altered the gene pool of the Sherpas, we would like to have at least a rough idea of how long their ancestors have lived under these conditions. The longer this period has been, the greater the likelihood that selection has been able to change their gene pools.

We cannot be very precise about this estimate, because uncertainties abound. Very little genetic information about Tibetan populations is available, and the human fossil record in this region ranges from sparse to nonexistent. The Tibetans have a strong genetic and physical resemblance to the peoples who currently inhabit the steppes to the north of the plateau, in the area around Dunhuang and elsewhere. That region is likely to be the primary origin of the peoples of Tibet.

But if the origin of the Tibetans is shrouded in mystery, so is the origin of their ancestors. Those puzzling Caucasians of four thousand years ago, so different from the present-day peoples of the northern steppes, are unlikely to have been the first arrivals in the area. Indeed, the first arrivals on the steppes, and perhaps even the first to venture into the Tibetan highlands, might not even have been members of our own species.

Early hominids,[2] in particular our immediate forerunner *Homo erectus*, likely inhabited Central Asia for a very long time. Although fossil hominid sites in Central Asia are few and far between, two different very ancient sites have been discovered that (very loosely) bracket the Tibetan Plateau. Fragmentary remains of *Homo erectus* from both of these sites have been dated to almost two million years ago. One of the sites is far to the west of Tibet, in the Caucasus Mountains; the other is located to its east, in the upper valley of the Yangtze.

Such old sites have not yet been found in Central Asia. But if bands of *H. erectus* did trudge across the vast windy space that separates these two known sites, it hardly seems likely that they did so only once. Much more probably, during this immense span of time, they migrated back and forth many times across what would eventually become western China and Kirgiziya. In doing so, they would have anticipated Marco Polo and the other much later travelers belonging to our own species, for they would have been following the route of the Silk Road—long before there was any silk or presumably even any concept of a road.

Of course, since no fossil record of such migrations exists, all this is sheer speculation. We also have no evidence that tribes of *H. erectus* ventured into the mountains that they would have glimpsed far to the south of their migratory path. If they had done so, they would probably have taken the most accessible routes, from the northeast and the southeast, in order to avoid crossing the vast Gobi Desert. But we do have evidence that, about half a million years ago, they were living close to the plateau itself. The evidence comes from a discovery made in a cave near the village of Yuanmou, not far to the southeast of the plateau's edge between Chengdu and Kunming. The scattering of teeth and tools found there belonged to *H. erectus* and have been tentatively dated to 500,000–600,000 years ago, though they may be younger.

It may not be coincidental that these traces of *H. erectus* happen to have been found near a well-worn trading route into Tibet that has been used extensively during historic times. There is no doubt that this difficult but negotiable route leading to the high plateau would have been open to these predecessors of modern humans. I find it hard to imagine that some of them, impelled by curiosity or the need to escape from enemies, did not venture into the mountains.

If *H. erectus* reached high altitudes and stayed there for any time, they would have become adapted to the conditions there. Then when they were displaced—and perhaps driven to extinction—by later arrivals, those adaptations may have disappeared with them. But perhaps not.[3]

The much more recent migrations through this area of our own species, *Homo sapiens,* are also mostly shrouded in mystery. For centuries the plateau has lured traders who have entered through routes that snake over the towering passes and lead into Tibet proper. Up until the time of the Chinese Revolution, endless files of Chinese peasants, bent almost double under eighty-kilogram bales of tea leaves, toiled up from Chengdu into the southeastern part of the plateau, in order to slake the Tibetans' great thirst for tea. Nineteenth- and twentieth-century travelers tell of endless lines of porters stumbling up slopes that would challenge a trained mountaineer, numb and empty-faced because they were unable to withstand the cold and fatigue without the aid of opium.

But these traders left few records. Essentially nothing is known of Tibet's history prior to the seventh century A.D., although Paleolithic tools dated to about fifty thousand years ago have been found on the northern part of the plateau. So we have no idea when the earliest modern humans might have arrived, whether they found the plateau already inhabited, and what might have happened to any earlier inhabitants. But we do know that, in spite of the strong physical and genetic resemblance of the present-day Tibetans to the peoples who inhabit the steppes to the north, they did not come from that area alone. The physical resemblance does not extend to the languages they speak, which have an affinity with those of the Burmese, to the southeast. This discordance between appearance and language suggests that the peoples of the plateau have had many long-term cultural contacts with a variety of peoples who lived at lower altitudes, and that the Tibetans must be an amalgam of many different migrations.

Thus it seems reasonable to suppose that, along with new languages and trade goods, new genes have been repeatedly infused into the gene pool of the Tibetans. The genes could have come from the tribes of the northern steppes, from peoples who lived in the ever-more-populous river valleys to the east that would eventually become China, and from the diverse inhabitants of the foothills of the Himalayas. However, if the genes already carried by the earlier settlers that aided high-altitude survival were sufficiently advantageous, they might have remained in the gene pool and spread in numbers even in the face of an influx of new genes from the outside.

While we cannot identify precisely the period of years that the Tibetans have had to adapt to high altitude, it is certainly in the thousands and probably in the tens of thousands. If *H. erectus* really did leave some genes behind in Tibet before vanishing, there is a slim possibility that this adaptive period might even have extended over hundreds of thousands of years!

To get a clearer idea of the impact that this long period of adaptation has had on the Tibetans, we can compare them with lowlanders who have lived at high altitudes for only a matter of months or years. Although lowlanders such as the Han Chinese settlers tend to be much less well adapted, it can always be argued that this is simply because they were not born and brought up under such extreme conditions. If a lowlander couple were to migrate to the Tibetan plateau and have a baby, then by the time that baby grows up, it might be just as well adapted as the Tibetans who have lived there for generations.

We do not know if this is the case. The Han Chinese who now live in Lhasa and elsewhere in Tibet do so for only part of the year, and pregnant Chinese women almost always descend to lower altitudes to give birth. So it is difficult to attribute any differences between Tibetans and these lowlanders to a genetic cause.

One way to disentangle true genetic change from mere physiological adaptation would be to examine another group, who have lived at altitudes as high as the Tibetans but for fewer generations. If the evolutionary scenario is correct, these people should have adapted to their environment less thoroughly than the Tibetans, since there would have been less time for new genes and new combinations of genes to appear in their gene pool. Luckily, such a group can be found. They inhabit the second greatest roof of the world.

BEFORE THE INCAS

The human history of that other roof, the great cordillera of the Andes, has almost certainly been briefer than that of the Tibetan Plateau. The Andes were also formed by a collision of tectonic plates, though not as massive as the one that took place between India and Asia. Here the encounter was between unequals. As the thin oceanic plates of the eastern Pacific encountered the massive plate that makes up the western edge of the South American continent, they were forced to bend down, pushing up the coastal rim in the process. This relatively mild encounter has not crushed and folded the Amazon basin, which lies to the east of the collision zone. Instead, it formed the Andes, an immensely tall but relatively narrow range of mountains: the world's second tallest after the Himalayas.

The ancestors of the Quechua and Aymara Indians who inhabit the high valleys of the Andes must have made their way up into these regions a relatively short time ago, probably five or six thousand years. For one thing, human occupation in the South American mountains was dependent on the development of crops that could support them. Further, because of the shorter distances involved, the Andean altiplano was far more accessible to

lowlanders than the huge and remote Tibetan Plateau. Throughout the history of the Inca empire, and undoubtedly in earlier times, there was much migration from low to high altitudes and back.

Nonetheless, during this short history, these peoples have managed astonishing things. Their accomplishments were not, as is generally supposed, all due to the Incas. The Inca empire did its best to foster this notion by carefully destroying any records of the achievements of earlier civilizations. But we know now that they were responsible only for putting some finishing touches on a vast network of roads and bridges that stretched from northern Ecuador to a point south of present-day Santiago in Chile, extending eastward into Bolivia and Argentina. This network, one of the most remarkable construction feats in the preindustrial world, was actually the result of the efforts of many different cultures.

Along these roads, in the days of the Inca empire, relays of specially trained runners called *chasqui* could carry verbal messages, or messages coded in a knotted string, from Quito to Cuzco in five days. For long stretches the *chasqui* had to run at altitudes well above four thousand meters.

The problems faced by the first colonizers of the Andean altiplano, like those that faced the first venturers into Tibet, were more challenging than a simple lack of oxygen. For most of the year, nighttime temperatures in the Andes fall below freezing. The extreme dryness of the air and the lowered vapor pressure suck moisture from the body fairly quickly. The blood literally thickens, and the brain is deprived of essential oxygen, leading to the blinding headaches, dizziness, and sleepiness—and sometimes the edema and internal bleeding—of mountain sickness.

When I arrived for the first time in Cuzco, the magnificent ancient capital of the Incas, I was advised by friends to drink as much liquid as I could manage for at least the first twenty-four hours. By following this good advice, I was able to avoid the worst of the altitude effects that often incapacitate unprepared tourists. But the first arrivals in these high desert valleys had no such warning. Their children were particularly at risk.

Life has always been severe in this region. Studies of mummified human remains from several different early cultures, ranging from 1300 B.C. to

A.D. 1400, show that fifteen percent of the women had died in childbirth or immediately post-partum. Even today, among the Indians of remote areas in southern Peru, disease and the effects of the rigorous environment kill three hundred out of every thousand babies during the first year of life.

The Aymara and Quechua have developed ingenious methods for preserving the lives of their fragile children. The youngest babies are wrapped in layer after layer of cloth, rendering them immobile. This conserves heat, moisture, and the child's energy. The child in its bundle is then placed in a carrying cloth or *manta*. The amount of oxygen reaching its lungs is reduced by all the layers, but because it cannot move very much, any damage from anoxia is presumably minimized. The baby is kept tightly wrapped for the first three months, but as it grows the wrappings are gradually loosened.

How much selection for sheer survival must have taken place before this effective method of protection was invented? Cumulatively, it must have been very great. Before infant mortality was reduced to its present, albeit still brutally high, level, uncounted tiny bodies were buried or interred in the stone mausoleums on the cliffs surrounding the altiplano valleys. Not all these deaths had a genetic effect on the population, but the fraction that did, over the millennia, had the cumulative result of increasing the likelihood of survival of each generation.

It is striking and perhaps significant that Tibetan mothers swaddle their babies as well, but the babies' heads are kept freer of clothing so that they can breathe more easily. Does this mean that a Tibetan baby is better able to withstand the fierce high-altitude conditions than a baby in the altiplano? As we will see, there is evidence that it is.

A RUSH OF BLOOD

Mark Twain remarked that even though history never repeats itself, it does tend to rhyme. So does evolution. Selection for different genes and combinations of genes must have occurred in the two adventurous peoples who colonized the Tibetan plateau and the Andean altiplano. Although the Andeans have adapted less well, both groups have acquired the ability to live under these extreme conditions.

So far, scientists have made only limited comparative genetic investigations of these two groups. They have yet to track down any specific genetic changes that have contributed to their adaptation. But it is almost certainly only a matter of time before some are found.

Perhaps the most telling indication of true genetic differences between the two populations comes from an examination of the weights of their babies at birth. In virtually all parts of the world, high altitude has a strong and significant negative effect on birth weight, even when babies are carried to normal term. The effect is detectable even when the differences in altitude are relatively small. On average, for every thousand meters of altitude, the birth weight of full-term babies decreases by about one hundred grams.

This pattern turns out to hold true for the Andean Indians: their babies weigh about four hundred grams less than babies born at sea level—for the metrically challenged, this translates into a difference of a pound or so. Such a large reduction in birth weight must contribute to the high infant mortality. Babies of acclimatized parents weigh a little more than unacclimatized babies born at the same altitude, but not much.

This pattern emphatically does not hold true for Tibetan babies. In a notable exception to the worldwide trend, their birth weight at term is the same as that of babies born at sea level.

These high birth weights are not some special property of conditions on the Tibetan plateau. Chinese mothers who have lived in Lhasa throughout their pregnancies obey the birth-weight-altitude law. Even though they usually descend to lower altitudes to give birth, they have smaller babies than do Chinese mothers who live at sea level.

How do Tibetan mothers manage to nourish their babies so efficiently at high altitude? To find out, Lorna Moore of the University of Colorado visited Tibet a number of times from 1983 to 1992. Although recent political upheavals have now made further work difficult, during that window of opportunity Moore and her coworkers carried out a number of important experiments on Tibetan volunteers. Using as controls some Han Chinese living in Lhasa who had spent long periods of time at high altitude, they found that, in vivid contrast to the Han women, Tibetan women excel at supplying oxygen to their babies during pregnancy.

Using Doppler ultrasound, it was possible to measure the rate of flow in the arteries that supply blood to the lungs and to the uterus. In most people low levels of oxygen cause the pulmonary arteries, which supply blood to the lungs, to constrict, which is exactly the reverse of what they should do. This turns out to be a reflex, an echo of the moment when we are born. As a fetus grows in the womb, the pulmonary arteries are small and little blood flows to the lungs, but at the moment of birth oxygen rushes into the lungs and the pulmonary arteries expand. We are now cursed with the reverse of this reflex—when oxygen drops, our pulmonary arteries contract in a physiological memory of fetal life. Moore and her coworkers found that this does not happen in Tibetans—soon after birth, they lose that dangerous reflex.

The rate of blood flow in the uterine arteries of the Tibetan women is very high for a different reason—their arteries are unusually large. These two factors combined mean that Tibetan women retain high rates of flow under hypoxic conditions.

After birth, other unusual adaptations are exhibited by the Tibetan babies themselves. During the period shortly after birth, Moore found that Tibetan babies had ten percent more oxygen in their arterial blood than babies born to Han Chinese parents who had lived at the same altitude. This difference persisted and actually grew more pronounced during the first weeks of life. Right from birth the newborn Tibetan babies were able to extract more oxygen from the thin air that surrounded them.

THE BODY'S PERCEPTION OF THE HIGH-ALTITUDE WORLD

The fact that Tibetan mothers can reverse the effects of high altitude and give birth to babies of normal weight, while Andean mothers cannot, is the most powerful argument for real genetic differences between the two populations. But Moore and her coworkers discovered other things about their physiologies that also undoubtedly have a ge-

netic component. Although these phenomena are complex and interrelated, they show that Tibetans have by far the best set of adaptations to high altitude of any human group so far examined—including even the Tibetans' neighbors, the high-altitude peoples who live in Ladakh at the northern tip of India. The people of Ladakh, like those of the Andes, ventured to these extreme altitudes more recently than the people of Tibet.

Both the similarities and the differences are informative. The lungs of both Tibetans and Andean natives have more of the tiny thin-walled sacs called alveoli, in which the blood is brought in close contact with air. But such adaptations to high altitude life are to be expected—even lowlanders can eventually develop them.

Another obvious accommodation to high altitudes is shown by the Andeans: They have more red blood cells, and higher levels of hemoglobin, than lowlanders. Lowlanders, too, tend to increase the number of red cells in their blood as they become acclimatized to high-altitude life. Remarkably, however, Tibetans show neither of these adaptations. In fact, they have slightly fewer red blood cells, and slightly less hemoglobin, than people living at sea level. This is not due to an increase in blood volume, which is the same as that of altitude-adapted Han. Further, when Tibetans climb to even more extreme altitudes than those at which they normally live, the hemoglobin in their blood does not increase to the same extent as it does in the blood of lowlanders when they become adapted to the same altitude. Recently suggestions have been made that an allele among Tibetans may control the rate of saturation of hemoglobin with oxygen, though hard biochemical evidence is as yet lacking. Oddly, the statistical analysis suggests that all Tibetans do not have this allele.

In the Tibetans increased blood flow is enough to overcome their deficiency in red blood cells. And their thinner blood has other consequences, the most important of which is protection against high-altitude pulmonary edema.

This severe illness constitutes the greatest danger to adult survival. When lowlanders climb quickly to high altitudes, their arterial pressure shoots up, especially the pressure in the pulmonary arteries. In mountaineers and others under severe stress, fluid is sometimes actually forced out of the circulation and into the lungs.

More insidious is chronic mountain sickness, in which the increased pressure forces blood out of the capillary beds into the tissues. A great variety of symptoms can result, some taking years to develop, including bleeding under the skin and gastrointestinal hemorrhage. The symptoms of the disease are obvious even to the casual observer: the faces of the victims are a darkened mahoganylike color, stained with the blood that has become trapped.

This slowly developing disease is common in people who have lived at high altitudes for long periods, or even for many generations. Surprisingly, it often develops in Peruvian highlanders, who one might have thought would have evolved resistance.

Chronic mountain sickness is also widespread among the Han Chinese living in Lhasa, who make it worse by incessant smoking. But it is almost never seen among Tibetans, even those who smoke heavily. Their cheeks remain pink and healthy without the telltale broken vessels or dark engorgement suffered by the lowland Chinese.

Resistance to the effects of dehydration may be the key to resistance to mountain sickness. Recall the remark of Tenzing Norgay's that I quoted at the beginning of this chapter. Tibetans may lose less moisture from perspiration, although this has not been systematically studied. In addition, the fact that Tibetans have a relatively small number of red blood cells means that their blood should not be as affected by dehydration. Even when they do lose fluids through exertion at high altitude, their blood will retain its normal low viscosity for longer. This too has yet to be studied in detail.

Yet another Tibetan adaptation, almost invisible but very effective, has to do with the way their bodies perceive the high-altitude world. They respond differently to the stresses of living at the edge of space.

When people who have spent their lives at sea level are first transported to a high altitude, their rate of breathing does the reverse of what one might expect—it actually slows down. This lowers the amount of oxygen in the blood and increases the amount of carbon dioxide, which can worsen the symptoms of mountain sickness. With time, as these newcomers become acclimatized, their breathing rates return to normal levels. Remarkably, the Quechua of the Andes, even after many generations at high altitude, always show a pattern of slow breathing, even though they are presumably thoroughly acclimatized. This may help to explain why chronic mountain sickness is so prevalent among them. They show what seems to be an inappropriate physiological response to their extreme conditions.

If you expect the Tibetans to show a different response from the Andeans, you will not be disappointed. At high altitude Tibetans breathe at the same rate as acclimatized newcomers. They do this because their bodies are sensitive to changes that are largely invisible to the rest of us.

In the laboratory it is possible to manipulate the amount of oxygen in the air supply that an experimental subject is breathing through a mask, and to do so in such a way that the subject gets no hint of what is going on. When oxygen is lowered to about two-thirds of normal, Tibetans react very differently from either Quechua or lowlanders. Their heartbeat rises rapidly from seventy to a hundred beats a minute. The Quechua show a much smaller response, and lowlanders show almost no change at all. It takes a further substantial reduction in oxygen before their hearts begin to respond.

The bodies of the Tibetans, it appears, are far better than those of the rest of us at measuring oxygen levels. Their ability to sense conditions on the edge of space has been extended by the process of evolution, in just the direction that is needed to enhance their survival.

THE COEVOLUTION OF HUMANS AND YAKS

Tibetans are not alone in their superb adaptation to the high-altitude world. They share many of these adaptations with yaks, the high-altitude cattle of the Tibetan plateau. Yaks, too, have large and unusually thin-walled pulmonary arteries. This means that, under hypoxic conditions, the hearts of both Tibetans and their cattle do not have to work as hard as the hearts of lowland humans or lowland cattle to achieve the same results.

Just when the yaks first came to occupy the high-altitude plateau of Tibet is as much of a puzzle as the history of the first human occupation of the area. We do know that yaks have been plentiful in Tibet for a long time, long enough for people to have invented all sorts of uses for them. They pull plows in the high-altitude fields and carry huge loads over passes as high as six thousand meters. One recent traveler described "their great lungs inhaling and exhaling in puffs like a blowing locomotive." Indeed, they are so thoroughly adapted to high altitude that they tend not to do well below about three thousand meters.

In Tibet it is not sensible to waste anything. Every part of each yak is utilized. The hide has many uses, from clothing to coverings for the boats in which the Tibetans navigate the high lakes. The long and massive horns have been ground into powder for medication and have even been employed as building materials—in Lhasa, crushed yak horn is often used to reinforce masonry, and intact horns are inserted at intervals along the resulting walls for decoration. Yak oil is essential for lamps, and the butter is used to flavor tea, which the Tibetans drink in immense quantities to counteract the severe liquid loss at high altitude. Slabs of yak butter are often carved into intricate sculptures. So honored is the yak that two stuffed carcasses hang from the ceiling of the great monastery that overlooks the remote town of Gyantse, southwest of Lhasa. Perhaps they are a relic of the time before Buddhism when the Tibetans worshipped a pantheon that included yak-headed gods.

Their long coarse hair gives yaks a very different appearance from lowland cattle. The differences extend to their internal organs as well. Their lungs are enormous—three times a heavy as the lungs of the cattle that live in nearby Inner Mongolia, which is a far greater difference than that seen between the lungs of human Tibetans and lowlanders. And, like human Tibetans, yaks have surprisingly little hemoglobin in their blood—less than in lowland cattle.

In spite of these and many other differences, however, one can think of yaks, without much loss of precision, as simply cattle with lots of hair. Zoologists have put them into a separate species (currently most authorities call them *Bos grunniens*), but their gene pool is not clearly separated from that of cattle. Because purebred yaks tend to be ill-tempered and balky beasts, for centuries the Tibetans have hybridized them with lowland cattle in order to produce animals that are a little more manageable. These hybrids turn out to be perfectly healthy, although there have been reports that they are not fully fertile.

All this hybridization has, however, made the task of disentangling the relationship between yaks and domestic cattle difficult. The best way to determine just how genetically separate they are is to compare the DNA of the two species. But it is difficult to find genetically pure yaks. Many animals exhibited as yaks in zoos are actually mixtures. Rather than venturing into the vastnesses of Tibet, scientists have understandably tended to obtain blood from these zoo animals, so they may have been misled into concluding that yaks and cattle are more closely related than they really are.

Still, the general position of yaks on the family tree of cattle and their relatives is undisputed: all the molecular studies show that yaks are by far the closest relatives of domestic cattle that have yet been found. They are much closer to cattle than the Indian gaur and the Javanese banteng, both of which have been suggested as ancestors of domestic cattle breeds. But exactly how much closer they are will remain problematical until this matter of genetic admixture has been straightened out. We may never know, for after centuries or millennia of forced interbreeding with cattle and escape of hybrids into the wild, it is possible that truly pure wild yaks no longer exist.

Further, artificial selection may have been imposed on top of their natural adaptation. The original wild yaks, grazing peacefully on their high-altitude grasslands, probably had no need for such giant lungs and extreme physiology. But when people began capturing them and forcing them to carry immense burdens over the high passes and pull heavy primitive plows through stony soil in the thin air, the yaks best able to carry out these grueling tasks must have been selected.

Selection, whether natural or artificial, is much more likely to proceed rapidly when a population is full of genetic variation. The numerous hybridizations of yaks with domestic cattle could have provided some of this variation, resulting in a kind of evolutionary kick-start.

Humans, may have benefited from the same sort of kick-start. As we have seen, the introduction of genes from lowland human populations into the Tibetan highlands may have helped provide evolutionary fuel for their adaptation to extreme conditions.

There is no doubt that selection is continuing in humans as well as yaks. While infant mortality is slowly decreasing in both Nepal and the Peruvian altiplano (we currently have only fragmentary information from Tibet itself), the rigors of high-altitude life remain severe. The Tibetans, the Quechua, the people of Ladakh, the yaks, and all the other human groups and human-associated species living at the edge of space will continue to evolve better mechanisms to survive these conditions for as long as they continue to inhabit this extreme environment.

It may not be long before some of the genes involved in high-altitude adaptation are tracked down. It recently has been found that one of the two common alleles in the English population for a gene controlling blood pressure is more frequent in people who are able to perform severe physical labor. It is particularly frequent in mountain climbers. Is this allele also frequent in the Tibetan population and less so in the Andean? Or do the Tibetans have yet another allele of this gene that adapts them even better to high-altitude living? The answers will soon be forthcoming.

This is the kind of natural selection that we can easily understand: severe conditions that select for new adaptations absolutely necessary for survival. But what about the rest of us? We are not faced daily with lung-freezing cold or a paucity of oxygen. Still, our lives are not risk-free. Many of us are faced with a different set of dangerous problems that require continuing adaptation. We are only beginning to see just how pervasive selective pressures are, and how difficult or impossible it will be to free ourselves entirely from their rigors. We have not, as many assume, overcome these selective pressures—far from it. Some of them are pressures connected with disease, which are far more pervasive and subtle than we had thought even a few years ago. The next chapter provides a glimpse of some of the difficulties that we still face in our fight for survival against the multitude of organisms that prey on us, and how we have evolved and continue to evolve in response.

NOTES

1. Earlier printed books are known, in particular books from Korea that probably date from before A.D. 750, but the *Diamond Sutra* is the first printed text that can be dated with precision.

2. Hominids include our own species and our very closest relatives, all of which are extinct—the Australopithecines, Homo erectus, the Neandertals, and so on. Hominoids, on the other hand, are the result of a wider cast of the taxonomic net and include our closest living relatives—the chimpanzees, bonobos, gorillas and orangutans.

3. I will do my best to ignore the persistent rumors of the yeti, or Abominable Snowman. This mysterious hairy creature figures in elaborate legends told by the Sherpas, who claim that it dines on fungi found at high altitude. Footprints and supposed samples of yeti hair have all, when carefully investigated, been traced to other animals. Still, one cannot help but wonder what the origins of the legend might be!

13 THE CO-EVOLUTION OF PEOPLE, PLANTS, AND PARASITES: BIOLOGICAL AND CULTURAL ADAPTATIONS TO MALARIA

Nina L. Etkin

Like the harsh environments described in the previous selection, disease organisms can act as agents of natural selection. A classic example is a group of blood cell disorders such as sickle-cell anemia that provide protection against malaria. The prevalence of these disorders is high in areas under long-term exposure to the disease (see Livingstone 1958; Wiesenfeld 1967).

The fact that nonhuman primates are also hosts for malaria suggests that humans have been in contact with the disease since the earliest times. However, it was the advent of agriculture, and the ecological and demographic changes it involved, that allowed the disease to become a common health threat in areas that also host the necessary mosquito species. This means that human genetic adaptations are relatively recent. In this selection, Etkin points out that these so-called balanced polymorphisms are expensive adaptations because they cause a considerable amount of sickness and suffering to homozygotes (with two copies of the gene in question) at the same time as they protect heterozygote carriers (with one copy).

Comparing antimalarial plants used around the world, Etkin shows that indigenous medical systems include substances that are effective against malaria parasites and disease symptoms. She proposes a single mechanism for the antimalarial action of both cultural defenses, such as plant foods and medicines, and malaria-protective blood cell disorders, such as thalassemia and G6PD deficiency. In both cases, the resulting oxidation within red blood cells adds to that caused by the parasite itself to cause the destruction of red blood cells and the release of parasites before they are viable. This explains why antioxidant drugs and foods such as vitamins A and E reduce the effectiveness of antimalarial drugs, whereas oxidizing substances such as dietary iron, fava beans, or spices such as nutmeg and clove increase it.

Populations around the world have been found to use oxidant foods and medicines most during seasons of peak malaria risk. In addition, these populations deny such substances to people with disorders such as G6PD deficiency, protecting them from the dangerous anemia that could occur because their red blood cells are unable to withstand oxidant stress—the same mechanism by which their disorder protects them from the disease. Oxidants therefore are a central feature of both human genetic adaptations to malaria plasmodia and broad-spectrum defenses used by plants against the insects, microbes, animals, and other plants that threaten them.

Questions to keep in mind

How does the malaria plasmodium's life cycle relate to the symptoms of malaria in humans?

How did malaria first spread among humans, and why has it increased in prevalence and geographical range in recent years?

How does Etkin's discussion of the limitations of biomedical knowledge about medicinal plants compare with selection 6?

What are some examples of cultural adaptations working in concert with biological adaptations to malaria?

Source: Etkin, N. L. "The Co-Evolution of People, Plants, and Parasites: Biological and Cultural Adaptations to Malaria." Originally published in *Proceedings of the Nutrition Society* (2003), 62(2):311–317. Reprinted with permission from the author.

MALARIA IN HUMAN POPULATIONS

Malaria infection has strained the biological (immunoprotective) and cultural (medicinal) resources of human populations since antiquity, and is today still one of the world's most devastating diseases. Anopheline mosquitoes are the obligate intermediary host and vector of malaria parasites, species of the sporozoan genus Plasmodium. The four human-specific species are *P. vivax, P. ovale, P. malariae,* and *P. falciparum.* The origins of human malaria are traced to infections of other vertebrate, and later non-human primate, hosts hundreds of thousands (perhaps millions) of years ago. Of the more than 100 plasmodia species that infect vertebrates, only a few of the simian parasites can also infect humans. This marked host specificity confirms that the association between humans and malaria is of long duration, long enough to suggest considerable pressure for both biological and cultural adaptations. The advent of agriculture during the Neolithic period (8000–5000 BCE) was critical in establishing malaria infection in human populations. Animal and plant domestications fostered the increased population size and density that could support "crowd infections" such as malaria. Furthermore, agriculture was assisted by forest clearing and related environmental modifications that both encouraged mosquito breeding and destroyed the habitats of non-human primates who formerly served as the anopheline feeding targets and plasmodium hosts. The increasingly transformed environments of the modern era continue to support malaria at a very high rate of transmissibility.

Malaria Life Cycle and Transmission

The complex plasmodial life cycle begins with gametocytes that are ingested as part of the female mosquito's blood meal, and that initiate sexual reproduction in the mosquito's stomach. The motile zygote (ookinete) migrates through and encysts to the outer surface of the stomach wall (as an oocyst). Asexual division (sporogony) within this oocyst produces large numbers of sporozoites, which migrate to the salivary glands, and from there are injected into a vertebrate host when the mosquito takes another blood meal.

In the vertebrate host asexual reproduction (schizogony) occurs first in the liver, the asymptomatic phase, and later in circulating erythrocytes. Each sporozoite invades a single hepatic cell and produces thousands of merozoites that burst out of the liver cell and invade erythrocytes. The intra-erythrocytic trophozoite (the "ring" stage) reproduces to form a multinucleated schizont, which contains a species-determined number of merozoites. When the schizont matures, the erythrocyte ruptures and releases merozoites that infect new erythrocytes. Completing the cycle, the sexual gametocytes that develop from some of the trophozoites are infective to the mosquito.

Pathophysiology of Malaria

The characteristic periodic fevers that are the signature of malaria are precipitated by synchronous parasite development and erythrocyte rupture, which releases new merozoites, malaria antigens and toxic metabolites. *P. vivax* and *P. ovale* are relatively benign infections that present with 48 h (tertian) periodicity. *P. malariae,* also benign, has a 72 h (quartan) periodicity. *P. falciparum,* malignant tertian malaria, evinces the most severe symptoms and highest mortality, and is the principal target of anti-malarial drug research. (Quotidian malaria with 24 h periodicity is usually a double tertian infection by two distinct groups of *P. vivax* or two generations of *P. falciparum,* or a mixed *P. vivax* and *P. falciparum* infection.) Early signs of malaria are fever and chills accompanied by tachycardia (rapid bounding pulse), nausea, vomiting, frequent urination and "flu-like" symptoms. Interfebrile episodes are characterized by leucopaenia and thrombocytopaenia (abnormally low numbers of leucocytes and platelets). Later developments include haemolytic anaemia and kidney and other organ dysfunction, including hepatosplenomegaly and jaundice. In the terminal stages, *P. falciparum* becomes "cerebral malaria" and "blackwater fever" (haemoglobinuria). Where malaria is endemic, children younger than 5 years bear the burden of morbidity and mortality, while older children and adults may develop an "immunity tolerance," a protection against superinfection (Taylor-Robinson, 2002).

Malaria Epidemiology and Anti-Malarial Drugs

Today, malaria is virulently resurgent, with increased severity and epidemicity. The number of malaria deaths and geographic distribution are more extensive than three decades ago. More than half the world's population lives in malaria-endemic areas, where each year an estimated two billion are exposed, 500 million cases occur and infection results in more than two million deaths (Hoffman *et al.* 2002; Warhurst, 2002). What was heralded as the "imminent arrival" of a malaria vaccine 20 years ago still has not materialized (Rabinovich, 2002). Existing anti-malarial drugs are less effective, and insecticide resistance among anopheline vectors is a growing problem. Consequently, the options are fewer, and more expensive. Once optimistic, the WHO has in the last 10 years downgraded its objectives and shifted its rhetoric from "eradication" to "control" (Najera, 2001).

NATURAL PRODUCTS AND MALARIA THERAPY

The urgency generated by plasmodial resistance to a growing number of pharmaceutical agents has accelerated malaria drug research over the last two decades, with a substantial amount of that effort devoted to natural products. A MEDLINE search for articles published during just the last 5 years located several hundred dealing specifically with anti-plasmodial plants. (Research on insecticides based on natural products, an important corollary to this work, is not addressed in the present paper.) These publications range across studies of single species, groups of plants from indigenous pharmacopoeias, isolated constituents, reversal of drug-resistance and influence on anti-malarial pharmaceutical agents. These articles published in the last 12 months are representative:

1. single species: crude extracts of *Uvaria klaineana* Engler and Diel (Annonaceae) are active against chloroquine-resistant *P. falciparum* (Akendengue *et al.* 2002); extracts of *Solanum nudum* Dunal (Solan-

aceae) have anti-falciparum activity (Pabon *et al.* 2002);

2. indigenous anti-pyretics: thirteen species from the islands of São Tomé and Príncipe (Gulf of Guinea, off the west coast of Africa) show strong *in vitro* anti-falciparum activity, including against both hepatic and erythrocyte forms, and several species are effective *in vivo* against murine *P. berghei* (do Ceu de Madureira *et al.* 2002); various combinations of these Mali plant substances act synergistically against malaria: *Mitragyna inermis* (Willd.) *O. Kuntze* (Rubiaceae), *Nauclea latifolia* (Sm.) (Rubiaceae), *Guiera senegalensis* (Gmel.) (Combretaceae) and *Feretia apodanthera* (Del.) (Rubiaceae; Azas *et al.* 2002);

3. constituents: the alkaloids febrifugine-1 and isofebrifugine-2 from the root of *Dichroa febrifuga* Lour. have strong activity against *P. falciparum* (Kikuchi *et al.* 2002); dioncophylline E, the novel naphthylisoquinoline alkaloid from *Dioncophyllum thollonii* (Dioncophyllaceae), is active against chloroquine-sensitive and -resistant *P. falciparum* (Bringmann *et al.* 2002);

4. reversal of drug-resistance: the monoindole alkaloids isoretuline and icajine from *Strychnos* spp. (Loganiaceae) reverse chloroquine resistance (Frederich *et al.* 2001); artemisinin from *Artemisia annua* L. (Asteraceae) reverses chloroquine resistance (Pradines *et al.* 2001);

5. influence on anti-malarial pharmaceutical agents: the monoindole alkaloid icajine from *Strychnos* spp. acts synergistically with mefloquine (Frederich *et al.* 2001); artemisinin from *A. annua* acts synergistically both with anti-malarial pharmaceutical agents (e.g. mefloquine) and with other plant-derived anti-malarial substances (e.g. quinine from *Cinchona* spp. (Rubiaceae); Gupta *et al.* 2002; Nosten & Brasseur, 2002).

Although many of these studies are based on plants identified in indigenous pharmacopoeias, they provide only minimal ethnographic depth. Typically, the findings are presented as decontextualized catalogues of plants and lists of phytoconstituents. This information provides valuable baseline data, but disappoints from the standpoints of both practice and theory. Few of these studies offer insights into the experience of real people in specific cultural and eco-political settings; and none projects the findings against some higher level of abstraction.

To fill some of those gaps, the present paper draws attention to the larger context in which plant use occurs. Specifically, emphasis is given to how the use of plants in more than one application (principally as medicines and foods), and in particular ways (in combinations, in particular doses and sequences), can affect human health. Further, consideration is given to how the selection of medicinal plants has evolved over millennia as part of the larger human effort to mediate illness. The objective is to present co-evolution as a theoretical link to illuminate how medical cultures manage the relationships among humans, plants, herbivores and their respective pathogens. A theory-driven integrated research programme should take the place of "hit-and-miss" strategies for identifying new drugs. This issue is approached by introducing the anti-malarial plant *Artemisia annua,* in many ways a quintessential indigenous medicine: its history as a Chinese fever medicine is thousands of years old; its active principle and its derivatives produce the most rapid parasitological and clinical responses; it has the broadest stage specificity; it is non-toxic and active by all routes of administration; it potentiates pharmaceutical agents such as chloroquine and mefloquine; it is effective against multi-drug-resistant strains of malaria (Li & Wu, 1998; Balint, 2001; Christen & Veuthey, 2001; Gupta *et al.* 2002).

THE CHEMICAL BASIS OF ANTI-MALARIAL ACTION

Artemisia annua and Oxidation

My specific interest in A. *annua* lies in what has been called its unique mode of action, oxidation (for example, see Price, 2000). It will be argued that oxidation is not a novel bioactivity, and that mode of action will be put forward as the framework for the theoretical co-evolutionary model.

The active constituent in this plant is artemisinin, a compound distinguished by a dioxygen (endoperoxide) bridge that connects two parts of the C skeleton. Biochemically, then, artemisinin is an "oxidant." It kills plasmodia by shifting the intracellular redox balance to a more electro-positive mode. Redox refers to linked reduction and oxidation reactions in which reducing agents are H donors and oxidants are H acceptors.

The importance of oxidation for malaria is that erythrocytes depend on suppression of chemical equilibrium with O_2 at the same time that O_2 transport is their principal function. Increased, and not compensated, oxidation eventuates in cell damage, which releases immature parasite forms that cannot transfer the infection to new erythrocytes. Intra-erythrocytic oxidation may increase as a consequence of ordinary metabolic fluctuations, genetic anomalies and some foods and drugs. Oxidation also is increased by certain pathologies, including plasmodial infection. This situation is apparent in malaria-infected erythrocytes that contain up to five times the normal concentration of methaemoglobin, an oxidized form of haemoglobin. Additional evidence for oxidation during malaria infection includes elevated levels of the coenzymes NAD and NADP, and glutathione (oxidized form) relative to their reduced counterparts (NADH, reduced glutathione). Other signs of oxidation are lipid peroxidation, spontaneous generation of oxygen radical species and parasite appropriation of host superoxide dismutase. These indicators reflect intraerythrocytic oxidation of parasite origin and erythrocyte response, as well as activation of leucocyte defence (Etkin, 1997; Scott & Eaton, 1997; Schwartz *et al.* 1999; Kemp *et al.* 2002).

The oxidant action of artemisinin accelerates oxidative erythrocyte senescence and premature destruction, and release of immature parasites. Oxidation also affects the parasite directly through damage to membranes surrounding the nucleus, food vacuole, mitochondria and endoplasmic reticulum (Dhingra *et al.* 2000). The oxidizing effect of artemisinin finds analogues in pharmaceutical anti-malarial agents (e.g. primaquine, dapsone, divicine, alloxan, menadione) whose action is mediated by activated oxygen species such as H_2O_2, hydroxyl and superoxide radicals, and singlet oxygen.

Other Oxidizing Plants

The mode of action of several other plants with demonstrated anti-malarial activity is also attributed to constituents that promote erythrocyte oxidation. This partial list illustrates the botanical and ecological diversity of species that share this particular biochemical profile (Etkin, 1997): *Cyperus rotundus* L. (Cyperaceae), mixed auto-oxidation products of β-selinene; *Chenopodium ambrosioides* L. (Chenopodiaceae), ascaridole which is an endoperoxide; *Gossypium* spp. (Malvaceae), gossypol; *Bidens pilosa* L. (Asteraceae), phenylhepatrine; *Hypericum japonicum* (Guttiferae), japonicine A.

Research on northern Nigerian anti-malarial plant medicines and food species suggests that the efficacy of those plants in the prevention and treatment of malaria is attributed at least in part to oxidant action. Extracts of these species are particularly compelling (Etkin & Ross, 1997): *Acacia nilotica* Del. (Fabaceae); *Azadirachta indica* A. Juss (Meliaceae); *Cassia occidentalis* L. (Fabaceae); *C. tora* L. (Fabaceae); *Guiera senegalensis* JF Gmel (Combretaceae).

Oxidants have been identified and chemically characterized in other plants, e.g. *Allium cepa* L. (Liliaceae), *Cinnamomum verum* J. Presl. (Lauraceae), *Myristica fragrans* Houtt. (Myristicaceae), *Ocimum basilicum* (Lamiaceae), *Syzygium aromaticum* Merr. & Perry (Myrtaceae). Although anti-malarial activity has not been reported for these species, they all play a prominent role in the medicines and cuisines of diverse human cultures. No doubt other oxidant plant substances can be identified as well, and all fit the comprehensive model developed herein for oxidant anti-malarial substances.

Drug–Food Synergy

Populations are exposed to plant substances not only in medicine, but also in other contexts, most prominently in the diet. There is great potential for both synergy and antagonism in the interactions among drugs and foods. Vitamins A and E, which occur widely in nature, are powerful antioxidants. In that way they antagonize oxidant anti-malarial drugs and contribute to higher parasite counts in malaria infection. Conversely, deficiencies of vitamins A and E protect against fulminant infection. Riboflavin and Se deficiencies also contribute to oxidation and suppress human and animal malarias. As transition metals, Fe and Cu can mediate the production of free radicals; foods high in those nutrients are potential oxidants with anti-plasmodial effects. Dietary Fe over-sufficiency is a proposed adaptation in some malaria-endemic areas, where high intake is linked to cultural practices such as fermenting beer in iron containers. Total body stores of Fe and Cu can be further affected by Zn, which itself is redox inactive, but it competes with Fe and Cu for binding sites and, thus, diminishes the risk of oxidant stress. The potential effects of Fe, Zn and other divalent cations are further mediated by phytates, tannins and other chelating agents that occur as ordinary constituents in foods, medicines and other non-food items (Levander & Ager, 1993; Greene, 1997; Adelekan & Thurnham, 1998; Akompong *et al.* 2000; Shankar, 2000).

The oxidant plants mentioned earlier include clove, nutmeg, cinnamon, basil and onion. As these aromatics are both common fever medicines in indigenous pharmacopoeias and important flavour principles, anti-malarial effects can be anticipated. The view that they are "merely" spices reflects a Western bias and may overlook the deliberate addition of these flavourings for their medicinal qualities.

Research on Hausa plants in northern Nigeria revealed substantial overlap and suggests that the seasonally-patterned use of oxidant plants in both food and medicine protects against fulminant malaria infection. Specifically, most of the Hausa plants that demonstrate oxidant and anti-malarial activities are prominent in the diet during the highest malaria risk period (Etkin & Ross, 1997). Building on this principle, other researchers have recently begun to explore nutrient-based interventions as low-cost adjuncts to current methods of malaria prevention and treatment (Levander & Ager, 1993; Shankar, 2000).

COMPREHENSIVE CO-EVOLUTIONARY PERSPECTIVES

Discussion up to this point has established that plants offer substantial promise for the development of new anti-malarial substances, and that oxidation provides a cogent unifying principle for identifying candidate new drugs. Oxidation also provides focus for understanding how other uses of the same plants expand exposure to biodynamic activities. Food plants are especially important as they tend to be consumed in larger volume and regularly. Other plant uses (cosmetics, hygiene, dyes and craft manufacture) also afford contact with constituents that have pharmaco-dynamic potential.

From a human-centered, or even animal-centered, perspective, it might seem paradoxical that plants generate oxidants. After all, oxidants are detrimental to most life forms. It might also seem curious that taxonomically-diverse plants share this chemical signature. However, in a broad co-evolutionary model we can understand the production of these metabolites as protective; e.g. some oxidants act as toxins and anti-feeding agents to discourage insects and herbivores, others are anti-microbial and protect against plant pathogens and other oxidant compounds are allelo-chemicals that suppress the growth of competing plants (Howe & Westley, 1988; Harborne, 1993). In these ways the anti-malarial action of oxidant plants is an artifact of broad-spectrum botanical defence systems. (These relationships are not unidirectional or otherwise simple, most are multitrophic (Dicke, 2000). While one species produces anti-feeding agents and allelo-chemicals, other plants and animals evolve mechanisms of chemo-detection, neutralization and detoxification. Still other organisms have saved themselves the energy required to maintain elaborate chemo-defences by evolving the visual or other organoleptic appearance of the defensive species.)

In the larger scheme it makes sense that humans have learned to take advantage of such chemo-defensive phenomena for their own purposes. The conventional view of agriculture is that the domestication of plants focused not only on greater yield and ease of harvesting, but also on palatability and diminished toxicity, so that contemporary food cultivars are mere chemical shadows of their wild counterparts. Recent research illustrates that this is not the case, even the most common foods have great potential to influence health beyond the standard nutrient measures of vitamins, protein etc. (for example, see Johns, 1996; Prendergast *et al.* 1998; Wildman, 2000).

ANTI-PLASMODIAL OXIDANT GENOTYPES

Discussions of the pharmaco-dynamics of drug and food plants typically ignore human biological variability, resonating a biomedical paradigm that projects a generic human biology. Stepping outside that template, the model will be expanded once more by noting that elevated erythrocyte oxidation not only explains how some anti-malarial plants, foods and pharmaceutical agents "work," but also the adaptive importance of several malaria-protective genotypes. These erythrocyte anomalies are classic examples of Darwinian evolution, occurring in high frequency in populations who have experienced considerable selective pressure from malaria. While the distribution of these polymorphisms is familiar terrain in anthropology and human genetics, their shared mode of anti-malarial action is not widely appreciated. The following discussion juxtaposes these inherited aspects of malaria protection to the human management of oxidant plants.

Glucose-6-Phosphate Dehydrogenase Deficiency

Glucose-6-phosphate dehydrogenase (G6PD) deficiency is biochemically the best characterized of the malaria-protective genotypes. It is inherited as an X-linked recessive gene (tens of alleles are known and are characterized by similar phenotypes that vary primarily in the extent to which enzyme activity is diminished). As G6PD is the first, thus rate-limiting, enzyme of the pentose phosphate pathway, low enzyme activity results in cells that cannot adequately respond to oxidant stress. In the presence of malaria infection the integrity of G6PD-deficient erythrocytes is compromised and parasite development is interrupted. Drug-induced erythrocyte destruction in the more severe G6PD variants was linked first to anti-malarial agents such as primaquine, and has since been expanded to embrace oxidant-generating drugs generally. Medicinal and food plants also have been implicated in oxidant erythrocyte destruction and the anaemia that accompanies it (Greene & Danubio, 1997; Ruwende & Hill, 1998).

Where G6PD is relatively common, this association between consumption of certain plants and anaemia has been assimilated into local explanatory models. This knowledge allows us to pose interesting questions regarding the cultural construction of G6PD deficiency, malaria and its treatment. For example, since the earliest recorded history Mediterranean variants of G6PD deficiency have been linked to "favism," a severe haemolytic reaction to oxidants in fava beans (*Vicia fava* L., Fabaceae). In some populations food taboos prohibit G6PD-deficient individuals from eating fava beans because of their association with anaemia. Similarly, for high-risk groups like children, fava beans are prepared by removing the seed coat, which contains the highest concentration of oxidants. Fava beans are also used medicinally; the malaria-protective effects of G6PD deficiency can be potentiated by fava consumption, and for G6PD-normal individuals the cultivation of fava beans is deliberately configured so that consumption coincides with periods of peak malaria risk. In this way both enzyme-deficient and enzyme-normal individuals are afforded protection through increased erythrocyte oxidation due to ingestion of fava beans. Oxidant plants recognized in other cultures where G6PD deficiencies occur are also subject to customs that govern who can or cannot use that species, how it should be harvested and prepared, and the timing of consumption. In another cultural spin some Chinese populations divide medicinal plants into cold or yin oxidant species and hot or yang antioxidants (Lin *et al.* 1995). In both the Mediterranean and Chinese examples cultural dicta have a bearing on the biophysiology of both G6PD deficiency and the various plants that interact with it.

Haemoglobinopathies and Other Inherited Protections

Several haemoglobin disorders also occur as malaria-protective balanced polymorphisms. Haemoglobins S (sickle cell), C and E are inherited as autosomal recessive structural abnormalities, each allele coding for a single amino acid substitution in the β chain of the haemoglobin protein. The α- and β-thalassemias are also autosomal recessive traits, the result of underproduction of either α or β haemoglobin chains respectively. In each case, like G6PD deficiency, the selective advantage lies with the heterozygous individual who is pro-

tected against fulminant malaria infection and has no, or fewer, clinical signs associated with the disorder. The anti-malarial effects of these erythrocyte anomalies also are explained by elevated intra-erythrocytic oxidation in infected cells, evidenced by high concentrations of methaemoglobin, NAD, NADP and the oxidized form of glutathione relative to their reduced counterparts (haemoglobin, NADH, NADH and reduced glutathione), lipid peroxidation and the presence of oxygen radical species. As in the case of G6PD deficiency, increased oxidation interferes with parasite development and survival, accelerates infected erythrocyte clearance by phagocytosis and may impede parasite entry into the erythrocyte (Chan *et al.* 1999; Destro-Bisol *et al.* 1999; Tesoriere *et al.* 2001).

CONCLUSION: CO-EVOLUTION, GENETIC AND CULTURAL ADAPTATIONS

The erythrocyte abnormalities discussed earlier represent the most expensive mode of adaptation, in which protection is conferred on a particular genotype. Conversely, the cultural management of medicines and foods is less expensive in the sense that it is not genetically "hard-wired" but changeable and reversible within one lifetime. Culture affords us considerably more flexibility in achieving therapeutic and preventive objectives. In the case of managing oxidant medicines and foods, human cultures have refined the biological templates represented by G6PD deficiency and the malaria-protective haemoglobinopathies. In eventually developing pharmaceutical agents such as primaquine, humans duplicated the folk therapeutic models based in oxidant plants, which are themselves molecular mimics of the genetic adaptations.

In the scientific literature oxidation is typically portrayed as detrimental; for example, its roles in carcinogenesis and cardiovascular disease are emphasized. This knowledge has been transposed in abbreviated form to the lay public, many of whom know they want antioxidants, although they are not sure why. Various lines of inquiry that converge to demonstrate the benefit of oxidation in malaria prevention and therapy have been presented. The characterization of oxidants, their basis in the chemical defences of plants and their interaction with malaria offers insights into the complexity of malaria prevention and cure.

This discussion offers a theoretical perspective for understanding how medical cultures mediate the intersection of co-evolutionary modes that involve humans, plants, herbivores and all their respective pathogens. Ultimately, this perception allows us to appreciate that human adaptation to malaria is complex and profoundly biocultural. On the practical side this insight suggests a paradigmatic shift in the way that plants can be evaluated for anti-malarial potential. On a more abstract level, following the theme of oxidation, we see continuity in the face of a shifting dynamic of biology and culture, stretching back as far as the Neolithic period.

REFERENCES

Adelekan DA & Thurnham DI (1998) Glutathione peroxidase (*EC* 1.11.1.9) and superoxide dismutase (*EC* 1.15.1.1) activities in riboflavin-deficient rats infected with *Plasmodium berghei* malaria. *British Journal of Nutrition* 79, 305–309.

Akendengue B, Ngou-Milama E, Roblot F, Laurens A, Hocqquemiller R, Grellier P & Frappier F (2002) Antiplasmodial activity of *Uvaria klaineana*. *Planta Medica* 68, 167–169.

Akompong T, Ghori N & Haldar K (2000) In vitro activity of riboflavin against the human malaria parasite *Plasmodium falciparum*. *Antimicrobial Agents and Chemotherapy* 44, 88–96.

Azas N, Laurencin N, Delmas F, Di GC, Gasquet M, Laget M & Timon-David P (2002) Synergistic in vitro antimalarial activity of plant extracts used as traditional herbal remedies in Mali. *Parasitological Research* 88, 165–171.

Balint GA (2001) Antemisinin and its derivatives: an important new class of antimalarial agents. *Pharmacology and Therapeutics* 90, 261–265.

Bringmann G, Messer K, Wolf K, Muhlbacher J, Grune M, Brun R & Louis AM (2002) Dioncophylline E from *Dioncophyllum thollonii*, the first 7,3-coupled dioncophyllaceous naphthylisoquinoline alkaloid. *Phytochemistry* 60, 389–397.

Chan AC, Chow CK & Chiu D (1999) Interaction of antioxidants and their implication in genetic anemia. *Proceedings of the Society for Experimental Biology and Medicine* 222, 274–282.

Christen P & Veuthey JL (2001) New trends in extraction, identification and quantification of artemisinin and its derivatives. *Current Medicinal Chemistry* 15, 1827–1839.

Destro-Bisol G, D'Aloja E, Spedini G, Scatena R, Giardina B & Pascali V (1999) Brief communication: resistance to Falciparum malaria in α-thalassemia, oxidative stress, and hemoglobin oxidation. *American Journal of Physical Anthropology* 109, 269–273.

Dhingra V, Rao KV & Narasu ML (2000) Current status of artemisinin and its derivatives as antimalarial drugs. *Life Sciences* 66, 279–300.

Dicke M (2000) Chemical ecology of host–plant selection by herbivorous arthropods: a multitrophic perspective. *Biochemical Systematics and Ecology* 28, 601–617.

do Ceu de Madureira M, Paula Martins A, Gomes M, Paiva J, Proenca da Cunha A & Rosario V (2002) Antimalarial activity of medicinal plants used in traditional medicine in S. Tome and Principe Islands. *Journal of Ethnopharmacology* 81, 23–29.

Etkin NL (1997) Plants as antimalarial drugs: relation to G6PD deficiency and evolutionary implications. In *Adaptation to Malaria: The Interaction of Biology and Culture*, pp. 139–176 [LS Greene and ME Danubio, editors]. New York: Gordon and Breach Publishers.

Etkin NL & Ross PJ (1997) Malaria, medicine and meals: a biobehavioral perspective. In *The Anthropology of Medicine*, 3rd ed., pp. 169–209 [L Romanucci-Ross, DE Moerman and LR Tancredi, editors]. New York: Praeger Publishers.

Frederich M, Hayette MP, Tits M, De Mol P & Angenot L (2001) Reversal of chloroquine and mefloquine resistance in *Plasmodium falciparum* by the two monoindole alkaloids, icajine and isoretuline. *Planta Medica* 67, 523–527.

Greene LS (1997) Modification of antimalarial action of oxidants in traditional cuisines and medicines by nutrients which influence erythrocyte redox status. In *Adaptation to Malaria: the Interaction of Biology and Culture*, pp. 139–176 [LS Greene and ME Danubio, editors]. New York: Gordon and Breach Publishers.

Greene LS & Danubio ME (editors) (1997) *Adaptation to Malaria: the Interaction of Biology and Culture*. New York: Gordon and Breach Publishers.

Gupta S, Thapar MM, Wernsdorfer WH & Bjorkman A (2002) In vitro interactions of artemisinin with atovaquone, quinine, and mefloquine against *Plasmodium falciparum*. *Antimicrobial Agents and Chemotherapy* 46, 1510–1515.

Harborne JB (1993) *Introduction to Ecological Biochemistry*, 4th ed. New York: Academic Press.

Hoffman SL, Subramanian GM, Collins FH & Venter JC (2002) Plasmodium, human and Anopheles genomics and malaria. *Nature* 415, 702–709.

Howe HF & LC Westley (1988) *Ecological Relationships of Plants and Animals.* New York: Oxford University Press.

Johns T (1996) *The Origins of Human Diet and Medicine.* Tucson, AZ: University of Arizona Press.

Kemp K, Akanmori BD, Adabayeri V, Goka BQ, Kurtzhals JA, Behr C & Hviid L (2002) Cytokine production and apoptosis among T cells from patients under treatment for *Plasmodium falciparum* malaria. *Clinical and Experimental Immunology* 127, 151–157.

Kikuchi H, Tasaka H, Hirai S, Takaya Y, Iwabuchi Y, Ooi H, Hatakeyama S, Kim HS, Watays Y & Oshima Y (2002) Potent antimalarial febrifugine analogues against the plasmodium malaria parasite. *Journal of Medicinal Chemistry* 45, 2563–2570.

Levander OA & Ager AL (1993) Malaria parasites and oxidant nutrients. *Parasitology* 107, S95–S106.

Li Y & Wu YL (1998) How Chinese scientists discovered quing-haosu (artemisinin) and developed its derivatives. What are the future perspectives? *Medecine Tropicale: Revue du Corps De Santé Colonial* 58, 9–12.

Lin WS, Chan WCL & Hew CS (1995) Superoxide and traditional Chinese medicines. *Journal of Ethnopharmacology* 48, 165–171.

Najera J (2001) Malaria control: achievements, problems and strategies. *Parassitologia* 43, 1–89.

Nosten F & Brasseur P (2002) Combination therapy for malaria: the way forward? *Drugs* 62, 1315–1329.

Pabon A, Carmona J, Maestre A, Camargo M & Blair S (2002) Inhibition of *P. falciparum* by steroids from *Solanum nudum. Phytotherapy Research* 16, 59–62.

Pradines B, Fusai T, Rogier C, Keundjian A, Sinou V, Merckx A, Mosnier J, Daries W, Torrentino M & Parzy D (2001) Prevention and treatment of malaria: in vitro evaluation of new compounds. *Annales Pharmaceutiques Francaise* 59, 319–323.

Prendergast HDV, Etkin NL, Harris DR & Houghton PJ (editors) (1998) *Plants for Food and Medicine. Proceedings of the Joint Conference of the Society for Economic Botany and the International Society for Ethnopharmacology, London.* London: Royal Botanic Garden.

Price RN (2000) Artemisinin drugs: novel antimalarial agents. *Expert Opinion on Investigational Drugs* 9, 1815–1827.

Rabinovich NR (2002) Are we there yet? The road to a malaria vaccine. *Western Journal of Medicine* 176, 82–84.

Ruwende C & Hill A (1998) Review: Glucose-6-phosphate dehydrogenase deficiency and malaria. *Journal of Molecular Medicine* 76, 581–588.

Schwartz E, Samuni A, Friedman I, Hempelmann E & Golenser J (1999) The role of superoxide dismutation in malaria parasites. *Inflammation* 23, 361–370.

Scott MD & Eaton JW (1997) Parasite-mediated progeria: a possible mechanism for antimalarial action of G-6-PD deficient erythrocytes. In *Adaptation to Malaria: the Interaction of Biology and Culture*, pp. 89–102 [LS Greene and ME Danubio, editors]. New York: Gordon and Breach Publishers.

Shankar AH (2000) Nutritional modulation of malaria morbidity and mortality. *Journal of Infectious Diseases* 182, S37–S52.

Taylor-Robinson AW (2002) A model of development of acquired immunity to malaria in humans living under endemic conditions. *Medical Hypotheses* 58, 148–156.

Tesoriere L, D'Arpa D, Buters D, Allegra M, Renda D, Maggio A, Bongiorno A & Livrea MA (2001) Oral supplements of vitamin E improve measures of oxidative stress in plasma and reduce oxidative damage to LDL and erythrocytes in beta-thalassemia intermedia patients. *Free Radical Research* 34, 529–540.

Warhurst DC (2002) Resistance to antifolates in *Plasmodium falciparum*, the causative agent of tropical malaria. *Science Progress* 85, 89–111.

Wildman EC (2000) *Handbook of Nutraceuticals and Functional Foods.* Boca Raton, FL: CRC Press.

14   THE VITAL ROLE OF THE SKIN IN HUMAN NATURAL HISTORY

Bruce A. Cohn

This selection presents a unifying theory to explain why the human skin is the way it is, in terms of hair, sweat glands, and color. These characteristics are very different between humans and other primates. According to Cohn, they allowed early hominids to exploit the savannah environment, with its warm temperatures and abundant sunshine. Plentiful sweat glands allow for highly efficient heat loss, favored further by generally small hair follicles and wispy short hairs that allow moisture to evaporate from the skin. At the same time, high melanin content in the dark skin of early hominids in Africa, while favoring heat absorption, played a crucial role in protecting against the damaging impacts of ultraviolet light, including burns and increased risk of infection, cancer, and immunosuppressive effects. In contrast, in Eurasia, light skin with little melanin evolved as an adaptation to the low exposure to ultraviolet light that would result in low vitamin D production if the skin were dark.

The evolutionary scenario relating to skin color, sweat glands, and body hair is linked to a second classic example of coevolution besides the malaria-protective anemias: the development of lactose tolerance in populations in which dairying was practiced over many generations (see selection 14; Kretchmer 1978), with a parallel in changes to the gene pool of domestic cattle in these same cultures (Beja-Pereira et al. 2003). The continued production of the enzyme lactase in the small intestine after childhood is a genetic adaptation that is relatively rare across the world's populations and unknown among other mammals. It allows for the absorption of the lactose in milk and also favors calcium absorption. Combined with light skin, it allowed humans to settle in geographical areas with little sunlight or vegetation without suffering from bone deficiencies. However, during the Industrial Revolution, when pollutants reduced the amount of sunlight yet further, rickets became a common disease of children. Current cultural practices limiting children's exposure to the sun seem to be causing new cases of the disease in the United States.

Questions to keep in mind

How is the distribution of sweat glands in humans different from that of other primates and other mammals?

Why are sweat glands so important to humans, and what happens if they do not function?

What are some properties and functions of hair, and how do the advantages of tiny hairs outweigh the loss of the benefits of large ones?

What are some of the dangers and benefits of sunlight, and how might climate change impact exposure and human health?

Why is it the genetic norm *not* to be able to digest milk after childhood? What might this suggest about the diet of most humans over time and around the world today?

Source: Cohn, B. A. 1998. "The Vital Role of the Skin in Human Natural History." *International Journal of Dermatology* 37(11):821–824. With permission from the publisher.

The role of the skin in human natural history has been crucial. Various imaginative beliefs have been presented to define this role, such as that hair loss represented a response to an existence in some primordial aquatic environment,[1] and that a main function of melanin was to act as a camouflage to protect against being seen by either predators or prey,[2,3] or to enhance heat absorption.[3,4] Rather, it seems likely that, in natural history, three features of human skin, namely diffuse thermoregulatory eccrine sweat glands, generalized loss of hair, and skin color, evolved as a functional complex to meet the challenges of the savanna mosaic of Africa in order to enable early hominids to survive.[5]

THE AFRICAN SAVANNA MOSAIC HABITAT

The spread of the savanna mosaic, following the fragmentation of the once continuous equatorial forests across central Africa, began in the middle Miocene. The savanna mosaic habitat is characterized by warm daytime temperatures, distinct seasons regulated by rainfall rather than by temperature, and a long dry season. Plants are often drought resistant, and vegetation is variable, patchily distributed, and includes low bushes and shrubs, gallery forests around lakes and rivers, and open grasslands. The varieties of trees are found in discontinuous stands or clumps. Unlike forests, savanna temperatures show substantial daily fluctuation and can be quite high during the day and during the dry season. Shade and humidity are less readily available than in forests.[6]

ECCRINE SWEATING

In most mammals, eccrine sweat glands are either absent or limited to the friction surfaces of the digital pads. In all primates, they are found on the palms and soles. In some New World monkeys, they occur on the ventral surface of the prehensile tail, and in African apes, on the knuckle pads.[7] Eccrine sweat in these sites permits the skin to be more supple for purposes such as walking, grasping, climbing, and tactile discrimination. In addition, a role for eccrine sweating in humans in the axillae, and possibly in the anogenital area, as a source to bathe and disperse apocrine sweat gland pheromones, has been postulated.[8]

The development of diffuse thermoregulatory eccrine sweat glands, however, was absolutely essential in natural history to allow the survival of early bipedal hominids as they left the habitat of the forests and woodlands of their ancestors to seek their sustenance in the hot days of the savanna mosaic environment of eastern and southern Africa some 3–4 million years ago.

The survival of these hominids in this new environment depended at least upon their ability to deal with the effects of heat from the sun, as well as from heat internally generated from muscular activity.[6] This eccrine sweating development to control against hyperthermia provided these early bipeds with the opportunity for long distance travel each day throughout the year under the hot sun and with the presence sometimes of the added burden of carrying extra weight such as babies and food.

Significant thermoregulation in humans is only possible because of the large number of eccrine sweat glands, more than 2 million, that are distributed over the entire body surface.[9] This heat regulatory function through evaporation is a critical channel available to the human body for maintaining body temperature within acceptable limits. Evaporation normally accounts for only about 25% of heat loss in humans.[10] When necessary, however, eccrine sweating can deliver up to about 2 L of water per hour to the skin surface for evaporation, and each gram of evaporated water can dissipate 0.585 cal into the air.[10] In 1 h, therefore, evaporation of eccrine sweat can carry off almost 1200 cal of heat from the skin. Survival each day in the hot savanna mosaic of Africa was dependent on the essential heat loss that could occur through the functioning of the diffuse eccrine sweat glands and in the taking in of sufficient water and salt to replenish that lost through sweating.

Human eccrine sweating is a much more effective method to dissipate heat than panting, which occurs when rapid and shallow respirations deliver water for evaporative heat loss. In a hot environment, a dog, even with maximum panting, needs to rest in the shade substantially more than does a human. A mouse may spread saliva over its skin, and an elephant may spray water over its skin with its trunk, but these are much less efficient methods of evaporative heat loss than that of human eccrine sweating.

Except for tree shrews, the prosimians and most of the New World monkeys lack eccrine glands throughout their hairy skin.[7] Old World monkeys and apes have eccrine glands in their hairy skin,[7] but thermoregulatory eccrine sweating approaching the significant quantities observed in humans may be present only in the African savanna-dwelling patas monkeys.[11,12] These monkeys are adapted for high-speed running. The apparent convergence in eccrine sweating of these two savanna-dwelling primates in natural history underscores the roles of both the environment and of the primate morphologic potential.

Because chimpanzee and gorilla eccrine glands do not contribute to significant thermoregulatory sweating, these apes are confined to a more restricted habitat than were early hominids. Studies on chimpanzees living in the Mt. Asserik region of Senegal have demonstrated this obstacle to mobility.[13,14] The region consists of gallery forest, woodland, bamboo and grassland, and short grass plateau. During the wet season, these chimpanzees move through the grasslands. In the early dry season, they eat several types of seeds in the woodland areas, and in the dry season they are confined to the gallery forest. They travel freely therefore only during the wet season when water and food are abundant and air temperatures are tolerable. During the dry season, the chimpanzees are restricted to areas that have standing water and shade.

There are situations that demonstrate the incapacitating health consequences that can result from inadequate eccrine sweat gland functioning in humans. Eccrine sweat glands do not develop at all, or are sparse or rudimentary, in hereditary anhidrotic (hypohidrotic) ectodermal dysplasia. Tropical anhidrotic asthenia, due to the ductal occlusion of miliaria profunda, has occurred in military troops in the tropics after they have been subjected to a large stimulus to sweat for a prolonged time. In this situation, the overstimulated eccrine sweat glands are prevented from delivering a sufficient volume of sweat to the skin surface for adequate evaporative heat loss. In both of these conditions, hyperthermia can easily occur in a hot environment, especially if there is physical exertion, with resultant fatigue, weakness, collapse, and potentially death.

HAIR LOSS

Hair, with its many important functions, is a unique feature of mammals. Hair assists in retaining heat in a cold climate and in keeping out heat in a hot environment. It protects the body against trauma and irritation, and against UV light damage from the sun. Hair has tactile and communicative functions, as in piloerection, signals in social display, and in fright or attack. Hair color may serve as a visual camouflage. In nonhuman primates, hair provides the means for young to cling to with prehensile hands and feet while being transported about by their mothers. Because hair serves so many functions, its generalized loss in early hominids in the African savanna mosaic must have had important survival value.[6]

The reduction of hair cover in these early hominids probably occurred as a secondary development to eccrine sweat gland functioning.[5] Although ape hair is relatively sparse compared with that of other primates, when compared with that of humans the hair shafts are quite prominent. In humans, much of the hair is miniaturized so that the skin appears to be naked. There are, nevertheless, about 60 hairs/cm^2 on much of the human naked skin.[9] Most of these hairs are very small and nonpigmented. The human situation is not so much a loss in the number of hairs that an individual possesses as a reduction in the size of most hair follicles, with resultant tiny hairs.

Hair reduction enhanced the effectiveness of these early hominids' temperature regulation through sweating evaporative heat loss.[6] Water, as it goes from the liquid phase into the gaseous phase, carries heat into the atmosphere. Water molecules evaporate from the human naked skin and hairy surfaces. The nonhairy skin creates no significant barrier to evaporation, whereas the presence of prominent hairs significantly reduces the rate of evaporative heat loss. After submergence in water, naked human skin dries faster than does the hairy scalp.

The reduction of all body hair was not necessary to achieve an effective heat regulatory mechanism. There are specific sites of significant human hair retention.[8] Humans can have much hair on the scalp, which is important in preventing too-direct UV light damage, and also the scalp hair may assist in stabilizing the temperature of the brain.

The hair retention in the axillae and anogenital area may be involved in apocrine sweat gland pheromonal functioning. The eyebrows and the lashes may prevent foreign materials and sweat from getting into the eyes. The male beard and some of the male body hair might only be assumed to have the social role of emphasizing the difference between the sexes. Human populations are variable in the amount of body hair present, but in all of them the skin surface is still hairless enough to permit efficient heat loss from eccrine sweating.[6]

The ability of these early hominids to forage during the day and throughout the year in the African savanna mosaic depended upon their capacity to lose excess body heat. The benefit of effective eccrine sweating through hair reduction in order to offset the heat of the day must have outweighed the need to retain hair for enhancing warmth during the cool African nights.[6]

SKIN COLOR AND VITAMIN D

The presence of dark skin was needed in the savanna mosaic of Africa in the early times of human natural history to protect these hominids from damaging UV light as they began to seek survival in their unique way under the sun.[15] Although various differences have been found to be present between dark and light skin,[16] dark skin must have been selected throughout the world in human natural history whenever populations were exposed to significant UV light.[6]

The melanin pigment in the skin provides significant protection against the damaging effects of UV light.[15] Acute sun exposure to light skin can be fierce, with resultant intense redness, swelling, and blistering, which can be incapacitating. Any denuded skin that results from a sunburn can increase the susceptibility to a variety of infections. UV light from sun exposure is a major cause of both squamous cell and basal cell carcinomas, and seems to contribute to the production of some melanomas. In addition, UV light can have immunosuppressive effects.

In the most recent Ice Age in northern Eurasia, light skin evolved simply because it was needed to increase vitamin D production in the skin.[17] This, in turn, led to increased internal formation of the active vitamin D that was needed to permit the presence of adequate calcium in the circulation for the purpose of making stronger bones. Individuals with light skin form more vitamin D from a given amount of UV light than do individuals with darker skin.[18]

This glaciation often presented with such cold temperatures that northern Eurasian humans usually had to be fully and heavily clothed. These Ice Age humans therefore had to maximize their ability to produce vitamin D in their skin in a setting in which UVB exposure often was limited to a small amount of uncovered skin, such as the face.[17]

In past times, there must have been human populations that could not receive adequate amounts of vitamin D in their diet. If they lived in areas of abundant UVB exposure, they would have been able to form sufficient vitamin D even with the darkest skin. On the other hand, if populations were deficient in vitamin D in their diet, and lived in areas where UVB exposure was less, light skin could have compensated for this dietary deficiency.[6] In the environment of the higher latitudes, with less UVB available, light skin had a distinct advantage.[17]

Because dark skin may absorb more heat than light skin, the belief has been presented that dark skin was an adaptation to increase heat absorption in the early hominids.[3,4] On the contrary, diffuse thermoregulatory eccrine sweat glands, with accompanying hair loss, evolved in order to enable the dissipation of the large heat load to which these early hominids were continually being presented as they were adapting to spend a significant amount of time under the hot African sun.

Solely from the point of view of heat absorption, therefore, dark skin was a theoretical disadvantage in the hot ancient African days in the savanna mosaic, but would have been a theoretical advantage in the very few warm northern Eurasian Ice Age days. The protective function against UV that caused dark skin to be the situation in Africa, and the increased vitamin D production that caused light skin to be the situation in northern Eurasia, however, were much more important survival needs than anything related to the relative heat absorbing properties of the different shades of skin.

Therefore, in spite of the heat and UV light in the African savanna mosaic, this new environment offered substantial opportunities to the naked and uncamouflaged hominids to exploit the sometimes widely scattered available resources. The adaptive response of the skin in allowing these hominids to leave the forests and woodlands of their ancestors and to be able to accomplish this exploitation and survive in this new environment was crucial.

The amount of skin pigmentation among populations may have shifted several times during the course of human natural history in response to changes in latitude, diet, body covering, and shelter. The variations in skin pigmentation among populations may have occurred relatively quickly, in a few thousand years or less.[8]

THE PARALLEL DEVELOPMENT OF LACTOSE TOLERANCE

In the most recent Ice Age of northern Europe, it was the development of lactose tolerance, as well as the creation of light skin, that helped to allow the presence of adequate calcium in the body to prevent the occurrence of weak bones. Modern northern Europeans are the only major group of people in which most of the population is lactose tolerant into adulthood, this situation being due to the persistence into adulthood of a significant quantity of the enzyme lactase in the small intestine. This enzyme is needed to hydrolyze the ingested lactose into the absorbable glucose and galactose. In most other people, and in all land mammals, lactase is only significantly present in childhood, in which it serves the essential purpose of allowing the intake of milk as a major source of calcium during the nursing of the young. In addition, the presence of lactose in the small intestine increases calcium absorption.[19] These Ice Age northern Europeans must have had a continual supply of milk from dairying to ingest in adulthood.

SOME PERSPECTIVES FOR THE NEW MILLENNIUM

At this time, there is the belief that ozone depletion, with its human contributory factors, has permitted an increase in UVB exposure in the southern and northern latitudes. In spite of this, human action to eliminate these factors has been lacking in universal support, even though the adverse effects of the increased UVB exposure are well known.

There has also been a diminution of UVB exposure from human causes, with resultant significant adverse consequences. This happened in the Industrial Revolution in England, Scotland, and Wales, in which there was so much burning of coal in many of the cities that the skies became continuously clouded by soot. The resultant decrease in UVB reaching the Earth's surface caused rickets to become prevalent among the children of these cities.

A little more than a century ago, Theobald Palm, a physician who had practiced medicine extensively in Japan for more than 9 years without having seen more than a few cases of rickets, requested the observations of several physicians in various nonindustrialized countries as to the incidence of rickets in those countries.[20]

Once he had obtained this information, which attested to the rarity of rickets in nonindustrialized countries, he was able to reason that it was solely the lack of adequate sunlight exposure that had caused rickets to be frequent in British cities. His deduction to allow adequate sunlight exposure led to the saving of many lives. His recommendation that urban and generally poor rachitic children should be routinely transferred out of the cities for sunshine exposure was a model of social responsibility for future generations.

The burning of coal in the Industrial Revolution, in addition to the production of soot, emitted heat-trapping carbon dioxide into the atmosphere. It was this activity that started the significant human contribution to the intensification of the natural greenhouse effect, and therefore to all of the perils of global warming.

The Industrial Revolution was extraordinary in initiating with unparalleled force human interaction with the environment. The technological achievements from that time have set the stage for the vast, but still unpredictable, accomplishments that are expected to be a major feature of the new millennium.

How *Homo sapiens* will handle the challenges of balancing the vast technological potential with the much needed respect and preservation of nature remains for time to tell.

NOTES

1. Morgan E. *The Aquatic Ape.* New York: Stein and Day, 1982.

2. Cowles RB. Some ecological factors bearing on the origin and evolution of pigment in the human skin. *Am Nat* 1959; 93: 283–293.

3. Morison WL. What is the function of melanin? *Arch Dermatol* 1985; 121: 1160–1163.

4. Hamilton WJ III, Heppner F. Radiant solar energy and the function of black homeotherm pigmentation: an hypothesis. *Science* 1967; 155: 196–197.

5. Zihlman AL, Cohn BA. Response of human skin to the savanna. *S Afr J Sci* 1986; 82: 89–90.

6. Zihlman AL, Cohn BA. The adaptive response of human skin to the savanna. *Hum Evol* 1988; 3: 397–409.

7. Montagna W. The skin of nonhuman primates. *Am Zool* 1972; 12: 109–124.

8. Cohn BA. In search of human skin pheromones. *Arch Dermatol* 1994; 130: 1048–1051.

9. Szabo G. The regional anatomy of the human integument with special reference to the distribution of hair follicles, sweat glands and melanocytes. *Philos Trans R Soc Lond B Biol Sci* 1967; 252: 447–485.

10. Kuno Y. *Human Perspiration.* Springfield, IL: Thomas, 1956: 23, 340.

11. Mahoney SA. Cost of locomotion and heat balance during rest and running from 0 to 55°C in a patas monkey. *J Appl Physiol* 1980; 49: 789–800.

12. Gisolfi CV, Sato K, Wall PT, Sato F. In vivo and in vitro characteristics of eccrine sweating in patas and rhesus monkeys. *J Appl Physiol* 1982; 53: 425–431.

13. McGrew WC, Baldwin PJ, Tutin CEG. Chimpanzees in a hot, dry and open habitat; Mt. Asserik, Senegal, West Africa. *J Hum Evol* 1981; 10: 227–244.

14. Baldwin PJ, McGrew WC, Tutin CEG. Wide-ranging chimpanzees at Mt. Asserik, Senegal. *Int J Primatol* 1982; 3: 367–385.

15. Cohn BA. The significance of dark skin in photoprotection. *J Am Acad Dermatol* 1992; 26: 281–282.

16. Berardesca E, Maibach H. Racial differences in skin pathophysiology. *J Am Acad Dermatol* 1996; 34: 667–672.

17. Cohn BA. The effect of the ice age on skin color. *Arch Dermatol* 1991; 127: 1586–1587.

18. Clemens TL, Henderson SL, Adams JS, Holick MF. Increased skin pigment reduces the capacity of skin to synthesize vitamin D$_3$. *Lancet* 1982; 1: 74–76.

19. Schuette SA, Knowles JB, Ford HE. Effect of lactose or its component sugars on jejunal calcium absorption in adult man. *Am J Clin Nutr* 1989; 50: 1084–1087.

20. Palm TA. The geographical distribution and aetiology of rickets. *Practitioner* 1890; 45: 270–279, 321–342.

■ ■ ■ ■ ■ ■ ■ ■ ■

15 WHY GENES DON'T COUNT (FOR RACIAL DIFFERENCES IN HEALTH)

Alan H. Goodman

The previous three selections have provided illustrations of human plasticity and variation. The current selection explains why this variation cannot be captured by racial categories, which have little power to explain disease differences across individuals and groups. Goodman does not deny the existence of human biological variation, but shows that the way to think about differences is not to try to make them fit into unscientific, static typologies that are at complete odds with the complex, changing nature of human variation and with evolutionary theory itself. Race does not represent biological reality, but is a real cultural construct. Its social and politico-economic utility is what keeps the concept alive in the face of contrary theory and evidence. In short, the true threats to human health are not race-based differences in susceptibility, but racialization (through differential access to social, economic, and health resources) and the experience of racism.

Source: Goodman, A. 2000. "Why Genes Don't Count (for Racial Differences in Health)." *American Journal of Public Health* 90(11):1699–1702. © The American Public Health Association. With permission from the publisher.

One of the main characteristics of biological variation is nonconcordance; that is, most genetic traits are inherited independently. Using the examples of sickle cell anemia (see selection 13) and lactose intolerance (see selection 14), Goodman illustrates how groups united by high frequencies of the alleles for these conditions do not fit established racial categories. For example, Eastern and Southern Africans, Southern Europeans, Japanese, and Native Americans have high frequencies of lactase deficiency. Nonconcordance, together with other characteristics of biological variation, makes it impossible to devise or use with any degree of precision a consistent classificatory scheme, especially one based on external appearance. As a scientific tool in health research, race is inadequate because there is little agreement about what it means. For some it may be a proxy for genes; for others it may be a way to put people into groups to assess the effects of racism.

Goodman analyzes the high rates of non-insulin-dependent diabetes among Native North Americans to illustrate how race can confuse scientific research and social action to prevent or treat disease. The hypothesis of a race-based metabolic syndrome often overrides evidence of great variability within the category of Native North Americans and the fact that the same phenomenon has been observed in nearly every population to undergo a similar lifestyle transition (see selections 42 and 43). Moreover, the devotion of scientific resources to a search for the "genes for" a complex and multifactorial syndrome unlikely to be explained in terms of genes alone, much less single ones, leads people to resign themselves to their presumed genetic destiny. It diverts attention away from the large role of changeable lifestyles as causes of disease and clues to prevention and treatment.

Questions to keep in mind

How do the previous three selections illustrate Goodman's point that race is not a useful way to characterize human biological variation?

In what ways does the concept of race conflict with evolutionary theory?

How does the idea that racial differences in disease are due to genetic variation between races fail both in theory and practice?

What are some ways that racialization and the experience of racism may affect health and disease?

In 1973, I took a course titled "Introduction to Physical Anthropology" with Professor George Armelagos. In the course, he taught that "race" was once a core worldview in anthropology and that it had spread to other sciences and practices such as medicine and public health. Natural historians in the 18th and 19th centuries thought in terms of idealized and unchanging types of objects, including human beings. The big question of the time concerned the degree and significance of racial differences. The church's monogenetic position held that the "races" were created together as a species with clear subspecies. Men of science such as Philadelphia physician George Morton and Cambridge natural historian Louis Agassiz supported a polygenetic position, asserting that the races were separately created species.

Professor Armelagos explained that human biological variation is continuous, complex, and ever changing. As a static and typological concept, race is inherently unable to explain the complex and changing structure of human biological variation. As in the decennial census, individuals will always fail to fit neatly into racial boxes. Moreover, the placement of an individual in a given box says little about his or her biology: the racial mean is meaningless. To begin to comprehend the human biological variation, one needed an evolutionary theory that focused on gradual change and populations rather than on race. Professor Armelagos went on to say that although race is still real, it is not biologically based; rather, it is social with biological consequences.

Students' responses ranged from disbelief to transformation. After having long assumed the biological basis of race, many in the room could not accept his claims. Others misunderstood his message, thinking he was denying the reality of biological variation itself. Still others were transformed forever by this new idea.

I recollect that it made almost instant sense to me that human races are social constructions. Although I saw Professor Armelagos as a White man, his birth certificate stated that he was Greek. I had grown up in a working-class family in a town composed mostly of second-generation immigrants from Italy and Ireland, and as a boy I was aware of being perceived as Jewish and different from my Irish and Italian friends in some fundamental way. Yet when I began attending a more diverse university, something striking happened: I became "White." I was no longer perceived as very distinct from other students of European descent. It was then that I learned about the fluidity of race and how social and political–economic processes were constantly changing color lines.

Professor Armelagos hinted at a powerful lesson: that scientific ideas can endure and be made to seem real if they have social and political–economic utility. An evolutionary framework that explained human variation had been established for more than a century, ever since the publication of Darwin's *Origin of Species*.[1] In the 1940s, Montagu used the "new evolutionary synthesis" to explain clearly why race was a biological myth.[2,3] Yet the idea of race as biology persists today in science and society.[4]

I was aware of the power of race as a worldview in 1973. But what I understood less was the idea's ability to persist after it had been proven unscientific. If I had been asked in the 1970s whether race would survive as a way to think about human biological variation in 2000, I would have answered emphatically, "No!" I was naive to the durability of an economically useful idea.

Acceptance of the notion of race-as-biology declined in anthropology throughout the late 1970s and early 1980s.[5,6] Yet, during the past decade, racialized notions of biology have made a comeback.[4,7] This is especially true in human genetics, a field that, paradoxically, once drove the last nail into the coffin of race-as-biology.

In this commentary, I explain why race should not be used as a proxy for genetic or biological variation. I then explain and illustrate the 2 unfounded assumptions that are needed for an acceptance that racial differences in disease are due to genetic differences among races.

THE MYTH OF RACE AS BIOLOGY

The first of 6 reasons why race is an inadequate and even harmful way to think about human biological differences is based on the history and theoretical underpinnings of the idea of race. The next 3 have to do with the structure of human biological variation. The last 2 pertain to the use of race in practice.

1. *The concept of race is based on the idea of fixed, ideal, and unchanging types.* Race was first a European folk concept from an era in which the world was seen as fixed and unchanging.[8,9] Such an idea, however, is completely incompatible with evolutionary theory. In response, some who still adhere to the concept of race might say that as it is now used in science, it is dynamic, flexible, and even evolutionary.[10,11] But the new race is the old race, typological and ideal. Like a chameleon changing its color to better hide in a chromatically different environment, race changes superficially to fit into a new intellectual environment.

2. *Human variation is continuous.* Allele frequencies tend to vary gradually. Therefore, there is no clear place to designate where one race begins and another ends. Skin color, for example, slowly changes from place to place. Templeton has shown that most human variation is explained by geographic distance[12]: individuals tend to be most similar to those who live nearby and least similar to those who live farthest away.

3. *Human variation is nonconcordant.* Traits tend to vary independently of other traits. Race classifications vary, therefore, by the traits used in the classification. A classification based on sickle cell trait might include equatorial Africans, Greeks, and Turks, while another based on lactase enzyme deficiency might include eastern and southern Africans along with southern Europeans, Japanese, and Native Americans. There is no possibility for consistency. Because skin color correlates with only a few other phenotypic traits such as hair and eye color, it is true that "race is only skin deep."

4. *Within-group genetic variation is much greater than variation among "races."* Starting with Lewontin,[13] studies have statistically apportioned variation in different genetic systems to different levels, among "races" and within "races" and smaller populations such as the Hopi, the Ainu, and the Irish.[14] Lewontin collected data on blood group polymorphisms in different groups and races.[13] He found that blood group variation among races statistically explained about 6% of the total variation.[13] The implication of Lewontin's results is that if one is to adopt a racial paradigm, one must acknowledge that race will statistically explain only a small proportion of variations. These variations are better explained by geographic distance.[12]

5. *There is no way to consistently classify by race.* Race is impossible to define in a stable and universal way because race-as-biology varies with place and time, and the socially determined color line is even more dynamic. A problem with race classification is that there is no agreed-upon "race scale" as there are hat and shoe size scales. Ideas about race are fluid and based on different phenotypic cues; the salient cues change over time, place, and circumstance. One study of infants who died in their first year showed that 37% of infants classified as Native American on their birth certificates were classified as some other race on their death certificates.[15] If race "changes" so quickly in less than a year, one can only imagine the degree of misclassification that could occur over decades and across regions.

6. *There is no clarity as to what race is and what it is not.* Other key methods of classification involve inconsistencies as well. For example, definitions of socioeconomic class vary widely. Although always imperfect, they begin to provide a glimpse of the underlying processes by which social and economic positions affect lived experiences and health. Race differs critically from other classification methods in the breadth of potential interpretations of the underlying processes. Some individuals view racial differences in disease as owing to genes, while others see race differences as the consequence of the lived experience of "racing"—the taxonomic practice of assigning individuals to races—and of racism. Obviously, this confusion has serious implications for theory and practice: One cannot practice predictive science on the basis of a changing and undefinable cause.

Probably none of these reasons is by itself sufficient to throw race onto the scrap heap of surpassed scientific ideas. But considered together, they clearly suggest that race-as-biology is obsolete. Just as we have moved beyond thinking that the sun revolves around the moon and that a fully-formed, tiny human lives in sperm, so too it is time to move beyond believing that race is a valid method for classifying human biological differences.

THE DOUBLE ERROR INHERENT IN GENETIC EXPLANATIONS OF RACIAL DIFFERENCES

Two errors—2 leaps of illogic—are necessary for acceptance of the idea that racial differences in disease are due to genetic differences among races. The first leap is a form of geneticization, the belief that most biology and behavior are located "in the genes."

Genes, of course, are often a part of the complex web of disease causality, but they are almost always a minor, unstable, and insufficient cause. The presence of Gm allotype, for example, might correlate to increased rates of diabetes in Native Americans,[16] but the causal link is unknown. In other cases, the gene is not expressed without some environmental context, and it may interact with environments and other genes in nonadditive and unpredictable ways.

The second necessary leap of illogic is a form of scientific racialism, the belief that races are real and useful constructs. Importantly, this leap propels one from explaining disease variation as caused by genetic variation to explaining that racial differences in disease are caused by genetic variation among races. To accept this logic, one needs to also accept that genetic variation occurs along racial divides: that is, most variation occurs among races. However, we know from Lewontin's work that this assumption is false for simple genetic systems.[13] For a disease of complex etiology, genetics is an illogical explanation for racial differences.

WHY RACE-AS-GENES FAILS IN PRACTICE

Scientifically, race-as-biology has been and is still used both as a means of identification and classification and as a means of explanation. As the former, it is often applied in the forensic sciences. As the latter, it requires the former and, depending on what is to be explained, may be used in many fields, including biological anthropology, exercise physiology, psychology, and public health.

Identification of humans from skeletal remains provides a clear example of the poor performance of a racial model of human variation.[4] The most widely referenced method for identifying race from the skeleton is Giles and Elliot's discriminant function for determining race from cranial remains.[17] In the original study of crania of individuals of known "race" and sex, Giles and Elliot were able to correctly classify about 85% of individuals as members of 1 of 3 races—Native American, White, or Black. This rate of correct racial classification is often cited in texts and popular articles.[18,19] However, in 4 retests of the method's ability to correctly classify Native Americans, the rate dropped to an average of approximately 33%.[4] In other words, the retest performance was about what one would expect by random assignment. Failure to extend the method to other times and places illustrates the nature of temporally and geographically changing color lines and biologies.

The attribution of racial differences in disease to genetic differences illustrates both geneticization and scientific racialism. For example, the rise in diabetes among some Native Americans is often thought to be caused by a genetic variation that separates Native Americans from European Americans.[17,20,21] Type II diabetes, along with obesity, gallstones, and heart disease, is part of what has been called "New World Syndrome."[21] The designation of a panracial syndrome may fix in one's mind the idea of homogeneity within race and the notion that the syndrome is innate.

Contemporary variation in diabetes rates among Native North American groups is tremendous, however, and the rise in diabetes rates is a relatively recent phenomenon.[22] Other groups experiencing shifts from complex carbohydrates to colas, from fast-moving foods to fast foods, and from exercise to underemployment have experienced very similar increases in diabetes rates. Rather than accept that diabetes is "in our blood," as articulated by the Pima,[23] it might be more productive to locate diabetes in changeable lifestyles.

FROM STUDIES OF RACE-AS-GENETICS TO STUDIES OF RACIALISM AND RACISM

As the 19th century turned into the 20th century, anthropology was united in viewing race as a powerful explanation for biology, culture, and behavior. As the 20th century turns to the 21st, anthropologists have begun to reach a consensus on the limits and significance of race. As is illustrated in the recently ratified American Anthropological Association statement on race, the new consensus maintains that

- Human biological variation should not be reduced to race. It is too complex and does not fit this outdated idea.
- Race is real. Rather than being based on biology, it is a social and political process that provides insights into how we read deeper meaning into phenotypes.
- Racialization and racism come about because, in a racialized culture, we read meaning into skin color and other phenotypic variants. Rather than biology affecting behavior, ideology and behavior affect individuals "under the skin."

The 20th century was a highly racialized century. All signs suggest that the 21st may be, too. A central confusion about race—one that is reflected in census debates and the use of census data—is that we use the concept differently. Although the Office of Management and Budget Directive 15 makes no claim that race is a scientific term or is biological in meaning, this disclaimer is hidden in the small type of an official document.

Until there are no racial distinctions in aspects of life such as access to employment and health care, a society that purports to be just, such as our own, needs to track racial differences and the political–economic consequences of a racial system. Professor Armelagos and others like him, extending back to Montagu, Franz Boas, W.E.B. Du Bois, and Frederick Douglass, paved the way toward rejecting race-as-biology. The symposium that follows will help us move beyond simply rejecting an outworn perspective and toward clarity about the ways in which being racialized and experiencing racism can affect health.

NOTES

1. Darwin C. *On the Origin of Species by Means of Natural Selection or the Preservation of Favored Races in the Struggle for Life.* London, England: John Murray; 1859.

2. Montagu MFA. The concept of race in the human species in light of genetics. *J Hered.* 1941; 32: 243–247.

3. Montagu MFA. *Man's Most Dangerous Myth: The Fallacy of Race.* New York, NY: Columbia University Press; 1942.

4. Goodman AH. Bred in the bone? *The Sciences.* March/April 1997:20–25.

5. Lieberman L, Stevenson BW, Reynolds LT. Race and anthropology: core concept without consensus. *Anthropol Educ Q.* 1989;20(2):67–73.

6. Barkan E. *The Retreat of Scientific Racism.* New York, NY: Cambridge University Press; 1992.

7. Goodman AH, Armelagos GJ. Race, racism and the new physical anthropology. In: Reynolds LT, Lieberman L, eds. *Race and Other Misadventures: Essays in Honor of Ashley Montagu in His Ninetieth Year.* Dix Hills, NY: General Hall Inc; 1996:174–186.

8. Smedley A. *Race in North America: Origin and Evolution of a World View.* 2nd ed. Boulder, Colo: Westview Press; 1999.

9. Stepan N. *The Idea of Race in Science: Great Britain, 1800–1960.* London, England: Macmillan Press; 1982.

10. Gill GW. A forensic anthropologist's view of the race concept. In: Abstracts of the 46th Annual Meeting of the American Academy of Forensic Sciences, 1996.

11. Brues AM. The objective view of race. In: Gordon CC, ed. *Race, Ethnicity and Applied Bioanthropology.* Richmond, Va: American Anthropological Association; 1993:74–78. NAPA bulletin 13.

12. Templeton A. Human races: a genetic and evolutionary perspective. *Am Anthropologist.* 1998; 100: 632–650.

13. Lewontin RC. The apportionment of human diversity. *Evol Biol.* 1972;6:381–398.

14. Nei M, Roychoudhury AK. Genetic relationship and evolution of human races. In: Hecht M, Wallace B, Prance G, eds. *Evolutionary Biology.* Vol 14. New York, NY: Plenum Press; 1982:1–59.

15. Hahn R, Mulinare J, Teutsch S. Inconsistencies in coding race and ethnicity between birth and death in US infants. *JAMA.* 1992;267:259–263.

16. Knowler WC, Williams RC, Pettitt DJ, Steinberg AG. Gm and type 2 diabetes mellitus: an association in American Indians with genetic admixture. *Am J Hum Genet.* 1988;43:520–526.

17. Giles E, Elliot O. Race identification from cranial measurements. *J Forensic Sci.* 1962;7:247–257.

18. St. Hoyme LE, Iscan MY. Determination of sex and race: accuracy and assumptions. In: Iscan MY, Kennedy KAR, eds. *Reconstruction of Life From the Skeleton.* New York, NY: Alan R Liss; 1989:53–93.

19. Sauer N. Forensic anthropology and the concept of race: if races don't exist, why are forensic anthropologists so good at identifying them? *Soc Sci Med.* 1992;34:107–111.

20. Weiss K. Transitional diabetes and gallstones in Amerindian peoples: genes or environment? In: Swedlund AC, Armelagos GJ, eds. *Disease in Populations in Transition.* Hadley, Mass: Bergen & Garvey; 1992: 105–123.

21. Weiss K, Ferrell R, Hanis CL. A new world syndrome of metabolic diseases with a genetic and evolutionary basis. *Yearbook Phys Anthropol.* 1984;27:153–178.

22. Young TK. *The Health of Native Americans.* New York, NY: Oxford University Press Inc; 1994.

23. Kozak D. Surrendering to diabetes: an embodied response to perceptions of diabetes and death in the Gila Indian community. *Omega J Death Dying.* 1996; 35: 347–359.

16 EVOLUTION AND THE ORIGINS OF DISEASE

Randolph M. Nesse and George C. Williams

In contrast to the tendency of biomedicine to focus on the proximal level of disease causation, this selection proposes an overarching framework from evolutionary biology to search for ultimate causes. Nesse and Williams analyze the universal characteristics of the human body that make it vulnerable to disease and to seemingly meaningless reactions to external threats. They explain that responses such as coughing, vomiting, diarrhea, and pain are, in fact, natural defenses. Fever helps the body fight infection, while anemia caused by diversion of iron to the liver keeps the iron from bacteria that need it. According to the "smoke detector principle," these mechanisms are automatic and may be set off by relatively innocuous threats to ensure that the real ones are not missed. As a result, they often may be suppressed without apparent damage, but in many cases the length and severity of an illness may be increased. On the other hand, some microbes reproduce more efficiently thanks to defenses such as fever and reduced availability of iron (see Ewald 1994), illustrating the need for further research.

A second focus of evolutionary medicine is the coevolution of humans and their diseases. The microbes that infect humans are constantly changing, trading genes with one another, and responding to human cultural adaptations such as antibiotics. Pathogens may become more or less virulent as their environmental circumstances change. For example, diseases that are spread by vectors, such as malaria spread by mosquitoes, are often relatively virulent because they are able to spread even when the host is immobilized. Cholera bacilli use polluted waterways in the same way as insect vectors, such that highly virulent strains give way to more benign forms when the water supply is purified.

Overall, humans have more or less the same genetic constitution as they did before the rise of agriculture. This indicates that the human body is not adapted to certain conditions prevailing today. The discordance in terms of diet, physical activity, alcohol and tobacco consumption, and reproductive patterns is the subject of selections 17 and 18 and helps to explain the rise of chronic degenerative diseases in the industrialized societies and increasingly in the rest of the world. Trade-offs such as that between sickle-cell anemia and protection against malaria (see selection 13), or active immune system function in youth and deterioration in older age due to consequent tissue damage, also illustrate the utility of an evolutionary approach. Such an approach can help bring improved understanding of human susceptibilities and of possible benefits to apparent drawbacks.

Questions to keep in mind

Why has natural selection not made us invulnerable to disease?

Do cultural vectors—such as hospital personnel and poor sanitation systems—that mimic the actions of insect vectors tend to favor increased or decreased microbial virulence, and why?

What lessons does evolutionary medicine suggest about how to think about or deal with bodily defenses, virulent infectious diseases, and widespread chronic degenerative diseases?

Why do you think evolutionary medicine is not already a part of mainstream medical education and research?

Source: Nesse, R. M. and G. C. Williams 1998. "Evolution and the Origins of Disease." *Scientific American* 279(5):86–93. Reprinted with permission.

Thoughtful contemplation of the human body elicits awe—in equal measure with perplexity. The eye, for instance, has long been an object of wonder, with the clear, living tissue of the cornea curving just the right amount, the iris adjusting to brightness and the lens to distance, so that the optimal quantity of light focuses exactly on the surface of the retina. Admiration of such apparent perfection soon gives way, however, to consternation. Contrary to any sensible design, blood vessels and nerves traverse the inside of the retina, creating a blind spot at their point of exit.

The body is a bundle of such jarring contradictions. For each exquisite heart valve, we have a wisdom tooth. Strands of DNA direct the development of the 10 trillion cells that make up a human adult but then permit his or her steady deterioration and eventual death. Our immune system can identify and destroy a million kinds of foreign matter, yet many bacteria can still kill us. These contradictions make it appear as if the body was designed by a team of superb engineers with occasional interventions by Rube Goldberg.

In fact, such seeming incongruities make sense but only when we investigate the origins of the body's vulnerabilities while keeping in mind the wise words of distinguished geneticist Theodosius Dobzhansky: "Nothing in biology makes sense except in the light of evolution." Evolutionary biology is, of course, the scientific foundation for all biology, and biology is the foundation for all medicine. To a surprising degree, however, evolutionary biology is just now being recognized as a basic medical science. The enterprise of studying medical problems in an evolutionary context has been termed Darwinian medicine. Most medical research tries to explain the causes of an individual's disease and seeks therapies to cure or relieve deleterious conditions. These efforts are traditionally based on consideration of proximate issues, the straightforward study of the body's anatomic and physiological mechanisms as they currently exist. In contrast, Darwinian medicine asks why the body is designed in a way that makes us all vulnerable to problems like cancer, atherosclerosis, depression and choking, thus offering a broader context in which to conduct research.

The evolutionary explanations for the body's flaws fall into surprisingly few categories. First, some discomforting conditions, such as pain,

fever, cough, vomiting and anxiety, are actually neither diseases nor design defects but rather are evolved defenses. Second, conflicts with other organisms—*Escherichia coli* or crocodiles, for instance—are a fact of life. Third, some circumstances, such as the ready availability of dietary fats, are so recent that natural selection has not yet had a chance to deal with them. Fourth, the body may fall victim to trade-offs between a trait's benefits and its costs; a textbook example is the sickle cell gene, which also protects against malaria. Finally, the process of natural selection is constrained in ways that leave us with suboptimal design features, as in the case of the mammalian eye.

EVOLVED DEFENSES

Perhaps the most obviously useful defense mechanism is coughing; people who cannot clear foreign matter from their lungs are likely to die from pneumonia. The capacity for pain is also certainly beneficial. The rare individuals who cannot feel pain fail even to experience discomfort from staying in the same position for long periods. Their unnatural stillness impairs the blood supply to their joints, which then deteriorate. Such pain-free people usually die by early adulthood from tissue damage and infections. Cough or pain is usually interpreted as disease or trauma but is actually part of the solution rather than the problem. These defensive capabilities, shaped by natural selection, are kept in reserve until needed.

Less widely recognized as defenses are fever, nausea, vomiting, diarrhea, anxiety, fatigue, sneezing and inflammation. Even some physicians remain unaware of fever's utility. No mere increase in metabolic rate, fever is a carefully regulated rise in the set point of the body's thermostat. The higher body temperature facilitates the destruction of pathogens. Work by Matthew J. Kluger of the Lovelace Institute in Albuquerque, N.M., has shown that even cold-blooded lizards, when infected, move to warmer places until their bodies are several degrees above their usual temperature. If prevented from moving to the warm part of their cage, they are at increased risk of death from the infection. In a similar study by Evelyn Satinoff of the University of Delaware, elderly rats, who can no longer achieve the high fevers of their younger lab companions, also instinctively sought hotter environments when challenged by infection.

A reduced level of iron in the blood is another misunderstood defense mechanism. People suffering from chronic infection often have decreased levels of blood iron. Although such low iron is sometimes blamed for the illness, it actually is a protective response: during infection, iron is sequestered in the liver, which prevents invading bacteria from getting adequate supplies of this vital element.

Morning sickness has long been considered an unfortunate side effect of pregnancy. The nausea, however, coincides with the period of rapid tissue differentiation of the fetus, when development is most vulnerable to interference by toxins. And nauseated women tend to restrict their intake of strong-tasting, potentially harmful substances. These observations led independent researcher Margie Profet to hypothesize that the nausea of pregnancy is an adaptation whereby the mother protects the fetus from exposure to toxins. Profet tested this idea by examining pregnancy outcomes. Sure enough, women with more nausea were less likely to suffer miscarriages. (This evidence supports the hypothesis but is hardly conclusive. If Profet is correct, further research should discover that pregnant females of many species show changes in food preferences. Her theory also predicts an increase in birth defects among offspring of women who have little or no morning sickness and thus eat a wider variety of foods during pregnancy.)

Another common condition, anxiety, obviously originated as a defense in dangerous situations by promoting escape and avoidance. A 1992 study by Lee A. Dugatkin of the University of Louisville evaluated the benefits of fear in guppies. He grouped them as timid, ordinary or bold, depending on their reaction to the presence of smallmouth bass. The timid hid, the ordinary simply swam away, and the bold maintained their ground and eyed the bass. Each guppy group was then left alone in a tank with a bass. After 60 hours, 40 percent of the timid guppies had survived, as had only 15 percent of the ordinary fish. The entire complement of bold guppies, on the other hand, wound up aiding the transmission of bass genes rather than their own.

Selection for genes promoting anxious behaviors implies that there should be people who experience too much anxiety, and indeed there are. There should also be hypophobic individuals who have insufficient anxiety, either because of genetic tendencies or antianxiety drugs. The exact nature and frequency of such a syndrome is an open question, as few people come to psychiatrists complaining of insufficient apprehension. But if sought, the pathologically nonanxious may be found in emergency rooms, jails and unemployment lines.

The utility of common and unpleasant conditions such as diarrhea, fever and anxiety is not intuitive. If natural selection shapes the mechanisms that regulate defensive responses, how can people get away with using drugs to block these defenses without doing their bodies obvious harm? Part of the answer is that we do, in fact, sometimes do ourselves a disservice by disrupting defenses.

Herbert L. DuPont of the University of Texas at Houston and Richard B. Hornick of Orlando Regional Medical Center studied the diarrhea caused by *Shigella* infection and found that people who took antidiarrhea drugs stayed sick longer and were more likely to have complications than those who took a placebo. In another example, Eugene D. Weinberg of Indiana University has documented that well-intentioned attempts to correct perceived iron deficiencies have led to increases in infectious disease, especially amebiasis, in parts of Africa. Although the iron in most oral supplements is unlikely to make much difference in otherwise healthy people with everyday infections, it can severely harm those who are infected and malnourished. Such people cannot make enough protein to bind the iron, leaving it free for use by infectious agents.

On the morning-sickness front, an antinausea drug was recently blamed for birth defects. It appears that no consideration was given to the possibility that the drug itself might be harmless to the fetus but could still be associated with birth defects, by interfering with the mother's defensive nausea.

Another obstacle to perceiving the benefits of defenses arises from the observation that many individuals regularly experience seemingly worthless reactions of anxiety, pain, fever, diarrhea or nausea. The explanation requires an analysis of the regulation of defensive responses in terms of signal-detection theory. A circulating toxin may come from something in the stomach. An organism can expel it by vomiting, but only at a price. The cost of a false alarm—vomiting when no toxin is truly present—is only a few calories. But the penalty for a single missed authentic alarm—failure to vomit when confronted with a toxin—may be death.

Natural selection therefore tends to shape regulation mechanisms with hair triggers, following what we call the smoke-detector principle. A smoke alarm that will reliably wake a sleeping family in the event of any fire will necessarily give a false alarm every time the toast burns. The price of the human body's numerous "smoke alarms" is much suffering that is completely normal but in most instances unnecessary. This principle also explains why blocking defenses is so often free of tragic consequences. Because most defensive reactions occur in response to insignificant threats, interference is usually harmless; the vast majority of alarms that are stopped by removing the battery from the smoke alarm are false ones, so this strategy may seem reasonable. Until, that is, a real fire occurs.

CONFLICTS WITH OTHER ORGANISMS

Natural selection is unable to provide us with perfect protection against all pathogens, because they tend to evolve much faster than humans do. *E. coli*, for example, with its rapid rates of reproduction, has as much opportunity for mutation and selection in one day as humanity gets in a millennium. And our defenses, whether natural or artificial, make for potent selection forces. Pathogens either quickly evolve a counterdefense or become extinct. Amherst College biologist Paul W. Ewald has suggested classifying phenomena associated with infection according to whether they benefit the host, the pathogen, both or neither. Consider the runny nose associated with a cold. Nasal mucous secretion could expel intruders, speed the pathogen's transmission to new hosts or both [see "The Evolution of Virulence," by Paul W. Ewald; *Scientific American,* April

1993]. Answers could come from studies examining whether blocking nasal secretions shortens or prolongs illness, but few such studies have been done.

Humanity won huge battles in the war against pathogens with the development of antibiotics and vaccines. Our victories were so rapid and seemingly complete that in 1969 U.S. Surgeon General William H. Stewart said that it was "time to close the book on infectious disease." But the enemy, and the power of natural selection, had been underestimated. The sober reality is that pathogens apparently can adapt to every chemical researchers develop. ("The war has been won," one scientist more recently quipped. "By the other side.")

Antibiotic resistance is a classic demonstration of natural selection. Bacteria that happen to have genes that allow them to prosper despite the presence of an antibiotic reproduce faster than others, and so the genes that confer resistance spread quickly. As shown by Nobel laureate Joshua Lederberg of the Rockefeller University, they can even jump to different species of bacteria, borne on bits of infectious DNA. Today some strains of tuberculosis in New York City are resistant to all three main antibiotic treatments; patients with those strains have no better chance of surviving than did TB patients a century ago. Stephen S. Morse of Columbia University notes that the multidrug-resistant strain that has spread throughout the East Coast may have originated in a homeless shelter across the street from Columbia-Presbyterian Medical Center. Such a phenomenon would indeed be predicted in an environment where fierce selection pressure quickly weeds out less hardy strains. The surviving bacilli have been bred for resistance.

Many people, including some physicians and scientists, still believe the outdated theory that pathogens necessarily become benign after long association with hosts. Superficially, this makes sense. An organism that kills rapidly may never get to a new host, so natural selection would seem to favor lower virulence. Syphilis, for instance, was a highly virulent disease when it first arrived in Europe, but as the centuries passed it became steadily more mild. The virulence of a pathogen is, however, a life history trait that can increase as well as decrease, depending on which option is more advantageous to its genes.

For agents of disease that are spread directly from person to person, low virulence tends to be beneficial, as it allows the host to remain active and in contact with other potential hosts. But some diseases, like malaria, are transmitted just as well—or better—by the incapacitated. For such pathogens, which usually rely on intermediate vectors like mosquitoes, high virulence can give a selective advantage. This principle has direct implications for infection control in hospitals, where health care workers' hands can be vectors that lead to selection for more virulent strains.

In the case of cholera, public water supplies play the mosquitoes' role. When water for drinking and bathing is contaminated by waste from immobilized patients, selection tends to increase virulence, because more diarrhea enhances the spread of the organism even if individual hosts quickly die. But, as Ewald has shown, when sanitation improves, selection acts against classical *Vibrio cholerae* bacteria in favor of the more benign EI Tor biotype. Under these conditions, a dead host is a dead end. But a less ill and more mobile host, able to infect many others over a much longer time, is an effective vehicle for a pathogen of lower virulence. In another example, better sanitation leads to displacement to the aggressive *Shigella flexneri* by the more benign *S. sonnei*.

Such considerations may be relevant for public policy. Evolutionary theory predicts that clean needles and the encouragement of safe sex will do more than save numerous individuals from HIV infection. If humanity's behavior itself slows HIV transmission rates, strains that do not soon kill their hosts have the long-term survival advantage over the more virulent viruses that then die with their hosts, denied the opportunity to spread. Our collective choices can change the very nature of HIV.

Conflicts with other organisms are not limited to pathogens. In times past, humans were at great risk from predators looking for a meal. Except in a few places, large carnivores now pose no threat to humans. People are in more danger today from smaller organisms' defenses, such as the venoms of spiders and snakes. Ironically, our fears of small creatures, in the form of phobias, probably cause more harm than any interactions with those organisms do. Far more dangerous than predators or poisoners are other members of our own species.

We attack each other not to get meat but to get mates, territory and other resources. Violent conflicts between individuals are overwhelmingly between young men in competition and give rise to organizations to advance these aims. Armies, again usually composed of young men, serve similar objectives, at huge cost.

Even the most intimate human relationships give rise to conflicts having medical implications. The reproductive interests of a mother and her infant, for instance, may seem congruent at first but soon diverge. As noted by biologist Robert L. Trivers in a now classic 1974 paper, when her child is a few years old, the mother's genetic interests may be best served by becoming pregnant again, whereas her offspring benefits from continuing to nurse. Even in the womb there is contention. From the mother's vantage point, the optimal size of a fetus is a bit smaller than that which would best serve the fetus and the father. This discord, according to David Haig of Harvard University, gives rise to an arms race between fetus and mother over her levels of blood pressure and blood sugar, sometimes resulting in hypertension and diabetes during pregnancy.

COPING WITH NOVELTY

Making rounds in any modern hospital provides sad testimony to the prevalence of diseases humanity has brought on itself. Heart attacks, for example, result mainly from atherosclerosis, a problem that became widespread only in this century and that remains rare among hunter-gatherers. Epidemiological research furnishes the information that should help us prevent heart attacks: limit fat intake, eat lots of vegetables, and exercise hard each day. But hamburger chains proliferate, diet foods languish on the shelves, and exercise machines serve as expensive clothing hangers throughout the land. The proportion of overweight Americans is one third and rising. We all know what is good for us. Why do so many of us continue to make unhealthy choices?

Our poor decisions about diet and exercise are made by brains shaped to cope with an environment substantially different from the one our species now inhabits. On the African savanna, where the modern human design was fine-tuned, fat, salt and sugar were scarce and precious. Individuals who had a tendency to consume large amounts of fat when given the rare opportunity had a selective advantage. They were more likely to survive famines that killed their thinner companions. And we, their descendants, still carry those urges for foodstuffs that today are anything but scarce. These evolved desires—inflamed by advertisements from competing food corporations that themselves survive by selling us more of whatever we want to buy—easily defeat our intellect and willpower. How ironic that humanity worked for centuries to create environments that are almost literally flowing with milk and honey, only to see our success responsible for much modern disease and untimely death.

Increasingly, people also have easy access to many kinds of drugs, especially alcohol and tobacco, that are responsible for a huge proportion of disease, health care costs and premature death. Although individuals have always used psychoactive substances, widespread problems materialized only following another environmental novelty: the ready availability of concentrated drugs and new, direct routes of administration, especially injection. Most of these substances, including nicotine, cocaine and opium, are products of natural selection that evolved to protect plants from insects. Because humans share a common evolutionary heritage with insects, many of these substances also affect our nervous system.

This perspective suggests that it is not just defective individuals or disordered societies that are vulnerable to the dangers of psychoactive drugs; all of us are susceptible because drugs and our biochemistry have a long history of interaction. Understanding the details of that interaction, which is the focus of much current research from both a proximate and evolutionary perspective, may well lead to better treatments for addiction.

The relatively recent and rapid increase in breast cancer must be the result in large part of changing environments and ways of life, with only a few cases resulting solely from genetic abnormalities. Boyd Eaton and his colleagues at Emory University reported that the rate of breast cancer in today's "nonmodern" societies is only a tiny fraction of that in the U.S. They hypothesize that the amount of time between menarche and first pregnancy is a crucial risk factor, as is the related issue of total lifetime number of menstrual cycles. In hunter–gatherers, menarche occurs at about age 15 or later, followed within a few years by pregnancy and two or three years of nursing, then by another pregnancy soon after. Only between the end of nursing and the next pregnancy will the woman menstruate and thus experience the high levels of hormones that may adversely affect breast cells.

In modern societies, in contrast, menarche occurs at age 12 or 13—probably at least in part because of a fat intake sufficient to allow an extremely young woman to nourish a fetus—and the first pregnancy may be decades later or never. A female hunter–gatherer may have a total of 150 menstrual cycles, whereas the average woman in modern societies has 400 or more. Although few would suggest that women should become pregnant in their teens to prevent breast cancer later, early administration of a burst of hormones to simulate pregnancy may reduce the risk. Trials to test this idea are now under way at the University of California at San Diego.

TRADE-OFFS AND CONSTRAINTS

Compromise is inherent in every adaptation. Arm bones three times their current thickness would almost never break, but *Homo sapiens* would be lumbering creatures on a never-ending quest for calcium. More sensitive ears might sometimes be useful, but we would be distracted by the noise of air molecules banging into our eardrums.

Such trade-offs also exist at the genetic level. If a mutation offers a net reproductive advantage, it will tend to increase in frequency in a population even if it causes vulnerability to disease. People with two copies of the sickle cell gene, for example, suffer terrible pain and die young. People with two copies of the "normal" gene are at high risk of death from malaria. But individuals with one of each are protected from both malaria and sickle cell disease. Where malaria is prevalent, such people are fitter, in the Darwinian sense, than members of either other group. So even though the sickle cell gene causes disease, it is selected for where malaria persists. Which is the "healthy" allele in this environment? The question has no answer. There is no one normal human genome—there are only genes.

Many other genes that cause disease must also have offered benefits, at least in some environments, or they would not be so common. Because cystic fibrosis (CF) kills one out of 2,500 Caucasians, the responsible genes would appear to be at great risk of being eliminated from the gene pool. And yet they endure. For years, researchers mused that the CF gene, like the sickle cell gene, probably conferred some advantage. Recently a study by Gerald B. Pier of Harvard Medical School and his colleagues gave substance to this informed speculation: having one copy of the CF gene appears to decrease the chances of the bearer acquiring a typhoid fever infection, which once had a 15 percent mortality.

Aging may be the ultimate example of a genetic trade-off. In 1957 one of us (Williams) suggested that genes that cause aging and eventual death could nonetheless be selected for if they had other effects that gave an advantage in youth, when the force of selection is stronger. For instance, a hypothetical gene that governs calcium metabolism so that bones heal quickly but that also happens to cause the steady deposition of calcium in arterial walls might well be selected for even though it kills some older people. The influence of such pleiotropic genes (those having multiple effects) has been seen in fruit flies and flour beetles, but no specific example has yet been found in humans. Gout, however, is of particular interest, because it arises when a potent antioxidant, uric acid, forms crystals that precipitate out of fluid in joints. Antioxidants have antiaging effects, and plasma levels of uric acid in different species of primates are closely correlated with average adult life span. Perhaps high levels of uric acid benefit most humans by slowing tissue aging, while a few pay the price with gout.

Other examples are more likely to contribute to more rapid aging. For instance, strong immune defenses protect us from infection but also inflict continuous, low-level tissue damage. It is also possible, of course, that most genes that cause aging have no benefit at any age—they simply never decreased reproductive fitness enough in the natural environment to be selected against. Nevertheless, over the next decade research will surely identify specific genes that accelerate senescence, and re-

searchers will soon thereafter gain the means to interfere with their actions or even change them. Before we tinker, however, we should determine whether these actions have benefits early in life.

Because evolution can take place only in the direction of time's arrow, an organism's design is constrained by structures already in place. As noted, the vertebrate eye is arranged backward. The squid eye, in contrast, is free from this defect, with vessels and nerves running on the outside, penetrating where necessary and pinning down the retina so it cannot detach. The human eye's flaw results from simple bad luck; hundreds of millions of years ago, the layer of cells that happened to become sensitive to light in our ancestors was positioned differently from the corresponding layer in ancestors of squids. The two designs evolved along separate tracks, and there is no going back.

Such path dependence also explains why the simple act of swallowing can be life-threatening. Our respiratory and food passages intersect because in an early lungfish ancestor the air opening for breathing at the surface was understandably located at the top of the snout and led into a common space shared by the food passageway. Because natural selection cannot start from scratch, humans are stuck with the possibility that food will clog the opening to our lungs.

The path of natural selection can even lead to a potentially fatal cul-de-sac, as in the case of the appendix, that vestige of a cavity that our ancestors employed in digestion. Because it no longer performs that function, and as it can kill when infected, the expectation might be that natural selection would have eliminated it. The reality is more complex. Appendicitis results when inflammation causes swelling, which compresses the artery supplying blood to the appendix. Blood flow protects against bacterial growth, so any reduction aids infection, which creates more swelling. If the blood supply is cut off completely, bacteria have free rein until the appendix bursts. A slender appendix is especially susceptible to this chain of events, so appendicitis may, paradoxically, apply the selective pressure that maintains a large appendix. Far from arguing that everything in the body is perfect, an evolutionary analysis reveals that we live with some very unfortunate legacies and that some vulnerabilities may even be actively maintained by the force of natural selection.

EVOLUTION OF DARWINIAN MEDICINE

Despite the power of the Darwinian paradigm, evolutionary biology is just now being recognized as a basic science essential for medicine. Most diseases decrease fitness, so it would seem that natural selection could explain only health, not disease. A Darwinian approach makes sense only when the object of explanation is changed from diseases to the traits that make us vulnerable to diseases. The assumption that natural selection maximizes health also is incorrect—selection maximizes the reproductive success of genes. Those genes that make bodies having superior reproductive success will become more common, even if they compromise the individual's health in the end.

Finally, history and misunderstanding have presented obstacles to the acceptance of Darwinian medicine. An evolutionary approach to functional analysis can appear akin to naive teleology or vitalism, errors banished only recently, and with great effort, from medical thinking. And, of course, whenever evolution and medicine are mentioned together, the specter of eugenics arises. Discoveries made through a Darwinian view of how all human bodies are alike in their vulnerability to disease will offer great benefits for individuals, but such insights do not imply that we can or should make any attempt to improve the species. If anything, this approach cautions that apparent genetic defects may have unrecognized adaptive significance, that a single "normal" genome is nonexistent and that notions of "normality" tend to be simplistic.

The systematic application of evolutionary biology to medicine is a new enterprise. Like biochemistry at the beginning of this century, Darwinian medicine very likely will need to develop in several incubators before it can prove its power and utility. If it must progress only from the work of scholars without funding to gather data to test their ideas, it will take decades for the field to mature. Departments of evolutionary biology in medical schools would accelerate the process, but for the most part they do not yet exist. If funding agencies had review panels with evolutionary expertise, research would develop faster, but such panels remain to be created. We expect that they will.

The evolutionary viewpoint provides a deep connection between the states of disease and normal functioning and can integrate disparate avenues of medical research as well as suggest fresh and important areas of inquiry. Its utility and power will ultimately lead to recognition of evolutionary biology as a basic medical science.

■ ■ ■ ■ ■ ■ ■ ■ ■

17 EVOLUTIONARY HEALTH PROMOTION

S. Boyd Eaton, Beverly I. Strassman, Randolph M. Nesse, James V. Neel, Paul W. Ewald, George C. Williams, Alan B. Weder, Stanley B. Eaton III, Staffan Lindeberg, Melvin J. Konner, Iver Mysterud, and Loren Cordain

The previous selection introduced the "discordance hypothesis," referring to the mismatch between an ancestral human genome adapted to life in Paleolithic times and a modern lifestyle far different in terms of diet, physical activity, reproductive patterns, infant and child care, and social organization. Other selections described some major genetic changes (hemolytic anemias, lactose tolerance, and possibly physical adaptations to high altitude) that have taken place since the adoption of agriculture some ten

Source: Reprinted from *Preventive Medicine*, Vol. 34, Eaton, S. B. et al. 2002. "Evolutionary Health Promotion," Pages 109–118, Copyright (2002), with permission from Elsevier.

thousand years ago, but these are rare compared to overall stability in the human genome. Indeed, human migrations and cultural innovations may have dampened the environmental variability that might otherwise have favored genetic changes.

The following two selections explore the impacts of the discordance between the genome and its current environment in terms of chronic degenerative diseases, including heart disease, hypertension, and cancer, which make up the major causes of morbidity and mortality in the industrialized countries today. The hypothesis may explain other conditions as well, from hearing loss to dental caries, substance abuse to anxiety disorders. All these health problems are rare or absent in modern-day foraging populations, whose lifestyle and physical condition are the closest available approximation to those prevailing over most of human history. Older foragers do not show many of the signs that we consider inevitable results of aging, such as insulin resistance or increased blood pressure and body fat with decreased lean muscle mass. These same biomarkers, together with reduced physical strength and aerobic power, are present in a significant and rising proportion of young people in industrialized societies. It is not age alone that accounts for the chronic diseases.

The evolutionary perspective provides an overarching framework for research on and analysis of current diseases. It also unifies a great deal of existing scientific knowledge about links between factors such as nutrition or physical activity and prevention and treatment of overweight–obesity and specific diseases. An anthropological approach to health promotion could help counter the widespread public dismay over ever-changing and often contradictory health recommendations.

Questions to keep in mind

Why are people drawn to things that are not good for them, such as inactivity and energy-rich foods?

What features of the human ancestral lifestyle contributed to low rates of the psychosocial problems mentioned in this article and the previous selection (substance abuse, anxiety, depression, attention deficit/hyperactivity, teenage pregnancy)?

How does the evolutionary perspective help make sense of the confusion surrounding the proposed link between sodium intake and hypertension?

What are some potential weaknesses of the arguments made in this selection?

INTRODUCTION

In 1930 gastric carcinoma was the most lethal American neoplasm, while lung cancer ranked seventh. Subsequently their rankings exchanged places: mortality from bronchogenic neoplasms increased 10-fold as deaths from stomach malignancies fell to 20% of their previous rate [1]—contrasting trajectories that reflect altered tobacco use and food preservation practices more than medical interventions [2]. Similarly, increasing prevalence of type 2 diabetes (nominally up 3-fold since 1935) [3] and the 20th century's rise in coronary heart disease rates [4–6] have resulted mainly from changes in how people live their daily lives. Preventable disorders make up approximately 70% of the American illness burden and its associated costs [7]; in some studies individuals with high-risk health habits have had annual medical claims eight times those of individuals with low-risk behavior [8]. Logically such considerations should generate palpable enthusiasm for preventive medicine among both health professionals and the general public. Instead, our view of prevention is jaundiced: Health conscious Americans

. . . increasingly find themselves beset with contradictory advice. No sooner do they learn the results of one research study than they hear of one with the opposite message. N Engl J Med 1994;331:189–90

The news about health risks comes thick and fast these days and it seems almost constitutionally contradictory. Science 1995;269:164–9

Advice to the public about what to eat . . . and basically how to live, seems to do an about-face every time a new study is published in a medical journal. New York Times 1998 Mar 22:WK 4

Respected opinion-shapers are not alone in recognizing health promotion disarray; ordinary moviegoers applaud with ironic appreciation when Woody Allen awakes, in *Sleeper,* to find that beefsteak has become a health food. Part of the problem with prevention is media-fostered misunderstanding of the epidemiological research process, but much results, we suggest, because there is no overall conceptual framework for this field. Here we consider whether evolutionary, or Darwinian, medicine [9,10] may provide a solid foundation for health promotion research and eventually for public recommendations. The central premises are straight-forward: (1) Our gene pool was shaped by natural selection for optimal function in past environments far different from the ones in which we now live [11,12]. (2) There have been some genetic changes since the beginnings of agriculture, but natural selection is slow so most of our genome remains adapted for ancestral conditions. (3) The resulting mismatch between our ancient bodies and the circumstances of modern life in affluent Western nations fosters development of chronic degenerative diseases. If correct, these theses should provide a parsimonious, plausible basis for health promotion.

EVOLUTIONARY FOUNDATIONS FOR PREVENTION

Since 1800, life expectancy has doubled in industrialized nations, partly from improvements in medical care, but more from public health measures and general economic prosperity [13]. Over this period, the nature of disease has changed. As prime causes of mortality, infectious illnesses have been superseded by the degenerative disease now endemic in Western societies. While longevity plays a role, a Darwinian perspective suggests that such conditions are not the inevitable consequence of longer life spans. More important is dissonance between "Stone Age" genes and "Space Age" circumstances [14–16], with resulting disruption of ancient, complex homeostatic systems [17].

Evidence for this contention comes from studies of hunter–gatherers and other peoples who continue critical aspects of Paleolithic life experience. While they undergo age-related bodily deterioration as do Westerners—albeit, in some respects (vision [18], hearing [19]), more slowly—their overall health pattern is quite different. With the exception of osteoarthritis, they rarely develop "chronic degenerative diseases" [20–22]. Biomarkers of incipient illness such as rising blood pressure [23], increasing adiposity [24], deficient lean body mass [25] hypercholesterolemia [15,26] nonocclusive atheromata [27], and insulin resistance [28–32] are quite infrequent among foragers and other traditional peoples compared with their prevalence in similar-aged Western populations. These observations suggest that many chronic degenerative disorders are not unavoidable concomitants of aging, but conditions that develop frequently when behavioral and environmental circumstances differ from those under which our ancestors evolved.

Cardinal goals of evolution-based prevention, then, are to (1) characterize differences between patterns of life in ancient and modern environments, (2) identify which of these are involved in the initiation and progression of specific diseases, (3) use this information to design innovative studies of the "proximate" pathophysiology, and (4) integrate epidemiological, mechanistic, and genetic data with evolutionary principles to create an overarching "ultimate" [33] formulation upon which to base persuasive, consistent, and effective public recommendations.

THE HUMAN EVOLUTIONARY PAST

Our genome is a temporal collage. Most of its components are far older than our genus, while some have changed recently, even since the latest Ice Age [11,12]. However, many of the characteristics that make us unique among primates (brain size, maturation schedule, daily foraging range, limb proportions, relative gut segment length, speech, etc.) reflect genetic change during the 2 million years since emergence of the first *Homo* species [34,35]. Evolution can be "rapid" [36,37], especially for traits affecting survival in early life, but overall rates of change are constrained by the complexity of the systems involved [38,39]. Disorders determined by single-gene mutations (e.g., hemoglobinopathies protective against malaria) are often used to illustrate the potential rapidity of natural selection, but they are imperfect models for chronic degenerative diseases, whose clinical manifestations chiefly affect older individuals (i.e., at ages heretofore uncommonly attained) and whose pathophysiology involves tens to hundreds of genes [40].

Some human genetic alteration since the appearance of agriculture reflects the effects of pathogens. To the extent that microorganisms influence chronic disease etiology, such changes may have altered the natural history of disorders until recently considered "noninfectious" (see below). Otherwise, however, evolution since the last Ice Age is unlikely to have systematically affected the gene pool in ways that could alter genetic susceptibility to cancer, atherosclerosis, osteoporosis, and like illnesses. As it relates to such conditions, our genome remains largely adapted for Paleolithic existence [41,42]. While there was no one specific past environment that can be considered uniquely "natural" for humankind [12], an appreciation of what late Stone Age life generally entailed should nonetheless be highly useful in our attempts to explicate environmental factors influencing chronic degenerative disease incidence.

Nutrition

There is surprisingly little overlap between current foods and those of the Paleolithic [43]. We get most of our calories from grains, domesticated livestock, dairy products, and refined sugars, but preagricultural humans ate naturally occurring plant foods and wild game. They used almost no cereal grains and had no dairy foods, no separated oils, no commercial processing, and no sources of "empty calories." People in the Stone Age consumed more animal protein than do current Westerners [43]. The proportion of total fat in Paleolithic diets varied considerably, chiefly with latitude; however, intake of serum-cholesterol-raising fat was nearly always far less than at present, and there was more dietary long-chain (C20 and above) polyunsaturated fatty acid (LCPUFA) [44,45]. The preagricultural essential fatty acid ratio (ω-6: ω-3) approached unity [44]; for average Americans it approximates 15:1 [45A]. Dietary cholesterol content roughly equaled current U.S. levels [45]. Carbohydrate consumption also varied with latitude, but in all cases came chiefly from fruits and vegetables, not from cereals, refined

sugars, and dairy products [43]. Compared with the typical American pattern, Paleolithic diets generally provided less sodium but more potassium, fiber (soluble and insoluble), micronutrients, and, probably, phytochemicals [43].

These differences are pertinent to several areas of current nutrition-related research, e.g., ω-3 fatty acids and depression [46–48]; ω-6:ω-3 ratios and coronary heart disease [49,50]; fruits, vegetables, and phytochemicals as cancer preventive agents [51,52]; optimal vs minimal requirements of vitamins and minerals [53] dietary sodium, hypertension, and overall mortality[54,55]; and the appropriate contribution of fats to dietary energy [56].

Physical Exertion

Through nearly all human evolution physical exertion and food procurement have been inextricably linked. Hierarchical social stratification uncoupled this relationship for elites; industrialization and mechanization have completed the dissociation for practically everyone. Prior to the industrial era humans are estimated to have expended a total of about 3000 kcal (12 MJ) daily [57]; for current affluent populations comparable estimates are 2000 kcal (8 MJ) or less [58]. This change has resulted from decreased energy expenditure through physical exertion: about 20 kcal/kg/day (84 kJ) for hunter–gatherers versus < 5 kcal/kg/day (21 kJ) for sedentary Westerners—a fourfold differential [59].

Exercise has important effects on aerobic power [22], muscular strength [22], and skeletal robusticity [60,61], all of which were substantially greater for ancestral populations. Exercise likely affects the incidence of age-related fractures [62], some cancers [63], and atherosclerosis [63]. Obligatory exertion promoted greater lean body mass while attenuating adipose tissue, thereby reducing type 2 diabetes risk for our ancestors [64].

Reproduction

Studies of women in foraging [65] and other traditional settings [66] suggest substantial differences between patterns of ancestral and modern reproduction [65–67]. For preindustrial women menarche was later (16 vs 12.5 years) and first birth earlier (~ 19 years) so that the nubility (menarche to first birth) interval was only 3 years, versus about 12 years for average Americans and Europeans. Foragers who lived through their full reproductive span had high parity: typically 6 live births vs 1.8 for Americans. Nursing was obligatory, intensive (on demand, not on schedule), and commonly lasted 3 years. Only about 50% of American babies are nursed at all and mean nursing duration is barely 3 months [64]. Age at menopause is hard to ascertain for forager women, but menses apparently ceased somewhat earlier than in affluent societies.

New reproductive patterns and the associated ovulatory differential (three times as many ovulations for Westerners not using oral contraceptives) [65,66] are associated with increased risk for cancers of the breast [68], endometrium, and ovary [65]. For example, immature breast lobules form at puberty; their rapidly dividing cells are relatively susceptible to natural mutation, genotoxic carcinogens, and clonal promotion (but see [69]). At first full-term pregnancy most lobules differentiate into mature forms whose cells divide more slowly and are hence more resistant. Prolonged nubility thus extends a period of high susceptibility to carcinogenesis [65,70,71].

Infection

Relationships between humans and microbes were altered by the rise of agriculture. Higher population density, frequent long-distance contacts, settled living, and interactions with domesticated animals vastly increased pathogen transmission [72]. As a result, certain infections assumed greater importance, becoming selective forces that have subsequently affected the human genome (e.g., malaria [73], typhoid fever [74]). More recently, improved sanitation has reduced transmission, a pivotal contribution to the past 2 centuries' increase in average life expectancy [13]. Discovery of antibiotics had dramatic impact, but intensive usage, including incorporation into animal feeds, has led to emergence of resistant organisms. Consequently, "preventive" anti-infective chemotherapy must now aim at minimizing resistance as well as attaining clinical efficacy. To this end, mathematical models integrating classic pharmacological approaches with the principles of evolutionary biology may help optimize treatment protocols given inherent conflict between the "within host" and

overall epidemiological contexts [75]. Attempts to reduce pathogen virulence may also benefit from Darwinian considerations. For example, vaccines directed against virulence-enhancing microbial antigens might disproportionately affect dangerous strains and promote their displacement by milder variants [76,77].

While adequate food, public health measures, and medical interventions have lowered infectious disease mortality during the past century, the megapolitan crowding and unparalleled mobility in current affluent nations have probably increased transmission of certain organisms, especially those spread by sexual and respiratory contact. This phenomenon could affect chronic disease prevalence: there are well-established relationships between viral infections and certain cancers [78,79] as well as intriguing hints of a causal link between microbes and atherosclerosis [80-82]. Epidemiological correlation between infectious exposure rates and incidence of chronic "noninfectious" degenerative diseases might ultimately open new avenues for preventive intervention via evolution-based antibiotic prophylaxis and/or vaccine development.

Growth and Development

In Western nations, less frequent and severe childhood infection, sharply reduced exercise requirements, and unprecedented caloric availability result in rapid bodily growth and early sexual maturation. Average adult height is asymptotically approaching a maximum [83] while age at menarche has fallen to about 12.5 years [84], probably near the population's genetic limit. Most recent hunter–gatherers have been short-statured, reflecting the nutritional stress of foraging in marginal environments, but average height for Paleolithic humans appears to have equaled or even exceeded that at present [85,86]. Nevertheless, maturation may have been slower, as it is for athletic young women in Western nations [87,88]. Traditional North African pastoralists—who have sufficient dietary protein, limited fat intake, little access to empty calories, and high levels of physical exertion—may simulate the ancestral standard. They experience later puberty and slower growth in height than do Westerners, attaining full stature only in their early 20s; still, their average adult height equals that of Europeans [89,90].

Rapid growth is usually interpreted as a sign of societal health, but maximal is not necessarily optimal. The current experience of puberty 3 years earlier than the hunter–gatherer average may result in dissociation between psychological and sexual maturation, thus contributing to unwanted teenage pregnancies [91]. Both early menarche [92] and youthful attainment of adult stature [93] are associated with increased breast cancer risk. Rapid bodily growth may also affect blood pressure regulation if renal development is unable to keep pace allometrically, thus requiring compensatory blood pressure elevation to maintain homeostasis and possibly establishing a pathophysiological trajectory toward subsequent hypertension[17]. And, in laboratory animals at least, slower growth during adolescence and early adulthood is associated with increased longevity—apparently independent of any effect on chronic disease susceptibility [94].

Psychosocial Factors

Genes affecting human behavior are ancient and probably coevolved with our life history characteristics. For example, prolongation of childhood during hominid evolution may have facilitated learning and correlated with brain expansion occurring over the same period [95,96]. But, like current sedentism and diet, the social circumstances of contemporary existence are novel [64,97]. Many factors believed to exert important influence on psychological development and interpersonal relations are profoundly different from what they are thought to have been during our evolutionary past. Average birth spacing is now closer, while nursing and physical contact between infants and adults is much reduced. In most affluent societies, babies do not sleep with their mothers— a break from general primate experience dating back many millions of years [98]. Ancestral childhood and adolescence were almost certainly characterized by multiage play groups, less restrictive supervision, and intense small group interpersonal dynamics quite different from the age-segregated, more structured routines of contemporary schools and little leagues. Based on what we know about hunter–gatherers, Paleolithic teenagers had relatively clear societal expectations, not the exciting-

but-daunting array of life choices that confronts young people today. For adults, a global society has advantages, but it differs radically from the more human-scale experience of our ancestors who lived, found their roles, and developed self-esteem in bands of 15–50 people, most of whom were relatives [98A]. We have little concrete evidence, but it seems likely that these differences and others—frequent contact with strangers, conflicting social roles, wage labor, working in bureaucracies, reduced support from kin, and education that questions social beliefs and ideologies—may contribute to syndromes such as attention deficit/hyperactivity, depression, anxiety disorders, and substance abuse [99,100].

HUMAN PREFERENCES AND PREVENTION

As every physician knows, providing accurate health advice is less than half the battle; at least as important is achieving patient compliance. Providing an explanation for health promotion based on a coherent theory of how disease arises from the mismatch between our original design and our current circumstances should help. Perhaps equally valuable, however, will be understanding why we so often prefer what is harmful to our health. Much public resentment about health promotion comes because physicians' recommendations are perceived as moralistic prohibitions, which deny people basic pleasures. Unfortunately, there is a grain of truth in this—health advice often counters "natural" inclinations. Humans like foods high in fat, salt, and sugar and they regularly avoid exercise. The explanations for these tendencies also lie in our evolutionary heritage. Polyunsaturated fatty acids and sodium are required nutrients, but on the African savanna they were sometimes in short supply, so taste preferences for them were advantageous; there was active selection against wasting calories on unproductive exercise. These and similar insights are not magic bullets, but at least they explain why we have innate propensities which, in today's circumstances, tend to promote disease and why health practices that forestall chronic illness are actually in accord with ancestral experience.

A RESEARCH AGENDA

In order to provide an evolutionary foundation for preventive recommendations, the most pressing research need is to identify, contact, interview, and examine remaining hunter–gatherers and other traditional peoples throughout the world. Few such groups still live in their original settings, but the information they can provide about relevant living patterns is an irreplaceable and rapidly vanishing resource. This comparatively inexpensive undertaking might return disproportionately valuable health benefits. Of similar importance is the need to discover mechanisms by which cultural changes cause specific diseases: the general hypothesis that our genes and lifestyles have become discordant can lead to "euphenic" [17,101] health recommendations only after detailed scientific evaluation. To this end, evolutionary insight must generate falsifiable predictions amenable to well-designed mechanistic and epidemiological investigation.

Pregnancy and Birth Weight

There is persuasive [102,103], albeit not universally accepted [104], evidence linking low birth weight with adult susceptibility to Syndrome X conditions (insulin resistance, type 2 diabetes, obesity, hypertension, coronary heart disease, etc.). The responsible mechanisms could be complex and may involve trade-offs, but an evolutionary perspective suggests that optimal gestational circumstances will resemble those of our ancestors. Limited maternal intake of simple carbohydrate in the first trimester and substantial third-trimester animal protein may be beneficial [105], as may generous intake of folate [106], zinc [107], and LCPUFA, especially docosahexaenoic acid [DHA (C22:6, ω-3)] [43,108–110]. Such prenatal nutrition is consistent with the typical pregnancy experience of women in ancestral conditions [43,44].

Breast Cancer

Mathematical modeling suggests that if American women's reproductive experiences could somehow be made to resemble those of women prior to the demographic transition, breast cancer incidence could be lowered—perhaps by an order of magnitude [65,71,111]. Societal and demographic constraints preclude reinstitution of the actual preindustrial pattern, but interventional endocrinology [65,112–114] (viz. menarcheal delay, early pseudopregnancy, and oral contraception that reduces average serum estrogen levels) could simulate the ancestral hormonal milieu. This approach may seem intrusively artificial, as did oral contraception in 1960, but primate testing and eventual clinical trials could expand currently limited preventive options for high-risk individuals.

Neurological Development

Bottle feeding infants, a manifestly unnatural innovation, may adversely affect intelligence. Nursing is associated with higher cognitive scores and improved scholastic performance among children [115]. This relationship probably reflects multiple factors, but nutritional input is a likely contributor [108,109,115,116]. In evolutionary perspective, breast milk composition represents a compromise between infant needs for nutrition and maternal needs to conserve resources for future reproduction [117]. This competition becomes less critical when essential constituents are relatively abundant in the maternal diet [118]. Over 90% of all LCPUFA in mammalian brain gray matter is composed of arachidonic acid [AA (C20:4, ω-6)] docosatetraenoic acid [DTA (C22:4, ω-6)], and DHA—nutrients found exclusively in foods of animal origin and not in plants. From a largely vegetarian primate baseline, dietary intake of these nutrients increased fivefold as hunting and/or scavenging assumed prominence during human evolution—coincident with a threefold expansion of cranial capacity [44]. Brain enlargement in the hominid line was probably driven by social complexity [119]; however, increasing availability of AA, DTA, and DHA may have been a contributing factor. While humans can synthesize these three LCPUFAs from 18 carbon precursors available in plant foods, the process appears too slow to supply amounts needed for optimal brain growth during fetal development and infancy [44,109]. For now, the evidence justifies studying possible benefits of AA and DHA supplementation in maternal diets and infant formulas.

Type 2 Diabetes

The relationship between obesity and insulin resistance is well recognized, but evolutionary considerations suggest that relative skeletal muscle deficiency may also be important. Contemporary Westerners are distinguished from ancestral humans by sarcopenia [25] and decreased physical fitness [15,25,59] as well as hyperadiposity. These altered factors distort the physiological milieu for insulin action compared with circumstances existing when the relevant genetic selection occurred. An evolution-based prediction is that functional insulin resistance, in its earliest stages, is directly proportional to fat mass, but inversely proportional to the mass and metabolic activity of skeletal muscle. This relationship might reflect competition between the insulin receptors of myocytes and those of adipocytes for available insulin molecules. The initial effect would be repetitive episodes of transient hyperglycemia and hyperinsulinemia. In genetically susceptible individuals further metabolic deterioration could result from secondary down-regulation of insulin receptors, glucose transporters, and intracellular enzymatic sequences, leading ultimately to glucose intolerance and type 2 diabetes [64].

Serum Cholesterol

According to The National Cholesterol Education Project, serum cholesterol levels (TC) below 200 mg/dl (5.2 mmol/L) are "desirable," yet many myocardial infarctions occur in persons with TC between 150 (3.9 mmol/L) and 200 mg/dl. When TC is below 150 mg/dl clinical coronary artery disease is rare, but aggressive behavior and depression are more common [120,121].

Also, several studies have shown an inverse association between hemorrhagic stroke and TC [122]. Notwithstanding, an evolutionary perspective suggests that optimal human TC is below 150 mg/dl, a value exceeding the mean for free-living nonhuman primates [109 mg/dl (2.8 mmol/L)], hunter–gatherers [123 mg/dl (3.2 mmol/L)], and other traditional peoples [134 mg/dl (3.5 mmol/L)] [15,45]. However, the diets of modern Western individuals whose TC falls below 150 mg/dl are different from those of hunter–gatherers with comparable values—paleolithic humans almost certainly consumed more animal protein, more dietary cholesterol, and more LCPUFA (with a more balanced ω-6:ω-3 fatty acid ratio). Furthermore, hypertension is almost nonexistent among hunter–gatherers, whereas the linkage between "low" TC and hemorrhagic stroke is largely restricted to hypertensive individuals [122]. The relationship of these factors to the putative adverse effects of "low" TC in affluent nations bears investigation.

DARWIN'S RAZOR

Evolutionary insights provide an independent perspective when conventional biomedical investigations yield inconclusive or contradictory results. For example, dietary sodium has been a major focus of hypertension research, but epidemiological studies regarding salt intake, blood pressure, and overall mortality have aroused fierce disagreement [123]. Theodosius Dobzhansky contended that "Nothing in biology makes sense except in the light of evolution" [124]. Can an evolutionary perspective shed light on this dispute?

Contemporary humans are the only free-living primates who habitually consume more sodium than potassium, the only ones to obtain sodium over and above that intrinsic to naturally occurring foods, and also the only ones to commonly develop hypertension [55]. Daily sodium intake for ancestral humans is estimated to have been less than 1000 mg/day (17 mEq) [43] and data from the Intersalt Study [125] suggest a threshold blood pressure effect just above this level [126]. Ecological surveys have identified numerous normotensive traditional populations who, like Paleolithic humans, lacked access to commercial salt [15,23]. However, such groups differed from Westerners in many ways so that variables in addition to salt may have affected blood pressure differences. Observations of acculturating societies [127–130] (and chimpanzees [131]) with graded salt availability suggest that sodium is a necessary, but not sufficient, factor in hypertension pathophysiology. Epidemiological analyses of sodium–blood pressure relationships may be frustrated because almost all contemporary humans consume far more sodium than their ancestors, well above the hypertension threshold indicated by Intersalt data. In this range sodium may exhibit a permissive rather than a direct relationship to hypertension so even the most ambitious meta-analysis has difficulty distinguishing the evolutionary theme amid other epidemiological factors. These additional influences—obesity, insulin resistance, poor physical fitness, over-rapid growth, alcohol, and deficiencies of potassium, calcium, fruits, and vegetables—all reflect environmental and behavioral differences that have appeared or intensified since the rise of agriculture [13,15,22,28–32].

An evolution-based prediction, consistent with prior investigative findings, is that individuals who habitually consume a nutritionally adequate diet providing less than 1000 mg sodium per day will be free from essential hypertension. Above this intake level the prevalence of high blood pressure will be more closely related to the other influences noted above than to sodium intake per se.

GENES AND VARIATION

Future research will gradually sort out the contributions of inheritance, environment, and behavior in chronic disease pathophysiology, but evolutionary considerations argue against blanket categorization of the genes involved as "defective." Alleles, which may have been neutral or beneficial in ancestral environments, can now promote disease because they interact with novel modern conditions. Recent foragers—the best available, if inexact, surrogates for preagricultural humans—have been largely free from atherosclerosis, diabetes, and hypertension, implying that the underlying genetic factors probably had little adverse effect during the Paleolithic. This highlights the fundamental principle, still widely misunderstood, that all phenotypes are formed by the interactions of a genotype with the environment and likewise, that degenerative diseases arise from one degree or another of genetic predisposition interacting with operative circumstances. Through nearly all human evolution genetic adaptation was closely coupled with environmental alterations. Now, however, cultural change comes too rapidly for genetic accommodation to keep pace [132,133]. We still carry genes that were selected for their utility in the past, but that in the novel circum-

stances of contemporary life confer increased susceptibility to chronic illnesses. Labeling such alleles "defects" implies an underlying misinterpretation of the body as a designed machine, instead of an organism assembled by whatever genes best get copies of themselves into future generations.

CONCLUSION

The 20th century's extraordinary medical advances eliminated previous scourges such as polio and small-pox and have ameliorated the effects of many other illnesses, but chronic degenerative disease incidence has been little affected [134]. For example, mammography, chemotherapy, radiation therapy, and breast-conserving surgery have improved breast cancer survivorship, but increasing incidence leaves age-adjusted mortality from this malignancy near its 1930 level [1]. We can hope that future tertiary prevention, such as gene therapy, will be more efficacious, but daunting ethical, economic, and technical obstacles may be difficult to overcome [135–137].

Prevention research based on attempts to isolate and identify individual causal factors has contributed much to our knowledge, but reductionism encounters problems when addressing multifactorial degenerative illnesses, the salt–hypertension controversy being a case in point. Furthermore, epidemiological studies of American nurses, traditional Mediterraneans, and the East Asians of 1960 may be limited because such groups lack optimal controls: the lifestyles of nearly all their members differ dramatically from those of our ancestors. Valuable data can be derived from investigating health differences within and between contemporary populations, but we suggest that some of the most potentially rewarding research involves contrasts between present and previous humans. Evidence arising from analyzing the biomedical implications of these differences should allow physicians to offer increasingly valid preventive advice and also to communicate recommendations more coherently and consistently because of their solid theoretical foundation. "Evolution is now widely recognized as the organizing principle at all levels of life." [138] The authors maintain that evolutionary principles can provide health promotion with a consistent, persuasive logic, which may, in turn, advance realization of its full potential.

NOTES

1. Landis SH, Murray T, Bolden S, Wingo PA. Cancer statistics, 1998. *CA Cancer J Clin* 1998;48:6–29.

2. Bailar JC, Gornik HL. Cancer undefeated. *N Engl J Med* 1997;336:1569–74.

3. American Diabetes Association. Diabetes 1996 vital statistics. Alexandria (VA): *Am Diabetes Assoc* 1996:14–5.

4. Levy RL, Bruenn HG, Kurtz D. Facts on disease of the coronary arteries based on a survey of the clinical and pathological records of 762 cases. *Am J Med Sci* 1934;187:376–90.

5. White PD. The historical background of angina pectoris. *Med Concepts Cardiovasc Dis* 1974; 43:109–12.

6. Hunink MGM, Goldman L, Tosteson ANA, et al. The recent decline in mortality from coronary heart disease, 1980–1990. The effect of secular trends in risk factors and treatment. *JAMA* 1997;277:535–42.

7. Fries JF, Koop CE, Beadle CE, et al. Reducing health care costs by reducing the need and demand for medical services. *N Engl J Med* 1993;329:321–5.

8. Yen LT, Edington DW, Witting P. Associations between health risk appraisal scores and employee medical claims costs in a manufacturing company. *Am J Health Promot* 1991;6:46–54.

9. Stearns SC, editor. *Evolution in health and disease.* Oxford: Oxford Univ. Press, 1999.

10. Trevathan WR, Smith EO, McKenna JJ, editors. *Evolutionary medicine.* Oxford: Oxford Univ. Press, 1999.

11. Strassmann BI, Dunbar R. Stone age legacies and modern medicine. In: Stearns SC, editor. *Evolution in health and disease.* Oxford: Oxford Univ. Press, 1999: 91–101.

12. Irons W. Adaptively relevant environments versus the environment of evolutionary adaptedness. *Evol Anthropol* 1998;6:194–204.

13. McKeown T. A basis for health strategies. A classification of disease. *Br Med J* 1983;287:594–6.

14. Neel JV. Medicine's genetic horizons. *Ann Intern Med* 1958; 49:472–6.

15. Eaton SB, Konner M, Shostak M. Stone agers in the fast lane: chronic degenerative diseases in evolutionary perspective. *Am J Med* 1988;84:739–49.

16. Williams GC, Nesse RM. The dawn of Darwinian medicine. *Q Rev Biol* 1991;66:1–21.

17. Neel JV, Weder AB, Julius S. Type II diabetes, essential hypertension, and obesity as "syndromes of impaired genetic homeostasis": the "thrifty genotype" hypothesis enters the 21st century. *Perspect Biol Med* 1998;42:44–74.

18. Salanzo FM, Neel JV. New data on the vision of South American Indians. *Bull Pan Am Health Organ* 1976; 10:1–8.

19. Rosen S, Bergman M, Plester D, El-Mofty A, Satti MH. Presbycusis study of a relatively noise-free population in the Sudan. *Ann Otol* 1962;71:727–43.

20. Trowell HC, Burkett DP, editors. *Western diseases: their emergence and prevention.* Cambridge (MA): Harvard Univ. Press, 1981:xiii–xvi.

21. Lindeberg S, Lundh B. Apparent absence of stroke and ischaemic heart disease in a traditional Melanesian population: a clinical study in Kitava. *J Intern Med* 1993;233:269–75.

22. Shephard RJ, Rode A. *The health consequences of modernization: evidence from circumpolar peoples.* Cambridge (UK): Cambridge Univ. Press, 1996: 101–8.

23. Blackburn H, Poineas R. Diet and hypertension: anthropology, epidemiology, and public health implications. *Prog Biochem Pharmacol* 1983;19:31–79.

24. Glanville EV, Geerdink RA. Skinfold thickness, body measurements and age changes in Trio and Wajana Indians of Surinam. *Am J Physiol Anthropol* 1970;32:455–62.

25. Rode A, Shephard RJ. The physiological consequences of acculturation: a 20-year study in an Inuit community. *Eur J Appl Physiol* 1994;69:16–24.

26. Lindeberg S, Nilsson-Ehle P, Terént A, Vessby B, Schersten B. Cardiovascular risk factors in a Melanesian population apparently free from stroke and ischaemic heart disease: the Kitava study. *J Intern Med* 1994;236:331–40.

27. Vint FW. Post-mortem findings in the natives of Kenya. *East African Med J* 1937;13:332–40.

28. Joffe BI, Jackson WPU, Thomas ME, et al. Metabolic response to oral glucose in the Kalahari bushmen. *Br Med J* 1971;4:206–8.

29. Merimee TJ, Rimoin DL, Cavalli-Sforza LL. Metabolic studies in the African pygmy. *J Clin Invest* 1972;51:395–401.

30. Kuroshima A, Itoh S, Azuma T, Agishi Y. Glucose tolerance test in the Ainu. *Int J Biometerol* 1972;16:193–7.

31. Spielmann RS, Fajans SS, Neel JV, Pek S, Floyd JC, Oliver WJ. Glucose tolerance in two unacculturated Indian tribes of Brazil. *Diabetology* 1982;23:90–3.

32. Lindeberg S, Eliasson M, Lindahl B, Ahren B. Low serum insulin in traditional Pacific Islanders—the Kitava study. *Metabolism* 1999; 48:1216–9.

33. Mayr E. Cause and effect in biology. *Science* 1961;134:1501–6.

34. Ruff CB, Trinkhaus E, Holliday TW. Body mass and encephalization in Pleistocene Homo. *Nature* 1997;387:173–6.

35. Wood B, Collaid M. The human genus. *Science* 1999;284:65–71.

36. Carroll RL. Rates of evolution. In: Carroll RL. *Patterns and processes of vertebrate evolution.* Cambridge (UK): Cambridge Univ. Press, 1997: 72–80.

37. Williams GC. *Natural selection: domains, levels, and challenges.* New York: Oxford Univ. Press, 1992:127–36.

38. Waxman D, Peck JR. Pleiotropy and the preservation of perfection. *Science* 1998;279:1210–3.

39. Wagner G. Complexity matters. *Science* 1998; 279:1158–9.

40. Sing CF, Haviland MB, Reilly SL. Genetic architecture of common multifactorial diseases. In: Chadwick D, Cardew G, editors. *Variation in the human genome* (Ciba Foundation Symposium 197). Chichester: Wiley, 1996:211–32.

41. Tattersall I. *Becoming human. Evolution and human uniqueness.* New York: Harcourt Brace, 1998:239.

42. Johanson D. Reading the minds of fossils. *Sci Am* 1998;278:102–3.

43. Eaton SB, Eaton SB III, Konner MJ. Paleolithic nutrition revisited: a twelve-year retrospective on its nature and implications. *Eur J Clin Nutr* 1997;51: 207–16.

44. Eaton SB, Eaton SB III, Sinclair AJ, Cordain L, Mann NJ. Dietary intake of long-chain polyunsaturated fatty acids during the Paleolithic. *World Rev Nutr Diet* 1998;83:12–23.

45. Eaton SB. Humans, lipids and evolution. *Lipids* 1992;27:814–21.

45A. Simopoulos AP. Evolutionary aspects of diet and essential fatty acids. *World Rev Nutr Diet* 2001;88:18–27.

46. Adams PB, Lawson S, Sanigorski A, Sinclair A.J. Arachidonic to eicosapentaenoic acid ratio in blood correlates positively with clinical symptoms of depression. *Lipids* 1996;31:S167–76.

47. Hibbeln JR, Umhau JC, George DT, Salem N Jr. Do plasma polyunsaturates predict hostility and depression? *World Rev Nutr Diet* 1997;82:175–86.

48. Stoll AL, Severus WE, Freeman MP, et al. Omega 3 fatty acids in bipolar disorder. A preliminary double-blind, placebo-controlled trial. *Arch Gen Psychol* 1999;56:407–12.

49. Lands WE, Libelt B, Morris A, et al. Maintenance of lower proportion of (*n*-6) eicosanoid precursors in phospholipids of human plasma in response to added dietary (*n*-3) fatty acids. *Biochem Biophys Acta* 1992; 1180:147–62.

50. Kang JX, Leaf A. Antiarrhythmic effects of polyunsaturated fatty acids. *Circulation* 1996;94:1774–80.

51. Block G, Patterson B, Subar A. Fruit, vegetables, and cancer prevention: a review of the epidemiological evidence. *Cancer* 1992;18:1–29.

52. World Cancer Research Fund, American Institute for Cancer Research. Food, nutrition, and the prevention of cancer: a global perspective. Washington: *Am. Inst. Cancer Res.*, 1997:506–7.

53. Levine M, Dhariwal KD, Welch RW, Wang Y, Park JB. Determination of optimal vitamin C requirements in humans. *Am J Clin Nutr* 1995;62(Suppl): 1347S–56S.

54. Alderman MH, Cohen H, Madhavan S. Dietary sodium intake and mortality: the national health and nutrition examination survey (NHANES1). *Lancet* 1998;351:781–5.

55. McCarron DA. Diet and blood pressure—the paradigm shift. *Science* 1998;281:933–4.

56. Conner WE, Conner SL, Katan MB, Grundy SM, Willett WC. Should a low-fat, high-carbohydrate diet be recommended for everyone? *N Engl J Med* 1997; 337:562–7.

57. Åstrand P-O. Whole body metabolism. In: Horton ES, Terjung RL, editors. *Exercise, nutrition and energy metabolism.* New York: Macmillan, 1988:1–8.

58. National Research Council. *Diet and health. Implications for reducing chronic disease risk.* Washington: National Academy Press, 1989:140, 142.

59. Cordain L, Gotshall RW, Eaton SB, Eaton SB III. Physical activity, energy expenditure and fitness: an evolutionary perspective. *Int J Sports Med* 1998;19: 1–8.

60. Ruff CB, Trinkaus E, Walker A, Larsen CS. Postcranial robusticity in Homo. I. Temporal trends and mechanical interpretations. *Am J Phys Anthropol* 1993;91:21–53.

61. Larsen CS. *Bioarchaeology. Interpreting behavior from the human skeleton.* Cambridge (UK): Cambridge Univ. Press, 1997:225.

62. Cooper C, Barker DJP. Risk factors for hip fracture. *N Engl J Med* 1995;332:814–5.

63. U.S. Department of Health and Human Services. *Physical activity and health: a report of the Surgeon General.* Atlanta (GA): U.S. Department of Health and Human Services, Centers Disease Control and Prevention, 1996:85–172.

64. Eaton SB, Eaton SB III. The evolutionary context of chronic degenerative diseases. In: Stearns SC, editor. *Evolution in health and disease.* Oxford: Oxford Univ. Press, 1999:251–9.

65. Eaton SB, Pike MC, Short RV, et al. Women's reproductive cancers in evolutionary context. *Q Rev Biol* 1994;69:353–67.

66. Strassman BI. The biology of menstruation in *Homo sapiens:* total lifetime menses, fecundity, and nonsynchrony in a natural fertility population. *Curr Anthropol* 1997;38:123–9.

67. Short RV. The evolution of human reproduction. *Proc R Soc London B* 1976;195:3–24.

68. Coe K, Steadman LB. The human breast and the ancestral reproductive cycle. *Hum Nat* 1995; 6:197–220.

69. Farber E. Cell proliferation as a major risk factor for cancer: a concept of doubtful validity. *Cancer Res* 1995;55:3759–62.

70. Russo J, Tay LK, Russo IM. Differentiation of the mammary gland and susceptibility to carcinogenesis. *Breast Cancer Res Treat* 1982;2:5–73.

71. Colditz GA, Frazier AL. Models of breast cancer show that risk is set by events of early life: prevention efforts must shift focus. *Cancer Epidemiol Biomarkers Prev* 1995;4:567–71.

72. Cohen MN. *Health and the rise of civilization.* New Haven (CT): Yale Univ. Press, 1989:32–54.

73. Weatherall DJ. The genetics of common diseases: the implications of population variability. In: Chadwick D, Cardew G, editors. *Variation in the human genome* (CIBA Foundation Symposium 197). Chichester: Wiley, 1996:300–11.

74. Pier GB, Grout M, Zaidi T, et al. Salmonella typhi uses CFTR to enter intestinal epithelial cells. *Nature* 1998;393:79–82.

75. Levin BR, Anderson RM. The population biology of anti-infective chemotherapy and the evolution of drug resistance. In: Stearns SC, editor. *Evolution in health and disease.* Oxford: Oxford Univ. Press, 1998:125–137.

76. Ewald PW. *Evolution of infectious disease.* Oxford: Oxford Univ. Press, 1994:207–12.

77. Ewald PW. Using evolution as a tool for controlling infectious diseases. In: Trevathan WR, Smith EO, McKenna JJ, editors. *Evolutionary medicine.* New York: Oxford Univ. Press, 1999:245–69.

78. Zur Hausen H. Viruses in human cancers. *Science* 1991;254:1167–73.

79. Parsonnet J, editor. *Microbes and malignancy. Infection as a cause of human cancers.* New York: Oxford Univ. Press, 1999.

80. Libby P, Egan D, Skarlatos S. Role of infectious agents in atherosclerosis and restenosis. An assessment of the evidence and need for future research. *Circulation* 1997;96:4095–103.

81. Danesh J, Collins R, Peto R. Chronic infections and coronary heart disease: is there a link? *Lancet* 1997;350:430–6.

82. Meier CR, Derby LE, Jick SS, Vasilakis C, Jick H. Antibiotics and risk of subsequent first-time acute myocardial infarction. *JAMA* 1999;281:427–31.

83. Van Wieringen JC. Secular growth changes. In: Falkner F, Tanner JM, editors. *Human growth. A comprehensive treatise. Vol. 3, Methodology. Ecological, genetic, and nutritional effects on growth.* 2nd ed. New York: Plenum, 1986:307–31.

84. Dann TC, Roberts DF. End of a trend? A 12-year study of age at menarche. *Br Med J* 1973;2:265–7.

85. Angel JL. Health as a crucial factor in changes from hunting to developed farming in the Eastern Mediterranean. In: Cohen MN, Armelagos GJ, editors. *Paleopathology at the origins of agriculture.* New York: Academic Press, 1984:51–74.

86. Walker A. Perspectives on the Nariokotome discovery. In: Walker A, Leakey R, editors. *The Nariokotome Homo erectus skeleton.* Cambridge (MA): Harvard Univ. Press, 1993:411–30.

87. Merzenich H, Boening H, Wahrendorf J. Dietary fat and sports activity as determinants for age at menarche. *Am J Epidemiol* 1993;138:217–24.

88. Cummings DC, Wheeler GD, Harber VJ. Physical activity, nutrition, and reproduction. *Ann N Y Acad Sci* 1994;709:55–70.

89. Little MA. Human biology of African pastoralists. *Yearbook Phys Anthropol* 1989;32:215–47.

90. Galvin KA. Nutritional ecology of pastoralists in dry tropical Africa. *Am J Hum Biol* 1992;4:209–21.

91. Konner MJ, Shostak MJ. Adolescent pregnancy and childbearing: an anthropological perspective. In: Lancaster JB, Hamburg BA, editors. *School-age pregnancy and childbearing: biosocial dimensions.* New York: Aldine, 1986:325–46.

92. Brinton LA, Schairer C, Hoover RN, Fraumeni JF. Menstrual factors and breast cancer. *Cancer Invest* 1988;6:245–54.

93. Li CI, Malone KE, White E, Daling JR. Age when maximum height is reached as a risk factor for breast cancer among young U.S. women. *Epidemiology* 1997;8:559–65.

94. Turturro A, Blank K, Murasko D, Hart R. Mechanisms of caloric restriction affecting aging and disease. *Ann N Y Acad Sci* 1994;719:159–70.

95. Bogin B. *Patterns of human growth.* 2nd ed. Cambridge (UK): Cambridge Univ. Press, 1999:188–9.

96. Leigh SR, Park PB. Evolution of human growth prolongation. *Am J Phys Anthropol* 1998;107:331–50.

97. Hewlett BS. Demography and childcare in preindustrial societies. *J Anthropol Res* 1991;47:1–37.

98. McKenna J, Mosko S, Richard C. Breast feeding and mother–infant cosleeping in relation to SIDS prevention. In: Trevathan WR, Smith EO, McKenna JJ, editors. *Evolutionary medicine.* Oxford: Oxford Univ. Press, 1999:53–74.

98A. Konner MJ. The natural child. In: Eaton SB, Shostak M, Konner MJ, editors. *The paleolithic prescription.* New York: Harper & Row, 1988:200–28.

99. Nesse RM. Testing evolutionary hypotheses about mental disorders. In: Stearns SC, editor. *Evolution in health and disease.* Oxford: Oxford Univ. Press, 1999:260–6.

100. Nesse R. What Darwinian medicine offers psychiatry. In: Trevathan WR, Smith EO, McKenna JJ, editors. *Evolutionary medicine.* Oxford: Oxford Univ. Press, 1999:351–73.

101. Lederberg J. Molecular biology, eugenics, and euphenics. *Nature* 1963;198:428–9.

102. Barker DJP. Fetal growth and adult disease. *Br J Obstet Gynaecol* 1992;99:275–6.

103. Waterland RA, Garza C. Potential mechanisms of metabolic imprinting that lead to chronic disease. *Am J Clin Nutr* 1999;69:179–97.

104. Joseph KS, Kramer MS. Review of the evidence on fetal and early childhood antecedents of adult chronic disease. *Epidemiol Rev* 1996;18:158–74.

105. Godfrey K, Robinson S, Barker DJP, Osmond C, Cox V. Maternal nutrition in early and late pregnancy in relation to placental and fetal growth. *Br Med J* 1996;312:410–3.

106. MRC Vitamin Study Research Group. Prevention of neural tube defects: results from the Medical Research Council Vitamin Study. *Lancet* 1991;338:131–7.

107. Goldenberg RL, Tamura T, Neggers Y, et al. The effect of zinc supplementation on pregnancy outcome. *JAMA* 1995;274:463–8.

108. Farquharson J, Cockburn F, Ainslie-Patrick W, Jamieson EC, Logan RW. Infant cerebral cortex phospholipid fatty-acid composition and diet. *Lancet* 1992;340:810–3.

109. Woods J, Ward G, Salem N Jr. Is docosahexaenoic acid necessary in infant formula? Evaluation of high linolinate diets in the neonatal rat. *Pediatr Res* 1996;40:687–94.

110. Birch EE, Hoffman DR, Uauy R, Birch DG, Prestidge C. Visual acuity and the essentiality of docosahexaenoic acid and arachidonic acid in the diet of term infants. *Pediatr Res* 1998;44:201–9.

111. Strassman BI. Menstrual cycling and breast cancer: an evolutionary perspective. *J Women Health* 1999;8:193–201.

112. Russo IH, Korszalka M, Russo J. Comparative study of the influence of pregnancy and hormonal treatment on mammary carcinogenesis. *Br J Cancer* 1991;64:481–4.

113. Henderson M. Current approaches to breast cancer prevention. *Science* 1993;259:630–1.

114. Spicer DV, Krecker EA, Pike MC. The endocrine prevention of breast cancer. *Cancer Invest* 1995;13:495–504.

115. Horwood LJ, Fergusson DM. Breastfeeding and later cognitive and academic outcomes. *Pediatrics* 1998;101:e9.

116. Willatts P, Forsyth JS, DiModugno MK, Varma S, Colvin M. Effect of long-chain polyunsaturated fatty acids in infant formula on problem solving at 10 months of age. *Lancet* 1998;352:688–91.

117. Haig D. Genetic conflicts of pregnancy and childhood. In: Stearns SC, editor. *Evolution in health and disease.* Oxford: Oxford Univ. Press, 1998:77–90.

118. Francois CA, Connor SL, Wander RC, Conner WE. Acute effects of dietary fatty acids on the fatty acids of human milk. *Am J Clin Nutr* 1998;67:301–8.

119. Dunbar RIM. The social brain hypothesis. *Evol Anthropol* 1998;6:178–90.

120. Erickson MT. Lowered serum cholesterol, famine and aggression: a Darwinian hypothesis. *Soc Sci Inform* 1997;36:211–22.

121. Kaplan, JR, Klein KP, Manuck SB. Cholesterol meets Darwin: public health and evolutionary implications of the cholesterol–serotonin hypothesis. *Evol Anthropol* 1997;6:28–37.

122. Iso H, Jacobs DR, Wentworth D, Neaton JD, Cohen J. Serum cholesterol levels and six-year mortality from stroke in 350,977 men screened for the multiple risk factor intervention trial. *N Engl J Med* 1989;320:904–10.

123. Taubes G. The (political) science of salt. *Science* 1998;281:898–907.

124. Dobzhansky T. Nothing in biology makes sense except in the light of evolution. *Am Biol Teacher* 1973;35:125–9.

125. Intersalt Cooperative Research Group. Intersalt: an international study of electrolyte excretion and blood pressure. Results for 24 hour urinary sodium and potassium excretion. *Br Med J* 1988;297:319–28.

126. Carvallo JJM, Baruzzi RG, Howard PF, et al. Blood pressure in four remote populations in the Intersalt Study. *Hypertension* 1989;14:238–46.

127. Page LB, Vandevert DE, Nader K, Lubin NK, Page JR. Blood pressure of Qash'qai pastoral nomads in Iran in relation to culture, diet, and body form. *Am J Clin Nutr* 1981;34:527–38.

128. Kasteloot H, Ndam N, Sasaki S, Kowo M, Seghers V. A survey of blood pressure distribution in Pygmy and Bantu populations in Cameroon. *Hypertension* 1996;27:108–13.

129. Hallenberg NK, Martinez G, McCullough M, et al. Aging, acculturation, salt intake and hypertension in the Kuna of Panama. *Hypertension* 1997;29:171–6.

130. Page LB, Danion A, Moellering RD. Antecedents of cardiovascular disease in six Solomon Islands societies. *Circulation* 1974;49:1132–46.

131. Denton D, Weisinger R, Mundy NI, et al. The effect of increased salt intake on blood pressure of chimpanzees. *Nat Med* 1995;1:1009–16.

132. Klein RG. *The human career. Human biological and cultural origins.* Chicago: Univ. Chicago Press, 1999;494, 514, 590.

133. Wilson EO. *Consilience. The unity of science.* New York: Knopf, 1998:171, 182.

134. Burkitt DP. *The Bower science lecture.* Philadelphia: Franklin Inst., 1993 Jan 15.

135. Williams GC. Pleiotropy, natural selection, and the evolution of senescence. *Evolution* 1957;11:398–411.

136. Mysterud I. Gener, atferd og sykdom: En skeptikers syn pá genkartlegging o'g genterapi. [Genes, behavior and disease: A skeptics view of gene mapping and gene therapy]. *J Norwegian Med Assoc* 1995;115:2114–9.

137. Neel JV. Looking ahead: some genetic issues of the future. *Perspect Biol Med* 1997;40:328–47.

138. Bull J, Wichman H. A revolution in evolution. *Science* 1998;281:1959.

18 EVOLUTIONARY HEALTH PROMOTION: A CONSIDERATION OF COMMON COUNTERARGUMENTS

S. Boyd Eaton, Loren Cordain, and Staffan Lindeberg

This selection addresses possible objections to the evolutionary arguments presented in the previous selection and shows that questions about life expectancy, genetic change, and human adaptability support rather than challenge the evolutionary model. The selection adds important pieces to the picture of human health history developed in this book and explains a number of key concepts concerning changing disease patterns. One such concept is life expectancy. As noted by Lock in selection 2, the rise in life expectancy since the 1800s does not mean that the human life span has increased, or that there are now old people, whereas in the past there were none. Instead, higher life expectancy rates indicate that fewer people die as infants or children and more people live into old age. Another point this selection clears up is the meaning of the apparent confinement of the impact of modern lifestyles to the older age ranges, which may give the impression that people can adapt biologically to the altered environment. However, the seeds for degenerative disease are planted in youth, although signs such as atherosclerosis or elevated blood pressure may be hidden.

The change in life expectancy that accompanied the rapid decline in mortality rates and the shift in the major causes of death from infectious to chronic degenerative diseases in the industrialized societies has been a historically and geographically limited phenomenon. There is more than one kind of epidemiologic transition, and the Western one cannot be considered complete, given that recently there has been a rise in mortality from infectious disease. Finally, the idea of transition should not be taken to mean that population health has only improved over time. Life expectancy among modern-day foragers and probably among Paleolithic humans is around age 40, whereas the adoption of agriculture brought significant reductions in life expectancy to around 20 years (see selections 19 and 20). Values in the low 20s and 30s were common in Europe until the late 1800s, such that subsequent improvements related to economic growth represented a reversal of the negative health impacts of the first transition to agriculture. Overall, it was mainly economic and public health changes behind the mortality decline, although specific medical treatments had some impact and now play a larger role in the health transitions occurring in less-developed countries.

Questions to keep in mind

Why is higher life expectancy not a valid argument against the evolutionary paradigm?

What are the features of the human "environment of evolutionary adaptedness" in terms of exercise and diet, social and political organization, and reproduction and child care?

On what basis can we conclude that there has been little genetic change in humans since the adoption of agriculture?

If the scenario in these two selections is correct, what public health interventions and behavioral changes might it support?

Source: Reprinted from *Preventive Medicine*, Vol. 34, Eston, S.B. et al. 2002. "Evolutionary Health Promotion: a Consideration of Common Counter-Arguments," Pages 119–123, Copyright (2002), with permission from Elsevier.

INTRODUCTION

Evolutionary health promotion is based on three propositions:

- Since the appearance of behaviorally modern humans perhaps 50,000 years ago and particularly since the Neolithic Revolution of 10,000 years ago, cultural evolution has proceeded more rapidly than has genetic evolution, thereby producing ever-greater dissociation between the way we actually live and the lifestyle for which our genome was originally selected.
- This discordance fosters the chronic degenerative diseases that cause most morbidity and mortality in contemporary affluent nations.
- A logical model for prevention research (and, potentially, for health recommendations) is an amalgamation of the lifestyles prevailing among early, behaviorally modern humans, before agriculture accelerated genetic–cultural evolutionary divergence.

On initial consideration, these premises commonly evoke one or more of several seemingly valid reservations concerning comparative life expectancy, potential genetic change since agriculture, the heterogeneity of ancestral environments, and/or human adaptability. Such stumbling blocks sometimes interfere with objective assessment of evolutionary health promotion's strengths and weaknesses, so it seems reasonable to address these issues in some detail.

LIFE EXPECTANCY[1]

The most intuitive, most frequently expressed criticisms of the evolutionary hypothesis involve comparative life expectancy. In the first place, if Paleolithic diet, physical activity, reproductive experience, and so forth, were really healthier than they are in contemporary affluent nations, why do people now live so much longer? And second, chronic degenerative diseases are age-related, so longer-lived populations would be expected to manifest more such disease; Stone Agers just didn't live long enough for these conditions to become clinically evident.

Lifestyle and Longevity

Healthy lifestyle choices can improve an individual's weight, body composition, strength, and endurance. They can minimize risk of stroke, heart attack, diabetes, and cancer. What they cannot achieve is major impact on a population's average life expectancy. Completely eliminating the major known risk factors for nine leading chronic diseases [2] would increase life expectancy at birth by only 4 years [1]. While desirable, a 4-year gain pales when compared to the near 60-year increase that has occurred in Western nations over the past three centuries [2].

The reason that reducing chronic disease frequency has relatively little effect on average life expectancy is straightforward: these conditions are typically causes of late-life mortality. Whether a person dies at 80 as opposed to 75 has far less influence on average longevity measures than does infant and childhood mortality. Circumstances that increase likelihood of surviving potentially lethal infectious illnesses at age 2 are representative of factors capable of substantially impacting a population's average length of life. Whether the Paleolithic lifestyle is healthier than that common in contemporary affluent nations should be judged on its ability to affect parameters other than average life expectancy.

Age and Chronic Disease

A population with a life expectancy of 40 at birth will inevitably have much lower mortality from cancer, heart disease, diabetes, and stroke than will a population with an average life expectancy of 75. To this extent comparisons between recently studied hunter–gatherers [3] and citizens of affluent Western nations are invalid. Of course age-related diseases will cause more deaths in a society with a greater proportion of older individuals.

This coin has another side, however. While chronic degenerative diseases generally produce mortality in later life, they begin much earlier, often in childhood. This allows comparison between age-matched younger members of industrial and technologically primitive societies. Biomarkers of developing abnormality such as obesity, rising blood pressure, nonobstructive coronary atherosclerosis, and insulin resistance are common among the former, but rare in the latter [3,4]. Measurements of muscular strength and aerobic power reveal similar discrepancies [5], again favoring individuals whose lives more closely resemble the ancestral pattern. About 20% of hunter–gatherers reach age 60 or beyond [6,7], but even in this age bracket, individuals from foraging and other technologically primitive cultures appear almost completely free from manifestations of most chronic degenerative diseases [8,9] (osteoarthritis is an exception). Together, these observations strongly suggest that it is current Western lifestyle rather than age alone that promotes those "afflictions of affluence," the prevention of which is a major goal of contemporary health promotion efforts.

Why Do We Live Longer Now?

Life expectancy estimates for recently studied forager populations converge on a figure of about 40 years [6,7,10,11], and it seems reasonable to extrapolate a similar value for preagricultural, behaviorally modern Stone Agers. The adoption of farming and settled living is commonly considered an advance for humanity, but the new conditions appear to have adversely affected longevity, precipitating a substantial decline to about 20 years [12]. Mortality profiles thereafter remained relatively stable (as late as 1667 average life expectancy in London was estimated to have been 18) [2] and it seems likely that from the Neolithic Revolution until the late 18th century, expectation of life in "civilized" nations seldom or never exceeded 25 years. Thereafter, technological breakthroughs in food production, manufacturing, transportation, trade, communications, and energy generation gave rise to what economists call *modern economic growth* [13,14]. A major component of this transformation was sustained increase in per capita income, a measure that reflects human productivity and determines average purchasing power. In Britain, per capita income doubled between 1780 and 1860, and then multiplied a further sixfold between 1860 and 1990 [15]. Shelter, transportation, clothing, and food became progressively less expensive in terms of the time and energy necessary to obtain them.

At the most basic level, increased human productivity equates to more efficient food energy acquisition: more calories are gained for a given effort. This improved efficiency makes more energy available for bodily requirements other than physical work.

$$\text{Food Energy Intake} = \begin{array}{l} \text{Physical Energy Expenditure} \\ + \\ \text{Resting Metabolism} \\ \text{Specific Dynamic Action} \\ \text{Pathogen Resistance} \\ \text{Growth} \\ \text{Reproduction} \\ \text{Energy Storage} \end{array}$$

Of these, the most important, vis-à-vis life expectancy, has been pathogen resistance [16,17]. The Industrial Revolution so significantly enhanced productivity per hour of human effort that human health improved even as population soared, thereby defying Malthusian expectations. This was an unprecedented development. Ten thousand years earlier the comparably significant Agricultural Revolution increased productivity per unit of land area, making more total food energy available so that population growth accelerated. However, productivity per hour of effort actually may have diminished: around this time average final height declined while skeletal markers of infection and nutritional stress became more common [18,19]. Modern economic growth reversed the agricultural era's negative effects on individual energy balance, thus promoting biological phenomena, such as greater adult stature, earlier puberty, and increased energy storage (as adipose tissue), which have characterized the past 200 years. The new energy balance also extended human life expectancy, another of the past two centuries' bio-phenomenal hallmarks. Greater energy availability enhanced potential for repairing the effects of trauma, meeting the energetic requirements of childbearing, and combating the onslaught of harmful microbes. Because infectious diseases had previously been the paramount causes of mortality, the latter was of special importance for longevity [16,17].

Life expectancy was negatively affected by population shifts from the countryside to urban areas where crowd diseases were prevalent. Also, increases were observed earlier among the upper classes, which received a greater proportion of the Industrial Revolution's initial benefits [13]. Nevertheless, between 1700 and 1900 overall British life expectancy increased 34 years—from 18 to 52 [2,16]. Between

1890 and 1990 real income (inflation adjusted) for the poorest 20% of households increased 19-fold so that the health effects of industrialization have become more equitably distributed [13], with the result that average life expectancy now exceeds 75 years in many Western nations.

Although they obviously make an irreplaceable contribution to individual health and quality of life, there is surprising consensus "that specific therapeutic medical treatments have had little impact on mortality reduction" [20]. On the other hand, there is increasing agreement that public health achievements such as better sanitation (purer water, adequate sewage disposal), safer food, effective systems of quarantine, and immunizations have exerted a critically important influence on longevity. Whether economic considerations or public health measures have had greater impact is disputed [16,20,21], but their effects have clearly been complementary, especially since the mid-19th century. It is the combination of these societal developments rather than individual lifestyle choices which have led to an average life expectancy twice that of any prior human society.

GENETIC CHANGE SINCE AGRICULTURE

During the past 10,000 years there have been approximately 400 to 500 human generations. Given sufficient selective pressure, this many generations afford ample opportunity for very significant genetic evolution. For example, Wrangel Island mammoths, isolated from the Siberian mainland by rising sea levels at the end of the last Ice Age became dwarfed (to about one-third the size of their ancestors) over a period of "only" 5,000 to 7,000 years [22]. In light of this and similar documented instances of rapid mammalian evolution, important post Stone Age changes in the human gene pool cannot be excluded. Perhaps these have adapted us for the conditions of life in affluent Western nations.

However, from the standpoint of evolutionary theory an expanding population, increasing interregional travel, and cultural innovations capable of dampening environmental variability should reduce the likelihood of genetic novelties becoming established [23]. That is, they should retard the rate of genetic evolution. Respected geneticists [24], paleoanthropologists [25], biologists [26], and evolutionary theorists [27] concur that, genetically, contemporary humans differ little from our Stone Age ancestors. This contention can be tested by comparing the genetic makeup of existing populations. If agriculture and "civilization" have significantly altered the human genome, groups like the Kalahari San, arctic Inuit, and Australian Aborigines, whose ancestors were hunter–gatherers until recent centuries, should differ, genetically, in some systematic, identifiable way from Near Easterners, Chinese, and New Guineans, whose ancestors adopted farming millennia ago. There is no evidence for any such distinction [28]. While there is genetic variation between different human populations, some of which affects disease susceptibility, little of this variation can be ascribed to the effects of cultural developments during the past ten millennia. (Lactose and gluten tolerance, as well as several hemolytic anemias, are possible exceptions.) There has been ample time for important changes in the human gene pool since the Neolithic Revolution, but comparative genetic data provide compelling evidence against the contention that long exposure to agricultural and industrial circumstances has distanced us, genetically, from our Stone Age ancestors.

THE ENVIRONMENT OF EVOLUTIONARY ADAPTEDNESS

This infelicitous term designates that evolutionary time segment during which selective pressures operating in our ancestors' physical and psychological environments led to the appearance of distinguishing modern human traits. Of course past circumstances varied with time period and geographical location and this inconstancy has been held by some to invalidate any "Paleolithic prescription." If there was no one universal ancestral lifestyle pattern, how can past experience provide a model for health recommendations in the present?

The answer is that differences between ancestral environments across time and space were minor compared with their essential similarities, especially when contrasted with human experience in the affluent present. Whether Stone Agers lived in the arctic or the tropics, vigorous physical exertion was essential; for foragers living 500,000 or 50,000 years ago food was derived from naturally occurring vegetation and wild game. Age at first pregnancy, nursing patterns, and birth intervals varied little among prehistoric hunter–gatherers but, in general, differed markedly from the reproductive experiences of most women in contemporary affluent nations [29]. If the social organization of recently studied foragers can be extrapolated into the past—which is probably valid at least back to the appearance of behaviorally modern humans—nomadic Stone Agers lived in small groups whose members knew each other intimately, not in megapolitan aggregations of strangers and casual acquaintances. Politically they were egalitarian, not hierarchical [30], and economically there must have been more equitable resource allocation than at any time subsequent to the appearance of chiefdoms during the Neolithic [31].

Ancestral lifeways during the environment of evolutionary adaptedness were indeed heterogeneous, but their core essentials were basically similar and differed strikingly from those of the present. These central characteristics can be utilized to create a legitimate, defensible basis for meaningful research and potentially, for health recommendations.

HUMAN ADAPTABILITY

Humans are among the most adaptable of all mammalian species; indeed, some theorists speculate that an important thrust of our evolutionary trajectory has been toward maximizing that adaptability [32]. In addition, our purely biological versatility is extended by culture, the behaviorally modern human capacity to manipulate environment through technology. Given this unique faculty for adjusting to differing conditions, is it not possible, or even likely, that we are acceptably suited to life amid affluent Western conditions? After all, there are now approximately 500 people alive for every single individual living at the end of the Stone Age; an estimated 10 to 15 million 10,000 years ago versus 6 billion at present. Doesn't that indicate how well we've adapted to changing circumstances?

There's no doubt that adaptability has been an important factor in human demographic expansion subsequent to agriculture. Some might question whether our species' explosive growth has been beneficial for the world's biome generally, or even whether it has exerted a positive influence on the individual lives of average humans. Nevertheless, our capacity for physical adaptation and cultural innovation has clearly allowed humans to survive and multiply in many different environmental settings.

However, this is not to say that our biology operates optimally in all these environments. As a rule, biological organisms are healthiest when their life circumstances most closely approximate the conditions for which their genes were selected. In many cases our intrinsic adaptive capacity allows us to accommodate deviations with little immediate effect on health. But ultimately, beyond currently undefined limits, an individual organism's adaptation may sacrifice future health for short-term survival. Conditions tolerable or even beneficial in early life may lead, eventually, to chronic degenerative diseases.

Suboptimal circumstances take varying time periods to induce ill effects. Lack of oxygen is lethal in minutes, scurvy develops after months of inadequate vitamin C intake, and insufficient dietary calcium commonly takes decades to produce clinical osteoporosis. Deviations from our ancestral lifestyle—in nutrition, exercise, reproduction, etc.—can produce ill effects during early life, but many individuals appear outwardly healthy well into middle adulthood and even beyond. However, if preagricultural lifeways are truly those for which humans remain genetically programmed, we can expect that, despite our adaptability, most of us will eventually have to pay the piper. The evolutionary hypothesis proposes that chronic degenerative diseases are the price.

CONCLUSION

These counterarguments are important because the intuitive appeal of the issues they address sometimes biases consideration of evolutionary health promotion's real nature and possible significance. Proponents of this emerging discipline do not, necessarily, oppose modern economic growth and are certainly not against the achievements of medicine and public health. Their argument is that, in the area of individual lifestyle choices relative to prevention of chronic degenerative disease, the pertinent aspects of Paleolithic experience [33] should be considered an attractive, potentially fruitful candidate paradigm that deserves discussion and research evaluation. No theory can become a paradigm until investigation and hypothesis achieve accord, but any rejection of evolutionary health promotion should be based on its falsification by experiment or because another theory fits better with known facts—not because of unjustified preconceptions about genetic evolution since agriculture, human adaptability, nor the heterogeneity of Paleolithic environments. And certainly not because we live longer than did Stone Agers. Contemporary longevity reflects modern economic structure in conjunction with public health measures. It is neither an endorsement of our current individual lifestyle choices nor a valid argument against evolutionary health promotion.

NOTES

1. Although technically imprecise, this article uses "life expectancy," "longevity," and similar expressions interchangeably to indicate the probable average number of years of life expected, at birth, for members of the entire population under consideration.
2. Stroke, coronary heart disease, diabetes, chronic obstructive pulmonary disease, lung cancer, female breast cancer, cervical cancer, colorectal cancer, and chronic liver disease/cirrhosis.
3. Imperfect, but the best available surrogates for prehistoric Stone Agers.

REFERENCES

1. Hahn RA, Teutsch SM, Rothenberg RB, Marks JS. Excess deaths from nine chronic diseases in the United States, 1986. *JAMA* 1990;264:2654–9.
2. Lancaster HO. *Expectation of life: a study in the demography, statistics and history of world mortality.* New York: Springer-Verlag. 1990:25.
3. Eaton SB, Konner M, Shostak M. Stone Agers in the fast lane: chronic degenerative diseases in evolutionary perspective. *Am J Med* 1988;84:739–49.
4. Eaton SB, Eaton SB III. The evolutionary context of chronic degenerative diseases. In: Stearns SC, editor. *Evolution in health and disease.* Oxford: Oxford Univ Press, 1999:251–9.
5. Shephard RJ, Rode A. *The health consequences of modernization: evidence from circumpolar peoples.* Cambridge: Cambridge Univ. Press, 1996:101–8.
6. Howell N. *Demography of the Dobe !Kung.* New York: Academic Press, 1979:30.
7. Hill K, Hurtado AM. *Ache life history. The ecology and demography of a foraging people.* New York: Aldine De Gruyter, 1996: 193,194,206.
8. Lindeberg S, Lundh B. Apparent absence of stroke and ischaemic heart disease in a traditional Melanesian population: a clinical study in Kitava. *J Int Med* 1993;233:269–75.
9. Trowell HC, Burkett DP, editors. *Western diseases: their emergence and prevention.* Cambridge, MA: Harvard Univ. Press, 1981:xiii–xvi.
10. Headland T. Population decline in a Phillipine Negrito hunter–gatherer society. *Am J Hum Biol.* 1989;1:59–72.
11. Blurton Jones N, Smith L, O'Connell J, Hawkes K, Kamusora CL. Demography of the Hadza, an increasing and high density population of savanna foragers. *Am J Physiol Anthropol* 1992; 89:159–81.
12. Angel JL. Health as a factor in the changes from hunting to developed farming in the eastern Mediterranean. In: Cohen MN, Armelagos GJ. editors. *Paleopathology at the origins of agriculture.* New York: Academic Press, 1984:51–73.
13. Fogel RW. *The fourth great awakening and the future of egalitarianism.* Chicago: Univ. Chicago Press, 2000:48, 137–75.
14. Kuznets S. *Modern economic growth: rate, structure, and spread.* New Haven: Yale Univ. Press, 1966:8–16.
15. Landes DS. *The wealth and poverty of nations.* New York: Norton, 1998:194.
16. McKeown T, Brown RG, Record R. An interpretation of the modern rise of population in Europe. *Population Studies* 1972;26: 345–82.
17. Scrimshaw NS. Infection and nutrition: synergistic interactions. In: Kiple KF, Ornelas KC, editors. *The Cambridge world history of food, Vol. 2.* Cambridge: Cambridge Univ. Press, 2000:1397–1411.
18. Cohen MN, Armelagos GJ. Editor's summation. In: Cohen MN, Armelagos GJ, editors. *Paleopathology at the origins of agriculture.* New York: Academic Press, 1984:585–601.
19. Larsen CS. Dietary reconstruction and nutritional assessment of past peoples: the bioanthropological record. In: Kiple KF, Ornelas KC, eds. *The Cambridge world history of food, Vol. 1.* Cambridge: Cambridge Univ. Press, 2000:13–34.
20. Kim JM. Nutrition and the decline of mortality. In: Kiple VF, Ornelas KC, eds. *The Cambridge world history of food. Vol. 2.* Cambridge: Cambridge Univ. Press, 2000:1381–9.
21. Szreter S. The McKeown thesis. *J Health Services Res Policy* 2000;5:119–21.

22. Carroll RL. Rates of evolution. In: Carroll RL, ed. *Patterns and processes of vertebrate evolution.* Cambridge: Cambridge Univ. Press, 1997:52, 72–80.

23. Tattersall I. *Becoming human.* New York: Harcourt Press, 1998:239.

24. Neel JV. *Physician to the gene pool.* New York: Wiley, 1994:302, 315.

25. Klein RG. *The human career.* Chicago: Univ. Chicago Press, 1999: 549.

26. Wilson, EO. *Consilience.* New York: Knopf, 1998: 171, 182, 296.

27. Gould SJ. *The panda's thumb.* Toronto: McLeod, 1980:83.

28. Cavilli-Sforza LL, Menozzi P, Piazza A. *The history and geography of human genes.* Princeton: Princeton Univ. Press, 1994: 73–83.

29. Eaton SB, Eaton SB III. Breast cancer in evolutionary perspective. In: Trevathan WR, Smith EO, McKenna JJ, eds. *Evolutionary medicine.* Oxford: Oxford Univ. Press, 1999:429–42.

30. Boehm C. *Hierarchy in the forest. The evolution of egalitarian behavior.* Cambridge, MA: Harvard Univ. Press, 1999:31–8.

31. Diamond J. *Guns, germs, and steel.* New York: Norton, 1997: 265–92.

32. Schlicting CD, Pigliucci M. *Phenotypic evolution. A reactive norm perspective.* Sunderland, MA: Sinauer, 1998:51–84.

33. Eaton SB, Strassmann BI, Nesse RM, et al. Evolutionary health promotion. *Prev Med,* doi:10.1006/pmed.2001.0876.

■ ■ ■ ■ ■ ■ ■ ■ ■ ■

19   EMERGING AND RE-EMERGING INFECTIOUS DISEASES: THE THIRD EPIDEMIOLOGIC TRANSITION

Ronald Barrett, Christopher W. Kuzawa, Thomas McDade, and George J. Armelagos

This selection expands on the historical changes in mortality described in the previous selections. By comparing disease patterns and their human contexts across four periods (Paleolithic, Neolithic, Industrial Revolution, and contemporary), the authors outline three epidemiologic transitions. The first epidemiologic transition was associated with the adoption of agriculture by populations that formerly made a living by foraging (see selection 20). This means that "the" epidemiologic transition, involving a rapid decline in mortality rates and a shift from infectious to chronic diseases as major causes of death, is really a second major transition and one that is not and can never be complete. Microbes are a constant feature of human existence. Indeed, many "emerging" diseases such as tuberculosis are new only in the sense that they are drawing increasing attention because of their renewed presence in wealthy countries (see selections 22, 34; Farmer 1999).

This selection provides extensive detail about the modes of subsistence and social structures that favored some diseases over others in various time periods and their effects on the disease and death rates of different age, gender, and social groups. This detail shows that the transition to agriculture and greater sociopolitical complexity tended to bring an increase in violence. It also brings up interesting connections between the diseases affecting humans and nonhuman primates and the degree to which disease

Source: Barrett, R., C. W. Kuzawa, T. McDade, and G. J. Armelagos 1998. "Emerging and Re-Emerging Infectious Diseases: The Third Epidemiological Transition." *Annual Review of Anthropology* 27:247–271. Reprinted, with permission, from the *Annual Review of Anthropology,* Volume 27 © 1998 by Annual Reviews www.annualreviews.org.

burdens are related to nutritional practices such as raising animals as opposed to handling and eating wild meat. The continued relevance of this connection is seen in the case of HIV and simian immunodeficiency viruses and the practice of eating bushmeat in parts of Africa (see Hahn et al. 2000).

From the point of view of the microbe, it is easy to see how human activities shape ecological conditions and contact with potential hosts. Today, there is an increasing confluence of disease ecologies through international movements of humans and goods. A third epidemiologic transition is under way in which infectious diseases that were considered to be under sufficient control are resurfacing and eluding efforts to control them. Antibiotic resistance is appearing in more and more varieties of pathogens, and new previously unidentified microorganisms are causing increasing rates of disease and death. Meanwhile, in many countries the second transition to chronic degenerative diseases as a major cause of death is taking place as it has in the wealthy countries, but the decline in mortality from infectious diseases has occurred incompletely and unevenly.

Questions to keep in mind

What are some criticisms of the original epidemiological transition model?

What were the social, demographic, economic, ecological, and behavioral factors involved in the first epidemiological transition?

What changes in health did it bring? How do these causes and consequences compare to those of the second and third transitions?

How has the second transition been different between the wealthy industrialized nations and the rest of the world?

What does the model proposed by Nesse and Williams (selection 16) suggest for dealing with today's infectious diseases?

INTRODUCTION

The problem of emerging infectious disease has recently captured the public's imagination and the attention of the scientific community. Popular books (e.g. Preston 1994) and movies (e.g. *Outbreak,* released in 1995) tell grisly tales of hapless victims bleeding from all orifices, prey to mutating microbes that challenge the supremacy of Western biomedical progress. A number of books aimed at an educated general audience chronicle the scientific research effort to understand these deadly pathogens (Garrett 1994; Rhodes 1997; Ryan 1993; Ryan 1997). Recent academic conferences (Lederberg et al 1992; Morse 1994) have brought together researchers in microbiology, public health, and biomedicine to survey the seriousness of the problem; they report an ominous resurgence of morbidity and mortality from new and old infectious diseases. These reports warn of the eroding efficacy of antimicrobial therapies in the face of growing multidrug resistance (Lewis 1994; Swartz 1994; Vareldzis et al 1994). They

note the first rise in infectious disease deaths in affluent postindustrial nations since the Industrial Revolution: In the US, age-adjusted mortality from infectious disease has increased by 40% from 1980 to 1992 (Pinner et al 1996). For its part, the US Centers for Disease Control and Prevention (CDC) has compiled a list of 29 pathogens that have emerged since 1973 (Satcher 1995), and has initiated an online journal—*Emerging Infectious Diseases*—to address this growing problem.[1]

The current spate of attention belies the fact that emerging infections are not a recent phenomenon but have always played a major role throughout human history (Armelagos & McArdle 1975; Boyden 1970; Cockburn 1971; Fenner 1970; Lambrecht 1985; Polgar 1964). We seek to contextualize these recent emerging infectious disease trends within an evolutionary and historical perspective, using an expanded framework of epidemiologic transition theory. By tracing the emergence of disease in the Paleolithic Age, the Neolithic Age, the Industrial Revolution, and contemporary global society, we argue for the existence of three distinct epidemiologic transitions, each defined by a unique pattern of disease that is intimately related to modes of subsistence and social structure. We suggest that current trends—the re/emergence of infectious disease in the industrialized world and an increasingly globalized disease ecology (Colwell 1996; Elliot 1993; Gubler 1996; Patz et al 1996)—herald the arrival of a qualitatively distinct third epidemiologic transition in human health.

Recognizing the complexity of the diverse sociocultural processes involved in the re/emergence of infectious disease, many researchers in biology, medicine, and public health are calling for input from the social and behavioral sciences (Sommerfeld 1995). With its integrative approach to complex biocultural issues, anthropology is well positioned to make significant theoretical and practical contributions.

In the sections that follow, we provide a brief overview of epidemiologic transition theory and propose an expanded framework to consider the recurring social, political, and ecological factors implicated in emerging disease patterns from the late Paleolithic era to the Industrial Revolution. We apply this broader framework to explain the most recent pattern of emerging disease as part of a third, qualitatively distinct, epidemiologic transition.

AN OVERVIEW OF EPIDEMIOLOGIC TRANSITIONS

The concept of the epidemiologic transition was first formulated by Omran as a model for integrating epidemiology with demographic changes in human populations (Omran 1971). Omran stated that this model "focuses on the complex change in patterns of health and disease and on the interactions between these patterns and the demographic, economic, and sociological determinants and consequences." Omran described the epidemiologic transition as occurring in three successive stages, or "ages": 1. of pestilence and famine; 2. of receding pandemics; and 3. of degenerative and manmade diseases. The third age described the shift in age-specific disease mortality from infectious diseases to chronic degenerative diseases in England and Wales following the Industrial Revolution.

Classically associated with the concept of the epidemiologic transition as a whole, this particular sequence of events represented an important tradeoff between mortality and morbidity as a result of the interaction between epidemiological and demographic processes. On one hand, decreased child and maternal mortality resulting from declining infectious diseases resulted in an overall increase in population size. On the other hand, a subsequent increase in life expectancy entailed an aging population with increasing mortality because of chronic degenerative diseases associated with the latter years of life.

Important criticisms have been made concerning this initial framing of the epidemiologic transition. Akin to assumptions of unilinear evolutionary progress in early models of cultural evolution, this framework implies that each stage of the transition is more advanced and desirable than previous stages. Because epidemiologic transition theory focuses solely upon trends in mortality, debates surrounding the ramifications of increased longevity for quality of life and well-being are not addressed by the model. It has been argued that the increase in life expectancy associated with the shift from acute infectious to chronic disease may be gained at the expense of increased total suffering and ill-health (Johansson 1992; Riley 1992; Riley & Alter 1989). However, others contend that populations undergoing the epidemiologic transition may eventually experience a delay in the age of onset of chronic disabilities and disease (Fries 1980; Olshansky & Ault 1986).

Second, although this framework emphasizes socioeconomic and ecological factors as chief determinants in disease mortality transition, the use of whole nations as units of analysis has been criticized for burying the differential experience of these events according to race, gender, and class within population statistics (Gaylin & Kates 1997). A parallel criticism has been made of "emerging infectious diseases," a classification which may not signify the emergence of new pathogens as much as a re-emerging awareness among affluent societies of old problems that never went away (Farmer 1996). These critiques underscore the need to expand this model to account for the heterogeneity of disease experience within populations undergoing epidemiologic transitions.

While Omran accounted for accelerated, delayed, and transitional variants of his "classical" model of epidemiologic transition in Europe and North America (Omran 1971, 1983), more recent modifications have improved its applicability to a broader array of contexts and issues. Bobadilla and colleagues adapted the model to fit observations in "middle income" nations such as Mexico, where trends in chronic disease have increased despite a persistence of infectious disease morbidity and mortality, resulting in what they describe as an overlap of eras (Bobadilla et al 1993). Popkin suggests that some chronic conditions have entered a refractory stage in populations such as in the United States, where individuals have changed their diet and lifestyle in an effort to prolong a healthy lifespan (Popkin 1994). This is akin to an additional stage of the epidemiologic transition proposed to explain the delayed onset of the symptoms and ill-health associated with chronic conditions in some industrial nations (Olshansky & Ault 1986).

Even with these modifications, however, the epidemiologic transition is restricted to a particular set of historical circumstances in the recent shift from infectious to chronic disease mortality. Yet, by further expanding this framework to include multiple transitions from the Paleolithic Age to the present day, we are able to illustrate how recurring sociohistorical and ecological themes have had an important influence on shifting disease patterns throughout modern human evolution. In this manner, we have reset the baseline for three distinct epidemiologic transitions to the conditions that existed just prior to the widespread changes that occurred with the adoption of agriculture in human populations.

EPIDEMIOLOGIC TRANSITIONS: FROM THE LATE PALEOLITHIC AGE TO THE INDUSTRIAL REVOLUTION

Paleolithic Age Baseline

During much of our evolutionary history, hominid ancestors of modern humans roamed the African savanna as small, nomadic bands of foragers. Early hominid populations likely were too small and dispersed to support many of the acute communicable pathogens common in densely populated sedentary communities (Burnet 1962), especially those for which human populations are the only disease pool (Cockburn 1971; Polgar 1964). Acute upper respiratory infections decline soon after being introduced to isolated communities, suggesting that they would have been absent from the dispersed populations of the Paleolithic era (Popkin 1994). Similarly, pathogens such as smallpox, measles, and mumps were unlikely to afflict early hominid groups (Cockburn 1967a).

Hominid social organization and demographics would have presented less of a barrier to the transmission and perpetuation of pathogens with long periods of latency or low virulence. Viruses such as chickenpox and herpes simplex may survive in isolated family units, suggesting that they could have been sustained in early dispersed and nomadic populations. The current distribution of parasite species common to human and nonhuman primates provides evidence for longstanding hominid–parasite relationships that predate the divergence of the hominid lineage (Cockburn 1967b; Kliks 1983). Sprent (1969b) coined the apt term "heirloom species" to describe such parasites, which he distinguished from the "souvenir" parasites contracted through chance encounters with infected nonhuman hosts or vectors.

Long-term coevolutionary relationships between hominids and a heirloom parasite imply a good match between the parasite's mode of transmission, virulence, and life cycle, and the lifestyle and demographics of early foraging bands (Sprent 1962, 1969a). As one example, the gregarious behavior, nesting habits, and frequency of hand-to-mouth contact typical of hominoid primates likely favored the persistence of the pinworm *Enterobius vermicularis* in hominid evolution, which continues to inflict contemporary human populations (Kliks 1983). Similarly, ectoparasites such as head and body lice (*Pediculus humanus*) and enteric pathogens such as *Salmonella* would likely have infested early hominids (Cockburn 1971; Polgar 1964).

Hominids would have contracted novel, or souvenir, parasites in their daily rounds of collecting, preparing, and eating raw plants, insects, meat, and fish (Audy 1958; Bennett & Begon 1997). The distribution and characteristics of these pathogens would have placed constraints on the ecosystems open to hominid exploitation. Lambrecht contends that the trypanosomiasis parasite carried by the tsetse fly opened ecological niches for hominid exploitation by eliminating trypanosome-susceptible fauna (Lambrecht 1980). Because modern humans are trypanosome-susceptible and thus have not developed genetic resistance to the disease, Lambrecht argues that early hominids must have adapted culturally and behaviorally to tsetse by residing in fly-free areas, and perhaps through the advent and use of fire. Similarly, Kliks argues that particularly problematic and ubiquitous helminths, such as those associated with schistosomiasis and onchocerciasis, may have limited access to productive niches, much as they do throughout large tracts of Africa today (Kliks 1983).

The distinction between the heirloom and souvenir parasites afflicting early hominid bands underscores the antiquity of disease "emergence" in human populations, which is as old as the hominid lineage itself (Sprent 1969a, b). Then as today, the environment provided the pool of potential emerging infections or parasites, and the social, demographic, and behavioral characteristics of hominid adaptation provided the opportunity for disease emergence. The rate of emergence may have increased as tool use allowed exploitation of novel ecological niches (Kliks 1983), and as ecological zones shifted with climate change during glacial and interglacial periods (Lambrecht 1980). The eventual movement of hominid populations out of Africa into Europe, Asia, and beyond would have exposed migrating bands to novel ecologies and parasites, increasing the rate of emergence at least temporarily in such groups. However, it is likely that disease ecologies in these new habitats would have remained qualitatively similar, owing to the continuation of a nomadic foraging adaptation and low population densities.

The First Epidemiologic Transition

Beginning about 10,000 years ago, a major shift occurred in most human populations, from a nomadic hunting and gathering lifestyle to sedentism and primary food production. This shift involved major changes in human social organization, diet, demographics, and behavior that created conditions favorable for zoonotic infections to make the

transition to human hosts, and for pre-existing human pathogens to evolve to more virulent forms. We describe the subsequent increase in infectious disease mortality that arose in the context of these changes as the first epidemiologic transition.

The shift to permanent settlements created larger aggregates of potential human hosts while increasing the frequency of interpersonal contact within and between communities, likely fostering the spread and evolution of more acute infections (Ewald 1994). In addition, accumulation of human waste would have created optimal conditions for dispersal of macroparasites and gastrointestinal infections. Skeletal remains from archaeological sequences spanning this cultural transition generally show an increase in the prevalence of infectious lesions as populations shifted from foraging to sedentism and food production (Cohen & Armelagos 1984), adding empirical support to these expectations.

The appearance of domesticated animals such as goats, sheep, cattle, pigs, and fowl provided a novel reservoir for zoonoses (Cockburn 1971). Tuberculosis, anthrax, Q fever, and brucellosis could have been readily transmitted through the products of domesticated animals such as milk, hair, and skin, as well as increased ambient dust (Polgar 1964). In these contexts, it should not be surprising that many contemporary human infections have their origins in the zoonoses of domesticated animals (Bennett & Begon 1997).

Agricultural practices increased contact with nonvector parasites such as schistosomal cercariae, contracted in irrigation work, and intestinal flukes, which were acquired through use of feces as fertilizer (Cockburn 1971). With the advent of food storage, the threat of contamination and widescale outbreaks of food poisoning increased (Brothwell 1972). Breaking the sod during cultivation may expose workers to insect bites and diseases such as scrub typhus (Audy 1961). Other vectors developed dependent relationships with human habitats, as in the case of the yellow and dengue fever-carrying mosquito, *Aedes aegypti*, which breeds preferentially in artificial containers (Thompson & O'Leary 1997; Whiteford 1997).

Reliance upon staple crops and a decline in dietary diversity may have predisposed Neolithic populations to nutritional problems similar to those experienced by subsistence-level agrarian communities in developing nations today (Harrison & Waterlow 1990). Most staple crops are efficient producers of calories capable of supporting more dense populations yet often lack critical micro- or macronutrients. Nutrient deficiencies are thus common in agrarian societies and are often exacerbated during periods of seasonal hunger or periodic droughts (Chambers et al 1981). Skeletal evidence suggests that such nutritional problems were typical in early agrarian communities and increased with agricultural intensification in some areas (Cohen & Armelagos 1984), and may have contributed to a more vulnerable host population.

Skeletal analyses demonstrate that women, children, and—with development of stratified societies—the lower classes suffered disproportionately from the first epidemiologic transition. Female remains among Neolithic populations indicate higher frequencies of bone loss and nutritional anemia (Martin & Armelagos 1979). Comparisons between agricultural populations and their foraging predecessors show greater mortality, dental defects, and impaired bone growth among infants and young children for populations in transition (Cohen & Armelagos 1984). Artifacts indicating social status differences correlate positively with nutrition and bone-growth among Lower Illinois Valley males during the Middle Woodland Period, emphasizing the role of early social stratification in the differential experience of disease (Buikstra 1984). Related issues of political organization also had health implications, as in the case of Nubian populations during the Neolithic period, in which life expectancies were inversely related to the degree of political centralization (Van-Gerven et al 1990).

The severity of disease outbreaks during the first epidemiologic transition intensified as regional populations increased and aggregated into urban centers. The crowded, unsanitary living conditions and poor nutrition characteristic of life in these early cities fostered rapid and devastating regional epidemics (Flinn 1974; McNeill 1976; McNeill 1978). The establishment of large cities increased problems of supplying clean water and removing human waste, while facilitating spread of more virulent pathogens in enclosed and densely crowded habitations (McNeill 1976; Risse

1988). Cholera contaminated water supplies, epidemics of vector-borne disease such as plague and typhus devastated populations, and outbreaks of measles, mumps, smallpox, and other viral infections were increasingly common (Knapp 1989). Unlike the infectious disease mortality common in early Neolithic populations, adults were frequently the target of epidemic outbreaks, paralyzing societies economically in their wake. As a dramatic example, tuberculosis routinely killed one third of all adults in many European communities, and by the end of the nineteenth century had claimed an estimated 350 million lives (Knapp 1989). Similarly, the Black Death of the 1300s is estimated to have eliminated at least a quarter of the European population in a decade (Laird 1989).

McNeill (1976) also discusses two important historical trends that initiated the global spread of pathogens across previously intractable geographic boundaries. First, increasing migration and trade between state-level societies in Eurasia led to the convergence of regional infectious disease pools beginning in the fifth century CE. Second, expansion of these networks into the New World through exploration and conquest brought European populations with acquired immunity to childhood infections into contact with Native Americans with no history of exposure to these pathogens (Black 1990). This contact resulted in massive pandemics of smallpox and typhoid that killed millions of people and facilitated the colonial domination of two continents (McNeill 1976, Dobyns 1993). It also probably resulted in the introduction of treponemal infections to Europe (Baker & Armelagos 1988), where sexual promiscuity in crowded urban centers may have favored a venereal mode of transmission in the form of syphilis (Hudson 1965). These historical events illustrate how the globalization of state-level societies has provided opportunities for pathogens to cross considerable social and geographic boundaries.

The Second Epidemiologic Transition

The second epidemiologic transition roughly coincided with the Industrial Revolution in mid-nineteenth century Europe and North America. It is distinguished by a marked decline in infectious disease mortality within developed countries. This decline is the major focus of the second proposition in Omran's model of epidemiologic transition: "a long-term shift in mortality and disease patterns whereby pandemics of infection are gradually displaced by degenerative and manmade disease as the chief form of morbidity and primary cause of death" (Omran 1971:516).

The decline of infectious diseases in the nineteenth and twentieth centuries has often been cited as an objective landmark in the progress of modern civilization—a product of developments in medical science and technology in the industrialized world that would eventually diffuse to less-developed societies. Garrett shows how early successes in the eradication of polio and smallpox influenced Western medical establishments in their confident forecast for the imminent demise of infectious diseases before the end of this century (Garrett 1994). However, these projections did not consider that the larger secular trend of declining infectious disease mortality was already well under way before the advent and application of antimicrobial technologies (McKeown 1976).

Based largely upon data from Scandinavia, Germany, France, Italy, and England, Schofield & Reher roughly estimated the decline in European infectious disease mortality to have occurred in three major phases beginning in the late seventeenth century (Schofield & Reher 1991). The first phase, lasting from the late seventeenth century to the beginning of the nineteenth century, is characterized by a flattening of crisis mortality peaks owing to sporadic epidemics of diseases such as plague, smallpox, and typhus. Beginning in the mid-nineteenth century, the second phase was characterized by an overall secular decline in mortality that, although subject to significant regional variation, contributed to an increased life expectancy by more than three decades, resulting in a major overall population increase despite concurrent fertility declines. The third phase began with the advent of antimicrobial therapies in the 1940s, representing a more modest decline in infectious disease mortality in more affluent nations that continued until the early 1980s.

McKeown argued for the primacy of nutritional factors in declining European mortality (McKeown 1976). However, McKeown has been criticized for weighing nutritional inferences beyond the resolution of available data (Schofield & Reher 1991; Johansson 1992). While evidence suggests that the creation of an international grain market may have spurred improved agricultural yields and distribution networks, the relative importance of other factors such as pasteurization, public hygiene, and home-based primary health care deserve further evaluation (Kunitz 1991; Woods 1991). Moreover, there is little disagreement that certain biomedical innovations such as the worldwide vaccination campaigns against smallpox played a significant role in mortality decline.

The decrease in infectious disease in industrialized nations and the subsequent reduction in infant mortality has had unforeseen consequences for human health. Namely, the subsequent extension of life expectancy has also brought increased morbidity from chronic diseases (Riley & Alter 1989). These so-called "diseases of civilization" include cancer, diabetes, coronary artery disease, and the chronic obstructive pulmonary diseases (Kaplan & Keil 1993). Other health tradeoffs of the second transition concern the role of industrial technology in the creation of artificial environments that have influenced the appearance of chronic diseases. Particularly in urban environments, increasing water and air pollution subsequent to industrialization has been linked to significantly higher rates of cancer (Anwar 1994; Dietz et al 1995), allergies (Barnes et al 1998), birth defects (Palmer 1994), and impeded mental development (Perrera 1993). These issues are compounded by the psychosomatic effects of urbanization, which is correlated with increased levels and incidences of hypertension (Grossman & Rosenthal 1993), as well as depression and anxiety (Harpham 1994).

As in the cases of the Paleolithic-era baseline and the first epidemiologic transition, social inequalities account for many of the differences in the way the second transition has been experienced within and between populations. Within more industrialized societies, socioeconomic, ethnic, and gender differences are strongly associated with differences in morbidity and mortality for both chronic and infectious diseases (Arriaga 1989; Blair 1993; Dressler 1993). Buried within national statistics, and temporarily masked by antibiotics, the conditions selected for the first transition persisted among the poorest people of the richest nations in the second.

Following the Second World War, the second epidemiologic transition made a more modest appearance in many less-developed nations and was marked by improvements in child survival and life expectancy at birth (World Bank 1993). Unlike the epidemiologic transitions experienced in the United States and Europe, which largely preceded the advent of modern biomedical innovation, biomedical fixes such as oral rehydration therapy, immunizations, and antibiotics played a pivotal role in the initial successes in mortality reduction in these societies (Gwatkin 1980; Hill & Pebley 1989; Ruzicka & Kane 1990). While variability of these declines between countries and their possible deceleration since the 1960s has been a source of controversy (Gwatkin 1980; United Nations 1982), there is little doubt that the second transition has fallen short of optimistic projections for the developing world (Gobalet 1989). Rapid urbanization combined with marked social inequalities and a continued lack of public health infrastructure have led to communicable diseases among the urban poor, with chronic degenerative diseases among the affluent and slowly emerging middle classes (Muktatkar 1995). In middle-income countries such as Mexico and Brazil, socioeconomic status now relates inversely to important chronic disease risk markers like obesity and hypertension (Popkin 1994), akin to similar associations in the United States, the United Kingdom, and other affluent nations (Kaplan & Keil 1993).

THE THIRD EPIDEMIOLOGIC TRANSITION

The current phenomenon of emerging infectious diseases indicates a third epidemiologic transition characterized by three major trends. First, an unprecedented number of new diseases have been detected over the last 25 years that are becoming significant contributors to adult mortality. Second, there is an increased incidence and prevalence of preexisting infectious diseases that were previously thought to have been under better control. Third, many of these reemerging pathogens are

generating antimicrobial-resistant strains at a faster rate than safe new drugs can be developed. These three trends are occurring within the broader context of an increasing globalization, involving not only international trade, migration, and information networks, but also the convergence of human disease ecologies.

Recently Emerging Infections

The Centers for Disease Control and Prevention (CDC) has compiled a list of 29 newly emerging pathogens since 1973 (Satcher 1995). It is possible that the overall size of this list is more a function of increased detection than the actual emergence of new pathogens in human populations. Such is the case of the *Legionella* bacterium responsible for the high-mortality pneumonia known as Legionnaire's Disease. Following its initial detection during a 1976 outbreak in a convention of American World War II veterans (Fraser et al 1977), environmental and retrospective patient cultures subsequently indicated that *Legionellae* had long been responsible for 2000 to 6000 deaths previously diagnosed as pneumonias of unknown etiology (McDade et al 1977), many of which were attributed to the exposure of susceptible elderly hosts to contaminated large-scale air conditioning units (Miller 1979; Morris et al 1979; Saravolatz et al 1979).

Despite possible increases in detection rates, it cannot be denied that at least some of these new diseases are making unprecedented contributions to adult mortality. The most dramatic example of this is the Human Immunodeficiency Virus (HIV). Although retrospective studies have detected cases in Europe and Africa going back as far as 1959 (Huminer et al 1987; Nahmias et al 1986), HIV has more recently become the second leading cause of death among adult males aged 25–40 years of age in the United States, and the chief contributor to a 40% increase in infectious disease mortality over the past 15 years (Pinner et al 1996). With the exception of the flu pandemic of 1918, this trend marks the first of such increases in affluent societies since the Industrial Revolution.

Phylogenetic analyses of HIV and related retroviruses indicate a recent evolution from a simian virus of Central African origin (Essex & Kanki 1988). Yet biological evolution alone does not account for the rampant spread of this disease, nor its unequal distribution within and between populations (Ewald 1994; Feldman 1990; MacQueen 1994). Throughout Asia, Africa, and the Americas, high HIV and sexually transmitted disease (STD) prevalence rates have been indices of deeper sociohistorical issues such as neocolonialism (Alubo 1990), the disintegration of poor families because of seasonal labor migrations (Hunt 1995), sexual decision-making strategies (Bolton 1992; Waddell 1996), and the gendered experience of poverty (Connors 1996; Daily et al 1996; Farmer et al 1993; MacQueen et al 1996; McCoy et al 1996). Yet, neither is this simply a case of the poor transmitting their problems to the affluent. For example, contrary to the myth of Haitian origin following the initial discovery of AIDS, evidence suggests an earlier transmission to urban Haiti by more affluent Westerners engaging in sex tourism (Farmer 1992).

The social history of AIDS provides a prototype for similar issues surrounding the transmission of other infectious diseases. Outbreaks of Ebola hemorrhagic fever have received much attention in the popular press, which has mainly focused on the gory aspects of its clinical manifestations, high mortality rates, and fears of airborne transmission accentuated with images of "virus hunters" running around in spacesuits (Preston 1994). Contrary to these dramatized accounts, however, the instances of possible airborne transmission was restricted to very close contact between unprotected healthcare workers and patients in the late stages of this disease (Garrett 1994). The Ebola outbreaks along Kinshasa Highway of Central and Eastern Africa in the 1970s mainly involved transmission via the commercial sex trade and the reuse of dirty syringes by untrained Western missionaries and underequipped healthcare workers (Garrett 1994). Regarding fears of transmission across national borders, the appearance of the closely related filoviruses detected in Reston, Virginia, and Marburg, Germany, were caused by the importation of primates for drug research, which ironically included the development of vaccines for other viruses (Bonin 1971; Morse 1993, 1995).

Ebola and Marburg are but two examples of a much larger set of recently discovered hemorrhagic diseases. Recent outbreaks of these diseases in the New World have been linked to climatic

fluctuations and ecological disruption. In 1993, a sudden outbreak of a virulent hemorrhagic fever in the Four Corners region of the American Southwest was quickly identified as a novel strain of hantavirus spread through the excreta of the deer mouse, *Peromyscus maniculatus,* but not before infecting 98 individuals in 21 states and claiming 51 lives (Weigler 1995). The 1993 outbreak was associated with abnormal weather patterns (Epstein 1995), and oral histories of local American Indian healers describe three clusters of similar outbreaks that coincide with identifiable ecological markers (Chapman & Khabbaz 1994), supporting the idea that this disease has long coexisted with and periodically afflicted human populations across the United States without detection by the medical community (Weigler 1995). The initial outbreaks of Argentinian hemorrhagic fever, or Junin, were traced to ecological disruption associated with the spread of maize agriculture and increasing rodent vector habitats (Benenson 1995).

First identified in the mid 1970s, tick-borne Lyme disease has since surfaced in all 50 states as well as overseas (Jaenson 1991), and has rapidly become the most often reported anthropod-borne disease in the United States (Oliver 1996). Regrowth of Eastern forests felled in the eighteenth and nineteenth centuries to make way for agricultural fields has greatly expanded the habitat of deer, mice, and their *Ixodes* tick parasites, which carry the disease-causing *Borrelia* spirochete (Walker et al 1996). Residential housing has expanded into forested areas, bringing populations into contact with the ticks and their wild-animal reservoirs. As exemplified by diseases as distinct as HIV, Ebola virus, and Lyme disease, pathogens are often provided the opportunity to jump the "species barrier" (Lappe 1994) by a combination of ecological disruption or change, and increased contact between humans and wild reservoir species. The size and mobility of human populations increases the potential for the pathogen to escape its geographic barrier (Armelagos 1998).

Re-Emerging Infections. Ecological disruption has also been cited as a major factor in re-emerging infectious diseases as well. Warmer climates have led to increased coastal blooms of algae, creating favorable environments for the proliferation of *Vibrio cholerae,* and inland changes in temperature and humidity are increasing the reproduction of malaria vectors (Martens et al 1995; Patz et al 1996). In addition, climactic fluctuations such as El Niño are thought to have significant effects on pathogen and disease vector environments (Bouma & Dye 1997; Colwell 1996).

While acts of nature may account for changing disease patterns, most of these ecological changes have anthropogenic origins (Brown 1996; Coluzzi 1994; de Zulueta 1994). In the last 15 years, dengue fever has shown a dramatic resurgence in Asia and Latin America, where poorly developed urban environments have led to the proliferation of the *Aedes egypti* mosquito vectors in open water pools (Chinery 1995; Whiteford 1997), contributing as well to sporadic outbreaks in the Southwestern United States (Gubler & Clark 1995). The practice of combined swine-duck agriculture in Southern China as well as commercial swine and turkey farming in the United States is thought to contribute to the genetic adaptability of flu viruses (Shortridge 1992; Shu et al 1994; Wright et al 1992). Bradley critically reviewed the practice of "third-world dumping" by multinational corporations, in which industrial production facilities are "outsourced" into developing countries with cheap labor pools and greatly relaxed environmental regulations, resulting in localized climate changes (Bradley 1993a, b). Increases in mosquito populations have compounded the problem of malaria and dengue in places where poor living conditions and the unequal distribution of health resources have already contributed to higher levels of preventable mortality (Brown et al 1996; Gubler & Clark 1995).

Among the re-emerging infectious diseases, tuberculosis (TB) is the greatest contributor to human mortality, and it is estimated that nearly a third of the world's population has been latently infected with the mycobacterium (Malin et al 1995). After more than a century of steady decline, the incidence of reported TB cases in the United States increased by more than 20% from 1985 to 1992. This trend is particularly unsettling given that the previous decline of TB was the single largest contributor to North American and European declines in infectious disease mortality during the middle stages of the second epidemiologic transition (Caselli 1991; Puranen 1991).

The resurgence of tuberculosis in affluent nations was preceded by decreased public health expenditures, becoming a forgotten disease in the context of overly optimistic predictions for its continued decline (Ryan 1993). Yet TB has remained the leading cause of infectious disease mortality in developing countries, where 95% of all cases occur (Raviglione et al 1995). Notoriously endemic to populations living under conditions of malnutrition, poor sanitation, and inadequate housing, tuberculosis has long been considered to be the classic disease of poverty (Darbyshire 1996). While HIV comorbidity is implicated in the most recent first world resurgence of TB, especially among young adults, higher rates of both diseases among the urban homeless indicate that socioeconomic issues play much the same etiological role in the re/emergence of infectious diseases today as they have in centuries past (Barclay et al 1995; Barnes et al 1996; Farmer 1997; Zolopa 1994).

Antimicrobial Resistance.   The history of antimicrobial resistance is almost as long—or rather, as short—as the widespread use of the drugs themselves. The first recorded instance of drug resistance occurred in 1917 during the initial trials of Optochine in the treatment of pneumococcal pneumonia (Moellering 1995; Moore 1917). Three years after the 1941 introduction of penicillin for clinical use against gram-positive "staph" infections,[2] new strains of *Staphylococcus aureus* began to emerge with penicillin-destroying beta lactamase enzymes (Neu 1992). The lessons of emerging resistance were well known even before the DDT fumigation campaigns to eradicate malaria-carrying *Anopheles* mosquitoes, in which warnings of impending insecticide susceptibility accompanied strong recommendations for a single major international campaign (Brown 1996; Olliaro et al 1996; Roberts & Andre 1994). These unheeded warnings would prove correct, not only for the vectors, but for the quinine and chloroquine-resistant plasmodium parasite itself (de Zulueta 1994; Longworth 1995; Roberts & Andre 1994).

At present, more than 95% of *S. aureus* strains are resistant to most forms of penicillin, and strains resistant to methycilline (MRSA) have become endemic to US nursing homes and acute-care settings around the world (Jacoby 1996). Last year, the first strains of *S. aureus* possessing intermediate resistance to vancomycin were identified in Japan and the United States (Centers for Disease Control 1997), joining the ranks of already emerging *Enteroccoci* with full resistance to this antibiotic (Nicoletti & Stefani 1995; Rice & Shlaes 1995; Swartz 1994). In many cases, vancomycin represents the last in the line of "magic bullet" defenses against these kinds of pathogens (Gruneberg & Wilson 1994; Nicoletti & Stefani 1995; Rice & Shlaes 1995). As such, the emergence of vancomycin-resistant pathogens hails the beginning of what has been called "The Post-Antimicrobial Era" (Cohen 1992).

In many ways, biological evolution provides the ultimate critique of biomedicine by demonstrating the inevitability of genetic adaptations of microorganisms to the selective conditions posed by human technology and behaviors (Lederberg 1997). Beyond this, however, predictions of specific resistance patterns have been problematic. *Streptococcus pneumoniae* provides a good example of this problem. Long since ranked among the pneumonias known as "the old man's friend" in affluent nations (Garrett 1994), *S. pneumoniae* has also been the microbial source of more than 1,000,000 annual deaths of children under five years of age (Obaro et al 1996). In the last five years, drug-resistant strains of this bacteria have emerged worldwide (Gerber 1995; Goldstein & Garau 1994; Jernigan et al 1996), with reported frequencies as high as 50% among clinical isolates (Obaro et al 1996). Yet there is no theoretical explanation for why it took more than 40 years for this organism to develop antibiotic resistance, while other drug-resistant species emerged in less than a decade (Bartlett & Froggatt 1995).

Bartlett & Froggatt outline three general themes in the emergence of antimicrobial resistance: 1. that high-grade resistant organisms are typically foreshadowed by low-grade resistant intermediates; 2. that resistant strains are typically resistant to more than one antibiotic; and not surprisingly, 3. that resistance develops under conditions of extensive antibiotic use (Bartlett & Froggatt 1995). The overuse of antibiotics by both trained and untrained health providers throughout the world is a major factor in the evolution of antimicrobial-resistant pathogens (Kollef 1994; Kunin 1993; Kunin et al 1987).

Besides the practices of health providers, the patients themselves have created selective conditions for antimicrobial resistance by early termination of prescribed courses of antibiotics, providing additional generation time for partly reduced organism populations within the host (Appelbaum 1994). This is especially problematic for diseases such as tuberculosis, which requires up to a year of medication adherence in the absence of detectable symptoms to completely eliminate the mycobacterium (Barnes & Barrows 1993). Acquired resistance owing to incomplete adherence to TB regimens is partly responsible for the emergence of multi-drug–resistant tuberculosis (MDRTB) (Jacobs 1994; Nunn & Felten 1994)—a situation compounded by issues of access and conflicting explanatory models between patients and healthcare providers (Dedeoglu 1990; Menegoni 1996; Rubel & Garro 1992; Sumartojo 1993; Vecchiato 1997).

Host susceptibility is another major factor in the evolution of antimicrobial-resistant pathogens (Morris & Potter 1997). The large majority of MDRTB outbreaks in the United States occurred in the context of comorbidity among HIV-infected patients (Crawford 1994; Zolopa 1994). Multi-drug–resistant nosocomial infections are predominantly found among elderly and immunocompromised patients in long-term and acute-care hospital settings (Hayden & Hay 1992; Koll & Brown 1993; Kollef 1994; Rho & Yoshikawa 1995; Schentag 1995; Toltzis & Blumer 1995). The emergence of the eighth cholera pandemic, involving the drug-resistant 0139 Bengal strain, has been found among populations of refugees and the poorest inhabitants of the fourth world already susceptible to the effects of unsanitary water sources (Martin et al 1994; Siddique et al 1995; Islam et al 1995; Toole 1995; Weber et al 1994).

The overuse of antibiotics in industrial animal husbandry also contributes to the rise of multi-drug–resistant strains of food-borne pathogens (Tauxe 1997). Nontyphoid strains of *Salmonella* have been on the rise in the United States since the Second World War, where it is currently the most common food-borne infection. Overuse of antibiotics in chickens has contributed to the emergence of *Salmonella* strains resistant to all known drug therapies. These were recently identified in British travelers returning from the Indian subcontinent (Rowe et al 1997). In Europe, the emergence of strains of *Campylobacter* resistant to enrofloxacin increased in parallel to the use of this antibiotic among poultry (Endtz et al 1991). Similarly, the use of avoparicin as a growth-promoter in European livestock is believed to have created selective conditions for the emergence of vancomycin-resistant enterococci (VRE), which are transmitted to human hosts through fecal-contaminated animal products (McDonald et al 1997).

While antibiotics have played a relatively minor role in the latter stage of the second epidemiologic transition, the erosion of these human cultural adaptations in the face of more rapid genetic adaptations of microorganisms forces us to confront major issues without the aid of technological crutches. We will discover to what degree these magic bullets may have subsequently obscured the relative efficacy of primary prevention in both affluent and underdeveloped societies.

Influenza and the Globalization of Human Disease Ecologies. Had the historical precedents of influenza been given closer consideration, previous projections for the continued decline in infectious diseases might not have been so optimistic. With an estimated worldwide mortality of over 20,000,000, the Spanish influenza pandemic of 1918–1919 killed more human beings than any previous war or epidemic in recorded history (Crosby 1989). This was followed by the less-virulent pandemics of 1957, 1968, and 1977 (Wiselka 1994), each bringing the millennialist promise of another major outbreak at some unknown year to come (Glezen 1996; Webster et al 1993).

Noting the rapidity with which the Spanish Flu spread throughout the world in the days of steamships and isolationism, Garrett grimly suggested how such an outbreak could spread in the present age of international economics and jet travel (Garrett 1994), a timely subject given the recent appearance of a potentially lethal influenza strain in Hong Kong poultry markets with H5 antigens, to which humans have no known history of previous exposure (Cohen 1997; Shortridge 1995). With revolutionary changes in transportation technology (Reid & Cossar 1993; Wilson

1996), worldwide urbanization (Muktatkar 1995; Phillips 1993), and the increasing permeability of geopolitical boundaries (Farmer 1996), human populations are rapidly converging into a single global disease ecology (McNeill 1976).

McNeill (1976) cites the early effects of transnationalism on the transmission of infectious diseases with the establishment of extensive Eurasian trade networks in the fifth century CE. Intercontinental shipping routes provided for the transport of pathogens as well as trade goods and organized violence. The European conquests of the new World presented a dramatic example of this trend, in which adult carriers of childhood diseases endemic to post-first transition populations suddenly infected unexposed Native American populations, resulting in massive pandemics of smallpox and typhus. Neither was this a one-way trade, as returning sailors brought syphilis and tobacco back to the European continent with them.

The current trend of accelerated globalization challenges us to consider the health implications not just of converging microbial ecologies, but also of the international flow of ideologies, behavior patterns, and commodities that underlie human disease patterns. This broader picture of globalization, involving the international exchange of *memes* (units of cultural information) as well as microbes, entails a convergence of both chronic and infectious disease patterns. This is evidenced in the many developing societies that are suffering what has been called the "worst of both worlds"— the postwar rise in chronic degenerative diseases among the poor without significant declines in infectious disease mortality (Bradley 1993a), while these infections re-emerge in post-second transition societies (Armelagos et al 1996).

CONCLUSION

Buoyed by early successes in the control of scourges such as polio and smallpox in the 1950s and 1960s, the Western medical establishment claimed that it was time to close the book on infectious diseases and focus research attention on the growing problem of chronic degenerative disease (Garrett 1993). Unfortunately, the book on infectious disease remains very much open, and new chapters continue to be added at an alarming pace. We address this issue from an evolutionary perspective, using the concept of epidemiologic transition theory as an organizing framework. Our discussion of epidemiologic transitions during the course of human evolution reveals that disease "emergence" is not new but has been a dynamic feature of the interrelationships between humans and their sociocultural and ecological environments since the Paleolithic period.

The initial formulations of the epidemiologic transition provided a useful interdisciplinary framework for macrolevel analyses of demographic changes associated with major declines in infectious disease mortality in Europe and North America in the wake of the Industrial Revolution (Omran 1971). Despite later modifications, however, interpretations of this framework still remained largely restricted to a single set of events at a particular period of human history (Omran 1983). The subsequent particularism of this transition fueled notions of unilinear progress, resulting in falsely optimistic projections for the continued decline and eventual elimination of infectious disease in human populations (Garrett 1994). Our expanded framework of multiple epidemiological transitions avoids these pitfalls by providing a broader historical and evolutionary perspective that highlights common themes that pervade changing human-disease relationships throughout modern human evolution.

In our review of epidemiologic transitions, we have highlighted the socioecological, technological, and political factors involved in human disease dynamics. The US Institute of Medicine has identified six principal factors contributing to the current problem of re/emerging infectious diseases: 1. ecological changes; 2. human demographics and behavior; 3. international travel and commerce; 4. technology and industry; 5. microbial adaptation and change; and 6. breakdown in public health measures (Lederberg et al 1992; Morse 1995). The degree to which these factors are fundamentally anthropogenic cannot be overstated, nor can the influence of socioeconomic inequalities across these factors.

Recognizing the complexity of these sociobehavioral dynamics, many researchers in biology, medicine, and public health are calling for greater involvement of social and behavioral scientists in addressing infectious disease issues (Morse 1995; Satcher 1995; Sommerfeld 1995). By taking a holistic approach to these important human issues, anthropologists are well positioned to make significant theoretical and practical contributions within interdisciplinary research settings. For example, 40 years ago, Livingstone described the emergence of malaria following the introduction of agriculture in sub-Saharan Africa in what has become a classic example of the ability of humans to shape their physical environments—with unforeseen health consequences (Livingstone 1958).

Anthropologists have explored the health implications of (*a*) sexual behaviors (Lindenbaum 1991; MacQueen et al 1996; Waddell 1996); (*b*) funerary practices (Lindenbaum 1990); (*c*) ethnic conflict and genocide (Tambiah 1989); and (*d*) population displacement (Bisharat 1995; Malkki 1995; Toole 1995). Recent work in transnationalism identifies the political, economic, and social trends that are increasingly integrating the world's diverse populations (Kearney 1995). The emerging paradigm of evolutionary medicine demonstrates the applicability of evolutionary principles to contemporary health issues (Armelagos 1997), and emphasizes the ability of humans to shape their environment through pathogen selection (Lederberg 1997). Finally, anthropologists have critiqued the political–economic constraints that limit access to health care and basic public-health needs (Farmer 1996; Inhorn & Brown 1990; Risse 1988). Given this range of issues impacting human–disease relationships, even anthropologists not directly concerned with infection can make significant contributions to an improved understanding of disease emergence.

NOTES

1. Full text articles from CDC's *Emerging Infectious Diseases* and *Morbidity and Mortality Weekly Report* can be accessed electronically using the CDC's Web site at http://www.edc.gov.
2. Although Alexander Fleming first identified a staphylocidal substance in *Penicillium notatum* molds in 1928, the actual development and distribution of penicillin for clinical use took another 13 years.

REFERENCES

Alubo SO. 1990. Debt, crisis, health and health services in Africa. *Soc. Sci. Med.* 31:639–48

Anwar WA. 1994. Monitoring of different populations at risk by different cytogenetic points. *Environ. Health Perspect.* 4:131–34

Appelbaum PC. 1994. Antibiotic-resistant pneumococci—facts and fiction. *J. Chemother.* 6(S4):7–15

Armelagos GJ. 1997. Disease, Darwin and medicine in the third epidemiological transition. *Evol. Anthropol.* 5(6):212–20

Armelagos GJ. 1998. The viral superhighway. *Sciences* 38:24–30

Armelagos GJ, Barnes KC, Lin J. 1996. Disease in human evolution: the re-emergence of infectious disease in the third epidemiological transition. *AnthroNotes* 18(3):1–7

Armelagos GJ, McArdle A. 1975. Population, disease, and evolution. In *Population Studies in Archaeology and Biological Anthropology: A Symposium,* ed. AC Swedlund, pp. 57–70. Soc. Am. Archaeol. *Am. Antiq.* 40(2) Part 2, Mem. 30

Arriaga EE. 1989. Changing trends in mortality decline during the last decades. In *Differential Mortality: Methodological Issues and Biosocial Factors,* ed. L. Ruzicka, G Wunach, P Kane, 1:105–29. Oxford: Clarendon

Audy JR. 1958. The localization of diseases with special reference to the zoonoses. *Trans. R. Soc. Trop. Med. Hyg.* 52:308–34

Audy JR. 1961. The ecology of scrub typhus. In *Studies in Disease Ecology: Studies in Medical Geography,* ed. JM May, pp. 389–432. New York: Hafner

Baker B, Armelagos GJ. 1988. Origin and antiquity of syphilis: a dilemma in paleopathological diagnosis and interpretation. *Curr. Anthropol.* 29(5):703–37

Barclay DM III, Richardson JP, Fredman L. 1995. Tuberculosis in the homeless. *Arch. Fam. Med.* 4(6):541–46

Barnes KC, Armelagos GJ, Morreale SC. 1998. Darwinian medicine and the emergence of allergy. In *Evolutionary Medicine,* ed. W Trevethan, J McKenna, EO Smith. New York: Oxford Univ. Press.

Barnes PF, Barrows SA. 1993. Tuberculosis in the 1990s. *Ann. Intern. Med.* 119(5):400–10

Barnes PF, Elhajj H, Preston-Martin S, Cave MD, Jones BE, et al. 1996. Transmission of tuberculosis among the urban homeless. *J. Am. Med. Assoc.* 275(4):305–7

Bartlett JG, Froggatt JW III. 1995. Antibiotic resistance, *Arch. Otolaryngol. Head Neck Surg.* 121(4):392–96

Benenson A. 1995. *Control of Communicable Disease Manual.* Washington, DC: Am. Public Health Assoc.

Bennett M, Begon ME. 1997. Virus zoonoses—a long-term overview. *Comp. Immunol. Microbiol. Infect. Dis.* 20(2):101–9

Bisharat G, ed. 1995. *Mistrusting Refugees.* Berkeley: Univ. Calif. Press

Black FL. 1990. Infectious disease and the evolution of human populations: the examples of South American forest tribes. See Swedlund & Armelagos 1990, pp. 55–74

Blair A. 1993. Social class and the contextualization of illness experience. In *Worlds of Illness: Biographical and Cultural Perspectives on Health and Disease,* ed. A Radley, pp. 114–47. New York: Routledge

Bobadilla JL, Frenk J, Lozano R, Frejka T, Stern C, et al. 1993. Cardiovascular disease. In *Disease Control Priorities in Developing Countries,* ed. DT Jamison, WH Mosley, AR Measham, JL Bobadilla, pp. 51–63. Oxford, UK: Oxford Univ. Press

Bolton R. 1992. AIDS and promiscuity: muddles in the models of HIV prevention. *Med. Anthropol.* 14(2–4):145–223

Bonin O. 1971. *Marburg Virus: Consequences for the Manufacture and Control of Virus Vacine,* ed. GA Martini, R Siegert. New York: Springer-Verlag

Bouma MJ, Dye C. 1997. Cycles of malaria associated with El Niño in Venezuela. *J. Am. Med. Assoc.* 278(21):1772–74

Boyden SV, ed. 1970. *The Impact of Civilization on the Biology of Man.* Toronto: Univ. Toronto Press

Bradley DJ. 1993a. Environmental and health problems of developing countries. In *Environmental Change and Human Health. Ciba Found. Symp.* 175:234–46. Chichester, UK: CIBA Found.

Bradley DJ. 1993b. Human tropical diseases in a changing environment. See Bradley 1993a, pp. 147–70

Brothwell D. 1972. The question of pollution in earlier and less developed societies. In *Population and Pollution,* ed. PR Cox, J Peel, pp. 15–27. London: Academic

Brown PJ. 1996. Culture and the global resurgence of malaria. In *The Anthropology of Infectious Disease: International Health Perspective,* ed. MC Inhorn, PJ Brown, pp. 119–44. Amsterdam: Gordon & Breach

Brown PJ, Inhorn M, Smith D. 1996. Disease, ecology and human behavior. In *Medical Anthropology: Contemporary Theory and Methods,* ed. CF Sargent, TM Johnson, pp. 183–218. Westport, CT: Praeger

Buikstra JE. 1984. The lower Illinois river region: a prehistoric context for the study of ancient diet and health. See Cohen & Armelagos 1984, pp. 217–36

Burnet FM, 1962. *Natural History of Infectious Disease.* Cambridge, UK: Cambridge Univ. Press

Caselli G. 1991. Health transition and cause-specific mortality. See Schofield et al 1991, pp. 68–96

Centers for Disease Control. 1997. *Staphylococcus aureus* with reduced susceptibility to vancomycin—United States, 1997. *Morbid. Mortal. Wkly. Rep.* (46):765–66

Chambers R, Longhurst R, Pacey A. 1981. *Seasonal Dimensions to Rural Poverty.* London: Osmun

Chapman LE, Khabbaz RF. 1994. Etiology and epidemiology of the Four Corners hantavirus outbreak. *Infect. Agents Dis.* 3(5):234–44

Chinery WA. 1995. Impact of rapid urbanization on mosquitoes and their disease transmission potential in Accra and Tema, Ghana. *Afr. J. Med. Med. Sci.* 24(2):179–88

Cockburn TA. 1967a. The evolution of human infectious diseases. See Cockburn 1967b, pp. 84–107

Cockburn TA. 1967b. Infections of the order primates. In *Infectious Diseases: Their Evolution and Eradication,* ed. TA Cockburn. Springfield, IL: Thomas

Cockburn TA. 1971. Infectious disease in ancient populations. *Curr. Anthropol.* 12(1):45–62

Cohen J. 1997. The flu pandemic that might have been. *Science* 277(5332):1600–1

Cohen ML. 1992. Epidemiology of drug resistance: implications for a post-antimicrobial era. *Science* 257(5073):1050–55

Cohen MN, Armelagos GJ, eds. 1984. *Paleopathology at the Origins of Agriculture.* New York: Academic

Coluzzi M. 1994. Malaria and the afrotropical ecosystems: impact of man-made environmental changes. *Parassitologia* 36(1–2):223–27

Colwell RR. 1996. Global climate and infectious disease: the cholera paradigm. *Science* 274(5295):2025–31

Connors M. 1996. Sex, drugs, and structural violence: unraveling the epidemic among poor women in the United States. See Farmer et al 1996, pp. 91–123

Crawford JT. 1994. The epidemiology of tuberculosis: the impact of HIV and multidrug-resistant strains. *Immunobiology* 191:337–43

Crosby AW. 1989. *The Forgotten Pandemic: The Influenza Pandemic of 1918.* Cambridge, UK: Cambridge Univ. Press

Daily J, Farmer P, Rhatigan J, Katz J, Furin J, et al. 1996. Women and HIV infection. See Farmer et al 1996, pp. 125–45

Darbyshire J. 1996. Tuberculosis—out of control? The Mitchell Lecture 1995. *J. R. Coll. Physicians London* 30(4):352–59

Dedeoglu N. 1990. Health and social inequities in Turkey. *Soc. Sci. Med.* 31(3):387–92

de Zulueta J. 1994. Malaria and ecosystems: from prehistory to posteradication. *Parassitologia* 36(1–2):7–15

Dietz A, Senneweld E, Maier H. 1995. Indoor air pollution by emissions of fossil fuel single stoves. *J. Otolaryngol. Head Neck Surg.* 112(2):308–15

Dobyns HF. 1993. Disease transfer at contact. *Annu. Rev. Anthropol.* 22:273–91

Dressler W. 1993. Health in the African American community: accounting for health inequalities. *Med. Anthropol. Q.* 7(4):325–35

Elliot P. 1993. Global epidemiology. In *Environmental Change and Human Health, Ciba Found. Symp.* 175, pp. 219–33. Chichester, UK: Wiley

Endtz HP, Ruijs GJ, Vankling B, Jansen WH, Vanderreijden T, Mouton RP. 1991. Quinolone resistance in campylobacter isolated from may and poultry following the introduction of fluoroquinolones in veterinary medicine. *J. Antimicrob. Chem.* 27(2):199–208

Epstein P. 1995. Emerging diseases and ecosystem instability: new threats to public health. *Am. J. Public Health* 85(2):168–72

Essex M, Kanki PJ. 1988. The origin of the AIDS virus. *Sci. Am.* 259(4):64–71

Ewald PW. 1994. *Evolution of Infectious Disease.* New York: Oxford Univ. Press

Farmer P. 1992. *AIDS and Accusation: Haiti and the Geography of Blame.* Berkeley: Univ. Calif. Press

Farmer P. 1996. Social inequalities and emerging infectious diseases. *Emerg. Infect. Dis.* 2(4):259–69

Farmer P. 1997. Social scientists and the new tuberculosis. *Soc. Sci. Med.* 44(3):347–58

Farmer P, Connors M, Simmons J, eds. 1996. *Women, Poverty, and AIDS: Sex, Drugs, and Structural Violence.* Monroe, ME: Common Courage

Farmer P, Lindenbaum S, Good MJ. 1993. Women, poverty and AIDS: an introduction. *Cult. Med. Psychiatry* 17(4):387–97

Feldman DA. 1990. *Assessing Viral, Parasitic, and Socioeconomic Cofactors Affecting HIV—I Transmission in Rwanda,* ed. DA Feldman, pp. 45–54. New York: Praeger

Fenner F. 1970. The effects of changing social organization on the infectious diseases of man. In *The Impact of Civilization on the Biology of Man,* ed. SV Boyden. Canberra: Aust. Natl. Univ. Press

Flinn MW. 1974. The stabilization of mortality in preindustrial Western Europe. *J. Eur. Econ. Hist.* 3:285–318

Fraser DW, Tsai TR, Orenstein W, Parkin WE, Beecham HJ, et al. 1977. Legionnaires' disease: description of an epidemic of pneumonia. *N. Engl. J. Med.* 297(22):1189–97

Fries JF. 1980. Aging, natural death, and the compression of morbidity. *N. Engl. J. Med.* 303(3):130–35

Garrett L. 1994a. *The Coming Plague: Newly Emerging Diseases in a World Out of Balance.* New York: Farrar Straus & Giroux

Garrett L. 1994b. Human movements and behavioral factors in the emergence of diseases. *Ann. NY Acad. Sci.* 740:312–18

Gaylin DS, Kates J. 1997. Refocusing the lens: epidemiologic transition theory, mortality differentials, and the AIDS pandemic. *Soc. Sci. Med.* 44(5):609–21

Gerber MA. 1995. Antibiotic resistance in group *A* streptococci. *Pediatr. Clin. North Am.* 42(3):539–51

Glezen WP. 1996. Emerging infections: pandemic influenza. *Epidemiol. Rev.* 18(1):64–76

Gobalet JG. 1989. *World Mortality Trends Since 1870.* New York: Garland

Goldstein FW, Garau J. 1994. Resistant pneumococci: a renewed threat in respiratory infections. *Scand. J. Infect. Dis. Suppl.* 93:55–62

Grossman E, Rosenthal T. 1993. Effect of urbanization on blood pressure in Ethiopian immigrants. *J. Hum. Hypertens.* 7(6):559–61

Gruneberg RN, Wilson APR. 1994. Anti-infective treatment in intensive care: the role of glycopeptides. *Intensive Care Med.* 20(S4):S17–22

Gubler DJ. 1996. The global resurgence of arboviral diseases. *Trans. R. Soc. Trop. Med. Hyg.* 90(5):449–51

Gubler DJ, Clark GG. 1995. Dengue/dengue hemorrhagic fever: the emergence of a global health problem. *Emerg. Infect. Dis.* 1(2):55–57

Gwatkin DR. 1980. Indications of change in developing country mortality trends: the end of an era? *Popul. Dev. Rev.* 33(2): 615–44

Harpham T. 1994. Urbanization and mental health in developing countries: a research role for social scientists, public health professionals, and social psychiatrists. *Soc. Sci. Med.* 39(2):233–45

Harrison G, Waterlow S, eds. 1990. *Diet and Disease in Transitional and Developing Societies.* Cambridge, UK: Cambridge Univ. Press

Hayden FG, Hay AJ. 1992. Emergence and transmission of influenza *A* viruses resistant to amantadine and rimantadine. *Curr. Top. Microbiol. Immunol.* 176:119–30

Hill K, Pebley LR. 1989. Child mortality in the developing world. *Popul. Dev. Rev.* 15(4):657–87

Hudson EH. 1965. Treponematosis and man's social evolution. *Am. Anthropol.* 67:885–901

Huminer D, Rosenfeld JB, Pitlik SD. 1987. AIDS in the pre-AIDS era. *Rev. Infect. Dis.* 9:1102–8

Hunt CW. 1995. *Migrant Labor and Sexually Transmitted Disease: AIDS in Africa,* ed. ER Bethel, pp. 137–56. Boston: Allyn & Bacon

Inhorn MC, Brown PJ. 1990. The anthropology of infectious disease. *Annu. Rev. Anthropol.* 19:89–117

Islam MS, Siddique AK, Salam A, Akram K, Majumdar RN, et al. 1995. Microbiological investigations of diarrhoea epidemics among Rwandan Refugees in Zaire. *Trans. R. Soc. Trop. Med. Hyg.* 89:506

Jacobs RF. 1994. Multiple-drug-resistant tuberculosis. *Clin. Infect. Dis.* 19(1):1–8

Jacoby GA. 1996. Antimicrobial-resistant pathogens in the 1990s. *Annu. Rev. Med.* 47:169–79

Jaenson TGT. 1991. The epidemiology of Lyme borreliosis. *Parasit. Today* 7:39–45

Jernigan DB, Cetron MS, Breiman RF. 1996. Minimizing the impact of drug-resistant *Streptococcus pneumoniae* (DRSP): a strategy from the DRSP working group. *J. Am. Med. Assoc.* 275(3):206–9

Johansson SR. 1992. Measuring the cultural inflation of morbidity during the decline in mortality. *Health Transit. Rev.* 2(1):78–89

Kaplan G, Keil J. 1993. Socioeconomic factors and cardiovascular disease: a review of the literature. *Circulation* 88:1973–98

Kearney M. 1995. Local and the global: the anthropology of globalization and transnationalism. *Annu. Rev. Anthropol.* 24:547–65

Kliks MM. 1983. Paleoparasitology: on the origins and impact of human-helminth relationships. In *Human Ecology and Infectious Disease,* ed. NA Croll, JH Cross, pp. 291–313. New York: Academic

Knapp VJ. 1989. *Disease and its Impact on Modern European History,* Vol. 10. Lewiston, NY: Mellen

Koll BS, Brown AE. 1993. The changing epidemiology of infections at cancer hospitals. *Clin. Infect. Dis.* 17(Suppl. 2):S322–28

Kollef MH. 1994. Antibiotic use and antibiotic resistance in the intensive care unit: are we curing or creating disease? *Heart Lung* 23(5):363–67

Kunin CM. 1993. Resistance to antimicrobial drugs—a worldwide calamity. *Ann. Intern. Med.* 118(7):557–61

Kunin CM, Lipton HL, Tupasi T, Sachs T, Schekler WE, et al. 1987. Social, behavioral, and practical factors affecting antibiotic use worldwide: report of Task Force 4. *Rev. Infect. Dis.* 9(3):270–84

Kunitz SJ. 1991. The personal physician and the decline of mortality. See Schofield et al 1991, pp. 248–62

Laird M. 1989. Vector-borne disease introduced into new areas due to human movements: a historical perspective. In *Demography and Vector-Borne Diseases,* ed. MW Service, pp. 17–33. Boca Raton, FL: CRC

Lambrecht FL. 1980. Paleoecology of tsetse flies and sleeping sickness in Africa. *Proc. Am. Philos. Soc.* 124(5):367–85

Lambrecht FL. 1985. Trypanosomes and hominid evolution. *BioScience* 35(10):640–46

Lappe M. 1994. *Evolutionary Medicine: Rethinking the Origins of Disease.* San Francisco: Sierra Club Books

Lederberg J. 1997. Infectious disease as an evolutionary paradigm. *Emerg. Infect. Dis.* 3(4):417–23

Lederberg J, Shope RE, Oaks SC Jr, eds. 1992. *Emerging Infection: Microbal Threats to Health in the United States.* Washington, DC: Inst. Med., Natl. Acad. Press

Lewis K. 1994. Multidrug resistance pumps in bacteria: variations on a theme. *Trends Biochem. Sci.* 19(3):119–23

Lindenbaum S. 1990. The ecology of kuru. See Swedlund & Armelagos 1990

Lindenbaum S. 1991. Anthropology rediscovers sex. Introduction. *Soc. Sci. Med.* 33(8):865–66

Livingstone FB. 1958. Anthropological implications of sickle-cell distribution in West Africa. *Am. Anthropol.* 60:533–62

Longworth DL. 1995. Drug-resistant malaria in children and in travelers. *Pediatr. Clin. North Am.* 42(3):649–64

MacQueen KM. 1994. The epidemiology of HIV transmission: trends, structure, and dynamics. *Annu. Rev. Anthropol.* 23:509–26

MacQueen KM, Nopkesorn T, Sweat MD. 1996. Alcohol consumption, brothel attendance, and condom use: normative expectations among Thai military conscripts. *Med. Anthropol. Q.* 10(3):402–23

Malin AS, McAdam KP, Keith PW. 1995. Escalating threat from tuberculosis: the third epidemic. *Thorax* 50:S37–42

Malkki LH. 1995. Refugees and exile: from "refugee studies" to the national order of things. *Annu. Rev. Anthropol.* 24:495–523

Martens WJM, Niessen LW, Rotman J, Jetten TH, McMichael AJ. 1995. Potential impact of global climate change on malaria risk. *Environ. Health Perspect.* 103(5):458–64

Martin AA, Moore J, Collins C, Biellik R, Kattel U, et al. 1994. Infectious disease surveillance during emergency relief to Bhutanese refugees in Nepal. *J. Am. Med. Assoc.* 272(5):377–81

Martin DL, Armelagos GJ. 1979. Morphometrics of compact bone: an example from Sudanese Nubia. *Am. J. Phys. Anthropol.* 51:571–78

McCoy CB, Metsch LR, Inciardi JA, et al. 1996. Sex, drugs, and the spread of HIV/AIDS in Belle Glade, Florida. *Med. Anthropol. Q.* 10(1):83–93

McDade JE, Shepard CC, Fraser DW, Tsai TR, Redus MA, et al. 1977. Legionnaires' disease: isolation of a bacterium and demonstration of its role in other respiratory disease. *N. Engl. J. Med.* 297(22):1197–203

McDonald LC, Kuehnert MJ, Tenover FC, Jarvis WR. 1997. Vancomycin-resistant enterococci outside the health care setting, prevalence, sources and public health implications. *Emerg. Infect. Dis.* 3:311–17

McKeown T. 1976. *The Modern Rise of Population.* New York: Academic

McNeill WH. 1976. *Plagues and People.* Garden City, NY: Anchor/Doubleday

McNeill WH. 1978. Disease in history. *Soc. Sci. Med.* 12:79–81

Menegoni L. 1996. Conceptions of tuberculosis and therapeutic choices in Highland Chiapas, Mexico. *Med. Anthropol. Q.* 10(3):381–401

Miller RP. 1979. Cooling towers and evaporative condensers. *Ann. Intern. Med.* 90(4):667–70

Moellering RC Jr. 1995. Past, present, and future of antimicrobial agents. *Am. J. Med.* 99(6A):29

Moore HF. 1917. A study of ethylhydrocpreine (optochin) in the treatment of acute lobar pneumonia. *Arch. Intern. Med.* (19):611

Morris GK, Patton CM, Feeley JC, Johnson SE, Gorman G, et al. 1979. Isolation of the Legionnaires' disease bacterium from environmental samples. *Ann. Intern. Med.* 90(4):664–66

Morris JG, Potter M. 1997. Emergence of new pathogens as a function of changes in host susceptibility. *Emerg. Infect. Dis.* 3(4):435–41

Morse SS. 1994. Prediction and biological evolution. Concept paper. *Ann. NY Acad. Sci.* 740:436–38

Morse SS. 1995. Factors in the emergence of infectious diseases. *Emerg. Infect. Dis.* 1(1):7–15

Muktatkar R. 1995. Public health problems of urbanization. *Soc. Sci. Med.* 41(7):977–81

Nahmias AJ, Weiss J, Yao X, Lee F, Kodsi R, et al. 1986. Evidence for human infection with an HTLV-III-LAV-like virus in central Africa, 1959. *Lancet* 1:1279–80

Neu HC. 1992. The crisis in antibiotic resistance. *Science* 257(5073):1064–73

Nicoletti G, Stefani S. 1995. Enterococci: susceptibility patterns and therapeutic options. *Eur. J. Clin. Microbiol. Infect. Dis.* 14(1):S33–37

Nunn P, Felten M. 1994. Surveillance of resistance to antituberculosis drugs in developing countries. *Tuberc. Lung Dis.* 75(3):163–67

Obaro SK, Monteil MA, Henderson DC. 1996. The pneumococcal problem. *Br. Med. J.* 312(7045):1521–25

Oliver JH. 1996. Lyme borreliosis in the southern United States: a review. *J. Parasitol.* 82(6):926–35

Olliaro P, Cattani J, Wirth D. 1996. Malaria, the submerged disease. *J. Am. Med. Assoc.* 275(3):230–33

Olshansky SJ, Ault AB. 1986. The fourth stage of the epidemiologic transition: the age of delayed degenerative diseases. *Milbank Mem. Fund Q.* 64(3):355–91

Omran AR. 1971. The epidemiologic transition: a theory of the epidemiology of population change. *Millbank Mem. Fund Q.* 49(4):509–37

Omran AR. 1983. The epidemiologic transition theory: a preliminary update. *J. Trop. Pediatr.* 29(6):305–16

Palmer JR. 1994. Advances in the epidemiology of gestational trophoblastic disease. *J. Reprod. Med.* 39(3):155–62

Patz JA, Epstein PR, Burke TA, Balbus JM. 1996. Global climate change and emerging infectious diseases. *J. Am. Med. Assoc.* 275(3):217–23

Perrera F. 1993. Prevention of environmental pollution: good for our health. *Environ. Health Perspect.* 101(7):562–63

Phillips DR. 1993. Urbanization and human health. *Parasitology* 106(107):S93–107

Pinner R, Teutsch SM, Simonsen L, Klug LA, Graber JM, et al. 1996. Trends in infectious diseases mortality in the United States. *J. Am. Med. Assoc.* 275(3):189–93

Polgar S. 1964. Evolution and the ills of mankind. In *Horizons of Anthropology*, ed. S Tax, pp. 200–11. Chicago: Aldine

Popkin BM. 1994. The nutrition transition in low-income countries: an emerging crisis. *Nutr. Rev.* 52(9):285–98

Preston R. 1994. *The Hot Zone*. New York: Random House

Puranen B. 1991. Tuberculosis and the decline of mortality in Sweden. In *The Decline of Mortality in Europe*, ed. R Schofield, D Reher, A Bideau, pp. 68–96. Oxford, UK: Clarendon

Raviglione MC, Snider DE, Kochi A. 1995. Global epidemiology of tuberculosis: morbidity and mortality of a worldwide epidemic. *J. Am. Med. Assoc.* 273: 220–26

Reid D, Cossar JH. 1993. Epidemiology of travel. *Br. Med. Bull.* 49(2):257–68

Rho JP, Yoshikawa TT. 1995. The cost of inappropriate use of anti-infective agents in older patients. *Drugs Aging* 6(4):263–67

Rhodes R. 1997. *Deadly Feasts: Tracking the Secrets of a Terrifying New Plague*. New York: Simon & Schuster

Rice LB, Shlaes DM. 1995. Vancomycin resistance in the enterococcus. Relevance in pediatrics. *Pediatr. Clin. N. Am.* 42(3):601–18

Riley JC. 1992. From a high mortality regime to a high morbidity regime: is culture everything in sickness? *Health Transit. Rev.* 2(1):71–78

Riley JC, Alter G. 1989. The epidemiologic transition and morbidity. *Ann. Demogr. Histor.* 1989:199–213

Risse GB. 1988. Epidemics and history: ecological perspectives and social responses. In *AIDS: The Burdens of History*, ed. E Fee, DM Fox, pp. 33–66. Berkeley: Univ. Calif. Press

Roberts DR, Andre RG. 1994. Insecticide resistance issues in vector-borne disease control. *Am. J. Trop. Med. Hyg.* 50(6):21–34 (Suppl.)

Rowe B, Ward LR, Threlfall EJ. 1997. Multidrug-resistant *Salmonella typhi*: a worldwide epidemic. *Clin. Infect. Dis.* 24(Suppl. 1):S106–9

Rubel AJ, Garro LC. 1992. Social and cultural factors in the successful control of tuberculosis. *Public Health Rep.* 107(6):626–35

Ruzicka L, Kane P. 1990. Health transition: the course of morbidity and mortality. In *What We Know About Health Transition: The Cultural, Social, and Behavioral Determinants of Health*, ed. J Caldwell, S Findley, P Cadwell, G Santow, W Cosford, J Braid, D Broers Freeman, pp. 1–24. Proc. Int. Workshop. Canberra: Health Transit. Cent.

Ryan F. 1993. *The Forgotten Plague: How the Battle against Tuberculosis Was Won—and Lost*. Boston: Little Brown

Ryan F. 1997. *Virus X: Tracking the New Killer Plagues: Out of the Present into the Future*. Boston: Little Brown

Saravolatz LD, Burch KH, Fisher E, Madhavan T, Kiani D, et al. 1979. The compromised host and Legionnaires' disease. *Ann. Intern. Med.* 90(4):533–37

Satcher D. 1995. Emerging infections: getting ahead of the curve. *Emerg. Infect. Dis.* 1(1):1–6

Schentag JJ. 1995. Understanding and managing microbial resistance in institutional settings. *Am. J. Health Syst. Pharm.* 52 (Suppl. 2):S9–14

Schofield R, Reher D. 1991. The decline of mortality in Europe. See Schofield et al 1991, pp. 1–17

Schofield R, Reher D, Bideau D, eds. 1991. *The Decline of Mortality in Europe*. Oxford, UK: Clarendon

Shortridge KF. 1992. Pandemic influenza: a zoonosis? *Semin. Respir. Infect.* 7(1):11–25

Shortridge KF. 1995. The next pandemic influenza virus? *Lancet* 346(8984):1210–12

Shu LL, Lin YP, Wright SM, Shortridge KF, Webster RG. 1994. Evidence for interspecies transmission and reassortment of influenza *A* viruses in pigs in southern China. *Virology* 202(2):825–33

Siddique AK, Salam A, Islam MS, Akram K, Majumdar RN, et al. 1995. Why treatment centres failed to prevent cholera deaths among Rwandan refugees in Goma, Zaire. *Lancet* 345(8946):359–61

Sommerfeld J. 1995. Emerging and resurgent infectious diseases: a challenge for anthropological research. *Proc. Annu. Meet. Am. Anthropol. Assoc., 94th, Washington, DC*

Sprent JFA. 1962. Parasitism, immunity and evolution. In *The Evolution of Living Organisms*, ed. GS Leeper, pp. 149–65. Melbourne: Melbourne Univ. Press

Sprent JFA. 1969a. Evolutionary aspects of immunity of zooparasitic infections. In *Immunity to Parasitic Animals*, ed. GJ Jackson, 1:3–64. New York: Appleton

Sprent JFA. 1969b. Helminth "zoonoses": an analysis. *Helminthol. Abstr.* 38:333–51

Sumartojo E. 1993. When tuberculosis treatment fails: a social behavioral account of patient adherence. *Am. Rev. Respir. Dis.* 147:1311–20

Swartz MN. 1994. Hospital-acquired infections: diseases with increasingly limited therapies. *Proc. Natl. Acad. Sci. USA* 91(7):2420–27

Swedlund AC, Armelagos GJ, eds. 1990. *Diseases in Population in Transition: Anthropological and Epidemiological Perspectives*. New York: Bergin & Garvey

Tambiah S. 1989. Ethnic conflicts in the world today. *Am. Ethnol.* 16:335–49

Tauxe RV. 1997. Emerging foodborne diseases: an evolving public health challenge. *Emerg. Infect. Dis.* 3(4):425–34

Thompson CS, O'Leary JP. 1997. The discovery of the vector for "yellow jack." *Am. Surg.* 63(5):462–63

Toltzis P, Blumer JL. 1995. Antibiotic-resistant gram-negative bacteria in the critical care setting. *Pediatr. Clin. N. Am.* 42(3):687–702

Toole MJ. 1995. Mass population displacement. A global public health challenge. *Infect. Dis. Clin. N. Am.* 9(2):353–66

United Nations. 1982. *Levels and Trends in Mortality Since 1950: A Joint Study by the United Nations and the World Health Organization.* New York: UN

VanGerven DP, Hummert J, Pendergast Moore K, Sanford MK. 1990. Nutrition, disease and the human life cycle: a bioethnography of a medieval Nubian community. In *Primate Life History and Evolution*, ed. CJ deRousseau, pp. 297–324. New York: Wiley-Liss

Vareldzis BP, Grosset J, Dekantori I, Crofton J, Laszlo A, et al. 1994. Drug-resistant tuberculosis: laboratory issues. World Health Organization recommendations. *Tuber. Lung Dis.* 75(1):1–7

Vecchiato NL. 1997. Sociocultural aspects of tuberculosis control in Ethiopia. *Med. Anthropol. Q.* 11(2):183–201

Waddell C. 1996. HIV and the social world of female commercial sex workers. *Med. Anthropol. Q.* 10(1):75–82

Walker DH, Barbour AG, Oliver JH, Lane RS, Dumler JS, et al. 1996. Emerging bacterial zoonotic and vector-borne diseases: ecological and epidemiological factors. *J. Am. Med. Assoc.* 275(6):463–69

Weber JT, Mintz ED, Canizares R, Semiglia A, Gomez I, et al. 1994. Epidemic cholera in Ecuador: multidrug-resistance and transmission by water and seafood. *Epidemiol. Infect.* 112(1):1–11

Webster RG, Wright SM, Castrucci MR, Bean WJ, Kawaoka Y. 1993. Influenza—a model of an emerging virus disease. *Intervirology* 35(1–4):16–25

Weigler BJ. 1995. Zoonotic hantavirus; new concerns for the United States. *J. Am. Veterin. Med. Assoc.* 206(7):979–86

Whiteford LM. 1997. The ethnoecology of dengue fever. *Med. Anthropol. Q.* 11(2): 202–23

Wilson ME. 1996. Travel and the emergence of infectious diseases. *Emerg. Infect. Dis.* 1(2):39–46

Wiselka M. 1994. Influenza: diagnosis, management, and prophylaxis. *Br. Med. J.* 308(6940):1341–45

Woods R. 1991. Public health and public hygiene: the urban environment in the late nineteenth and early twentieth centuries. See Schofield et al 1991, pp. 233–47

World Bank. 1993. *World Development Report 1993: Investing in Health.* Oxford, UK: Oxford Univ. Press

Wright SM, Kawaoka Y, Sharp GB, Senne DA, Webster RG. 1992. Interspecies transmission and reassortment of influenza *A* viruses in pigs and turkeys in the United States. *Am. J. Epidemiol.* 136(4):488–97

Zolopa AR. 1994. HIV and tuberculosis infection in San Francisco's homeless adults. *J. Am. Med. Assoc.* 272(6):455–61

20   HEALTH CONDITIONS BEFORE COLUMBUS: PALEOPATHOLOGY OF NATIVE NORTH AMERICANS

Debra L. Martin and Alan H. Goodman

This selection provides substantive detail regarding the health impacts of the first epidemiologic transition that accompanied the adoption of agriculture by foraging populations. It shows how anthropologists assess health status, physical strength and functional limitation, and infectious and nutritional disease stress through analysis of bone lesions in skeletal remains. The selection describes the kinds of information that specific lesions can reveal about the living conditions of the person who bore them. It shows

Source: Martin, D. L. and A. H. Goodman 2002. "Health Conditions before Columbus: Paleopathology of Native North Americans." *Western Journal of Medicine* 176(1):65–68. With permission from the BMJ Publishing Group.

how comparative analysis of bones from different populations can provide insights into the impacts on health of changes in subsistence modes and living conditions.

In addition to confirming the overall picture presented in previous selections concerning the negative health effects of the transition to agriculture—increased infectious disease, iron deficiency anemia, infant mortality, and adult female mortality, and decreased stature and life expectancy—the analysis provides insights into the devastating impact of contact with Europeans. Yet, although while the effect on Native American mortality was enormous, involving mainly acute and epidemic diseases, precontact Americans did not live in a sterile environment. Rather, they were beset by a number of infectious diseases, although these tended to be of chronic and episodic type (see selection 19 on why the foraging lifestyle favored these kinds of diseases, and selection 16 on the relationship among vectors, disease organisms, and human populations). As we have seen, humans and microbes are locked in a timeless, never-ending embrace, but the shape of the relationship depends on a complex set of ecological, behavioral, and socioeconomic factors.

Questions to keep in mind

How do the lifestyle changes described for Native North American populations in transition compare to those outlined in the previous selection?

What do the bone lesions discussed in this selection reveal about disease, nutritional status, and physical strain?

What specific health changes accompanied the transition to agriculture in the groups considered in this study?

How were the negative health impacts of increasing reliance on agriculture unevenly distributed across gender and age groups?

Information about the health status of the earliest inhabitants of North America provides a chronology of health problems that spans more than a thousand years. Studies of disease in ancient times add an important dimension to our understanding of the life struggles of a largely unknown past. In this article, we provide a brief overview of health conditions and quality of life in North America before contact and colonization.

Data on health in ancient societies are inferred from the analysis of a wide range of archaeologic materials, but human bones and teeth form by far the largest body of evidence. For several regions in the United States, there are health chronologies spanning hundreds of years. For example, Walker, using a multimethod approach involving the analysis of skeletal lesions and detailed reconstruction of the environment, demonstrated that Indians of southern California who lived in marginal island environments (about 800 BC to AD 1150) showed greater evidence of health problems than those who lived on the mainland, where food was more abundant and diverse.[1] He also showed increased rates of infectious diseases over time.

There has been a shift toward conducting population-level analyses that shed light on epidemiologic characteristics of the health of ancient societies by providing frequencies and patterning of disease within and between populations.[2] Much of the recent paleopathology literature emphasizes temporal and spatial variability in patterns of disease and the shift in many parts of North America at different times from an economy based on gathering and hunting to agriculture. Although not all groups in North America adopted full-blown maize agriculture, many did, and it has been the focus of intense debate.[2]

The study of North American archaeologic remains has been under protest by native groups because historically they have had little say over the excavation and curatorship of their ancestors' remains.[3] These protests led to legislation passed in 1990 entitled the Native American Graves Protection and Repatriation Act (US Public Law

101-601). This law ensures that Native Americans have the final say regarding the nature of studies that rely on ancestral and historic human remains. In many ways, this legislation has redefined the nature of archaeologic research in the United States and has opened new venues of study as Native Americans and anthropologists have begun working together to reconstruct the past.[4]

AN ANALYSIS OF DISEASE IN ANCIENT POPULATIONS

Because skeletal tissue typically responds in non-specific ways to disease, the diagnosis of a specific cause is often difficult. Fortunately, what has the greatest explanatory power is not the specific agent but, rather, the severity, duration, and temporal course of generalized physiologic perturbations. These general stressors, as they may be read and deciphered from skeletal lesions, can provide a means for assessing the health status and degree of functional impairment that an individual experienced.

To elucidate this general health stress perspective, a model was developed to apply to studies of health in the past.[5] With its focus on relationships between environment, culture, and biologic conditions, this model has proved useful in considering past adaptive struggles and the centrality of health (Figure 20.1). Analysis of past health begins with understanding the environmental context within which people lived. The environment greatly influences how successful groups are at procuring food and what the constraints may be in providing food, clothing, and shelter. If groups are to thrive, they must adapt to climate, excess heat or cold, high altitude, parasites, and predators.

In terms of ancient health, understanding the cultural patterns helps us to understand which cultural customs buffered against poor health and which customs may have promoted disease. For example, enclosed rock shelters in Colorado offered protection from the elements and predators, but they also facilitated the exchange of communicable diseases.[6] The development of agriculture in North America allowed greater production of calories relative to human expenditure[7] and, thus, would seem to have provided a buffer against undernutrition. However, the resulting increased population density, along with other ecologic and demographic changes associated with intensified farming, had a profound influence on health, with statistically significant increases in infectious diseases and iron deficiency anemia.

The response to disease stress is often a stereotypic physiologic change that results from the effort to adjust and overcome the stress, and this is frequently manifest in relatively permanent osteologic indicators. Although paleopathologists may be limited by the amount of information that can be gleaned from archaeologic remains, a multidisciplinary approach has allowed the integration of forensic, medical, and epidemiologic methods to reconstruct health conditions.

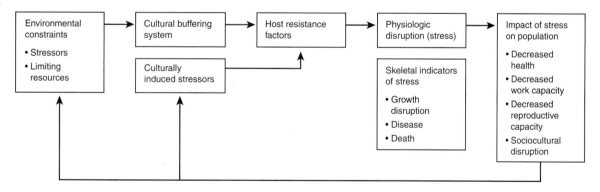

Figure 20.1   Model depicting variables necessary for delineating precontact group adaptation. The feedback loop can be used only when the archaeologic context of the human remains is well documented.

PREVALENT HEALTH PROBLEMS IN PRE-COLUMBIAN TIMES

Iron Deficiency Anemia

Porotic hyperostosis is a descriptive term for lesions primarily found on the parietal and orbital bones of the cranium, produced by bone marrow proliferation diagnostic of anemia. The lesion generally takes the form of a raised, porous area that develops when the trabecular portion of the cranial bone (diploë) expands and the outer table of bone becomes thinner, exposing the inner diploë. Anemias can potentially affect any bone of the skeleton that is involved in the production of red blood cells, but the most frequently affected bones are those of the cranium.

Porotic hyperostosis is a skeletal indicator of nutritional stress that has been extensively studied in archaeologic populations.[8] Nearly all cases in North America seem to be due to iron deficiency, and the presence of low iron stores is likely to occur concomitantly with other health problems and nutritional deficiencies. Although these lesions can also be caused by hereditary hemolytic anemia and other disorders, iron deficiency is accepted as the primary cause of porotic hyperostosis for the vast majority of documented prehistoric cases.[9]

Iron deficiency anemia appears to have been widespread and ubiquitous in most ancient populations in the New World.[8] The general distribution of the lesion corresponds with increasing reliance on agricultural products such as maize, which are low in bioavailable iron. For example, Lallo and co-workers evaluated changes in rates of porotic hyperostosis for ancient Mississippians in Illinois living in the 12th century and found that its prevalence increased dramatically in the transition from hunting and gathering to agriculture.[10] They suggested that this was due to an overreliance on maize in the diet and that the lesions were most pronounced in younger children because of diarrheal disease during weaning, combined with poor diet.

Infectious Diseases

Infectious diseases are among the most significant selective forces in human evolution[11] and, combined with undernutrition, continue to be the largest contributor to morbidity and mortality worldwide. Although most infectious diseases leave no diagnostic markers, it is fortunate for paleopathologists that some affect the skeleton, changing the structure of bone tissue. The most frequent causes of infectious diseases in prehistory have been estimated to be common microorganisms such as staphylococcus and streptococcus, with conditions such as tuberculosis and venereal and nonvenereal syphilis relatively rare and more controversial to diagnose.[12] The chronic (typically nonlethal) conditions are important to track at the community level because these illnesses perhaps shed the most light on everyday occurrences of poor diet, transmissible diseases, and the state of waste disposal and hygiene.

Osteomyelitis results from the introduction of pyogenic infection, and the skeletal response involves the periosteum, cortex, and medullary cavity. Osteitis is another form of this phenomenon, but the reaction is primarily localized within the cortical bone. Periostitis occurs when the reaction is restricted to the outer shaft, or periosteum. It can occur as a direct response to a skin infection, through trauma, through systemic bacterial invasions, or from other soft tissue infections. Diagnosis and identification of the cause of the infection are difficult, and paleopathologists have now advocated using general descriptive categories for classifying the skeletal changes observed.[13] Referred to as nonspecific infectious lesions, the skeletal manifestations are categorized as periosteal reactions because most of the infectious conditions seen on prehistoric bones tend to fall in this category. Specific diagnoses are attempted by paleopathologists when there are lesions that seem to fit the pattern reported for treponemal or tubercular infections, although the number of these in pre-Columbian individuals is relatively rare.

Lallo and colleagues noted that the severity of periosteal reactions among Mississippian burials increased nearly fourfold during the period spanning the hunter–gatherer phase through intensive agriculture.[10] The increase in infectious diseases in the intensive agriculturalists was thought to be related to increased population density and sedentary behavior, coupled with low dietary quality and overreliance on maize. Other trends in infectious diseases demonstrated that adult women had higher rates than did men and that individuals with infections died at an earlier age. Individuals had a high rate of co-occurrence of porotic hyperostosis and infections, suggesting that iron deficiency may have predisposed children to infectious diseases by lowering resistance.

Osteoarthritis

Osteoarthritis is among the oldest and most commonly known diseases that affect humans. Measuring the amount of arthritic involvement with skeletal remains is sometimes difficult because of the potentially large number of areas to be assessed (each vertebra and all joint systems) and the range of variation in bony response among individuals. Although many factors may contribute to the breakdown of skeletal tissue, the primary cause of osteoarthritis is related to biomechanical wear and tear and functional stress.[14] Biomechanical stress is most apparent at the articular surfaces of long bone joint systems and is referred to as degenerative joint disease. There may be a relationship between such disease and other health problems. For example, a study correlating the incidence of degenerative joint disease and infection was undertaken for a Mississippian population from Illinois (AD 1000–1200). Individuals with multiple joint involvement demonstrated a statistically higher percentage of periosteal reactions. The prevalence of both infectious lesions and degenerative joint disease increased with age, and women demonstrated greater frequencies of disease in the shoulder and elbows than did age-matched men.

In general, early Native Americans appeared to sustain osteoarthritis at rates comparable with individuals today, although the earlier rate of onset and decreased life span of early Native Americans may have served to compress the observable cases into a shorter time frame within the life span. Much work in the area of osteologic correlates of occupational stress and weapon use suggest strong associations between lifestyle and patterns of osteoarthritic and other bone changes.[15]

DEMOGRAPHY AND DISEASE AT CONTACT

There is wide agreement about the effects of diseases and epidemics associated with European contact.[16,17] The first well-documented, widespread epidemic in what was to become New Mexico was smallpox in 1636. Shortly thereafter, measles entered the area, and many Pueblos lost as many as a quarter of their inhabitants.[18] After the founding of Spanish settlements and missions, there was substantially more contact, and throughout the 17th century, epidemic disease was repeatedly imported.

Osteologic data demonstrate that native groups were most definitely not living in a pristine, disease-free environment before contact. Although New World indigenous disease was mostly of the chronic and episodic kind, Old World diseases were largely acute and epidemic. Different populations were affected at different times and suffered varying rates of mortality.[19] Diseases such as treponemiasis and tuberculosis were already present in the New World, along with diseases such as tularemia, giardia, rabies, amebic dysentery, hepatitis, herpes, pertussis, and poliomyelitis, although the prevalence of almost all of these was probably low in any given group.[14] Old World diseases that were not present in the Americas until contact include bubonic plague, measles, smallpox, mumps, chickenpox, influenza, cholera, diphtheria, typhus, malaria, leprosy, and yellow fever.[19] Indians in the Americas had no acquired immunity to these infectious diseases, and these diseases caused what Crosby referred to as "virgin soil epidemics," in which all members of a population would be infected simultaneously.[20]

It is important to look not only at the effects of specific events like epidemic outbreaks but also at longer-term processes that influence the age and mortality structure of populations. Kunitz and Euler stated that "one does not need to invoke large-scale dramatic epidemics; prosaic entities like malnutrition and infectious diarrhea are more than sufficient to do the job."[6] Neel likewise cautioned that, to understand the influence of introduced diseases on indigenous peoples, we must first know the longer history and "epidemiologic profile" of the populations.[21] This points to the value of incorporating the information on precontact health as a precursor to understanding the effects of contact.

CONCLUSIONS: LESSONS FROM THE PAST

The importance of understanding health within a broad historical framework is illustrated by the following example, which draws on recent collaborative investigations into endemic health problems of the indigenous groups who call themselves the Pima and Tohono O'odham in southern Arizona. High rates of diabetes, hypertension, and obesity have plagued members of these groups since the 1940s. Recent multidisciplinary efforts to understand the etiology of these patterns have combined oral history and anthropologic, archaeologic, and epidemiologic information on diet and health to better understand the progression of these health problems over time.[22] Some Pima Indians have begun to incorporate traditional foods such as lima beans, tepary beans, mesquite pods, and maize into their diet, with positive health results.[23] Research such as this examines the larger interacting sphere of culture, environment, and life processes, and such studies of ancestral menus and ancestral health trends may continue to provide important dues to today's health problems.

NOTES

1. Walker PL. Integrative approaches to the study of ancient health: an example from the Santa Barbara area of Southern California. In: Pérez-Pérez A, ed. *Notes on Population Significance of Paleopathological Conditions.* Barcelona: Fundació Uriach; 1996:6–98.

2. Cohen MN, Armelagos GJ, eds. *Paleopathology at the Origins of Agriculture.* New York: Academic Press; 1984.

3. Echo-Hawk RC. Working together: exploring the ancient world. *Soc Am Archacol Bull* 1993;11:5–6.

4. Barrios P. Native Americans and archaeologists working together toward common goals in California. *Soc Am Archacol Bull* 1993;11:6–7.

5. Martin DL, Goodman AH, Armelagos GJ, et al. *Black Mesa Anasazi Health: Reconstructing Life from Patterns of Death and Disease.* Carbondale: Southern Illinois Press; 1991.

6. Kunitz SK, Euler RC. *Aspects of Southwestern Paleoepidemiology. Prescott College Anthropological Reports 2.* Prescott, AZ: Prescott College Press; 1972.

7. Wetterstrom W. *Food, Diet and Population at Prehistoric Arroyo Hondo Pueblo, New Mexico.* Santa Fe, NM: School of American Research Press; 1986.

8. Mensforth RP, Lovejoy CO, Lallo JW, et al. The role of constitutional factors, diet, and infectious disease in the etiology of porotic hyperostosis and periosteal reactions in prehistoric infants and children. *Med Anthropol* 1978;2:1–59.

9. Stuart-Macadam P. Porotic hyperostosis: new evidence to support the anemia theory. *Am J Phys Anthropol* 1987;74:521–526.

10. Lallo J. Armelagos GJ, Rose JC. Paleoepidemiology of infectious disease in the Dickson Mounds population. *Med College Va Q* 1977;14:17–23.

11. Armelagos GJ, Dewey JR. Evolutionary response to human infectious disease. In: Logan MH, Hunt EE, eds. *Health and the Human Condition.* North Scituate, MA: Duxbury Press; 1970:101–106.

12. Ormer DJ, Tyson R. *Human Paleopathology and Related Subjects: An International Bibliography.* San Diego: San Diego Museum of Man; 1997.

13. Buikstra J, Ubelaker D, eds. *Standards for Data Collection from Human Skeletal Remains,* Chicago: Field Museum of Natural History; 1994.

14. Ormer DJ, Purschar WGJ. *Identification of Pathological Conditions in Human Skeletal Remains.* Washington, DC: Smithsonian Institution Press; 1981.

15. Kennedy KAR, Skeletal markers of occupational stress. In: Iscan MY, Kennedy KAR, eds. *Reconstruction of Life from the Skeleton.* New York: Alan R Liss; 1989:129–160.

16. Dobyns HF. *Their Number Became Thinned.* Knoxville: University of Tennessee Press; 1983.

17. Ramenofsky AF. *Vectors of Death: The Archaeology of European Contact.* Albuquerque: University of New Mexico Press; 1987.

18. Chavez A. *Archives of the Archdioceses of Santa Fe. Publications of the Academy of American Franciscan History Bibliographical Series 8.* Washington, DC: Academy of American Franciscan History; 1957.

19. Larsen CS. In the wake of Columbus: native population biology in the postcontact Americas. *Yearbook Phys Anthropol* 1994;37:109–154.

20. Crosby AW Jr. Virgin soil epidemics as a factor in the aboriginal depopulation in America. *William Mary Q* 1976;33:289–299.

21. Neel JV. Health and disease in unacculturated Amerindian populations. *Ciba Found Symp* 1997;49(ns):155–177.

22. Smith CJ, Schakel SF, Nelson RG. Selected traditional and contemporary foods currently used by the Pima Indians. *J Am Diet Assoc* 1991;91:338–341.

23. Cowen R. Seeds of protection: ancestral menus may hold a message for diabetes-prone descendants. *Sci News* 1990;137:350–351.

21   A COMPARISON OF HEALTH COMPLAINTS OF SETTLED AND NOMADIC TURKANA MEN

Nanette L. Barkey, Benjamin C. Campbell, and Paul W. Leslie

There is abundant evidence that the settlement of foraging groups brings negative impacts on health, both in the past and today. Similar changes occur when nomadic groups settle, with some qualifications related to the fact that nomads tend to be in frequent, direct contact with herded animals and to consume a diet relatively high in animal products such as meat, milk, and blood. This selection proposes that, as is the case with newly settled foragers, settled nomads experience lower nutritional status and a higher disease burden due in large part to increased infectious disease. This effect has already been demonstrated in women and children (see Fratkin et al. 1999), so the present research focuses on men. The results are discouraging given that people in permanent settlements supposedly have the benefit of greater access to medical care, education, and employment, and a reliable and more ample food supply.

Some of the major differences in lifestyle pattern for settled men include a reduction in physical activity, even though there may be greater physical strain in agricultural labor; a diet based on cereals and legumes with relatively little animal protein; life in a stable, large group of relatives who, if nomadic, would splinter and reunite many times over the course of the year; and disruption of the relations of reciprocity that prevail among nomadic groups. The latter two factors may lead to increased conflict and violence, as has been documented in paleopathological studies on past populations undergoing settlement and social stratification. These factors, together with the loss of their herds (the main reason most of the men settled) and the fact that they are not always able to procure their own food and must accept food aid, contribute to increased psychosocial stress and lower subjective health.

As predicted, the study found that settled men generally report experiencing a range of ailments at a much higher frequency than nomadic men. This shows that the impact of settlement can be rapid, for the men were all born into nomadic groups but gave up the pastoral life as teenagers or adults. It also raises questions about the ethics of forcing nomadic and foraging people into settlements through encroachment on their lands or by governmental action.

Questions to keep in mind

What are the strengths and weaknesses of using local disease categories and self-reporting?

What are some exceptions to the pattern of more frequent and severe health complaints among the settled men? What might be the reason for them?

What do the specific health complaints reveal about living conditions and activities of settled and nomadic men?

Why was the study unable to establish a link between nutritional status (as opposed to dietary intake) and the finding of more health complaints among the settled Turkana, or between nutritional status and the types of complaints shared by both groups?

Source: Barkey, N. L., B. C. Campbell, and P. W. Leslie 2001. "A Comparison of Health Complaints of Settled and Nomadic Turkana Men." ©2001 by the American Anthropological Association. Reprinted from *Medical Anthropology Quarterly* Vol. 15 No. 3 pp. 39–408, by permission.

The impact of cultural transitions and their attendant lifestyle changes on health is a topic of widespread interest in anthropology. While medical anthropologists have studied the impact of acculturation and culture contact on the health of living populations (cf. Kunitz 1994), archaeologists and physical anthropologists have sought diachronic reconstructions of the health of historic and prehistoric peoples based on skeletal remains (cf. Swedlund and Armelagos 1990). Central to the larger anthropological endeavor has been an interest in joining these two bodies of knowledge toward gaining an understanding of the health impact of the transition from a mobile to a more sedentary lifestyle (Chabasse et al. 1985; Larsen 1995; Lindtjorn et al. 1993; Nathan et al. 1996).

This article compares the health complaints and nutritional status of nomadic and settled Turkana men of northwestern Kenya in an attempt to document more generally the health effects of sedentarization on African pastoral nomadic men. While most previous work has focused on the health of women and children, there is a need to understand the impact of sedentarization on the health of males as well. Not only may the impact differ by gender, but the ways it differs also may have implications for male contribution to subsistence in newly sedentarized communities.

BACKGROUND

There is overwhelming evidence from prehistoric populations to support the contention that sedentarization has deleterious health consequences, as suggested by Cohen and Armelegos (1984; see also Armelegos 1990; Cohen 1989). Most anthropologists agree that among groups adopting a sedentary lifestyle, infectious and zoonotic disease increases, while nutritional status and physical stature decrease (cf. Cohen and Armelagos 1984). Cohen (1989) highlights several potential pathways to poorer health and nutritional status. These include increased group size and density, the building of permanent structures, accumulation of human wastes, maintenance of weaker members by the community, contamination of water sources, sustained contact with a greater number of people, changes in dietary composition, and increased numbers of pathogens requiring human hosts.

Studies of living populations also suggest an increased level of infectious disease with the sedentarization of nomadic or seminomadic hunter–gatherer groups, such as the !Kung San of the Kalahari. Susan Kent (1989, 1991) and colleagues (Kent and Lee 1992) have followed a group of San as they became semisedentary. They found that in contrast to nomadic San groups, the semisedentary group was characterized by a high pathogen load, anemia, and higher rates of self-reported ill health (Kent 1991; Kent and Lee 1992). They concluded that, despite evidence of a sufficient diet (Kent 1991), recently settled San appear to suffer from higher rates of morbidity.

Though increases in population density should have a similar impact on disease processes during the transition to settled life, nomadic pastoralists may experience different changes in their mortality and morbidity patterns than hunter–gatherers. Unlike hunter–gatherers, pastoralists are accustomed to sustained contact with domesticated or semidomesticated animals, are more able to manage these animals, and consume proportionally more calories from animal than from plant products. However, like hunter–gatherers, pastoralists have developed intricate systems of socioeconomic reciprocity that allow them to survive in a harsh and somewhat unpredictable environment. These strategies may not be transferable to an agriculture-based, settled lifestyle (McCabe 1990a).

Previous studies of African pastoral nomads have reported changes in nutrition and morbidity with sedentarization. Chabasse et al. (1985) report higher rates of bilharzia, nemotodes, and malaria among settled as compared with pastoral groups in Mali. Among the Ariaal Rendille of northern Kenya, Fratkin and co-workers (Fratkin et al. 1999; Nathan et al. 1996) report higher rates of malnutrition but no difference in rates of morbidity among settled and nomadic children, despite better access to health care and higher rates of vaccination among the former. Whether such results can be generalized to apply to men is not known.

THE TURKANA

The Turkana of northwest Kenya are a nomadic population making the transition to a sedentary life. Traditional Turkana pastoralists inhabit an arid ecosystem, herding camels, goats, sheep, and cattle (Little and Leslie 1999). Yet many Turkana are forced to settle because they have lost their herds to livestock disease, raiding, drought, bad luck, or poor management (Campbell et al. 1999). Estimates of the proportion of Turkana living a settled lifestyle range from 15 to 30 percent (Galvin 1985; Lowenthal and Pe'er 1991; McCabe 1990b; Norconsult 1990). It is likely that the trend toward sedentism will continue.

HEALTH AMONG THE TURKANA

A recent overview of health and morbidity among the Ngisonyoka Turkana cites studies that show nomadic groups to be "remarkably healthy, even. . . at the end of a long drought" when compared with neighboring pastoralist groups and with settled Turkana (Shell-Duncan et al. 1999:228). However, this conclusion may be true primarily for cardiovascular health. Men, in particular, are reported to be in good cardiovascular health, as indicated by low serum lipid and blood pressure levels (1999:228). Blood pressure readings for adult nomadic Turkana (Mugambi and Little 1983) were extremely low, lower than those previously recorded for semisettled Turkana (Shaper et al. 1969). On the other hand, recent research on the health of Turkana children has documented a high prevalence of infectious diseases, including malaria, acute respiratory infections, and gastroenteritis (Shell-Duncan et al. 1999).

The main health problems highlighted by research on both settled (Brainard 1986, 1990a) and traditional nomadic Turkana (Little et al. 1988; Mugambi and Little 1983; Shell-Duncan 1993, 1994; Shelley 1985) include malaria, respiratory diseases, and eye infections. Among the 58 nomadic adults she examined, Shelley (1985) found numerous cases of otitis, enlarged or painful spleen, and anemia. She attributed the latter two conditions to chronic malaria. Brainard (1986, 1990a, 1990b) found similar patterns of health complaints among Turkana who had settled around the Nakwamoru irrigation project. The top five health problems among cases treated at the Nakwamoru clinic were malaria, cough/chest, eye problems, vomiting/diarrhea, and tuberculosis (Brainard 1990b).

Chronic undernutrition among the Turkana has been well documented by studies of growth, body composition, and diet (Galvin 1985; Leslie et al. 1999; Little 1989; Little and Gray 1990; Little et al. 1999) and may contribute to disease susceptibility. Shell-Duncan (1993) found depressed levels of cell-mediated immunity (CMI) in 52 children during a year-long study and concluded that it was indicative of morbidity and nutritional stress. Seasonal variation in immune function among children was not evident despite the highly seasonal nature of the Turkana environment.

The lack of seasonal variation in CMI among Turkana children can be partially explained by a lack of variation in nutritional status due to limited environmental variation during the study period and the moderate malnutrition of all of the children in the study. Turkana parents attempt to protect their children from seasonal fluctuations in food availability by giving them preferential access to resources during lean periods (Galvin 1985). Adult Turkana experience extreme seasonal weight loss as a result of this practice (Little et al. 1988), which, in turn, may suppress immune function more in adults than Shell-Duncan observed in children.

Differences between Nomadic and Settled Turkana

Nomadic and settled Turkana have strikingly different dietary consumption, physical activity, and social organization. Because most settled Turkana own only a few animals, they consume primarily cereals and legumes, with a small proportion of their diet coming from animal sources (Campbell et al. 1999). Conversely, the nomads consume primarily animal foods, most notably, milk, meat, and blood (Galvin 1985, 1992; Little et al. 1988).

There are several different types of settlement among the Turkana (see Campbell et al. 1999). Morelum, the site of an irrigation scheme in existence since 1981, is occupied by Turkana who have recently made the transition from nomadic to settled life. Nearly all of those living at Morelum report settling there because of the loss of their herds (Campbell et al. 1999). However, many men still retain some livestock, and a few may have families who continue to live nomadically. Nonetheless, the settled residents of Morelum are clearly subjected to different ecological, dietary, and social conditions than nomads.

Turkana men engaged in pastoralism spend varying amounts of time in rigorous herding activities, with those aged 15 through 35 being the most physically active (Galvin 1985). Those in this age group are responsible for finding food and water for the most active animals, and the physical demands on them increase during the dry season when they must graze the animals farther from the main camp and travel further for water. A study of maximal aerobic work capacity (Curran-Everett 1994) compared the aerobic fitness of various categories of nomadic herders aged 20–44. Turkana men who were actively herding had significantly higher maximal oxygen uptake compared with those who had attained the status of herd-owner and were no longer expected to herd (Curran-Everett 1994). Similar information on physical activity patterns of settled Turkana men is not available, although agricultural work in the fields may mean that they utilize their upper bodies more than do nomads.

Settlement results in changes in social context as well as diet and physical activity. Nomadic Turkana live in extended family groupings *(awi),* and small groups may splinter off from and rejoin such groupings up to 15 times over the course of each year, depending on the availability of food and water (Little 1988). While the basic social unit among Turkana settled in agricultural communities is similar, it is situated throughout the year, sometimes permanently, in a context that includes more distantly related or nonrelated people. Thus, the process of sedentarization places social demands on the Turkana that include, but are not limited to, the need to, first, establish new forms of handling disputes and aggression (Kent 1991); second, develop alternatives to reciprocity networks and strategies for replacing lost herds (McCabe 1990b); and, third, cope with their reliance on food aid (Bush 1995).

As groups of Turkana move from a nomadic, pastoral lifestyle to a sedentary one, they present us with an opportunity to directly examine the health effects of such a transition. This form of "natural experiment" allows for the comparison of illness patterns between settled and nomadic Turkana and preliminary investigation into the factors contributing to the general health of both

groups. Some health differences between the two groups may be related to differential access to health care. However, access to care is poor for both groups; only very limited biomedical services are available at a health clinic in Lokori, approximately 10 kilometers from Morelum.

In this article we first present data on the general pattern of health complaints among Turkana men. We then examine differences between the nomadic and sedentary groups and factors contributing to the differences. Specific hypotheses that guided the analysis are:

1. the settled Turkana men will suffer from a greater disease burden than the nomadic men;
2. the majority of this increase will be related to infectious disease; and
3. nutritional differences will be an indirect cause of morbidity among the settled men.

METHODS

The data considered in this article are derived from a larger study of male reproductive ecology within the South Turkana Ecosystem Project (STEP). The nomadic men ($n = 152$) were interviewed in July and August 1992. The settled men ($n = 124$) were interviewed in April 1993 at the Morulem settlement. In total, 155 nomads and 129 settled Turkana men were interviewed, but those men for whom we do not have their age are excluded from most analyses.

While data collection took place in different seasons, seasonal differences were mitigated by a severe drought. The settled Turkana were attempting to rely on irrigation agriculture for subsistence but were primarily dependent on food aid at the time of the study. Food supplementation in the form of maize, beans, oil, and soya milk was supplied by World Vision, both as direct aid and in the context of a food-for-work program. DeLuca (1997) estimates that women enrolled in both of these forms of aid were receiving approximately 90 kilograms of maize, 26 kilograms of beans, 3 liters of oil, and a variable amount of soya milk per month for their households.

The data were collected using four different instruments. The primary data are responses to a

Table 21.1   Turkana Disease Categories and English Equivalents.

Term	English Equivalent
Etid	Discomfort or sharp pains in left abdomen—spleen
Loriwo	Abdominal pain or swelling, liver related
Lokou	Serious headache, often with sweating and dizziness
Akurut	Diarrhea
Eguru	Backache
Erarum	Chest pains lasting at least 5 days, cough, and fever
Arukum	Common cold of a few days duration, with cough
Lomeskin	Swelling of the joints and jaundice
Angakonyen	Literally "eyes," refers to all eye problems; irritation, infection, etc.
Ngipeeli	Tapeworm or threadworm
Lokud	"Whooping cough"

(Adapted from Shelley 1985)

health questionnaire based on Turkana disease categories taken from Shelley 1985 (Table 21.1). Participants were first asked to describe current health problems or problems experienced in the past month. Each man was then read a list of 11 Turkana disease categories (TDCs) and asked if he had suffered from any of these conditions in the preceding month. TDCs were used to improve reliability and validity by avoiding the problems of intertranslator variation in terminology and the use of unfamiliar biomedical terms. Optimum recall time for medical conditions is two weeks, although one-month recall can also be accurate (Bernard et al. 1984). There is no evidence to suggest that the settled and nomadic men differed significantly in the accuracy of their recall of illness.

Age was estimated using an event calendar (Leslie et al. 1999), which was part of a general demographic questionnaire. All participants were at least 14 years of age at the time of the study. Multiple measures of weight, height, and body composition were recorded on an anthropometric data sheet. Dietary intake was estimated using a 48-hour dietary recall.

Data Management

The data were coded, entered into an SPSS database, and the computerized data checked against the raw data. Several variables were created from the original data. Body Mass Index (BMI) was calculated as weight/height,^{2} ten-year age categories were created, and the six skinfold measurements (triceps, midaxillary, periumbilical, midcalf, subscapular, and suprailiac) were summed into an index. Three skinfold measurements (midaxillary, subscapular, and suprailiac) were used to compute an estimate of body fat (Durnin and Wormsley 1974).

The sample was more or less evenly distributed among ten-year age groups, as shown in Table 21.2.

Responses to questions on general health at the time of the interview and over the previous month

Table 21.2   Sample Size by Age Group and Residency.

Age Group	Nomads (n = 152)	Settled (n = 124)
14–24	35	37
25–34	19	15
35–44	40	16
45–54	27	27
55–64	11	13
65+	20	16

were coded according to severity (0 = no complaints reported; 1 = only mild complaints suggestive of isolated symptoms [e.g., eye infection, headache, backache]; 2 = moderate complaints suggestive of more general problems [e.g., chest pains, edema]). Responses to the two sets of questions were coded independently by two of the authors according to the severity of each condition and the number of conditions a respondent reported. The scores were compared, and in three cases where different severity scores had been assigned, the reasons were discussed and the differences reconciled. The severity scores for the two time periods (day of interview and previous month) were collapsed into one score (range 0–5) to provide a global score for the self-report of general health.

RESULTS

Overall Pattern of Health Complaints

The frequency of specific health complaints is summarized in Table 21.3. The most commonly cited illnesses were cold with cough (62.4 percent), eye infection (36.9 percent), and chest infection (43.5 percent). Spleen pain was reported by 34.4 percent of the men. Rates of chest infection, eye infection, and spleen complaints are consistent

with the high frequencies of these conditions found by previous researchers.

The low reported incidences of diarrhea (19.1 percent) and worms (7.1 percent) are inconsistent with expectations of high rates of gastrointestinal (GI) infection in the Turkana, which were based on earlier studies reporting significant GI problems among Turkana children (Brainard 1990b; Shell-Duncan 1994, 1995). Among other nomadic groups living in arid ecosystems, like the San, worms and diarrhea are reported infrequently (Kent and Lee 1992).

Turkana men often reported backache and headache (63.1 percent and 49.8 percent, respectively). Since both are general symptoms that may be associated with a wide variety of conditions, the results are difficult to interpret. Previous health researchers among the Turkana do not report on headache and backache, with the exception of Shelley (1985), who briefly mentions them in her general discussion of the local disease categories.

Differences between the Settled and Nomadic Men

As predicted in hypothesis 1, the settled Turkana men reported significantly more serious health complaints than the nomads on the day of the interview ($p = .002$) and for the past month ($p = .007$; Kruskal-Wallis test for nonparametric data).

Table 21.3   Percentage Reporting Suffering from Each Turkana Disease Category.

(IN PAST MONTH)	Nomads (n = 155)	Settled (n = 129)	Combined (n = 284)[*]	p
Chest infection (*erarum*)	22.4	48.8	43.5	.0000
Cold with cough (*arukum*)	41.2	87.6	62.4	.0000
Eye (*edeke angakonen*)	26.1	49.6	36.9	.0000
Backache (*eguru*)	52.9	75.2	63.1	.0001
Whooping cough (*lokud*)	10.5	18.6	14.2	.05
Worms (*ngipeeli*)	9.8	3.9	7.1	.053
Liver (*loriwo*)	29.4	22.4	26.2	.18
Spleen (*etid*)	31.3	37.9	34.4	.24
Headache (*lokou*)	52.6	46.5	49.8	.31
Edema (*lomeskin*)	19.6	16.3	18.1	.46
Diarrhea (*akurut*)	19.6	18.6	19.1	.83

[*] All cases were considered, regardless of whether we knew the survey participants' ages.

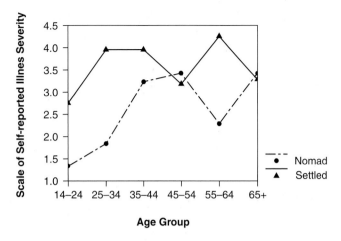

Figure 21.1   Severity of Health Complaints by Age:
Settled Versus Nomadic Turkana Men.

Scores of self-reported general health status across the six age-groups are shown in Figure 21.1. The severity of the health complaints increases with age among the 14–44 year olds. The settled men report more severe complaints than nomads in all but one age category; in the 45–54 age group, the reverse is the case. In the oldest age category (65+), the scores for the two groups converge, perhaps indicative of a survivor effect.

Related to hypothesis 2, the settled Turkana men reported significantly more eye infection, chest infection, backache, and cough/cold

(arukum) than the nomads. Conversely, the nomads reported slightly more cases of worms. Cough or cold lasting fewer than five days was indicated by nearly 88 percent of the settled group and by 100 percent of settled men aged 55–64 reporting the condition within the past month (see Figure 21.2) In further confirmation of the seriousness of chest problems among the Turkana, complaints of chest *pain* (rather than infection) were reported spontaneously by 31 percent of the settled and five percent of the nomadic men during discussions of their general health.

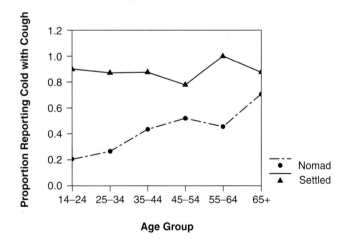

Figure 21.2   Complaints of Cold with Cough by Age
Group: Settled Versus Nomadic Turkana Men.

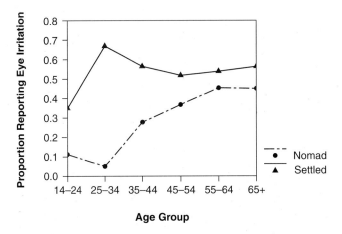

Figure 21.3 Complaints of Eye Irritation by Age Group: Settled Versus Nomadic Turkana Men.

Figure 21.3 shows the trend in eye complaints across age groups. Eye problems were reported by nearly 50 percent of the settled men, while only 26 percent of the nomadic men voiced this complaint. The rates of eye complaints among the settled Turkana increase with age. The contrast between the two groups is most striking among 25–34 year olds. In this age group, almost 70 percent of the settled men said they suffered from eye problems, compared with just five percent of the nomadic men. This may be due in part to the large numbers of flies in the settlement, which spread eye infection and cause irritation.

Asked about the TDC for worms (*ngipeeli*), nomadic men reported a slightly higher rate than settled men. The difference between the groups was small, yet marginally significant ($p = .053$). The settled men were expected to suffer more from worms due to increased transmission in the settlements, yet this was not the case.

Malaria was not specifically queried as a TDC because of the difficulty in self-diagnosis and frequent confusion of its symptoms with those of other diseases; however, 10 percent of the settled men and five percent of the nomads spontaneously reported that they had suffered from malaria in the past month. The TDC of spleen pain *(etid)*, considered a sequela of chronic or acute malaria (following Shell-Duncan 1994, 1999; Shelley 1985), was reported by 38 percent of the settled and 31 percent of nomadic men. These results are roughly equal to the 28 percent Shelley (1985) found in her sample of adult men and women. Figure 21.4 shows how spleen pain generally decreases with age for the nomadic men, while increasing among younger to middle-aged settled men.

Impact of Nutrition

Table 21.4 reports mean body composition measures and age for settled and nomadic Turkana men and for the two samples combined. All of the Turkana men in this study are at the extreme lean end of the body composition continuum (mean BMI = 17.26, triceps skinfold = 4.74 millimeters, sum of the six skinfold measures = 32.2 millimeters), even when compared with samples from other African and developing countries.

The settled Turkana were shorter than the nomadic men ($p = .009$). The two groups were almost identical with respect to body weight (50.77 kilograms and 50.78 kilograms). The higher BMI for the settled men was due to the difference in height ($p = .013$). The two groups differed greatly in still other measures of body composition. The mean triceps skinfold measure was 4.1 millimeters for the nomadic sample and 5.5 millimeters for the settled one. The sum of the six skinfold measures also shows a difference between subgroups, with significantly higher scores for the settled men (37.9 millimeters) than the nomads (27.3 millimeters).

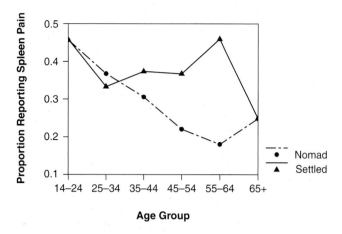

Figure 21.4   Spleen Complaints by Age Group: Settled Versus Nomadic Turkana Men.

Based on the 48-hour recall there is a striking difference in energy intake and dietary composition between the two groups. Twenty percent of the nomadic men reported eating nothing at all the day before the interview or simply drinking tea provided by the research team, yet none of the settled men reported having eaten nothing during the previous 24 hours. The nomads in this study consume a typical Turkana diet, high in protein and low in calories. Thirteen percent reported drinking milk, 51 percent ate meat, and 33.5 percent ingested animal blood in the 48 hours prior to interview. The sedentary Turkana diet consists mostly of maize and beans, with smaller amounts of milk, oil, and tea. Estimates of dietary intake, based on 48-hour recall, indicate that total caloric intake for

the settled Turkana males was approximately twice that of the nomadic males (1,830 versus 772 kcals/day). Total fat and dietary intake is indistinguishable between the two groups, with estimates of 52 grams of protein and 14 grams of fat for the nomads and 52 grams of protein and 15 grams of fat for the settled males (Muhlenbein 1998).

To determine the association between body composition and health reports, logistic regression analyses were run for each of the TDCs and for the general health rankings. Separate models were estimated for BMI, sum of six skinfold measures, mid-upper arm circumference, and triceps skinfold, controlling for age. We excluded men under age 25 in order to control for the fact that Turkana men continue to grow into their early twenties

Table 21.4   Age and Body Composition Indicators for Nomadic and Settled Turkana Men. Mean and (S.D.)

	Nomadic (n = 155)	Settled (n = 129)	Combined (N = 284)[*]	p
Age	40.5 (17.2)	40.3 (18.8)	40.44 (17.9)	.9
Height (cm)	172.23 (9.7)	169.04 (10.6)	170.78 (10.2)	.009
Weight (kg)	50.77 (8.8)	50.76 (9.6)	50.76 (9.2)	.993
Body mass index (kg/m^2)	16.99 (1.86)	17.58 (2.14)	17.26 (2.0)	.013
Triceps skinfolds (mm)	4.1 (.91)	5.5 (1.8)	4.74 (1.5)	.000
Sum of 6 skinfolds (mm)	27.3 (3.9)	37.9 (10.4)	32.2 (9.3)	.000

[*] All cases were considered, regardless of whether we knew the survey participants' ages.

(Little and Gray 1990), which could potentially confound growth patterns with nutritional status.

There was no association between general health status or the TDCs with measures of body fat among either the settled or nomadic group. In fact, none of the measures of body composition were significantly predictive of the 11 local disease categories. While the settled men have more fat on average, this does not appear to directly predict their reports of specific diseases. This finding is curious because we predicted that even a small energy reserve in the form of body fat would be protective against disease. The extreme leanness of both groups of Turkana men may mean that they are unable to mobilize sufficient energy resources to resist disease.

DISCUSSION

The general pattern of disease in the Turkana men reported here confirms the findings of previous studies based primarily on women and children (Brainard 1986, 1990a, 1990b; Shell-Duncan 1994, 1995; Shell-Duncan and Wood 1997; Shelley 1985). The most commonly cited health problems are eye complaints, chest infection, cough, and spleen pain. Backache and headache are symptoms frequently reported by both nomadic and settled Turkana.

The settled Turkana men report more ill health than their nomadic counterparts, both in general health self-assessments and when prompted by specific disease categories. Disease complaints increase with age for both groups, although rates for the settled men are generally higher than those for the nomads. The settled Turkana's report of significantly more backaches may be a reflection of work activities specifically related to agriculture.

A detailed discussion of the most important diseases affecting the Turkana men—malaria, chest infection, and eye infection—follows.

The World Health Organization (WHO) recommends that researchers use spleen enlargement to evaluate the frequency of malaria in endemic areas (WHO 1963, cited in Shelley 1985). Thus, complaints of spleen pain by the Turkana may be interpreted as sequelae to malaria, as Shelley (1985), Shell-Duncan (1994, 1999), and Brainard

(1990b) have suggested. Shelley (1985) has confirmed the association between self-reports of spleen pain and clinically assessed spleen enlargement. However, malaria itself is difficult to assess from self-reports because confusion of its symptoms with those of other illnesses results in overreporting.

The burden of malaria begins early for the Turkana, and, by all reports, it is a major health problem (American Medical and Research Foundation [AMREF] 1982; Shell-Duncan 1994, 1995; Shell-Duncan et al. 1999; Shelley 1985). Twenty percent of the children (aged 2–9) examined by Shelley had enlarged spleens. She observed that "this rate of spleen abnormalities among the southern nomadic population corresponds to the 10–49 percent range which the WHO has defined as mesoendemic" (Shelley 1985:246). In the present study, reports of spleen complaints declined with age, in contrast to other local disease categories, which tended to increase with age. Increasing protective immunity with age for malaria has been documented for other parts of Africa (Nkuo-Akenji et al. 1993; Oloo et al. 1996). It is highly likely that both settled and nomadic Turkana men acquire protective immunity for malaria as they age, suffering fewer attacks and experiencing less spleen involvement.

Turkana men also reported high rates of cough/cold (arukum), and *erarum*, literally "chest." The respiratory tract is one of the most common sites for infection, along with the GI tract, and Turkana men appear to suffer from substantial levels of respiratory distress. The high rate of chest infection for the Turkana (settled 49 percent versus nomads 22 percent) undoubtedly has several underlying causes. Both Shelley (1985) and Shell-Duncan (1994, 1995) have suggested tuberculosis to be an important contributor to the Turkana's chest problems. The Turkana, particularly the nomads, drink large quantities of untreated milk, which could infect them with the *Mycobacterium bovis* strain of TB (Cosivi 1995; Vecchiato 1997; WHO 1994). Increased crowding among settled men may contribute to higher rates of respiratory complaints, as both TB and colds are known to spread via close human contact.

The high rates of eye complaints found in the present study are consistent with prior findings for the Turkana (Lowenthal and Pe'er 1991; Shell-

Duncan 1995; Shell-Duncan et al. 1999; Shelley 1985). Settled men reported almost double the rate of eye problems of nomadic men. The marked contrast in rates of eye complaints in the present study is puzzling, particularly in the 25–34-year-old age group (68 percent for the settled group versus five percent for the nomadic group). Shelley (1985) found extremely high rates of *Xerosis conjunctivae* (drying of the conjunctivae), affecting 90 percent among the nomads (over age 15) that she studied. This condition is often associated with vitamin A deficiency, and Shelley thought it was also possibly linked to the "arid environment with blowing dust" (1985:230).

While the patterns of disease complaints among Turkana males reported here are generally consistent with our understanding of the men's environmental exposure to disease, our data allow us to say much less about the role of host susceptibility factors. We failed to find an association between nutrition status and any specific disease categories, despite indications of compromised nutritional status presumably sufficient to cause immunosuppression and contribute to disease susceptibility. We attribute this to a lack of individual variation in nutritional status within both nomadic and settled groups.

This is especially notable in the case of chest infection, which, we have argued, is most likely related to TB, an infection prototypically controlled by cell-mediated immunity (Haas and Des Pres 1995). Fifteen percent of individuals infected with TB develop active cases, although immunosuppressed individuals are more likely to experience the onset of an active case (Bell 1995). Again, we have no direct evidence of suppressed immune function, but the poor nutritional status of the Turkana men surveyed could be associated with an inability to fight off chest infections, including TB.

The lack of impact of nutritional status on differences in disease reports between the two groups requires further consideration. Skinfold measures show that the settled males have significantly more body fat than the nomads. These apparently greater energy reserves do not appear to buffer the settled men from ill-health, as might be expected. The settled men are of shorter stature than the nomads, which suggests poorer long-term health. Since almost all of the settled males were originally

nomads, their shorter stature presumably reflects conditions prior to settling rather than a direct effect of the settled environment. Thus, prior nutritional status may contribute to greater disease susceptibility among the settled population.

Almost all of the settled men cited the loss of their herds through drought or raiding as the event precipitating their settlement. The loss of animals for the Turkana males represents not only the loss of economic livelihood, but also a significant loss of identity, autonomy, and authority. These conditions may lead to psychosocial stress, which has been shown to suppress immune function (Glaser et al. 1991, 1994; Herbert and Cohen 1994), thus contributing to increased disease susceptibility among settled males.

Dietary composition and quality also may contribute to observed differences in disease complaints between the settled and nomadic groups. Striking contrasts were found in dietary composition and intake, and it may be that a higher-protein diet promotes growth and disease resistance among the nomadic men.

CONCLUSION

Self-reports of general health and local disease categories in the present study suggest that settled Turkana men suffer from significantly higher rates of ill-health when compared to nomadic men, despite their having higher food intake and, possibly, better access to biomedical care. These results are consistent with earlier reports of increased infectious disease and decreased growth inferred from skeletal samples in populations undergoing sedentarization and stand as confirmation of Cohen and Armelegos's model of the impact of sedentarization on health (Armelegos 1990; Cohen 1989; Cohen and Armelegos 1984). We were unable to document any effect of nutritional status on health in this study, but several other independent factors, including changes in diet, host susceptibility, increased pathogen exposure, and crowding, might contribute to higher rates of ill-health among the sedentary Turkana.

The interpretation of our findings, while consistent with changes in actual disease status in the two subpopulations, is nonetheless limited by the nature of self-reports. At this point, we cannot rule out the possibility that differences in health complaints are the result of increased likelihood of complaining among the settled population, a tendency first suggested some 500 years ago (Ibn Khaldun 1967). Thus, further research, including more objective measures of assessment of health, particularly prospective research, will be helpful in confirming the differences we have found. Such research would also help to pinpoint the relative contribution of the various factors to ill health in recently settled nomadic populations.

REFERENCES

African Medical and Research Foundation. 1982. *Turkana Survey Report on Epidemiology, Nutrition, Health-Related Social Anthropology and Radio Communication.* Nairobi: African Medical and Research Foundation.

Armelegos, George J. 1990. Health and Disease in Prehistoric Populations. In *Disease in Populations in Transition: Anthropological and Epidemiological Perspectives.* Alan C. Swedlund and George J. Armelegos, eds. Pp. 127–144. New York: Bergin and Garvey.

Bell, Dion R. 1995. *Tropical Medicine.* Oxford: Blackwell.

Bernard, H. Russell, Peter D. Killworth, David Kronenfeld, and Lee Sailer. 1984. The Problem of Informant Accuracy: The Validity of Retrospective Data. *Annual Review of Anthropology* 13:495–517.

Brainard, Jean M. 1986. Differential Mortality in Turkana Agriculturists and Pastoralists. *American Journal of Physical Anthropology* 70:525–536.

———. 1990a. Nutritional Status and Morbidity on an Irrigation Project in Turkana District, Kenya. *American Journal of Human Biology* 2:153–163.

———. 1990b. *Health and Development in a Rural Kenyan Community.* New York: Peter Lang.

Bush, J. 1995. The Role of Food Aid in Drought and Recovery: OXFAM's North Turkana (Kenya) Drought Relief Program, 1992–94. *Disasters* 19(3): 247–259.

Campbell, Benjamin C., Paul W. Leslie, Michael A. Little, Jean M. Brainard, and Michael Anthony DeLuca. 1999. The Settled Turkana. In *Turkana Herders of the Dry Savanna: Ecology and Biobehavioral Response of Nomads to an Uncertain Environment.* Michael A. Little and Paul W. Leslie, eds. Pp. 333–352. Oxford: Oxford University Press.

Chabasse, D., C. Roure, A. Rhaly, P. Ranque, and M. Quilici. 1985. The Health of Nomads and Semi-Nomads of the Malian Gourma: An Epidemiological Approach. In *Population, Health and Nutrition in the Sahel.* Allan G. Hill, ed. Pp. 319–339. London: Routledge and Kegan Paul.

Cohen, Mark N. 1989. *Health and the Rise of Civilization.* New Haven, CT: Yale University Press.

Cohen, Mark N., and George J. Armelegos. 1984. *Paleopathology at the Origins of Agriculture.* Orlando, FL: Academic Press.

Cosivi, O., F. X. Meslin, C. J. Daborn, and J. M. Grange. 1995. Epidemiology of *Mycobacterium bovis* Infection in Animals and Humans, with Particular Reference to Africa. *Revue Scientifique et Technique* 14(3):733–746.

Curran-Everett, Linda S. 1994. Accordance between VO2 max and Behavior in Ngisonyoka Turkana. *American Journal of Human Biology* 6(6):761–771.

DeLuca, Michael Anthony. 1997. *Reproductive Ecology and Pregnancy Loss in a Settled Turkana Population.* Ph.D. dissertation, Department of Anthropology, State University of New York at Binghamton.

Durnin, J. V. G. A., and J. Womersley. 1974. Body Fat Assessed from Whole Body Density and its Estimation from Skinfold Thickness. *British Journal of Nutrition* 32:77–97.

Fratkin, Elliot M., Eric Abella Roth, and Martha A. Nathan. 1999. When Nomads Settle: The Effects of Commodization, Nutritional Change, and Formal Education on Ariaal and Rendille Pastoralists. *Current Anthropology* 40:729–735.

Galvin, Kathleen A. 1985. *Food Procurement, Diet, Activities and Nutrition of Ngisonyoka, Turkana Pastoralists in an Ecological and Social Context.* Ph.D. dissertation, Department of Anthropology, State University of New York at Binghamton.

———. 1992. Nutritional Ecology of Pastoralists in Dry Tropical Africa. *American Journal of Human Biology* 4:209–221.

Glaser, R., D. K. Peark, J. H. K. Kiecolt-Glaser, and W. B. Malarkey. 1994. Plasma Cortisol Levels and Reactivation of Latent Epstein-Barr Virus in Response to Examination Stress. *Psychoneurondocrinology* 19:765–772.

Glaser, R., G. R. Pearson, R. H. Bonneau, B. A. Esterling, C. Atkinson, and J. K. Glaser. 1991. Stress-Related Activation of Epstein-Barr Virus in Healthy Medical Students. *Health Psychology* 12(6):435–442.

Haas, D., and R. Des Pres. 1995. *Mycobaterium tuberculosis.* In *Principles and Practice of Infectious Disease.* 4th edition. Gerald L. Mandell, John E. Bennet, and Raphael Dolin, eds. Pp. 2213–2242. New York: Churchill Livingston.

Herbert T. B., and S. Cohen. 1994. Stress and Immunity in Humans: A Meta-Analytic Review. *Psychosomatic Medicine* 55:364–379.

Ibn Khaldun. 1967. *The Muqaddimah.* Frans Rosenthal, trans., N. Dawood, ed. Princeton, NJ: Princeton University Press.

Kent, Susan. 1989. And Justice for All: The Development of Political Centralization Among Newly Sedentary Foragers. *American Anthropologist* 91:703–712.

———. 1991. The Shift to Sedentism as Viewed from a Recently Sedentary Kalahari Village. *Nyame Akuma* 35:2–11.

Kent, Susan, and Richard Lee. 1992. A Hematological Study of !Kung Kalahari Foragers. In *Diet, Demography and Disease: Changing Perspectives on Anemia.* P. Stuart-Macadam and Susan Kent, eds. Pp. 173–200. New York: Aldine de Gruyter.

Kunitz, Stephen J. 1994. *Disease and Social Diversity: The European Impact of Health on Non-Europeans.* New York: Oxford University Press.

Larsen, C. S. 1995. Biological Change in Human Population with Agriculture. *Annual Review of Anthropology* 24:185–213.

Leslie, P. W., R. Dyson-Hudson, E. A. Lowoto, and J. Munyesi. 1999. Appendix 1, Ngisonyoka Event Calendar. In *Turkana Herders of the Dry Savanna: Ecology and Biobehavioral Response of Nomads to an Uncertain Environment.* Michael A. Little and Paul W. Leslie, eds. Oxford: Oxford University Press.

Lindtjorn, B., T. Alemu, and B. Bjorvatn. 1993. Nutritional Status and Risk of Infection among Ethiopian Children. *Journal of Tropical Pediatrics* 39: 76–82.

Little, Michael A. 1989. Human Biology of African Pastoralists. *Yearbook of Physical Anthropology* 32: 215–247.

Little, Michael A., Kathleen Galvin, K. Sheeley, B. R. Johnson, and M. Mugambi. 1998. Resources, Biology, and Health of Pastoralists. In *Arid Lands Today and Tomorrow.* E.E. Whitehead, C.F Hutchinson, B.N. Timmermann, and R.C. Varady, eds. Pp. 713–726. Boulder, CO: Westview Press.

Little, Michael A., and Sandra J. Gray. 1990. Growth of Young Nomadic and Settled Turkana Children. *Medical Anthropology Quarterly* 4:296–314.

Little, Michael A., Sandra J. Gray, I.L. Pike, and M. Mugambi. 1999. Infant, Child and Adolescent Growth, and Adult Physical Status. In *Turkana Herders of the Dry Savanna: Ecology and Biobehavioral Response of Nomads to an Uncertain Environment.* Michael A. Little and Paul W. Leslie, eds. Pp. 187–204. Oxford: Oxford University Press.

Little, Michael A., and Paul W. Leslie, eds. 1999. *Turkana Herders of the Dry Savanna: Ecology and Biobehavioral Response of Nomads to an Uncertain Environment.* Oxford: Oxford University Press.

Lowenthal, R. and J. Pe'er. 1991. Traditional Methods Used in the Treatment of Ophthalmic Diseases among the Turkana Tribe in Northwest Kenya. *Journal of Ethnopharmacology* 33:227–229.

McCabe, J.T. 1990a. Turkana Pastoralism: A Case Against the Tragedy of the Commons. *Human Ecology* 18(1):81–103.

———. 1990b. Success and Failure: The Breakdown of Traditional Drought Coping Institutions among the Pastoral Turkana of Kenya. *Journal of Asian and African Studies* 25(3–4): 146–160.

Mugambi, A., and Michael. A. Little. 1983. Blood Pressure in Nomadic Turkana Pastoralists. *East African Medical Journal.* 60(12):863–869.

Muhlenbein, M. 1998. *The Ngisonyoka of Turkana: Environment, Nutrition, and Disease in Northwest Kenya.* Senior Honors Thesis, Department of Environmental Sciences, Northwestern University.

Nathan, Martha A., Elliot Fratkin, and Eric Abella Roth. 1996. Sedentism and Child Health among Rendille Pastoralists of Northern Kenya. *Social Science and Medicine* 43:503–515.

Nkuo-Akeni, T., J. E. Deas, R. G. Leke, and J. L. Ngu. 1993. Correlation between Serum Levels of Antibodies to the 96-kD Antigen of *Plasmodium falciparum* and Protective Immunity in Cameroon: A Longitudinal Study. *American Journal of Tropical Medicine and Hygiene* 49(5):566–573.

Norconsult. 1990. Environmental Study of Turkana District, vol. 2. Environmental Impact of Settlements in Turkana. Nairobi: Norconsult.

Oloo, A. J., J. M. Vulule, and D. K. Koech. 1996. Some Emerging Issues on the Malaria Problem of Kenya. *East African Medical Journal* 73(1):50–53.

Shaper, A. G., D. H. Wright, and J. Kyobe. 1969. Blood Pressure and Body Build in Three Nomadic Tribes of Northern Kenya. *East African Medical Journal* 46:273.

Shell-Duncan, Bettina. 1993. Cell-Mediated Immunocompetence among Nomadic Turkana Children. *American Journal of Human Biology* 5:225–235.

———. 1994. *Determinants of Infant and Childhood Morbidity among Nomadic Turkana Pastoralists of Northwest Kenya.* Ph.D. dissertation, Department of Anthropology, Pennsylvania State University.

———. 1995. Impact of Seasonal Variation in Food Availability and Disease Stress on the Health Status of Nomadic Turkana Children. *American Journal of Human Biology* 7:339–355.

Shell-Duncan, Bettina, and J.W. Wood. 1997. The Evaluation of Delayed-Type Hypersensitivity Responsiveness and Nutritional Status as Predictors of Gastro-Intestinal and Acute Respiratory Infection: A Prospective Field Study among Traditional Nomadic Kenyan Children. *Journal of Tropical Pediatrics* 43:25–32.

Shell-Duncan, Bettina, J. Kareh Shelley, and Paul W. Leslie. 1999. Health and Morbidity among Ngisonyoka

Turkana: Ethnomedical and Epidemiological Perspectives. In *Turkana Herders of the Dry Savanna: Ecology and Biobehavioral Response of Nomads to an Uncertain Environment.* Michael A. Little and Paul W. Leslie, eds. Pp. 207–229. Oxford: Oxford University Press.

Shelley, J. Karen. 1985. *Medicines for Misfortune: Diagnosis and Health Care among Southern Turkana Pastoralists of Kenya.* Ph.D. dissertation, Department of Anthropology, University of North Carolina, Chapel Hill.

Swedlund, Alan C., and George J. Armelegos, eds. 1990. *Disease in Populations in Transition: Anthropological and Epidemiological Perspectives.* New York: Bergin and Garvey.

Vecchiato, Norbert L. 1997. Sociocultural Aspects of Tuberculosis Control in Ethiopia. *Medical Anthropology Quarterly* 11:183–201.

World Health Organization. 1994. Zoonotic Tuberculosis *(Mycobacterium bovis). Weekly Epidemiologic Record* 19:139–140.

■ ■ ■ ■ ■ ■ ■ ■ ■ ■

22   THE RESURGENCE OF DISEASE: SOCIAL AND HISTORICAL PERSPECTIVES ON THE "NEW" TUBERCULOSIS

Matthew Gandy and Alimuddin Zumla

The failure to control malaria discussed in previous selections has a parallel in the history of tuberculosis, which remains the largest infectious cause of death in the world. Both diseases present difficulties to chemical treatment given that the pathogens hide within human cells. The resistance developed by mosquito vectors and malaria plasmodia has been paralleled by the emergence of drug-resistant strains of tuberculosis. In both cases, humans may host the disease organism for decades.

A major difference is that in the case of tuberculosis there are already effective treatments. Nevertheless, the disease continues to infect as much as one-third of the world's population because of a number of technical, logistical, and social factors related to diagnosis and treatment delivery. This proportion is a grim reminder that medical advances alone are not sufficient to eradicate disease.

This selection compares tuberculosis in Europe in the nineteenth and early twentieth centuries against the "new" tuberculosis of the past few decades, to show that politico-economic forces were central to the decline of the disease in the first case and its rise in the second. Tuberculosis is a disease of poverty. In industrializing Europe, however, economic and political forces worked together to improve the well-being of the poor and control the spread of tuberculosis. Today, beyond the emergence of drug-resistant strains and the impact of coinfection with HIV, poverty is deepening in the developing world, public health systems are breaking down, and there are mass movements of people due to wars and other crises that lead to settlements with hygienic conditions similar to those of early industrial Europe.

The emphasis on the individual as opposed to the social level of disease that is a central feature of biomedicine (see Part I) deflects attention from these broader conditions and leads to the blaming of treatment failures on inadequate patient compliance. In reality, these failures are due principally to problems in treatment delivery (see selection 34). Such problems are related in large part to the current political climate justifying the economic rationalization and commodification of health care (see selection 10). However, as the authors show, even from an economic point of view, the shortsightedness of current ap-

Source: Reprinted from *Social Science and Medicine,* Vol. 55, Gandy, M. and A. Zumla, "The Resurgence of Disease: Social and Historical Perspectives on the 'New' Tuberculosis," Pages 385–396, Copyright (2002), with permission from Elsevier.

proaches to health-care provision (or lack thereof) is increasing exponentially the costs of controlling tuberculosis, not to mention the losses to national economies through the reduced productivity of the sick.

Questions to keep in mind

What factors contribute to drug resistance among tuberculosis strains (see also selections 16 and 19)? Why is multi-drug-resistant tuberculosis so much more expensive to treat than it is to prevent?

In what ways do historical and new tuberculosis strains, and their social contexts, differ and in what ways are they alike?

By what mechanisms does infection with HIV favor the development of active disease in people with quiescent tuberculosis?

How do gender and ethnicity affect vulnerability to tuberculosis infection?

What aspects of historical European tuberculosis control efforts might we do well to avoid today?

INTRODUCTION

In 1993 the World Health Organization took the unprecedented step of declaring a tuberculosis global emergency, yet the number of cases worldwide has continued to rise. Decades after cheap and proven methods of treatment have been developed, tuberculosis remains the world's leading cause of preventable illness and is now more prevalent than in any previous period of human history. The World Health Organization has calculated that around one third of the world's human population has been infected by the tuberculosis bacterium. Approximately three million people now die of tuberculosis each year. These deaths are mostly young adults but also include about 100,000 children under the age of 5 years. Current morbidity data show that tuberculosis is the most prevalent infectious cause of death, being responsible for 1 in 7 adult deaths and 1 in 4 preventable adult deaths worldwide. Only around 15 per cent of patients worldwide receive adequately supervised therapy and as this is a chronic disease there are between 16 and 20 million persons with active tuberculosis at any given time. About half of these patients are infectious and each infects between 2 and 20 persons annually which adds a further 100 million to the total numbers of infected people each year.

The discovery of streptomycin by Selman Waksman and Albert Schatz in 1944 led to the widespread use of effective anti-tuberculosis drugs. This opened the door to the potential con-

quest of tuberculosis and led to the development of the effective drug treatments available today. Further advances in the early 1970s with the use of rifampicin allowed the development of shorter and more convenient forms of treatment. Not only has such therapy been convincingly shown to be highly effective but it has been calculated that it is among the most cost-effective of all therapeutic interventions (Murray, Styblo, & Rouillon, 1990). In the 1950s it was widely believed that TB could be virtually eradicated but over the last fifteen years there has been a resurgence in reported cases in both developed and developing countries. Both the UK and the USA, for example, have seen a sharp rise in TB morbidity since the early 1980s (Brudney and Dobkin, 1991b; Farmer, 1997; Ryan, 1993). In much of the developing world the return of TB has been even more dramatic and threatens to overwhelm existing medical facilities (Bloom & Murray, 1992; Young, 1998). There is growing recognition that the conquest of this disease cannot be achieved by medical advances alone. Little progress can be made in tackling the crisis unless there is political willingness to address gross inequalities in healthcare provision (Benatar, 1995; Farmer, 1997; Zumla & Grange, 1998, 1999). This is why bio-medical research must be complemented by work from within the social and historical sciences.

The study of TB from within the social sciences includes the contributions of history, social anthropology, spatial science and social policy. What is currently lacking, however, is a detailed analysis of the interaction between regional shifts in TB incidence and wider social and economic developments at different spatial scales. This requires an interdisciplinary approach capable of moving beyond disciplinary specialisms towards a fully integrated and contextual form of analysis employing the kind of insights derived from historical studies which have revealed so much about the incidence of TB and other diseases in the past (see Ranger & Slack, 1992). This article suggests that whilst some aspects to the crisis are biological we cannot restrict our explanation to the bio-medical sciences alone. What we are confronted with is a complex interplay between political, social, economic, cultural and biological factors.

We begin the article by outlining the main characteristics of the "new" tuberculosis in order to emphasize the combination of biological and socio-economic developments which have contributed to the spread of disease. Secondly, we explore some of the key debates surrounding the decline and resurgence of tuberculosis. We suggest that although the decline of TB in the twentieth century has been widely studied, the emergence of the "new" tuberculosis is much less well understood. Finally, we turn to a series of conceptual and theoretical themes which may illuminate a more productive kind of approach to the understanding of the evolving relationship between disease and society. A series of critical themes is identified which require further investigation as part of an interdisciplinary research agenda capable of combining advances in the biophysical sciences with insights derived from the social and historical sciences.

THE "NEW" TUBERCULOSIS

Recent research into the epidemiology of the "new" tuberculosis has revealed a number of different contributory factors. It is useful to distinguish between three principal developments: the emergence of drug-resistant strains of TB; the prevalence of co-infection with HIV; and social and economic developments affecting access to medical care. In order to make sense of the contemporary crisis we need to consider a range of interrelationships between these contributory factors in order to build a full picture of the global dynamics of disease. The emergence of drug resistance is thought to be responsible for around 10 per cent of new TB cases (Neville, Bromberg, & Bromberg, 1994; Nolan, 1997; Small, Shafer, & Hopewell, 1993; Small & Moss, 1993; Simone & Dooley, 1998). The problem of drug resistance was encountered soon after the discovery of streptomycin and other anti-tuberculosis drugs and led to the universal recognition of the need to use multi-drug treatment programmes. The emergence of worldwide drug resistance has been caused by a variety of factors including the poor supervision of therapy, the use of badly prepared combination preparations, inconsistent prescribing practices, erratic drug supplies, and unregulated over-the-counter sales of drugs (including cough mixtures containing isoniazid) (see Okeke, Lamikanra, & Edelman, 1999). The most commonly encountered resistance is to a single drug, usually streptomycin or isoniazid, and most patients with such resistance respond adequately to a multi-drug treatment programme. The emergence of resistance to rifampicin is much more serious as this is the most powerful anti-tuberculosis drug with the ability to sterilize lesions by destroying near-dormant "persister" bacilli. Furthermore, most rifampicin-resistant strains are also resistant to isoniazid and, by convention, tuberculosis due to strains resistant to these two agents, with or without additional resistances, is said to be multi-drug resistant. The use of standard short-course treatment becomes not only ineffectual but may even be positively harmful as resistance to other drugs such as pyrazinamide and ethambutol also develops as part of the so-called "amplifier effect" (see Farmer & Kim, 1998). In Russia, for example, mutant forms of TB, variously referred to as multi-drug resistant tuberculosis (MDR-TB), have been rapidly spreading in response to chronic overcrowding in the prison system and severe cutbacks in primary health care (Meek, 1998). The problems and costs of managing each case of MDR-TB are enormous. Successful therapy requires prolonged courses of less effective, more expensive, and more toxic drugs, under long-term supervision (Kochi, Vareldzis, & Styblo, 1993). The incidence of MDR-TB in New York has been reduced by such a strategy, although at a very great cost: the management of a single case can exceed US$250,000 (Farmer & Kim, 1998). In the case of New York the spread of MDR-TB was facilitated by reductions in public health expenditure but the city ended up having to spend ten times more than they saved in order to bring TB under control (Boseley, 1999). There is little prospect that these kind of expensive and complex medical interventions could be widely applied on a worldwide scale, yet it is the breakdown in existing disease control programmes which is facilitating the emergence of a far more serious public health crisis to be faced in the future. A significant barrier to the control of MDR-TB is the lack of good epidemiological data on the prevalence and distribution of such resistance and the lack of adequate laboratory facilities for its detection, evaluation and monitoring. In order to tackle this dimension to the problem the World Health Organization, together with the International Union Against Tuberculosis and Lung Disease, has undertaken a global survey which has found very wide regional variations in the incidence and monitoring of MDR-TB (World Health Organization, 1997b; 1999).

A second factor is the pandemic of HIV infection and AIDS which is estimated to have contributed towards 8–10 per cent of TB cases worldwide. In Africa, however, HIV is responsible for at least 20 per cent of TB cases (Hart, Beeching, & Duerden, 1996; Kumaresan, 1996; Murray & Lopez, 1996; Schulzer, Fitzgerald, Enarson, & Grzybowski, 1992; Zumla, Johnson, & Miller, 1997). Given that a third of the world's population carry quiescent TB infection the effects of immune system damage can be expected to have devastating consequences: the most recent data suggest that in parts of sub-Saharan Africa, for example, a quarter of the adult population are now infected with HIV (Altman, 1998). Infection by HIV is currently the most important predisposing factor for the development of overt tuberculosis in those infected by *M. tuberculosis* before or after becoming HIV positive (Chretien, 1990; Coker & Miller, 1997). In the absence of immunosuppression, people who have overcome primary tuberculosis have about a 5 per cent chance of developing post-primary tuberculosis at some time during the remainder of their lives. HIV-positive persons have an 8 per cent chance annually of developing tuberculosis rising to a total of 50 per cent during the remainder of their shortened life span (Dolin, Raviglione, & Kochi, 1994). By late 1997, there were an estimated 30 million HIV-infected persons worldwide and, assuming that one third had been infected with *M. tuberculosis*, there would have been around 10 million co-infected persons. The burden of HIV-associated tuberculosis has also particularly affected women and children. One study found that HIV seroprevalence rates in Zambia among hospitalised children with tuberculosis rose from 18 to 67 per cent over an eight year period, while remaining at a constant 10 per cent among children admitted with surgical conditions (Chintu & Zumla, 1995). In Zambia, at least 1 in 4 pregnant women are HIV positive and tuberculosis has overtaken direct obstetric complications as a cause of pregnancy-related mortality (Ahmed et al., 1999; Fylkesnes, Musonda, & Kasumba, 1997). The increasing recognition of links between TB and HIV among patients has also had the adverse effect of adding to the stigma of TB symptoms and has hindered cooperation between patients, health care workers and local communities (Van Cleef & Chum, 1995).

A third factor covers what we might term social and economic "disruption." Mass movements of people in response to war, economic insecurity, community disruption and other factors have been involved in the spread of TB and other infectious diseases associated with crowding, makeshift housing and poor sanitation (Farmer, 1997; McKenna, McCray, & Onorato, 1995; Mutatkar, 1995; Smallman-Raynor & Cliff, 1991, 1998). In addition to short-term disruption we must consider longer term social and economic shifts which have emerged over the post-war period and particularly since the early 1970s. There is now increasing evidence that growing poverty, infrastructural decay and declining health services have facilitated the spread of TB (Brudney & Dobkin, 1991a, b; Elender, Bentham, & Langford, 1998; Greenberg, Schneider, & Martell, 1995; Lewontin & Levins, 1996; Snider, 1997; World Health Organization, 1996; Zumla & Grange, 1998). An emerging theme is the extent to which the resurgence of TB can be related to contemporary processes of social and economic restructuring in response to changes within the global economy since the late 1960s and early 1970s associated with a shift towards neoliberal patterns of policy making. A more market-orientated approach to public policy making has sharply altered the rationale and distribution of health care services. A substantial body of evidence suggests that tuberculosis has a disproportionate impact on the economically poor: 95 per cent of all TB cases and 98 per cent of TB deaths occur in the developing world where problems of ill-health contribute towards vicious cycles of economic hardship in the context of high unemployment and weak social security and health care provision. Even in developed economies such as the United Kingdom, the current increase of the disease can be attributed to widening social inequalities. Between 1980 and 1992, for example, there was a 35 per cent increase in the incidence of tuberculosis among the poorest 10 per cent of the population of England and Wales, a 13 per cent increase among the next poorest 20 per cent but no significant increase among the remaining 70 per cent of the population (Bhatti, Law, & Morris, 1995). The latest figures for the UK suggest that the prevalence of the disease has continued to rise during the 1990s with the rate of infections increasing from 9.4 to 10.9 per 100,000 people over the decade (Boseley, 1999). It is in developing countries, however, where the poverty-disease cycle is most striking. The poor have few health advocates, either in their own communities or in the wealthier nations, and in comparison with other major health afflictions the disease remains relatively neglected: the funding of tuberculosis control worldwide, for example, continues to be very low in comparison with other infectious disease with just 8 dollars of external aid spent for each patient death compared with 137 dollars for malaria, 925 for AIDs and over 38,000 for leprosy (World Health Organization, 1994).

TUBERCULOSIS IN HISTORICAL CONTEXT

There is an extensive literature on the decline of tuberculosis over the twentieth century (see, for example, Bates, 1992; Bryder, 1988; Johnston, 1995; Packard, 1989; Smith, 1988). Historical studies have emphasized the role of advances in medical science, along with more general improvements in nutrition, housing and other indicators of social well-being. The precise contribution of these different developments is the subject of con-

tinuing scholarly debate (see Barnes, 1992; Chretien, 1993; Guerrand, 1984; Mitchell, 1992; Ranger & Slack, 1992; Wilson, 1990; Szretzer, 1988) but there is little doubt that the decline of TB can be clearly related to a set of identifiable social, political, economic and scientific developments. A critical divide exists in the historical literature between those accounts which attribute declining mortality from TB to economic growth (variously referred to as the demographic or epidemiological transition) and alternative views which stress the variety of different paths towards higher living standards under the influence of contrasting political responses and institutional arrangements for sanitation and public health.

An influential view is the so-called McKeown thesis whereby the decline of infectious diseases and high mortality rates is attributed to general improvements in nutrition and welfare associated with economic development. These ideas have been developed in relation to the history of tuberculosis by the use of empirical evidence to show that the disease was in decline before the widespread use of sanatoria and other public health measures. In contrast, alternative perspectives developed by Simon Szreter, Constance Nathanson and others emphasize the critical importance of institutional and legislative change fostered by the political salience of public health advocates (Nathanson, 1996; Szreter, 1997). An emphasis on public health advocacy reveals the significance of specific measures aimed against tuberculosis such as effective patient segregation, housing improvements and the control of bovine tuberculosis (see Fairchild & Oppenheimer, 1998). This is an important distinction because the former position tends to downplay the politically contested nature of historical outcomes in public health whereas the latter position draws our attention to the diversity of possible outcomes. For Constance Nathanson, a critical dimension to the politics of public health is the capacity of the state to intervene on behalf of a putative public interest. She argues that where states are strong and clearly centralized this facilitates the coordination and implementation of public health policies. A variety of studies have illustrated this across diverse fields such as prenatal health care, water fluoridation, and the modernization of sanitation practices. In other words, the advance and retreat of disease is not only related to the broader dynamics of economic growth but is also affected by the outcome of political conflict and social reform. In the case of Glasgow, for example, historical research has revealed that the decline of tuberculosis was closely related to political efforts to improve overcrowded and inadequate housing rather than the outcome of more general nutritional improvements (McFarlane, 1989; see also Castells, 1983; Chapman, 1971; Dubos & Dubos, 1992; Gauldie, 1974; Melling, 1980).

Research into the contemporary resurgence of tuberculosis has repeatedly emphasized behavioural and biological aspects to the epidemiology of TB to the relative neglect of social and historical context. Individual (behavioural) approaches have focused on non-compliance with treatment regimes as the main barrier to the control of TB (see, for example, Bayer & Dupuis, 1995; Menzies, Rocher, & Vissandjee, 1993). Much research suggests that non-compliance with therapy is the major cause of the failure to control tuberculosis. Unfortunately, the word "non-compliance" implies that the fault lies with the patient, while in fact most breakdowns in therapy are due to failure on the part of the health care provider (Chintu & Zumla, 1995; Chowdhury, Chowdhury, & Islam, 1997; Gittler, 1994). Common faults include poor prescribing practices, an interrupted supply of drugs, demands (sometimes clandestine) on patients for payment for the drugs, arrogant and patronising behaviour of health care staff, and a requirement for excessive traveling to health care facilities (see Ellner et al., 1983; Needham, Godfrey-Faussett, & Foster, 1998; Saunderson, 1995). Much of the existing literature has adopted the analytical approach of "bio-medical individualism" with respect to the epidemiology of disease through an emphasis on qualitative ethnographic accounts of individual patients or a quantitative scaling up from individual patient history (see Fee & Krieger, 1994). Yet accounts which focus on individual patients fail to advance any overall conception of the dynamics of disease epidemiology as part of a broader set of social processes (see Benatar, 1995). If we take the example of MDR-TB, the growth of drug resistance is related to changing patterns of health care provision and cannot be explained in bio-medical terms alone or simply by blaming patients for non-compliance.

The emergence of the World Health Organization's directly observed therapy (DOTS) strategy is based on ensuring patient compliance through a closely monitored programme of treatment (see, for example, Wilkinson & Davies, 1997). Although the DOTS strategy is a crucial element in any coordinated response to TB there remain significant difficulties in relation to funding, staff recruitment, and the fear of stigma by patients who are reluctant to regularly meet health workers in the clinic, workplace or home. The DOTS strategy is approaching the limits of what can be achieved without more fundamental changes in public health policies as part of a wider programme to tackle poverty and social inequality (see Dievler & Pappas, 1999; Gittler, 1994; Young, Rachal, Bailey, Tate, & Nelson, 1997). Beyond individual non-compliance with treatment programmes the two most common explanations to be found in the bio-medical literature for the return of tuberculosis are the advent of HIV and the emergence of TB strains resistant to drugs (Farmer, 1997). These two factors are routinely used in reference to the "new" tuberculosis yet they constitute only part of the changing picture. The most decisive set of changes contributing towards the re-emergence of this disease lie at a structural level in society rather than at the level of the individual patient or TB bacillus. As the microbiologist René Dubos has argued: "Tuberculosis is a social disease . . . its understanding demands that the impact of social and economic factors on the individual be considered as much as the mechanisms by which tubercle bacilli cause damage to the human body" (quoted in Farmer, 1997, p. 348). By shifting our analytical emphasis from the individual to society an individualized mode of explanation is replaced by a structural framework within which we can trace changing patterns of disease as a broader set of "bio-social" processes.

Some of the most innovative insights into the relationship between the individual patient and their social context have been derived from anthropological studies of disease. Extensive anthropological research has examined the mis-match between (Western) medical belief systems and alternative traditional forms of knowledge held by local cultures (see, for example, Caldwell, Orubuloye, & Caldwell, 1992; de Villiers, 1991; Ingstadt, 1990; Moloantoa, 1982; Vecchiato, 1997).

In developed economies, by contrast, a discourse of "non-compliance" has emerged to differentiate between different categories of patients and their degree of cooperation with medical authorities (Lerner, 1997). In order to advance our understanding of the "new" tuberculosis we need to make the methodological and analytical leap between individual and society. In altering the scope of our analysis a series of further issues are raised. How, for example, can we account for the changing epidemiology of tuberculosis? Under what material conditions has the disease been able to spread so rapidly over the last twenty years? In what ways must we alter our conceptions of the relationship between disease and modern societies in order to formulate an adequate explanation and policy response for this public health crisis?

RETHINKING THE EPIDEMIOLOGY OF DISEASE

Changing patterns of economic and social investment have contributed towards a new geography of wealth and poverty with significant implications for the epidemiology of disease. This presents a very different picture from the political dynamics of disease prevention in the nineteenth-century city where different social classes lived in much closer proximity. With the advent of more diffuse patterns of urbanization and the greater mobility of capital investment it has become far easier for public health crises to be effectively ignored where they present no generalized threat to the overall well-being of an increasingly globalized economic system. Indeed, the combined impact of the greater marketization of health care and the growth of new insurance based financial derivatives is making the management of health risk increasingly remote from democratic forms of government. In order to make sense of the global dynamics of the tuberculosis epidemic, we need an analytical framework within which we can explore nested scales of causality and interdependence linking the dynamics of urban and regional change to processes of global economic restructuring (Table 22.1). These insights can be used to explore the interaction between processes of institutional change, shifting public health discourses, and the social production of the human environment.

What is clearly needed is some kind of conceptual vocabulary which allows us to integrate the analysis of disease into the broader dynamics of social and political change associated with post-war fluctuations in the global economy. Much scholarly attention has been devoted to establishing what kind of social and economic structures are emerging from the ashes of the relatively stable era of economic growth which was experienced in Western economies from the late 1940s until the early 1970s (see, for example, Amin, 1994; Brenner, 1998; Lipietz, 1985). This period saw significant improvements in fields such as education, health care and employment and was marked by sustained advances in the arena of public health. There has been little attempt, however, to trace substantive connections between twentieth-century economic history and changing patterns of public health.

The resurgence of disease in the so-called "de-developing" enclaves of urban America and the poverty stricken cities of the former Soviet Union can only be fully understood with reference to the dynamics of global post-war political and economic change (see Tulchinsky & Varavikova, 1996; Wallace, Wallace, Andrews, Fullilove, & Fullilove, 1995; Wallace, Wallace, & Andrews, 1997; Wallace, Wallace, Ullman, & Andrews, 1999; Whiteis, 1997; 1998). This suggests an implicit challenge to the emerging literature on the "healthy city" which explores quality of life issues in an intellectual context which is divorced from the underlying dynamics of urban change (see, for example, Milewa & de Leeuw, 1996). In the case of New York City, for example, we can identify an interconnection between disease epidemiology and urban decline. In the wake of the city's 1975 fiscal crisis there was a dramatic fall in public health expenditure on the control of tuberculosis which led to cuts in the number of health care workers and a cessation of patient tracking to ensure compliance with treatment. The disruption of treatment and very limited detention of non-compliant patients contributed towards the emergence of MDR-TB in the 1980s. Coupled with growing poverty and high levels of HIV infection the stage was set for a dramatic return of tuberculosis (Brudney & Dobkin, 1991a, b; Lerner, 1993). This observation is taken further by Wallace (1997) and Wallace et al. (1999) who argue that the legacy of neo-liberal

Table 22.1   The "new" tuberculosis: a typology of contributory factors

General Categories	Specific Outcomes
Bio-medical factors	The evolution of MDR-TB
	The dynamics of co-infection with HIV
	The creation of "ecological niches" for the spread of disease
Political factors	The transition towards neo-liberal (market driven) patterns of public policy making since the 1970s
	The shift from collective to more individualized approaches to health care
	Cuts in social expenditure
	War, political instability and mass movements of refugees
Cultural factors	The continuing stigmatization of tuberculosis
	The impacts of racism
	The impacts of gender inequalities
	Tensions between different systems of medical knowledge
Economic factors	Global economic changes since the 1970s leading to widening international and regional disparities in wealth and income
	Unprecedented levels of global poverty and inequality
	New patterns of urban and regional change with deteriorating sanitation and housing conditions for the world's poor
	Unprecedented levels of capital mobility with new patterns of investment in financial derivatives and other non-productive commodities

policy making has created an "ecological niche" within which disease can spread through American inner cities and that only a systematic "integrated ecsosystem intervention" can tackle the root causes of persistent and pervasive ill-health. We need to re-integrate the control of disease with a progressive social agenda since narrow bio-medical interventions can only tackle surface manifestations of the problem.

A range of historical studies have highlighted the crucial significance of public health issues in contributing towards the emergence of new kinds of institutional structures during the nineteenth century (see Barnes, 1995; Craddock, 1998; Evans, 1987, 1992; Pickstone, 1992; Rosne, 1992). A critical theme for investigation is whether the contemporary threat of disease is sufficient to challenge current approaches to public health in a similar fashion to the impacts of cholera, typhoid and other diseases in the past. A distinction must be drawn here between the impact of short-term epidemics such as plague and cholera and the longer term impact of chronic illnesses such as syphilis and tuberculosis (Slack, 1992). The changing character of urbanization is crucial since the spatially compressed industrial cities of the nineteenth century were a key motor behind the

modernization of public health and social policy more generally. In contrast, contemporary patterns of urbanization are marked by systematic social and spatial discontinuities which facilitate the mobility of capital investment rather than regional resolutions to chronic problems of social and environmental underinvestment. This is a decisive difference between past and present processes of urbanization which necessitates a new kind of theorization of the relationships between disease, urbanization and political change. In particular, we need to know why a long period of relative stability and progression in public health care from the middle decades of the nineteenth century until the late twentieth century has come to an abrupt end. This radical break in the incidence of TB cannot be explained by economic change alone but involves a complex interaction between social, cultural and biological factors which are widely neglected within political-economy research into health and the urban environment.

Issues of poverty, gender inequality, disease stigmatization and the adequacy of medical services are central elements in any full explanation of the contemporary resurgence of this disease. In developing countries, for example, the treatment of tuberculosis is closely linked with pregnancy and childbirth as one of few instances when many women come into contact with modern health services. The incidence of tuberculosis-related maternal mortality is in turn related to pervasive gender inequalities in access to health care (Connolly & Nunn, 1996; Holmes, Hausler, & Nunn, 1998; Miller & Miller, 1996; Mofenson, Rodriguez, & Hershow, 1995). The interaction between race and tuberculosis is also striking. In the case of South Africa, for example, the nineteenth-century spread of tuberculosis was closely related to patterns of industrialization and the over-crowded conditions endured by migrant workers. The South African state sought to cover up the extent of TB among miners and intensified race-based health inequalities through its Apartheid legislation (Andersson, 1990; Collins, 1982; Packard, 1989). Recent research has highlighted the interaction between race, gender and place in contributing towards differential vulnerability towards disease (see Hudelson, 1996; Nair, George, & Chacko, 1997; Packard, 1989; Warren, 1997). The analytical challenge is to combine an understanding of the diversity of local contexts for disease transmission with a wider intellectual framework engaged with processes of global economic and political change.

A further omission in much of the existing social science literature is any detailed consideration of the interaction between bio-physical and social systems. How, for example, can we integrate biological changes such as mutations in TB strains with social and historical modes of analysis? Recent interdisciplinary scholarship drawn from both the biological and social sciences has advocated a historical approach to understanding relations between social and bio-physical systems where nature itself is perceived as a social product (see Cronon, 1983; Harvey, 1996; Levins & Lewontin, 1985). The highly fragmentary methodologies of the bio-physical sciences tend to not only split nature from society but also divide physical reality into ever smaller units of analysis. The study of disease requires a combination of small-scale molecular and experimental insights with a full appreciation of the social context in which the understanding of human health has developed in modern societies. We need to recognize that tuberculosis is as much a social as a biological phenomenon: ever since the emergence of tuber-

culosis with the domestication of cattle some 7000 years ago the disease has undergone a series of transformations. In the modern era, however, the relationship between tuberculosis and society has entered a new and more complex phase.

CONCLUSIONS

The spread of tuberculosis is a multi-faceted phenomenon comprising many different dimensions ranging from neo-liberal policy making to the evolution of bacterial resistance to drugs. In view of the seriousness of the global emergency of tuberculosis and the increasing impact of the HIV/AIDS pandemic and the spread of multi-drug resistance, a radical revision of control strategies is essential. From a social perspective, the effective control of tuberculosis requires attention to the gross global inequalities in wealth and living standards which limit access to adequate health care. To improve treatment compliance and to standardize the various national tuberculosis programmes the World Health Organization has advocated the so-called DOTS strategy which involves not only direct observation of patients but also government commitment to a national tuberculosis programme, case detection through sputum smear microscopy, short-course drug treatments, adequate medical infrastructure to ensure an uninterrupted supply of drugs, and regular monitoring and evaluation of the programme. Yet only about 15 per cent of TB patients globally have been able to receive treatments which meet the DOTS criteria. Although there is evidence that the DOTS strategy has begun to make a real impact in parts of China, India and Bangladesh, there remain formidable social, cultural and economic barriers to its effective worldwide implementation. Even in developed economies the advocacy of a more integrated approach has not been without difficulty. In the UK, for example, there is a shortage of clinical nursing staff specialized in the treatment of tuberculosis and it is doubtful whether district nurses would be willing to take on this additional responsibility (Coker & Miller, 1997).

There is now a wealth of empirical data to demonstrate the changing incidence of tuberculosis over the last twenty years. In order to account for this shift we need to find out what changes have occurred in the field of public health policy which have contributed towards the resurgence of disease. In particular, we need to know to what extent the failure of public agencies to intervene effectively is due to changing socio-economic circumstances. Since tuberculosis is a disease of poverty we need to know whether existing institutional arrangements for disease control are genuinely powerless to prevent the spread of disease. In order to investigate this theme we need to relate the changing epidemiology of disease to shifting relations between government agencies, the economy and civil society. A key challenge is to relate changing patterns of TB infection to broader social and economic processes operating at different spatial scales and across different historical periods. This will involve the identification of structural as opposed to individual or behavioural barriers to the control of TB as part of nested hierarchy of causality ranging from local to global scales of analysis.

In the late nineteenth century and early twentieth century the control of tuberculosis was closely related to public health advocacy in order to improve the living conditions of the poor: the links between poverty and ill health were clear and unambiguous. With scientific advances in the twentieth century, however, there has been a shift away from this holistic advocacy approach towards a bio-medical emphasis on individual patients (see Lerner, 1993). The increasing use of out patient drug treatments has reduced the need for institutional interventions such as sanatoria and indirectly led to shifting priorities in public health policy. The early success of new medical interventions such as the BCG, isoniazid, and rifampicin, disguised the complexity of tuberculosis epidemiology and masked the continuing interconnections between poverty and ill-health. Yet to return to the highly moralistic public health discourses of the past with their emphasis on segregation and control raises another set of dilemmas around the stigmatization of illness which cannot contribute to more effective public health policies (see Abel, 1997). The principal motor behind the resurgence of tuberculosis has been the sharp rise in global poverty which has undermined many of the public health advances of the twentieth century. The challenge for scholars, public health advocates and health care workers is to build a coherent and persuasive policy agenda which lays bare the interconnections between tuberculosis and social injustice in order to galvanize political action.

REFERENCES

Abel, E. K. (1997). Taking the cure to the poor: Patients responses to New York City's tuberculosis program, 1894–1918. *American Journal of Public Health, 87,* 1808–1815.

Ahmed, Y., Mwaba, P., Chintu, C., Grange, J. M., Ustianowski, A., & Zumla, A. (1999). A study of maternal mortality at the University Teaching Hospital, Lusaka, Zambia: The emergence of tuberculosis as a major non-obstetric cause of maternal death. *The International Journal of Tuberculosis and Lung Disease, 3,* 675–680.

Altman, L. K. (1998). Parts of Africa showing HIV in 1 in 4 adults. *The New York Times,* June 24.

Amin, A. (1994). Post-Fordism: Models, fantasies and phantoms of transition. In A. Amin (Ed.), *A postfordist reader* (pp. 1–39). Oxford and Cambridge MA: Blackwell.

Andersson, N. (1990). Tuberculosis and social stratification in South Africa. *International Journal of Health Studies, 20,* 141–165.

Barnes, D. S. (1992). The rise or fall of tuberculosis in belle-époque France: A reply to Allan Mitchell. *Social History of Medicine, 5,* 279–290.

Barnes, D. S. (1995). *The making of a social disease: Tuberculosis in nineteenth-century France.* Berkeley, CA: University of California Press.

Bates, B. (1992). *Bargaining for life: A social history of tuberculosis 1876–1938.* Philadelphia: University of Philadelphia Press.

Bayer, R., & Dupuis, L. (1995). Tuberculosis, public health and civil liberties. *Annual Review of Public Health, 16,* 307–326.

Benatar, S. (1995). Prospects for global health: Lessons from tuberculosis. *Thorax, 50,* 487–489.

Bhatti, N., Law, M. R., & Morris, J. K., et al. (1995). Increasing incidence of tuberculosis in England and Wales: A study of the likely causes. *British Medical Journal, 310,* 967–969.

Bloom, B., & Murray, C. (1992). Tuberculosis: Commentary on a resurgent killer. *Science, 257,* 1055.

Boseley, S. (1999). Warning as TB cases increase. *The Guardian,* 14 December.

Brenner, R. (1998). The economics of global turbulence: A special report on the world economy, 1950–98. *New Left Review, 229,* 1–264.

Brudney, K., & Dobkin, J. (1991a). A tale of two cities: Tuberculosis control in Nicaragua and New York City. *Seminars in Respiratory Infections, 6,* 261.

Brudney, K., & Dobkin, J. (1991b). Resurgent tuberculosis in New York City: Human immunodeficiency virus, homelessness, and the decline of tuberculosis control programs. *American Review of Respiratory Disease, 144,* 745.

Bryder, L. (1988). *Below the magic mountain: A social history of tuberculosis in twentieth-century Britain.* New York: Oxford University Press.

Caldwell, J. C., Orubuloye, I. O., & Caldwell, P. (1992). Under-reaction to AIDS in Sub-Saharan Africa. *Social Science and Medicine, 34,* 1169–1182.

Castells, M. (1983). *The city and the grassroots: A cross-cultural theory of urban social movements.* Berkeley, CA: University of California Press.

Chapman, S. D. (Ed.) (1971). *The history of working class housing.* Newton Abbot: David and Charles.

Chintu, C., & Zumla, A. (1995). Childhood tuberculosis and infection with the Human Immunodeficiency Virus. *Journal of the Royal College of Physicians of London, 29,* 92–94.

Chowdhury, A. M. R., Chowdhury, S. A., & Islam, M. N., et al. (1997). Control of tuberculosis through community health workers in Bangladesh. *Lancet, 350,* 160–172.

Chretien, J. (1990). Tuberculosis and HIV. The cursed duet. *Bulletin of Intenational Union against Tuberculosis and Lung Diseases, 65*(1), 25–28.

Chretien, J. (1993). La contribution francaise à la chute contre la tuberculose et sa maitrise. *Histoire des Sciences Médicales, 27,* 241–248.

Coker, R., & Miller, R. (1997). HIV associated tuberculosis. *British Medical Journal, 314,* 1847.

Collins, T. F. B. (1982). The history of southern Africa's first tuberculosis epidemic. *South African Medical Journal, 62,* 780–788.

Connolly, M., & Nunn, P. (1996). Women and tuberculosis. *World Health Statist Quart, 49,* 115–119.

Craddock, S. (1998). Tuberculosis, tenements and the epistemology of neglect: San Francisco in the nineteenth century. *Ecumene, 5,* 53–80.

Cronon, W. (1983). *Changes in the land: Indians, colonists, and the ecology of New England.* New York: Hill and Wang.

de Villiers, S. (1991). Tuberculosis in anthropological perspective. *South African Journal of Ethnology, 14,* 69.

Dievler, A., & Pappas, G. (1999). Implications of social class and race for urban public health policy making: A case study of HIV/AIDS and TB policy in Washington, DC. *Social Science and Medicine, 48,* 1095–1102.

Dolin, P. J., Raviglione, M. C., & Kochi, A. (1994). Global tuberculosis incidence and mortality during 1990–2000. *Bulletin of the World Health Organization, 72,* 213–220.

Dubos, R., & Dubos, J. (1992). *The white plague: Tuberculosis, man and society.* New Brunswick, NJ: Rutgers University Press.

Elender, F., Bentham, G., & Langford, I. (1998). Tuberculosis mortality in England and Wales during 1982–1992: Its association with poverty, ethnicity and AIDS. *Social Science and Medicine, 46,* 673–681.

Evans, R. J. (1987). *Death in Hamburg: Society and politics in the cholera years 1830–1910.* Oxford and New York: Oxford University Press.

Evans, R. J. (1992). Epidemics and revolution: Cholera in nineteenth-century Europe. In T. Ranger, & P. Slack (Eds.), *Epidemics and ideas: essays on the historical perception of pestilence* (pp. 149–173). Cambridge: Cambridge University Press.

Fairchild, A. L., & Oppenheimer, G. M. (1998). Public health nihilism versus pragmatism: History, politics, and the control of tuberculosis. *American Journal of Public Health, 88,* 1105–1117.

Farmer, P. (1997). Social scientists and the new tuberculosis. *Social Science and Medicine, 44,* 347–358.

Farmer, P., & Kim, J. Y. (1998). Community based approaches to the control of multidrug resistant tuberculosis: Introducing DOTS-plus. *British Medical Journal, 317,* 671–674.

Fee, E., & Krieger, N. (1994). "What's class got to do with health? A critique of biomedical individualism." Paper presented to the Meeting of the Society for the Social Studies of Science, New Orleans (12–16 October). In Haraway, D. J. (Ed.) 1997. *Modest witness: feminism and technoscience.* London and New York: Routledge.

Fylkesnes, K., Musonda, R. M., & Kasumba, K., et al. (1997). The HIV epidemic in Zambia: Socio-demographic prevalence patterns and indications of trends among childbearing women. *AIDS, II,* 339–345.

Gauldie, E. (1974). *Cruel habitations: A history of working class housing, 1780–1918.* London: George Allen and Unwin.

Gittler, J. (1994). Controlling resurgent tuberculosis: Public health agencies, public policy, and law. *Journal of Health Politics, Policy and Law, 19,* 107–147.

Greenberg, M., Schneider, D., & Martell, J. (1995). Health promotion priorities of economically stressed cities. *Journal of Health Care for the Poor and Underserved, 6,* 10–22.

Guerrand, R.-H. (1984). Guerre a la tuberculose. *Histoire, 74,* 78–81.

Hart, C. A., Beeching, N. J., & Duerden, B. I. (1996). Tuberculosis into the next century: Proceedings of a symposium held on 4 February 1995 at the Liverpool School of Tropical Medicine. *Journal of Medical Microbiology, 44,* 1.

Harvey, D. (1996). *Justice, nature and the geography of difference.* Oxford and Cambridge, MA: Basil Blackwell.

Holmes, C. B., Hausler, H., & Nunn, P. (1998). A review of sex differences in the epidemiology of tuberculosis. *International Journal of Tuberculosis and Lung Diseases, 2,* 96–104.

Hudelson, P. (1996). Gender differentials in tuberculosis. *Tubercle and Lung Disease, 77,* 391–400.

Ingstadt, B. (1990). The cultural construction of AIDS and its consequences for prevention in Botswana. *Medical Anthropology Quarterly, 4,* 28.

Johnston, W. (1995). *The modern epidemic: A history of tuberculosis in Japan.* Harvard East Asian Monographs.

Kochi, A., Vareldzis, B., & Styblo, K. (1993). Multidrug-resistant tuberculosis and its control. *Research in Microbiology, 144,* 104–110.

Kumaresan, J. A. (1996). Tuberculosis. In C. J. L. Murray, & A. D. Lopez (Eds.), *The global epidemiology of infectious diseases.* Cambridge, MA: Harvard University Press.

Lerner, B. H. (1993). New York City's tuberculosis control efforts: The historical limitations of the war on consumption. *American Journal of Public Health, 83,* 758–766.

Lerner, B. H. (1997). From careless consumptives to recalcitrant patients: The historical construction of noncompliance. *Social Science and Medicine, 45,* 1423–1431.

Levins, R., & Lewontin, R. (1985). *The dialectical biologist.* Cambridge, MA: Harvard University Press.

Lewontin, R., & Levins, R. (1996). The return of old diseases and the appearance of new ones. *Capitalism, Nature, Socialism: A Journal of Socialist Ecology, 7,* 103–107.

Lipietz, A. (1985). *Miracles et mirages. Problèmes de lindustrialisation dans le Tiers-Monde.* Paris: La Découverte.

McFarlane, N. (1989). Hospitals, housing and tuberculosis in Glasgow, 1911–51. *Social History of Medicine, 2,* 59–85.

McKenna, M. T., McCray, E., & Onorato, I. (1995). The epidemiology of tuberculosis among foreign-born persons in the United States, 1986–1993. *New England Journal of Medicine, 332,* 1071–1076.

Meek, J. (1998). Killer TB threat to the world. *The Guardian,* 23 September.

Melling, J. (Ed.) (1980). *Housing, social policy and the state.* London: Croom Helm.

Menzies, R., Rocher, I., & Vissandjee, B. (1993). Factors associated with compliance in treatment of tuberculosis. *Tubercle and Lung Disease, 74,* 32.

Milewa, T., & de Leeuw, E. (1996). Reason and protest in the new urban public health movement: An observation on the sociological analysis of political discourse in the healthy city. *British Journal of Sociology, 47,* 657–670.

Miller, K. S., & Miller, J. M. (1996). Tuberculosis in pregnancy: Interactions, diagnosis and management. *Clinical Obstetrics and Gynecology, 39,* 120–142.

Mitchell, A. (1992). Tuberculosis statistics and the McKeown thesis: A rebuttal to David Barnes. *Social History of Medicine, 5,* 291–296.

Mofenson, L. M., Rodriguez, E. M., & Hershow, R., et al. (1995). Mycobacterium tuberculosis infection in pregnant and non-pregnant women infected with HIV in the woman and infants study. *Archives of Internal Medicine, 155,* 1066–1072.

Moloantoa, K. E. (1982). Traditional attitudes towards tuberculosis. *South African Medical Journal, 17,* 29–31.

Murray, C. J. L., & Lopez, A. D. (Eds.) (1996). *The global burden of disease.* Cambridge, MA: Harvard University Press.

Murray, C. J. L., Styblo, K., & Rouillon, A. (1990). Tuberculosis in developing countries: burden, intervention, and cost. *Bulletin of International Union against Tuberculosis and Lung Diseases, 65,* 2–20.

Mutatkar, R. K. (1995). Public health problems of urbanization. *Social Science and Medicine, 41,* 977–981.

Nair, D. M., George, A., & Chacko, K. T. (1997). Tuberculosis in Bombay: New insights from poor urban patients. *Health Policy and Planning, 12,* 77–85.

Nathanson, C. A. (1996). Disease prevention as social change: Toward a theory of public health *Population and Development Review, 22*(4), 609.

Needham, D. M., Godfrey-Faussett, P., & Foster, S. D. (1998). Barriers to tuberculosis control in urban Zambia: the economic impact and burden on patients prior to diagnosis. *International Journal of Tuberculosis and Lung Disease, 2,* 811–817.

Neville, K., Bromberg, A., & Bromberg, R., et al. (1994). The third epidemic—multidrug-resistant tuberculosis. *Chest, 105,* 45–48.

Nolan, C. M. (1997). Nosocomial multidrug-resistant tuberculosis—global spread of the third epidemic. *Journal of Infectious Diseases, 76,* 748–751.

Okeke, I. N., Lamikanra, A., & Edelman, R. (1999). Socio-economic and behavioural factors leading to acquired bacterial resistance to antibiotics in developing countries. *Emerging Infectious Diseases, 5,* 18–27.

Packard, R. M. (1989). *White plague, black labor: Tuberculosis and the political economy of health and disease in South Africa.* Berkeley, CA: University of California Press.

Pickstone, J. (1992). Dearth, dirt and fever epidemics: Rewriting the history of British public health, 1780–1850. In T. Ranger, & P. Slack (Eds.), *Epidemics and ideas: essays on the historical perception of pestilence* (pp. 125–148). Cambridge: Cambridge University Press.

Ranger, T., Slack, P. (Eds.) (1992). *Epidemics and ideas: Essays on the historical perception of pestilence.* Cambridge: Cambridge University Press.

Rosner, D. (Ed.) (1992). *Hives of sickness: Public health and epidemics in New York City.* New Brunswick, NJ: Rutgers University Press.

Ryan, F. (1993). *The forgotten plague: How the battle against tuberculosis was won and lost.* Boston: Little Brown.

Saunderson, P. R. (1995). An economic evaluation of alternative program designs for tuberculosis control in rural Uganda. *Social Science and Medicine, 40,* 1203–1212.

Schulzer, M., Fitzgerald, J. M., Enarson, D. A., & Grzybowski, S. (1992). An estimate of the future size of the tuberculosis problem in sub-Saharan Africa resulting from HIV infection. *Tubercle and Lung Disease, 73,* 52–58.

Simone, P. M., & Dooley, S. W. (1998). Drug resistant tuberculosis in the USA. In P. D. O. Davies (Ed.), *Clinical Tuberculosis* (2nd ed.) (pp. 265–2287). London: Chapman and Hall.

Slack, P. (1992). Introduction. In T. Ranger, & P. Slack (Eds.), *Epidemics and ideas: Essays on the historical perception of pestilence* (pp. 1–20). Cambridge: Cambridge University Press.

Small, P., & Moss, A. (1993). Molecular epidemiology and the new tuberculosis. *Infections and Agents of Disease, 2,* 132.

Small, P., Shafer, R., & Hopewell, P. (1993). Exogenous reinfection with multidrug-resistant *Mycobacterium tuberculosis* in patients with advanced HIV infection. *New England Journal of Medicine, 328,* 1137.

Smallman-Raynor, M., & Cliff, A. (1991). Civil war and the spread of AIDS in Africa. *Epidemiology and Infection, 107,* 69–79.

Smallman-Raynor, M., & Cliff, A. (1998). The Philippines insurrection and the 1902–4 cholera epidemic: Part I—Epidemiological diffusion processes in war. *Journal of Historical Geography, 24,* 69–89.

Smith, F. B. (1988). *The retreat of tuberculosis, 1850–1950.* Croom Helm: New York.

Snider, G. L. (1997). Tuberculosis then and now: A personal perspective on the last fifty years. *Annals of Internal Medicine, 126,* 237–243.

Szreter, S. (1988). The importance of social intervention in Britain's mortality decline c. 1850–1914: A reinterpretation of the role of public health. *Social History of Medicine, 1,* 1–37a.

Szreter, S. (1997). Economic growth, disruption, deprivation, disease and death: On the importance of the politics of public health for development. *Population and Development Review, 23*(4), 693.

Tulchinsky, T. H., & Varavikova, E. A. (1996). Addressing the epidemiologic transition in the former Soviet Union: Strategies for health system and public health reform in Russia. *American Journal of Public Health, 86,* 313–320.

Van Cleef, M. R. A., & Chum, H. J. (1995). The proportion of tuberculosis cases in Tanzania attributable to human immunodeficiency virus. *International Journal of Epidemiology, 24,* 637–642.

Vecchiato, N. L. (1997). Socio-cultural aspects of tuberculosis control in Ethiopia. *Medical Anthropology Quarterly, 11,* 183–201.

Wallace, R. (1997). The destruction of US minority urban communities and the resurgence of tuberculosis. *Environment and Planning A, 29,* 269–291.

Wallace, R., Wallace, D., & Andrews, H. (1997). AIDS, tuberculosis, violent crime, and low birthweight in eight US metropolitan areas: Public policy, stochastic resonance, and the regional diffusion of inner city markers. *Environment and Planning A, 29,* 525–555.

Wallace, R., Wallace, D., Andrews, H., Fullilove, R., & Fullilove, M. T. (1995). The spatiotemporal dynamics of AIDS and TB in the New York metropolitan region from a sociogeographic perspective: Understanding the linkages of central city and suburbs. *Environment and Planning A, 27,* 1085–1108.

Wallace, R., Wallace, D., Ullman, J. E., & Andrews, H. (1999). Deindustrialization, inner-city decay, and the hierarchical diffusion of AIDS in the USA: How neoliberal and cold war policies magnified the ecological niche for emerging infections and created a national security crisis. *Environment and Planning A, 31,* 113–139.

Warren, C. (1997). Northern chills, southern fevers: Race-specific mortality in American cities, 1730–1900. *Journal of Southern History, 63,* 23–56.

Whiteis, D. G. (1997). Unhealthy cities: Corporate medicine, community economic underdevelopment, and public health. *International Journal of Health Services, 27,* 227–242.

Whiteis, D. G. (1998). Third World medicine in First World cities: Capital accumulation, uneven development and public health. *Social Science and Medicine, 47,* 795–808.

Wilkinson, D., & Davies, G. R. (1997). Coping with Africa's increasing tuberculosis burden: Are community supervisors an essential component of the DOT strategy? *Tropical Medicine and International Health, 2,* 700–704.

Wilson, L. G. (1990). The historical decline of tuberculosis in Europe and America: Its causes and significance. *Journal of the History of Medicine and Allied Sciences, 45,* 366–396.

World Health Organization. (1994). *TB-a global emergency.* Geneva: WHO.

World Health Organization. (1996). *Tuberculosis in the Era of HIV. A deadly partnership.* Geneva: World Health Organization.

World Health Organization. (1997a). *Global Tuberculosis Control. WHO Report 1997.* Geneva: World Health Organization Global Tuberculosis Programme. (WHO/TB/97.225).

World Health Organization. (1997b). *Anti-tuberculosis drug resistance in the world. The WHO/IUATLD global project on anti-tuberculosis drug resistance surveillance.* Geneva: World Health Organization.

World Health Organization. (1999). *Global tuberculosis control.* Geneva: World Health Organization.

Young, D. B. (1998). Blueprint of the white plague. *Nature, 393,* 537–544.

Young, R. C., Rachal, R. E., Bailey, S. B. C., Tate, H. L., & Nelson, B. (1997). Strategies for suppression, containment, and eradication of resurgent tuberculosis. *Journal of Health Care for the Poor and Underserved, 8,* 424–436.

Zumla, A., & Grange, J. M. (1998). Establishing a united front against the injustice of tuberculosis. *The International Journal of Tuberculosis and Lung Disease, 2*(3), 1–4.

Zumla, A., & Grange, J. M. (1999). The global emergency of tuberculosis. *Proceedings of the Royal College of Physicians Edinburgh, 29,* 104–115.

Zumla, A., Johnson, M., & Miller, R. F. (Eds.) (1997). *AIDS and respiratory medicine.* London: Chapman and Hall.

■ ■ ■ ■ ▧ ▧ ▨ ■ ■

23   IMPLICATIONS OF PANDEMIC INFLUENZA FOR BIOTERRORISM RESPONSE

Monica Schoch-Spana

The Spanish flu pandemic of 1918–1919 is one example of what can happen when disease pools converge (see selection 19). It serves as a warning that similar disease episodes are possible and even likely in an increasingly interconnected world. Because of its rapidity and violence, the Spanish flu pandemic also provides an historical model of social, medical, and governmental responses that can be utilized to develop recommendations in the event of an intentionally created epidemic.

Flu viruses come in many types and circulate through a number of reservoirs in addition to humans. They change their characteristics rapidly, such that immune protection against one strain is ineffective against another. Since the Spanish flu, there have been several pandemics of the disease, and in the past decade there has been a rise in the number of new subtypes of the virus and its animal and bird hosts (see Webby and Webster 2003).

This selection describes how airborne transmission allowed the disease to spread rapidly in 1918–19 and affect much of the world's population. There was confusion in the United States about the causal agent, fueling public fears. The epidemic had impacts on the economy, government, health and safety services, and transportation and communications. There were not enough health-care and funeral sector workers or appropriate spaces to deal with the volume of people stricken with the disease. This led to some ingenious solutions but also to situations that conflicted with accepted ways of doing things and contributed to an atmosphere of instability and dismay.

By examining the impact of the epidemic through a broad sociohistorical lens, Schoch-Spana shows that beyond developing the public health system to be able to provide adequate reporting, delivery of supplies, institutional care, and home treatment, it will be necessary to prepare for handling a potential bioterrorist attack in ways that respect social mores, calm public fears, attend to social class differences

Source: Schoch-Spana, M. 2000. "Implications of Pandemic Influenza for Bioterrorism Response." *Clinical Infectious Diseases* 31(6):1409–1413. Published by the University of Chicago Press. ©2000 by the Infectious Diseases Society of America. All rights reserved.

and inequalities, and ensure public commitment to emergency control measures. Even if medical research and development are successful, it is unlikely that vaccines and other supplies could be delivered efficiently on a mass scale for a well-known pathogen like influenza virus, much less an unknown one. The kind of breakdown in public health provision due to financial constraints and lack of political investment described by Gandy and Zumla in the previous selection has already taken place, as evidenced in recent large-scale outbreaks of flu in the United States. These crises bring to light the degree to which epidemic diseases strain health-care systems and disrupt social systems.

Questions to keep in mind

How do influenza viruses change such that they are not recognized by the immune system?

What were some of the public health, governmental, and social responses to the Spanish flu epidemic in the United States?

Which ones were effective, and which were not?

What does the Spanish flu pandemic suggest about how to prepare for and deal with a bioterrorist attack?

At its peak, the 1918–1919 influenza pandemic (Spanish flu) incapacitated American cities and paralyzed the health care system. A 20th century outbreak of disease with calamitous effects in this country, Spanish flu is an apt case to influence current bioterrorism planning efforts. This article presents a set of principles meant to assist medical, public health, and government leaders as they construct a response to the potential mass casualties and social turmoil initiated by a bioterrorist attack.

INFLUENZA: EVOLVING PATHOGENS AND PROFOUND HEALTH BURDEN

Throughout human history, global influenza outbreaks have sickened large numbers of people, claimed many lives, and dramatically disrupted social and economic relations [1, 2]. The most infamous episode is the 1918–1919 influenza pandemic, which altered World War I battle plans and peace talks and made almost 1 billion people (one-half the world's population) ill, killing from 21 to 40 million [3, 4]. In interpandemic years, flu still exacts a harsh toll: excess deaths, in the aggregate, approach pandemic levels [2, 5, 6]. Influenza's destructive capacity resides in the pace and unpredictability of the evolution of the virus, which can subvert the body's immune response and outstrip society's efforts at containment [7, 8].

Influenza viruses infect human host cells (typically, epithelial cells that line the respiratory tract) and reproduce [9, 10]. Flu's characteristic structure is a sphere that contains RNA material and is studded with protein surface antigens: hemagglutinin that binds the virus to the host cell, initiating replication, and neuraminidase that frees up newly manufactured virions from the host cell, facilitating virus spread. Three types of influenza virus exist: type A, isolated from humans, birds, pigs, horses, and sea mammals; and types B and C, found only in humans. Influenza A viruses are subtyped according to the unique surface antigens that they manifest (e.g., H1N1 and H3N2). Fifteen different types of hemagglutinin and 9 types of neuraminidase have been observed.

Influenza A and B viruses are genetically and structurally more similar to each other than either are to influenza C viruses, and they contribute to a greater proportion of human disease than does influenza C virus [10, 11]. Epidemics of influenza A tend to affect all age groups but especially children and the elderly, spread widely across regions and continents, and exhibit significant excess mortality rates. About 1% of all US deaths from 1972 through 1992 could be attributed to influenza (9.1 deaths per 100,000 population per season), most occurring when influenza A (H3N2) viruses were prevalent [5]. Characteristic of influenza B outbreaks are mild respiratory disease that tends to target children, potentially high attack rates among concentrated groups (e.g., schools), regional distribution of cases, and limited excess mortality despite high incidence. Influenza C infrequently causes mild respiratory disease, mainly in young children.

Recurrent human influenza virus infection and potential for severe outbreaks are a result of the virus' penchant for change [9–11]. In antigenic "drift," simple genetic mutations gradually transform the surface proteins (primarily hemagglutinin) to which the host produces antibodies. Vulnerability to infection arises with the increasing "mismatch" between antibodies and surface antigens: immunity developed during one flu season to a particular strain may have no or limited future value. In antigenic "shift," a profound change in surface proteins occurs, rendering the virus unrecognizable to the circulating antibodies in most people. Influenza B viruses evolve slowly through antigenic drift. Influenza A viruses transform more quickly, through both antigenic drift and shift.

A new influenza A virus subtype, produced through antigenic shift, sets the stage for a possible pandemic. Two forms of genetic reassortment have been hypothesized to generate pandemic virus. First, a commingling of gene segments from the prevailing human influenza virus and an avian influenza virus may occur, as is thought to have produced the 1957 Asian flu and the 1968 Hong Kong flu [10]. In some parts of Asia, pigs serve as animal intermediaries facilitating the exchange of viruses between bird and human hosts [10, 12]. A second mechanism involves reassortment of subtypes from prior human outbreaks within a human host [10, 13]. An alternate theory of emergence is that an avian or mammalian virus becomes infectious for humans and capable of person-to-person transmission, a possible scenario for Spanish flu [10].

A typical case of influenza causes high-grade fever, cough, sore throat, rhinitis, muscle ache, headache, and extreme fatigue with a 2-week recovery unless pneumonia or a secondary medical condition develops; complications are potentially fatal [14]. The collective burden of influenza in a community can be substantial, depending upon seasonal prevalence of infections, proportions and virulence of circulating strains, and population resistance [15]. Excess hospitalizations averaged 50 per 100,000 Americans per season in the early 1970s to mid-1990s [5, 16]. The number of deaths beyond what is typically expected during an outbreak of influenza-like illness (i.e., "excess death") have been substantial during pandemics: 1918 Spanish flu, 218.4 deaths per 100,000 Americans; 1957 Asian flu, 22 deaths per 100,000 population; 1968 Hong Kong flu, 13.9 deaths per 100,000 population [2]. Flu's direct costs (hospitalizations, medical fees, drugs, tests, and equipment) were estimated in 1986 at $1 billion annually; indirect costs were estimated from $2 to $4 billion (lost productivity and wages) [17]. Without a mass vaccination campaign, the cost of the next pandemic is projected at $71.3 to $166.5 billion in 1995 US dollars (inpatient and outpatient care, self-treatment, and lost work days and wages) [18].

SPANISH FLU: UNPARALLELED LETHALITY AND SOCIAL DISTRESS

In early spring 1918, an influenza A (H1N1) virus began a global campaign, producing a moderate outbreak among US military recruits in the Midwest and Southeast before moving into the civilian population and then by troopships to Europe and beyond [3, 4, 19, 20]. By summer's end, this first wave had circled the world and earned the name Spanish flu after receiving much publicity in Spain, a neutral country without news censorship. This outbreak caused disproportionately high mortality rates among young adults, presaging the disastrous autumn when a related, more virulent form of the virus began to circulate. By late August, epidemics of unprecedented lethality had broken out in ports in France (Brest), the United States (Boston), and Sierra Leone (Freetown), after which the pathogen blanketed the globe, aided by ship, railroad, and by war-induced migrations of civilians and military personnel. Dispersed episodic outbreaks during winter and spring (1918–1919) comprised a third wave.

The course of disease during fall 1918 was often swift. Convalescence in survivors was protracted, with fatigue, weakness, and depression frequently lasting for weeks [3, 20–23]. Symptoms presented suddenly: high-grade fever and rigors, severe headache and myalgias, cough, pharyngitis, coryza, and in some cases epistaxis. Some patients had mild illness and recuperated without incident. Other patients were stricken quickly and severely, with symptoms and signs consistent with hemorrhagic pneumonia, and died within days and sometimes hours. Autopsies revealed inflamed hemorrhagic lungs. Still other patients with more typical flu developed severe superinfection with bacterial pneumonia, resulting in death or a laborious recovery. Unusually lethal, Spanish flu was also distinct in killing what was typically the cohort least vulnerable to influenza, 20- to 40-year-olds.

The disease's incidence, severity, and pattern of spread baffled laypeople and experts alike [3, 4, 20, 21]. Doctors debated possible pathogens, with no final consensus: Pfeiffer's bacillus (presumed cause of influenza since the 1889–1990 pandemic but rarely isolated from 1918 victims); *Yersinia pestis* (because of migrating laborers from China, the site of pneumonic plague outbreaks in 1910–1917); *Streptococcus* species, *Streptococcus pneumoniae,* and *Staphylococcus* species (cultured from specimens from patients with Spanish flu); and a hypothesized "filtrable virus" (based on experiments that produced an infectious filtrate after removing known microorganisms) were all suggested as possible etiologies. Popular explanations included the foul atmosphere conjured by the war's rotting corpses, mustard gas, and explosions; a covert German biological weapon; spiritual malaise due to the sins of war and materialism; and conditions fostered by the European conflict and overall impoverishment.

During the fall, the disease moved swiftly through US cities. Acute absenteeism among critical personnel strained industrial production, government services (e.g., sanitation, law enforcement, fire fighting, postal delivery), and maintenance of basic infrastructure (e.g., transportation, communications, health care, food supply) [3, 22, 24]. Given the incomplete disease reporting, inaccurate diagnoses, and circumscribed census practices of the day, morbidity and mortality figures are conservative estimates [3, 19]. Twenty-eight percent of Americans became ill, and there were 550,000 deaths in excess of what is normally expected during influenza season [3]. The case-fatality rate associated with Spanish flu has been estimated at 2.5% [20], but this rate more likely represents the experience of the developed world. Africa and Asia had fall death rates an order of magnitude higher than those of Europe and North America (e.g.,

India, 4200–6700 deaths per 100,000 population; England, 490 deaths per 100,000 population) [19].

BIOTERRORISM RESPONSE: LESSONS FROM THE 1918–1919 INFLUENZA PANDEMIC

A catastrophic epidemic that would severely tax society's ability to care for the sick and dying and to contain disease is the scenario of greatest concern to medical, public health, and political leaders charged with developing a response to bioterrorism [25]. Surveying the prominent issues that arose during Spanish flu's fall peak in 1918 provides a number of lessons on how the suffering and social disruption caused by a large-scale lethal epidemic might be reduced. The following recommendations are meant to advance conversations among health professionals and policymakers about what constitutes an effective medical and public health reaction to a bioterrorist act and to inform planning for any large-scale infectious disease emergency (e.g., pandemic flu).

Build Capacity to Care for Mass Casualties

US cities sustained most influenza cases and deaths over 3–4 weeks in autumn 1918, crippling the health care system. Baltimore incurred 2 of every 3 pandemic-related deaths (3110 people or 0.5% of its population) in October alone [3]. Acute demand for medical, nursing, hospital, and pharmacy services exceeded supply. Over one-third of physicians and even more nurses were serving overseas [4], and hospitals found it difficult to fill every position (e.g., orderlies, custodians, and cooks) [3]. Influenza further reduced the pool of health care workers by infecting caregivers, pharmacists, and laboratory workers and other personnel [3, 21, 24] and by creating fear of contagion among some [23]. Community doctors faced tremendous caseloads, and public health nurses were frequently surrounded by throngs of tenement dwellers requesting help [22, 26]. Druggists struggled to fill demands for prescription medications, and customers, desperate for protection or relief, emptied pharmacy shelves of over-the-counter remedies (author's unpublished data).

Few in number, nurses were critical in alleviating the distress of Spanish flu: they provided comfort measures and reassurance, instructed families in basic care, and assisted with daily needs (e.g., laundry and cooking) [3, 22, 26]. Appealing to retired, private, and student nurses and women with any nursing experience, the Red Cross readied a network of professionals and volunteers for deployment in collaboration with the US Public Health Service and state health chiefs [3, 27]. To ameliorate the physician shortage, the US Public Health Service dispatched its Volunteer Medical Service Corps, a reserve of civilian doctors unable to serve overseas [3, 27]. States compensated for the lack of doctors by authorizing dentists as physicians, graduating medical students early, and expediting medical board examinations [4]. Without antibiotics or medical treatments for flu, however, physicians had very little to offer patients [3, 4], and conflicting reports about the effectiveness of different vaccines made most practitioners hesitant to use them [28].

Already inundated with patients, hospitals frequently turned people away for want of space and personnel. Facing extraordinary demand, hospitals lengthened staff hours, tasked student doctors and nurses with professional duties, discharged the least ill, accepted only urgent admissions, and prepared makeshift accommodations in halls, offices, porches, and tents [3, 26]. Basic supplies (e.g., linens, mattresses, bedpans, and gowns) were sometimes difficult to obtain [23]. Gymnasiums, state armories, parish halls, and other spaces served as emergency hospitals [3, 4, 26]. Many people languished at home, having neither strength nor opportunity to go to the hospital; social workers, visiting nurses, and Red Cross volunteers provided home health care as well as food, child care, and burial assistance to these patients and their families [26, 29].

Extrapolating from 1918, we can identify several elements that are likely to be critical to the capacity to handle mass casualties from a bioweapon among civilians. Health care workers, from least to most technically expert, would be a critical asset that should be protected, at minimum, by preventing secondary infection and by educating and reassuring them about the infectious disease outbreak. Hospitals, actual and symbolic loci of care, should have contingency plans in place and receive government support to endure a period of crisis as people converge on them. Decentralized delivery of aid (e.g., home care) would be indispensable in the context of overburdened health facilities or a contagious disease whose management dictates home isolation. In the context of a disease outbreak for which limited or no curative or preventive therapies were available, compassionate supportive care of the sick would be one of the few and most essential measures provided by the health care system.

Respect Social Mores Relating to Burial Practices

At the climax of the Spanish flu pandemic, the numerous and rapid deaths overwhelmed undertakers and gravediggers (many of whom were ill) and exhausted supplies of caskets and burial plots (author's unpublished data; [3, 4, 23]). Corpses remained unburied at home as relatives searched for the virtually unobtainable: a willing mortician, an affordable yet "decent" coffin, and a prepared grave. Some funeral homes and cemeteries were accused of price gouging, and local leaders were accused of not doing enough to help the bereaved. With body disposal interrupted, city and hospital morgues exceeded capacity, in some cases 10-fold, prompting a search for auxiliary space. Cities took desperate measures: Philadelphia commissioned coffins from local woodworkers, Buffalo produced its own, and Washington, DC, seized railroad cars with coffins en route to Pittsburgh, where the demand was equally desperate. Emergency internment measures such as mass graves and families digging graves themselves undermined the prevailing sense of propriety. Bodies stranded at home and coffins accumulating at cemeteries provided powerful symbols of the country's inability to function normally during the fall of 1918. Proper treatment of the dead during an infectious disease emergency would require expeditious handling of corpses to prevent public health threats while avoiding mortuary practices seen to be dehumanizing.

Characterize Outbreak Accurately and Promptly

Poor disease reporting systems seriously hampered the ability of public health officials to keep the public informed and to manage the outbreak. Influenza was not a reportable condition before the outbreak, and no well-developed system existed through which federal, state, and local health entities could sketch the course of the disease [3]. With a crisis evident, the US Surgeon General urged weekly reports from state and municipal health departments [27]. Preoccupied with vast patient loads, doctors did not register cases quickly [3, 19], and public health officers recognized their own inability to evaluate efforts to prevent influenza's spread (author's unpublished data). Death certificates poorly reflected flu's impact: physicians frequently cited preexisting conditions (e.g., heart disease) as the cause of death [3, 19], and overworked health departments could not analyze the multitude of death reports at the outbreak's peak (author's unpublished data). Despite the uncertainty of official counts, some newspapers relentlessly reported new cases and deaths, fueling public speculation as to whether the epidemic was retreating or advancing (author's unpublished data).

Faced with the uncertainties that accompany an epidemic (e.g., whom will it claim and when and how will it end), people need a way to measure and describe it. Health officials and clinicians need the means to judge the efficacy of interventions. Communities must have a way to make sense of individual and collective losses. An effective medical and public health response to bioterrorism would include the capacity to count cases and deaths accurately and promptly, measure the success of epidemic controls, and communicate with the public as the epidemic unfolds.

Earn Public Confidence in Emergency Measures

Some community members embraced public health measures to control Spanish flu; others resisted orders seen as inconsistent, burdensome, or contrary to common sense or deeply held values. At the US Surgeon General's October behest, state and local health officials suspended public gatherings: entertainment centers, schools, and churches were closed, meetings were postponed, funerals were banned, and retail hours were curtailed [3, 4, 27]. Gauze masks and sanitation ordinances (e.g., hosing of walkways and prohibition of spitting) complemented closures [4, 27]. Health department directives evoked strong criticism in Baltimore. The public argued that the order to keep streetcar windows open in the cold fall weather was promoting disease and not preventing it. Closed churches and open saloons revealed the arbitrariness of closures. Lay and religious observers loudly protested church closures, arguing that an exclusively medical perspective of human suffering ignored a more spiritual one, depriving residents of solace (author's unpublished data). Most San Franciscans ignored a mandate to redon masks during the winter/spring wave: civil libertarians railed against the tyranny of compulsory behavior; business owners, about a veiled public afraid to shop; and Christian Scientists, about trampled personal liberties [3].

Neither support nor resistance to public health recommendations by the community, a critical ally, should be taken for granted. A successful plan for managing an epidemic would convey consistent and meaningful messages, serve audiences with diverse beliefs and languages, and acknowledge citizen concerns and grievances.

Guard Against Discrimination and Allocate Resources Fairly

Spanish flu fostered both social cohesion and distance. Through a common enemy and shared sacrifices of war, many Americans had a well-developed sense of fellowship when the epidemic struck [3]. At risk to themselves, neighbors nursed one another, fed the sick, helped with daily tasks, and joined the volunteer ranks [4]. Nonetheless, fear of contagion interrupted normal displays of intimacy (e.g., kissing, shaking hands, and huddling to gossip) [4] and pitted groups against one another in an effort to assign blame or to protect access to limited resources. Rumors circulated in the United States that German spies, some disguised as doctors and nurses, were spreading flu and that Bayer aspirin, a German product, was infected with flu germs [3, 27]. Baltimore hospitals, during Jim Crow segregation, were closed to blacks at their moment of dire need, and once the epidemic passed, an official defended the city's poor public health record by attributing high mortality rates to the number of black residents (author's unpublished data).

As evident during Spanish flu and other historic outbreaks, explanations of disease often convey prejudice and serve to reinforce existing social schisms and inequalities. In a bioterrorist scenario, medical, public health, and political leaders should protect against social discrimination and assure fair allocation of resources.

CONCLUSION: SIGNS OF UNPREPAREDNESS IN 2000

Influenza's lessons for bioterrorism planners do not end with an 80-year-old crisis. The 1999–2000 flu season, which the Centers for Disease Control and Prevention did not consider unusually severe, stymied US hospitals in ways that parallel 1918. At the season's peak, hospitals faced acute shortages of staff, beds, and equipment; patients confronted long delays in care. The disruption was the result, not of an especially virulent virus, but a health care system unable to cope with a nominal upswing in demand [30]. Hospitals have had to employ strategies (e.g., fewer staffed acute beds) to assure survival in a harsh fiscal climate (e.g., slim profit margins, managed care demands for cost reduction, and mandated yet uncompensated care for the uninsured), leaving the country ill-prepared to deal with a mass casualty scenario [31, 32].

Research and development needs in the control of influenza virus, a familiar if elusive pathogen, are substantial (e.g., accelerated manufacturing processes and development of alternate vaccines and antivirals) [6, 8], raising the question as to the vast research and development challenges posed by the more unusual pathogens identified as likely bioterrorist agents [33]. The logistics and time frame for manufacture and administration of the conventional killed influenza virus vaccine (6 months from identification of a strain to vaccine production and distribution and 1–2 months for delivery en masse) would inhibit the availability of vaccine before the first wave of a pandemic [2, 6, 8]. A comparably long production timetable character-

izes the new live attenuated virus vaccines, which nonetheless promise broader immune response as well as easier administration and social acceptance through intranasal delivery [9]. Antiviral compounds may have limited value amidst pandemic conditions due to costs associated with prolonged use, the potential for drug resistance, and the short time in which demand would exceed supply [6, 8].

Medical, public health, and policy communities should attend to the warnings of influenza, in its pandemic form and during interpandemic years, about the potential frailty of populations and institutions in the face of an infectious disease emergency, particularly one initiated by a deliberately released pathogen.

NOTES

1. Ghendon Y. Introduction to pandemic influenza through history. *Eur J Epidemiol* 1994; 10:451–3.

2. Glezen WP. Emerging infections: pandemic influenza. *Epidemiol Rev* 1996; 18:64–76.

3. Crosby A. *America's forgotten pandemic: the influenza of 1918.* New York: Cambridge University Press, 1989.

4. Iezzoni I. *Influenza 1918: the worst epidemic in American history.* New York: TV Books, 1999.

5. Simonsen L. The global impact of influenza on morbidity and mortality. *Vaccine* 1999; 17(Suppl 1):3–10.

6. Gross PA. Preparing for the next influenza pandemic: a re-emerging infection. *Ann Intern Med* 1996; 124:682–5.

7. Cox NJ. Prevention and control of influenza. *Lancet* 1999; 354:30.

8. Patriarca PA, Cox NJ. Influenza pandemic preparedness plan for the United States. *J Infect Dis* 1997; 176(Suppl 1):4–7.

9. Laver WG, Bischofberger N, Webster RG. Disarming flu viruses. *Sci Am* 1999; 280:78–87.

10. Webster RG, Bean WJ, Gorman OT, et al. Evolution and ecology of influenza A viruses. *Microbiol Rev* 1992; 56:152–79.

11. Langmuir AD, Schoenbaum SC. The epidemiology of influenza. *Hosp Pract* 1976; 11:49–56.

12. Webster RG. Predictions for future human influenza pandemics. *J Infect Dis* 1997; 176(Suppl 1):14–9.

13. Oxford JS. Influenza A pandemics of the 20th century with special reference to 1918: virology, pathology and epidemiology. *Rev Med Virol* 2000; 10:119–33.

14. Centers for Disease Control and Prevention. Influenza fact sheet. Available at: www.cdc.gov/ncidod/diseases/flu/fluinfo.htm. Accessed 14 January 2000.

15. Izurieta HS, Thompson WW, Kramarz P. et al. Influenza and the rates of hospitalization for respiratory disease among infants and young children. *N Engl J Med* 2000; 342:232–9.

16. Simonsen L, Fukuda K, Schonberger LB, et al. The impact of influenza epidemics on hospitalizations. *J Infect Dis* 2000; 181:831–7.

17. Schoenbaum SC. Economic impact of influenza: the individual's perspective. *Am J Med* 1987; 82:26–30.

18. Meltzer MI, Cox NJ, Fukuda K. The economic impact of pandemic influenza in the United States: priorities for intervention. *Emerg Infect Dis* 1999; 5:659–71.

19. Patterson KD, Pyle GF. The geography and mortality of the 1918 influenza pandemic. *Bull Hist Med* 1991; 65:4–21.

20. Kolata G. *Flu: the story of the great influenza pandemic of 1918 and the search for the virus that caused it.* New York: Farrar, Straus, & Giroux, 1999.

21. Nuzum JW, Pilot I, Stangl FH, et al. 1918 pandemic influenza and pneumonia in a large civil hospital. *IMJ III Med J* 1976; 150:612–6.

22. Keen-Payne R. We must have nurses: Spanish influenza in America 1918–1919. *Nurs Hist Rev* 2000; 8:143–56.

23. McCord CP. The purple death: some things remembered about the influenza epidemic of 1918 at one army camp. *J Occup Med* 1966; 8:593–8.

24. Straight WM. Florida and the Spanish flu. *J Fla Med Assoc* 1981; 68:644–54.

25. Inglesby TV, O'Toole T, Henderson, DA. Addressing the challenge of biological weapons. *Clin Infect Dis* 2000; 30:926–9.

26. Robinson KR. The role of nursing in the influenza epidemic of 1918–1919. *Nurs Forum* 1990; 25:19–26.

27. Gernhart G. A forgotten enemy: PHS's fight against the 1918 influenza pandemic. *Public Health Rep* 1999; 114:559–61.

28. Heagerty JJ. Influenza and vaccination. *CMAJ* 1991; 145:481–2.

29. Kerson TS. Sixty years ago: hospital social work in 1918. *Soc Work Health Care* 1979; 4:331–43.

30. Schoch-Spana M. Hospitals buckle during normal flu season: implications for bioterrorism response. *Biodefense Quarterly* 2000; 1:1–2, 8.

31. Espinal D. *California health care 1999–2005: view of the future, the turn of the millennium.* Sacramento, CA: California Healthcare Association, 1999.

32. Moore Jr JD. Understaffed in California: state report urges added ER capacity for flu season. *Mod Healthc* 1998; 28:64, 6.

33. Committee on R&D Needs for Improving Civilian Medical Response to Chemical and Biological Terrorism Incidents, Health Science Policy Program, Institute of Medicine, and Board on Environmental Studies and Toxicology, Commission on Life Sciences, National Research Council. Chemical and biological terrorism: research and development to improve civilian medical response. Washington, DC: National Academy Press, 1999.

■ ■ ■ ■ ■ ■ ■ ■ ■

24   HEALTH IMPLICATIONS OF MODERN AGRICULTURAL TRANSFORMATIONS: MALARIA AND PELLAGRA IN ITALY

Peter J. Brown and Elizabeth D. Whitaker

This selection concerns the direction of health impacts of agricultural transformations and ties in with the previous selections on the prehistory and history of human health. It also connects to the following selection on ecology and environment by describing human modifications of the landscape that affect animal and microbe habitats as well as the availability and variety of foodstuffs. The authors suggest that whereas the initial transformation from foraging to agriculture probably brought mostly negative health impacts most of the time, subsequent agricultural transformations have led to both positive and negative health impacts. Moreover, the impacts may be different over the short and long term and may not be spread evenly across social groups. Even in the first transition from relatively egalitarian foraging societies to increasingly stratified agrarian societies, the differential health effects on various social classes were soon evident (see selections 19, 20).

In the two case studies considered in this selection, agricultural practices were at the heart of both the rise and fall of the diseases analyzed. On the island of Sardinia, deforestation, imported labor, and large-scale farming beginning more than two thousand years ago provided the conditions necessary for mosquitoes to breed more efficiently and malaria to be introduced and take hold among the lowland populations. Over the nineteenth and early twentieth centuries, government-supported agricultural intensification, together with specific control measures, led to better water control, prevention of illness, and eventually elimination of the mosquito vector.

In north-central Italy, corn cultivation and consumption spread widely over the eighteenth and nineteenth centuries, but without the New World cultural practices that protect against nutritional deficiency. This led to the rise of the disease pellagra among the rural populations. Over many decades, a combination of international market forces, demographic changes, industrial growth, development of infrastructure, and labor organization led to a variegated pattern of disease across space and social class that brought shifts in prevalence rates and eventually the decline and disappearance of the disease.

As noted by Gandy and Zumla in selection 22, improvement of population health was a priority of European governments in the eighteenth and nineteenth centuries. This is evident in the Italian government's promotion of intensified agriculture in both Sardinia and north-central Italy, although in the latter case it was not supplemented by sufficient or effective health measures. Such contrasts between the two cases highlight the need for detailed analyses of health transitions related to agricultural change.

Questions to keep in mind

What are some causes of agricultural transformations? Why is it important to examine them over the long term?

How do subsistence farmers get drawn into market economies? What impacts does this have on their health?

What are some examples of health impacts resulting from changes in land use, markets, and demographic pressures in the two case studies and other places mentioned in this selection?

How did lifestyle, economic conditions, and health change over time for the main social categories in the two case studies?

In *Health and the Rise of Civilization* (1989), Cohen uses data from archaeology, paleopathology, and epidemiology to reach the conclusion that the prehistoric transition from food foraging to farming caused a marked decline in nutrition and health. Early agriculturalists had shorter stature, more nutritional stress, and more disease than their hunter–gatherer ancestors. The take-home message is simple and clear—early agrarian transformations made people's health and nutrition worse. This idea is not new. Cohen and Armelagos's collection of 23 case studies of the health changes associated with the neolithic revolution (1984) showed a concurrent health decline in most archaeological sites when agriculture was introduced or intensified, but there was a significant minority of sites that showed little or no health change. Nevertheless, there has been a tendency of scholars to overgeneralize from these findings. For example, Diamond calls the origin of agriculture "the worst mistake in the history of the human race" (1987:64), and blames a litany of human problems (such as war, over-population, and sexual discrimination) on that mistake. In a similar vein, Eaton, Shostak, and Konner (1988) have linked the emergence of the chronic diseases in Western societies to patterns of diet and lifestyle related to the constant overnutrition and low level of physical activity permitted by continued agricultural transformation involving intensification, mechanization, improved food storage and preparation, and stabilization of distribution and transportation networks. They challenge established dietary norms with unconventional recommendations of diet and lifestyle which imitate those of living and past hunter–gatherer societies where the chronic diseases are rare.

Such analyses suffer from the problems of oversimplification and an anthropological romanticism about the past. Goodman (1990, 1991) has argued that the basic argument in Cohen's book—that agriculture always caused a decline of health—is a simplistic reversal of the unilineal evolutionist and progressivist view of history that agriculture and civilization always made things better. The archaeological data possibly lend themselves to this conclusion, and consequently confuse the differences between ancient and modern agricultural transformations. In this selection, we argue that evidence pertaining to the question of agricultural change and health, particularly historical evidence, does *not* lead to a simple unidirectional answer. Whether agricultural transformations improve health or increase rates of disease and malnutrition depends on particular ecological and political–economic contexts of change.

This selection explores the connection between agricultural change and health through the social history of two diseases that were once highly prevalent in Italy—malaria in Sardinia and pellagra in Emilia-Romagna. These historical examples illustrate that the relationship between agricultural change and health is complex. Both positive and negative health outcomes are possible, and more importantly there may be differences between short-term and long-term effects of agricultural change. The inadequacy of Cohen's universal model stems from its dependence on the short-term perspective and its failure to consider the differential effects of economic change for distinct social classes. Rather than using a simple cause–effect epistemology, our historical analysis emphasizes the complex political economic variables that initiate and shape the character of agrarian change and its consequences. This is important to keep in mind when considering agricultural transformation and health in contemporary third world countries.

These historical cases stand in sharp contrast to most examples from applied anthropology because they demonstrate a long-term *positive* association between agricultural transformation and health,

even when the initial health outcomes were negative (Brown and Inhorn 1990). Both the expansion of agricultural production and the improvement of the health of agricultural populations were important political goals in the emerging modern nation of Italy. There are important advantages in using historical data for understanding this question rather than depending entirely on ethnography. Doing so allows for a comparison of the health effects of different types of agricultural change (e.g., mechanization, crop selection, land reclamation) over significant stretches of time. It therefore becomes possible to distinguish between the short-term and long-term effects of diverse agrarian or economic policies. The impact of agricultural transformations on ecology, for example, take time to play themselves out and may operate differently for people of different social classes.

MACRO CONTEXTS AND LOCAL FACTORS IN AGRARIAN TRANSFORMATIONS

Agricultural transformation is neither a universal nor a monolithic process. There are multiple and complex factors that vary according to local conditions and broader political–economic contexts, including the underlying causes of the agricultural change, its technological character, the historical and political–economic contexts of agrarian change, and the differential impact of the change on different social groups. This variability in the causes and characteristics of agricultural transformations means that there is also variability in the economic and health consequences of that change.

Three categories of underlying causes for agricultural change have been suggested: population pressure, international political–economic pressures, and national or regional political–economic pressures. Since Boserup's *Conditions of Agricultural Growth* (1966), population pressure has been considered a primary factor in the intensification of pre-industrial agricultural systems. In fact, population pressure may be an abstract label for *hunger*, a powerful biological incentive for the adoption of technological innovations even when they require greater labor inputs. Population pressure may result in a change in crop choice and diet through substitution of a foodstuff with more calories but poorer overall nutritional value, a major reason for the adoption of cassava in much of West Africa (McElroy and Townsend 1989) or for the process by which corn became the exclusive food crop in northern Italy during the 18th century. Population growth and agricultural intensification can interact in an autocatalytic process that may have serious health ramifications.

In general, subsistence farmers are drawn into market economies because of a need for money to purchase food and manufactured goods to meet basic needs. Common patterns of change are increased wage work and agricultural commercialization or the production of either non-food crops or specialized food to be sold on the regional or international market. Both patterns add to farmers' dependence on the vagaries of the market, an exogenous factor that can seem less predictable than the weather.

International political economic pressures may take the form of changing prices for commodities, sometimes lowered by foreign imports or increased by tariffs. For farm families who must sell their cash crops in order to buy food for their table, lower food prices because of imports can mean greater chance of hunger at home. As in the case of northern Italy discussed below, this situation is complicated by the uneven availability of wage labor and low wages. National political policies affecting patterns of land ownership can also change the agricultural system. For example, the expropriation of land from Irish peasants due to the Corn Laws in 19th century Ireland exacerbated linked problems of population pressure, dietary dependence on the potato, and susceptibility to famine (Ross 1986). The disentailment of Church and common lands in nineteenth-century northern Italy had similar effects, reducing public access to grazing land and wild foods and thereby increasing dietary dependence on corn. The ultimate health consequence in both cases was disaster. In contrast, political economic change in land reform can result in improved agricultural production and health. In the case of Sardinia described below, political policies aimed at agricultural development coincided with health improvements.

Along with the causes of agricultural transformations, the technological character of change and its social and ecological correlates are important. The availability of technology is a necessary but

not sufficient condition for agricultural change, which is why it has been important for anthropologists to study the processes of agricultural decision making (Barlett 1987). The two most important choices involve which crops to grow and whether to adopt technological innovations, such as mechanization or irrigation. Agricultural intensification generally includes monocropping, growing non-food crops, irrigation and drainage control, mechanization, and the use of fertilizers. In the pre-industrial setting, a common character of agricultural change is changing land use patterns, including the building of terraces for rice farming. All such technological changes carry the potential of altering a population's disease ecology. This linkage can be direct, as, for example, when irrigation increases transmission of schistosomiasis (Brown and Inhorn 1990), or indirect, as in the case of monocropping leading to increased malnutrition and susceptibility to infectious disease (DeWalt 1983; Scrimshaw, Taylor, and Gordon 1968).

The ultimate health consequences of agricultural change depend upon an individual's position in the social structure. Modern agricultural transformations may enrich some people while impoverishing others, and these different groups may live in the same community or in different hemispheres. For this reason, it is necessary to specify which social sectors are being considered in discussions of health outcomes. Under conditions of poverty, agricultural decisions are usually limited by the immediate concerns of the current crop and farm survival—consideration of longer term issues of ecology or health is a luxury. In political economic contexts where the population is forced to change its economic base to industry or the service sector, the character of agricultural change is one of decline or abandonment, and farming can be transformed into a hobby.

The creation or abandonment of irrigation systems can drastically change local ecology, affecting breeding sites for insects that transmit diseases such as malaria, yellow fever, schistosomiasis, and trypanosomiasis. Such ecological change can have either a positive or negative effect upon health. Livingstone's classic work on the history of the sickle cell gene in West Africa (1958) shows how the introduction of swidden horticulture changed the ecology of anopheline breeding sites, and increased mortality from malaria. Chapin and Wasserstrom

(1981) have shown that intensified use of chemical pesticides for cotton production in India and Latin America resulted in the evolution of insecticide-resistant strains of anopheles mosquitoes and contributed to the resurgence of malaria. In contrast to these negative examples, agricultural intensification in Italy, described below, reduced the risk of malaria by reducing the focolai where anopheles mosquitoes could breed (Brown 1983; Hackett 1937).

Health outcomes of agrarian change should be compared across time (to the historical antecedents before agricultural transformations) and across social categories. In the context of sweeping social and economic change, it is valuable to distinguish between short-term and long-term health implications: in the historical example of northern Italy, the industrialization of agriculture brought short-term misery and increased disease rates, but the long-term health outcome was much more positive. In Sardinia, the intensification of plains agriculture first increased malaria but later played an important role in its decline.

MALARIA IN SARDINIA

Many historians of Italy, including Celli (1933), Bianchini (1964), and Jones, Ross, and Ellet (1908) have argued that there has been an inverse correlation between the severity of malaria and agricultural productivity, not only in Sardinia but in other areas such as the Agro Romano and the Pontine marshes. This situation is the result of the intensification of agriculture, resulting in better control of standing water and hence lower densities of anopheline mosquitoes and malaria. The inverse correlation between agricultural productivity and malaria was particularly the case for dry crops like grains, grapes, and vegetables.[1] This ecological relationship is reflected in the Italian proverb, "Malaria flees before the plow."

The historical rise and fall of malaria in Sardinia is inextricably linked to changes in agricultural production. Malaria was introduced to the lowland areas of the island in the second century BCE and became endemic during the periods of Carthaginian and Roman colonization (Brown 1984). This early colonial domination established the character of lowland agriculture on the island and changed

the ecology to increase malaria. Two factors combined to introduce and spread the disease. First, severe deforestation of the inland hills region (Marghine, Monte Ferru, Sarcidano) resulted in poor water control and an increase in swamplands on the Campidano plain. Second, state-run plantations were created in the lowlands, using imported slave labor from the eastern Mediterranean and North Africa who probably brought the disease to the island. Since the anopheles mosquito that transmits the disease was already present, malaria soon became a severe health problem for the lowland populations. The malaria problem in Roman Sardinia was so bad that the island was a favorite location for exiling political enemies of the emperor because exile to Sardinia was tantamount to a death sentence.

By the 18th and 19th centuries, malaria prevalence on the island was as high as in many tropical zones, at least by reputation. At the turn of the century malaria was the largest single cause of death, and according to Fermi (1925) the disease was indirectly associated with half of the deaths on the island. The first thorough epidemiological survey of malaria on the island was conducted in the 1930s (Fermi 1934, 1938), and found that more than half of the 336 communities still had populations in which 60% of the inhabitants suffered from malaria each year, even after a decade of early malaria control efforts. The burden of malaria during most of the Sardinian history was obviously severe.

By the mid-19th century and the unification of Italy, Sardinia was characterized by three interrelated problems: low agricultural productivity, low population, and severe malaria. Together, these problems were discussed as "the Sardinian Question," since the new nation of Italy was faced with quite opposite difficulties of overpopulation (Brown 1983). The majority of the indigenous Sardinian population lived as sheep pastoralists in the highland zone, La Barbagia, which also supported banditry aimed against other shepherds and occasionally against lowland agricultural settlements (Ledda 1971). There is evidence that these highland populations, despite their extreme poverty, enjoyed relatively better health than lowland agriculturalists. Nineteenth century efforts by the central government to reform the miserable socioeconomic conditions of the island emphasized the development of mixed agriculture in the lowland plain, the Campidano (Lei-Spano 1922). The most radical of reform plans involved the importation of entire peasant communities from northern Italy to the lowlands of Sardinia. When over 90% of the families in the new community were stricken by malaria in 1838, some programs shut down and others switched to use "inferior" Sardinian labor (Tyndale 1849). Other reforms, like the abolition of communal land tenure in the 1860s, were also aimed at increasing lowland agricultural productivity.

By the 1880s, reform efforts to increase agricultural productivity, largely based on extensive water control projects, were successful. Although the productivity of Sardinian agriculture increased markedly, it still lagged behind that of mainland Italy or Sicily. This continued discrepancy was largely the result of Sardinia's low population density. Infrastructural investment in the agricultural areas of the island were part of a central government strategy for solving the problems of regional demographic imbalances and national agricultural self-sufficiency (Carta-Raspi 1971). At the same time, political policies actively discouraged the traditional pastoral economy. From the mid-19th century until the Fascist era, malaria was seen by government planners as an agricultural problem as much as it was a health problem, because it sapped the strength of the agricultural labor force during critical periods of the agricultural cycle.

From 1880 to 1900, malaria morbidity and mortality rates steadily decreased, largely because intensified agriculture and better water control meant that there was less standing water near habitations (Brown 1983). National anti-malaria legislation was an integral part of government plans for the intensification of agriculture in Sardinia. The national legislation of 1900 and 1902 focused on making quinine readily available in malarious areas; quinine was distributed at a very low price through the system of state monopoly stores, which also sold tobacco and salt. The availability of quinine reduced malaria mortality by over 70% over a 20 year period. (In fact, this may have been one of the most cost effective public health programs in the historical record.) Malaria morbidity, however, still remained very high and was only controlled through anti-anopheline programs introduced in the 1920s. The complete eradication of the disease occurred in 1951 as the result of a massive post-war pilot project using DDT and organized by the Rockefeller International Health Foundation (Logan 1953).

This example illustrates the relationship between agricultural change and health in two ways. First, the deforestation and latifundia system initiated by the Carthaginians and continued by the Romans changed the island's ecology so that swamps were expanded and malaria became widespread. It was a form of international colonial exploitation that forced an agricultural transformation, worsened health, and reduced natural resources. In this epidemiological context, the pre-colonial subsistence economy of pastoralism was associated with better general health than the agricultural economy. Second, agricultural intensification related to governmental development efforts between 1895 and 1940 changed the ecology through better water control and reduced densities of the malaria vector. This initiative had the expected result of lower malaria rates and coincided with a general improvement in health. Both the increase in agricultural productivity and the improvement in health were part of a domestic political economic policy.

PELLAGRA IN EMILIA-ROMAGNA

The second example concerns pellagra, a sometimes fatal disease resulting from niacin deficiency, and historically associated with diets consisting chiefly of corn. Pellagra is known as the disease of the four d's: dermatitis, diarrhea, dementia, and death. Meat and dairy products protect against the disease by providing an amino acid precursor for niacin, while processing corn with lime as in the production of tortillas makes niacin more available, helping to prevent the deficiency disease. Corn was widely adopted in Europe in the 18th and 19th centuries but without its New World processing technique. Pellagra soon became endemic in northern and central Italy, Spain, and southern France, as well as in cotton growing areas of the southern United States. Corn became the predominant food for northern and central Italy and its introduction coincided with a surge of population growth.

In Italy, pellagra was linked to the socioeconomic transformations associated with the development of industrial production and modern intensified agriculture (Whitaker 1992). Corn cultivation increased while earlier economic structures dissolved, including small farms, sharecropping arrangements, and common and church lands, which were replaced with large agricultural enterprises during the 18th and 19th centuries especially in the tracts of fertile land in the Po River Valley regions of Lombardy, Veneto, and Emilia-Romagna.

Dietary dependence upon corn flour, and therefore pellagra, was the price of this economic transformation; it was paid entirely by the rural population, according to the expression "pellagra stops at the city gates" (Bell 1979:137), and largely by a growing rural population of landless day laborers.[2] In 1887, there were 31 reported *pellagrosi* per 1000 population in Lombardy and Veneto, 23 in Emilia-Romagna, and between 0 and 6 in the other regions (Garzanti Ravasi 1931:21). Nationally, there were over 100,000 reported cases of pellagra in 1881, with some 3,400 deaths per year (Porisini 1974:3). However, these numbers understated the prevalence of pellagra by at least three times (DeBernardi 1984:99, 109). Indeed, in one of the lesser-affected regions, Le Marche, two-thirds of the entire population was said to suffer from pellagra in 1845 (DeBernardi 1984:99). At first, peasant families who retained sharecropping arrangements were protected from the disease because the sharecropping system was resistant to specialization or conversion to wage labor. When pellagra began to decline late in the 19th century, however, the disease became characteristic of these sharecroppers and reflected economic stagnation rather than transformation. Day-laborers moved into the growing industrial sector, emigrated, or participated in a growing labor movement, eventually bringing about significant improvements in farm work and its compensation. Sharecroppers, on the other hand, suffered from high taxation requiring the production of cash crops, exploitative contracts, and the elimination of padronal responsibilities in providing medical care and an adequate diet to workers. Pellagra did not disappear among the sharecroppers of the mountainous areas of the central and northern regions until the First World War, when a reduced labor supply led to an increase in wages and corn was replaced by potatoes and greens (DeBernardi 1984; Porisini 1974).

The history of pellagra in Emilia-Romagna, in particular, highlights these changes in political economy and nutrition during two centuries of economic and ecological transformation. Compared with the other two regions of the "pellagra triangle," Lombardy and Veneto, Emilia-Romagna was relatively late in developing endemic pellagra. When the state ordered reports on the pellagra phenomenon soon after unification in 1861, it found that an explosion of cases and deaths was occurring primarily in Emilia-Romagna (DeBernardi 1984). Subsequent reports on rural economic and health conditions led to some provisions regarding housing, corn quality and distribution, and promotion of rabbit farming in the 1880s, but such governmental responses reflect more an awareness of the poverty and misery of the countryside than a willingness to intervene with effective measures. Hospitals and soup kitchens were generally located in population centers far from those who needed them, while the regulations on corn quality and distribution made matters worse by raising the price of well-dried and matured corn so that farmers sold their better corn and subsisted on what remained. The law for prevention and treatment of pellagra in 1902 provided for the free distribution of calcium salts, but by this time cases of pellagra had already declined by one-half. Only in 1900 did the efforts of sympathetic members of parliament achieve an expenditure of 100,000 lire for the campaign against pellagra. In 1891, the government had spent 300,000 lire to acquire one stallion for the improvement of its stock of race horses (DeBernardi 1984:173).

While common lands and communal land-use rights had long been abolished in favor of private ownership in Lombardy and Veneto, in Emilia-Romagna these lands and usages survived along with the old sharecropping system until the 1860s. Soon after unification in 1861, the new government outlawed the feudal-like rights and obligations of the sharecropping system, while also ordering the disentailment of church and common lands. Small farms were then bought up by large agricultural enterprises when they failed because of high taxation or the lack of capital for intensification. These processes, combined with rapid population growth, created an expansion of the population of landless day-laborers (*braccianti*), which, together with the increased tendency to pay workers in corn during the 1860s and 1870s, caused the explosion of pellagra cases and deaths.

Beginning in the early 1880s, pellagra began a rapid decline in Italy. This trend was linked to the shrinkage of land cultivated in corn and a combination of social and economic changes ushering in the industrial era. State and financial sector cooperation brought about the growth of the industrial and service sectors in the northern regions, especially Lombardy (Forgacs 1990). Massive emigration also led to increased incomes for those remaining in Italy, especially in Veneto. In Emilia-Romagna, the agricultural system was transformed through irrigation and land reclamation projects, mechanization, application of fertilizers, careful seed selection, and the cultivation of new crops including tobacco, tomatoes, beets, and forage. These changes caused intensified production and increased employment.

In addition to industrialization, emigration, and agricultural modernization, northern and central Italy experienced a rapid rise in labor organization and agitation, which brought about improvements in wages and working conditions, particularly a decline in the proportion of the salary paid in kind, that is, corn. During the 1880s and 1890s the importation of inexpensive grain from the United States, Russia, and India led to an agricultural crisis and a fall in commodity prices. Lower agricultural prices were not accompanied by a fall in wages, thanks to the contraction of the labor supply through emigration (De-Bernardi 1984). There was a consequent rise in real incomes among those paid in money rather than kind, including day-laborers. Meanwhile, the state completed several rail, road, and harbor development projects, contributing to the delocalization of food production and distribution, as well as an improvement in the variety and stability of the food supply.[3]

These processes led to a change in the social epidemiological distribution of pellagra between day-laborers and sharecroppers in Emilia-Romagna. The day-laborers had previously been particularly susceptible, but now that they had higher real incomes and greater access to varied foodstuffs, they were protected against the disease. Sharecroppers, on the other hand, worked relatively infertile land and continued to cultivate corn

for home consumption alongside cash crops for necessities and taxes. This difference helps to explain a puzzling rise in pellagra deaths and pellagra patients hospitalized for dementia despite a dramatic fall in the death rate (deaths as a proportion of population size) during the late 1880s and the 1890s (Whitaker 1992). Despite the decline in the incidence of pellagra, there was a rise in the severity of the disease among chronically ill sharecroppers who continued to subsist on corn. This rise, reflected in a high number of deaths and hospitalizations for dementia, highlights the contrast between the new industrial–agricultural regime and the stagnant economy of the sharecropping areas.

The case of pellagra in Emilia-Romagna and the other regions of Italy illustrates the complex interrelationship between agrarian change and health in two ways. First, the new crop of corn, along with population growth and a change in the organization of land and labor, resulted in a dietary change that imperiled the health of the rural poor. Second, the modern transformation of industrial agriculture, embedded in a larger political economic transformation, had divergent short-term and long-term effects as well as divergent effects on different labor categories. Changes in agriculture initially brought about increased poverty and poor living conditions among those who were detached from the land. Landless laborers, however, later experienced increased access to foods other than corn for a variety of reasons including industrial and service sector growth, intensified cultivation of new crops in place of corn, emigration, the rural labor movement, and a real decline in food prices without a proportional decline in wages. Meanwhile, sharecroppers suffered from pellagra because they continued to cultivate corn for home consumption. Finally, conditions for sharecroppers improved due to employment associated with the First World War, better sharecropping contracts, participation in the labor movement, and the cultivation of a wider variety of foods.

The transformation of agriculture in Italy initially had tragic consequences in widespread niacin deficiency, but the longer-term term effect has been an improvement in the availability and stability of a varied food supply. Moreover, the history of pellagra illustrates how agricultural change is entangled in other components of political economic transformations that influence health. Finally, not all of the health ramifications of modern agricultural and economic transformation have been positive, as contemporary Sardinia and Emilia-Romagna, like other Western societies, are faced with epidemics of overnutrition and its related consequences in the chronic diseases.

CONCLUSION

In conclusion, there is no constant and unidirectional relationship between agrarian change and health outcomes. Agrarian transformations are highly variable in their social, technological, ecological and health consequences. This variation needs to be studied with an historical frame of reference, with attention to the political, ecological and economic context. Universal historical "laws," like the analysis of Cohen in *Health and the Rise of Civilization* (1989), ignore this most important variation. This is especially the case in the failure to assess the variation in health that was concurrent with the increased social differentiation that accompanied the neolithic revolution. Later stages of agrarian change and intensification have not only affected local ecology, diet, population size and density but—as surplus production and surplus extraction increased—also the social differentiation in wealth and health. It is too simple to argue that modern agricultural change always results in poorer health for rural populations. What needs to be emphasized is the political economic context of agrarian change and the way in which changes in health are distributed for different social strata.

As seen in the historical examples from Italy, the health effects of agricultural change can be positive or negative, and there can be discrepancies between long-term and short-term effects. In both of the examples from Italy, the short-term health effects were negative, but as the agrarian transformations played themselves out they were ultimately associated with significant health improvements. These improvements took place in the context of a new industrializing nation–state consciously trying to improve rural economic conditions, but whereas in the first case direct governmental intervention with respect to rural health conditions was effective, in the second it was rela-tively inconsequential if not counterproductive. Therefore, the impact of agricultural transformation on health can be mediated to both positive and negative effect by governmental initiatives. Thus, the health impacts of historical agricultural transformations have emerged through a complex interaction of many factors over time, with differential outcomes among social strata and between time periods.

NOTES

1. An important exception was wet rice agriculture in central Italy and the Po River Valley (Sorcinelli 1979).
2. In the towns, the only *pellagrosi* were the very poorest or newcomers (Mastri 1855:7).
3. For a discussion of the delocalization of food production and distribution in Europe, see Pelto and Pelto (1983).

REFERENCES

Barlett, P. F. 1987. Industrial Agriculture in Evolutionary Perspective. *Cultural Anthropology* 2:137–154.

Bell, R. 1979. *Fate and Honor, Family and Village: Demographic and Cultural Change in Rural Italy since 1800.* Chicago: University of Chicago Press.

Bianchini, A. 1964. *La malaria e la sua incidenza nellia storia e nell economia della regione pontine.* Latina: Amministrazione Provinciale Latii Adiecti Documenta.

Boserup, E. 1966. *The Conditions of Agricultural Growth.* Chicago: Aldine.

Brown, P. J. 1983. Demographic and Socioeconomic Effects of Disease Control: The Case of Malaria Eradication in Sardinia. *Medical Anthropology* 7:63–87.

———. 1984. Malaria in Nuragic, Punic and Roman Sardinia: Some Hypotheses. In *Studies in Sardinian Archaeology* I. M. S. Balmuth and R. J. Rowland, eds. Pp. 209–235. Ann Arbor: University of Michigan Press.

Brown, P. J. and M. C. Inhorn. 1990. Disease, Ecology, and Human Behavior. In *Medical Anthropology: A Handbook of Theory and Method.* T. Johnson and C. Sargent, eds. Pp. 187–214. New York: Praeger Scientific.

Carta-Raspi, R. 1971. *Storia della Sardegna.* Milan: U. Mursia.

Celli, A. 1933. *The History of Malaria in the Roman Campagna.* London: John Bale, Sons, and Danielson.

Chapin, G. and R. Wasserstrom. 1981. Agricultural Production and Malaria Resurgence in Central America and India. *Nature* 293:181–185.

Cohen, M. N. 1989. *Health and the Rise of Civilization.* New Haven, CT: Yale University Press.

Cohen, M. N. and G. J. Armelagos, eds. 1984. *Paleopathology at the Origins of Agriculture.* New York: Academic Press.

DeBernardi, A. 1984. *Il Mal della Rosa: Denutrizione e Pellagra nelle Campagne Italiane fra '800 e '900.* Milan: Franco Angeli Editore.

Dewalt, K. M. 1983. Income and Dietary Adequacy in an Agricultural Community. *Social Science and Medicine* 23:1877–1886.

Diamond, J. 1987. The Worst Mistake in the History of the Human Race. *Discover* (May): 64–66.

Eaton, S. B., M. Shostak, and M. Konner. 1988. *The Paleolithic Prescription.* New York: Harper and Row.

Fermi, C. 1925. La malaria in Sardegna, cause e rimedi: nota riassuntiva. *Studi Sassaresi,* serie II, vol. 3, no. 3.

———. 1934. *Regioni malariche, decadenza, risanamento e spesa: Sardegna.* Volume 1, Provincia di Sassari. Rome: Tipografia dello Stato.

———. 1938. *Regioni malariche, decadenza, risanamento e spesa: Sardegna.* Volume 2, Provincia di Nuoro. Volume 3, Provincia di Cagliari. Rome: Tipografia dello Stato.

Forgacs, D. 1990. *Italian Culture in the Industrial Era, 1880–1980: Cultural Industries, Politics, and the Public.* Manchester: University Press.

Garzanti Ravasi, S. 1931. *Inchiesta sulle condizioni dell'infanzia: La Lombardia.* Florence: Vallecchi.

Goodman, A. H. 1990. *The Paleolithic Prescription: A Guide to Modern Living?* Paper presented at the Sixth International Conference on Hunting and Gathering Societies, Fairbanks, Alaska.

———. 1991. Review of *Health and the Rise of Civilization. Ethnicity and Disease* 1:305–308.

Hackett, L. W. 1937. *Malaria in Europe: An Ecological Study.* London: Oxford University Press.

Jones, W., R. Ross, and R. Ellet. 1908. *Malaria: A Neglected Factor in the History of Greece and Rome.* Naples: Dethen and Rocholl.

Ledda, A. 1971. *La civiltà fuorilegge: natura e storia del banditismo sardo.* Milan: Mursia.

Lei-Spano, G. M. 1922. *La Questione Sarda.* Sassari: Libreria Editrice Dessi.

Livingstone, F. B. 1958. Anthropological Implications of the Sickle-Cell Gene Distribution in West Africa. *American Anthropologist* 60:533–562.

Logan, J. A. 1953. *The Sardinia Project.* Baltimore: Johns Hopkins University Press.

Mastri, S. 1855. *Discorso sulla pellagra.* Forlì: Tipografia Casali.

McElroy, A. and P. K. Townsend. 1989. *Medical Anthropology in Ecological Perspective.* Boulder, CO: Westview.

Pelto, G. H. and P. J. Pelto. 1983. Diet and Delocalization: Dietary Changes Since 1750. *Journal of Interdisciplinary History* 14:507–528.

Porisini, G. 1974. Agricoltura, alimentazione, e condizioni sanitarie. Prime ricerche sulla pellagra in Italia dal 1880 al 1940. *Quaderni Internazionali di Storia Economica e Sociale,* n.3. Bologna: Cooperativa Libraria Universitaria Editrice.

Ross, E. B. 1986. Potatoes, Population, and the Irish Famine: The Political Economy of Demographic Change. In *Culture and Reproduction.* P. Handwerker, ed. Pp. 196–220. Boulder, CO: Westview.

Schrimshaw, N. S., C. E. Taylor, and J. E. Gordon. 1968. *Interactions of Nutrition and Infection.* Geneva: WHO.

Sorcinelli, P. 1979. *Miseria e Malattie nel XIX Secolo.* Milan: Franco Angeli Editore.

Tyndale, J. W. 1849. *The Island of Sardinia.* London: Richard Bently.

Whitaker, E. D. 1992. Bread and Work: Pellagra and Economic Transformation in Turn-of-the-Century Italy. *Anthropological Quarterly* 65:80–90.

25   ECOLOGY AND ETHNOMEDICINE: EXPLORING LINKS BETWEEN CURRENT ENVIRONMENTAL CRISIS AND INDIGENOUS MEDICAL PRACTICES

Charles Anyinam

All medical systems rely on natural products as inputs for healing (see selections 6, 13). Consequently, environmental degradation has direct impacts on the ability of people and healers to manage sickness. Modification of the landscape through agriculture, mining, and lumbering, together with industrial and agricultural pollution, contributes to the loss of trees and other vegetation, animals, insects, and microorganisms. Populations who move away from their homeland lose contact with familiar flora and fauna as well as sacred places, revealing another dimension of the impacts of forced settlement described in previous selections (19, 20, 21).

This selection shows that traditional medicine use must be viewed in relation to an overall cultural system in which healing is intimately linked to religion, even if in Western biomedicine the two tend to be kept separate. Plant and animal products are used as medicines, worn for protection against spiritual and bodily harm, and incorporated into rituals, festivals, and ceremonies. Ethnomedical systems include not just knowledge about the properties of plants and animals, but also reverence for or perhaps a fear of particular features of the natural environment considered capable of promoting healing or causing harm. Such features are protected or left unexploited (see selections 27, 29).

A religious ecological understanding tends to promote the conservation and preservation of the natural environment, as does the low level of harvesting that prevails when medicines are consumed locally. On the other hand, although ethnomedical practices are shaped by the availability of plants and animals in the nearby environment, these same practices in turn influence ecological systems. This is especially so as more people turn to traditional medicines and healers sell their preparations in larger regional and international markets, which may lead to overexploitation of plants and animals to the point of endangerment. The mining of dirt used as a food/medicine (see selection 44) may also cause significant damage to local landscapes and habitats.

While indigenous practices can be significant sources of environmental harm, the largest internal threat to local ecologies may be ongoing cultural changes toward a secular view of nature. The latter undermines the management of resources under spiritual/religious ethnomedical systems. Together with ongoing environmental degradation and loss of ethnomedical knowledge, such cultural changes may weaken humanity's ability to treat disease, discomfort, and spiritual distress.

Questions to keep in mind

What are some examples of the use of plant and animal products and features of the landscape in healing?

How do changes in the way people conceive of the relationship between humans and nature affect their use of natural resources?

Why would you expect non-Western ethnomedical systems to be more effective at conserving and preserving natural resources than Western societies with Judeo-Christian traditions?

In what ways might climate change worsen the ecological degradation described in this selection?

Source: Reprinted from *Social Science and Medicine,* Vol. 40, Anyinam, C., "Ecology and Ethnomedicine: Exploring the Links between Current Environmental Crisis and Indigenous Medical Practices," Pages 321–329, Copyright (1995), with permission from Elsevier.

INTRODUCTION

There is a growing number of publications on the links between religion and environmental crisis [1–6]. Much of the discussion, however, has centred on links between ecology and Christianity and other major religions, with very little attention being given to the role of indigenous religion (what some describe as, "paganism" or "animism") practised among many societies in developing nations. There is no explicit discussion of the relationships between paganism as a religion and the environment. More so, very limited research has been undertaken to investigate relationships between natural ecosystems and the practice of ethnomedicine which is intricately intertwined with the practice of indigenous religion. The fact that traditional medicine is intimately related to biotic and abiotic environments, makes it imperative that a discussion of the links between religion and environmental crisis should include that of ethnomedicine. In the existing literature, explicit discussion of ecological dimensions of ethnomedicine is almost nonexistent even though, to a large extent, the practice of ethnomedicine is an important vehicle for understanding indigenous societies and their relationships with nature.

Ethnomedicine, as defined by Foster and Anderson, is the totality of health, knowledge, values, beliefs, skills and practices of members of a society including all the clinical and nonclinical activities that relate to their health needs [7]. The link between ethnomedicine and ecology is exemplified by a long tradition of healing powers associated with the earth's natural systems, whether this entails medicinal plants and animal species, the ambient salubrious air, spring water or the natural scenery. The pharmacopocia of folk societies as well as professional medical systems like Chinese, Ayurvedic, Unani and biomedicine contain thousands of medicines made from leaves, herbs, roots, bark, animal, mineral substances and other materials found in nature. In addition, practitioners of ethnomedicine employ methods based on the ecological, socio-cultural and religious background of the people to provide health care [8, 9].

The study of such links requires, on the one hand, investigations into how environmental characteristics influence the practice of ethnomedicine, and, on the other hand, how traditional medicine affects the quality and sustainability of natural systems [10]. Both ecology and culture evolve and change and each produces alterations in the other. Recent decades have seen significant changes occurring within several aspects of ethnomedicine (especially changes in availability and use of medicinal plants, perceptions and etiology of diseases, and indigenous value systems) as a result of environmental degradation and tremendous changes in modern social and economic systems. As well, over the years, the practice of ethnomedicine has had both positive and negative impacts on local natural ecosystems.

The objective of this paper is to explore the nature of the links that do exist between ethnomedicine and ecology, focusing particularly on the relationships between ethnomedical practices and environmental degradation as well as conservation of biotic communities. The paper firstly, examines the extent to which ethnomedicine is dependent on local ecosystems for its pharmacoepia and healing. Secondly, it assesses the extent to which environmental degradation and destruction have affected the practice of traditional medicine in terms of procurement and preparation of medicinal plants, the use of sacred space, and reduction in ethnomedical knowledge of plants and healing practices over the years. Thirdly, the paper examines how ethnomedical practices have adversely impacted on local natural ecosystems, and fourthly, the contributions made by the practice of ethnomedicine towards ecological sustainability are assessed. Many of the examples cited in the paper come from developing societies.

ETHNOMEDICINE AND BIOTIC AND ABIOTIC RESOURCES

Indeed, there are close links between ethnomedicine and ecology. Not only are plant and animal species used for medicinal purposes, but also they are of cultural and religious importance, especially for rituals and festivals. From time immemorial, human-kind has depended and still largely depends on plants in treating all forms of ailments. Plants have always had an important role to play in medicine and public health [11–14]. According to an estimate of the WHO, approx. 88% of people in developing countries rely chiefly on traditional medicines (mostly plant extracts) for their primary health care needs [15, 16]. In China where there is one of the most sophisticated and extensive medical traditions, more than 5000 plants have been catalogued and 1700 of them are in common use. In other places like India, at least 2500 plants, out of 18,000 recorded in the country are utilized for medicinal purposes (together with other applications, e.g. aromatic properties). There are about 46,000 licensed pharmacies manufacturing the traditional remedies of Indian systems of medicine and homeopathy [17]. Probably the region that makes the widest use of herbal preparations is Africa where people reputedly depend on plants, via ethnomedicine, for as much as 95% of their drug needs [18].

Spiritual or magico-religious healers, herbalists, technical specialists (e.g. bone-setters), and traditional birth attendants employ diverse forms of herbs, roots, leaves, bark, mammals and birds in the preparation of medicine [19]. Wild animals and their by-products (hooves, skins, bones, feathers and tusks), for example, form important ingredients in the preparation of curative, protective and preventive medicine. More importantly for some, they are used to perform rituals and invoking and appeasing gods and witches [20]. Belts, necklaces and bangles made of wild animal by-products (e.g. skins of leopards, lions, gorillas and monkeys) embedded with herbs are commonly utilized in some societies for preventive and protective measures against witches and for immunity from bad luck, diseases and enemies. Wildlife species and their parts are also utilized for aphrodisiacs and potency purposes. In addition, a variety of wild animals form an integral part of cultural and religious festivals and ceremonies, some of which seek to promote the good health of local people and their communities [21]. During the performance of some rituals and festivals, for example, certain specific wild animals may be sacrificed. In some communities, parts of animals (e.g. feathers of parrots) are used as special "tools" for making masks for masquerades. Tusks and skins of elephant, lion and leopard are used for the installation of traditional rulers and are worn during cultural festivals in some parts of Africa. American Indians, for example, are known to express special relationship with animals in ceremonies

and by using eagle feathers as symbols of power and authority.

Apart from ethnomedicine's reliance on flora and fauna of local ecosystems, some natural features have religious significance to local people and practitioners of ethnomedicine. The magico-spiritual and religious aspects of ethnomedicine have particularly had much impact on space in areas where people assign religious values to natural phenomena. In many indigenous societies where the practice of ethnomedicine is predominant local people assign sanctity to certain portions of their natural landscape and regard them as worthy of devotion, loyalty, dignity and worship. Some natural objects like mountains, peaks, lakes and rivers and their surroundings are personified in gods, deities and spirits and such ecological features are believed to emanate power. Sacred-healers, in particular, live as close as possible to these features which they regard as "sacred spaces" and where they communicate with their gods and obtain greater access to supernatural powers for the purpose of medical practices. This kind of devotion and loyalty to natural objects is termed by Wright as "geopiety" [22].

The areal extent of such "sacred spaces" varies from infinite to a finite point. As well, the cared view or esteem associated with them varies according to their roles. The relative permanence of a sacred space is also a function of the event associated with its recognition as a unique place and the permanence of the ideas which gave rise to the perception of its sanctity. Thus, while certain sacred spaces have lost their sacredness due to loss of belief in the efficacy of the "spirit world", often the combined effects of modernization, Christianization and formal education, others remain to function in respective cultures as "places" of reverence and worship.

Shrine cults in Zambia and many other African countries, for example, tend to have a strong ecological emphasis and hills, imposing trees, caves, streams, falls and rapids become associated with invisible entities and become objects of veneration [23]. The personification of such objects in the physical environment and the intuitive rapport which both practitioners of ethnomedicine and lay people establish with their natural landscape are the way in which the ecology becomes clothed with some divine qualities still displayed in many societies in developing countries.

As the next section illustrates, current environmental degradation has had much impact on the links between ethnomedicine and biotic and abiotic elements of local ecosystems.

ECOLOGICAL DEGRADATION AND THE PRACTICE OF ETHNOMEDICINE

During the last century, the scale of human activities has been such that ecosystems of developed and developing countries have been degraded, resulting in several forms of ecological problems. Millions of distinct species and a variety of habitats and biotic communities are threatened. The integrity, diversity, and productivity of natural systems have been damaged by several forms of pollution over the years. Our planet is witnessing rapid changes in the composition of plant and animal species through over-exploitation of natural resources [24]. Agricultural, lumbering and mining activities have particularly contributed to significant habitat loss. Deforestation, in particular, has had tremendous ramifications for the practice of ethnomedicine in many areas. In 1950, while 30% of the world's surface was covered by forests, by 1975 the forest areas had shrunk to a mere 12%. The destruction continues at an estimated rate of some 10,000 trees a minute [25]. The loss of animal and microbial life is also incalculable. Existing estimates of species extinction differ and range from 1 to 50 per day, a total of 365 to 18,250 each year. Of the estimated 250,000 known plant species, about 25% are expected to be extinct by the year 2050 [26].

Most medicinal plants as well as animals have restricted habitats, usually confined to geographic sites like seasides, riversides, highlands, forest, and savanna zones [27]. In his study of wild life utilized for healing and preventive medicine in Nigeria, Adeola, for example, observed marked differences among the rain forest, deciduous, and savanna ecological zones regarding use of animals for healing and preventive medicine [21]. At the broader level, some species are endemic to particular countries. For example, of the 10,000 or so plant species that grow on the Madagascar island,

half are endemic, i.e. they are found no where else in the global ecosystems. Reports indicate that many of the species are almost extinct due to extensive deforestation and marked soil erosion facing the island [28].

Transformation of local ecosystems wrought through human economic activities has been exercising severe constraints on the availability and accessibility of specific types of plant and animal species used for medicinal purposes. As forests are degraded into woodland savannas, savanna to scrublands and bushes, and scrublands to desert characteristics in many parts of the Third World, certain species of plants are disappearing altogether. Such a situation poses problems for the future practice of indigenous medicine; with a few exceptions, all medicines are made from concoctions prepared with plants, plant organs or their secreted products [27]. The procurement of plant and animal species needed by indigenous medical practitioners currently requires long distance travel. This affects not only operational costs of providing traditional medical services particularly in urban areas, but also the forms of herbal medicine prepared. For example, freshly prepared herbal medicines are increasingly being replaced by different concoctions, tinctures and powdered forms even in rural areas in order that they can be stored for longer periods without losing their potency or getting spoiled [29].

Degradation and destruction of the natural systems also pose a threat to sacred sites and spaces designated by local healers and people. Many sacred lands are being desecrated and their spiritual value destroyed. Forest enclaves which traditionally served effectively as "sacred spaces" used by religious healers and consequently were prevented from exploitation, have been cultivated, wiping away the dignity, devotion and fear usually attached to such symbolic landscapes. The desecration of such landscapes dispell their sacral aura, resulting in a new relationship that usually leads to severe abuse especially by a large percentage of the new generation of population which has little or no knowledge of such hierophanes in their localities. In such cases, the fear of local gods has been "extracted" from the natural environment.

Like the current spasm of plant and animal species extinction, the practitioners of ethnomedicine (especially herbalists and cult healers) appear to be at a greater risk of extinction than even forests and other biomes. Knowledge of the use of plants is disappearing faster than the plants themselves. The destruction of tropical forests has meant, in many parts of the tropical region, increasing disappearance of native peoples who have been living in these areas and who have accumulated a compendium of folk knowledge about the usefulness of plants for curing various diseases. The diminishing number of indigenous people in many parts of Latin America illustrates the problems of disappearing societies. When discovered by Europeans in the fifteenth century, the Amazon, had an indigenous population estimated at six million or more [30–32]. Approximately 250,000 remain today, distributed among more than 200 ethnic groups [33]. One-third of the Amazonian tribes known to exist in 1900 are now said to be extinct [34]. Amazonian Ecuador supported 17 distinct ethnic groups before European contact but today, only seven remain. As part of their objective to christianize the indigenous populations, the rich ethnobotany of the Aztecs and other precolonial Meso American cultures was deliberately and systematically destroyed by the Spanish invaders [35].

Policies to "decimate" typical indigenous societies continue to occur today. In West Africa, the government of Cameroon, for example, is criticized for its policy of socio-economic integration of the country's forest peoples—the Baku and Bakola people. The government has placed emphasis on the need to, as it calls it, "disinfect the socio-economic life of the hunter-gatherers of the forest region of the country so that they can become productive members of society" [36]. The existence of these groups of people actually has contributed immensely to saving the tropical forest from capitalist exploitation. The attempts to "sedentarize" 20,000–35,000 Baka people in Cameroon's south-eastern forests and about 3500 Bakola people dispersed in the coastal forests of south-west Cameroon fail to recognize the value of indigenous forest knowledge and the economic contribution of their use of forest resources on a sustainable basis [37]. Undoubtedly, with the disappearance of the human cultures that the "forest peoples" have developed in and around the tropical forest, gone also will be the habitats and traditions and knowledge concerning medically useful plants from the tropical rain forest regions.

In addition, European missionary activities have led to the rejection of traditional beliefs, rituals and other non-Christian observations which form integral part of ethnomedicine. This has seriously undermined the prestige accorded ethnomedicine and the influence wielded by its practitioners. Over time, Christian teachings and Western civilization have created new attitudes, value systems and expectations among potential adherents of ethnomedical principles, and this has led to significant shifts in traditional beliefs of both the educated and uneducated. The denigration of folk cultures and the disappearance of indigenous people not only pose a problem for the future practice of ethnomedicine, but also the protection of biotic communities which serve as sources of indigenous medicine.

Loss of indigenous knowledge has impact also on development of modern medicine. Medicinal folklore over the years has proved to be an invaluable guide in the present day screening of drugs. Many important modern drugs (e.g. digitoxin, reserpine, tubocurarine, ephedrine, to name a few) have been discovered by following leads from folk uses. As Farnsworth points out, about 74% of the 121 biological active plant-derived compounds currently in use worldwide have been discovered through follow-up research to verify the authenticity of information concerning the folk or ethnomedical uses of the plants [16]. As indigenous cultures become increasingly fragmented and threatened by modern development pressures in developing countries folk knowledge may be lost for ever. Suzuki is right in his observation that once the indigenous people have disappeared, their body of priceless thought and medicinal knowledge painstakingly acquired over thousands of years, will disappear forever [38].

The foregoing does not, however, mean that the practice of ethnomedicine is wholly environmentally benign. While environmental degradation and other factors have impacted on several aspects of ethnomedicine, ethnomedical practices do have adverse effects on local natural environments.

ETHNOMEDICINE AND ENVIRONMENTAL DEGRADATION

For centuries, healers and indigenous people have been collecting medicines from local plants and animals without threatening the population dynamics of the species because of the low level of harvesting. Commoditization of plant medicine and animal parts was an insignificant aspect of the practice of ethnomedicine. In the last few decades, however, there has been a marked increase in the sale of herbal remedies, precipitating large-scale harvesting of medicinal plants, factory-like production of herbal drugs, and animal poaching in many parts of developing countries.

A large number of healers engage in mass production of herbal medicine both for their own practice and for sale to city herbal pharmacies which supply the needs of urban dwellers who continue to rely on ethnomedicine for their health care. In addition, herbal medicine peddlers buy from healers at discount rates and sell them to the general public at lorry parks, in buses, in trains, towns and cities. In some countries, the production and sale of herbal preparations are important sources of income. In a report by World Health Organization, for example, the production of traditional plant remedies in China was valued at U.S. $571 million and the country-wide sales of crude plant drugs at U.S. $1.4 billion annually [39]. In India, the collection of medicinal plants for sale in the markets forms an important part of the livelihood of the local inhabitants in the forested areas or traders who send their own workers into the forests to collect medicinal plants [17]. The sale of herbal medicine is also well developed in South Africa and is on a scale that is causing concern among conservation organizations and rural herbalists [40–43]. Currently, over 400 indigenous species and 20 exotic species are commercially sold to Zulu people as herbal medicines [44]. Unavailability as well as high cost of imported Western pharmaceuticals, coupled with increasing population and the continued faith in the potency of herbal preparations underlie the surge in the demand of locally-prepared medicine.

Apart from internal trade in herbal drugs, there is an increase in international trade in traditional pharmacoepoeia. A vigorous trade exists among many West African countries (for example, Nigeria, Benin, Togo and Ghana). Singapore, Hong Kong, Canada, United States, Switzerland and Germany are destinations for large amounts of packaged herbal medicines. In these countries, numerous herbal stores have mushroomed in the cities. In the early 1980s, India exported phyto-

chemical (plant-derived) materials, primarily medicinals and pharmaceuticals, worth over U.S. $55 million. In most western industrialized cities, there is a slow but steady shift away from the synthetic in favor of natural substances; thus, encouraging a proliferation of natural health foods shops and herbal remedy stores with a variety of dietary regimes based on macrobiotics, whole-foods, health foods and vitamins [45]. There is, therefore, a profitable trade in all kinds of herbs and botanicals which are sold as tea, extracts, elixirs, powders and oils, and are employed as diuretics, laxatives, sedates, stimulants, tranquilizers and tonics.

Harvesting and gathering of herbs from the wild which has become a boom industry in the Third World have, therefore, led to the impoverishment of various biotic communities in many areas. The exploitation of wild-growing *Rauvolfia serpentina* in India for export exhausted the supply to a point where the Indian government several years ago placed an embargo (which remains in place today) on the export of this plant [46]. Another example of a plant that has been over-exploited in India for export to other Asian countries is *Coptis teeta*, which is now considered an endangered species in India [17]. In Indonesia, the over-harvesting of medicinal plant locally known as *gaharu* collected from wild sources in primary forest has led to its depletion in the country. The plant, traded through a series of middlemen, is used in Chinese and Malay pharmacopoeias to treat a variety of ailments, particularly those associated with pregnancy and childbirth. In Indonesian cities it sells around U.S. $100 per kg [47]. The problem with the harvesting of the *gaharu* plant is that its occurrence of valuable grades is sporadic and many trees must be felled to obtain a small amount of medicine. Excessive harvest of roots, bulbs, seeds and flowers which are essential to the survival of the plants themselves often leads to the premature death of individual trees. A good example is the root barks of *Rauvolfia vomitoria*, the main source for the manufacture of reserpine and ajmaline [48].

In addition to the loss of medicinal plant species, the worldwide market for animal parts and their medicinal derivatives is contributing to loss of some species. The increased use of medicinal animals has led to over-exploitation of species like rhinos, tigers, musk deer, bears, monkeys and pangolins. All the five species of rhinocerous, one of the world's oldest mammals, are being threatened with extinction because of poaching. In spite of international regulations and several national laws against poaching and heavy penalties for culprits, the extremely high prices offered for the parts of some species serve as strong incentives for illegal trade in animal parts to flourish. Rhinocerous parts are used to provide relief against tuberculosis, fever, skin lesions, snake bite, ear ache and stomach ache. Asian rhino horns are the most prized animal parts and trade in their parts is very lucrative. Such horns can fetch as much as U.S. $28,600 a kilogram [49]. Rhino horn are smuggled to China and other parts of Asia where they are sliced or ground into powder for use as medicine and a centuries-old aphrodisiac [49]. Tiger parts are also in high demand. They are used for skin disease, to provide courage, to immunize against bullets, to drive away centipedes, to cure laziness, to cure abscesses on hands and feet, to stop persistent watering of the eyes and to cure convulsions [50]. Other highly valued animal parts are bear gall bladders used as medicine for chronic fatigue, digestive problems, inflammation, blood impurities, hemorrhoids and various liver, stomach and intestinal ailments. Gall bladders are priced U.S. $200 per 3-oz [50].

The international trade in animal parts for medicinal purposes is primarily controlled by a network of professional poachers tied to the markets in China, Japan, Korea, Hong Kong and Taiwan. Some endangered species in North America have fallen victim to this illegal trade. South Korea appears to be the largest consumer of these North American bear parts. The current dependence upon North American bear and other species is due to the disappearance of bears in the Asian natural environment, the result of incessant demand and use of bear gall bladders in Chinese medicine over the past thousand years.

Another example that can be cited in relation to environmental degradation through ethnomedical practice is the issue of geophagy. Though limited in its geographic scale of impact, the practice of geophagy (i.e. eartheating) as related to ethnomedicine is an environmental concern in some areas where it occurs. Eartheating, a habitual consumption of earth materials which has been going on for at least 2000 years in many parts of the world, is a practice that meets the physiological and psycho-

logical needs of addicts [51–54]. The eating of clay, for example, is said to be an effective treatment for certain diseases and parasites [55]. It is believed clay provides the needed nutrients for pregnant women. The practice is deeply ingrained in many cultures and is widespread in Africa and concentrated among rural blacks and whites in the American south [51]. In one form or another, geophagy has been observed also among northern Europeans, Mediterraneans, Central Americans, Australian aborigines and Pacific Islanders [51]. Geophagy is also part of the traditional pharmacopoeias in many areas where religious significance of geophagical clay objects at shrines is recognized (e.g. that of Our Lady of Esquipulas, the Black Christ of Guatemala) [56]. The clay material is usually "mined" in large quantities from river valleys and roadsides. The increased extraction tends to create unwanted excavations, leading to serious erosion and disfigurement along rivers noted for their fine clay.

Notwithstanding the foregoing selected examples of ways in which the practice of ethnomedicine can be environmentally unsustainable, traditional medical practices do contribute to conservation and preservation of local ecosystems.

ETHNOMEDICINE AND ECOSYSTEM PRESERVATION AND CONSERVATION

Unlike the beliefs of the Judeo-Christian humanistic tradition which generated the view of the universe that sharply separated God and the world and humanity and nature, encouraging, thus, attitudes of conquest and exploitation in relation to nature, the religious aspects of ethnomedicine generally encourage indigenous people to relate to natural phenomena with reverence and dignity. As mentioned earlier, various traditions within indigenous societies have intricate relationships with nature which reflect a keen sense of the interdependence of human culture and nature and involve a holistic ethic of respect for nature. This conception of reality is a form of world view in which most indigenous people structure their world and experiences. Knowledge of animals and their ways, particularly those of utilitarian value as well as knowledge of plants, especially edible and medicinal ones, are well-known and much respected dimensions of ethnomedicine.

From the ecological point of view, sacred spaces are jealously protected from any forms of human pollution and environmental degradation and thus, contribute to the preservation of nature. In typical indigenous societies, the bonds existing between people, the bio-physical environment, and spiritual world exercise some restrictions on where to engage in such activities as farming and fishing. The shaman, in some indigenous communities, is a powerful force in the control and management of resources. The role of the shaman interferes quite directly with hunting, fishing, gathering and most other harvesting activities. For example, in shamanistic practice among the Tukano Indians of the Columbian Northwest Amazon, illness is taken to be the consequence of a person's upsetting a certain aspect of the ecological balance [57]. Overhunting is regarded as a common cause and so are harvesting activities in which some relatively natural scarce resources have been wasted. As Reichel-Dolmatoff reports, a shaman can personally control quantity and concentration of fish-poison to be used on a certain stretch of a river. He/she will decide on a suitable harvesting strategy for the gathering of wild fruits [58].

In Africa, for example, cult organizations in some areas contribute to the preservation of nature. In their studies of indigenous people, Schoffeleers and van Binsbergen have argued that shrine activities and ecological processes are mirror images of each other [23, 59]. As Schoffeleers reports of the Malawians, the indigenous people maintain "a ritually directed ecosystem." Cult organizations regulate significant practical activities of the people. Large areas of wilderness are, for example, ritually protected from burning. Cults issue and enforce directives with regard to a community's use of its environment. Cult mediums could, at times, compel people to plant particular crops and restrict fishing and grazing so as to protect fragile resources [59]. Schoffeleers describes an instance in the 1930s in which the Mbona cult pressured part of the population of the Lower Shire Valley to emigrate in order to relieve conditions of overcrowding [59]. Certain environmental settings are usually outside the cycle of ecological transformations and do not serve any direct utilitarian pur-

pose for the people in the locality [23]. In many African societies, cults which function for the whole community, what Schoffeleers calls "territorial cults" are known to perform rituals which they believe could counteract droughts, floods, blights, pests and epidemic diseases [23].

There is also an existence of a plethora of spirit beings or "divinities" with special moral and practical functions satisfying human natural needs. In some indigenous societies, prohibitions on the use of certain species of wildlife exist to protect animal species. Squirrels, for example, are considered sacred to the Afana people [60]. Certain wild animals may not be killed or touched because of formal religious dicta, taboos or prejudices. For example, among the Tukano Indians of the Colombian Northwest Amazon, occasionally, the shaman might completely prohibit the killing of certain animals in a restricted area of the local forest. The shaman's role as a protector of game and plant-life explains why some animals and plants figure so prominently as his/her spirit-helpers [58]. In some sense, therefore, as Reichel-Dolmatoff rightly puts it, the shaman plays the role of an "ecological broker" [58].

The religious aspects and belief systems related to ethnomedicine tends also to instill some fear in local people about certain natural landscapes. In Uganda, for example, among some lowland communities, mountains are feared because they are believed to harbour supernatural spirits and diseases brought about by the spirits of the mountains. In such areas, mountain resources are consequently often left unexploited [60, 61]. In the Kwahu district of the eastern region of Ghana, an inselberg in the local landscape whose surroundings are thickly forested is very much revered by the inhabitants of the area because it is regarded as the "home" of one of the most powerful gods in the district. This forested peak and its surroundings remained unexploited for decades until relatively recently. There are several other examples in African environment where fears of certain physical features have tended to influence the use of rivers, shorelines, forests and other features. In other places like the Indian Himalayas, the collection of certain plants continues to be restricted to certain days of the year and during religious festivals in some districts [62]. That the practice of ethnomedicine can safeguard natural phenomena is undeniable, though the resultant conservation and preservation advantages may be limited in their geographic scale. It is also worth noting that with increased population pressure and economic hardships, the protective tendencies of ethnomedical practices and indigenous culture in general are being weakened.

CONCLUSION

It is undeniable that culture influences the way people perceive and use the resources of their environment [63]. The practice of ethnomedicine as an integral part of the culture of indigenous people in many parts of the world has a close interface with local ecosystems. The nature of the interrelationships and interactions between ethnomedicine and ecology can be both positive and negative on each other. Though the above discussion is exploratory, it is quite clear that the practice of ethnomedicine is not immuned to the current environmental crisis facing our planet. Significant changes in forests, savannas and other vegetational types have impacted on the procurement and preparation, as well as the cost of plant medicine. Desecration of spiritual spots, sacred spaces, and grooves has tended to reduce the dignity of such "landscapes" and to encourage their abuse.

While ethnomedicine, expecially its religious elements which generally do shape the value systems, attitudes and behaviour of indigenous people towards a positive relationship with nature, modern developments appear to be steadfastly eroding the "core of respect" that is bestowed on nature. Indigenous cultures are increasingly being fragmented and threatened by development pressures. Folk knowledge, painstakingly acquired over thousands of years is also steadily disappearing. Threats to, and desecration of, sacred sites and spaces are destroying their spiritual value. The sacral aura of these "places" are dissipating, resulting in a new relationship with nature that threatens the future sustainability of ecosystems upon which the practice of ethnomedicine is dependent. In some cases, however, ethnomedical practices also do contribute to the process of environmental degradation and disruption. The commercialization of the ingredients required for the preparation

of herbal medicine is contributing to the extinction of certain animal and plant species. The continued adherence of indigenous people, however, to traditional cultural principles and values of ethnomedical systems contributes to the preservation and conservation of several biotic communities.

Preservation of the world's indigenous cultures and practices may contribute to the preservation and conservation of the remaining undisturbed forests and other biotic communities. It is very encouraging that, in the last few years, the issue of culture and ecology has become a "respected" academic topic worthy of investigation. The news media, the publishing "world" and academics are beginning to promote indigenous knowledge and culture and its relevance for the sustainability of the earth's ecosystems. Increasingly, the roles that indigenous cultures (and their ethnomedical practices, in particular) could play in the preservation of nature are being investigated. The recent conference on the need for the conservation of medicinal plants by World Health Organization, the International Union for the Conservation of Nature and World Wildlife Fund is a step in the right direction. This international consultation on the conservation of medicinal plants brought together leading experts in different fields to exchange views on the problems, determine priorities, and make recommendations for action [64]. This paper is a contribution to that effort and the purpose here is to highlight links that exist between ecology and a particular cultural practice. Hopefully more detailed studies will be undertaken within specific geographic settings to shed more light on the broader question of the relationship between culture and ecology.

NOTES

1. Rockfeller S. C. and Elder J. C. (Eds) *Spirit and Nature: Why the Environment is a Religious Issue?* Beacon Press. Boston, 1992.

2. Bowman D. C. *Beyond the Modern Mind: The Spiritual and Ethnical Challenge of the Environmental Crisis.* The Pilgrim Press, New York, 1990.

3. Carmody J. *Ecology and Religion: Toward a New Christian Theology of Nature.* Paulist Press, New York, 1983.

4. Hargrove E.C. (Ed.) *Religion and Environmental Crisis.* The University of Georgia Press, Athens and London, 1986.

5. Knudtson P. and Suzuki D. *Wisdom of the Elders.* Stoddart Publishing Co, Ltd, 1992.

6. Schofeleers J. M. (Ed.) *Guardians of the Land: Essays on Central African Territorial Cults.* Mambo Press, Gwelo, 1978.

7. Foster G. M. and Anderson B. G. *Medical Anthropology.* John Wiley and Sons Ltd, New York, 1978.

8. Good C. Ethno-medical Systems in Africa and the LDCs: Key Issues in Medical Geography. In *Conceptual and Methodological Issues in Medical Geography* (Edited by Meade M.S.) University of North Carolina at Chapel Hill. Studies in Geography No. 5: 93–116, 1980.

9. Gesler W. M. Therapeutic landscapes: medical Issues in Light of the new cultural geography. *Soc. Sci. Med.* 34, 735, 1992.

10. "Ethnomedicine" is used interchangeably with "Traditional Medicine."

11. The plant kingdom has offered biomedicine a broad range of medicinal and pharmaceutical products. In developed industrialised countries today, about 25% of drug prescriptions come from natural products while another 25% are from substances derived from modification of a natural product.

12. Farnsworth N. R. The role of ethnopharmacology in drug development. In *Bioactive Compounds from Plants* (Edited by Chadwick D. J. and Marsh J.), pp. 2–21. John Wiley and Sons Ltd. Chichester, 1990.

13. Myers N. Plant and Medicine. *A Wealth of Wild Species Storehouse for Human Welfare.* Chap. 6, pp. 89–141. West View Press Boulder, CO, 1983.

14. Myers N. Plants as Sources of Anticancer Drugs. *A Wealth of Wild Species Storehouse for Human Welfare,* Chap. 7. West View Press Boulder, CO, 1983.

15. WHO Global Medium-Term Programme (Traditional Medicine) Covering a Specific Period 1990–1995 (WHO Document TRM/MTP/87.1).

16. Farnsworth N. R. *et al.* Medicinal plants therapy. *Bull. WHO* 63, 965, 1985.

17. Alok S. K. Medicinal plants in India: Approaches to Exploitation and Conservation. In *The Conservation of Medicinal Plants* (Edited by Akerele O. *et al.*) Proceedings of an International Consultation 21–27 March 1988 held at Chiang Mai, Thailand, pp. 295–303. Cambridge University Press, Cambridge, 1991.

18. Iwu M. M. *Handbook of African Medicinal Plants.* CRC Press, London, 1993.

19. Odu M. The art of traditional healing in Nigeria. *National Concord* July 17, 5, 1987.

20. Ajayi S. S. *The Utilization of Tropical Forest Wildlife: State of Knowledge and Research Priorities,* 8th World Forestry Congress, Jarkata, Indonesia, 1978.

21. Adeola M. O. Importance of Wild Animals and their Parts in the Culture, Religious Festivals and Traditional Medicine in Nigeria. *Environ. Conservation* 19, 125, 1992.

22. Wright J. K. *Human Nature in Geography.* Harper and Row, New York, 1966.

23. Schoffeleers J. M. *Guardians of the Land: Essays on Central African Territorial Cults* 47, 1978.

24. Kaufman D. G. and Franz C. M. *Biosphere 2000: Protecting Our Global Environment.* Harper Collins College Publishers, 1993.

25. Mkali H. Traditional medicine under the spotlight. *Africa Hlth* 10, 36, Dec. 1987/Jan 1988.

26. Fellows L. What are the forests worth? *The Lancet* 339, 1330, 1992.

27. Kerharo J. Traditional Pharmacopoieas and Environment. *African Environ.* 1, 30, 1975.

28. Jolly A. and Landting G. Man against nature: time for a truce in Madagascar. *Nat. Geograph.* 171, 160, 1987.

29. Anyinam C. A. *Persistence with Change: A Rural-Urban Study of Ethno-Medical Practices in Contemporary Ghana.* PhD dissertation, Queen's University, Kingston, Ontario, 1987.

30. Bunker S. G. *Understanding the Amazon: Extraction, Unequal Exchange, and the Failure of the Modern State.* University of Chicago Press, Chicago, 1985.

31. Carneiro R. L. Indians of the Amazonian Forest. In *People of the Tropical Rainforest* (edited by Denslow J. S. and Padoch C.). University of California Press, Berkeley, 1988.

32. Denevan W. M. The Aboriginal Population of Amazonia. In *The Native Population of the Americas in 1492* (edited by Denevan W. M.), pp. 205–234. University of Wisconsin Press, Madison 1976.

33. Schreider H. and Schreider F. *Exploring the Amazon.* National Geographic Society. Washington D.C., 1970.

34. Hecht S. and Cockburn A. *The Fate of the Forest: Developers, Destroyers, and Defenders of the Amazon.* Verso, London, 1989.

35. Diaz J. L. Ethnopharmacology of sacred-psycoactive plants used by the Indians of Mexico. *A. Rev. Phacol. Toxic.* 17, 647, 1977.

36. Ministere des Affaires Sociales et de la Condition Feminine. *Synopsis of Project for the Socio-Economic Integration of the Baka/Bakola Peoples.* Yaoude, 1989/90.

37. Agland P. *Baka: People of the Rainforest.* Broadcasting Support Services, London, 1988.

38. Knudtson, P. and Suzuki D. *Wisdom of the Elders.* Stoddart Publishing Co, Ltd. 1992.

39. Li Chaojin Management of Chinese Traditional Drugs. In *The Role of Traditional Medicine in Primary Health Care in China* (Edited by Kerele O. *et al.*) *Am. J. Chin. Med.* Suppl. No. 1 39–41, 1987.

40. Cunningham A. B. Medicinal plants and witch-doctors: are we barking up the wrong tree? *African Wildlife* 38, 247, 1984.

41. Gerstner J. Some factors affecting the perpetuation of our indigenous flora *J. S. African Forestry Assoc.* 13, 4, 1946.

42. MacDonald L. A. W. Witchdoctors versus wildlife in southern Africa. *African Wildlife* 38, 4, 1984.

43. Selincourt K. de. Good hope for cape's endangered medicinal plants. *New Scientist* 7, 4 Jan. 1992.

44. Cunningham A. B. Development of a conservation policy on commercially exploited medicinal plants: a case study from Southern Africa. In *The Conservation of Medicinal Plants* (edited by Akerele O. *et al.*). Proceedings of an International Consultation 21–27 March 1988 held at Chiang Mai, Thailand. Cambridge University Press, pp. 337–358, 1991.

45. Anyinam C. A. Alternative medicine in western industrialized countries: an agenda for Medical geography. *Can. Geographer* 34, Spring, 69–76, 1990.

46. Akerele O. *et al.* (Ed) *The Conservation of Medicinal Plants.* Proceedings of an International Consultation 21–27 March 1988 held at Chiang Mai, Thailand. Cambridge University Press, Cambridge, 1991.

47. Padoch C. *et al.* Complexity and conservation of medicinal plants: anthropological cases from Peru and Indonesia. In *The Conservation of Medicinal Plants* (Edited by Akerele O. *et al.*). Proceedings of an International Consultation 21–27 March 1988 held at Chiang Mai, Thailand. Cambridge University Press, pp. 321–327, 1991.

48. Bonati A. Industry and the Conservation of Medicinal Plants. In *The Conservation of Medicinal Plants* (Edited by Akerele O. *et al.*). Proceedings of an International Consultation 21–27 March 1988 held at Chiang Mai, Thailand. Cambridge University Press, pp. 141–145, 1991.

49. Miller T. G. *Environmental Science: Sustaining the Earth.* Wadsworth Publishing Company, Belmont, CA, 1993.

50. McNeely J. A. and Thorsell J. W. Enhancing the Role of Protected Areas in Conserving medicinal Plants. In *The Conservation of Medicinal Plants* (Edited by Akerele O. *et al.*). Proceedings of an International Consultation 21–27 March 1988 held at Chiang Mai, Thailand. Cambridge University Press, pp. 199–210, 1991.

51. Frate D. A. Last of the earth eaters. *The Sciences* Nov-Dec, 34–38, 1984.

52. Vermeer D. E. and Frate D. A. Geophagy in a Mississippi county. *Ann. Assoc. Am. Geograph.* 65, 414, 1975.

53. Vermeer D. E. Geophagy among the Tiv of Nigeria. *Ann. Assoc. Am. Geograph.* 56, 197, 1966.

54. Vermeer D. E. Geophagy among the Ewe of Ghana. *Ethnology* 10, 1971.

55. Hunter J. M. Geophagy in Africa and the United States: As culture–nutrition hypothesis. *Geograph. Rev.* 63, 170, 1973.

56. Hunter J. M. and DeKleine R. Geophagy in Central America. *Geograph. Rev.* 74, 1984.

57. Bennet B. C. Plants and people of the Amazonian Rainforests. *BioScience* 42, 599, 1992.

58. Reichel-Dolmatoff G. Cosmology as Ecological analysis: a view from the rain forest. *Man* 11, 307, 1976.

59. van Binsbergen W. H. J. Explorations into the History and Sociology of Territorial Cults in Zambia. In *Guardians of the Land: Essays on Central African Territorial Cults* (Edited by Schoffeleers J. M.), pp. 47–88, 1978.

60. Messenger J. G. Ididio drama. *Africa* 12, 208, 1971.

61. Vos A. de. Game as food: a report on its significance in Africa and Latin America. *Unasylva,* FAO, Rome 29, 2, 1978.

62. Gadgil M. Social restraints on resource utilization: The Indian experience. In *Culture and Conservation: The Human Dimension in Environmental Planning* (Edited by McNeely J. J. and Pin D.). pp. 125–154, JUCN Load on Croom Hel

63. Cohn J. P. Culture and Conservation. *BioScience* 38, 450, 1988.

64. The proceedings of the international consultation appear in *The Conservation of Medicinal Plants* (Edited by Akerele O. *et al.*). Proceedings of an International Consultation 21–27 March 1988 held at Chiang Mai. Thailand, Cambridge University Press, 1991.

Part III

Culture-Oriented Approaches

The aim of this part of the book is to present the main culture-oriented theoretical approaches and concepts in medical anthropology and related fields. The first two selections focus explicitly on theory. The remaining selections are united by themes such as mind-body-universe connections, or race and racism. Parts III and IV contain many selections that provide detail about ethnographic and other social science methods and should be read critically with regard to research questions and strategies (see also selection 7).

Most of the selections in this book draw on a number of theoretical approaches. For example, selections in all four parts discuss and use political economic or "critical medical anthropology" (CMA) approaches (see selection 1; Baer et al. 1997; Farmer 1999, 2003; Scheper-Hughes 1992; Scheper-Hughes and Sargent 1999). CMA focuses on large-scale structures and forces that produce or maintain inequalities in power and wealth and shape conditions of health and disease. Such conditions include not just exposure to disease but also the organization of medical care, access to health services, and the character of patient–healer relationships. Like other social systems, medical systems have defined roles, hierarchies of authority and prestige among practitioners, and inequalities between healers and patients and their families (see selections 10, 34).

Given that many if not most medical anthropologists today incorporate politico-economic approaches into their work, critical medical anthropology is not singled out in a separate section. Similarly, selections that concern applied social science (such as 32, 33, 36, 37) are not set apart from those that are more theoretical, given the interchange of concepts and data between applied and basic research. Finally, selections on sex and gender could have been included in this part of the book but are placed in the next one because they fit within a sequence of ideas and topics in Part IV.

Part I introduced interpretive approaches to understanding people's illness experience, including the concept of "explanatory models" or cultural beliefs about what causes illness and other kinds of misfortune, how the body works, and how the body and spirit are related. The selections in Part II applied evolutionary theory to disease patterns in the past and present and to relationships between humans and stresses including pathogens and environmental challenges. The historical perspective brought to light the importance of social inequality, lifestyle change, and human modifications of the environment in affecting disease patterns. These lessons have implications for understanding and managing health problems today.

The distinguishing characteristic of Part III is a focus on culture. Cultural beliefs are learned through life in a group and come to be accepted as natural and obvious. This can make it difficult both to recognize one's own ethnocentric notions and to perceive the logic of another culture. Selection 26, by Linda C. Garro, illustrates how intensive, long-term ethnographic research allows the researcher to piece together the structure of healing systems and health beliefs in a given setting. Garro compares healing traditions in two societies in terms of three common typologies used in medical anthropology. Although the selection highlights some difficulties in fitting real-world cultural systems into classificatory schemes, it also reveals the benefits of making comparisons based on detailed knowledge.

The selection by Nancy Scheper-Hughes and Margaret M. Lock turns the spotlight on Western ways of conceptualizing nature, the mind–body interface, and personhood. It compares these ideas to alternative ways of thinking from pre-Cartesian times and other cultures around the world. The selection draws attention to the body as an object of social and cultural elaboration as well as scholarly inquiry and shows how Western concepts of the individuo-centered, autonomous, impermeable body/self are cultural constructs rooted in a particular social-historical context (but see Kusserow 1999 on the overlap between Western and Eastern, individuo-centric and socio-centric concepts of personhood).

In Part I, we saw that not all cultures share the same ideas about health, disease, and "normal" biological processes. There is wide variation in the recognition of culturally significant symptoms of disease or in the definition of disability (see Ingstad and Whyte 1995). Even countries sharing a common biomedical system differ in the way diseases are defined and medicine is practiced (see Part I). For example, in countries where physicians often play a paternalistic or protective role, such as Japan and Italy, it is common for terminally ill patients not to be told the truth about their condition. This is believed to be the best way to maintain or engender hope. By contrast, in the U.S. there is usually full disclosure and clinical narratives center around a combination of planning of treatment and discussion of statistics and probabilities (Good 1995; see selection 28). In Germany heart medicines are used six times more frequently than in the United Kingdom, even though rates of heart disease are similar, reflecting different cultural concepts about the vulnerability of the heart and its role in maintaining health. French people use fewer antibiotics but more nutritional supplements and thermal and homeopathic cures than people in the United States, reflecting an emphasis on the constitution or "terrain" rather than microbes threatening from the outside (Payer 1996).

The sick role refers to a special status that sets the sick person outside normal social, family, and work obligations and brings support from healers, relatives, and friends. On the other hand, it brings duties such as complying with advice and treatment from experts and others and getting well promptly. The symbolic meanings associated with specific sicknesses, meanwhile, influence the experience of illness and the response of others to the person's assumption of the sick role (see selections 32, 36). For example, whether a sickness is considered treatable influences the likelihood of recovery. New sickness labels such as posttraumatic stress disorder (see Young 1995) or functional somatic syndromes including multiple chemical sensitivity and fibromyalgia (see Barsky and Borus 1999) allow for creative construction of meaning and the possibility that the sickness becomes a defining part of the afflicted person's identity.

The sick role is available only where a disease label exists, so that variation in disease labels across cultures brings variation in illness experience. Interestingly, the incorporation of local communities into regional and global systems tends to bring more disease labels, a proliferation of explanatory models rather than the replacement of old ones with new ones, and more health complaints (see selections 21, 28–31). In the industrialized societies, the culture of risk management and the quantitative reading of nature fuels a rising enthusiasm for testing and screening but creates new sources of anxiety over an ever-expanding range of health risks (see selection 28; Douglas 1992; Finkler 2003).

Selections 28 and 29 by Margaret M. Lock and Shelley R. Adler, respectively, indicate that expectations of illness can bring about the very malady that is feared, by way of what is known as the nocebo effect. The inverse is the better-known placebo effect. The placebo effect refers to a broad psychophysical phenomenon by which symbolic mechanisms used in some form or other by all medical systems envelop patients and families in systems of meaning that can improve the effectiveness of medical treatments or independently bring about healing (see also selections 8, 9; Moerman 2002). On the other hand, Michelle M. Alexander and J. Anthony Paredes show in selection 31 that some remedies considered to act only by way of a placebo effect may actually be pharmacologically active.

In fact, in most cases of illness it is not biomedical treatments but time and what Daniel E. Moerman and Wayne B. Jonas (selection 30) call the meaning response that bring about recovery. This means that in the past, when medical treatments were of little efficacy, the care itself that was given by physicians may have been effective. Consequently, the importance of medicine in the second epidemiologic transition may have been underestimated (see Part II). At the same time, in many patients today the meaning response is strengthened by the tendency of biomedicine to encourage a distanced relationship between patients and physicians, deny the existence of ritual behavior in hospitals and medical personnel, and reject the placebo effect as well as psychological and spiritual factors in general. Hence, for some people current attempts to weaken the authority of physicians and reduce the social distance between patients and healers may have a counterproductive effect.

Elucidating explanatory models can show how people's behavior makes sense in a particular sociocultural context and improve communication between patients and healers. However, there is a common assumption that patients will learn physicians' explanatory models and that patient understandings are useful only in terms of overcoming barriers to compliance. Yet, some physicians express a willingness to accept or adopt their patients' explanatory models, as seen in selection 11 and as Schoenberg and Drew (2002) report regarding patients' beliefs in silent symptoms of hypertension.

In selection 32 on biomedical and indigenous beliefs and practices concerning Ebola in Uganda, Barry S. Hewlett and Richard P. Amola show how there can be within-culture variation in explanatory models and a mixing of explanatory models held simultaneously (see also Part I; selections 26, 32, 34; Dressler et al. 1995). Trisha Greenhalgh et al. consider humoral medical principles about ailments caused by imbalances of temperature, humidity, or physical or mental exertion (see selections 3, 4, 26). These beliefs coexist with biomedical beliefs in much of the world today, but sometimes the two come into conflict. In selection 33, the authors explain that biomedical recommendations for treatment of diabetes in Bangladeshi immigrants to London may not be followed if the prescribed foods, such as uncooked or grilled vegetables, are considered indigestible and therefore debilitating. It is important to consider humoral explanatory models in each cultural context, given that there is great variation across space and time with regard to the values of particular foods, behaviors, and medicines.

Emphasizing culture does not mean ignoring the fact that social stratification by socioeconomic class, gender, and ethnicity is the primary factor explaining the distribution of disease, differential access to health services, and outcomes of illness (see selection 28). It is also important to recognize that individual behavior may be shaped by material conditions of life, irrespective of beliefs, as Paul Farmer argues in selection 34.

For example, in the case of tuberculosis, inadequate nutrition, poor hygienic conditions, exposure to diverse pathogens such as HIV, and erratic availability of medicines are forces beyond the control of people living in poverty. These factors make the reactivation of tuberculosis infection more likely, the progression of the disease more rapid, and the result of treatment less favorable. Further, conditions of poverty and inequality are rooted in local to global forces that directly impact on people's ability to comply with medical treatment and challenge prevailing ideas about agency, or the freedom of individuals to behave as they see fit. The concept of agency raises questions about ethics and universal standards of care, given that politico-economic factors favor reliance on expensive technological treatments in contexts of plenty but circumscribe the therapeutic options of individual practitioners and patients in contexts of scarcity (see selections 22, 34; Farmer 1999; Mackenbach and Howden-Chapman 2003).

Selection 35, by Maria B. Olujic, weaves together several strands from earlier articles. It illustrates Scheper-Hughes and Lock's principles concerning the body politic through an analysis of politically motivated and politically meaningful violence (see also Ajmer and Abbink 2000; Das et al. 2001; Kleinman et al. 1997; Sluka 2000). The selection illustrates the power of symbols to destroy as well as heal. Olujic's informants also raise the issue of stigma. Stigma refers to the attachment of negative value to an individual because of a deviation from culturally defined normality, such as disease, disability, or in the case at hand, the experience of sexual violence (see Das et al. 2001; Goode 1994; Silla 1998). As L. I. Remennick shows through the case of radiation exposure from the Chernobyl accident (selection 36), stigmatization can have profound social, health, and economic impacts over a long period of time.

Selection 37 by Elisabeth A. Faxelid and Kristina M. Ramstedt compares the notification process used to interrupt the spread of sexually transmitted infections in Zambia and Sweden. The authors find that resource constraints and cultural beliefs affect the process and its success in both settings. Even in Sweden, where the notification process is highly organized and well supported, and cultural beliefs construe notification as a civic duty, stigma continues to keep some patients from participating. In selection 38 on AIDS, Christopher J. M. Whitty argues that although stigma is generally a negative concept, there are times when it may be employed in positive, health-promoting ways.

The final three selections of Part III concern race and racism (see also Braun 2002; selection 15). In selection 39, Vanessa Northington Gamble explores the impact of racism in the United States on health disparities and people's experiences of health care. Gamble argues that the Tuskegee study should be seen not as a closed episode in history but rather as an incident that forms part of a pattern which continues to shape people's expectations concerning medical treatment.

Ethnicity is a term that explicitly expresses self-identification with a cultural group. Ethnic identity can provide stability and a sense of belonging. On the other hand, Olujic shows that ethnic identity can form the basis of violent conflict. Discrimination and stigmatization by the majority population or more powerful groups can deepen socioeconomic class differences that intersect with ethnic differences and manifest themselves in health disparities. These health disparities are real, although it is difficult to measure and characterize them accurately. There is a lack of agreement on the categories that should be used—some classification systems include both racial and ethnic groups and some systems depend on self-identification, whereas others allow observers to make a selection—and people may change their ethnic affiliation over time.

The difficulties of classification and measurement do not mean that the health impacts of racism and racialization elude scientific scrutiny. To the contrary, as selection 40 by Nancy Krieger shows, greater precision in the use of terms and a more explicit approach to racism can lead to improved understanding of health disparities. These differences are the result of racism and socioeconomic inequalities, not inherent biological differences. Yet, some physicians and researchers continue to use racial thinking, closing their eyes to social, economic, and political factors. Selection 41, by Jonathan Kahn, traces the social construction and manipulation of a statistic that turns out to be wrong but has become the basis of an effort to create the first "ethnic drug." It is a case study of the damage that can be caused by misplaced faith in quantitative data, particularly when the data are interpreted through a theoretical paradigm that has an aura of scientific objectivity but is fundamentally a product of culture (see also selection 28).

Suggested films

Chelyabinsk: The Most Contaminated Spot on the Planet. 1994. Slawomir Grunberg, producer. 58 min.

Plagued, 1992. Janet Bell, producer. (NY: Filmmakers Library). [Part IV, Will We Ever Learn, 52 min.]

Playing with Poison. 2001. John Ritchie and Rob Bromley, producers (Discovery Health Channel/CBC). 46 min.

The Lost Children of Rockdale County. 1999. Rachel Dretzin and Barak Goodman, producers (Frontline). 90 min.

The Deadly Deception (Tuskegee Study). 1993. Denisce Diiane, producer (Nova). 56 min.

26 CULTURAL MEANING, EXPLANATIONS OF ILLNESS, AND THE DEVELOPMENT OF COMPARATIVE FRAMEWORKS

Linda C. Garro

This selection introduces three frameworks for comparing beliefs about disease and the treatment of illness. Garro applies the frameworks to two case studies and demonstrates some strengths and weaknesses of each. Her analysis focuses on the general population rather than healers, but it also describes the types of healers in each setting and illustrates the principle of medical pluralism examined in Part I. This selection is explicit about how the research was done and the kinds of information generated by specific research methods. Attention to methodology will be useful for the selections that follow.

One of the frameworks, Foster's division of non-western medical traditions into naturalistic or personalistic systems, was discussed in Part I. A second framework proposes a distinction between internalizing and externalizing systems and has room for biomedicine as an ethnomedical system. A third proposes a dozen illness theories divided into two main categories of natural versus spiritual causation and sets them all against the standard of Western biomedicine.

Garro provides examples showing that although the three frameworks help to order information and encourage comparisons and contrasts, they have trouble capturing the complexity and variable internal logic of individual healing systems. For example, she finds humoral beliefs in Pichátaro, Mexico, but discovers that witchcraft is a seldom-invoked explanation limited to illness rather than a broad range of misfortunes. Moreover, several common ailments are considered to derive from emotional causes, which cannot be placed confidently in either the naturalistic or personalistic category.

In an Anishinaabe community in Canada, Garro discovers that the indigenous language expresses a way of thinking about disease that emphasizes causes and experiences over diagnostic labels. By allowing for a great deal of ambiguity and contingency, the language itself keeps the range of causal possibilities open. These possibilities include equilibrium, contagion, and the destruction of traditional ways of life as agents of disease. In addition, problems in social relationships cause certain indigenous sicknesses, but the cause of the illness may be a failure to meet an obligation to a benevolent being that has no home in any of the three frameworks.

Questions to keep in mind

How do the case studies illustrate the strengths and weaknesses of the comparative frameworks introduced in the selection?

Why do you need local knowledge to design structured interview questions and other research tools (see also selection 21)?

What kinds of information are elicited by studying how people respond to illness and seek remedies, as opposed to following actual illness episodes and their management?

How do beliefs about equilibrium in the two cases resemble or differ from others presented so far?

In what ways do witchcraft/sorcery beliefs and practices converge with or diverge from those described in other selections?

Source: Garro, Linda 2000. "Cultural Meaning, Explanations of Illness, and the Development of Comparative Frameworks." *Ethnology* 39(4):305–334. With permission from the publisher.

Illness and suffering are universal human experiences which come to be endowed with cultural meaning. As such, the domain of explanatory frameworks for illness is an appropriate one for cross-cultural comparative research. How illness is understood and dealt with in diverse cultural settings is addressed by a large number of medical anthropology studies. In addition, several general schemes for categorizing theories of illness causation across cultures exist. Three of the better-known proposals (Murdock 1980; Young 1976; Foster 1976) are reviewed here. Although these schemes have been around for some time, their continued relevance is attested to by recent medical anthropology textbooks that organize discussions of cross-cultural variability in etiological understandings with reference to one or more of these schemes (e.g., Anderson 1996:82–86; Loustanau and Sobo 1997:91–103; Brown 1998:15, 110).

The ethnographic material considered here is drawn from two field studies. One site is Pichátaro, a town in the highlands of the west-central Mexican state of Michoacán, where both Purépecha (Tarascan) and Spanish are spoken. (Most of this work was carried out in conjunction with James C. Young.) The other site is an Ojibwa community in Manitoba, Canada. This choice was influenced by A. Irving Hallowell's insightful writings (e.g., Hallowell 1942, 1955, 1976), which led to an appreciation that the Ojibwa might be an illuminating contrast with Pichátaro. (Rather than "Ojibwa," the terms Anishinaabe, or its plural Anishinaabeg, will be used, as this is how people refer to themselves.) Research in the Anishinaabe community was explicitly designed to be comparative with my earlier work in Pichátaro. Adopting a cognitive anthropological approach, the intent was to make comparisons at the level of cultural meaning. In both sites, the focus was on discovering the nature of cultural knowledge brought to the occurrence of illness, how this knowledge is applied in evaluating illness, and what considerations are brought to bear in making treatment decisions; i.e., how illness forms part of these meaningful worlds. Cultural understandings are resources which may be variably drawn upon to help make sense of one's own or another's experiences (Garro 2000). Thus, cultural understandings do not function in a top-down deterministic manner but rather are better seen as tools (which both enable and constrain interpretive possibilities) available to navigate the ambiguity surrounding illness and other troubling experiences.

COMPARATIVE FRAMEWORKS FOR THEORIES ABOUT ILLNESS

Murdock (1980) coded the ethnographic literature from 139 societies to examine the cross-cultural distribution of twelve illness theories. These theories are of two main types; natural causation and supernatural causation. Theories of natural causation he defined as "any theory, scientific or popular, which accounts for the impairment of health as a physiological consequence of some experience of the victim in a manner that would appear reasonable to modern medical science" (Murdock 1980:9). Four distinct types of theories are coded in this category: infection, stress, organic deterioration, and accident. The contrasting set of supernatural causation theories "fall into three readily distinguishable groups" but are viewed as having "little in common other than that they all rest on supernatural assumptions which modern medical science does not recognize as valid" (Murdock 1980:17). These descriptions clearly bear the imprint of the outside observer and an underlying ethnocentric assumption that modern medical science sets the standard by which other theories are assessed. The eight supernatural causation theories are of three types: mystical causation (encompassing fate, ominous sensation, contagion, and mystical retribution); magical causation (sorcery, witchcraft); and animistic causation (soul loss, spirit aggression).

Using a four-point scale to rate each theory's importance as a cause of illness within a specific culture at a given time, Murdock provides codes for 139 societies in the Standard Cross-Cultural Sample (Murdock and White 1969). For the Saulteaux (Ojibwa), Murdock dates the period at approximately 1930 and bases his codes on Hallowell's writings, assigning positive ratings to three theories of supernatural causation (mystical retribution, spirit aggression, and sorcery). The use of labels such as supernatural causation and spirit aggression conflicts with Hallowell's contention that the supernatural/natural distinction is not made by the Ojibwa and that imposing such a scheme "distorts their world view and makes it impossible to understand their actual behavioral environment" (Hallowell 1992:63). Still, by applying an external framework and a detailed coding scheme, Murdock was able to examine the distributional patterning of these theories and show that illness theories are not randomly distributed across world regions or linguistic phyla. He finds, for example, that theories based on witchcraft (as distinct from sorcery) are prevalent among those living in the circum-Mediterranean region and among speakers of three large linguistic phyla. Additional intriguing patterns and tests of hypotheses are presented by Murdock (1980) and in later studies using the same coded data (Moore 1988; Gray 1998).

The frameworks of Foster (1976) and Young (1976) are based on polar typologies and are fairly comprehensive. Even so, the fit between the real world and the prototype may only be approximate as each author allows for some fuzziness. The publications are mainly descriptive and the authors do not systematically code a sample of societies using the schemes. Lacking a systematic comparative analysis, they seem to aim for similarities and contrasts in theories and associated practices across diverse settings. Foster (1976:778) writes,

> Obviously, a dual taxonomy for phenomena as complex as worldwide beliefs about causes of illness leaves many loose ends. But it must be remembered that a taxonomy is not an end in itself, something to be polished and admired; its value lies rather in the understanding of relationships between apparently diverse phenomena that it makes possible . . . [throwing] into sharp perspective correlations in health institutions and health behavior that tend to be overlooked in descriptive accounts.

Foster (1976:773) concentrates on "disease etiologies in non-Western medical systems." These are of two basic types, naturalistic and personalistic. In naturalistic systems, illness is explained in "impersonal, systemic terms," with disease resulting from "such *natural forces or conditions* as cold, heat, dampness, and, above all, by an upset in the balance of the basic body elements" (Foster 1976:775). Intervention is therapeutically oriented toward achieving bodily equilibrium and individuals can maintain good health by avoiding disease-producing situations and/or behavior. Personalistic sys-

tems (unlike naturalistic ones) view illness as "*but a special case in the explanation of all misfortune*" (Foster 1976:776) which can be attributed to the "*active, purposeful intervention* of an *agent*, who may be human (witch or sorcerer), nonhuman (ghost, ancestor, evil spirit), or supernatural (a deity or other very powerful being)" (Foster 1976:775). In such systems, there may be considerable overlap between what might be labeled as religion, magic, and medicine. Intervention is primarily centered on determining who is responsible. While it is important to "make sure that one's social networks" with all possible agents "are maintained in good working order," generally the onset of sickness is beyond the ill individual's control. Foster in this account makes no reference to Murdock's broad category of mystical causation; i.e., a "*theory which accounts for the impairment of health as the automatic consequence of some act or experience of the victim mediated by some putative impersonal causal relationship rather than by the intervention of a human or supernatural being*" (Murdock 1980:17).

Foster regards much of Latin America as participating in a naturalistic system. Indeed, his characterization of naturalistic medical systems appears to be grounded in distinguishing humoral/balance-type theories from the bodily based explanations found within biomedicine. The principal examples he provides of a "loose end" in his dichotomous scheme are illnesses attributed to emotional upsets (common throughout Latin America). He concludes that they conform to the naturalistic principle because it is hard to "identify purposive action on the part of an agent intent on causing sickness" (Foster 1976:776). He does not acknowledge, however, that this resolution effectively transforms his scheme into one based in an opposition between "personalistic" and "non-personalistic." Murdock also has difficulty dealing with emotion in his framework. He (Murdock 1980:8) writes, "If a cause described in the ethnographic literature suggests emotional tension, I classify it under 'stress' even though it fails to accord precisely with any recognized psychiatric definition."

The organizing distinction in Young's (1976) scheme is between "externalizing" and "internalizing" systems. (Where a system falls between the two poles is a matter of emphasis, not of absolutes.) Internalizing systems rely upon physiological explanations and conceptions of internal mechanisms "which make it possible for people to order events within the sick person's body from the onset of symptoms to the conclusion of the sickness episode" (Young 1976:147). With illness inside a sick person, therapeutic practices depend on the "healer's ability to restore physiological equilibrium" (Young 1976:148), concentrating efforts "on decoding the symptomatic expressions of intrasomatic events" (Young 1976:149). Rather than standing apart, in this scheme Western medicine is one instance of an internalizing system. (Hereafter, the term "biomedicine" will be used rather than "Western medicine.") Externalizing systems, in contrast, depend on etiological explanations for "serious sickness" (Young 1976:148) which take the "form of narratives in which at least some medically important events take place outside the sick person's body" (Young 1976:147). Sickness is "a symptom of disrupted relations" (Young 1976:149) and "pathogenic agencies are usually purposive and often human or anthropomorphized. Diagnostic interests concentrate on discovering what events could have brought the sick person to the attention of the pathogenic agency . . . Often only gross symptomatic distinctions are made, since the intrasomatic link between aetiological events and sequences of biophysical signs is either ignored or not elaborated" (Young 1976:148).

All three frameworks have strengths, drawbacks, and tradeoffs. A strength of Foster and Young (not shared by Murdock) is the recognition that, in many societies, illness is not a discrete and relatively independent domain but subsumed under widely applicable explanatory frameworks for various kinds of misfortune. Young's positioning of biomedicine as just one medical system among many is a step in the right direction, a step that also extends the range of the framework to encompass the existing variability. With reference to Foster's framework, there is no a priori reason why personalistic and naturalistic explanations should be mutually exclusive. Foster does not address the implications of societies where multiple explanatory frameworks are present or how this affects classification. Young does allow for some gradations in distinctiveness, as his work with the Amhara of Ethiopia illustrates (Young 1976:149). Young is not explicit, however, on how to deter-

mine whether internalizing or externalizing explanatory frameworks predominate in specific settings or how to deal with intracultural variability within "mixed" societies. In addition, concentrating on serious illness at the expense of the full range of illness events is likely to needlessly restrict the basis for comparisons across cultures. Generally, anthropological accounts tend to privilege the more unusual and dramatic episodes of illness over the more commonplace ones, and this tendency may become reified through efforts to code materials in ethnographies.

Murdock's model has an advantage in that it remains open to coding the presence of any number of the twelve illness theories for each culture. The coding is not limited to a single dimension but oriented toward a summary tendency for each of the twelve theories he sees as comprising the cross-cultural variability. In an effort to be comprehensive, Murdock includes among his theories explanations like "organic deterioration," "accident," and "overt human aggression." The detailed coding scheme allows Murdock to carry out much more fine-grained comparisons among the societies studied than would be possible using either of the polar typologies. Using Murdock's codes as a rough guide, it seems that most societies would be classified as best corresponding to the profiles of personalistic and externalizing. While dichotomies highlight meaningful differences and patterns at a general level, reducing each society to a single descriptor leaves out much of the variability Murdock reports and likely glosses over the range of meaningful explanations within a cultural setting.

For contemporary research, an almost unavoidable complication in applying any of the three schemes is the widespread acceptance of biomedical explanations, although the form they take may vary greatly. Further, many colonized peoples have experienced "new" forms of sickness and some explanations for these conditions pose a challenge to existing frameworks.

Perhaps a more fruitful approach than listing the shortcomings of each of the three frameworks, though admittedly of much more modest scope, is to offer methods that would assist both in determining the range of explanatory frameworks in a particular setting and in making comparisons between settings. By working in a bottom-up manner in relatively diverse settings, it may be possible to help build a comparative framework that remains open to ethnographic possibilities. This article explores how this process might be started by sketching the parameters of such an undertaking for two locations. The focus in both settings is on community members, rather than healing specialists, with the intent of portraying how individuals within these "behavioral environments" (Hallowell 1955) are oriented to interpret and act in response to situations of illness. It is worthwhile to underscore (in terms of the existing comparative schemes) that the two settings examined here might be expected to show few points of correspondence. Thus, they provide a good starting point for such an endeavor.

ILLNESS EXPLANATIONS IN PICHÁTARO

Field research in Pichátaro was carried out principally from 1975 to 1977, with shorter visits in 1981 and 1982. Pichátaro is situated about 30 kilometers from the regional market and administrative center of Pátzcuaro. Pichátaro's population was almost 3,000 during the 1975–1977 period; mostly maize farmers, with fruit growing, resin collecting, some craft production, and temporary migrant wage labor as secondary occupations. Families generally viewed four principal treatment alternatives as available: 1) home treatments such as herbal remedies, locally sold commercial remedies, and dietary avoidances: 2) treatment by folk curers (*curanderas*), who used *remedios caseros* (herbal remedies and other folk curing methods) exclusively; 3) treatment by *practicantes* (local unlicensed practitioners of biomedicine who claim varying amounts of informal or formal medical training) who dispensed a variety of *remedios médicos* ("doctor's remedies" which are typically prescription-type medications); and 4) treatment by a physician. Since there was no physician in Pichátaro, consultations most often took place in Pátzcuaro with private practitioners or at a government-run health center.

This cognitively oriented study attempted to provide an account of what people do when faced with illness and why. Central to the research design was the building of a decision model using interview data and other information primarily obtained from one sample and then evaluating the decision model using treatment actions taken in illness case histories obtained from a second, independent sample of families who were visited on a regular basis over a six-month period. The research relied upon structured data-collection methods as well as more traditional ethnographic methods. Fieldwork yielded numerous opportunities to observe illness episodes that enriched, corroborated, and challenged understandings and hypotheses about what people do when faced with illness.

Here, attention is given to one of the structured interview methods (the term-frame interview) because of its potential for use in comparative research (Garro 1988b:691–92; D'Andrade, Quinn, Nerlove, and Romney 1972). The question frames (also known as attribute frames) and illness terms were based on what had been learned during fieldwork, mostly from earlier informal interviews which began by asking informants to list the illnesses (*enfermedades*) they knew. This task was interspersed with talk aimed at learning about the characteristics of the illnesses mentioned, including ways of dealing with them, and their relationships with other illnesses. Statements selected from these interviews were later recast as yes/no question frames and a set of illness terms selected. Each illness term was placed in each frame and the informant was asked whether the resulting statement was true or not.

A term-frame questionnaire is useful for discriminating between and illustrating the nature of relationships among a set of named illnesses. Although not intended to be exhaustive of understandings about illness, a term-frame questionnaire should be representative of what matters to informants when they talk about illness and the range of illnesses covered. Thus, to successfully carry out this type of research, an anthropologist must be well grounded in a given cultural setting and have a representative corpus of informants' statements about illness that can be used to create this type of structured interview. At the same time, a questionnaire need not touch on all of the commonly used explanations that would form part of an account used for cross-cultural comparisons. For example, in Pichátaro the questionnaire did not need to include conditions like burns, broken bones, bruises, sprains, and cuts or other wounds, as these are easily identified, are seen to directly result from trauma, and require specific treatments. Another general concept which underlies a number of frames, without being the focus of specific attention, is that of *fuerza* (strength or vigor). One's fuerza is stronger or weaker depending on one's physical condition. How regularly and what one eats contribute to fuerza and extreme emotional upsets can weaken one's fuerza. Working too hard or experiencing too much exertion at any task can diminish one's fuerza and lower one's ability to resist (*resistir*) illness. Typically, men are thought to have more fuerza than women, adults more than children, and in aging one gradually loses the fuerza to resist illness, until one dies. For Pichátaro, a long version (43 sentence frames and 34 illness terms resulting in 1,462 questions) was used with ten informants to help ensure relative comprehensiveness, and a short version (22 sentence frames and eighteen illness terms for a total of 396 questions) was used for testing specific hypotheses about intracultural variability (e.g., extent of sharing between curers and noncurers).

A variety of data reduction tools (e.g., hierarchical cluster analysis, multidimensional scaling analysis, entailment analysis) can be used to discover patterning across responses. The patterning is more easily seen in a multidimensional scaling analysis when the illness terms and the frames are both present in the same scaling plot, as long as the total number of data points is not too large (Garro 1983, 1986). The overall patterning in a multidimensional scaling plot is determined by similarity. Illnesses that share similar attributes with other illnesses are placed closer together and attribute frames that have similar responses in terms of illnesses are also in proximity to each other. How closely illnesses are associated with attribute frames is also spatially represented in the scaling plot. Because there is a high level of correspondence across the long and short versions. for ease of discussion and visual presentation only the two-dimensional scaling plot for the shorter version is presented here (see Garro 1983:53 for the two-dimensional depiction of the longer version).

The eighteen illness terms and 22 question frames used in the shorter version appear in Tables 26.1 and 26.2. The scaling plot in Figure 26.1 has a total of 40 data points, one for each illness term and question frame. Illness terms are given in Spanish and appear in capitals; attribute frames appear in lowercase letters and are identified through English keywords highlighted in Table 26.2. The data represented come from a study of twenty women, ten curers and ten noncurers (Garro 1986). A general finding was a single cul-

Table 26.1 Illness Terms

Term	Translation
Enfermedad de corazón	heart illness
Empacho	blocked digestion
Cólico	colic, sharp stomach pains
Mollera caída	fallen fontanelle; displacement of a section of the top of the skull
Disenterla	dysentery
Calor subido	risen heat
Gripa	grippe, cold, flu
Deposiciones	diarrhea
Sofoca del estómago	bloated stomach
Latido	"palpitations" brought about by eating delay
Broncomonía	bronchopneumonia
Anginas	swollen glands in the neck
Bilis	"bile," illness resulting from strong emotions
Punzadas	sharp headache around the temples
Pulmonía	pneumonia
Mal de ojo	evil eye
Fogazo	fever sores
Bronquitis	bronchitis

Table 26.2 Attribute Frames

1. Can _____ come from *anger?*
2. Does _____ come from the *"heat"?*
3. Are there pains in the *chest* with _____?
4. When you leave a warm place and enter into the *cold air,* can you get _____?
5. Can you get _____ from eating lots of *"hot" things?*
6. Does _____ come from an *air?*
7. With _____ does the *head* hurt?
8. Can you cure _____ with *folk* remedies?
9. Does _____ come from *germs?*
10. Does _____ come from *not eating* "by the hours"?
11. With _____ do you lose your *appetite?*
12. Can you get _____ from eating lots of *cold things?*
13. With _____ is there a *temperature?*
14. When you get *wet,* can you get _____?
15. With _____ is there pain in the *stomach?*
16. Does _____ come from the *"cold"?*
17. Does _____ come by *contagion* from other people?
18. Can _____ come from *witchcraft?*
19. Does _____ come from walking about without *shoes?*
20. When you have _____, do you have to take *"hot"* remedies to be cured?
21. Can you cure _____ with *"doctors'* remedies"?
22. Can _____ come from a *fright?*

Note. The word(s) italicized in each frame appear in the multidimensional scaling plot (Figure 26.1)

tural knowledge system for the domain of illness common to both curers and noncurers. It is thus appropriate to represent the findings in a single plot and to consider understandings about illness as being generally shared.

In addition to multidimensional scaling plots, other approaches for finding patterning in the data contribute to the interpretation of the findings presented here. Rather than going through details available elsewhere (e.g., Young and Garro 1994: ch. 4; and Garro 1983:61–67), the main findings regarding illness causation are highlighted by pointing to patterns observable in Figure 26.1.

First, causal explanatory frameworks appear to play a major role in structuring the illness domain (Garro 1983:62). Three basic groupings in the plot correspond to the ways that Pichatareños talk about and respond to illness (one on the left side, another on the right, and a third in the bottom middle portion). While the discussion of these groupings is at a somewhat higher level of abstraction than individual explanatory principles, the analysis does not stray far from perceived similarities among possible causes of illness. Although Figure 26.1 provides a useful guide, it is important

not to assume too literal a correspondence between location in the plot and interpretation. Especially when reduced to a two-dimensional solution, some ambiguities arise. Also, this brief summary cannot do justice to the full complexity of illness-related knowledge in Pichátaro.

Returning to the major groupings, on the left side of Figure 26.1 are the external causes of illness, the illnesses themselves (e.g., *gripa, broncomonía*), and their symptoms. The illnesses located in this section are primarily attributed to contact with "cold" agents in the environment that upset the body's internal balance. Remedies with a "hot" quality are thought to restore the internal balance and cure such illnesses. In Pichátaro, illness is often attributed to changes in weather, especially cold and wet weather. "Contagion," although rarely mentioned, usually refers to illnesses affecting large numbers of people at one time and as due to many people being exposed to the same conditions. In other cases, illnesses may be linked to "carelessness" (*un descuido*), implying that the victim bears some responsibility for contacting a cold environmental agent. For example, a person who was sleeping in a warm location and got up

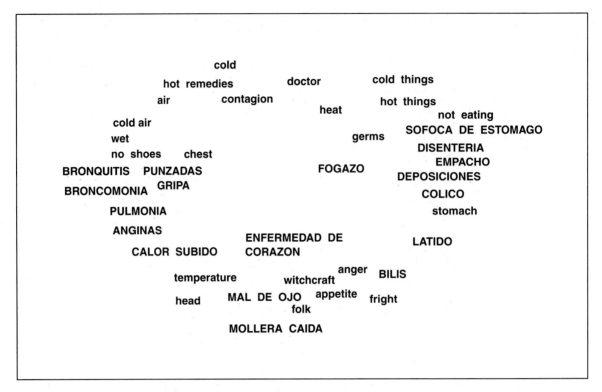

Figure 26.1 Two-Dimensional Scaling Plot of Illness Terms and Attribute Frames (Stress = .235)

quickly, her feet suddenly contacting the cold ground, could have her body heat displaced upward, resulting in symptoms of red, burning eyes and *anginas* (swollen glands).

On the right side of Figure 26.1 are stomach-based illnesses seen as caused by a diet that fails to maintain a healthy internal balance. Not eating (e.g., skipping a regular meal or not having enough to eat), eating too much, eating an injudicious mixture of "hot" and "cold" foods, or eating too many "hot" or "cold" things are common explanations for these illnesses. Again, individuals are expected to assume some responsibility to prevent such conditions. In Pichátaro, the idea of *microbios* (germs) seldom comes up in illness discussions (and was never cited as a cause in any of the 323 actual illness case histories obtained as part of this research). When mentioned, microbios are equated with dirtiness and are thought to cause stomach problems and diarrhea when present in food, which explains why they are present in this section of the plot. These first two groupings

are consistent with Foster's description of a naturalistic system, including the charge that individuals are responsible for trying to maintain good health by avoiding disease-producing situations and/or behavior.

An internal equilibrium disruption also accounts for the presence of a number of the illnesses and frames located in the lower middle section, but here the disruption is tied to an intense emotion. According to Pichatareños, experiencing strong emotions (such as anger, joy, fright, desire, sorrow, humiliation, and sadness) may lead to illness. Diffuse and nonspecific somatic complaints, referred to as *bilis* (bile), are seen as a consequence of the release of bile. Anginas may be attributed to not crying when you feel you must. *Mollera caída* (fallen fontanelle), an illness of infants, may be caused by a strong fright or more often is attributed to a fall. Stomach-based illnesses, especially those located closest to the bottom grouping (e.g., *latido, cólico,* and *deposiciones*), may also be caused by emotional upsets. Unlike the two other major groupings, persons who experience such illnesses are regarded as victims of situations which are for the most part beyond their control and often inevitable.

Although not captured in the scaling plot, emotional experiences that upset the internal balance and cause illness may be transferred from mothers to children in the womb or through breastfeeding. *Mal de ojo* (evil eye) occurs when an adult seeing a child or infant has a strong emotional reaction to the child. The younger the child, the greater is its vulnerability to mal de ojo. The illnesses located in this lower middle section are often considered curable through remedios caseros (folk curing methods and herbal remedies), although only a few illnesses, such as evil eye, fallen fontanelle, and witchcraft-related illnesses, are considered incurable with remedios médicos.

The explanatory framework centering on *brujería* or *hechicería* (witchcraft) is limited to illness and is not used as general explanation for other types of misfortune. To refer to an illness as *mala enfermedad* (bad illness) or *enfermedad de brujería* (witchcraft-caused illness) implies the intentional, malevolent, and covert actions of someone to bring about illness in another (sorcery in Murdock's framework). These illnesses are either chronic and prolonged or recurrent illnesses and defy treatment. Rather than being based on identifying the person seen as causing harm, a diagnosis of mala enfermedad is usually made by a process of elimination, after a host of treatments have been tried and have failed. Such illnesses are considered grave and/or as causing considerable suffering. The specialists who can best treat cases of mala enfermedad charge extremely high fees for their services and are referred to as witches (*brujos;* the same term is applied to those who can cure as well as those who can cause this illness).

Through posing questions about ways of responding to and dealing with different types of illnesses, the term-frame interview format helps illuminate the relationship between cultural knowledge and what people do when faced with illness. But more than this is needed. Following actual illness cases and attending to the cultural resources that are used when a family is faced with illness provide a means of ascertaining the relative importance of various illness theories and a vantage point for gaining an appreciation of the be-

havioral environment. In Pichátaro, a large corpus of case histories was recorded during visits every two weeks over a six-month period to a randomly selected sample of 62 families (referred to below as the case collection sample). Actions taken to deal with a particular episode of illness reveal how the illness is framed within the Pichatareño behavioral environment (Garro 1998a). The way an illness is understood may change, often as a consequence of an unsuccessful treatment outcome, with the new interpretation setting in motion a different course of action. Although the data summary presented below focuses only on the final designations (sufficient for current purposes) and thus has a static quality, it must be emphasized that the evaluation of a particular illness episode is emergent and often shifting, reflecting a dynamic process of applying cultural and personal knowledge.

In the complete set of 323 episodes, more than 60 different diagnoses comprise the set of final designations, even though *gripa* (grippe, cold, flu) and *calentura* (a "temperature" or fever) make up almost one-third of all cases. The ascribed cause of nearly 40 per cent of the cases involved external environmental agents, with "the cold" and "airs" most frequently named. Around 20 per cent of the cases were attributed to dietary causes, and almost 10 per cent to emotional causes (excluding mal de ojo). There were numerous examples of illnesses thought to be best treated by remedios caseros (including instances of mal de ojo, mollera caída, enfermedad de corazón, and bilis). A smaller percentage of cases were blamed on physical trauma; other cases on overexertion. For many of the remaining cases, informants said they did not know the cause or were not sure of it, more commonly when the sufferers were under five years of age.

There was not a single instance of mala enfermedad or a causal attribution of brujería across the case collection sample, suggesting that while this is a plausible explanatory framework, it is infrequently used. An alternative possibility is that individuals were unwilling to relate such cases, given the sensitivity that surrounds this topic in Pichátaro. This reticence may indeed exist, but it is unlikely to be the whole of the explanation, as members of some families in the case collection sample told about previously occurring cases of mala enfermedad. More generally, the identification of particular community members as brujos was an acceptable topic of conversation, and we were warned about interacting with those who were reputed witches. Also, families who were not part of the case collection sample told us of past illnesses involving witchcraft, but we were not told of any suspicions that brujería was involved in any of the illnesses that we observed and followed more informally in these families. That brujería is not prominent is supported by two additional considerations. First, it is highly unusual for it to be suspected early in an illness. Second, almost every illness comes to some resolution before witchcraft is actively considered.

As has been seen, culturally shared explanatory frameworks and illness labels serve as resources when illness occurs. The name conferred upon an illness carries information about possible causes, and what Pichatareños know about illness causation structures the way they deal with a given episode. In addition to direct physical trauma, the main explanatory frameworks are oriented around the permeability and vulnerability of the physical body to environmental dangers, dietary disturbances, and emotional upsets. Reaching a provisional diagnosis so treatment can proceed involves assessing the relevance of cultural and personal knowledge. An epistemological claim supporting a diagnosis is initially based on the way similar cases were effectively treated in the past and later supported when treatment is judged to be successful. Brujería as an explanation comes into play only in a small minority of cases. The epistemological claim that an illness is one of brujería can only be supported once alternative claims have been tested and have failed.

With the findings from Pichátaro it is possible to ask about the extent of correspondence with the comparative schemes presented earlier. The explanatory frameworks uncovered pose challenges to all three schemes. First, none of Murdock's five theories of natural causation (i.e., "in a manner that would appear reasonable to modern medical science") comes close to capturing the three main imbalance-related explanations, and only sorcery as a theory of supernatural causation can be linked with brujería. In Murdock's framework, evil eye is considered a form of witchcraft, but this is inappropriate for mal de ojo in Pichátaro (Young and Garro 1994:64) and there is no suitable alternative placement. However, there are some discernible

parallels between the concept of fuerza and Murdock's theory of "organic deterioration." And while reference to microbios (germs) might on the surface suggest correspondence with Murdock's naturalistic causation theory of infection, the cultural meaning behind the use of microbios suggests otherwise. Second, while Foster's division into naturalistic and personalistic theories does not mesh well with the concept of intense emotion leading to illness, perhaps the substitution of "bodily imbalance" for "naturalistic" would resolve the difficulty in the Pichátaro case. Unfortunately, this revision, as the findings from the Anishinaabe case study will indicate, runs into as much difficulty in providing comprehensive coverage as the original personalistic and naturalistic dichotomy does. Finally, while the emphasis on physiological equilibrium in Pichátaro is consistent with Young's "internalizing" endpoint, some accounts, especially those involving emotional experiences, share the characteristic of "externalizing" systems by taking the "form of narratives in which at least some medically important events take place outside the sick person's body" (Young 1976:147). In addition to the distinctive conditions through which mal de ojo arises, a couple of illness narratives are illustrative. The first concerns a case of dysentery reported by a 70-year-old man:

> I've had it, two days ago—the day before yesterday, and yesterday too. It came from *sentimiento* [sorrow], when my ox died I had lots of pity—I lost a lot of money. It was like a bilis. My wife cooked me a remedy and with this I got well fast

Even more problematic for the internalizing-externalizing scheme are cases like the following:

> We had a girl that died of la bilis. This happened two years ago. It started when the girl was five months old Her mother had a *coraje* [anger], and then she gave her the breast, and from this the bilis started. She was real sick—vomiting and with diarrhea.

The main point here is not to belabor the difficulties of developing a comprehensive scheme, but to suggest that it might be best to start by looking at the range of explanatory frameworks and their epistemological and ontological underpinnings in diverse settings and then address the issue of developing a comparative framework.

EXPLANATORY FRAMEWORKS FOR ILLNESS IN THE ANISHINAABE COMMUNITY

The Anishinaabe community of around 2,000 people is located in southwestern Manitoba, Canada. Ojibway or Saulteaux may be used as descriptors when communicating in English with individuals from outside the community. While some children and young adults speak only English, a substantial majority of adults still speak their own language, Anishinaabemowin, and prefer to use it in most social settings. There is insufficient land on the reserve or surrounding it to allow a subsistence or trapping-based means of livelihood for any but a few fishermen. Unemployment is high, and many individuals depend on some form of social assistance. Housing is crowded and substandard; more than 80 per cent of the houses are without indoor plumbing. A health center on the reserve is staffed by visiting physicians approximately three afternoons a week. Other physicians and hospitals are located in towns approximately an hour's drive distant. All expenses of biomedical care, including transportation costs and prescription drugs, are covered by universal health insurance or the Canadian government.

Two general types of Anishinaabe curers are important sources of care. The first, usually women, are those who "know how to make medicine." They make herbal preparations, the special knowledge for which is learned from another healer, typically a family member. This type of curer will be referred to here as a herbalist.

Curers of the second type are regarded as "gifted" (Garro 1990). They may sometimes also be asked for herbal remedies for specified conditions. More often they are consulted because of their gift for communicating with those whom Hallowell (1955, 1960) refers to as "other-than-human persons." Hallowell (1960:380–81) describes the domain of "persons" as encompassing more than just human beings. Attributes of personhood do not depend on outward appearance but on "an inner vital part which is enduring," and include self-awareness, understanding, personal identity, volition, autonomy, speech, and memory. Human beings, both living and dead, and other-than-human persons are differentiated on the basis of power, with other-than-human persons occupying the "top rank in the power hierarchy of ani-

mate being" (Hallowell 1960:377; see also Black 1977a, 1977b). Contemporary Anishinaabe medicine persons depend upon the relationships they have established with more powerful beings, which may be realized through dreams, visions, or other altered states of consciousness, to diagnose, establish cause, and prescribe remedial actions. At a very general level, individuals call on Anishinaabe medicine persons to help them make sense of what is happening, and to request guidance and assistance in interpreting and/or responding to the situation at hand. While locally referred to as "medicine men" when speaking in English (and the majority were men), I call them Anishinaabe medicine persons, or simply medicine persons.

In Pichátaro, the term-frame interview along with other data converged to support a basic assumption that community members participated in the same understandings about illness and its care (although the application to a particular case could be variable). It was only when an illness could be a consequence of brujería that a few openly expressed reservations. The situation is much more complicated in the Anishinaabe community, especially with regard to explanations that Foster would categorize as personalistic and Young as externalizing. For these types of explanations, some individuals expressed strong disbelief and rejected the possibility that Anishinaabe medicine persons could have any competence in dealing with illness. While it is possible to say at a general level that community members share knowledge of a variety of theories about the causes of illness and misfortune, there is considerable intracultural variation in the extent to which individuals espouse these theories, use them to evaluate events, and the extent to which such understandings can be said to have motivational force (D'Andrade and Strauss 1992) for treatment decisions. Divergent opinions may be held by members of the same household.

As noted earlier, the research intent was essentially to implement the same approach used successfully in Pichátaro. As in Pichátaro, families were visited regularly to ask about ongoing illnesses and those that had occurred since the last visit. These cases illuminate the extent to which culturally available explanatory frameworks are relied on to make sense of illness experiences.

As patterns of care-seeking in the Anishinaabe community are diverse and complex (Garro 1998b), a brief summary of case histories is a useful general orientation. Thirteen separate visits were made to 61 randomly selected families over a six-to-eight-month period. Thirty-eight households (62 per cent) reported visiting a medicine person during the case collection period. Out of a total of 468 illness cases, 189 (40 per cent) were treated at home without recourse to any other source of care. Among the remaining 279 cases, 225 (81 per cent) were seen by a physician, 98 (35 per cent) were seen by medicine persons consulted in their role as mediators with other-than-human persons, 21 (8 per cent) sought remedies from a herbalist, and ten (4 per cent) consulted another type of practitioner (non-Anishinaabe herbalist, chiropractor, acupuncturist, psychologist). The percentages add up to more than 100 because some cases involved multiple treatment alternatives outside the home. Of the 225 cases seen by a physician, 66 (29 per cent) also consulted a medicine person. In some cases where only physicians were seen, family members made remarks indicating that consulting a medicine person was actively being considered. In cases where both physicians and medicine persons were consulted, physicians tended to be seen first. Thirty-two cases only resorted to a medicine person and not to a physician. In the 22 cases where neither a physician nor a medicine person was consulted, herbalists and other types of practitioners were seen. At a closing interview held during the final household visit, all but thirteen families reported consulting a medicine person in the past five years. When asked about all consultations with medicine persons, six families (10 per cent) reported never seeing one. During the first visit to the families, nine made statements indicating disbelief in the powers of medicine persons, though sometimes these statements referred specifically to medicine persons living in the community.

As in the Pichátaro study, early in the fieldwork I informally asked individuals to list the different illnesses they knew and followed up with questions about the nature and characteristics of the illnesses mentioned. Participants responded using Anishinaabemowin or English, and most often used both to varying degrees. The research objective was to use this information to design a term-frame questionnaire that would allow comparing understandings about illness between the two communities. Just as in the Pichátaro study, I hoped to discover group-

ings of illness terms and attribute frames that correspond to the ways that people talk about and respond to illness. Because a questionnaire's content reflects local cultural understandings and illness terminologies, a comparison of findings between Pichátaro and the Anishinaabe community would not be direct but rather based on interpretations of the relationships among illness terms and attribute frames for each of the two sites.

To my initial surprise, the free-listing part of the interview fell flat. Typically, only a small number of illness names were mentioned before the individual claimed to be unable to recall more (the most frequently mentioned included cold, flu, fever, high blood pressure, diabetes, and cancer; illnesses receiving somewhat less mention were rheumatism/arthritis, gallstones, stroke, polio, tuberculosis, and measles). Aches in parts of the body (e.g., headaches, stomachaches, backaches) might also come up during the course of the interview. The information obtained did not provide sufficient material to construct a truly representative term-frame interview format, Informal conversations about illness apart from the interviews indicated that the interview data did not come close to approaching the range of illness-related understandings in the community. As will be mentioned, illness talk outside of the interview context tended to be descriptions of how individuals were feeling (without illness labels) and discussions of the circumstances surrounding ill health, including its possible association with other instances of misfortune.

In retrospect, the free-listing interview did not proceed in the manner intended because, first, a noun-based free-listing task is at odds with the verb-based structure of Anishinaabemowin. In Anishinaabemowin a rich descriptive vocabulary is available to convey somatic experiences. In everyday talk, descriptions, which allow individuals to impart the particularities of their personal experience or what can be observed in others (e.g., children) are more common than illness labels. Yet the free-list interview asked for names and those that were given tended to be in English, a language which organizes reality in discrete chunks. Second, when someone is ill, making sense of the condition does not depend so much on determining the best label but rather on assessing the likely causes, especially if there are grounds for suspecting that a physician's treatment may not be sufficient. Talk about a specific illness episode may suggest a likely cause while still being framed in such a way as to leave causal possibilities open. Anishinaabe-mowin is a language with fine gradations in uncertainty and the expression of ambiguity. It is grounded in an awareness that others may perceive a situation differently and in an openness to the possibility of future change in one's present understanding of a situation, even after an illness situation has been resolved. Remaining at the level of describing symptoms is one way of maintaining an openness to alternative causes. In contrast, to refer to an illness by one of the labels seen as having been introduced by biomedical practitioners (as with high blood pressure or diabetes) essentially sets a boundary around the range of causal possibilities and implicitly conveys that the illness is best treated by a physician.

It is, however, incorrect to think that the free-listing interview provided little useful information. The following discussion develops themes first raised in the initial interview, supplemented with material from other interviews and from case histories. Once again, the objective is not to provide an exhaustive list but one that is relatively comprehensive for the explanatory frameworks serving to make sense of illness. It should go without saying that, despite its rural location, the Anishinaabe community does not stand apart from the broader societal contexts of Canada and North America. Among other influences, physicians, other bio-medical health professionals, schools, television, printed material, radio, and alternative forms of medicine have all influenced local understandings. In addition, it was not at all uncommon for community members to set up a contrast between the health-sustaining characteristics of the foods and lifestyle of the Anishinaabe past and sickness-inducing propensities of contemporary ways of living from which the Anishinaabeg cannot escape.

One strong impression from the free-listing interview was the profound level of concern about the number of people diagnosed with diabetes and high blood pressure in recent years. The comments made about these illnesses helped develop a structured interview format similar to a term-frame interview but dealing with only one illness (one for high blood pressure and a parallel one for

diabetes). Both these systematically structured questions and a series of open-ended questions were asked in a set of interviews with community members previously diagnosed with one of these two conditions. The range of explanatory principles raised pertain to other conditions as well and a summary of the findings are in the discussion that follows.

Many of the explanations proffered in the Anishinaabe community are also widely found throughout Canada and the United States and some resemble those from Pichátaro. For example, most instances of bruises and sprains, cuts or other wounds, toothaches, burns, and broken bones are seen as requiring no additional explanation. Similarly, as in Pichátaro and throughout North America, dietary upsets can lead to illness. That is, stomachaches or diarrhea can result from overeating or from food that has spoiled. However, while details of how illness can arise through the specific conditions of what and when one eats receive considerable elaboration by Pichatareños, the same did not hold in the Anishinaabe community, where simple matter-of-fact statements for transitory illnesses were the norm. However, there were numerous reflections on the long-term consequences of what one ate, often with differing emphases on what had the potential to lead to illness.

Another area sharing some correspondence with Pichátaro and more broadly with North America is the role played by contact with "cold" agents in the environment, although not at the same level of elaboration as in Pichátaro. Colds, fevers, and respiratory conditions like bronchitis and sometimes tuberculosis may be attributed to exposure to excessive cold or to being overheated and catching a chill. A minor illness like a cold may leave one in a weakened state and thus more susceptible to the effects of cold and the danger of having the illness worsen into pneumonia or bronchitis. Rheumatism and arthritis were also attributed to frequently getting wet or being exposed to the cold; fishermen were considered to be particularly vulnerable to these conditions. Women are considered vulnerable to the effects of cold during their menstrual periods. This malady, which can be fatal, is also considered something that physicians are unable to recognize or treat and is typically diagnosed by women (either the sufferer or a relative) and treated with a specific herbal remedy.

Unlike Pichátaro but similar to general lay models in Canada and the United States, the potential for illnesses to be passed from one to another is commonly accepted as a potential cause. Colds, flu, and tuberculosis were all talked about as something caught from someone and transmitted by means of "a bug," germs, or a virus. Similarly, measles was talked about as a common childhood illness which could spread to anyone. An unchecked illness could develop into something more serious, such as a child's fever developing into convulsions. Another concept likely based in biomedical teachings (and not characteristic of Pichátaro) is that of an illness being inherited through the family. Reference to genes was rare but talk about the possibility that an illness could run in the family was generally understood. At the same time, heredity appears not to be an explanatory notion of widespread saliency or application (Garro 1995, 1996).

Within the Anishinaabe community, there are a number of things which, if in a state of excess, have the potential to overstress the body and tip the balance toward ill health. Smoking too much can lead to cancer and other problems involving breathing and the lungs; eating too many greasy foods can lead to gallstones; drinking too much precipitates a variety of problems, including liver damage and birth defects such as fetal alcohol syndrome; and being under too much emotional stress can cause sickness and exacerbate most illnesses. High blood pressure, for example, is commonly seen to result from many sources of bodily imbalance (Garro 1988a). Although the most frequently cited cause is too much emotional stress or having too many worries, other catalysts include overexertion or working too hard, drinking too much alcohol, eating too much salty or greasy food, and being overweight. That these can act singly or jointly suggests that they are seen to work in analogous fashion to affect the body, even though the pathophysiological mechanisms are not specified. The same set of multicausal possibilities may explain diabetes. The possibility of a combinatory impact from quite diverse sources contrasts with the modified humoral-balance system operative in Pichátaro, which depends on the identification of specific sources of imbalance. Further, and consistent with the probabilistic character of Anishinaabemowin as well as the am-

biguity conveyed by biomedical practitioners, conversational deliberations concerning specific cases of diabetes or high blood pressure may be framed in terms of possibilities (or probabilities) rather than established certainties.

There are a couple of basic and generally applicable terms in Anishinaabemowin which indicate the state of being sick. Assigning a name, describing symptoms, or assessing probable cause are all ways of contextualizing and adding specificity to a state of ill health. Another way to add meaning is to modify a basic term in a way that connects with a broad causal category, as when a condition is referred to as an example of a "white man's sickness." White man's illnesses are seen as occurring after Europeans came to North America. Although potentially any number of illness episodes may come to be understood as white man's sickness, this phrase is commonly (although not routinely) coupled with well-known illnesses such as measles, chicken pox, tuberculosis, high blood pressure, diabetes, and cancer. To use such a label is to make a statement, at times with political overtones, about the social epidemiology of these diseases by embedding their presence in the community within the continuing disruption and destruction of the Anishinaabe way of life. Reference to measles, chicken pox, and tuberculosis as white man's sicknesses affirms that they were introduced by European settlers. Health problems linked to alcohol may also be referred to as white man's sickness when one intends to indicate that alcohol was once not a presence in the Anishinaabe community. Discussions about diabetes, high blood pressure, and cancer often highlighted strongly articulated contrasts between the healthy and fortifying foods obtained through Anishinaabe subsistence activities in the past and the comparatively unhealthy reliance on the store-bought foods of the present. For some, it was simply the inferiority of the present-day foods that predisposed one to illness, whereas "wild food" was inherently fortifying. Although several commentators deplored the large amount of junk food and sugar-laden foods eaten by Anishinaabeg today, by far the most commonly cited source of bodily disturbance associated with white man's sickness was the contaminating and insidious omnipresence of "poisons" in comestibles. These included chemicals and other substances sprayed on crops and injected into animals as well as those added during food processing and canning. For some, these substances were unavoidable due to widespread environmental contamination affecting all things ingested, including tobacco, water, and wild foods. Referring to diabetes, high blood pressure, or cancer as white man's sickness shifts responsibility away from the individual (e.g., for eating too much sugar or too much salt, smoking too much, or worrying too much) to a societal etiology that is based in actions essentially occurring outside the Anishinaabe community. This is more than a rhetorical claim, however, as actions taken in response to diabetes relate to how the condition is understood, including when diabetes is understood as exclusively a white man's sickness. Still, few individuals consistently affirmed the primacy of white man's sickness in accounting for a given illness. It was more common to mix this explanation with other potential sources of bodily imbalance, such as those mentioned in the preceding paragraph (Garro 1995, 1996, 2000).

A subsequent structured interview held with 35 individuals (mostly women) provided a different outlook on Anishinaabe illness theories. The interview was organized around a set of contrastive questions inquiring when a given treatment would be used. For example, a participant would be asked when she would consult a physician rather than a medicine person or when she would consult a medicine person rather than a physician. All possible combinations of home-based treatment, herbalists, Anishinaabe medicine persons, and physicians were contrasted. Following this, past illness cases in the household were discussed. Almost all reported using each of the different treatment alternatives, and this was reflected in their illness case histories.

Responses given to some of the contrastive questions highlight the perceived link between behavior and explanatory frameworks. The majority of illnesses are initially assumed to be treatable either at home or by physicians (whose care and remedies are provided free of charge). Sometimes herbalists or medicine persons are contacted and asked for a specific remedy. An example of this is a request for a herbal remedy said to dissolve gallstones, eliminating future pain and avoiding the need for further medical procedures. Often, such requests were reported as occurring after a visit to a physician for diagnosis.

By far the most common reason given for seeking the assistance of a medicine person was to ascertain whether an illness was one that can only be resolved through the mediation of a medicine person with other-than-human persons. These other-than-human persons may bestow a variety of "gifts," "blessings," "knowledge," "medicine," or "powers" on human beings, who then can accomplish things that would not otherwise be possible (Hallowell 1955:104; Black 1977a). Taking many forms, including superior prowess in hunting or warfare, one of these gifts is the ability to confer with and gain otherwise unattainable knowledge from these other-than-human persons. If truly gifted, medicine persons act as intermediaries or mediums on behalf of those who seek assistance.

One goes to a medicine person to learn why otherwise unexplainable troubles have occurred and what can be done to stop their recurrence or to remedy the situation. Medicine persons may advise whether a condition is a treatable one and whether a physician is an appropriate source of care. Some problems can only be dealt with properly under a medicine person's guidance, even though a physician or other biomedical practitioner may be able to treat the surface manifestations. If nothing can be done to rectify the present situation (e.g., a death or an abnormality present at birth), the medicine person may be able to advise on how to prevent future problems stemming from the same source. Conditions fitting one of the latter two descriptions are referred to as "Anishinaabe sickness," and this is the other main way (in addition to white man's sickness) in which a basic term indicating the state of being ill may be modified. Anishinaabe sickness may be suspected when a physician is unable to cure an illness or if the illness does not seem to be an ordinary one (i.e., one that seems to be satisfactorily accounted for with reference to one or more of the explanations presented in the preceding paragraphs). Informants explained that only a medicine person might be consulted, or consulted first, if certain features of the illness or illness context aroused forebodings about Anishinaabe sickness. In the illness case histories, multiple instances of this type were recounted, showing what led families to suspect Anishinaabe sickness for what might otherwise be considered straightforward injuries or an uncomplicated illness. In some instances, these suspicions, even though voiced, did not lead directly to consultations with a medicine person, leaving the perceived causal ambiguity unresolved. If troubles persist, suspicions about earlier events may be revisited and motivate resort to a medicine person.

When one seeks the aid of a medicine person, the combination of available clues and cultural knowledge often points in the direction of Anishinaabe sickness. Without the certainty of direct communication with other-than-human persons, however, these appearances may be deceiving. Even if one were relatively certain about causation, guidance would still be needed with regard to the course of action required to ensure that the trouble is brought to an end. The epistemological stance is one where the most certain route for acquiring knowledge about the etiology of troubling experiences and their treatment is through direct interaction with other-than-human persons, which typically occurs through private experiences of dreams and visions. Yet the majority of individuals have not been gifted in ways that allow for these direct interactions on a routine basis. In seeking the help of a medicine person, one seeks to enter into relationships that a medicine person has already established with other-than-human persons. In this relational epistemology, what is communicated by other-than-human persons to medicine persons through dreams, visions, or other means provides a privileged vantage point for elucidating the essence of an illness experience and transmitting counsel concerning the most appropriate course of action. The act of consulting with a medicine person signals a conviction in the ontological reality of the Anishinaabe behavioral environment. Further, those seeking assistance must have complete confidence in the medicine person's gifts. The same is not true for treatment by a herbalist. Lack of conviction by one seeking help, at either a general level or in terms of a specific individual, can be used to explain the seeming inability of a medicine person to cure an illness or the failure to provide an accurate prognosis. In some of the illnesses recorded, help was sought from a medicine person without any knowledge or involvement on the part of the afflicted individual or, in the case of a child, the parents. Because conviction is important to achieving a cure, it is counterproductive to involve individuals who do not share a positive stance toward the powers of medicine persons. For cases of Anishinaabe sickness, the afflicted person often does not need to have direct interaction with a medicine person to be successfully treated.

A feature of Anishinaabe illness is that it is grounded in discrete and identifiable, or potentially knowable, actions of human beings, alive or dead, and understood with reference to tenets governing social relationships. According to Hallowell (1963:410), "causes of illness are sought by the Ojibwa within their web of interpersonal relations, rather than apart from it. This is consistent with a world view in which the interrelations of *persons* are of paramount importance." For example, one type of Anishinaabe illness mentioned in the contrastive questioning was brought about by a dead person's desire to be joined by another family member, usually a beloved child. The dead person's efforts to bring this about result in the living person's enduring despondency over the preceding death and in the individual's recurring dreams of the dead person. These indicators of the dead person's continued presence in the living person's daily life suggest the need for the intercession of a medicine person, lest the dead person's desire be realized. Only someone gifted with the ability to intercede with other-than-human persons can shed light on what is going on and what is an appropriate response.

Most visits to a medicine person take place when one or both of two explanatory frameworks are under active consideration. Both involve violations of a proper Anishinaabe way of life. The first is "bad medicine" (Hallowell's "sorcery" [1955:173] and "witchcraft" [1992:96]). The "harming powers" of bad medicine "include the ability to cause another's death, illness, or misfortune without being present or in physical contact" (Black 1977a:149). Although bad medicine often strikes the intended target, there is some unpredictability in its use; victims may accidentally come into contact with bad medicine and suffer unintended consequences. Bad medicine can be used to covertly influence other people, objects, or events in order to benefit the user or to harm others. Jealousy, envy, anger, laziness, greed, desire for revenge or retaliation, desire to avoid privation, and lust are seen to motivate individuals to resort to bad medicine. Even when bad medicine causes no direct harm to others (e.g., influencing a courtroom judge to dismiss charges or to impose a lesser sentence for a victimless offense; or winning a competition), its use is a profound violation of norms governing social relationships between human beings. As bad medicine causes others to "perform acts or enter into a state they wouldn't have if left to their own autonomy" (Black 1977a:150), its use contravenes the high cultural value on an individual's right to self-determination.

Although a medicine person conveys information about the cause of illness, there is a general proscription against divulging the source of bad medicine. The ability to wield bad medicine is hidden and not advertised; it is understood that a skilled user's private evil intent may be masked by public amiability. Hallowell (1960:378) characterizes the Ojibwa as having a general cognitive orientation toward the perceptual world which accepts the possibility that appearances may be misleading. In many instances, sufferers are not sure who is to blame or may consider themselves to be accidental victims. Even when sufferers feel certain they know who is responsible, confirmation is elusive and an element of doubt remains. Also, there is significant diversity among community members in the extent to which Anishinaabe sickness is considered a credible account.

In the illness case histories collected, misfortunes ultimately attributed to bad medicine took myriad forms and included flat tires, equipment and vehicle malfunctions, losing a talent contest, a house fire, relatively minor physical problems, striking alterations in an individual's behavior, loss of a spouse's affection, seemingly accidental injuries (ranging from a broken finger to quite serious injuries incurred in a car crash), acute and prolonged illnesses, "twisted mouth," a miscarriage, and a couple of sudden deaths. A series of misfortunes, not always involving illness, may be linked as stemming from the same underlying cause. Even relatively minor illnesses and/or events may raise suspicions of bad medicine. The suspicions may not be acted upon immediately, but kept in mind and re-evaluated in the future in light of other events (Garro 1998b). This is different from Pichátaro, where the effects of brujería are localized in individual bodies and where brujería tends to be the explanation of last resort.

The second major explanatory framework links illness and other problems to transgressions that lie outside the realm of everyday and observable interactions between normal living humans. Everyday difficulties do not necessitate the assistance of other-than-human persons; such problems may be addressed through human means. But illness and misfortune, as Hallowell (1992:24) puts it, often indicate that "there had been some departure from the accepted values that served to channel the relations of human beings" with other persons. Proper Anishinaabe behavior requires that one enter into respectful relationships with other animate beings, with obligations to behave appropriately toward sources of power. In addition, it is imperative that obligations to other-than-human persons be fulfilled. When these respectful relations and obligations are breached, illness and misfortune may result. The term *ondjine* is used to indicate an illness or misfortune occurring "for a reason," attributable to something that someone once did. This infraction may occur without intent, unknowingly, or even in an attempt to be helpful. There is typically a time lag, often spanning years, between the act and the eventual illness, and offspring may suffer the consequences of their parents' misdeeds.

With one exception, all the explanations for ondjine provided here are based on material from the illness case history data, but limited to five diverse yet representative examples. The first is that of an infant who cries and cannot be comforted. There are a number of possible reasons—teething, a temperature, or simply that a child is just "born that way." But often the fussiness of a "colicky" infant is seen to signal the need for the child to be given an Anishinaabe name (and the parents' failure to carry out this responsibility). An Anishinaabe name confers some protection on the infant and establishes its relationships with other-than-human persons. The power to bestow names is a gift given to some individuals; an exception to the general rule that Anishinaabe sickness requires the attention of a medicine person (although medicine persons often have this gift).

A different example involves an infraction of appropriate behavior by women, especially when they are menstruating, but whether this type of illness is considered to be ondjine is not clear. Menstrual blood can cause illness in males and there were several cases in the household data involving young boys who were inadvertently affected. Women are expected to respect this power through appropriate behavior; all women, and especially menstruating women, should not step over a male or even over a piece of clothing that will be worn by a male, and should take care that males do not use their bath towels.

Yet another reason for illness results from the failure of individuals to fulfill an obligation promised to or imposed by other-than-human persons. For example, as part of obtaining the assistance of other-than-human persons, one might incur the obligation of holding an annual feast and preparing offerings. If an obligation is overlooked or not done properly, illness or misfortune may result. As well, any item that is associated with other-than-human persons must be treated respectfully and in a manner to ensure that damage does not occur. This includes offerings (e.g., colored ribbons tied on a tree), items prepared under the direction of a medicine person, and any implements used by a medicine person.

The fourth explanation for ondjine is consistent with this obligational ethos, but no illness case histories are available. Ondjine from this source is suspected of some but admitted by no one, so all of the cases in my field notes are inferred rather than reported. Ondjine is an inevitable consequence of the use of bad medicine. The violation of another individual's autonomy through bad medicine is an inappropriate use of power. Eventually, this abuse of power boomerangs, bringing illness and misfortune to the user or to members of his or her family. Any crippling illness or painful death is likely to be seen by someone in the community as a confirmation of his or her suspicions concerning the use of bad medicine by the afflicted individual or a close family member (Garro 1990; Hallowell 1942:77).

The final explanation is by far the mostly frequently encountered and the majority of all cases reported were of this type. It also is grounded in Anishinaabe expectations about proper relationships, but this time between humans and animals. That humans need to kill animals to sustain life is acceptable, but this should be done gratefully and without causing undue suffering. Otherwise, animals should be left alone and it is inappropriate for human beings to interfere with their autonomy. Ondjine can occur if an animal is injured or killed for sport, or when an animal is killed and only a small part of the animal is used with the rest left to decay. If, even when hunting for subsistence, a hunter merely injures an animal and it escapes, ondjine may be an eventual consequence. Why this happens—bad luck, a poor shot, carelessness—is irrelevant. Further, attempting to assist an injured or orphaned animal can also result in ondjine, as can an injury to an animal that occurs without intent to harm. A high proportion of the ondjine cases recorded involved interactions with animals during childhood (with the affliction often visited on the transgressor's offspring or grandchildren many years later).

While some of the explanatory frameworks for illness are similar to those present more widely within Canadian society, much of the preceding discussion has drawn attention to the embedding of illness and misfortune within the webs of relationships that constitute the Anishinaabe behavioral environment. Talk about white man's sickness extends these relationships beyond the Anishinaabe community into the broader Canadian and North American context. Such talk often contains an explicit critique of the changes that have been imposed on the community and places the responsibility for illness outside the Anishinaabe community while highlighting the perception that contemporary Anishinaabeg are powerless to reverse such trends. The Anishinaabe imputation of a social origin for the ever-increasing rates of diabetes and high blood pressure must be recognized by any effort that aspires to make cross-cultural comparisons at the level of cultural meaning. White man's sickness cannot be divested of the social and historical relations seen to produce illness.

The overview of the culturally based rationale for Anishinaabe sickness underscores the importance of interpersonal relationships and how they enter into explanations of illness and misfortune. Special consideration is given to what may transpire when certain normative expectations are breached, even if this occurs without the knowledge of the transgressor. Indeed, in cases of ondjine, the individual responsible typically gains insight about the infraction only under the guidance of a medicine person. The individual who is considered to be aware of doing wrong (i.e., the self-serving perpetrator of bad medicine) also receives the strongest negative sanction. Accepting the reality of Anishinaabe sickness requires adoption of their relational epistemology, obligational ethos, and ontological assumptions.

With regard to the comparative frameworks of Murdock, Foster, and Young, the findings from the Anishinaabe community pose some challenges. As noted previously, accommodating white man's sickness and the explanations associated with it is problematic for all three frameworks. In addition, the polar typologies are overwhelmed by the complexity and diversity of illness explanations. It is also of interest to note that both Foster in his personalistic system and Young in his externalizing system posit intentional pathogenic agents who cause illness. This would certainly fit the situation of bad medicine. But ondjine presents more difficulty. As Hallowell first pointed out, other-than-human persons "are not characterized by any punishing role" (Hallowell 1963:411); "their relations to man are benevolent" (Hallowell 1966:462). An illness "thought to eventuate from the violation of moral obligations" to other-than-human persons "cannot be interpreted as stemming from their anger" (Hallowell 1963:418). There is no retributive pathogenic agent for illness referred to as ondjine. Indeed, it can be plausibly argued that the whole concept of a punishing agency (who sits in judgment of another person's behavior) runs counter to the deeply ingrained ethos of individual autonomy and self-determination.

Murdock, relying exclusively on Hallowell's writings, did include the Saulteaux (around 1930) as one of the 139 cultures coded in his 1980 study. Examining Murdock's coding scheme and how it applies in this instance, before looking at his actual determinations, indicates that the presence and importance of sorcery, despite the aforementioned reservations about the use of the term "supernatural," can be easily supported by Hallowell's work, as well as in the contemporary community. In addition, Hallowell (1963:409) distinguished between "serious cases of sickness," which called for explanation, and other "ailments like colds, headaches, disturbances of digestion and so forth, which are considered inconsequential." In an early essay, Hallowell (1939:181) referred to "fortuitous circumstances which may result in broken limbs, cuts, wounds, colds, minor ailments." These conditions are captured under Murdock's theories of natural causation as "accident" and coded as minor or relatively unimportant.

What about ondjine? Within Murdock's scheme, there are two possible options, but neither is truly satisfactory. One, that or spirit aggression, which Murdock (1980:20) describes as "the attribution of illness to the direct hostile, arbitrary or punitive action of some malevolent or affronted supernatural being," has already been raised and rejected. The second is that of mystical retribution, which is defined as "acts in violation of some taboo or moral injunction when conceived as causing illness directly" (Murdock 1980:18) and is part of the larger category of theories of mystical causation which account "for the impairment of health as the automatic consequence of some act or experience of the victim mediated by some putative impersonal causal relationship" (Murdock 1980:17; italics omitted). For the Saulteaux, Murdock characterizes this theory as an important auxiliary cause. At first glance, this description might seem apropos for ondjine. Hallowell refers often to a "disease sanction" based in the "belief that illness will invariably follow deviations from established codes of conduct" (1942:86). If, for example, a human being fails to fulfill any obligation to an other-than-human person, "sickness 'follows him' as a matter of course" (Hallowell 1966:462). At the same time, the idea that this disease sanction is perpetuated through an "impersonal causal relationship" is at odds with the social relational aspect of ondjine that is so integral to its conceptualization and remedy. Hallowell goes so far as to deny the cultural appropriateness of a concept or impersonal force: "All the effective agents of events throughout the entire behavioral environment of the Ojibwa are selves—my own self or other selves. *Impersonal* forces are never the causes of events. *Somebody* is always responsible" (Hallowell 1955:181). This is the kind of disjunction that needs to be addressed in an effort to develop a comparative framework that takes cultural meaning seriously. One issue to be resolved is whether this could be accomplished through careful attention to use of language and significant modification of the existing classificatory unit (as well as the overarching group in which it is embedded), or whether something more sweeping is required.

There are several additional observations regarding Murdock's framework that are not found in Hallowell's writings but come out of the contemporary research in the Anishinaabe community. First, although illness seen as linked to a behavioral infraction by women, especially while menstruating, has been discussed here as ondjine, there is no consensus in the community about this label. Murdock's framework would code this illness theory as one of contagion ("coming into contact with some purportedly polluting object, substance, or person"), and notes that "menstrual blood or menstruating women" as a source of contagion "preponderates in North America" (1980:18). In a cross-cultural comparative study, placing this as indicative of a theory based on inappropriate behavior toward a source of power or a theory of contagion would involve a judgment call (and likely an explanatory footnote). A second observation relates to the attribution of illness to a dead person's desire to be joined by a living family member. This explanation does not fit within any of Murdock's existing categories. although it would not be difficult to modify, rename, and broaden what he refers to as "soul loss" (without the overarching framework of "animistic causation") to encompass the Anishinaabe theory. Finally, as has been discussed, there are several illness theories that stand apart from interrelationships among animate beings. Some of these (infection, accident, stress) are found within Murdock's framework, but others (such as "running in the family," environmental exposure, and diverse sources of bodily imbalance) do not easily fit within the scheme.

CONCLUDING COMMENTS

This examination of comparative schemes for explanations of illness within two distinctive cultural settings has revealed shortcomings in all three conceptual frameworks. Implicit assumptions underlying each limit their utility. While this seems especially problematic for Murdock's scheme, which most clearly projects onto other cultures' ontological premises and "categorical abstractions derived from Western thought" (Hallowell 1955:88), such as supernatural, natural, animistic, and mystical, the other two frameworks examined are also problematic in this regard. In addition, none of the three is able to encompass the full range of understandings in either of the sites. Even when frameworks aspire to a very high level of generality, as with the two polar typologies, this accomplishment can only be achieved by glossing over major differences between cultures. What is truly gained by lumping biomedicine and the situation described for Pichátaro as examples of internalizing systems, or by contrasting both systems with the externalizing system as exemplified by Hallowell's description of the Ojibwa? Yet even at this level of abstraction, it has not been possible to come up with a single dimension of contrast along which societies can be positioned. Also problematic for the dichotomies is the presence of diversity within a cultural setting, so clearly seen in the Anishinaabe community. The development of a comparative scheme that illuminates meaningful differences and similarities across cultural settings is a demanding and complex task that requires more than a simple contrast set.

At the same time, it is important to stress that while I advocate a wholesale revision at a lexical as well as conceptual level, I am not recommending a wholesale rejection of the existing frameworks. It is possible to productively use the tension between existing comparative schemes and an effort to understand illness theories at the level of cultural meaning to inform the process of making cross-cultural comparisons. Any effort to organize and present cultural data carries the imprint of the observer; this is unavoidable. However, confronting the implications of the three schemes examined did compel me to consider more carefully the grounding for my analytic and ethnographic claims. In itself, even without a comparative agenda, this would seem a useful exercise for any effort to communicate cultural understandings about illness. Attempting to grasp the epistemological and ontological assumptions underpinning illness understandings in Pichátaro and the Anishinaabe community provided a useful counterpoint when thinking through assumptions present in the comparative schemes. The highlighting of areas of correspondence in explanations of illness between Pichátaro and the Anishinaabe community, such as the presence of sorcery or the link between emotion and illness, forces an appraisal of how much generalization is acceptable (e.g., how should mal de ojo in Pichátaro be handled?).

A significant component of the research described here is attention to how individuals in specific cultural settings make sense of and deal with illness. It is critical that the focus not be on representing the knowledge of healing specialists but on understanding the range of explanatory frameworks commonly relied upon by those with no specialized knowledge about the treatment of illness. In both Pichátaro and the Anishinaabe community, structured data collection methods were used to accomplish this aim and to gain an appreciation of the extent of intracultural variability. If ethnographically feasible, the benefits of collecting data that allow for direct comparisons across informants should not be underestimated. Still, as the discussion of the free-listing task and the term-frame interview in the Anishinaabe community illustrates, these tools themselves are based in assumptions about the nature of reality. There is no methodological recipe that will fit all settings. An absolutely essential feature of the research design in both locations, however, was to follow actual illness cases in a systematic manner. Without this information it would be impossible to assess the relative importance of available explanatory frameworks as cultural resources when dealing with illness.

REFERENCES

Anderson, R 1996. *Magic, Science and Health: The Aims and Achievements of Medical Anthropology.* Fort Worth.

Black. M. B. 1977a. Ojibwa Power Belief System. *The Anthropology of Power: Ethnographic Studies from Asia, Oceania, and the New World,* eds. R. D. Fogelson and R. N. Adams. pp. 141–51. New York.

———. 1977b. Ojibwa Taxonomy and Percept Ambiguity, *Ethos* 5:90–118.

Brown, P. J (ed.) 1998. *Understanding and Applying Medical Anthropology.* Mountain View CA.

D'Andrade, R. G, N. R. Quinn, S. B. Nerlove, and A. K. Romney. 1972. Categories of Disease in American-English and Mexican Spanish. *Multidimensional Scaling: Theory and Applications in the Behavioral Sciences,* Vol. 2, eds. A. K. Romney, R. N. Shepard, and S. B. Nerlove, pp. 9–54. New York.

D'Andrade, R., and C. Strauss (eds). 1992. *Human Motives and Cultural Models.* Cambridge.

Foster, G. M. 1976. Disease Etiologies in Non-Western Medical Systems. *American Anthropologist* 78:773–82.

Garro, L. C. 1983. *Variation and Consistency in a Mexican Folk Illness Belief System.* Unpublished Ph.D, dissertation, University of California, Irvine.

———. 1986, Intracultural Variation in Folk Medical Knowledge: A Comparison between Curers and Non-Curers, *American Anthropologist* 88:351–70.

———. 1988a. Explaining High Blood Pressure: Variation in Knowledge about Illness. *American Ethnologist* 15:98–119.

———. 1988b. Commentary on Paper by C. H. Browner, B. R. Ortiz, and A. J. Rubel, "A Methodology for Cross-Cultural Ethnomedical Research." *Current Anthropology* 29:691–92.

———. 1990. Continuity and Change. The Interpretation of Illness in an Anishinaabe (Ojibway) Community. *Culture, Medicine and Psychiatry* 14:417–54.

———. 1995. Individual or Social Responsibility? Explanations of Diabetes in an Anishinaabe (Ojibway) Community. *Social Science and Medicine* 40:37–46.

———. 1996. Intracultural Variation in Causal Accounts of Diabetes: A Comparison of Three Canadian Anishinaabe Communities. *Culture, Medicine and Psychiatry* 20:381–420.

———. 1998a. On the Rationality of Decision Making Studies: Part 1: Decision Models of Treatment Choice. *Medical Anthropology Quarterly* 12:319–40.

———. 1998b. On the Rationality of Decision Making Studies: Part 2. Divergent Rationalities. *Medical Anthropology Quarterly* 12:341–55.

———. 2000. Remembering What One Knows and the Construction of the Past: A Comparison of Cultural Consensus Theory and Cultural Schema Theory, *Ethos* 28(3):275–319.

Gray, J. P. 1998. Regional Patterning in Illness Theories: Analyses with Different Types of Optimal Scaling. *Cross-Cultural Research* 32:3–36.

Hallowell, A I 1939. Sin, Sex and Sickness in Saulteaux Belief. *British Journal of Medical Psychology* 18, Part 2:191–97.

———. 1942. *The Role of Conjuring in Saultcaux Society.* Philadelphia.

———. 1955. *Culture and Experience.* Philadelphia.

———. 1960. Ojibwa Ontology, Behavior and World View. *Culture in History: Essays in Honor of Paul Radin,* ed. S. Diamond, pp. 19–52. New York.

———. 1963. Ojibwa World View and Disease. *Man's Image in Medicine and Anthropology,* ed I. Galdston, pp. 258–315. New York.

———. 1966. The Role of Dreams in Ojibwa Culture. *The Dream and Human Societies,* eds. G. E. von Grunebaum and R. Caillois, pp. 267–92. Berkeley.

———. 1976. *Contributions to Anthropology: Selected Papers of A. Irving Hallowell,* Chicago.

———. 1992. *The Ojibwa of Berens River, Manitoba: Ethnography into History,* ed. J. S. H. Brown. Fort Worth.

Loustaunau, M. O., and E. J. Sobo. 1997. *The Cultural Context of Health, Illness, and Medicine,* Westport CT.

Moore, C. C. 1988. An Optimal Scaling of Murdock's Theories of Illness Data—An Approach to the Problem of Interdependence. *Behavior Science Research* 22:161–79.

Murdock, G. P. 1980. *Theories of Illness: A World Survey.* Pittsburgh.

Murdock, G. P., and D. R. White, 1969. Standard Cross-Cultural Sample. *Ethnology* 8:329–69.

Rogers, E. S. 1962. The Round Lake Ojibwa. University of Toronto, Royal Ontario Museum, Art and Archaeology Division, Occasional Paper no. 5. Toronto.

Rubel, A. J., C. W. O'Nell, and R. Collado-Ardón. 1984. *Susto: A Folk Illness.* Berkeley.

Waldram, J. B. 1997. *The Way of the Pipe: Aboriginal Spirituality and Symbolic Healing in Canadian Prisons.* Petersborough.

Young, A. 1976. Internalizing and Externalizing Medical Belief Systems: An Ethiopian Example. *Social Science and Medicine* 10:147–56.

Young, J. C., and L. C. Garro, 1994. *Medical Choice in a Mexican Village.* Prospect Heights.

■ ■ ■ ■ ■ ■ ■ ■ ■

27   THE MINDFUL BODY: A PROLEGOMENON TO FUTURE WORK IN MEDICAL ANTHROPOLOGY

Nancy Scheper-Hughes and Margaret M. Lock

The previous selection presented three comparative frameworks and showed how cross-cultural studies highlight the complexity of cultural models for thinking about illness and how to manage it. This selection is a keystone in critical medical anthropology that analyzes accepted scientific categories and assumptions underlying scholarly research and interpretation. In particular, the selection focuses on the epistemological tradition of Cartesian dualism that divides the spirit from matter, the mind from the body, and the subjective from the objective (see selections 3 and 11). As we saw in the last selection, although these divisions may continue to influence Western scholarship, they are not cultural universals. Indeed, there are many examples of philosophical traditions that emphasize inclusiveness or complementarity rather than exclusiveness or opposition, such as Chinese yin/yang cosmology.

The selection takes the body as a tool for analyzing cultural constructs related to health and well-being. By examining three conceptual and epistemological levels synthesized in the notions of the individual body, social body, and body politic, the authors suggest a model that does not depend on Cartesian dualisms for comparing beliefs and practices across cultures. The authors are self-reflexive about social and politico-economic contexts for scientific categories and the broader cultural concepts in which they are embedded, so that biomedical ways of thinking may be deconstructed without criticizing those who operate under them. They suggest that greater attention to human emotions could help to bridge the mind–body, nature–culture gap. As the following selections indicate, feelings generated by meaningful symbols and experiences can play significant roles in both causing and curing illness (see also selections 8 and 9).

Questions to keep in mind

Why was the separation of body from mind or soul in Descartes' time so important to the development of the natural sciences?

Why do the authors feel that it is important to challenge it now?

Source: Scheper-Hughes, N. and M. Lock 1987. "The Mindful Body: A Prolegomenon to Future Work in Medical Anthropology." © by the American Anthropological Association. Reprinted from *Medical Anthropology Quarterly* Vol. 1 No. 1 pp. 6–41, by permission.

How do cultural concepts of personhood relate to ideas about disease causation?

What are some examples of body symbolism, and how do these differ from the body as symbol?

Have you have observed examples of the body politic exercising control over individual bodies?

How does the discussion of the medical gaze and the training of biomedical professionals to disregard suffering and social context in this selection compare to the selections by Malone (selection 10) and Davenport (selection 11)?

How does the discussion of emotion connect with Garro's observations about the way emotion-caused illness in Mexico defies classification under the schemes developed by Western anthropologists?

The body is the first and most natural tool of man
—*Marcel Mauss (1979[1950])*

Despite its title this article does not pretend to offer a comprehensive review of the anthropology of the body, which has its antecedents in physical, psychological, and symbolic anthropology, as well as in ethnoscience, phenomenology, and semiotics. Rather, it should be seen as an attempt to integrate aspects of anthropological discourse on the body into current work in medical anthropology. We refer to this as a prolegomenon because we believe that insofar as medical anthropology has failed to problematize the body, it is destined to fall prey to the biological fallacy and related assumptions that are paradigmatic to biomedicine. Foremost among these assumptions is the much-noted Cartesian dualism that separates mind from body, spirit from matter, and real (i.e., visible, palpable) from unreal. Since this epistemological tradition is a cultural and historical construction and not one that is universally shared, it is essential that we begin our project in medical anthropology with a suspension of our usual belief and cultural commitment to the mind/body, seen/unseen, natural/supernatural, magical/rational, rational/irrational, and real/unreal oppositions and assumptions that have characterized much of ethnomedical anthropology to date. We will begin from an assumption of the body as simultaneously a physical and symbolic artifact, as both naturally and culturally produced, and as securely anchored in a particular historical moment.

In the following pages we will critically examine and call into question various concepts that have been privileged in Western thinking for centuries and which have determined the ways in which the body has been perceived in scientific biomedicine and in anthropology. This article is descriptive and diagnostic. Its goal is both the definition of an important domain for anthropological inquiry and an initial search for appropriate concepts and analytic tools.

. . .

THE THREE BODIES

Essential to our task is a consideration of the relations among what we will refer to here as the "three bodies."[1] At the first and perhaps most self-evident level is the individual body, understood in the phenomenological sense of the lived experience of the body-self. We may reasonably assume that all people share at least some intuitive sense of the embodied self as existing apart from other individual bodies (Mauss 1985[1938]). However, the constituent parts of the body—mind, matter, psyche, soul, self, etc.—and their relations to each other, and the ways in which the body is received and experienced in health and sickness are, of course, highly variable.

At the second level of analysis is the social body, referring to the representational uses of the body as a natural symbol with which to think about nature, society, and culture, as Mary Douglas (1970) suggested. Here our discussion follows the well-trodden path of social, symbolic, and structuralist anthropologists who have demonstrated the constant exchange of meanings between the "natural" and the social worlds. The body in health offers a model of organic wholeness; the body in sickness offers a model of social disharmony, conflict, and disintegration. Reciprocally, society in "sickness" and in "health" offers a model for understanding the body.

At the third level of analysis is the body politic, referring to the regulation, surveillance, and control of bodies (individual and collective) in reproduction and sexuality, in work and in leisure, in sickness and other forms of deviance and human difference. There are many types of polity, ranging from the acephalous anarchy of "simple" foraging societies, in which deviants may be punished by total social ostracism and consequently by death (see Briggs 1970; Turnbull 1962), through chieftainships, monarchies, oligarchies, democracies, and modern totalitarian states. In all of these polities the stability of the body politic rests on its ability to regulate populations (the social body) *and* to discipline individual bodies. A great deal has been written about the regulation and control of individual and social bodies in complex, industrialized societies. Foucault's work is exemplary in this regard (1973, 1975, 1979, 1980a). Less has been written about the ways in which preindustrial societies control their populations and institutionalize means for producing docile bodies and pliant minds in the service of some definition of collective stability, health, and social well-being.

The "three bodies" represent, then, not only three separate and overlapping units of analysis, but also three different theoretical approaches and epistemologies: phenomenology (individual body, the lived self), structuralism and symbolism (the social body), and poststructuralism (the body politic). . . .

THE INDIVIDUAL BODY

How Real Is Real?
The Cartesian Legacy

A singular premise guiding Western science and clinical medicine (and one, we hasten to add, that is responsible for its awesome efficacy) is its commitment to a fundamental opposition between spirit and matter, mind and body, and (underlying this) real and unreal. We are reminded of a grand rounds presentation before a class of first-year medical students that concerned the case of a middle-aged woman suffering from chronic and debilitating headaches. In halting sentences the patient explained before the class of two hundred that her husband was an alcoholic who occasionally beat her, that she had been virtually housebound for the past five years looking after her senile and incontinent mother-in-law, and that she worries constantly about her teenage son who is flunking out of high school. Although the woman's story elicited considerable sympathy from the students, many grew restless with the line of clinical questioning, and one finally interrupted the professor to demand "But what is the *real* cause of the headaches?"

The medical student, like many of her classmates, interpreted the stream of social information as extraneous and irrelevant to the *real* biomedical diagnosis. She wanted information on the neurochemical changes which she understood as constituting the true causal explanation. This kind of radically materialist thinking, characteristic of clinical biomedicine, is the product of a Western epistemology extending as far back as Aristotle's starkly biological view of the human soul in *De Anima*. As a basis for clinical practice, it can be found in the Hippocratic corpus (ca. 400 B.C.). Hippocrates[2] and his students were determined to erradicate the vestiges of magico-religious thinking about the human body and to introduce a rational basis for clinical practice that would challenge the power of the ancient folk healers or "charlatans" and "magi," as Hippocrates labeled his medical competitors. In a passage from his treatise on epilepsy, ironically entitled "On the Sacred Disease," Hippocrates (Adams 1939: 355–356) cautioned the Greek *iatros* (physician) to treat only what was observable and palpable to the senses:

> I do not believe that the so-called Sacred Disease is any more divine or sacred than any other disease, but that on the contrary, just as other diseases have a nature and a definite cause, so does this one, too, have a nature and a cause. . . . It is my opinion that those who first called this disease sacred were the sort of people that we now call 'magi.' These magicians are vagabonds and charlatans, pretending to be holy and wise, and pretending to more knowledge than they have.

The natural/supernatural, real/unreal dichotomy has taken many forms over the course of Western history and civilization, but it was the philosopher-mathematician Rene Descartes (1596–1650) who most clearly formulated the ideas that are the immediate precursors of contemporary biomedical conceptions of the human organism. Descartes was determined to hold nothing as true until he had established the grounds of evidence for accepting it as such. The single category to be taken on faith, as it were, was the intuited perception of the body-self, expressed in Descartes's dictum: *Cogito, ergo sum*—I think, therefore I am. From this intuitive consciousness of his own being, Descartes proceeded to argue the existence of two classes of substance that together constituted the human organism: palpable *body* and intangible *mind*. In his essay, "Passions of the Soul," Descartes sought to reconcile material body and divine soul by locating the soul in the pineal gland whence it directed the body's movements like an invisible rider on a horse. In this way Descartes, a devout Catholic, was able to preserve the soul as the domain of theology, and to legitimate the body as the domain of science. The rather artificial separation of mind and body, the so-called Cartesian dualism, freed biology to pursue the kind of radically materialist thinking expressed by the medical student above, much to the advantage of the natural and clinical sciences. However, it caused the mind (or soul) to recede to the background of clinical theory and practice for the next three hundred years.

The Cartesian legacy to clinical medicine and to the natural and social sciences is a rather mechanistic conception of the body and its functions, and a failure to conceptualize a "mindful" causation of somatic states. It would take a struggling psychoanalytic psychiatry and the gradual development of psychosomatic medicine in the early 20th century to begin the task of reuniting mind and body in clinical theory and practice. Yet, even in psychoanalytically informed psychiatry and in psychosomatic medicine there is a tendency to categorize and treat human afflictions as if they were either wholly organic or wholly psychological in origin: "it" is *in* the body, or "it" is *in* the mind. In her astute analysis of multidisciplinary case conferences on chronic pain patients, for example, Corbett (1986) discovered the intractability of Cartesian thinking among sophisticated clinicians. These physicians, psychiatrists, and clinical social workers "knew" that pain was "real" whether or not the source of it could be verified by diagnostic tests. Nonetheless, they could not help but express evident relief when a "true" (i.e., single, generally organic) cause could be discovered. Moreover, when diagnostic tests indicated some organic explanation, the psychological and social aspects of the pain tended to be all but forgotten, and when severe psychopathology could be diagnosed, the organic complications and indices tended to be ignored. Pain, it seems, was *either* physical *or* mental, biological *or* psycho-social—never both nor something not-quite-either.

As both medical anthropologists and clinicians struggle to view humans and the experience of illness and suffering from an integrated perspective, they often find themselves trapped by the Cartesian legacy. We lack a precise vocabulary with which to deal with mind-body-society interactions and so are left suspended in hyphens, testifying to the disconnectedness of our thoughts. We are forced to resort to such fragmented concepts as the bio-social, the psycho-somatic, the somato-social as altogether feeble ways of expressing the myriad ways in which the mind speaks through the body, and the ways in which society is inscribed on the expectant canvas of human flesh. As Kundera (1984:15) recently observed: "The rise of science propelled man into tunnels of specialized knowledge. With every step forward in scientific knowledge, the less clearly he could see the world as a whole or his own self." Ironically, the conscious attempts to temper the materialism and the reductionism of biomedical science often end up inadvertently recreating the mind/body opposition in a new form. For example, Leon Eisenberg (1977) elaborated the distinction between disease and illness in an effort to distinguish the biomedical conception of "abnormalities in the structure and/or function of organs and organ systems" *(disease)* from the patient's subjective experience of malaise *(illness)*. While Eisenberg and his associates' paradigm has certainly helped to create a single language and discourse for both clinicians and social scientists, one unanticipated effect has been that physicians are claiming *both* aspects of the sickness experience for the medical domain. As a result, the "illness" dimension of human distress (i.e., the social relations of sickness) are being medicalized and individualized, rather than politicized and collectivized (see Scheper-Hughes and

Lock 1986). Medicalization inevitably entails a missed identification between the individual and the social bodies, and a tendency to transform the social into the biological.

Mind/body dualism is related to other conceptual oppositions in Western epistemology, such as those between nature and culture, passion and reason, individual and society—dichotomies that social thinkers as different as Durkheim, Mauss, Marx, and Freud understood as inevitable and often unresolvable contradictions and as natural and universal categories. Although Durkheim was primarily concerned with the relationship of the individual to society (an opposition we will discuss at greater length below), he devoted some attention to the mind/body, nature/society dichotomies. In *The Elementary Forms of the Religious Life* Durkheim wrote that "man is double" (1961[1915]:29), referring to the biological and the social. The physical body provided for the reproduction of society through sexuality and socialization. For Durkheim society represented the "highest reality in the intellectual and moral order." The body was the storehouse of emotions that were the raw materials, the "stuff," out of which mechanical solidarity was forged in the interests of the collectivity. Building on Durkheim, Mauss wrote of the "dominion of the conscious [will] over emotion and unconsciousness" (1979 [1950]:122). The degree to which the random and chaotic impulses of the body were disciplined and restrained by social institutions revealed the stamp of higher civilizations.

Freud introduced yet another interpretation of the mind/body, nature/culture, individual/society set of oppositions with his theory of dynamic psychology: the individual at war within himself. Freud proposed a human drama in which natural, biological drives locked horns with the domesticating requirements of the social and moral order. The resulting repressions of the libido through a largely painful process of socialization produced the many neuroses of modern life. Psychiatry was called on to diagnose and treat the dis-ease of wounded psyches whose egos were not in control of the rest of their minds. *Civilization and its Discontents* may be read as a psychoanalytic parable concerning the mind/body, nature/culture, and individual/society oppositions in Western epistemology.

For Marx and his associates the natural world existed as an external, objective reality that was transformed by human labor. Humans distinguish themselves from animals, Marx and Engels wrote, "as soon as they begin to produce their means of subsistence" (1970:42). In *Capital* Marx wrote that labor humanizes and domesticates nature. It gives life to inanimate objects, and it pushes back the natural frontier, leaving a human stamp on all that it touches.

Although the nature/culture opposition has been interpreted as the "very matrix of Western metaphysics" (Benoist 1978:59) and has "penetrated so deeply . . . that we have come to regard it as natural and inevitable" (Goody 1977:64), there have always been alternative ontologies. One of these is surely the view that culture is rooted *in* (rather than against) nature (i.e., biology), imitating it and emanating directly from it. Cultural materialists, for example, have tended to view social institutions as adaptive responses to certain fixed, biological foundations. M. Harris (1974, 1979) refers to culture as a "banal" or "vulgar" solution to the human condition insofar as it "rests on the ground and is built up out of guts, sex, energy" (1974:3). Mind collapses into body in these formulations.

Similarly, some human biologists and psychologists have suggested that the mind/body, nature/culture, individual/society oppositions are natural (and presumed universal) categories of thinking insofar as they are a cognitive and symbolic manifestation of human biology. Ornstein (1973), for example, understands mind/body dualism as an overly determined expression of human brain lateralization. According to this view, the uniquely human specialization of the brain's left hemisphere for cognitive, rational, and analytic functions and of the right hemisphere for intuitive, expressive, and artistic functions *within the context of left-hemisphere dominance* sets the stage for the symbolic and cultural dominance of reason over passion, mind over body, culture over nature, and male over female. This kind of biological reductionism is, however, rejected by most contemporary social anthropologists who stress, instead, the cultural sources of these oppositions in Western thought.

We should bear in mind that our epistemology is but one among many systems of knowledge regarding the relations held to obtain among mind, body, culture, nature, and society. We would point, for example, to those non-Western civilizations that have developed alternative epistemologies that tend to conceive of relations among similar entities in monistic rather than in dualistic terms.

Representations of Holism in Non-Western Epistemologies

In defining relationships between any set of concepts, principles of exclusion and inclusion come into play. Representations of holism and monism tend toward inclusiveness. Two representations of holistic thought are particularly common. The first is a conception of harmonious wholes in which everything from the cosmos down to the individual organs of the human body are understood as a single unit. This is often expressed as the relationship of microcosm to macrocosm. A second representation of holistic thinking is that of *complementary* (not opposing) dualities, in which the relationship of parts to the whole is emphasized.

One of the better known representations of balanced complementarity is the ancient Chinese yin/yang cosmology, which first appears in the *I Ching* somewhat before the 3rd century B.C. In this view, the entire cosmos is understood as poised in a state of dynamic equilibrium, oscillating between the poles of yin and yang, masculine and feminine, light and dark, hot and cold. The human body is likewise understood as moving back and forth between the forces of yin and yang—sometimes dry, sometimes moist, sometimes flushed, and sometimes chilled. The evolving tradition of ancient Chinese medicine borrowed the yin/yang cosmology from the Taoists and from Confucianism a concern with social ethics, moral conduct, and the importance of maintaining harmonious relations among individual, family, community, and state. Conceptions of the healthy body were patterned after the healthy state: in both there is an emphasis on order, harmony, balance, and hierarchy within the context of mutual interdependencies. A rebellious spleen can be compared to an insubordinate servant, and a lazy intestine compared to an indolent son. In the *Nei Ching, The Yellow Emperor's Classic of Internal Medicine*, the Prime Minister counsels: "the human body is an imitation of heaven and earth in all its details" (Veith 1966:115). The health of individuals depends on a balance in the natural world, while the health of each organ depends on its relationship to all other organs. Nothing can change without changing the whole. A conception of the human body as a mixture of yin and yang, forces of which the entire universe is composed, is altogether different from Western body conceptions based on absolute dichotomies and unresolvable differences. In ancient Chinese cosmology the emphasis is on balance and resonance; in Western cosmology, on tension and contradiction.

Islamic cosmology—a synthesis of early Greek philosophy, Judeo-Christian concepts, and prophetic revelations set down in the Qur'an—depicts humans as having dominance over nature, but this potential opposition is tempered by a sacred world view that stresses the complementarity of all phenomena (Jachimowicz 1975; Shariati 1979). At the core of Islamic belief lies the unifying concept of *Towhid*, which Shariati argues should be understood as going beyond the strictly religious meaning of "God is one, no more than one" to encompass a world view that represents all existence as essentially monistic. Guided by the principle of *Towhid* humans are responsible to one power, answerable to a single judge, and guided by one principle: the achievement of unity through the complementarities of spirit and body, this world and the hereafter, substance and meaning, natural and supernatural, etc.

The concept in Western philosophical traditions of an observing and reflexive "I," a mindful self that stands outside the body and apart from nature, is another heritage of Cartesian dualism that contrasts sharply with a Buddhist form of subjectivity and relation to the natural world. In writing about the Buddhist Sherpas of Nepal, Paul suggests that they do not perceive their interiority or their subjectivity as "hopelessly cut off and excluded from the rest of nature, but [rather as] . . . connected to, indeed identical with, the entire essential being of the cosmos" (1976:131).

In Buddhist traditions the natural world (the world of appearances) is a product of mind, in the sense that the entire cosmos is essentially "mind." Through meditation individual minds can merge with the universal mind. Understanding is reached not through analytic methods, but rather through an intuitive synthesis, achieved in moments of transcendence that are beyond speech, language, and the written word. For, the essence of world meaning is unspeakable and unthinkable. It is experientially received as a perception of the unity of mind and body, self and other, mind and nature, being and nothingness.

. . .

Person, Self, and Individual

The relation of individual to society, which has occupied so much of contemporary social theory, is based on a perceived "natural" opposition between the demands of the social and moral order and egocentric drives, impulses, wishes, and needs. The individual/society opposition, while fundamental to Western epistemology, is also rather unique to it. Geertz has argued that the Western conception of the person "as a bounded, unique . . . integrated motivational and cognitive universe, a dynamic center of awareness, emotion, judgement, and action . . . is a rather peculiar idea within the context of the world's cultures" (1984:126). In fact, the modern conception of the individual self is of recent historical origin, even in the West. It was really only with the publication in 1690 of John Locke's *Essay Concerning Human Understanding* that we have a detailed theory of the person that identifies the "I" or the self with a state of permanent consciousness that is unique to the individual and stable through the life span and physical change until death (Webel 1983:399).

. . .

In all, Japan has been repeatedly described as a culture of "social relativism," in which the person is understood as acting within the context of a social relationship, never simply autonomously (Lebra 1976; Smith 1983). One's self-identity identity changes with the social context, particularly within the hierarchy of social relations at any given time. The child's identity is established through the responses of others; conformity and dependency, even in adulthood, are not understood as signs of weakness, but rather as the result of inner strength (Reischauer 1977:152). One fear, however, which haunts many contemporary Japanese is that of losing oneself completely, of becoming totally immersed in social obligations.

One protective device is a distinction made between the external self *(tatemae)*—the persona, the mask, the social self that one presents to others—versus a more private self *(honne)*, the less controlled, hidden self. Geertz has described a similar phenomenon among the Javanese and Balinese (1984:127–128).

Read argues that the Gahuku-Gama of New Guinea lack a concept of the person altogether: "Individual identity and social identity are two sides of the same coin" (1955:276). He maintains that there is no awareness of the individual apart from structured social roles, and no concept of friendship—that is, a relationship between two unique individuals that is not defined by kinship, neighborhood, or other social claims. Gahuku-Gama seem to define the self, insofar as they do so at all, in terms of the body's constituent parts: limbs, facial features, hair, bodily secretions and excretions. An assault on any part of the body (stealing feces, for example) is tantamount to an attack on the person, as occurs in sorcery accusations. Of particular significance is the Gahuku-Gama conception of the social skin, which includes both the covering of the body *and* the person's particular social and character traits. References to one's "good" or "bad" skin indicate a person's moral character or even a person's temperament or mood. This is compatible with a society in which social relationship is expressed in touching, fondling, stroking, holding, and other immediate physical manifestations. Gahuku-Gama seem to experience themselves most intensely when in contact *with others* and *through their skins* (see also LaFontaine 1985:129–130).

Such sociocentric conceptions of the self have been widely documented for many parts of the world (see Shweder and Bourne 1982; Devisch 1985; Fortes 1959; Harris 1978) and have relevance to ethnomedical understanding. In cultures and societies lacking a highly individualized or articulated conception of the body-self it should not be surprising that sickness is often explained or attributed to malevolent social relations (i.e., sorcery), or to the breaking of social and moral codes, or to disharmony within the family or the village community. In such societies therapy, too, tends to be collectivized. Lévi-Strauss (1963) has noted that in transcendental and shamanic healing, the patient is almost incidental to the ritual, which is focused on the community at large. The !Kung of Botswana engage in weekly healing trance-dance rituals that are viewed as both curative and preventive (Katz 1982). Lorna Marshall has described the dance as "one concerted religious act of the !Kung [that] brings people into such union that they become like one organic being" (1965:270).

In contrast to societies in which the individual body-self tends to be fused with or absorbed by the social body, there are societies that view the individual as comprised of a multiplicity of selves. The Bororo (like the Gahuku-Gama) understand the individual only as reflected in relationship to other people. Hence, the person consists of many selves—the self as perceived by parents, by other kinsmen, by enemies, etc. The Cuna Indians of Panama say they have eight selves, each associated with a different part of the body. A Cuna individual's temperament is the result of domination by one of these aspects or parts of the body. An intellectual is one who is governed by the head, a thief governed by the hand, a romantic by the heart, and so forth.

. . .

While in the industrialized West there are only pathologized explanations of dissociative states in which one experiences more than one self (schizophrenia, multiple personality disorder, borderline, etc.), in many non-Western cultures individuals can experience multiple selves through the normative practice of spirit possession and other altered states of consciousness. In Haiti and Brazil, where the spirits of voodoo or condomblé are believed to have distinct personalities that are expressed both in food, drink, and clothing preferences and in particular behavioral traits, those in training as "daughters of the saints" must learn how to change their own behavior in order to "invite" possession by particular saints. Once possessed and in trance, the spirit visitors are free to come and go, appear and disappear at will, much to the pleasure and entertainment of all present. Such ritualized and controlled experiences of possession are sought after throughout the world as valued forms of religious experience and therapeutic behavior. . . .

Body Imagery

Closely related to conceptions of self (perhaps central to them) is what psychiatrists have labeled "body image" (Schilder 1970[1950]; Horowitz 1966). Body image refers to the collective and idiosyncratic representations an individual entertains about the body in its relationship to the environment, including internal and external perceptions, memories, affects, cognitions, and actions. . . .

Some of the earliest and best work on body image was contained in clinical studies of individuals suffering from extremely distorted body perceptions that arose from neurological, organic, or psychiatric disorders (Head 1920; Schilder 1970[1950]; Luria 1972). The inability of some so-called schizophrenics to distinguish self from other, or self from inanimate objects has been analyzed from psychoanalytic and phenomenological perspectives (Minkowski 1958; Binswanger 1958; Laing 1965; Basaglia 1964). Sacks (1973[1970], 1985) has also written about rare neurological disorders that can play havoc with the individual's body image, producing deficits and excesses as well as metaphysical transports in mind-body experiences. . . .

While profound distortions in body imagery are rare, neurotic anxieties about the body, its orifices, boundaries, and fluids are quite common. Fisher and Cleveland (1958) demonstrated the relationship between patients' "choice" of symptoms and body image conceptions. The skin, for example, can be experienced as a protective hide and a defensive armour protecting the softer and more vulnerable internal organs. In the task of protecting the inside, however, the outside can take quite a beating, manifested in skin rashes and hives. Conversely, the skin can be imagined as a permeable screen, leaving the internal organs defenseless and prone to attacks of ulcers and colitis. . . .

Particular organs, body fluids, and functions may also have special significance to a group of people. The liver, for example, absorbs a great deal of blame for many different ailments among the French, Spanish, Portuguese, and Brazilians, but to our knowledge only the Pueblo Indians of the Southwest suffer from "flipped liver" (Leeman 1986). In their national fantasy about the medical significance of the liver the French have created a mystical "phantom organ," one altogether fierce in its tyranny over the rest of the body and its ability to inflict human suffering (Miller 1978:44). The English and the Germans are, by comparison, far more obsessed with the condition and health of their bowels. Dundes takes the Germanic fixation with the bowels, cleanliness, and anality as a fundamental constellation underlying German national character (1984), while Miller writes that "when an Englishman complains about constipation, you never know whether he is talking about his regularity, his lassitude, or his depression" (1978:45).

Once an organ captures the imagination of a people, there appears to be no end to the metaphorical uses to which it may be put. Among "old stock" American Midwestern farmers, for example, the backbone has great cultural and ethnomedical significance. When illness strikes at these industrious and "upright" people, being forced off their feet comes as a grave blow to the ego. Even among the elderly and infirm, well-being is defined as the ability to "get around," to be on one's feet. Obviously, the ability to stay "upright" is not confined to the mere technical problems of locomotion; it carries symbolic weight as well. . . . Among rural Midwesterners laziness is a most serious moral failing, and "spinelessness" is as reviled as godlessness. It is little wonder that a therapy concerned with adjusting perceived malalignments of the spine—chiropractic medicine—would have its origins in middle America (Cobb 1958).

Blood, on the other hand, is a nearly universal symbol of human life, and some peoples, both ancient and contemporary, have taken the quality of the blood, pulse, and circulation as the primary diagnostic sign of health or illness. The traditional Chinese doctor, for example, made his diagnosis by feeling the pulse in both of the patient's wrists and comparing them with his own, an elaborate ritual that could take several hours. The doctor was expected to take note of minute variations, and the *Nei Ching* states that the pulse can be "sharp as a hook, fine as a hair, taut as a musical string, dead as a rock, smooth as a flowing stream, or as continuous as a string of pearls" (Majno 1975:245). Snow (1974) has described the rich constellation of ethnomedical properties and significances attached to the quality of the blood by poor black Americans, who suffer from "high" or "low," fast and slow, thick and thin, bitter and sweet blood. Linke (1986) has analyzed the concept of blood as a predominant metaphor in European culture, especially its uses in political ideologies, such as during the Nazi era. Similarly, the multiple stigmas suf-

fered by North American AIDS patients include a preoccupation with the "bad blood" of diseased homosexuals (Lancaster 1983).

Hispanic mothers from southern Mexico to northern New Mexico focus some of their body organ anxieties on the infant's fontanelle. Open, it exposes the newborn to the evil influences of night airs, as well as the envious looks and wishes of neighbors. Until it closes over, there is always the threat of *mollera caida*, "fallen fontanelle," a life-threatening pediatric disorder (Scheper-Hughes and Stewart 1983).

In short, ethnoanatomical perceptions, including body image, offer a rich source of data both on the social and cultural meanings of being human and on the various threats to health, well-being, and social integration that humans are believed to experience.

THE SOCIAL BODY

The Body as Symbol

Symbolic and structuralist anthropologists have demonstrated the extent to which humans find the body "good to think with." The human organism and its natural products of blood, milk, tears, semen, and excreta may be used as a cognitive map to represent other natural, supernatural, social, and even spatial relations. The body, as Mary Douglas observed, is a natural symbol supplying some of our richest sources of metaphor (1970:65). Cultural constructions of and about the body are useful in sustaining particular views of society and social relations.

. . .

Ethnobiological theories of reproduction usually reflect the particular character of their associated kinship system, as anthropologists have long observed. In societies with unilineal descent it is common to encounter folk theories that emphasize the reproductive contributions of females in matrilineal and of males in patrilineal societies. The matrilineal Ashanti make the distinction between flesh and blood that is inherited through women, and spirit that is inherited through males. The Brazilian Shavante, among whom patrilineages form the core of political factions, believe that the father fashions the infant through many acts of coitus, during which the mother is only passive and receptive. The fetus is "fully made," and conception is completed only in the fifth month of pregnancy. As one Shavante explained the process of Maybury-Lewis, while ticking the months off with his fingers: "Copulate. Copulate, copulate, copulate, copulate a lot. Pregnant. Copulate, copulate, copulate. Born" (1967:63).

Similarly, the Western theory of equal male and female contributions to conception that spans the reproductive biologies of Galen to Theodore Dobzhansky (1970) probably owes more to the theory's compatibility with the European extended and stem bilateral kinship system than to scientific evidence, which was lacking until relatively recently. The principle of one father, one mother, one act of copulation leading to each pregnancy was part of the Western tradition for more than a thousand years before the discovery of spermatozoa (in 1677), the female ova (in 1828), and before the actual process of human fertilization was fully understood and described (in 1875) (Barnes 1973:66). For centuries the theory of equal male and female contributions to conception was supported by the erroneous belief that females had the same reproductive organs and functions as males, except that, as one 6th-century Bishop put it, "*theirs* are *inside* the body and not outside it" (Laquer 1986:3). To a great extent, talk about the body and about sexuality tends to be talk about the nature of society.

Of particular relevance to medical anthropologists are the frequently encountered symbolic equations between conceptions of the healthy body and the healthy society, as well as the diseased body and the malfunctioning society. Janzen (1981) has noted that every society possesses a utopian conception of health that can be applied metaphorically from society to body and vice versa. One of the most enduring ideologies of individual and social health is that of the vital balance, and of harmony, integration, and wholeness that are found in the ancient medical systems of China, Greece, India, and Persia, in contemporary Native American cultures of the Southwest (Shutler 1979), through the holistic health movement of the 20th century (Grossinger 1980). Conversely, illness and death can be attributed to social tensions, contradictions, and hostilities, as manifested in Mexican peasants' image of the limited good (Fos-

ter 1965), in the hot–cold syndrome and symbolic imbalance in Mexican folk medicine (Currier 1969), and in such folk idioms as witchcraft, evil eye, or "stress" (Scheper-Hughes and Lock 1986). Each of these beliefs exemplifies the link between the health or illness of the individual body and the social body.

The Embodied World

One of the most common and richly detailed symbolic uses of the human body in the non-Western world is to domesticate the spaces in which humans reside. Bastien has written extensively about the Qollahuaya-Andean Indians' individual and social body concepts (1978, 1985). The Qollahuayas live at the foot of Mt. Kaata in Bolivia and are known as powerful healers, the "lords of the medicine bag." Having practiced a sophisticated herbal medicine and surgery since A.D. 700, Qollahuayas "understand their own bodies in terms of the mountain, and they consider the mountain in terms of their own anatomy" (1985:598). The human body and the mountain consist of interrelated parts: head, chest and heart, stomach and viscera, breast and nipple. The mountain, like the body, must be fed blood and fat to keep it strong and healthy. Individual sickness is understood as a disintegration of the body, likened to a mountain landslide or an earthquake. Sickness is caused by disruptions between people and the land, specifically between residents of different sections of the mountain: the head (mountain top), heart (center village), or feet (the base of the mountain). Healers cure by gathering the various residents together to feed the mountain and to restore the wholeness and wellness that was compromised. "I am the same as the mountain," says Marcelino Yamahuaya the healer, "[the mountain] takes care of my body, and I must give food and drink to Pachemama" (Bastien 1985:597). Bastien concludes that Qollahuaya body concepts are fundamentally holistic rather than dualistic. He suggests that

> The whole is greater than the sum of the parts. . . . Wholeness (health) of the body is a process in which centripetal and centrifugal forces pull together and disperse fluids that provide emotions, thoughts, nutrients, and lubricants for members of the body. [1985:598]

Possibly, however, the most elaborate use of the body in native cosmology comes from the Dogon of the Western Sudan, as explained by Ogotemmeli to Marcel Griaule (1965) in his description of the ground plan of the Dogon community. The village must extend from north to south like the body of a man lying on his back. The head is the council house, built in the center square. To the east and west are the menstrual huts which are "round like wombs and represent the hands of the village" (1965:97). The body metaphor also informs the interior of the Dogon house:

> The vestibule, which belongs to the master of the house, represents the male part of the couple, the outside door being his sexual organ. The big central room is the domain and the symbol of the woman; the store-rooms each side are her arms, and the communicating door her sexual parts. The central room and the store rooms together represent the woman lying on her back with outstretched arms, the door open, and the woman ready for intercourse. [1965:94–95]

. . .

Manning and Fabrega (1973) have summarized the major differences between most of these non-Western ethnomedical systems and modern biomedicine. In the latter body and self are understood as distinct and separable entities; illness resides in either the body or the mind. Social relations are seen as partitioned, segmented, and situational—generally as discontinuous with health or sickness. By contrast, many ethnomedical systems do not logically distinguish body, mind, and self, and therefore illness cannot be situated in mind or body alone. Social relations are also understood as a key contributor to individual health and illness. In short, the body is seen as a unitary, integrated aspect of self and social relations. It is dependent on, and vulnerable to, the feelings, wishes, and actions of others, including spirits and dead ancestors. The body is not understood as a vast and complex machine, but rather as a microcosm of the universe.

As Manning and Fabrega note, what is perhaps most significant about the symbolic and metaphorical extension of the body into the natural, social, and supernatural realms is that it demonstrates a unique kind of human autonomy that seems to have all but disappeared in the "modern," industrialized world. The confident uses of the body in speaking about the external world conveys a sense that humans are in control. It is doubtful that the Colombian Qollahuayas or the Desana or the Dogon experience anything to the degree of body alienation, so common to our civilization, as expressed in the schizophrenias, anorexias, and bulemias, or the addictions, obsessions, and fetishisms of "modern" life in the postindustrialized world.

. . .

However, the mind/body dichotomy and the body alienation characteristic of contemporary society may also be linked to capitalist modes of production in which manual and mental labors are divided and ordered into a hierarchy. Human labor, thus divided and fragmented, is by Marxist definition "alienated," and is reflected in the marked distortions of body movement, body imagery, and self-conception that E. P. Thompson (1967), among others, has described. Thompson discusses the subversion of natural, body time to the clock-work regimentation and work discipline required by industrialization. He juxtaposes the factory worker, whose labor is extracted in minute, recorded segments, with the Nuer pastoralist, for whom "the daily timepiece is the cattle clock" (Evans-Pritchard 1940:100), or the Aran Islander, whose work is managed by the amount of time left before twilight (Thompson 1967:59).

. . .

In contrast, the world in which most of us live is lacking a comfortable and familiar human shape. At least one source of body alienation in advanced industrial societies is the symbolic equation of humans and machines, originating in our industrial modes and relations of production and in the commodity fetishism of modern life, in which even the human body has been transformed into a commodity. . . .

We rely on the body-as-machine metaphor each time we describe our somatic or psychological states in mechanistic terms, saying that we are "worn out" or "wound up," or when we say that we are "run down" and that our "batteries need recharging." In recent years the metaphors have moved from a mechanical to an electrical mode (we are "turned off," "tuned in," we "get a charge" out of something), while the computer age has lent us a host of new expressions, including the all-too-familiar complaint: "my energy is down."

Our point is that the structure of individual and collective sentiments down to the "feel" of one's body and the naturalness of one's position and role in the technical order is a social construct. Thomas Belmonte described the body rhythms of the factory worker:

> The work of factory workers is a stiff military drill, a regiment of arms welded to metal bars and wheels. Marx, Veblen and Charlie Chaplin have powerfully made the point that, on the assembly line, man neither makes nor uses tools, but is continuous with tool as a minute, final attachment to the massive industrial machine. [1979:139]

. . .

Non-Western and nonindustrialized people are "called upon to think the world with their bodies" (O'Neill 1985:151). Like Adam and Eve in the Garden they exercise their autonomy, their power, by naming the phenomena and creatures of the world in their own image and likeness. By contrast, we live in a world in which the human shape of things (and even the human shape of humans with their mechanical hearts and plastic hips) is in retreat. While the cosmologies of nonindustrialized people speak to a constant exchange of metaphors from body to nature and back to body again, our metaphors speak of machine to body symbolic equations. O'Neill suggests that we have been "put on the machine" of biotechnology, some of us transformed by radical surgery and genetic engineering into "spare parts" or prosthetic humans (1985:153–154). Lives are saved, or at least deaths are postponed, but it is possible that our humanity is being compromised in the process.

THE BODY POLITIC

The relationships between individual and social bodies concern more, however, than metaphors and collective representations of the natural and the cultural. The relationships are also about power and control. Douglas (1966) contends, for example, that when a community experiences itself as threatened, it will respond by expanding the number of social controls regulating the group's boundaries. Points where outside threats may infiltrate and pollute the inside become the focus of particular regulation and surveillance. The three bodies—individual, social, and body politic—may be closed off, protected by a nervous vigilance about exits and entrances. Douglas had in mind witchcraft crazes and hysterias from the Salem trials through contemporary African societies and even political witch hunts in the United States. In each of these instances the body politic is likened to the human body in which what is "inside" is good and all that is "outside" is evil. The body politic under threat of attack is cast as vulnerable, leading to purges of traitors and social deviants, while individual hygiene may focus on the maintenance of ritual purity or on fears of losing blood, semen, tears, or milk.

Threats to the continued existence of the social group may be real or imaginary. Even when the threats are real, however, the true aggressors may not be known, and witchcraft can become the metaphor or the cultural idiom for distress. Lindenbaum (1979) has shown, for example, how an epidemic of Kuru among the South Fore of New Guinea led to sorcery accusations and counteraccusations and attempts to purify both the individual and collective bodies of their impurities and contaminants. Mullings suggests that witchcraft and sorcery were widely used in contemporary West Africa as "metaphors for social relations" (1984:164). In the context of a rapidly industrializing market town in Ghana, witchcraft accusations can express anxieties over social contradictions introduced by capitalism. Hence, accusations were directed at those individuals and families who, in the pursuit of economic success, appeared most competitive, greedy, and individualistic in their social relations. While Foster (1972) might label such witchcraft accusations a symptom of envy among the less successful, Mullings argues that witchcraft accusations are an inchoate expression of resistance to the erosion of traditional social values based on reciprocity, sharing, and family and community loyalty. Mullings does not, of course, suggest that witchcraft and sorcery are unique to capitalist social and economic formations, but rather that in the context of increasing commoditization of human life, witchcraft accusations point to the social distortions and dis-ease in the body politic generated by capitalism.

When the sense of social order is threatened, as in the examples provided above, the symbols of self-control become intensified along with those of social control. Boundaries between the individual and political bodies become blurred, and there is a strong concern with matters of ritual and sexual purity, often expressed in vigilance over social and bodily boundaries. Individuals may express high anxiety over what goes in and what comes out of the two bodies. In witchcraft-fearing societies, for example, there is often a concern with the disposal of one's excreta, hair cuttings, and nail parings. In small, threatened, and therefore often conservative peasant communities, a similar equation between social and bodily vigilance is likely to be found. For example, in Ballybran, rural Ireland, villagers were equally guarded about what they took into the body (as in sex and food) as they were about being "taken in" (as in "codding," flattery, and blarney) by outsiders, especially those with a social advantage over them. Concern with the penetration and violation of bodily exits, entrances, and boundaries extended to material symbols of the body—the home, with its doors, gates, fences, and stone boundaries, around which many protective rituals, prayers, and social customs served to create social distance and a sense of personal control and security (Scheper-Hughes 1979).

In addition to controlling bodies in a time of crisis, societies regularly reproduce and socialize the kind of bodies that they need. Aggressive (or threatened) societies, for example, often require fierce and foolhearty warriors. The Yanomamo, who, like all Amerindian peoples living in the Amazon, are constantly under siege from encroaching ranching and mining interests, place a great premium on aggressivity. The body of Yanomamo males is both medium and message: most adults' heads are criss-crossed by battle scars into which red dyes are rubbed. The men's mutilated crowns are kept clean and shaved for display; their scars are endowed with a religious as well as a political significance—they represent the rivers of blood on the moon where Pore, the Creator-Spirit of the Yanomamo, lives (Brain 1979:167–168). In creating a fine consonance among the physical, material, political, and spiritual planes of existence, many Yanomamo men are encouraged to put their bodies—especially their heads—in the service of the body politic. . . .

. . .

In our own increasingly "healthist" and body-conscious culture, the politically correct body for both sexes is the lean, strong, androgenous, and physically "fit" form through which the core cultural values of autonomy, toughness, competitiveness, youth, and self-control are readily manifest (Pollitt 1982). Health is increasingly viewed in the United States as an achieved rather than an ascribed status, and each individual is expected to "work hard" at being strong, fit, and healthy. Conversely, ill health is no longer viewed as accidental, a mere quirk of nature, but rather is attributed to the individual's failure to live right, to eat well, to exercise, etc. We might ask what it is our society "wants" from this kind of body. DeMause (1984) has speculated that the fitness/toughness craze is a reflection of an international preparation for war. A hardening and toughening of the national fiber corresponds to a toughening of individual bodies. In attitude and ideology the self-help and fitness movements articulate both a militarist and a Social Darwinist ethos: the fast and fit win; the fat and flabby lose and drop out of the human race (Scheper-Hughes and Stein 1987). Crawford (1980, 1985), however, has suggested that the fitness movement may reflect, instead, a pathetic and individualized (also wholly inadequate) defense against the threat of nuclear holocaust.

Rather than strong and fit, the politically (and economically) correct body can entail grotesque distortions of human anatomy, including in various times and places the bound feet of Chinese women (Daly 1978), the 16-inch waists of antebellum Southern socialites (Kunzle 1981), the tuberculin wanness of 19th-century Romantics (Sontag 1978), and the anorexics and bulemics of contemporary society. Crawford (1985) has interpreted the eating disorders and distortions in body image expressed in obsessional jogging, anorexia, and bulimia as a symbolic mediation of the contradictory demands of postindustrial American society. The double-binding injunction to be self-controlled, fit, and productive workers, and to be at the same time self-indulgent, pleasure-seeking consumers is especially destructive to the self-image of the "modern," "liberated" American woman. Expected to be fun-loving and sensual, she must also remain thin, lovely, and self-disciplined. . . .

Cultures are disciplines that provide codes and social scripts for the domestication of the individual body in conformity to the needs of the social and political order. Certainly the use of physical torture by the modern state provides the most graphic illustration of the subordination of the individual body to the body politic. Foucault (1979) argued that the spectacle of state-mandated torture of criminals and dissidents—brutal, primitive, and utterly public—was compatible with the political absolutism of the French monarchy. A more gentle way of punishment (through prisons, reform schools, and mental institutions) was more compatible with republicanism and a "democratization" of power. Torture addressed the soul through the vehicle of the body; contemporary psychiatry, medicine, and "corrections" address the body through the soul and mind of the patient or inmate. Both, however, serve the goal of producing "normal" and "docile" bodies for the state. Torture offers a dramatic lesson to "common folk" of the power of the political over the individual body. The history of colonialism contains some of the most brutal instances of the political uses of torture and the "culture of terror" in the interests of economic hegemony (Taussig 1984; Peters 1985). Scarry suggests that torture is increasingly resorted to today by unstable regimes in an attempt to assert the "incontestable reality" of their control over the populace (1985:27).

The body politic can, of course, exert its control over individual bodies in less dramatic and mundane, but no less brutal, ways. Foucault's (1973, 1975, 1979, 1980b) analyses of the role of medicine, criminal justice, psychiatry, and the various social sciences in producing new forms of power/knowledge over bodies are illustrative in this regard. The proliferation of disease categories and labels in medicine and psychiatry, resulting in ever more restricted definitions of the normal, has created a sick and deviant majority, a problem that medical and psychiatric anthropologists have been slow to explore. Radical changes in the organization of social and public life in advanced industrial societies, including the disappearance of traditional cultural idioms for the expression of individual and collective discontent (such as witchcraft, sorcery, rituals of reversal and travesty), have allowed medicine and psychiatry to assume a hegemonic role in shaping and responding to human distress. Apart from anarchic forms of random street violence and other forms of direct assault and confrontation, illness somatization has become a dominant metaphor for expressing individual

and social complaint. Negative and hostile feelings can be shaped and transformed by doctors and psychiatrists into symptoms of new diseases such as PMS (premenstrual syndrome) or Attention Deficit Disorder (Martin 1987; Lock 1986a; Lock and Dunk 1987; Rubinstein and Brown 1984). In this way such negative social sentiments as female rage and schoolchildren's boredom or school phobias (Lock 1986b) can be recast as individual pathologies and "symptoms" rather than as socially significant "signs." This funnelling of diffuse but real complaints into the idiom of sickness has led to the problem of "medicalization" and to the overproduction of illness in contemporary advanced industrial societies. In this process the role of doctors, social workers, psychiatrists, and criminologists as agents of social consensus is pivotal. As Hopper (1982) has suggested, the physician (and other social agents) is predisposed to "fail to see the secret indignation of the sick." The medical gaze is, then, a controlling gaze, through which active (although furtive) forms of protest are transformed into passive acts of "breakdown."

. . .In the following passage, recorded by Bourdieu (1977:166), an old Kabyle woman explains what it meant to be sick before and after medicalization was a feature of Algerian peasant life:

> In the old days, folk didn't know what illness was. They went to bed and they died. It's only nowadays that we're learning words like liver, lung . . . intestines, stomach . . ., and I don't know what! People only used to know [pain in] the belly; that's what everyone who died died of, unless it was the fever. . . . Now everyone's sick, everyone's complaining of something. . . . Who's ill nowadays? Who's well? Everyone complains, but no one stays in bed; they all run to the doctor. Everyone knows what's wrong with him now.

Or *does* everyone? We would suggest the usefulness to the body politic of filtering more and more human unrest, dissatisfaction, longing, and protest into the idiom of sickness, which can then be safely managed by doctor–agents.

An anthropology of relations between the body and the body politic inevitably leads to a consideration of the regulation and control not only of individuals but of populations, and therefore of sexuality, gender, and reproduction—what Foucault (1980a) refers to as bio-power. Prior to the publication of Malthus's *An Essay on the Principle of Population* in 1798, there existed a two-millennia-old tradition of interpreting the health, strength, and reproductive vigor of individual bodies as a sign of the health and well-being of the state (Gallagher 1986:83). Following Malthus, however, the equation of a healthy body with a healthy body politic was recast: the unfettered fertility of individuals became a sign of an enfeebled social organism. The power of the state now depended on the ability to control physical potency and fertility; "the healthy and, consequently *reproducing* body [became]. . . the harbinger of the disordered society full of starving bodies" (Gallagher 1986:85).

In short, the healthy human body, including its appetites and desires, became problematized beginning in the 19th century, and various disciplines centering around the control of human (especially female) sexuality have come to the fore. B. Turner (1984:91) suggests that the government and regulation of female sexuality involves, at the institutional level, a system of patriarchal households for controlling fertility; and at the individual level, ideologies of personal asceticism. Thus, late marriage, celibacy, and religious ideologies of sexual puritanism were a structural requirement of European societies until the mid-19th century (Imhof 1985) and of rural Ireland through the late 20th century (Scheper-Hughes 1979).

. . .

EMOTION: MEDIATRIX OF THE THREE BODIES

An anthropology of the body necessarily entails a theory of emotions. Emotions affect the way in which the body, illness, and pain are experienced and are projected in images of the well or poorly functioning social body and body politic. To date, social anthropologists have tended to restrict their interest in emotions to occasions when they are formal, public, ritualized, and "distanced," such as the highly stylized mourning of the Basques (W. Douglas 1969) or the deep play of a Balinese cock fight (Geertz 1973). The more private and idiosyncratic emotions and passions of individuals have tended to be left to psychoanalytic and psychobiological anthropologists, who have reduced them to a dis-

course on innate drives, impulses, and instincts. This division of labor, based on a false dichotomy between cultural sentiments and natural passions, leads us right back to the mind/body, nature/culture, individual/society epistemological muddle with which we began this article. We would tend to join with Geertz (1980) in questioning whether any expression of human emotion and feeling—whether public or private, individual or collective, whether repressed or explosively expressed—is ever free of cultural shaping and cultural meaning. The most extreme statement of Geertz's position, shared by many of the newer psychological and medical anthropologists, would be that without culture we would simply not know how to feel.

Insofar as emotions entail both feelings and cognitive orientations, public morality, and cultural ideology, we suggest that they provide an important "missing link" capable of bridging mind and body, individual, society, and body politic. As Blacking (1977:5) has stated, emotions are the catalyst that transforms knowledge into human understanding and that brings intensity and commitment to human action. Rosaldo (1984) has recently charged social and psychological anthropologists to pay more attention to the force and intensity of emotions in motivating human action.

. . . It is sometimes during the experience of sickness, as in moments of deep trance or sexual transport, that mind and body, self and other become one. Analyses of these events offer a key to understanding the mindful body, as well as the self, social body, and body politic.

Elaine Scarry claims to have discovered in the exploration of pain (especially pain intentionally inflicted through torture) a source of human creativity and destructiveness which she refers to as the "making and unmaking of the world" (1985). Pain destroys, disassembles, deconstructs the world of the victim. We would offer that illness, injury, disability, and death likewise deconstruct the world of the patient by virtue of their seeming randomness, arbitrariness, and hence their absurdity. Medical anthropologists are privileged, however, in that their domain includes not only the unmaking of the world in sickness and death, but also the remaking of the world in healing, especially during those intensely emotional and collective experiences of trance-dance, sings, and charismatic faith healing.

John Blacking (1977) refers to the "waves of fellow-feeling" that wash over and between bodies during rituals involving dance, music, movement, and altered states of consciousness. These "proto-rituals" occur, Blacking suggests, in a special space that is "without language, without symbols," drawing upon experiences and capacities that are species specific. The language of the body, whether expressed in gesture or ritual or articulated in symptomatology (the "language of the organs") is vastly more ambiguous and overdetermined than speech. Blacking's insight is reminiscent of Jean-Paul Sartre's observation (1943) that language, insofar as it represents above all a being-for others, presupposes a prereflexive relationship with other human beings. We might, perhaps, think of those essentially wordless encounters between mother and infant, lover and beloved, mortally ill patient and healer, in which bodies are offered, unreservedly presented to the other, as prototypical. In collective healing rituals there is a merging, a communion of mind/body, self/other, individual/group that acts in largely nonverbal and even prereflexive ways to "feel" the sick person back to a state of wellness and wholeness and to remake the social body.

"Belief kills; belief heals," write Hahn and Kleinman (1983:16) although they might as accurately have stated it "feelings kill; feelings heal." Their essay is part of that tradition in psychiatry, psychosomatic medicine, and medical anthropology that seeks to understand human events in that murky realm (close to religion and parapsychology) where the causes of "sudden death" or of "miraculous cure" cannot be explained by conventional biomedical science.[3] At the one pole for Hahn and Kleinman is "culturogenic" death involving voodoo, bone pointing, evil eye, sorcery, fright, "stress," and other states involving strong and pathogenic emotions. These they label "nocebo" effects. At the other, and therapeutic, pole are unexplained cures attributed to faith, suggestion, catharsis, drama, and ritual. These they label placebo effects. Moerman (1983), reporting on remarkable improvements in coronary bypass surgery patients (in which the surgery was a technical failure), attributes cause to the powerfully metaphoric effects of the operation as a cosmic drama of death and rebirth. His analysis strikes many chords of resonance with previous interpretations of the "efficacy of symbols" in shamanic and other ethnomedical cures (e.g., Lévi-Strauss 1967; Edgerton 1971; Herrick 1983). What is apparent is that nocebo and placebo effects are integral to *all* sickness and healing, for they are concepts that refer in an incomplete and oblique way to the interactions between mind and body and among the three bodies: individual, social, and politic.

CONCLUDING OBSERVATIONS

We would like to think of medical anthropology as providing the key toward the development of a new epistemology and metaphysics of the mindful body and of the emotional, social, and political sources of illness and healing. Clearly, biomedicine is still caught in the clutches of the Cartesian dichotomy and its related oppositions of nature and culture, natural and supernatural, real and unreal. If and when we tend to think reductionistically about the mind-body, it is because it is "good for us to think" in this way. To do otherwise, using a radically different metaphysics, would imply the "unmaking" of our own assumptive world and its culture-bound definitions of reality. To admit the "as-ifness" of our ethnoepistemology is to court a Cartesian anxiety—the fear that in the absence of a sure, objective foundation for knowledge we would fall into the void, into the chaos of absolute relativism and subjectivity (see Geertz 1973: 28–30).

We would conclude by suggesting that while the condition may be serious, it is far from hopeless. Despite the technologic and mechanistic turn that orthodox biomedicine has taken in the past few decades, the time is also one of great ferment and restlessness, with the appearance of alternative medical heterodoxies. And, as Cassell (1986:34) has recently pointed out, there is hardly a patient today who does not know that his mind has a powerful effect on his body both in sickness and in health. We might also add, with reference to our combined experience teaching in medical schools, that most clinical practitioners today know (although often in a nontheoretical and intuitive way) that mind and body are inseparable in the experiences of sickness, suffering, and healing, although they are without the vocabulary and concepts to address—let alone the tools to probe—this mindful body (Lock and Dunk 1987).

In our experience, most clinicians today know that back pain is real, even when no abnormalities appear under the penetrating gaze of the x-ray machine. And many are aware, further, of the social protest that is often expressed through this medium. Most surgeons know not to operate on a patient who is sure she will not survive what may be a rather minor surgical procedure. And, while most psychiatrists know that the effectiveness of tricyclic antidepressants has something to do with their effects on brain transmitters, few believe that chemical abnormalities are the sole causes of depression. Therefore, they invariably explore the painful life events and difficulties of their patients.

Consequently, physicians are increasingly looking to medical anthropology and to the other "softer" disciplines of cultural psychiatry, medical sociology, and psychiatric epidemiology for the answers to the ultimate and persistent existential questions that are not reducible to biological or to material "facts." Why *this* person, of all people? Why this particular disease? Why this particular organ or system? Why this "choice" of symptoms? Why now?

What we have tried to show in these pages is the interaction among the mind/body and the individual, social, and body politic in the production and expression of health and illness. Sickness is not just an isolated event, nor an unfortunate brush with nature. It is a form of communication—the language of the organs—through which nature, society, and culture speak simultaneously. The individual body should be seen as the most immediate, the proximate terrain where social truths and social contradictions are played out, as well as a locus of personal and social resistance, creativity, and struggle.

NOTES

1. Mary Douglas refers to "The Two Bodies," the physical and the social bodies in *Natural Symbols* (1970). More recently John O'Neill has written a book entitled *Five Bodies: The Human Shape of Modern Society* (1985), in which he discusses the physical body, the communicative body, the world's body, the social body, the body politic, consumer bodies, and medical bodies.

We admit that this proliferation of bodies had our decidedly nonquantitative minds stumped for a bit, but the book is nonetheless a provocative and insightful work. We are indebted to both Douglas and O'Neill but also to Bryan Turner's *The Body and Society: Explorations in Social Theory* for helping us to define and delimit the tripartite domain we have mapped out here.

2. We do not wish to suggest that Hippocrates's understanding of the body was analogous to that of Descartes or of modern biomedical practitioners. Hippocrates's approach to medicine and healing can only be described as organic and holistic. Nonetheless, Hippocrates was, as the quote from his works demonstrates, especially concerned to introduce elements of rational science (observation, palpation, diagnosis, and prognosis) into clinical practice and to discredit all the "irrational" and magical practices of traditional folk healers.

3. See also "The Surgeon As Priest" in Selzer (1974).

REFERENCES

Adams, F., transl. 1939. *Hippocrates: The Genuine Works of Hippocrates.* 2 vols. Baltimore: Williams & Wilkins.

Barnes, J. A. 1973. Genitrix:Genitor::Nature:Culture? In *The Character of Kinship.* Jack Goody, ed. Cambridge: Cambridge University Press.

Basaglia, Franco. 1964. Silence in the Dialogue With the Psychotic. *Journal of Existentialism* 6(21):99–102.

Bastien, Joseph. 1978. *Mountain of the Condor: Metaphor and Ritual in an Andean Ayllu.* St. Paul, MN: West Publishing.

———. 1985. Qollahuaya-Andean Body Concepts: A Topographical-Hydraulic Model of Physiology. *American Anthropologist* 87:595–611.

Belmonte, Thomas. 1979. *The Broken Fountain.* New York: Columbia University Press.

Benoist, Jean. 1978. *The Structural Revolution.* London: Weidenfeld and Nicolson.

Binswanger, Ludwig. 1958. Insanity as Life-History Phenomenon. In *Existence: A New Dimension in Psychiatry and Psychology.* Rollo May, Ernest Angel, and Henri Ellenberger, eds. New York: Simon & Schuster.

Blacking, John. 1977. Towards an Anthropology of the Body. In *The Anthropology of the Body.* John Blacking, ed. Pp. 1–27. New York: Academic Press.

Blacking, John, ed. 1977. *The Anthropology of the Body.* New York: Academic Press.

Bourdieu, Pierre. 1977. *Outline of a Theory of Practice. Cambridge Studies in Social Anthropology,* Vol. 16. Cambridge: Cambridge University Press.

Brain, Robert. 1979. *The Decorated Body.* New York: Harper & Row.

Briggs, Jean. 1970. *Never in Anger: Portrait of an Eskimo Family.* Cambridge, MA: Harvard University Press.

Cassell, Eric. 1986. Ideas in Conflict: The Rise and Fall and Rise and Fall of New Views of Disease. *Daedalus* 115:19–42.

Cobb, Beatrix. 1958. Why do People Return to Quacks? In *Patients, Physicians, and Illness.* E. Gartly Jaco, ed. Pp. 283–287. New York: Free Press.

Corbett, Kitty King. 1986. *Adding Insult to Injury: Cultural Dimensions of Frustration in the Management of Chronic Back Pain.* Ph.D. dissertation, Department of Anthropology, University of California, Berkeley.

Crawford, Robert. 1980. Healthism and the Medicalization of Everyday Life. *International Journal of Health Services* 10:365–388.

———. 1985. A Cultural Account of Health: Self Control, Release, and the Social Body. In *Issues in the Political Economy of Health Care.* J. McKinlay, ed. London: Tavistock.

Currier, Richard. 1969. The Hot-Cold Syndrome and Symbolic Balance in Mexican and Spanish-American Folk Medicine. In *The Cross-Cultural Approach to Health Behavior.* L. R. Lynch, ed. Pp. 255–273. Madison, NJ: Fairleigh Dickinson University Press.

Daly, Mary. 1978. *Gyn/Ecology.* Boston: Beacon Press.

deMause, Lloyd. 1984. *Reagan's America.* New York: Creative Books.

Devisch, Renaat. 1985. Symbol and Psychosomatic Symptom in Bodily Space-Time: The Case of the Yaka of Zaire. *International Journal of Psychology* 20:589–616.

Dobzhansky, Theodosius. 1970. Heredity. *Encyclopedia Britannica* 11:419–427.

Douglas, Mary. 1966. *Purity and Danger.* New York: Praeger.

———. 1970. *Natural Symbols.* New York: Vintage.

Douglas, William. 1969. *Death in Murelaga: Funerary Ritual in a Spanish Basque Village.* Seattle: University of Washington Press.

Dundes, Alan. 1984. *Life is Like a Chicken-Coop Ladder.* New York: Columbia University Press.

Durkheim, Emile. 1961[1915]. *The Elementary Forms of the Religious Life.* Joseph Ward Swain, transl. New York: Collier.

Edgerton, Robert. 1971. A Traditional African Psychiatrist. *Southwestern Journal of Anthropology* 27:259–278.

Eisenberg, Leon. 1977. Disease and Illness: Distinctions Between Professional and Popular Ideas of Sickness. *Culture, Medicine and Psychiatry* 1:9–23.

Evans-Pritchard, E. E. 1940. *The Nuer.* Oxford: Oxford University Press.

Fisher, S., and S. Cleveland. 1958. *Body Image and Personality.* Princeton, NJ: D. Van Nostrand.

Fortes, Meyer. 1959. *Oedipus and Job in West African Religion.* Cambridge: Cambridge University Press.

Foster, George. 1965. Peasant Society and the Image of the Limited Good. *American Anthropologist* 68: 210–214.

———. 1972. The Anatomy of Envy: A Study in Symbolic Behavior. *Current Anthropology* 13(2):165–186.

Foucault, Michel. 1973. *Madness and Civilization: A History of Insanity in the Age of Reason.* New York: Vintage.

———. 1975. *The Birth of the Clinic: An Archeology of Medical Perception.* New York: Vintage.

———. 1979. *Discipline and Punish: The Birth of the Prison.* New York: Vintage.

———. 1980a. *The History of Sexuality,* Vol. 1: An Introduction. New York: Vintage.

———. 1980b. *Power/Knowledge: Selected Interviews and Other Writings.* New York: Pantheon.

Gallagher, Catherine. 1986. The Body Versus the Social Body in the Works of Thomas Malthus and Henry Mayhew. *Representations* 14:83–106.

Geertz, Clifford. 1973. *The Interpretation of Cultures.* New York: Basic Books.

———. 1980. *Negara: The Theatre-State in Nineteenth Century Bali.* Princeton: Princeton University Press.

———. 1984. From the Native's Point of View: On the Nature of Anthropological Understanding. In *Culture Theory.* Richard Shweder and Robert LeVine, eds. Pp. 123–136. Cambridge: Cambridge University Press.

Goody, Jack. 1977. *The Domestication of the Savage Mind.* Cambridge: Cambridge University Press.

Grraule, Marcel. 1965. *Conversations with Ogotemmeli.* Oxford: Oxford University Press.

Grossinger, Richard. 1980. *Planet Medicine: From Stone Age Shamanism to Post-Industrial Healing.* New York: Doubleday.

Hahn, Robert, and Arthur Kleinman. 1983. Belief as Pathogen, Belief as Medicine. *Medical Anthropology Quarterly* 14(4):3, 16–19.

Harris, Grace. 1978. *Casting Out Anger: Religion among the Taita of Kenya.* Cambridge: Cambridge University Press.

Harris, Marvin. 1974. *Cows, Pigs, Wars and Witches.* New York: Vintage.

———. 1979. *Cultural Materialism: The Struggle for a Science of Culture.* New York: Random House.

Head, Henry. 1920. *Studies in Neurology.* 2 vols. London: H. Frowde: Hodder Stoughton.

Herrick, James. 1983. The Symbolic Roots of Three Potent Iroquois Medicinal Plants. In *The Anthropology of Medicine.* Lola Romanucci-Ross, Daniel Moerman, and L. Tancredi, eds. Pp. 134–155. New York: Bergin & Garvey.

Hopper, Kim. 1982. Discussant comments following the organized session, "The Lure and Haven of Illness." 81st annual meeting of the American Anthropological Association, Washington, D.C.

Horowitz, M. J. 1966. Body Image. *Archives of General Psychiatry* 14:456–461.

Imhof, Arthur. 1985. From the Old Mortality Pattern to the New: Implications of a Radical Change from the Sixteenth to the Twentieth Century. *Bulletin of the History of Medicine* 59:1–29.

Jachimowicz, Edith. 1975. Islamic Cosmology. In *Ancient Cosmologies*. Carmen Blacker and Michael Lowe, eds. London: George Allen and Unwin.

Janzen, John. 1981. The Need for a Taxonomy of Health in the Study of African Therapeutics. *Social Science and Medicine* 15B:185–194.

Katz, Richard. 1982. *Boiling Energy*. Cambridge: Harvard University Press.

Kundera, Milan. 1984. The Novel and Europe. *New York Review of Books* 31:15–19.

Kunzle, David. 1981. *Fashion and Fetishism: A Social History of the Corset, Tight-Lacing, and Other Forms of Body-Sculpture in the West*. London: Rowan and Littlefield.

LaFontaine, J. S. 1985. Person and Individual. In *The Category of the Person: Anthropology, Philosophy, History*. M. Carrithers, S. Collins, and S. Lukes, eds. Pp. 123–140. Cambridge: Cambridge University Press.

Laing, R. D. 1965. *The Divided Self*. Harmondsworth: Penguin.

Lancaster, Roger Nelson. 1983. What AIDS Is Doing to Us. *Christopher Street* 7(3):48–52.

Laquer, Thomas. 1986. Orgasm, Generation, and the Politics of Reproductive Biology. *Representations* 14:1–41.

Lebra, Takie Sugiyama. 1976. *Japanese Patterns of Behavior*. Honolulu: University Press of Hawaii.

Leeman, Larry. 1986. Pueblo Models of Communal Sickness and Wellbeing. Paper read at the Kroeber Anthropological Society Meetings, Berkeley, March 8.

Lévi-Strauss, Claude. 1963. The Sorcerer and His Magic. In *Structural Anthropology*. Pp. 167–185. New York: Basic Books.

———. 1967. The Efficacy of Symbols. In *Structural Anthropology*. Garden City, NY: Doubleday.

Lindenbaum, Shirley. 1979. *Kuru Sorcery: Disease and Danger in the New Guinea Highlands*. Palo Alto, CA: Mayfield.

Linke, Uli. 1986. *Where Blood Flows, a Tree Grows: A Study of Root Metaphors and German Culture*. Ph.D. dissertation, Department of Anthropology, University of California, Berkeley.

Lock, Margaret. 1986a. Castigations of a Selfish Housewife: National Identity and Menopausal Rhetoric in Japan. Paper read at the American Ethnological Society Meetings, Wrightsville Beach, North Carolina.

———. 1986b. Plea for Acceptance: School Refusal Syndrome in Japan. *Social Science and Medicine* 23:99–112.

Lock, Margaret, and Pamela Dunk. 1987. My Nerves are Broken: The Communication of Suffering in a Greek-Canadian Community. In *Health in Canadian Society: Sociological Perspectives*. D. Coburn, C. D'Arcy, P. New, and G. Torrence, eds. Toronto: Fitzhenry and Whiteside.

Luria, A. R. 1972. *The Man With a Shattered Sword*. New York: Basic Books.

Majno, Guido. 1975. *The Healing Hand: Man and Wound in the Ancient World*. Cambridge, MA: Harvard University Press.

Manning, Peter, and Horatio Fabrega. 1973. The Experience of Self and Body: Health and Illness in the Chiapas Highlands. In *Phenomenological Sociology*. George Psathas, ed. Pp. 59–73. New York: Wiley.

Marshall, Lorna. 1965. The !Kung Bushmen of the Kalahari Desert. In *Peoples of Africa*. J. L. Gibbs, ed. New York: Holt, Rinehart & Winston.

Martin, Emily. 1987. *The Woman in the Body*. Boston: Beacon Press. (In press.)

Marx, Karl, and Frederick Engels. 1970. *The German Ideology*. New York: International Publishers.

Mauss, Marcel. 1979[1950]. *Sociology and Psychology: Essays*. London: Routledge & Kegan Paul.

———. 1985[1938]. A Category of the Human Mind: The Notion of the Person, the Notion of the Self. In *The Category of the Person: Anthropology, Philosophy, History*. M. Carrithers, S. Collins, and S. Lukes, eds. Pp. 1–25. Cambridge: Cambridge University Press.

Maybury-Lewis, David. 1967. *Akwe-Shavante Society*. Oxford: Clarendon Press.

Merchant, Carolyn. 1980. *The Death of Nature: Women, Ecology, and the Scientific Revolution*. New York: Harper & Row.

Merleau-Ponty, Maurice. 1962. *The Phenomenology of Perception*. London: Routledge and Kegan Paul.

Miller, Jonathan. 1978. *The Body in Question*. New York: Vintage.

Minkowski, Eugene. 1958. Findings in a Case of Schizophrenic Depression. In *Existence: A New Dimension in Psychiatry and Psychology*. Rollo May, Ernest Angel, and Henri Ellenberger, eds. Pp. 127–138. New York: Simon & Schuster.

Moerman, Daniel. 1983. Physiology and Symbols: Anthropological Implications of the Placebo Effect. In *The Anthropology of Medicine*. Lola Romanucci-Ross, Daniel Moerman, and L. Tancredi, eds. Pp. 156–167. New York: Bergin & Garvey.

Mullings, Leith. 1984. *Therapy, Ideology, and Social Change*. Berkeley: University of California Press.

O'Neill, John. 1985. *Five Bodies: The Human Shape of Modern Society*. Ithaca: Cornell University Press.

Omstein, R. E. 1973. Right and Left Thinking. *Psychology Today* May:87–92.

Paul, Robert. 1976. The Sherpa Temple as a Model of the Psyche. *American Ethnologist* 3:131–146.

Peters, Edward. 1985. *Torture*. London: Basil Blackwell.

Pollitt, K. 1982. The Politically Correct Body. *Mother Jones* May:66–67.

Read, Kenneth E. 1955. Morality and the Concept of the Person Among the Gahuku-Gama. *Oceania* 25:233–282.

Reischauer, Edwin O. 1977. *The Japanese.* Cambridge, MA: Harvard University Press.

Rosaldo, Renato. 1984. Grief and the Headhunter's Rage: On the Cultural Force of Emotions. In *Text, Play, and Story.* Edward Bruner, ed. Pp. 178–195. Washington, DC: American Ethnological Society.

Rubinstein, Robert A., and Ronald T. Brown. 1984. An Evaluation of the Validity of the Diagnostic Category of Attention Deficit Disorder. *American Journal of Orthopsychiatry* 54(3):398–414.

Sacks, Oliver. 1973[1970]. *Migraine: The Evolution of a Common Disorder.* Berkeley: University of California Press.

———. 1985. *The Man Who Mistook His Wife For a Hat and Other Clinical Tales.* New York: Summit Books.

Sartre, Jean-Paul. 1943. *L'Etre et le Neant.* Paris: Gallimard.

Scarry, Elaine. 1985. *The Body in Pain: The Making and Unmaking of the World.* Oxford: Oxford University Press.

Scheper-Hughes, Nancy. 1979. *Saints, Scholars, and Schizophrenics: Mental Illness in Rural Ireland.* Berkeley: University of California Press.

Scheper-Hughes, Nancy, and Margaret Lock. 1986. Speaking Truth to Illness: Metaphors, Reification, and a Pedagogy for Patients. *Medical Anthropology Quarterly* 17(5):137–140.

Scheper-Hughes, Nancy, and Howard Stein. 1987. Child-Abuse and the Unconscious. In *Child Survival: Anthropological Approaches to the Treatment and Maltreatment of Children.* Nancy Scheper-Hughes, ed. Dordrecht: Reidel. (In press.)

Scheper-Hughes, Nancy, and D. Stewart. 1983. Curanderismo in Taos County, New Mexico: A Possible Case of Anthropological Romanticism? *Western Journal of Medicine* 139(6):71–80.

Schilder, Paul. 1970[1950]. *The Image and Appearance of the Human Body.* New York: International Universities Press.

Selzer, Richard. 1974. *Mortal Lessons: Notes on the Art of Surgery.* New York: Simon & Schuster.

Shariati, Ali. 1979. *On the Sociology of Islam.* Hamid Algar, transl. Berkeley, CA: Mizan Press.

Shweder, Richard, and Edmund J. Bourne. 1982. Does the Concept of the Person Vary Cross-Culturally? In *Cultural Conceptions of Mental Health and Therapy.* Anthony J. Marsella and Geoffrey M. White, eds. Pp. 97–137. Dordrecht: Reidel.

Shutler, Mary Elizabeth. 1979. Disease and Curing in a Yaqui Community. In *Ethnic Medicine in the Southwest.* E. Spicer, ed. Tucson: University of Arizona Press.

Smith, Robert V. 1983. *Japanese Society: Tradition, Self, and the Social Order.* Cambridge: Cambridge University Press.

Snow, Loudell. 1974. Folk Medical Beliefs and Their Implications for Care of Patients: A Review Based on Studies Among Black Americans. *Annals of Internal Medicine* 81:82–96.

Sontag, Susan. 1978. *Illness as Metaphor.* New York: Farrar, Strauss and Giroux.

Taussig, Michael. 1984. Culture of Terror—Space of Death: Roger Casement's Putumayo Report and the Explanation of Torture. *Comparative Studies in Society and History* 26(3):467–497.

Thompson, E. P. 1967. Time, Work, Discipline, and Industrial Capitalism. *Past and Present* 38:56–97.

Turnbull, Colin. 1962. *The Forest People.* New York: Simon & Schuster.

Turner, Bryan. 1984. *The Body and Society: Explorations in Social Theory.* Oxford: Basil Blackwell.

Veith, Ilza. 1966. *The Yellow Emperor's Classic of Internal Medicine.* Berkeley: University of California Press.

Webel, Charles P. 1983. *Self: An Overview.* International Encyclopedia of Psychiatry, Psychoanalysis, Psychobiology, and Neurology. Benjamin Wolman, ed. Pp. 398–403. New York: Aesculepius Press.

28 BREAST CANCER: READING THE OMENS

Margaret M. Lock

The selections thus far have outlined historical processes that have brought a shift in Western societies from a culture of resignation to a culture of planning and control, and from a model of medicine that had room for social and spiritual dimensions of illness to one that has trouble conceiving of mind–body interactions. These historical processes include a dramatic decline in birth and death rates, which coincided with the processes of industrialization, urbanization, and national political and cultural unification. This selection explains that these changes brought a new concept of time as linear as opposed to cyclical, while industrial rationalization and a revolution in mathematics meant that nature came to be seen in quantitative terms.

These demographic and cultural changes are the backdrop for the modern culture of risk, which entails an entirely disenchanted view of the world. Yet, as Lock explains, attempts by modern science to avert misfortune by "reading the genetic code" or quantifying the health risks of certain behaviors continue to resemble traditional practices of divination. Both inevitably lead to further uncertainties and ambiguities (see selection 9; Good 1995).

Furthermore, the discourse of risk is a moral one. The popular penchant for viewing diseases as direct products of single genes contributes to a tendency to view illness at the individual level and to ignore complex environmental, social, and politico-economic factors (see selection 27). Rather than being the unlucky target of chance, God's will, or a malevolent spirit, individuals are held responsible for managing risks inherent in their own and their children's genes or deriving from their own lifestyle choices. High false-positive rates and unnecessary and possibly harmful further tests and treatments seem not to dampen the public enthusiasm for this kind of risk management. A recent study found that 41% of U.S. adults agree that an 80-year-old woman is irresponsible if she fails to submit for screening mammography, and 32% feel the same way about 80-year-olds who do not receive regular colonoscopies (Schwartz et al. 2004).

Screening for disease or genetic risk can have serious consequences in terms of employment and insurance. In addition, screening raises doubts about one's status as a healthy person and can provoke extreme anxiety about the future. As selections 29 and 30 indicate, worry and apprehension can actually bring about the very illness that one fears. Thus, as Førde (1998) suggests, the spread of risk-oriented thinking to other countries or subgroups within industrialized societies could be seen as a form of cultural imperialism with far-reaching moral and health impacts.

Questions to keep in mind

How is time manipulated in both divination and the discourse of probability and risk?

Why is being a woman considered a risk in itself? How is this message brought home to women throughout their lives?

Is it a good idea to use screening tests if there is no acceptable preventive or curative treatment?

Why do cancer societies often exaggerate risks? Do you think they are justified in doing so in order to increase screening rates or gain financial support?

Source: Lock, M. 1998. "Breast Cancer: Reading the Omens." *Anthropology Today* 14(4):7–16. With permission from the publisher.

When Azande ask about health or marriage or hunting they are seeking information about the movement of psychic forces which might cause them misfortune. They do not attempt simply to discover the objective conditions at a certain point of time in the future, nor the objective results of a certain action, but the inclination of mystical powers, for those conditions and the result depend upon them. . . . Hence when the oracle paints a black horizon for a man he is glad to have been warned because now that he knows the dispositions of witchcraft he can get into touch with it and have the future changed to be more favourable to him. . . . [A] man's future health and happiness depend on future conditions that are already in existence and can be exposed by the oracles and altered. The future depends on the disposition of mystical forces that can be tackled here and now. Moreover, when the oracles announce that a man will fall sick, . . . his 'condition' is therefore already bad, his future is already part of him.

E.E. Evans-Pritchard, Witchcraft,
Oracles, and Magic among the Azande
(Oxford: Clarendon Press 1937)

The art and science of divination has been a preoccupation of people everywhere, and continues to exert a hold over perhaps the majority of the world's population. Whether its practice concerns an examination of the entrails of sacrificed birds or animals, or the patterns of cracks in heated animal bones, the lining up of yarrow stalks according to the rules of the I Ching (*The Book of Changes*), or consultation with oracles in trance-like states, divination produces knowledge not readily available to ordinary people, knowledge that forms the basis for action. Historical and anthropological research suggests that a primary concern during divinatory proceedings addresses explanations for what has already taken place, for it is in the reconstruction of past events that causes of misfortune are uncovered and moral responsibility is assigned, on the basis of which, suitable action can be determined (Reynolds White 1997:6).

Divination does not, however, simply link the past to the present. Omens for the future are also central to many divinatory practices. Nadia Serematakis's research in the Inner Mani reveals how 'warnings'—the interpretations by gifted women of divinatory practices and of their own dreams—permit the bringing together of events, people and meanings usually separated by time and space in everyday life, because dreams and divination do not comply with a lineal temporality. Exactly where and on whom the danger will alight is not usually foretold by the women, but in re-telling their dreams, they frequently speculate about whom the dream 'targets' (1991: 61–63).

The new technology of genetic testing permits us to divine our past, and to make that heritage—in the form of genes—into omens for the future. In this article on breast cancer and the concept of risk, I will argue that although genetic testing permits us to speculate with more precision than was previously the case about who may be struck with misfortune, a characteristic feature of divination nevertheless remains, namely that in seeking to avoid misfortune we create new ambiguities and uncertainties (Lambek 1993; Reynolds White 1997; Wikan 1990). Second, this powerful new technology encourages us to concentrate on a style of reasoning (Hacking 1992) for which we in EuroAmerica have a great proclivity, namely that of biological reductionism (in this case in the form of genetic determinism).[1] By focusing on genetics, other factors that contribute to cancer—environmental, social, and political—are eclipsed, allowing us to understand this disease as though it were entirely an individual misfortune.

The common idiom of being 'at risk' from a given disease, in particular a so-called genetic disease, encourages a heightened anxiety about what the future may hold in store. While knowledge about the possibility of contracting a disease may, at times, encourage an individual to act so as to try to avoid or control that disease, this information is inevitably compounded with uncertainty and ambiguity. Further, misrepresentation of probability estimates are common in the media, and at times in professional discourse, usually with the result that the odds of becoming diseased are estimated as greater than is warranted, thus heightening public anxiety. Being known as someone 'at risk' may also have direct social and political ramifications, particularly in connection with employment and access to health insurance. With these points in mind, it seems appropriate that before widespread testing and screening for genes are institutionalized, some of the confusion and dangers associated with this new technology of divination should be widely aired.[2]

FROM DANGER TO PROBABILITY

Serematakis, following Aries (1981), notes the gradual disappearance of beliefs in omens and warnings in Europe over the past three hundred years, associated with the expansion of commodification, the rationalization of community and daily life, and especially with the linearization of time. In their place Hacking (1990) argues that a 'professional lust for measurement' emerged during the Industrial Revolution. Historians disagree as to whether a direct link exists between this 'avalanche of numbers' and earlier forms of mechanical divination, gambling and lotteries, in which the idea of probability is inherent (Daston 1988). For Hacking, links with the past are not important. He acknowledges the presence of gambling in Imperial Rome, and that a scientific approach to probability almost certainly originated in the Arab world (1975). He is also aware that techniques of quantification were highly sophisticated by the 15th century (see also Crosby 1997), but insists that what must be explained is not a continuity with the past, but rather the partial erosion of the science of determinism, so dominant during the 16th and 17th centuries, culminating in 'the philosophical success story of the first half of the twentieth century' (1990: 4) namely, probability mathematics.

Hacking argues that it was the recognition of statistical regularities that permitted us to gain a thoroughly quantitative feel for nature. At the same time, a space was created in which the manipulation of chance became a possibility. This 'taming of chance' required the production of new social categories—the 'making up' of people and of populations exhibiting statistical regularities, and the discovery of the idea of normalcy (Canguilhem 1991). Hacking suggests that today we are obsessed with the 'chances of danger' and with finding ways to change the odds, an obsession descended directly from a nineteenth century desire to achieve control through the application of statistics.

There is good evidence that the early Chinese with their complex divinatory practices were preoccupied with prediction and the avoidance of misfortune and danger (Loewe 1981), and Evans-Pritchard leads us to believe that something similar might have been the case among the Azande (1976). But it is the scale of what is happening today, and the efficiency of the dissemination and promotion of the use of statistics through governmental bodies, professional organizations and the media (Burchell et al. 1991) that sets us apart.

Our thoughts about control have recently turned to the world of molecular genetics, where information is being amassed at an alarming rate. For example, in September 1997 the opening of a new private fertility clinic was announced in Toronto: in the words of one newspaper reporter. 'Canada's first commercial enterprise to offer parents the chance to weed out genetically defective embryos before they are implanted in the mother's uterus' (*Globe and Mail* 1997a). The doctor who founded this clinic describes its opening as a 'huge advance in human development' adding that, 'this is the beginning of the end of genetic disease.' Among the conditions this physician plans to eliminate are breast cancer and other multifactorial, 'adult onset' diseases (in the medical idiom). An era which claims to eliminate 'bad' genes has commenced, not simply those genes that we are convinced will cause deadly diseases during infancy or early childhood, but those that put our offspring at a greatly increased risk (we are often told) of getting one or more diseases in adult life.

The physician and writer Lewis Thomas pointed out more than a decade ago that we live today with an 'epidemic of anxiety,' caused in large part by the ceaseless assault from the media of messages informing us that we are at risk for everything imaginable (1983). In widely publicized clinics such as the one in Toronto, and the many others like it springing up around the world, the fruits of the powerful, reductionistic sciences of molecular genetics and cell biology, coupled with the probability sciences of biometrics and population genetics, permit us to manipulate chance in entirely new ways. This new divinatory space creates a highly potent zone of anxiety, in which the thought of one's genetic heritage as a ticking time-bomb becomes a motive for action.

Yoxen notes that the availability of genetic testing has brought about a shift in public perception, one in which our genes have come to be understood as 'quasi-pathogens.' People tend to assume that if a predisposing gene is identified, this indicates the presence of disease at conception, even when the gene is associated with an illness that manifests itself late in life (1982). It has been argued that, because of a widespread assumption that genetics determine disease, we are 'at risk,' of making up yet another stigmatized class of people—the pre-symptomatic ill. Every one of us will in effect be part of this underclass given that, as Francis Collins, the current director of the National Center for Human Genome Research in Washington, points out, 'we are all at risk for something' (Beardsley 1996:102).

THE REALITY OF VARIATION

The concept of risk is not at all self-evident, and predictions about risk must be translated from statistical probabilities to 'fit' with the circumstances of individual lives. Moreover, health care professionals, their patients and clients, and involved families, may weight these contextual variables quite differently. For instance, Stephen J. Gould the biologist has written (1985) of the acute anxiety he experienced on being diagnosed with abdominal mesothelioma, a deadly cancer. The literature could not have been more 'brutally clear' in Gould's words, in that the disease is incurable, and has a median mortality of about eight months after diagnosis. Gould set about questioning what a median mortality of about eight months actually signifies. He suggests that to most people it would mean, 'I will probably be dead in eight months,' but this is exactly the conclusion that should be avoided, Gould insists. We tend to view medians and means as hard 'realities' and forget the most important thing, the variation that permits their calculation. Thus, Gould argues, if the median is the reality and the variation around the median just a device for its calculation, then 'I will probably be dead in eight months' may pass as a reasonable interpretation. But it is actually the medians and means that are the abstractions, and the *variation* that is the reality. Gould estimated where, in all probability, he was located amidst the variation, and found himself, not surprisingly given his socio-economic status and his self-described positive attitude, in a 'right skewed tail,' indicating that he was among that group of diagnosed individuals who remain alive, often for many years beyond the median point.

Gould's case makes it clear how easy it is to misinterpret numbers—a process that we witness everyday in media reporting of numerous scientific articles involving probablity calculations, which are then uncritically incorporated into public knowledge. In his article, Gould also reminded readers that the proliferation of cancer cells in a human body is a complex, multi-causal process in which the immune system plays a key role, something about which we now have plenty of incontrovertible evidence, but which usually passes unnoted in the current literature on cancer (see review article by Bolles et al., 1982[3]).

Of all the cancers, it is breast cancer that is currently portrayed as a woman's bane, in large part through extensive media coverage. The resultant escalating anxiety of women exposed almost daily to this media coverage may well serve to actually increase the incidence of the disease, including among those up to 7% of women carrying one or other of the genes thus far located that experts agree predispose individuals to breast cancer. 'Predispose' is, of course, the significant word here; it cannot be repeated too often that genes do not 'cause' cancer in any predetermined way, and further that in the case of breast cancer, more than 90% of its incidence, it seems, is not associated with genetics, but with a complex array of other environmental and social factors.

TREATING BREAST CANCER GENES

In a recent article in the *New Yorker* entitled 'Decoding Destiny' (1998), Jerome Groopman, a physician, recounts with great sensitivity the story of one of his patients and how she fought with uncertainty. Karen's mother had died of breast cancer, and her sister is currently being treated for the same disease, which had spread to other parts of her body before it was detected. Karen's sister tested positive for a BRCA mutation, that is for a breast cancer gene, after she had been diagnosed with the disease. Because her life was completely disrupted by anxiety, and despite her father's opposition, Karen, a married woman with children, came to Dr Groopman's office asking for the test.

At the Boston hospital where Jerome Groopman works, test results revealing genetic information are strictly confidential, and no third party can ever get access to the results (we will see shortly why this is so important).

Five weeks after having the test, Karen's doctor told her that the result was positive. Her immediate response was to demand a straight answer from him about her belief that she should have her breasts and ovaries removed. Dr Groopman was suitably cautious in explaining to Karen that, despite the presence of the gene, she was not necessarily 'destined' to get cancer. Her body was not the same as that of her sister and mother, he pointed out, and genes must be modified during one's lifetime before they can contribute to the onset of the disease. Karen's choices, both unsatisfactory, were clear: either to have the surgery, or have frequent, minute surveillance for the rest of her life. The surgery, although it would greatly reduce the risk, would not make her chances zero. Neither double prophylactic mastectomy nor oophorectomy [removal of the ovaries] eliminates the possibility of future disease entirely, because some tissue inevitably remains after surgery. On the other hand, intensive surveillance, although often very effective, and with much improved outcomes lately through early detection and therapy (Lopez and Porter 1996), does not ensure that the disease will be discovered before it has spread to other parts of the body. Jerome Groopman told Karen that most women opt for the 'conservative' approach.

Karen decided that day that she could not go through with surgery, but Groopman makes it clear in recounting his story that he hoped that Karen would make this her choice. Despite his position, the only indirect pressure he placed on her was to insist that Karen wait for a week before making the final decision. When she returned to the doctor's office Karen had changed her mind: she had decided to go through with the surgery, both a double mastectomy and an oophorectomy (the odds for Karen of contracting ovarian cancer were about 20%). Her husband, and especially her sister, had helped her reach this decision, which was based perhaps more than anything else on a wish to see her children grow up. One of Karen's children is a thirteen year old girl who will now have to decide whether or not to be tested for the BRCA genes. It is clear that Jerome Groopman was deeply unsettled by this case, and no doubt other similar ones he has had to deal with. He writes about 'new genetic terrors,' of 'genetic time bombs,' of 'twilit terror.' He remains unsure if we benefit by trying to predict the future and concludes that perhaps 'the hope that sustains us comes from the belief that our future is yet to be created, and is created in part by us' (1998:47).

Requests for 'cancer susceptibility information' [that is, for genetic testing] when a tumour is first detected are increasingly common in North America and Europe (Friend 1996). Some women, like Karen, opt for 'prophylactic mastectomies' in an effort to avoid cancer. Not surprisingly, it is among 'cancer dense' families like that of Karen where surgery is carried out most often. One woman whose great-grandmother, grandmother, and mother all had breast cancer (we are not told if they died of the disease) was offered a double mastectomy at aged 18. She declined, but recently, aged 38, tested positive for a breast cancer gene and then decided to have both her breasts removed, a decision that she reports was clearly the right choice for her (Friend 1996). In Vancouver, a psychiatric nurse whose elder sister died from breast cancer at aged 42 also has a twin sister in remission from breast cancer. She was informed at the counselling service she attended that the high proportion of female relatives who had breast cancer from the paternal side of her family was of particular significance. This woman, even though she did not undergo genetic testing, opted for a double mastectomy about which she has no regrets because 'it would go a long way towards removing [my] 80% risk of getting breast cancer' (*Globe and Mail*, 1997b). In England, a genetic counsellor who comes from a family with a history of both female and male cancer, and who has an identical twin sister who contracted breast cancer at aged 38, was given an estimate that she had a 94% chance of having inherited one of the two known breast cancer genes. Her colleagues advising her took careful account of her life history, and reasoned that she was in the lower range of risk among those with a genetic predisposition for breast cancer: a 60% chance for becoming diseased by age 70. On the basis of this information, the counsellor chose to have a double prophylactic mastectomy about which she too has no regrets (Eeles et al. 1996).

Given that all four of these women witnessed close relatives suffering and often dying from cancer, their decision to undergo major disfiguring surgery is understandable. It is also clear, as Karen pointed out to her doctor, that none of us can put ourselves in the places of these women, and presume what might be best for them. One is tempted to wonder, however, if Stephen J. Gould had been the counsellor, might one or two of them have made a different decision? As a master of probability theory, and the father of a young son when he was faced with death, his advice would surely have been of value.

Thus far, aside from case reports such as the above, very little has been published on subjective responses to the new knowledge about the genetics of breast cancer. Clearly anthropology has a contribution to make here, although Pat Kaufert has cautioned that women have already proved themselves well able to voice their own concerns about and experiences with breast cancer, without the anthropologist as intermediary (1998:289). However, an important contribution would be to focus on the knowledge, beliefs and practices of researchers and clinicians in relation, on the one hand to politics and the media, and on the other hand to patients and the public at large.

THE MORAL DISCOURSE OF RISK

Mary Douglas has characterized the idea of 'risk' as a central cultural construct of our time (1986); a construct that did not exist in a technical sense prior to the end of the last century. The 'philosophy of risk' as Ewald notes, incorporates a secularized approach to life, where God is removed from the scene, leaving the control of events entirely in human hands. This approach is a logical outcome of understanding life as a rational enterprise to be actively orchestrated by societies and individuals (Ewald 1991). In contemporary society, events, barring those that we continue to label as accidents, are believed to be governed by physical laws, or by the dictates of probability, although individual activities, conscious or unconscious, may obviously provide modifying forces. Thus, events can be predicted and potentially controlled, provided that individuals do not stretch the limits of acceptable risk. However, the break with divina-

tory practices prevalent before the development of modern science is not complete, because the idea of risk retains not only uncertainty about the future, but also permits the creation of a moral discourse.

Douglas argues that use of the word 'risk,' rather than 'danger' or 'hazard,' has the rhetorical effect of creating an aura of neutrality, of cloaking the concept in scientific legitimacy. Paradoxically, this permits statements about risk to be readily associated with the moral approbation of individuals, perhaps more directly so than was the case in the past. Danger, reworded as risk, is removed from the mediating domain of the supernatural or the divine and is placed squarely, in EuroAmerica at least, on the shoulders of responsible individuals. Risk becomes, in Douglas's words, 'a forensic resource' whereby individuals can be held accountable (1990).

Even where externalized, environmental risk is clearly implicated in the workplace, management tends to focus on those employees whom they define as at high risk, at the expense of considering other factors. Draper quotes a worker employed at a major auto manufacturing corporation: 'For years, companies have been saying that workers' diseases are not caused by what we work with in the plants, but by smoking, diet, lack of exercise, and other problems with our life-style. Now they're saying it's the workers' genetic heritage' (1991:59). A production employee in a chemical manufacturing firm informed Draper that: 'By weeding out the so-called susceptibles, industry will presume the workplace is safe' (1991:59). When legal suits are brought against companies in connection with occupational hazards, efforts are frequently made by defence lawyers to throw social responsibility back onto individual workers, employees, or family members, and the epidemiological 'expert' has been made use of at times to back up such claims (Draper 1991). Someone deemed 'at risk' is a liability in a competitive work environment.

In Euro/America we live in societies in which we are encouraged to conceptualize health as a condition that should be sustained largely through individual effort. This approach to health has its roots in the philosophical tradition of the past several centuries, and is not evident in the same form in other societies, even those with complex technologies (Conrad 1994; Crawford 1979; Lock

1998).[4] It is not surprising, therefore, that much of the current professional literature pertaining to health care starts out with an assumption that individuals should be made responsible for behaviours believed to place them 'at risk' for contracting disease. However, making individuals responsible for their own health, and for the birth of healthy infants and their continued well being, is the product of a moral discourse, one which although it may appear entirely reasonable, is in part politically motivated. In her book *Hidden Arguments,* Tesh asserts that a health policy which consists mainly of exhorting individuals to change their behaviour is not only shortsighted but, more ominously, indirectly protects those institutions that threaten individual health through discrimination, exploitation, pollution or iatrogenesis (1988; see also Lupton 1995; Lock 1998a).

Details were published recently about a Harvard School of Public Health report which stated that smoking, 'poor diet', and what in one newspaper was described as 'sloth' leads to 70% of 'cancer deaths' (*Globe and Mail* 1996). This report argues that we have become preoccupied with 'minor' risks such as environmental pollution and genetics, which have been 'sensationalized' at the cost of thinking about individual life styles. Reports such as this, while they are no doubt correct to criticize the excessive emphasis given to the relationship of individual genetic makeup to disease incidence, nevertheless place responsibility for health firmly with the individual, and in effect ignore the social and political origins of most ill health. Poverty more than any other variable has repeatedly been associated with a wide range of diseases, including both the incidence of and survival from breast cancer (Schrijvers et al. 1995). Poverty is, of course, also associated with poor diet, but to focus on eating habits is to miss the broader political message entirely. Critics of an approach that calls for a focus on self-responsibility rarely deny that individuals would do well to exhibit some care for their own health, but want to emphasize that a large array of so-called 'risk factors' lie well outside the realm of individual control, and that many have their origins in the hazardous social arrangements and environments in which we live (Gorey and Vena 1995).

With our rapidly expanding ability to test and screen for individual genotypes, we are witnessing an expansion of the discourse about health and self-responsibility into new territory. The current politics of breast cancer, for example, appears to be moving in a direction in which individuals are increasingly being offered a chance to take responsibility for assessing and controlling the risks to which their genetic inheritance may expose both them and their potential offspring. With the hype associated with the newly discovered gene mutants BRCA1 and BRCA2 (others genes are in the pipeline), risk is internalized, medicalized and geneticized (to use Lippman's term 1992), and social factors fade into the background. Unlike the carefully controlled testing available at the Boston hospital cited above, private enterprises such as Myriad Genetics in Colorado are springing up in many places. For a fee of $2,400, Myriad is prepared to test every American woman who has been diagnosed with breast cancer, in order that she may then, if found to carry a breast cancer gene, encourage other members of her family to undergo testing. This company is also discussing the implementation of 'hereditary susceptibility testing,' in order to routinely screen populations of 'presymptomatic' women. Myriad provides no medical or counselling services, simply a test, the results of which can take several months to be made known. Since, as we have seen, the only medical 'treatment' available prior to the onset of cancer is a highly invasive prophylactic mastectomy, the value of such testing and screening is debatable (Beardsley 1996).

In contrast to Myriad, the Toronto clinic discussed above, and similar enterprises involved with reproductive technologies, focus on the next generation. Through the application of preimplantation genetic diagnosis, such clinics offer women and their partners, those who can afford to pay between Can$6,500 and nearly Can$10,000, a chance to 'select out' those embryos deemed to be 'at risk' from future disease, and to bring only 'healthy' embryos to term. The success rate for in vitro fertilization (IVF), which must be made use of to make such diagnoses, is very low, often as low or lower than 15%, depending upon the clinic, but this information is not broadcast nearly as loudly by involved practitioners as is the offer to 'sift out bad genes.' Consumers, it is claimed, are being given an unsurpassed opportunity through genetic testing to divine the future, to name the omens, and to take control and responsibility in connection with reproduction, by working to change the odds.[5]

WOMEN AS RISK

Susan Sontag warned us, when she contracted breast cancer more than two decades ago, about the 'punitive and sentimental fantasies' concocted in connection with certain illnesses. She was concerned about the way in which images about illnesses are put to social use and about the various stereotypes which come to be associated with certain of them throughout history. Sontag insisted that the 'most truthful way of regarding illness— and the healthiest way of being ill—is the one most purified of, most resistant to, metaphoric thinking.' She was particularly concerned, not surprisingly, with research current at that time which claimed to have established a statistically significant association between a given personality type and the incidence of breast cancer (1977).

Sontag was justly outraged, given the inadequate way in which the research had been constructed, with biases and confounding factors built into it. However, metaphor cannot be stripped away, either from the production of scientific knowledge, or from the experience of illness to reveal the 'truth' laid bare underneath. Contingent factors are implicated in the production of scientific knowledge about disease (Casper and Koenig 1996; Lock and Gordon 1988; Nelkin 1996; Wright and Treacher 1982), and meanings associated with the experience of illness should not be ignored: if for no other reason than that diagnosed disease does not stand in a one to one relationship with the subjective experience of illness—a fact that deeply affects patient care, as the cases described above make clear (Eisenberg 1977).

Sontag is right, however, in that a goodly portion of metaphorical thinking is indeed destructive, and should be dissected out and disposed of. Today, in connection with health, we are bombarded with value-laden figures about individuals at risk, figures that become iconic of what can be expected to occur to certain populations as they mature and age. It is most often women in all their variation who are subsumed into categories of risk, which then come to stand in place of real people.

The 'making up' (in Hacking's words) of women as adolescent smokers, pregnant teenagers, single mothers, or as post-menopausal, signals impending disaster in one form or another. Increasingly, despite having on average a longer life expectancy than men, simply being a woman is deemed a risk, not because of high mortality during pregnancy and birth, as was formerly the case, but by virtue of the numerous hazards that certain behaviours, characteristics, or the unavoidable processes of ageing are thought to create for individual health and the health of one's offspring.

Few would dispute that some of these activities, such as smoking, are bad for physical well being, but to decontextualize smoking, substance abuse, becoming pregnant and so on, and to individualize and psychologize such behaviours simply as risk taking, is to prematurely assign moral blame, usually at the expense of considering social and political ramifications. We have now entered an era where it is possible to apportion blame to women who select to carry a pregnancy to term when genetic testing indicates that the foetus may be predisposed to one or more diseases some time after birth. Here we see a collapsing of time, a juxtaposition of events—of a pregnancy and of possible disease often many decades hence—in order that manipulation of the future may be facilitated through surveillance of women's bodies; a task made relatively easy by the prevalent notion of individual responsibility for the occurrence of disease in oneself and one's children, before and after birth. As we move into an era of testing and screening for genetic susceptibility to breast cancer, one can be quite certain that numerous women will demand testing for themselves. In some cases they will also want their frozen embryos tested, as is indeed already happening.

THE TICKING TIME BOMB

The media, in their efforts to keep the public informed, have kept up a regular barrage of articles about recent discoveries in connection with genetics and cancer. However, epidemiologists have found it necessary to criticize figures that are repeated so often in newspaper articles: namely that women with BRCA gene mutations have an 80% to 90% lifetime risk of getting breast cancer. Epidemiologists point out that these are average probabilities and that, as with Stephen Gould, the cases of individual women must be placed in the variation distributed around these figures. BRCA1 and possibly BRCA2 appear to be tumour-suppresser genes, whose task is to protect against cancer when functioning appropriately. Both copies of such genes acquired from one's parents must be lost or inactivated in order for this type of breast cancer to become a probability. An inherited mutation usually eliminates only one copy, and the contribution made from the second parent must be affected by other factors, in all probability environmental, before an individual's risk is greatly increased (Kahn 1996). It has been suggested that mammography may act as this trigger, but pesticide exposure and other factors may also be involved.

Richards argues that we should not use the term 'familial breast cancer,' as is done in much of the professional literature, but rather hereditary breast cancer, to refer to the approximately 7% of women where genes appear to play a powerful role in disease incidence. He makes this point because much of the breast cancer that occurs among family members can be shown to be due to shared environmental exposure rather than to a shared genetic heritage (1993). Cross cultural and historical variation in the prevalence and incidence of cancers makes it quite clear that, in addition to genetic differences among biological populations, environmental, toxic, and nutritional factors are implicated in by far the majority of cancers, and are controllable once we have access to a better knowledge base. Although the contribution of genetics to breast cancer must not be minimized, and genetics appears to play a greater role in breast cancer than it does in, for example, lung cancer, research and policy making in connection with environmental issues should not be eclipsed by the current focus on genetics. A major impact on mortality from breast cancer will only be brought about by systematic attention to the environment and related social and political variables.

A further difficulty is that risk estimates in connection with BRCA 1 and 2 have been based on 'cancer dense' families, that is, families such as those described above, where numerous cases of breast cancer, and in many instances, ovarian and prostate cancer in addition, have been found. Before extravagant claims based on these estimates were ever made about risk of hereditary breast cancer for all women, research should have been carried out in which the population at large was surveyed. Until such time as this is done, we live with these terrifying, badly constructed figures which, it is easy to understand, play havoc with the imagination, particularly in those families designated at high risk. Professional journals are not above criticism either. A recent article, concerned to highlight imprecise statistical and histologic terminology in several professional journals, pointed out that the cumulative risk of any one woman is not simply a multiplication of the relative risk factors by other factors, and went on to note that even when familiar cancer is present, the cumulative lifetime risk for a 35-year-old whose mother and one sister have breast cancer is about 15% (Lopez and Porter 1996), but it is the figures of 80% and over that capture everyone's imagination.

The question of penetrance (the estimation of the frequency with which a specific gene will produce the expected effect in a given organism) is frequently reassessed, adding further confusion. Environmental and/or lifestyle factors, together with other genes, affect phenotypic expression, and play an important role in the avoidance of or, alternatively, the onset of cancer (Kahn 1996), but as yet we understand very little of just how this works. For example, the 80% to 85% increased average risk for breast cancer associated with some mutations has recently been re-estimated and lowered by as much as half (Struewing et al. 1997). However, when asked, geneticists indicated that they believe that clinicians probably continue to advise women in terms of very high risk (Bassett, pers. comm.). Friend argues that 'beyond the delicate issues of applying the statistics of susceptibility to the individual, the presence of modifier genes represents the wild-card not placed on the table of statistical averages. For the particular individual, this wild-card may determine what might be their correct course of action' (1996). A highly reliable estimation of probabilities about the outlook for any one woman in connection with breast cancer is, therefore, impossible.

The insurmountable difficulties of interpreting risk in connection with breast cancer, whether a suspect gene is identified or not, suggests that for the time being a headlong rush towards widespread genetic testing and screening may cause more harm than good. Further, the complexity of the subject would indicate that the recent claim of

Myriad that their genetic test for breast cancer will empower women, is both premature and highly irresponsible (*San Francisco Chronicle* 1996).

Lupton reminds us that the certainty with which 'risk factors' and 'risk relationships' are set out for both the public and institutions implicated in one way or another with health care, obscures the ongoing, complex, and often fraught medical and epidemiological debates about what exactly research results signify (1995). Epidemiological knowledge is under continual dispute and reconstruction, but this goes unmarked in popular publications, and even at times in professional literature. Perhaps the best current example of this ignorance is in connection with hormone replacement therapy (Lock 1993), but the breast cancer debate presents another striking case of a premature transformation of 'possible' probabilities, often based on poorly constructed studies, into 'certain' probabilities and then, further, into 'certainties,' in the minds of many members of the public and a large number of researchers, employers, insurance underwriters, lawyers, and others.

In making calculations about disease probabilities, epidemiology can never catch up with the decontextualized findings of basic science. Epidemiology works in a time frame requiring years of longitudinal research to establish the contribution of various factors to human health and illness. Nevertheless, the public is increasingly being asked to subject itself prematurely to screening and testing programmes, on the assumption that the results produced by such tests will unequivocally point individuals towards appropriate preventive measures. Diviners are usually careful not to make extravagant claims about the management of omens. Today, however, certain interested parties forge ahead under the twin banners of probability theory and molecular genetics, offering certainty and control through the manipulation of genes.

FROM RISK TO DANGER

Risk discourse in public health can be divided into three main perspectives: first, risk as a health danger posed to populations by environmental hazards; second, risk which arises as the consequence of life style choices, that is, internally rather than externally imposed risk. Third, social groups may be understood as at risk either because of their position in society, or because of their lack of access to health care resources (Lupton 1995). Each of these approaches to risk has built into it possible courses of avoidance action. Clearly one's genetic inheritance, no longer simply estimated through Mendelian probabilities, but now further 'tamed' and exposed through laboratory representation and manipulation, can be considered as a fourth type of risk, that cuts across the other three perspectives. Molecular genetics, in penetrating one of the facets of nature remaining in the world of chance, facilitates the incorporation of population genetics into a zone of risk analysis with greater precision than was formerly the case.

It is clear, however, that our methods of mastering the omens themselves represent a form of danger: a new kind of forensic risk. When (not if) employers and insurance companies are given access to the results of genetic tests, or unilaterally demand that such tests are carried out, an insidious form of discrimination is exerted over an increasingly large segment of the population. We know from a recent survey reported in *Science* based on a sample of over 300 members of genetic support groups in the United States, that 25% of respondents believe that they have been refused life insurance on the basis of genetic testing; 22% believe that they were refused health insurance, and 13% believe they were denied employment or dismissed from a job. Fear of genetic discrimination resulted in 9% of respondents or family members refusing genetic tests (another study showed that people use false names when they undergo such tests), 18% did not reveal genetic information to insurers, and 17% did not inform employers (Lapham et al. 1996). Given that we are dealing in the case of breast cancer with an almost exclusively female population, one can predict an unholy combination of gender and genetic discrimination being brought to bear on occasion.

SCREENING AND TESTING FOR EMBODIED DANGER

From the time when mammography was first institutionalized, there is evidence of poor medical practice in connection with the promotion of screening programmes for breast cancer, and also in connection with the dissemination of information about these programmes. For example, the anxiety associated with cancer has at times been capitalized upon in recruitment advertising. An Australian advertisement ran as follows: 'no woman needs to die of breast cancer if she reads and heeds the leaflets of the cancer societies and has her breasts examined regularly' (Skrabanek 1985:316). Such advertising suggests that screening protects one from the actual disease, while at the same time in essence making women fully responsible, in that those who do not go for screening take an undue risk with their lives.

Services are usually promoted under the banner of rights of access to good health care, something in which many women's groups actively participate, on the assumption that resort to preventive measures will decrease their ultimate dependency on medicine. But the contrary is usually the case, whether it be genetic screening, mammography, amniocentesis, bone scans, or use of hormone replacement therapy. False positives alone, extremely high in the case of mammograms, result in elevated anxiety levels. Regular monitoring, questionable results, repeat tests, and the daily imbibing of pills, ensure that women cannot put the fallible, treacherous body out of mind; this never-ending surveillance creates a vicious cycle of anxiety from which there is no escape—a culturally enhanced anxiety, one particularly evident in North America, which encourages many middle class women, at least, to see the body as inherently weak and ever in need of protection and modification through technological intervention. Screening programmes also present major difficulties associated with the interpretations and explanations given in connection with risk to which I have alluded above, and to which I now return.

In professional circles, health related risk is usually assumed to be a unidimensional, technical concept that simply refers to a numerical probability value (Hansson 1989). Obviously, in popular usage other meanings are associated with risk, which often have implications for everyday life. At issue, therefore, is a major difficulty in connection with commensurability, that is, with the translation of meanings between the professional and the popular domains. Integral to this lack of commensurability are not simply the gulf between techni-

cal and lay language, but judgmental decisions and the assigning of blame (Nelkin 1985); also difference in status and power relations and, of over-riding importance, the difference between objectivity and subjectivity: between calculated assessment and individual experience.

For some years now, in part as a result of the requirement of informed consent, there has been an increased sensitivity in the medical world to the importance of paying at least some attention to the patient's point of view in medical encounters, but this insight is rarely followed through adequately. It is often perverted, in fact, in that attending to patient concerns can provide a means of coercing patients into compliance while leaving the assumptions, values and obfuscating language of medicine unexamined and unexplained. Professional genetic counsellors have self-consciously tried to combat this tendency by making 'non-directional' counselling the lynch-pin of their practice.

Gifford argues that the very act of transposing the concept of risk from the probabilities of epidemiology into clinical practice means that risk is made into the specific property of individuals: it is now something that a patient suffers (1986). This creation of an 'at risk patient' has two immediate outcomes: first, the clinician, rather than being able to formulate a satisfactory diagnosis on which to base treatment, must make judgments grounded in clinical uncertainty. Second, those at risk, the presymptomatic ill, internalize a state of being which is one of waiting with dread for what the future holds in store. As Yoxen noted, it is difficult for such individuals to think of themselves as healthy; thus, being labelled with an at-risk diagnosis, being made aware of the omens, in itself becomes a risk.

Gifford's ethnographic study from the early 1980s showed how different surgeons respond to a state of clinical uncertainty. A self-described compulsive surgeon, for example, wanted all breast lumps removed, because he could not deal with his own anxiety about not being able to distinguish with absolute certainty between a cyst and a lump. Earlier, remarkable differences were demonstrated between rates of tonsillectomy, hysterectomy and prostatectomy within the state of Vermont: differences that were attributed to surgeon personality more than to any other variable (Wennberg and Gittelsohn 1982). In her study, Gifford found a surgeon who not only recommended prophylactic mastectomies where a family history of breast cancer was evident, but also in cases where patients had what he described as 'extremely difficult breasts to follow.' Similarly, we may assume, I think, that certain physicians, driven by their own anxieties, compulsions, and perhaps curiosity, will tend to encourage women to undergo genetic testing. It is, after all, a simple test with no danger involved. These same physicians may well be the ones to encourage prophylactic mastectomies on the basis of positive test results, even though we know that this drastic action does not necessarily eliminate a later occurrence of cancer. Women on their part, similarly motivated by what, in North America at least, approaches an obsession with 'being in control' (Crawford 1984), may well collude with physicians into opening the door to testing, even when they are not thought to be at high risk. Alternatively, certain women may bully sceptical physicians into making available a procedure about which the physician may have serious reservations.

Given the tenuous state of current knowledge, genetic testing for breast cancer, a disease for which we have no preventative measures other than mastectomy, can potentially have disastrous results for psychological well-being, and for family and community relationships. We know that both positive and negative test results can cause havoc. Survivor guilt and shame have already been demonstrated among those members of families with hereditary breast cancer who test negative (MacDonald et al., 1996). Negative results may also create a sense of false security, since such results by no means rule out the occurrence of cancer at a future date. On the other hand, positive results may elevate anxiety to exceedingly high levels, and the knowledge that not everyone who tests positive gets cancer will provide little alleviation. In addition, as we have seen, there may well be other unforeseen effects in connection with employment and health insurance. Entrepreneurs involved with the marketing of genetic tests and with efforts to patent genes simply counter concerns expressed by the American Society of Human Genetics, the National Breast Cancer Coalition, and other groups and individuals, by asserting that individual women have the right to make their own choices in this matter.

It has been argued that a ban on free access to testing would be patronizing to women (Wadman 1996:573), but we do not argue that individuals should have unrestricted access to drugs or diagnostic tests, and in any case we (usually) keep such products out of the market until such time as they have been rigorously tested. Appropriate testing of thalidomide or diethylstilboestrol (DES) could have saved indescribable suffering. Obviously the technology of genetic testing is not in itself dangerous, but the uncertainties, ambiguities and ignorance associated with the dissemination and interpretation of such test results are vast. Some control over the dissemination of false, misleading or patently unclear information is very nearly as important as is the regulation of dangerous drugs, although obviously it is difficult, if not impossible, to implement such control.

It is of note that the National Action Plan on Breast Cancer (NAPBC) in the United States argues that, for the present, genetic testing for hereditary susceptibility for breast and ovarian cancer should only be offered through 'hypothesis-driven, institutional review board approved, research studies designed to address specific questions' (Department of Health and Human Services 1996), and that the findings of such tests should be kept strictly private. Francis Collins, past director of the Human Genome Project, is co-director of the working group that produced this document.

CANCER AND THE ENVIRONMENT

Although scientific knowledge about breast cancer genes is without doubt of great significance, with promise of more to come, there is a great danger that these remarkable 'breakthroughs' are deflecting attention away from the major contributing causes of breast cancer: those associated with social and environmental variables. Here too, risk language is predominant in research, but confusion is also common when this kind of data is interpreted by the media. The epidemiologist Philip Cole was quoted in a recent issue of *Science* as pointing out that in the history of epidemiology only a dozen or so environmental agents have been repeatedly and strongly associated with cancer. Among them are 'cigarette smoke, alcohol, ionizing radiation, a few drugs, a handful of occupational carcinogens, such as asbestos, and perhaps three viruses—hepatitis B, human T cell leukaemia, and human papillomavirus' (Taubes 1995). Nevertheless we are peppered with new findings about the dangers of the environment almost every day in the media. The *Science* article informs us that:

> most epidemiologists interviewed by *Science* said they would not take seriously a single study reporting a new potential risk of cancer unless it reported that exposure to the agent in question increased a person's risk by at least a factor of 3—which is to say it carried a risk ratio of 3. Even then, they say, skepticism is in order unless the study was very large and extremely well done and biological data support the hypothesized link. (Taubes 1995:165)

Taubes lists 25 studies reported in professional journals over the previous eight years, and then picked up by the popular press, in which risk factors for cancer, most of them for breast cancer, have been identified. He notes that most of the studies made use of small samples, and few have come close to fulfilling the criteria noted above, including a significant risk ratio, but they have nevertheless added to the current epidemic of anxiety about breast cancer because of decontextualized reporting by the media. Among the factors that have been shown to be associated with breast cancer in these studies are the following: high-fat diet (rr = 2); weight of 3.6 kilograms or more at birth (rr = 1.3); pesticide exposure indicated by high blood residues (rr = 4); occupational exposure to electromagnetic fields (rr = 1.38); smoking two packs of cigarettes a day (rr = 1.74 for fatal breast cancer); eating red meat twice a day (rr = 2); abortion (rr = 1.5) (this finding was later retracted); having shorter or longer on average menstrual cycles (rr = 2); consuming olive oil only once a day or less (rr = 1.25) (Taubes 1995:165). Surprisingly, use of hormone replacement therapy among post-menopausal women does not appear on this list, even though several frequently cited studies have shown an association between use of this medication and an increased risk for breast cancer. Taubes concludes that pesticide exposure is the one factor that has been studied sufficiently and with large enough samples to be considered as a risk to the health of individual women. However, a recent publication disputes even this finding, and one of the involved doctors accuses 'paparazzi science' of setting agendas before the evidence is in (Immen 1997c).

When we add to these disconcerting messages the most powerful image of all currently circulating in connection with breast cancer, namely that 1 in 9 women will get breast cancer in their lifetime (1 in 8 in some reports), and that 1 in 25 women will die of this disease, it should come as no surprise that anxiety prevails. This figure is exceedingly misleading, but repeated incessantly, stripped of context. Risk estimates are made in different ways, and do not necessarily take into account the same variables, thus causing confusion. One in nine is the cumulative probability of contracting breast cancer over an entire lifetime, that is, somewhere between birth and age 110; even for elderly women, the probabilities at any one time are never as high as 1 in 9. As Ruth Hubbard and others have pointed out, once this figure is broken down by age, a very different impression is created (Hubbard and Wald 1993); but it is cumbersome to recite these figures. For example, one newspaper states that 'if you are 30 today, you have one chance in 5,000 of breast cancer developing in the next year, and one chance in 238 of it developing in the next 10 years; if you are 35, you have one chance in 2,500 of the disease developing in the next year, and if you are 45, you have one chance in 714' (*Globe and Mail*, 1994). A second newspaper more recently announced a different set of figures: 'By age 35, a woman has one chance in 622 of developing breast cancer. The risk rises to one in 93 by age 45, one in 33 by age 55 and one in 17 by age 65 (*New York Times* 1997).

Because these figures are calculated in different ways, and different time spans are taken into account, they are confusing, but they nevertheless present a more accurate picture than the 1 in 9 mantra. Both make use of age cohorts rather than cumulative probability, and reveal that at no time in her life is any one woman's chance of getting breast cancer within the next ten years as high as 1 in 9. However, we can be sure that doctors regularly tell their patients that their chances are 1 in 9 of contracting breast cancer, and that they do this to encourage women to undergo annual mammograms and to foster self-responsibility for health. No doubt most women, after hearing this omen, leave the doctor's office, stunned, to sit in the park, look at the eight women nearest them, and think despairingly: 'one of us will soon be dead of cancer.'

No wonder that so many women demand increased access to mammography, even when its worth, especially to women under 50, has been thoroughly questioned, and the number of false positives is astounding. It is also not surprising that demand for genetic testing is on the increase. However, reading the omens and transmitting this complex, inconclusive knowledge wild-cards and all, so that people do not panic, is an art that it is likely very few have mastered.

We have at least five issues to sort out post-haste which have relevance to all multifactorial diseases in which genetics are sometimes implicated, including prostate cancer and heart disease, among others. First, how to put in place enforceable regulatory measures in connection with facilities that provide genetic testing and screening. Second, how to prevent discrimination against individuals both in the work place and by insurance companies on the basis of genetics. Third, we should reconsider our current devotion to the ideas of individual choice, and to self-responsibility for maintaining health as being more important than other factors. Fourth, we (the media, the public and many health care professionals) must become better acquainted with probability mathematics if we are to interpret risk analyses. And fifth, it is urgent that we disabuse ourselves of genetic determinism.

NOTES

1. Over the centuries, particularly in Europe and North America, we have witnessed biological determinism of one kind and another. Today's new wave of genetic determinism promises to be particularly powerful and potentially dangerous because it is so tightly associated with large-scale entrepreneurial endeavours; further, it is gaining recognition at a time when governments in many countries are unloading responsibilities for large segments of health care onto the private sector.

2. My interest in and knowledge about this subject has been informed greatly by participation in a Canadian national committee known as the Medical, Ethical, Legal and Social Issues committee of the Canadian Genome Analysis and Technology Programme. This entire programme, both the scientific and the much smaller ethics section, is now defunct due to government cut-backs.

3. These findings should not be interpreted to mean that emotional states or 'personality types' cause cancer, as had been argued at times. Rather, they indicate that the immune and neuroendocrinological systems are inter-dependent and, further, that throughout the life course, the environment, physical and social, is in a dialectical relationship with individual biology.

4. Obviously there is variation among European and North American countries with respect to ideas about how much individual effort is required to sustain health and, further, actual practices vary considerably from one country to another. I well recall the father of an American family being outraged by Norwegian adolescents when they started to smoke on a train going from Bergen to Oslo, but his loud complaints about the danger these adolescents were posing to the health of the American family were simply ignored. Similarly, I have observed smokers in restaurants in Italy respond with anger when North American tourists asked if they would stub out their cigarettes. It is quite possible that America represents an extreme case in arguments for individual responsibility, and the lack of a socialized health care system certainly reinforces this type of thinking.

5. In making these arguments I have reviewed literature produced in the United States and Canada, and, to a lesser extent Australia. Unlike the U.S., Canada and Australia both have socialized health care systems, but, thus far, most genetic testing and reproductive technologies are not incorporated into these systems. The situation may be different in European countries.

REFERENCES

Aries, Philippe. 1981. *The Hour of our Death*. New York: Alfred A. Knopf.

Beardsley, Tim. 1996. Vital data. *Scientific American* 274: 100–105

Bolles. R. C. and M. S. Fanselow. 1982. Endorphins and behaviour. *Annual Review of Psychology* 33: 87–101.

Burchell, Graham, Colin Gordon and Peter Miller. 1991. *The Foucault Effect: Studies in Governmentality*. Chicago: U. of Chicago P.

Canguilhem, Georges. 1991. *The Normal and the Pathological*. New York, Zone Books.

Casper. Monica J. and Barbara A. Koenig. 1996. Reconfiguring nature and culture: Intersections of medical anthropology and technoscience studies. *Medical Anthropology Quarterly* 10(4): 523–536.

Conrad, Peter. 1994. Wellness as virtue: Morality and the pursuit of health. *Culture, Medicine and Psychiatry* 18: 385–401.

Crawford, Robert. 1979. Individual Responsibility and Health Politics in the 1970s. In Susan Reverby and David Rosner (eds) *Health Care in America: Essays in Social History*. Philadelphia: Temple U.P., pp. 247–268.

———. 1984. A Cultural Accident of Health: Self Control, Release and the Social Body. In John McKinlay (ed) *Issues in the Political Economy of Health Care*. London: Tavistock, pp. 60–103.

Crosby, Alfred W. 1997. *The Measure of Reality: Quantification and Western Society, 1250–1600.* Cambridge: Cambridge U.P.

Daston, Lorraine. 1988. *Classical Probability in the Enlightenment.* Princeton: Princeton U.P.

Douglas, Mary. 1986. *Risk Acceptability according to the Social Sciences.* London: Routledge and Kegan Paul.

———. 1990. Risk as a forensic resource. *Daedalus* 119: 1–16.

Draper, Elaine. 1991. *Risky Business: Genetic Testing and Exclusionary Practices in the Hazardous Workplace.* Cambridge: Cambridge U.P.

Eeles, R., T. Cole, R. Taylor, P. Lunt and M. Baum. 1996. Prophylactic mastectomy for genetic predisposition to breast cancer: The Proband's story. *Clinical Oncology* 8: 222–225.

Eisenberg, Leon. 1977. Disease and illness: Distinctions between professional and popular ideas of sickness. *Culture, Medicine and Psychiatry* 1: 9–23.

Evans-Pritchard, E. E. 1937. *Witchcraft, Oracles and Magic among the Azande.* Oxford: Clarendon P.

Ewald, F. 1991. Insurance and Risk. In G. Burchell, C. Gordon and P. Miller (eds) *The Foucault Effect: Studies in Governmentality.* Hemel Hempstead: Harvester Wheatsheaf, pp. 197–210.

Friend, Stephen H. 1996. Breast cancer susceptibility testing: Realities in the post-genomic era. *Nature Genetics* 13: 16–17.

Gifford, Sandra. 1986. The Meaning of Lumps: A Case Study of the Ambiguities of Risk. In C. R. Janes, R. Stall and S. M. Gifford (eds) *Anthropology and Epidemiology: Interdisciplinary Approaches to the Study of Health and Disease.* Dordrecht: Reidel Publishers, pp. 213–246.

Globe and Mail. 1994. How to assess the risk of breast cancer, 24 January.

———. 1996. Report lifts major cancer risks, 20 November.

———. 1997a. Clinic to sift out bad genes, 24 September.

———. 1997b. Betsy Lewthwaite's genetic odyssey, 14 June.

Gorey, Kevin M. and John E. Vena. 1995. The association of near poverty status with cancer incidence among black and white adults. *Journal of Community Health* 20(4): 359–366.

Gould, Stephen Jay. 1985. The median isn't the message. *Discover,* June.

Groopman, Jerome, 1998. Decoding destiny. *New Yorker,* 9 February, pp. 42–47.

Hacking, Ian. 1975. *The Emergence of Probability.* Cambridge: Cambridge U.P.

———. 1982. Language, Truth and Reason. In Martin Hollis and Steven Lukes (eds) *Rationality and Relativism.* Cambridge, MA.: MIT Press, pp. 48–66.

———. 1990. *The Taming of Chance.* Cambridge: Cambridge U.P.

Hansson, S. E. 1989. Dimensions of risk. *Risk Analysis* 9(1): 107–112.

Hubbard, Ruth and Elijah Wald. 1995. *Exploding the Gene Myth.* Boston: Beacon P.

Immen, Wallace. 1997. Breast cancer, pesticides not linked, study says. *Globe and Mail,* 30 October.

Kahn, Patricia. 1996. Coming to grips with genes and risk. *Science* 274: 496–498.

Kaufert, Patricia. 1998. Women, Resistance and the Breast Cancer Movement. In Margaret Lock and Patricia Kaufert (eds) *Pragmatic Women and Body Politics.* Cambridge: Cambridge U.P., pp. 287–309.

Lambeck, Michael. 1993. *Knowledge and Practice in Mayotte: Local Discourses of Islam, Sorcery, and Spirit Possession.* Toronto: U. of Toronto P.

Lapham, E. Virginia, Chahira Kozma and Joan O. Weiss. 1996. Genetic discrimination: Perspectives of the consumer. *Science* 274: 621–624.

Lippman, Abby. 1992. Prenatal genetic testing and screening: Constructing needs and reinforcing inequities. *American Journal of Law and Medicine* 17: 15–50.

Lock, Margaret. 1993. *Encounters with Aging: Mythologies of Menopause in Japan and North America.* Berkeley: U. of California P.

—and Deborah Gordon (eds). 1988. *Biomedicine Examined.* Dordrecht: Kluwer Academic Publishers.

—(forthcoming). Situating Women in the Politics of Health. In Susan Sherwin (ed) *Agency, Autonomy, and Politics in Women's Health.* Temple U.P.

Loewe, Michael. 1981. China. In Michael Loewe and C. Blacker (eds) *Oracles and Divination.* Boulder, CO.: Shambhala Publications.

Lopez, Marvin J. and Kathleen A. Porter. 1996. The current role of prophylactic mastectomy. *Surgical Clinics of North America* 76(2): 231–239.

Lupton, Deborah. 1995. *The Imperative of Health: Public Health and the Regulated Body.* London: Sage Publications Inc.

Macdonald, Kathleen G., Brian Doan, Merrijoy Kelner and Kathryn M. Taylor. 1996. A sociobehavioural perspective on genetic testing and counselling for heritable breast, ovarian and colon cancer. *Canadian Medical Association Journal* 154(4): 457–464.

National Action Plan on Breast Cancer (NAPBC). 1996. *Position Paper: Hereditary Susceptibility Testing for Breast Cancer.* Washington, Department of Health and Human Services, March.

Nelkin, Dorothy. 1996. The social dynamics of genetic testing: The case of fragile-x. *Medical Anthropology Quarterly* 10(4): 537–550.

New York Times. 1997. Reducing the risk of disease, 19 October.

Richards, M. P. M. 1993. The new genetics: Some issues for social scientists. *Sociology of Health & Illness* 15(5): 567–586.

San Francisco Chronicle. 1996. Another genetic test for breast cancer on the market, 11 November.

Schrijvers, C. T. M., J. P. Mackenback. J.-M., Lutz, M. J. Quino and M. P. Coleman. 1995. Deprivation and survival from breast cancer. *British Journal of Cancer* 72: 738–743.

Serematakis, C. Nadia. 1991. *The Last Word: Women, Death, and Divination in Inner Mani*. Chicago: U. of Chicago P.

Skrabanek, P. 1985. False premises and false promises of breast cancer screening. *Lancet* ii: 316–320.

Sontag, Susan. 1978. *Illness as Metaphor*. New York: Farrar, Straus and Giroux.

Struewing, Jeffrey P., Patricia Hartge, Sholom Wacholder, Sonya M. Baker, Martha Berlin, Mary McAdams, Michelle M. Timmerman, Lawrence C. Brody and Margaret A. Tucker. 1997. The risk of cancer associated with specific mutations of BRCA1 and BRCA2 among Ashkenazi Jews. *The New England Journal of Medicine* 336(20): 1401–1408.

Taubes, Gary. 1995. Epidemiology faces its limits. *Science* 269(14 July): 164–169.

Tesh, Sylvia Noble. 1988. *Hidden Arguments: Political Ideology and Disease Prevention Policy*. New Brunswick, NJ: Rutgers U.P.

Thomas, Lewis. 1983. *The Youngest Science: Notes of a Medicine-Watcher*. New York: The Viking Press.

Wadman, Meredith. 1996. Panel softens cancer gene test warning. *Nature* 380: 573.

Wennberg, John and Alan Gittelsohn. 1982. Variations in medical care among small areas. *Scientific American* 246: 120–133.

Whyte, Susan Reynolds. 1997. *Questioning Misfortune: The Pragmatics of Uncertainty in Eastern Uganda*. Cambridge: Cambridge U.P.

Wikan, Uni. 1990. *Managing Turbulent Hearts: A Balinese Formula for Living*. Chicago: Chicago U.P.

Wright, Peter W. G. and Andrew Treacher (eds). 1982. *The Problem of Medical Knowledge: Examining the Social Construction of Medicine*. Edinburgh: U. of Edinburgh P.

Yoxen, Edward. 1982. Constructing Genetic Diseases. In P. Wright and A. Treacher (eds) *The Problem of Medical Knowledge: Examining the Social Construction of Medicine*. Edinburgh: U. of Edinburgh P., pp. 144–161.

■ ■ ■ ■ ■ ■ ■ ■ ■

29   REFUGEE STRESS AND FOLK BELIEF: HMONG SUDDEN DEATHS

Shelley R. Adler

This selection argues that mortal harm can come from the displacement of an explanatory model from one behavioral environment to another (see also selection 26). Adler's analysis of the mass relocation of Hmong refugees from Laos to the United States highlights the psychophysical stress experienced by people living under conditions of extreme insecurity and violence who flee to new locations with new sources of anxiety and uncertainty (see also selection 33). The sudden death of seemingly healthy people provides an extreme illustration of the nocebo effect, or the power of belief to cause disease and death, not just healing (see Hahn 1997; selections 27, 28, 30).

The Hmong in this study live in conditions that are radically different from those left behind. Previously, they were more certain of their cultural and social identity, their geographical and historical position, and their relationship to the spirit world and the topography and specific natural features associated with it (see selections 25, 26, 27). Uprooted from this circle of life, detached from previously stable social support systems, and impeded in the practice of their religion—if not converted to the mainstream one

Source: Reprinted from *Social Science and Medicine*, Vol. 40, Adler, S. R., "Refugee Status and Folk Belief: Hmong Sudden Deaths," Pages 1623–1629, Copyright (1995), with permission from Elsevier.

of their new home—these refugees experience a disjuncture that can bring on nightmares and apparently sudden death as well.

Adler describes a universal nightmare phenomenon rooted in human anatomy and physiology and elaborated in various ways across cultures. For the Hmong, the nocturnal pressing spirit was well known back home, but could be appeased through the intervention of a shaman and prescribed actions to rectify a transgression. In the United States, this spirit comes more frequently and with deadly force, as people worry about failing in their religious obligations, on top of struggling with daily economic and social difficulties.

The deaths of healthy people in the prime of life seem to defy explanation in biomedical terms. Adler suggests that the underlying reason is psychological distress deriving from a worldview that does not separate the human from the spirit world, the mind from the body, but which has been displaced into a social context where religious obligations are difficult to meet and life is stressful overall. In this scenario, repeated visits from an evil nighttime spirit can literally press the life out of a person.

Questions to keep in mind

Is the universal nightmare phenomenon explainable by concepts from laboratory sleep research, and if so, how?

In what ways is this universal phenomenon shaped specifically by Hmong culture?

Why are Hmong men more susceptible to nightmare and SUNDS than Hmong women?

In what ways does the Hmong worldview and mind–body construction converge with anthropological understandings about the role of belief in illness?

With the fall of the capital city of Vientiane in 1975, thousands of Hmong fled their native Laos and—often after extended delays in Thai refugee camps—began arriving in the United States. The Hmong are more widely known in the West than other Laotian ethnic groups because of their efforts on behalf of the United States during the war in Viet Nam, particularly after it spread to Laos and Cambodia. Thousands of Hmong were funded directly and secretly by the Central Intelligence Agency to combat the Communist Pathet Lao. Hmong men served as soldiers, pilots, and navigators, and their familiarity with the mountain terrain helped make them remarkable scouts and guerrilla fighters [1]. By the end of the civil war, the Hmong had suffered casualty rates proportionally ten times higher than those of Americans who fought in Viet Nam [2]; it is estimated that nearly one-third of the Laotian Hmong population lost their lives [1]. When the Laotian government changed hands after the departure of American troops, large groups of Hmong were forced to flee Laos rather than chance "re-education" camps or possible death under the new Communist regime.

There are currently over 110,000 Hmong living in the United States, with 70,000 in California's Central Valley alone [3]. The city of Fresno is now home to the largest single community of Hmong in existence. The relocation of this large number of refugees from Laos to the United States has been characterized by extraordinary difficulties.

These displaced and resettled Hmong, while finding welcome freedom from persecution and physical annihilation, are nevertheless going through a grave cultural crisis, immersed as they are, an infinitesimal minority, in overwhelmingly dominant majority modes of living, norms of behavior, beliefs and values. Everywhere they face the possibility of cultural annihilation and struggle to maintain for themselves and their children, a clear idea of who they are, of their identity as Hmong, of their place in history and in the cosmic realm of spirits, ancestors' souls and human societies [4].

The Hmong who have fled Laos leave behind them a homeland ravaged by war, but in their transition to the West they are met with new and unique problems. Those Hmong who have come to the United States find themselves suspended between worlds, in a place where their religion, language and skills are de-contextualized and where their previous social support system is greatly weakened [5]. In particular, for many Hmong the relocation marks the end of the prevalent form of their traditional religious beliefs and practices.

In the traditional Hmong worldview, the natural world is alive with spirits. Trees, mountains, rivers, rocks and lightning are all animated by distinctive spirits. Ancestor spirits not only remain around the living, but play an essential role in complex rituals of reciprocity with their living descendants.

> The Hmong celebrate their humanity not as a discrete and impenetrable part of the natural order, but as part of the circle of life of all creation—caught up in the rotation of the seasons, and deeply connected with the configuration of the mountains, and the reincarnation of life from generation to generation, even from species to species. Life, in its myriad forms, is intimately articulated through souls and spirits [6].

In interviews with refugees, it became clear that many Hmong feared that the ancestor spirits who protected them from harm in Laos would be unable to travel across the ocean to the United States and thus could not shield them from spiritual dangers. Solace was taken, however, in the conviction that the myriad evil spirits who challenged Hmong well-being in Laos would also be prevented from following the Hmong to their new home. Among these evil spirits assumed to have been left behind was the nocturnal pressing spirit *dab tsog* (pronounced 'da cho') [7]. It soon became frighteningly apparent, however, that this notorious evil spirit had made the journey to America as well.

HMONG SUDDEN UNEXPECTED NOCTURNAL DEATH SYNDROME

Since the first reported case, which occurred in 1977, more than 100 Southeast Asians in the United States have died from the mysterious disorder that is now known as SUNDS, the Sudden Unexpected Nocturnal Death Syndrome [8]. The sudden deaths have an unusually high incidence among Laotians, particularly male Hmong refugees. All but one of the victims have been men, the median age is 33, the median length of time living in the United States before death is 17 months [9], all were apparently healthy, and all

died during sleep. The rate of death from SUNDS has reached alarming proportions: at its peak in 1981–1982, the rate of death among 25–44-year-old Hmong men (92/100,000) [10] was equivalent to the sum of the rates of the five leading causes of natural death among United States males in the same age group [11].

Despite numerous studies of SUNDS, medical scientists have not been able to determine exactly what is causing the deaths of these seemingly healthy people in their sleep [12]. Biomedical studies have taken into account such varied factors as toxicology [13–17], heart disease [12, 18, 19], genetics [14, 15, 20, 21], metabolism [15], and nutrition (particularly thiamine deficiency [22]), but are no nearer to a comprehensive answer. Current medical opinion appears to favor the role of abnormalities of the cardiac conduction system, although a 1988 report from the Centers for Disease Control indicates the incompleteness of this solution: "Only at night, in times of unusual stress, and possibly in conjunction with other, as yet undefined, factors are these people at risk of developing abnormal electrical impulses in the heart that result in ventricular fibrillation and sudden death" [9].

THE NIGHTMARE SPIRIT

Biomedicine thus provides no adequate answer to the question of what causes SUNDS; from my vantage point in the social sciences, however, I propose that an investigation of Hmong traditional belief can reveal the event that triggers the fatal syndrome. The focus of this research is a supranormal nocturnal experience that I refer to as the 'nightmare' and that is familiar to the Hmong. I use the word 'nightmare' not in the modern sense of a bad dream, but rather in its original denotation as the nocturnal visit of an evil being that threatens to press the very life out of its terrified victim [23–25].

According to descriptions of the Nightmare spirit [26], the sleeper suddenly becomes aware of a presence close at hand. Upon attempting to investigate further, the victim is met with the horrifying realization that he or she is completely paralyzed. The presence is usually felt to be an evil one, and often this impression is confirmed by a visual perception of the being, which places itself on the sleeper's chest and exerts a pressure great enough to interfere with respiration. The classic nightmare experience, then, is characterized by the following symptoms: the impression of wakefulness, immobility, sensation of pressure on the chest, realistic perception of the environment, and intense fear. (To avoid confusion, I use *Nightmare* [upper case] to refer to the spirit or demonic figure to which these nocturnal assaults are attributed and *nightmare* [lower case] to refer to the basic experience; that is, the impression of wakefulness, immobility, realistic perception of the environment, and intense fear [27]).

The case definition presented in the *Final Report of the SUNDS Planning Project* [15] emphasizes the need to observe closely people "who fit the demographic characteristics of SUNDS" and who have transient nocturnal events that include

"1. a sense of panic or extreme fear,

2. paralysis (partial or complete);

3. a sense of pressure on the chest;

4. a sense that there is an alien being (animal, human, or spirit) in the room; [and]

5. a disturbance in sensation (auditory, visual or tactile)."

This list of five symptoms of SUNDS-related events is identical to the characteristics of the nightmare experience as it is known in countless folk traditions, including those of the Hmong. Since the conditions described by Holtan *et al.* as "SUNDS-related" are consistent with the symptoms of a Nightmare attack, I decided to investigate the possibility that SUNDS is initiated by such a confrontation.

Based on preliminary fieldwork and a review of previous research, I developed the hypothesis that the supranormal nocturnal experience traditionally known as the nightmare and familiar to the Hmong acts as a trigger for the sudden nocturnal deaths [28]. In order to study the prevalence of the nightmare phenomenon and the role of the nightmare in traditional Hmong culture, I interviewed a representative sample of 118 Hmong in Stockton, California. In the course of research it was necessary to establish the veracity of a series of facts: first, that the Hmong supranormal experience that I had isolated was in fact a culture-specific manifestation of the universal nightmare phenomenon; second, that Hmong belief regarding the experience forms a collective tradition; third, that the

Hmong nightmare, in specific contexts, causes cataclysmic psychological stress; and fourth, by drawing on the growing medical and anthropological literature on ethnomedical pathogenesis, that intense psychological stress can cause sudden death.

The nightmare syndrome appears to be universal in its occurrence. There are innumerable instances of the nightmare throughout history and in a multitude of cultures; from the ancient Greek *ephialtes* (= leap upon) and Roman *incubus* (= lie upon) to contemporary examples such as French *cauchemar* (from La. *calcare* = to trample upon, squeeze), German *Alpdruck* (= elf pressure), Newfoundland "Old Hag" [23, 24, 29], Polish *zmora*, and Mexican *pesadilla* [30]. The nightmare's significance and impact vary considerably in different cultural settings, but the core nightmare phenomenology appears to be stable cross-culturally [31].

THE NIGHTMARE AND SLEEP RESEARCH

The consistent features of the nightmare are better understood with the assistance of concepts from laboratory sleep research. Somnologists distinguish between two major divisions of sleep: active sleep (or REM) and quiet sleep. REM sleep is characterized by brain waves resembling those of wakefulness. Unlike the waking state, however, the body is paralyzed, apparently to keep the sleeper from acting out his or her dreams [32]. In rare instances, this normal muscle inhibition or atonia occurs during partial wakefulness. This condition is known as 'sleep paralysis,' a stage in which the body is asleep, but the mind is not. Often sleep paralysis is accompanied by hypnagogic hallucinations, which consist of complex visual, auditory, and somatosensory perceptions occurring in the period of falling asleep and resembling dreams [33].

Sleep paralysis and hypnagogic hallucinations are products of 'sleep-onset REM,' a REM stage that occurs earlier than usual, when the individual is still partially conscious [24, 30, 34] Sleep-onset REM accounts for the subjective impression of wakefulness, the feeling of paralysis, and, as a result, the tremendous anxiety that mark the nightmare experience. Researchers have shown convincingly that sleep-onset REM accounts for the subjective impression of wakefulness, the feeling of paralysis, and, as a result, the tremendous anxiety that mark the nightmare experience [23, 24, 27] I extend these explanations of nightmare symptoms to include the fact that the sense of oppression or weight on the chest and the attendant feature of lying in a supine position are a result of the fact that when the sleeper is lying on his or her back, the atonic muscles of the tongue and esophagus collapse the airway. The relaxed muscles not only hinder breathing, but actually create a sensation of suffocation, strangulation or pressure on the chest of the terrified sleeper [35]. The connection between Nightmare attacks and sleep paralysis is highlighted by the fact that Hmong women report that some men, fearing that deep sleep might bring about their deaths, set their alarm clocks to awaken them every 20 or 30 minutes [15]. Ironically, this type of sleep disruption may actually cause sleep-onset REM and nightmares (through the mechanism of 'REM pressure' [36–38]).

THE HMONG NIGHTMARE

In the Hmong language, the Nightmare spirit is referred to as *dab tsog* ('da cho'). *Dab* is the Hmong word for spirit, and is often used in the sense of an evil spirit. *Tsog* is the specific name of the Nightmare spirit, and also appears in the phrase used to denote a Nightmare attack, *tsog tsuam* ('cho chua'). *Tsuam* means "to crush, to press, or to smother" [39].

In the sample of Stockton Hmong, a total of 58% (36 men, 33 women) had experienced at least one nightmare. The interviews and the personal narratives they elicited clarified that the Hmong supranormal experience that I had isolated was in fact a cultural manifestation of the Nightmare phenomenon. The following is a portion of a narrative from a 33-year-old Hmong man who had a nightmare experience shortly after his arrival in the United States:

> First, I was surprised, but right away, I got real scared. I was lying in bed. I was so tired, because I was working very hard then. I wanted to go to school, but I had no money. I kept waking up, because I was thinking so much about my problems. I heard a noise, but when I turned—tried—I could not move. My bedroom looked the same, but I could see—in the corner, a dark shape was coming to me. It came to the bed, over my feet, my legs. It was very heavy, like a heavy weight over my whole body, my

legs, my chest. My chest was frozen—like I was drowning, I had no air. I tried to yell so someone sleeping very close to me will hear. I tried to move—using a force that I can—a strength that I can have. I thought, "What if I die?" After a long time, it went away it just left. I got up and turned all the lights on. I was afraid to sleep again.

With regard to the emic term for the nightmare experience, 97% of the informants used either *dab tsog* or *tsog tsuam*. All of those who were able to provide a name for the nocturnal encounter could also define it. This widespread awareness of the Nightmare tradition clearly established that Hmong belief regarding the nightmare forms a collective tradition.

DAB TSOG AND HMONG RELOCATION

Since Hmong who maintain their traditional religious beliefs and practices and those who have converted to Christianity both die of SUNDS, the testing of the hypothesis of a belief-triggered disorder necessitated an exploration of the influence of the Nightmare on Hmong of both religions. In the sample, 54% of traditional Hmong and 72% of Christian Hmong had experienced at least one nightmare. The interview data reveals that psychological stress regarding religious practice is present among both traditional and Christian Hmong refugees in the United States and also that this stress is exacerbated in both groups by the supranormal nocturnal assaults. Traditional Hmong face great difficulty in practicing their religion as they had done in Laos. The inability to obtain animals for slaughter, disruption of clan ties and the scarcity of shamans all contribute to the problem of performing expected religious duties. Many Christian Hmong also retain traditional beliefs and have anxieties about not fulfilling their religious requirements. Some Christian Hmong converted out of a sense of obligation to church sponsors and many experience peer disapproval and clan ostracization. Although the more devout Christians I spoke with denied any ambivalence, many of the Christian Hmong informants described ways in which they combined the two religions in order to prevent incurring the Hmong spirits' wrath. It is striking that of the informants who offered an explanation for the cause of SUNDS, 74% suggested an etiology that was directly spirit-related or involved the absence of traditional religion and ritual from their lives.

I have noted an increased incidence of nightmares during informants' times of stress. (Emotional stress, physical exhaustion and sleep deprivation have been shown to be predisposing factors for sleep-onset REM, see [27,40–42].) According to the traditional belief informants described, *tsog tsuam* assaults are rarely, if ever, fatal on the first encounter.

> It is believed that once you have one of those nightmares—you are visited by one of the *dab tsog* evil spirits—once you are seen by one of those evil spirits, often they will come back to you, until you have the worst nightmare and probably die.

Usually the lethal potential manifests only after an individual has been given time to rectify a situation, but chooses not to, or is unable to, appease the intruding spirit. As one informant explains, because of traditional countermeasures undertaken in Laos, SUNDS deaths did not occur prior to the Hmong exodus: "There were nightmares, but the sudden death was unheard of. It might have happened, but I never heard of it." None of the informants I interviewed recalled incidents of SUNDS deaths in Laos [43].

DAB TSOG AND HMONG SUNDS

Aside from the conflict between Hmong traditional religion and Christianity, Hmong refugees have experienced a host of hardships including language and employment problems, changing generational and gender roles [44], survivor guilt [45] and trauma-induced emotional and psychological disorders [46–48]. These changes can affect all Hmong immigrants in varying degrees, but Hmong men, in particular, have had their roles dramatically altered. This gender dichotomy is mirrored by the vast discrepancy in the ratio of male to female SUNDS deaths.

Since both Hmong men and women suffer from Nightmare attacks, however, why are SUNDS deaths almost exclusively male? The answer lies in the meaning of Nightmare attacks in traditional

Hmong culture. Hmong informants explained that among other religious requirements, one's ancestor spirits must be fed annually. If the ancestor spirits are neglected, they become angry, deserting the individual, the head-of-household, and leaving him vulnerable to evil spirit attacks. Most of the Hmong informants perceived a direct causal relationship between failure to perform traditional Hmong rituals and Nightmare attacks. (Etiologies related to either traditional spirits or to the lack of traditional religious practice constituted 81% of all the nightmare causes suggested.) One Hmong man summarized the widely held belief as follows:

> At least once a year those evil spirits must be fed. If someone forgets to feed them, then they will come back and disturb you. If you have *tsog tsuam*, the ancestor spirit is supposed to protect you. If you feed the ancestors regularly, then whenever you have *tsog tsuam*, the ancestor spirits will protect you. Usually the father, the head-of-household, is responsible for feeding the evil spirits. Women have nightmares, too, but not as often as men. The evil spirit would first attack the head-of-household. Coming to this country, people tend to forget to do the rituals. A lot of people either ignore or forget to practice their religious belief. . . . Men are the ones who are responsible for feeding both the evil spirits and the ancestor spirits. Since they are not doing their part, it is logical that their soul should be taken away.

This explanation clearly has great significance for the investigation of SUNDS etiology in that it contains a matter-of-fact description of the precise manner in which a man's failure to fulfil traditional religious obligations can result in his death. The inability to fulfill roles and responsibilities with regard to religion (as well as in their lives generally) has a calamitous impact on the psyche of many Hmong males.

Although Hmong women do experience Nightmare attacks and are aware of the roles of both spirits and the absence of traditional religious practices in SUNDS deaths, they also know that *dab tsog* will seek out their husbands, fathers or brothers as the individuals held accountable. As one Hmong informant recalled of her own nightmare experience "Even though I was very, very scared, I thought it was good my husband wasn't there, so the spirit wouldn't hurt him." Several informants suggested that the one woman who died of SUNDS must have been unmarried or widowed and therefore, as the head of her household, the individual who was held accountable by the spirits.

If the nightmare is usually a transient, non-pathological phenomenon, how can it trigger a fatal disorder among Hmong refugees? Nightmare assaults occurred in Laos, but none of the informants I interviewed recalled incidents of SUNDS deaths in their homeland. I propose that the differences between the Hmong way of life in pre-war Laos and their current situation in the United States are responsible for this phenomenon. The various resettlement stresses I have discussed manifest most strongly during the initial arrival period, thus explaining the overwhelming preponderance of deaths in the two-year period following resettlement in the United States [49].

The subject of intense emotional stress as the cause of sudden death is a motif well-represented in world folklore throughout history and has also been a topic of serious biomedical investigation. A number of anthropological and biomedical studies suggest a link between psychological stress and sudden death, see for example [50–55]. In the medical anthropological and ethnomedical literature, the notion of beliefs playing a significant role in illness causation (nocebo effect) or its remedy (placebo effect) is widely held [56]. Robert A. Hahn and Arthur Kleinman's notion of the pathogenic effects of belief or "ethnomedical pathogenesis,' is a particularly useful concept for the study of the role of traditional belief in SUNDS. Significantly, the concept of ethnomedicogenic illness and healing, with its emphasis on the relationship between the mind/spirit and body, is compatible with the holistic traditional Hmong worldview regarding health.

Since Nightmare assaults and other spirit-related problems did occur in Laos, it is significant that Hmong refugees in the United States attribute SUNDS to traditional spirits. I believe that the differences between the Hmong way of life in pre-war Laos and their current situation in the United States are responsible for this phenomenon. Traditional Hmong culture has sustained a severe disruption. The Hmong have undergone a seemingly endless series of traumatic experiences: the war in Laos, the Pathet Lao takeover and subsequent Hmong persecution (including the threat of genocide), the harrowing nighttime escapes through jungles and across the Mekong River, the hardships of refugee camps in Thailand, and finally re-

settlement in the United States, with not only housing, income, language and employment concerns, but the separation of families and clans, inability to practice traditional religion, and hasty conversions to Christianity, among many others. These recent changes appear to account for the fact that, while SUNDS deaths occur in the United States, no informant I interviewed was aware of any SUNDS deaths in pre-migration Laos.

When *dab tsog* tormented sleepers in Laos, it did so in a sociocultural context that sustained a fundamental structure of support. Hmong shamans conducted prescribed rituals designed to ascertain the nature of the individual's transgression and sought to appease the angry spirits in order to prevent the possibility of the sleeper's death during a subsequent nocturnal encounter. In the United States, while the majority of Hmong retain many of their traditional beliefs, in many instances they have lost their religious leaders and ritual responses. The insular communities that characterized Hmong life in Laos appear to have fostered traditional cultural practices whose presence alleviated, but whose subsequent loss provokes, feelings of terror and impending death associated with negative supranormal encounters. Therefore, although the *dab tsog* attack in Laos was akin to the worldwide Nightmare tradition, the peculiar stresses of the recent Hmong refugee experience have transformed its outcome. In conclusion, the power of traditional belief in the nightmare—compounded with such factors as the trauma of war, migration, rapid acculturation, and the inability to practice traditional healing and ritual—causes cataclysmic psychological stress that can result in the deaths of male Hmong refugees from SUNDS [57].

NOTES

1. Quincy K. *Hmong: History of a People.* East Washington University Press, Cheney, 1988.

2. Cerquone J. *Refugees from Laos: In Harm's Way.* U.S. Committee for Refugees, Washington, DC, 1986.

3. *Profiles of the Highland Lao Communities in the United States.* United States Department of Health and Human Services, Washington, DC, 1988.

4. Johnson C. *Dab Neeg Hmoob: Myths, Legends, and Folktales from the Hmong of Laos.* Macalester College, St. Paul, MN, 1985.

5. Muecke M. A. In search of healers: southeast Asian refugees in the American health care system. *Western J. Med.* 139, 835–840, 1983.

6. Conquergood D. *I am a Shaman: A Hmong Life Story with Ethnographic Commentary.* pp. 45–46. University of Minnesota, Minneapolis, 1989.

7. Hmong was an exclusively oral language until the 1950s when Christian missionaries in Laos developed a written form using the Roman alphabet. In this essay, italicized Hmong terms represent words in the Hmong language written in the Roman Popular Alphabet (RPA). For ease of pronunciation I provide an English transliteration in quotation marks.

8. The disorder is also known by the acronym SUDS, Sudden Unexplained Death Syndrome. I think that both the unpredictable nature of the syndrome and the fact that 98 percent of the deaths occurred between 10:00 P.M. and 8:00 A.M. [9] warrant the inclusion of both the words 'unexpected' and 'nocturnal' in the label. Thus, Sudden *Unexpected Nocturnal* Death Syndrome is a more accurate description of the disorder. My use of the term SUNDS is consistent with that of The SUNDS Planning Project at Saint Paul-Ramsey Medical Center.

9. Parrish R. G. Death in the Night: Mysterious Syndrome in Asian Refugees. In *1989 Medical and Health Annual* (Edited by Berstein E. and Tomchuck L.), pp. 286–290. Encyclopedia Britannica, Chicago, 1988.

10. Baron R. C. and Kirschner R. H. Sudden nighttime death among south-east Asians too. *The Lancet* 8327, 764, 1983.

11. Munger R. G. Sudden death in sleep of Laotian-Hmong refugees in Thailand: a case-control study. *Am. J. Pub. Hlth* 77, 1187, 1987.

12. Beginning in 1981, a number of researchers began to note similarities between SUNDS and the sudden deaths of Filipino and Japanese men from disorders known respectively as *bangungut* and *pokkuri* e.g. Refs [10, 18, 19, 49]. These findings are significant in illustrating that despite peculiar cultural manifestations and elaborations, the phenomenon of SUNDS (like the nightmare itself [31]), appears to be consistent across unrelated cultures.

13. Baron R. C., Thacker S. B., Gorelkin L., Vernon A. A., Taylor W. R. and Choi K. Sudden deaths among southeast Asian refugees: an unexplained nocturnal phenomenon. *J. Am. Med. Assoc.* 250, 2947, 1983.

14. Bissinger H. G. More cities report death syndrome. *St. Paul Pioneer Press* 6 February, F1, 4, 1981.

15. Bliatout B. T. *Hmong Sudden Unexpected Nocturnal Death Syndrome: A Cultural Study.* Sparkle Publishing, OR, 1982.

16. Holtan N., Carlson D., Egbert J., Mielke R. and Thao T. C. *Final Report of the SUNDS Planning Project.* St Paul-Ramsey Medical Center, St Paul, MN, 1984.

17. Pyle J. Death stalking refugees. *The News Tribune* (Tacoma, Washington). 16 April: C1, 1981.

18. Kirschner R. H., Eckner F. A. O. and Baron R. C. The cardiac pathology of sudden, unexplained, nocturnal death in southeast Asian refugees. *J. Am. Med. Assoc.* 256, 2700, 1986.

19. Otto C. M., Tauxe R. V., Cobb L. A., Greene H. L., Gross B. W., Werner J. A., Burroughs R. W., Samson W. E., Weaver D. and Trobaugh G. B. Ventricular fibrillation causes sudden death in southeast Asian immigrants. *Ann. Intern. Med.* 100, 45, 1984.

20. Marshall E. The Hmong: dying of culture shock? *Science* 212, 1008, 1981.

21. Munger R. G. and Hurlich M. G. Hmong deaths. *Science* 213, 952, 1981.

22. *Refugee Health Issues Quarterly.* Update: sudden unexplained death syndrome among southeast Asian refugees. 4, 1, 1989.

23. Hufford D. J. A new approach to the "Old Hag": the nightmare tradition reexamined. In *American Folk Medicine: A Symposium* (Edited by Hand W. D.), pp. 73–85. University of California Press, Berkeley, 1976.

24. Hufford D. J. *The Terror That Comes in the Night.* University of Pennsylvania Press, PA, 1982.

25. Ward D. The little man who wasn't there: encounters with the supranormal. *Fabula: J. Folklore Stud.* 18, 213, 1977.

26. The word *mara*, from which "nightmare" is derived, can be traced to a proto-Indo-European root that most likely referred to a nocturnal pressing spirit. (Kluge F. *Etymologisches Wörterbuch der Deutschen Sprache.* Walter de Gruyter, Berlin, 1960.)

27. I am indebted to David J. Hufford for his characterization of the nightmare in *The Terror That Comes in the Night* (1982). Although I have altered his configuration slightly [based on the results of my own fieldwork in Jerusalem (1987–88) and Los Angeles (1986–87)] Hufford's criteria, which are unique in the literature on the subject, remain the foundation of the minimal requirements for the nightmare experience as I present them.

28. Adler S. R. Sudden unexpected nocturnal death syndrome among Hmong immigrants: examining the role of the "nightmare". *J. Am. Folklore* 104, 54, 1991.

29. Ness R. C. The old hag phenomenon as sleep paralysis: a biocultural, interpretation. *Culture, Med. Psychiat.* 2, 15, 1978.

30. Foster G. M. Dreams, character, and cognitive orientation in Tzintzuntzan. *Ethos* 1, 106, 1973.

31. Hufford D. J. Inclusionism versus reductionism in the study of culture-bound syndromes. *Culture, Med. Psychiat.* 12, 503, 1988.

32. Dement W. C., Frazier S. H. and Weizman E. D. *The American Medical Association Guide to Better Sleep.* Random House, New York, 1984.

33. Hartmann E. *The Nightmare: The Psychology and Biology of Terrifying Dreams.* Basic Books, New York, 1984.

34. Parkes J. D. *Sleep and Its Disorders.* W. B. Saunders, London, 1985.

35. Kellerman H. *Sleep Disorders: Insomnia and Narcolepsy.* Brunner/Mazel, New York, 1981.

36. Rechtschaffen A. and Dement W. C. Narcolepsy and Hypersomnia. In *Sleep: Physiology and Pathology* (Edited by Kales A.), pp. 119–130. J. B. Lippincott, PA, 1969.

37. Riley T. C. *Clinical Aspects of Sleep and Sleep Disturbances.* Butterworth Publishers, Boston, 1985.

38. Takeuchi T., Miyasita A., Sasaki Y., Inugami M. and Fukuda K. Isolated sleep paralysis elicited by sleep interruption. *Sleep* 15, 217, 1992.

39. Heimbach E. E. *White Hmong-English Dictionary.* Cornell University Press, Ithaca, 1979.

40. Hishikawa Y. Sleep Paralysis. In *Narcolepsy: Proceedings of the First International Symposium on Narcolepsy, Advances in Sleep Research* (Edited by Guilleminault C., Dement W. C. and Passouant P.), Vol. 3, pp. 97–124. Spectrum Publications, New York, 1976.

41. Rechtschaffen A. and Dement W. C. Narcolepsy and hypersomnia. In *Sleep: Physiology and Pathology* (Edited by Kales A.), pp. 119–130. J. B. Lippincott, PA, 1969.

42. Riley T. C. *Clinical Aspects of Sleep and Sleep Disturbances.* Butterworth Publishers, Boston, 1985.

43. Despite the uniformity of opinion among informants regarding the absence of SUNDS deaths in premigration Laos, it is important to note that the forensic diligence to account for unusual death in Laos is not comparable to that of the United States, particularly in the isolated rural villages in which the Hmong lived. Although it is therefore impossible to know with certainty whether SUNDS deaths occurred in Laos, the conviction on the part of Hmong immigrants that the deaths were absent is a significant element in their dichotomization of experience between premigration Laos and post-resettlement America.

44. Donnelly N. D. The changing lives of refugee Hmong women. University of Washington doctoral dissertation. University Microfilms International, Michigan, 1989.

45. Tobin J. J. and Friedman J. Spirits, shamans, and nightmare death: survivor stress in a Hmong refugee. *Am. J. Orthopsychiat.* 53, 439, 1983.

46. Westermeyer J. Hmong deaths. *Science* 213, 952, 1981.

47. Westermeyer J. Prevention of mental disorder among Hmong refugees in the U.S.: lessons from the period 1976–1986. *Soc. Sci. Med.* 25, 941, 1987.

48. Westermeyer J. A matched pairs study of depression among Hmong refugees with particular reference to predisposing factors and treatment outcome. *Soc. Psychiat. Psychiat. Epidemiol.* 23, 64, 1988.

49. Parrish R. G., Tucker M., Ing R., Encarnacion C. and Eberhardt M. Sudden unexplained death syndrome in southeast Asian refugees: a review of CDC surveillance. *Morbidity and Mortality Weekly Rev.* 36, 43, 1987.

50. Brodsky M. A., Soto D. A., Iseri L. T., Wolff L. J. and Allen B. J. Ventricular tachyarrhythmia associated with psychological stress: the role of the sympathetic nervous system. *J. Am. Med. Assoc.* 257, 2064, 1987.

51. Cannon W. Voodoo death. *Am. Anthropol.* 44, 169, 1942.

52. Engel G. L. Sudden and rapid death during psychological stress: folklore or folk wisdom? *Ann. Intern. Med.* 74, 771, 1971.

53. Greene W. A., Goldstein S. and Moss A. J. Psychosocial aspects of sudden death: a preliminary report. *Arch. Intern. Med.* 129, 725, 1972.

54. Lown B., Verrier R. and Corbalan R. Psychologic stress and threshold for repetitive ventricular response. *Science* 182, 834, 1973.

55. Rahe R. H., Romo M., Bennett L. and Siltanen P. Recent life changes, myocardial infarction, and abrupt coronary death. *Arch. Intern. Med.* 133, 221, 1974.

56. Hahn R. A. and Kleinman A. Belief as pathogen, belief as medicine: "voodoo death" and the "placebo phenomenon" in anthropological perspective. *Med. Anthrop. Q.* 14, 6, 1983.

57. Given that myriad cultures possess traditions of evil Nightmare spirits, do nightmare experiences precipitate similar disorders among other peoples? Although those affected by SUNDS are overwhelmingly Laotian Hmong men, individuals belonging to other groups, notably Filipinos, Thai, Khmu and Cambodians, have died of what appears to be SUNDS. A detailed discussion of these potentially parallel phenomena is beyond the aim of the present paper, but it is important to note that my preliminary investigation of Khmu and Thai sudden deaths indicates that individuals of both groups perceive a connection between Nightmare spirit attacks and sudden deaths in situations of extreme psychological stress. Any definitive statement regarding a correlation between these Nightmare spirits and SUNDS, however, requires an in-depth study of the type presented in this paper that focuses on the beliefs and experiences of the non-Hmong groups affected.

30 DECONSTRUCTING THE PLACEBO EFFECT AND FINDING THE MEANING RESPONSE

Daniel E. Moerman and Wayne B. Jonas

Like the rising medical and popular interest in alternative medicine, there is growing interest in mind–body interactions that influence the course of disease and the effectiveness of treatment. This selection argues that biomedical concepts are limited in their ability to grasp such interactions, especially when placebos are defined narrowly as inert substances, and placebo effects are seen as inconvenient and difficult-to-measure noise in studies of treatment efficacy. The inadequacy of current models is evident in the fact that even treatments considered to work only by a placebo effect, such as acupuncture to relieve pain, can be obstructed by chemical means.

Every aspect of healing encounters, from physician dress and manner to the form and administration of drugs or other treatments, is embedded in symbols and meanings (see selection 8). These meanings can have negative as well as positive impacts, expressed in nocebo and placebo effects or what Moerman and Jonas call the "meaning response" (see selections 27, 28, 29). In addition, there seems to be a range of variation in individual suggestibility to external influences that may make some people more likely to experience strong nocebo or placebo effects (see Spiegel 1997). Finally, the meaning response appears to be stronger for some ailments, such as nausea or pain, than others, such as toxin-induced diarrhea or inflammation related to an insect bite. Interestingly, as shown in other selections in this book, many indigenous belief systems categorize illnesses into those that are more or less spiritual in aspect, perhaps reflecting awareness of the meaning response.

It does not seem to be possible for people to work placebo effects on themselves. Indeed, it may only add a psychological burden to urge patients to try to maintain a positive outlook, as the authors of a study on lung cancer patients argue in light of their finding that optimism had no effect on survival—although they point out that this may not be the case for other cancers (Schofield et al. 2004). Moerman and Jonas offer an evolutionary explanation based on the social nature of human life in general and healing in particular. The intervention of someone else indicates a level of social support that triggers the meaning response and the investment of psychophysiological resources it entails. Such a theory is borne out on the social level, for community health is favored where physical and social structures promote mutual support and a sense of belonging and investment in social relationships among individuals (Lomas 1998).

Questions to keep in mind

What are some meanings that influence patient perceptions and the outcome of medical treatments and procedures?

How is the term "meaning response" an improvement over placebo or nocebo effects?

What does this selection suggest about the relationship between the meanings associated with traditional medicines as opposed to Western pharmaceuticals and the effectiveness of the two kinds of medicine (see selections 6 and 25)?

How do SUNDS (selection 29) and Chinese beliefs about birth year relate to Lock's concept of local biologies (selection 2)?

Source: Moerman, D. E. and W. B. Jonas 2002. "Deconstructing the Placebo Effect and Finding the Meaning Response." *Annals of Internal Medicine* 136(6):471–476. With permission from the publisher.

[The cure for the headache] was a kind of leaf, which required to be accompanied by a charm, and if a person would repeat the charm at the same time that he used the cure, he would be made whole; but that without the charm the leaf would be of no avail.

— *Socrates, according to Plato (1)*

There is a renewed interest in placebos and the placebo effect—on their reality, their ethics, their place in medicine, or not, both in and out of the clinic and academy. The U.S. National Institutes of Health recently sponsored a large conference called "Science of the Placebo" (2). At least five serious books on the subject (3–7) plus a book of poetry (8) and a novel (9)—each titled *Placebo Effect*—have been published since 1997. In the past 10 years, the National Library of Medicine has annually listed an average of 3972 scholarly papers with the keywords "placebo," "placebos," or "placebo effect," with a low of 3362 papers in 1992 and a high of 4814 in 2000. During the fall of 2000, a discussion of the effect of new "drag free" suits, which might give an edge to Olympic swimmers, appeared in *US News and World Report*: "[S]wimming officials aren't convinced this is anything more than the placebo effect. Swimmers excel because they *think* they've got an edge" (10). One widely reported study, which concluded that placebos were powerless (11), or represented the Wizard of Oz, (12) occasioned a blizzard of criticism (13–25) and some support (26). It's in the papers (27, 28). It's in the air.

Yet the most recent serious attempt to try logically to define the placebo effect failed utterly (30). Given the ways people have gone about it, this seems unsurprising. Arthur K. Shapiro, MD, who spent much of his career as a psychiatrist studying the placebo effect, recently wrote:

A placebo is a substance or procedure . . . that is objectively without specific activity for the condition being treated . . . The placebo effect is the . . . therapeutic effect produced by a placebo. (30)

If we replace the word "placebo" in the second sentence with its definition from the first, we get: "The placebo effect is the therapeutic effect produced by [things] objectively without specific activity for the condition being treated." This makes no sense whatsoever. Indeed, it flies in the face of the obvious. The one thing of which we can be absolutely certain is that placebos *do not* cause placebo effects. Placebos are inert and don't cause anything.

Moreover, people frequently expand the concept of the placebo effect very broadly to include just about every conceivable sort of beneficial biological, social, or human interaction that doesn't involve some drug well-known to the pharmacopoeia. A narrower form of this expansion includes identifying "natural history" or "regression to the mean" (as we might observe them in a randomized, controlled trial) as part of the placebo effect. But natural history and regression occur not only in the control group. Nothing in the theory of regression to the mean (30) hints that when people are selected for being extreme on some measure (blood pressure or cholesterol, for example), they are immune to regression if they receive active treatment. Such recipients are as likely (or unlikely) to move toward homeostasis as are control group patients. So, regression to the mean is in no meaningful way a "placebo effect." Ernst and Resch (31) took an important step in trying to clarify this situation by differentiating the "true" from the "perceived" placebo effect. But "true placebo effect" hasn't really caught on as a viable concept.

The concept of the placebo effect has been expanded much more broadly than this. Some attribute the effects of various alternative medical systems, such as homeopathy (32) or chiropractic (33), to the placebo effect. Others have described studies that show the positive effects of enhanced communication, such as Egbert's (34), as "the placebo response without the placebo" (7).

No wonder things are confusing.

MEANING AND MEDICINE

We suggest thinking about this issue in a new way. A group of medical students was asked to participate in a study of two new drugs, one a tranquilizer and the other a stimulant (35). Each student was given a packet containing either one or two blue or red tablets; the tablets were inert. The students' responses to a questionnaire indicated that 1) the red tablets acted as stimulants while the blue ones acted as depressants and 2) two tablets had more effect than one. The students were not responding to the inertness of the tablets. Moreover, these responses cannot be easily accounted for by natural history, regression to the mean, or physician enthusiasm (presumably the experimenters were as enthusiastic about the reds as the blues). Instead, they can be explained by the "meanings" in the experiment: 1) Red means "up," "hot," "danger," while blue means "down," "cool," "quiet" and 2) two means more than one. These effects of color (36–39) and number (40, 41) have been widely replicated.

In a British study, 835 women who regularly used analgesics for headache were randomly assigned to one of four groups (42). One group received aspirin labeled with a widely advertised brand name ("one of the most popular" analgesics in the United Kingdom that had been "widely available for many years and supported by extensive advertising"). The other groups received the same aspirin in a plain package, placebo marked with the same widely advertised brand name, or unmarked placebo. In this study, branded aspirin worked better than unbranded aspirin, which worked better than branded placebo, which worked better than unbranded placebo. Among 435 headaches reported by branded placebo users, 64% were reported as improved 1 hour after pill administration compared with only 45% of the 410 headaches reported as improved among the unbranded placebo users. Aspirin relieves headaches, but so does the knowledge that the pills you are taking are "good" ones.

In a study of the benefits of aerobic exercise, two groups participated in a 10-week exercise program. One group was told that the exercise would enhance their aerobic capacity, while the other group was told that the exercise would enhance aerobic capacity and psychological well-being. Both groups improved their aerobic capacity, but only the second group improved in psychological well-being (actually "self-esteem"). The researchers called this "strong evidence . . . that exercise may enhance psychological well-being via a strong placebo effect" (43).

In the red versus blue pill study, we can correctly (if not very helpfully) classify the responses of the students as "placebo effects" because they did indeed receive inert tablets; it seems clear, however, that they responded not to the pills but to their colors. In the second study, the presence of

the brand name enhanced the effect of both the inert and the active drug. It doesn't seem reasonable to classify the "brand name effect" as a "placebo effect" because no placebos are necessarily involved. Meanwhile, calling the consequences of authoritative instruction to the exercisers a "placebo effect" could come only from someone who believes that words do not affect the world, someone who has never been told "I love you" or who has never read the reviews of a rejected grant proposal. It seems reasonable to label all these effects (except, of course, of the aspirin and the exercise) as "meaning responses," a term that seeks, among other things, to recall Dr. Herbert Benson's "relaxation response" (44). Ironically, although placebos clearly cannot do anything themselves, their meaning can.

We define the *meaning response* as the physiologic or psychological effects of meaning in the origins or treatment of illness; meaning responses elicited after the use of inert or sham treatment can be called the "placebo effect" when they are desirable and the "nocebo effect" (45) when they are undesirable. This is obviously a complex notion with several terms that would be challenging to unpack ("desirable," "effect," "meaning," "treatment," "illness")—an exercise that cannot be carried out here. Note that this definition excludes several elements that are usually included in our understanding of the placebo effect, such as natural history, regression, experimenter or subject bias, and error in measurement or reporting. Note as well that the definition is not phrased in terms of "nonspecific" effects; although many elements of the meaning response or placebo effect may seem nonspecific, they are often quite specific in principle after they are understood.

Meaning Permeates Medical Treatment

Insofar as medicine is meaningful, it can affect patients, and it can affect the outcome of treatment (46–48). Most elements of medicine *are* meaningful, even if practitioners do not intend them to be so. The physician's costume (the white coat with stethoscope hanging out of the pocket) (49), manner (enthusiastic or not), style (therapeutic or experimental), and language (50) are all meaningful and can be shown to affect the outcome; indeed, we argue that both diagnosis (51) and prognosis (52) can be important forms of treatment.

Many studies can be cited to document aspects of the therapeutic quality of the practitioner's manner (53). In one, a strong message of the effect of a drug (an inert capsule) substantially reduced the patients' report of the pain of mandibular block injection compared with the pain after a weak message. Patients who received the weak message reported less pain than a group that received no placebos and no message at all (54). In another study, 200 patients with symptoms but no abnormal physical signs were randomly assigned to a positive or a negative consultation. In a survey of patients 2 weeks later, 64% of patients in the positive consultation group said they were all better, while only 39% of those who had negative consultations thought they were better (55).

Although there is strong evidence for such "physician effects," little evidence shows that "patient effects" are very important. A mass of research in the 1970s designed to identify "placebo reactors" produced only inconsistent and contradictory findings (56–58).

Meaning Can Have Substantial Physiologic Action

Placebo analgesia can elicit the production of endogenous opiates. Analgesia elicited with an injection of saline solution can be reversed with the opiate antagonist naloxone and enhanced with the opiate agonist proglumide (59). Likewise, acupuncture analgesia can be reversed with naloxone in animals (60) and people (61). To say that a treatment such as acupuncture "isn't better than placebo" does not mean that it does nothing.

Meaning and Surgery

The classic example of the meaningful effects of surgery comes from two studies of ligation of the bilateral internal mammary arteries as a treatment for angina (62, 63). Patients receiving sham surgery did as well—with 80% of patients substantially improving—as those receiving the active procedure in the trials or in general practice. Although the studies were small, the procedure was no longer performed after these reports were pub-

lished. Of note, these effectiveness rates (and those reported by the proponents of the procedure at the time) are much the same as those achieved by contemporary treatments such as coronary artery bypass or β-blockers.

Some observers have suggested that the success of transmyocardial laser revascularization, a procedure without a clear mechanism, may be explained by what they call the placebo effect (64) but what we call the meaning response. This is a plausible interpretation of a recent trial showing dramatic improvement in very sick people in both participant groups of a control trial of transmyocardial laser revascularization (Leon MB, Baim DS, Moses JW, Laham RJ, Knopf W. A randomized blinded clinical trial comparing percutaneous laser myocardial revascularization [using Biosense LV Mapping] vs. placebo in patients with refractory coronary ischemia. Presented at American Heart Association Scientific Session, 12–15 November 2000).

Surgery is particularly meaningful: Surgeons are among the elite of medical practitioners; the shedding of blood is inevitably meaningful in and of itself. In addition, surgical procedures usually have compelling rational explanations, which drug treatments often do not. The logic of arthroscopic surgery ("we will clean up a messy joint") is much more sensible and understandable (and even effective (65), especially for people in a culture rich in machines and tools, than is the logic of non-steroidal anti-inflammatory drugs (which "inhibit the production of prostaglandins which are involved in the inflammatory process," something no one would ever tell a patient). Surgery clearly induces a profound meaning response in modern medical practice (66–68).

MEANING, CULTURE, AND MEDICINE

Anthropologists understand cultures as complex webs of meaning, rich skeins of connected understandings, metaphors, and signs. Insofar as 1) meaning has biological consequence and 2) meanings vary across cultures, we can anticipate that biology will differ in different places, not because of genetics but because of these entangled ideas; we can anticipate what Margaret Lock has called "local biologies"(69, 70); Lock has shown dramatic cross-cultural variation in the existence and experience of "menopause" (69, 70). Moreover, Phillips has shown that "Chinese Americans, but not whites, die significantly earlier than normal (1.3 to 4.9 y) if they have a combination of disease and birth year which Chinese astrology and medicine consider ill fated" (71). Among Chinese Americans whose deaths were attributed to lymphatic cancer ($n = 3041$), those who were born in "Earth years"—and consequently were deemed by Chinese medical theory to be especially susceptible to diseases involving lumps, nodules, or tumors—had an average age at death of 59.7 years. In contrast, among those born in other years, age at death of Chinese Americans with lymphatic cancer was 63.6 years—nearly 4 years longer. Similar differences were also found for various other serious diseases. No such differences were evident in a large series of "whites" who died of similar causes in the same period. The intensity of the effect was shown to be correlated with "the strength of commitment to traditional Chinese culture." These differences in longevity (up to 6% or 7% difference in length of life!) are not due to having Chinese genes but to having Chinese ideas, to knowing the world in Chinese ways. The effects of meaning on health and disease are not restricted to placebos or brand names but permeate life.

One of us has shown variation in the response of control groups to inert medication in diverse cultures for the same conditions (ulcers, hypertension, and anxiety) (41). Figure 30.1 shows the relationship between control group and active treatment group healing for endoscopically diagnosed duodenal ulcer treated with antisecretory medication. Control group healing and active treatment group healing seem functionally related in these studies. The correlation between control and active healing rates is 0.49; as the placebo group's healing rate increases, so does the rate of the active treatment group. Although the average control group healing rate in five German studies has been 62.4%, the healing rate was 16.7% in three studies from neighboring Denmark and the Netherlands. The number needed to treat for benefit (NNT_B), to obtain ulcer healing, can be calculated; for ulcer patients treated with placebo, the NNT_B for those who are German (not Danish or Dutch) is 2.

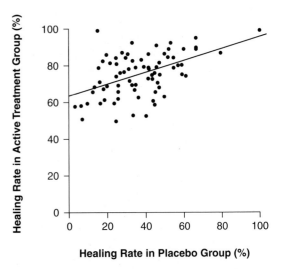

Figure 30.1 Data from 83 Studies of the Use of Cimetidine or Ranitidine for Duodenal Ulcer Disease.

In all cases, ulcers and ulcer healing were diagnosed endoscopically. Most studies lasted 4 weeks; a few were a bit shorter or longer. Sample sizes ranged from 12 to 210 participants (mean, 58). The quality of these studies was generally good for the era in which they were conducted (mostly between 1976 and 1986), although probably not fully adequate by contemporary standards. This analysis differs from the ordinary, in which placebo and active treatments are combined in an odds ratio, relative risk, or risk difference. The point of this analysis is not, however, to determine whether antisecretory medication is effective; clearly it is. The issue is the relationship between the pharmacologic and the meaningful dimensions of treatment. (A detailed account of these studies is available elsewhere (41).)

CONCLUSIONS

Practitioners can benefit clinically by conceptualizing this issue in terms of the meaning response rather than the placebo effect. Placebos are inert. You can't do anything about them. For human beings, meaning is everything that placebos are not, richly alive and powerful. However, we know little of this power, although all clinicians have experienced it. One reason we are so ignorant is that, by focusing on placebos, we constantly have to address the moral and ethical issues of prescribing inert treatments (72, 73), of lying (74), and the like. It seems possible to evade the entire issue by simply avoiding placebos. One cannot, however, avoid meaning while engaging human beings. Even the most distant objects—the planet Venus, the stars in the constellation Orion—are meaningful to us, as well as to others (75).

Yet, a huge puzzle remains: Obviously the meaning response is of great value to the sick and the lame. For example, eliciting the meaning response requires remarkably little effort ("You will be fine, Mr. Smith"). So why doesn't this happen all the time? And why can't you do it to yourself? Psychologist Nicholas Humphrey has suggested that this conundrum may have evolutionary roots: Healing has its benefits but also its costs (76). (For example, relieving pain may encourage premature activity, which could exacerbate the injury. Moreover, immune activity is metabolically very demanding on an injured system.) Perhaps only when a friend, relative, or healer indicates some level of social support (for example, by performing a ritual) is the individual's internal economy able to act. Moreover, as we have clarified, routinized, and rationalized our medicine, thereby relying on the salicylates and forgetting about the more meaningful birches, willows, and wintergreen from which they came—in essence, stripping away Plato's "charms"—we have impoverished the meaning of our medicine to a degree that it simply doesn't work as well as it might any more. Interesting ideas such as this are impossible to entertain when we discuss placebos; they spring readily to mind when we talk about meaning.

NOTES

1. Jowett B. *Dialogues of Plato.* Chicago: Univ Chicago Pr; 1952.

2. "The Science of the Placebo: Toward an Interdisciplinary Research Agenda." National Institutes of Health, Bethesda, Maryland. 19–20 November 2000. Available at placebo.nih.gov. Accessed on 25 January 2002.

3. Harrington A. ed. *The Placebo Effect: An Interdisciplinary Exploration.* Cambridge, MA: Harvard Univ Pr; 1997.

4. Shapiro AK, Shapiro E. *The Powerful Placebo: From Ancient Priest to Modern Physician.* Baltimore: Johns Hopkins Univ Pr; 1997.

5. Spiro HM. *The Power of Hope: a Doctor's Perspective.* New Haven: Yale Univ Pr; 1998.

6. Kirsch I. ed. *How Expectancies Shape Experience.* Washington, DC: American Psychological Association; 1999.

7. Brody H, Brody D. *The Placebo Response: How You Can Release the Body's Inner Pharmacy for Better Health.* New York: Cliff Street Books; 2000.

8. Beaumont JM. *Placebo Effects: Poems.* New York: W.W. Norton; 1997.

9. Russell G. *Placebo Effect.* New York: BBC Worldwide Americas; 1998.

10. Clark K, Milliken R. Today, it's "May the best swimsuit win." *US News and World Report.* 21 August 2000: 55.

11. Hrobjartsson A, Gotzsche PC. Is the placebo powerless? An analysis of clinical trials comparing placebo with no treatment [Review]. *N Engl J Med.* 2001;344:1594–602. [PMID: 11372012]

12. Bailar JC 3rd. The powerful placebo and the Wizard of Oz. *N Engl J Med.* 2001;344:1630–2. [PMID: 11372017]

13. Beldoch M. Is the placebo powerless? *N Engl J Med.* 2001;345:1278; discussion 1278–9. [PMID: 11680460]

14. DiNubile MJ. Is the placebo powerless? *N Engl J Med.* 2001;345:1278; discussion 1278–9. [PMID: 11680459]

15. Kupers R. Is the placebo powerless? *N Engl J Med.* 2001;345:1278; discussion 1278–9. [PMID: 11680457]

16. Eicarson TE, Hemels M, Stolk P. Is the placebo powerless? *N Engl J Med.* 2001;345:1277; discussion 1278–9. [PMID: 11680456]

17. Kaptchuk TJ. Is the placebo powerless? *N Engl J Med.* 2001;345:1277; discussion 1278–9. [PMID: 11680455]

18. Miller FG. Is the placebo powerless? *N Engl J Med.* 2001;345:1277; discussion 1278–9. [PMID: 11680454]

19. Lilford RJ. Braunholtz DA. Is the placebo powerless? *N Engl J Med.* 2001;345:1277–8; discussion 1278–9. [PMID: 11680453]

20. Spiegel D, Kraemer H, Carlson RW. Is the placebo powerless? *N Engl J Med.* 2001;345:1276; discussion 1278–9. [PMID: 11680452]

21. Ader R. Much ado about nothing. *Advances in Mind-Body Medicine.* 2001;17:293–95.

22. Brody H, Weismantel D. A challenge to core beliefs. *Advances in Mind-Body Medicine* 2001;17:296–8.

23. Greene PJ, Wayne PM, Kerr CE, Weiger WA, Jacobson E, Goldman P, et al. The powerful placebo: doubting the doubters. *Advances in Mind-Body Medicine.* 2001;17:298–307.

24. Kirsch I, Scorboria A. Apples, oranges, and placebos: heterogeneity in a meta-analysis of placebo effects. *Advances in Mind-Body Medicine* 2001; 17:307–9.

25. Wickramasekera I. The placebo efficacy study: problems with the definition of the placebo and the mechanisms of placebo efficacy. *Advances in Mind-Body Medicine.* 2001;17:309–12.

26. McDonald CJ. Is the placebo powerless? *N Engl J Med.* 2001;345:1276–7; discussion 1278–9. [PMID: 11680451]

27. Talbor M. The placebo prescription. *New York Times Magazine.* 9 January 2001;34–9, 44, 58–60.

28. Rubin R. 'Eat one. You'll feel better.' *USA Today,* 16 January 2001:D1.

29. Gotzsche PC. Is there logic in the placebo? *Lancet.* 1994;344:925–6. [PMID: 7934350]

30. McDonald CJ, Mazzuca SA, McCabe GP Jr. How much of the placebo 'effect' is really statistical regression? *Star Med.* 1983;2:417–27. [PMID: 6369471]

31. Ernst E, Resch KL. Concept of true and perceived placebo effects. *BMJ.* 1995;311:551–3. [PMID: 7663213]

32. Ernst E, Pittler MH. Efficacy of homeopathic arnica: a systematic review of placebo-controlled clinical trials. *Arch Surg.* 1998;133:1187–90. [PMID: 9820349]

33. Curtis P. Spinal manipulation: does it work? *Occup Med.* 1988;3:31–44. [PMID: 2963390]

34. Egbert LD, Battit GE, Welch CE, Barden MK. Reduction of postoperative pain by encouragement and instruction of patients. A study of doctor-patient rapport. *N Engl J Med.* 1964;270:825–7.

35. Blackwell B, Bloomfield SS, Buncher CR. Demonstration to medical students of placebo responses and non-drug factors. *Lancet.* 1972;1: 1279–82. [PMID: 4113531]

36. Schapira K, McClelland HA, Griffiths NR, Newell DJ. Study on the effects of tablet colour in the treatment of anxiety states. *Br Med J.* 1970;1:446–9. [PMID: 5420207]

37. Honzak R, Horackova E, Culik A. Our experience with the effect of placebo in some functional and psychosomatic disorders. *Activa Nervosa Superior* (Prague). 1971;13:190–1.

38. Cattaneo AD, Lucchilli PE, Filippucci G. Sedative effects of placebo treatment. *Eur J Clin Pharmacol.* 1970;3:43–5.

39. de Craen AJ, Roos PJ, Leonard de Vries A, Kleijnen J. Effect of colour of drugs: systematic review of perceived effect of drugs and of their effectiveness. *BMJ.* 1996;313:1624–6. [PMID: 8991013]

40. de Craen AJ, Moerman DE, Heisterkamp SH, Tytgar GN, Tijssen JG, Kleijnen J. Placebo effect in the treatment of duodenal ulcer. *Br J Clin Pharmacol.* 1999;48:853–60. [PMID: 10594490]

41. Moerman DE. Cultural variations in the placebo effect: ulcers, anxiety, and blood pressure. *Med Anthropol Q.* 2000;14:51–72. [PMID: 10812563]

42. Branthwaite A, Cooper P. Analgesic effects of branding in treatment of headaches. *Br Med J (Clin Res Ed).* 1981;282:1576–8. [PMID: 6786566]

43. Desharnais R, Jobin J, Còté C, Lévesque L, Godin G. Aerobic exercise and the placebo effect: a controlled study, *Psychosom Med.* 1993;55:149–54. [PMID: 8475229]

44. Benson H, Klipper MZ. *The Relaxation Response.* New York: Wings Books 1992.

45. Hahn RA. The nocebo phenomenon: concept, evidence, and implications for public health. *Prev Med.* 1997;26:607–11. [PMID: 9327466]

46. Levi-Strauss C. *The Effectiveness of Symbols. Structural Anthropology:* Garden City, NY: Anchor Books; 1967.

47. Moerman DE. Anthropology of symbolic healing. *Current Anthropology.* 1979;20:59–80.

48. Kirmayer LJ. Healing and the invention of metaphor: the effectiveness of symbols revisited. *Cult Med Psychiatry.* 1993;17:161–95. [PMID: 7693395]

49. Blumhagen DW. The doctor's white coat. The image of the physician in modern America. *Ann Intern Med.* 1979;91:111–6. [PMID: 88917]

50. Uhlenhuth EH, Rickels K, Fisher S, Park LC, Lipman RS, Mock J. Drug, doctor's verbal attitude and clinic setting in the symptomatic response to pharmacotherapy. *Psychopharmacologia.* 1966;9:392–418. [PMID: 4872909]

51. Brody H, Waters DB. Diagnosis is treatment. *J Fam Pract.* 1980;10:445–9. [PMID: 7354290]

52. Christakis NA. *Death Foretold: Prophecy and Prognosis in Medical Care.* Chicago: Univ Chicago Pr; 1999.

53. Gracely RH. Charisma and the art of healing: can nonspecific factors be enough? In: Devor M, Rowbotham MC, Wiesenfeld-Hallin Z. eds. Proceedings of the 9th World Congress on Pain, Seattle: *IASP Pr.* 2000:1045–67.

54. Gryll SL, Karahn M. Situational factors contributing to the placebos effect. *Psychopharmacology* (Berl), 1978;57:253–61. [PMID: 97705]

55. Thomas KB. General practice consultations: is there any point in being positive? *Br Med J (Clin Res Ed).* 1987;294:1200–2. [PMID: 3109581]

56. Moerman DE. Edible symbols: the effectiveness of placebos. *Ann N Y Acad Sci.* 1981; 364:256–68.

57. Fisher S. The placebo reactor thesis, antithisis, synthesis and hypothesis. *Dis Nerv Syst.* 1967; 28:510–5. [PMID: 6048413]

58. Liberman RP. *The elusive placebo reactor.* In: Brill H, ed. Neuro-Psycho-Pharmacology: Proceedings of the Fifth International Congress of the Collegium Internationale Neuro-Psycho-Pharmacologicum. Amsterdam: Excerpta Medica Foundation. 1967; 557–66.

59. Benedetti F. Amanzio M. The neurobiology of placebo analgesia: from endogenous opioids to cholecystokinin. *Prog Neurobiol.* 1997;52:109–25. [PMID: 9185235]

60. Pomeranz B. Chiu D. Naloxone blockade of acupuncture analgesia: endorphin implicated. *Life Sci.* 1976;19:175–62. [PMID: 187888]

61. Mayer DJ, Price DD, Rafii A. Antagonism of acupuncture analgesis in man by the narcotic antagonist naxalone. *Brain Res.* 1977;121:368–72. [PMID: 832169]

62. Cobb L, Thomas GI, Dillard OH, Merendino KA, Bruce RA. An evaluation of internal-mammary artery ligation by a double blind technic. *N Engl J Med.* 1959;260:1115–8.

63. Dimond EG. Kittle CF. Crockett JE. Comparison of internal mammary ligation and sham operation for angina pectoris, *Am J Cardiol.* 1960;5:483–6.

64. Lange RA, Hillis LD. Transmyocardial laser revascularization [Editorial]. *N Engl J Med.* 1999; 341:1075–6. [PMID: 10502599]

65. Moxeley JB Jr. Wray NP. Kuykendall D. Willis K. Landon G. Arthroscopic treatment of osteoarthritis of the knee: a prospective, randomized, placebo-controlled trial. Results of a pilot study. *Am J Sports Med.* 1996;24:28–34. [PMID: 8638750]

66. Beecher HK. Surgery as placebo. A quantitative study of bias. *JAMA.* 1961;176:1102–7

67. Johnson AG. Surgery as a placebo. *Lancet,* 1994;344:1140–2. [PMID: 7034500]

68. Kaptchuk TJ. Goldman P. Stone DA. Stason WB. Do medical devices have enhanced placebo effects? *J Clin Epidemiol.* 2000;53:786–92. [PMID: 10942860]

69. Lock MM. *Encounters with Aging: Mythologies of Menopause in Japan and North America.* Berkeley Univ California Pr. 1993.

70. Lock M. Menopause: lessons from anthropology. *Psychosom Med.* 1998;60:410–9. [PMID: 9710286]

71. Phillips DP, Ruth TE, Wagner LM. Psychology and survival. *Lancet.* 1993;342:1142–5 [PMID: 7901476]

72. Macklin R. The ethical problems with sham surgery in clinical research. *N Engl J Med.* 1999;341:992–6. [PMID: 10498498]

73. Reynolds T. The ethics of placebo-controlled trials. *Ann Intern Med.* 2000;133:491. [PMID: 10975985]

74. Evans M. Justified deception? The single blind placebo in drug research. *J Med Ethics.* 2000; 26:188–93. [PMID: 10860211]

75. McCleary TP. *The Stars We Know. Crow Indian Astronomy and Lifeways.* Prospect Heights, IL: Waveland Pr. 1997.

76. Humphrey N. Great expectations: The evolutionary psychology of faith-healing and the placebo response. In: Humphrey N. ed. *The Mind Made Flesh: Essays from the Frontiers of Evolution and Psychology.* Oxford: Oxford Univ Pr. 2002: Chapter 19.

■ ■ ■ ■ ■ ■ ■ ■ ■ ■

31   POSSIBLE EFFICACY OF A CREEK FOLK MEDICINE THROUGH SKIN ABSORPTION: AN OBJECT LESSON IN ETHNOPHARMACOLOGY

Michelle M. Alexander and J. Anthony Paredes

This selection shows that even substances or treatments that seem to be inert stimuli of placebo or meaning responses may in fact be chemically efficacious. The authors propose a pharmacologically active substance and a likely means of absorption for a remedy used by Poarch Creek Indian people in Alabama to treat teething in infants. This topic connects to readings in Parts I and II on the rise in interest in pharmaceutically useful substances from non-Western healing traditions, and on the principle that such healing traditions are rooted in local plant and animal products and involve knowledge of how to use poisonous plants safely. The selection is comparative in its review of the cross-cultural use of the same plant and others in its family for similar or related ailments. It highlights the possibility that plants used against the skin (such as belts, necklaces, or armbands) for ritual or protective purposes may not be just magical substances but medicinal ones also.

Source: Alexander, M. M. and J. A. Paredes 1998. "Possible Efficacy of a Creek Folk Medicine through Skin Absorption: An Object Lesson from Ethnopharmacology." *Current Anthropology* 39(4):545–549. ©1998 by The Wenner-Gren Foundation for Anthropological Research. With permission from the University of Chicago Press.

The remedy in question is a necklace of nine beads made from the roots of the treadsash briar. This plant is from a family of plants used around the world as sedatives and pain killers and as treatments for respiratory ailments and toothache. Poarch Creek medical tradition maintains that the necklace relieves the pain of teething and dries overactive mucous membranes that cause a runny nose in infants. Skin absorption is a plausible mechanism used also in biomedicine, in the form of nicotine patches, topical analgesics, nitroglycerin for angina, and hormones for birth control.

The necklace appears to belong to an indigenous category of spiritual or magical cures known as "old Indian rules" that commonly involve a mixture of ritual components and material objects from plants or animals. Even though there is doubt about its effectiveness and appropriateness within the community itself, the necklace holds a lesson for medical anthropologists. It would be wise to keep the "magical" and medicinal dimensions together in any analysis of healing practices, in order not to miss either the meaning responses described in the last selection or the chemical action that might underlie treatments such as those analyzed in this one.

Questions to keep in mind

What does this study indicate about the possibility of finding new pharmacologically active substances by studying the whole range of objects used in traditional medical/religious systems?

Would you expect the meaning response to be more powerful among older or younger Poarch Creek people?

What procedures help minimize the toxicity of the necklace and maximize its effectiveness as a remedy?

What additional information, if any, would you need to be convinced that the necklace is effective for its stated purpose?

Successes in the use of transdermal nicotine patches to treat tobacco addiction (Daughton et al. 1991; see *Time,* December 23, 1991, p. 52) encourage us to share with a wider audience our ideas on the possible efficacy of a Poarch Creek Indian folk medicine relying on the same therapeutic mechanism. These ideas were first presented orally nearly 20 years ago (Alexander and Paredes 1978). We believe that they may be widely applicable in the search for pharmacologically useful substances in the medical lore of tribal and folk peoples, a subject of renewed popular as well as scholarly interest.

The Poarch Creeks constitute a federally recognized tribe numbering approximately 2,000 members with headquarters near the town of Atmore, Alabama (Paredes 1992). They are the descendants of mixed-blood Creeks who were allowed to remain in extreme southern Alabama when the main body of Creeks was "removed" to Indian Territory, now the state of Oklahoma. They are currently engaged in efforts to recapture a portion of their native Creek cultural heritage and taking part in intertribal Pan-Indian activities as well. Until about the 1950s the Poarch Creek way of life was one that Paredes (1975) has characterized as a "folk culture" (see Redfield 1941:338–69), containing a few distinctly Indian elements but more accurately described as an amalgam of several southern U.S. folk traditions. The Poarch Creek folk culture included a variety of medicinal cures and prophylactics.

No systematic ethnoscientific elicitation of medicines was conducted with Poarch Creeks, but from general descriptions by older informants it appears that they recognized two types of folk medicines. First, there were those involving some materia medica taken internally or applied to lesions and sores; as the older Creeks would say, "people had to doctor themselves with weeds and things they'd find growing in the woods." In addition to plant remedies that were common knowledge, there were others known only to those recognized by the Poarch Creeks as herbal specialists, "Indian doctors," the last of whom survived until the late 1970s. A second kind of Poarch Creek remedy was part of popular lore and generally did not involve the use of herbs. Among these remedies were placing a quail's head in an infant's mouth to ensure that the child would speak well and reciting a particular verse to relieve the pain of a burn. Some late-middle-aged Creeks of the early 1970s seemed to have this kind of remedy most in mind as an example of what they called "old Indian rules." Even for this latter kind of remedy, however, the older Creeks had a rather pragmatic attitude, though some of these beliefs were tinged with ritualism and supernaturalism. It was this latter type of medicine about which some younger Creeks sometimes seemed rather dubious if not a little embarrassed when talking about the beliefs and practices of their elders.

Whatever emic ("native") distinctions there might have been among kinds of Poarch Creek folk medicine, from an outsider point of view many of the Poarch Creek traditional cures—especially those that used no herbs—would popularly be regarded as "magical" (Paredes 1975:100). At least two of these so-called magical remedies in fact employed botanical substances. One was an aphrodisiac; the other is the subject of this selection. In field interviews, some informants seemed to describe these two medicines—sometimes with a smile or a chuckle—as a sort of cognitive bridge between the purely herbal prescriptions and the "old-Indian-rules," or magical, kind of folk remedies. It now appears, however, that one of these so-called magical herbals may, in fact, have the chemical properties and was applied in such a way as to produce *pharmacologically* efficacious results. Moreover, since the remedy was used on infants and toddlers, a placebo effect hardly seems indicated.

The Poarch Creek remedy in question consisted of nine beads, each about a half-inch long, made from the roots of the treadsash briar *(Solanum carolinense)*,[1] strung on ordinary sewing thread and tied snugly about an infant's neck to alleviate teething pain and accompanying discomforts such as a runny nose. Alternative remedies for the same purposes described by Poarch Creeks were a necklace of nine hog teeth or nine shirt buttons. The consistent prescription of the number nine and specification of nonvegetal substitutes for *S. carolinense* may have misled the ethnographer, Paredes, and perhaps some young Creeks themselves into erroneously classifying the whole set of remedies as magical, lacking any pharmeceutically active basis for effecting relief.

In field interviews none of the older Creeks ventured any theory to explain how the teething remedy worked but merely asserted that it did, *particularly in its treadsash briar form*. Though the ethnographer collected descriptions of the remedy from several informants, he saw it in use only once. In the summer of 1973 a 60-year-old woman prepared a treadsash briar necklace for her grandson; she asserted that it reduced his discomfort from teething and, perhaps more important, the upper respiratory symptoms of a cold within only a few hours. Ironically, a young woman then active in local Indian cultural affairs recalled the frequent use of the treadsash briar remedy in the past and remarked to Paredes, "I wouldn't have a string of those dirty old beads around one of my younguns' neck." She too may have erred in not taking more seriously the possible objective pharmacologically therapeutic value of a necklace of *S. carolinense* beads.

A chance reading of a discussion of a Comanche herb medicine involving a species of *Solanum* (Vogel 1970:328) prompted a reexamination of the possible efficaciousness of the Poarch Creek use of *S. carolinense*. Alexander has reviewed the botanical literature on *S. carolinense* and compiled examples of the medicinal uses of this and related plants. This report is devoted to the presentation of inferential evidence that a string of treadsash briar beads around a baby's neck may indeed have functioned as a mild sedative and had other therapeutic effects (e.g., drying mucous membranes) through the mechanism of skin absorption. No attempt will be made to explain the importance of the number nine or the alternative forms of the remedy. Nor will any attempt be made to account for the ethnological origins of this remedy, even though Puckett (1926) and Hamel and Chiltoskey (1975:46) report an almost identical remedy in southern black and North Carolina Cherokee folk cultures respectively. Our concern here is with the possible efficacy of one of those medicines, without regard for whether the usage was native to the Creeks or borrowed from some other cultural tradition.

THE SOLANACEAE AND THEIR USES

S. carolinense belongs to the Solanaceae, one of the world's largest plant families. The family "is strongly centered in the Americas, south of the

United States," but "species are found over most of the world" (D'Arcy 1968:3). It includes many economically important plants, such as potatoes, tomatoes, peppers, eggplants, and tobacco, as well as such medicinal plants as belladonna, mandrake, henbane, jimsonweed, and night-shade. Plants in this family are particularly "rich in alkaloids, containing more basic types than any other family except the Leguminosae" (Alston and Turner 1963:342). Important drugs found in the Solanaceae include nicotine, hyoscyamine, atropine, belladonna, scopolamine, and solanine....

· · ·

In summary, the family Solanaceae includes a variety of plants containing medicinal drugs that affect the nervous system, glandular systems, and mucous membranes.

The Solanaceae family derives its name from the genus *Solanum*, which, like others in the family, includes plants that can be poisonous. Indeed, the principal drug of this genus, solanine, is known primarily for its toxic effects (Morton 1971:24). Nonetheless, *S. nigrum*, deadly nightshade, was used by the Sotho of Africa to treat lumbago, in Italy as an antispasmodic and sedative, and mixed with honey in certain parts of Africa as a treatment for tuberculosis (Watt and Breyer-Brandwijk 1962:16, 996). The Houmas of Louisiana "used the boiled roots of *Solanum nigrum* for an infusion given to babies with worms; the green leaves were crushed and mixed with grease to produce a poultice that was used on sores. The Rappahannocks of Virginia used a weak infusion of the leaves to cure insomnia" (Vogel 1970: 328). A *Solanum* species was used by Comanche as a general tonic and as a remedy for tuberculosis. According to Stern (1985:474) deadly nightshade is "one of the best-known medicinal drug producers . . . of Europe," the source of belladonna and of atropine, scopolamine, and hyoscyamine. Stern continues, "Atropine is used . . . for relief of pain, to dilate eyes, and to counteract muscle spasms. Scopolamine is used as a tranquilizer, and hyoscyamine has effects similar to those of atropine."

In view of the Creek use of *S. carolinense* as a teething remedy it is perhaps significant that at least five other species of *Solanum (S. indicum, S. panduraeforme, S. surattense, S. verbascifolium, and S. merkeri)* have been used to treat toothache and other oral discomforts by various peoples of Africa, India, and the Solomon Islands (Lewis and Elvin-Lewis 1977:257, 261, 265, 302).

S. carolinense is an erect or spreading woody perennial growing to 60 cm. The stems are green to purple with 1-cm spines. The plants have deep horizontal rhizomes with cylindrical tubers. The leaves range from simple to lanceolate margins entire to sinuate and have 2–5 lobes on each side of the midvein. Both sides of the leaf are covered with 4–8-rayed hairs, and there are spines on the major veins. The flowers are mauve, blue, or white and 2–3.5 cm in diameter. *S. carolinense* fruits are white, ripening to green mottled and then yellow. The plant dies to the ground in the winter and survives by means of its tuberous roots, resprouting near the end of March. It is probably native to the southeastern United States (D'Arcy 1974:840; Duncan and Foote 1975:164).

Despite a concerted search, no complete chemical analysis of *S. carolinense* could be found in the literature (but see, e.g., Evans and Somanabandhu 1977, 1980). It is, however, reported to contain solanine (Rigg 1924:167; Kingsburg 1964:289), mainly in its leaves (Bonner and Varner 1965:704). The amount of solanine present depends on factors such as soil type, genetic strain, and maturity (Lampe and Fagerstrom 1968:71–78). Poisoning by solanine is evidenced by a variety of possible symptoms, including nausea, fever, sweating, slowing of the heart, dilation of the pupils, and mental confusion (Kingsburg 1964:289). The plant has been reported poisonous and even fatal to livestock (Kingsburg 1964:289). Solanine is found not only in *S. carolinense* but also in such species as *S. nigrum, S. dulcamara,* and *S. tuberosum,* the "Irish potato" (Youngken 1938:87).

Even though *S. carolinense* contains the toxin solanine, it has been used for a variety of medicinal purposes. In addition to the aforementioned use of the plant by southern rural blacks and North Carolina Cherokees as a teething remedy like that of the Poarch Creeks, Grime (1976:183) and Morton (1974:148) report that the root of *S. carolinense* was used as an aphrodisiac by some African-Americans in South Carolina. Moerman (1977:78) also lists the root as being used as an aphrodisiac but adds that a decoction of the root was used as an anticonvulsive. Coon (1974:247) states that the root of *S. carolinense* acts as a sedative to the central nervous system and has been used to treat asthma and bronchitis. In colonial times the "juice of five or six berries, taken daily in increasing quantities, was used to treat tetanus" (Krochmal and Krochmal 1973:207). According to Morton (1974:148), "French scientists have demonstrated the value of the fruit of *Solanum carolinense* in treating tetanus." The berries have been used to promote urination and to relieve pain and nervous tension (Krochmal and Krochmal 1973:207). The dried fruit has been collected in the United States and exported to Europe for pharmaceutical use as an anodyne, antispasmodic, and diuretic (Morton 1974:148). In 1916 *S. carolinense* was listed as a pharmaceutical by the *National Formulary*, which has been published by the American Pharmaceutical Association since 1888 and has been the official U.S. compendium of standards for drugs in use since the Federal Food and Drug Act of 1906 (Grollman and Grollman 1970:36). In 1930 the U.S. Department of Agriculture listed *S. carolinense* as a "medicinal plant of commercial importance" (Sievers 1930).

The foregoing information is sufficient to suggest strongly that members of the Solanaceae family, the genus *Solanum*, and *S. carolinense* itself contain drugs with the sedative, analgesic, and mucous-drying properties that would be effective in alleviating the infant teething symptoms for which the Creeks have used *S. carolinense*. (It must be borne in mind, of course, that no detailed chemical analysis of *S. carolinense* has yet been uncovered and that the plant is poisonous; perhaps it is noteworthy that the Creeks used its root and not its leaves, where the solanine is synthesized.) In addition to the chemical evidence, ethnological data provide inferential support for the idea that the Poarch Creek usage of *S. carolinense* is therapeutically beneficial. Many peoples of the world have used plants of the Solanaceae family as sedatives, analgesics, and decongestants, thus suggesting that through either diffusion or independent invention human beings in many places and times have discovered their medicinal values.

SKIN ABSORPTION

It remains to be shown how Creek babies obtained the suggested benefits, since the plant was neither ingested nor applied directly to the gums. It is ten-

tatively proposed here that the drugs were absorbed through the skin into the nervous system, the bloodstream, or both.

In their survey of methods of administration of drugs, Grollman and Grollman (1970:31) state that "drugs may be applied to the skin for their general as well as for their local action." Passage through the entire thickness of the skin is an extremely complex matter depending on the chemical composition and concentration of the drugs involved and other factors (e.g., Adriani and Naraghi 1977). Even so, it is well established that in some cases local analgesics such as Aspercreme™ (*Physicians' Desk Reference*, 32d edition, p. 1666) may be used to provide temporary relief from the pain of arthritis and rheumatism merely by application to the skin. Likewise, since the 1970s skin absorption has been relied upon for the administration of certain medications for the control of systemic conditions. When an ointment containing nitroglycerin is spread on the skin, "the active ingredient (nitroglycerin) is continuously absorbed through the skin into the circulation, thus exerting prolonged vasodilator effect. Nitroglycerin ointment is effective in the control of angina pectoris, regardless of the site of application" (*Physicians' Desk Reference*, 32d edition, p. 1070).

More recently, various other medicinal substances have been prepared for administration transdermally or topically. For present purposes, those employing chemicals found in plants of the Solanaceae family are of special interest. A skin patch for the control of motion sickness may be worn behind the ear for delivery of a continuous dose of scopolamine for up to three days (*Physicians' Desk Reference*, 40th edition, pp. 820–21). Daughton and associates (1991) have used transdermal patches for administering nicotine to reduce tobacco withdrawal symptoms, and within months of the publication of their findings advertisements for commercial nicotine patch products were already appearing in popular magazines (e.g., *Time*, February 24, 1992, pp. 38–39), even though available only by physician's prescription. Finally, Harris (1974:217–20), citing Harner (1972), has suggested that medieval European witches obtained the hallucinatory effects of atropine by applying to the skin and to the genitalia a salve concocted of solanaceous plants (hence the association of witches with broom-sticks).

Obviously, careful experimental research would be required to demonstrate that any therapeutic drugs that *S. carolinense* might contain could be absorbed effectively through the skin. Nonetheless, recent successes of transdermal patches in Western scientific medicine certainly tend to support the skin absorption hypothesis. Perhaps it is also significant that the traditional Creek *S. carolinense* necklace is attached snugly about the baby's neck in such a way that the beads transect the major blood vessels to the mouth, nose, and throat lying just beneath the skin. Also, the more permeable roots rather than stems of *S. carolinense* are used to make the necklace. In making a replica of a treadsash briar necklace Alexander observed that the *S. carolinense* roots exuded a mucilaginous substance that possibly might promote effective adhesion and, thus, absorption through the skin.

CONCLUDING REMARKS

Because *S. carolinense* contains a highly poisonous substance, solanine, there remains the possibility that Poarch Creek usage of the plant had negative effects on children. Nonetheless, the circumstantial evidence for the objective medicinal value of the *S. carolinense* necklace as once used by Poarch Creeks through the mechanism of skin absorption is sufficiently convincing as to constitute a general lesson of anthropological significance.

The medicinal and ritual practices of tribal and folk peoples around the world include a host of vegetable substances that are placed in contact with the skin in the form of ointments, poultices, amulets, belts, armbands, necklaces, and talismans. Many of these that earlier ethnographers and folklorists have considered solely *materia magica* and, at best, effective only through psychosomatic mechanisms should be reexamined for their possible systemic pharmaceutical effectiveness through skin absorption. We hope that this report will encourage others to undertake such examinations.

NOTES

1. Identification of the plant was done by staff of the Florida State University Herbarium from a field specimen collected by Paredes. Perhaps the most

widely used common name for *S. carolinense* is horse nettle.

REFERENCES

ADRIANI, JOHN, AND MOHAMMED NARAGHI. 1977. "The pharmacologic principles of regional pain relief," in *Annual review of pharmacology and toxicology*, vol. 17. Edited by Henry W. Elliott, Robert George, and Ronald Opun. Palo Alto: Annual Reviews/Alston and Turner.

ALEXANDER, MICHELLE, AND J. ANTHONY PAREDES. 1978. *Solanum carolinense:* A possible natural sedative in the folk medicine of the Eastern Indians of Alabama. Paper presented at the 30th annual meeting of the Florida Anthropological Society, Ft. Walton Beach, Fla., April 1–2.

ALSTON, RALPH E, AND BILLIE LEE TURNER. 1963. *Biochemical systematics.* Englewood Cliffs: Prentice-Hall.

BONNER, JAMES, AND J. E. VARNER. 1965. *Plant biochemistry.* New York: Academic Press.

COON, NELSON. 1974. *The dictionary of useful plants.* Emmaus, Pa.: Rodale Press.

D'ARCY, WILLIAM GERALD. 1968. A taxonomic study of the genus *Solanum lato* in Florida and neighboring areas. Master's thesis, University of Florida, Gainesville, Fla.

———. 1974. *Solanum* and its close relatives in Florida. *Annals of the Missouri Botanical Garden* 61:819–67.

DAUGHTON, DAVID M., ET AL. 1991. Effect of transdermal nicotine delivery as an adjunct to low-intervention smoking cessation therapy. *Archives of Internal Medicine* 151:749–52.

DUNCAN, WILBUR, II, AND LEONARD E. FOOTE. 1975. *Wildflowers of the Southeastern United States.* Athens: University of Georgia Press.

EVANS, WILLIAM C., AND AIMON SOMANABANDHU. 1977. Bases from the roots of *Solanum carolinense.* *Phytochemistry* 16:1859–60.

———. 1980. Nitrogen-containing non-steroidal secondary metabolites of *Solanum, Cyphomandra, Lycianthes,* and *Margaranthus. Phytochemistry* 19: 2351–56.

GRIME, WILLIAM E. D. 1976. *Botany of the black American.* St. Clair Shores, Mich.: Scholarly Press.

GROLLMAN, ARTHUR, AND EVELYN FRANES GROLLMAN. 1970. *Pharmacology and therapeutics.* Philadelphia: Lea and Febiger.

HAMEL, PAUL B., AND MARY U. CHILTOSKEY. 1975. *Cherokee plants.* Sylva, N.C.: Herald.

HARNER, MICHAEL. 1972. "The role of hallucinogenic plants in European witchcraft," in *Hallucinogens and shamanism.* Edited by Michael Harner. New York: Oxford University Press.

HARRIS, MARVIN. 1974. *Cows, pigs, wars, and witches: The riddles of culture.* New York: Vintage Books.

KINGSBURG, JOHN M. 1964. *Poisonous plants of the United States and Canada.* Englewood Cliffs: Prentice-Hall.

————. 1965. *Deadly harvest: A guide to common poisonous plants.* New York: Holt, Rinehart and Winston.

KROCHMAL, ARNOLD, AND CONNIE KROCHMAL. 1973. *A guide to the medicinal plants of the United States.* New York: Quadrangle New York Times Book Company.

LAMPE, KENNETH, AND RUNE FAGEISTROM. 1968. *Plant toxicity and dermatitis: A manual for physicians.* Baltimore: Williams and Watkins.

LEWIS, WALTER, AND MEMORY P. F. ELVIN-LEWIS. 1977. *Medical botany: Plants affecting man's health.* New York: John Wiley.

MOERMAN, DANIEL E. 1977. *American medical ethnobotany: A reference dictionary.* New York: Garland.

MORTON, JULIA. 1971. *Plants poisonous to people in Florida and other warm areas.* Miami: Hurricane House.

————. 1974. *Folk remedies of the low country.* Miami: Seamann.

PAREDES, J. ANTHONY. 1975. "The folk culture of the Eastern Creek Indians," in *Indians of the Lower South: Past and present.* Edited by John K. Mahon. Pensacola: Gulf Coast History and Humanities Conference.

————. 1992. "Federal recognition and the Poarch Creek Indians," in *Indians of the Southeastern United States in the late 20th century.* Tuscaloosa: University of Alabama Press.

PUCKETT, NEWBELL NILES. 1926. *Folk beliefs of the Southern Negro.* Chapel Hill: University of North Carolina Press.

REDFIELD, ROBERT. 1941. *The folk culture of Yucatan.* Chicago: University of Chicago Press.

RIGG, GEORGE B. 1924. *The pharmacists' botany.* New York: Macmillan.

SIEVERS, A. F. 1930. *American medicinal plants of commercial importance.* U.S. Department of Agriculture Miscellaneous Publication 77.

STERN, KINGSLEY R. 1985. 3d edition. *Introductory plant biology.* Dubuque: William C. Brown.

VOGEL, VIRGEL J. 1970. *American Indian medicine.* Norman: University of Oklahoma Press.

WATT, JOHN MITCHELL, AND MARIA GERDINA BREYER-BRANDWIJK. 1962. *The medicinal and poisonous plants of Southern and Eastern Africa.* Edinburgh: E. and S. Livingston.

YOUNGKEN, HEBER W. 1938. *A college textbook of pharmaceutical botany.* Philadelphia: Blakiston.

■ ■ ■ ■ ■ ■ ■ ■ ■

32   CULTURAL CONTEXTS OF EBOLA IN NORTHERN UGANDA

Barry S. Hewlett and Richard P. Amola

This selection examines explanatory models surrounding Ebola among people as well as healers in Uganda (see selection 26). It shows how different groups of people may interpret the causes of disease and the treatment of illness differently. The selection serves as a reminder not to assume that people outside the industrialized societies (or subpopulations within them) are "empty vessels" with faulty medical knowledge or none at all, who need only be taught the correct biomedical explanatory models to learn to best care for their health.

The authors of this selection do not limit themselves to characterizing indigenous explanatory models for the purpose of improving the effectiveness of biomedical control measures during emergency situations such as an epidemic (see selection 23). Their work shows that biomedical measures in fact may be

Source: Hewlett, B. S. and R. P. Amola 2003. "Cultural Contexts of Ebola in Northern Uganda." *Emerging Infectious Diseases* 9(10): 1242–1248.

unhelpful and that indigenous understandings may contribute to effective prevention and treatment. Indeed, the indigenous protocol for dealing with contagion indicates that Western health experts may learn from people who have knowledge gained through long experience of epidemic disease. The fact that spiritual and social concerns dovetail with several of the measures in the protocol makes this no less true. Moreover, as seen in selection 23 about Spanish flu, when religious and social issues are ignored the chaos and confusion associated with an epidemic may be felt more acutely.

This selection, along with previous ones, shows that indigenous healing systems may categorize illnesses on a graded scale of spiritual content, but in the absence of a mind–body, spirit–matter opposition. During the Ebola epidemic, ritual measures were taken only when it was evident that the disease was not an infection treatable by indigenous herbal or biomedical remedies, or a malady that could be removed by consultation with a traditional healer. The analysis also shows that indigenous healing systems are flexible and adaptable, as seen in recent changes in object removal practices in Uganda (see also selections 8 and 9). Far from being stuck in their ways, local healers were very willing to assist in control efforts during the Ebola epidemic. Hewlett and Amola argue that the exclusion of these healers, together with other missteps such as hospital burials without family notification, may have worsened the impact of the disease and contributed to the unusually extreme stigmatization (see selections 36, 37, 38) of the recovered.

Questions to keep in mind

What did the researchers do in this study, and in what order? How did these activities connect to the research questions? What are some limitations of the study and the methods used?

What are the three explanatory models that emerged during the epidemic, and why did people not see them as contradictory?

How did caregiving and burial practices change when the disease was categorized as *gemo*?

What mistakes made by international health authorities might have been prevented if they had had more knowledge about religious beliefs and practices, burial customs, and indigenous healing?

Many emerging disease specialists are sensitive to and acknowledge the potential importance of social science in disease control, but seldom is this perspective considered when organizing response efforts. In part, this situation exists because so little research in this area has been conducted. The special issue on Ebola in The Journal of Infectious Diseases (1) does not include any articles on the behavioral aspects of the disease. However, World Health Organization (WHO) technical guidelines for responding to Ebola hemorrhagic fever (EHF) state that, in conducting epidemiologic surveillance, "Special attention must be given to the actual perception of the outbreak by the community. In particular, specific cultural elements and local beliefs must be taken into account to ensure proper messages, confidence, and close cooperation of the community"(2).

We describe the first systematic sociocultural study of an outbreak of EHF. The outbreak occurred in several locations in northern Uganda in 2000 to 2001. We conducted this research in villages and neighborhoods in and around Gulu during the last month of the outbreak. The field study aimed to: 1) describe local explanatory models of EHF; 2) provide understanding of topics of concern to WHO (i.e., burial practices, patients' fear of going to the hospital, the role of traditional healers in disease transmission); and 3) identify local and international beliefs and practices that enhanced or were detrimental to the control of EHF. An "explanatory model" refers to a person's or culture's explanations and predictions regarding a particular illness. Some of the questions asked when trying to understand an explanatory model include: How do persons refer to the illness? How do they explain it (i.e., cause)? What do they see as appropriate treatments? What do they do to prevent the illness? Patients, physicians, healthcare workers, and local residents in different parts of the world each have explanatory models for different illnesses. Providing care and treatment for a particular disease is often based on negotiating these different models.

BACKGROUND

The 2000–2001 Uganda outbreak was one of the largest EHF outbreaks to date, with 425 presumptive cases and 224 deaths (case-fatality rate 53%). Most patients were women (269 or 63%). The earliest reported presumptive case-patient had disease onset on August 30, 2000, and the last case began on January 9, 2001 (3).

The Gulu EHF outbreak was relatively unusual in comparison to other recent EHF outbreaks (e.g., Democratic Republic of Congo [DRC], Gabon) in that the disease affected primarily one ethnic group, the Acholi, and most of the district medical staff and decision makers (e.g., district medical officer, director of health education) were also from this ethnic group. Also, most (60%) EHF cases occurred in the urban area of Gulu town. Gulu District has approximately 470,000 people, primarily Acholi, and 60% of the population live in protected villages because of rebel activity.

Most Acholi are agro-pastoralists and have a social organization strongly influenced by patrilineal descent and patrilocal postmarital residence (4). Other researchers have written about Acholi and other Nilotic peoples' health beliefs (5–7), but none has described cultural responses to epidemic diseases.

METHODS

Qualitative and quantitative methods were used. The first 2 weeks of the research emphasized open-ended and focus group interviews as well as document review (e.g., health education materials, reports). The last few days emphasized the development of systematic questionnaires. Open-ended interviews were conducted with the following: 1) 10 persons and four focus groups in villages or neighborhoods with large numbers of early cases of EHF; 2) 8 persons and one focus group with survivors of EHF (both healthcare workers and community members); 3) four focus groups with male and female elders (two meetings with each gender); 4) 3 persons and two focus groups of chil-

dren; 5) 4 persons and two focus groups with healthcare workers responsible for the isolation unit and counseling survivors; and 6) 4 persons and one focus group with traditional healers. Focus group meetings usually had 5–8 participants, with the exception of the survivor focus group meeting, which had 35 participants.

Questionnaires were administered to 85 Gulu High School students 15–21 years of age (all members of three senior classes; 33 men, 52 women). Precoded questionnaires were administered to 49 adults in Gulu (25 women, 24 men; an adult from every third house from two randomly selected Gulu neighborhoods) and 60 EHF survivors (22 men, 38 women; all survivors were located through a survivors' organization). We also examined existing documents, such as field reports and health education materials used in the outbreak (e.g., posters, brochures, music cassettes, videos).

RESULTS

Explanatory Models

Table 32.1 summarizes three primary explanatory models identified by the Acholi. The third model is biomedical. Biomedical models have existed in the area for ≥ 100 years, and all Acholi know these models well and use them often. In the early phases of the outbreak, many families, thinking the disease was a bacterial infection or malaria, turned to tetracycline or chloroquine. Most early case-patients went to the hospital seeking biomedical treatment. The biomedical model for EHF was introduced in late October by the Ugandan Ministry of Health. The health education program was multidimensional (e.g., posters, radio shows, videos, brochures) and transmitted this model effectively. However, by the time the EHF biomedical model was introduced, local people had already used two other indigenous explanatory models.

Both of these models require an understanding of the concept of *jok*, which is common to many Nilotic-speaking peoples, including the Acholi. *Jok* are spirits or gods (8). Many different types of *jok* exist; they have names and reportedly are often found near bodies of water, mountains, and natural salt licks for cattle. *Jok* are generally benevolent, as they provide and control resources, but

Table 32.1 **Explanatory models for Ebola hemorrhagic fever (EHF) among the Acholi**

Terms	Yat	Gemo	Disease of Contact; Ebola
Description	"Medicine" or substance that enters the body and causes illness	Bad spirit that comes suddenly and rapidly and effects many people	EHF, biomedical description
Signs and symptoms	Starts with pain inflammation but can have many other signs in later stages	Mental confusion, rapid death, high fever	High fever, vomiting, headache
Causes	Bad "medicine" (poison) goes into body	Lack of respect for _jok_, sometimes no reason	Filovirus, but host reservoir unknown
Transmission	Step on it, cat it, catching it, somebody sends, just looking at a person	Physical proximity, easy for _gemo_ to catch you	Physical contact with bodily fluids of patients
Pathophysiology	Inflammation and pain in area touched by or location of _yat_	Attacks all of body	Damage to major organs
Treatment	_Tak_—techniques of healers who use their _jok_ to identify and remove _yat_ from body or environment	Talk to _jok_ via traditional healer, give whatever wants, gifts of food to _jok_	None, hydrate (ORS)[a], control vomiting
Prevention and control	Protective bracelets	See protocol in text, _chani labolo_, _ryemo gemo_	Do not touch patients, barrier nursing
Prognosis	Good if removed from body; otherwise death	Not good, no cure	Not good, no cure
Risk groups	Very smart, successful, salaried people; anybody	Caregivers close to patients (women), families that do not respect _jok_, families that do not follow protocol	Unprotected healthcare workers, caregivers of patients, people that wash or touch dead victims
Political	Infected troops returning from DRC[a] sent to Gulu	Infected troops returning from DRC sent to Gulu	Infected troops returning from DRC sent to Gulu

[a]DRS, oral rehydration salts; DRC, Democratic Republic of Congo.

they can also cause harm if they are not respected. Deference to and respect for others are central values in Acholi life, and spiritual life reflects and reinforces these values. These spirits are like elders in the community; the Acholi listen to what they have to say, do what they say without question, and give them gifts to show respect.

Traditional healers (_ajwaka_), who are primarily women, obtain their powers to heal from specific _jok_ that they have acquired through time. Most healers acquire as many as 10 such spirits during their lifetime. Each spirit has a name and a specific kind of knowledge (e.g., treatments for mental confusion or infertility).

At first, many persons treated the symptoms of EHF as a regular illness and sought a variety of both biomedical (i.e., malarial drugs or antibiotics) and indigenous cures (i.e., herbs, traditional heal-

ers). In late September 2000, the heads of families in neighborhoods with many deaths asked a traditional healer to locate poisons (_yat_) in and around the lineage household that might be causing the illness and death (Table 32.1, first explanatory model). The healers used their _jok_ and special spears to locate poisoned objects (e.g., roots, bones) in the neighborhood. The healer's _jok_ was also called on to communicate with the spirit associated with a particular poison and to determine if burning the object and sacrificing goats and sheep was necessary to demonstrate respect. Once the poison was removed and respect demonstrated, the healers said the deaths would stop. But the deaths continued. _Yat_ removal is not cheap; each EHF-affected family paid 150,000 Ugandan shillings (U.S.$88), four to five goats or sheep, and one chicken (about half the annual income for a rural Acholi family). The families pointed out that in addition to the enormous loss of loved ones, an incredible amount of family assets was lost in trying to treat the ill.

In early October, residents began to realize that this outbreak was more than a regular kind of illness and began to classify it as *two gemo* (two [illness] gemo [epidemic]), the second explanatory model in Table 32.1. *Gemo* is a bad spirit (type of *jok* that comes suddenly and causes a mysterious illness and death in many people within a very short period of time). *Gemo* reportedly comes like the wind in that it comes rapidly from a particular direction and affects many people, but the wind itself does not necessarily bring it. Acholi have experienced other types of *gemo* (e.g., measles and smallpox). Forty-nine of 50 adults interviewed indicated a belief that Ebola was a type of *gemo*. The term *two gemo* was also used in health education posters and music.

Gemo is said to be mysterious in that it just comes on its own, but several people indicated that it comes because of lack of respect and honor for the gods. Elders indicated that in the past, lack of respect for *jok* of *tura* (hills, mountains, bodies of water) was the major cause of *gemo*. People talk about *gemo* catching you, so if someone is close to a person with *gemo* it is easier for *gemo* to catch you. Once an illness is identified as *gemo,* a protocol for its prevention and control is implemented that is quite different from the treatment and control of other illnesses.

When an illness has been identified and categorized as a killer epidemic (*gemo*), the family is advised to do the following: 1) Quarantine or isolate the patient in a house at least 100 m from all other houses, with no visitors allowed. 2) A survivor of the epidemic should feed and care for the patient. If no survivors are available, an elderly woman or man should be the caregiver. 3) Houses with ill patients should be identified with two long poles of elephant grass, one on each side of the door. 4) Villages and households with ill patients should place two long poles with a pole across them to notify those approaching. 5) Everyone should limit their movements, that is, stay within their household and not move between villages. 6) No food from outsiders should be eaten. 7) Pregnant women and children should be especially careful to avoid patients. 8) Harmony should be

increased within the household, that is, there should be no harsh words or conflicts within the family. 9) Sexual relations are to be avoided. 10) Dancing is not allowed. 11) Rotten or smoked meat may not be eaten, only eat fresh cattle meat. 12) Once the patient no longer has symptoms, he or she should remain in isolation for one full lunar cycle before moving freely in the village. 13) If the person dies, a person who has survived *gemo* or has taken care of several sick persons and not become ill, should bury the persons; the burial should take place at the edge of the village.

From a biomedical perspective, this protocol constitutes a broad-spectrum approach to epidemic control. Isolation and identification of the patient's home and village were emphasized by all groups interviewed, but sexually transmitted and foodborne transmissions were also frequently listed. Elders were adamant that this protocol existed before the arrival of Europeans in the late 1800s. Although historic research is needed to verify this claim, the facts that an indigenous term (*gemo*) is associated with the behaviors, the belief is integrated into the religious system (*jok*), and the protocol is common knowledge to children who do not learn it in school suggest that many rules existed in pre-Colonial times.

Several other ways exist to try to control *gemo,* including driving it away to the Nile by noisemaking (*ryemo gemo*). This procedure was conducted several times during the outbreak and is conducted every December 31 to chase away any potential *gemo* before the New Year begins. Another local custom is *chani labolo*, which consists of wearing a dried banana leaf bracelet for 3 days (for men) or 4 days (for women) to protect and chase away *gemo*. Some healers have *jok* that is supposedly specific for *gemo,* and three of the four traditional healers interviewed indicated their *jok* told them about the impending *gemo* before it arrived (i.e., back in August 2000).

Most local residents saw a political dimension to the explanatory models of EHF (Table 32.1). Many felt that EHF came from infected Ugandan soldiers returning from DRC. Residents felt that the current government has little interest in the North so when Ugandan soldiers became infected in the DRC, the decision was made to send them to military bases in Gulu. Although some of the first female victims of EHF had relationships with men in the military, existing epidemiologic evidence does not support the DRC origin hypothesis. The origin of this outbreak is not known. Political dimensions to disease, killer epidemics, in particular, are common. The first author's visit to Gabon during the 1996 EHF outbreak indicated that local people believed that the French military, which had military exercises in the area just before the outbreak, were partially responsible for introducing the disease. In addition, the 2003 Congo outbreak was linked, in part, to activities of Euro-Americans conducting research in a national park there.

Many informants and healthcare workers indicated that fleeing the village or neighborhood was common, in particular in locations with the highest number of infected persons. Fleeing is not an explicit part of the explanatory models but makes some sense because the *gemo* or biomedical models indicate the illness is a rapid killer transmitted by close contact with infected persons.

Most persons involved in this outbreak were familiar with all three explanatory models and did not necessarily see them as contradictory. Healthcare workers emphasized the biomedical model, but many Acholi healthcare workers participated in *ryemo gemo* when it passed through the community. Some persons and villages turned to the *yat* and *gemo* explanatory models but did not hesitate to purchase tetracycline and other medicines to treat cases of EHF. The first two explanatory models may seem strange to international health workers, but they reflect a holistic and social view of illness common to many people in the world. Acholi are aware of the biomedical model but view illness as having social, spiritual, and biological dimensions. The epidemic control protocol is a good example. Family members refrain from sex and quarreling to show respect to *jok* (spiritual) and increase family harmony and peace (social).

ISSUES OF CONCERN

Funerals and Burials

National and international healthcare workers were concerned that burial practices contributed to the amplification of EHF. A brief study indicated that once a person died, his or her paternal aunt (father's sister) was called to wash and prepare the body for burial. If the father did not have a sister, an older woman in the victim's patriline was asked to prepare the body. Generally, the woman removed the clothes from the body, washed the body, and dressed the deceased in a favorite outfit. At the funeral, all family members ritually washed their hands in a common bowl, and during open casket all were welcome to come up to deceased person and give a final touch on the face or elsewhere (called a love touch). The body was then wrapped in a white cloth or sheet and buried. The person was buried next to or near their household. This practice is the normal system of burial.

However, when disease is classified as *gemo*, burial practices change. The body is not touched and is buried outside or at the edge of the village. The designated caregiver, someone who has survived the outbreak or an older woman, is responsible for washing and preparing the body for burial.

Various activities associated with burial practices contributed to transmission of EHF (Table 32.2). Washing the body was a possible means of infection for women only, while a touch was a more common means of infection among men. The fact that 63% of the survivors in this study

Table 32.2   How Survivors Thought They Contracted Ebola Hemorrhagic Fever (EHF)[a]

How survivors felt they acquired Ebola	%	
	Men (n = 22)	Women (n = 38)
Washing body of EHF victim	0	21
Love touch	32	11
Transporting EHF patient to hospital	5	16
Caregiving of EHF patient	27	53

[a]More than one response possible per informant.

had their first symptoms in October implies that they probably became infected before laboratory tests confirmed EHF and before the disease was designated as a type of *gemo* in many communities. Caregiving, especially by women, contributed substantially to many cases, which explains, in part, why 63% of all presumptive EHF cases in Uganda were in women.

WHO was also concerned that local persons were not coming to the hospital when symptoms first emerged. Healthcare workers theorized that patients were afraid of being buried at the airfield if they died. Persons were running and hiding when the ambulance arrived to take them to hospital. Later interviews indicated, however, that the airfield burial was not the problem. As described in the protocol, once an illness is identified as a killer epidemic, burial at the edge of the village is expected. Rather, sources indicated, many persons ran from the ambulance and did not seek treatment quickly because they feared they would never see their family once they were admitted to the hospital. A fear of Euro-Americans buying and selling body-parts is common in many parts of central Africa but was especially pronounced in Gulu hospitals because bodies were placed in body bags and taken to the airfield to be buried without relatives being notified. Relatives were not always around at the time of death, and healthcare workers were required to dispose of the body as quickly as possible. The anger and bad feelings about not being informed were directed toward healthcare workers in the isolation unit. This fear could have been averted by allowing family members to see the body in the bag and allowing family members to escort the body to the burial ground.

Traditional Healers

The term traditional healers is used here because it is commonly used by WHO and other international agencies. In the Gulu area, however, such healers are often referred to as witchdoctors. Both terms misrepresent the nature of what they do. The term traditional gives the impression that their practices have not changed since time immemorial, when, in fact, such healers are always changing their practices. For instance, as mentioned, they no longer suck out *yat* with their mouths because some healers who did so con-

tracted and died from HIV/AIDS. Today such healers use a local sponge or type of grass to extract *yat*. The term witchdoctor is even more misleading because witches (called night dancers or *lajok*) are relatively uncommon in this area by comparison to the Bantu-speaking areas to the south, and few healers know how to treat witchcraft. Indigenous healer may be a more appropriate term.

Before this study was conducted, WHO and other international and national health workers felt that traditional healing practices of some healers led to the amplification of the outbreak. A female healer and some of the earliest EHF patients were often mentioned as examples. In September, a healer traveled from Gulu town to her rural village a few days after treating a known EHF patient. The healer became ill and reportedly treated patients by cutting and sucking poisons, such as *yat,* from ill patients, and thus infecting her patients with her bodily fluids. The healer died, and ≥ 10 deaths were subsequently associated with her healing. But village sources indicated that she did not treat people in the rural village and she did not have any of her healing tools (e.g., spear and rattle) because rebels in the rural areas kill healers caught with these implements (rebels view the work of healers as contrary to the ways of God). Rather, the healer infected many people because she was a prominent and powerful healer. Consequently, when she became ill in the rural area, many people assisted in her care, several different persons slept with her during the night to watch after her, and once she died, several persons assisted in the traditional washing of her body. This case occurred early in the outbreak, and misunderstanding led health authorities to ban all traditional healing. Traditional healers were stigmatized, which may have been unfortunate as all those we interviewed wanted to help in control efforts. As mentioned above, healers rarely cut the skin to remove *yat* or to insert medicines or herbs because of HIV/AIDS health education programs and the loss of several healers to that infection.

Stigmatization

Independent research on stigmatization was conducted by Kabananukye (9) so only a limited number of results from our study will be described.

Adults were asked when they would feel comfortable touching a person who survived Ebola: on the day of hospital release, after 2 weeks, after 1 month, or after >1 month. The most common response (49%) was 1 month after hospital release. This response is consistent with the epidemic control protocol described previously, but many survivors experienced stigmatization long after this 1-month period, in part, because they continued to experience other illnesses (e.g., vision problems, fatigue, leg pains).

Many survivors experienced intense stigmatization. Some were not allowed to return home, many had all their good clothes burned, and some were abandoned by their spouses. Their children were told not to touch them, and wives were told to go back to their home villages. The discrimination also extended to family and village members. For instance, community members from one of the first rural villages affected were regularly turned away at the marketplace and watering hole. One man eventually committed suicide, in part, because he had lost his wife to EHF but also reportedly because of the stress of rejection, harassment, and discrimination in public because of his association with EHF. The survivors' questionnaires suggested that women experienced somewhat greater stigmatization than men. Table 32.3 summarizes some of these findings.

DISCUSSION

Several limitations apply to our study: 1) it was conducted within a relatively short period of time (16 days); 2) researchers were not allowed to live in a village as participant observers because of political insecurity, and 3) the study was conducted at the end of the outbreak. Given these limitations, the study nevertheless provided useful data for control efforts.

Fred Dunn, (10) a physician and anthropologist, developed a simple framework for integrating anthropologic work into disease control efforts. The framework is useful because it emphasizes identifying both health-enhancing and health-lowering beliefs and practices of both the local, national, and international communities. Many sociocultural studies tend to focus only on how local beliefs and practices amplify the disease (e.g., how traditional burial practices contribute to disease transmission); little attention is given to how local peoples' beliefs and practices might contribute to control efforts. Many models also do not examine the beliefs and practices of the biomedical community. The data from this limited study are placed in Dunn's framework in Tables 32.4 and 32.5. These data indicate that local, national, and international actions contributed to the control of this outbreak. All of the health-lowering activities in the community were targeted for change by health educators. Most of the health-lowering activities of the na-

Table 32.3   Ways and Location in which Ebola Survivors Felt Stigmatized

Location in which Survivors Felt Stigmatized	% of Yes Responses	
	Men (*n* = 22)	Women (*n* = 38)
Feared by others when you returned to the community	55	82
Rejected at market or store	36	58
Rejected at well or borehole	32	58
Rejected when walking through neighborhood	55	76

Table 32.4   Community Beliefs and Practices that Enhanced and Lowered Health of Some Persons during Gulu Ebola Hemorrhagic Fever Outbreak

Health Enhancing	Health Lowering
Indigenous protocol for epidemics (see text)	Some aspects of burial and funeral practices: washing of body, dressing the body, love touches, and ritual washing of hands in common bowl of water
Elders sought to help organize the community	Transporting sick or dead by bike, cart, or other means
	Some aspects of traditional healing practices, such as cutting of body to insert medicines

Table 32.5   Beliefs and Practices of the National and International Healthcare Professionals that Enhanced and Lowered Health of some Persons during Gulu Ebola Hemorrhagic Fever (EHF) Outbreak

Health-enhancing Beliefs and Practices	Health-lowering Beliefs and Practices
Most national government health workers and decision makers spoke local language and had an understanding of local cultures	Unintended consequences of WHO[a] health education video: burning of houses of survivors
Establishment of isolation unit and use of barrier nursing	Taking bodies to burial ground before family members could verify the death. This practice led to sick persons hiding from family and health workers; family members being afraid to take sick persons to hospital; persons running away from the ambulance; and stories of Europeans selling body parts
Providing gloves and bleach to local communities	Omitting traditional healers from control efforts; they were ready and willing as a group to help mobilize the community
Medical care of Ebola victims including rehydration, control of vomiting, other drugs/medications	Early stages only: 1) nurses and healthcare nurses lacked training about barrier nursing, protective gear, and education about the transmission and nature of the disease; 2) lack of transport for sick patients; 3) international health workers not familiar with naming, kinship system, household organization of local communities
Multidimensional health education	Taking blood samples for research only or blood taken without reporting results back to persons or communities' increased distrust of healthcare workers
Suspension of the following activities: handshaking upon greeting, cutting by traditional healers, schools, discos, public funerals, traditional beer drinking	International team members conducting EHF studies for research only. This diverted time and energy from control efforts
Diagnostic laboratories for Ebola	
Ambulances to transport patients to hospital to isolate	
Reallocation of tasks of health workers to focus on EHF	
Use of mobile teams to follow all contacts and provide health education, support for survivors and impacted families	

[a]WHO, World Health Organization.

tional and international teams were recognized shortly after they occurred. Many beliefs and practices are neutral in that they do not help or hinder transmission of EHF. For instance, chasing away *gemo* by using *ryemo gemo* or *chani labolo* did not clearly help or hinder disease transmission.

Most national and international physicians, nurses, and healthcare workers are supportive of sociocultural studies, but most do not have the time, especially in outbreak situations, or tool kits to conduct the kinds of studies that might be useful. In the short term, social scientists can contribute to: 1) epidemiologic studies (how to identify persons, personal naming systems, kinship terms, clan names); 2) doctor–patient relations (international healthcare workers understanding of local explanatory models); 3) control efforts (cultural practices and beliefs that may be amplifying outbreak, identifying and mobilizing existing cultural institutions); and 4) health education (which cultural practices and beliefs to build upon, where to focus change).

Many national and international healthcare workers tend to view cultural practices and beliefs as something to overcome, and certain cultural burial practices (washing the body and love touches) did initially amplify EHF in Uganda. However, once people realized that EHF killed rapidly and classified it as *gemo,* a different set of cultural practices and beliefs were implemented. One reason the health education program worked so well was that it was in many ways consistent with indigenous epidemic control measures (isolation, suspension of greetings, dances, public funerals). Even the burying of victims at the airfield, while a bit dramatic for some, was consistent with burying *gemo* victims outside or at the edge of the village

Sensitivity to cultural factors associated with the control of chronic infectious and parasitic disease has increased in the past 20 years, but little attention has been given to cultural factors associated with emerging infectious diseases, especially diseases such as EHF that cause rapid death. The urgent context of these outbreaks often leads to the neglect of local people's feelings and knowledge. The general impression is that, without Western intervention, the epidemic would kill hundreds and spread to all parts of the world; local practices and beliefs are perceived only as amplifying the outbreaks. Our study was the first systematic sociocultural study of EHF. It showed that some cultural practices did indeed amplify the outbreak. However, an important finding was that local people have beliefs and practices in place that can be useful to control rapid epidemics, such as EHF, with high fatalities. Because local people have lived with high mortality rates and serious epidemics for some time, their knowledge may be useful to national and international teams in their efforts to control emerging diseases.

NOTES

1. Special issue on Ebola hemorrhagic fever. *J Infect Dis* 1999;179(Suppl 1).

2. World Health Organization. *WHO recommended guidelines for epidemic preparedness and response: Ebola haemorrhagic fever (EHF).* Geneva: the Organization; 1997.

3. World Health Organization. Outbreak of Ebola haemorrhagic fever, Uganda, August 2000–January 2001. *Wkly Epidemiol Rec* 2001;76:41–8.

4. Atkinson RR. Acholi. In: Middleton J, Rassam A, editors. *Encyclopedia of world cultures: Africa and the Middle East.* Boston: GK Hall; 1995.

5. Geissler PW. Worms are out life. Part I: understandings of worms and the body among the Luo of Western Kenya. *Anthropology and Medicine* 1998;5:63–79.

6. Geissler PW. Worms are our life. Part II: Luo children's thoughts about worms and illness. *Anthropology and Medicine* 1998;5:133–44.

7. Cohen J. Deep denial. *Sciences* 2001;41:20–5.

8. Evans Pritchard EE. *The Nuer.* Oxford (UK): Clarendon; 1956.

9. Kabananukye KIB. *Denial, discrimination and stigmatisation: the case of Ebola epidemic in some districts,* Uganda: Ugandan Ministry of Health, National Ebola Task Force; 2001.

10. Dunn FL. Social determinants in tropical disease. In: Warren KS, Mahmoud ADF, editors. *Tropical and geographical medicine.* New York: McGraw-Hill; 1985.

■ ■ ■ ■ ■ ■ ■ ■

33   HEALTH BELIEFS AND FOLK MODELS OF DIABETES IN BRITISH BANGLADESHIS: A QUALITATIVE STUDY

Trisha Greenhalgh, Cecil Helman, and A. Mu'min Chowdhury

This selection compares a group of recent British Bangladeshi immigrants to a sample of Londoners to show that the explanatory models the immigrants express in relation to diabetes may be used productively in health promotion (see also selection 32). Among the British Bangladeshis in the study, there is a mixing of old and new ideas and similarities as well as differences with mainstream British health beliefs.

Source: Greenhalgh, T., C. Helman, and A. M. Chowdhury 1998. "Health Beliefs and Folk Models of Diabetes in British Bangladeshis: A Qualitative Study." *British Medical Journal* 316(7136):978–983. With permission from the BMJ Publishing Group.

Humoral ideas about equilibrium and flow of bodily substances (see selections 4, 26) merge with understandings of diabetes as fundamentally caused by the Western diet with its excess of sugar (although other factors such as stress or heredity are also recognized). Religious resignation in the face of misfortune is tempered by the idea that individuals are accountable for following their doctors' orders and making every effort to control the disease.

A main point of the study is that while religious restrictions and cultural barriers to exercise or appropriate nutrition persist and may make it difficult for the immigrant group to adopt new behaviors, structural and material barriers such as unsafe urban environments and poor housing and economic conditions overall are at least if not more important in shaping choices and actions. These barriers indicate how inappropriate it is to invoke the notion of patient noncompliance to explain treatment failures (see selections 22, 34). Moreover, the study finds that Bangladeshi patients, in contrast to the control group, view physicians as authority figures not to be bothered by questions. This may help to explain why diabetes prevention and care seem not to be well understood.

One of the strengths of this selection is its attention to the advantages and disadvantages of the methods used. The authors explain how respondents were recruited and how this allowed for breadth of characteristics but limited the study to people who were under biomedical treatment. The research moved from open-ended interviews to focus groups and the use of a structured vignette to elicit responses in a culturally sensitive manner (see Box 33.2). Such strategies should be considered both when reading studies and when planning one's own research projects.

Questions to keep in mind

How do the changes in living conditions and social relations, and related health impacts, experienced by the Bangladeshis in this selection compare to those described in selections 26 (Anishinaabe in Manitoba) and 29 (Hmong refugees in California)?

How would you categorize the explanatory models in this study in light of the classificatory schemes presented in selection 26?

How do British Bangladeshi beliefs about the qualities of foods (strong vs. weak, quantity, balance, digestibility) affect the likelihood that patients will eat the foods recommended by health professionals?

How do British Bangladeshi beliefs about sweating and exercise relate to notions about the causes and care of diabetes?

What are some conditions that affect people's ability to practice behaviors that favor diabetes control and prevention?

INTRODUCTION

Successful management of diabetes requires that we understand the lifestyle, beliefs, attitudes, and family and social networks of the patients being treated.[1] Qualitative methods are particularly useful when the subject of research is relatively unexplored and the research question is loosely defined or open ended.[2] With two recently published exceptions[3,4] and a small British study based entirely on individual interviews,[5] such methods have rarely been used in the study of diabetes.

Anthropological analysis accepts that there are three levels of cultural behaviour: what people say they do (for example, during an interview), what they are actually observed to do, and the underlying belief system which drives that behaviour (Hall's "primary level culture"[6]). In addition, consideration must be given to the wider context in which the behaviour takes place. In particular, the British Bangladeshi informants in this study must be viewed as members of an atomistic rural society living as recent immigrants in a socio-economically deprived urban environment (see Box on page 364).

Bangladeshi population of East London

The frontiers of present day Bangladesh were drawn after the second world war, when British India was partitioned. The Muslim majority of Bengal, along with Sylhet district in the far north east, came to form East Pakistan. In 1971 Bengal seceded from Pakistan and became the separate state of Bangladesh. The country is flat, with a monsoon climate, prone to flooding, and served mainly by inland waterways. The economy is pre-industrial, and most people live in scattered homesteads with an atomistic social organisation (that is, the family is the dominant unit with no effective social organisation or hierarchy beyond the family). The staple crop is rice, and the diet is largely fish, rice, and vegetables. Although about 95% of the population is Muslim, the society contains vestiges of its Buddhist and Hindu cultural roots. In the 1960s and '70s, large numbers of economic migrants came to Britain, particularly from certain villages in rural Sylhet. Men tended to emigrate several years before their wives followed.

Data from the 1991 census suggest that British Bangladeshis account for about 0.3% of the population of England and Wales,[7] and about a quarter of the population of lower Hamlets (East London and City Health Authority; unpublished estimates for 1997 based on projections from 1991 census data).

Qualitative methods used in study

Audiotaped narrative in which subject "tells the story" of his or her diabetes (all subjects)

Semistructured interview in which defined domains are covered (all subjects), including

  Personal medical history

  Psychological reaction to diagnosis of diabetes

  Knowledge about causes, complications and treatment objectives in diabetes

  Body image and beliefs about physiological and pathological processes

  Attitude to dietary restriction

  Attitude to physical exercise

  Perceived social constraints resulting from diabetes

  Satisfaction with current diabetes service

  Experience of and attitude to health professionals

Focus group discussion of 6–9 participants grouped by sex, in which similar topics are covered and areas of controversy and dissent within the group specifically explored (total of 24 subjects)[8]

  Construction of genogram ("family tree") (all subjects) *Pile sorting exercises,* (all subjects), comprising

  Disease ranking—Diabetes is ranked against 10 other medical conditions (heart attack, gastric ulcer, flu, asthma, gall stones, back pain, tuberculosis, cancer, stroke, and malaria)

  Foods—Raw foodstuffs are grouped into "permitted" and "not permitted" and the classification then discussed

  Meal menus—Above exercise is repeated with complete meals

  "Preferred" and "healthy" body size—A selection of eight photographs of Bangladeshis (all of similar age and same sex as informant but of varying body mass index) is sorted into "most [aesthetically] preferred" through to "least preferred" and again into "most healthy" through to "least healthy"

Structured vignette method (see text for details) (18 subjects)

Feedback of preliminary constructs to focus groups, in which responses were videotaped (eight subjects) *Study of patients' general practice case notes* (the "Lloyd George" record), which also contain correspondence about hospital admissions and outpatient visits (all subjects)

SUBJECTS AND METHODS

Subjects

After gaining approval from local research ethics committees, we recruited patients from three general practices in east London known to have a high proportion of Bangladeshi patients. Using computerised diabetes registers where available, and otherwise by manual search of case notes, we identified patients with diabetes and approached them to request a tape recorded interview. Recruitment was usually by letter followed up by telephone call, but in one practice we recruited opportunistically through practice receptionists when patients came to book appointments or collect prescriptions. In all, 40 of the 44 Bangladeshi subjects we approached agreed to be interviewed.

We interviewed these 40 Bangladeshis and a control group of eight white British and two Afro-Caribbean subjects who lived in east London and had similar socioeconomic background. We used purposive sampling methods (that is, we intentionally sought to interview subjects with certain characteristics) to ensure a range of demographic variables and experiences (see Table 33.1).

Table 33.1   Characteristics of Subjects Interviewed in Qualitative Study

	Bangladeshi (n = 40)	Non-Bangladeshi (n = 10)
Age (years):		
21–40	6	0
41–60	23	5
61–80	11	5
Education:		
None	13	0
<3 years school	15	0
>3 years school	10	10
Higher	2	0
Employment:		
Employed	1	2
Unemployed	16	3
Housewife	15	1
Pensioner	8	4
Housing:		
Owner occupied	2	1
Council rented	38	9
Language:		
Sylheti only	24	0
Sylheti plus standard Bengali	8	0
Sylheti plus standard Bengali plus English	8	0
English only	0	10
Type of diabetes (method of control):		
Diet alone	6	1
Diet plus tablets	32	6
Diet plus insulin	2	3
Generation of immigrant:		
Indigenous	0	9
First	39	1
Second	1	0
Extended family in United Kingdom:		
Yes	33	8
No	7	2
Known diabetes complications:		
Yes	21	4
No	19	5
Missing data	0	1
Type of care:		
General practitioner only	15	3
Shared (general practitioner plus hospital)	25	7
Hospital only	0	0

Methods

The research methods used are summarised in the Box on page 364. We allowed the subjects to tell their story in their own words and in no particular order, but we used a checklist of semistructured prompting questions to make sure that the domains listed in the box were covered at some stage by all subjects.

Translation.   Interviews with Bangladeshi subjects were conducted in Sylheti, a dialect of Bengali spoken as a first language by all our Bangladeshi subjects.

Since Sylheti has no written form, the interviews were simultaneously translated and transcribed by an independent translator and were all checked by AMC (a Sylheti anthropologist), who listened to the original recording while reading the draft translation.

Analysis. Transcripts were analysed with NUDIST software. The entire text of the interview was entered onto a computer database and text blocks were coded into 11 broad categories of statement such as body image, information sources, professional roles, and so on.

The objective of the analysis was to identify constructs—that is, provisional inferences about primary level culture drawn from statements and observations.[9] Using the powerful cross referencing facility of the software, we considered together all statements relevant to each construct and modified the construct accordingly.

Validation. An important technique for demonstrating the validity of qualitative findings is triangulation—comparing data obtained by one method with similar data obtained by another method.[10] After developing the constructs, we presented them to a smaller sample of the subjects to determine whether our interpretation of the initial interviews had been correct. For this, we used two methods, the first being a further set of sex specific focus groups in which we presented our initial constructs and recorded the group's responses on videotape. In the second, we developed the new qualitative technique of structured vignette.

Structured Vignette. We presented our constructs in the form of a story recorded on tape about Mr (or Mrs) Ali, a person with diabetes. The story was first played in full and then played back slowly, sentence by sentence. After each sentence, the tape was stopped and the subject asked: "Do you agree that this person would have [acted in this way/thought this/etc]?" (A sample paragraph of the vignette is reproduced in the appendix.) The vignette included some deliberately incorrect statements to check that subjects were not simply agreeing with all the statements. This method was developed to avoid the problems, which have been well documented in non-European cultures,[11] of asking informants to respond to closed questions about their own beliefs or behaviour, which would require them to challenge directly statements made by the interviewer. We performed the structured vignette study on a sample of 18 subjects, and repeated it on 10 of these same subjects after an interval of two months. The internal reliability of the technique was high (overall, 89%, of questions received identical answers on repeat interview).

RESULTS

Sources of Explanatory Models

The desire of the informants to understand and explain the onset and experience of illness was often strong. However, it tended not to lead to a systematic search for professional or scientific explanations but rather to a reflection on personal experience and the experiences of friends and relatives. Lay sources of information were frequently cited as a major influence on behaviour. In the structured vignette study, 17 of the 18 informants agreed that the best way to find out about diabetes was to ask friends and relatives.

While strong religious (Muslim) views were held by all the Bangladeshi informants and explanations often given in terms of "God's will," such views were usually held in parallel with acceptance of individual responsibility and potential for change. Indeed, both stoicism and adherence to particular dietary choices were perceived as the duty of the ill person.

Constructs

Body Concepts.   Youth and health were usually viewed as virtually synonymous, and physical degeneration and weakness as an inevitable consequence of aging—"Once you are 40 eyes tend to give trouble. I am almost 55. So I am expected to have bad eyesight" (Bangladeshi man).

In contrast, Crawford's study of white women in the United States indicated that "health" for them was not merely the absence of illness but had to be earned by taking positive action in terms of diet and exercise in leisure time.[12]

Both men and women chose photographs of large individuals when asked to "pick out the healthiest person." Large body size was generally viewed as an indicator of "more health" and thinness with "less health," but many also perceived that "too much health" (that is, too large a body size) was undesirable, especially if the body is weakened by diabetes. Airhihenbuwa has discussed the phenomenon of immigrants holding simultaneously both "traditional" constructs (deeply rooted values and perceptions drawn from the culture of origin) and "recent" ones (drawn from the host culture and less likely to be enduring in the long term).[13]

Origin and Nature of Diabetes. Illness was generally attributed to events or agents outside the body rather than to primary failure of an organ within it. This model may reflect the predominance of acute infectious illness in the recent cultural history of this group. All informants believed that the primary cause of diabetes, and that of poor diabetic control, was too much sugar and, to a lesser extent, other features of a Western diet, both of which feature strongly in folk models of other cultural groups.[2,4,14,15]

Other aetiological factors mentioned by the Bangladeshi informants included heredity (the notion of an agent transmitted through "shared blood" rather than an inherited predisposition) and germs. Many informants mentioned physical or psychological stress, either as a perceived cause of diabetes or simply when reporting the experience of daily life—especially in relation to economic difficulties, poor housing, and fear of crime.

Impact of Diabetes. The diagnosis of diabetes was generally seen as devastating, and the expression "I was spoiled" was used by several informants. Virtually all felt that diabetes was a chronic, incurable condition and a potential threat to life. They feared acute complications (collapse and "dropping dead"), and a minority volunteered specific long term sequelae in the heart, eyes, and kidneys. Control of diabetes (and therefore reduction in disability and prolongation of life) was felt to lie in restoring the body's internal balance via taking particular foods and fighting the "germ" with medicine.

Many informants expressed difficulty obtaining food that was both acceptable and palatable. Other practical difficulties included confusion over sickness benefits; language barriers when speaking to professionals, especially the use of children as interpreters; and the inability to understand leaflets, either because of the concepts presented or because the leaflets were printed in standard Bengali (some informants said they were better able to understand the English alphabet, such as in road signs or notices, than standard Bengali).

Diet and Nutrition. In the pile sorting exercise, foods were not grouped according to Western notions of nutritional content but in terms of their perceived strength (nourishing power) and digestibility. "Strong" foods, perceived as energy giving, included white sugar, lamb, beef, ghee (derived from butter), solid fat, and spices. Such foods were considered health giving and powerful for the healthy body and suitable for festive occasions, but liable to produce worsening of illness in the old or debilitated. "Weak" foods, preferred in the everyday menu and for the old or infirm, included boiled (pre-fluffed) rice and cereals.

Raw foods, and those that had been baked or grilled, were considered indigestible, as were any vegetables that grew under the ground. Foods of low digestibility were considered unsuitable for elderly, debilitated, or young people. Thus, the recommendation for diabetic patients to bake or grill foods rather than fry them may not accord with cultural perceptions of digestibility.

The structured vignette study showed almost universal agreement that strong foods, solid fat, and ghee should be avoided in diabetes. All 18 agreed that Mr Ali should not eat spicy foods because of his diabetes and that a person with diabetes should eat a different diet from the rest of the family.

Some informants indicated that body components may be linked to certain foods because of physical similarity. For example, sugar, butter, ghee, body fat, bone marrow, semen, and white vaginal discharge were perceived by some to be the same fundamental entity, because their colour is the same and they all solidify when cool and liquefy when heated. Eight of 18 informants in the structured vignette study thought that molasses (a dark form of raw sugar, liquid at room temperature) was an acceptable substitute for sugar in the diet.

"Sugar is the white substance that is stored in the bone marrow, is it not? From this semen is produced. Since I have diabetes, I have come to think that [it is] because of using the semen more. When the 'calcium' inside the bone is exhausted at that time our diabetes starts" (Bangladeshi man in focus group). This statement brought general agreement in the focus group. These findings are consistent with Lambert's work on the traditional South Asian "humoral" concepts of health, which centre on the ecological flow of substances and qualities between the environment, food, and the human body.[16]

Many informants believed that the same amount of rice could be taken as frequent small meals since it was imbalance, rather than total quantity, that mattered. In the structured vignette study, 16 of 18 informants agreed that Mr Ali's doctor had underestimated the amount of rice he needed when advising him to reduce his food intake, and all 18 agreed he should take biscuits or other snacks between meals to sustain his strength. Only five thought that such snacks could cause any harm.

In Bangladeshi society, feasts, festivals, and social occasions are common, culturally important, and centre on eating sweet and rich food. A calculated compromise between dietary compliance and social duty was usually made.

Smoking. Of our Bangladeshi informants, nine of the 23 men and none of the 17 women smoked; only a few took paan (chewing tobacco) regularly, and those who did acknowledged that it was harmful and expressed a desire to quit. In the structured vignette study, only four of 18 informants disagreed that tobacco was harmful.

Concepts of Balance. Many cultures equate balance with health and imbalance with illness.[17] There was a strong and almost universal belief among the Bangladeshi informants that both the onset and the control of diabetes depended on the balance of food entering the body and on balanced emission of body fluids such as sweat, semen, urine, menstrual blood, etc. Excess emission was perceived to deplete the internal stock, low quantity of emissions to indicate inner build up and putrefaction, and thin quality a weakening of the internal stock. Weakness (as in diabetes) was perceived to occur as a result of such depletion or weakening.

Absence of sweating (due to the cold British climate and lack of physical labour) on immigration to Britain was commonly cited as a cause of diabetes and a reason why the condition improved or

disappeared on return to hot countries. In the structured vignette study, 14 of 18 informants agreed that if Mr Ali returned to Bangladesh his diabetes might be cured.

Exercise. Exercise in the context of health and fitness seemed to have little cultural meaning for the Bangladeshi informants, even though they often recalled specific advice on this topic from their doctor. Exercise was viewed as potentially exacerbating illness or physical weakness. The association between sweating (see above) and exercise in leisure time was not made by any informant, but ritual Muslim prayers (namaz) were often cited as a worthy and health giving form of exercise.

The Sylheti language has no expression for physical activity that has the same connotations of vitality, improvement in body condition, social desirability, and inherent "moral" value as the word "exercise." Sports and games are not generally pursued by adults in Bangladesh[18] or by Bangladeshis in Britain.[19] The closest translation for the word "exercise" is "beyam," a word of obscure etymology. Interestingly, the prefix "bey" in Sylheti often has negative connotations—for example, "beyaram" (meaning illness, literally "no comfort") or "beytamiz" (poor etiquette, literally "no manners")—and we were struck by the lack of positive connotations accorded to the concept by our Bangladeshi informants compared with the white British and Afro-Caribbeans.

Some informants gave physical or material constraints to taking exercise. In particular, many of the women rarely left their house, apparently through fear of physical attack. Some informants lived in high rise flats with no working lift, and some commented on the absence of parks, dirty pavements, and street crime.

Professional Roles. The doctor was viewed as a busy, authoritative and knowledgeable person who rarely makes mistakes and has full understanding of the conditions he or she treats. Several informants felt that the doctor's instructions should always be obeyed, and 12 of 18 in the structured vignette study agreed that "Mr Ali's doctor [general practitioner] knows everything about diabetes." Twelve also agreed that it would be impertinent for Mr Ali to ask the doctor any questions. In contrast, both white British and Afro-Caribbean informants were openly assertive and critical of health professionals. Nurses were sometimes viewed in a traditional caring and technical role but were sometimes recognised as providers of information and advice.

Diabetic Monitoring. Informants generally tested their urine regularly, and all who did so seemed to understand the importance of a change in the colour of the test strip. Most informants seemed to believe that, in the absence of symptoms, diabetes was well controlled. The need for regular surveillance when asymptomatic was rarely acknowledged, and only one of 18 informants in the structured vignette study thought that Mr Ali should ever visit the doctor if he did not feel ill. Preventive care was not well understood—"He [the doctor] explained to me and said before complications start, start wearing glasses. This is because your eyes are all right. The diabetes may affect either your eyes or your feet. So if you take the glasses, your eyes may be spared" (Bangladeshi man).

DISCUSSION

Strengths and Limitations of the Study

This study addressed an important and previously underexplored subject in health research.[20] We used a wide range of qualitative techniques on a sample that is likely to have included the least acculturated members of British Bangladeshi society, since we recruited from practices with Bangladeshi general practitioners, nurses, or advocates, we required neither literacy (in any language) nor spoken English or Bengali for participation in the study (indeed, 24 of the 40 informants spoke only the Sylheti dialect), and the response rate for the individual interviews was high (91%). Furthermore, our main field worker was an experienced anthropologist who has worked with this community for 25 years and speaks Sylheti as his first language.

The sample does, however, have limitations. In recruiting subjects from general practices, we failed to access those who do not seek or receive Western medicine in any form. We recruited only one second generation Bangladeshi, probably for demographic reasons. We did not assess any measure of

diabetic control in our informants (such as glycated haemoglobin, which was inconsistently recorded in case notes) so we were unable to relate individual perceptions or experiences to level of control.

Implications for Policy and Practice

Although the differences in body image and illness maps shown here are of considerable anthropological interest, we believe that our findings support the notion that the similarities in health beliefs and health related behaviours (for example, failed attempts to lose weight or give up smoking) between minority groups and the host culture are often understated and may be of more practical importance than their differences.[21]

A recurring theme in this research was that of structural and material barriers to improving health. Poor housing, unsafe streets, and financial hardship were at least as important in preventing certain outcomes (such as taking regular exercise) as religious restrictions or ethnic customs, a finding noted by other researchers in this area.[21,22] It is not within the remit of this paper to expand on the profound socioeconomic disadvantage of many British Bangladeshis, nor on the literature linking poverty with health inequalities in general,[23] but

---

Constructs which might be used as starting points for culturally sensitive diabetes education in British Bangladeshis

- Diabetes is caused by sweet things, a Western diet, and stress
- Diabetes is chronic and incurable, but its effects can be lessened by changes in lifestyle
- Dietary modification is essential for diabetes control, and effort must be made to prepare special food for the family member with diabetes
- A person with diabetes should aim to lose weight if overweight
- Physical labour which produces sweat is beneficial to health
- Sugar, fatty food, and solid fat (including ghee derived from butter) are harmful
- Complications may occur if diabetes is poorly controlled
- Poor diabetic control can be detected by change in the colour of the urine testing strip

the importance of this factor as a barrier to health gain should not be ignored.

Health education that concords with people's "lay epidemiology" and folk models is more likely to lead to changes in behaviour than that which seems to contradict such models. Airhihenbuwa and colleagues, in the context of AIDS prevention, have exposed the fallacy of the assumption that health education is merely a matter of determining "deficiencies" in knowledge and meeting those deficiencies with educational material such as leaflets, teaching seminars, or mass media programmes. Instead, educators must centralise the cultural experiences of those who have hitherto been marginalised.[13,24] Given that the Bangladeshis in this study indicated a high regard for oral explanations from informal sources (friends, relatives, and other patients with diabetes), we think that the potential for learning via oral sources within Bangladeshi culture is high.

Hence, rather than designing an education programme to be delivered externally to rectify "deficiencies" in knowledge or "incorrect" behaviour,[25] we suggest that health promotion programmes attempt to build on those beliefs, attitudes, and behaviours already existing in Bangladeshi culture that promote good diabetes control, prevent complications, and improve quality of life, and address practical barriers to positive health behaviours such as non-availability of particular foodstuffs. The Box on page 369 lists examples of constructs which, though not universally held, are sufficiently

Table 33.2   Examples of Bangladeshi Patients' Perceptions, Structural and Material Barriers, and Reinforcing Factors Affecting Acceptance of a Behavioural Priority in Diabetes Education—"People with Diabetes Should take Regular Sustained Low-intensity Physical Exercise"

	Implications for Health Education and Health Policy
Perceptions	
Loss of body sweat, such as occurs during physical labour, is good for health	Recommendations for physical exercise should focus on the potential for producing sweat in ways other than physical labour
Prayers (namaz) are a form of physical exercise	Educators should be aware of the perceived association of prayer with exercise
Sport and organised physical exercise have no cultural meaning and are inappropriate for women and older men. Sports clothing and footwear are "not appropriate for our community"	Non-sporting activities that do not require special clothing or footwear may be more acceptable than pressure to become involved in sport
Walking is an acceptable form of exercise, but fast walking is inappropriate, especially for women and those of high social status	Promotion of walking and other indigenous activities may allow activity level to be increased in a culturally acceptable way, at least for males
Women should generally remain within the home, dress modestly, and remain demure. Young children should remain with their mother or grandmother at all times	Activities that can be done discretely and in private (such as home exercise videos) may be more acceptable to women
Structural and material factors	
Walking in the street is considered unsafe, particularly for women and elderly people, because of fear of crime and harassment	Effective local and national policies on crime and racial harassment, and community policing in particular, are required on health as well as social grounds
Opportunities for exercise in daily living often go unrecognised	Health promotion campaigns should encourage walking to school and shops rather than using motor transport
Reinforcing factors	
Advice from educators and health professionals is held in high regard	Even though physical exercise is not part of the culture, it should be encouraged in individual doctor–patient encounters
Approval or disapproval by family seems to strongly influence lifestyle choices	Involvement of key family members in education for exercise is likely to improve its success

prevalent in Bangladeshi culture to form the starting point for successful culturally sensitive health education and promotion.

Table 33.2 draws on a framework developed by Danial and Green to identify perceptual, structural, and reinforcing factors that influence specific behavioural outcomes in health promotion.[26] We have used the recommendation for regular, low intensity, physical exercise as an example of a desired behavioural priority for people with diabetes. As Table 33.2 shows, many of the constructs identified in our fieldwork have direct implications for educators working on an individual or public health level. In addition, however, this framework highlights both the broader social and political context within which behaviour change in minority ethnic groups must be placed, and the danger of assuming that "non-compliance" with such advice about lifestyle is always attributable to "cultural factors."

NOTES

1. Bradley C, Gamsu DS, for the Psychological Wellbeing Working Group of the WHO/IDF St Vincent Declaration Action Programme for Diabetes. Measures of psychological well-being and treatment satisfaction developed from the responses of people with tablet-treated diabetes. *Diabet Med* 1994;7:510–6.

2. Helman CG. Research in primary care—the qualitative approach. In: Norton PG, Stewart M, Tudiver F, Bass MJ, Dunn E, eds. *Primary care research: traditional and innovative approaches.* London: Sage Publications, 1991:105–24.

3. Gittelsohn J, Harris SB, Burris KI, Kakegamic L, Landman L, Sharma A, et al. Use of ethnographic methods for applied research on diabetes among the Ojibway-Cree in Northern Ontario. *Health Educ Q* 1996;23:365–82.

4. Grams G, Herbert C, Heffernan C, Calam B, Wilson MA, Grzybowski S, et al. Haida perspectives on living with non-insulin-dependent diabetes. *Can Med Assoc J* 1996;155:1563–8.

5. Kelleher D, Islam S. "How should I live?" Bangladeshi people and non-insulin dependent diabetes. In: Kelleher D, Hillier S, eds. *Researching cultural differences in health.* London: Routeledge, 1996:220–37.

6. Hall ET. *Beyond culture.* New York: Anchor Books, 1977.

7. Balarajan R, Soni Raleigh V. The ethnic populations of England and Wales: the 1991 census. *Health Trends* 1992;24:113–6.

8. Kitzinger J. The methodology of focus groups: the importance of interaction between research participants. *Sociol Health Illness* 1994;16:104–21.

9. Hayes BE. How to measure empowerment. *Qual Progress* 1994;Feb.41–6.

10. Denzin NK, Lincoln YS, eds. *Handbook of qualitative research.* London: Sage Publications, 1994.

11. Helman C. *Culture, health and illness.* 3rd ed. Oxford: Butterworth-Heinemann, 1994.

12. Crawford R. A cultural account of "health": control, release and the social body. In: McKinley JB, ed. *Issues in the political economy of health care.* London: Tavistock, 1984:60–103.

13. Airhibenbuwa CO. Developing culturally appropriate health programs. In: *Health and culture: beyond the Western paradigm.* London: Sage Publications, 1995:25–43.

14. Pierce MB. Non-insulin dependent diabetes and its complications—beliefs, perceptions and prospects for risk reduction [thesis]. London: University of London, 1997.

15. Garro L. Individual or societal responsibility? Explanations of diabetes in an Anishaabe (Ojibway) community. *Soc Sci Med* 1995;40:37–46.

16. Lambert H. The cultural logic of Indian medicine: prognosis and etiology in Rajastani popular therapeutics. *Soc Sci Med* 1992;34:1069–76.

17. Helman C. Balance and imbalance. In: *Culture, health and illness.* 3rd ed. Oxford: Butterworth-Heinemann, 1994:21–4.

18. Chowdhury AM. Household kin and community in a Bangladesh village [thesis]. Exeter: University of Exeter, 1986.

19. Health Education Authority. *Health and lifestyles survey: black and minority ethnic groups in England.* London, HEA, 1994.

20. Greenhalgh PM. Diabetes in British south Asians—nature, nurture and culture. *Diabet Med* 1997;11:10–4.

21. Lambert H, Rose H. Disembodied knowledge? Making sense of medical science. In: Irwin A, Wynne B, eds. *Misunderstanding science: Making sense of science and technology within everyday life.* Cambridge: Cambridge University Press, 1996:65–83.

22. Anderson JM, Wiggins S, Rajwani R, Holbrook A, Blue C, Ng M. Living with a chronic Illness: Chinese-Canadian and Euro-Canadian women with diabetes—exploring factors that influence management. *Soc Sci Med* 1995;41:181–95.

23. Calman KC. Equity, poverty, and health for all. *BMJ* 1997;314:1187–91.

24. Airhihenbuwa CO, Di Clemente RJ, Wingwood GM, Lowe A. HIV/AIDS education and prevention among African-Americans: a focus on culture. *AIDS Educ Prev* 1992;4:267–76.

25. Becker MH. The tyranny of health promotion. *Public Health Rev* 1986;14:15–25.

26. Danial M, Green LW. Application of the precede-proceed model in prevention and control of diabetes: a case illustration from an aboriginal community. *Diabet Spectrum* 1995;8:80–123.

Appendix   Sample Section from Structured Vignette

Statement	Agree	Disagree	Not Sure	Comment
Mr Ali thought that living in Britain had caused his diabetes. He thought that if he went back to Bangladesh the diabetes might be cured				
He thought that the lack of sweating in Britain was unhealthy and that it predisposed people to get diabetes				
He also thought that diabetes was caused by something that got into his body, like a germ or some other bad thing from outside				

■ ■ ■ ■ ■ ■ ■ ■ ■

34   SOCIAL SCIENTISTS AND THE NEW TUBERCULOSIS

Paul Farmer

The previous two selections explored explanatory models and their relationship to behavior. The current selection emphasizes large-scale national and international structures that place limits on the ability of individuals to act in ways that protect their health. To Farmer, these forces represent a form of violence against the poor, who are disproportionately exposed both to disease and to inadequate or inappropriate medical care. Insufficient food, miserable hygienic conditions, and lack of health services combine to make malnutrition and disease more common in poor people. Diseases such as tuberculosis and HIV/AIDS progress more rapidly and outcomes are worse (see selection 22).

Farmer suggests that inequality favors the spread of reemerging or persistent diseases, as evidenced in the greater susceptibility of the poorest socioeconomic categories and of women and certain ethnic groups within the ranks of the poor. Likewise, microbial resistance follows steep grades of inequality. Where all are poor, antibiotics are absent; where all are well off, the disease is controlled; where there is inequality, antibiotics are available unevenly and unpredictably (see Farmer 1999).

Yet, rather than pointing to structural forces and inadequacies of medical care, physicians and other authorities blame these unfavorable conditions on the poor themselves through the notion of patient noncompliance. This is a common manifestation of the Western emphasis on the individual, which directs attention away from social forces and toward personal failures in disease prevention and treatment. In addition, academic research on explanatory models may also contribute to the lack of awareness of the politico-economic level through an overemphasis on culture. Farmer finds that, in fact, patients who attribute their disease to sorcery or folk illnesses are just as likely to comply with chemotherapy as those

Source: Reprinted from *Social Science and Medicine,* Vol. 44, Farmer, P. E., "Social Scientists and the New Tuberculosis," Pages 347–358, Copyright (1997), with permission from Elsevier.

who do not, for access to medicines and economic resources is the principal factor in determining whether a patient completes a course of drug treatment.

Farmer compares studies from around the world that focus on local culture and seem to fail to grasp the fact that local to large-scale forces make treatment by world medical standards inaccessible to the majority of people sick with tuberculosis. As selection 25 shows, most people in the developing world have no choice but to rely on indigenous herbal medicines. Farmer warns against romanticizing folk healing when biomedical remedies of demonstrated effectiveness exist but remain largely out of the reach of those who need them. His arguments remind us that anthropologists have an important role not just in eliciting the patient's point of view, but also in exploring the wider socioeconomic and political contexts that shape patterns of disease and medical care.

Questions to keep in mind

What are some examples of limits on personal agency that affect an individual's ability to comply with treatment?

Do you think Farmer's criticism of anthropologists is overly severe? Is it justified in the case of most medical anthropologists?

Why do you think that international health authorities emphasize educational interventions?

What can anthropology and other social sciences contribute to efforts to prevent and treat tuberculosis?

INTRODUCTION

"It seems almost incredible that during this century and the previous one, a single disease, tuberculosis, was responsible for the deaths of approximately a thousand million human beings" [1]. So begins a somewhat breathless recounting of the search for a cure for tuberculosis (TB), a search that was to prove fruitful, according to the author, with the 1943 discovery of streptomycin. The book, subtitled *How the battle against tuberculosis was won—and lost*, argues that "Throughout the developed world, with the successful application of triple therapy and the enthusiastic promotion of prevention, the death rate from tuberculosis came tumbling down." But was this claim of causality ever documented? Granted, hundreds of thousands of deaths have been prevented by effective therapies, but TB mortality in the wealthy world was "tumbling down" well before their discovery. In the rest of the world, and in pockets of the United States, TB remained undaunted by ostensibly effective drugs, which are used too late, inappropriately, or not at all. A recent review of the world epidemiology of tuberculosis has led to the conclusion that it remains the leading infectious cause of

preventable deaths in the world [2]. "It is sufficiently shameful," notes one of the world's leading authorities on TB "that 30 years after recognition of the capacity of triple-therapy . . . to elicit 95% + cure rates, tuberculosis prevalence rates for *many* nations remain unchanged" [3].

. . .

This unsetting reversal has only become more pronounced since 1991. Why has the promise of the 1950s—when TB, it was declared, would soon be a disease of the past—failed to come to fruition? Why, if effective chemotherapy exists, does TB remain a leading killer of young adults? Two factors are commonly cited to explain this setback: the advent of HIV, the virus that causes AIDS, and the emergence of TB strains resistant to multiple drugs. Both AIDS and MDR TB, as we shall see, are often held by social scientists to be linked to the "behavioral problems" of individuals and groups held to be at risk for these disorders. The advent of HIV and MDR TB have had sufficient impact to warrant several of the field's leaders to speak of "the new tuberculosis" [4].

. . .

Who is falling ill with these deadly strains of TB? In spite of the theoretical risk to the "general population," the majority of U.S. cases to date have been registered among the inner-city poor, with significant outbreaks confined to prisons, homeless shelters, and public hospitals. This strikingly patterned occurrence of MDR TB speaks to some of the "large-scale" forces at work in the pandemic. The two factors central to the new TB—the development of drug-resistant strains and the advent of HIV—are ostensibly biological in nature, but are in fact best understood as *sociomedical* phenomena. Arguing that drug-resistant TB is a socially-produced biological phenomenon should not be controversial, since it refers to the induction of resistance to chemotherapeutic agents recently created by humans. But the rapid spread of HIV among certain populations has also been shaped by social (political, economic, and cultural) processes—the same processes, in large part, that led to the emergence of MDR TB.

Anthropologists and other social scientists have long argued that tuberculosis will not be eradicated without attention to these fundamentally social forces. In this sense, then, the advent of MDR TB is a terrible vindication for the sociomedical sciences. But there is less consensus among the social scientists than meets the eye. *Which* social forces might be involved in the persistence of TB and the emergence of MDR TB? How might these forces be differentially weighted? By what mechanisms, precisely, do large-scale and impersonal forces come to be embodied as individual pathology? As epidemic disease? More to the point, what is the significance of such analyses to interventions to prevent and treat MDR TB?

· · ·

Indeed, for researchers in a host of disciplines, the emergence of MDR TB poses new challenges and also forcefully reposes a number of old questions. In addition to those just raised are the inevitable and thorny "compliance" questions. "The word compliant," notes Sumartojo in a recent, sophisticated review of the topic, "has the unfortunate connotation that the patient is docile and subservient to the provider" [5]. Even more unfortunately, the term exaggerates patient agency, for it suggests that *all* patients possess the ability to comply—or refuse to comply—with antituberculous therapies. This makes no sense, if the World Health Organization is correct: as many as half of all cases of active TB are never even diagnosed [6]. Experience across boundaries of time and place have shown that there are radical differences in the ability of different populations to comply with demanding therapies, whether they be admonitions to move to "consumptive climes," as in the past century, or exhortations to take a year's worth of several drugs.

More can be said. The poor have no options but to be at risk for TB, and are thus from the outset victims of "structural violence" [7]. For many populations, chances of acquiring infection, developing disease, and lacking access to care are structured by a series of forces that we can now identify. In South Africa, say, these forces include poverty and racism; in other settings, gender inequality conspires with poverty to lead to a higher incidence of TB in poor women [8]. Throughout the United States, increased indices of economic inequity seem to favor epidemics in blighted inner cities, already ravaged by related epidemics of AIDS, injection drug use, homelessness, and racism. Overt political violence and war, themselves usually a reflection of structural violence, have well-known associations with increased rates of TB.

I would like to examine the relationship between structural violence and the emergence of drug-resistant TB by presenting data from Haiti, which currently serves, sadly, as a natural laboratory for the ill-effects of such violence on the health of a population. Although TB has usually been termed the leading cause of death in autopsy series of Haitian adults between 15 and 50 years of age [9], MDR TB has not yet been reported in Haiti. Indeed, in the only large study in which drug susceptibilities were tested, we read that "no significant resistance to drugs other than isoniazid was seen even though streptomycin and thiacetazone have been widely used" [10].

But the hypotheses generated above would lead us to predict that such strains are present, and that they will emerge first among the poor. The case of Robert David, examined in detail below, shows that this prediction has already come true.

CASE STUDY

In August of 1986, Robert David, then 19 years old, noted the onset of a non-productive cough, night sweats, and intermittent fevers and chills that were more marked in the evenings. Like most peasant families living in poverty, the Davids lived in fear of tuberculosis, in part because of its high mortality, and in part because of its tendency to leave survivors—or surviving kin—saddled with unpayable debts [11]. And so Robert attempted, at first, to self-treat with readily available herbal remedies. But when his cough gave way to dyspnea and marked weight loss, Robert's parents brought him to a referral hospital in the city of Hinche, the district seat of Haiti's central plateau. There Robert was diagnosed with pulmonary TB and placed on an unknown two-drug regimen that probably included isoniazid.

In order to receive care in this public facility, Robert had to commute from his home village. By truck, this took 2 hours; by donkey or on foot, it was an overnight trek. In spite of heroic efforts to keep appointments, which included a full day of waiting once inside the clinic, Robert did not respond promptly. In June 1987, he sought care in a large market town closer to his home village. He was then treated for 18 months, initially with a three-drug regimen (isoniazid, ethambutol, streptomycin). During this second course of therapy, Robert recalled that he had organisms in his sputum on "several" occasions, but his regimen was never altered. Throughout this period, he had great difficulty acquiring his medications, even though family members made enormous financial sacrifices—including selling more than half of their land—in order to buy the prescribed items.

Robert terminated one and one-half years of irregular treatment in December 1988, but continued to experience the same symptoms. In January of 1989, he had an episode of massive hemoptysis, but essentially received no biomedical care for this life-threatening complication. "We didn't have any money," he responded, when asked why he did not seek care, "and the bleeding had stopped by the time we borrowed some."

The other symptoms persisted. In May 1990, Robert traveled to Port-au-Prince, the capital city, where he was admitted to a sanatorium for 6 months of directly observed therapy with isoniazid, ethambutol, pyrazinamide, and rifampin. He was discharged to complete a total of 8 months of this regimen, followed by 2 more months of isoniazid and ethambutol. Due to political difficulties—including but not limited to the destruction of a key pharmacy by a bomb—Robert was unable to obtain many of his medications. He did, however, feel "much better" for over 1 year.

Robert returned to central Haiti, where he remained until June 1992, when most of his symptoms (cough, weight loss, night sweats) recurred. In September, he was again admitted to a Port-au-Prince sanatorium, where he received only thiazina, the combination of isoniazid and thiacetazone. His symptoms did not lessen substantially, and, again, Robert was often unable to acquire medication due to political disruptions in the capital.

These same political upheavals drove Robert back to the central plateau and, eventually, to the Clinique Bon Sauveur. When we first met him, in January 1993, Robert explained that he had been unable to obtain his medications because he had no money. He reported to the clinic seeking relief of his chronic cough, night sweats, and weight loss. A thin young man with minimally labored breathing, Robert then weighed 110 pounds. Physical examination revealed temporal wasting, pale conjunctiva, and severe oropharyngeal candidiasis. His neck was supple with no cervical lymphadenopathy. Examination of his lungs revealed abolition of breath sounds at the left apex. The remainder of his exam was unremarkable. Laboratory studies included examination of his sputum, which was laden with acid-fast bacilli (AFB), and a rapid serologic test for HIV, which was negative. A lack of electricity meant that mycobacterial cultures could not be performed.

We found Robert to be a highly motivated young man who wished desperately to recover from his refractory TB. He had made every attempt, he noted, to comply with his physicians' orders. MDR TB was raised as a possibility, although it had not been previously reported in Haiti. The only antituberculous drugs available in Haiti are isoniazid, thiacetazone, pyrazinamide, PAS, streptomycin, and rifampin, all of which are stocked at the Clinique Bon Sauveur. Reasoning that the patient developed floridly positive sputum on thiazina, it was elected to give him a cocktail of *all* of the other drugs, although we were aware that PAS was the only drug he had not yet received.

On February 9, 1994, then, Robert began this difficult regimen. The streptomycin was stopped when he complained of a buzzing in his ears; this symptom abated shortly thereafter. In both March and May, Robert had negative sputum exams, but continued to lose weight and his pulmonary symptoms diminished only slightly. He attributed his nausea and abdominal pain to the enormous number of pills he was taking each day. A repeat HIV test was again negative.

In August, Robert's sputum was again laden with AFB. A sputum specimen was collected for culture and sensitivity testing, which was performed in the United States. These isolates were found to be resistant to isoniazid, rifampin, ethambutol, streptomycin, and pyrazinamide. The isolate was sensitive to kanamycin, cycloserine, capreomycin, ethionamide, and ciprofloxacin. As noted, none of these drugs is readily available in Haiti; arrangements were made to import them, and Robert was eventually started on a four-drug regimen consisting of cycloserine, kanamycin, ethionamide, and ciprofloxacin.

Robert showed marked clinical improvement— weight gain, decreased shortness of breath and coughing—within 2 months. His sputum became free of AFB 2 months after initiation of this therapy and remained so for 6 months. In August of 1994, however, Robert again began losing weight and coughing. He continued his treatment, in spite of side effects including epigastric pain and, at one point, an abscess at an intramuscular injection site. Repeat tests showed that his MDR TB recurred, and had furthermore become resistant to kanamycin. The organism continued to destroy his lungs in spite of his religious compliance with a brutal regimen. In December, 1995, Robert David died in his sister's home [12].

DISCUSSION: POVERTY AND MDR TB

Robert's story is explored in some depth in the hope that the complex interplay of individual agency and structural violence—central to the emergence of drug resistance—is best illuminated by considering the gritty details of biography. How does his experience speak to the central thesis of this selection, that the "emergence" of MDR TB (and of the "new" TB in general) is inextricably linked to structural violence? How representative of others' experience of MDR TB was Robert's?

First, how does the biomedical literature explain the emergence of resistance? To cite an influential review recently published in the *New England Journal of Medicine:*

> In the circumstances of monotherapy, erratic drug ingestion, omission of one or more of the prescribed agents, suboptimal dosage, poor drug absorption, or an insufficient number of active agents in a regimen, a susceptible strain of *M. tuberculosis* may become resistant to multiple drugs within a matter of months [13].

In this sentence, Iseman lists a host of "risk factors" for MDR TB; each of these is inescapably a part of the lives of millions like Robert David— poorly nourished adults who develop reactivation TB, which is treated, when it is treated, with a small number of erratically available drugs. There is, then, a "political economy of MDR TB." That is, there are large-scale forces that make monotherapy and erratic drug ingestion much more likely to happen in settings such as Haiti or Harlem, say, than in the affluent communities where MDR TB has not become a problem.

Like most patients with MDR TB, Robert had been previously treated for TB. He was treated inappropriately—started on a two-drug regimen that he could ill-afford. When he relapsed, he was not started on a regimen consisting of drugs that he had never received before. Again, he was "noncompliant"—but how useful is such a term in describing the experience of a young man whose family was willing to sell all of its land to treat him? Even while in a sanatorium, he was unable to purchase his medications, a problem rendered worse by the incessant political violence of the period.

Robert David's lamentable experience brings into relief the complicated relationship between individual agency and structural violence. In most settings where TB is prevalent, the degree to which patients are able to comply is significantly limited by forces quite beyond their control. In reading the biomedical literature, one detects a certain delicacy in discussing this problem. In the largest Haitian series in which drug susceptibilities were examined, we read only that "primary drug resistance in Haiti has many probable causes, including the availability of isoniazid without prescription, past inclusion of isoniazid in cough remedies and a high default rate"[14]. Nowhere do we read about the insurmountable barriers to effective biomedical care faced by the overwhelming majority of Haitians.

In theory, MDR TB can often be cured, at least in HIV-negative patients like Robert David. What do the experts recommend as therapy? Empirical five- or six-drug regimens, followed by multidrug regimens after sensitivity data are available. The recommended duration of these therapies is 18–36 months. Careful monitoring of all drug levels is strongly advised, as are directly observed therapy, universal precautions for all those in close contact with patients, and the use of ultraviolet light to protect health-care workers. But to whom are these recommendations addressed? Leaving aside the millions now dying, for lack of therapy, from *susceptible* strains of TB, it must be pointed out that these recommendations for the treatment of MDR TB cannot possibly be addressed to those without access to laboratories, masks, electricity, and up to $250,000 worth of medical care. In other words, the recommendations are not relevant to precisely those persons most likely to acquire MDR TB.

Just as the poor are "at risk" of finding themselves likely to develop or acquire MDR TB, so too are they "at risk" of being unable to find adequate therapy for this disease. In places like Haiti, one sadly concludes, active MDR TB is likely to be fatal.

SOCIAL SCIENCE AND IMMODEST CLAIMS OF CAUSALITY

How have social scientists discussed the various forces that conspire to render certain groups susceptible to TB, while shielding others? Although there is a large sociomedical literature on TB, we have yet to comment on the "new" TB. Let us examine, then, a handful of studies of TB published in the sociomedical or anthropological presses. Each of these studies was conducted in a poor country, and each makes certain "claims of causality" by attempting to explain both non-compliance and the persistence of TB as a major cause of mortality in the setting under study. Often, the former is held to explain the latter.

In important research conducted in southern Haiti and published in *Social Science and Medicine*, Weise allots most of the discussion to the "health beliefs" of TB patients and their families, which are certainly a legitimate preoccupation for

an anthropologist. She further argues that the failure of a TB-control program in the region was largely the result of "the clinic's lack of knowledge about the local culture and consequent failure to operate within it" [15].

It could more easily be argued that TB-control programs in Haiti have failed not through cultural insensitivity but rather through a lack of commitment to the destitute sick. In a study conducted in the central plateau, we interviewed 100 TB patients regarding their own understanding of their illness, which most agreed to be TB. Many patients felt that sorcery might have caused their illness. Because both the medical anthropological literature and the Haitian physicians queried predicted that these individuals would be those most likely to abandon anti-tuberculous therapy, we followed all of these patients for more than 18 months. We found that patients' etiologic beliefs did not predict their compliance with chemotherapy. Similar disjunctions are reported elsewhere in the literature. For example, Rubel reported high rates of compliance among migrant tuberculous Mexican farmworkers in California, who attributed their symptoms to disorders ranging from bronchitis to "folk illnesses" such as *susto*. "Interestingly, interviews with these patients show a continued denial of their diagnosis of tuberculosis despite faithful adherence to lengthy treatment regimens and extensive education by clinical staff members" [16].

In Haiti's central plateau, what *did* predict adherence to therapy? Among patients offered free and convenient care, compliance and outcome were strongly related only to whether or not patients had access to supplemental food and income. We were led to conclude that cultural, political, and economic factors, although inevitably important, cannot be of equal significance in all settings. Whereas cultural considerations, such as the nearly universal stigma attached to TB, may very well be of overriding significance in settings in the industrialized countries, we would argue that they are often less so in Haiti, where so many factors (initial exposure to mycobacteria, reactivation of exogenous TB infection, complications, access to therapy, length of convalescence, development of resistance, degree of tissue destruction, and finally, mortality) are determined chiefly by economic factors [17].

To take an example from South Africa, where blacks of all ethnic backgrounds have much higher rates of TB than do whites, a recent anthropological study identified several reasons for the high default rate seen among Xhosa-speaking patients with TB. Chief among these were the "deep-seated mystical beliefs" of the people under study. These beliefs include the understanding that TB may be caused by witchcraft and is thus best treated with the help of a diviner who can explain *who* caused the sickness. The author listed several other reasons as well, from the side effects of the medications to the "carelessness" of certain patients, but nowhere was there any mention of the poverty of South African blacks or of apartheid and its effects on the delivery of services. Small wonder, then, that the investigator's conclusions focus so exclusively on patients' cognitive profiles:

> As an anthropologist it is therefore possible to plead that health care personnel who treat black patients with tuberculosis be aware that their patients' perceptions of the disease may differ from their own, that the patient may already have consulted a nonwestern practitioner, or that they are merely seeking time before they embark on a different strategy for seeking a solution for what troubles them [18].

One could argue instead that, for South African blacks, the proximate cause of increased rates of morbidity and mortality is not their "mystical beliefs," but rather lack of access to resources, as a study by a team of physicians recently concluded: "Poverty remains the primary cause of the prevalence of many diseases and widespread hunger and malnutrition among black South Africans. The role of apartheid in creating and maintaining this poverty has been well documented" [19].

Even here, more rigorous social analysis is necessary, for TB is closely linked to a "racial capitalism" far older than apartheid itself. In an important study of TB in South Africa, the historian Randall Packard shows that institutionalized apartheid does not in and of itself explain the skewed incidence of the disease. Indeed, these patterns were emerging well before the enactment of apartheid laws, which are merely decades old:

> It is not enough to invoke apartheid, racial discrimination, and black poverty, for they themselves are symptoms of more fundamental political and economic transformations that have been associated with the rise of industrial capitalism in South Africa.

Ultimately the answer to why TB remains such a serious problem in South Africa lies in understanding the history of these transformations [20].

Another study, set in Honduras and published in *Medical Anthropology*, begins with a telling vignette:

> One day, in an important health center in Tegucigalpa, the capital city of Honduras, Central America, the general practitioner identified ten patients suffering from symptoms of tuberculosis. He asked them to go up to the laboratory, which was one floor above, then get the authorization for laboratory exams. Only five of them arrived at the laboratory; of those, only three brought the sputum sample the following day. Only one of them returned to pick up his result: it was negative. The results of the other two, who had given false addresses, were positive. They were suffering from tuberculosis. They were never located [21].

A team of investigators set off to interview some 500 Hondurans to uncover the reasons for this noncompliance; the study began with the formulation of six hypotheses that might explain it. None of these hypotheses linked treatment failure to a failure of the public health system, or to Honduran society at large; none of these hypotheses mentioned poverty or social inequality at all, although those surveyed, in contrast, correctly associated TB with "extreme poverty, filth, and malnutrition" [22].

The researchers found the patients and public to be full of strange "knowledge, attitudes, and behaviors" as well as a "great lack of education about the disease." When patients were interviewed, many "maintained a careful distance when speaking to the investigators, and seemed fearful and distrustful" (they had, speculates the author, "feelings of isolation . . . accompanied by guilt"). Above all, of course, the patients were non-compliant, "refus[ing] to accept [TB's] existence, and attempt[ing] to remedy the symptoms with self-prescribed medications." Some of the patients were downright refractory, "and obstinately refused the visits of health personnel." "Even when the patient can no longer ignore the evidence of his symptoms," adds Mata, "he is willing to die rather than undergo treatment" [23].

Fortunately, consultants like the author were able to remedy the situation. They designed a flip-chart explaining "the measures that should be taken by the patient and his family," and had sputum cups "printed with attractive and clear illustrations." Sadly enough, "the Ministry [of Health] had not yet improved its tuberculosis program services, and the necessary sample cups were not available in time," nor were the flip-charts. But a series of radio spots, posters, and a pamphlet served to "clear up the patient's immediate confusions about the disease" [24]. The author seemed confident that Honduras—which in his account sounds more like Sweden than one of the poorest countries in Latin America—is well on its way to solving its TB problem.

Even in a more thoughtfully conceived investigation, with more robust data, the same circular logic is easily discerned. Working in Wardha District in central India, Barnhoorn and Adriaanse compared 52 compliant with 50 non-compliant patients in an effort to determine what factors might be responsible for failure to take medications. They found that "three socioeconomic variables, i.e. the monthly income per capita in a family, the type of house in which a family lived, and the monthly family income" were the strongest predictors of compliance with antituberculous chemotherapy. "It is noteworthy," the authors add, "that the highest ratings were followed by three additional socioeconomic variables, i.e. place of residence, fuel used and education" [25].

Etiological beliefs about TB did not have striking relevance to compliance. A number of "health beliefs" were, however, felt to be strong predictors of compliance—but these "beliefs" also sound much more like indirect socioeconomic indicators: "Compliers also tended to clean their body, ate good foods, visited a Primary Health Centre, whereas noncompliers tended to isolate themselves and prayed to God for a cure." Similarly, other items classified under "family attitudes" include having someone to prepare meals and "eating breakfast regularly" [26].

In essence, the researchers found that the only strong predictors of compliance were fundamentally economic, not cognitive or cultural. However, their conclusions would seem otherwise: "Concerns with the determinants of [noncompliance] might improve the care of tuberculosis patients by giving directions for *educational interventions.*" And although Barnhoorn and Adriaanse insist that socioeconomic obstacles to treat-

ment do exist and are fundamental, they become, in much of the discussion, secondary: "before obstacles to a treatment regimen can be cleared away, patients have to develop health beliefs and social norms consistent with it." When the investigators call for the patients to be "liberated," it is not from the structural violence that creates and sustains a significant and growing TB epidemic among the world's poor. Instead, they propose that "future health education programmes aimed at the public at large should be focused on the liberation of the masses from false thoughts and burdens" [27].

In another paper published in *Social Science and Medicine,* a prominent anthropologist reported that, in one city in the Philippines, children's respiratory symptoms are often attributed to *piang,* a folk illness best treated by traditional healers: "Such a lay diagnosis *leads to* long delays before tubercular children are brought to a physician" [28]. If this claim is true, then little short of changing the culture should lead to a change in compliance. But Valeza and McDougall, working in a nearby area, were able to double compliance with antituberculous medications by merely making drugs readily available and easy to take [29]. In East Africa, another region characterized by extreme poverty, a weak medical infrastructure, and high rates of TB, "attribution of tuberculosis symptoms to witchcraft or other folk illnesses is associated with delays in seeking professional treatment as well as remarkably high rates of default once treatment has begun" [30]. As noted, similar claims are often made in Haiti, where we found no association, except in the minds of most physicians surveyed, between sorcery and TB *outcomes*—although even compliant patients often attributed their TB to sorcery.

It is inappropriate, of course, to generalize based on such a small number of papers. But a more thorough review of the sociomedical literature on compliance with antituberculous therapy does little to gainsay the impressions made upon reading the above articles. Such research tends to be conducted in settings—called "cultures" in many of these studies—characterized by high rates of tuberculosis and by extreme poverty, which a *priori* calls into question conclusions regarding the impact, on treatment failures, of the cultures of the patients in question. These patients do not share culture or language. What they share is tuberculosis and poverty. They also share, often enough, spectacularly bad TB services, such as those described by Friemodt-Möller, working in rural India:

> The treatment began when a sufficient number of patients had been collected to justify sending out a drug-issue team the long distances. To begin with, there was an interval of 2 months from the time the sputum was found positive until treatment began. Forty-seven patients died before the treatment could begin, 14 left the towns, 20 refused treatment from the beginning, 26 stopped after the first or second drug issue, two preferred to take their own drugs [31].

Strenuous insistence on the causal role of culture or personality in explaining treatment failures runs the risk of conflating cultural (or psychological) difference with structural violence, leading to the immodest claims of causality evident above. *Throughout the world, those least likely to comply are those least able to comply.* In theory, it would be necessary to ensure full and facile access to all persons before ascribing failure to complete treatment to patient-related shortcomings. And in none of the places in which the above-cited research was conducted is full and facile access ensured. On the contrary, these settings are crying out for measures to improve the quality of care, not the quality of the patients [32].

Curiously, many of these studies take it as a matter of faith that educational interventions will have significant effects on rates of TB in a particular population. But no one, as far as I know, has ever shown this to be true. Historical reviews, such as that by McKeown, would suggest that, in England and Wales at least, death rates from TB have varied quite independently of patients'—and healers'— understandings about the disease.

In each of the sociomedical studies critiqued, a well-intentioned effort to incorporate the patients' points of view has served, paradoxically, to shift the blame onto the sick-poor by exaggerating their agency. In so doing, researchers have echoed the received wisdom of many physicians and other providers. Their explanations, as noted, tend to focus on local actors—most notably, on patients—and local factors. "The most serious problem hampering tuberculosis treatment and control," note three pulmonologists in a recent review, "is patient non-compliance with therapy." There is no mention of any structural barriers to therapy. "Potential determinants of compliance," they continue, "include personal characteristics of patients, features of the disease and/or treatment, and patients' beliefs and attitudes" [33].

Sociomedical research shows not merely the expected divorce between patients' and healers' etiologic conceptions of TB, but also great dissensus regarding treatment failure [34]. Collando reported that, when Mexican district health officials were asked, "To what do you contribute the problematic nature of tuberculosis control in your jurisdiction?" those surveyed "overwhelmingly laid the blame at the door of their patients' shortcomings: 'poverty,' 'lack of education,' 'poor motivation,' 'superstition,' and 'failure to comprehend the importance of compliance with treatment recommendations'" [35]. A similiar pattern was described in a San Francisco chest clinic, where in the 1960s up to 34% of patients failed to keep their appointments. Again, providers and the patients had very discrepant ideas about this failure. The physicians and nurses tended to focus on the patients' shortcomings—"the social and cultural characteristics of the user population"—while the patients listed structural barriers ranging from the inconvenience of the clinic's hours and location and a "rigidity in taking patients in order of registration regardless of extenuating circumstances" to a failure to treat affected families as a unit, with adults and children seen on different days and by different physicians [36]. Addressing these structural problems by moving the clinics to more convenient times and places, as well as "an improved attitude on the part of the professional staff," led to a decrease in missed appointments from 34% to 6% after 5 years [37].

Anthropologists and other social scientists have long complained that their perspectives have not been incorporated into TB-control efforts. While it is true that physicians and their biomedical colleagues have been guilty of underplaying the significance of social forces at work in the changing epidemiology of TB, a review of the biomedical literature increasingly reveals a willingness to incorporate social factors into their explanations of why TB control has failed. Indeed, specialists from the CDC and from academic departments are all likely, these days, to speak of social and economic determinants. For example, the following assessment is by two TB specialists writing in the journal *Seminars in Respiratory Infections:* "Regaining control of epidemic tuberculosis will be difficult and will require effective approaches to hardcore issues also common to the AIDS epidemic: poverty, homelessness, and substance abuse" [38].

Medical anthropologists have often been less willing to incorporate basic biomedical insights, including the following: untreated TB disease may have a case fatality rate of over 80%; in drug-susceptible TB, at least, over 95% can be cured with appropriate therapy. However, drug-susceptible TB will kill millions in the coming years, and it will kill them slowly, so that they may serve as culture media for the induction of resistant strains. The obscenity of late twentieth-century TB lies precisely in this, and not in a failure to incorporate the concept of culture—or the opinions of anthropologists—in efforts to prevent or treat the disease.

These assertions are rooted in the hopeful belief that social science may well hold some of the keys to halting the spread of these new pandemics. But if we are to be other than academic Cassandras, we would do well to acknowledge the largely structural causes of persistent TB and to take stock of why we have not had much influence in past attempts to prevent or treat it. In other words, the research tasks before us might be more likely to be accomplished if we can avoid the traps of the past. Examining my own field—similar exercises would be welcome in each of the sociomedical sciences—five such pitfalls come quickly to mind, and these are discussed in the following subsections.

Conflating Structural Violence with Cultural Difference

Each of the sociomedical sciences—medical anthropology, medical sociology, health economics, etc.—has tended to stake out "turf" to be regarded as the bailiwick of that particular subspecialty. Representatives of these fields have then tended to claim that their disciplinary focus is of paramount importance in explaining the phenomenon under scrutiny—regardless of what that phenomenon happens to be. In medical anthropology, often enough, *culture* is held up as the determinant variable. Surely these immodest claims of causality amount to inadequate phenomenology, and are underpinned by inadequate social theory. Because culture is merely one of several potentially impor-

tant factors, anthropologists and other researchers who cite cognitivist "cultural" explanations for the poor health of the poor have been the object of legitimate critiques:

> Medical anthropologists and sociologists have tended to elevate the cultural component into an omnibus explanation. The emphasis is on cultural determination. Even when social relations receive more than reflexive recognition, medical social scientists restrict the social relations to small "primary" group settings, such as the family, and factions at the micro unit. . . Little or no attempt is made to encompass the totality of the larger society's structure [39].

One of the side-effects of such cognitivist approaches to culture, as noted, is a conflation of structural violence and cultural difference. Related trends are easily discerned in medical psychology, where personality attributes—the turf of that field—are held to explain risk for such disorders as AIDS, alcoholism, and addiction to drugs.

Minimizing the Role of Poverty

Many anthropologists, regarding their turf to be the "cultural piece," have also tended to underplay economic barriers to effective care. Poverty has long been the chief risk factor for both acquiring and dying from TB, and this was true long before MDR strains appeared. . . . Tuberculosis has retreated in certain populations, maintained a steady state in others, and surged forth in still others, remaining, at this time of writing, the world's leading infectious cause of preventable deaths [40]. Thus tuberculosis has not really emerged so much as *emerged from the ranks of the poor.* One of the implications, clearly, is that one place for diseases to "hide" is among poor people, especially when the poor are socially and medically segregated from those whose deaths might be considered more significant.

Almost unexamined has been the relationship between the social reproduction of inequalities and the persistence of TB. Our failure to discern a political economy of risk for both the development of MDR TB and also for suboptimal treatment may be related to a desire to link our (perfectly legitimate) investigations of the shaping of personal experience by culture to (inaccurate) claims of causality.

Exaggeration of Patient Agency

The praiseworthy effort to incorporate patients' points of view can serve, at times, to obscure the very real constraints on agency experienced by most, but not all, patients with TB. . . . In tuberculosis clinics throughout the world, patient-related factors top providers' lists of reasons to explain treatment failures. These lists, as Sumartojo politely and acutely notes, reflect providers' "observations and experience, but [they] exclude environmental, structural, and operational factors that are beyond the patient's control" [41]. Calls to change "lifestyle and behavior" are often made to precisely those persons whose agency is most constrained. The same exaggerations took place in earlier eras, as the historian Barbara Rosenkrantz has noted in examining the elaborate treatment protocols of the turn of the century: "The disease-oriented hygienic regimen dictated by bacteriologic research came to grief when a patient's poverty made it unlikely that such advice would be followed" [42].

Exaggeration of patient agency is particularly marked in the biomedical literature, in part because of medicine's celebrated focus on individual patients, which is inevitably desocializing. But it is social science that has underlined the importance of contextualization, and so our failure to complement clinicians' views with more robustly contextualized ones is all the more significant. . . .

Romanticism about "Folk Healing"

A strong vein of commentary in medical anthropology depicts folk healing as somehow superior to biomedical therapies. Although these claims have been called into question by some within the field, they have since assumed importance far beyond the boundaries of anthropology [43]. But non-biomedical treatments for active pulmonary or extrapulmonary TB have thus far proven to be spectacularly ineffective. They do not change case fatality rates. If folk healing were so effective, the world's wealthy would be monopolizing it. When the privileged do use folk healing and other non-biomedical modalities, it is as adjunctive therapy, often for chronic illnesses refractory to biomedical intervention. (As an aside, I cannot count the number of Haitian folk healers that I have personally treated for TB and malaria.) We live in an increasingly interconnected world. Robert David's use of herbal remedies to treat tuberculosis is emblematic not of cultural integrity, but of an unfair distribution of the world's resources.

Persistence of Insularity

Medical anthropologists, like other subspecialists, are usually familiar with the arcane debates of our own field. Yet we are too often unwilling to learn the basics of infectious disease or epidemiology, even when they are related to our chosen arenas of intervention. This sectarian approach to research can be costly when examining pandemics with demonstrable relation to both biological and social forces. . . .

CONCLUSION: FUTURE RESEARCH ON MDR TB

The emergence of MDR TB is a terrible vindication for those who predicted that a social disease would not be eradicated without social responses. But this clairvoyance is no occasion for celebration, nor is it a time for concern about the advancement of our own particular subspecialties. MDR TB is a biologically and socially complex development. To check it, we must understand the forces promoting and retarding its advance. How, more precisely, might anthropology (and the other social sciences) make meaningful contributions to efforts to control the new scourge of MDR TB?

Several research tasks come to mind. First, who better than social scientists to discern the precise mechanisms by which social forces (ranging from racism to political violence) promote or retard the transmission or recrudescence of TB? . . .

Second, ethnographic research will be important in identifying and, again, *ranking*, the barriers preventing those afflicted with MDR TB from having access to the best care available. . . .

Third, social scientists should become more engaged in multidisciplinary research and trials. We would have much to offer those seeking to design programs that will increase access to optimal therapies. . . .

Fourth, research that exposes—and deplores—the precise mechanisms by which entrenched medical inequities are buttressed may help to redress these inequities. In so doing, we would no doubt also be exposing the real co-factors in this emerging epidemic of "social disease."

These suggestions are more crassly utilitarian than those usually heard in calls for social science research, but it is clear that we should act quickly to make common cause with those on the side of the sick-poor, regardless of profession—whether we are community health workers, or folk healers, or physicians, or bench scientists. Certainly, some of these will be stop-gap measures, but such measures matter a great deal to those sick with tuberculosis. "It is useful to remember," remarks Rosenkrantz, "that a 'social disease' typically affects the socially marginal, who can ill-afford to wait for the fundamental insights and social transformations that challenge the well-established associations of disadvantage and disease" [44].

NOTES

1. Ryan, F. (1993) *The Forgotten Plague: How the Battle Against Tuberculosis Was Won—and Lost*. Little, Brown, Boston.

2. Bloom, B. and Murray, C. (1992) Tuberculosis: commentary on a resurgent killer. *Science* 257, 1055.

3. Iseman, M. (1985) Tailoring a time-bomb. *American Review of Respiratory Diseases* 132, 735.

4. Snider, D. and Roper, W. (1992) The new tuberculosis. *New England Journal of Medicine* 326, 703.

5. Sumartojo, E. (1993) When tuberculosis treatment fails: a social behavioral account of patient adherence. *American Review of Respiratory Disease* 147, 1311. Dr Sumartojo prefers the term "adherence."

6. World Health Organization (1991) *Guidelines for Tuberculosis Treatment in Adults and Children in National Tuberculosis Programmes*. World Health Organization, Geneva.

7. Farmer, P. (1996) On suffering and structural violence—a view from below. *Daedalus* 125, 261.

8. Margono, F., Garely, A., Mroueh, J. and Minkoff, H. (1993) Tuberculosis among pregnant women—New York City, 1985–1992. *Morbidity and Mortality Weekly Report* 42, 605.

9. For a review of these data, see Farmer, P., Robin, S., Ramilus, St.-L. and Kim, J. Y. (1991) Tuberculosis, poverty, and "compliance": lessons from rural Haiti. *Seminars in Respiratory Infections* 6, 254.

10. Scalcini, M., Carre, G., Jean-Baptiste, M., Hershfield, E., Parker, S., Wolfe, J., Nelz, K. and Long, R. (1990) Antituberculous drug resistance in central Haiti. *American Review of Respiratory Disease* [Suppl.] 142(3), 508.

11. For a more in-depth discussion of Haitian understandings of TB, see Farmer, P. (1992) *AIDS and Accusation: Haiti and the Geography of Blame*. University of California Press, Berkeley.

12. The case of Robert David led us to search more aggressively for other cases of MDR TB. Two other patients were also discovered to be infected with multiply-resistant strains. The resistance patterns were different from the strain infecting Robert David.

13. Iseman, M. (1993) Treatment of multidrug-resistant tuberculosis. *New England Journal of Medicine* 9, 784.

14. Scalcini *et al*. [10], p. 509.

15. Weire, H. J. C. (1974) Tuberculosis in rural Haiti. *Social Science and Medicine* 8, 359.

16. Rubel, A. and Garro, L. (1992) Social and cultural factors in the successful control of tuberculosis. *Public Health Report* 107, 626.

17. Farmer *et al*. In *The Time of AIDS*, eds. G. Herdt and S. Lindenbaum. Sage, Los Angeles. p. 259.

18. de Villiers, S. (1991) Tuberculosis in anthropological perspective. *South African Journal of Ethnology* 14, 69.

19. Nightingale, E. O., Hannibal, K., Geiger, H. J., Hartmann, L., Lawrence, R. and Spurlock, J. (1990) Apartheid medicine. Health and human rights in South Africa. *Journal of the American Medical Association* 264(16), 2097.

20. Packard, R. (1989) *White Plague, Black Labor: Tuberculosis and the Political Economy of Health and Disease in South Africa*. University of California Press, Berkeley.

21. Mata, J. I. (1985) Integrating the client's perspective in planning a tuberculosis education and treatment program in Honduras. *Medical Anthropology* 9(1), 57.

22. Mata [21], p. 59.

23. Quotations drawn from Mata [21], pp. 62, 60, 61, 58.

24. Mata [21], pp. 62-63.

25. Barnhoorn, F. and Adriaanse, H. (1992) In search of factors responsible for noncompliance among tuberculosis patients in Wardha District, India. *Social Science and Medicine* 34, 291.

26. Barnhoorn and Adriaanse [25], pp. 299, 302.

27. Barnhoorn and Adriaanse [25], pp. 291, 301, 302.

28. Rubel and Garro [16], p. 630 (emphasis added), referring to a paper by Lieban R. (1976) Traditional medical beliefs and the choice of practitioners in a Philippine city. *Social Science and Medicine* 10, 289.

29. Cited in Sumartojo [5], p. 1314.

30. Rubel and Garro [16], p. 630.

31. Friemodt-Möller, J. (1968) Domiciliary drug therapy of pulmonary tuberculosis in a rural population in India. *Tubercle* 49 [Suppl.], 22.

32. Chaulet puts this sharply in an editorial castigating health care professionals for *their* non-compliance: "It is only after these general measures have been applied that we can turn our attention to improving compliance." Chaulet, P. (1987) Compliance with anti-tuberculosis chemotherapy in developing countries. *Tubercle* [Suppl.] 68, 19.

33. Menzies, R., Rocher, I. and Vissandjoe, B. (1993) Factors associated with compliance in treatment of tuberculosis. *Tubercle and Lung Disease* 74, 32.

34. For sharply divergent interpretations of TB control, see the disturbing essay by Steven Nachman, an anthropologist who briefly worked among Haitians detained by the U.S. Immigration and Naturalization Service: Nachman, S. (1993) Wasted lives: tuberculosis and other health risks of being Haitian in a U.S. detention camp. *Medical Anthropology Quarterly* 7, 227. Nachman offers compelling ethnography without making immodest claims of causality. For a review stressing the importance of patients' perspectives, see Conrad, P. (1985) The meaning of medications: another look at compliance. *Social Science and Medicine* 20, 29. Too few of the papers reviewed underline the enormous difference between failure to adhere to an INH prophylaxis regimen and failure to adhere to treatment for active disease.

35. Cited in Rubel and Garro [16], p. 627.

36. Rubel and Garro [16].

37. Sumartojo [5], p. 1316.

38. Brudney, K. and Dobkin, J. (1991) A tale of two cities: tuberculosis control in Nicaragua and New York City. *Seminars in Respiratory Infections* 6, 261.

39. Onoge, O. (1975) Capitalism and public health: a neglected theme in the medical anthropology of Africa. In *Topias and Utopias in Health,* eds., S. Ingman and A. Thomas. Mouton, The Hague.

40. Bloom and Murray [2].

41. Sumartojo [5], p. 1312.

42. Rosenkrantz, in her excellent introduction to Dubos, R. and Dubos, J. (1992) *The White Plague: Tuberculosis, Man, and Society,* 2nd edition. Rutgers University Press. p. xxi.

43. See, for example, Patel, M. (1987) Problems in the evaluation of alternative medicine. *Social Science and Medicine* 25, 669.

44. Rosenkrantz [42], p. xxxiv.

■ ■ ■ ■ ■ ■ ■ ■ ■

35   EMBODIMENT OF TERROR: GENDERED VIOLENCE IN PEACETIME AND WARTIME IN CROATIA AND BOSNIA-HERZEGOVINA

Maria B. Olujic

Violence is an uncomfortable and distressing reality with serious impacts upon individual and population health (see Das et al. 2001). State-sponsored violence, political oppression, and resistance are phenomena through which the power of the state is inscribed on the body, leaving long-term psychosocial and physical marks. Yet, organized violence is not limited to states. In internal ethnic conflicts, the individual-state opposition is relatively meaningless, and violence occurs in a context of social and moral disorder and absence of control that is the inverse of state repression. Moral disintegration apparent in the form of the violence and the composition of its perpetrators (nonsoldiers, children) calls for special attention to the degree to which culture shapes behavior, while the resulting demoralization requires consideration of the resilience of culture over time and through violent disruption.

Source: Olujic, M. B. 1998. "Embodiment of Terror: Gendered Violence in Peacetime and Wartime in Croatia and Bosnia-Herzegovina." © 1998 by the American Anthropological Association. Reprinted from *Medical Anthropology Quarterly* Vol. 12 No. 1 pp. 31–50, by permission.

This selection explores connections between ethnic violence in the former Yugoslavia and preexisting cultural meanings surrounding sexuality and reproduction. It argues that sexual violence during the conflict was not a random manifestation of individuals acting on unlicensed aggressive impulses, but rather an organized effort to destroy an enemy ethnic group. The form the violence took was one that resonated with peacetime cultural concepts to maximize its effectiveness as a weapon of terror and torture. As a central symbolic locus of male competition in a shared patrilineal, patriarchal family and economic system (see also selection 50), the female body became an object on which acts of genocide and ethnic cleansing were directed during the war. The individual body, the social body, and the body politic (see selection 27) intersected in the cultural meanings surrounding individual experiences of violence, collective acts of torture, and political manipulations of information to conceal shame or garner outside military support.

This selection shows how a body of anthropological literature on a particular geographical area may provide conceptual tools for an analysis of local folklore and cultural idioms operating in current times and modified under novel circumstances. During the war, the sexual tensions and suppressed violence expressed through cultural concepts surrounding shaving, cutting, and blood assumed new meanings but grew out of preexisting forms that gave them their power to inflict maximum harm. Olujic's analysis helps us focus on the concept of culture in the disordered context of terror, chaos, and mortal danger and to separate it from ethnicity. The study also considers the subject of stigma (see selection 32), which is the focus of the next three selections.

Questions to keep in mind

In what ways does the wartime sexual violence against both women and men resonate with peacetime sexual ideology?

How do the stigma and shame borne by women relate to peacetime cultural concepts about femininity and family?

What does the creation of a child through violence mean to the aggressors, and why are these children symbols of ethnic identity crisis?

What connections do you see between the individual body and the social body, and the individual body and the body politic?

Violence against women is not restricted to war; its roots are well established in peaceful times. And use of violence against women in war cannot be understood without first examining its cultural meanings in peace, meanings that utilize metaphors of the body, sexuality, and honor to manipulate the social order. Unlike the work of the theorists who describe wartime rape as an aberration (cf. Brownmiller 1975), my research shows that wartime gender violence highlights preexisting sociocultural dynamics. Indeed, war rapes in the former Yugoslavia would not be such an effective weapon of torture and terror if it were not for concepts of honor, shame, and sexuality that are attached to women's bodies in peacetime. War rape would not work as well as a policy of terror were it not for the cultural salience within the honor/shame complex generalized in the southeastern European cultural area.

BRIEF POLITICAL BACKGROUND

The political dissolution of Eastern Europe at the end of 1980s exposed military disputes and caused long-term social, political, and economic upheaval. The greatest fallout is evidenced by the political collapse of the Socialist Federative Republic of Yugoslavia (SFRY).

Socialist Yugoslavia (1945–91) was a federation of six republics: Croatia, Bosnia-Herzegovina, Serbia, Slovenia, Macedonia, and Montenegro. In June 1991, after referendums in both republics, Croatia and Slovenia declared their independence;

war broke out shortly thereafter. Bosnia-Herzegovina followed suit in March of 1992 and war broke out one month later. All three states were admitted to the United Nations (UN) in May 1992. Macedonia voted independence in September 1991, but was not admitted into the UN until April 1993. The remaining two republics, Serbia and Montenegro, formed a union and to this day refer to themselves as the "Federal Republic of Yugoslavia," or simply "Yugoslavia."

Although the war "officially ended" in Croatia in 1992, the occupied Croatian territories (about one-fourth of the country) were under Serbian occupation and were liberated in May and August of 1995. After the Croatian offensive the international community decided to send International Forces (IFOR) troops into Bosnia. As of this writing (1996), IFOR is still in Bosnia.

RESEARCHER IN A WAR SITUATION

In December 1991 to May 1993, when the war was at its peak, I went to Croatia as the deputy minister of Science and Technology. During my tenure there, I was fully enmeshed in all aspects of day-to-day living in a wartime situation (Olujic 1995a), spending time in bomb shelters and carrying a gas mask (see also Robben and Nordstrom 1995). Since the summer of 1993, I have conducted anthropological research as a H. F. Guggenheim Fellow on violence against women—specifically, war rapes in Bosnia-Herzegovina and Croatia.

As both the deputy minister of Science and as a researcher, I was confronted with numerous difficulties in regard to the war and political situation. I was both an insider and an outsider, a U.S.-educated anthropologist and also a Croatian who was thereby expected, because of my ancestry and history, to have a particular allegiance, one subjectively based, in this conflict. Yet no researcher could remain completely unmoved by the horrifying stories told by survivors of tortures. The stories in this article are difficult to read; they were even more difficult to hear in person.

To understand the public violence in former Yugoslavia requires insight not only of a wartime "culture of violence" (Desjarlais and Kleinman 1994:11), but also of the "culture of peacetime." The two are inextricably interlinked. Desjarlais

and Kleinman (1994) point out that the notion of "culture" has been problematic when applied to situations where violent disorder persists. I argue along with them that theorists must link collective action with individual experience to find "a space where the social body and the physical body intersect" (Desjarlais and Kleinman 1994:11). In the former Yugoslavia, explanation for the dynamics, meaning, and experience of violence requires analysis of the context—peace, war, or postwar time—of violence and honor in gender relations.

METHODOLOGY AND FIELD SITE

My methods included semistructured interviews with victims–survivors, family member(s), health officials, and religious leaders. Informants included Bosnian and Croatian refugees of both sexes. In sum, I collected 75 in-depth, open-ended interviews, which I call *testimonies*. I refer to these interviews as testimonies because they bear direct witness to wartime violence. Interviews typically lasted for several hours and were often done over a period of several months. Some were series of dialogues that took place between 1992–96. Interviews elicited demographic data and information about informants' lives before and during the war. All of the interviews were tape-recorded in the Croatian language and then transcribed. Interview data were supplemented with life-history accounts and by observations. For example, as most of the interviews were done in people's homes, I also observed interactions with members of the household.

In addition, I used an attitude survey of 1,060 informants that also included refugees and internally displaced persons, which focused on questions about the war in Croatia and Bosnia, war rapes, victims, and perpetrators. The survey was a broadly based, short questionnaire that asked questions about respondents' background and opinion of the war in Croatia and Bosnia-Herzegovina. Questions were aimed to elicit opinions or attitudes about the perpetrators of war atrocities, especially war rapes; who respondents blamed for the war; and how respondents would punish perpetrators of war rapes. Analysis of some of the findings from the survey questionnaire have been published elsewhere (Rijavec et al. 1996). Two open-ended questions referred to subjects' beliefs about *causes* of sexual violence in peacetime and in wartime.

Interviewees lived in border areas where fighting had taken place and where there were no sharp cultural distinctions among the combatant groups. The folklore of all three groups—Croat, Serb, and Muslim—reflected similar motifs, and these motifs remained constant across versions and genres in the folklore of the regions. Despite these cultural similarities, however, interviewees' ethnic self-identities were distinctive.

TRADITIONAL CULTURE IN PEACETIME: GENDER RELATIONS AND FAMILY STRUCTURE

Gendered violence in war draws on peacetime meanings of sexuality. In peacetime, even as we near the end of the 20th century, control of women by men and protection of their sexuality continue to be convenient means of justifying the domination of women by men in southeastern Europe.

The dynamic of male protection of female honor is embedded in the complex traditional cultures of the Slavic peoples in southeastern Europe. Here, the center of the patriarchal regime is the extended family, called *zadruga,* a corporate family unit under which all holdings—for example, property, livestock, and land—are held communally by the patrilineage (Byrnes 1976; Hammel 1968, 1972; Tomasevich 1976). Zadruga ideology has persisted for centuries and is the crux of Yugoslavian *cultural* ideologies.

Women marry into their husband's families and are thus outside of the core social unit. They are valued as sex objects, mothers, and workers (Denich 1974; Stein Erlich 1966). This pattern is familiar to much of the Mediterranean: women represent the code of *honor* of the family and the code of shame via the blood revenge for nonfamily member's transgressions, which along with a male-dominated strict hierarchy, provide many behavioral norms and unity (Boehm 1984; Davis 1977; Simic 1983; Woodward 1985).

The honor/shame dichotomy is evident in the highly guarded aspects of women's virginity, chastity, marital virtue, and especially fertility. For women, honor and shame are the basis of morality and underpin the three-tiered hierarchy of sta-

tuses: husband, family, and village. In the former Yugoslavia, these traditional values regarding sexual behavior, which condoned rape through honor/shame constraints, took precedence over economic transformations, state policy commitments under communism, and male migration (Olujic 1990).

PEACETIME METAPHORS OF SEXUALITY AND THE BODY

Sexuality, Courtship, and Reproduction

One must understand the constructions of sexual violence in peacetime in order to understand the meanings of wartime sexual tortures. In the former Yugoslavia peacetime gender interactions are illustrated in songs, jokes, and stories, which, though different in different geographical regions, have similar messages (cf. Knezevic 1996). A Croatian form of epic singing called *ganga* conveys its meaning through symbolism: "plowing" means intercourse, a cluster of wool symbolizes the vagina, a rifle represents the penis.

Ganga is performed by a group of men or women and communicates messages of love and betrayal between young men and young women. Songs are not sung directly to women, but womenhood, especially the sexuality of women, is the main focus. Men generally sing songs about their virility and masculinity. They portray themselves as wanting sex and portray women as withholding it; men depict women as hypocritical objects and depict themselves as powerful subjects. In ganga, men express their view of women as sexual objects through symbolic language. For example, in the following ganga verse, which draws on the metaphor of baking, a man shows his manly dominance by shaving and cutting a woman's pubic hair on the hearth.

> *Ja sam moju i brija i sisa*
> *na kominu di se pura misa.*

> I shaved and cut her [pubic hair] I shaved and cut [my woman]
> On the open hearth where the polenta [cornmeal] is mixed.

Placing a woman on the hearth symbolizes her sexual "hotness" or readiness for penetration, according to the man. The mixing of polenta is also a sexual image. Crucial to making good polenta is artful stirring with a long wooden (phallic) stick *(misac)*. When polenta is not properly cooked, it is offensive to eat it or to offer it to guests. Thus in the verse a man's stick/penis is depicted as controlling a woman's sexual being.

The images of shaving and cutting the pubic hair in the verse quoted above are complicated symbols that men and women interpret differently. For example, male informants interpreted this verse to mean that "the man is able to do what he wants with a woman," that "he's boasting to other men that he is not a chicken, but a macho guy," or that "this means that he is a man." Female informants, in contrast, interpreted the verse to mean that "the man even took the opportunity for sexual intercourse on a *hot* hearth," that "the man was only thinking about sex," or that "sperm is equivalent to foam and his penis is a razor, so he has the ability to shave a woman—get her sexually."

In the current war, the words *shave* and *cut* mean to kill someone. A spray of machine gun fire, for example, is said to "shave" the enemy. Historically, shaving hair, especially women's hair, has also been used to signify dishonor. During World War II if a woman was thought to be a spy, Yugoslavian partisans shaved her head. During the recent war, another metaphor was associated with hair. The word *procesljati,* which means "to comb through," also refers to liquidating the enemy. Soldiers often state that "First we combed the forest, then the village." Because of the ritual importance of cutting a boy's hair, shaving symbolizes a man's coming of age and circumcision in Muslim areas (Eugene A. Hammel, personal communication, April 14, 1995). In sum, cutting and shaving suggest male power and male sexual prowess.

Another folk song that uses metaphors of polenta making includes the common expression, "blood is not polenta" *(krv nije pura).* This song and conventional phrase warns against mixing together ethnic groups as if they were polenta. The same expression can be used to praise the strength of blood relative ties, similar to the English saying, "Blood is thicker than water."

Images of blood with polenta also make reference to the physically thick *(gusta)* property of polenta. While male blood is considered thick or coagulated *(tvrda or gusta)* like polenta, female blood is thin (runny) and soft *(rijetka, meka)* like poorly made polenta. Women's blood is thin because they marry out and leave their lineage; men's blood is thick and lumpy because it remains part of the lineage and is passed on to offspring. This is why people of the region consider daughters to be "alien bone" *(tudja kost)* or "alien fate" *(tudja sreca).* They are viewed as the property of another lineage and are therefore seen as valueless to the natal family. The expressions "blood is not polenta" and "blood is not like water" *(krv nije voda)* make reference to not only the importance of the "pure blood" of kinship but also to the superior blood of males.

Historically, in ballads about the distress of war, heroes wrote letters in their blood or wept tears of blood in their fury, which expressed love. In many ceremonies blood is used as a sign of allegiance or bonding. A person may suck the blood from another's finger in the ceremony of "sworn brotherhood" or may scratch his face until it bleeds as an expression of grief. A wrongful act is avenged by "blood revenge" by killing a member of a transgressor's "blood kin." In addition, first brides into a family may assert their rank over later brides by saying, "I spilled my blood here before you did." This is a reference to the blood that virgins are believed to shed on their wedding nights.

The tight control over the expression of women's sexuality in southeastern European cultures does not obviate the widespread discussion of sexuality by both men and women in the form of jokes, songs, aphorisms, and other folklore phrases. Similar to ganga songs, jokes and other forms of folklore express the ideas that women are secretly and ardently sexual, that priests are secretly lustful, and that men are publicly sexually powerful, strong, and boastful (cf. Brandes 1980).

Men are preoccupied with their own as well as women's sexuality. They literally "measure" their own sexuality and ways to "measure up" to each other by resorting to various public displays of virility or sexual prowess. For example, men publicly boast to each other about their sexual affairs—imaginary or real—in order to show their manliness and power. Male informants, even from different generations, share in common "competitive games." "As teenagers," one man stated, "while shepherding cows, or just playing around in the woods, we would gather in groups and would compete with each other to see which one of us could ejaculate the furthest. There were also competitions to see which one of us had the longest penis." Another informant added that "There was no ruler, so we devised various measuring techniques. We would use our hand. The distance between the thumb and the index finger when stretched out was *(rogusa),* the thickness or width of one, two, or three fingers *(prst),* the length of the thumb *(palac),* or the area of the palm of a hand *(dlan)."* Men viewed these activities as competitive but nonaggressive games for determining which one of them was the most sexually capable.

Another competitive game involved comparing stories of seeing naked women. "To see a naked woman, especially her bare breasts and her pubic hair, was a desire," said one man, "of every young man. We all strived to visibly accomplish this feat." Another male informant stated that he and his buddies went to a lot of trouble to see a naked woman:

> We all knew that each Sunday before Mass the women had to change from their everyday clothes into their Sunday best. We, of course, knew how long the walk took from the village to the church, and approximately how long it would take the women to get dressed. We would peek through the window to get a glimpse of a woman's naked body while she was changing her clothes. Another method was standing below a ladder and watching underneath her skirts when she climbed up. Another method, less common, was putting a piece of mirror on the floor where the woman was standing and performing some labor intensive task. Some men also placed a piece of mirror on the tip of their own shoes.

Measurements were also used to evaluate a women's past sexual experiences. Men told me that they could tell, even without sleeping with a woman, whether or not she was a virgin. One way to "measure" her chastity was to assess her breasts: If she had soft breasts *(meka sisa),* in other words, if they were "hanging," it meant that someone else already perforated her *(probusit).* Another way to decipher whether or not a woman was a virgin was to secretly listen to the sound of her flowing urine. If she "pissed wide" *(siroko pisa),* it meant that she had been pierced *(probijena).*

Rape and symbolic or "play rape" have historically been a part of some marriage rituals in southeastern Europe. Marriage by capture *(otmica),* in which a man kidnaps a woman and takes her to the mountains to sexually express his right over her as his wife, often took place without the consent of the woman or her male kin. Today, the otmica is sometimes a form of elopement, allowing a young couple to marry without the approval of the bride's parents. The theme is also played out in a form of courtship called "chasing" *(gonjanje),* which became especially common after World War II. Male teenagers would run after a woman, knock her down, jump on top of her, pin her onto the floor, roll her over, and then pinch her breasts or grab at her genital region. In public, this physical assault aroused the cheers of men and motivated women to yell out and pull the man off the victim. I was told by women informants that men openly chased women as a way of publicly boasting to other men of their accomplishments *(pohvaliti se).* Since the attacked women usually rejected the men's advances, the play rape became a way for a man to publicly save face and publicly humiliate a woman for rejecting him. In short, it was a game of status in which men had to be on top.

Conversely, if an unmarried woman attracted the attention of a young man, her face or cheek *(obraz)* was dishonored *(sramota),* which in turn ruined the honor *(cast)* of her entire family. The term *shameful (bezobrazluk)* literally means "faceless act," and the expression "to sit on one's own face" *(sjesti na svoj obraz)* means to disgrace oneself by an immoral act. Courtship contained an intrinsic undercurrent of dangerous, violent sexuality. While male teenagers had almost unlimited rights of expression, female teenagers were frequently told publicly to contain [barricade] themselves. Mothers might publicly yell lengthy and insulting instructions at daughters suspected of flirting. An example of such a "cool down" instruction is, "If you are so incandescent *(uzarena),* heat up *(mase)* coal pliers or an ash scooper *(ozeg)* and put it in yourself. If you are burning. . . ." These instructions of self-violence demonstrate the extent to which women are expected to keep themselves in control and avoid men's public control over them.

Distrust of female sexuality before marriage is also illustrated by the custom of publicly demonstrating proof of virginity after the wedding night. The blood-stained sheets of the wedding night are traditionally displayed publicly for all to witness. The ubiquitousness of this custom is reflected in the numerous stories and jokes of women who resort to using animal blood or red paint to stain the sheets. One particular joke comes to mind: before the sun came up, a woman displayed her blood-stained sheets during the early dawn. The pitch darkness outside obscured the actual color of the paint she had grabbed, which was green. Two nuns walking by early that morning were the first ones to see the displayed sheets. One nun looked at the other and said, "Oh, my God! Poor woman, this one [man] even penetrated/punctured her gall bladder!"

A woman's blood also reflects men's antagonistic attitudes toward women. Virgin blood, for example, is neutral; menstrual blood is unclean *(necista krv)*. When a child is born deformed, such as a baby with cleft palate, it is said that the woman conceived in dirty blood *(zanijela u necistoj krvi)*. This statement implies that a woman's sexual activities during menstruation negatively impact her child's physical genetic well-being. Nature thus supposedly determines or judges women's behavior.

Given the importance and value placed on women's chastity, monogamy, and fertility, it is understandable why women, and by extension family and lineage, constitute critical targets in the current war in Croatia and Bosnia-Herzegovina. Aggression or violence against women is a means by which combatants show who controls the "sexual property" and political process through traditional honor/shame ideology. Women's honor reflects that of men's, which, in turn, reflects that of the nation.

RECIPE FOR TERROR, CULTURE OF FEAR: SETTING THE STAGE FOR THE WAR

In the Summer of 1990, a preplanned sequence of intimidation and *tactics of fear* became a recipe for terror: roads were barricaded, JNA or Yugoslav People's Army helicopters and bombers flew very low over villages and civilians, and individual arrests, tortures, and massacres of small groups of people took place (cf. Suarez-Orozco 1990). In the Summer of 1991, these events culminated in full-scale war.

Before the actual fighting started in 1990–91, the most common form of terror was selection and roundup of the civilian population. Although some individuals testified that the local police and army units merely arrested them and took them to various locations for an "informative conversation" *(informativni razgovor)*, most people were beaten and tortured, and many were killed. By the end of the Summer of 1991, an all-out assault with the heaviest artillery—tanks, cannons, bombs, and missiles—began. By April 1992, the war had become vicious and this viciousness persisted until the IFOR were deployed in Bosnia in January 1996. Most of the fighting took place in Bosnia and in the disputed border areas of Croatia.

At the onset of the war in Croatia, ganga was used as a means to communicate images of warfare. Ganga songs and jokes became very popular:

Mala moja, materina bona,
 Biz 'po da me, eto aviona.

My little one, mama's little sweetheart,
 Quickly, run [hide] underneath me there is a bomber airplane [coming].

Da su na nebu sve zvizdice pizdice
 Svi bi momci bili zrakoplovci.

If all the stars in the sky were pussies,
 Then all the men would be airmen.

The sexual content, especially the analogy of violent attacks and sexual behavior, is apparent in the ganga songs.

On the eve of the war in Bosnia, a number of popular jokes revealed apprehension and anxiety about expected sexual violence. Before fighting or war-related sexual violence began, the following joke was popular: "Haso told his wife Fata 'The tanks are rolling into Bosnia, so go out and lay down on the street to stop them!' Fata replied, 'No, I'll wait for the foot soldiers.' " Haso commands Fata to use her sexuality as a weapon to stop the tanks. Fata's reply implies anticipation of sexual violence as though it were pleasurable. The joke hides the reality that her sexuality does not stop the soldiers, but becomes their weapon.

A second joke, which was current after the war started, reflected the growing recognition that rape is a weapon: "Fata came home naked and Haso asked her, 'What happened to you?' She responded, 'A sniper got me' " The meaning of the joke is that the worst fears of Haso have been realized—his wife came home naked—which could only mean that she had sexual intercourse with another man. The joke does not make clear whether or not the sexual relation was consensual. The irony in the joke is that Fata had a sexual relationship with someone other than her husband and that it was her fault for being "taken by the sniper."

These jokes represent the merger of images of sex and combat and illustrate the importance of rape as both a physical and a symbolic form of terror. The jokes portray women as the objects of men's military/political aims (Enloe 1992; Farmanfarmaian 1992).

GENDERED VIOLENCE IN WARTIME

The presence of everyday sexual violence in peacetime is absent in most of the literature about sexual coercion. The current literature treats rape in peacetime as a crime against an *individual* woman, and only rape in wartime as a tactic of terror against women in general (Brownmiller 1975, 1993; Nordstrom 1994; Stiglmayer 1994).

In previous wars, rape did not receive the widespread publicity that it does in the ongoing war in former Yugoslavia, and it was not studied by social scientists. The focus on rape in Bosnia-Herzegovina and Croatia by the media provides a unique opportunity to study rape in the context of conflict. In this context rape constitutes a physical and moral attack against women, as well as an attack by humiliation and dishonor on the husbands, brothers, fathers, and sons of the victims. Rape demonstrates men's inability to protect their women. Thus, in wartime, violation of female honor is a weapon used by the men of one ethnic group against those of another. This type of humiliation is especially intense in southeastern Europe where the honor/shame complex is strong and female chastity is central to family and community honor (Boehm 1984; Davis 1977; Schneider 1971).

Men suffer the shame of their failure to protect their property that includes women, family, bloodlines, and soil. Women suffer through their duty to endure the *private stigma of shame*. Their suffering is protection of men's public shame. Public admission of sexual victimization means public defeat of

the honor of the men: the loss of their public, status-focused face *(obraz);* the public admission of loss of their bloodline *(krv);* and the loss of their soil/nation *(zemlja).*

In war individual bodies become metaphoric representatives of the social body, and the killing or maiming of that body symbolically kills or maims the individual's family and ethnic group. War rapes reinforce the cultural notions of cleanliness and dirtiness associated with sexuality and ethnic affiliation. Through forced pregnancy resulting from rape, aggressors can "purify the blood" of the attacked group by creating "ethnically cleansed" babies belonging to the group of the invading fathers.

In the former Yugoslavia, because meanings of rape are shared by the three ethnic groups (Croats, Muslims, and Serbs), sexual violence is especially salient as a weapon of torture (Olujic 1995b). Elaine Scarry (1985:56–58), in her discussion of the political construction of pain under torture, identifies the creation of state hegemony as part of the torture process, which is based on detachment and transfer of political meaning and significant capacities from the body of the tortured to the instruments of torture that become fetishized symbols of the state. Like Foucault (1977), Scarry sees vestiture and divestiture of the body as modes of domination when performed by the state (cf. Aretxaga 1993; Feldman 1991).

WAR RAPES IN CROATIA AND BOSNIA-HERZEGOVINA (1990–95)

Dimensions of Violence

Nobody knows the actual number of the victims of rape and sexual torture in the war in former Yugoslavia (Brecic and Loncar 1995). According to the figures released by the Bosnian government at the end of September 1992, almost 15 percent of the population of approximately one and a half million or 200,000 individuals, had been confined in concentration camps (*New York Times* 1993). Men and women were held separately. Individuals of both sexes were physically and sexually tortured. Tortures included rape and sexual mutilation. Men were forced to watch their female relatives raped multiple times. The same report stated that the number of women who had been raped was at least 14,000. Because it is a shame and dishonor to admit rape, however, many victims probably remained silent. It was estimated that among all the female rape victims 14 percent were girls between the ages of 7 and 18, 57 percent were between the ages of 18 and 35, 21 percent were between the ages of 35 and 50, and 7 percent were above the age of 50 (*New York Times* 1993).

In another report compiled by a fact-finding mission of the European Community in December 1992, Bosnian Serb soldiers were reported to have raped 20,000 women, mostly of Muslim ethnicity. The report noted, "in recent months this was part of a deliberate pattern of abuse [where] rapes cannot be seen as incidental to the main purposes of the aggression but as serving a strategic purpose in itself" (European Community Investigation Mission into the Treatment of Muslim Women in the Former Yugoslavia n.d.: 18). War rapes are one of the forms of "ethnic cleansing" (1992: 18). The Bosnian Ministry of the Interior places the number of women rape victims at 50,000. While the reported number of rapes varies, all reports agree that rape has been used as a genocidal tool used against ethnic populations.

Concentration Camps: Rapists' Attack Centers

Many mass rapes in Bosnia-Herzegovina have occurred in what the Bosnian government terms *rape camps*, where Serbian soldiers forcibly held and raped the conquered women, who faced either of two cruel fates: to survive repeated rapes and tortures, or to be killed immediately.

The names and locations of rape camps reflect preexisting attitudes toward sexuality and courtship, but in a cruel new context. Rape camps were former coffeehouses and restaurants whose names symbolize both the traditional and the modern, such as "Vilina Vlas" (Nymph's Tresses) and "Kafana Sonja" (Coffeehouse Sonja). To a weary traveler in this part of the world, these names previously symbolized a traditional, quaint, and poetic place of pleasure (Olujic 1995a). The names currently mean brothels, not detention camps, in which women willingly satisfy men's desires. The

names of these camps thus blame women for their own victimization.

For women, these places are *pakao na zemlji* (hell on earth). In many camps, the majority of the female victims have been murdered, dying from gunshot wounds, bleeding as a consequence of gang rape, or dying by suicide motivated by shame.

Although rapes have been committed by Croatian as well as Muslim soldiers, such instances were fewer in number without "preplanned rape camps and women were not imprisoned until they became pregnant," according to one male soldier. Moreover, rape was not a systematic policy among the Croatians and Muslims, as evidenced from the testimonies collected during the research period.

Systematic Violence

The atrocities committed by Serbian soldiers were systematic. Unwilling Serbian soldiers were sometimes coerced by superior officers to rape or help rape women. One Serbian soldier, for example, recounted that his commander instructed them to rape and then kill Muslim women because it was "good for raising the fighters' morale" (*New York Times* 1992:1). The purpose of systematic rape was to "clean" women of their ethnic identity and humiliate their male kin.

There are also accounts, although not as common, of forced sexual relations or rapes among related male prisoners. Forced sexual atrocities, especially oral sex among siblings and between fathers and sons, are documented (Brecic and Loncar 1995). For example, Brecic and Loncar, both of whom are medical doctors, cataloged four categories of sexual abuse against men:

1. Injuries of testicles with blunt objects (44% of their sample)
2. Castrations and semi-castrations (24% of their sample)
3. Rape (20% of their sample)
4. Perverse sexual acts (12% of their sample)

Rape was the most difficult trauma for men to deal with because they associated male rape with homosexuality. They believed that a man who rapes another man is a homosexual and that only homosexual males are victims of rape. Such beliefs lead men to question the core of their sexual identity. Their homophobia often lead to a prolonged process of healing.

My research points out that among relatives, more common were instances where male relatives were forced to physically torture each other. The following is a translation of an excerpt from a testimony given by a Muslim man during 1993 while he was a refugee living in Croatia:

> In their second wave of interrogation *(nalet)*, the Serbian soldiers asked [the prisoners] if there were families amongst ourselves. A father and a son stood up. The soldiers said, "Hit yourselves. Fight each other." They started slapping each other. The soldier said: "It's no good. Why isn't it good? Because there is no blood." The father and the son then started to hit each other harder. The soldier again said: "It's still not good. There is no blood. This is the way you have to do it." The soldiers started beating up the son so hard that he fell down unconscious. Then randomly the soldiers asked one of the prisoners: "What is your name?" As soon as the prisoner identified himself, the soldier said: "So, that's you, mother fucker. Cut his throat." Five soldiers then jumped on top of him. The man started screaming. They didn't kill him—they cut off his ears. . . . The man is screaming, the blood is hissing all over us, they are still on top of him—laughing. . . . All of us who were around there, they ordered us to lick the blood that was [spilled] on the wooden floor.

There was a deliberate attempt to impregnate women and hold them as prisoners until it was too late to abort—usually through the second trimester of pregnancy. Today the raped women and their children from rape are constant reminders of suppression and domination. The following is a lengthy and a very difficult translation from Sanela (pseudonym), a 19-year-old woman:

> The four Serbian soldiers asked me if I ever had a man [sexually] and I told them that I never was with a man because we are forbidden [to have sexual intercourse] before marriage. . . .
>
> The soldiers told me "You are a spy, not a Muslim. Muslims are shaven down there/below" [pubic hair]. My mother and those older ladies shaved down there, that was some kind of custom, but the younger women didn't shave, it wasn't mandatory. At this point, a soldier grabbed me down there [genital area] and started pulling out [the pubic hairs] and said

> "See you are not a Muslim, if you were a Muslim you wouldn't have that [pubic hair]. . . ."
>
> And he continued, "You're not a Muslim, admit who you are." I said, "I am a Muslim, I swear to God, I swear on my mother, let me go." "No you're not." "Yes I am." He said, "If you are a Muslim, then we will shave you *(obrijati)*." And then he took out that knife which he carried and threw me down and pinned me on the floor and called the others to come and help him. They were all laughing and yelling, "shave," "shave her," "cut that." They proceeded to shave me, but it can't be called that. He was plucking, waving the knife, cutting across my body and over my breasts. . . . That was not accidental. Yes it was almost dark, but he was cutting me on purpose [the cutting was not accidental due to darkness]. They are holding me. One sat on my stomach, he was lifting my legs and I couldn't move. They shoved some kind of rag in my mouth so that I wasn't able to yell, and every time he plucked [my pubic hair] my body jerked and then he would kick me and pluck even harder. Later when I saw [my genital area] everything was bloody, red, all around, hurting, it was bleeding, and then all night they. . . .

The testimony continues with details of other forms of torture committed by the four Serbian "hero soldiers." Grazing her breasts with a knife, they told her to get up so that they could better see her. Then they ordered her, like a Playboy bunny or model showing off her body, to turn around, sit, stand, move, lie down, get up, and so on. They wanted her to pose in order to emphasize the tortured body. She was pleading with them to let her go and to give her a piece of cloth to stop the bleeding from the cuts inflicted earlier. Instead of giving her a cloth to stop the bleeding, one of the soldiers told her

> Blood is bloody, and you have not even felt what it means to have your blood running. But you will feel it, just you wait a little. And now, you are a real Muslim, beautiful, you have no hair [pubic hair], now you are proper [complete]. And do you know what I do with such types? I slit their throats. And I will also cut, slowly, so that you can truly feel how it is when the blood is running.

Sanela lived to report these terrifying acts and words. The remainder of her testimony reveals more tortures, beatings, and acts of oral sex, which she was forced to perform on all of the men that day. She was also forced to go outside and to lie naked on the cold branches and leaves. She was raped by each of the four soldiers. One of the soldiers told her, "Lie down and shut-up. So, you were never with a man? No? Well, now you will see what is a man, a real man. And not one of yours. . . . Peeled [oguljeni]. . . . [this refers to the Muslim practice of circumcision]." Sanela survived their rapes and tortures and was released in a prisoner exchange. She terminated her pregnancy and is now living in a refugee camp in Croatia.

There is a deeper significance of the Serbian soldier's remark to his Muslim victim about circumcision. Instead of using the word *circumcised (sunet/obrezat),* he chose the word *peeled (ogulit),* a word more commonly used in connection to bananas and other fruit, implying that unlike the deformed, incomplete, or mutilated circumcised penis of a Muslim, his Serbian penis was whole. His cruel remarks also implied that he regarded his rape of Sanela as a favor rather than an assault. And finally, his remarks also implied that the true object of his torture was her fiancé, who was robbed of his right to take his lover's virginity himself, and who was demeaned as phallically inferior. Sanela's account calls to mind the ganga, only here cutting and shaving is literal rather than metaphoric.

In the foregoing testimony, the use of the body as a means of justifying domination of male over female and Serb over Muslim is apparent when, for example, the soldiers "shave and cut" Sanela in order to make her body physically resemble their stereotype of a Muslim woman. They inscribe visible markers of "ethnicity" onto her physical body. The inscription of ethnicity relates directly to the particular tensions of the region, where people believe that they are of different "bloods," but recognize that they are unable to tell the difference between ethnicities through physical examination. Here, the fear of women being secretly impregnated and fooled into raising a child of another ethnicity is especially strong because people are not ordinarily able to recognize that a child has been parented by an invader.

Pain is often used (or administered) as a symbolic substitute for death in many cultures. "Physical pain always mimes death and the infliction of physical pain is always a mock execution," according to Scarry (1985:31). In a similar vein,

Theweleit (1993) argues that the effect of torture is double-sided; namely, its purpose is that

> The effect of the torture is double-sided: to destroy the victim, to eliminate a "threat" the victim embodies; and to construct the torturer as a new person. The production of a dead person on the one hand is matched by the production of a newborn person on the other. The torturer gets a new body while the body of the tortured is brought into shapes of vexation, the view of which the torturer needs for his own transformation. [Theweleit 1993:300]

Military rapists bind themselves together ethnically by separating their male and female victims through a multitude of sexually violent acts. By acting as a group and by systematically imposing their methods through acts and words of brutality, rapists are a social body that acts against another social body. In short, a purpose of ethnically organized rape is to destroy another ethnic group.

TRANSFORMATION DURING THE WAR CULTURE

War transforms the political uses of rape. Although the first rapes of women in this conflict occurred during 1991 in Croatia, the Croatian government kept silent. In the spring of 1992, I was told by a gynecologist at a teaching hospital in Croatia that an "ethics committee" in Croatia was discussing the problem of pregnant Croatian women who could not abort their fetuses because they were "too far into the pregnancy." This information, he said, was a "private secret" and to be withheld from the press. When the same atrocities on a larger scale occurred in Bosnia-Herzegovina, the matter became a "public secret" (cf. Taussig 1987). Why the difference in the treatment? At first it may seem obvious: the atrocities occurred in greater numbers in Bosnia-Herzegovina than in Croatia. Also, Muslim women were valued more in Bosnia than Christian women in Croatia. But these answers fail to reveal the complexity of the relevant cultural expressions and interactions.

Lack of official disclosure about war rapes of Croatian women enabled Croatian men to publicly retain their honor and their face. Public admission would have required an admission of male weaknesses. There is an expression in the Croatian language that refers to men who are "feminized," made weaker (*naprviti pizdu od muskarca*—"to make a pussy out of man"). Indeed, when Serb forces burned and pillaged the villages around Dubrovnik, they left signs that read: *Gdje ste sada Ustaske picke?* (Where are you now Ustasha pussies?).

War rapes in Bosnia symbolized an assault on the Muslim social body. While both Croatian and Muslim women were raped by military men in Bosnia, the bulk of the victims were Muslim. The sheer scale of the violence against women and against Muslim women made it impossible initially to hide the reality of these atrocities.

Furthermore, the Bosnian government profited politically from publicizing the aggression against its "own" women. Bosnian women who were victims of mass rapes in Serb-run Bosnian rape camps became bargaining tools of the Bosnian government to entice or persuade the West to intervene militarily. Raped women were also used to manipulate the media and other governments' actions by male members of the Bosnian government who in effect confiscated the identity of these women, thereby becoming rapists of another sort.

Although divorced women were more likely to talk about their experiences than single or married women, they did not have the same stake in virginity or marital fidelity and therefore did not have the same potential to bring public shame to their families, even though they told me that they could never return to their villages after the violence. The shame of their ordeal was too much to share with family. Like the young girls who are chastised for being "too hot" in peacetime, these women were seen as having brought dishonor to their families through their sexuality. In the ideology of honor and shame, it does not matter whether or not a woman consents to sexual intercourse (cf. Rebhun 1995). What matters is simply that sexual penetration has taken place. And it is through the penetration of a woman's corporeal body that the social body of her family is permanently and irretrievably damaged.

Some women learned to use their own bodies in ways that deflected their shame. For example, discussion of their "menstrual blood" deterred or spared them from being raped by the Serb soldiers. Statements such as, "I was spared [not raped] be-cause I had my period," or "it was my time so no one touched me" echoes through several testimonies. The significance of the linkages these women created between wartime and peacetime images and beliefs about blood cannot be overstated. Individual embodiment and its connections to the social body are visible in the desperate attempt of refugee Bosnian women to use their "live blood" to stop the "bloodshed" in the ongoing war: They donated their own blood, which was mixed with the printers ink of the *Suddeutsche Zeitung* (a German daily newspaper from Munich, on November 19, 1993) in a desperate attempt to draw the attention and intervention of the West in stopping the war.

But rape-induced pregnancies present the ultimate crisis of ethnic identity. Women raped refer to rape-produced babies (born and unborn) as *Chetniks* (Serbian extremists from World War II). Many state that they do not want to hold or see their infants for fear that overwhelming hatred would lead them to strangle the babies. These pregnancies also create a crisis for religious leaders. While the head of the Croatian Catholic Church, Cardinal Franjo Kuharic, has expressed his belief that mothers' love should overcome such feelings, a prominent Muslim leader from Egypt urged Bosnian Muslim officials to pass a religious decree (*fadwa*) to allow abortion after the fourth month and to proclaim raped Muslim women as religious martyrs.

The Shifting of Violence

In both peacetime and wartime, the meanings inscribed on women's bodies constantly shift between individual and social meanings (cf. Scheper-Hughes and Lock 1987). In peacetime, on the one hand, women's bodies are the symbolic repository of their men's honor, the symbolic terrain of male competition. By controlling women's bodies and invading the bodies of other men's women, either symbolically through folkloric boasts, or physically through kidnap and rape, men play out masculine competitions. They achieve status among themselves by stripping women of status (cf. Ortner 1981). Because a woman's body is a microcosm of her lineage, and the body's weak points being its orifices (cf. Douglas 1982[1970]), by dishonoring a woman, a man symbolically dishonors the whole lineage. This is partly due to women's reproductive power. Underlying the whole honor complex is the fear that somehow a man from another group will impregnate a woman and make fools of the whole group by forcing them to raise an "alien" child. In this way the competing lineage would have permanently invaded the victim's lineage.

Raping women and forcing them to bear "Chetnik" babies is the logical extension of the unconscious fears that underlie the honor complex. What the soldiers are doing is making the worst fears of their victims come true: unstated but deep-seated fears are now stated openly and have become a reality.

On a larger scale, in the context of war the concept of lineage can be extended to include an entire ethnic group. In this political context in the former Yugoslavia all ethnic lineages—Croats, Serbs and Muslims—were antagonists. The symbolic "body" of these lineages became a geographic territory in terms of both land and the physical bodies that the military groups were able to hold. "Ethnic cleansing" became a way of "devirginizing" their national territory and then holding it safe from the symbolic rape of invasion. In sum, the rapes of individual women were microcosms of the larger invasions of territory.

DISCUSSION

Rather than being an aberration, the use of rape as a weapon of war comes directly out of southern European concepts of sexuality and honor, and without an understanding of these concepts in peacetime culture, wartime behavior is not understandable. It is precisely because the ideology of honor/shame was shared by Croats, Muslims, and Serbs that war rapes became such an effective weapon in the former Yugoslavia.

Returning to Desjarlais and Kleinman's comment cited in the beginning of this article, our notion of "culture" is problematic when applied to situations of extreme violence, terror, and uncertainty. This article has attempted to reveal links between collective action and individual tendencies. Further, it has illustrated that metaphors are expressions of the tendencies embodied within a

culture, and that they manifest themselves differently during peacetime and wartime. Specifically, the individual body of peacetime, especially its essences—sexuality and reproduction—are the symbols of everyday domination and aggression (cf. Csordas 1994). War transforms the individual body into the social body as seen in genocidal rapes, ethnic cleansing, and purifying of the bloodlines. Further, medical, religious, and government institutions reinforce the wartime process by manipulating the individual body into a body politic, thereby controlling and defining "human/life" and the political uses of rapes in order to entice Western military intervention (Scheper-Hughes and Lock 1987).

The origin of war rape and particular motifs of sexual torture in local folklore in no way excuses or condones the behavior of either individual soldiers or army policy makers. Sexual torture magnifies the suffering of people already uprooted, terrified, and acutely grieving.

The greatest atrocity of all, as in all wars and in peacetime, is that individuals are absorbed by the collective actions of the social/political fantasy. The tragedy is that people are tortured, torn apart. Their lives are destroyed and then discarded as the collective fantasy proceeds.

REFERENCES

Aretxaga, Begona. 1993. Dirty Protest: Symbolic Overdetermination and Gender in Northern Ireland Ethnic Violence. *Ethos* 23:123–148.

Boehm, Christopher. 1984. *Blood Revenge: The Enactment and Management of Conflict in Montenegro and Other Tribal Societies.* Philadelphia: University of Pennsylvania Press.

Brandes, Stanley. 1980. *Metaphors of Masculinity: Sex and Status in Andalusian Folklore.* Philadelphia: University of Pennsylvania Press.

Brecic, Petra, and Mladen Loncar. 1995. Characteristics of Sexual Violence against Men during the War in Croatia and Bosnia-Herzegovina. Paper presented at the conference entitled *"(En)Gendering Violence: Terror, Domination, Recovery."* Zagreb, Croatia, October 27–28, 1995.

Brownmiller, Susan. 1975. *Against Our Will: Men, Women, and Rape.* New York: Bantam Books.

———. 1993. Making Female Bodies the Battlefield: Alas for Women, There Is Nothing Unprecedented about Mass Rape in War. *Newsweek,* January 4:37.

Byrnes, Robert F., ed. 1976. *Communal Families in the Balkans: The Zadruga.* Notre Dame, IN and London: University of Notre Dame Press.

Csordas, Thomas J. ed. 1994. *Embodiment and Experience: The Existential Ground of Culture and Self.* Cambridge: Cambridge University Press.

Davis, J. 1977. *The People of the Mediterranean: An Essay in Comparative Social Anthropology.* London: Routlege.

Denich, Bettie. 1974. Sex and Power in the Balkans. In *Women, Culture, and Society.* Michelle Rosaldo and Louise Lamphere, eds. Pp. 243–262. Stanford: Stanford University Press.

Desjarlais, Robert, and Arthur Kleinman. 1994. Violence and Demoralization in the New World Disorder. *Anthropology Today* 10(5):9–12.

Douglas, Mary. 1982[1970]. *Natural Symbols: Explorations in Cosmology.* New York: Pantheon Books.

Enloe, Cynthia. 1992. The Gendered Gulf. In *Collateral Damage: The New World Order at Home and Abroad.* Cynthia Peters, ed. Pp. 111–138. Boston: South End Press.

European Community Investigation Mission into the Treatment of Muslim Women in the Former Yugoslavia N.d. Unpublished internal report. December 1992.

Farmanfarmaian, Abouali. 1992. Did You Measure Up?: The Role of Race and Sexuality in the Gulf War. In *Collateral Damage: The New World Order at Home and Abroad.* Peters, ed. Pp. 111–138. Boston: South End Press.

Feldman, Allen. 1991. *Formations of Violence: The Narrative of the Body and Political Terror in Northern Ireland.* Chicago: University of Chicago Press.

Foucault, Michel. 1977. *Power/Knowledge: Selected Interviews and Other Writings.* New York: Pantheon Books.

Hammel, Eugene A. 1968. *Alternative Social Structures and Ritual Relations in the Balkans.* New Jersey: Prentice-Hall, Inc.

———. 1972. The Zadruga as Process. In *Household and Family in Past Time.* Peter Laslett and Richard Wall, eds. Pp. 335–373. Cambridge: Cambridge University Press.

Knezevic, Anto. 1996. *The Woman in the Eyes of Patriarchal Male Refugees: An Analysis of Some Recently Created Bosnian Folk Songs.* Department of Philosophy, University of Zagreb, unpublished MS.

New York Times. 1992. A Killer's Tale: One Serbian Fighter Leaves Trail of Brutality. November 27:1.

———. 1993. European Inquiry Says Serbs' Forces Have Raped 20,000. January 9:1.

Nordstrom, Carolyn. 1994. Rape: Politics and Theory in War and Peace. Working Paper, 146. The Australian National University Research School of Pacific Studies, Peace Research Center.

Olujic, Maria B. 1990. Economic and Demographic Change in Contemporary Yugoslavia: Persistence of Traditional Gender Ideology. *East European Quarterly* 23(4):477–485.

———. 1995a. Coming Home: The Croatian War Experience. In *Fieldwork under Fire.* Carolyn Nordstrom and Antonius Robben, eds. 186–204. Berkeley: University of California Press.

———. 1995b. Sexual Coercion and Torture in Former Yugoslavia. In *Women and War.* Special issue. *Cultural Survival Quarterly* (Spring):43–54.

Ortner, Sherry B. 1981. Gender and Sexuality in Hierarchical Societies. In *Sexual Meanings: The Social Construction of Gender and Sexuality.* Sherry Ortner and Harriet Whitehead, eds. Pp. 359–409. Cambridge: Cambridge University Press.

Rebhun, Linda-Anne. 1995. Edible Women: Ascribed Sexual Availability in Northeast Brazilian Women. Paper presented to the 94th Annual Meeting of the American Anthropological Association, Washington, DC, November.

Rijavec, Majda, Zora Raboteg-Saric, and Maria Olujic. 1996. Living under War Stress: Some Qualitative Aspects of Adolescents' Experiences. *Nordic Journal of Psychiatry* 50(2): 109–115.

Robben, Antonius, and Carolyn Nordstrom. 1995. The Anthropology and Ethnography of Violence and Sociopolitical Conflict. In *Fieldwork under Fire: Contemporary Studies of Violence and Survival.* Carolyn Nordstrom and Antonius Robben, eds. Pp. 1–32. Berkeley: University of California Press.

Scarry, Elaine. 1985. *The Body in Pain: The Making and Unmaking of the World.* New York: Oxford University Press.

Scheper-Hughes, Nancy, and Margaret M. Lock. 1987. The Mindful Body: A Prolegomenon to Future Work in Medical Anthropology. *Medical Anthropology Quarterly* 1(1):6–41.

Schneider, Jane. 1971. Of Vigilance and Virgins: Honor, Shame and Access to Resources in Mediterranean Societies. *Ethnology* 10(1): 1–24.

Simic, Andrei. 1983. Machismo and Cryptomatriarchy: Power, Affect and Authority in the Contemporary Yugoslav Family. *Ethos* 11:66–86.

Stein Erlich, Vera. 1966. *Family in Transition: A Study of 300 Yugoslav Villages.* Princeton, NJ: Princeton University Press.

Stiglmayer, Alexandra, ed. 1994. *Mass Rape: The War against Women in Bosnia-Herzegovina.* Lincoln and London: University of Nebraska Press.

Suarez-Orozco, Marcelo. 1990. Speaking the Unspeakable: Toward a Psychological Understanding of Responses to Terror. *Ethos* 18-353-383.

Taussig, Michael. 1987. *Shamanism, Colonialism, and the Wild Man: A Study in Terror and Healing.* Chicago: University of Chicago Press.

Theweleit, Klaus. 1993. The Bomb's Womb and the Gender of War (War Goes on Preventing Women from Becoming the Mothers of Invention). In *Gendering War Talk.* Cooke and Wollacott, eds. Pp. 283–315. Princeton, NJ: Princeton University Press.

Tomasevich, Jozo. 1976. The Tomasevich Extended Family on the Peninsula Peljesac. In *Communal Families in the Balkans: Zadruga.* Robert F. Byrnes, ed. Pp.

187–200. Notre Dame, IN and London: University of Notre Dame Press.

Woodward, Susan L. 1985. The Rights of Women: Ideology, Policy, and Social Change in Yugoslavia. In *Women, State, and Party in Eastern Europe.* Sharon L. Wolchik and Alfred G. Meyer, eds. Pp. 234–254. Durham, NC: Duke University Press.

■ ■ ■ ■ ■ ■ ■ ■ ■ ■

36 IMMIGRANTS FROM CHERNOBYL-AFFECTED AREAS IN ISRAEL: THE LINK BETWEEN HEALTH AND SOCIAL ADJUSTMENT

L. I. Remennick

As we saw in the last selection, the experience of violence and other kinds of extreme disorder can result in demoralization, stigmatization, and physical and psychosocial harm (see Das et al. 2001). The current selection shares this focus as well as an emphasis on social adjustment related to relocation (see selections 29 and 33). It introduces the concept of cumulative adversity resulting from a combination of stress due to resettlement and past, present, and future psychophysical harm through radiation exposure and "radio-phobia" related to the experience of the Chernobyl disaster. Radiation survivors experience higher rates of a range of diseases and disorders that reach well beyond the expected set of cancers, reproductive and genetic disorders, and thyroid dysfunctions, to include immune system, cardiovascular, and developmental disorders. In addition, radiation survivors are susceptible to the psychosomatic manifestations of having experienced a disaster and having continued to live in the same area for years afterward. The effects appear to vary in proportion to the amount of exposure to radiation.

The study compares immigrants to Israel from Chernobyl-affected areas to immigrants from other parts of Russia to demonstrate how the combination of exposure to Chernobyl and emigration brings not only a higher burden of disease but also less-satisfactory integration into the new occupational and social environment. One significant outcome is a greater degree of downward occupational mobility, reflecting the effects of self-victimization, poor perceived health, and anxiety about future disease on the ability of immigrants to pursue economic and social goals. Remennick explains that perceptions of radiation exposure, poor health, and stigma may be as relevant to the etiology of disease conditions and somatoform disorders as the radiation itself. This is what the nocebo effect or meaning response would predict (see selection 30), but it would be difficult to determine the relative importance of each. In the meantime and in concert with the arguments made by Farmer (selection 34), the study shows that it is important to provide for the immediate needs of radiation survivors, whose condition may be made worse by the failure of health services to recognize the dual nature of their health and social problems.

Source: Reprinted from *Social Science and Medicine,* Vol. 54, Remennick, L. I., "Immigrants in Chernobyl-Affected Areas in Israel: The Link between Health and Social Adjustment," Pages 309–317, Copyright (2002), with permission from Elsevier.

Questions to keep in mind

How might the experience of ecological emigration be different from that of emigration for reasons of political oppression or economic necessity?

Why is it important to assess self-reported health and psychosocial well-being?

How might perceptions about being a victim and about current and future health affect people's ability to adjust to new social and occupational environments?

What gender differences did the study find? What do they indicate about the experience of Chernobyl and emigration?

In what ways are Israeli health services inadequate to the needs of the immigrants in the study? How would you suggest making them more accessible and appropriate?

INTRODUCTION

The concept of *cumulative adversity* has recently emerged as a promising way of exploring the association between traumatic life events and health outcomes (Turner & Lloyd, 1995). The experiences of international refugees and other migrants who undergo resettlement under chronic stress caused by wars, natural disasters, and other mass-scale hardships may be the most striking example of adjustment to cumulative adversity (Martic, Spoljar, & Rudan, 1996). Several studies among first generation migrants from Asian and Latin American countries in the US and Canada have shown their increased mental health risks and higher somatic morbidity, suggesting a synergistic effect from the past traumas and current acculturation stress (Lipson, 1993; Gil & Vega, 1996; Tran & Ferullo, 1997). This study focuses on the special case of immigrants who underwent a chronic traumatic life event before emigration, namely, a long-term exposure to radiation. It shows that cumulative adversity among recent immigrants may manifest not only in poor physical and mental health, but also in lower levels of social and economic accommodation in the new country.

The explosion at the Chernobyl atomic power plant on April 26, 1986 has signified technological, managerial and political failure of communism, and effectively marked the beginning of the downfall of the Soviet regime. The catastrophic scale of this accident and its health implications for millions of Soviet people (as well as some segments of the European population outside the USSR) resulted from Chernobyl's location in the midst of the densely populated industrial and agricultural area of Ukraine only 90 km north of the capital Kiev. Since western parts of the European USSR have been the traditional area of Jewish settlement, the Chernobyl disaster has affected many Soviet Jews. At the first opportunity, which showed in the wake of Glasnost' in the late 1980s and early 1990s, these people fled their homes and became 'ecological immigrants,' mainly in Israel and in the US.

Due to secrecy, initial paralysis and subsequent inefficiency of the late Soviet administration in the crisis management, evacuation of the surrounding towns and villages was long delayed, and no personal precautions (such as oral iodine intake) have been taken by the population. Millions of people have been exposed to high doses of cesium, iodine and other radioactive elements during the initial post-explosion months. These included the estimated 600,000 of salvage workers and soldiers (the so-called 'liquidators') who cleaned up the burnt reactor and built a concrete sarcophagus above it. The majority of the liquidators subsequently died of acute leukemia and other radiation-induced conditions (WHO, 1995). The state could not organize relocation, housing and jobs for the millions living outside of the immediate 'dead zone' around the reactor, leaving them for years under chronic secondary exposure via contaminated water, food chain, buildings, etc. The unwilling participants of this huge live experiment on the long-term effects of ionizing radiation embraced the entire three million living in Kiev and surrounding towns, as well as several cities in Belorus, western Russia and the Baltic region (IAEA, 1991).

During the initial post-catastrophe years, the authorities granted some monetary and housing benefits to those survivors who received the formal status of 'Chernobyl victims.' Local health facilities offered periodic check-ups and available treatment of radiation-induced diseases, especially to the liquidators and residents of specific towns known for the highest levels of contamination. People with unascertained 'victim status' and/or non-specific health problems did not get even such limited support. Over the post-communist years of market reforms, special benefits for Chernobyl survivors gradually vanished in most places (Bebeshko, 1996; Viel, 1997).

Like no prior nuclear accident, Chernobyl provided epidemiologists and specialists in nuclear medicine with ample research data. In almost 15 years after the accident, tens of cooperative studies involving former Soviet and western experts have assessed the immediate and cumulative effects of ionizing radiation on humans. Although most attention centered on the traditional triplet of malignant disease, thyroidal dysfunction and reproductive/genetic disorders (IAEA, 1991; WHO, 1995), the range of health hazards from chronic radiation exposure proved to be much wider than was formerly assumed. Controlled studies have shown that the incidence of many conditions formerly not linked to radiation (e.g., cardiovascular, auto-immune, neurological, vision and hearing problems) was significantly higher in Chernobyl survivors (Kordysh et al., 1995; Cwikel, Abdelgani, Goldsmith, Quastel, & Yevelson, 1997a, Cwikel, Goldsmith, Kordysh, Quastel, & Abdelgani, 1997b). Women who had lived in the contaminated areas had higher prevalence of repeated miscarriages, complicated pregnancies, low weight and various congenital defects (from severe to minor) in the newborn. Even children born relatively healthy manifested slower growth, more allergic tendencies, and poorer immunity (i.e. higher rates of childhood infections), compared to children born outside the affected zone (WHO, 1995; Bebeshko, 1996; Whitcomb & Sage, 1997).

After the initial focus on the somatic effects of radiation, more recent studies addressed the psychological aftermath of living through a nuclear disaster, usually via the lens of post-traumatic stress disorder (PTSD) (Davidson, 1993; Havenaar, 1996). Both adult and young survivors—while living in the contaminated areas and after fleeing them—suffered from multiple psychosomatic manifestations of the so-called radio-phobia. Surrounded by the constant invisible hazard, get-ting no reliable information and guidance from the authorities, and having no feasible way for defense or escape, many Chernobyl survivors developed depression, cancer-related anxiety, sleep disturbances and chronic fatigue. Common somatic complaints included headaches, limb tremors, cardiac arrhythmia, gastro-intestinal disorders, skin rashes and vaguely located pains (Havenaar, 1996; Bebeshko, 1996; Viel, 1997). Since individual measurement of cesium doses absorbed by the body was non-feasible on a mass scale (IAEA, 1991), most survivors were uncertain as to their actual risks and often tended to exaggerate the extent of their exposure. Yet, imagined or real, this lingering sense of victimization gradually took its toll for the people most affected. Commenting on the results of the International Conference on Radiation and Health held in 1996 in Israel, Julie Cwikel emphasized that psychological responses to the disaster may be at least as important source of higher morbidity as direct effects of radiation. On top of anxiety, fear and lack of control over modern technology, survivors may suffer from social stigma for many years after the event. More cross-cultural research on the psychosocial hazards of radiation exposure and effective ways of assistance to survivors was called for (Cwikel, 1997).

Among some 800,000 former Soviet Jewish immigrants who moved to Israel after 1989, the estimated 150–170 thousand come from the Chernobyl-affected areas (CBS, 1998). About 200 Jewish engineers and technicians who had worked on the site as liquidators were among these newcomers. For the majority of these immigrants, the wish to escape the radiation-contaminated environment and to improve their impaired health was the single most important motive for emigration. In the early 1990s, immigrants from the Chernobyl-affected area established several advocacy groups (of which the largest one was called "SOS Chernobyl") for the promotion of their cause of getting a special status and entitlements in the health and welfare systems in Israel. Their activity yielded few results: Israeli authorities argued in response that compensations should be claimed from the responsible party (i.e., the no longer existing Soviet or newly formed Ukrainian governments). The state of Israel did its best by providing immigrants with citizenship, health insurance and chances for rehabilitation and a healthier future for their children. Since there is no sound way of measuring individual exposure or linking health problems to radiation, special medical procedures cannot be justified and funded. Hence, the best Chernobyl survivors can do is forget their past and get on with their new lives in Israel—went the response from the Ministries of Health and Immigrant Absorption. Many Chernobyl activists, who continued to think of themselves as victims, were strongly disappointed by the alleged 'indifference' of the Jewish state to their cause.

However, this advocacy campaign has attracted the attention of physicians and medical researchers and led to the inception of several epidemiological studies among Chernobyl survivors in Israel. One on-going project based on Haifa's Rambam hospital follows up oncological morbidity in the cohort of immigrants from the defined locales in the Ukraine and Belorus with high radio-contamination. Research teams in Beer-Sheba's Ben-Gurion University conducted a series of comparative studies trying to link individual body burdens (Quastel, Kramer, & Goldsmith, 1995) and/or residence-related estimates of exposure (Kordysh et al., 1995; Cwikel et al., 1997b) to various health outcomes. Both study groups reported that the prevalence of chronic disease among Chernobyl survivors significantly exceeds general population rates. Among their common ailments are thyroidal malfunction, hypertension, heart disease, diabetes, rheumatic, visual and hearing disorders, and many other non-specific conditions. Studies by Cwikel et al. have demonstrated the psychosomatic nature of many health problems among Chernobyl survivors, linking higher rates of blood pressure and heart disease to stress and PTSD. A dose–response relationship between the level of exposure and chronic morbidity has also been demonstrated (Cwikel et al., 1997a). One study of psychological distress among recent Russian immigrants has found increased demoralization scores among those who immigrated from the area within a radius of up to 150km from Chernobyl (Zilber & Lerner, 1996).

Yet, most Israeli studies have focused on epidemiological aspects of the Chernobyl experience, while the call for more psychosocial and sociological studies (Cwikel, 1997) has largely remained unmet. Trying to contribute to this stream of research, the current study addressed the influence of perceived somatic and mental health status on the immigration experience, social adjustment and general well-being of Chernobyl survivors in Israel. Immigrants from the Chernobyl-affected area combine two features of interest for medical sociologists: self-victimization bred on past traumas—due to actual radiation exposure and/or radio-phobia—plus the distress involved in the resettlement process in Israel. Do these past and present stressors act in synergy, merging into cumulative adversity syndrome and compromising the general social adjustment of immigrants from radiation-affected areas? In light of this question, the study centered on two main goals: (1) to assess self-rated health status, psychosomatic morbidity and the utilization of health services among Chernobyl survivors vs. other former Soviet immigrants; and (2) to explore the influence of health status and self-awareness as 'Chernobyl victims' on the social and occupational integration of this group of immigrants in Israel.

STUDY POPULATION AND METHODS

The study was based on a questionnaire administered in two groups of the post-1989 Russian immigrants of working age (30–59): 180 persons who came from Chernobyl-affected areas and 200 persons from other areas of the former Soviet Union. During fall-winter of 1997, respondents were recruited in three main geographic areas of Israel: North, Center and South. Since regular residential sampling proved to be very costly and ineffective (due to high residential mobility of recent immigrants), a combined approach to sampling was utilized. The study group was recruited via snowballing that was started from the mentioned Chernobyl advocacy organizations, using the list of Soviet cities and towns with established levels of radio-contamination (IAEA, 1991) as an eligibility criterion. Respondents for the control group were contacted in different places of immigrants' gathering—retraining courses, shopping and entertainment centers, school meetings, etc.

Although both samples were formed on casual or ad hoc basis, interviewers (Russian-speaking graduate students of sociology) were instructed to recruit similar numbers of men and women and balance the groups by age (similar proportions of those aged 30–39, 40–49 and 50–59 years). The bottom age limit of 30 was chosen so that respondents in the Chernobyl group had been at least 18–19 years old at the time of the accident and were still in the age of active family formation at the time of the study. Another entry criterion was at least a three year tenure in Israel, so that the initial crisis of resettlement was behind our respondents and their interim social integration could be assessed. Respondents filled the questionnaire in the presence, and with the assistance, of interviewers. Response rates in the Chernobyl group was higher (over 85%), probably reflecting the personal importance of the topic for this group of immigrants. In the control group around 60% of those approached agreed to participate.

. . .

FINDINGS

Socio-demographics of the Sample

The characteristics of the study population reflected the general demographic and socio-economic profile of working age immigrants from the former Soviet Union (Table 36.1).

The comparison between the two groups of immigrants reveals significant similarity in their demographics and pre-emigration social background. Most were married, had the average of 1.6 children and belonged to the category of educated urban professionals or white-collar workers. The most striking change in their life as immigrants, after some 5–6 years in Israel, was occupational downgrading. Only one-third worked as professionals, and another 24% had skilled white-collar jobs, while the rest were in blue-collar occupations (33%) or unemployed. This pattern is typical for post-1989 Russian immigrants at large (Lithwick & Habib, 1996). Women and older immigrants of either gender experienced especially dramatic downward occupational mobility (Remennick, 1999). Looking at the current occupational profile of the two groups, one can notice that the share of professional and white-collar occupations in the Chernobyl group (26% and 19%) is significantly lower than in the comparison group (42% and 25%, respectively), while the share of unskilled jobs and unemployment is higher (in both cases, $P < 0.005$). Given the lack of a major difference in the pre-emigration education and occupational make up of the two groups, this finding points to the poorer occu-

pational adjustment of the immigrants from the Chernobyl-affected areas.

Social Mobility, Integration and General Well-being

The findings reported in this section are based on closed-ended questions, Likert-type and open-ended items (Table 36.2). As was expected, persons from the radiation-affected areas were generally doing worse as immigrants in Israel, whatever measures of accommodation were used. They had lower income and job satisfaction, as well as poorer housing conditions. They scored lower in self-rated knowledge of the Hebrew language, had fewer contacts and friends among the locals, and often tended to self-isolation within Russian-speaking community.

Many survivors were disappointed by the Israeli society generally and its 'unfriendly' attitudes towards the immigrants specifically, of which 'lack of interest in and support of Chernobyl survivors' was just one example. Negative feelings about Israel must have contributed to their lower motivation for improving Hebrew and more persistent search for professional jobs. In turn, the lack of occupational success further reinforced their grudge against the host society. As a result of this vicious circle, many respondents succumbed to their downward socio-economic mobility, after several years of futile attempts to make it in Israel. Although such moods and attitudes were found in both groups, they were certainly more common among Chernobyl survivors. Some of them explained their lack of success by the inherent social stigma of 'radiation-induced defectiveness' they expected to carry for their lifetime. This hidden stigma, of which most Israelis are oblivious (few know the details of the Chernobyl disaster, which cities were affected, etc.), was nevertheless very detrimental to our respondents' self-esteem and precluded them from social self-advancement. As expected, many respondents from the study group linked their poor adjustment in Israel to their impaired health.

Self-rated Health Status

Respondents marked their health problems using the list of 25 common chronic conditions. Most respondents from the study group reported poorer

Table 36.1   Socio-demographic Profiles of the Two Study Groups (%)

	Survivors (n = 180)	Others (n = 200)
Age		
30–39	34	31
40–49	36	34
50–59	30	35
Gender		
Men	46	44
Women	54	56
Marital status		
Married	70	74
Divorced or widowed	23	18
Single	7	8
Mean number of children	1.4	1.8
Tenure in Israel		
3–4 years	19	27
5–6 years	38	34
7 years or more	43	39
Places of origin in the FSU		
Capitals or large cities	44	48
Smaller cities and towns	49	50
Rural areas	7	2
Education (years of study)		
Secondary (10)	12	9
Technical (10–12)	28	22
Higher (13+)	60	69
Pre-emigration occupation		
Engineers, technicians and scientists	41	36
Teachers, doctors, nurses	21	25
Economists, accountants	14	17
Culture, journalism, the arts	10	15
White collar workers	14	7
Current occupation		
Professional	26	42
Skilled white-collar	19	25
Skilled blue-collar	23	16
Unskilled	21	10
Unemployed	11	7

general state of their health and a greater number of ailments, which typically had appeared or aggravated after the Chernobyl disaster. The composition of chronic morbidity was similar in both groups (with heart disease, hypertension and thyroidal dysfunction being most common) but the prevalence of all conditions was much higher among the survivors. Their ailments significantly hampered their daily functioning (Table 36.3).

Mental Health and Somatization

As was mentioned, the questionnaire included several general items on affective disorders, usually in the form of 5-point Likert scales. We were mainly interested in depression, cancer-related anxiety and somatization (i.e. somatic expression of mental disturbances). Depression was assessed via describing its common symptoms and asking if this state of mind occurred during the last year, whether it was

Table 36.2 Self-rated Indicators of Economic and Social Well-being (Means on 5-point Scales; all Differences Significant at P < 0.005 Level)

	Survivors (n = 180)	Others (n = 200)
Income (from very low to very high)	2.7	4.1
Housing conditions (from very poor to very good)	2.9	4.0
Hebrew language command (from very poor to fluent)	2.8	4.0
Job satisfaction (from very low to very high)	2.6	4.7
Satisfaction with children's life in Israel (from very low to very high)	3.8	4.6
Contacts/friends among Israelis (from none to many)	2.1	3.6
Extent to which respondent's pre-emigration expectations were met (from not at all to completely)	2.6	4.1

clinically diagnosed and treated, and to what extent depressive symptoms thwarted normal functioning of respondents. Cancer anxiety was measured by a composite index based on two items: (1) *How would you estimate your own risks for developing a malignant disease (from negligible to high)* and (2) *How often do you think about cancer as applied to you and your family members* (from never to very often). Somatization was assessed by several related items, of which the central one was: *"After you moved to Israel, did it happen that you consulted your doctor with bothering symptoms (the list of common symptoms enclosed) and, upon the series of medical tests, the doctor found no specific disease? Did your symptoms persist after that?"*

On all these scales, Chernobyl survivors scored significantly higher than other immigrants. While often being emotionally troubled, survivors did not seek psychological or psychiatric counseling more often than other immigrants (16% and 12%, respectively). Some statistically significant findings are presented in Table 36.4.

Utilization of Health Services and Patient Satisfaction

Several commonly used items were included in this questionnaire (Table 36.5).

As expected, Chernobyl survivors used more medical services, both conventional and alterna-

Table 36.3 Self-rated Health Status, Chronic Ailments and Daily Functioning (all Differences Significant at P < 0.005)

Item	Survivors (n = 180)	Others (n = 200)
State of health (5-point scale from very poor to excellent)	2.6	4.3
Most common chronic ailments (%)		
Heart disease	30	11
Hypertension	39	18
Thyroidal dysfunction	23	7
Diabetes	18	7
Asthma/chronic bronchitis	15	4
Gastro-intestinal disorders	13	7
Arthritis or rheumatism	11	6
Skin diseases	9	5
Migraine	10	4
Gynecol./urological diseases	9	3
Mean No of chronic conditions	2.3	0.6
Extent to which chronic morbidity limits daily functioning (5-point scale from not at all to very much)	2.4	0.8

Table 36.4   Indicators of Mental Health and Somatization (all Differences Significant at *P* < 0.005)

Item	Survivors (n = 180)	Others (n = 200)
Depression episode(s) during the last year (%)		
Self-reported	36	12
Clinically diagnosed	15	8
Anti-depressant medication (%)		
During the last year	17	5
Ever after immigration	26	12
Depression's interference with daily functioning (among those depressed) (5 points from not at all to strongly)	3.1	1.4
	(n = 58)	(n = 33)
Cancer anxiety (composite index from 1 to 5)	2.8	0.6
Somatization, % reporting:	44	21
One episode		
Recurrent episodes	27	9
Seeking professional help, % (counselor, psychiatrist, self-help groups)	16	12

tive. More survivors had a regular internist and the routine of preventive check-ups. While having more intense contact with the medical system, immigrants from the Chernobyl-affected areas were less satisfied with the quality of the services and providers' attitudes. As indicated by the open-ended item asking respondents to explain their opinion of Israeli health care, Chernobyl survivors were upset by the lack of sensitivity and effort on the part of providers who failed to meet their perceived special needs (e.g., more frequent screening tests, lifestyle advice).

Table 36.5   Selected Measures of Health Services Utilization and Satisfaction (Differences Significant at *P* < 0.005, Except Those Marked with "NS")

	Survivors (n = 180)	Others (n = 200)
Mean No of annual visits to:		
GP or internist	9.5	5.5
Gynecologist (for women)	2.7	0.7
Pediatrician (with children)	4.3	2.1
% of respondents reporting visits for preventive purposes:		
Annually	34	12
Once every few years	57	41
Seldom or never	13	47
% having a regular GP	69 ns	60 ns
Use of alternative medicine in Israel (%)		
Never	56	77
Once or twice	19 ns	21 ns
Several times	25	2
No of hospitalizations in Israel	0.7	0.3
Satisfaction with health services (5-point scale from low to high)		
GP or internist	3.2	4.4
Specialist care	3.1	4.7
Hospital experience	4.6 ns	4.4 ns
(for those reporting hospitalization)	(n = 43)	(n = 25)

Clinical encounters around psychosomatic symptoms were especially unpleasant for the survivors, whose suffering was not granted a medical label and hence ostensibly defined as malingering.

. . .

Correlation between Health Status and Social Integration in Israel

In line with our leading hypothesis, poorer physical and mental health was associated with lower levels of occupational and social integration in both groups of immigrants. Allowing for differences in age and education, Pearson's correlation coefficient r between the self-rated physical health and occupational success (measured by having a professional or white-collar job) was equal to 0.31; r between the composite index of mental health (based on depression and somatization items) and occupational success was 0.35 (both significant at $p < 0.01$, two-tailed test). Since Chernobyl survivors as a group scored worse by most indicators of self-rated health, this factor must have seriously compromised both their practical achievements and their general sense of well-being in the new country. The opposite causality (i.e., the deterioration of their health as a result of unemployment, poor living conditions and other immigration-related stressors) cannot be excluded, but it can hardly explain all the observed differences between the groups. Most survivors dated their ailments back to the late 1980s and *arrived* in Israel being less healthy. In the qualitative analysis of the open-ended items, the lingering sense of stigma, self-victimization and difficulties in solving daily problems were expressed more often by Chernobyl survivors than by other immigrants. As a 50 year old woman from Gomel (the most contaminated city in Belarus) bitterly pointed out, "The shadow of Chernobyl will hang over our lives forever, you cannot run from it—to Israel, America or elsewhere. When your blood and bone are poisoned by radiation you become different, and somehow it shows. There is this morbid spirit of hopelessness around you. Chernobyl victims live here under a double stigma—as Russian immigrants and as radio-zombies. . ."

DISCUSSION

. . .

This study contributes to two current research streams. One is the analysis of psychosocial and health effects of cumulative adversity—in our case, the combination of past radiation exposure with the pressures of immigration. At the same time, the case under study facilitates understanding of long-term systemic consequences of radiation exposure for survivors of nuclear accidents. First, it shows that, even many years after leaving the hazardous area, the shadow of self-victimization and health anxiety precludes the survivors from effective pursuit of their life goals. When faced by dramatic lifestyle changes and challenges of resettlement, Chernobyl survivors manifested lower levels of accommodation and achievement. As expected, the past traumas and current hardships of resettlement acted synergistically, resulting in chronic distress and social maladjustment. This trend was most vividly expressed by the lower share of Chernobyl survivors (many of whom had higher education and good professional record) who worked in professional or white-collar jobs, 4–6 years after moving to Israel. The extent of their social integration in the host society—as measured by the Hebrew language command and numbers of local contacts/friends—was also lower than in the rest of the Russian immigrants. Chernobyl-area immigrants were also less satisfied with their children's lives in Israel, suggesting a possible carry-over of the victimization moods on to the younger members of these families. A few follow-up studies of Chernobyl survivors in the Soviet successor states have also shown their lower propensity for adaptation to dramatic changes of the economic and social environment under market reforms (Bebeshko, 1996; Mironov, Kalmykova, Tereshenko, & Kogan, 1998).

Our findings fully support the assertion that psychological trauma and lingering radio-phobia experienced by survivors may emerge as a more potent source of morbidity and social maladjustment than direct physical hazards of radiation (Havenaar, 1996; Cwikel, 1997). While the perceived state of health and daily functioning of the immigrants from the contaminated areas were significantly worse than in other immigrants, in practice it is hard to disentangle the relative roles of radiation-induced somatic conditions and stress-related psychosomatic disorders.

Seen from another angle, this study offers some insights about the relations between victims of mass disasters and health care systems. The fact that survivors, including those who had not suffered direct damage, tend to seek medical care more often than others, has been well-documented (WHO, 1995; Whitcomb & Sage, 1997). In our study too, immigrants from the Chernobyl area reported more intense contacts with doctors at all levels of the system (outpatient and hospital). Compared to other immigrants, they also demonstrated a more regular and proactive approach to preventive matters, probably reflecting their former special status in the Soviet medical system. Yet, their satisfaction with the available services (other than hospital) was rather moderate. This disappointment led many survivors to seek alternative health care, often provided in Israel by former Russian doctors and healers (Remennick & Ottenstein, 1998).

As elsewhere, mainstream Israeli epidemiologists and physicians share rigid definitions of radiation-induced diseases and fail to respond to a broader range of nonspecific and psychosomatic health problems experienced by survivors. Given the psychosocial nature of many complaints, it is also crucial to offer survivors easy access to counseling and various outlets of self-help. In our case, these services ought to be provided in immigrants' native language and in a culturally relevant mode. The fact that only 16% of the immigrants from the Chernobyl area ever addressed Israeli psychological or psychiatric services (while about two-thirds reported recurrent or chronic emotional problems) points to the failure of these services to reach Chernobyl survivors and alleviate their crises. Admittedly, a special effort of social and medical services is needed here, given the stigma of mental illness and suspicious attitudes of most former Soviets to the mental health establishment inherited from their past (Zilber & Lerner, 1996).

Finally, a note on the gender aspect of our findings is due. Since in most sets of analysis the differences between Chernobyl survivors and other immigrants were much stronger than those between men and women within the groups, it was decided not to split the tables also by sex. However, some gender differences still surfaced, including more dramatic occupational down-grading of women in both groups, previously reported in Israeli studies among Russian immigrants (Remennick, 1999). While self-ratings of health and mean numbers of chronic ailments in men and women within the groups were rather similar, women more often used preventive health services, psychological or social counseling and alternative treatments of psychosomatic problems. These findings are also in line with known and fairly universal gender differences in health care use (Lorber, 1997). Yet, at odds with the established patterns, the prevalence of emotional distress, anxiety and somatization was similar in men and women. Moreover, our impression was that women from the Chernobyl group manifested greater resilience and propensity for social adjustment than their male counterparts. Women's overall satisfaction with their and their children's life in Israel was also higher and they often stressed positive aspects of their life in Israel, while men tended to mourn their loss of social status and economic assets in the FSU.

To conclude, this study sheds more light on the long-term ramifications of nuclear disasters for the survivors. Since many survivors experience resettlement (inside or outside their country) with concomitant dramatic changes in social and cultural contexts, the experiences of the Russian immigrants from Chernobyl-affected areas described in this study may be of a broad relevance. On the practical side, it is important for the future studies that local health authorities in various host countries keep the record of Chernobyl survivors to make possible representative sampling and follow-up projects. Such population and health registers can also facilitate better preventive services for the survivors and faster clinical application of new research that can mitigate their ailments.

REFERENCES

Bebeshko, V. K. (1996). Psychosocial status and psychosomatic health of adolescent victims of the Chernobyl disaster. *Public Health Reviews, 24*(3–4), 350.

CBS—Central Bureau of Statistics of Israel (1998). Annual Statistical Abstract. Jerusalem: CBS Press.

Cwikel, J. (1997). Comments on the psychosocial aspects of the international conference on radiation and health. *Environmental Health Perspectives, 105*(Suppl. 6), 1607–1608.

Cwikel, J., Abdelgani, A., Goldsmith, J. R., Quastel, M., & Yevelson, I. I. (1997a). Two-year follow-up study of stress-related disorders among immigrants to Israel from the Chernobyl area. *Environmental Health Perspectives, 105*(Suppl. 6), 1545–1550.

Cwikel, J., Goldsmith, J. R., Kordysh, E., Quastel, M., & Abdelgani, A. (1997b). Blood pressure among immigrants from areas affected by the Chernobyl disaster. *Public Health Reviews, 25,* 317–335.

Davidson, J.R.T. (Ed.) (1993). *Posttraumatic stress disorder: DSM-IV and beyond.* Washington: American Psychiatric Press.

Gil, A. G., & Vega, W. A. (1996). Two different worlds: Acculturation stress and adaptation among Cuban and Nicaraguan families. *Journal of Social and Personal Relationships, 13*(3), 435–456.

Havenaar, J.M. (1996). *After Chernobyl: Psychological factors affecting health after a nuclear disaster.* Ph.D. thesis, Utrecht University, Utrecht.

IAEA—International Atomic Energy Agency (1991). *The international Chernobyl project: An overview. Assessment of radiological consequences and evaluation of protective measures.* Report by an International Advisory Committee. IAEA, Vienna.

Kordysh, E., Goldsmith, J. R., Quastel, M., Poljak, S., Merkin, L., & Gorodischer, R. (1995). Health effects in a casual sample of immigrants to Israel from areas contaminated by the Chernobyl explosion. *Environmental Health Perspectives, 103*(10), 2–9.

Lipson, J. G. (1993). Afghan refugees in California: Mental health issues. *Issues in Mental Health Nursing, 14*(4), 411–423.

Lithwick, I., & Habib, J. (1996). *Absorption of immigrants from the former Soviet Union into the labor force.* Jerusalem: JDC-Brookdale Institute of Gerontology and Human Development (Hebrew).

Lorber, J. (1997). *Gender and the social construction of illness.* New York, London: Sage.

Martic, B. S., Spoljar, V. S. M., & Rudan, V. (1996). Anthropological and psychodynamic characteristics of family life of displaced persons and refugees. An example from the Island of Hvar (Croatia). *Collegium Antropologicum, 20*(2), 301–308.

Mironov, V. A., Kalmykova, Z. N., Tereshenko, & A. I., Kogan, P. P. (1998). Social and economic adjustment of migrants from Chernobyl-affected areas 10 years after the resettlement. In Golub', V. V., & Kuz'menkova L. I. (Eds.), *Problems of internal migration in Russia.* Novosibirsk: Academic Press (in Russian).

Quastel, M. R., Kramer, G. H., & Goldsmith, J. R., et al. (1995). Radiocesium body burdens in immigrants to Israel from areas of the Ukraine, Belarus, and Russia near Chernobyl. *Health Physics, 68,* 102–112.

Remennick, L. I., & Ottenstein, N. (1998). Reaction of new Soviet immigrants to primary health care services in Israel. *International Journal of Health Services, 28*(3), 555–574.

Remennick, L. I. (1999). Women with a Russian accent in Israel. On the gender aspects of immigration. *The European Journal of Women's Studies, 6*(4), 441–461.

Tran, T. V., & Ferullo, D. N. (1997). Indochinese mental health in North America: Measures, status and treatments. *Journal of Sociology and Social Welfare, 24*(2), 3–20.

Turner, R. J., & Lloyd, D. L. (1995). Lifetime traumas and mental health: The significance of cumulative adversity. *Journal of Health and Social Behavior, 36*(4), 360–376.

Viel, J. F., Curbakova, E., & Dzerve, B., et al. (1997). Risk factors for long-term mental and psychosomatic distress of Latvian Chernobyl liquidators. *Environmental Health Perspectives, 105*(Suppl. 6), 1539–1544.

Whitcomb, R.C., Jr., & Sage, M. (1997). Nuclear reactor incidents. In: E.K. Noji (Ed.). *The public health consequences of disasters.* London: Oxford University Press.

WHO—World Health Organization (1995). *Health consequences of the Chernobyl accident. Results of the IPHECA pilot projects and related national programmes.* Geneva: WHO.

Zilber, N., & Lerner, Y. (1996). Psychological distress among recent immigrants from the former Soviet Union to Israel. I. Correlates of level of distress. *Psychological Medicine, 26,* 493–501.

37 PARTNER NOTIFICATION IN CONTEXT: SWEDISH AND ZAMBIAN EXPERIENCES

Elisabeth A. Faxelid and Kristina M. Ramstedt

The previous selection and several others have brought up the topic of stigma. This selection focuses on sexually transmitted infections, a health concern that tends to be highly stigmatized due to cultural tensions and ambiguities about sexuality, gender, and power. Like other diseases, sexually transmitted infections are not evenly patterned across space or across social categories such as gender and class. They are caused by a variety of persistent, emerging, and reemerging pathogens that take advantage of opportunities for transmission and may change their characteristics in response to environmental conditions (see Part II; selections 32, 34). This selection aims to improve the effectiveness of social means of interrupting transmission and preventing health complications of sexually transmitted infections. It illuminates factors that facilitate or impede the notification of sexual partners and seeks ways of improving notification rates.

Partner notification is a central component of the biomedical approach to disease control, and like the notion of compliance discussed in previous selections, it is one that may tend to bring attention to individual failures rather than larger contexts that may affect its feasibility. To illustrate, this selection compares two countries with similar population sizes and numbers of clinics dedicated to sexually transmitted infections, but different resources and approaches to partner notification. The details regarding diagnostic equipment, personnel and patient loads, reporting and registration systems, availability of medicines, and infrastructure for locating people show very clearly that the same biomedical standards cannot be met in all settings, due to material and other constraints (see selection 34). Moreover, particular sociocultural contexts may make compulsory notification or provider referral acceptable in one place but unthinkable in another. Even in Sweden, where conditions are highly favorable to partner notification and patient confidentially is ensured, stigma continues to induce some people to circumvent state health services and remain outside the notification process.

Questions to keep in mind

What are the advantages and disadvantages of patient referral, provider referral, and conditional referral?

What are some similarities and differences between the two countries in terms of types of common sexually transmitted infections, organization of health services, and referral practices?

Why do you think people in Sweden tend to accept compulsory notification?

Why might the time period used in determining which sexual partners to notify vary from one individual or social context to another?

Source: Reprinted from Social Science and Medicine, Vol. 44, Faxelid, E. A. and K. M. Ramstedt, "Partner Notification in Context: Swedish and Zambian Experiences," Pages 1239–1243, Copyright (1997), with permission from Elsevier.

INTRODUCTION

Sexually transmitted diseases (STDs) are a global health problem. They are the most common group of notifiable infectious diseases in many countries. In the Western world the incidence of classical bacterial STDs such as gonorrhoea, syphilis and chancroid has decreased. These diseases have been replaced by a second generation of STDs, caused by Chlamydia trachomatis, Herpes genitalis, human papilloma virus (HPV) and HIV. Bacterial STDs are still a considerable problem in many developing countries where the second generation of STDs has also entered the scene [1,2].

Partner notification is a public health activity to notify, counsel, examine and treat sexual partners of STD patients. The purpose of partner notification is to decrease the frequency of STD in society by breaking the chain of transmission and to prevent reinfections and complications in the patient and his/her sexual partners [3, 4]. Strategies for partner notification are *patient referral,* where the patient informs his/her partner(s), *provider referral,* where the health care provider informs the partner(s), and *conditional referral,* a combination of patient and provider referral. Written information, a so-called contact slip, is sometimes sent or handed over to the partner(s).

Partner notification has been a component of STD control programmes in industrialized countries for a long time [5–8]. There are few studies on partner notification in less affluent countries and the available study results show a poor outcome in form of number of partners traced [9,10]. This is partly explained by the lack of resources, particularly shortage of staff and facilities, and an unwillingness of the patients to cooperate due to social and cultural reasons [11].

In 1990, a World Health Organization (WHO) study group[†] stated that partner notification should be voluntary, confidential and only undertaken when appropriate support services are available to index patient and partners. Patient referral should be the natural starting point, while provider referral should only be used for selected index patients and partners [4].

Partner notification is considered an important part of the biomedical approach to preventing STD. For most people, however, it is a difficult and sensitive task to notify and inform sexual partners. Norms and values determine if and how patients notify their partners. Therefore, knowledge from medical as well as social sciences is needed in the analysis of the process. The authors of this paper have different professional backgrounds[‡] and use perspectives which complement each other.

The aims of this paper are to communicate experiences gained from studies on partner notification in Sweden and Zambia and emphasize the need for a contextualized approach to partner notification.

STD EPIDEMIOLOGY AND HEALTH CARE STRUCTURE

Sweden

Sweden has a population of nine million. The most common STDs in Sweden are chlamydial infection and HPV. In 1988 37,928 cases of chlamydia were reported. Many resources have been put into the health care system to improve STD management including partner notification. There are approximately 50 STD clinics with specially trained physicians and counsellors/social workers in Sweden. Patients with STD are also treated in many other settings, however. Every physician who suspects a patient to have an STD has access to relevant diagnostic equipment.

In 1994 13,592 cases of chlamydia were reported. Approximately 300 cases of gonorrhoea and 100 cases of syphilis are reported each year. Approximately 350 people are reported with HIV each year [12]. Most of these patients are infected abroad, which means that the possibility of find-

---

[†]This study group consisted of STD experts from England, the U.S.S.R., Jamaica, Chile, Sri Lanka, the U.S., Tanzania and Papua, New Guinea.

[‡]E. Faxelid is a teacher in midwifery with a licentiate degree from studies on STD in Sweden and Zambia; K. Ramstedt is a social worker with a Ph.D in STD epidemiology and contact tracing in Sweden.

ing the source of infection is limited. However, partner notification still has its role to limit the spread of the infection within the country.

Sweden has had an STD legislation since the beginning of the 20th Century. According to the law, each person who suspects an STD is obliged to seek health care. Partner notification is compulsory. There is also a compulsory reporting system regarding chlamydial infections, chancroid, gonorrhoea, syphilis and HIV/AIDS. All STD cases are reported with a special code to ensure confidentiality. The treating physician is responsible for asking the patient about sexual contacts and ensuring that all reported contacts are examined. Confidentiality is considered a cornerstone in the partner notification process and a patient's identity is never revealed to a partner.

Zambia

Sexually transmitted diseases, including HIV, are a major public health problem in Zambia, where the population is approximately eight million. These diseases and related complications are the third most common cause for hospital attendance [13]. Up to 10% of outpatient visits are related to STD. This might even be an underestimation since STDs are not included among those infectious diseases that have to be reported according to legislation. Between 13 and 30% of pregnant women and as many as 50–60% of STD patients are found to be seropositive for HIV [14].

In 1980 the Zambian government launched an STD programme. One component was the training of clinical officers in STD management. Today approximately 50 clinics with at least one specially trained clinical officer are established around the country. However, many STD cases are treated outside these clinics, in health centres, by private practitioners and traditional healers [15,16].

The diagnosis is made from the patient's history and clinical observations as many health centres do not have, or have but do not use, diagnostic equipment [17]. The STD control programme has produced guidelines for the management of STD patients [18]. These guidelines include flowcharts starting with a symptom. Partner notification is recommended. Some clinics practice the rule "no

partner no treatment." This is not sanctioned by the STD programme since the patients might as a result seek treatment elsewhere. Patient referral is the most commonly used method to notify partners. Patients are told to bring only one partner. Sometimes a contact slip is used. This is always handed over by the patient.

METHODS

Nine studies on partner notification in Sweden and Zambia are reviewed [19–27]. . . .

FINDINGS AND DISCUSSION

STD Legislation

Partner notification is compulsory in Sweden. The STD legislation is thus not fully in line with the WHO's recommendations that it be voluntary. The ethics that justify the coercion is that protection of the society is more important than the freedom of the individual. Advantages and disadvantages with compulsory partner notification have been discussed in Sweden. However, most people seem to accept the idea of compulsory prevention for the good of society. After chlamydial infections were included in the STD legislation in 1988, fewer partners refused examination [21]. The only change in management was that the health care worker told the patient that she/he had to make sure that all partners attended for examination and information.

There is no STD legislation in Zambia today. Although partner notification is recommended in the STD guidelines, it is not compulsory. If partner notification was made compulsory, it would require a registration/reporting system which does not exist today. Furthermore, there are cultural structures that refrain men in Zambia from informing their partners about STD. Men, who participated in focus group discussions, expressed fear of being brought to court by the wife and her family for bringing an STD into the home. Therefore, some men treated their STD problems without informing their wives [26].

Quality of Care

Sweden has put a lot of resources into STD/HIV prevention and health care. This means that a person who enters the STD health care system will meet skilled staff who wish to give the patient all the time needed as well as access to adequate diagnostic equipment. Pharmaceuticals are available, free of charge. Furthermore, all STD clinics have one or more specially trained counsellor to support and help the patients.

Despite the well-functioning system in Sweden, not all sexual partners are identified [19–22], e.g. due to lack of information about the partners' identities. This is true for Zambia as well [23, 24]. However, there are additional reasons that partners are not treated in Zambia. Lack of counselling and insufficient information to the STD patients about partner notification are examples [23, 25]. Individual counselling of men for 10–20 minutes in combination with written information to their partners significantly increased the number of partners traced and treated [24]. Other studies have also shown that if more time and effort are spent on counselling the index patients, more infected partners are identified [28–30]. However, most health care providers in Zambia are not trained in communication and counselling.

The lack of privacy and confidentiality at the Zambian health centre forced some people who suspected an STD to seek care from private practitioners or traditional healers [26]. Those providers seldom asked the patients to bring their partners, which was considered to be an advantage, according to the group participants. In Sweden too; many STD patients are diagnosed outside the STD clinics e.g. by private physicians, gynaecologists and family doctors. The reason for not seeking care at the STD clinic might be the same in Sweden as in Zambia.

Shortage of appropriate drugs at the Zambian clinics forces patients to buy expensive drugs at the pharmacy. This affects partner notification since men, rather than women, are supposed to pay for their partners' drugs [26]. Furthermore, some health care providers expressed negative feelings towards STD patients [27], which might influence the patient's compliance with partner notification.

Provider Referral

In Sweden, patients are offered provider referral if they do not wish to contact their partners themselves. Most partners are, however, traced through patient referral [20, 22].

In one of the Zambian studies, the patients said that they would not be able to inform as many as 43% of the partners they actually knew by name and address [23]. Theoretically, these partners could be traced through provider referral. But provider referral is difficult to carry out in settings without telephones and reliable addresses. The health care provider would have to make a personal visit to the partner's house, flat, or working place which would raise curiosity among neighbours, relatives and workmates. Confidentiality would be difficult to maintain. Those STD patients who said they could not inform their partners were offered provider referral. Since no-one accepted the offer, provider referral might not be an appropriate strategy in Zambia [24].

Partner notification, especially provider referral, is time-consuming. Time needs to be spent on building a trustful relationship between counsellor and patient, and in most health care settings, providers do not have enough time for provider referral. If time is scarce, it might be better to use patient referral in combination with some kind of contact slip [31].

Contact Slips

In Sweden contact slips are used if the patient so wishes. The letter is either mailed or handed over by the patient. The partner is informed about the disease but also that she/he is obliged to come for examination according to the law.

When contact slips are used in Zambia they are always handed over by the patient. Since there is no STD law the information is limited to advice on the importance of seeking health care to reduce the risk of complications. Handing out contact slips is an inexpensive strategy that has been found to be useful in Zambia and Zimbabwe [24, 32]. The use of contact slips in settings where some people are illiterate might, however, pose ethical problems since a literate friend or relative might be asked to read the information to the person receiving the letter. Some patients expressed fear that the information could be used as evidence in a court situation [26]. To avoid this risk, explicit confirmation of an STD might be omitted.

Time Period for Tracing Partners

In Zambia it is common, at least for men, to have more than one regular partner simultaneously.

Few STD patients are, however, asked by the health care provider to bring more than one partner [23, 25]. A study from Sweden showed that if only the current partner was traced, as many as 41% of the infected partners would have been missed [20]. This shows the importance of encouraging not only the regular partner(s) but also the occasional partners to come for treatment.

There is limited work done to standardize how far back in time (time period) partners should be traced. The optimal period during which most infected partners are to be found varies from STD to STD and depends, for example, on the time between the infection and the onset of symptoms (incubation period). The time period needs to be contextualized according to the disease and to what is feasible in specific settings and for different individuals. Examples from Sweden and Zambia could illustrate this. In Sweden most clinics use a time period of three months for chlamydial infections. Since many people with Chlamydia trachomatis are asymptomatic, partner notification could be seen as a screening method to find partners at risk. When appropriate laboratory facilities are available only the partners that are found to be infected need to be treated. In Zambia, where there are no laboratory facilities to confirm a chlamydial infection, all identified partners should be treated. In Sweden the tracing process for patients with gonorrhoea stops when one negative partner, whom the patient had sexual contact with before the suspected source of infection, is found. The time period is thus different from individual to individual. This approach requires laboratory facilities and is not possible to use in Zambia. In Sweden, a patient with trichomoniasis is given treatment and a prescription to bring to her/his regular partner. Compulsory partner notification is not carried out since this type of infection is not included in the STD legislation. In the Zambian setting it is important to recognize that there might be several regular partners, wives and girlfriends who need to be treated. The patients in Zambia are not given drugs/prescriptions to bring to their partner(s), as the risk that the drugs may be sold to someone else or saved for another time is considered too high. Furthermore, it would be difficult to have different time periods for various STDs in Zambia since the diagnosis is made from clinical observations and often not confirmed by laboratory tests. A syndromic approach, which means that patients with STD symptoms are treated for more than one STD at the same time, is recommended in the STD control programme [18]. We recommend that three months should be taken as the time period for all STD patients in Zambia. This would, according to what is known, cover most partners at risk [7, 33, 34].

CONCLUSION

Despite many resources, it is not possible to notify all sexual partners of a patient in Sweden due to lack of information about the partners' identities and the patient's unwillingness to cooperate. In Zambia there are additional problems, such as lack of time and basic resources in the health care settings, which make partner notification even more difficult. Furthermore, social and economic factors deter some patients in Zambia from informing their partners. Provider referrals seem to be a good complementary strategy in Sweden but are not feasible in Zambia, where it is necessary to rely on patient referral. Contact slips with culturally relevant and sensitive information could be useful tools to increase the number of partners traced and treated both in Sweden and Zambia. The time period from which to notify partners needs to be adjusted according to the context. Finally, health care providers in Zambia need more training in communication and counselling to be able to improve the outcome of partner notification.

NOTES

1. Aral, S. O. and Holmes, K. K. (1990) Epidemiology of sexual behavior and sexually transmitted diseases. In *Sexually Transmitted Diseases*, eds K. K. Holmes *et al.*, pp. 19–36. McGraw-Hill, New York.
2. De Schryver, A. and Meheus, A. (1990) Epidemiology of sexually transmitted diseases: the global picture. *Bulletin of the World Health Organization* 68, 639–654.
3. World Health Organization (WHO) (1989) *Consensus Statement from Consultation on Partner Notification for Preventing HIV Transmission.* WHO, Geneva.
4. World Health Organization (WHO) (1991) *Management of Patients with Sexually Transmitted Diseases. Report from a WHO Study Group.* WHO Technical Report Series 810, WHO, Geneva.
5. Wigfield, A. S. (1972) 27 years of uninterrupted tracing: the Tyneside scheme. *British Journal of Venereal Disease* 48, 37–50.
6. Rothenberg, R. B. and Potterat, J. J. (1990) Strategies for management of sex partners. In *Sexually Transmitted*

Diseases, eds K. K. Holmes *et al.*, pp. 1081–1086. Mc-Graw-Hill, New York.

7. Potterat, J. J., Meheus, A. and Gallwey, J. (1991) Partner notification: operational considerations. *International Journal of STD and AIDS* 2, 411–415.

8. Oxman, A. D. *et al.* (1994) Partner notification for sexually transmitted diseases: an overview of the evidence. *Canadian Journal of Public Health* 85(1), 41–47.

9. Asuzu, A. C., Ogunbanjo, B. O., Ajayi, I. O., Oyediran, A. B. O. and Osoba, A. O. (1984) Contact tracing in the control of STD in Ibadan, Nigeria. *British Journal of Venereal Disease* 60, 114–116.

10. Jethá, C. and Falcato, J. (1991) Factors influencing simplified STD contact tracing in a Mozambican health centre. Paper presented at the Seventh Regional Conference on STD, Lusaka, Zambia.

11. Rotowa, N. A., Ajayi, I. O. and Osoba, A. O. (1986) Casual contacts of the infective type—an infective pool of gonorrhoea in a developing country. *African Journal of STD* 0, 16–18.

12. Smittskyddsinstitutet (1994) *Statistical Report.* Smittskyddsinstitutet, Stockholm.

13. Hira, S. K. (1986) Sexually transmitted diseases—a menace to mothers and children. *World Health Forum* 7, 243–247.

14. World Health Organization (1992) Global programme on AIDS, HIV sentinel surveillance. *Weekly Epidemiology Record*, 67, 221–227.

15. Sajiwandani, J. and Baboo, K. (1987) Sexually transmitted diseases in Zambia. *Journal of Research in Social Health* 107, 183–186.

16. Bond, V. A. and Ndubani, P. (1993) *Community Capacity to Prevent, Manage and Survive HIV/AIDS. Indicators of Health in Chiawa.* Working Paper No. 3, University of Hull/University of Zambia/Karolinska Institutet, London.

17. Hanson, S., Sunkutu, R. M. and Höjer, B. (1993) STD control in Central Province, Zambia. Would an integrated approach change the situation? Poster presented at the Eighth International Conference on AIDS in Africa and Eighth African Conference on Sexually Transmitted Diseases, Marrakech, Marocko.

18. Ministry of Health, Zambia (1991) *Sexually Transmitted Diseases (STD) Guide-lines for Diagnosis and Management.* Ministry of Health, Lusaka, Zambia.

19. Ramstedt, K., Forssman, L. and Giesecke, J. (1991) Epidemiologic characteristics of two different populations of women with Chlamydia trachomatis infection and their male partners. *Sexually Transmitted Diseases* 18, 205–210.

20. Skoglösa, I., Lindgren, E. and Lundberg, M. (1993) *Projekt STD-SYD.* National Institute of Public Health, Stockholm.

21. Ramstedt, K., Forssman, L. and Johannisson, G. (1991) Contact tracing in the control of genital Chlamydia trachomatis infection. *International Journal of STD and AIDS* 2, 116–118.

22. Faxelid, E. and Krantz, I. (1993) Experiences of disease and treatment among chlamydia patients. *Scandinavian Journal of Caring Science* 7, 169–173.

23. Faxelid, E., Ndulo, J., Ahlberg, B. M. and Krantz, I. (1994) Behaviour, knowledge and reactions concerning sexually transmitted diseases: implications for partner notification in urban Lusaka. *East African Medical Journal* 71, 118–121.

24. Faxelid, E., Tembo, G., Ndulo, J. and Krantz, I. (1996) Individual counselling of STD patients—a way to improve partner notification in the Zambian setting? *Sexually Transmitted Disease* 23, 289–292.

25. Ndulo, J., Faxelid, E. and Krantz, I. (1995) Quality of care and sexually transmitted diseases in Zambia. The patients' perspective. *East African Medical Journal* 72, 641–644.

26. Tembo, G., Tembo, E. and Faxelid, E. (1993) Factors influencing health seeking behaviour of STD patients. Focus group discussions with patients attending a health care centre in Lusaka. Paper presented at the Second Workshop on HIV/AIDS Prevention in Africa, Lusaka, Zambia.

27. Faxelid, E., Ahlberg, B. M. and Krantz, I. (submitted) Quality of STD care in an urban Zambian setting. The providers' perspective.

28. Mulenga, D., Msiska, R., Sichone, M., Raja, S. and Sipatunyana, J. (1995) Maternal syphilis screening programme in Lusaka—urban Zambia: can partner notification be improved? Poster presented at the Ninth International Conference on Aids and STD in Africa, Kampala, Uganda.

29. Potterat, J. J., Phillips, L., Rothenberg, R. B. and Darrow, W. W. (1980) Gonococcal pelvic inflammatory disease: case-finding observations. *American Journal of Obstetrics and Gynecology* 138, 1101–1104.

30. Capinsky, T. Z. and Urbanczyk, J. (1970) Value of reinterviewing in contact tracing. *British Journal of Venereal Disease* 46, 130–140.

31. Parra, W., Drotman, D. P., Siegel, K., Esteves, K. and Baker, T. (1990) Patient counseling and behavior modification. In *Sexually Transmitted Diseases*, eds K. K. Holmes *et al.*, pp. 1057–1068. McGraw-Hill, New York.

32. Winfield, J. and Latif, A. S. (1985) Tracing contacts of persons with sexually transmitted diseases in a developing country. *Sexually Transmitted Disease* 12, 5–7.

33. Phillips, L., Potterat, J. J., Rothenberg, R. B., Pratts, C. and King, R. D. (1980) Focused interviewing in gonorrhoea control. *American Journal of Public Health* 70, 705–708.

34. Starcher, E. T., Kramer, M. A., Carlota-Orduna, B. and Lundberg, D. F. (1983) Establishing efficient interview periods for gonorrhoea patients. *American Journal of Public Health* 73, 1381–1384.

38 ERASMUS, SYPHILIS, AND THE ABUSE OF STIGMA

Christopher J. M. Whitty

In contrast to the more data-driven selections presented so far, this is an essay written from the perspective of a practicing physician in Blantyre, Malawi. Many of Whitty's points resonate with those raised in other selections, such as the tendency for people to blame outsiders or foreigners for grave health problems (see selections 23, 32, and 34) or to deny their existence (see selection 35). Whitty distinguishes between stigmatizing a behavior pattern and stigmatizing individuals suffering from sickness or medical problems and shows how in some cases the former may be a justifiable and successful public health strategy. On the other hand, to demonize people as disease transmitters is not likely ever to be helpful. It causes greater suffering in the sick and their loved ones and blinds people to the fact that the disease is transmitted by ordinary people and not just the deviants described by moralists and some health authorities.

This selection indicates how important it is to look objectively at the concept of stigma and not assume that it has only one meaning and one impact. This lesson comes through an historical example and an ancient piece of wisdom brought to bear on an epidemic in a vastly different time and place.

Questions to keep in mind

When might it be helpful to stigmatize a particular behavior pattern?

What is the difference between stigmatizing behavior and stigmatizing individuals who are sick?

In the case of sexually transmitted infections, at what point does stigmatizing a behavior pattern change from being useful for impeding transmission to interfering with attempts to stop the spread of the disease?

How might working with a highly stigmatized disease and patient population pose ethical problems for health professionals?

A man who has never had syphilis, wrote the devout Catholic humanist Erasmus in 1516, could be considered *ignobilis et rusticans*—loosely translatable as a bit of a country bumpkin.[1] He was writing at a time when a terrible new sexually transmitted disease was devastating his continent, and his flippant attitude has shocked pious historians ever since. It was certainly in stark contrast to the stern lectures from most of the political, medical, and religious leaders then and now; then and now from a public-health perspective he was taking absolutely the right line. In this continent of Africa, facing a sexually transmitted disease even more catastrophic than syphilis was to Europe in the 16th century, we have much to learn from this most upright of religious thinkers. AIDS is destroying the economies here, and more than decimating the populations—the destruction to societies cannot be overstated. Reactions to this crisis have been entirely natural, often hysterical, and largely counter-productive. The problem comes from a muddled understanding of the uses, and abuses, of stigmatising certain behaviour as a public-health message.

The near-automatic response of moral leaders down the years to sexually transmitted diseases is either to ignore their existence or to go in for rousing denunciations of the wickedness of certain members of society who transmit this filthy disease by their immoral ways. For tackling AIDS

Source: Whitty, C. J. M. 1999. "Erasmus, Syphilis, and the Abuse of Stigma." Reprinted with permission from Elsevier *(The Lancet,* 1999, Vol. 354 No. 9196, pages 2147–2148).

many of our political leaders in Africa and elsewhere have taken the first line, which is inexcusable, or at best acknowledged HIV exists but implied it is a "foreign" problem. This attitude is not new, of course; again taking the example of syphilis, the British initially referred to the French Pox or the Spanish disease (depending who was more out of favour), the French called it the Neopolitan disease, and so on. The surprisingly common belief that even spending time with foreigners causes people to contract unpleasant social diseases may be misplaced, but is not always unhelpful. At an individual level it sometimes allows people to get round the stigma of disease. On hearing a friend has HIV people here will nod wisely and say "of course, doctor, he was once in Mozambique," in much the same way as relative of a Vietnamese patient can point knowingly to the trip to Cambodia, and British patients will remember that American or German boyfriend. Blaming foreigners can occasionally provide a smokescreen behind which real issues can be discussed. Blaming the immoral ways of those who spread the disease, which is in a sense more in keeping with the facts, is far more destructive.

Politicians, who seldom like bad news, may have tried to ignore the issue or blame it on outsiders. By contrast, most religious and other moral leaders here stated clearly there is a problem from early in the epidemic, although some (particularly senior members of the Catholic Church) have had difficulties, partly because to acknowledge that this is one of the most important challenges for their congregations would raise awkward questions about their attitude to issues such as barrier contraceptives. The majority of those not in the religious hierarchy have, however, tackled the issue with commendable force. The message from pulpits in churches and mosques of every denomination is remarkable for its consistency, simplicity, and logical force. Viewed as a public-health message it is extremely powerful, and largely wrong. Complete abstinence is they say (correctly) the only 100% safe way to avoid the disease. There are wicked people who do not know they have the disease always on the lookout to prey on the innocent, and others who are actually going out deliberately to infect as many as possible. The solution is clear: with a bit of help from on high, stick to the tried

and tested formula Nice Girls Say No until marriage and you will be fine.

The drawback of this logically flawless scheme is that in the heat of the moment nice girls often say yes, and nice boys are generally no better. They do so feeling safe in the knowledge that HIV is a disease passed on by wicked ungodly people who hang around the bars, take drugs, and are clearly on the road to hell. The pleasant man or woman from a good family in the pew next door, pillar of the church or mosque, and clearly intent on a serious romantic relationship is definitely not the sort of person all the priests, newspapers, and posters in the mission hospital are talking about.

Public health is not a branch of morality, and should attempt to protect the health of as many people as possible by the most effective means available. Taking a stern moral line can sometimes be highly effective. We should differentiate sharply here between stigmatising a behaviour pattern, which can often be justified on public-health grounds, and stigmatising an individual with a medical problem (say alcoholism or drug addiction), which is almost always inappropriate and unhelpful. Any doctor who claims we should never use stigma to try to back up a public-health message is being profoundly naïve, and there are many examples where it has worked excellently as part of an overall strategy. Stigmatising drink driving has had a significant impact on attitudes of the young (if not the old); addictive drugs, smoking, and female circumcision are all medical issues that have been tackled by taking up the cudgels of outraged morality. Fiery denunciations of wicked behaviour from the pulpit have been central to the destruction of slavery, the reform of prisons, the campaign against child labour, and relief for the poor. As a force for potential good it has its place, and while our liberal medical education makes most of us feel queasy to accept the possibility, where HIV began in groups with a very clearly defined behaviour pattern which is seriously stigmatised this may well have played a role in delaying spread to the general population. A great deal of unnecessary misery was caused at an individual level to people with the disease by the stigma that went with it, and even from a strictly utilitarian standpoint it probably did more harm than good overall. It is, nevertheless, a fact that societies where, for example, visiting prostitutes is less heavily stigmatised and more common were open to faster spread within the general heterosexual community.

Once a disease like HIV has moved into the general community spread by entirely "normal" behaviour, however, this stigma becomes a serious barrier to tackling the spread of the disease effectively. It is obviously a serious handicap in managing the medical and social problems of those living with HIV, a point widely recognised by the many religious groups who combine a moralistic line on the causes of transmission with selfless care for those who have contracted AIDS. People in their final dying months thrown out of families, shunned by friends, and denounced in public if they are known to have the disease are too depressingly common worldwide for it to be worth labouring the tragic effect of stigma at an individual level. It is the counter-productive effect on *transmission* of demonising behaviour that passes on HIV which has not yet been grasped by most of those in a position to alter public perceptions.

It is now so firmly established in the public mind that bad people with promiscuous behaviour spread AIDS almost nobody accepts they know close friends or relatives who are dying from it, and medical staff are understandably reluctant to disabuse at an individual level. The people coming to visit patients on my wards come to see a favourite uncle dying of chronic malaria, a sister dying of gastroenteritis, a daughter dying with tuberculosis, a loved spouse dying of meningitis. They all know that there is a lot of HIV about; most governments have finally stopped pretending it is a myth put about by detractors of Our Great Nation, but the people on the radio saying their friends are dying of AIDS are western pop-stars, not the girl, or even popular icon, next door. It remains firmly a disease of other people, either bad, foreign, or both. It definitely would never, could never, happen to their loved ones. Glib suggestions that we should be taking every opportunity to educate ignore the fact that in this part of the world people are usually coming in their last few weeks or months; to choose this moment to call into question their moral worth in the eyes of their family for some perceived greater good is not ethically defensible medicine.

Maybe the only way to combat this false perception that HIV is passed on by abnormally bad behaviour is to go on a serious publicity drive for the virus. The fact we have to broadcast is that people with HIV are often the most attractive, socially successful, sexy people in town; that, after all, is why they got the disease in the first place. They are no more wicked than the next man or woman, just a bit less lucky. In this society HIV is the disease of the beautiful and the rich. The handsome, charming, caring boy who everybody wants to marry because he is so nice is, for exactly those reasons, the most likely to be a bit of a hazard. It is the disease of happy people who are having fun, and in the context of most countries where HIV is a serious problem they are usually being a bit naughty by generally accepted standards (at worst) or behaving exactly like everybody else their age (more commonly). People who have to pay or cheat to get HIV are generally a small minority—most normal people here get it for free, as a token of affection within a genuine relationship, a gift for being so lovable. Anybody who argues this is not the case is going to have to work very hard to explain away the fact that in this typical small, peaceful African city over a third of respectably married pregnant women my age have the virus, and it is higher still in some neighbouring countries.

Once people believe it is a disease caught by normal behaviour with ordinary friends it will be on its way out. A society where admitting to having no friends with HIV was tantamount to admitting to a sad, dull, backward life might seem a sick society to some. It would also be a society where behaviour would inevitably change, probably in ways even the most sternly moralistic would approve of. Let us follow Erasmus, the clearest moral thinker of his day, and proclaim that AIDS is the disease that all the best people have, their only error being to love not wisely, but too well.

NOTES

1. Erasmus D, *Opera Omnia* vol 5, col 346, quoted in Temkin I, The Double Face of Janus and other essays in the history of medicine. Baltimore: Johns Hopkins University Press, 1977: 475.

39   UNDER THE SHADOW OF TUSKEGEE: AFRICAN AMERICANS AND HEALTH CARE

Vanessa Northington Gamble

The selections in this part of the book, together with several others in Parts I and II, illustrate how disease patterns and health outcomes vary among socioeconomic and ethnic groups. The next three selections focus explicitly on race and racism as factors affecting health. The first of these analyzes the infamous Tuskegee syphilis study and its historical and social context. On a positive note, revelations about the study brought attention to the presence of racism in medical research and led to the creation of rules guiding the conduct of research and clinical practice. However, as Gamble argues, to view the study as a single, closed event is to explain away certain fears and health-related behaviors of African Americans and to miss the larger historical and socioeconomic context that provided the backdrop for the study and that continues to influence people's attitudes about and interactions with health professionals.

Both real and imagined medical mistreatment of African Americans from the times of slavery through the present, together with persistent disparities in mortality and morbidity rates between ethnic groups, may be experienced as evidence that American society values Black people less than White people. It is little wonder that the mistrust turns to fear of genocide with respect to interpreting both the Tuskegee study and current health issues such as birth control and epidemic disease. The experience of being treated with disrespect and viewed through racial stereotypes may reinforce the mistrust and apprehension associated with submission to medical care or experimentation. This is the larger historical and social context that needs to be clarified to bring greater understanding of the effects of racism on the health of African Americans.

Questions to keep in mind

Do fear and mistrust of health workers and governments among African Americans and other people around the world seem misplaced in our times? Can you think of examples that justify the fear and mistrust?

Was the Tuskegee study a single anomalous event in the United States or part of a pattern?

What is the meaning of persistent differences in mortality rates between ethnic groups in a given society?

In what ways do racial stereotypes surface in the patient–healer relationship? How might health professionals learn to guard against them?

INTRODUCTION

On May 16, 1997, in a White House ceremony, President Bill Clinton apologized for the Tuskegee Syphilis Study, the 40-year government study (1932 to 1972) in which 399 Black men from Macon County, Alabama, were deliberately denied effective treatment for syphilis in order to docu-ment the natural history of the disease.[1] "The legacy of the study at Tuskegee," the president re-marked, "has reached far and deep, in ways that hurt our progress and divide our nation. We cannot be one America when a whole segment of our na-tion has no trust in America."[2] The president's comments underscore that in the 25 years since its public disclosure, the study has moved from being a singular historical event to a powerful metaphor. It has come to symbolize racism in medicine, mis-conduct in human research, the arrogance of physicians, and government abuse of Black people.

Source: Gamble, V. 1997. "Under the Shadow of Tuskegee: African Americans and Health Care." *American Journal of Public Health* 87(11):1773–1778. © The American Public Health Association. With permission from the publisher.

The continuing shadow cast by the Tuskegee Syphilis Study on efforts to improve the health status of Black Americans provided an impetus for the campaign for a presidential apology.[3] Numerous articles, in both the professional and popular press, have pointed out that the study predisposed many African Americans to distrust medical and public health authorities and has led to critically low Black participation in clinical trials and organ donation.[4]

The specter of Tuskegee has also been raised with respect to HIV/AIDS prevention and treatment programs. Health education researchers Dr Stephen B. Thomas and Dr Sandra Crouse Quinn have written extensively on the impact of the Tuskegee Syphilis Study on these programs.[5] They argue that "the legacy of this experiment, with its failure to educate the study participants and treat them adequately, laid the foundation for today's pervasive sense of black distrust of public health authorities."[6] The syphilis study has also been used to explain why many African Americans oppose needle exchange programs. Needle exchange programs provoke the image of the syphilis study and Black fears about genocide. These programs are not viewed as mechanisms to stop the spread of HIV/AIDS but rather as fodder for the drug epidemic that has devastated so many Black neighborhoods.[7] Fears that they will be used as guinea pigs like the men in the syphilis study have also led some African Americans with AIDS to refuse treatment with protease inhibitors.[8]

The Tuskegee Syphilis Study is frequently described as the singular reason behind African-American distrust of the institutions of medicine and public health. Such an interpretation neglects a critical historical point: the mistrust predated public revelations about the Tuskegee study. Furthermore, the narrowness of such a representation places emphasis on a single historical event to explain deeply entrenched and complex attitudes within the Black community. An examination of the syphilis study within a broader historical and social context makes plain that several factors have influenced, and continue to influence, African Americans' attitudes toward the biomedical community.

Black Americans' fears about exploitation by the medical profession date back to the antebellum period and the use of slaves and free Black people as subjects for dissection and medical experimentation.[9] Although physicians also used poor Whites as subjects, they used Black people far more often. During an 1835 trip to the United States, French visitor Harriet Martineau found that Black people lacked the power even to protect the graves of their dead. "In Baltimore the bodies of coloured people exclusively are taken for dissection," she remarked, "because the Whites do not like it, and the coloured people cannot resist."[10] Four years later, abolitionist Theodore Dwight Weld echoed Martineau's sentiment. "Public opinion," he wrote, "would tolerate surgical experiments, operations, processes, performed upon them [slaves], which it would execrate if performed upon their master or other whites."[11] Slaves found themselves as subjects of medical experiments because physicians needed bodies and because the state considered them property and denied them the legal right to refuse to participate.

Two antebellum experiments, one carried out in Georgia and the other in Alabama, illustrate the abuse that some slaves encountered at the hands of physicians. In the first, Georgia physician Thomas Hamilton conducted a series of brutal experiments on a slave to test remedies for heatstroke. The subject of these investigations, Fed, had been loaned to Hamilton as repayment for a debt owed by his owner. Hamilton forced Fed to sit naked on a stool placed on a platform in a pit that had been heated to a high temperature. Only the man's head was above ground. Over a period of 2 to 3 weeks, Hamilton placed Fed in the pit five or six times and gave him various medications to determine which enabled him best to withstand the heat. Each ordeal ended when Fed fainted and had to be revived. But note that Fed was not the only victim in this experiment; its whole purpose was to make it possible for masters to force slaves to work still longer hours on the hottest of days.[12]

In the second experiment, Dr J. Marion Sims, the so-called father of modern gynecology, used three Alabama slave women to develop an operation to repair vesicovaginal fistulas. Between 1845 and 1849, the three slave women on whom Sims operated each underwent up to 30 painful operations. The physician himself described the agony associated with some of the experiments[13]: "The first patient I operated on was Lucy. . . . That was before the days of anaesthetics, and the poor girl, on her knees, bore the operation with great heroism and bravery." This operation was not successful, and Sims later attempted to repair the defect by placing a sponge in the bladder. This experiment, too, ended in failure. He noted:

> The whole urethra and the neck of the bladder were in a high state of inflammation, which came from the foreign substance. It had to come away, and there was nothing to do but to pull it away by main force. Lucy's agony was extreme. She was much prostrated, and I thought that she was going to die; but by irrigating the parts of the bladder she recovered with great rapidity.

Sims finally did perfect his technique and ultimately repaired the fistulas. Only after his experimentation with the slave women proved successful did the physician attempt the procedure, with anesthesia, on White women volunteers.

EXPLOITATION AFTER THE CIVIL WAR

It is not known to what extent African Americans continued to be used as unwilling subjects for experimentation and dissection in the years after emancipation. However, an examination of African-American folklore at the turn of the century makes it clear that Black people believed that such practices persisted. Folktales are replete with references to night doctors, also called student doctors and Ku Klux doctors. In her book, *Night Riders in Black Folk History*, anthropologist Gladys-Marie Fry writes, "The term 'night doctor' (derived from the fact that victims were sought only at night) applies both to students of medicine, who supposedly stole cadavers from which to learn about body processes, and [to] professional thieves, who sold stolen bodies—living and dead—to physicians for medical research."[14] According to folk belief, these sinister characters would kidnap Black people, usually at night and in urban areas, and take them to hospitals to be killed and used in experiments. An 1889 *Boston Herald* article vividly captured the fears that African Americans in South Carolina had of night doctors. The report read, in part:

> The negroes of Clarendon, Williamsburg, and Sumter counties have for several weeks past been in a state of fear and trembling. They claim that there is a white man, a doctor, who at will can make himself invisible, and who then approaches some unsuspecting darkey, and having rendered him or her insensible with chloroform, proceeds to fill up a bucket with the victim's blood, for the purpose of making medicine. After having drained the last drop of blood from the victim, the body is dumped into some secret place where it is impossible for any person to find it. The colored women are so worked up over this phantom that they will not venture out at night, or in the daytime in any sequestered place.[15]

Fry did not find any documented evidence of the existence of night riders. However, she demonstrated through extensive interviews that many African Americans expressed genuine fears that they would be kidnapped by night doctors and used for medical experimentation. Fry concludes that two factors explain this paradox. She argues that Whites, especially those in the rural South, deliberately spread rumors about night doctors in order to maintain psychological control over Blacks and to discourage their migration to the North so as to maintain a source of cheap labor. In addition, Fry asserts that the experiences of many African Americans as victims of medical experiments during slavery fostered their belief in the existence of night doctors.[16] It should also be added that, given the nation's racial and political climate, Black people recognized their inability to refuse to participate in medical experiments.

Reports about the medical exploitation of Black people in the name of medicine after the end of the Civil War were not restricted to the realm of folklore. Until it was exposed in 1882, a grave robbing ring operated in Philadelphia and provided bodies for the city's medical schools by plundering the graves at a Black cemetery. According to historian David C. Humphrey, southern grave robbers regularly sent bodies of southern Blacks to northern medical schools for use as anatomy cadavers.[17]

During the early 20th century, African-American medical leaders protested the abuse of Black people by the White-dominated medical profession and used their concerns about experimentation to press for the establishment of Black-controlled hospitals.[18] Dr Daniel Hale Williams, the founder of Chicago's Provident Hospital (1891), the nation's first Black-controlled hospital, contended that White physicians, especially in the South, frequently used Black patients as guinea pigs.[19] Dr Nathan Francis Mossell, the founder of Philadelphia's Frederick Douglass Memorial Hospital (1895), described the "fears and prejudices" of Black people, especially those from the South, as "almost proverbial."[20] He attributed such attitudes to southern medical practices in which Black people," when forced to accept hospital attention, got only the poorest care, being placed in inferior wards set apart for them, suffering the brunt of all that is experimental in treatment, and all this is the sequence of their race variety and abject helplessness."[21] The founders of Black hospitals claimed that only Black physicians possessed the skills required to treat Black patients optimally and that Black hospitals provided these patients with the best possible care.[22]

Fears about the exploitation of African Americans by White physicians played a role in the establishment of a Black veterans hospital in Tuskegee, Ala. In 1923, 9 years before the initiation of the Tuskegee Syphilis Study, racial tensions had erupted in the town over control of the hospital. The federal government had pledged that the facility, an institution designed exclusively for Black patients, would be run by a Black professional staff. But many Whites in the area, including members of the Ku Klux Klan, did not want a Black-operated federal facility in the heart of Dixie, even though it would serve only Black people.[23]

Black Americans sought control of the veterans hospital, in part because they believed that the ex-soldiers would receive the best possible care from Black physicians and nurses, who would be more caring and sympathetic to the veterans' needs. Some Black newspapers even warned that White southerners wanted command of the hospital as part of a racist plot to kill and sterilize African-American men and to establish an "experiment station" for mediocre White physicians.[24] Black physicians did eventually gain the right to operate the hospital, yet this did not stop the hospital from becoming an experiment station for Black men. The veterans hospital was one of the facilities used by the United States Public Health Service in the syphilis study.

During the 1920s and 1930s, Black physicians pushed for additional measures that would battle medical racism and advance their professional needs. Dr Charles Garvin, a prominent Cleveland

physician and a member of the editorial board of the Black medical publication *The Journal of the National Medical Association,* urged his colleagues to engage in research in order to protect Black patients. He called for more research on diseases such as tuberculosis and pellagra that allegedly affected African Americans disproportionately or idiosyncratically. Garvin insisted that Black physicians investigate these racial diseases because "heretofore in literature, as in medicine, the Negro has been written about, exploited and experimented upon sometimes not to his physical betterment or to the advancement of science, but the advancement of the Nordic investigator." Moreover, he charged that "in the past, men of other races have for the large part interpreted our diseases, often tinctured with inborn prejudices."[25]

FEARS OF GENOCIDE

These historical examples clearly demonstrate that African Americans' distrust of the medical profession has a longer history than the public revelations of the Tuskegee Syphilis Study. There is a collective memory among African Americans about their exploitation by the medical establishment. The Tuskegee Syphilis Study has emerged as the most prominent example of medical racism because it confirms, if not authenticates, long-held and deeply entrenched beliefs within the Black community. To be sure, the Tuskegee Syphilis Study does cast a long shadow. After the study had been exposed, charges surfaced that the experiment was part of a governmental plot to exterminate Black people.[26] Many Black people agreed with the charge that the study represented "nothing less than an official, premeditated policy of genocide."[27] Furthermore, this was not the first or last time that allegations of genocide have been launched against the government and the medical profession. The sickle cell anemia screening programs of the 1970s and birth control programs have also provoked such allegations.[28]

In recent years, links have been made between Tuskegee, AIDS, and genocide. In September 1990, the article "AIDS: Is It Genocide?" appeared in *Essence,* a Black woman's magazine. The author noted: "As an increasing number of African-Americans continue to sicken and die and as no cure for AIDS has been found some of us are beginning to think the unthinkable: Could AIDS be a virus that was manufactured to erase large numbers of us? Are they trying to kill us with this disease?"[29] In other words, some members of the Black community see AIDS as part of a conspiracy to exterminate African Americans.

Beliefs about the connection between AIDS and the purposeful destruction of African Americans should not be cavalierly dismissed as bizarre and paranoid. They are held by a significant number of Black people. For example, a 1990 survey conducted by the Southern Christian Leadership Conference found that 35% of the 1056 Black church members who responded believed that AIDS was a form of genocide.[30] A *New York Times*/WCBS TV News poll conducted the same year found that 10% of Black Americans thought that the AIDS virus had been created in a laboratory in order to infect Black people. Another 20% believed that it could be true. [31]

African Americans frequently point to the Tuskegee Syphilis Study as evidence to support their views about genocide, perhaps, in part, because many believe that the men in the study were actually injected with syphilis. Harlon Dalton, a Yale Law School professor and a former member of the National Commission on AIDS, wrote, in a 1989 article titled, "AIDS in Black Face," that "the government [had] purposefully exposed Black men to syphilis."[32] Six years later, Dr Eleanor Walker, a Detroit radiation oncologist, offered an explanation as to why few African Americans become bone marrow donors. "The biggest fear, she claimed, is that they will become victims of some misfeasance, like the Tuskegee incident where Black men were infected with syphilis and left untreated to die from the disease."[33] The January 25, 1996, episode of *New York Undercover*, a Fox Network police drama that is one of the top shows in Black households, also reinforced the rumor that the US Public Health Service physicians injected the men with syphilis.[34] The myth about deliberate infection is not limited to the Black community. On April 8, 1997, news anchor Tom Brokaw, on "NBC Nightly News," announced that the men had been infected by the government.[35]

Folklorist Patricia A. Turner, in her book *I Heard It through the Grapevine: Rumor and Resistance in African-American Culture*, underscores why it is important not to ridicule but to pay atten-

tion to these strongly held theories about genocide.[36] She argues that these rumors reveal much about what African Americans believe to be the state of their lives in this country. She contends that such views reflect Black beliefs that White Americans have historically been, and continue to be, ambivalent and perhaps hostile to the existence of Black people. Consequently, African-American attitudes toward biomedical research are not influenced solely by the Tuskegee Syphilis Study. African Americans' opinions about the value White society has attached to their lives should not be discounted. As Reverend Floyd Tompkins of Stanford University Memorial Church has said, "There is a sense in our community, and I think it shall be proved out, that if you are poor or you're a person of color, you were the guinea pig, and you continue to be the guinea pigs, and there is the fundamental belief that Black life is not valued like White life or like any other life in America."[37]

NOT JUST PARANOIA

Lorene Cary, in a cogent essay in *Newsweek*, expands on Reverend Tompkins' point. In an essay titled "Why It's Not Just Paranoia," she writes:

> We Americans continue to value the lives and humanity of some groups more than the lives and humanity of others. That is not paranoia. It is our historical legacy and a present fact; it influences domestic and foreign policy and the daily interaction of millions of Americans. It influences the way we spend our public money and explains how we can read the staggering statistics on Black Americans' infant mortality, youth mortality, mortality in middle and old age, and not be moved to action.[38]

African Americans' beliefs that their lives are devalued by White society also influence their relationships with the medical profession. They perceive, at times correctly, that they are treated differently in the health care system solely because of their race, and such perceptions fuel mistrust of the medical profession. For example, a national telephone survey conducted in 1986 revealed that African Americans were more likely than Whites to report that their physicians did not inquire sufficiently about their pain, did not tell them how long it would take for prescribed medicine to work, did not explain the seriousness of their illness or injury, and did not discuss test and examination findings.[39]

A 1994 study published in the *American Journal of Public Health* found that physicians were less likely to give pregnant Black women information about the hazards of smoking and drinking during pregnancy.[40]

The powerful legacy of the Tuskegee Syphilis Study endures, in part, because the racism and disrespect for Black lives that it entailed mirror Black people's contemporary experiences with the medical profession. The anger and frustration that many African Americans feel when they encounter the health care system can be heard in the words of Alicia Georges, a professor of nursing at Lehman College and a former president of the National Black Nurses Association, as she recalled an emergency room experience. "Back a few years ago, I was having excruciating abdominal pain, and I wound up at a hospital in my area," she recalled. "The first thing that they began to ask me was how many sexual partners I'd had. I was married and owned my own house. But immediately, in looking at me, they said, 'Oh, she just has pelvic inflammatory disease.'"[41] Perhaps because of her nursing background, Georges recognized the implications of the questioning. She had come face to face with the stereotype of Black women as sexually promiscuous. Similarly, the following story from the *Los Angeles Times* shows how racism can affect the practice of medicine:

> When Althea Alexander broke her arm, the attending resident at Los Angeles County–USC Medical Center told her to "hold your arm like you usually hold your can of beer on Saturday night." Alexander who is Black, exploded. "What are you talking about? Do you think I'm a welfare mother?" The White resident shrugged: "Well aren't you?" Turned out she was an administrator at USC medical school.

This example graphically illustrates that health care providers are not immune to the beliefs and misconceptions of the wider community. They carry with them stereotypes about various groups of people.[42]

BEYOND TUSKEGEE

There is also a growing body of medical research that vividly illustrates why discussions of the relationship of African Americans and the medical profession must go beyond the Tuskegee Syphilis Study. These studies demonstrate racial inequities in access to particular technologies and raise critical

questions about the role of racism in medical decision making. For example, in 1989 *The Journal of the American Medical Association* published a report that demonstrated racial inequities in the treatment of heart disease. In this study, White and Black patients had similar rates of hospitalization for chest pain, but the White patients were one third more likely to undergo coronary angiography and more than twice as likely to be treated with bypass surgery or angioplasty. The racial disparities persisted even after adjustments were made for differences in income.[43] Three years later, another study appearing in that journal reinforced these findings. It revealed that older Black patients on Medicare received coronary artery bypass grafts only about a fourth as often as comparable White patients. Disparities were greatest in the rural South, where White patients had the surgery seven times as often as Black patients. Medical factors did not fully explain the differences. This study suggests that an already-existing national health insurance program does not solve the access problems of African Americans.[44] Additional studies have confirmed the persistence of such inequities.[45]

Why the racial disparities? Possible explanations include health problems that precluded the use of procedures, patient unwillingness to accept medical advice or to undergo surgery, and differences in severity of illness. However, the role of racial bias cannot be discounted, as the American Medical Association's Council on Ethical and Judicial Affairs has recognized. In a 1990 report on Black–White disparities in health care, the council asserted:

> Because racial disparities may be occurring despite the lack of any intent or purposeful efforts to treat patients differently on the basis of race, physicians should examine their own practices to ensure that inappropriate considerations do not affect their clinical judgment. In addition, the profession should help increase the awareness of its members of racial disparities in medical treatment decisions by engaging in open and broad discussions about the issue. Such discussions should take place as part of the medical school curriculum, in medical journals, at professional conferences, and as part of professional peer review activities.[46]

The council's recommendation is a strong acknowledgment that racism can influence the practice of medicine.

After the public disclosures of the Tuskegee Syphilis Study, Congress passed the National Research Act of 1974. This act, established to protect subjects in human experimentation, mandates institutional review board approval of all federally funded research with human subjects. However, recent revelations about a measles vaccine study financed by the Centers for Disease Control and Prevention (CDC) demonstrate the inadequacies of these safeguards and illustrate why African Americans' historically based fears of medical research persist. In 1989, in the midst of a measles epidemic in Los Angeles, the CDC, in collaboration with Kaiser Permanente and the Los Angeles County Health Department, began a study to test whether the experimental Edmonston—Zagreb vaccine could be used to immunize children too young for the standard Moraten vaccine. By 1991, approximately 900 infants, mostly Black and Latino, had received the vaccine without difficulties. (Apparently, 1 infant died for reasons not related to the inoculations.) But the infants' parents had not been informed that the vaccine was not licensed in the United States or that it had been associated with an increase in death rates in Africa. The 1996 disclosure of the study prompted charges of medical racism and of the continued exploitation of minority communities by medical professionals.[47]

The Tuskegee Syphilis Study continues to cast its shadow over the lives of African Americans. For many Black people, it has come to represent the racism that pervades American institutions and the disdain in which Black lives are often held. But despite its significance, it cannot be the only prism we use to examine the relationship of African Americans with the medical and public health communities. The problem we must face is not just the shadow of Tuskegee but the shadow of racism that so profoundly affects the lives and beliefs of all people in this country.[31]

NOTES

1. The most comprehensive history of the study is James H. Jones, *Bad Blood,* new and expanded edition (New York: Free Press, 1993).

2. "Remarks by the President in Apology for Study Done in Tuskegee," Press Release, the White House, Office of the Press Secretary, 16 May 1997.

3. "Final Report of the Tuskegee Syphilis Study Legacy Committee," Vanessa Northington Gamble, chair, and John C. Fletcher, co-chair, 20 May 1996.

4. Vanessa Northington Gamble, "A Legacy of Distrust: African Americans and Medical Research," *American Journal of Preventive Medicine* 9 (1993): 35–38; Shari Roan, "A Medical Imbalance," *Los Angeles Times,* 1 November 1994; Carol Stevens, "Research: Distrust Runs Deep; Medical Community Seeks Solution," *The Detroit News,* 10 December 1995; Lini S. Kadaba, "Minorities in Research," *Chicago Tribune,* 13 September 1993; Robert Steinbrook, "AIDS Trials Shortchange Minorities and Drug Users," *Los Angeles Times,* 25 September 1989; Mark D. Smith, "Zidovudine: Does It Work for Everyone?" *Journal of the American Medical Association* 266 (1991): 2750–2751: Charlise Lyles, "Blacks Hesitant to Donate; Cultural Beliefs, Misinformation, Mistrust Make It a Difficult Decision," *The Virginian-Pilot,* 15 August 1994; Jeanni Wong, "Mistrust Leaves Some Blacks Reluctant to Donate Organs," *Sacramento Bee,* 17 February 1993; "Night-line," ABC News, 6 April 1994; Patrice Gaines, "Armed with the Truth in a Fight for Lives," *Washington Post,* 10 April 1994; Fran Henry. "Encouraging Organ Donation from Blacks," *Cleveland Plain Dealer,* 23 April 1994; G. Marie Swanson and Amy J. Ward, "Recruiting Minorities into Clinical Trials: Toward a Participant-Friendly System," *Journal of the National Cancer Institute* 87 (1995): 1747–1759; Dewayne Wickham, "Why Blacks Are Wary of White MDs," *The Tennessean,* 21 May 1997, 13A.

5. For example, see Stephen B. Thomas and Sandra Crouse Quinn, "The Tuskegee Syphilis Study, 1932 to 1972: Implications for HIV Education and AIDS Risk Education Programs in the Black Community," *American Journal of Public Health* 81 (1991): 1498–1505; Stephen B. Thomas and Sandra Crouse Quinn, "Understanding the Attitudes of Black Americans," in *Dimensions of HIV Prevention. Needle Exchange,* ed. Jeff Stryker and Mark D. Smith (Menlo Park, Calif.: Henry J. Kaiser Family Foundation, 1993), 99–128; and Stephen B. Thomas and Sandra Crouse Quinn, "The AIDS Epidemic and the African-American Community: Toward an Ethical Framework for Service Delivery," in *"It Just Ain't Fair": The Ethics of Health Care for African Americans,* ed. Annette Dula and Sara Goering (Westport, Conn.: Praeger, 1994), 75–88.

6. Thomas and Quinn, "The AIDS Epidemic and the African-American Community," 83.

7. Thomas and Quinn, "Understanding the Attitudes of Black Americans," 108–109; David L. Kirp and Ronald Bayer, "Needles and Races," *Atlantic,* July 1993, 38–42.

8. Lynda Richardson, "An Old Experiment's Legacy: Distrust of AIDS Treatment," *New York Times,* 21 April 1997, Al, A7.

9. Todd L. Savitt, "The Use of Blacks for Medical Experimentation and Demonstration in the Old South," *Journal of Southern History* 48 (1982): 331–348; David C. Humphrey, "Dissection and Discrimination: The Social Origins of Cadavers in America, 1760–1915," *Bulletin of the New York Academy of Medicine* 49 (1973): 819–827.

10. Harriet Martineau, *Retrospect of Western Travel*, vol. 1 (London: Saunders & Ottley; New York: Harpers and Brothers; 1838), 140, quoted in Humphrey, "Dissection and Discrimination," 819.

11. Theodore Dwight Weld, *American Slavery As It Is: Testimony of a Thousand Witnesses* (New York: American Anti-Slavery Society, 1839), 170, quoted in Savitt, "The Use of Black," 341.

12. F. N. Boney, "Doctor Thomas Hamilton: Two Views of a Gentleman of the Old South, *Phylon* 28 (1967): 288–292.

13. J. Marion Sims, *The Story of My Life* (New York: Appleton, 1889), 236–237.

14. Gladys-Marie Fry, *Night Riders in Black Folk History* (Knoxville: University of Tennessee Press, 1984), 171.

15. "Concerning Negro Sorcery in the United States," *Journal of American Folk-Lore* 3 (1890): 285.

16. Ibid., 210.

17. Humphrey, "Dissection and Discrimination," 822–823.

18. A detailed examination of the campaign to establish Black hospitals can be found in Vanessa Northington Gamble, *Making a Place for Ourselves: The Black Hospital Movement, 1920–1945* (New York: Oxford University Press, 1995).

19. Eugene P. Link, "The Civil Rights Activities of Three Great Negro Physicians (1840–1940)," *Journal of Negro History* 52 (July 1969): 177.

20. Mossell graduated, with honors, from Penn in 1882 and founded the hospital in 1895.

21. "Seventh Annual Report of the Frederick Douglass Memorial Hospital and Training School" (Philadelphia, Pa.: 1902), 17.

22. H. M. Green, *A More or Less Critical Review of the Hospital Situation among Negroes in the United States* (n.d., circa 1930), 4–5.

23. For more in-depth discussions of the history of the Tuskegee Veterans Hospital, see Gamble, *Making a Place for Ourselves*, 70–104; Pete Daniel, "Black Power in the 1920's: The Case of Tuskegee Veterans Hospital," *Journal of Southern History* 36 (1970): 368–388; and Raymond Wolters, *The New Negro on Campus: Black College Rebellions of the 1920s* (Princeton, NJ: Princeton University Press, 1975), 137–191.

24. "Klan Halts March on Tuskegee," *Chicago Defender*, 4 August 1923.

25. Charles H. Garvin, "The 'New Negro' Physician," unpublished manuscript, n.d., box 1. Charles H. Garvin Papers, Western Reserve Historical Society Library, Cleveland, Ohio.

26. Ronald A. Taylor, "Conspiracy Theories Widely Accepted in U.S. Black Circles," *Washington Times*, 10 December 1991, Al; Frances Cress Welsing, *The Isis Papers: The Keys to the Colors* (Chicago: Third World Press, 1991), 298–299. Although she is not very well known outside of the African-American community, Welsing, a physician, is a popular figure within it. *The Isis Papers* headed for several weeks the best-seller list maintained by Black bookstores.

27. Jones, *Bad Blood*, 12.

28. For discussions of allegations of genocide in the implementation of these programs, see Robert G. Weisbord, "Birth Control and the Black American: A Matter of Genocide?" *Demography* 10 (1973): 571–590; Alex S. Jones, "Editorial Linking Blacks, Contraceptives Stirs Debate at Philadelphia Paper," *Arizona Daily Star*, 23 December 1990, F4; Doris Y. Wilkinson, "For Whose Benefit? Politics and Sickle Cell," *The Black Scholar* 5 (1974): 26–31.

29. Karen Grisby Bates, "Is It Genocide?" *Essence*, September 1990, 76.

30. Thomas and Quinn, "The Tuskegee Syphilis Study," 1499.

31. "The AIDS 'Plot' against Blacks," *New York Times*, 12 May 1992, A22.

32. Harlon L. Dalton, "AIDS in Blackface," *Daedalus* 118 (Summer 1989): 220–221.

33. Rhonda Bates-Rudd, "State Campaign Encourages African Americans to Offer Others Gift of Bone Marrow," *Detroit News*, 7 December 1995.

34. From September 1995 to December 1995, *New York Undercover* was the top-ranked show in Black households. It ranked 122nd in White households. David Zurawik, "Poll: TV's Race Gap Growing," *Capital Times* (Madison, Wis), 14 May 1996, 5D.

35. Transcript, "NBC Nightly News," 8 April 1997.

36. Patricia A. Turner, *I Heard It through the Grapevine: Rumor in African-American Culture* (Berkeley: University of California Press, 1993).

37. "Fear Creates Lack of Donor Organs among Blacks," *Weekend Edition*, National Public Radio. 13 March 1994.

38. Lorene Cary, "Why It's Not Just Paranoia: An American History of 'Plans' for Blacks," *Newsweek*, 6 April 1992, 23.

39. Robert J. Blendon, "Access to Medical Care for Black and White Americans: A Matter of Continuing Concern, *Journal of the American Medical Association* 261 (1989): 278–281.

40. M. D. Rogan et al., "Racial Disparities in Reported Prenatal Care Advice from Health Care Providers," *American Journal of Public Health* 84 (1994): 82–88.

41. Julie Johnson et al., "Why Do Blacks Die Young? *Time*, 16 September 1991, 52.

42. Sonia Nazario, "Treating Doctors for Prejudice: Medical Schools Are Trying to Sensitize Students to 'Bedside Bias.'" *Los Angeles Times,* 20 December 1990.

43. Mark B. Wenneker and Arnold M. Epstein, "Racial Inequities in the Use of Procedures for Patients with Ischemic Heart Disease in Massachusetts," *Journal of the American Medical Association* 261 (1989): 253–257.

44. Kenneth C. Goldberg et al., "Racial and Community Factors Influencing Coronary Artery Bypass Graft Surgery Rates for All 1986 Medicare Patients," *Journal of the American Medical Association* 267 (1992): 1473–1477.

45. John D. Ayanian, "Heart Disease in Black and White," *New England Journal of Medicine* 329 (1993): 656–658; J. Whittle et al., "Racial Differences in the Use of Invasive Cardiovascular Procedures in the Department of Veterans Affairs Medical System." *New England Journal of Medicine* 329 (1993): 621–627; Eric D. Peterson et al., "Racial Variation in Cardiac Procedure Use and Survival following Acute Myocardial Infarction in the Department of Veterans Affairs," *Journal of the American Medical Association* 271 (1994): 1175–1180; Ronnie D. Horner et al., "Theories Explaining Racial Differences in the Utilization of Diagnostic and Therapeutic Procedures for Cerebrovascular Disease," *Milbank Quarterly* 73 (1995): 443–462; Richard D. Moore et al., "Racial Differences in the Use of Drug Therapy for HIV Disease in an Urban Community," *New England Journal of Medicine* 350 (1994): 763–768.

46. Council on Ethical and Judicial Affairs, "Black-White Disparities in Health Care," *Journal of the American Medical Association* 263 (1990): 2346.

47. Marlene Cimons, "CDC Says It Erred in Measles Study," *Los Angeles Times,* 17 June 1996, A 11; Beth Glenn, "Bad Blood Once Again." *St. Petersburg Times,* 21 July 1996, 5D.

■ ■ ■ ■ ■ ■ ■ ■ ■ ■

40   DOES RACISM HARM HEALTH? DID CHILD ABUSE EXIST BEFORE 1962? ON EXPLICIT QUESTIONS, CRITICAL SCIENCE, AND CURRENT CONTROVERSIES: AN ECOSOCIAL PERSPECTIVE

Nancy Krieger

The previous selection raised the issue of persistent public health problems related to racial/ethnic disparities in both disease patterns and medical treatment. This selection emphasizes the importance of thinking clearly about racism and framing research questions based on precise definitions and principles. Krieger makes an analogy between doing this for the emerging scientific field of study on the effects of racism and the way in which the naming of child abuse, through an influential article published in the early 1960s, rendered that preexisting health concern more concrete and tangible. It is not that the problem did not exist before it was named, or that people were unaware of it or did nothing to attempt to resolve it. Rather, the establishment of a comprehensive framework helped to unify diverse approaches so that further research could proceed.

In order to examine the pathways toward negative health impacts that racism may take, it is necessary to be clear about definitions, methods, and research questions. For example, biological manifestations of the experience of racism must be distinguished from racialized interpretations of biology. Arbitrary biological traits are often taken to be coterminous with genetic characteristics shared by a particular population, but the two do not follow hand in hand, as Goodman explains through the example of lactose intolerance (selection 15). Moreover, even where gene frequencies may unite a group, gene expression is

Source: Krieger, N. 2003. "Does Racism Harm Health? Did Child Abuse Exist before 1962? On Explicit Questions, Critical Science, and Current Controversies: An Ecosocial Perspective." *American Journal of Public Health* 93(2):194–199. © The American Public Health Association. With permission from the publisher.

highly variable, as seen in the case of the West African diaspora and the rapid rise in obesity, hypertension, and diabetes in new socioeconomic and ecological contexts (see selections 42 and 43). Race/ethnicity is a social category, but this is not the same thing as saying it is not real, or that biology has no connection to health.

Like nuclear radiation described in selection 36, racism affects health both through exposure to it and perceptions of exposure. Research methods accordingly must be of both direct and indirect type. Self-reported and observed responses to the experience of racism are one prong, while epidemiological analysis of health impacts of racial inequalities are another. On the surface racism may seem elusive as a causal mechanism, but it is of the same order as other social determinants of health and therefore amenable to similar research methods. What is needed is willingness to face the empirical reality of ongoing physical and psychosocial impacts of racism, in the same way that scientific scrutiny has been brought to bear on other discomforting but previously veiled problems such as child abuse or economic inequality.

Questions to keep in mind

What is racism as opposed to race?

What is the difference between gene frequency and gene expression?

Why would it be an error to do away with racial/ethnic classifications in health research?

What are some specific ways in which racism affects people's health? Which should be studied directly and which indirectly?

Why might you expect direct analysis of the harmful effects of racism on health to be controversial?

Did child abuse exist before 1962, when C. Henry Kempe and coauthors published the now classic article "The Battered-Child Syndrome"?[1] Certainly.[2-5] Did it harm health? Yes, if current research is any guide.[2-7] Before the Kempe et al. article catapulted the issue onto the mainstream US medical and public health agenda, had anyone previously raised concerns about child abuse? Absolutely. Since the early 1800s, numerous individuals and organizations—many in fields that came to be known as public health, medicine, social work, philanthropy, and criminal justice—had attempted to investigate, raise public awareness about, and ameliorate problems of family violence.[2,3,5] Public and scientific attention to the issue, however, waxed and waned in concert with broader societal concerns.[2,3]

Kempe's article in a prominent scientific journal nevertheless was and remains enormously influential. Why? In part, because it explicitly named—and simultaneously highlighted the health consequences of—a volatile societal problem then hidden from view by dominant beliefs about the sanctity of family life. The unnamable problem, once named, became less nebulous and more tangible, something that could be more rigorously documented, monitored, and analyzed, bolstered by the belief that—with adequate will and resources—it could ultimately be rectified.[4-7]

Forty years later, in 2002, we are reaching a similar juncture: the unnamable is again becoming named, and explicit investigation of racism as a harmful determinant of population health is gaining entry into mainstream public health and medical discourse. At issue are the myriad ways in which racism—and other forms of social inequality and discrimination—can adversely affect health across the life course via varied, intertwined economic, environmental, psychosocial, and iatrogenic pathways.[8-12] The scientific question "Does racism harm health?" prompts a plenitude of hypotheses, each meriting serious scientific attention and resources.

Is it, however, novel to posit that racial/ethnic disparities in health arise from inequitable race relations? Surely not.[13,14] Are we the first to suggest that health is harmed not only by heinous crimes against humanity, such as slavery, lynching, and genocide, but also by the grinding economic and social realities of what Essed has aptly termed "everyday racism"?[15] Once again, no. In the mid-1800s, leading US abolitionists and physicians, Black and White alike, challenged convention by arguing that the poorer health of the Black relative to the White population resulted not from innate inferiority but rather White privilege, enforced via slavery in the South and legal racial discrimination in the North.[13,14]

The Choctaw and Cherokee nations, forcibly evicted from their homelands after the US Congress passed the Indian Removal Act in 1830, likewise understood that their health was being decimated by not only territorial but also cultural dispossession, justified in the name of White supremacy.[16–18] Concerns about health consequences of racism clearly are not new; to suggest otherwise is to misstate the historical record. Rather, reflecting the historical impact of racial inequality on not only health but also health sciences, the stark reality is that, despite long-standing awareness of the problem, the serious scientific study of racism as a determinant of population health remains in its infancy.

One way to move to the next stage is to consider current conceptual issues in the field, given that scientific knowledge is more often spurred by clarification of our thinking than by technological breakthroughs.[19,20] In this spirit, I address 3 interrelated issues from the vantage of an epidemiologist guided by an ecosocial perspective[21–23]: (1) links between racism, biology, and health, including recognition of biological expressions of race relations and racialized expressions of biology; (2) methodological controversies over how to study the impact of racism on health; and (3) debates over whether racism or class underlies racial/ethnic disparities in health.

RACISM, BIOLOGY, AND HEALTH

Clarity of terminology is critical for any science. A first step for analyzing the contribution of racism to racial/ethnic disparities in health is being explicit about definitions of racism, race/ethnicity,

and the link between these concepts.[8,23] In essence, both are interdependent expressions of inequitable and institutionalized societal race relations.[24–26] More specifically, *racism* refers to institutional and individual practices that create and reinforce oppressive systems of race relations whereby people and institutions engaging in discrimination adversely restrict, by judgment and action, the lives of those against whom they discriminate.[8,15]

Race/ethnicity, in turn, is a social rather than a biological category, referring to social groups, often sharing cultural heritage and ancestry, that are forged by oppressive systems of race relations justified by ideology. One group benefits from dominating other groups and defines itself and others through this domination and the possession of selective and arbitrary physical characteristics (e.g., skin color).[8,9] Although once trumpeted as scientific "fact," the notion that "race" is a valid, biologically meaningful a priori category has long been—and continues to be—refuted by work in population genetics, anthropology, and sociology.[26–34] The fact that we know what "race" we are says more about our society than it does our biology.[35]

Why do these sorts of explicit definitions matter? Because they provide a conceptual foundation for integrating thinking about racism *and* biology as a means of understanding and investigating the impact of racism on health. Both matter. Two diametrically opposed constructs are at issue, constructs that nevertheless are routinely conflated in the scientific literature. The first is *biological expressions of race relations;* the second is *racialized expressions of biology.*[8,23,36] The former draws attention to how harmful physical and psychosocial exposures due to racism adversely affect our biology, in ways that ultimately are embodied and manifested in racial/ethnic disparities in health. The latter refers to how arbitrary biological traits are erroneously construed as markers of innate "racial" distinctions.

Consider skin color. The biology of pigmentation and its direct relationship to certain skin-related disorders is real.[37,38] Whether or not racism existed, people with lighter vs darker skin (i.e., less vs more dispersed melanosomes) would be at higher risk of malignant melanoma, given sufficient exposure to sunlight (and especially bad sunburns before puberty).[38,39] By contrast, damage resulting from adverse use of skin lightening products,[38] as prompted by the ideology that lighter is better, would constitute a biological expression of race relations.

Skin color, in turn, would become a racialized expression of biology if, absent any evidence, it were treated as a valid marker for other unspecified genetic traits, reflecting a presumption that the biology of "race" equals the biology of gene frequencies. This was the logic of the flawed research agenda egregiously exemplified by the Tuskegee syphilis study, unnaturally intended to determine whether the "natural history" of untreated syphilis in Blacks was the same as that previously observed in Whites, in light of hypothesized differences in their nervous systems.[40,41]

As Cruickshank[42] has recently pointed out, however, drawing on lessons from the Human Genome Project and systems biology,[43,44] it is a logical and biological fallacy to assume that gene expression is equivalent to gene frequency. Consider the recent, rapid secular changes in obesity, hypertension, and diabetes among populations of West African descent living in the United Kingdom, the Caribbean, and the United States, as well as in West Africa,[45–51] to use but one diasporic example. Only changes in gene expression, not gene frequency, can explain the speed of these trends. Even so, myriad epidemiological studies continue to treat "race" as a purely biological (i.e., genetic) variable or seek to explain racial/ethnic disparities in health absent consideration of the effects of racism on health.[8–11,52]

By clearly distinguishing between and emphasizing the importance of taking into account both racism and biology, these 2 constructs make clear that we can never study human biology—or behavior—in the abstract. Exemplifying that we instead study people in context is Sapolsky's cautionary tale[53]: If adrenal glands are studied only among cadavers of the poor, long since hypertrophied as a result of excess excretion of cortisol, then—as occurred in the early 20th century—the wealthy will be diagnosed with adrenal deficiency disorders. Simplistic divisions of the social and biological will not suffice.[54] The interpretations we offer of observed average differences in health status across socially delimited groups reflect our theoretical frameworks, not ineluctable facts of nature.

METHODOLOGICAL CONTROVERSIES

How then, methodologically, can we test the hypothesis that racism harms health? Addressing this scientific question raises several critical questions and controversies. At issue is the need for—and strengths and limitations of—studies that directly and indirectly assess the impact of racism on health, whether employing quantitative or qualitative methods.[8–12,55] By direct, I mean health studies explicitly obtaining information on people's self-reported experiences of—and observing people's physiological and psychological responses to—real-life or experimental situations involving racial discrimination.[8] By indirect, I mean studies that investigate racial/ethnic disparities in distributions of deleterious exposures or health outcomes and explicitly infer that racism underlies these disparities.[8] Each approach has its flaws, and both are necessary, addressing questions the other cannot.

Highlighting why both direct and indirect approaches are necessary are 5 key pathways through which racism can harm health, by shaping exposure and vulnerability to the following: (1) economic and social deprivation: (2) toxic substances and hazardous conditions; (3) socially inflicted trauma (mental, physical, and sexual, directly experienced or witnessed, from verbal threats to violent acts); (4) targeted marketing of commodities that can harm health, such as junk food and psychoactive substances (alcohol, tobacco, and other licit and illicit drugs); and (5) inadequate or degrading medical care.[8] Also relevant are health consequences of people's responses to discrimination. These responses—each with its own set of potential health impacts—can range from internalized oppression and harmful use of psychoactive substances to reflective coping, active resistance, and community organizing to end discrimination and promote human rights and social justice.[8–12,15,26,55]

From this perspective, the direct approach is necessary for investigating pathways pertaining to socially inflicted trauma. There is no substitute. The caveat, well recognized in the enormous body of literature on "stress" and health, is that such research must reckon with not only exposures but perceptions of these exposures, as well as cognitive issues pertaining to memory and disclosure.[8,12,55–57] The scientific task is therefore to understand how various threats to validity can affect investigations relying on self-report data. Potential solutions include the following: research on what constitutes valid self-report measures of racial discrimination[8,58]; experimental studies (as conducted in the areas of housing and job discrimination) that employ "testers" of the same age, gender, and physical size, equipped with identical resumes but differing in terms of their race/ethnicity[59,60]; or psychological and criminal justice studies investigating differences in perception of and responses to designated scenarios.[61–63]

Notably, conduct of such studies requires appraisal of participants' racial/ethnic identity. Recent suggestions, however well intentioned, to "abandon" use of racial/ethnic categories in public health research, on grounds that "race" is not a valid scientific concept,[64,65] err on 2 accounts.[36,66,67] First, such an argument implies that only biological, and not social, variables are "real" and can be studied scientifically. Second, it presumes that the race/ethnicity of persons reporting experiences of racial discrimination is irrelevant, thereby rendering it impossible to distinguish between—or evaluate the health effects of—racial discrimination reported by people of color and that reported by White people.

The indirect approach, in turn, is necessary for most of the other pathways listed, precisely because they involve exposures that extend beyond individual perception.[8,9] Knowledge of racial discrimination in wages, for example, can be obtained only if one knows what others are paid.[59] Similarly, knowledge of racial inequality in the provision of medical care, above and beyond disrespectful interpersonal interactions, can be obtained only by comparing the types of treatment offered to groups that exhibit equivalent morbidity rates but differ in regard to their race/ethnicity.[68,69]

Herein lies the rub. A claim recently advanced by some social epidemiologists, notably Cooper and Kaufman, is that we cannot make causal inferences based on studies comparing health outcomes across different racial/ethnic groups.[70–72] Why? Because, they argue, such studies violate the counterfactual criterion of exchangeability. That is, people who are "exposed" should, in principle, be capable of being "unexposed." Using this logic, their debatable example is that smokers differ from nonsmokers only because they smoke[72]; in principle, the "treatment" of smoking could be randomized.

By contrast, according to Cooper and Kaufman, there is no way a White person could ever be or become a Black person or have the lifetime set of related experiences contingent upon being Black. The exposure of "race" is thus nonexchangeable and also, in their examples, uniform.[72] Because commonly used statistical tests presume exchangeability, they assert that parameter estimates for racial/ethnic contrasts have no valid causal interpretation, including in relation to racial discrimination.

The fallacy of their argument is contained within their counterfactual propositions. Cooper and Kaufman in effect relegate "race" to an intrinsic trait.[73–75] They confuse the fact that people cannot simply "choose" their race/ethnicity, in that it is conditioned by the racial/ethnic relations of the society into which they are born, with the consequences of experiencing differential—and variable—treatment by virtue of inequitable race relations. The appropriate counterfactual is thus as follows: What would happen if people were randomized to discriminatory treatment, as occurs with racial discrimination? As is often the case in epidemiology, we cannot perform such an experiment to test this hypothesis regarding racial/ethnic disparities in health across the life course and instead must rely on observational studies.

More broadly, the counterfactual contrast is of a world with and without racism.[74] In the latter, people with darker vs lighter skin would in fact be "exchangeable"—as human beings—and thus equally at risk for all ailments other than those directly involving skin color (e.g., melanoma, vitiligo[38,39]). This contrast, premised upon a common humanity, underlies the "tester" studies alluded to earlier regarding housing and job discrimination. It also underlies inferences made comparing health outcomes across birth cohorts;

obviously, someone born in 1910 cannot be "exchanged" with or have the same set of experiences as a person born in 1940 or in 1970.[74] Birth cohort comparisons of both rates of disease and exposures, however, are critical for assessing whether cross-sectional associations—even those derived from randomized clinical trials—can in fact explain secular changes in health.[22,76]

As with any scientific research, poorly specified counterfactuals are what threaten causal interpretation,[77–80] and all observational studies—not only those concerned with social determinants of health—must consider carefully their motivating counterfactuals.[77–79] Even the smokers and non-smokers of Cooper and Kaufman's example would, after all, violate a strict "exchangeability" criterion, because the fact and process of being a smoker brings with it an array of other correlated exposures and life histories.[81,82]

RACISM OR SOCIAL CLASS: THE LIMITS OF "EITHER/OR" LOGIC

The third and final conceptual controversy builds on the first and second. It is the debate over whether "racism" or "social class" explains racial/ethnic disparities in health and, relatedly, which is causally prior.[8–14,52,65,67,70–75,83,84] Typically argued with reference to the Euro-American legacy of colonization and the slave trade, the logical and historical fallacy is to frame this debate as "either/or" rather than as "both/and." As attested to by reams of sociological and historical research, class and race relations are in fact intertwined.[26,33,34,85–88] Since the global expansion of European power and economies in the mid-15th century and contingent territorial conquest and intercontinental slave trade, people have lived in a world of racialized class relations and class-contingent race relations.[26,33,34,85–88] It logically follows that racial/ethnic inequalities are shaped and fostered by class inequalities, and vice versa.

The same holds for other types of discrimination that render people socially and economically vulnerable (e.g., discrimination based on gender or sexuality).[8,88–90] Translated to health research, it is therefore an empirical question, not a philosophical principle, whether pathways involving economic deprivation and/or noneconomic manifestations of racial discrimination contribute to racial/ethnic disparities in health. Or, put simply, the answer to the crude question "Which matters—race or class?" can be one, the other, neither, or both. This is why we need scientific research: to test competing hypotheses.

BEING EXPLICIT ABOUT RACISM: A SCIENTIFIC NECESSITY

In conclusion, recalling the example of child abuse, the point of explicitly naming and scientifically investigating racism as a determinant of population health is to generate valid knowledge to guide actions designed to improve public health. It is not to imply that racism is solely a public health or medical problem or that solutions will come primarily from public health or medical initiatives.[91,92] Nor is health research required to "prove" that racism is "bad"; it is, by definition, and in many instances it is illegal as well.[8] Rather, the point is that neglecting study of the health impact of racism means that explanations for and interventions to alter population distributions of health, disease, and well-being will be incomplete and potentially misleading, if not outright harmful.[93,94] Of course, work in this field will, inevitably, be fraught with controversy, because the exposure raises important themes of accountability, agency, and human rights.[8,95–98]

That there are legal, political, and economic consequences of attributing disparities in health status to racial discrimination is, however, no more or less germane than it is for research on any other determinant of societal health, whether child abuse,[1–7] ambient air pollution,[99,100] tobacco,[101,102] or food.[46,103] The canard that research on health consequences of racism is "political" rather than "scientific"[104] is blatantly incorrect: it is in fact political and unscientific to exclude the topic from the domain of legitimate scientific inquiry and discourse.[92,94,105] Nor is this insight new: James McCune Smith and John Rock, 2 of the first credentialed African American physicians in the United States, said as much a century and a half ago.[13,14,106,107] Rather, the task at hand is to bring the knowledge and methods available in our generation to the pressing public health problem of persistent racial/ethnic disparities in health.

NOTES

1. Kempe CH, Silverman FN, Steele BF, Droegemueller W, Silver HK. The battered-child syndrome. *JAMA*. 1962;181:17–24.

2. Gordon L. *Heroes Of Their Own Lives: The Politics and History of Family Violence. Boston, 1880–1960.* New York, NY: Viking; 1988.

3. Asbhy L. *Endangered Children: Dependency, Neglect and Abuse in American History.* New York, NY: Twayne Publishers; 1997.

4. Merrick J. Browne KD. Child abuse and neglect—a public health concern. *Public Health Rev.* 1999; 27:279–293.

5. Lynch MA. Child abuse before Kempe: an historical literature review. *Child Abuse Negl.* 1985;9:7–15.

6. Margolin G, Gordis EB. The effects of family and community violence on children. *Annu Rev Psychol.* 2000;51:445–479.

7. MacMillan HL. Child maltreatment: what we know in the year 2000. *Can J Psychiatry.* 2000;45:702–709.

8. Krieger N. Discrimination and health. In: Berkman L. Kawachi I, eds. *Social Epidemiology.* Oxford, England: Oxford University Press Inc; 2000:36–75.

9. Krieger N. Rowley DL, Herman AA, Avery B, Phillips MT. Racism, sexism, and social class: implications for studies of health, disease, and well-being. *Am J Prev Med.* 1993;9(suppl):82–122.

10. Williams DR. Race, socioeconomic status, and health: the added effects of racism and discrimination. *Ann N Y Acad Sci.* 1999;896:173–188.

11. Lillie-Blanton M. LaVeist T. Race/ethnicity, the social environment, and health. *Soc Sci Med.* 1996;43:83–92.

12. Clark R. Anderson NB, Clark VR, Williams DR. Racism as a stressor for African Americans: a biopsychosocial model. *Am Psychol.* 1999;54:805–816.

13. Krieger N. Shades of difference: theoretical underpinnings of the medical controversy on black-white differences. 1830–1870. *Int J Health Serv.* 1987; 17:258–279.

14. Byrd WM, Clayton LA. *An American Health Dilemma: The Medical History of African Americans and the Problem of Race.* Vol 1. New York, NY: Routledge; 2000.

15. Essed P. *Understanding Everyday Racism: An Interdisciplinary Theory.* Newbury Park, Calif: Sage Publications; 1991.

16. Akers DL. Removing the heart of the Choctaw people: Indian removal from a native perspective. In: Trafzer CD, Weiner D, eds. *Medicine Ways: Disease,* *Health and Survival Among Native Americans.* Walnut Creek, Calif: Altamira Press; 2001:1–15.

17. Nabovok P, ed. *Native American Testimony: A Chronicle of Indian-White Relations From Prophecy to the Present, 1492–1992.* New York: Viking; 1991.

18. Zinn H. *A People's History of the United States, 1492–Present.* New York, NY: HarperPerennial; 1995:124–146.

19. Fleck L. *Genesis and Development of a Scientific Fact.* Chicago, Ill: University of Chicago Press; 1979.

20. Ziman JM. *Real Science: What It Is, and What It Means.* Cambridge, England: Cambridge University Press; 2000.

21. Krieger N. Epidemiology and the web of causation: has anyone seen the spider? *Soc Sci Med.* 1994;39: 887–903.

22. Krieger N. Theories for social epidemiology in the 21st century: an ecosocial perspective. *Int J Epidemiol.* 2001;30:668–677.

23. Krieger N. A glossary for social epidemiology. *J Epidemiol Community Health.* 2001;55:693–700.

24. Marshall G, ed. *The Concise Oxford Dictionary of Sociology.* Oxford, England: Oxford University Press Inc; 1994:125–126.

25. Jary D, Jary J, eds. *Collins Dictionary of Sociology.* 2nd ed. Glasgow, Scotland: HarperCollins Publishers; 1995:169.

26. Winant H. Race and race theory. *Annu Rev Sociol.* 2000;26:169–185.

27. Graves JL Jr. *The Emperor's New Clothes: Biological Theories of Race at the Millenium.* New Brunswick, NJ: Rutgers University Press; 2001.

28. Cavalli-Sforza LL, Menozzi P, Piazza A. *The History and Geography of Human Genes.* Princeton. NJ: Princeton University Press; 1994.

29. Harris B, Ernst W, eds. *Race, Science, and Medicine, 1700–1960.* London, England: Routledge; 1999.

30. American Association of Physical Anthropology. AAPA statement on biological aspects of race. *Am J Phys Anthropol.* 1996;101:569–570.

31. American Association of Anthropology. AAA statement on race. *Am Anthropologist.* 1999;100:712–713.

32. Armelagos GJ, Goodman AH. Race, racism, and biology. In: Goodman AH, Leatherman TL, eds. *Building a New Biocultural Synthesis: Political-Economic Perspectives on Human Biology.* Ann Arbor, Mich: University of Michigan Press; 1998:359–377.

33. Banton MP. *Racial Theories.* 2nd ed. Cambridge, England: Cambridge University Press; 1998.

34. Cox OC. *Race: A Study in Social Dynamics. 50th Anniversary Edition of "Caste, Class, and Race."* New York, NY: Monthly Review Press; 2000.

35. Krieger N, Bassett M. The health of black folk: disease, class and ideology in science. *Monthly Rev.* 1986;38:74–85.

36. Krieger N. Refiguring "race": epidemiology, racialized biology, and biological expressions of race relations. *Int J Health Serv.* 2000;30:211–216.

37. Sturm RA, Box NF, Ramsay M. Human pigmentation genetics: the difference is only skin deep. *Bioessays.* 1998;20:712–721.

38. Taylor SC. Skin of color: biology, structure, function, and implications for dermatologic disease. *J Am Acad Dermatol.* 2002;45(suppl 2):S41–S62.

39. Armstrong BK, Kricker A. The epidemiology of UV induced skin cancer. *J Photochem Photobiol B.* 2001; 63:8–18.

40. Jones JH. *Bad Blood: The Tuskegee Syphilis Experiment.* New York, NY: Free Press; 1993.

41. Reverby SM, ed. *Tuskegee's Truths: Rethinking the Tuskegee Syphilis Study.* Chapel Hill, NC: University of North Carolina Press; 2000.

42. Cruickshank JK. Ethnic health, "ecological balance," the environment, and genes. *Ethn Dis.* 2001; 11:378–384.

43. Kitano H. Systems biology: a brief overview. *Science.* 2002;295:1662–1664.

44. Keller EF. *The Century of the Gene.* Cambridge, Mass: Harvard University Press; 2000.

45. Cruickshank JK, Mbanya JC, Wilks R, Balkas B, McFarlane-Anderson N, Forrester T. Sick genes, sick individuals or sick populations with chronic disease? The emergence of diabetes and high blood pressure in African-origin populations. *Int J Epidemiol.* 2001; 30:111–117.

46. Luke A, Cooper RS, Prewitt TE, Adeyemo AA, Forrester TE. Nutritional consequences of the African diaspora. *Annu Rev Nutr.* 2001;21:47–71.

47. James PT, Leach R, Kalamara E, Shayeghi M. The worldwide obesity epidemic. *Obes Res.* 2001;9(suppl 4):228S–233S.

48. Seidell JC. Obesity, insulin resistance and diabetes—a worldwide epidemic. *Br J Nutr.* 2000;83 (suppl 1):S5–S8.

49. Cooper R, Rotimi C, Ataman S, et al. The prevalence of hypertension in seven populations of West African origin. *Am J Public Health.* 1997; 87:160–168.

50. Rosenthal T, Shamiss A. Migration, acculturation and hypertension. In: Bulpitt CJ, ed. *Handbook of Hypertension: Vol. 20, Epidemiology of Hypertension.* Amsterdam, the Netherlands: Elsevier; 2000:230–248.

51. Cooper RS, Rotimi CN, Kaufman JS, et al. Prevalence of NIDDM among populations of the African diaspora. *Diabetes Care.* 1997;20:343–348.

52. Muntaner C, Nieto FJ, O'Campo P. The bell curve—on race, social class, and epidemiologic research. *Am J Epidemiol.* 1996;144:531–536.

53. Sapolsky RM. Poverty's remains. *Sciences.* 1991;31: 8–10.

54. Krieger N. Commentary: society, biology, and the logic of social epidemiology. *Int J Epidemiol.* 2001;30: 44–46.

55. Williams DR, Neighbors H. Racism, discrimination and hypertension: evidence and needed research. *Ethn Dis.* 2001;11:800–816.

56. Stone AA, Turkkan JS, Bachrach CA, Jobe JB, Kurtzman HS, Cain VS, eds. *The Science of Self-Report: Implications for Research and Practice.* Mahwah, NJ: Lawrence Erlbaum Associates; 2000.

57. Cohen S, Kessler RC, Gordon LU. *Measuring Stress: A Guide for Health and Social Scientists.* New York, NY: Oxford University Press Inc; 1995.

58. Utsey SO. Assessing the stressful effects of racism: a review of instrumentation. *J Black Psychol.* 1998; 24:269–288.

59. Fix M, Struyk R, eds. *Clear and Convincing Evidence: Measurement of Discrimination in America.* Washington, DC: Urban Institutes Press; 1993.

60. Ayers I. *Pervasive Prejudice? Unconventional Evidence of Race and Gender Discrimination.* Chicago, Ill: University of Chicago Press; 2001.

61. Guyll M, Matthews KA, Bromberger JT. Discrimination and unfair treatment: relationship to cardiovascular reactivity among African American and European American women. *Health Psychol.* 2001;20:315–325.

62. Lynch M, Haney C. Discrimination and instructional comprehension: guided discretion, racial bias, and the death penalty. *Law Hum Behav.* 2000; 24:337–358.

63. McConnell AR, Leibold JM. Relations among the Implicit Association Test, discriminatory behavior, and explicit measures of racial attitudes. *J Exp Soc Psychol.* 2001;37:435–442.

64. Fullilove MT. Comment: abandoning "race" as a variable in public health research—an idea whose time has come. *Am J Public Health.* 1998;88:1297–1298.

65. Stolley PD. Race in epidemiology. *Int J Health Serv.* 1999;29:905–909.

66. Krieger N, Williams D, Zierler S. Whiting-out white privilege will not advance studying how racism harms health [letter]. *Am J Public Health.* 1999; 69:782–783.

67. LaVeist TA. On the study of race, racism, and health: a shift from description to explanation. *Int J Health Serv.* 2000;30:217–219.

68. van Ryn M. Research on the provider contribution to race/ethnicity disparities in medical care. *Med Care.* 2002;40:140–151.

69. Smedley BG, Stith AY, Nelson AR, eds. *Unequal Treatment: Confronting Racial and Ethnic Disparities in Health Care.* Washington, DC: National Academy Press; 2002.

70. Kaufman JS, Cooper RS, McGee DL. Socioeconomic status and health in blacks and whites: the

problem of residual confounding and the resiliency of race. *Epidemiology*. 1997;8:621–628.

71. Kaufman JS, Cooper RS. Seeking causal explanations in social epidemiology. *Am J Epidemiol*. 1999;150:113–120.

72. Kaufman JS, Cooper RS. Commentary: considerations for the use of racial/ethnic classification in etiologic research. *Am J Epidemiol*. 2001;154:291–298.

73. Muntaner C. Invited commentary: social mechanisms, race, and social epidemiology. *Am J Epidemiol*. 1999;150:121–126.

74. Krieger N, Davey Smith G. Re: "Seeking causal explanations in social epidemiology" [letter]. *Am J Epidemiol*. 2000;151:831–832.

75. Jones CP. Invited commentary: "race," racism, and the practice of epidemiology. *Am J Epidemiol*. 2001;154:299–304.

76. Davey Smith G, Gunnell D, Ben-Shlomo Y. Lifecourse approaches to socio-economic differentials in cause-specific adult mortality. In: Leon D, Walt G, eds. *Poverty, Inequality, and Health: An International Perspective*. Oxford, England: Oxford University Press Inc; 2001:88–124.

77. Robins JM, Greenland S. Comment on Dawid. *J Am Stat Assoc*. 2000;95:431–435.

78. Winship C, Morgan SL. The estimation of causal effects from observational data. *Annu Rev Sociol*. 1999;25:659–707.

79. Little RJ, Rubin DB. Causal effects in clinical and epidemiological studies via potential outcomes: concepts and analytic approaches. *Annu Rev Public Health*. 2000;21:121–145.

80. Victora CG, Hutly SR, Fuchs SC, Olinto MTA. The role of conceptual frameworks in epidemiologic analysis: a hierarchical approach. *Int J Epidemiol*. 1997;26:224–227.

81. Graham H. Smoking prevalence among women in the European community 1950–1990. *Soc Sci Med*. 1996;43:243–254.

82. Heslop P, Smith GD, Macleod J, Hart C. The socioeconomic position of employed women, risk factors and mortality. *Soc Sci Med*. 2001;53:477–485.

83. Navarro V. Race or class versus race and class: mortality differentials in the United States. *Lancet*. 1990;336:1238–1240.

84. Davey Smith G. Learning to live with complexity: ethnicity, socioeconomic position, and health in Britain and the United States. *Am J Public Health*. 2000;90:1694–1698.

85. Williams E. *Capitalism and Slavery*. New York, NY: Capricorn Books; 1944.

86. Marable M. *How Capitalism Under-developed Black America: Problems in Race, Political Economy, and Society*. Boston, Mass: South End Press; 1983.

87. Cooper F. Back to work: categories, boundaries and connections in the study of labor. In: Alexander P, Halpern R, eds. *Racializing Class, Classifying Race: Labour and Difference in Britain, the USA, and Africa*. New York, NY: St. Martin's Press; 2000.

88. Rothenberg PS, ed. *Race, Class, and Gender in the United States: An Integrated Study*. 5th ed. New York, NY: WH Freeman; 2001.

89. Rives JM, Yousefi M, eds. *Economic Dimensions of Gender Inequality: A Global Perspective*. Westport, Conn: Praeger; 1997.

90. Badgett LMV. *Money, Myths, and Change: The Economic Lives of Lesbians and Gay Men*. Chicago, Ill: University of Chicago Press; 2001.

91. Meyer IH, Schwartz S. Social issues as public health: promise and peril. *Am J Public Health*. 2000;90: 1189–1191.

92. Krieger N. The ostrich, the albatross, and public health: an ecosocial perspective—or why an explicit focus on health consequences of discrimination and deprivation is vital for good science and public health practice. *Public Health Rep*. 2001;116:419–423.

93. Schwartz S, Carpenter KM. The right answer for the wrong question: consequences of type III error for public health research. *Am J Public Health*. 1999;89:1175–1180.

94. Krieger N. Questioning epidemiology: objectivity, advocacy, and socially responsible science. *Am J Public Health*. 1999;89:1151–1153.

95. Gruskin S, Tarantola D. Health and human rights. In: Detels R, McEwen J, Beaglehole R, Tanaka K, eds. *The Oxford Textbook of Public Health*. 4th ed. New York. NY: Oxford University Press Inc. 2001; 311–335.

96. *Universal Declaration of Human Rights*. New York, NY: United Nations; 1948.

97. United Nations International Convention on the Elimination of all Forms of Racial Discrimination. Available at: http://www.unhchr.ch//html/menu3/b /d_icerd.htm. Accessed April 21, 2002.

98. United Nations General Assembly. Report of the World Conference against Racism, Racial Discrimination, Xenophobia and Related Intolerance, Durban, 31 August–8 September 2001. Available at: http:// www.unhchr.ch/huridocda/huridoca.nsf/(Symbol)/A .Conf.189.12. En? Opendocument. Accessed March 11, 2002.

99. McNeill JR. *Something New Under the Sun: An Environmental History of the Twentieth-Century World*. New York, NY: WW Norton & Co; 2000.

100. Dewey SH. *Don't Breathe the Air: Air Pollution and U.S. Environmental Politics, 1945–1970*. College Station, Tex: Texas A&M University Press; 2000.

101. Wellcome Institute for the History of Medicine, History of Twentieth Century Medicine Group. *Ashes to Ashes: The History of Smoking and Health*. Amsterdam, the Netherlands: Rodopi; 1998.

102. Kluger R. *Ashes to Ashes: America's Hundred-Year Cigarette War, the Public Health, and the Unabashed*

Triumph of Philip Morris. New York, NY: Vintage Books; 1997.

103. Schlosser E. *Fast Food Nation: The Dark Side of the All-American Meal.* Boston. Mass: Houghton Mifflin Co; 2001.

104. Satel SL. *PC. M.D.: How Political Correctness Is Corrupting Medicine.* New York, NY: Basic Books; 2000.

105. Muntaner C. Gomez MB. Antiegalitarianism, legitimizing myths, racism, and "neo-McCarthy-ism" in social epidemiology and public health: a review of Sally Satel's *PC. M.D.: How Political Correctness Is Corrupting Medicine. Int J Health Serv.* 2002;32:1–17.

106. Levesque GA. Boston's Black Brahmin: Dr. John S. Rock. *Civil War Hist.* 1980;54:326–346.

107. Smith JM. On the fourteenth query of Thomas Jefferson's notes on Virginia. *Anglo-African Magazine.* 1859;1:225–238.

■ ■ ■ ■ ■ ■ ■ ■ ■ ■

41 GETTING THE NUMBERS RIGHT: STATISTICAL MISCHIEF AND RACIAL PROFILING IN HEART FAILURE RESEARCH

Jonathan Kahn

This is a case study that points to some potentially negative consequences of failing to think clearly about race and racism (see the previous selection). This selection also provides a detailed illustration of the misinterpretation of statistics and the lack of standards and accountability in publishing them on the part of journalists, physicians, medical researchers, and pharmaceutical companies (see selection 28). For example, a widely cited statistic holds that mortality rates from heart disease are twice as high among Blacks as among Whites. This difference has been used to justify the development of an "ethnic drug" designed specifically on the basis of a thinly veiled concept of race. Kahn argues that this approach both diverts attention away from complex socioeconomic, behavioral, and psychosocial factors and favors the tendency to construe race as a biological category. He explains that thinking of diseases in terms of racial susceptibility continues to attract adherents despite a consensus within anthropology and genetics about the disutility of such a construct (see Graves 2001).

This selection shows that the search for pharmaceutical solutions to a presumed biological deficiency in Blacks is based on an incorrect statistic. In reality the difference in mortality rates between Blacks and Whites is very small, although it apparently was larger about two decades ago. Both the current lack of a significant difference and the rapidity of change in the discrepancy between mortality rates of the two groups suggest that the disparity is due to anything but innate biological differences. In contrast, the heart study examined in this selection involves physicians and researchers who seem to believe that the "natural history" of heart disease may be different in Blacks and Whites, or that it is indeed a different disease.

The idea of natural history has arisen in other selections including 39 on the Tuskegee study. It implies that each disease takes a given course that can be generalized across cases. However, the responsiveness of disease processes to social and cultural forces makes such a concept rather illusory and misleading (see Brody 1983). It may be more appropriate to speak of the unnatural history of disease, for political and economic forces like those described in previous selections are powerful determinants

Source: Kahn, Jonathan. "Getting the Numbers Right: Statistical Mischief and Racial Profiling in Heart Failure Research." *Perspectives in Biology and Medicine* 46:4 (2003), 473–483. © The Johns Hopkins University Press. Reprinted with permission of The Johns Hopkins University Press.

of the progression of disease in populations and individuals. Kahn suggests that in a context of scarce resources it would be more fruitful to examine the impacts of racial inequality and the experience of racism than to search for biological mechanisms underlying ethnic disparities in disease distributions and outcomes (see also selections 39, 40).

Questions to keep in mind

What kinds of scientific reasoning are shared between the heart drug trial and the Tuskegee study (selection 39)?

What are some dangers of overemphasizing genetics even for health conditions that correlate well with racial/ethnic groups?

How might the organization of biomedicine (see Part I) favor recourse to genetic explanations as the default setting of physicians and researchers?

What does selection 28 by Margaret M. Lock indicate about categorizing heterogeneous sets of people such as women or ethnic groups as being at risk because of a presumed biological similarity?

The claim that African Americans die from heart failure at a rate twice that of white Americans is widely cited in both medical literature and popular media. This 2:1 mortality ratio has been invoked by medical researchers to guide the search for race-based drug development and therapy for heart failure; by biotech corporations and financial journals exploring the economic potential of such drugs; by professional associations seeking to advise their constituents; and, of course, by scholars and commentators of all stripes arguing over the appropriate use of racial categories in science and medicine. Nonetheless, this statistic is wrong. The most current available data place the age-adjusted ratio of black:white mortality from heart failure at approximately 1.1:1 (CDC 1998, n.d.).[1] Uncritical acceptance and promulgation of inaccurate data may be distorting current efforts to address the real health problems associated with heart failure and also lends credence to those who argue that race can and should be used as a biological category.

BIDIL®: A "RACE-SPECIFIC" THERAPY FOR HEART FAILURE?

BiDil®, a combination of two vasodilators (hydralazine and isosorbide dinitrate), is currently undergoing a trial for FDA approval as the first drug specifically to treat heart failure in African Americans—and only in African Americans (Franciosa et al. 2002).[2] A-HeFT, the African American Heart Failure Trial, aims to enroll 600 to 800 African Americans with heart failure and is likely to be completed by the end of 2003. In March 2001, NitroMed, the privately held biotech firm holding the rights to market BiDil, issued a press release announcing the receipt of a letter from the FDA "describing the regulatory status and ultimate approvability of BiDil" as a new drug (NitroMed 2001a). The release declared that "death rates from heart failure are more than twice as high in black patients than in white patients" and heralded BiDil as presenting an opportunity to address "the disparity in outcomes for African American heart failure patients." NitroMed posited that the disparity might be due to "a pathophysiology found primarily in black patients that may involve nitric oxide (NO) insufficiency." A follow-up press release announcing the initiation of A-HeFT reiterated both the 2:1 mortality ratio and the proposition that "observed racial disparities in mortality and therapeutic response rates in black patients may be due in part to ethnic differences in the underlying pathophysiology of heart failure" (NitroMed 2001b). Clearly, the reported disparity in mortality rates played a central role in suggesting the existence of biological differences in the pathophysiology of heart failure between blacks and whites, and in justifying the creation of a race-specific drug trial.

Soon the word was out. News of a new "ethnic drug" traveled far and wide, with the distinctive speed and lack of nuance of any report that may possibly be (mis)construed as "proving" a biological difference between the races. The issue has been taken up by organizations ranging from the lunatic right to the Revolutionary Communist Progressive Labor Party. More importantly, however, was the extensive coverage of BiDil and the racial difference in mortality from heart failure in mainstream media, including ABC, the BBC, the *Wall Street Journal*, the *New York Times, Business Week*, and the *Financial Times*. In an article about the use of racial categories in evaluating heart drugs in the *Chronicle of Higher Education*, Guterman (2001) reported the 2:1 ratio and asserted that "statistically, the higher rate of heart failure among black people is undeniable." The author provided no citation for this "undeniable" fact. It had simply entered the commonsense realm of accepted reality—as one would not need to cite Copernicus for the proposition that the earth traveled around the sun.

Among scientific and professional publications, *Science* (Editors 2001; Marshall 2001), the newsletter of the American Medical Association (Elliot 2001), and *Today in Cardiology* (2001) all repeated the 2:1 statistic in reports about the initiation of A-HeFT. The Association of Black Cardiologists (2002) reiterated the statistic as recently as 31 July 2002, in a follow-up press release encouraging further enrollment in the trials.

It soon became evident that the 2:1 mortality statistic was framing much of the coverage of BiDil in both the popular and professional literature. The logic implicit in the story seemed to be as follows: (1) blacks die from heart failure at a rate twice that of whites; (2) given this great disparity there must be some underlying biological (as opposed to "merely" social or environmental) factor accounting for the difference; (3) therefore, a response that addresses this different biology of blacks is called for; (4) enter BiDil, a pharmaceutical response to the statistical disparity that appears to have a selectively beneficial effect on blacks at the molecular level.

HISTORY OF THE 2:1 MORTALITY RATIO

From where, then, did this statistic come? I began my search with the most immediate source—NitroMed. In response to my queries, NitroMed provided a press kit that contained some news articles and press releases that cited the 2:1 mortality ratio but did not provide any reference to support this statistic. Likewise, the Association for Black Cardiologists did not have the evidence ready to hand, but they directed me to Feinstein and Kean Healthcare, a subsidiary of Ogilvy PR Worldwide, one of the world's largest public relations firms. Feinstein and Kean, it turns out, was handling the publicity for the A-HeFT trials.

The people at Feinstein and Kean also did not have a reference readily available, but assured me they would look for it. After several weeks, my contact at Feinstein and Kean was pleased to have a citation for me. A study that considered race as a variable in heart failure had just been published in the *New England Journal of Medicine,* and a *Wall Street Journal* article reporting on the study had cited the 2:1 mortality statistic (Small et al. 2002; Zimmerman 2002). While this was a helpful lead, it was not what I was looking for. I was expecting a reference that provided the basis for the original press releases, not a newspaper story published a year and a half later.

The *Wall Street Journal* reporter referred me to the web site of the National Heart, Lung, and Blood Institute (NHLBI). One page on this web site, "Facts About Heart Failure," stated: "Heart failure mortality is about twice as high for African Americans as whites for all age groups" (NHLBI 1995). And yet, while providing ample justification for the *Journal* reporter, the NHLBI itself provided no citation to any underlying study to support its own use of this statistic.

The NHLBI fact sheet was apparently based on data from the National Health and Nutrition Examination Survey (NHANES; Striar 2002). The NHANES data were collected from 1988 to 1991; they were over 10 years old, and those intervening years had seen great strides in the treatment of heart failure. Moreover, NHANES data provide information about the *prevalence* of disease in a population, not about mortality. These are two very different things. Of course, using a study of prevalence to make claims about mortality rates is a gaffe of the first order.

The NHLBI web site contains another page, "Data Fact Sheet: Congestive Heart Failure in the United States: A New Epidemic" (NHLBI 1996). Here, citing the *Vital Statistics of the United States,* NHLBI states: "the death rate for CHF in 1993 was nearly 1.5 times higher in black men and women than in white men and women." (In fact, the graph accompanying this statement shows a black:white mortality ratio of about 1.4:1. It isn't clear why these data differ from those of the CDC [1998]; according to the CDC, the black:white mortality ratio in 1993 was close to 1.1:1.) A third page on the NHLBI web site, "Morbidity and Mortality: 2002 Chart Book on Cardiovascular, Lung, and Blood Diseases," states (citing data from the CDC [n.d.]): "In 1999, [age-adjusted] death rates for CHF within sex groups were *slightly higher* in blacks than in whites" (NHLBI 2002). The same government web site provided statistics of race-based differentials in mortality that ranged from 2:1, to nearly 1.5:1, to "slightly higher" (i.e., 1.12:1). And yet, the only statistic with a firm grounding in current mortality data from the CDC is the third.

The confusing profusion of web-based data available at the NHLBI appears to provide some justification for those in the public media who disseminated the incorrect 2:1 statistic. But what of the doctors and medical researchers who develop therapies and publish papers in peer reviewed journals? The first mention of the statistic in the medical literature related to the development of BiDil came in 1999. An article by Dries, et al., published in the *New England Journal of Medicine* presented a retrospective analysis of data gathered largely in the 1980s from the Studies of Left Ventricular Dysfunction (SOLVD) that purported to identify "racial differences in the outcome of left ventricular dysfunction, [a central component of heart failure]." The authors set their story against the backdrop of "population-based studies [that] have found that black patients with congestive heart failure have a higher mortality rate than white patients with the same condition" (p. 609). This initially posited statistical disparity led them to hypothesize "racial differences in the natural history of left ventricular dysfunction." Thus,

from the outset, the statistic was being used to rationalize a search for race-based biological differences. It was paving the way for reconceptualizing race in biological terms.

In the opening paragraph, the authors present their own version of the statistic: "The population-based mortality rate from congestive heart failure is 1.8 times as high for black men as for white men and 2.4 times as high for black women as for white women" (Dries et al. 1999, p. 609). To document the racial difference in mortality from heart failure, Dries and colleagues cite two editorials by Richard Gillum (1987, 1996), from the National Center for Health Statistics. While the authors note that "not all studies . . . have found a higher mortality among blacks than whites with heart failure," they dismiss these studies and base their research on Gillum's analysis.

Gillum's 1987 editorial, which was based on examination of both published and unpublished data from the National Center for Health Statistics, does state: "the ratio of age adjusted [mortality] rates in blacks and whites was 1.8 for men and 2.4 for women." But this is not a complete reference. The whole sentence reads: *"For persons aged 35 to 74 years,* the ratio of age adjusted rates in blacks and whites was 1.8 for men and 2.4 for women" (emphasis added). Gillum notes that "the ratio of black-to-white [mortality] rates was highest under age 65, approaching 1 [i.e., 1:1] in persons 75 years of age and older." According to Gillum's data, the 35-to-74 age group contains approximately 50 percent of heart failure deaths in blacks but only 30 percent of that in whites. Blacks may have earlier onset and mortality from heart failure—but this is not the same as a higher mortality rate. Moreover, the data in Gillum (1987) represent mortality rates in 1981, 18 years before the publication of the Dries paper. Gillum's more recent editorial (1996) does not provide new data. Not only do Dries and colleagues misquote Gillum (1987) and conflate mortality in the 35–to–74 age group with population-wide mortality, but they also ignore more recent data showing that the overall black:white ratio of age-adjusted mortality rates from heart failure had declined to about 1.1:1 (CDC 1998). Indeed, this documented decline in the disparity between mortality rates over so short a time would seem to support the counter-hypothesis, that the disparity is due more to social, economic, or environmental factors than to any inherent biological difference between the races.

Shortly after the publication of Dries, et al. (1999), Carson and colleagues (1999) claimed to demonstrate a race-based differential response to the BiDil drugs—hydralazine and isosorbide dinitrate; specifically, these authors argued that blacks responded more favorably than whites to the BiDil drug combination. (One of the co-authors was Jay Cohn, the cardiologist who, with Carson, holds the relevant patents concerning BiDil that have been licensed to NitroMed.) Carson, et al. (1999), cite the Dries paper—Carson was a co-author of that paper—and note that the racial differentials observed in the analysis of the SOLVD trials buttress its own findings and "lend credence to the suggestion that therapy for heart failure might appropriately be racially tailored" (Carson et al. 1999, p. 186).

Carson, et al., presented a retrospective analysis of the Vasodilator–Heart Failure Trials (V-HeFT), two trials conducted during the 1980s that studied the efficacy of the BiDil drug combination in treating heart failure (Cohn et al. 1986, 1991). Both V-HeFT I and II, however, tested the efficacy of the BiDil drugs without a specific focus on race. In 1996, when BiDil was first brought to the FDA for approval, it was presented as a drug to treat heart failure in *all* patients—no mention of race was made. It was only after the FDA rejected BiDil in 1997—because the retrospective analysis of the V-HeFT data was insufficiently powered to meet the FDA's threshold for statistical significance—that the BiDil researchers went back to the 1980s V-HeFT data and analyzed it by race. Only then did they find a racial difference in response (Carson et al. 1999).[3] Some of these same researchers, together with NitroMed, then went to the FDA to request approval for the A-HeFT trial. Thus was born BiDil, the "ethnic" drug.

THE USE OF RACIAL CATEGORIES IN MEDICAL RESEARCH

Since Richard Lewontin's (1972) path-breaking work on blood group polymorphisms in different groups and races in the 1970s, scientists have understood that race will statistically explain only a small portion of genetic variations. As a recent editorial in *Nature Genetics* put it, "scientists have long been saying that at the genetic level there is more variation between two individuals in the same population than between populations and that there is no biological basis for 'race'" (Editorial 2001). Yet, as anthropologist Alan Goodman (2000) cautions, during the past decade racialized notions of biology have made a comeback. The story of the 2:1 mortality statistic shows how even well-meaning professionals can contribute to that comeback.

The medical literature is replete with well-documented health disparities that correlate with social categories of race (HHS 2000; IOM 2002). Addressing such disparities is not only legitimate, it is imperative. But connecting these disparities to biological and/or genetic differences is an enterprise fraught with peril. Certain genetic variations may well correlate with groups whose ancestors lived in particular regions (e.g., the sickle-cell trait is found in areas of western Africa, the Mediterranean, and southeast India where malaria has long been prevalent). These correlations can help in identifying and treating diseases. Directly correlating genetic differences to social categories of race may, in the short run, help to address certain health problems. In the long run, however, it opens the door to a wide range of potentially devastating discriminatory practices—some overt, others subtle and hard to see or anticipate. Noting such perils, Lee, Mountain, and Koenig (2001) consider the example of genetic research on breast cancer that targets individuals of Ashkenazi Jewish descent. Such research, they argue, could possibly have two unintended consequences: "stigmatizing the population through the creation of a new racialized disease, while at the same time contributing to the idea that this population is somehow racially distinct" (p. 64).

To the extent that there are real health disparities that correlate with racial groups, an over-emphasis on genetics as an explanation for the disparity can lead to a misallocation of intellectual and material resources. For example, hypertension (a primary cause of heart failure) is caused by a wide array of factors, some social and environmental, some genetic. There are disparities in the incidence of hypertension between blacks and whites. The drive to reduce such racial disparities to a function of genetic variation fuels a logic that would concentrate resources needed to redress disparities on pharmaceutical interventions that work at the molecular level, rather than addressing larger issues of diet, behavior, racism, and economic inequality that also play significant roles in hypertension (Dressler 1990; Klag et al. 1991; Krieger and Sidney 1996; Raphael 2002; Williams 1992). The 2:1 statistic undergirds an approach that assumes a disparity of such magnitude must have a substantial genetic component. In answer to the question, "Do we need to address larger issues of social and economic inequality to redress such health disparities?" such an approach contains the implicit response, "Maybe, but first let's fix the molecules instead of fixing society."

Clyde Yancy, a cardiologist on the steering committee of A-HeFT, has published several articles arguing, "heart failure in blacks is likely to be a *different disease*" (Yancy 2002, p. 224, emphasis added; see also Yancy 2000, 2001). Yancy posits that this "likely" difference is probably based on "physiological explanations." Specifically, he considers certain possible sites for genetic polymorphisms and asserts, "the emerging field of genomic medicine has provided insight into potential mechanisms to explain racial variability in disease expression and response to medical therapy" (Yancy 2002). Elsewhere, Yancy states that the aims of A-HeFT include looking for a genetic pattern among African American patients that may suggest a molecular basis for understanding differential outcomes in heart failure etiology and treatment (UTSMCD 2002).

While surely motivated by a laudable desire to develop better therapies to serve African American communities, Yancy's articles have effectively constructed race as a genetic category. If pressed, Yancy (like many in the field) might say that he was merely using race as a surrogate category to identify different degrees of prevalence among certain groups. But in practice, he has recast the social category of race in genetic terms. This is more than a mere rhetorical gaffe. It opens the door to new forms of discrimination that are based neither wholly on race nor exclusively on genetics but on the subtle and insidious conflation and intermingling of the two. As Braun (2002) has noted, this disjunction between a rhetorical acknowledgment of racial categories as social, and the continued

practical use of such categories as, in effect, genetic, is all too common in biomedical research.

Yancy (2000) begins an editorial on "Heart Failure in African Americans" by noting "a striking incidence of hypertension as a plausible cause of heart failure," and goes on to cite the black:white mortality ratios from Dries, et al. (1999). Yancy argues that the data from the SOLVD trials "do not support socioeconomic factors as important contributors to the excess mortality rate seen in African Americans affected with heart failure." What remains, then, is only to consider the "true physiological differences that may in fact contribute to this pathology."

At first blush, the logic here seems reasonable enough: there is a major race-based health disparity, and since socioeconomic factors do not account for this disparity it must have a physiological (read "genetic") basis. There are several problems with this. First, although Yancy focuses on hypertension as a key precursor to heart failure, he ignores the vast medical and public health literature connecting racial differences in hypertension to everything from diet, to environment, to exercise, to stress (Dressler 1990; Klag et al. 1991; Williams 1992). Many of these social factors correlate strongly with race; for example, the stress of experiencing racism may itself elevate blood pressure (Krieger and Sidney 1996). The more recent of the two editorials by Gillum cited by Dries, et al. (1999), actually argues that current reports "indicate a real heterogeneity in the patterns of death from cardiovascular disease among black Americans," and suggests that "further research must now define the socioeconomic, cultural, behavioral, and ethnic determinants of these differences" (Gillum 1996). Finally, Dries and colleagues claimed to "control" for non-biological variables that might affect differential rates of heart failure mortality by ascertaining the participants' level of education and asking them to report "yes" or "no" and "major financial distress" at any time during the 12 months before enrollment. As the numerous studies of hypertension and Gillum's own admonition show, this represents a remarkably thin conception of the social, economic, and environmental factors that might influence heart failure. As one letter in response to the article noted: "Obviously, it is impossible to control perfectly for the complex and somewhat nebulous concept of socioeconomic status in any study, and Dries et al.

appropriately advise caution in the interpretation of their results. By focusing, however, on biological factors as the fallback explanation for their findings, the authors pay inadequate attention to the environmental, psychosocial, and economic factors that are just as likely, if not more likely, explanations of racial differences in health" (Saha 1999).

The question then becomes how and why these workers so readily came to biology as the "fallback explanation for their findings." First, they are cardiologists, trained to look inside the body to explain disease. They may be aware that social, economic, and environmental factors affect "their" disease, but medical education and the incentives of biomedical research do not provide them with the tools or the inclination to explore such issues in depth. They diagnose pathophysiological processes and deliver therapies to individual patients. The traditional and longstanding divisions between the professions of medicine and public health go a long way toward explaining what questions get asked and which data get analyzed. Secondly, the large apparent mortality ratio between blacks and whites frames the entire analysis of the problem. Given the magnitude of the difference in mortality rates, it may seem to make sense to look at biology as a major factor contributing to this disparity. Perhaps the statistic was so readily and unquestioningly accepted precisely because it comported well with the institutionalized biomedical perspective to look first and foremost for inherent biological, even genetic, explanations for disease. Without this statistic, the impetus to find a biological explanation for differences between blacks and whites is lost.

Heart failure is a serious disease affecting millions of Americans. The cardiologists working on A-HeFT and other related trials have blazed trails toward new therapies that have undeniably provided immense benefits to those suffering from this condition. The A-HeFT trials may well establish the efficacy of BiDil in African Americans. If so, this new drug will undoubtedly benefit the African American community. BiDil, however, may be similarly efficacious in many non–African Americans. The trials won't tell us that. Instead, driven by the 2:1 mortality statistic, they are already providing fodder for those who argue that new links between race and biology must be recognized and acted upon. As the drive to approve

BiDil as an ethnic drug fuels the search for genetic bases for health disparities, it may come to direct the future allocation of resources to address health disparities away from larger social and economics and environmental considerations. It need not be an either/or situation, but given limited resources, we must be wary of the potential consequences of an over-emphasis on genetics as the be-all and end-all of health research. Thus, in the context of broader issues of racial politics, approving BiDil as an ethnic drug may be an example of good intentions paving a perilous road, a road that may lead to something more complicated and potentially more harmful than the "ethnic" drug developers realize.

NOTES

1. In 1998, the CDC report, "Changes in Mortality from Heart Failure—United States, 1980–1995," noted a steady narrowing in the disparity in mortality from heart failure between blacks and whites. Considering individuals 65 and older (among whom approximately 94 percent of heart failure deaths occurred in 1994), the CDC observed, "Because of greater declines in death rates from heart failure among black adults, from 1980 to 1995 the black:white ratio for men narrowed from 1.3:1 to 1.1:1 and for women from 1.4:1 to 1.1:1." More recently, the CDC (n.d.) reported that age-adjusted mortality rates for heart failure (ICD codes 150.0–150.9) in 1999 were 22.7 per 100,000 for blacks and 20.3 per 100,000, a ratio of 1.12:1.

2. Congestive heart failure (CHF) and heart failure (HF) are often used interchangeably, although technically the former is a subset of the latter. Nonetheless, CHF mortality comprises the vast majority of all HF mortality. BiDil is specified for treatment of CHF.

3. To be fair, in presenting their new drug application before the relevant FDA advisory committee in 1997, they had made a passing reference to a potential racial differential, but had not made much of it.

REFERENCES

Association of Black Cardiologists. 2002. Press release, 31 July. <http://biz.yahoo.com/bw/020731/312249_1.html>. Accessed 10 Oct. 2002.

Braun, L. 2002. Race, ethnicity, and health: Can genetics explain disparities? *Perspect. Biol. Med.* 45(2):159–74.

Carson, P., et al. 1999. Racial differences in response to therapy for heart failure: Analysis of the vasodilator-heart failure trials. *J. Card. Fail.* 5(3):178–87.

Centers for Disease Control (CDC). 1998. Changes in mortality from heart failure—United States, 1980–1995. *Mor. Mortal. Wkly. Rep.* 47(30). <http://www.cdc.gov/mmwr/preview/mmwrhtml/00054249.htm>.

Centers for Disease Control (CDC). n.d. CDC Wonder. <http://wonder.cdc.gov>. Accessed 20 Nov. 2002.

Cohn, J. N., et al. 1986. Effect of vasodilator therapy on mortality in chronic congestive heart failure: Results of a veterans administration study (V-HeFT). *N. Engl. J. Med.* 314:1547–52.

Cohn, J. N., et al. 1991. A comparison of enalapril with hydralazine-isosorbide dinitrate in the treatment of chronic congestive heart failure. *N. Engl. J. Med.* 325:303–10.

Department of Health and Human Services (HHS). 2000. *Healthy people 2010: Understanding and improving health,* 2d ed. <http://www.healthypeople.gov/document/>. Accessed 4 Dec. 2002.

Dressler, W. W. 1990. Lifestyle, stress and blood pressure in a Southern black community. *Psychosom. Med.* 52:182–98.

Dries, D. L., et al. 1999. Racial differences in the outcome of left ventricular dysfunction. *N. Engl. J. Med.* 340(8):609–16.

Editorial, 2001. Genes, drugs and race. *Nat. Genet.* 29:239–40.

Editors, 2001. Trials for "ethnic" drug. *Science* 291:2547

Elliot, V. S. 2001. FDA may approve new heart drug for Blacks. Amednews.com (26 March). <http://www.ama-assn.org/sci-pubs/amnews/pick_01/hlsc0326.htm>. Accessed 12 Dec. 2002.

Franciosa, J. A., et al. 2002. African-American heart failure trial (A-HeFT): Rationale, design, and methodology. *J. Card. Fail.* 8:128–35.

Gillum, R. F. 1987. Heart failure in the United States, 1970–1985. *Am. Heart J.* 113:1043–45.

Gillum, R. F. 1996. The epidemiology of cardiovascular disease in black Americans. *N. Engl. J. Med.* 335:1597–99.

Goodman, A. J. 2000. Why genes don't count (for racial differences in health). *Am. J. Pub. Health* 90:1699–1702.

Guterman, G. 2001. Shades of doubt and fears of bias in the doctors office. *Chron. High. Ed.* (25 May). <http://chronicle.com/free/v47/i37/37a01601.htm#race>. Accessed 16 Dec. 2002.

Institute of Medicine (IOM). 2002. *Unequal treatment: Confronting racial and ethnic disparities in health care.* Washington, DC: National Academies Press.

Kevles, D. 1995. *In the name of eugenics: Genetics and the uses of human heredity.* Cambridge: Harvard Univ. Press.

Klag, P., et al. 1991. The association of skin color with blood pressure in U.S. blacks with low socioeconomic status. *JAMA* 265:599–602.

Krieger, N., and S. Sidney. 1996. Racial discrimination and blood pressure: The CARDIA study of young black and white adults. *Am. J. Pub. Health* 86: 1370–78.

Lee, S. S.-J., J. Mountain, and B. A. Koenig. 2001. The meanings of "race" in the new genomics: Implications for health disparities research. *Yale J. Health Policy Law Ethics* 1:33–68.

Lewontin, R. C. 1972. The apportionment of human diversity. *Evol. Biol.* 6:381–98

Marshall, E. 2001. Trial for "ethnic" therapy. *Science Now* (26 March). <http://sciencenow.sciencemag.org/cgi/content/full/2001/326/2>. Accessed 12 Dec. 2002.

National Heart, Lung, and Blood Institute. (NHLBI). 1995. Facts about heart failure. <http://www.nhlbi.nih.gov/health/public/heart/other/hrtfail.htm>. Accessed 3 Dec. 2002.

National Heart, Lung, and Blood Institute. (NHLBI). 1996. Data fact sheet: Congestive heart failure in the United States: A new epidemic. <http://www.nhlbi.nih.gov/health/public/heart/other/CHF.htm>. Accessed 3 Dec. 2002.

National Heart, Lung, and Blood Institute. (NHLBI). 2002. Morbidity and mortality: 2002 chart book on cardiovascular, lung, and blood diseases, at 39. <http://www.nhlbi.nih.gov/resources/docs/02_chtbk.pdf>. Accessed 3 Dec. 2002.

NitroMed. 2001a. Press release, 8 March. <http://www.nitromed.com>. Accessed 4 Dec. 2002.

NitroMed. 2001b. Press release, 17 March. <http://www.nitromed.com>. Accessed 4 Dec. 2002.

Raphael, D. 2002. *Social justice is good for our hearts: Why societal factors—not lifestyles—are major causes of heart disease in Canada and elsewhere.* Toronto: CSJ Foundation for Research and Education.

Saha, S. 1999. Letter to the editor. *N. Engl. J. Med.* 341: 287.

Small, K. M., et al. 2002. Synergistic polymorphisms of beta 1 and alpha 2C adrenergic receptors and the risk of congestive heart failure. *N. Engl. J. Med.* 347: 1135–42.

Striar, D., Senior Press Liaison, National Heart, Lung, and Blood Institute. 2002. Personal communication, 15 Oct.

Today in Cardiology. 2001. HF drug trial planned for Black patients. (July). <http://www.cardiologytoday.com/200107/frameset.asp?article=AHeFT.asp>. Accessed 20 Aug. 2002.

University of Texas Southwestern Medical Center at Dallas (UTSMCD). 2002. News release, 15 May. Disparities in black Americans' response to heart failure therapies may signal different disease. <http://www.newswise.com/articles/2002/5/BLACKHRT.SWM.html>. Accessed 4 Dec. 2002.

Williams, D. R. 1992. Black-white differences in blood pressure: The role of social factors. *Ethn. Dis.* 2:126–41.

Yancy, C. W. 2000. Editorial. Heart failure in African Americans: A cardiovascular enigma. *J. Card. Fail.* 6(3):183–86

Yancy, C. W. 2001. Heart failure in blacks: Etiological and epidemiological differences. *Curr. Card. Rep.* 3:191–97.

Yancy, C. W. 2002. The role of race in heart failure therapy. *Curr. Card. Rep.* 4:218–25.

Zimmerman, R. 2002. Pair of genes is said to increase risk of heart failure in blacks. *Wall Street J.* (10 Oct.).

Part IV

Special Topics and Case Studies

The previous selections presented a range of theoretical perspectives and topical interests in medical anthropology and related fields. The selections in this final part of the book apply concepts and approaches from earlier selections to case studies, essays, and research reports grouped according to topic or issue. The first two selections focus on non-insulin-dependent diabetes, or NIDDM, a health concern also discussed in other selections (see 15, 17, 33, 40). The purpose is to consider how a chosen theoretical perspective or level of analysis shapes the research questions that are asked and limits the range of evidence that is considered relevant.

The first selection in the pair, by Jared Diamond, takes an evolutionary approach, whereas selection 43, by Robyn McDermott, is more cultural in emphasis but informed by attention to biological issues as well. Together, they unite many arguments that appear elsewhere in the book. For example, the discordance hypothesis is at the center of Diamond's argument, and he also considers specific historical events that may have favored especially "thrifty" genes in some populations. Both selections consider the difference between gene frequency and gene expression. McDermott discusses cultural beliefs about NIDDM and how they influence the perceptions and behavior of health professionals and patients. In particular, she examines the process of geneticization and medicalization in industrialized society (see selection 28) and a form of racial thinking in Australia that construes Aborigines as genetically predisposed to NIDDM (see selections 40, 41). Echoing many other selections, McDermott argues that social and economic factors are of primary importance in accounting for epidemics of NIDDM in many locations around the world.

The second group of selections concerns the topic of food and food use. Food is a powerful cultural and religious symbol, a central instrument of social exchange, a valuable commodity and focus of economic activity, and a material product that wends its way through politico-economic systems. As we have seen in Part II, changes in food procurement systems have been associated with major changes in health patterns. Food connects people, land, water, and plant and animal life (see selection 54). Not surprisingly, there is tension between the expansion of industrialized, globalized agricultural production and commodity markets and social movements reacting against biotechnology, massive agricultural input companies, and governmental and other institutions that favor the delocalization of food production and consumption (see Parts II and III; Lentz 1999; Nestle 2002, 2003; Ungar and Teaford 2002).

Selection 44 is about geophagy, the consumption of dirt as food or medicine. Gerald N. Callahan reviews biological and cultural reasons for a practice that biomedicine considers an expression of psychopathology. He describes some important developmental and physiological mechanisms related to ingestion of soil components and suggests that geophagy is an example of coevolution. The selection builds on the evolutionary, ethnopharmacological, and interpretive approaches discussed elsewhere in the book. In selection 45, William Jankowiak and Dan Bradburd draw on cross-cultural comparisons to trace the use of drug foods as labor inducers and enhancers in a large number of social and historical contexts. Their argument has links to various selections on political economy and on plant use interspersed throughout this book. Selection 46 shifts the focus more directly to culture, examining meanings associated with vegetarianism. Marjaana Lindeman's research on vegetarians, semivegetarians, and omnivores explores connections between chosen systems of nutrition and identity, happiness, worldview, and eating-disordered behavior.

Infant and child health is the subject of the next group of selections. Biocultural anthropologists are interested in infant and child health because of the impact of living conditions on development (see Part II on human plasticity). Scholars and practitioners in public health often focus on maternal, infant, and child health because relatively simple and inexpensive interventions can make a large difference to population health. These interventions include oral rehydration therapy for diarrhea, promotion of breast-feeding, and immunization. However, unrelenting poverty, lack of infrastructure such as clean water systems, and persistent infectious diseases result in "double burdens" of both undernutrition and over-nutrition/obesity, and both chronic and infectious disease, in developing countries and in the poor socioeconomic strata of wealthy countries. Children's health is also affected by violence, sexual abuse, child labor, and the use of child soldiers (Scheper-Hughes and Sargent 1999). Another important area of research is children's health beliefs and explanatory models of disease (see Solomon and Cassimatis 1999).

Selection 47 concerns infant feeding practices and their health impacts on infants and mothers. Elizabeth D. Whitaker considers the biological consequences of breastfeeding in ways different from those practiced by humans in preagricultural societies. The selection traces the demographic and cultural changes that have led to the medicalization of childbirth and breastfeeding in industrialized societies and contributed to an abbreviation or elimination of breastfeeding (see Davis-Floyd and Dumit 1998; DeVries et al. 2001; Rapp 1999; Whitaker 2000; selections 2, 11, 27, 28). Selection 48, by Patricia Bustos et al., is a report on research from Chile showing that ethnicity is less salient than poverty as a factor affecting children's growth. This conclusion challenges prevailing views that some "races" are genetically destined to being short (or tall), recalling the selections on human variation in Part II and on racism in Part III.

The focus turns next to the topic of sex and gender, an area that intersects with issues such as inequality, demography, cultural construction of disease categories, stigma, and patient–healer relationships. Often, when people talk about gender and health, they imply that what is at issue is women's health. This is in part because men's physiology and health have long been taken for granted as the human standard, so that it has been necessary to call attention to women's health as well. However, the study of women's health continues to be shaped by political and cultural forces. Medical and moral discussions often essentialize girls and women as reproducers, focusing attention on sexual and reproductive concerns to the exclusion of other health issues. One illustration is the lag in awareness of heart disease among women compared to the abundant attention given to breast cancer. Another is the dedication of scientific and public health resources to controlling the fertility of women as opposed to men. A third is the blaming of women for sexually transmitted infections from the time of syphilis to the era of AIDS, to the detriment of recognizing or even acknowledging the role of men.

Just as women should not be considered a uniform category (see selection 28), neither should men's particular and variable living conditions and experiences be ignored. Moreover, the fact that men are taken for granted as the biological standard does not mean that gender roles and expectations do not apply to them (see Bledsoe et al. 2000; Campbell 1995). Accordingly, the selections in this part of the book consider both women and men, together and separately.

Many gender-related topics are not covered directly. These include demography (see Greenhalgh 1995), sexually transmitted disease (see Hutchinson 2001; Parker 2001), and fertility/infertility, contraception, and reproduction (see Becker 2000; Ellison 2001; Ginsburg and Rapp 1995; Inhorn and van

Balen 2002; Russell et al. 2000). Also not included is a selection on female circumcision. This is a phenomenon that is too complex, cross-culturally variable, and controversial for a short review, especially because it would be appropriate to also consider male circumcision (see Caldwell et al. 1997; Gruenbaum 2001).

Selection 49, by Nancy Krieger, explains how biological sex and culturally constructed gender both can impact on exposure to disease, access to and experience of health services, and the progression of sickness (see Doyal 1995). Krieger develops and applies a model for analyzing the direction and quality of these impacts, laying the groundwork for the selections that follow. Barbara D. Miller's comparative analysis of female-selective abortion relates sex and gender to cultural beliefs and politico-economic structures in patriarchal systems that privilege male births. She shows how the rise of new imaging technologies has converged with social and economic changes and preexisting cultural beliefs to favor the spread of the practice in many areas.

Selection 51, by Alean Al-Krenawi, considers marriage and family and the effect of the type of marriage relationship on the mental health and material well-being of women. Al-Krenawi finds that first wives in polygamous marriages in patriarchal Bedouin society suffer greater psychological distress and reduced social and economic well-being compared to women in monogamous marriages (on comparative mental health and psychiatric treatment, see Desjarlais et al. 1995; Kleinman 1980; Littlewood 2002). The form and meaning of the marriage relationship differs between the two types of marriage relationship, with repercussions on wives and their children.

Julie Park's selection on hemophilia in New Zealand turns our attention to men's experiences as sons, husbands, and fathers. The selection focuses on rugby as a central cultural value that can become an idiom of either distress or normality for hemophiliac boys and men, depending on whether or not their disease prevents them from participating in the sport. Park's analysis of rugby unpacks the hegemonic gender constructions the sport has expressed and conveyed over time and their continuing impacts on both men and women. The performance aspect of gender bridges Park's work with that of Joan Cassell in selection 53. Cassell analyzes the culture of the predominantly male medical specialization of surgery (see also Katz 1999), and the gender-specific behavioral expectations of women and men that are enforced by physicians and nurses through everyday interactions. Cassell emphasizes gender as expression rather than essence, echoing the message of Krieger and the other authors in this group of selections, and recalling the performance aspects of healing roles discussed in Part I.

The final set of selections on biotechnology and bioethics begins with an essay by David Ehrenfeld on the use of hormones to increase milk yields in dairy cows. Selection 54 illustrates how the questions one asks circumscribe the kind of information that is considered important and that can be generated by research (see also selection 7). It connects with the themes in the food and food use section, as well as selections throughout the book on topics such as agriculture, the body, and biotechnology in general and medical technology in particular (see Browdin 2000; Lock et al. 2000; selections 27, 28).

The selection by Ehrenfeld is followed by a selection on organ transplantation that continues the discussion of technology and cultural values. The possibility of transplanting organs has arisen through both technological advancements of the past few decades, and a contemporaneous redefinition of death. Central to organ transfer is the idea that brain death represents true death, making it possible to remove organs from a body that otherwise appears alive and is kept alive through technological means. The concept of brain death has a particular, recent history and is not a cultural universal. Even where it is scientifically and publicly accepted, as in the U.S., it still generates considerable unease among both patients and health professionals. The criteria used for measuring brain death vary across states and among hospitals within the same state, contributing to ambiguity and uncertainty and making it clear that the setting of standards is a moral domain. Alongside its potential to save lives, the tansfer of most organs depends upon death and consequently generates complex and often deeply troubling emotions for donor families, organ recipients, and procurement professionals (see Joralemon 1995; Lock 2002; Sharp 2001).

Selection 55 by Nancy Scheper-Hughes concerns the largely illegal international transfer of kidneys from economically desperate live donors to wealthy recipients. Scheper-Huges examines this practice in light of global politico-economic structures and new symbolic constructs concerning displaceable organs and the meaning of human life itself. The practice raises questions about the validity of Western-oriented medical ethics applied to international settings and even within the industrialized nations themselves (see Hoffmaster 2001). In particular, Scheper-Huges questions the relevance of ideas about individual agency and market freedom to a practice by which poor people's bodily integrity is compromised for the sake of short-term survival. It is worth noting that also within the United States, socio-economic inequalities create both a greater disease burden and reduced access to organs among disadvantaged classes (see Koch 2002).

Part IV concludes with selection 56 by Finn Bowring on ethics in relation to therapeutic and reproductive cloning. Bowring suggests that the true danger of cloning is less the creation of an unattainable biological product than the emergence of an ill-advised way of thinking about personal identity and the shaping of children's destiny. As selections 28 and 50 indicate, there does not seem to be any end to people's enthusiasm for testing and screening. A likely result is increasing social disapprobation of people who refuse to submit to screening and any resulting medical interventions, including expectant parents (see Parens and Asch 2000). The specter of cultural conceits about humanity's ability to predetermine traits and the expectations of behavior that feed and are reinforced by such beliefs invites us to consider what it means to be human and brings us back to the mind–body, biology–culture nexus at the heart of this book.

Suggested Films

Diet Wars. 2004. Jon Palfreman, producer (Frontline). 60 min.

Making Babies. 1996. Produced by Doug Hamilton and Sarah Spinks, producers (Frontline). 60 min.

Harvest of Fear. 2001. Jon Palfreman, producer (Frontline). 120 min.

Organ Farm. 2001. Frank Simmonds and Ben Loeterman, producers (Frontline). 120 min.

■ ■ ■ ■ ■ ■ ■ ■ ■

42 THE DOUBLE PUZZLE OF DIABETES

Jared Diamond

This is the first of a pair of selections presenting different theoretical approaches leading to different research questions and diverse ideas about the management of Type II diabetes. This first selection emphasizes the interaction between genetic susceptibility factors and lifestyle characteristics as the mechanism explaining the distribution of the disease. Diamond's analysis illustrates Krieger's point about the difference between gene frequency and gene expression (selection 40) and Goodman's argument about distinguishing between groups of people sharing high frequencies of certain genes and groups of people classified according to cultural concepts of race (selection 15).

The selections in Part II followed the radical changes in diet and activity that have occurred over the past millennia with the advent of agriculture, and later, industrial manufacturing. The mismatch between our Paleolithic physiology and new conditions of overnutrition and insufficient exercise has led to diseases characteristic of societies practicing a Western lifestyle. More recent changes carry us along the same path. For example, the change in agricultural practices that began a century ago in the United States and resulted in livestock being kept in pens and fed cereals has had the intended effect of fattening the animals and the meat we eat. It should come as no surprise that recent food industry practices and governmental dietary recommendations emphasizing grains as the basis of human nutrition have contributed to an epidemic of obesity in both adults and children (Sears 2001).

Diamond argues that it is not just our universal human metabolism adapted to a diet low in fat and sugar, but specific historical events that make some populations especially prone to diabetes. The "thrifty genes" of survivors of events such as perilous migrations protect against famine by causing more efficient food use and storage, but in conditions of plenty result in the elevated blood sugar levels that characterize diabetes. One example is Native Americans, whose ancestors spent a period of time in the extreme north after the first migration and were forced to subsist on meat with few carbohydrate foods. The genetic adaptations of survivors now lead to a metabolic syndrome involving obesity, diabetes, and other disorders. Diamond suggests that Pima Indians suffered a more recent stressful event when European colonists diverted their water supply in the late nineteenth century, which then selected out the people who did not have the benefit of thrifty genes. The result is an even higher susceptibility to diabetes than that of other Native American groups. Diamond suggests that by identifying such groups, it might be possible to devise specific interventions to prevent the disease.

Questions to keep in mind

What additional evidence would support the hypothesis that genetic factors cause high rates of diabetes in certain populations?

How are selection pressures different for foraging societies than agricultural ones (see selections 17–21)?

Should advice about the health impacts of a Western lifestyle be given only to groups with high frequencies of identified susceptibility factors?

What do you think are the most important directions for future research on diabetes?

Source: Diamond, J. "The Double Puzzle of Diabetes." Reprinted from *Nature* 423(6940):599–602 copyright 2003 MacMillan Publishers Ltd.

Type 2 diabetes mellitus exacts a huge toll in money and human suffering. For instance, it accounts for more than 100 billion dollars of health-care costs annually in the United States, or 15% of costs due to all diseases combined. The number of cases worldwide is estimated at 150 million. But this is a minimum number because, for each diagnosed case, there is thought to be one undiagnosed case in First World countries and eight in the Third World.[1] Despite its other name of adult-onset diabetes, the disease is becoming more common in young people.[2,3] At its present rate of increase, within a few decades it will be one of the world's commonest diseases and biggest public-health problems,[2,4] with an estimated minimum of half-a-billion cases.[5] This explosion in prevalence is occurring especially in the Third World, at about 50% per decade; and because the epidemic is just beginning in the world's two most populous countries, India and China, by the year 2010 more than half of the world's diabetics will be Asians.[2,3,5]

There are two main forms of diabetes mellitus, and the principal characteristics are outlined in the Box. But this is the story of type 2, not only because it is much more common and rising steeply in prevalence, but because that rise is doubly puzzling. Not only would the disease seem to be highly disadvantageous in terms of natural selection, but some human populations are much more affected than others.

The geographical variations are shown in Figure 42.1. The lowest prevalences, of practically zero, are in rural Third World areas, whereas the highest, 37–50%, are among Nauru Islanders of the tropical Pacific.[6,7] Pima Indians in Arizona[8] and urban Wanigela people in Papua New Guinea.[9] Most of the world's broad geographical groupings of people include populations of both very low and very high prevalence—for instance, Mapuche Indians versus Arizona Pima Indians, and rural New Guineans versus the urban Wanigela. Populations undergoing increases in the incidence of type 2 diabetes include not only Asian Indians and Chinese, but also Japanese, Aboriginal Australians, Hispanic Americans and Afro-Americans.[2,4,10] A conspicuous exception is the absence of any comparable explosion, or very-high-prevalence population, among people of European ancestry. Thus, the puzzling aberrations

The Diversity of Diabetes Mellitus

The term "diabetes mellitus" covers a wide variety of conditions that are linked only by shared symptoms arising from high levels of blood sugar. That diversity may be crudely partitioned[2,3,11,12] into type 2 (adult-onset) and the less-common type 1 (juvenile-onset). The respective prevalences among diabetics in the United States are 90–95% and 5–10%. Both diseases centre on the hormone insulin, which is responsible for mediating the uptake by cells of glucose from the blood.

Type 1 diabetes (insulin-dependent diabetes mellitus) is an autoimmune disease in which autoantibodies destroy the pancreatic-islet cells that synthesize insulin. Patients are thin, produce little or no insulin, and are prone to ketosis, a particular metabolic imbalance. They carry certain gene types—the HLA alleles *DR3*, *DR4* or both—that encode particular components of the immune system. Type 2 diabetes (non-insulin-dependent diabetes mellitus) involves altered insulin secretion and insulin resistance. Patients are often obese and are not subject to ketosis. They do produce insulin but become insulin-resistant—that is, unable to respond effectively to it.

Distinguishing the two forms can be complicated, however, because there is early-onset type 2 and late-onset type 1. Type 2 diabetes is itself very heterogeneous, both genetically and in the associated pathological and physiological symptoms. The disease arises from at least 60 identified genetic disorders, united only by the common feature of high blood-glucose levels due to insulin resistance. This heterogeneity reinforces the evolutionary puzzle: genes that predispose the bearer to type 2 diabetes must really convey some advantage because they have evidently been preserved independently many times by natural selection. The "thrifty gene" hypothesis, according to which such genes allow efficient food utilization in times of plenty, in preparation for famine, provides a possible explanation.

J.D.

are not Nauruans and Pimas, as usually assumed; they are merely the extreme examples. Instead, the aberration demanding explanation is Europe.

As an evolutionary biologist, I have long been puzzled by these differences. In this article I shall suggest a hypothesis for why we are not seeing nearly as much of an explosion among Europeans as among other populations. The evidence comes

Population grouping	Region	Percentage prevalence
Europeans	Britain	2
	Germany	2
	Australia (1981)	2
	Australia (2002)	8
	United States	8
Native Americans	Chile Mapuche	1
	US Hispanic	17
	US Pima	50
Pacific Islanders	Nauru (1952)	0
	Nauru (2002)	41
New Guineans	Rural	0
	Urban	37
Aboriginal Australians	Traditional	0
	Westernized	23
Middle East	Yemen, traditional	4
	Yemenite Jews in Israel	13
	Lebanon, westernized	14
Black Africans	Rural Tanzania	1
	Urban South Africa	8
	United States	13
Chinese	Rural China	0
	Urban Singapore	9
	Urban Taiwan	12
	Urban Mauritius	13
Asian Indians	Rural India	0
	Urban Tanzania	11
	Urban India	12
	Urban Singapore	17
	Urban Mauritius	17
	Urban Fuji	22

Figure 42.1   Age-standardized prevalence of type 2 diabetes mellitus.

Among the main features are the low prevalence among groups of European origin, especially those remaining in Europe; the high prevalence among Pima Indians and urban New Guineans, and among Nauruans today; and the higher prevalence in urban or westernized groups, compared with their rural or traditional counterparts. Because type 2 prevalence in a given population increases with age, it would be misleading to compare raw values of prevalence between two populations that differ in their age distribution; the raw values would be expected to differ merely as a result of the different age distributions, even if prevalences at a given age were identical between the two populations. Instead, one measures the prevalence in a population as a function of age, then calculates what the prevalence would be for that whole population if it had a certain standardized age distribution.[30] (From refs 5, 30 and other sources.)

initially from food history, and tests of it may come from medicine, medical history and molecular biology.

GENETICS AND LIFESTYLE

Genetics

The high prevalence of type 2 diabetes in any large population poses a further evolutionary question. Why is the disease so common, when it should disappear as those genetically susceptible to it are removed by natural selection? (Readers who answer, "Because it kills only older individuals whose child-bearing or child-rearing years are behind them" will find this objection answered below.) The disease certainly has a genetic component,[11,12] as is evident from the following.

- There is a concordance in diagnosis of nearly 100% for monozygotic twins (those that develop from the same fertilized egg, and so have identical genetic constitutions), but only 20% for dizygotic twins. The latter figure is comparable to that for non-twin siblings, suggesting that factors in the uterus play a quantitatively minor role (without denying the existence of such factors[3,13]).

- The prevalence of diabetes among Hispanic Americans varies according to their proportion of Native American genetic ancestry.[10]

- Many specific genetic susceptibility factors have been identified.[11,12] Because the highest mutation rates for any human gene are only around 10^{-5} per generation, the expectation is that only deleterious genes with prevalences below 10^{-5} could be sustained within a population by recurrent mutations alone. The actual incidence of type 2 diabetes is up to 50,000 times higher. And the high prevalence of the disease in many large, ancient, well-mixed populations rules out explanations in terms of the founder effect or genetic drift. These, respectively, are instances where there was only a very limited initial genetic variability, or where random processes such as selective extinction operated, and they tend to affect only small populations. Hence, the high prevalences of type 2 diabetes, like the

prevalence of sickle-cell anaemia in certain groups, must be sustained by some compensating advantage that offsets the obvious morbidity and mortality (in the case of sickle-cell disease, the compensating advantage is a certain resistance to malaria).

Lifestyle

In addition to that genetic component, type 2 diabetes also involves environmental and lifestyle risk factors—especially high calorie intake and low exercise.[2,11,12,14] For example:

- Disease prevalence is 5–10 times higher in obese people than in those of normal weight.

- The metabolic abnormalities and symptoms of diabetes can often be reversed by dieting and exercise.

- The symptoms decline or disappear in populations under starvation conditions—as, for instance, they did in French diabetics under the food rationing imposed during the 1870–71 siege of Paris.[3]

- Prevalence of diabetes increases within about two decades[1,15] in populations that have adopted a high-calorie, low-exercise lifestyle as a result of emigration: for instance, when Yemenite Jews were airlifted to Israel, and when there was a burst of Japanese emigration to the United States. Other examples are groups of emigrant Asian Indians in Fiji, Mauritius, Singapore, Tanzania, the United States and Britain,[3,4,16] and of emigrant Chinese in Hong Kong, Mauritius, Singapore and Taiwan.[2,3,17]

- Prevalence similarly rises rapidly in a population that remains in the same geographical area but in which calorie intake increases and exercise decreases. Examples include the Nauru Islanders, Arizona Pima Indians, white Australians, urban Aboriginal Australians, urban black Africans in Cape Town,[1] urban Samoans, Chinese, Asian Indians and Japanese.

- In Japan, graphs against time of the incidence of type 2 diabetes and of economic indicators are parallel—down to details of year-to-year wiggles. That's because people eat more, and so risk developing diabetic symptoms, when they have more money.[3]

- As I learned while serving on the Animal Regulation Committee of the Los Angeles Zoo, there is now a diabetes epidemic among captive populations of many primate species whose zoo lifestyle approximates the high-calorie, low-exercise lifestyle of urban humans in the First World. It will be instructive to see whether or not our primate relatives share genes conferring susceptibility to diabetes with us.

All in all, the basis of type 2 diabetes can be summarized as follows[3]: it "is a lifestyle disorder with the highest prevalence seen in populations that have a heightened genetic susceptibility; environmental factors associated with lifestyle unmask the disease."

NAURU

Nauru is a remote island in the Pacific that was colonized by the Micronesians in prehistoric times. It was annexed by Germany in 1888, occupied by Australia in 1914 and eventually achieved independence in 1968. It is the world's smallest republic, but it also has a less welcome distinction. The island is the site of a grimly instructive epidemic of diabetes, which illustrates a rarely documented phenomenon—an epidemic of a genetic disease.[6,7] Epidemics of infectious diseases wax when transmission of the infectious agent increases; they then wane when the number of susceptible potential victims falls, due both to acquired immunity of the survivors and to differential mortality of those who are genetically susceptible. An epidemic of a genetic disease waxes because of a rise in environmental risk factors, and then wanes when the number of susceptible potential victims falls (but only because of the preferential deaths of those who are genetically more susceptible).

The traditional lifestyle of Nauruans was based on agriculture and fishing, and involved frequent episodes of starvation because of droughts and the island's poor soil. Early European visitors nevertheless noted that Nauruans were plump, and that they admired big, fat people and put girls on a diet

to fatten them and so make them more attractive. In 1906 it was discovered that most of Nauru consists of high-quality phosphate rock that could be used for fertilizer, and in 1922 the mining company extracting the rock began to pay royalties to the islanders. As a result of this new wealth, average sugar consumption by Nauruans reached a pound per day by 1927, and labourers were imported because Nauruans disliked working as miners.

During the Second World War the island was occupied by Japanese military forces, who imposed forced labour, reduced food rations to half-a-pound of pumpkin per day, and then deported most of the population to Truk, where half of them died of starvation. When the survivors returned, they regained their phosphate royalties, and resumed eating sugar and other store-bought food. They abandoned agriculture almost completely, became sedentary, and came to rely on motor vehicles to travel around their 20-km^2 island. Following independence in 1968, per capita phosphate royalties rose to A\$37,500 (US\$22,500) annually, making Nauruans among the world's richest people. Today they are the most obese and have the highest blood pressure of all peoples in the Pacific; their average body weight is half as much again as that of Australians of European origin.

Although colonial European physicians on Nauru knew how to recognize type 2 diabetes, and diagnosed it there in non-Nauruan labourers, the first case in Nauruans was not noted until 1925. The second was recorded in 1934. After 1954, however, the prevalence of the disease rose steeply and it became the commonest cause of non-accidental death. One-third of all Nauruans over the age of 20, two-thirds of those over age 55, and 70% of those few who survive to the age of 70, are diabetics. Within the past decade, prevalence of the disease has begun to fall, not because of mitigation of environmental risk factors (obesity and the sedentary lifestyle are as common as ever), but presumably because those who are genetically most susceptible have died. If this interpretation is correct, then Nauru provides the most rapid instance known to me of natural selection in a human population—an occurrence of detectable population-wide selection within less than 40 years.

The case of Nauru also illustrates why, earlier in this article, I dismissed the usual objection that type 2 diabetes lacks selective impact because it supposedly affects people only when their reproductive years are behind them. In fact, although the disease appears mainly after age 50 in Europeans, in Nauruans and other non-Europeans it affects people of reproductive age in their twenties and thirties, especially pregnant women, whose fetuses and newborn babies are also at increased risk. For instance, in Japan today, more children suffer from type 2 than type 1 diabetes, despite the latter's popular name of juvenile-onset diabetes. Moreover, in traditional human societies, unlike modern First World societies, no old person is truly "post-reproductive" and selectively unimportant, because grandparents contribute crucially to the food supply, social status and survival of their children and grandchildren.[18]

THRIFTY GENES

The leading evolutionary theory for the possible benefits of genes predisposing to type 2 diabetes is James Neel's "thrifty gene" hypothesis.[13,14,19,20] Neel postulated the existence of metabolically thrifty genes: these permit more efficient food utilization, fat deposition and rapid weight gain at occasional times of food abundance, thereby making the gene-bearer better able to survive a subsequent famine. Examples of thrifty genes would include those resulting in high levels of insulin or of leptin (a hormone released by fat cells that regulates appetite), or in hair-triggered insulin release. Such genes would be advantageous under the conditions of unpredictably alternating feast and famine that characterized the traditional human lifestyle, but they would lead to obesity and diabetes in the modern world when the same individuals stop exercising, begin foraging for food only in supermarkets, and consume three high-calorie meals day in, day out. Following Arthur Koestler, Zimmet refers to the spread of this lifestyle to the Third World as "coca-colonization."[3,4]

So accustomed are we in the First World to regular meals that we find it hard to imagine the fluctuating food availability that was formerly the norm and remains so in some parts of the world. I often encountered such fluctuations during my fieldwork among New Guinea mountaineers still subsisting by farming and hunting. For example, some years ago, in a memorable incident, I hired a dozen men to carry heavy equipment all day over a steep trail up to a mountain campsite. We arrived just before sunset, expecting to meet another group of porters with food, and instead found that they had not arrived because of a misunderstanding. Faced with hungry, exhausted men and no food, I expected to be lynched. Instead, my carriers just laughed and said, *"Orait, i samting nating, yumi slip nating, enap yumi kaikai tumora"* ("OK, it's no big deal, we'll sleep on empty stomachs tonight and wait till tomorrow to eat"). Conversely, on other occasions when pigs were slaughtered for a feast, the New Guineans would consume prodigious amounts of food. This anecdote illustrates an accommodation to the pendulum of feast and famine that was very necessary in times when that pendulum swung often but irregularly—a situation that was much more typical of our evolutionary history than the state of plenty to which we are accustomed.

Two lines of human evidence and two animal models support the plausibility of Neel's thrifty gene hypothesis. Non-diabetic Nauruans and Arizona Pima Indians have postprandial levels of plasma insulin (in response to an oral glucose load) that are triple those of Europeans.[14] And given ample food, diabetes-prone populations of Pacific Islanders, Native Americans and Aboriginal Australians do exhibit more propensity to obesity than Europeans: first they gain weight, then they develop diabetes. As to the animal examples, laboratory rats carrying genes predisposing them to type 2 diabetes and obesity survive starvation better than do normal rats, illustrating the advantage of these genes under occasional conditions of famine.[16] And the Israeli sand rat, which is adapted to a desert environment with frequent scarcities of food, develops high levels of leptin and insulin, and insulin resistance, obesity and diabetes, when maintained in the laboratory on a "westernized rat diet" with abundant food. But those symptoms reverse when its food is restricted.[21]

NATURAL SELECTION

The thrifty gene hypothesis provides an explanation for why humans in general become prone to diabetes under a westernized lifestyle. But why, in light of this hypothesis, are Nauruans and Arizona Pima Indians experiencing especially severe epidemics of type 2 diabetes while European populations—in Europe and elsewhere—have uniquely low prevalences?

Nauru Nauruans suffered two extreme bouts of natural selection for thrifty genes, followed by an extreme bout of coca-colonization.[7] First, like other Pacific Islanders—but unlike the inhabitants of continental regions—their population was founded by people who undertook inter-island canoe voyages lasting several weeks. In numerous attested examples of such lengthy voyages, many or most of the canoe occupants died of starvation, and only those who were originally the fattest survived. That is why Pacific Islanders in general tend to be heavy people. Second, the Nauruans were then set apart from most other Pacific Islanders by their extreme starvation and mortality during the Second World War, leaving the population presumably even more enriched in diabetes susceptibility genes. After the war, their new-found wealth, superabundant food and diminished need for physical activity led to exceptional obesity.

The Pimas

Like other Native Americans, Arizona Pima Indians were formerly peasant farmers and hunter–gatherers who had a physically vigorous lifestyle and were at periodic risk of starvation. Their extra bout of natural selection possibly came during the late nineteenth century, when European immigrants diverted the headwaters of the rivers on which the Pimas depended for irrigation water. The result was crop failures, widespread starvation and the likely enrichment of the surviving population in thrifty genes.[8,22]

Europe

Europeans are unique among the modern world's populations in the relatively low prevalence of type 2 diabetes. Although prevalence of the disease is increasing, it is still lower than in any non-European population matched for lifestyle, even though Europeans—in Europe itself, and throughout the world—are the richest and best-fed people in the world, and the originators of the Western lifestyle. As Figure 42.1 shows, even compared with the European population with the highest prevalence (white Australians, 8%), almost all other major population groupings (Native Americans, Pacific Islanders, Aboriginal Australians, East Asians and South Asians of the Indian subcontinent) include populations with much higher prevalences of 15–50%.

This uniquely low occurrence of type 2 diabetes among Europeans is curious. Several experts in the study of the disease have suggested to me informally that perhaps Europeans traditionally had little exposure to famine, so that they would have undergone little selection for a thrifty genotype. But this is not the case—there is abundant documentation of famines that have caused widespread and severe mortality in medieval and Renaissance Europe.[23–27] So lack of exposure to famine seems unlikely to be an answer.

Instead, a more promising hypothesis is based on Europe's recent food history (see also ref. 28 for another view). The periodic widespread and prolonged famines that used to wrack Europe, like the rest of the world, disappeared between about 1650 and 1900 at different times in different parts of Europe—the late 1600s in Britain and the Netherlands, for example, and the late 1800s in southern France and southern Italy.[23–27] With one famous exception, Europe's famines were ended by a combination of three or four factors: increasingly efficient state intervention that rapidly redistributed any surplus grain to famine areas; increasingly efficient food transport by land and especially by sea; increasingly diversified agriculture after AD 1492, a consequence of the advent of crops, such as potatoes and corn (maize), which were brought back by European voyagers and broadened the base of European agriculture, thereby reducing the risk of starvation from failure of a single crop; and finally perhaps, Europe's reliance on "rain agriculture," which reduced the risk of a crop failure that was too widespread to be solved by food transport within Europe, rather than (as in many populous areas outside Europe) "irrigation agriculture." The famous exception is, of course, the Irish potato famine of the 1840s. But this may be the exception that proves the rule. The potato famine was due to a disease of one crop in an economy that was unusual in Europe in its reliance on that single crop, and it occurred on an island governed by a state centred on another island.

A Cryptic Epidemic in Europe?

A corollary of this view based on Europe's food history is that, several centuries before the advent of modern medicine, Europeans, like modern Nauruans, should have undergone an epidemic in type 2 diabetes that resulted from the new reliability of adequate food supplies and eliminated most diabetes-prone bearers of the thrifty genotype. However, there would have been big differences between that postulated earlier European epidemic and the well-documented modern epidemics among Nauruans and among so many other peoples today. In the modern epidemics, abundant and continually reliable food arrived suddenly, within a decade for the Nauruans and within just a month for the Yemenite Jews. The result was a sharply peaked surge in prevalence to 20–50% that occurred right under the eyes of modern diabetologists. That increase will probably wane quickly, as individuals with the thrifty genotype become eliminated by natural selection within a mere generation or two. In contrast, Europe's food abundance would have increased gradually over the course of several centuries, and the result, between the 1400s and 1700s, would have been a slow rise in type 2 prevalence long before there were diabetologists to take note.

A possible victim of this postulated cryptic epidemic of diabetes was the composer Johann Sebastian Bach (1685–1750). Bach's medical history is too poorly documented to permit certainty as to the cause of his death. Nonetheless, the corpulence of his face and hands in the sole authenticated portrait of him, the accounts of deteriorating vision in his later years, and the evident deterioration of his handwriting, possibly secondary to his failing vision, are consistent with a diagnosis of type 2 diabetes. The disease certainly occurred in Germany during Bach's lifetime, being known as *"honigsüsse Harnruhr"* (honey-sweet urine disease).[29]

TESTS OF THE HYPOTHESES

These ideas about the evolution of type 2 diabetes can be tested. Here are some of the questions that can be asked, and predictions that can be tested.

- How much evidence is there for the postulated epidemic of diabetes in late medieval and Renaissance Europe, either in individual biographies (as that of Bach) or in contemporary medical treatises? Did the timing of the epidemic vary locally with the different times for the disappearance of famines in different parts of Europe? Was a diabetes epidemic evident after the Black Death, when human population declined much more rapidly than did food availability?

- The prevalence of type 2 diabetes in European immigrants of British and German ancestry to the United States and Australia is reported as 7–8%, much higher than the 2% for British and German people still living in Europe today under similar lifestyles. This difference is consistent with the socially stratified emigration often discussed by historians. The Europeans who stayed at home tended to be richer than those who emigrated; in the former group, the genotype predisposing the bearer to type 2 diabetes may have already been selected out by centuries of abundant food, whereas those who emigrated may have been the starvation-prone poor who still carried the thrifty genotype.[3] This possibility could be tested by controlled comparison of modern Europeans still living in Europe with overseas Europeans whose ancestors' country of origin and date of emigration are known. As a specific example, are overseas descendants of Irish emigrants in the 1840s more susceptible to diabetes than are Ireland's inhabitants today?

- In pre-modern times, the risk of famine was higher in the drought- and flood-prone northern areas of China than in the south. Is there a corresponding difference in predisposition to diabetes? And did China's famines during the Great Leap Forward of the late 1950s produce additional selection for thrifty genes?

- Were the risks of famine, and so selection for thrifty genes, higher in societies that depended heavily on fishing and hunting-and-gathering (Nauruans, Pimas and Aboriginal Australians, for instance) than in farming societies in which food storage had become the norm (Europe and China)?

- Are genetic susceptibility factors for type 2 diabetes especially evident in Nauruans, Yemenite Jews and other populations showing recent surges of the disease?

- Anecdotal accounts suggesting that there were other modern epidemics of diabetes deserve investigation. For instance, a colleague whose grandfather was from northern Iran recounts that improved food transport there in the early 1900s reduced the frequency of starvation and triggered a diabetes epidemic, especially among rich people—hence the local term "the rich man's disease."

- Medical geneticists seek to identify and preemptively counsel people carrying susceptibility factors for specific diseases. Can Third World populations, whose history of marked swings between food and starvation puts them at risk of diabetes with the spread of coca-colonization, be likewise identified and preemptively counselled by public-health officials? That might spare them the fate of the Nauruans, Arizona Pima Indians and Wanigela. The evolutionary history and geography of type 2 diabetes would then have provided us not only with a double puzzle, but also with insights that could potentially help save millions of people from premature death.

NOTES

1. Levitt, N. *et al. Diabetes Care* 16, 601–607 (1993).

2. Zimmet, P., Alberti, K. & Shaw. J. *Nature* 414, 782–787 (2001).

3. Zimmet, P. in *The Medical Challenge: Complex Traits* (eds Fischer, E. & Moller, G.) 55–110 (Piper, Munich, 1997).

4. Zimmet, P. *J. Intern. Med.* 247, 301–310 (2000).

5. King, H., Aubert, R. & Herman, W. *Diabetes Care* 21. 1414–1431 (1998).

6. Dowse, G., Zimmet, P., Finch, C. & Collins, V. *Am. J. Epidemiol* 133, 1093–1104 (1991).

7. Rubinstein, H. & Zimmet, P. *Phosphate. Wealth, and Health in Nauru: A Study of Lifestyle Change* (Brolga. Gundaroo, 1993).

8. Knowler, W., Pettitt, D., Saad, N. & Bennett, P. *Diabetes Metab. Rev.* 6, 1–27 (1990).

9. Dowse, G. *et al. Med. J. Aust.* 160, 767–774 (1994).

10. Gardner, L. *et al. Diabetes* 33, 86–92 (1984).

11. Elbein, S., Chiu, K. & Permutt, M. In *The Genetic Basis of Common Diseases* 2nd edn (eds King. R., Rotter, J. & Motulsky, A.) 457–480 (Oxford Univ. Press, 2002).

12. Raffel, L. & Rotter, J. in *Principles and Practice of Medical Genetics* Vol. 2. 4th edn (eds Rimoin, D., Connor, J. & Pyeritz, R.) 2231–2276 (Churchill Livingston, London, 2001).

13. Hales, C. & Barker, D. *Diabetologia* 35, 595–601 (1992).

14. Zimmet, P. *Diabetes Care* 15, 232–252 (1992).

15. Campbell, G. S. *Afr. Med. J.* 37, 1195–1207 (1963).

16. Coleman, D. *Science* 203, 663–665 (1979).

17. Dowse, G. K. *et al. Diabetes* 39, 390–396 (1990).

18. Diamond, J. *Nature* 410, 521 (2001).

19. Neel, J. *Am. J. Hum. Genet.* 14, 353–362 (1962).

20. Neel, J. in *The Genetics of Diabetes Mellitus* (eds Kobberling, J. & Tattersall, J.) 283–293 (Academic, New York, 1982).

21. Haines, H., Hackel, D. & Schmidt-Nielsen, K. *Am. J. Physiol.* 208, 297–300 (1965).

22. Russell, F. *The Pima Indians* (Univ. Arizona Press, Tucson, 1975).

23. Appleby, A. *Famine in Tudor and Stuart England* (Stanford Univ. Press, 1978).

24. Jordan, W. *The Great Famine: Northern Europe in the Early Fourteenth Century* (Princeton Univ. Press, 1996).

25. Monahan, W. *Year of Sorrows: The Great Famine of 1709 in Lyon* (Ohio State Univ. Press, Columbus, 1993).

26. Post, J. *Food Shortage. Climatic Variability and Epidemic Disease in Preindustrial Europe* (Cornell Univ. Press, Ithaca, 1985).

27. Rotberg, R. & Rabd, T. (eds) *Hunger and History: The Impact of Changing Food Production and Consumption Patterns on Society* (Cambridge Univ. Press, 1983).

28. McMichael, A. *Human Frontiers, Environments and Disease: Past Patterns on Certain Futures* (Cambridge Univ. Press, 2001).

29. Kranemann, D. *Bach Jahrbuch* 53–64 (1990).

30. King, H. & Rewers, M. *Diabetes Care* 16, 157–177 (1993).

43   ETHICS, EPIDEMIOLOGY AND THE THRIFTY GENE: BIOLOGICAL DETERMINISM AS A HEALTH HAZARD

Robyn McDermott

This selection places the research emphasis on genetic factors as the root cause of Type II diabetes in the context of what Lock calls "geneticization" (selection 28), or the rendering of human nature and morphology as uniform materials emerging directly from the genes. Such an emphasis also resonates with the cultural ideal of autonomous individualism evident in the biomedical focus on individual pathology. McDermott argues that this line of thinking is counterproductive and harmful because it places blame on individual patients and obscures the difference between "causes of cases" and "causes of incidence," or patterns of disease. Epidemics of diabetes are not limited to populations that are famous for extremely high rates of the disease, as the recent rise in diabetes rates among American and European children shows. Instead, epidemics of obesity and diabetes are the predictable, nearly universal responses of populations undergoing a transition to a Western lifestyle.

McDermott cites the case of Australian aborigines to illustrate how the idea that diabetes is a genetic disease characteristic of certain populations can lead to attitudes and behaviors in health professionals that result in poorer care and worse outcomes for patients. The previous selection gave ample evidence for the fact that genes alone are not sufficient to cause diabetes, and that the symptoms of the disease can be reversed through lifestyle changes. This makes it important to avoid misconceptions among physicians, nurses, and patients about the role of genes in causing the disease in individuals and populations.

This selection suggests that it is not necessary to have exact knowledge about the causes of diabetes, given that highly effective dietary and exercise interventions are already available and in use. This is not an antibiological stance, as seen in McDermott's explanation of the U-shaped relation between birth weight and adult obesity and diabetes, or her examination of the role of micronutrients in fresh fruits and vegetables in preventing and treating diabetes. These topics, meanwhile, highlight the importance of social and political inequality in making some people more susceptible to the disease than others. For many emigrant and indigenous populations, a childhood of insufficient nutrition, disease, and poverty, combined with an adulthood of continued poverty, lack of physical activity, and inappropriate nutrition, creates conditions favorable to obesity and diabetes.

The importance of understanding genetic susceptibility factors, physiological mechanisms, and socioeconomic factors supports the biocultural perspective of medical anthropology and serves as a reminder that complex multifactorial diseases do not lend themselves to simple explanations or racial categorizations.

Questions to keep in mind

What are the physiological mechanisms involved in impaired glucose metabolism, and how do these relate to the socioeconomic transformations discussed in these articles and in Part II?

Do you think that McDermott's and Diamond's perspectives are irreconcilable or complementary?

Source: Reprinted from *Social Science and Medicine*, Vol. 47, McDermott, R., "Ethics, Epidemiology, and the Thrifty Gene: Biological Determinism as a Health Hazard," Pages 1189–1195, Copyright (1998), with permission from Elsevier.

In what ways might an overemphasis on genetic factors impede the development of scientific knowledge about diabetes?

Where do you see the concepts of race and racism in these articles? How are these concepts related to diabetes?

INTRODUCTION

The vulgar error that confuses heritability and fixity has been, over the years, the most powerful single weapon that biological ideologues have had in legitimating a society of inequality. Since as biologists they must know better, one is entitled to at least a suspicion that the beneficiaries of a system of inequality are not to be regarded as objective experts (R. C. Lewontin).

The world is experiencing an epidemic of non-insulin dependent diabetes (NIDDM). This is not occurring evenly across the globe nor is its distribution within countries uniform; in developing countries the burden of NIDDM is apparently concentrated among newly prosperous groups while in industrialised countries NIDDM is increasingly a disease of socioeconomic disadvantage. Diabetes affects some ethnic groups disproportionately and spectacularly high prevalence has been observed in recent generations of indigenous groups in Australia, the Pacific Islands and North America (King and Rewers, 1993).

THE THRIFTY GENOTYPE HYPOTHESIS

In 1962, near the beginning of the epidemic, James Neel, an American population geneticist, postulated the existence of the "thrifty gene" in order to explain the apparent paradox of the high prevalence of diabetes, a disease with a "well-defined genetic basis" in the population when it clearly had an adverse effect on reproduction. This hypothesis suggested that, in the early years of life the diabetic genotype was "thrifty" in the sense of being exceptionally efficient in the utilisation of food. It would thereby confer a survival advantage in times of food shortages, as was presumably frequently the case in hunter–gatherer and pre-industrial agricultural societies (Neel, 1962). However, rapid westernisation occurring in many countries since world war II, including the substitution of high energy imported food to replace traditional low-fat, low nutrient-dense diets, has changed the environment from one of relative scarcity of food to one of plenty. The thrifty genotype in this new environment no longer confers a survival advantage, but renders its owners more susceptible to obesity and diabetes.

20 years later Neel revised the proposed physiological mechanisms for the thrifty gene in the light of new classifications for diabetes and confined his attention to NIDDM. He suggested large cohort studies beginning in very early childhood might elucidate the hypothesis and concluded with some circumspection: "All these speculations may be utterly demolished the moment the precise aetiologies of NIDDM become known. Until that time, however, devising fanciful hypotheses based on evolutionary principles offers an intellectual sweepstake in which I invite you all to join" (Neel, 1982).

The 35 years since Neel's first hypothesis have seen an extraordinary outpouring of research effort in human genetics, including the hugely expensive co-operative venture of the human genome project (HGP), some directed at finding the genes involved in NIDDM. The enormously successful marketing efforts of the HGP stemmed from the corporatisation of much genetic research and the need to sell the idea to US Congressional committees in charge of allocations to the National Institutes of Health, the main initial sponsor of the project (Davis, 1991). Much of this success was probably also at least partly due to the message falling on fertile soil in the public imagination, the foundations of which were laid in the 19th century where Darwinism and Mendelian theories combined to form a general theory of human nature which is unchangeable (in the short term at least and for individuals) and encoded in our genes. Biological determinism, the notion that all of our existence is controlled by DNA, has not confined itself subsequently to biology, but has had more sinister incarnations in Social Darwinism, phrenology and more recently in sociobiology, where even the political structures of society (competitive, hierarchical and entrepreneurial) are determined by DNA and are therefore immutable (Gould, 1981).

While few epidemiologists, medical researchers and practitioners subscribed to the more extreme claims of the sociobiologists, they were and are still to some extent operating within a paradigm of general disease theory which is heavily reductionist and deterministic, the more powerful for an almost unconscious acceptance by its practitioners. In diabetes research until recently this has been manifest in a preoccupation with finding genetic markers for NIDDM (Wang and Korc, 1995; Bate and Coleman, 1996). Despite this search of more than 30 years, the "genes for NIDDM" have not been found. This limited concept of causation and a monopoly of concern with pathogenesis and treatment almost completely ignore the need to attend to environmental factors, including the socioeconomic environment and prevention.

The consequences of this type of approach with respect to diabetes among Aborigines in Australia have been an unfortunate combination of curiosity-driven research with few interventions (Lake, 1992) and a common view among doctors and nurses that diabetes in Aborigines is "genetic" and therefore inevitable (Knight, 1992). This reification of an unproved theory among practitioners searching for simple explanations for this puzzling non-communicable outbreak has led to a kind of fatalism and therapeutic nihilism which is quickly transferred to patients and their relatives (Scrimgeour et al., 1997). This tends to reinforce the denial of agency of individuals and community in improving health outcomes. Indeed, even though the emergence of diabetes was first noticed among Torres Strait Islanders in 1960 (Winterbotham, 1961), only one intervention in Aborigines has found its way into the medical literature (Lee et al., 1995). The incidence of serious complications and premature mortality among Aboriginal diabetics, much of which is preventable with good clinical care, is higher than other diabetics, suggesting reduced access to effective care (Phillips et al., 1995). Other factors besides fatalism have clearly contributed to poor outcomes in Aboriginal diabetics, including reduced access to services of

all kinds including medical care, communication difficulties (both linguistic and cultural), continuing low education levels and poverty (Tsey, 1997). However, the belief system in which health care providers operate, especially doctors, is a powerful determinant of outcomes and outcomes in Australian Aborigines are now universally acknowledged to be uniquely poor when looked at in the context of gains made in indigenous health in comparable countries: New Zealand, Canada and the U.S.A. (Kunitz, 1994).

SO WHERE ARE THE EPIDEMIOLOGISTS IN THIS EPIDEMIC?

Weed describes the role of epidemiologists in this type of problem as two-fold: answering the epistemological question, is an exposure causal?, as well as the related moral question, should something be done about the exposure? (Weed, 1996). Below we look at evidence to support alternative hypotheses to the thrifty gene in the light of research so far reported, including the cohort studies prescribed originally by Neel, while acknowledging the ontological and epistemological problems of prediction and uncertainty. Then we discuss the ethical implications (in terms of public health action) of acceptance of each hypothesis and what this might mean for public health policy and practice in the light of the ethical principle; of beneficence, non-maleficence and utility.

First, what is the evidence so far to support the genetic theory for NIDDM: in particular, that indigenous people (and some other ethnic groups) have a genetic and therefore immutable, rather than merely an inherited (or metabolically adapted) and therefore changeable, susceptibility to NIDDM?

In the absence of the culprit gene(s), the genetic theory is based on epidemiological evidence. Early data pointed to NIDDM clustering in certain ethnic groups, especially the Pima Indians, Nauruans and Australian Aborigines (Knowles et al., 1990; Zimmett et al., 1990; O'Dea, 1992). This pattern fitted the hypothesis of the thrifty gene being "unmasked" in "primitive" groups by sudden exposure to increased sedentariness and an abundance of high energy food. However, as more and more people have been exposed to the western lifestyle of the late 20th century, it has become clear that obesity and NIDDM are a consistent response to this lifestyle transition. The emergence of NIDDM among adolescents in the U.S.A. is a case in point (Pinhas-Hamiel et al., 1996). The rise of diabetes in Australia among all groups has been recently documented, highlighting the spectacular increase in NIDDM among migrant groups to Australia from many countries where prevalence of NIDDM is very low (McCarty et al., 1996).

The second line of argument for the genetic theory rests on the fact that NIDDM is familial. In particular, NIDDM appears to be carried in the female line. It is in elucidating this pattern that the cohort studies suggested by Neel have been particularly valuable. In 1980 Norbert Freinkel hypothesised that a mechanism for the inheritability of diabetes might rest in a form of "fuel-mediated teratogenesis" during pregnancy, where the fetus exposed to hyperglycemia in utero has long term anthropometric and metabolic effects, including increased susceptibility to obesity and NIDDM (Freinkel, 1980). The large cohort studies in the Pima Indians tended to support this hypothesis. Pettit and colleagues reported that the 19–24 year-old offspring of Pima Indian women with NIDDM were more obese and had a much higher prevalence of diabetes (50%) than offspring of non-diabetic women (1.4%) or of women who developed diabetes after the pregnancy (8.6%). These effects persisted after controlling for age, fathers' diabetic status and age of onset of the mothers' diabetes. These data not only supported Freinkel's theory, but further suggested that the very early age of onset of diabetes in the female offspring of these diabetic mothers set up a vicious circle where this generation was exposing the next to a diabetogenic intrauterine environment thus amplifying the risk through the generations (Pettit et al., 1993).

While it could be said that the Pima studies are not generalisable to other populations due to the very high prevalence of (genetically determined) diabetes in this group, new data are emerging from other populations which support Freinkel's idea. A cohort study in Chicago of mixed race (mainly Caucasian) non-indigenous American women and their offspring has shown a significantly increased body weight in the offspring of diabetic mothers by the age of 8 years and a greatly increased risk of impaired glucose tolerance (IGT) by 10 years (Silverman et al., 1995). The significance of this study is that the risk of IGT was linked to fetal hyperinsulinemia (which is directly correlated with maternal hyperglycemia) rather than the type of the mother's diabetes, since most of the mothers had insulin-dependent diabetes mellitus (IDDM) while their offspring were showing a NIDDM syndrome (obesity and IGT).

Animal studies have shown that rhesus monkeys made hyperinsulinemic in utero by exogenous infusion of insulin (i.e. independently of the mother's glycemic status) develop abnormal glucose tolerance as pregnant adults and have macrosomic offspring (Susa et al., 1993). This suggests a teratogenic effect which can persist through to the third generation.

At the other end of the metabolic scale, in cohort studies from the U.K., Barker and colleagues have shown that poor nutrition and growth in utero or early infancy carry a significantly increased risk of diabetes (NIDDM) and cardiovascular disease later in life, especially when weight gain in adulthood is added to early undernutrition (Barker, 1992). They originally proposed that early undernutrition affected pancreatic beta-cell development which predisposed to beta-cell dysfunction and exhaustion later in life (the "thrifty phenotype" hypothesis) but more recent studies have suggested that the mechanism lies with the effects of insulin (predisposing to insulin resistance later in life) rather than on insulin secretion. Low birth weight and obesity in adulthood are both independently associated with insulin resistance, and individuals who were both thin as babies and obese as adults were the most insulin resistant. The precise physiological mechanism for this effect is still unclear, but may be related to changes in sensitivity to glucocorticoids, including those secreted from fat cells in the omentum (Bujalska et al., 1997). Barker has summarised his work thus: "Where differences in individuals' susceptibility to disease cannot be explained by differences in the adult environment. . . they have often been attributed to genetic causes, especially if the disease has a familial tendency. Part of what is now regarded as the genetic contribution to ischaemic heart disease (for example) may turn out to be the effect of the intrauterine or early post-natal environment" (Barker, 1992).

Animal studies suggest a mechanism for this effect. The offspring of rats fed low protein diets during pregnancy have reduced beta-cell proliferation and reduced islet size and vascularisation. When tested at 10 weeks of age, the offspring had impaired glucose tolerance and reduced insulin secretion (Dahri et al., 1993). Desai and co-workers have demonstrated the effects of protein deprivation in pregnancy on activity levels of glucoregulatory liver enzymes in the offspring. They concluded that the "enzymatic setting of the liver is biased by a factor of 400% towards the production rather than the utilisation of glucose" and that these effects were evident throughout adult life (Desai et al., 1995). The human counterpart to this experiment can be seen in the "Dutch famine" cohort of children who were exposed in utero to severe protein shortage at a critical stage in pregnancy and who as adults experienced higher than expected rates of diabetes and cardiovascular disease compared to genetically similar controls (Ravelli et al., 1998).

The Pima studies support both theories, showing a U-shaped relationship between birthweight and the prevalence of obesity and NIDDM in the offspring, with the highest rates in those individuals with the highest and those with the lowest birthweights (McCane et al., 1993).

It is interesting in the light of these new speculations (given the inadequacy of observational data on humans to date to attribute causality in a strictly Popperian sense) to contrast the explanations given for recent trends in diabetes prevalence among the Nauruans (who previously had one of the highest documented rates of NIDDM in the world) between those favouring the genetic hypothesis vs proponents of the "thrifty phenotype" theory. Dowse and co-workers found an apparent decline in the incidence of abnormal glucose tolerance in Nauru in recent years. They attributed this to a fall in population frequency of the thrifty genotype as a result of the higher mortality and lower fertility of diabetic Nauruans (Dowse et al., 1991). Barker suggested that the size and speed of the change were unlikely to be a eugenic effect of low reproduction among diabetics. As it was among the post-war generation that the improvements were seen, and in the absence of major be-

havioural or nutrition changes among adults, he attributed this transition as more likely to be due to improved fetal and infant nutrition after the war (Barker, 1992).

One of the criteria for causal inference is predictability. The predictions of the Barker hypothesis in Aboriginal populations would suggest that, if we are indeed seeing an age-cohort-period effect of poor childhood nutrition followed by over-nutrition and obesity, then either a public health intervention to improve maternal and child nutrition or a natural experiment in the better-nourished next generation would lead to a reduced prevalence of NIDDM in that successive cohort. Improved childhood nutrition combined with reduced obesity in adulthood would see further gains.

The "fuel-mediated teratogenesis" theory of Freinkel would predict that programs to prevent obesity and gestational diabetes mellitus (GDM) in young women, plus improved detection and management of those pregnant women with abnormal glucose metabolism would result in offspring with less risk of obesity and diabetes later in life.

At the current time, Aboriginal women are subject to the double jeopardy of poor antenatal nutrition and low birth weight babies plus a high and increasing rate of gestational diabetes mellitus. If the theories of Barker and Freinkel are correct, there is potentially great scope for public health intervention. If the genetic hypothesis is also true it does not negate the need for intervention but does not of itself suggest any specific action.

As Rose has pointed out, "ignorance of specific causes does not of itself rule out the possibility of preventive action. One recalls the dramatic benefits to public health achieved by reformers of the last century, whose measures to improve housing, working conditions and sanitation antedated knowledge of bacteria and toxicology. In a similar way today one may suppose that measures to improve national nutrition and to lessen socio-economic inequalities would bring corresponding benefits to the nation's health, for even though many of the specific explanations still elude us, we know that the major causes of ill-health bear a lot more heavily on those who are socially deprived" (Rose, 1992).

Rose here is urging action, not just for the sake of sick minorities (statistical outliers), whose problems are often considered as though their existence were independent of the rest of society, but for the betterment of everyone's health. This brings us to the nub of the ethical problem with how we approach a disease like NIDDM in a very marginalised group like Aborigines. The genetic paradigm seeks to emphasise the "independence" of the disorder and of the group, making it a "special problem" with no immediate ramifications for the rest of society or for specific interventions to improve the situation. It may also be simply wrong, in that what we are seeing in Aborigines has little to do with genetics but represents an extreme example of a physiological effect arising from past and continuing malnutrition (including adult obesity and lack of micronutrients), poverty and social marginalisation.

From the accumulating evidence of the effects of the social environment including the increasingly measurable effects of social class, education, income, poverty and racism on chronic diseases, especially heart disease and hypertension, there may be little left in the "race" variable so entrenched in epidemiological design (Cooper and David, 1986; Krieger, 1990; Muntaner, 1996). Recent evidence for the protective effects of micronutrients (particularly antioxidant vitamins found in fresh fruit and vegetables) against heart disease, cancer and now progression of diabetes and the insulin resistance syndrome (Paolissi et al., 1993) suggests yet another mechanism for the socio-economic distribution of health: poor people buy more energy-dense food (animal fats, sugar) than better-off folk who spend more on fresh produce, richer in micronutrients but lower in energy (James et al., 1997). Studies done so far on the availability of fresh fruit and vegetables in remote Aboriginal communities suggest that this group may be exceptionally deprived of micronutrients (Lee et al., 1995; Leonard et al., 1995).

The difficulty in allocating "true" attribution in real life complex situations of chronic disease in populations (as opposed to a controlled experimental design) between competing theories of causality highlights a major philosophical problem facing contemporary epidemiology: the lack of development of concepts and a framework within which we might examine the current and changing health status of human societies as opposed to a preoccupation with modelling complex relationships among individual risk factors, or "black box

epidemiology" (Susser, 1989; Terris, 1992; Krieger, 1994). The black box has been defended as a useful tool in generating hypotheses and even uncovering relationships which are unexpected and can then lead to a paradigm shift (Savitz, 1994). Increasingly, however, risk factor epidemiology has been criticised as "a reductionist approach (which) focuses on the individual, blames the victim and produces interventions which may be harmful" (Pearce, 1996). It also fails to distinguish between what Rose describes as "the causes of cases" rather than the "causes of incidence" (Rose, 1992). Krieger suggests that the implicit theoretical underpinnings of the black box approach lie in biomedical individualism, where only biological determinants of disease are emphasised which are amenable to intervention through the health care system, social determinants of disease are secondary if not irrelevant and populations are simply the sum of individuals where population patterns of disease simply reflect individual cases (Krieger, 1994). This approach had its roots in U.S. post-war history, where academic discourse about disease causation was shaped by the Cold War and McCarthyism and discussion about social class and social inequality were "subversive." Epidemiologists and others therefore sheltered in the safety of the biomedical model which considered individual risk only in the context of "lifestyle" and genetic predisposition (Susser, 1985). This rather dismal assay tends to support the assertion of Kuhn that it is the scientific community which determines what is to be considered in the analytical space, what is to be accepted and what is to be refuted (Kuhn, 1962).

The idea that causal inference is a sociological process has given rise to robust debate between subjectivists and objectivists. Where this has relevance to the causes of NIDDM in populations lies in the acceptance of the notion of continuing uncertainty and the possibility that none of these "speculations will be utterly demolished" but will continue to lie in a conjectural limbo. Weed suggests three approaches to dealing with uncertainty: belief, probability and criticism. Belief, or a "retreat to commitment," often results in a total cessation of critical inquiry. The use of probability as an alternative to certainty is also problematical in that assigning probabilities to hypotheses does not help us to decide where to look for more evidence or what evidence to ignore. Criticism is valuable in its "ability to bring weaknesses to the surface. These weaknesses are to be found in our public health actions, just as they are to be found in the hypotheses from which they arise. And, although such criticism will never make us certain, it will help us to avoid being more wrong than we need to be" (Weed, 1988).

The ethical question, "When is it appropriate to act, given our more or less uncertain knowledge of cause?" should be approached according to the general principles of beneficence (including acceptability to the community), non-maleficence and utility. MacMahon's invocation "to effect preventive measures, it is not necessary to understand causal mechanisms in their entirety . . . (since) wherever the chain is broken the disease will be prevented" (MacMahon et al., 1960) can be enacted in the light of the principles above and would give rise to the following kinds of interventions:

1. Community-based and -designed mother and child health programs aimed at reducing the incidence of low birth weight and failure to thrive in infancy.

2. Screening of all pregnant women for abnormal glucose tolerance and intensive management throughout pregnancy to avoid exposure of the fetus to hyperglycemia.

3. Ensuring the safe supply of good quality affordable food, particularly fresh fruit and vegetables, to all areas, particularly areas of low socioeconomic status.

4. Promotion of healthy eating habits, particularly among young women.

5. Strategies to prevent obesity at all ages, especially adolescence and young adulthood.

6. Education of health care providers in paradigms other than the biomedical model in general disease theory.

7. Public action aimed at reducing social inequality, including access to education and employment opportunities in disadvantaged populations.

CONCLUSION

Most problems have at least two kinds of history. The first is a narrative of the object of study and the second is the history of scientific thinking about the problem. This second history is determined not by "nature" but by the ways we think about and act upon "disease." These two histories are connected and it is often the paradigm operating at the second scientific level which will determine what goes into the narrative space of the first. Thus diabetes in Aborigines has been defined, by non-Aboriginal scientists, simply as a problem of "race" and "genes" in a changing environment. Race becomes a biological entity and an independent risk factor, reified over and over again in repeated studies of disease which take no account of socioeconomic status, history or culture. This uncritical association (and implicit attribution) of disease with "race" is dangerous on three counts: first, it impedes the advancement of science (one historical example was the delay in finding the causal agent of kuru in the Fore tribe of Papua due to the belief that it was a genetic disease). Second, it limits primary prevention and third, it perpetuates simplistic and inappropriate attributions to race which are really due to social factors.

If the first "epidemiological" narrative of diabetes in Aborigines is expanded to include social history, early life experiences of malnutrition, poverty and illness followed by later life experiences of welfarism, poverty, physical inactivity and obesity, explanations other than genetic ones might emerge. This is a picture which is common to many post-colonial indigenous populations and also often found among groups migrating from poor to wealthy countries. The island of Nauru is a case in point. Nauruans suffered terribly under Japanese rule during World War II with forced labour, exile and starvation. Post-war prosperity from phosphate exports was spectacular and accompanied by sedentariness, obesity and diabetes. The Nauruan diabetes epidemic was at the time attributed to the operation of the thrifty gene. Barker's reinterpretation of the "cause" of the epidemic to include the nutritional history of the diabetic cohort and the subsequent observation of a decline in prevalence of abnormal glucose intolerance in the next generation (better nourished in early life), not only enriches the story but explains the changes in prevalence over the space of two generations more satisfactorily than the genetic theory alone.

It appears that over the years, Neel's original idea had been changed in a way which isolated "the gene" to marginal, badly affected groups instead of its first conception as an explanation for an almost universal phenomenon. This process has served to reinforce the status quo and the general biomedical approach to disease theory, including large investments in genetic research, relative neglect of inquiry into social determinants of chronic disease and public health inaction. The dogged search for the elusive genes has continued despite evidence that NIDDM was appearing in every group exposed to western lifestyle. This search has been likened to looking for susceptibility genes to cholera in the middle of an outbreak (Perry, 1996).

Epidemiology is now said to be "in crisis," losing credibility and causing unjustified fears because it is trying to find subtle links between disease, diet, lifestyle and environmental factors (Taubes, 1995) and even contributing to public misunderstanding (Angell, 1996). This crisis points to the need to attend more to ontological and ethical, rather than just methodological, questions in epidemiology: a concern with meaning as well as technique. It may open the way to more explicit framing of theory to guide hypothesis generation and the elaboration of a more coherent approach to the complexity of patterns of health in society.

In the meantime, those who are concerned equally with public health action and good science must continue to criticise and advocate. Criticism of the genetic paradigm opens the way to other theories which can be tested and then in turn criticised, advocacy for good science which is ethical science followed by appropriate public action.

REFERENCES

Angell, M. (1996) *Science on Trial: The Clash of Medical Evidence and the Law in the Breast Implant Case.* WW Norton, New York.

Barker, D. J. P. (ed.) (1992) *Fetal and Infant Origins of Adult Disease. BMJ.*

Bate, K. and Coleman, P. G. (1996) New pieces in the puzzle of diabetes. *Lancet* 348 (Suppl. II), 4.

Bujalska, I. J., Kumar, S. and Stewart, P. M. (1997) Does central obesity reflect "Cushing's disease of the omentum"? *Lancet* 349, 1210–1213.

Cooper, R. and David, R. (1986) The biological concept of race and its application to epidemiology. *J. Health Politics Policy Law* 11, 87–116.

Dahri, S., Snoeck, A., Reusens-Billen, B., Ramacle, C. and Hoet, J. J. (1993) Islet function in offspring of mothers on low protein diet during gestation. *J. Physiol.* (London) 467, 292.

Davis, J. (1991) *Mapping the code: The Human Genome Project and the Choices of Modern Science.* Wiley, New York.

Desai, M., Crowther, N. J., Ozanne, S. E., Lucas, A. and Hales, C. N. (1995) Adult glucose and lipid metabolism may be programmed during foetal life. *Biochem. Soc. Trans.* 23, 331–335.

Dowse, G. K., Zimmett, P. Z., Finch, C. F. and Collins, V. R. (1991) Decline in incidence of epidemic glucose tolerance in Nauruans: Implications for the "Thrifty Genotype." *Am. J. Epidemiol.* 133, 1093–1104.

Freinkel, N. (1980) Of pregnancy and progeny. *Diabetes* 29, 1023–1035.

Gould, S. J. (1981) *The Mismeasure of Man.* Penguin, Canada.

James, W. P. T., Nelson, M., Ralph, A. and Leather, S. (1997) The contribution of nutrition to inequalities in health. *BMJ* 314, 1545–1549.

King, H. and Rewers, M. (1993) WHO *Ad Hoc* Diabetes Reporting Group. Global estimates for prevalence of diabetes and impaired glucose tolerance in adults. *Diabetes Care* 16, 157–177.

Knight, S. (1992) *The Ntaria Diabetes Project Final Report.* Menzies School of Health Research, Alice Springs.

Knowles, W. C., Pettit, D. J., Saad, M. F. and Bennett, P. H. (1990) Diabetes mellitus in the Pima Indians: incidence, risk factors and pathogenesis. *Diabetes/ Metabolic Rev.* 6, 1–27.

Krieger, N. (1990) Racial and gender discrimination: risk factors for high blood pressure? *Soc. Sci. Med.* 30, 1273–1281.

Krieger, N. (1994) Epidemiology and the web of causation: has anyone seen the spider? *Soc. Sci. Med.* 39, 887–903.

Kuhn, T. S. (1962) *The Structure of Scientific Revolutions*, 2nd edn. University of Chicago Press, Chicago.

Kunitz, S. J. (1994) *Disease and Social Diversity.* Oxford, New York.

Lake, P. (1992) A decade of Aboriginal health research. *Aboriginal Health Information Bulletin* 17, 12–16.

Lee, A. J., Bonson, A. P. V., Yarmir, D., O'Dea, K. and Matthews, J. D. (1995) Sustainability of a successful health and nutrition program in a remote Aboriginal community. *Med. J. Aust.* 162, 632–635.

Leonard, D., Beilin, R. and Moran, M. (1995) Which way kaikai blo umi? Food and nutrition in the Torres Strait. *Aust. J. Public Health* 19, 589–595.

Lewontin, R. C. (1992) *Biology as Ideology.* Harper, New York.

MacMahon, B., Pugh, T. F. and Ipsen, L. (1960) *Epidemiologic Methods.* Little Brown and Co., London.

McCane, D. R., Pettit, D. J. and Hanson, R. L. et al. (1993) Low birth weight and type 2 diabetes in Pima Indians. *Diabetologia* 36 (Suppl. 1)(A4), 8.

McCarty, D. J. et al. (1996) The rise and rise of diabetes in Australia, 1996: a review of statistics, trends and costs. *Diabetes Australia*, NSW.

Muntaner, C., Nieto, F. J. and O'Campo, P. (1996) The bell curve: on race, social class and epidemiologic research. *Am. J. Epidemiol. 144*, 531–536.

Neel, J. V. (1962) Diabetes mellitus: A "thrifty" genotype rendered detrimental by "progress"? *Am. J. Human Genet. 14*, 353–362.

Neel, J. V. (1982) The thrifty genotype revisited. In *The Genetics of Diabetes mellitus*, Serono Symposium No. 47, ed. J. Kobberling. Academic Press, London.

O'Dea, K. (1992) Diabetes in Australian Aborigines: impact of the western diet and lifestyle. *J. Int. Med. 232*, 103–117.

Paolissi, G., D'Amore, A. and Guigliano, D. et al. (1993) Pharmacologic doses of vitamin E improve insulin action in healthy subjects and NIDDM patients. *Am. J. Clin. Nutr. 57*, 650–656.

Pearce, N. (1996) Traditional epidemiology, modern epidemiology and public health. *Am. J. Public Health 86*, 678–683.

Perry, I. J. (1996) The causes of diabetes: a non-geneocentric view (letter). *Lancet 347*, 1489–1490.

Pettit, D. J., Nelson, R. G., Saad, M. F., Bennett, P. H. and Knowler, W. C. (1993) Diabetes and obesity in the offspring of Pima Indian Women with diabetes during pregnancy. *Diabetes Care 16*, 310–314.

Phillips, C. B., Patel, M. S. and Weeramanthri, T. S. (1995) High mortality from renal disease and infection in Aboriginal central Australians with diabetes. *Aust. J. Public Health 19*, 482–486.

Pinhas-Hamiel, O. et al. (1996) Increased incidence of NIDDM among adolescents. *J. Pediatr. 128*, 608–615.

Ravelli, A. C. J., van der Meulen, J. H. P., Michels, R. P. J., Osmond, C., Barker, D. J. P., Hales, C. N. and Bleker, O. P. (1998) *Lancet 351*, 173–177.

Rose, G. (1992) *The Strategy of Preventive Medicine*. Oxford, New York.

Savitz, D. A. (1994) In defense of black box epidemiology. *Epidemiology 5*, 550–552.

Scrimgeour, D., Rowse, T. and Lucas, A. (1997) *Too much sweet. The social relations of diabetes in central Australia.* Occasional Papers No. 3/97. Menzies School of Health Research, Alice Springs, NT.

Silverman, B. L., Metzger, B. E., Cho, N. H. and Loeb, C. A. (1995) Impaired glucose tolerance in adolescent offspring of diabetic mothers. *Diabetes Care 18*, 611–617.

Susa, J. B., Sehgal, P. and Schwartz, R. (1993) Rhesus monkeys made exogenously hyperinsulinemic in utero as foetuses, display abnormal glucose homeostasis as pregnant adults and have macrosomic foetuses. *Diabetes 42* (Suppl. 1), 86A.

Susser, M. (1985) Epidemiology in the United States after world war II: the evolution of technique. *Epidemiol. Rev. 7*, 147–177.

Susser, M. (1989) Epidemiology today: a "thought-tormented world". *Int. J. Epidemiol. 18*, 481–488.

Taubes, G. (1995) Epidemiology faces its limits. *Science 269*, 164–169.

Terris, M. (1992) The Society for Epidemiological Research (SER) and the future of epidemiology. *Am. J. Epidemiol. 136*, 909–915.

Tsey, K. (1997) Aboriginal self determination, education and health. *Aust. NZ J. Public Health 21*(1), 77–83.

Wang, P. H. and Korc, M. (1995) Searching for the holy grail: the cause of diabetes. *Lancet 346* (Suppl.), 4.

Weed, D. L. (1988) Causal criteria and Popperian refutation. In *Causal Inference,* ed. K. J. Rothman. Epidemiol Res., Massachusetts.

Weed, D. L. (1996) Epistemology and ethics in epidemiology. In *Ethics and Epidemiology*, eds. S. S. Coughlin and T. L. Beauchamp. OUP, New York.

Winterbotham, K. (1961) Diabetes mellitus in Mabuiag Island, Torres Straits (letter). *Med. J. Aust.*, May 27.

Zimmett, P., Dowse, G., Finch, C., Sargentson, S. and King, H. (1990) The epidemiology and natural history of NIDDM: lessons from the south Pacific. *Diabetes/Metab Rev. 6*, 91–124.

■ ■ ■ ■ ■ ■ ■ ■ ■

44   EATING DIRT

Gerald N. Callahan

Food and eating are central aspects of human existence, whose significance goes beyond individual survival to the realms of political economy, social exchange, and ritual and symbolic meaning-production (Counihan 1999; Counihan and Van Esterik 1997; Mintz and Du Bois 2002). This selection examines the practice of geophagy, or the eating of dirt. Many animals, including nonhuman primates, regularly consume dirt (see Diamond 1999), and human groups across the globe do so on a regular basis, whether unwittingly or deliberately. Eating dirt on purpose is considered a disease by Western biomedicine, illustrating the social construction of disease categories. This view has been an obstacle to understanding by researchers or physicians who consider such behavior quirky at best and pathological at worst.

Eating nonfood items (or pica) is in fact a manifestation of various psychological disorders, and it is the case that certain soils and microbes living in dirt can cause disease. However, Callahan explains that it is not clear how much dirt eating is pathological, while there are strong medicinal, nutritional, and immunological reasons that argue in favor of the practice. Dirt is used in food preparation for flavor, for nutrition in times of scarcity, and to remove toxins from certain animals and plants. In pregnant women it can help reduce nausea and provide calcium and other minerals. Even people in industrialized societies eat kaolin clay as medicine for gastric distress. As the example of antimalarial plant foods and medicines used by indigenous groups shows (see selection 13), the adaptive value of eating dirt may or may not be recognized by those who consume it.

The most important benefit of eating dirt may be the stimulation of the immune system by exposure of the lymphoid tissue in the gastrointestinal tract to microorganisms and inorganic substances such as aluminum. In small children, eating dirt favors the development of the immune system, and it may be important for the growth of normal intestinal flora (which assist in nutrition and defense against disease). Animal models and epidemiological studies indicate that lack of exposure to germs in childhood is linked to inadequate or inappropriate immune responses later in life.

Echoing many of the authors in Part II, Callahan points out that humans and microbes are intertwined in a never-ending dance and that training the immune system by exposure to relatively harmless germs seems to be necessary for people to deal with the dangerous ones. That traditional food and medical systems have ways of dealing with this problem should come as no surprise (see selection 6). What truly seems to need explanation is the Western aversion to germs and dirt.

Questions to keep in mind

If avoiding exposure to germs in childhood is maladaptive in terms of increasing risks of allergies and other health conditions, but eating dirt in a crowded, polluted world is dangerous, what can be done to bolster immunity in children?

What are some ways of making geophagy safer?

Does the metaphor of a waltz between humans and microbes describe the relationship better than military metaphors do?

Source: Callahan, G. N. 2003. "Eating Dirt." *Emerging Infectious Diseases* 9(8):1016–1021.

Please
This earth is blessed
Do not play in it

Sign on the wall of El Santuario
de Chimayo, New Mexico

This place feels old beyond human recollection. The carvings and paintings were surely done by human hands, but no one remembers whose hands those were. The work is striking, especially in the apse behind the altar. There, the colors of surrounding hills have been transferred onto nearly luminous wooden reredos full of Catholic symbolism. Above the altar hangs a most intricate ancient Christ crucified on a green cross. Overhead, the roof is held in place by massive carved wooden beams, big around as human bodies and blackened by nearly two centuries of incense and candle smoke. The air is rich with the memory of thousands of benedictions and baptisms. Threadbare trousers have polished the pews to a high varnish that this afternoon ripples with a low orange glow from dozens of votive candles burning purposefully in back of the church.

This is El Santuario de Chimayo, an old adobe-brick and stucco structure in the hills of northern New Mexico. This chapel was built in 1816, but a sanctuary has been at this site for much longer. The locals offer many legends about its origins, fanciful tales of miraculous crucifixes and Santo Niños. But the truth is buried beneath the murk of time. One thing is clear though, as beautiful as the sanctuary is and as striking as the crucifix (El Señor de Esquipalas) above the altar is, nearly none of those in the pews today have come to see the sanctuary or the crucifix. Instead, they have come from all over the world to this place in New Mexico to eat the dirt that lies beneath the adobe floor.

According to legend, that dirt is sacred, consecrated by Christ himself. Crutches cast off by the newly healed fill the anteroom, and on some days, the line of pilgrims stretches for blocks. Some call this place the Lourdes of America, but in Chimayo the miracle can be seen each day by anyone who peers into a low-ceilinged room off the main entrance. There, a hole (the *posito*), half a meter across, pierces the floor. Beside it, someone has left a plastic spoon to aid the faithful. Beyond the spoon, beneath the opening, lies only dirt, only the deep-red dirt of Chimayo.

Most of the faithful here today have come to eat that dirt. This religious tradition is practiced, as far as I know, only at one other place—a Catholic shrine in Esquipalas, Guatemala. But pilgrims to these shrines are not the only humans who eat dirt. Nor are religious reasons the only reasons to imagine that dirt may have special powers.

GEOPHAGY (EATING DIRT) AND ITS REASONS

Other than water, what little stuff we humans have inside us is largely dirt. Admittedly, this dirt is sometimes highly processed before we receive it, but most solids that make up humans and other creatures either are now or recently were dirt (the simple stuff that stripes the outer surface of our world, the thin paste that raises us above the rocks) transformed by sunlight into plants or animals. Most of us prefer the dirt we eat in the form of cows and sheep and carrots and squash and bison and sorghum. Other dirt we'd just as soon scrape from our feet and leave at the door.

But not everyone wishes to be so far removed from the stuff of mud pies and mucilage. On every continent (except, possibly, Antarctica), some of us intentionally eat dirt, and we are joined in this practice by a myriad of rats, mice, mule deer, birds, elephants, African buffalo, cattle, tapirs, pacas, and several species of primates (1). Most scientists consider animal geophagy "normal," probably because most soil consumption by animals has no obvious adverse effects and is sometimes beneficial (2); however, some of these same scientists consider most (or all) human geophagy "abnormal."

Abnormal Behavior

In the United States, many of us believe that humans should only eat food. We consider the consumption of nonfood items pathological, even though we know that what people define as "food" varies dramatically by region and ethnicity. We call the pathological act of eating nonfood items pica. Pica is a disease, but a disease different from polio or smallpox. No infectious agent is obviously associated with pica. Pica is a disease only because we believe normal "undiseased" persons would not eat anything but traditional human foods; some of those who do, some of the time, are at considerable risk because of their unusual appetites.

Pathological consumption of soil, "soil pica," is associated with several psychological abnormalities. But all ingestion of soil is not soil pica. How much soil a person has to eat to be considered ill is not known. One report described soil pica in a developmentally disabled person who regularly consumed more than 50 g of soil per day (3). Most of us would consider that level of geophagy at least potentially pathological, although I am not sure why.

In June 2000, the U.S. Agency for Toxic Substances and Disease Registry appointed a committee to review soil pica. The committee settled on pathological levels as consumption of more than 500 mg of soil per day but conceded that the amount selected was arbitrary (3). Soil consumption is defined as pathological according to the amount eaten (no normal person could possibly eat that much dirt) and the severity of health consequences (lead poisoning, parasites). Because underlying psychological or biologic abnormalities are not easy to establish, I explore only what appears to be nonpathological dirt eating in pregnant women (especially in sub-Saharan Africa), migrants from sub-Saharan cultures to other parts of the world (notably the United States), and children worldwide.

Inadvertent Exposure

Why is it, that in spite of all the times we've been told not to, we still eat dirt? This is a very complex question with many possible answers. And while each proposed answer has its advocates, no single answer seems satisfactory to all—except one. Almost everyone agrees on one cause of geophagy, inadvertent consumption of air-, water-, and food-borne dirt. Contaminated food, soiled hands, and inhaled dust add soil to our diets. Children ingest considerable amounts of soil in these ways. My children did. Of course, my children also ate dirt on purpose. But child or adult, each of us inadvertently eats a little dirt every day. This dirt can pose a health threat, especially near sites of industrial contamination, but dirt we eat intentionally poses a greater challenge. Intention may indicate something biologic that drives some of us (sometimes

regularly, sometimes religiously, sometimes ritually) to eat dirt.

Tradition and Culture

For centuries, indigenous peoples have routinely used clays (decomposed rock, silica and aluminum or magnesium salts, absorbed organic materials) in food preparation. The clays were used to remove toxins (e.g., in aboriginal acorn breads); as condiments or spices (in the Philippines, New Guinea, Costa Rica, Guatemala, the Amazon and Orinoco basins of South America); and as food during famine (4). Clays were also often used in medications (e.g., kaolin clay in Kaopectate). But the most common occasion for eating dirt in many societies (the only occasion in some societies) is pregnancy. When sperm and egg collide, the world changes. That is obvious. But why pregnant women eat dirt is not.

Wiley and Katz (5) have proposed that eating clay serves different purposes during different periods of pregnancy, soothing stomach upset during morning sickness in the first trimester and supplementing nutrients (especially calcium) during the second and third trimesters, when the fetal skeleton is forming. This type of geophagy occurs most commonly in cultures of sub-Saharan Africa and their descendants (5). The timing of dirt ingestion and amounts consumed vary with tribes and individual persons, but soil comes consistently from certain sites. In some cultures, well-established trade routes and clay traders make rural clays available for geophagy even in urban settings. Clays from termite mounds are especially popular among traded clays, perhaps because they are rich in calcium (5). Whatever the underlying reason, geophagy in Africa does not appear to be a recent cultural development; it may predate *Homo sapiens.*

Women eat dirt during the first, second, or third trimester or throughout pregnancy (5), often throughout the day, as a supplement rather than a meal. Most commonly consumed are subsurface clays, especially kaolin and montmorillonite (5), 30 g to 50 g a day (sometimes much more) (3). However, eating dirt is not always confined to pregnant women, even among the cultures of sub-Saharan Africa (4), nor is it limited to tribes with little or no access to dairy-derived calcium (5), so these hypotheses do not adequately explain local tastes for dirt.

Soil, including kaolinitic and montmorillonitic clays, contains considerable amounts of organic material, including many live microorganisms. The human gut is the largest area of direct contact between a person and the world. Gut-associated lymphoid tissue (GALT) is a major site of T-cell differentiation and selection in adults and of intense immunologic activity (including T lymphopoiesis) in children and adults (6–9). And while it is not entirely clear why some gut-introduced antigens promote tolerance of microorganisms and others immunize against them (10), it is clear that immunization via the gut is a major source of immunoglobulin (Ig)A, both locally and systemically (6–10).

Regular consumption of soil might boost the mother's secretory immune system. Monkeys that regularly eat dirt have lower parasite loads (1). In some cultures, clays are baked before they are eaten, which could boost immunity from previous exposures. For decades we have used aluminum salts, like those found in clays, as adjuvants in human and animal vaccines. Adjuvants are compounds that nonspecifically amplify immune response, probably because of their effects on innate defenses such as macrophages, dendritic cells, and the inflammatory response. Aluminum compounds make effective adjuvants because they are relatively nontoxic, the charged surfaces of aluminum salts absorb large numbers of organic molecules, and macrophages and dendritic cells readily phagocytose the particulates produced by the combination of the adjuvants and the organic compounds (11). The clays that pregnant women and others consume, which are rich in aluminum compounds, likely make at least passable immunologic adjuvants. For all these reasons, clays might act as vaccines. And the IgA antibodies produced against the associated organic antigens may appear in breast milk and have a major role in mucosal protection of newborns.

In pregnant women, this type of gut immunization might produce high levels of IgA against endemic pathogens and other antigens. All this IgA would appear shortly before birth in the breast milk and would provide protection for infants against precisely the pathogens encountered immediately after birth. Furthermore, IgA antibod-

ies prevent attachment of bacteria and some viruses at mucosal surfaces (12), the major contact between the infant and the infectious world. In humans, mucosal surfaces offer the only routes of natural immunization short of wounding, and dirt would seem to offer a potent vaccine containing many endemic pathogens—no needles, no sugar-cube, no gene gun.

Eating dirt, then, rather than being abnormal, may be an evolutionary adaptation acquired over millennia of productive and not-so-productive interactions with bacteria—an adaptation that enhances fetal immunity and increases calcium, eliminates gastric upset, detoxifies some plant and animal toxins, and perhaps boosts mothers' immunity at times when the hormones of pregnancy (13), factors produced by the fetus (14), changes in the complement system, replacement of MHC class I antigens in the trophoblast (15), and who knows what else suppress the mother's natural immunologic desire to destroy her fetus—a miracle, nearly.

Innate Tendency

My children ate dirt with surprising gusto, garden soil, road soil, leaf-mush soil, sod soil, bug-body soil—even gutter soil. As usual with my children, before I could talk them out of this behavior, they gave it up on their own—their behavior depending more on personal likes and dislikes than on my paternal concerns. I was pleased when they quit. Later I was reassured to discover from other parents that their children were just as taken with dirt as mine, some even more so. I felt less like the parent of a couple of dirt-eating, psychosis-ridden, nutritionally deprived children, even if my children were never quite "normal."

Eating dirt appears nearly universal among children under 2 years of age. When I asked my 2-year-old daughter why she ate dirt, she just stared at me, her eyes wide open, a thick moustache of loam limning her lips. She must have decided that either what I had asked was unfathomably abstract or her answer would be far beyond my comprehension.

Soil pica has been defined as eating 500 mg to > 50 g of soil per day (3). But the general applicability of these numbers is widely disputed (pregnant women in Africa eat far more soil than this). By inference, however, normal soil consumption must fall into the range of 0 mg to 500 mg per day per small mouth. Soils consumed by children may differ from those consumed by adults. Generally, children consume topsoils and not the deep (60 cm to 90-cm deep) clays adults regularly consume (5). And children are considerably less selective in the sites they choose for dirt to eat. But why children eat dirt remains largely obscure to all but children.

Children may eat soil for the same reasons pregnant women and some animals do (2,4,16–18). Because of their rapid growth, they have special nutritional needs and surface soils may serve as supplemental nutrients; detoxification of plant or animal toxins might be accelerated by geophagy—particularly in some parts of the world; or soil components, especially clays, may relieve gastric distress. But topsoils are probably not as effective as deep clays at gastric soothing.

Among children, too, it seems eating dirt might have immunologic consequences. Maternal immunoglobulins are secreted in breast milk shortly before birth and for 1 year or more afterwards. Children often begin eating dirt a year or two after birth. As maternal immunity wanes, eating dirt might "vaccinate" children who are losing their maternal IgA, which could stimulate production of nascent immunoglobulins, especially IgA. Eating dirt might also help populate intestinal flora.

But all of this remains speculative. No clear evidence supports a biologic benefit to geophagy among children. Its frequency and distribution, though, suggest a greater biologic involvement than the simple oral obsessions of children.

RISKS OF EATING DIRT

How dangerous is eating dirt? My mother was pretty certain about this—damn dangerous. Soils contaminated by industrial or human pollutants pose considerable threat to anyone who eats them. Reports abound of lead poisoning and other toxicities in children eating contaminated soils. Similarly, we do not have to look farther than the last refugee camp or the slums of Calcutta or Tijuana or Basra to find the dangers of soils contaminated with untreated human waste. But the inherent biologic danger of soil is difficult to assess. Soil unaffected by the pressures of overpopulation, industry, and agriculture may be vastly different from the soil most of us encounter routinely.

Using DNA-hybridization analyses, Torsvik et al. (19–20) found an estimated 4,600 species of prokaryotic microorganisms per gram of natural soil. Subsequent investigations, using more sophisticated techniques, found even more species (20), 700–7,000 g of biomass per cubic meter of soil. Soil is a considerable biologic sink, and certainly some organisms found in it are pathogenic in humans. Yet evidence of soil as a major cause of disease in humans and other animals is limited. And many reported diseases are the result of an abnormal situation, e.g., industrial pollution or untreated sewage.

Most infectious diseases acquired through eating dirt are associated with childhood geophagy, which routinely involves topsoils rather than deep clays. One recent report describes infection of two children at separate sites with raccoon roundworm (*Baylisascaris procyonis*) (21). The infection resulted in severe neurologic damage to both children, and one died. The roundworm was ingested along with soil in both cases. Eating dirt can have dire consequences.

In the United States, the most common parasitic infection associated with geophagy is toxocariasis, most often caused by the worm *Toxocara canis*. Seroprevalence is 4% to 8% depending on the region, but incidence of antibodies to *T. canis* is as high as 16%–30% among blacks and Hispanics. The most common route of infection is ingestion of soil contaminated with dog or cat feces (22). Even though, humans are only paratenic hosts of *T. canis*, under some circumstances (though severe cases are rare), the worm can cause considerable damage (visceral larva migrans, ocular larva migrans, urticaria, pulmonary nodules, hepatic and lymphatic visceral larva migrans, arthralgias) (22–24). Toxocara eggs persist in soil for years. As with soils contaminated by human wastes, soil consumption itself does not cause toxocariasis. And studies of seroprevalence do not distinguish between infection and immunization.

Among children in Nigeria, the most common parasitic infection associated with eating dirt is ascariasis (25). Ascarid worms infect as many as 25% of the world's population (more than 1.25 billion). *Ascaris lumbricoides* is the most common worm. Asymptomatic in many adults, infection is much more serious in children; intestinal obstruction is the most common symptom. Because the worms do not replicate in humans, reexposure is required to maintain infection beyond 2 years.

The correlation between geophagy and helminth infection varies with different helminths. Geissler et al. reported correlation between geophagy and ascariasis (especially caused by *A. lumbricoides*) and possibly trichuriasis but none between geophagy and reinfection with *Schistosoma mansoni, Trichuris trichiura,* or hookworm (26). All parasites that infest soil do not uniformly infect people who consume dirt. Nor do all who eat dirt routinely contract disease.

IMMUNOLOGIC DEVELOPMENT AND INFECTIOUS DISEASE

Many nonhuman animals regularly eat dirt, generally without ill effects and in many cases with some benefits. Even in humans, there are few reports of infections routinely associated with geophagy by pregnant women in sub-Saharan Africa, probably because women take clays from 60 cm to 90 cm below the soil surface and, at least some of the time, they bake the clays. But these factors seem inadequate to fully account for the frequent absence of overt ill effects.

Helminth infections associated with geophagy appear to affect the frequency of inflammatory bowel diseases, which occur most often in industrialized nations. The underlying cause of these diseases may be abnormal immune response to the contents of the gut or perhaps to the gut itself (27). Inflammatory bowel diseases occur at much lower rates in regions where helminth infections are common. Development of normal gut-associated immune response may be aided by the presence of worms.

In studies of healthy mice, *Trichinella spiralis* prevented colitis induced with tri-nitrobenzene sulfonic acid by redirecting a primarily Th-1 response to a Th-2 response (28). Preliminary studies indicate that helminth infection may also alter the course of inflammatory bowel disease in humans (29). Soil is a rich source of parasitic worms. Studies using a number of other animals have also, at least indirectly, associated dirt and microorganisms with normal immunity.

The Environmental Protection Agency estimates that children in the United States consume, on average, 200–800 mg of dirt per day. Some children regularly consume more than their allotment. Still, that doesn't seem like a lot of dirt. We parents have tried for years to put a stop to it. I don't know of an instance in which anybody has succeeded in keeping children away from dirt. But animals have been successfully raised in absolutely sterile environments. Rabbits, mice, guinea pigs, and rats have been raised under such conditions (30,31). In each case, the immune system failed to develop normally. Lymph nodes and GALT did not achieve the right shape or composition and could not initiate normal immune response. Reexposure to infection later in life does not work, at least not fully. There is a window when infection drives the immune system toward its proper end. After that, mice, rats, rabbits, and guinea pigs are at the mercy of the microbial world.

Evidence suggests that the results would be the same in children. In large families, children with many older brothers and sisters are less likely to have asthma, hay fever, or eczema. West African children who have had measles are half as likely to have allergies as children who never had measles. Italian students who recovered from infection with hepatitis A had fewer and less severe allergies than fellow students who were never infected. Children with Type I diabetes (an autoimmune disease) are less likely to have had infections before their fifth birthdays than healthy children of the same age. Children raised in rural areas, especially on farms, have fewer allergies and autoimmune diseases than children raised in cities. All of these notions have been referred to as the "hygiene hypothesis" (32).

Children exposed a little more to the infectious face of this world seem to fare better as adults. I do not mean to say that vaccination is inappropriate. Vaccination *is*, most often, infection, and vaccinations have done more to improve childhood survival rates that any other single bit of modern medicine. Nor are water purification and sewage treatment inappropriate. Water and sewage treatment have done even more than vaccination to eliminate disease in areas where human populations have exceeded the ability of the local environment to deal with human waste and the pathogens associated with it. But, evidence indicates that infection early in life is critical for the development of normal immune systems.

Exposure-dependent development is not limited to the immune system. Animals, humans included, must be exposed to the sights, sounds, feels tastes, and smells of this septic world. When we are not, our nervous systems do not develop normally, do not rewire, expand, and contract as they must to survive (33). For humans, as for rabbits, there is a window in childhood when our experiences, our infections, change everything, once and for all. Inside that window, infection causes lymph nodes and GALT to enlarge and reorganize, to separate into cortices and medullae, into primary lymphoid follicles, and develop T- and B-lymphocyte–rich regions of immune competence destined to someday be germinal centers, where our defenses will muster and the real battle will be fought. This window is a defining moment, when the simplest and lowest forms of life—the dirty, the infectious, the parasitic, and the septic—alter who we are.

We do not know which childhood infections are most important, but several studies implicate mycobacterial infections. A large group of bacteria, most of which cause no apparent disease, the mycobacteria, have strains that cause serious diseases (e.g., tuberculosis, leprosy). Mice injected with ovalbumin (the major protein in egg white) become allergic to ovalbumin. But mice first infected with mycobacteria and then injected with ovalbumin do not become allergic (34).

Early infection of children with some mycobacteria may promote strong immune systems, a normal sense of self, and a normal defense of that self. Mycobacteria are found in large numbers in dirt. And animals (probably including humans) kept from this dirt may lose the ability to recognize certain dangerous organisms as a threat, lose the ability to discriminate between self and not self, and lose the ability to distinguish the fatal from the innocuous.

THE "AGE OF BACTERIA"

For more than 3 billion years, microorganisms, especially bacteria, have ruled earth. As Stephen Jay Gould said, "We live now in the 'Age of Bacteria.' Our planet has always been in the 'Age of Bacteria' ever since the first fossils, bacteria of course, were entombed in rocks more than three and a half billion years ago" (35). And bacteria have done more than any other living group to alter the character of this earth (36). It has been estimated that more than 10^{29} bacteria live on this planet and as many as 10^{14} live on each one of us. Through all of history, we humans have waltzed with bacteria and the rest of the microscopic world. We had no choice. Bacteria outnumber, outweigh, out-travel, and outevolve us.

That bacteria cause so many human diseases is not astounding. It is astounding that so few bacteria cause human disease. Pathogenic bacteria are merely the microscopic tip of the largest of all biologic icebergs. How fortunate, we imagine. But fortune may have little or nothing to do with our survival. Billions of years of confrontation rather than luck were likely our benefactor. Through those confrontations and those eons, nearly all of us learned to coexist peacefully. Neither humans nor microorganisms benefit from fully destroying the other. Fatal infections seem, biologically at least, shortsighted. And even a brief course of antibiotics is enough to remind us that a world without bacteria would be a poorer world. This is not a war, as it has often been described, even though we have mustered an impressive array of weapons— bactericidal cribs and mattresses, toilet cleaners and counter tops, blankets, deodorants, shampoos, hand soaps, mouthwashes, toothpastes. This is not a war at all. If it were, we would have lost long ago, overpowered by sheer numbers and evolutionary speed. This is something else, something like a lichen, something like a waltz. This waltz will last for all of human history. We must hold our partners carefully and dance well.

Chimayo

Here beneath the old wood crucifix, as I watch the faithful leave the little chapel in Chimayo, I marvel with them at the miracle beneath this adobe floor, the same miracle buried beneath most every place human feet have trod.

NOTES

1. Krishnamani R, Mahaney WC. Geophagy among primates: adaptive significance and ecological consequences. *Animal Behavior* 2002;59:899–915.

2. Diamond J. Dirty eating for healthy living. *Nature* 1999;400:120–1.

3. Summary report for the ATSDR Soil-Pica Workshop, Atlanta, Georgia, 2000. Available from: URL: http://www.atsdr.cdc.gov/NEWS/soilpica.html

4. Johns T. *With bitter herbs they shall eat it: chemical ecology and the origins of human diet and medicine.* Tucson (AZ): University of Arizona Press; 1990.

5. Wiley AS, Solomon HK. Geophagy in pregnancy: a test of a hypothesis. *Current Anthropology* 1998; 39:532–45.

6. Guy-Grand D, Azogui O, Celli S, Darche S, Nussenzweig M, Kourilsky P, et al. Extrathymic T cell lymphopoiesis. *J Exp Med* 2003;197:333–41.

7. Heuy Ching W, Zhou Q, Dragoo J, Klein JR. Most murine CD8$^+$ intestinal intraepithelial lymphocytes are partially but not fully activated. *J Immunol* 2002;169:4717–25.

8. Lambolez F, Azogui O, Joret A, Garcia C, von Boehmer H, Di Santo J, et al. Characterization of T cell differentiation in the murine gut. *J Exp Med* 2002;195:437–49.

9. Poussier P, Julius M. Thymus independent T cell development and selection in the intestinal epithelium. *Annu Rev Immunol* 1994;12:521–53.

10. Mowat AM. Anatomical basis of tolerance and immunity to intestinal antigens. *Nature Rev Immunol* 2003;3:331–41.

11. Gupta RK. Aluminum compounds as vaccine adjuvants. *Adv Drug Deliv Rev* 1998;32:155–72.

12. Noguera-Obenza M. Ochoa TJ, Gomez HF, Guerrero ML, Herrera-Insua I, Morrow AL, et al. Human milk secretory antibodies against attaching and effacing *Eschericia coli* antigens. *Emerg Infect Dis* 2002;9:545–55.

13. Smith JL. Foodborne infections during pregnancy. *J Food Prot* 1999;62:818–29.

14. Munn DH, Shou M, Attwood JT, Bondarev I, Conway SJ, Marshall B, et al. Prevention of allogeneic fetal rejection by tryptophan catabolism. *Science* 1998; 281:1191–3.

15. Moffet-King A. Natural killer cells and pregnancy. *Nature Rev Immunol* 2002;2:656–61.

16. Abrahams PW. The chemistry and mineralogy of three Savanna lick soils. *J Chem Ecol* 1999; 25:2215–28.

17. Gilardi JD, Duffey SS, Munn CA, Tell L. Biochemical functions of geophagy in parrots: detoxification of dietary toxins and cytoprotective effects. *J Chem Ecol* 1999;25:897–922.

18. Johns T, Duquette M. Detoxification and mineral supplementation as functions of geophagy. *Am J Clin Nutr* 1991;53:448–56.

19. Torsvik V, Salte K, Sorheim R, Goksoyr J. Comparison of phenotypic diversity and DNA heterogeneity in population of soil bacteria. *Appl Environ Microbiol* 1990;56:776–81.

20. Kent A, Triplett EW. Microbial communities and their interactions in soil and rhizosphere ecosystems. *Annu Rev Microbiol* 2002;56:211–36.

21. Centers for Disease Control and Prevention. Racoon roundworm encephalitis—Chicago, Illinois, and Los Angeles, California, 2000. *MMWR Morb Mortal Wkly Rep* 2002;50:1153–5.

22. Laufer M, Toxocariasis. Available from: URL: http://www.emedicine.com/ped/topic2270.htm, 2002

23. Glickman LT, Schantz PM. Epidemiology and pathogenesis of zoonotic toxocariasis. *Epidemiol Rev* 1981;3:230–50.

24. Kazacos KR, Visceral and ocular larva migrans. Seminars in Veterinary Medicine and Surgery (Small Animal) 1991;6:227–35.

25. Ozumba UC, Ozumba N. Patterns of helminth infection in the human gut at the University of Nigeria Teaching Hospital, Enugu, Nigeria. *Journal of Health Science* 2002;48:263–8.

26. Geissler PW, Mwaniki D, Thiong F, Friis H. Geophagy as a risk factor for geohelminth infections: a longitudinal study of Kenyan primary schoolchildren. *Trans R Soc Trop Med Hyg* 1998;92:7–11.

27. Elliott DE, Li V, Blum A, Metawali A, Urban JF, Weinstock JV. Exposure to schistosoma eggs protects mice from TNBS-induced colitis. *Gastrointestinal and Liver Physiology* 2003;284:385–91.

28. Elliott DE, Urban JF, Curtis AK, Weinstock JV. Does the failure to acquire helminthic parasites predispose to Crohn's disease, *FASEB J* 2000;14: 1848–55.

29. Khan WI, Blennerhasset PA, Varghese AK, Chowdhury SK, Omsted P, Deng Y, Collins SM. Intestinal nematode infection ameliorates experimental colitis in mice. *Infect Immun* 2002;70:5931–7.

30. Lanning D, Sethupathi P, Rhee KJ, Zhai SK, Knight KL. Intestinal microflora and diversification of the rabbit antibody repertoire. *J Immunol* 2000, 165:2012.

31. Paul W, editor. *Fundamental immunology.* New York: Lippincott Raven; 1999.

32. Weiss ST. Eat dirt—the hygiene hypothesis and allergic disease. *N Engl J Med* 2002;347:930–1.

33. Callahan GN. *Faith, madness, and spontaneous human combustion: what immunology can teach us about self-perception.* New York: St. Martins Press; 2002.

34. Zuany-Amorim C, Elzbieta S, Manilu C, Le Moine A, Brunet LR, Kemeny DM, et al. Suppression of airway eosinophilia by killed *Mycobacterium vaccae*-induced allergen-specific regulatory T-cells. *Nat Med* 2002;8:625–9.

35. Gould, SJ. *Full house.* New York: Harmony Books; 1996.

36. Margulis L, Sagan D, Thomas L. *Microcosmos: four billion years of evolution from our microbial ancestors.* Berkeley (CA): University of California Press; 1997.

■ ■ ■ ■ ■ ■ ■ ■ ■

45   USING DRUG FOODS TO CAPTURE AND ENHANCE LABOR PERFORMANCE: A CROSS-CULTURAL PERSPECTIVE

William Jankowiak and Dan Bradburd

Dietary practices and the qualities of food are not just matters of nutrition. As previous selections have shown, major changes in food production and use have been linked historically to socioeconomic transformations. This selection uses a cross-cultural database to follow the spread of drug foods such as tobacco, alcohol, opium, and coffee in economic systems in transition (see also Jankowiak and Bradburd 2004; Mintz 1985). The argument is that drug foods may be used to enhance the productivity of workers or to induce people to provide more trade goods or new forms of labor than they otherwise would. The latter is more important during the early stages of contact, the former when production systems change in ways that require different kinds of work performance. The results of the study show that drug foods have been used in the expansion of nation–states in every area of the world.

The use of drug foods to deal with heavy labor is rare among foraging populations but more common among agricultural ones, in line with the evidence from Part II about agricultural labor being harder, longer, and more physically damaging that hunting, gathering, or fishing. Historically, in order for drug foods to be used on a large social and geographical scale, they had to be refined and packaged in ways not used by the societies in which they originated. This tended to make them more potent. As seen in selection 9 and Part II, in traditional societies mind-altering foods/drugs tend to be restricted to certain individuals such as shamans and used only in ritual or religious contexts. It has only been in recent centuries that humans have come to use these items on a mass scale, in unlimited quantities, and often in individual rather than social contexts. Although drug foods may be useful for coping with physical effort or mental fatigue, they tend to create physical and psychological dependencies that may bring negative health consequences.

Questions to keep in mind

Why are drug foods used to induce native populations to take on new economic relationships and forms of work?

How do you explain the relationship between use of drug foods as labor inducers, and level of political complexity?

Why do hallucinogenic drug foods tend not to be used as labor inducers or enhancers?

How might you fit the marketing of soft drinks and junk foods to developing countries into the framework presented in this selection?

Source: Jankowiak, William and Dan Bradburd 1996. "Using Drug Foods to Capture and Enhance Labor Performance: A Cross-Cultural Perspective." *Current Anthropology* 37(4):717–720. © 1996 by The Wenner-Gren Foundation for Anthropological Research. With permission from the University of Chicago Press.

The production and distribution of drug foods (i.e., pharmacologic agents that alter cortical stimulation, resulting in the modification of mental activity) have played a critical role in the expansion of trade within the emerging world economy (Marshall 1976, 1987; Marshall and Marshall 1979; Mintz 1985; Lindstrom 1982; van Onselen 1976; Wallerstein 1974; Wolf 1982). Mintz (1985), for example, documents the link between the rise of Britain's colonial empire, industrialization, and the increase in British consumption of sugar and tea. Similarly, the Marshall's study (1979:216–17) of the introduction of alcoholic beverages into eastern Micronesia examines the cultural impact of traders who relied on both alcoholic beverages and tobacco as trade goods. They demonstrate that alcohol was an important item in the trader's bag of goods on the Australian as well as the American frontier (see MacAndrew and Edgerton 1969, Steinberg and Hanner 1980). Clearly, especially in the early stages of cultural contact, drug foods were important trade items and in many instances the only ones acceptable to the native.

This scholarship has contributed to our understanding of the impact of the drug food trade on the development of European economies and indigenous societies. Yet, in focusing on the drug foods' impact on the development or destruction of specific social institutions we have overlooked their role in regulating the conditions of trade and labor productivity. In this paper we will explore three broad questions: (1) Do the biochemical properties of drug foods or the nature of their introduction account for their becoming such potent forces in opening or expanding trade? (2) Are the variant patterns of usage found in the historical and ethnographic literature related to a society's level of political complexity, or do they depend entirely upon the dynamics of cultural contact? and (3) Is there a relationship between the use of specific kinds of drug foods and the required tasks of labor?

DEFINING THE PROBLEM

As Lindstrom has pointed out, "If gifts make slaves just as whips make dogs . . . gifts of drugs are doubly dangerous. Commentators have frequently alluded to human 'inborn' desires to consume drugs in order to alter mood or state of human consciousness" (1987:5). Because the dominant drug foods—cacao, coffee, tea, tobacco, distilled alcohol, sugar, opium—are either analgesics or stimulants, habitual users tend to develop psychological or physiological dependency on them and, in turn, on the trader or merchant who provides them.

With the exception of alcohol, all of the drug foods in question occur in or can be processed into forms which are relatively easy to transport. Many of them can be and often are used in conjunction with others. Sugar, for example, is an excellent agent that is often taken together with bitter tropical drug foods such as coffee, tea, cacao, and, of course, alcohol. The products of European and Chinese expansion, most notably alcohol but also sugar, tobacco, and tea, are pharmacologically purer, more refined, and therefore more potent versions of traditional drug foods that were consumed before contact. Indeed, one might hypothesize a form of Gresham's Law for drug foods—that the purer, more concentrated forms of drug foods will drive out the indigenous forms. Drug foods, unlike other trade items such as metal and cloth, all share the singular and, from the perspective of the trader, convenient feature that their use encourages immediate consumption. They are therefore unlikely to be successfully hoarded or stored, and consumer demand and their exchange values are likely to remain constant if not to increase over time.

The record suggests that drug foods can be used together or separately in two ways—as "inducers" or "enhancers." As inducers, they encourage and compel members of the contacted culture to provide the trader or merchant with either goods or labor in return for the drug food and other desired goods. As enhancers they may be used to increase a laborer's work efficiency, intensity, and duration of effort. While these categories are heuristic and descriptive and may overlap, drug foods tend to be used as inducers under circumstances in which it is difficult to compel producers or workers to provide adequate quantities of trade goods or sustained labor activity. In practical terms, these circumstances are generally associated with early contacts by isolated traders operating beyond the frontiers of their own societies and contacts with mobile peoples exploiting difficult environments such as hunter–gatherers and nomadic pastoralists. In this way, drug foods often serve as an alternative to military force and are generally selected because they are more efficient, more economical, or easier to sustain. Once control has been institutionalized and the colonial power's infrastructure has been fully developed, the rationale for using drug foods shifts from attracting laborers or goods to maximizing production. There seems to be a clear relationship between the nature of the labor required to complete a task and a drug food's biochemical composition, with those (such as marijuana, hashish, opium, cocaine, nicotine, and alcohol) that increase or stimulate cortical alertness being preferred in a work context over those capable of producing delusions and hallucinations (such as peyote, jimsonweed, and morning glory).

METHODOLOGY

We drew our data primarily from Murdock and White's (1969) Standard Cross-Cultural Sample (SCCS) of 186 societies, supplementing it where necessary with more recent ethnographic and historical sources. We grouped drug foods that have similar effects on the central nervous system. Kola nuts, tea, and coffee, for example, were grouped together and coded as "caffeine." Honey, sugarcane, and refined sugar were coded as "sugar." Beverages that contained ethanol, either distilled or undistilled, were classified as "alcohol."

For lack of data on working conditions, laborers, or colonialist motives, 102 societies were eliminated from our sample, leaving 84 societies, and this sample was expanded with 10 societies for which an ethnographer had discussed the historical or contemporary use of drug foods in a work context.[1] Coding reliability was ensured by having two graduate students independently read the accounts and record whether the context illustrated labor inducement or enhancement or was unclear. Discrepancies were reanalyzed and recorded; in one instance no consensus could be established and the society was dropped from the sample.

RESULTS

An examination of the conjunction of the use of drug foods with the rise of the capitalist world market shows the following patterns:

The introduction of drug foods was such a common feature of nation–states' economic expansion that it warranted recognition as one of the primary forces employed in the expansion. Drugs were used as labor or trade inducers in every cultural area (Table 45.1). The drug foods most frequently used as labor inducers were alcohol and tobacco, followed by opium and caffeine. Significantly, it was rare for two or more alien drug foods to be used to attract a labor supply or establish an ongoing trade relationship in a specific culture area. Although tobacco, for example, was used throughout the world, it was in the Insular Pacific that it was most important (occurring in 15 of 19 societies). In every other cultural area, alcohol, a depressant that acts as a temporary stimulant, was the primary means of attraction. Narcotics such as opium were predominantly used in Eurasia by agents of both European and non-European nation-states.

The low frequency of drug use in the Circum-Mediterranean seems to be linked to the higher

Table 45.1   Labor and Trade Inducers by Cultural Area

Cultural Area	Drugs Used	Not Used	Opium	Caffeine	Tobacco	Alcohol	Marijuana	Coca
North America	20	2	0	1	2	17	0	0
South America	13	1	0	0	2	7	2	2
Insular Pacific	19	0	1	0	15	3	0	0
Africa	12	1	0	1	2	9	0	0
Circum-Mediterranean	6	6	0	1	1	5	1	0
Eurasia	10	4	3	2	2	5	2	0
Total	80	14	6	5	28	47	5	2

level of political complexity of the indigenous societies. Because other means of influence and coercion (e.g., taxes, corvée labor, bride-price, etc.) were already institutionalized, the creation of chemical dependency was probably unnecessary. There is in fact a close relationship between the level of political complexity and the use of drug foods as trade or labor inducers (see Table 45.2). About 85% (66 of 76) of independent and single-level communities (e.g., bands and tribes) exchange labor for a drug food compared with less than 50% (5 of 12) of the supercommunity and multilevel societies (e.g., chiefdoms and states).

There is also a clear relationship between the type of subsistence and the chemical stimulants used to enhance a laborer's work performance (Table 45.3). The more labor-intensive the subsistence system, the greater the likelihood that a drug food will function as a labor enhancer. Labor-enhancing drugs are not, then, a European contribution to world culture (Cooper 1949); they existed well before the advent of mercantilism or market capitalism. For forager and fishing societies there is little or no use of drugs to relieve physical toil. In contrast, cultivators often use drug foods to overcome muscle fatigue and thus enhance labor activity. Contemporary industrial societies use drug foods (especially tea, coffee, and cola drinks) to overcome mental fatigue.

As the nature of capitalist production shifted, there was a shift in drug foods promoted and permitted as labor enhancers away from drugs such as alcohol and (quite likely) opiates to less obviously harmful stimulants such as caffeine and nicotine. Alcohol was commonly used as a labor enhancer on plantations and haciendas, in the mines, in the merchant marine, in the armed forces, and, during the earliest phase of industrial capitalism, in factories. With the rise of industrial capitalism and its

Table 45.2 Use of Drugs as Labor and Trade Inducers by Level of Political Complexity

	Total	Labor	Trade
Independent	43	15	22
Single-level	33	12	17
Supercommunity	6	2	2
Three or more levels	12	4	1
Total	94	33	42

Table 45.3 Use of Drugs as Labor Enhancers by Subsistence Type

	Yes	No	Total
Fishing	1	11	12
Hunter–gatherer	3	8	11
Pastoralist	2	6	8
Simple horticulturalist	16	3	19
Advanced horticulturalist	8	4	12
Agriculturalist	27	0	27
Industrial	10	0	10

more sophisticated technology, the use of alcohol as a labor enhancer lost favor. Moreover, there was often pressure for regulation or even prohibition of its use, and it was replaced (or its use was tempered) by alternative drug foods such as coffee, tea, cocoa, and sugar—the latter consumed in combination with any of the above, alongside of them, or alone. Each drug food has specific chemical properties that are often manifested in very different behavior expressions. Those drug foods (e.g., marijuana, hashish, opium, cocaine, nicotine, and alcohol) that increase or stimulate cortical alertness are consistently preferred over drugs and drug foods (e.g., peyote, jimsonweed) capable of producing intense illusions and delusions. Of the 94 societies in our survey not a single one relies on hallucinogenic drug food(s) to alleviate hunger or enhance a labor activity.

CONCLUSION

The conjunction between the use of drug foods and the rise of the capitalist world market reveals the following pattern: the agents of colonialism (e.g., trader, merchant, and settler) initially lacked the means to compel native populations to perform new forms of labor. They were faced with the recurrent problem of motivating and organizing a population in new or more sustained forms of labor when that population did not need or embrace the status symbols of the colonial social order. The response to this dilemma was to foster chemical dependency. It was discovered and rediscovered time and again that drug foods contributed to the development of a one-sided but, from the point of view of the colonialists, highly beneficial social dependency.

The development of the capitalist world market system required the intensification of production of commodities. In this new global context, quality rather than quantity of output was encouraged. Labor efficiency became the ideal, and with this shift came a corresponding change in the drug foods deemed acceptable or unacceptable. An illustration of this shift is found in the remarks of a Mr. Johnson, a late-19th-century British Member of Parliament, in response to reports of the increasing frequency with which inebriated native African miners were being injured on the job, urging management to provide the African miners with a substance less harmful than alcohol, he suggested giving "the natives all the coffee they could drink."

NOTES

1. These societies were Cagaba, Costa Rica, Georgian Britain, Iroquois, Jamaica, Japan, Pawnee, Rajput, Tarahumara, and Zuin.

REFERENCES

Cooper, J. M. 1949. "A cross-cultural survey of South American Indian tribes: Stimulants and narcotics," in *Handbook of South American Indians*, vol. 5. Edited by Julian Steward, pp. 589–627. Bureau of American Ethnology Bulletin 143.

Hanner, J., and J. Steinberg. 1980. *Alcohol and native peoples of the North*. Washington, D.C.: University Press of America.

Johnson, H. 1911. Alcohol in Africa. *The Nineteenth Century*, September, pp. 476–81.

Lindstrom, L. 1982. "*Grog blong yumi*: Alcohol and *kava* on Tanna, Vanuatu," in *Through a glass darkly: Beer and modernization in Papua New Guinea*. Edited by M. Marshall. Boroko, Papua New Guinea: Institute of Applied Social and Economic Anthropology.

Macandrew, M., and R. Edgerton. 1969. *Drunken comportment*. Chicago: Aldine.

Marshall, M. 1976. "A review and appraisal of alcohol and *kava* studies in Oceania," in *Cross-cultural approaches to the study of alcohol*. Edited by M. Everett, J. Waddell, and D. Heath, pp. 103–18. Paris: Mouton.

———. 1987. *Weekend warriors*. Palo Alto: Mayfield.

———. 1990. *Silent voices speak*. Belmont: Wadsworth.

Mintz, S. 1985. *Sweetness and power*. New York: Penguin.

Murdock, G. P., and D. White. 1969. Standard cross-cultural sample. *Ethnology* 8:329–69.

Steinberg, J., and J. Hanner. 1980. "Introduction," in *Alcohol and native peoples of the North*. Edited by J. Hanner and J. Steinberg. Washington, D.C.: University Press of America.

Van Onselen, C. 1976. Randlords and rotgut 1886–1903. *History Workshop*, no. 2 (Autumn), pp. 33–89.

Wallerstein, I. 1974. *The modern world system: Capitalist agriculture and the origins of the European world-economy in the sixteenth century*. New York: Academic Press.

Wolf, E. 1982. *Europe and the people without history*. Berkeley: University of California Press.

■ ■ ■ ■ ■ ■ ■ ■ ■

46   THE STATE OF MIND OF VEGETARIANS: PSYCHOLOGICAL WELL-BEING OR DISTRESS?

Marjaana Lindeman

This selection explains that vegetarianism in industrialized societies is a way of life that for many practitioners connects directly to personal identity as well as social, moral, and political expression. Some studies have shown that vegetarians tend to report greater health and happiness on choosing vegetarianism as a

Source: "The State of Mind of Vegetarians" by Marjaana Lindeman, *Ecology of Food and Nutrition* 41(1):75–86. Copyright © 2002. Reproduced by permission of Taylor & Francis, Inc., http://www.taylorandfrancis.com.

way of life. In contrast, this selection points out that other research has found that vegetarian women tend to be very weight conscious and to show psychological and interpersonal symptoms of eating disorders such as anorexia nervosa. This connection is largely borne out in the first of two studies comparing omnivores to vegetarians and semivegetarians reported in the selection.

To get a better grasp on the level of happiness of vegetarians compared to omnivores, Lindeman then asks whether there might be a difference in perceptions of the world and people in general as fundamentally hospitable or hostile. On most measures the second study did find consistent differences, which makes it rather paradoxical that vegetarians experience an improvement in well-being after the lifestyle change. The reason may be that the difference between their happiness and that of omnivores is even greater beforehand. The selection suggests that vegetarians may manage their higher levels of fear and distress by practicing a way of life that gives meaning to and imposes order on a chaotic, dangerous, and unfair world, but in a socially and medically acceptable way. This adds another dimension to discussions of vegetarianism, which often revolve around nutritional aspects rather than meaning or personal identity.

Questions to keep in mind

What differences did the two studies find between omnivores and vegetarians (and semivegetarians)?

What are the strengths and limitations of the methods, instruments, and data analysis used in the two studies?

Are you satisfied with the studies' definitions and measurements of happiness?

Do you think that vegetarianism may be a socially acceptable way of dealing with the anxiety and distress underlying eating disorders or discomfort with living in the modern world?

Contemporary vegetarianism is a fascinating scientific phenomenon because it embodies strong medical, social and psychological aspects. In a similar way, empirical studies on vegetarianism can be classified into different categories that reflect different foci of investigation. The first line of research has addressed the beneficial and adverse effects of a vegetarian diet. The majority of these studies suggest that vegetarians are healthier than omnivores and that a vegetarian diet is a safe approach for the prevention and management of many diseases, such as obesity, diabetes, coronary heart diseases, and cancer (Key et al., 1999; Messina and Burke, 1997; Segasothy and Phillips, 1999; Willett, 1999).

The second category of studies has analyzed vegetarians' self-reports on their dietary motives and the implications of the diet for their personal well-being (Amato and Partridge, 1989; Beardsworth and Keil, 1992, 1993; Jabs et al., 1998; Kenyon and Barker, 1998; Santos and Booth, 1996; Watson and Clark, 1984; Willett, 1999; Worsley and Skrzypiec, 1998). These studies delineate most vegetarians as socially conscious individuals who, after their dietary change, have experienced improvements in physical health, psychological functioning, and quality of life.

However, the third line of studies, which has addressed the psychological characteristics of vegetarians, portrays a different picture of vegetarians. These studies show that vegetarian women are intensely preoccupied with being slim (Martins and Pliner, 1999; Worsley and Skrzypiec, 1997) and that they display clear symptoms of eating disorders (Lindeman et al., 2000). Moreover, vegetarian women have been shown to suffer from depression and anxiety (Cooper et al., 1985) and from maturity fears, ineffectiveness, and interpersonal distrust (Lindeman et al., 2000), which have been identified as fundamental aspects of the psychopathology of anorexia nervosa (Garner et al., 1983).

These findings raise a question that so far has not been addressed but will be examined in this study: Do vegetarians and omnivorous individuals differ in terms of psychological well-being? Psychological well-being is a broad category of phenomena that may be conceptualized both as a global judgment of life satisfaction or as separate affective states (e.g., depression) and domain satisfactions (e.g., self-esteem, body-image) (DeNeve and Cooper, 1998; Diener, 1984; Diener et al., 1999). In addition, although health, wealth, and other such conditions are not necessary parts of well-being, they are typically seen as potential influences on well-being. And finally, because it is a question of subjective feelings, psychological well-being is here equated with happiness (for similar notions, see DeNeve and Cooper, 1998; Diener et al., 1999).

Given that vegetarianism may be intertwined with pathological eating, symptoms of eating disorders and those indices of well-being that have been shown to differentiate healthy individuals from individuals with an increased risk for eating disorders, (i.e., depression, self-esteem, and body image) were included in the study (Halmi, 1995; Polivy and Herman, 1987; Szmukler et al., 1995). Consistent with the literature on vegetarians' psychological characteristics, it was hypothesized that vegetarians have lower well-being than omnivores.

STUDY 1

Participants

The participants were recruited from eight Summer University courses in the capital city of Finland, Helsinki. The questionnaire was delivered and filled in during their lecture time. Out of 370 questionnaires, 356 were returned. Because there were only a few semivegetarian ($N = 5$) and vegetarian ($N = 1$) men in the sample, only women were included. The final sample thus consisted of 308 women. Of them, 2.3% were in high school, 7.1% had finished school and were seeking admission for study, 63% were full-time university students from over 25 fields of study, 25.6% were working, and 1.3% were neither working or studying. The age of the participants varied from 13 to 74 years of age, with a mean age of 29 ($SD = 10.81$). The participants represented various eating status categories in the following way: 197 of the women were omnivorous, 69 avoided red meat or ate only fish and vegetarian dishes, and 42 were vegetarians. As in previous studies (Amato and Partridge, 1989; Martins and Pliner, 1999; Worsley and Skrzypiec, 1998), those who ate fish and avoided red meat were labeled semivegetarians.

Measures

Depression was measured with the short form of the Center for Epidemiologic Studies Depression Scale (Cronbach's $\alpha = .85$), which has been shown to be a valid and reliable measure both among younger and older individuals (Andresen and Malmgren, 1994; Shrout and Yager, 1989). The subjects were asked to rate 10 items in terms of the frequency with which each mood or symptom of depression (e.g., restless sleep or feelings of loneliness) occurred during the past week (0 = none of the time, 3 = most of the time). The possible range of scores is thus 0–30, with higher scores representing greater degrees of depressed moods.

Self-esteem was assessed by Rosenberg's (1979) Self-Esteem Scale (Cronbach's $\alpha = .85$). The subjects rated the ten items (e.g., "On the whole, I am satisfied with myself") on a five-point scale (1 = strongly disagree, 5 = strongly agree). The scores were averaged and the range of scores was thus 1–5, the highest scores indicating high self-esteem. In previous studies, Rosenberg Self-Esteem Scale has been shown to be a reliable and valid measure of global self-esteem (for a review, Gray-Little et al., 1997; Robins et al., 2001).

Appearance dissatisfaction and weight dissatisfaction were measured by Visual Analogue Scales (VAS) (Thompson, 1996). These two scales are 10 cm horizontal lines with the endpoints 0 (no appearance [weight] dissatisfaction) and 100 (extreme appearance [weight] dissatisfaction). The subjects were asked to mark with a slash their level of dissatisfaction on the two lines. The distance from 0, measured from the left in millimeters, indicated the level of dissatisfaction. The scale can be used as a quick and reliable measure of weight and size and overall appearance dissatisfaction (Thompson, 1996).

Symptoms of eating disorders were measured by the short form of the Eating Attitudes Test (EAT; Garner and Garfinkel, 1979; Garner et al., 1982). EAT (Cronbach's $\alpha = .80$) includes 26 items (e.g., "I am terrified about being overweight") which the participants answer on a six-point scale (1 = never, 6 = always). Subjects' raw scores were rescored along the lines recommended by Garner and Garfinkel (1979), that is scores 1–3 were rescored as 0, 4 as 1, 5 as 2, and 6 as 3. A cutoff point of 20 can be used to screen individuals with a high risk for eating disorders. The reliability and validity of EAT are well established (e.g., Garner and Garfinkel, 1979; Garner et al., 1982).

Results and Discussion

To analyze psychological well-being among the participants, analysis of variance (ANOVA) was conducted with the dietary practice (omnivores vs. semivegetarians vs. vegetarians) as between-subjects variable and depression, self-esteem, satisfaction with weight and appearance, and symptoms of eating disorders as dependent variables. Significant differences among the three dietary groups were found on all variables except satisfaction with weight (Table 46.1). Specific comparisons showed that semivegetarians were more satisfied with their appearance than omnivores and vegetarians, $t(303) = -3.06$, $p < .002$. In addition, semivegetarians and vegetarians had lower self-esteem, $t(306) = -3.09$, $p < .002$, and more symptoms of depression, $t(306) = 3.58$, $p < .001$, than omnivores. Semivegetarians and vegetarians also scored higher on EAT than omnivores, $t(306) = 3.09$, $p < .002$, indicating that they had more symptoms of eating disorders than omnivores. With the exception of body-image, the results thus supported the hypothesis in that both vegetarians and semivegetarians had a lower well-being than omnivores.

Besides daily problems and physical health, one major factor related to everyday well-being is one's assumptions of the world (Feist et al., 1995; Janoff-Bulman, 1989; Janoff-Bulman and Frieze, 1983). World assumptions consist of implicit assumptions about ourselves and about the benevolence and meaningfulness of the world. Longitudinal studies have shown that these assumptions are both a cause and an effect of well-being (Feist et al., 1995). For example, negative views of the world color interpretations of experiences as negative and thus lower well-being, whereas low well-being makes us perceive the world in negative terms. Because of the strong relation between world assumptions and well-being, and because of the increasing evidence of vegetarians' low well-being, the second study was designed to test the assumption that vegetarians have a more negative worldview than omnivores.

STUDY 2

Participants

The participants were recruited from four Open University courses at the University of Helsinki and from three senior high schools in the Helsinki area. Out of 400 questionnaires, 315 were returned. Again, there were only a few semivegetarian ($N = 4$) and vegetarian ($N = 2$) men in the sample, thus only women were included in the study. The sample consisted of 226 women. Of them, 26% were full-time university students from over 15 fields of study, 22% were working, and 52% were in high school. The age of the participants varied from 16 to 54, with a mean age of 22.3 ($SD = 8.68$). Of the participants, 148 were omnivorous, 60 were semivegetarians, and 17 were vegetarians.

Measures

To measure the participants' view of the world, the World Assumption Scale (WAS; Janoff-Bulman, 1989) was used. The scale consists of eight categories of assumptions of self and the world: benevolence of people, benevolence of the world, luck,

Table 46.1   Means and standard deviations (in parentheses) on well-being among the three dietary groups

	Omnivores	Semivegetarians	Vegetarians	F(2,306)
Dissatisfaction with weight	38.73 (30.22)	41.32 (31.93)	33.85 (30.82)	0.77
Dissatisfaction with appearance	32.76 (20.90)	41.57 (24.55)	30.90 (21.59)	4.73[**]
Self-esteem	3.85 (.64)	3.52 (.86)	3.62 (.79)	6.08[**]
Depression	9.65 (5.75)	12.16 (6.47)	12.56 (6.18)	7.03[***]
Symptoms of eating disorders	9.60 (7.32)	11.70 (9.91)	13.86 (8.98)	5.40[**]

[***] $p < .001$. [**] $p < .01$.

Note: Higher means indicate stronger dissatisfaction and depression, higher self-esteem, and more eating disorder symptoms.

justice, randomness, controllability, self-controllability, and self-worth. An example item from the Luck scale is "I am luckier than other people." Each subscale includes four items on which the participants indicated their agreement using a five-point scale (1 = strongly disagree, 5 = strongly agree). The scores were averaged and the possible range was thus 1–5. The higher the score the higher was the respondent's belief in benevolence of people, benevolence of the world, luck, justice, randomness, controllability, self-controllability, and self-worth, respectively. Previous studies have shown that the WAS has a consistent factor structure and a modest reliability (Janoff-Bulman, 1989). In this study, the reliabilities (Cronbach's α) of the scales ranged from .79 to .85.

Results

World assumptions among omnivores, semivegetarians and vegetarians were analyzed with a one-way ANOVA (Table 46.2). Significant differences between the three dietary groups were found on assumptions about the controllability of events, the benevolence of world, the benevolence of people, justice, and self-worth.

Specific comparisons showed that omnivores and semivegetarians did not differ in their world assumptions (all p's > .05). However, in comparison to vegetarians, omnivores and semivegetarians saw the world as more controllable, $t(221) = 2.94$, $p < .01$, and had more positive assumptions about the benevolence of the world, $t(221) = 2.72$, $p < .01$, the benevolence of people, $t(221) = 3.09$,

$p < .01$, justice, $t(221) = 2.46$, $p < .02$, and self-worth, $t(221) = 1.99$, $p < .05$. Other differences were not significant.

GENERAL DISCUSSION

The results of the two studies indicated that vegetarian and semivegetarian women had a lower self-esteem and more symptoms of depression and eating disorders than omnivorous women. In addition, vegetarian women regarded both people and the impersonal world as basically more malevolent and they saw outcomes as less distributed in accordance with a principle of justice than semivegetarian or omnivorous women. Nonetheless, vegetarians did not differ from others in body-image or in those world assumptions that focus on luck or randomness.

The results extend previous findings that vegetarian women display enhanced emotional distress and symptoms of eating disorders (Cooper et al., 1985; Lindeman et al., 2000; Worsley and Skrzypiec, 1997, 1998). Furthermore, if vegetarians typically experience increased psychological well-being after converting to vegetarianism, as many vegetarians have reported, it is possible that the differences between omnivores and future vegetarians' happiness is even stronger before individuals adopt vegetarianism. With longitudinal designs it would be possible to ascertain whether vegetarians are individuals who have indeed been able to decrease their psychological distress, at least to some extent, by adopting the current social ideals of environmental welfare, animal liberation, and social

Table 46.2   Means and standard deviations (in parentheses) on assumptions of world among the three dietary groups

	Omnivores	Semivegetarians	Vegetarians	F(2,221)
Controllability	2.53 (.62)	2.68 (.49)	2.17 (.55)	5.98[**]
Benevolence of world	2.98 (.79)	2.94 (.85)	2.40 (.74)	3.98[*]
Benevolence of people	3.82 (.61)	3.66 (.63)	3.26 (.51)	7.17[***]
Justice	2.03 (.57)	2.20 (.62)	1.75 (.39)	4.36[*]
Self-worth	3.51 (.69)	3.34 (.72)	3.06 (.82)	3.53[*]
Luck	3.40 (.83)	3.46 (.79)	2.99 (.68)	2.34
Randomness	2.87 (.67)	2.83 (.77)	2.69 (.72)	0.54
Self-control	3.08 (.69)	3.22 (.78)	2.79 (.72)	2.42

[***] $p < .001$. [**] $p < .01$. [*] $p < .05$.
Note: Higher means in the subscales indicate a stronger assumption.

justice, and by ending up with a life style that many nutritionists and medical scientists regard as satisfactory.

The present studies do not answer the question about the causal relations between low psychological well-being and negative views of the world on the one hand, and adopting a vegetarian diet on the other. However, it is plausible to assume that vegetarianism has not decreased well-being but that individuals who suffer from low well-being are more apt to adopt a vegetarian diet. If this is the case, the question arises why might low well-being generate an aspiration to convert to vegetarianism? One hypothesis that might direct future studies is based on terror management theory (Pyszczynski et al., 1997; Solomon et al., 1991): Vegetarianism may serve as an ideology with which one imbues the world with meaning, order, stability, and permanence, and by so doing, one buffers distress and anxiety. This hypothesis would also be in line with the suggestions of Beardsworth and Keil (1992) and Lawrence (1993) and with empirical findings (Lindeman and Stark, 1999) that vegetarianism is an ideology whose adoption is at root an exercise in the management of anxiety, the negotiation of identity, and the reestablishing of peace of mind.

It is important to note that our findings were obtained with a convenience sample consisting of Finnish women only. At least in Western societies, women are more concerned about food and eating than men (Chaiken and Pliner, 1987; Pliner and Chaiken, 1990). In addition, Finnish people are very homogeneous in religion (mostly Lutheran) and race, and therefore it is possible that different results would be obtained for other samples. Moreover, the conclusion that vegetarians have a lower well-being is inaccurate in that well-being is a broader category of affects and domain satisfactions (Diener et al., 1999) than mere depressive tendencies, self-esteem, and body-image. Finally, vegetarianism is pursued for a variety of reasons and it may be that low psychological well-being is not typical of all vegetarian subgroups. Therefore, future studies should validate the results by employing a more differentiated set of well-being measures and with larger and more heterogeneous samples of participants.

Existing literature on the psychological well-being of vegetarians is limited, and it is worth ex-

ploring this issue further. Thus, far, however, the available evidence suggests that although vegetarians may have a healthier lifestyle and a lower risk for some disease, they seem to live a less happy life than other individuals do.

REFERENCES

Amato, P. R. and S. A. Partridge (1989). *The new vegetarians: Promoting health and protecting life.* New York: Plenum Press.

Andresen, E. M. and J. A. Malmgren (1994). Screening for depression in well older adults: Evaluation of a short form of the CES-D. *Am. J. Prev. Med.,* 10, 77–84.

Beardsworth, A. and T. Keil (1992). The vegetarian option: Varieties, conversions, motives and careers. *Sociological Review,* 40, 253–293.

Beardsworth, A. D. and E. T. Keil (1993). Contemporary vegetarianism in the U.K.: Challenge and incorporation? *Appetite,* 20, 229–234.

Chaiken, S. and P. Pliner (1987). Women, but not men, are what they eat: The effect of meal size and gender on perceived femininity and masculinity. *Personality and Social Psych. Bull.,* 13, 166–176.

Cooper, C. K., T. Wise and L. S. Mann (1985). Psychological and cognitive characteristics of vegetarians. *Psychosomatics,* 26, 521–527.

DeNeve, K. M. and H. Cooper (1998). The happy personality: A meta-analysis of 137 personality traits and subjective well-being. *Psych. Bull.,* 124, 197–229.

Diener, E. (1984). Subjective well-being. *Psych. Bull.,* 95, 542–575.

Diener, E., E. M. Suh, R. E. Lucas, and H. L. Smith (1999). Subjective well-being: Three decades of progress. *Psych. Bull.,* 125, 276–302.

Feist, G. J., T. E. Bodner, J. F. Jacobs, M. Miles and V. Tan (1995). Integrating top-down and bottom-up structural models of subjective well-being: A longitudinal investigation. *J. Personality Social Psych.,* 68, 138–150.

Garner, D. M. and P. E. Garfinkel (1979). The Eating Attitudes Test: An index of the symptoms of anorexia nervosa. *Psych. Med.,* 9, 273–279.

Garner, D. M., M. P. Olmsted, Y. Bohr and P. E. Garfinkel (1982). The eating attitude test: Psychometric features and clinical correlates. *Psych. Med.,* 12, 871–878.

Garner, D. M., M. P. Olmstead and J. Polivy (1983). Development and validation of a multidimensional eating disorder inventory for anorexia nervosa and bulimia. *Int. J. Eating Disorders,* 2, 15–34.

Gray-Little, B., V. Williams and T. Hancock (1997). An item response theory analysis of the Rosenberg Self-Esteem Scale. *Personality Social Psych. Bull., 23,* 443–451.

Halmi, K. A. (1995). Current concepts and definitions. In G. I. Szmukler and C. Dare (Eds.), *Handbook of eating disorders: Theory, treatment and research.* Chichester: Wiley, pp. 29–42.

Jabs, J., C. M. Devine and J. Sobal (1998). Model of the process of adopting vegetarian diets: Health vegetarians and ethical vegetarians. *J. Nutrition Educ., 30,* 196–202.

Janoff-Bulman, R. (1989). Assumptive worlds and the stress of traumatic events: Applications of the schema construct. *Social Cognition, 7,* 113–136.

Janoff-Bulman, R. and I. H. Frieze (1983). A theoretical perspective for understanding reactions to victimization. *J. Social Issues, 39,* 1–17.

Kenyon, P. M. and M. E. Barker (1998). Attitudes towards meat-eating in vegetarian and non-vegetarian teenage girls in England—An ethnographic approach. *Appetite, 30,* 185–198.

Key, T. J., G. K. Davey and P. N. Appelby (1999). Health benefits of a vegetarian diet. *Proc. Nutrition Society, 58,* 271–275.

Lawrence, V. (1993). Is vegetarianism a diet or an ideology? *Can. Med. Assoc. J., 148,* 998–1002.

Lindeman, M. and K. Stark (1999). Pleasure, pursuit of health, or negotiation of identity? Personality correlates of food choice motives among young and middle-aged women. *Appetite, 33,* 141–161.

Lindeman, M., K. Stark, and K. Latvala (2000). Vegetarianism and eating-disordered thinking. *Eating Disorders, 8,* 157–165.

Martins, Y. and P. Pliner (1999). Restrained eating among vegetarians: Does a vegetarian eating style mask concerns about weight? *Appetite, 32,* 145–154.

Messina, V. K. and K. I. Burke (1997). Position of the American Dietetic Association: Vegetarian diets. *J. Am. Dietetic Assoc., 97,* 1317–1321.

Pliner, P. and S. Chaiken (1990). Eating, social motives, and self-presentation in women and men. *J. Exp. Social Psych., 26,* 240–254.

Polivy, J. and C. P. Herman (1987). Diagnosis and treatment of normal eating. *J. Consulting and Clinical Psych., 55,* 635–644.

Pyszczynski, T., J. Greenberg, and S. Solomon (1997). Why do we need what we need? A terror management perspective on the roots of human social motivation. *Psych. Inquiry, 8,* 1–20.

Robins, R. W., H. M. Hendin and K. H. Trzesniewski (2001). Measuring global self-esteem: Construct validation of a single-item measure and the Rosenberg Self-Esteem Scale. *Personality and Social Psych. Bull., 27,* 151–161.

Rosenberg, L. (1979). *Conceiving the self.* New York: Basic Books.

Santos, M. L. S. and D. A. Booth (1996). Influences on meat avoidance among British students. *Appetite, 27,* 197–205.

Segasothy, M. and P. A. Phillips (1999). Vegetarian diet: Panacea for modern lifestyle diets? *QJM, 92,* 531–544.

Shrout, P. E. and T. J. Yager (1989). Reliability and validity of screening scales: Effect of reducing scale length. *J. Clinical Epidem., 42,* 69–78.

Solomon, S., J. Greenberg, and T. Pyszcynski (1991). A terror management theory of social behavior: The psychological functions of self-esteem and cultural worldviews. *Adv. Exp. Social Psych., 24,* 93–159.

Szmukler, G.-I., C. Dare, and J. Treasure (Eds.) (1995). *Handbook of eating disorders: Theory, treatment and research.* Chichester: Wiley.

Thompson, J. K. (1996). Assessing body image disturbance: Measures, methodology, and implementation. In J. K. Thompson (Ed.), *Body image, eating disorders, and obesity.* Washington, DC: American Psychological Association, pp. 49–81.

Watson, D. and L. A. Clark (1984). Negative affectivity: The disposition to experience aversive emotional states. *Psych. Bull., 96,* 465–490.

Willett, W. C. (1999). Convergence of philosophy and science: The third international congress on vegetarian nutrition. *Am. J. Clinical Nutrition, 70* (3 Suppl.), 434–438.

Worsley, A. and G. Skrzypiec (1997). Teenage vegetarianism: Beauty or the beast? *Nutrition Research, 17,* 391–404.

Worsley, A. and G. Skrzypiec (1998). Teenage vegetarianism: Prevalence, social and cognitive contexts. *Appetite, 30,* 151–170.

■ ■ ■ ■ ■ ■ ■ ■ ■

47 BREASTFEEDING, BREAST CANCER, AND THE SUDDEN INFANT DEATH SYNDROME IN ANTHROPOLOGICAL PERSPECTIVE

Elizabeth D. Whitaker

As the first in a group on infancy and childhood, this selection considers the process of medicalization discussed in previous selections as it has affected the relationship between mothers and infants. The hospitalization of childbirth, guided by mechanical understandings and instrumental approaches, provides a clear example of the medicalization of a process that previously had been managed by relatives or traditional birth assistants (see Davis-Floyd and Sargent 1997). Although the role of the modern physician may seem paramount in medicalized childbirth, the presence of birth assistants is not new but has been a fact of human existence ever since the evolutionary step toward bipedalism. This step produced skeletal constraints that require the fetus to change direction during childbirth and emerge face downward, making it very difficult for women to give birth alone (Trevathan and Rosenberg 2000). Our biology is evidence of the social nature of human existence.

Hospital birth, the immediate separation of the infant from the mother, bottle feeding, and the use of cribs, strollers, and other devices that detach infants from their parents are evidence of both intense medical surveillance and direction, and the cultural ideal of individual autonomy that presumes that it is "natural" and fitting that infants and mothers not remain too attached to each other. This selection demonstrates that this is a cultural construct rather than a biological one. For most of human history the care and feeding of infants has emphasized the interdependence of mothers and infants rather than their autonomy. Like the selections in Part II, this selection hypothesizes health consequences of deviation from this type of relationship.

An ancestral pattern of breastfeeding may be inferred from the practices of contemporary foraging populations and is supported by evidence ranging from the composition of human milk to maternal hormones that prevent a subsequent pregnancy. Prolonged, intensive, and frequent breastfeeding brings significant benefits to both mothers and infants in terms of health and well-being. For infants, it contributes to physical, cognitive, and psychosocial development. Many of these benefits have been published widely in recent years, but without the biocultural framework that pieces them together and reveals the socioeconomic, demographic, and cultural conditions that interfere with breastfeeding and the mother–infant relationship.

Questions to keep in mind

What cultural beliefs have you been exposed to about how babies should be fed and cared for, and where they should sleep?

How does the biocultural perspective provide a framework for analyzing and understanding health concerns such as SIDS and women's reproductive cancers? What causal mechanisms does the framework suggest in each case?

What historical changes brought about the decline in breastfeeding in the industrialized societies?

Source: Whitaker, E. 1999. "Breastfeeding, Breast Cancer, and the Sudden Infant Death Syndrome in Anthropological Perspective." Originally published as "Ancient Bodies, Modern Customs, and Our Health: Breastfeeding, Breast Cancer, and the Sudden Infant Death Syndrome," in A. Podolefsky and P. Brown (eds.) *Applying Anthropology.* 4th edition. Mt. View, CA: Mayfield. Pp. 67–76.

What current conditions work against breastfeeding and make it difficult even for the most committed mothers?

Mothers and infants are physiologically interconnected from conception to the termination of breast-feeding. While this mutual biological relationship is obvious during pregnancy, to many people it is less clear in the period following birth. In Western society, individuals are expected to be autonomous and independent, and this ideal extends to mothers and their babies. Individual autonomy is a core value in our economy, society, and family life; it is a value that even shapes our understanding of health and disease. However, it is not a widely shared notion, as more *sociocentric* conceptions of personhood are very common in other cultures and have prevailed in other time periods (see Scheper-Hughes and Lock 1987). Until the Industrial Revolution, Western society also recognized the dependence relationships among individuals and families, and this matched an agrarian social structure involving mutual responsibilities and obligations. Mothers and infants were considered interdependent and there was relatively little cultural intervention in or manipulation of gestation or lactation.

Until a century ago, medical experts followed Aristotle, Hippocrates, and Galen in saying that *not* to breast-feed was to have half a birth, because mother's milk came from the same blood which nourished the fetus (see Whitaker 2000). Today, in many cultures around the world, infants are not expected to be independent of their mothers for as long as they breast-feed—that is, for at least the first few years of life. These beliefs reflect an appreciation of the fact that breast-feeding represents a physiological process for both mothers and infants and is more than a simple question of nutrition.

Cultural interventions in the mother–infant relationship are bound to bring significant biological outcomes. Common infant feeding practices in Western societies, such as timed, widely spaced meals, early weaning, pacifier use, and isolated infant sleep with few or no nighttime feedings, are very new and rare in human history, and do not reflect "natural" needs or optimal behaviors, as is commonly presumed. They result in partial or short-term breast-feeding that is very different from the "traditional" or ancient pattern humans have known over evolutionary time. This pattern involves frequent, exclusive, and prolonged breast-feeding, and brings the greatest benefits to mothers and infants. These benefits include reduced risk of breast cancer and the Sudden Infant Death Syndrome (SIDS), diseases which share a common thread in their history: the decline in breast-feeding in the Western industrial societies. By examining them together, we will try to overcome the assumption of individual autonomy, which is so entrenched in Western culture that studies on breast-feeding commonly focus on either the mother or child, but not both.

OLD GENES, NEW LIFESTYLES

Beyond the level of personal experience, breast-feeding concerns both biological processes and cultural interpretation and manipulation. Biocultural anthropology examines such a topic by bringing together cross-cultural comparison and evolutionary considerations. This can mean, for example, comparing human physiology and behavior to those of other primates, such as chimpanzees and gorillas, with whom we share common ancestors and diverge genetically by less than 2%. It also involves looking at different strategies for making a living among human populations. In particular, anthropologists are interested in comparing hunter–gatherers, or foragers, to agricultural or industrial societies. We study modern-day foragers such as the !Kung San of Botswana or the Gainj of Papua New Guinea because their diet, exercise, and health patterns roughly represent those of humans for the vast majority of evolutionary history (see Cohen 1989; Eaton, Konner, and Shostak 1988; Wood et al. 1985).

With a few exceptions, our genetic endowment has not changed since the first foraging groups began to practice settled agriculture and animal husbandry between 13,000 and 9,000 years ago (the Neolithic Revolution). From the start, the lifestyle change produced notable health consequences. Early agriculturists had shorter stature, greater nutritional stress, and higher infant mortality, especially at the age of weaning. Whereas foragers suffered annual seasonal food shortages, these were less severe than the famines that resulted when crops or livestock were lost. Although famines are rare now, especially in the wealthier countries, constant over-nutrition produces new health problems. At the same time, the diet in many impoverished countries remains scanter and less varied than the foraging diet.

In contrast to what we think of as proper nutrition, foragers subsist on a low-calorie diet made up exclusively of wild plant parts (roots, seeds, stalks, leaves, nuts, fruits) and game or fish. There are no dairy products (except mother's milk) or processed grains in their diet. Most of the food comes from plants, while meat is a less reliable but highly valued supply of concentrated protein, fat (though only one-seventh the amount in the meat of domesticated animals), and vitamins and minerals.

Foragers collect these foods over distances of 10 or more kilometers per day, often carried out in a pattern of one or two days of work for six to eight hours and one or two days of other activities. This averages out to more than 6½ kilometers per day. Women routinely carry up to 15 kilograms (almost 35 pounds) of food, a bundle which can reach half their body weight. They also carry children up to three or four years of age, adding up to another 15 kilograms. In addition to this physical activity, foragers move camp several times each year. Because they work outdoors and do not have climate control indoors, they are constantly exposed to the elements.

Unlike people in affluent societies, foragers do not experience any "natural" rise in blood pressure with age. They do not undergo hearing loss or overweight as inevitable consequences of aging, nor does their body mass increase. They are not free of disorders including accidents and injuries, degenerative bone disease, complications of childbirth, and infectious disease, but the major health problems of the Western societies are very rare. These "diseases of civilization" or "chronic diseases" include heart disease, hypertension, strokes, and cancer, as well as emphysema, cirrhosis, diabetes, and obesity and overweight.

While we all share a genetic propensity for the chronic diseases, it is our lifestyle and environment which cause their wide expression today (see Nesse and Williams 1994; Williams and Nesse 1991). Our biological characteristics are those of Stone Age humans practicing a hardy foraging lifestyle, making our bodies adept at storing fat against the likelihood of periodic food shortage. This helps to explain why overweight and obesity are so common wherever physical activity and exposure to the elements are minimal while food supplies are plentiful and steady.

Similarly, the perspective of evolutionary medicine helps us to understand cancer as the cost of the beneficial biological adaptation of tissue repair and regeneration through cell division. In all living things, the body's various ways of regulating and suppressing cell division become less effective in older age. However, over the past centuries, cancer rates have risen way beyond those which would result simply from the increase in the proportion of individuals living into old age. Beyond exposure to carcinogenic and viral agents, this can be explained in terms of changes in diet and lifestyle away from the foraging pattern. Our diet is scarce in protective micro-nutrients such as beta-carotene and selenium, but abundant in macro-nutrients such as fat, protein, and calories which, in themselves and in relation to body composition and size, promote cancer (Micozzi 1995).

MOTHERS AND INFANTS

When breast-feeding patterns are compared across mammals (from *mamma*, Latin for "breast"), nonhuman primates, and humans, "on-demand" or baby-fed feeding emerges as the evolutionary norm for our species. Many aspects of the ancestral pattern are shared by non-Western societies today and were common in Western populations until a few generations ago. A relationship of interdependence and mutuality is expressed in parent–infant co-sleeping and exclusive, unrestricted breast-feeding well beyond the first year.

The ancestral pattern involves frequent feedings (from several times an hour to once every hour or two) all day and night with no limit on their duration; no supplementary foods before six months and low to moderate use of pre-chewed foods or very ripe fruits thereafter; and complete weaning at 2½ to 4 years, when the child is able to walk long distances on its own. Mother's milk remains the principal food until 15 to 18 months, after which it continues to be a significant source of nutrition. When these conditions prevail, infants are more likely to survive, pregnancy is prevented for 2 to 3 years or more, and births are spaced 3 to 5 years apart (see Konner and Shostak 1987; Konner and Worthman 1980; Wood et al. 1985). In all but one family of primates, lactation implies anovulation (lack of ovulation). In our closest relatives, births are spaced as far as 5 (in chimpanzees) to 8 (in orangutans) years apart (Dettwyler 1995; Stuart-Macadam 1995).

In foraging societies such as the !Kung, the mother carries her child in a sling against her body, providing constant physical contact and access to the breast. Infants hardly ever cry for more than a moment or two. Their signs of distress bring an immediate response from their mother or another relative, but never with any kind of pacifier other than the breast. Infants are constantly cuddled and kissed all over the body, including the genitals. Parents are bewildered to hear that Western infants cry and are left alone in a crib, swaddled perhaps, to do so for long periods without being held or allowed to suckle. They do not share the idea that infants and children need to be denied what they want or they will grow up spoiled or dependent. Indeed, the opposition between independence and dependence has relatively little meaning in these societies.

Milk production and release are regulated by pituitary hormones secreted in response to nipple stimulation, the emptying of the breast, and psychological factors (see Cunningham 1995; Daly and Hartman 1995; Konner and Worthman 1980). Prolactin is released in response to suckling, stimulating the synthesis of milk in the lacteal cells within a couple of hours. Oxytocin is also released in response to nipple stimulation, and immediately causes the cells around the milk-producing bulbs and ducts to contract and secrete milk. This pathway can be affected by psychological factors in positive and negative ways. A thought, emotion, or sound or sight of an infant can cause the release of oxytocin. Contrariwise, fear and other stressful emotions lead to the secretion of epinephrine,

which impedes the circulation of oxytocin to breast tissue by constricting the blood vessels around it.

After the surge following nipple stimulation, prolactin levels drop off quickly, reaching baseline levels within two hours. Consequently, to maintain continuous milk production it is necessary to breast-feed at short intervals and keep prolactin levels high. Especially in the early months, more frequent feedings result in greater milk production. Milk that is not secreted but left in the breast has an independent dampening effect on production through both a substance in the milk and the mechanical pressure it exerts on the surrounding cells. This kind of control over milk production seems to apply in a preponderant way after the first two or three months, against a diminishing but still important background of hormonal regulation. Moreover, more frequent feedings and complete removal of milk lead to higher average fat and calorie content. Infants fed without restrictions are able to vary feed frequencies and the degree of breast-emptying and thereby regulate their nutrition very closely. They tend to be satiated and satisfied after feedings (Woolridge 1995).

High prolactin levels inhibit ovulation, so that infrequent feedings and reduced time at the breast lead to less effective suppression of fertility. In addition, other hormones involved in the menstrual cycle are affected by frequent breast-feeding, interfering with normal follicle growth, ovulation (should an egg mature), development of the endometrium, and implantation of a fertilized ovum. As women space feedings at wider intervals, introduce supplementary foods, and reduce nighttime feeding, the contraceptive effect of breast-feeding weakens and ovulation and menstruation resume (see Ellison 1995; Konner and Worthman 1980; Wood et. al 1985).

The composition of human milk also indicates that it is made to be given frequently. Unlike other mammals such as rabbits or tree shrews, who keep their young in nests and leave them all day or even longer, primates carry their babies and thereby provide them with transportation and temperature regulation, for which their milk is less fatty. Primate infants are born less mature and grow more slowly, explaining why protein is relatively scarce in the milk. Continuous breast-feeding and physical contact also protect the infant from predators, as well as illness. Contact with others is reduced, while exposure to the same diseases leads to the production of immunological substances, which are then transmitted in the mother's milk.

In recent years, there has been wide publication of the wonderful properties of breast-milk, from nutritional components to immunological factors, sedative substances to anti-allergenic properties (see Cunningham 1995; Riordan and Auerbach 1993). These benefits make breast-fed infants better able to resist and overcome infections, including those of the gastrointestinal and respiratory tract (which includes the middle ear). Breast-feeding promotes optimal growth and development of the body's systems, such as the cardiovascular, immune, nervous, and gastrointestinal systems. It also protects breast-fed infants from protein malnutrition, even in areas of the world in which it is common. This is because the quality of milk is remarkably constant across mothers, regardless of their diet or nutritional status (Cohen 1989).

The uniform quality of mother's milk, even in conditions of stress, brings up two points. It implies that we should focus upon infant demand and suckling behavior when there are problems in breast-feeding, but the tendency is instead to search for maternal causes. Secondly, by focusing on the benefits of breast-feeding in terms of the useful properties of the milk, we may fail to acknowledge the impacts of breast-feeding on the mother. Mothers who are overworked and poorly nourished may become depleted, their lives shortened by repeated cycles of gestation and lactation.

On the other hand, assuming good conditions breast-feeding has many positive effects on mothers (see Ellison 1995; Micozzi 1995). It helps the uterus to return to its normal size and shape after childbirth, hastens weight loss and moderates digestion, metabolism, blood circulation, and sensations of well-being. It favors bone consolidation, preventing osteoporosis and hip and other fractures in later life, and reduces the risk of women's reproductive cancers. In order to appreciate these benefits, we must go beyond looking at breast-milk as a mere product manufactured for the advantage of the child.

Whereas in foraging and agricultural societies mothers and their fetuses or infants are considered inseparable, even when physically divided after childbirth, in Western society they are considered independent even during gestation. In evolutionary biology, this is an appropriate concept since the interests of the child and the mother may conflict: for example, the fetus of humans and all placental animals taps into the mother's blood circulation, injecting fetal hormones into it and drawing nutrients from the mother's organs if they are not available through her diet. Yet, the biological concept of individuality simultaneously presumes physiological interdependence. The cultural concept of the autonomous individual denies it. After childbirth, the separation between mother and child is complete, and the physiological interrelationship in breast-feeding is obscured by a focus on the infant's nutritional and psychological independence. This has notable health outcomes for both mothers and infants, some of which we will now examine in light of an evolutionary perspective.

BREAST CANCER

Until the 19th century, European medical philosophers observed that well-off women who lived in cities were much more susceptible to breast cancer than women who lived in the countryside (Whitaker 2000). They attributed this difference to the abandonment of breast-feeding, which, they noted, caused numerous other maladies and grave health effects. Even today, not only is breast cancer more common in affluent societies, but within them it is more frequent among the wealthier classes.

The decline in breast-feeding has been part of a broad change in reproductive and child-rearing patterns since the Industrial Revolution. Urban women were the first to undergo the secular trend of earlier maturation and greater achieved stature. They experienced earlier puberty, delayed marriage and first birth, fewer pregnancies, and reduced or forsaken breast-feeding. Over time, these patterns diffused through the entire population.

Many of the things we consider "natural" are therefore more like aberrations or deviations from what evolution has produced (see Eaton et al. 1994; Micozzi 1995). To illustrate, a typical woman of a foraging or pre-industrial society reaches puberty and her first menstrual period (menarche) at the age of 16 to 18. She becomes pregnant within three or four years, breast-feeds for three or four years, and has a subsequent child four or five years after the first. This sequence repeats itself between four and six times before she reaches menopause at around the age of 45. As a result, she has about 150 ovulations in her lifetime, taking account of non-ovulatory cycles at the near and far end of her reproductive years. Periodic nutritional and exercise stress reduce the number of ovulations even more. Because only half of her children survive long enough to reproduce, population grows very slowly, as was the case until historical times. Lactation has represented humankind's main method of birth control for most of our existence.

In contrast, Western women enjoy a stable food supply, including foods concentrated in fat, protein, and calories, and experience very little stress from exercise and exposure. Over the past centuries, this has caused them, and men, to reach higher stature and lower age at puberty. Girls arrive at menarche at the age of 12 or 13, while menopause is delayed to 50 or 55 years. Significantly, the first birth is postponed for 13 or 14 years, to the age of 25 or 26, and the average number of births is reduced to two or three. The average Western woman breast-feeds for a few months, if at all. Because she spaces feedings at long intervals and supplements with other foods, breast-feeding does not inhibit ovulation for long. As a result, population growth was very rapid in Europe for several centuries (and in many developing countries today) not only because mortality rates were falling but also because women did not have a long interval of infertility associated with lactation.

If she does not take oral contraceptives, the average woman will ovulate around 450 times over her lifetime. Ovulation will rarely be suppressed due to physiological constraints associated with nutritional or exercise stress. This amounts to three or four times as many ovulations over the life-span, and some scholars have suggested that the proportion may be as high as nine times.

The differences in reproductive patterns between women in foraging as opposed to affluent societies match some of the currently known risk factors for women's reproductive cancers (breast, endometrium, ovary), including age at menarche and menopause, parity (number of births), and breast-feeding. Differences in diet and physical activity, as well as body composition, also agree with identified non-reproductive risk factors such as fat intake and percent body fat. Together with other factors, they give Western women, especially below the age of 60, at least 20 times the risk of reproductive cancer. The risk for breast cancer may be more than 100 times higher. In nonhuman primates, these cancers are extremely rare.

For all three cancers, earlier age at menarche and later age at menopause increase risk, while greater parity reduces risk. Like these factors, breast-feeding is protective against ovarian cancer because it inhibits ovulation. This reduces the monthly mechanical injury to the ovarian epithelium and the release of hormones by the follicle, which are considered the main elements in the etiology of ovarian cancer. For breast cancer, lactation and earlier first birth are also protective factors.

The breast's susceptibility to carcinogenesis is directly related to the rate of epithelial cell proliferation. Consequently, the lengthening of the period between menarche and first birth widens the window of time in which undifferentiated structures destined to become secretory glands are vulnerable to carcinogenic agents and therefore the initiation of tumors. In breast tissue, cell proliferation is promoted by exposure to estrogen, apparently in concert with progesterone, and cell division rates are highest during the first five years after menarche. With pregnancy and lactation, these structures differentiate and develop, devoting themselves less ardently to cell proliferation. Their cell cycle is longer, and they are more resistant to chemical carcinogens. Subsequent pregnancies may also be protective because they increase the proportion of fully differentiated secretory lobules, until in advanced age pregnancy increases risk by favoring the expansion of initiated tumors.

While the age at first pregnancy seems to be of primary importance and may even modulate the protective effect of breast-feeding and later pregnancies, breast-feeding in itself provides protection against breast cancer in step with the number of children breast-fed and the cumulative duration of breast-feeding. The reason some studies have found no effect or a weak one is that they were based upon the experiences of Western women, who do not generally conform to the ancient pattern of breast-feeding at close intervals for at least a year. Short periods of breast-feeding may in fact provide very little protection.

At the level of the breast fluid, there are lower levels of a potential carcinogen, cholesterol-epoxide, as well as cholesterol, in breast-feeding women, a reduction that persists for two years after childbirth or lactation. Estrogen levels are also lower, protecting the breast tissue directly as opposed to systemically through variations in blood estrogen levels. Breast-feeding also affects the turnover rate of substances in the breast fluid, so that prolonged breast-feeding reduces exposure of the breast epithelial tissue to potential exogenous carcinogens.

Exercise, high consumption of dietary fiber, and low fat consumption and percent body fat are all protective against breast and other cancers. High dietary levels of fat and protein (especially from animal sources) and total calories are associated with higher levels of breast cancer across populations and within subpopulations of single countries. Animal studies have shown that dietary protein promotes tumor development while restriction of protein intake inhibits tumor growth. The enzymes in adipose tissue convert precursor adrenal hormones into active estrogens. Dietary fat raises serum estrogen levels and promotes tumor development and may also play a role in originating tumors. In contrast to Western women, women in foraging societies have low serum estrogen levels.

Western women's skinfold thickness (a measure of the proportion of body fat) is almost twice that of pre-agricultural women. Compared to college athletes, women who are not athletic in college (and less active in adolescence and somewhat less active after college) have two to five times the rates of breast, uterine, and ovarian cancer. Women in affluent societies consume 40% or more of their calories in the form of fat, against 20 to 25% among pre-agricultural women, but only 20 as opposed to 100 grams of fiber per day. Dietary fiber is protective because it reduces free estrogen levels in the blood. It helps to prevent bowel dysfunction, which has been associated with breast cancer, and the severe constipation which can lead to the migration of mutagenic substances from the gastrointestinal tract to the breast fluid.

The protective effect of breast-feeding goes beyond the current generation to the next one, for early nutritional influences seem to have an important effect on later susceptibility to cancer. Breast-feeding contributes to the development and regulation of the immune system, which plays a central role in suppressing the initiation and growth of tumors. It prevents over-consumption of fat, protein, and calories. This influences body size and composition, the baseline against which nutrition works throughout life. That is, breast-feeding prevents the accelerated growth of muscles and fat stores associated with breast cancer risk factors: faster growth rates, earlier menarche, and greater achieved stature and size. Women who have been breast-fed themselves are less likely to develop breast cancer.

We have seen that breast-feeding benefits both the mother and child with respect to prevention of breast cancer. In the mother, breast-feeding according to the ancient pattern influences systemic hormone levels and the micro-environment of the breast tissue, reducing exposure to exogenous and endogenous carcinogens. In the child, breast-milk provides an appropriate balance of nutrients that prevents over-nutrition, rapid growth, and early maturation. This circular interaction of factors expresses and can be predicted by the concept of the mother-infant dyad as a biological interacting pair.

SUDDEN INFANT DEATH SYNDROME

From a global perspective, Western society's expectation that infants should sleep alone for long hours away from their parents stands out as anomalous, even if it fits well in its cultural context. One unfortunate consequence is that the diffusion of lone infant sleep over the past several generations may be related to the rise in the frequency of infant death from the Sudden Infant Death Syndrome (SIDS) (see Mckenna 1986; Mckenna and Mosko 1990).

The meaning of reproduction and child-rearing changed with the emergence of industrial society and its predominance of small, simple families (couples plus children). In this kind of society, the crib symbolizes the child's place and is usually placed in a separate room. By contrast, in rural pre-industrial Europe and in a survey of over 90 contemporary non-Western societies, infants invariably slept in the same bed or room as their parents. SIDS does not appear to exist in these societies, nor is it found among non-human primates or other mammals. In many Western societies, SIDS is the major cause of infant death, though rates are very low among sub-populations in which there is co-sleeping and nocturnal breast-feeding. Peak mortality is between the ages of two and four months, with 90% of all deaths occurring before the age of six months.

While there seem to be many intrinsic and secondary factors that affect infants in different ways to bring about SIDS events, one common factor is that SIDS usually happens during sleep. While breast-feeding in itself reduces risk, it is the frequent, intensive, prolonged breast-feeding implying mother–infant co-sleeping that may provide the best environment for avoiding the disease.

Co-sleeping infants lie on their backs or sides with their heads turned toward the breast and feed through the night, often without waking their mothers. Even newborns and very young infants are able to attach to the breast on their own, provided it is within reach. In non-industrialized societies, it is rare for infants younger than one year to sleep long hours with only a few arousals or feedings. They do not increase the length of their longest sleep episode within the first few months, nor do they stop feeding at night, as parents in Western societies expect.

These same patterns are observed in sleep laboratories, where mothers report waking up and feeding their child many times fewer than the number recorded on the monitors. They and their infants move through the various stages of sleep in synchrony, shifting between them more frequently and spending less time in the deep sleep which makes arousal more difficult. If in the laboratory the breast-feeding mother spends the night in a separate room from her child, on average she breast-feeds less than half as often. She also tends to put the child on its stomach when leaving it to sleep alone. Notably, breast-feeding mothers who routinely sleep in a separate room from their infants actually sleep for a shorter amount of time during the night, even though they feed their infants less often and for a shorter overall time period than mothers who co-sleep.

One factor common to a majority of cases is that the infant had been placed on its stomach to sleep: the opposite of the position used by infants who sleep with their mothers and breast-feed throughout the night. This may be due to suffocation because the child is unable to move out of pockets of its own carbon dioxide in puffy mattresses or bean bag cushions. It also may be the result of developmental changes related to a shift in the position of the larynx (windpipe) which takes place at four to six months.

At birth, the larynx is in contact with the back of the palate, allowing air inhaled by the nostrils to go by its own route to the lungs. It then begins to descend in the throat to a position below the back of the tongue, so that the two openings leading to the lungs and stomach lie side by side (which is why food sometimes "goes down the wrong tube"). During this shift, problems can occur if breathing through the nose (which infants greatly prefer) is impeded by a cold or other factor. Breathing through the mouth can be blocked by the uvula (the fleshy structure hanging over the back of the tongue) if it enters the descending larynx, especially if the child is lying at the wrong angle. Huge reductions in SIDS rates have taken place over the past decade in many European countries and the United Kingdom since the initiation of campaigns against the face-down position, and the U.S. is also beginning to show rapid improvement in SIDS rates.

There is more to the story than sleep position, which itself inculpates the crib since co-sleeping is associated with the safer position. More directly, the crib implies isolated, prolonged, deep sleep. Like adults, infants are able to fall into deep sleep, but they are less equipped to arouse themselves out of it. All people have temporary lapses in breathing during the night, but their brains generally respond to them appropriately. Infants are different, for they are born at a much earlier stage of neurological development than other primates, even our closest relatives.

During sleep, infants may need frequent arousals to allow them to emerge from episodes of apnea or cardiorespiratory crisis. External stimuli and parental monitoring from co-sleeping and breast-feeding give them practice at doing so, and keep them from spending long periods of time in deep stages of sleep. SIDS deaths peak at the same age at which the amount of deep sleep relative to REM sleep increases dramatically, at two to three months. Moreover, at this time infants begin to exercise more voluntary control of breathing, as parents notice in their more expressive cries. This is a step toward the speech breathing they will use later, but may complicate breathing in the short term.

The rhythm of sound and silence in the mother's breathing gives the infant auditory stimulation, while contact with her body provides tactile stimulation. The carbon dioxide which her breathing releases into the air they share induces the infant to breathe. Frequent waking for breast-feeding is a behavior common to primates and prevents hypoglycemia, which has been implicated in some SIDS deaths. Human milk also provides immunological protection against several infectious organisms (and preparations of them given as immunizations) considered responsible for some deaths. This protection is especially needed after two months, when inherited maternal antibodies become scarce but the infant's own immune system is not yet developed. Breast-feeding and constant physical contact prevent overheating and the exhausting crying spells which seem to be factors in the disease. In addition, the infant is sensitive to other aspects of its micro-environment, including temperature, humidity, and odors.

While many experts and parents advise against or avoid co-sleeping because they fear suffocating the infant, in fact this risk is very low, especially where people sleep on hard bedding or the floor. Modern bedding is dangerous because of the conformation of bed frames and the use of soft mattresses and heavy coverings. Yet, these factors are at least as relevant to cribs as parents' beds. On the other hand, some parents should not sleep with their infants, such as those who go to bed affected by drugs or alcohol. Cigarette smoke in the sleeping room could cancel the benefit of co-sleeping.

While isolated infant sleep may be consistent with parents' desires and the primacy of the conjugal bond and other Western values, it is a new behavioral norm in human history and does not represent a "natural" need. It is neither in the infant's best interest nor in conformity with behavioral patterns and biological conditions established long before our time. By contrast, parent–infant co-sleeping matches evolutionary considerations such as the need for temperature regulation, frequent nutrition, and protection from predators and disease. There may be some wisdom to the popular term, "crib death," or "cot death," for it points to the crib and the Western concept of infant independence as major factors in the disease.

SOCIAL AND CULTURAL INTERVENTION

We have seen that mothers and infants are physiologically bound together from conception to weaning, not just conception to birth. The Western ideal of the autonomous individual, even the neonate, is not shared by other societies today or by those of the past. The biocultural model shows that evolution has favored frequent, exclusive, and prolonged breast-feeding in humans. This entails constant physical contact, parent–infant co-sleeping, and nighttime breast-feeding. It leads to postpartum infertility and protects against SIDS and breast and other reproductive system cancers. Breast-feeding therefore has significant health outcomes, beyond the usual benefits of breast-milk which have been popularized in recent years.

Unfortunately, the health benefits of breast-feeding, especially for mothers, are generally overshadowed by assertions regarding the supposed convenience of bottle feeding and the nutritional adequacy of artificial milk. Even the promotion of breast-feeding on the basis of the milk's value to infants does not always induce women to breast-feed, since there is little if any mention of a benefit to them. To the contrary, there are many disincentives to breast-feeding, such as beliefs that it causes the breasts to sag and makes it difficult to lose weight, or that it makes the husband feel jealous and left out. The lack of familiarity with breast-feeding which has resulted from a couple of generations of preference for the bottle also discourages it. Many people have never seen a woman breast-feed, and would prefer not to.

The degree to which our culture has come to favor intervention in the fundamental relationship between nurslings and mothers is evident in the nearly-universal use of pacifiers. This has been promoted by the notion, sanctioned by professional medicine, that infants need to suckle, and better a scientifically designed object than the thumb or finger (the nipple is not even among the choices). However, in evolutionary perspective, a pacifier is completely unnecessary since infants who are breast-fed according to the ancient pattern are allowed to suckle to their heart's content. Not surprisingly, pacifier use has been found to reduce the duration of breast-feeding (Victoria et al. 1993).

The birthing process is focused upon the infant, while the mother is considered and often treated as an impediment to the physician's efforts to extract the child. Afterward, the medical care of the two is split between obstetricians and pediatricians, reflecting the conceptual splitting of the mother–infant relationship at birth. There is little or no breast-feeding (in the United States, only one half of all infants begin life feeding at the breast; see National Center for Health Statistics 1997: 97 tab. 19). Weaning takes place within a few months and almost always within the first year, and the mother resumes her menstrual cycle within a few months. Mothers are strongly encouraged to put their children on feeding schedules and eliminate nighttime feeding as quickly as possible, and to teach them to get to sleep and stay asleep on their own, in their own bed and room. Instead of being carried and cuddled throughout the day and night, infants are left in cribs, strollers, and playpens and are touched relatively rarely. They are expected to cry and left to do so, sometimes for hours. Often, the door to their room is closed at nap time and during the night.

On a social-structural level, cultural interference in breast-feeding seems to be more common in societies which are based upon vertical inheritance and the simple family structure, than societies in which families are wide and inheritance is lateral (see Maher 1992). In the former, the institution of marriage is emphasized over kin relationships. Women's sexual and conjugal duties take precedence over their role as kinswomen and mothers, while children are considered heirs rather than links in a kinship network. These conditions can make breast-feeding seem to interfere with sexuality, and pit the husband against the child in competition over the woman's sexualized breast.

Notably, our culture describes breasts as "secondary *sexual* characteristics," highlighting a tendency to regard them as objects of display rather than functional organs. In medieval to modern Europe, the post-partum taboo against sex during lactation was circumvented among the elite classes by wet-nursing, so that women could be available to their husbands instead of breast-feeding. This was subsequently replaced by formula feeding and practiced by a much wider segment of the population.

The rise of the modern nation–state over the past two centuries meanwhile has brought an expansion of the authority of medical experts. Beginning with early industrialization, the state and its emerging medical system sought to shape public morality and oppose traditional authority by reaching into the private, intimate world of the family. As a result, reproduction and child-rearing became medicalized well before professional medicine had much legitimate knowledge or expertise in these areas. As multiple families broke up due to socioeconomic changes, families became more dependent upon outside experts in areas which had previously been handled by older relatives or other authorities such as midwives and clerics.

By now, it is rare for anyone to question the authority of the medical community in questions such as birth control or infant feeding. This phenomenon has emerged hand-in-hand with the notion of the autonomous individual. By considering fetuses and infants as beings independent of their mothers, Western society has allowed and welcomed experts into the life of the dyad and granted them predominant authority in decisions regarding the care and upbringing of the young. Mothers are not encouraged to think of themselves as competent or knowledgeable enough to breast-feed without expert intervention and surveillance. This is reinforced by the regimen of evermore numerous obstetric and pediatric examinations before and after childbirth, and the literature directed at mothers by the medical and pharmaceutical communities.

In contrast to agricultural and foraging societies, in ours breast-feeding does not easily fit into women's work or social lives. Few professions allow women much flexibility in time scheduling, and there is a deep, underlying expectation that the new mother will immediately be independent from her child. Many working women are forced to pump their milk in bathrooms, often in secrecy. Women who do not work outside the home are targeted by formula manufacturers, who capitalize on cultural values such as work and efficiency by suggesting that formula feeding with an increasingly complex array of products demonstrates a woman's capability in scientific mothering.

Firms that sell formula, pacifiers, and other infant care products distribute samples and coupons through hospitals and physicians' offices, lending their products a medical stamp of approval that appeals to many parents. Often, they are able to "hook" babies even before they leave the hospital because the staff supplements the mother's milk with formula or sugar water, and the infant comes to prefer the easier flow of the bottle.

Thus, even when breast-feeding is promoted and women feel committed to it, social and cultural obstacles can make it difficult. A biocultural understanding of breast-feeding as an evolved, two-way process could help to make conditions more favorable. It would highlight the fact that women are normally able to breast-feed without medical approval, surveillance, and intervention and reduce the public's receptiveness to industrially produced formula and baby foods. Most importantly, the biocultural perspective would foster an appreciation of the intricate mechanisms linking mothers and infants together in a dynamic system of nutrition that benefits them both.

REFERENCES

Cohen, Mark Nathan. 1989. *Health and the Rise of Civilization*. New Haven: Yale University Press.

Cunningham, Allan S. 1995. Breast-feeding: Adaptive Behavior for Child Health and Longevity. In Patricia Stuart-Macadam and Katherine Dettwyler (eds.) *Breast-feeding: Biocultural Perspectives*. New York: Aldine de Gruyter.

Daly, S. E. J., and P. E. Hartmann. 1995. Infant Demand and Milk Supply. *Journal of Human Lactation* 11(1):21–37.

Dettwyler, Katherine. 1995. A Time to Wean. In Patricia Stuart-Macadam and Katherine Dettwyler (eds.) *Breast-feeding: Biocultural Perspectives*. New York: Aldine de Gruyter.

Eaton, S. Boyd, Melvin Konner, and Marjorie Shostak. 1988. *The Paleolithic Prescription*. New York: Harper and Row.

Eaton, S. Boyd, et al. 1994. Women's Reproductive Cancers in Evolutionary Perspective. *The Quarterly Review of Biology* 69(3):353–367.

Ellison, Peter. 1995. Breast-feeding, Fertility, and Maternal Condition. In Patricia Stuart-Macadam and Katherine Dettwyler (eds.) *Breast-feeding: Biocultural Perspectives*. New York: Aldine de Gruyter.

Konner, Melvin, and Marjorie Shostak. 1987. Timing and Management of Birth among the !Kung. *Cultural Anthropology* 2(1):11–28.

Konner, Melvin, and Carol Worthman. 1980. Nursing Frequency, Gonadal Function, and Birth Spacing among !Kung Hunter–Gatherers. *Science* 207: 788–791.

Maher, Vanessa (ed.). 1992. *The Anthropology of Breast-feeding*. Oxford: Berg.

McKenna, James. 1986. An Anthropological Perspective on the Sudden Infant Death Syndrome (SIDS): The Role of Parental Breathing Cues and Speech Breathing Adaptations. *Medical Anthropology* 10(1): 9–53.

McKenna, James, and Sarah Mosko. 1990. Evolution and the Sudden Infant Death Syndrome (SIDS). Part 3: Infant Arousal and Parent–Infant Co-Sleeping. *Human Nature* 1(3):291–330.

Micozzi, Marc. 1995. Breast Cancer, Reproductive Biology, and Breast-feeding. In Patricia Stuart-Macadam and Katherine Dettwyler (eds.) *Breast-feeding: Biocultural Perspectives*. New York: Aldine de Gruyter.

National Center for Health Statistics. 1997. *Health, United States 1996–97 and Injury Chartbook*. Hyattsville, MD: National Center for Health Statistics.

Nesse, Randolph M., and George C. Williams. 1994. *Why We Get Sick: The New Science of Darwinian Medicine*. New York: Random House.

Riordan, Jan, and Kathleen Auerbach. 1993. *Breast-feeding and Human Lactation*. Boston: Jones and Bartlett.

Scheper-Hughes, Nancy, and Margaret Lock. 1987. The Mindful Body: A Prolegomenon to Future Work in Medical Anthropology. *Medical Anthropology Quarterly* 1(1):6–41.

Stuart-Macadam, Patricia. 1995. Breast-feeding in Prehistory. In Patricia Stuart-Macadam and Katherine Dettwyler (eds.) *Breast-feeding. Biocultural Perspectives*. New York: Aldine de Gruyter.

Victoria, Cesar G., Elaine Tomasi, Maria Teresa A. Olinto, and Fernando C. Barros. 1993. Use of Pacifiers and Breastfeeding Duration. *Lancet* 341: 404–406.

Whitaker, Elizabeth D. 2000. *Measuring Mamma's Milk: Fascism and the Medicalization of Maternity in Italy*. Ann Arbor: University of Michigan Press.

Williams, George C., and Randolph M. Nesse. 1991. The Dawn of Darwinian Medicine. *The Quarterly Review of Biology* 66(1):1–22.

Wood, James W. et al. 1985. Lactation and Birth Spacing in Highland New Guinea. *Journal of Biosocial Sciences, Supplement* 9:159–173.

Woolridge, Michael W. 1995. Baby-Controlled Breast-feeding. In Patricia Stuart-Macadam and Katherine Dettwyler (eds.) *Breast-feeding: Biocultural Perspectives*. New York: Aldine de Gruyter.

■ ■ ■ ■ ■ ■ ■ ■ ■

48   GROWTH IN INDIGENOUS AND NONINDIGENOUS CHILEAN SCHOOLCHILDREN FROM THREE POVERTY STRATA

Patricia Bustos, Hugh Amigo, Sergio R. Muñoz, and Reynaldo Martorell

The growth and development of children is a central topic in the fields of public health and international health, for comparisons of height and weight are used to assess population health, living conditions including infectious disease burden, and nutrition and nutritional status. Although small differences due to genetic inheritance have been observed, scientific studies overwhelmingly demonstrate that social class and economic differences are the most salient factors determining variation in average height across populations and time periods. In fact, upper-class children are of similar stature worldwide. Groups that immigrate to wealthy countries experience gains in stature within the first generation and soon resemble the host population more than the population back home, including showing increased rates of obesity and related health problems (see Smith et al. 2002).

Nevertheless, it is often assumed that genetic ancestry is the reason for some populations' shorter stature, which would mean that variation from the international standard overestimates growth stunting in their children since they are destined to be "small but healthy" (see Martorell 1989). This selection argues that such reasoning is harmful because it leads to miscalculation of malnutrition and inadequate growth and thereby affects the allocation of resources. The authors address the problem of teasing apart the relation between social class and ancestry in Latin America—where there are few indigenous people in the upper classes—by comparing the height of indigenous (Mapuche) and nonindigenous (European-origin) children in south-central Chile across three socioeconomic levels. Average heights are calculated in terms of distance from international reference values and compared in relation to two measures of poverty.

The study is able to demonstrate the negative impacts of poverty on the growth of children, irrespective of their ethnicity. Overall, it shows that for each socioeconomic category, children in the two groups are similar in height. Where the level of poverty is lowest, the height of both groups of children is close to that of the international reference population. Where the level of poverty is great, the variation from the standard is significant. These results point to the preponderant effect of socioeconomic conditions as opposed to genetic ancestry in determining the average height of a group of children.

Questions to keep in mind

Have you seen pictures or texts expressing the assumption that particular groups of people are genetically short (or tall) in stature?

Is it acceptable to use standards based on a reference population of U.S. children for assessing the growth of children elsewhere?

Source: Bustos, P., H. Amigo, S. R. Muñoz, and R. Martorell 2001. "Growth in Indigenous and Nonindigenous Chilean Schoolchildren from Three Poverty Strata." *American Journal of Public Health* 91(10):1645–1649. ©The American Public Health Association. With permission from the publisher.

How does this study illustrate the concepts of human adaptation, plasticity, and variation discussed in Part II?

What are some mechanisms by which poverty causes stunting or growth retardation?

Many Latin American countries, such as Mexico, Guatemala, Bolivia, Peru, and Ecuador, have large indigenous populations. These groups are generally the poorest and least educated, as well as the most growth retarded or stunted.[1,2] The question arises whether the high levels of stunting recorded among indigenous peoples are a result of poverty or are also (or instead) indicative of bias introduced by using an inappropriate reference population—that is, by using the National Center for Health Statistics—World Health Organization curves, which are derived from studies of US children of Northern European ancestry.[3]

If the small size of children of indigenous origin relative to Northern Europeans is the result of genetic differences in growth potential, the use of the current reference may overestimate the extent of true stunting. This is an important question for many Latin American countries, because the prevalence of stunting is commonly used to define the problem of malnutrition, to identify the groups most affected, and to allocate resources.

The work of Habicht et al.[4] established that child stature at 7 years of age differs substantially between the highest and lowest socioeconomic levels of many countries. On the other hand, children of well-off families from various countries in Asia, Africa, and Latin America were found to be very similar in size to each other and to children of European origin. These authors concluded that differences in child size associated with social class were marked and many times larger than those that might be attributed to ethnic differences. This seminal article[4] provided strong justification for the use of the current reference to assess the status of children worldwide.

Guatemala was one of the countries included in the analyses. A criticism of the approach of Habicht and colleagues is that social class distinctions in Guatemala reflect differences not only in wealth but also in ancestry, which is largely Spanish at the top of the social order and largely indige-nous at the bottom. For Guatemala, as well as other Latin American countries, a more apt comparison would have been the growth of indigenous children vs that of nonindigenous children from families along the socioeconomic gradient. This was not done by Habicht et al., nor has it been done by anyone else, for the simple reason that few indigenous people have attained high socioeco-nomic status—a sobering social comment.

About 7% of the population of Chile is of indigenous ancestry, of which the Mapuche (also referred to as Araucanos) are the largest group.[5] The Mapuche inhabit the south central part of the country. Chile has experienced rapid economic and social development in recent years and this has brought significant improvements in the general standard of living.[6] Also, Chile has one of the best public health systems of the region, with many health and nutrition programs targeted at the poor.[7] Nevertheless, the Mapuche continue to be one of the poorest groups in the country, despite improved living conditions.

The situation in Chile permits studying the size of Mapuche children of various social classes. Consequently, the objective of this study was to compare the heights of indigenous and nonindige-nous children aged 6 to 9 years at various levels of the socioeconomic gradient. The general hypothe-sis tested was that poverty, not ancestry, accounts for the short stature of Mapuche children. The specific hypotheses tested were as follows.

1. Going from extreme to low levels of poverty, height increases among indigenous and nonindigenous groups.
2. Height does not differ between indigenous and nonindigenous children within poverty levels.
3. In areas with the lowest levels of poverty, the heights of indigenous and nonindige-nous children will not differ from that of the international reference population.

METHODS

The study was a cross-sectional comparison of indigenous (Mapuche) and nonindigenous children in the first and second grades living in areas of decreasing levels of poverty. We used UNICEF's poverty classification. This system, which is used widely in Chile to guide government programs, divides poverty into extreme, medium, and low levels on the basis of 17 indicators, such as the proportion of the population living in poverty, the infant mortality rate, and maternal education level[8], the 3 levels of poverty correspond to the highest, middle, and lowest quintiles, respectively, of UNICEF's poverty classification. Of the counties selected for study, 6 were classified as having an extreme level of poverty, 7 as having a medium level of poverty, and 19, in the metropolitan area of Santiago, as having a low level of poverty. The counties with extreme poverty were rural, in contrast with the urban counties with middle and low poverty levels.

In Latin America, it is customary for a person to use 2 surnames, derived from the parents' primary surnames. In the United States, this would be equivalent to using one's father's surname and mother's maiden name. Children were defined as Mapuche if all compound surnames of both father and mother were of Mapuche origin (i.e., all 4 surnames had to be of Mapuche origin). Nonindigenous children were defined as those whose 4 parental surnames were all of Spanish origin. Children with mixed Mapuche and Spanish surnames were omitted from the study, as were all those with "foreign" surnames (German, Italian, etc.). This process required screening a large number of children in many schools. A total of 41 rural schools, drawn at random from a larger list, were selected from areas of extreme poverty, and all 32 urban schools from areas of medium poverty were included. All 75 schools from low-poverty sectors in Santiago that were known to have Mapuche children were included.

Sample sizes were largely determined by resources and circumstances (i.e., nonprobabilistic sample selection). There were few nonindigenous children in the extreme-poverty group, so all children in this group who met the nonindigenous criteria was included (n = 103) For each such child, a Mapuche child of the same sex and within 6 months of the same age was selected. The Ma-

puches were least common in the medium-poverty group; all Mapuche children in this group were included (n = 134), along with a similar number of nonindigenous children. In the low-poverty group in Santiago, we could find only 90 children meeting the Mapuche definition. For convenience, we selected 3 nonindigenous children for every. Mapuche child. Only one child per family was selected in all areas.

Trained personnel (4 persons) measured the heights of children in 1997 and 1998 using standard methods.[9] The values were expressed as sex- and age-specific z scores, using the National Center for Health Statistics/World Health Organization reference.[10]

Home interviews also took place in which information about parental education and household wealth was collected by methods used previously in Chile.[11] A factor analysis of household information (i.e., possession of appliances such as televisions, refrigerators, or washing machines, and characteristics of the home such as type of materials used in construction, number of rooms, sanitation, parental education) was used to generate an index of household poverty. Households falling in the lowest tertile of the distribution of this index were classified as poor and all others as nonpoor. Thus, 2 measures of poverty were used: poverty level as defined by UNICEF[8] (county level) and household poverty as defined by household possessions and characteristics (family level).

Cases with complete data for age, sex, height, and household poverty were selected for analyses. Final sample sizes are given in Table 48.1 Values for indigenous and nonindigenous groups were compared within poverty levels, before and after adjustment for household poverty, by using multiple regression models (indigenous: 1 = yes, 0 = no; household poverty: 1 = yes, 0 = no). Age and sex were included as covariates in all models. A linear model was fitted to assess for linear trends in z score for height across poverty strata. Statistical significance was defined as P<.05.

RESULTS

The characteristics of the sample are given in Table 48.1. The 2 groups were similar in age and percentage of males. The percentage of households

Table 48.1 General Characteristics of Sample of Indigenous (Mapuche) and Nonindigenous Chilean Schoolchildren, by Poverty Strata: Chile, 1997–1999

| | | | | | | Poverty Strata | | | | | | | | |
| | Extreme | | | Medium | | | Low | | | |
Variable	Indigenous	Nonindigenous	P	Indigenous	Nonindigenous	P	Indigenous	Nonindigenous	P
n	92	92	…	124	124	…	84	252	…
Mean age ± SE, y	8.1 ± 0.07	8.1 ± 0.10	.9	7.7 ± 0.09	7.6 ± 0.06	.7	8.0 ± 0.08	8.00 ± 0.07	.9
Male, %	50	50	1	57.3	49.3	.7	47.4	47.6	.97
Household poverty, %	91.3	64.1	.001	51.6	14.5	.001	15.5	1.2	.001
Height z score ± SE	−1.10 ± 0.10	−0.70 ± 0.11	.04	−0.50 ± 0.08	−0.50 ± 0.08	.76	−0.21 ± 0.11	−0.37 ± 0.04	.15

classified as poor was greater for the Mapuche sample in all poverty strata. The z scores for mean height ranged from -1.1 for indigenous children living in areas of extreme poverty to -0.21 for indigenous children living in low-poverty areas. Differences in height between indigenous and nonindigenous groups were statistically significant only in the extreme-poverty level, with indigenous children being shorter.

In Figure 48.1, z scores for mean height indigenous and nonindigenous groups are given by poverty level. There was a linear trend for height to increase with decreasing levels of poverty in indigenous ($P<.001$) and nonindigenous ($P<.03$) groups. The z scores for mean height in areas of low poverty were -0.21 ± 0.11 for indigenous children and -0.37 ± 0.04 for nonindigenous children (Table 48.1). These values were not significantly different from 0 (i.e., from the reference value) for indigenous children ($P=0.6$) but were significantly different from 0 for nonindigenous children ($P<.01$).

Ethnic differences within a poverty level were examined before and after adjustment for household poverty (Table 48.2). For the extreme-poverty group, being of Mapuche ancestry was associated with a z score of -0.303 in the unadjusted model ($P<.05$); after adjustment, the z score was -0.225 and ceased to be significant ($P=.161$). For the medium- and low-poverty strata, ethnicity was not a significant predictor of z score for

height, either before or after adjustment. Household poverty was negatively related to height in all models but was significant only in the medium-poverty level.

DISCUSSION

Chilean history texts describe the Mapuches as being stocky in build and short in stature, with males averaging no more than 1.62 meters in height and females no more than 1.45 meters.[12] Studies published in Chile over the last few years report that Mapuches living in the "reservations" of the Araucania are shorter than the average Chilean of Spanish or mixed ancestry.[13] Only a few studies of Mapuche children have been carried out, but all report that indigenous children are shorter than the general Chilean population. During the 1980s, one study found that about a third of Mapuche children were stunted (<90% of height-for-age).[14] Finally, 2 UNICEF studies found that the prevalence of growth retardation in the geographical zone inhabited by the Mapuche was the highest in Chile.[8,15] In our study, the prevalence of stunting (z score <-2) was 17.4% and 3.6%, respectively, among Mapuche children of extreme- and low-poverty strata, compared with the national average of 4.6%.[15]

Previously, it was not possible to establish whether the short stature of Mapuche children, or

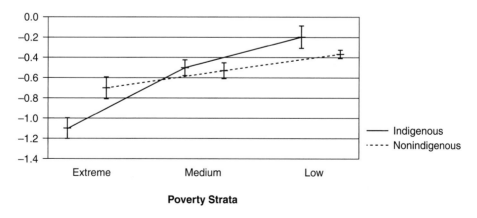

Note: Bars denote standard errors. The linear trend is significant for both groups (P <.05).

Figure 48.1 z scores for height-for-age among indigenous (Mapuche) and nonindigenous schoolchildren: Chile, 1997–1999.

Table 48.2 **Regression Coefficients for Ethnicity of Height *z* Scores by Poverty Strata, Before and After Adjustment for Household Poverty: Chile, 1997–1999**

Poverty Strata	Variable	Unadjusted Model		Adjusted Model	
		β	P	β	P
Extreme	Indigenous	−.303	.047	−.225	.161
	Household poverty	NA	NA	−.289	.135
Medium	Indigenous	−.037	.759	.157	.230
	Household poverty	NA	NA	−.323	.021
Low	Indigenous	.166	.151	.218	.072
	Household poverty	NA	NA	−.361	.142

Note. For both indigenous and household poverty, 1 = yes and 0 = no; NA = not applicable. Age and sex were included as covariates in both unadjusted and adjusted models.

of other children of indigenous ancestry in Latin America, is due to genetics or to poverty. In this report, we show that in the case of the Mapuche, it is poverty and not ancestry that causes stunting.

A strength of this study is the use of careful criteria for defining indigenous and nonindigenous ancestry. The use of surnames to identify ethnicity is a practical and valid approach in the Chilean context. Although there is no pretense of "racial purity" in the groups defined, the use of surnames undoubtedly improved the classification of ethnicity. Another strength of the study is the inclusion of children from extreme-, medium-, and low-poverty strata. This classification was developed by UNICEF for program planning use in Chile[8]; its validity was confirmed in our study by the fact that the percentage of poor households, defined in terms of data we collected for each household, varied as expected by poverty strata. For example, for the Mapuche sample, the percentage of poor households was 91%, 52%, and 16%, respectively, for extreme-, medium-, and low-poverty strata.

Limitations of the study include the lack of a well-to-do sample of Mapuche children from Santiago. Few Mapuche children live in the expensive neighborhoods of Santiago. In fact, it proved extremely difficult to find Mapuche children at all in 75 schools from low- to middle-class neighborhoods of Santiago; only 90 children met the Mapuche definition. Also, schoolchildren were chosen for the study because it was easy to locate and measure them. Ideally, younger children should have been targeted, because growth retar-

dation mainly occurs before 2 years of age. However, stunting among young schoolchildren is known to reflect prior malnutrition.[3] Finally, household poverty was measured at school age, about 5 years after the period of growth failure. Although changes may have occurred, it is unlikely that these were marked, because the poverty index is partly dependent on parental and household characteristics (parental education, size and type of home, water supply, and sewage), which are less likely to change in a 5-year period.

Three hypotheses were tested. First, we predicted that child stature would increase across the poverty gradient. We found this to be the case for both Mapuche and non-Mapuche groups. While the relationship between growth retardation and poverty is well established in the literature,[16,17,18] few studies have controlled for differences in ethnicity across socioeconomic groups. Because we used careful definitions of ethnicity, our results are less subject to this bias and permit us to assess the negative effect of poverty on child stature, independent of ethnicity.

Our second prediction was that there would be no differences in child stature between Mapuche and non-Mapuche children within poverty strata. Between the 2 groups, however, we found important differences in the percentage of poor households, even within poverty levels. In all 3 strata, the Mapuche were always the poorest. Consequently, ethnic comparisons of child stature within strata were adjusted for levels of household poverty. These analyses found that Mapuche and non-Mapuche children were similar within poverty strata. In the extreme-poverty group, the Mapuche children were shorter (z score $=-0.225$), but this difference was not significant. For medium- and low-poverty strata, the differences favored the Mapuche children (z score $=0.157$ and 0.218, respectively), but those differences were not statistically significant.

Our third prediction was that among children in Santiago, the heights of both Mapuche and non-Mapuche children would not differ from that of the reference population (i.e., from 0). We found that the mean height-for-age z score in Santiago was -0.21 for Mapuche children and -0.37 for non-Mapuche children. These values were significantly different from 0 only for non-Mapuche children. By contrast, mean z scores for the extreme-poverty groups were -1.1 and -0.7, respectively, for Mapuche and non-Mapuche groups, and values have been reported to be as high as -3.0 for indigenous groups in other parts of Latin America.[19]

What do we make of the fact that children measured in Santiago had negative scores? We think that these low- to middle-class children may have experienced mild growth retardation. Other studies have shown that the mean height-for-age z scores of Chilean children who attend private schools are in fact greater than 0.[20] As conditions in Santiago continue to improve, we would expect this minor deficit to eventually disappear among all classes.

CONCLUSION

Our study shows that the most important indigenous group in Chile, the Mapuche, has the potential to achieve heights similar to those of the reference population at ages 6 to 9 years. Thus, this is the first study to demonstrate that the short stature that had been observed in the past among Mapuche children[14] is due to poverty. On the other hand, this finding should not be extrapolated to growth during puberty, because we did not include adolescents in our study.

Our study supports the recommendation of Habicht et al.[4] that international reference data are appropriate for assessing the growth of young children worldwide, including the indigenous peoples of the Americas. We do not know whether our findings apply to all indigenous groups in the continent, but we believe that this should be assumed, unless subsequent studies show otherwise. The high levels of stunting generally found in the indigenous peoples of the Andean region and in Mesoamerica should be interpreted as reflective of their poverty, which leads to poor growth on account of poor diets, frequent infections, and deficient child care, and not as a genetic trait. For this reason, the high level of stunting found in indigenous peoples should be viewed as a marker of the need for socioeconomic development programs and effective public health measures.

NOTES

1. Psacharopoulos G, Patrinos H. *Indigenous People and Poverty in Latin America: An Empirical Analysis.* Washington, DC: World Bank; 1994.

2. Rivera-Dommarco J, González-Cosio T, Flores M, Hernández-Avila M, Lezama MA. Sepúlveda-Amor J. Déficit de talla y emaciación en menores de cinco años en distintas regiones y estratos en México. *Salud Publica Mex.* 1995;37:95–107.

3. *Physical Status: The Use and Interpretation of Anthropometry: Report of a WHO Expert Committee.* Geneva. Switzerland: World Health Organization; 1995. WHO Technical Series 854.

4. Habicht JP, Martorell R, Yarbrough C, Malina R, Klein R. Height and weight standards for preschool children: how relevant are ethnic differences in growth potential? *Lancet.* 1974; 1:611–614.

5. *Censo de población y vivienda Chile 1992: Resultados generales.* Santiago, Chile: Instituto Nacional de Estadisticas; 1994.

6. United Nations Development Programme. *Human Development Report 2000.* Madrid, Spain: Mundi Press; 2000.

7. Vial I, Muchnik E, Kain J. The evolution of Chile's main nutrition intervention programmes. *Food Nutr Bull.* 1991;14:170–175.

8. *Una propuesta de clasificación de las comunas del país según situación de la infancia.* Santiago, Chile: UNICEF; 1994.

9. Habícht JP. Estandarización de métodos epidemiológicos cuantitativos sobre el terreno, *Bol Of Sanit Panam.* 1974;76:375–384.

10. *Measuring Change in Nutritional Status. Guidelines for Assessing the Nutritional Impact on Supplementary Feeding Programmes for Vulnerable Groups.* Geneva, Switzerland: World Health Organization; 1983.

11. Alvarez ML, Wurgaft F, Salazar ME. Mediciones del nivel socioeconómico bajo urbano en familias con

lactante desnutrido. *Arch Latinoam Nutr.* 1982;32:650–662.

12. Frías, Valenzuela F. *Historia de Chile. Tomo 1. Los origenes.* Santiago, Chile: Editorial Nacimiento: 1984.

13. Valenzuela C, Rothhammer F, Chakraborty R. Sex dimorphism in adult stature in four Chilean populations. *Ann Hum Biol.* 1978;5:533–538.

14. Franco E, San Martin S, Bioley E, Rodriguez E, Novoa A. Situación nutricional de población Mapuche menor de 18 años: Cautin, Chile. *Rev Chil Nutr.* 1985; 13:19–27.

15. *Una propuesta de clasificación de las comunas del país según criterios de riesgo biomédico y socio económico para medir la vulnerabilidad infantil.* Santiago, Chile: UNICEF; 1990.

16. Kain J, Uauy R. Diaz M, Aburto AM. Height increase among school children assisting to first grade during the last decade in Chile. *Rev Med Chil.* 1999; 127:539–546.

17. Sinclair D, Dangerfield P. Environmental factors influencing growth and maturation. In: *Human Growth After Birth.* Oxford, England: Oxford University Press; 1998:155–170.

18. Frongillo EA Jr, de Onis M, Hanson KM. Socioeconomic and demographic factors associated with worldwide patterns of stunting and wasting of children. *J Nutr.* 1997;127:2302–2309.

19. Martorell R, Schroeder DG, Rivera JA, Kaplowitz HJ. Patterns of linear growth in rural Guatemalan adolescents and children. *J Nutr.* 1995;125(suppl): 1060S–1067S.

20. Amigo H, Bustos P, Radrigán ME, Ureta E. Nutritional status of school age children of differing socioeconomic levels. *Rev Med Chil.* 1995;123:1063–1070.

■ ■ ■ ■ ■ ■ ■ ■ ■ ■

49   GENDERS, SEXES, AND HEALTH: WHAT ARE THE CONNECTIONS, AND WHY DOES IT MATTER?

Nancy Krieger

As an introduction to the following selections on sex and gender, this selection takes up the task of defining these terms and illustrating how gender constructions and sex-linked biology can affect exposure to particular health conditions, the treatment of illness, and the outcome of sickness. Clarity in talking about sex and gender is necessary in light of popular and medical confusion about their meaning and the tendency of many researchers to use the terms interchangeably or to focus on only one or the other dimension in health research. In practice, people are both sexed and gendered, making it necessary to examine both levels together.

This selection is composed of a short text and a very detailed table. The table presents 12 health issues and the ways in which gender relations and sex-linked biology may influence exposures and outcomes, whether alone, together, or not at all. The table provides a model for outlining the direction of impact and distinguishing between sex and gender as determining factors. The model will be useful for reading the following selections and for analyzing many contemporary public health problems.

Questions to keep in mind

What is the difference between sex and gender (or sexes and genders)?

Do sex and gender matter for health only in trivial ways, or do they have an impact on serious diseases and mortality?

Source: Krieger, N. 2003. "Genders, Sexes, and Health: What Are the Connections—and Why Does It Matter?" *International Journal of Epidemiology* 32(4):652–657. By permission of Oxford University Press.

What are four health conditions presented in the table that illustrate how each of the following can affect exposure and outcome: sex, gender, both, neither? What are the pathways by which they do so in each case?

What are some other examples (not discussed in the table) of health differences between women and men, and how might you map them using Krieger's model?

Open up any biomedical or public health journal prior to the 1970s, and one term will be glaringly absent: *gender*. Open up any recent biomedical or public health journal, and two terms will be used either: (1) interchangeably, or (2) as distinct constructs: *gender* and *sex*. Why the change? Why the confusion?—and why does it matter?

As elegantly argued by Raymond Williams, vocabulary involves not only "the available and developing meaning of known words" but also "particular formations of meaning—ways not only of discussing but at another level seeing many of our central experiences" (ref. 1, p. 15). Language in this sense embodies "important social and historical processes", in which new terms are introduced or old terms take on new meanings, and often "earlier and later senses coexist, or become actual alternatives in which problems of contemporary belief and affiliation are contested" (ref. 1, p. 22).

So it is with "gender" and "sex".[2,3] The introduction of "gender" in English in the 1970s as an alternative to "sex" was expressly to counter an implicit and often explicit biological determinism pervading scientific and lay language.[2–8] The new term was deployed to aid clarity of thought, in a period when academics and activists alike, as part of and in response to that era's resurgent women's movement, engaged in debates over whether observed differences in social roles, performance, and non-reproductive health status of women and men—and girls and boys—was due to allegedly innate biological differences ("sex") or to culture-bound conventions about norms for—and relationships between—women, men, girls, and boys ("gender").

For language to express the ideas and issues at stake, one all-encompassing term—"sex"—would no longer suffice. Thus, the meaning of "gender" (derived from the Latin term "generare", to beget) expanded from being a technical grammatical term (referring to whether nouns in Latin and related languages were "masculine" or "feminine") to a term of social analysis (ref. 1, p. 285; ref. 4, p. 2; ref. 5, pp. 136–37). By contrast, the meaning of "sex" (derived from the Latin term *secus* or *sexus*, referring to "the male or female *section* of humanity" [ref. 1, p. 283]) contracted. Specifically, it went from a term describing distinctions between, and the relative status of, women and men (e.g. Simone DeBeauvoir's *The Second Sex*[9]) to a biological term, referring to groups defined by the biology of sexual reproduction (or, in the meaning of "having sex," to interactions involving sexual biology) (ref. 1 p. 285; ref. 4, p. 2; ref. 5, pp. 136–37).

As the term "gender" began to percolate into everyday use, however, it also began to enter the scientific literature,[3–8,10] sometimes with its newly intended meaning, other times as a seemingly trendy substitute for "sex"—with some articles[11] even including both terms, interchangeably, within their titles! Other studies, by contrast, have adhered to a strict gender/sex division, typically investigating the influence of only one or the other on particular health outcomes.[3–8,10] A new strand of health research, in turn, is expanding these terms from singular to plural by beginning to grapple with new constructs of genders and sexes now entering the scientific domain, e.g., "transgender," "transsexual," "intersexual," which blur boundaries not only *between* but also *within* the gender/sex dichotomy.[8] The net result is that although lucid analyses have been written on why it is important to distinguish between "gender" and "sex,"[4–8] epidemiological and other health research has been hampered by a lack of clear conceptual models for considering *both*, simultaneously, to determine their relevance—or not—to the outcome(s) being researched.

Yet, we do not live as a "gendered" person one day and a "sexed" organism the next; we are both, simultaneously, and for any given health outcome, it is an empirical question, not a philosophical principle, as to whether diverse permutations of gender and sex matter—or are irrelevant. Illustrating the importance of asking this question, conceptually and analytically, Table 49.1 employs an ecosocial epidemiological perspective[2,12] to delineate 12 examples,[13–24] across a range of exposure—outcome associations, in which gender relations and sex-linked biology are singly, neither, or both relevant as independent or synergistic determinants.[25] These examples were chosen for two reasons. First, underscoring the salience of considering these permutations for any and all outcomes, the examples range from birth defects to mortality, and include: chromosomal disorders, infectious and non-infectious disease, occupational and environmental disease, trauma, pregnancy, menopause, and access to health services. Second, they systematically present diverse scenarios across possible combinations of gender relations and sex-linked biology, as singly or jointly pertinent or irrelevant. In these examples, expressions of gender relations include: gender segregation of the workforce and gender discrimination in wages, gender norms about hygiene, gender expectations about sexual conduct and pregnancy, gendered presentation of and responses to symptoms of illness, and gender-based violence. Examples of sex-linked biology include: chromosomal sex, menstruation, genital secretions, secondary sex characteristics, sex-steroid-sensitive physiology of non-reproductive tissues, pregnancy, and menopause.

As examination of the 12 case examples makes clear, not only can gender relations influence expression—and interpretation—of biological traits, but also sex-linked biological characteristics can, in some cases, contribute to or amplify gender differentials in health. For example, as shown by case No. 9, not recognizing that parity is a social as well as biological phenomenon, with meaning for men as well as women, means important clues about why parity might be associated with a given outcome might be missed. Similarly, as shown by case No. 11, recognition of social inequalities among women (including as related to gender disparities between women and men) can enhance understanding of expressions of sex-linked biology, e.g. age at perimenopause. Because our science will only be as clear and error-free as our thinking, greater precision about whether gender relations, sex-linked biology, both, or neither matter for health is warranted.

NOTES

1. Williams R. *Keywords: A Vocabulary of Culture and Society. Revised Edn.* NY: Oxford University Press, 1983.

2. Krieger N. A glossary for social epidemiology. *J Epidemiol Community Health* 2001;55:693–700.

3. Krieger N, Fee E. Man-made medicine and women's health: the biopolitics of sex/gender and race/ethnicity. *Int J Health Serv* 1994;24:265–83.

4. Oudshoorn N. *Beyond the Natural Body: An Archeology of Sex Hormones.* London: Routledge, 1994.

5. Hubbard R. Constructing sex differences. In: Hubbard R. *The Politics of Women's Biology.* New Brunswick, NJ: Rutgers University Press, 1990, pp. 136–40.

6. Schiebinger L. *Nature's Body: Gender in the Making of Modern Science.* Boston: Beacon Press, 1993.

7. Doyal L. Sex, gender, and health: the need for a new approach. *BMJ* 2001;323:1061–63.

8. Fausto-Sterling A. *Sexing the Body: Gender Politics and the Construction of Sexuality.* New York, NY: Basic Books, 2000.

9. DeBeauvoir S. *The Second Sex.* NY: Vintage Books, 1974 (1952).

10. Institute of Medicine, Committee on Understanding the Biology of Sex and Gender Differences. Wizemann TM, Pardue M-L (eds). *Exploring the Biological Contributions to Human Health: Does Sex Matter?* Washington, DC: National Academy Press, 2001.

11. Boling EP. Gender and osteoporosis: similarities and sex-specific differences. *J Gend Specif Med* 2001;4:36–43.

12. Krieger N. Theories for social epidemiology in the 21st century: an ecosocial perspective. *Int J Epidemiol* 2001;30:668–77.

13. Ippolito G, Puro V, Heptonstall J, Jagger J, De Carli G, Petrosillo N. Occupational human immunodeficiency virus infection in health care workers: worldwide cases through September 1997. *Clin Infect Dis* 1999;28:365–83.

14. Liesegang TJ. Contact lens-related microbial keratitis: Part I: Epidemiology. *Cornea* 1997;16:125–31.

15. Ranke MG, Saenger P. Turner's syndrome. *Lancet* 2001;358:309–14.

16. Aoki Y. Polychlorinated biphenyls, polychlorinated dibenzo-p-dioxins, and polychlorinated dibenzofurans as endocrine disrupters—what we have learned from Yusho disease. *Environ Res* 2001;86:2–11.

17. Pickle LW, Gillum RF. Geographic variation in cardiovascular disease mortality in US blacks and whites. *J Natl Med Assoc* 1999;91:545–56.

18. Van Tongeren M, Nieuwenhuijsen MJ, Gardiner K *et al.* A job-exposure matrix for potential endocrine-disrupting chemicals developed for a study into the as-

Table 49.1 Selected examples of differential roles of gender relations and sex-linked biology on health outcomes: only gender, only sex-linked biology, neither, and both

Case	Diagrammed illustration	Exposure–outcome association	Relevance of: Gender relations	Relevance of: Sex-linked biology	Explication
1	gender relations sex-linked biology exposure → health outcome	Greater prevalence of HIV/AIDS due to needle-stick injury among female health care workers providing patient care[13]	Yes: for exposure	No	• Gender relations: determinant of risk of exposure (needle stick injury), via gender segregation of the workforce (e.g. greater likelihood of women being nurses) • Sex-linked biology: not a determinant of risk of exposure • Risk of outcome, given exposure: risk of seroconversion same among women and men
2	gender relations sex-linked biology exposure → health outcome	Greater prevalence of contact lens microbial keratitis among male compared with female contact lens wearers[14]	Yes	No	• Gender relations: determinant—among those wearing contact lenses—of risk of exposure to improperly cleaned contact lenses (men less likely to properly clean them than women) • Sex-linked biology: not a determinant of exposure • Risk of outcome, given exposure: risk of contact lens microbial keratitis same among women and men, once exposed to improperly cleaned contact lenses
3	gender relations sex-linked biology exposure → health outcome	Greater prevalence of short stature and gonadal dysgenesis among women with Turner's syndrome compared with unaffected women[15]	No	Yes: for exposure	• Gender relations: not a determinant of exposure (X-monosomy, total or mosaic, or non-functional X chromosome) • Sex-linked biology: determinant of exposure • Risk of outcome, given exposure: not influenced by gender relations
4	gender relations sex-linked biology exposure → health outcome	Both similar and different adverse health outcomes among women and men due to ubiquitous exposure to cooking oil contaminated by polychlorinated biphenyls (PCB) ('Yusho' disease)[16]	No	Yes: once exposed	• Gender relations: not a determinant of risk of exposure (ubiquitous exposure to the contaminated cooking oil, in staple foods) • Sex-linked biology: not a determinant of risk of exposure • Risk of outcome, given exposure: partly influenced by sex-linked biology, in that although both women and men experienced chloracne and other dermal and ocular lesions, only women experienced menstrual irregularities

Table 49.1 (Continued)

Case	Diagrammed illustration	Exposure–outcome association	Relevance of: Gender relations	Relevance of: Sex-linked biology	Explication
5	gender relations sex-linked biology exposure → health outcome	Higher risk of stroke among both women and men in the US "stroke belt" in several Southern states, compared with women and men in other regions of the US (as distinct from differences in risk for women and men within a given region)[17]	No	No	• Gender relations: not a determinant of risk of exposure (living in the US "stroke belt") • Sex-linked biology: not a determinant of risk of exposure • Risk of outcome, given exposure: neither gender relations nor sex-linked biology determine *regional variation* in stroke rates among men and among women (even as both may contribute to within-region higher risks among men compared with women)
6	gender relations sex-linked biology exposure → health outcome	Higher risk of hypospadias among male infants born to women exposed to potential endocrine-disrupting agents at work[18]	Yes: for exposure	Yes: once exposed	• Gender relations: a determinant of risk of exposure, via gender segregation of the work force (e.g. high level of phthalate exposure among hairdressers, who are mainly women) • Sex-linked biology: not a determinant of risk of exposure • Risk of outcome, given exposure: different for women and men, and for female and male fetus, as only women can be pregnant, and adverse exposure can lead to hypospadias only among fetuses with a penis
7	gender relations sex-linked biology exposure → health outcome	Geographical variation in women's rates of unintended pregnancy as linked to variation in state policies re family planning[19]	Yes: for exposure and once exposed	Yes: once exposed	• Gender relations: a determinant, at societal level, of risk of exposure, i.e. state policies and spending for family planning • Sex-linked biology: not a determinant, at individual level of the girl or woman at risk of pregnancy, of state policies and spending for family planning • Risk of outcome, given exposure: gender relations, at the individual level, influence women's access to—and ability to act on information obtained from—family planning programs, and sex-linked biology is a determinant of who can get pregnant

Table 49.1 (Continued)

Case	Diagrammed illustration	Exposure–outcome association	Relevance of: Gender relations	Relevance of: Sex-linked biology	Explication
8	gender relations, sex-linked biology → exposure → health outcome	Earlier age of human immunodeficiency virus infection among women compared with heterosexual men (in the US)[20]	Yes: for exposure	Yes: for exposure and once exposed	• Gender relations: a determinant of age of sexual partner and risk of unprotected sex (e.g. gender power imbalance resulting in sex between older men and younger women, the latter having a lesser ability to negotiate condom use) • Sex-linked biology: a determinant of exposure, via genital secretions • Risk of outcome, given exposure; sex-linked biology a determinant of greater biological efficiency of male-to-female, compared with female-to-male, transmission
9	gender relations, sex-linked biology → exposure (a) → health outcome; exposure(b)	Parity among both women and men associated with increased risk of melanoma[21]	Yes: for exposures	Yes: for exposure	• Gender relations: a determinant of parity (via expectations of who has children, at what age) • Sex-linked biology: a determinant of who can become pregnant and pregnancy-linked hormonal levels • Risk of outcome, given exposure: decreased risk of melanoma among nulliparous women and men indicates that non-reproductive factors linked to parity may affect risk among both women and men, even as pregnancy-related hormonal factors may also affect women's risk
10	gender relations, sex-linked biology → exposure → health outcome	Greater referral of men compared with women for interventions for acute coronary syndromes[22]	Yes: for exposure and once exposed	Yes: for exposure	• Gender relations: a determinant of how people present and physicians interpret symptoms of acute coronary syndromes • Sex-linked biology: a determinant of age at presentation (men are more likely to have acute infarction at younger ages) and possibly type of symptoms • Risk of outcome, given exposure: gender relations are a determinant of physician likelihood of referral for diagnostic and therapeutic interventions (women less likely to be referred, especially at younger ages)

Table 49.1 (Continued)

Case	Diagrammed illustration	Exposure–outcome association	Relevance of:		Explication
			Gender relations	Sex-linked biology	
11	gender sex-linked biology relations exposure → health outcome	Earlier age at onset of perimenopause among women experiencing greater cumulative economic deprivation over the life course[23]	Yes: for exposure	Yes: as outcome	• Gender relations: a determinant of poverty, across the life course, among women (via the gender gap in earnings and wealth) • Sex-linked biology: a determinant of who can experience perimenopause • Risk of outcome, given exposure: risk of earlier age at perimenopause among women subjected to greater economic deprivation across the life course, including non-smokers, may reflect impact of poverty on oocyte depletion
12	gender sex-linked biology relations exposure → health outcome	Greater rate of mortality among women compared with men due to intimate partner violence[24]	Yes: for exposure	Yes: for exposure and once exposed	• Gender relations: a determinant of likelihood of men versus women using physical violence against intimate partners, plus being encouraged to and having access to resources to increase physical strength • Sex-linked biology: a determinant of muscle strength and stamina, at a given level of training and exertion, and also body size • Risk of outcome, given exposure: risk of lethal assault related to on-average greater physical strength and size of men, and gender-related skills and training in inflicting and warding off physical attack

sociation between maternal occupational exposure and hypospadias. *Ann Occup Hyg* 2002;46:465–77.

19. Melvin CL, Rogers M, Gilbert BC *et al.* Pregnancy intention: how PRAMS data can inform programs and policy. *Matern Child Health J* 2000;4:197–201.

20. Hader SL, Smith DK, Moore JS, Holmberg SD. HIV infection in women in the United States: status at the Millennium. *JAMA* 2001; 285:1186–92.

21. Kravdal O. Is the relationship between childbearing and cancer incidence due to biology or lifestyle? Examples of the importance of using data on men. *Int J Epidemiol* 1995;4:477–84.

22. Feldman T, Silver R. Gender differences and the outcome of interventions for acute coronary syndromes. *Cardiol Rev* 2000;8:240–47.

23. Wise LA, Krieger N, Zierler S, Harlow BL. Lifetime socioeconomic position in relation to onset of perimenopause: a prospective cohort study. *J Epidemiol Community Health* 2002;56:851–60.

24. Watts C, Zimmerman C. Violence against women: global scope and magnitude. *Lancet* 2002;359: 1232–37.

25. Darroch J. Biological synergism and parallelism. *Am J Epidemiol* 1997;145:661–68.

■ ■ ■ ■ ■ ■ ■ ■ ■

50   FEMALE-SELECTIVE ABORTION IN ASIA: PATTERNS, POLICIES, AND DEBATES

Barbara D. Miller

This selection shows how gender differences in health can begin even before birth, in this case through female-selective abortion (FSA). At issue is a cultural system that affects females only, by way of both gender beliefs (male children are valued more than female children) and biological sex (only females get pregnant and bear the health consequences). In addition to clarifying the different impacts of sex and gender on health (see selection 49), the selection demonstrates the importance of contextualizing quantitative data with sociocultural and politico-economic analysis.

A cultural preference for male children is common among patriarchal societies worldwide and has been associated in various locations with increased childbearing, female infanticide, and fatal parental neglect of female babies and children. What has been different in the last 20 years is that widely available new technologies to influence or discover fetal sex permit parents to prevent the birth of females in the first place. The result has been increased frequency of FSA in countries such as India, China, and Taiwan, especially among the educated elite.

The use of FSA in these and other Asian countries is rooted in a widespread patriarchal culture that elevates males in every sphere (see selections 35, 51), leaving women dependent on their fathers and husbands and constructing female children as a burden and a financial loss to their families. Although there are exceptions, in most cases "modernization" has brought only a further reduction in women's status relative to men's. Parents consequently continue to prefer sons, and women may use FSA to benefit their own social and family status and long-term economic security. In so doing, they participate in a practice that reinforces the low economic, social, political, and ideological position of females. Miller points out that this raises questions about the appropriateness of concepts such as choice and agency (see Part III).

This selection suggests that the scale of FSA, its causes, and its consequences demand consideration of the moral and ethical aspects of the uses to which technological innovations are put (see selections

Source: Miller, B. D. 2001. "Female-Selective Abortion in Asia: Patterns, Policies, and Debates." ©2001 by the American Anthropological Association. Reprinted from *American Anthropologist* Vol. 103 No. 4 pp. 1083–1095, by permission.

54–56). Miller also argues for discussion of the wider social significance of male-biased sex ratios in engendering violence and expressing male violence toward women. Both reflect a lack of personal and public security. This is a reminder of the need to look beyond the level of the individual to the sociocultural and politico-economic context of health issues.

Questions to keep in mind

What are some social class differences in the use of FSA in the countries analyzed in this selection?

Why is it difficult to enforce laws that prohibit the use of ultrasound or other equipment for the purpose of determining sex?

Why is it insufficient to target financial incentives to prevent FSA or female infanticide only at low-income families?

How do people justify FSA, and how does Miller argue against them?

Why does a balanced sex ratio tend not to appear in discussions of public goods or human rights issues?

When concluding my 1981 book about unbalanced sex ratios among children in India, I commented on the implications of the possibility of prenatal sex selection of offspring: "If such a choice were ever made widely available to the Indian population, there is no doubt that people would opt for many more sons than daughters, particularly in the North" (1997a[1981]:168). Many scholars, during the 1980s, emphatically told me that my view was extremist and unnecessarily alarmist because sex-selection technology would never be widely available in India's rural areas or sufficiently affordable for most Indians. These critics were short sighted, and, unfortunately, my prediction was more correct than I had imagined. Fifteen year later, I was asked to write a paper for an international population conference, and I decided to examine the data on India and also on other Asian countries in the belief that comparisons can provide new insights.[1] In this article, building on that conference paper, I pursue a currently unusual approach for a cultural anthropologist in broad comparative analysis. I face the risks involved in the hope that lessons learned will more than compensate for lost particularities and that more localized studies will be done to help provide those.

This article's focus is the increasing use of sex-selective abortion in several Asian populations since the early 1980s. Estimates at the beginning of the year 2000 indicate that several million female fetuses were aborted in the last two decades of the twentieth century. After reviewing the available evidence, I discuss some features of Asian culture that support strong son preference. I then review related issues including the growing technological availability for prenatal sex selection and current national policies about sex selection. Next, I consider the varied positions taken regarding this issue by feminists, ethicists, and other thinkers. In the end, I suggest new ways that anthropologists can contribute to thinking about unbalanced sex ratios in order to bring greater policy attention to the increasing gender gap in many Asian populations.

FEMALE-SELECTIVE ABORTION IN ASIA

Female-selective abortion (FSA) is practiced predominantly but not exclusively in parts of Asia, especially China, Taiwan, the Republic of Korea, Pakistan, and India, and among some Asian immigrant populations in Canada, the United States, and probably elsewhere.[2] Given the limitations of the available information on FSA, this overview does not include all Asian countries and regions where son preference has been documented and demand for FSA is likely, such as Bangladesh, Nepal, and Vietnam. Beyond Asia, son preference has been documented, and thus demand for FSA is possible, in Central/West Asia, some Middle Eastern countries, and North Africa (Makinson 1986; Obermeyer 1996; Williamson 1976).[3] My review also excludes the puzzling case of Japan, for I was unable to find evidence of FSA in the literature. Contemporary Japan has a balanced juvenile sex ratio.[4] Yet a survey of more than 100 Japanese medical geneticists reveals that 32 percent had been directly approached by parents for prenatal sex information (Wertz and Fletcher 1998). This figure, while low compared with the 79 percent of medical geneticists approached in China and 70 percent in India, nonetheless indicates some parental interest in sex selection in Japan.

Data Constraints

Efforts to assess the extent of FSA in Asian cultures are constrained by lack of data. At this point, most reports provide figures aggregated at the national level. This lack means that we have no way of assessing regional and social variations that are likely to be important. Beyond sheer scarcity of data, data quality is often questionable. Underreporting of FSA is to be expected because sex-selective abortion has been banned or is in some way illegal in most countries. I have been unable to locate any systematic studies providing direct data about numbers of abortions performed because of fetal sex for any place or time.[5] Medical staff who perform female-selective abortions would be unlikely to record them as such.

The sex ratio at birth (SRB) is the usual basis for estimating the number of selective abortions, calculated on the basis of the assumed "normal" SRB of 105 males for 100 females. The generally accepted "norm" for SRBs is between 104 and 107 males per 100 females (Visaria 1967). This range is based on worldwide data from the 1950s and 1960s, before sex-selective abortion was available. Data indicating SRBs above the upper limit of 107 are interpreted as not "natural" but, rather, as culturally achieved primarily through FSA. An SRB of 117–120 boys per 100 girls, for example, in comparison with an international average of 106 boys per 100 girls, means that one of every seven–ten female fetuses has been selectively aborted.

National censuses conducted in countries with dependable birth statistics include those of the Republic of Korea, Taiwan, and China. A more dependable source of evidence of FSA comes from records of SRBs that occur in hospitals. The value of hospital data, compared with census data, lies in the total counting of births and avoidance of the possibility of underreporting of female births. Data from hospital births suffer from one bias, however. If parents have sought fetal sex testing and have aborted an unwanted female fetus, they may be more likely to seek a hospital delivery to ensure a safer delivery. These hospital SRBs would be more masculine than those of the population giving birth outside the hospital. Without comparative data on hospital births and nonhospital births, it is impossible to know how large this bias might be. In countries where most or all births take place in hospitals and are recorded, this data problem does not exist.

A final data limitation arises from the fact that most national censuses are conducted decennially. Census results from the year 2000 are at the time of this writing still unavailable. Localized surveys and other more recent data are used to update findings whenever possible in the following section.

The Republic of Korea

The increasing use of FSA in the Republic of Korea is clear from longitudinal data on sex ratios at birth. By 1980, the national SRB was 108.3 boys per 100 girls, and by 1985 it had risen to 110.4 boys. The government of the Republic of Korea outlawed the practice of sex-selective abortion in 1987. Since then the national annual report on vital statistics has shown an increase in the SRB, especially among higher parity females, that is, females born second, third, fourth, and so on in a sibship (Hong 1994). The SRB of second-born infants was 109 in 1987, 114 in 1988, 114 in 1989, 117 in 1990, and 114 in 1992. In 1992, the SRB for third children was 196, and it was 229 for fourth children. FSA is the only viable explanation for these distorted sex ratios at birth. Data from 1993 placed the Republic of Korea in the distinguished position of having the highest reported national sex ratio at birth in the world, at 115.6 boys per 100 girls (Anderson 1996).[6]

Within this relatively small nation of some 22 million-plus people, regional and class differences are likely to exist in son preference and resorting to FSA, but localized studies that might shed light on possible differences are rare. A landmark study of changes in the SRB in the Republic of Korea provides one paragraph and one table on variation in sex ratios of children under five years of age by geographic area from 1980 to 1990 (Park and Cho 1995). The authors comment that as of 1980, sex ratios among young children were within normal range throughout the country (1995:62). Beginning in 1985, some large cities had extremely high sex ratios. A journalistic report reveals that in the southeastern city of Taegu, the SRB of third-born children was 305 and that for fourth-born children was 582 (*The Economist* 1989), indicating that people in Taegu used FSA to a substantial degree. While urbanization in general appears to be associated with rising SRBs, rural areas are characterized by a parallel rise (Park and Cho 1995). Nevertheless, Taegu and its surrounding region bear special scrutiny as a possible "core" region of FSA in the Republic of Korea that may lead to sharper hypothesis formulation and policy focus.

China

Early analyses of China's 1990 population census firmly established that China's sex ratio at birth is also male biased. For the nation as a whole, the 1989 SRB was 114 boys per 100 girls (Gu and Li 1994). From a "normal" SRB of 106 in 1970, the SRB rose steadily, reaching 111 by 1985. As in the Republic of Korea, parity plays a strong role in FSA. In 1989 SRBs were 105 for first-order births 121 for second-order births, 124 for third-order births, and 132 for fourth-order births. Analysis of census data indicates that in 1990 nearly four million girls were "missing" because of FSA in China, taking into account possible undercounting, abandonment, and differential child mortality among girls (Banister 1996:19).

Some researchers claim that the primary explanation for China's "missing girls" is underreporting, and they adjust the data to account for this hypothesized error (Gu and Li 1994:7–11). Several factors weaken this position. First, no logical reason exists to explain why underreporting would be steadily increasing, especially because the highest (most masculine) SRBs are reported for some of the more "developed" regions where reporting would be more accurate. Second, the pattern of rising SRBs closely resembles that of the Republic of

Korea, for which no claims of underreporting are made. Most convincingly, data on live births from 945 Chinese hospitals between 1988 and 1991 reveal SRBs moving from 108 to 110 over the period of the study. These figures are only slightly lower than the national average SRB in 1989 of 111. Thus, the underreporting of female births as an explanation for male-biased SRBs lacks strength.

Within China, regional variations in SRBs are significant (Gu and Li 1994). The 1990 census showed that, of China's 30 provinces, 21 had SRBs clearly in the "abnormal" range of over 108 males per 100 females. The highest SRBs, of about 117, were found in Guangxi and Zhejiang Provinces. In contrast, Guizhou and Tibet have the lowest at around 103. Male-biased SRBs are most prominent in regions that are more involved in capitalistic economic development and have reduced fertility rates. This finding raises the question of the degree to which urbanization affects FSA. Shanghai, the most economically developed municipality, is a case in question. As of the mid-1990s, provincial-level data indicated that FSA appeared to be insignificant in China's most economically developed city, Shanghai, and in the capital city of Beijing (Banister 1996). Yet a journalistic report from 1989 indicates that FSA was practiced in Shanghai: "For many months, hospital delivery rooms in Shanghai have welcomed 125 squalling boy babies for every 100 girls" (*U.S. News and World Report* 1989:16).

Taiwan

Compared with those of the Republic of Korea and parts of China, Taiwan's sex ratios at birth from 1960 to 1986 indicate a "moderate" excess of boys over girls with an average SRB of 106.7 (Chang 1994). Since then, increases occurred with a rise to 108 in 1987 and then to slightly over 110 in 1990. Again, though, the SRB increased with parity. In 1987, the SRB was 107 for first births, 108 for second births, 110 for third births, and 114 for fourth births. SRBs in 1990 were similar for first and second births but increased for the third and fourth, with the SRB of fourth-born children rising to 128. These rising SRBs are, according to one scholarly interpretation, not due to underregistration of females but, rather, to the increased use of prenatal sex screening and abortion (Chang 1994:15–16).

India

Compared with the work on all other countries discussed in this section, more studies are available for India's sex ratio and regional and social variations in it, though the picture is by no means clearly established or agreed on among scholars. Estimates of India's national SRB in the early 1990s placed it "as high as 112" (Westley 1995:3). Beneath this national average, substantial regional and class variations are likely to exist, following patterns in the degree of son preference (Basu 1992; Dyson and Moore 1983) and differential treatment of children on the basis of gender (Miller 1997a [1981]). The general regional pattern of unbalanced juvenile sex ratios in India during the 1970s and 1980s was greater scarcity of girls in the northwestern plains compared with the eastern and southern regions. The general social pattern at that time was of greatest scarcity of girls relative to boys in the propertied groups of the northwestern plains (Miller 1997a [1981]). More recent trends show the diffusion of strong son preference and unwanted daughters to nonpropertied groups in the north and increasing evidence for such among some propertied and nonpropertied groups in the south, particularly among rural propertied groups in the state of Tamil Nadu (Chunkath and Athreya 1997; George et al. 1992).

Insight about change over time comes from a longitudinal study of SRBs conducted from 1983 to 1988 in several hospitals in the city of Ludhiana, Punjab, located in the part of northern India long characterized by high juvenile sex ratios (Sachar et al. 1990). SRBs increased from 105 in 1983 to 119 in 1988. Another study conducted in Ludhiana that examines social factors involved in FSA was based on interviews with mothers of 596 infants (Booth et al. 1994). The mothers were selected at random from those giving birth in or admitted to Brown Memorial Hospital between 1990 and 1991. The mothers' reported use of fetal sex determination was high: 14 percent of the mothers of boys had used fetal testing to learn the sex of the fetuses they were carrying. In contrast, only 2 percent (five cases) of the mothers of girls reported using fetal sex determination. The mothers who had used fetal testing but had given birth to girls were distinguished by two factors: either their pregnancies involved a set of twins of which one was male or the fetuses had been misdiagnosed as male. This study also shows that the presence of an older female sibling greatly increases the use of sex determination while the presence of an older brother greatly reduces the likelihood of sex determination. FSA in this sample increased with the level of household income and with the level of maternal education. Of the mothers with no formal education, none had undergone prenatal testing, whereas among the mothers with formal education, the frequency of FSA was constant.

Another, larger interview-based study involving over 1,000 study families in villages in the state of Haryana, which is located just east of Punjab, found a reported SRB of 127 males per 100 females among upper caste women, compared with 102 among the lowest caste women (George and Dahiya 1998). Upper caste women openly discussed the widespread practice of FSA with the interviewers, whereas women of the lowest caste category denied its practice.

Pakistan

The strength of son preference in Pakistan closely parallels that in the neighboring region of India's northwestern plains (Dyson and Moore 1983; Miller 1984). Thus, logically, demand for FSA in Pakistan would also be strong. Yet obtaining data to assess this possibility is especially difficult. Data inadequacy is the most prominent in Pakistan out of all the Asian countries discussed so far, and that includes the lack of census data, survey data, and local studies. Other factors that make the study of FSA in Pakistan especially difficult include the negative view of Pakistani Islam toward abortion in general and stronger denial by many experts that FSA is practiced in Pakistan compared with the countries discussed above.

A clear example of denial by experts appears in a paper presented at the Seoul meeting on sex preferences for children in the rapidly changing demographies of Asia, in which Karim (1994) notes sanguinely that the 1989 national reported SRB of 107 is "consistent with the accepted biological norm" but then follows this statement with data on very high sex ratios for first births: 137 in 1986,

116 in 1987, 133 in 1988, 124 in 1989, and 117 in 1990. He next suggests that the data on first-birth sex ratios are due to misreporting but offers no explanation for why people would be more likely to underreport births of daughters for first births than higher parity births. Karim also states that "abortion of female fetuses is a rarely practiced phenomenon" because people simply "continue to bear children until they achieve the desired number of sons" (1994:3). This comment ignores the fact of class differences in fertility in Pakistan: upper class people have fewer children than lower class people, in general. In addition to such misinterpretations, Karim's paper contains confusing and contradictory statements such as his comment that "even though in large cities, ultrasound has become an important tool to predict the sex of the fetus, in a personal communication with the secretary general of the society of ultrasound practitioners, it was pointed out, that whatever abortions take place in Pakistan, it is irrespective of the sex of the child to be born" (1994:3). How, one must wonder, can a scholar state in one breath that ultrasound is important in fetal sex determination and also state that it is not used for fetal sex determination?

Summary

Evidence from the various sources available indicates that FSA is widely practiced in many Asian contexts and that the use of FSA has increased substantially since the middle of the 1980s in all of the Asian countries discussed in this article, though with internal and social differences. Adequate information does not exist to provide a dependable idea of the total number of females aborted since the 1980s, but China alone is likely to account for about four million. Increased FSA appears to run parallel, especially in East Asia, with urbanization and economic growth. As a strategy within the microdemography of family building, people are generally more likely to use FSA for second and third births, especially if a family already has one daughter. Pakistan, however, may present a case of FSA for first-born daughters. At this point, the lack of localized studies prevents more nuanced generalizations about intranational patterns. There are some indications,

mostly anecdotal at this point, that some diaspora Asian populations seek FSA.[7]

Because a similar trend toward increasingly masculine sex ratios at birth occurred throughout patriarchal cultures of Asia during the 1980s and 1990s, a political economy approach seems plausible in general and in specific localities, such as the regions of China adjacent to Hong Kong where economic growth has been high and regions and classes of northern India most affected by economic development. Yet, if this hypothesis were borne out, it explains only the similarity in change during these decades but not why these cultures have long been patriarchal, though I again would favor an approach that begins with a political economy model (that is a good project for social and demographic historians). In sum, though, resorting to explanations for patterns that cross much of Asia that are grounded in regionally specific ideologies such as "Confucian values" or "Islamic values" does little to explain either the distant past or changes during the 1980s and 1990s.

ASIAN PATRIARCHAL DEMOGRAPHICS AND CHANGE

The countries discussed above could all be characterized as patriarchal, to varying degrees and with varying demographic results.[8] In using the word *patriarchal,* I am referring to cultural contexts in which males dominate economic, political, social, and ideological spheres.[9] Economic domination includes male control of and access to important forms of productive property, inheritance rights, and preferred employment. Females, in such cultural contexts, are economically dependent on males—either their fathers, husbands, or sons—because they themselves have no direct economic entitlements (Cain 1981, 1986, 1993; Sen 1981). Politically, male dominance means that men control leadership and decision making in both the public and private domains to the exclusion and disadvantage of female status and welfare (women leaders can and often do assume political roles in the public domain in male-dominated cultures, but most have not supported pro-female policies). Socially, one finds kinship systems that emphasize the importance of male relatives, solidarity among male kin and separation of female kin from each other through exogamy, and dowry systems that require heavy expenditures for the marriage of a daughter but not for a son. Ideologically, religious and philosophical systems elevate maleness to a level of purity and power and associate femaleness with impurity, danger, and the need to be controlled by males.[10]

Patriarchal Demographics

One possible demographic result of such patriarchal cultural systems is parental preferences—by mothers and fathers and in-laws—for sons.[11] A fertility preference (for sons or for daughters generally or, more specifically, for offspring of a particular gender to be the first born or the last born) will either increase fertility as parents attempt to achieve their preference, promote high rates of "wastage" of unwanted offspring through infanticide or fatal neglect, or result in a combination of overreproduction and high wastage.

This model holds at a general level, for example, when comparing regions of Asia such as Han China, the Republic of Korea, and northern India, which are strongly patriarchal, with Thailand, Indonesia, and Burma, which have less male-biased cultures. Localized variations exist, but many more local studies are needed to help map such differences. In addition to gaining a better understanding of local and regional social variations, it is also time to raise urgent questions about how, why, and with what effects patriarchal cultures change.

Modernity and Patriarchal Demographics

Popular thinking suggests that aspects of patriarchy will decline or even disappear with "modernization" (variously defined but usually including primarily capitalist economic growth, higher levels of income and consumerism, and increased access to Western-style education). To the contrary, substantial feminist research has documented since the 1970s that capitalist economic development and growth are likely to lower women's status relative to men's, either by undermining women's traditional roles and entitlements, by increasing men's entitlements relative to women's (for example, by targeting income-generating schemes toward men and bypassing women), or both.

"Modernization" (read: economic development, growth-driven capitalism) in patriarchal contexts is closely linked to both lowered fertility rates and increased use of FSA. When discussing the demographic impact of recent economic changes in China, demographers Gu and Li (1994) explain that the "early birds" who are gaining from economic reform have become increasingly concerned about who will inherit the property they have recently accumulated if they do not have sons. Whyte's (1993) research in Chengdu, the capital city of Sichuan Province, shows that the capitalist economic reforms have brought a resurgence of Confucian—patriarchal—family norms and strategies that strengthen the value of sons and decrease the value of daughters.

Modernity and Changing Marriage Costs

In India, especially in northern India's propertied classes and increasingly throughout the entire country, the prevalent practice is for the bride's family to provide large sums of money and costly goods that mostly go to the groom's family, not the newly married couple. This system should be called "groomwealth," as it is a near mirror image of bridewealth, which involves the giving of wealth and goods by the groom and his family to the bride's parents. Groomwealth is fast replacing other forms of marriage payments in India, its negotiated size is increasing, and it is only part of an increasingly expensive stream of gifts that flows from the bride's family to the groom's for many years following the marriage. Under this system, the birth of a daughter is a financial disaster for a family, especially if they have no son whose bride will bring in money and goods that can be used for the daughter's marriage. This fact, combined with the effects of the groomwealth system and other kinship rules such as hypergyny (the girl must marry a boy from a family with higher socioeconomic status than hers), ensures that skewed sex ratios in India will not lead to an increased "value" of daughters.

Consider, in contrast, the changes that have taken place in one area of Han China (Min and

Eades 1995). In Anhui Province, since the beginning of the responsibility system in 1980, female agricultural labor has become more valuable. More people are arranging marriages closer to home, so that daughters can move back and forth between natal and marriage homes during crucial periods of labor demand. At the same time, marriage payment patterns have changed dramatically. The heavier financial burden is now on the groom's side, and the bride's side has greater power in the negotiations and arrangements. What has emerged is not a bridewealth system but a new form of dowry system financed by the groom's side for the benefit of the newly married couple. Its size and contents are shaped by demands made from the bride's side. Several contrasts with the Indian pattern exist. First, the marriage market in Anhui is more "closed"—increasingly so with the preference for locally endogamous marriages. Second, hypergyny is not practiced; instead, value is placed on finding an isogamous match in which bride and groom are socioeconomic equals. In this context, the scarcity of brides created by unbalanced sex ratios does translate into greater bargaining power for parents of the bride. On the negative side, another trend is that parents are taking girls out of school sooner than before so that they can use their labor as much as possible before their marriage. The possible effects of these changes on parents' willingness to have daughters are not discussed by Min and Eades (1995), but one should not immediately jump to the conclusion that parents will now want daughters more than (or even as much as) sons. No bridewealth is involved, so parents of a bride "net" no wealth compared with parents of a groom in a groomwealth system. Other key questions are, Does the marital property go under the name of the husband and wife jointly or just the husband? Does a woman's agricultural labor give her high domestic status and decision-making power? Recent research indicates that as women become more important in agricultural labor, men are gaining more economic status and power through entrepreneurship—thus strengthening the importance of male economic roles to the detriment of female economic roles (Entwisle et al. 1995).

Economic, political, and kinship practices are changing rapidly throughout Asia, yet male control of the most lucrative and prestigious, and

newly emerging, economic roles remains strong and may be expanding as new opportunities, particularly in business, arise and are differentially taken up by males. Parents who contemplate their status in old age are likely to continue to use FSA to ensure the presence of a son to support them.[12]

THE TECHNOLOGICAL MODERNIZATION OF MALE-BIASED REPRODUCTION

In addition to these cultural dynamics, rapid innovation in reproductive technology since the late 1970s has brought the capability of choosing whether or not to have a daughter within reach of millions of people. Before the emergence of amniocentesis as a way of learning the sex of one's fetus, no method existed for prenatal sex selection. Sex selection of offspring had to be delayed until birth. Now, a variety of techniques exist for influencing fetal sex, including sperm separation and implantation of embryos of a particular sex, and for determining the sex of a fetus, including chorionic villi sampling and ultrasound (Steinbacher and Gilroy 1996).

Throughout Asia, ultrasound scanning has become the most widespread technique. In obstetrics, the ultrasound machine was originally used to scan the fetus for certain physical problems such as Down's syndrome. The technological ability to detect the sex of the fetus first emerged with amniocentesis in the mid-1950s (Elias and Simpson 1992). Amniocentesis became available in parts of Asia, especially the more urbanized and industrial areas of the Republic of Korea, Taiwan, and Hong Kong, by the mid-1970s (Williamson 1978). Chorionic villus sampling, which can be done earlier in the pregnancy but requires more sophisticated equipment, was developed in the late 1960s (Brambati 1992) and is available now mainly in Asia's large urban hospitals.

China

In China, emerging indications of male-biased sex ratios at birth in the later 1980s raised the question of the use of amniocentesis for FSA there, but scholarly denial in the United States of this trend remained strong until the early 1990s.[13] Ultrasound, however, has long been used to monitor women's use of IUDs and pregnancy in general in China, so the technology and technical expertise for widespread FSA is widely available (Zeng et al. 1993). Availability has continued to increase in recent years. As Zeng et al. comment, "With economic development and the concomitant improvements in medical technology in the 1980s, a large number of ultrasound B machines were introduced in China" (1993:291). China manufactured its own ultrasound B machine first in 1979 and was able to produce over 10,000 per year, "enough to provide every county in China with four machines" (Zeng et al. 1993:291). China continued to import high-quality machines with a peak in 1989 of over 2,000 machines. In sum, the number of ultrasound scanners greatly increased during the transition toward a more market-driven economy (*The Christian Science Monitor* 1995).

India

By the early 1980s, FSA based on amniocentesis had become available in some cities in India, mainly in the north but also in Bombay on the west coast. By the 1990s, ultrasound had replaced amniocentesis as the predominant means for determining the sex of the fetus in India. The profits from manufacturing and distributing ultrasound machines are huge, and the market is expanding. In India, ultrasound equipment constituted 20 percent of the total market in medical technology in 1993, and that market grew by 20 percent every year, with stiff competition among several international businesses including Siemens, General Electric (in a joint venture with Wipro Ltd.), Toshiba, and Philips (*Business Week* 1993:68). A new GE model offers most of the conventional functions in a 20-pound unit. The device can fit in the backseat of a car as a doctor makes rounds at remote clinics. Indian activists have been watchdogging this growth but appear to be unable to do more than that.

It is impossible to estimate how much of all ultrasound testing done in a particular country is for sex selection because ultrasound testing can be used for a range of diagnostic purposes, including for adults "virtually all biliary, gynaecological, and genitourinary lesions, abdominal and pelvic masses, thyroid, salivary gland, and lymph-node tumors, and scrotal lesions" and several purposes for children (*The Lancet* 1990:1225). When questioned about the sex-selection use of ultrasound technology in India, Vivek Paul, president of Wipro GE, responded defensively that sex determination is a "very, very small percentage of their usage" (*The Lancet* 1990:1225). It is difficult to imagine that the thousands of ultrasound machines in India, in areas where son preference is most extreme, are used primarily for purposes other than FSA, and it is equally difficult to imagine being able to obtain accurate data on actual uses of ultrasound machines in areas of high son preference.[14]

POLICIES REGARDING FSA

The Republic of Korea

In 1987, the government of the Republic of Korea banned fetal screening for sex identification. A few years later, it "imposed stiffer penalties for performing illegal abortions, and . . . firmly told doctors to desist" (*The Economist* 1989:42). In 1994, the medical code was strengthened by including a provision for revoking the medical licenses of doctors who disobey the law, imposing steep fines, and threatening possible imprisonment (*The Christian Science Monitor* 1995). I have no information on whether any, or how many, doctors have been penalized.

China

In 1993, the Chinese government banned hospitals from using ultrasound scanners to reveal the sex of a child (*The Christian Science Monitor* 1995). Another law went into effect in January 1995 that bans sex screening of fetuses through such technical means as ultrasound except when needed on medical grounds. Doctors who perform such tests could lose their licenses. When asked how the provision would be enforced, Health Minister Chen Minzhang replied that enforcement would depend on hospital staff or the person's relatives to report an illegal test. The government has also launched a campaign to change attitudes toward girl children and upgrade women's economic support and social status, including improving education and providing pension support in rural areas. Some provinces have made lowering the sex ratio a goal of family-planning efforts. In spite of government regulations against FSA, doctors reportedly perform FSA as a favor to friends and contacts or in response to a bribe:

> Couples who already have a daughter and who have a strong desire to have a son will try all means to have the sex of the fetus identified through personal connections or by bribing medical personnel. . . . Some medical personnel, disregarding government regulations, illegally use ultrasound B machines or other available technology for prenatal sex identification because they cannot turn down the request of a relative or friend, or cannot resist the temptation of money and gifts. [Zeng et al. 1993:291–292]

India

India has the longest history of activism and policy attention to FSA. In 1988 Maharashtra became the first state to ban amniocentesis for sex selection. Fines and prison terms were mandated for both those who administer the tests and the women who undergo them. Within the same year, serious doubts were raised about how effective the ban would be, especially given gaps in the legislation that leave the private sector unregulated. The lack of government action against a clinic that advertised sex-determination services was cited by an activist group, the Forum against Sex Determination and Sex Pre-Selection, as evidence of the ineffectiveness of the legislation. In 1994, Dr. Chayanika Shah of the Bombay Forum for Women's Health stated that as yet "no one has been convicted" (*Ms.* 1994a:17).

In India, the Maharashtra state policy provided the model for the Prenatal Diagnostic Techniques (Regulation and Prevention of Misuse) Bill that was enacted as of January 1, 1996 (*Deutsche Presse-Agentur* 1996). One difference is that the national bill requires that all institutions providing prenatal testing be registered. The intent is that such registration will allow for oversight and monitoring. Although this provision might have some effect on large institutions, it is completely useless for preventing FSA provided on the basis of tests obtained from the new portable ultrasound machine. It also says nothing about sex selection through

sperm separation, which is legally obtainable in Bombay.

Different states of India have adopted other policies and programs. The relatively progressive southern state of Tamil Nadu developed programs in response to recent discoveries of outright female infanticide in some districts. One of these includes an incentive program for parents of a daughter by promising a sum of money when she reaches a certain age. The northern state of Haryana, which has extremely unbalanced juvenile sex ratios, devised a scheme in 1994 that invests Rs 2,500 (about US$78) in the name of a newborn girl (*The Economist* 1995). When the girl reaches the age of 18, the investment will yield Rs 25,000. If she marries before that age, the money is not granted to her. This plan is restricted to families with annual incomes below Rs 11,000 and no more than two children. A plan that was designed for neighboring Rajasthan in 1993 is similar, but it is linked to having the girl's father or mother undergo sterilization. A serious design flaw of these programs is that they target lower income households. Given the findings of the Ludhiana, India, study cited above (Booth et al. 1994), FSA is practiced more among propertied (nonpoor) people who are completely bypassed by these programs.

DIVERGENT VIEWS ON FSA

Many, but not all, social scientists and other experts view FSA as a serious problem that deserves high priority from international and national policy makers. Those who consider it a serious problem disagree about how policy should seek to address it. This section first presents some of the divided views.[15]

Denial of Its Seriousness

Denial of FSA as a serious social problem often involves statements that FSA is not practiced to a "significant" degree or that it will not have a "significant" effect on the population. Visaria provides an example of this type of denial in her statement, "The analysis presented in this paper suggests that the small fluctuations in the sex ratio of the Indian population cannot by themselves be regarded as cause for great concern about increasing deficit of women. Nor is the sex-selective foeticide likely to alter the numerical balance of sexes in the population to any significant extent" (1994:16–17).

Studies of Chinese data often involve elaborate demonstrations of the insignificance of FSA in comparison to other factors, notably underreporting of female births (discussed above) or adopting out female infants. Johansson and Nygren argue for the adoption explanation and assert that FSA cannot account for a large proportion of the "missing girls" of the 1980s because "the medical technology for early diagnosis of the sex of the fetus to allow for differential abortion was not widely enough available to have had any impact" (1991:843).

Denial of numeric "significance" survives in spite of the fact that social scientists offered early warnings of the potential widespread use of FSA in patriarchal cultures beginning in the late 1970s and early 1980s (Williamson 1978). Since the 1980s, several activist groups have sought to increase awareness of the extent of the problem and to demand legal and other reforms, notably India's Forum against Sex Determination and Sex Pre-Selection, the Bombay Forum for Women's Health, and UNIFEM, an international group addressing the new reproductive technologies in general. At the same time, new research did show that discrimination against girls was a major part of the explanation of unbalanced sex ratios in northern India (Bardhan 1974; Miller 1997a[1981]). During the 1980s, more data accumulated on son preference and daughter neglect in Asia, but they did not attract much global attention until the early 1990s. Two events occurred at this time that helped promote awareness and undermine denial: Chinese census data became available on SRBs and respected economist-philosopher Amartya Sen (1990) published a lead article in *The New York Review of Books* on the "missing millions" of women and girls in Asia.

FSA Will Increase the Value of Women

Some commentators suggest that the practice of FSA is not urgently important because the future scarcity of women will eventually lead to their increased value and enhanced status. This crude "supply and demand" model is apparently very attractive, perhaps especially to people swayed by simpleminded "economic" formulae. For example, a simplistically optimistic editorial published in a prestigious international medical journal, *The Lancet,* comments: "If the use of sex selection were to increase the proportion of boys significantly, women would benefit from the wider choice of marriage partners and would acquire greater social value. The long-term outcome would be an increase in the birth of girls and restoration of balance" (1993:728). Those who argue for this model should consider the patriarchal context in which sheer scarcity is not likely to raise women's status. During the eighteenth century in some villages of northern India, people raised very few or no daughters (Miller 1997a[1981]). Brides were therefore scarce in the northwest, but women's status was not high. In China, the scarcity of females has led to an increase in the kidnapping of girls. Along this line, demographers Tuljapurkar, Li, and Feldman discuss the probability of continued high sex ratios in China's future and comment that over the long term, masculinization of births will "complicate efforts to increase the social and economic status of women and their control over reproductive decisions" (1995:876).

FSA as Preferable to Female Infanticide

Still others evaluate FSA as preferable to female infanticide or to girls being born who are unwanted and mistreated. Current levels of FSA, however, mean that far more females are being aborted than would ever have been born unwanted and treated less favorably than their brothers (Goodkind 1996). With FSA, unwanted daughters who—if allowed to be born—would survive disfavored treatment are being "more efficiently" excluded from the population. FSA, in other words, is not a "replacement" for infanticide or discrimination—it outdoes these forms. Additionally, this position all too easily slides into being one that "accepts" a certain amount of son preference and daughter disfavor and simply compares techniques on the basis of whether they are more or less "humane" toward the unwanted females.

FSA Reduces Population Growth

Another supposedly positive aspect of FSA, though rarely directly stated, is its effect on reducing rates of population growth. "Population bomb" theorists and lay thinkers are so terrified of population growth—especially in the Asian giants of India and China—that they would avoid criticizing the use of FSA because it serves as a quiet way to deal with "overpopulation" (Miller 1994).

FSA Represents Free Choice

The discussion of FSA is further complicated by the divergent views of certain ethicists, feminists, and other commentators concerning the question of "choice" about abortion in general and FSA in particular. Many, if not most, Western feminists regard a woman's free reproductive choice as a right that has been fought hard for in the West and is worth protecting from legal encroachments as to grounds (Renteln 1992). Other views of some feminists and ethicists say that abortion on gender grounds alone is morally wrong (Fletcher and Wertz 1992; Weiss 1995). The question of women's reproductive "freedom" in highly son-preferential cultures bears close attention. Strong son preference and other structural facts of patriarchy limit women's "freedom" to exercise choice even when it appears that they are doing so (Parikh 1990; Rothman 1986). This notion of "illusory choice" is important in relation to FSA in Asia. Is a woman who uses FSA in fact exercising free "choice"? Interviews with the woman might show that she was extremely anxious to have a son, that she voluntarily pursued FSA, and that she was pleased with its positive results. Some argue, then, that she exercised freedom of choice and that to state otherwise is to be "reckless" with the concept of choice itself (Fletcher and Wertz 1992). But if we avoid considering the structural limitations that patriarchy places on women's choices, we deny the fact that a woman in such a context is not "free" to choose to have a daughter instead of a son. She is "free" only to comply with the masculinist reproductive mandate, but she is not free to resist that mandate. Pure reproductive freedom is the complete absence of constraints and structured choice and should, therefore, logically result in equal sex ratios at birth. Conversely, unbal-anced SRBs can be taken as evidence of the lack of reproductive freedom.

BALANCED SEX RATIOS, PUBLIC GOODS, AND HUMAN RIGHTS

At the time of this writing, I know of no country in the world that places FSA high on its policy agenda, though the United Nations included prenatal sex selection as a form of discrimination in its 1994 Programme of Action following the Cairo Conference on Population and Development.[16] If policy experts were to take FSA seriously and place it high on their agendas, what kinds of directions are indicated or counterindicated? Clearly, no single policy will bring an end to FSA, as is the case with any form of massive and blatant discrimination. Legal reforms are an important step, but they must be implemented. Economic reform is required that equalizes female entitlements. Addressing women's job access, unequal pay scales, dowry systems, and legacies is crucial even though strong resistance is to be expected from forces protective of male dominance. A favored solution to gender inequities of many kinds through the decades has been increased levels of education and literacy. Of all these, people would be most likely to agree that progressive laws cannot, at least, increase levels of FSA, even though, if unimplemented, they are unlikely to decrease it.

In terms of economic reforms, most scholars of Indian demography agree that the only clear finding of all studies thus far is that high levels of female labor force participation are correlated with more equal sex ratios (Murthi et al. 1997:370).[17] Thus, any economic policies that reduce female labor force participation should be subject to critical scrutiny. Education is the most controversial factor because research in several contexts in India and Bangladesh reveals that higher levels of parental education are often correlated with more son preference and heightened survival levels of sons compared with that of daughters (Das Gupta 1987; Miller 1997b; Murthi et al. 1997), though this correlation is less apparent in less patriarchal contexts such as southern India (Basu 1992) and the Himalayan region of the far north of India, which typically deviates from patterns in the northern plains region (Cohen 2000; Miller 1997b). These findings mean that a simple policy of investing in education in patriarchal contexts could actually reduce girls' birth and survival relative to boys'.

A Balanced Sex Ratio as a Public Good

In general, however, the massive use of FSA in Asia requires massive amounts of research and informed policy thinking. Perhaps one way to help place the issue of unbalanced sex ratios in a more prominent place in academic research and policy is to see a balanced sex ratio as both a local and a global public good. The concept of a public good refers to something that is widely considered to be of value and should be made available to everyone in order to sustain and improve their quality of life. Economists tend to list things like clean water and air, streetlights, and sewage removal as local public goods. Global public goods include health, peace and security, and environmental and cultural heritage (Kaul et al. 1999).

A balanced sex ratio might be considered as both a local and a global public good that should be promoted and supported by national governments, multinational organizations including businesses, private institutions concerned with human development and welfare, and individual citizens. Why should such large-scale organizations be concerned about FSA? Intriguing studies, one several decades old and some others more recent, point to the need to draw the topic of violence into analyses of unbalanced sex ratios. A cross-cultural analysis of many "tribal" (nonagricultural) societies of the mid–twentieth century shows that male-biased sex ratios are correlated with high levels of intersocietal warfare (Divale and Harris 1976). More recently, a comparison of district-level sex ratios and violence in one state in northern India has revealed the same correlation: where sex ratios are high, violence is more frequent (Oldenburg 1992). A nationwide study of Indian murder rates has also found a strong correlation between high rates of murder and highly masculine sex ratios in district-level populations (Drèze and Khera 2000). Localized male violence toward women in India is another correlate of unbalanced sex ratios (Miller 1999[1992]).

These studies, while few in number and not detailed in terms of what actually occurs at an everyday level in high-violence contexts, suggest the need for further attention to the possibility that patriarchal and territorially aggressive cultures (including contemporary global capitalism) promote the reproduction of many males as boundary protectors and boundary expanders and, therefore, disvalue females and limit their numbers in the population through sex-selective infanticide, fatal neglect, or FSA. Such a distorted demography takes its toll first and most directly on females but also on males, whose survival may be impaired in their adult years through violence.[18] Unbalanced sex ratios can be seen, therefore, as both local and global "public bads," closely related to violence in the home and the public domain.

Unbalanced Sex Ratios as Indicators of Human Rights Violations

Another important future direction is to consider FSA and male-biased sex ratios as human rights issues because of their links to violence. If assurance of personal and public security (freedom from violence) is accepted as a human right, then societies in which FSA is practiced and in which male-biased sex ratios exist are more likely to be societies in which security as a right is not assured. Seeing female-selective abortion in these new ways will challenge cultural anthropologists to refocus future research to take into account global connections and local contexts in reproduction, gender, and violence and to bring their findings to the world of policy makers and activists working for gender equality and greater assurances of personal and public security.

NOTES

1. I take my lead from other cultural anthropologists' comparative analyses of Asian economic, political, and household systems, notably Goody 1976, 1996; and Skinner 1997. British sociologist Elisabeth Croll has recently written a comparative book-length study of discrimination against daughters in Asia (2000). Political scientist Valerie Hudson is also writing comparatively about patriarchal demographics and violence in Asia (two journal articles and a book-length manuscript under review).

2. Because sex-selective abortion in Asian cultures is almost completely directed at aborting female fetuses and preserving male fetuses, I use the specific term *female-selective abortion* instead of the general term *sex-selective abortion*.

3. Female-selective abortion is not practiced by Asian peoples only (Sohoni 1994). It has been documented as occurring for several years in the United States and Canada, though to an undocumented extent. Studies in the United States and Canada have probed opinions on female-selective abortion and people's willingness to seek them (e.g., Gilroy and Steinbacher 1991; Khatamee et al. 1989).

4. Balanced overall sex ratios can conceal the practice of sex-selective infanticide or abortion within families. Skinner's (1993) research on data from the Tokugawa period, between 1600 and 1868, shows that families in Japan practiced either female or male infanticide to achieve reproductive goals for offspring birth order. Mothers preferred a daughter first, and husbands preferred a son first.

5. Journalistic reports do exist, for example, noting that a recently opened ultrasound scanning center in a small Indian city performed 75 scans a month in 1996 with demand reportedly increasing (*Frontline* 1998).

6. Certain regions of India and China have higher SRBs than 115.4 males per 100 females, but their total national SRBs are lower because of averaging in data from regions of the country where FSA is less prominent, for example, Tibet in China and Kerala in India.

7. Scattered reports suggest that FSA is practiced in the United States and Canada and that there is demand for other forms of sex selection such as sperm separation. Occasional newspaper articles over the past decade have reported that some Asian Canadians practice FSA by using services provided in the United States. Dr. John Stephens, a U.S. doctor who operates two clinics near the Canadian border, one in Blaine, Washington, and the other in Buffalo, New York, advertises his ultrasound services, in English and Punjabi, in Canadian newspapers that serve primarily Indian Canadians (*Ms.* 1994b:17). Commuting between his two clinics, he has provided an unknown number of tests. Using the test results, a client may then seek an abortion from some other provider in the United States, presenting a gender-neutral excuse.

8. One anonymous reviewer raised the important question of why some patriarchal contexts are characterized by son preference and daughter disfavor while others, as in some parts of Africa, are not notably son preferential but have other practices that appear to be detrimental to women such as genital cutting. I cannot answer that question, certainly not in this article, but I believe that such broadly comparative "why" questions should impel research in and beyond cultural anthropology of the future.

9. I use the term *culture* to refer to all learned behavior and beliefs, not in the more limited Geertzian sense of symbols, thoughts, and motivations. Thus, culture includes economic, political, social, and ideological aspects of acting and thinking.

10. Care must be taken in applying this general model of patriarchy to any particular cultural context. For example, Spiro (1993) argues that Burmese culture assigns superiority to males in public power roles and in ideology but females dominate economically and in the private political domain of the household. Burmese people are not son preferential, and Burma's sex ratios are not male biased.

11. Son preference and unwanted daughters are not the only or necessary outcomes of patriarchal regimes. What many international feminists and others refer to as female genital mutilation (FGM) in some African cultures is another example of a patriarchally related practice. Why FGM occurs in some cultures and why FSA occurs in others is an important question that calls for even wider comparative analysis than this article attempts.

12. Anecdotal evidence emerges here, too. Starting in the late 1990s, I have heard several urban, educated northern Indians say that they can no longer depend on their sons to take care of them in their old age, especially because of international migration and the high likelihood that sons living in North America, Europe, or Australia may marry non-Indian women and fail to maintain their parental ties. Therefore, these people say that they may have to turn to depending on their daughters instead, a marked change from traditional North Indian kinship norms that prohibit old age care by a daughter.

13. The reluctance of scholars in the United States to consider the possibility of widespread FSA in China was influenced by the politics of research. The U.S. academic community was under considerable indirect pressure to avoid saying things that could be construed as negative by the Chinese government in order to not damage emerging relations between the two countries and opportunities for future U.S. research.

14. Although the sheer availability of prenatal fetal sex testing in patriarchal contexts may promote FSA, one anonymous reviewer raised the question of whether training more women doctors and medical technicians involved in prenatal testing would lower rates of FSA on the assumption that women would be less likely to condone FSA or to advertise FSA services. This question is eminently researchable, though I know of no one who has looked into it. Wertz and Fletcher (1991) conducted an analysis of gender differences in the responses of geneticists in 18 countries to several questions about counseling, such as paternity questions and various kinds of genetic disorders. Although they found significant differences in the responses of male and female geneticists, the study does not include the question of advice about fetal sex determination.

15. For another review of ethical questions related to prenatal sex selection, especially FSA and the effects of legislation to ban it, see Goodkind 1999.

16. In India, and perhaps elsewhere, numerous non-governmental organizations and other local humanitarian groups address FSA and female child discrimination in general. Their work is important, and a synthesis of their approaches and achievements would be helpful.

17. An analysis of the decline in sex ratios in India from 1890 to 1990 claims that women's labor force participation accounts for only a minor part of the change (Mayer 1999). Unfortunately, given the dramatic differences in the definitions of female labor force participation in India's decennial censuses, the attempt to seek correlations between sex ratio and labor force participation over time using census data is futile in the first place.

18. Some commentators take another tack on the negative consequences of FSA for men in terms of the scarcity of future brides. A 1994 article in The *New York Times* discusses the "bleak" situation for many Chinese males who cannot find brides: "The quandary of the lonely Chinese male is evident in the hangdog looks of the young men who gather on Saturday afternoons to watch the passing crowds along Wangfujing Street." One young man is quoted as saying, "This whole generation of Chinese men will become monks. And maybe then the women will feel sorry for us" (1994).

REFERENCES

Anderson, Barbara. 1996. Son Preference and Premature Death in Korea. *The Journal of the International Institute* 4(1).

Banister, Judith. 1996. China's Missing Girls: Provincial Variation in Cause and Effect. Paper presented at the Annual Meeting of the Population Association of America, New Orleans.

Bardhan, Pranab K. 1974. On Life and Death Questions. *Economic and Political Weekly* 9:1293–1303.

Basu, Alaka Malwade. 1992. *Culture, the Status of Women and Demographic Behaviour: Illustrated with the Case of India.* New York: Oxford University Press.

Booth, Beverly E., Manorama M. Verma, and R. Singh Beri. 1994. Fetal Sex Determination in Infants in Punjab, India: Correlations and Implications. *British Medical Journal* 309:1259.

Brambati, Bruno. 1992. Genetic Diagnosis through Chorionic Villus Sampling. In *Genetic Disorders and the Fetus: Diagnosis, Prevention, and Treatment.* Aubrey Milunsky, ed. Pp. 123–154. Baltimore: Johns Hopkins University Press.

Business Week. 1993. An Ultrasound Foothold in Asia. *Business Week*, November 8: 68–69.

Cain, Mead. 1981. Risk Insurance: Perspectives on Fertility and Agrarian Change in India and Bangladesh. *Population and Development Review* 7:435–474.

———. 1986. The Consequences of Reproductive Failure: Dependence, Mobility, and Mortality among the Elderly of Rural South Asia. *Population Studies* 40:375–388.

———. 1993. Patriarchal Structures and Demographic Change. In *Women's Position and Demographic Change.* Nora Federici, Karen Oppenheim Mason, and Søvi Sogner, eds. Pp. 43–60. Oxford University Press.

Chang, Ming-cheng. 1994. Sex Preference and Sex Ratio at Birth: The Case of Taiwan. Paper presented at the Smposium of Issues Related to Sex Preferences for Children in the Rapidly Changing Demographic Dynamics in Asia, Seoul, November 21–24.

The Christian Science Monitor. 1995. A Rush to Rob the Cradle—of Girls. *The Christian Science Monitor,* August 2.

Chunkath, Sheela Rani, and V. B. Athreya. 1997. Female Infanticide in Tamil Nadu. *Economic and Political Weekly,* April 26: WS21–WS28.

Cohen, Alex. 2000. Excess Female Mortality in India: The Case of Himachal Pradesh. *American Journal of Public Health* 90:1369–1371.

Croll, Elisabeth. 2000. *Endangered Daughters: Discrimination and Development in Asia.* New York: Routledge.

Das Gupta, Monica. 1987. Selective Discrimination against Female Children in Rural Punjab, North India. *Population and Development Review* 13:77–100.

Deutsche Presse-Agentur. 1996. *India Bans Sex-Determination Tests.* Deutsche Presse-Agentur, January 10.

Divale, William, and Marvin Harris. 1976. Population, Warfare, and the Male Supremacist Complex. *American Anthropologist* 78:521–538.

Drèze, Jean, and Reetika Khera. 2000. Crime, Gender, and Society in India: Insights from Homicide Data. *Population and Development Review* 26:335–352.

Dyson, Tim, and Mick Moore. 1983. On Kinship Structure, Female Autonomy, and Demographic Behavior in India. *Population and Development Review* 9:35–60.

The Economist. 1989. Where Have All the Flowers Gone? *The Economist* 313:42.

———. 1995. India's Rich Little Poor Girls. *The Economist* 334:40.

Elias, Sherman, and Joe Leigh Simpson. 1992. Amniocentesis. In *Genetic Disorders and the Fetus: Diagnosis, Prevention, and Treatment.* Aubrey Milunsky, ed. Pp. 33–57. Baltimore: Johns Hopkins University Press.

Entwisle, Barbara, Gail E. Henderson, Susan E. Short, Jill Bouma, and Zhai Fengying. 1995. Gender and Family Businesses in Rural China. *American Sociological Review* 60:36–57.

Fletcher, John C., and Dorothy C. Wertz. 1992. Ethics and Prenatal Diagnosis: Problems, Positions, and Proposed Guidelines. In *Genetic Disorders and the Fetus:*

Diagnosis, Prevention, and Treatment. Aubrey Milunsky, ed. Pp. 823–857. Baltimore: Johns Hopkins University Press.

Frontline. 1998. *Frontline,* magazine of the Hindu.

George, Sabu M., Rajaratnam Abel, and Barbara D. Miller. 1992. Female Infanticide in Rural South India. *Economic and Political Weekly,* May 30: 1153–1156.

George, Sabu M., and Ranbir S. Dahiya. 1998. Female Foeticide in Rural Haryana. *Economic and Political Weekly,* August 8: 2191–2198.

Gilroy, Faith D., and Roberta Steinbacher. 1991. Sex Selection Technology Utilization: Further Implications for Sex Ratio Imbalance. *Social Biology* 38:285–288.

Goodkind, Daniel. 1996. On Substituting Sex Preference Strategies in East Asia: Does Prenatal Sex Selection Reduce Postnatal Discrimination? *Population and Development Review* 22:111–125.

———. 1999. Should Prenatal Sex Selection Be Restricted? Ethical Questions and Their Implications for Research and Policy. *Population Studies* 53:49–61.

Goody, Jack. 1976. *Production and Reproduction: A Comparative Study of the Domestic Domain.* New York: Cambridge University Press.

———. 1996. Comparing Family Systems in Europe and Asia: Are There Different Sets of Rules? *Population and Development Review* 22:1–20.

Gu, Baochang, and Yongping Li. 1994. Sex Ratio at Birth and Son Preference in China. Paper presented at the Symposium on Issues Related to Sex Preferences for Children in the Rapidly Changing Demographic Dynamics in Asia, Seoul, November 21–24.

Hong, Moon Sik. 1994. Boy Preference and Imbalance in Sex Ratio in South Korea. Paper presented at the Symposium on Issues Related to Sex Preferences for Children in the Rapidly Changing Demographic Dynamics in Asia, Seoul, November 21–24.

Johansson, Sten, and Ola Nygren. 1991. The Missing Girls of China: A New Demographic Account. *Population and Development Review* 17:35–51.

Karim, Mehtab. 1994. Sex Preference in Pakistan. Paper presented at the Symposium on Issues Related to Sex Preferences for Children in the Rapidly Changing Demographic Dynamics in Asia, Seoul, November 21–24.

Kaul, Inge, Isabelle Grunberg, and Marc A. Stern, eds. 1999. *Global Public Goods: International Cooperation in the 21st Century.* New York: Oxford University Press.

Khatamee, Masood A., Anayansi Leinberger-Sica, Pater Matos, and Alvin C. Wesley. 1989. Sex Preselection in New York City: Who Chooses Which Sex and Why. *International Journal of Fertility* 34:353–354.

The Lancet. 1990. Clinical Ultrasound in Developing Countries. *The Lancet* 336:1225–1226.

———. 1993. Jack or Jill? *The Lancet* 341:727–728.

———. 1994. Legislation on Prenatal Sex-Determination in India. *The Lancet* 344:399.

Makinson, Carolyn. 1986. *Sex Differentials in Infant and Child Mortality in Egypt.* Ph.D. dissertation, Princeton University.

Mayer, Peter. 1999. India's Falling Sex Ratio. *Population and Development Review* 25:323–343.

Miller, Barbara D. 1984. Daughter Neglect, Women's Work, and Marriage: Pakistan and Bangladesh Compared. *Medical Anthropology* 8:109–126.

———. 1994. Unwanted Daughters in Northwest India: The Convergence of Household Interests and National Population Policy. In *Unwanted Pregnancies and Public Policy: An International Perspective.* Hector Correa, ed. Pp. 193–207. New York: Nova Science Publishers.

———. 1997a[1981]. *The Endangered Sex: Neglect of Female Children in Rural North India.* New Delhi: Oxford University Press.

———. 1997b. Social Class, Gender and Intrahousehold Food Allocations to Children in South Asia. *Social Science and Medicine* 44:1685–1695.

———. 1999[1992]. Wife Beating in India: Variations on a Theme. In *To Have and to Hit: Cultural Perspectives on Wife Beating.* Dorothy Counts, Judith Brown, and Jacquelyn Campbell, eds. Pp. 203–215. Champaign: University of Illinois Press.

Min, Han, and J. S. Eades. 1995. Brides, Bachelors and Brokers: The Marriage Market in Rural Anhui in an Era of Economic Reform. *Modern Asian Studies* 29:841–869.

Ms. 1994a. Right End, Wrong Means. *Ms.* 5:16–17.

———. 1994b. Unsound Ultrasound. *Ms.* 4:17.

Murthi, Mamta, Anne-Catherine Guio, and Jean Drèze. 1997. Mortality, Fertility and Gender Bias in India: A District-Level Analysis. In *Indian Development: Selected Regional Perspectives.* Jean Dreze and Amartya Sen, eds. Pp. 357–406. Delhi: Oxford University Press.

The New York Times. 1994. Chinese Bias against Girls Creates Glut of Bachelors. The *New York Times,* August 16.

Obermeyer, Carla M. 1996. Fertility Norms and Son Preferences in Morocco and Tunisia: Does Women's Status Matter? *Journal of Biosocial Science* 28:57–72.

Oldenburg, Philip. 1992. Sex Ratio, Son Preference and Violence in India: A Research Note. *Economic and Political Weekly* 27:2657–2662.

Parikh, Manju. 1990. Sex-Selective Abortions in India: Parental Choice or Sexist Discrimination? *Feminist Issues* 10:19–32.

Park, C. B., and N. H. Cho. 1995. Consequences of Son Preference in a Low Fertility Society: The Imbalance of Sex Ratio at Birth. *Population and Development Review* 21:59–84.

Renteln, Alison Dundes. 1992. Sex Selection and Reproductive Freedom. *Women's Studies International Forum* 15:405–426.

Rothman, Barbara. 1986. *The Tentative Pregnancy: Prenatal Diagnosis and the Future of Motherhood.* New York: Viking.

Sachar, R. K., J. Verma, V. Prakash, A. Chopra, R. Adlaka, and R. Sofat. 1990. Sex-Selective Fertility Control: An Outrage. *The Journal of Family Welfare* 36:30–35.

Sen, Amartya. 1981. *Poverty and Famines: An Essay on Entitlement and Deprivation.* New York: Oxford University Press.

———. 1990. More Than 100 Million Women Are Missing. *The New York Review of Books* 37:61–66.

Skinner, G. William. 1993. Conjugal Power in Tokugawa Families: A Matter of Life or Death. In *Sex and Gender Hierarchies.* Barbara D. Miller, ed. Pp. 236–270. New York: Cambridge University Press.

———. 1997. Family Systems and Demographic Processes. In *Anthropological Demography: Toward a New Synthesis.* David I. Kertzer and Tom Fricke, eds. Pp. 53–95. Chicago: University of Chicago Press.

Sohoni, Neera Kuckreja. 1994. Where Are All the Girls? *Ms.* 5:96.

Spiro, Melford E. 1993. Gender Hierarchy in Burma: Cultural, Social, and Psychological Dimensions. In *Sex and Gender Hierarchies.* Barbara D. Miller, ed. Pp. 316–333. New York: Cambridge University Press.

Steinbacher, Roberta, and Faith D. Gilroy. 1996. Technology for Sex Selection: Current Status and Utilization. *Psychological Reports* 79:728–730.

Tuljapurkar, Shripad, Nan Li, and Marcus W. Feldman. 1995. High Sex Ratios in China's Future. *Science* 267:874–876.

U.S. News and World Report. 1989. The Old Sexism in the New China. *U.S. News and World Report* 106:16.

Visaria, Leela. 1994. Deficit of Women, Son Preference and Demographic Transition in India. Paper presented at the Symposium on Issues Related to Sex Preferences for Children in the Rapidly Changing Demographic Dynamics in Asia, Seoul, November 21–24.

Visaria, Pravin. 1967. Sex Ratio at Birth in Territories with a Relatively Complete Registration. *Eugenics Quarterly* 14:132–142.

Weiss, Gail. 1995. Sex-Selective Abortion: A Relational Approach. *Hypatia* 10:202–217.

Wertz, Dorothy C., and John C. Fletcher. 1991. Ethical Decision Making in Medical Genetics: Women as Patients and Practitioners in Eighteen Nations. In *Healing Technology: Feminist Perspectives.* Kathryn Strother Ratcliff, Myra Marx Ferree, Gail O. Mellow, Barbara Drygulski Wright, Glenda D. Price, Kim Yanoshik, and Margie S. Freston, eds. Pp. 221–244. Ann Arbor: University of Michigan Press.

———. 1998. Ethical and Social Issues in Prenatal Sex Selection: A Survey of Geneticists in 37 Nations. *Social Science and Medicine* 46:255–273.

Westley, Sidney B.. 1995. Evidence Mounts for Sex-Selective Abortion in Asia. *Asia-Pacific Population and Policy* 34.

Whyte, Martin King. 1993. Wedding Behavior and Family Strategies in Chengdu. In *Chinese Families in the Post-Mao Era.* Deborah Davis and Stevan Harrell, eds. Pp. 189–218. Berkeley: University of California Press.

Williamson, Nancy. 1976. *Sons or Daughters: A Cross-Cultural Survey of Parental Preferences.* Beverly Hills: Sage Publications.

———. 1978. Boys or Girls? Parents' Preferences and Sex Control. *Population Bulletin* 33:1–35.

Zeng Yi, Tu Ping, Gu Baochang, Xu Yi, Li Bohua, and Li Yongping. 1993. Causes and Implications of the Recent Increase in the Reported Sex Ratio at Birth in China. *Population and Development Review* 19:283–302.

■ ■ ■ ■ ■ ■ ■ ■ ■

51 WOMEN FROM POLYGAMOUS AND MONOGAMOUS MARRIAGES IN AN OUT-PATIENT PSYCHIATRIC CLINIC

Alean Al-Krenawi

This selection considers the effect of living in patriarchal cultures on women's mental health, particularly for Bedouin Arab women who are first wives in a polygamous marriage. It shows that health issues need to be considered in a family and social context. By exploring women's living conditions in relation to their marriage relationships, the analysis connects with the previous selection on the social and politico-economic forces that induce people to favor sons over daughters in patriarchal cultures.

The aim of the study is to link specific psychological symptoms to structural features, socioeconomic conditions, and cultural factors related to Bedouin marriage relationships. Al-Krenawi explains that first marriages are often arranged or are the result of kin exchanges, whereas subsequent marriages often involve a greater element of choice and love. Women in polygamous marriages are much more likely than women in monogamous marriages to live in unrecognized villages without services. All women live in a gender-segregated, patriarchal culture in which their status depends directly on being married and rearing sons. Having too many daughters is considered a failure for which a woman's husband may take another wife.

Although wives in both polygamous and monogamous marriages report a variety of psychological symptoms at similar rates, a much larger percentage of the former report loneliness, low self-esteem, and symptoms of anxiety. The latter measures are linked to women's main explanations for their husbands' second marriage, which are having had too many daughters and being perceived as old and less attractive. The women also report poorer-quality relationships with their husbands, especially on the arrival of the second wife, and feeling neglected on all levels from the economic to the intimate. The impacts extend to their children, who receive reduced social and economic resources. This only worsens the psychological distress of the mothers, illustrating the wide impact of marriage systems on the health and well-being of entire families.

Questions to keep in mind

What roles, if any, do sex and gender play in the mental health issues considered in this article?

What are some connections between women's loneliness and self-esteem and the reasons they believe their husbands marry a second wife?

Why do you think there is such a large difference in the frequency of polygamous and monogamous wives living in unrecognized villages? How might this relate to their respective economic well-being?

What are some possible mental health impacts of marriage systems in other cultures, including your own?

Source: Reproduced with permission from Al-Krenawi, Alean. "Women from Polygamous and Monogamous Marriages in an Out-Patient Psychiatric Clinic." *Transcultural Psychiatry* 38(2):187–199. Copyright (©McGill University, 2001), by permission of Sage Publications Ltd.

Polygamy has long been associated with family stress and mental illness among women (Al-Issa, 1990; Al-Krenawi, 1998, 1999b; Al-Krenawi, Graham, & Al-Krenawi, 1997; Makanjuola, 1987). The practice can lead to co-wife jealousy, competition and unequal distribution of household resources (Al-Krenawi, 1998; Borgerhoff Mulder, 1992; Kilbride & Kilbride, 1990; Ware, 1979), creating acrimony between co-wives and between the children of different wives (Al-Krenawi, 1998; Ware, 1979). A greater prevalence of mental disorders has been found among women in polygamous than monogamous marriages (Leighton et al., 1963); and, relative to their number in the general population, higher proportions of women in polygamous marriages are psychiatric out-patients (Chaleby, 1987) and in-patients (Chaleby, 1985). Among psychiatric patients, polygamous marriage is associated with depressive disorders, anxiety states (Ghubash, Hamdi, & Bebbington, 1992), depression and somatization disorders (El-Islam, 1975). This study contributes further to the literature by comparing expressed symptomatologies and marital relationship satisfaction among a convenience sample of Bedouin-Arab women who were senior wives in a polygamous marriage, and those who were sole wives in a monogamous marriage. Those in polygamous marriages were also asked to identify perceived causes leading to the husband's remarriage. All subjects were out-patients in the psychiatric department of a medical clinic in Beer-Sheva, Israel.

POLYGAMY

Anthropologists typically define polygamy as "a marital relationship involving multiple wives" (Kottak, 1978, cited in Low, 1988, p. 189). There are three types of polygamy, but only the first is of concern in this article: polygyny (one husband is married to two or more wives; hereafter referred to as polygamy), polyandry (one wife married to two or more husbands) and polygynandry (a group marriage scenario in which two or more wives are simultaneously married to two or more husbands) (Sinha & Bharat, 1985, p. 697; Valsiner, 1989, p. 69). Of the three forms, the first is the most common worldwide. It is important to distinguish between wealth-increasing polygamy, in which

women's domestic labor generates wealth, and sororal polygamy, of concern in this article, in which the husband's wealth permits more than one wife (White, 1988). Polygamy is common in Africa, Asia, the Middle East and Oceana, but is also known to occur in western societies such as Europe and North America (Altman & Ginat, 1996; Broude, 1994). Within practicing cultures, attitudes toward polygamy vary within and between the sexes (see Adams & Mburugu, 1994; Low, 1988; White, 1988). Polygamous wives may live together, although they most commonly have independent households, in which each lives with her children (Broude, 1994, pp. 207–208). A senior wife is defined as any married woman "who was followed by another wife in the marriage." A "junior wife" is "the most recent wife joining a marriage" (Chaleby, 1985, p. 57). Among the Bedouin-Arab, like other Arab cultures, first-time marriages are commonly arranged by parents/parent substitutes, or are consanguineous or exchanges (where two men are married to each other's sister) (Al-Krenawi et al., 1997; Chaleby, 1985; El-Islam, 1989). Subsequent marriages are associated with both love and with greater propensity toward choice. Hence, second and subsequent wives often experience favored status with respect to economic resources, social support and attention (Al-Krenawi, 1998; Al-Krenawi et al., 1997).

BEDOUIN-ARABS

The Bedouin-Arab have lived in the Negev region for two millennia (*Hebrew Encyclopaedia*, 1954) and are one national, linguistic, political and geographic entity that ought to be considered as distinct from other non-Bedouin-Arab communities in Israel, and distinct from, although related to, Bedouin-Arab communities in other countries. Traditionally, the Bedouin-Arab, who are Muslim, were a nomadic people, but today they are undergoing a rapid and dramatic process of transition and change caused by sedentarization, urbanization and the influences of modernization. Fifty six percent of the Negev's 120,000 Bedouin-Arab already live in villages, whereas 44% still live in unrecognized villages and tent communities without basic infrastructures or services (Al-Krenawi, 1999a).

The society has been described as "high context" (Hall, 1976). Thus, both a slower pace of societal change and a higher sense of social stability predominate, and the collective is emphasized over the individual. To a considerable extent, social status, safety from economic hardship, and potential for personal development continue to be founded upon tribal identity. The larger the tribe, the more powerful it is in the Bedouin-Arab status hierarchy. Each tribe has a leader (*sheik*), and major decisions are made by forums of male elders representing the several extended families that constitute the tribe (Abu-Khusa, 1994; Marks, 1974).

Bedouin-Arab society is highly gender-segregated and patriarchal. Men lead the household and dominate the polity and economy. Women's physical and intellectual capacities tend to be devalued (Al-Sadawi, 1985; Attir, 1985; Chaleby, 1985; El-Islam, 1975), and their social status is strongly contingent upon being married and rearing children, especially boys. Women rarely leave the home unescorted, devote most of their time to family care, and tend not to have careers outside the home (Al-Krenawi, Maoz, & Reicher, 1994; Mass & Al-Krenawi, 1994). The culture controls women through such constructs as family honor, shame, female virginity, female sexuality, and, in some instances, female genital mutilation (Al-Krenawi & Graham, 1999; Al-Sadawi, 1985; Shalhoub-Kevorkian, 1997). A divorced woman's marital prospects are usually restricted to becoming the second wife of a married man, or the wife of a widower or of an older man (Al-Krenawi & Graham, 1998; Brhoom, 1987; Hays & Zouari, 1995).

METHOD

Setting and Sample

The study was conducted in the psychiatric clinic of the Soroka Medical Center, the main regional hospital in the Negev desert region of Israel. The clinic has a present catchment area of nearly 300,000 inhabitants, including the 120,000 Bedouin-Arabs of the Negev (Al-Krenawi, 1999a). The clinic mainly receives patients who are referred by general practitioners (GPs) or fam-

ily physicians working in community primary care clinics, the emergency room in Soroka hospital, and by privately practicing physicians. All patient-research subjects were referred by GPs, working in a community medical center serving Bedouin-Arab peoples. It should be noted that all Bedouin-Arabs of the Negev region belong to this psychiatric clinic of Soroka, regardless of their place of domicile.

A convenience sample of 92 Bedouin-Arab women newly referred to the clinic with a non-psychotic diagnosis was interviewed. Diagnoses included neurotic depression, anxiety, family problems, phobic disorders, conversion reaction and somatoform disorders. These diagnoses are considered reliable, although it should be noted that they were made by Jewish psychiatrists, most of whom were recent immigrants from Russia, and who were therefore unfamiliar with the patients' culture, language and religion. The sample was divided into two categories: senior wives in polygamous marriages (two wives only), women whose husbands had married a second wife within the last two years ($N = 53$); and a comparison group of wives in monogamous marriages ($N = 39$). Gwanfogbe, Schumm, Smith, and Furrow (1997) found that junior wives in rural Cameroon had higher life satisfaction than their senior wife counterparts, but older senior wives were more satisfied with marriage than were younger senior wives. Thus, the present study controlled for recency of the husband's second marriage (all occurring within the last two years) and senior wife status (all women in polygamous marriages were senior wives).

Procedure

Data were collected by the author over a three-month period in the summer of 1994, using a semi-structured, open-ended questionnaire written in an Arabic dialect familiar to the Bedouin-Arab population. Patient files were also consulted to exclude psychotic patients from the subject pool. Standard academic procedures of subject consent were followed. The questionnaire sought the following information:

1. Social demographic variables, such as age, education, employment, domicile and number of children. The subjects also were

asked about their economic situation, indicating poor (1) to excellent (5) on a 5-point Likert scale.

2. The perceived relationships between the wives and husbands using a 5-point Likert scale indicating poor (1) to excellent (5).

3. The perceived reasons for the husband's remarriage (asked of women in polygamous marriages only).

4. Major presenting symptoms, as described by the subjects. The subjects were asked to described their symptoms as they wished. Symptoms were not listed for them, and no instrument was used for this purpose. While the subjects were describing their symptoms they complained of symptoms that reflected their sense of self-esteem. Because of the level of the subjects' education, the questions were read for them, and explanations and clarifications of the questions were provided when they were needed.

RESULTS

Table 51.1 shows the differences between the two groups. The mean age for polygamous subjects was 31.9 years ($SD = 4.55$) and for monogamous women, 27.0 years ($SD = 4.34$; $t = 5.225$, $p < .0001$). There were no significant differences in the level of education between the two groups: ($M = 3.88$, $SD = 2.69$) for polygamous and monogamous ($M = 3.66$, $SD = 1.56$) women. None of the

polygamous women and only 2.5% of the monogamous women worked outside their homes, in accordance with Bedouin-Arab strictures on women's non-domestic labor. Women from polygamous marriages reported more economic problems than monogamous women ($M = 2.88$, $SD = 0.800$) versus ($M = 2.15$, $SD = 0.960$; $t = 3.98$, $p < .001$). Thus, there are economic consequences of polygamy. As shown in Table 51.1, 51% of polygamous women live in unrecognized villages (villages not recognized by the Israeli authorities as official settlements), compared with 23.1% of monogamous women. The mean number of children for polygamous women was 6.132 ($SD = 2.88$) and for monogamous women 5.07 ($SD = 1.47$; $t = 2.21$, $p < .05$).

Table 51.2 summarizes the major symptoms presented by the subjects. Low self-esteem was described by subjects in Arabic by phrases such as "I feel I am worth nothing," "I am not satisfied with myself," "I feel that I failed in my life" and "I feel that I am not equal to the rest of the women in the Bedouin-Arab community." Symptoms such as nervousness and somatization were frequent among the two groups. The women expressed their difficulties through various bodily ailments, using cultural terminology such as *colo boga'a* ("the pain swims in my body").

Table 51.1   Socio-Demographic Characteristics of the Sample

	Polygamy	Monogamy
Age (years)[***]	31.9	27.0
Education (years)	3.88	3.66
Economic situation[*]	2.88	2.15
Working outside of the house	0%	2.5%
Unrecognized villages	51%	23.1%
Villages	49%	76.9%
Number of children[***] (mean)	6.13	5.07

[*] $p < .05$; [***] $p < 0.001$.

Table 51.2   Frequency (%) of Symptoms among Senior Wives from Polygamous and Monogamous Families

Symptoms	Monogamy ($n = 39$)	Polygamy ($n = 53$)
Somatization	89.74	86.79
Nervous	89.74	86.79
Bad dreams[***]	97.43	45.28
Feeling fearful	7.69	16.98
Losing weight[*]	17.9	20.7
Pain in the chest[***]	17.9	86.8
Poor appetite[**]	89.7	66
Trouble remembering things[***]	92.3	60.3
Loneliness[***]	12.8	64.1
Shortness of breath[*]	12.8	35.8
Bad thoughts[***]	15.3	62.2
Hopelessness about the future[*]	15.3	33.9
Low self-esteem[***]	7.7	58.4

[*] $p < .05$; [**] $p < 0.01$; [***] $p < 0.0001$.

There were differences between the two groups on most of the symptoms with women in polygamous marriages generally reporting more despair. Of the polygamous subjects, 58.4%, compared with 7.7% of monogamous subjects, described feelings of low self-esteem (chi-squared = 28.11, df = 1, $p < .001$); a sense of loneliness was expressed by 64.1% of polygamous respondents, compared with 12.8% of monogamous subjects (chi-squared = 26.359, df = 1, $p < .001$).

Four main situations were described by polygamous subjects when they were asked to provide their perceived reasons that led their husbands to marry a second wife: (1) an exchange marriage ($n = 23$), in which two men are married to each other's sister; (2) the number of daughters the first wife had had ($n = 10$); (3) the age of the first wife, i.e. the idea that the husband considered her "old" ($n = 14$); and (4) other ($n = 6$), including situations in which the husband is persuaded to marry a woman from his extended family. When someone from another tribe considered by the extended family to be unsuitable or inferior wants to marry one of their women, the extended family tries to find a man from within the extended family or the tribe to marry her instead. By accepting the marriage, the man solves a family problem. Another

example is when a woman from the extended family becomes older and is still not married; in this case a married man may accept her as a wife in order to protect the family's honor.

Of those subjects with low self-esteem, 71% gave reason 2 (number of daughters) as the motivation for the husband taking a new wife; 100% of those who gave reason 3 (believe that their husband thinks they are old) reported low self-esteem (chi-squared = 34.47, df = 3, $p < .001$; see Table 51.3). All the women, regardless of the reasons for the remarriage of their husbands, reported somatic distress. It is culturally acceptable in Bedouin-Arab society, like other rural and relatively illiterate populations, for individuals to express their emotional difficulties through physical symptoms over which the person is assumed to have no control (Al-Krenawi, 1999a; El-Islam & Abu-Dagga, 1992; Marsella, Sartorius, Jablensky, & Fenton, 1985; Racy, 1985).

There were significant differences between the two groups in the perceived quality of relationship with the husbands, with polygamous respondents reporting poorer relationships ($M = 1.849$) versus ($M = 3.025$), ($F(1,90) = 39.004$, $p < .001$, $MSE = 31.102$). In addition, subjects said that they were now neglected by their husbands. Typical state-

Table 51.3 Relationship Between Women's Symptoms and Reasons for Husbands' Remarriage

Symptoms (%)	Reason for remarriage			
	Exchange ($n = 23$)	Number of girls ($n = 10$)	Woman's age ($n = 14$)	Other ($n = 6$)
Somatization	94	93	86	73
Nervous[*]	6	0	0	0
Bad dreams[*]	6	0	0	0
Feeling fearful	12	7	14	27
Losing weight	18	21	14	27
Pain in the chest	100	79	86	87
Poor appetite[*]	6	0	0	0
Trouble remembering things[*]	94	0	0	100
Loneliness[**]	94	14	0	100
Shortness of breath[**]	0	86	100	0
Bad thoughts[**]	100	0	14	100
Hopelessness[**]	6	79	86	0
Low self-esteem[**]	0	71	100	0

[*] $p < .01$; [**] $p < 0.001$.

ments from women of polygamous marriages were: "We are like divorced women. Nobody cares for us," "I consider myself a widow," "Since my husband married his second wife, for me he is dead," "Officially we have husbands, but in fact we have none." Some of the subjects complained that their husbands did not visit them and left them alone to deal with their children's problems and needs. These responses clearly indicate that these women feel neglected by their husbands physically, sexually, emotionally and instrumentally.

DISCUSSION

The socio-demographic characteristics of the sample revealed significant differences between the groups of women from polygamous and monogamous marriages in terms of age, economic situation and number of children. The women in polygamous marriages tended to be older, poorer and had more children. They were also more likely to come from unrecognized villages. All of these factors may have contributed to the mental health difficulties that the women of polygamous marriages reported.

In general, women from both types of marriages reported a wide variety of symptoms and comparably high incidences of somatization, nervousness, poor appetite and trouble remembering. Women in monogamous marriages reported a greater frequency of bad dreams, although close to half of the polygamous respondents also experienced bad dreams. There was a higher prevalence of various symptoms among polygamous respondents, including two of particular interest: low self-esteem and loneliness.

One of the more frequently cited definitions of self-esteem points to its psychosocial implications. Self-esteem is "the condition in which an individual feels 'good enough' and is a person of worth. Not unlike self-acceptance, an individual with high self-esteem has self-respect, feels worthy, does not consider himself or herself better or worse than others, recognizes personal limitations, and expects to experience personal growth and improvement over time" (Rosenberg, 1979; Rosenberg, Schooler, Schoenbach, & Rosenberg, 1995). There was a relationship between women's report

that their husband's reason for taking a second wife was the high number of female children and their own low self-esteem. In Bedouin-Arab society, women's social status is particularly elevated by bearing and raising male children who will carry on the husband's family name; female children are considered less prestigious (Abu-Lughod, 1985; Al-Sadawi, 1985). Sons contribute to a woman's social status throughout her life, and also contribute to her economic well-being. Thus, the presence of boys and the expectations of future good fortune, are inextricably linked. The culture deems a low number of sons, or an inability to have sons, as always the fault of the mother, not the father. This construction gives the husband leverage to marry a second wife. The inability to have a sufficient number of sons, and the husband's remarriage, in effect are double assaults on the senior wife's social status and sense of self (Al-Krenawi, 1999b).

Polygamous respondents who thought that they were perceived as old by their husbands also reported low self-esteem. Feminine youth is highly esteemed within Bedouin culture. In a general sense, like those in other cultures (Chaleby, 1985, 1987), respondents whose husbands took a second wife perceived themselves as having failed to meet their husband's and their community's expectations of a successful wife. The impact, therefore, is two-fold, involving both the immediate level of the personal and the broader levels of the family, extended family, and community (Al-Krenawi, 1998, 1999b).

Respondents from polygamous marriages reported poor relationships with their husbands. Polygamous women stated that they considered themselves as divorced women or widows; as one woman put it. "Since my husband married a second wife, for me he is dead." This is a culturally acceptable way for a woman to say that she has no sexual relationship with her husband. Many commented that their spousal relationships worsened after the husband's remarriage to a second wife. As is common cross-culturally (Topouzis, 1985), the senior wife in Bedouin families typically receives fewer economic resources and less emotional support from her husband (Al-Krenawi, 1998). The junior wife is invariably younger than her senior counterpart, and the husband's second marriage, unlike the first, could well be based on love, rather than an arranged, exchange or consanguineous union. These factors could also contribute to the senior wife's low self-esteem and marital dissatisfaction. Moreover, frequent, and often intense, competition and jealousy between the co-wives, and between the children of each wife, was widely described. This acrimony, in turn, could exacerbate marital tensions (Al-Krenawi, 1998; Al-Krenawi & Lightman, 2000).

Not surprisingly, circumstances encouraged polygamous respondents to withdraw from their social networks—or lead the networks to withdraw from them, particularly the husband or those closely associated with him. These factors explain, in part, polygamous respondents' frequent report of loneliness. A significant number of women who were lonely reported that theirs was an exchange marriage (in which two men are married to each other's sister). Many of these cases, in fact, were instigated by the woman's brother, who had taken on a second wife. The woman's husband had then experienced family pressure to do likewise, in order to maintain symmetry between the two families and hence pride within the brother's family. The women invariably experienced pressure, tension and decreased emotional support from her husband's family. Indeed, polygamous respondents had a significantly higher prevalence of bad thoughts (anxiety) and pain in the chest (understood in the Arab idiom as emotional distress) (Al-Krenawi, 1999a; El-Islam & Abu-Dagga, 1992). These dynamics, compounded by the woman's inability to resolve the sources of her problems, could reinforce feelings of isolation, hopelessness and loneliness.

The pressures experienced by polygamous respondents affect their children. Many women expressed anxiety regarding decreased economic and social resources for their children. Many also noted increased stresses between children and between mother and children. Not surprisingly, most respondents divulged feelings of hopelessness. Mothers' low self-esteem was associated with both psychological and interpersonal problems. Low parental self-esteem is known to be associated with children's behavioral problems (Finken & Amato, 1993) and children from polygamous families tend to have lower academic achievement and greater behavioral and social adjustment problems (Al-Krenawi & Lightman, 2000; Cherian, 1990;

Eapen, Al-Gazali, Bin-Othman, & Abu-Saleh, 1998).

CONCLUSION

Future research could elaborate the implications of the present findings to health professional practice. Practitioners need to appreciate the significance of polygamous marriage to women's mental health, particularly in terms of self-esteem and a sense of loneliness, as well as the interpersonal effects on senior wives and their children. From a systemic perspective, the second marriage upsets the equilibrium within the immediate and extended family systems. Moreover, these same structures continue to influence the women's well-being.

It is important to consider strategies for empowering women in polygamous marriages. One leverage point to motivate husbands is the children's well-being, because his social status and the children's successful functioning are interrelated (Al-Krenawi, 1998; Al-Krenawi et al., 1997). Change may also occur through educating women, the wider communities in which polygamy is practiced, and the helping professionals who provide services within these communities. Above all, polygamy should be reframed not as a deficiency of senior wives, as it is conceived by many polygamous respondents, but as a social practice that has deep and long-lasting negative implications for women and their children.

REFERENCES

Abu-Khusa, A. (1994). *The tribes of Beer-Sheva.* Amman: Al-Matbah Al-Wataniah. [In Arabic.]

Abu-Lughod, L. (1985). A community of secrets: The separate world of Bedouin women. *Signs: A Journal of Women in Culture and Society, 10*(4), 635–657.

Adams, B., & Mburugu, E. (1994). Kikuyu bride wealth and polygyny today. *Journal of Comparative Family Studies, 25*(2), 159–166.

Al-Issa, I. (1990). Culture and mental illness in Algeria. *International Journal of Social Psychiatry, 36*(3), 230–240.

Al-Krenawi, A. (1998). Family therapy with a multi-parental/multispousal family. *Family Process, 37*(1), 65–82.

Al-Krenawi, A. (1999a). Explanation of mental health symptoms by the Bedouin-Arabs of the Negev. *International Journal of Social Psychiatry, 45*(1), 56–64.

Al-Krenawi, A. (1999b). Women of polygamous marriages in primary health care centers. *Contemporary Family Therapy, 21*(3), 417–430.

Al-Krenawi, A., & Graham, J. R. (1998). Divorce among Muslim Arab in Israel. *Journal of Divorce and Remarriage, 29*(3/4), 103–119.

Al-Krenawi, A., & Graham, J. R. (1999). Social work practice and female genital mutilation. *Social Development Issue, 21*(1), 29–36.

Al-Krenawi, A., Graham, J. R., & Al-Krenawi, S. (1997). Social work practice with polygamous families. *Child and Adolescent Social Work Journal, 14*(6), 445–458.

Al-Krenawi, A., & Lightman, E. (2000). Learning achievement, social adjustment, and family conflict among Bedouin-Arab children from polygamous and monogamous families. *Journal of Social Psychology, 140*(3), 345–355.

Al-Krenawi, A., Maoz, B., & Reicher, B. (1994). Familial and cultural issues in the brief strategic treatment of Israeli Bedouin. *Family Systems Medicine, 12*(4), 415–425.

Al-Sadawi, N. (1985). Growing up female in Egypt. In E. W. Fernea (Ed.), *Women and the family in the Middle East: New voices of change* (pp. 111–120). Austin: University of Texas Press.

Altman, I., & Ginat, J. (1996). *Polygamous families in contemporary society.* Cambridge, UK: Cambridge University Press.

Attir, M. O. (1985). Ideology, value change, and women's social position in Libyan society. In E. W. Fernea (Ed.), *Women and the family in the Middle East: New voices of change* (pp. 121–133). Austin: University of Texas Press.

Borgerhoff Mulder, M. (1992). Women's strategies in polygamous marriage: Kipsigis, Dotoga, and East African cases. *Human Nature, 3*(1), 45–70.

Brhoom, M. (1987). The phenomenon of divorce in Jordan. *Derasaat, 13*(12), 189–205. [In Arabic.]

Broude, G. J. (1994). *Marriage, family, and relationships. A cross-cultural encyclopaedia.* Denver, CO: ABC-CLIO.

Chaleby, K. (1985). Women of polygamous marriages in an inpatient psychiatric service in Kuwait. *Journal of Nervous and Mental Disease, 173*(1), 56–58.

Chaleby, K. (1987). Women of polygamous marriages in outpatient psychiatric services in Kuwait. *International Journal of Family Psychiatry, 8*(1), 25–34.

Cherian, V. I. (1990). Academic achievement of children from monogamous and polygynous families. *Journal of Social Psychology, 130*(1), 117–119.

Eapen, V., Al-Gazali, L., Bin-Othman, S., & Abu-Saleh, M. (1998). Mental health problems among school children in United Arab Emirates: Prevalence and risk factors. *Journal of the American Academy of Child and Adolescent Psychiatry, 37*(8), 880–886.

El-Islam, M. F. (1975). Clinical bound neurosis in Qatari women. *Social Psychiatry, 10*(1), 25–29.

El-Islam, M. F. (1989). Collaboration with families for rehabilitation of schizophrenic patients and the concept of expressed emotion. *Acta Psychiatrica Scandinavica, 79*(4), 303–307.

El-Islam M. F., & Abu-Dagga, S. (1992). Lay explanation of symptoms of mental ill health in Kuwait. *International Journal of Social Psychiatry, 38*(2), 150–156.

Finken, L. L., & Amato, P. R. (1993). Parental self-esteem and behavior problems in children: Similarities between mothers and fathers. *Sex Roles, 28*(9–10), 569–582.

Ghubash, R., Hamdi, E., & Bebbington, P. (1992). The Dubai community psychiatric survey, I. Prevalence and socio-demographic correlates. *Social Psychiatry and Psychiatric Epidemiology, 27*(2), 53–61.

Gwanfogbe, P. N., Schumm, W. R., Smith, M., & Furrow, J. L. (1997). Polygyny and marital/life satisfaction, an exploratory study from rural Cameroon. *Journal of Comparative Family Studies, 28*(1), 55–71.

Hall, E. (1976). *Beyond culture.* New York: Doubleday.

Hays, P. A., & Zouari, J. (1995). Stress, coping, and mental health among rural village and urban women in Tunisia. *International Journal of Psychology, 30*(1), 69–90.

Hebrew Encyclopaedia, vol. 7 (1954). (pp. 624–630). Tel Aviv: Reshafim Press. [In Hebrew.]

Kilbride, P., & Kilbride, J. (1990). *Changing family life in East Kenya: Women and children at risk.* Philadelphia PA: University Park Press.

Leighton, A. H., Lembo, T. A., Hughes, C. C., Leighton, D. C., Murphy, J. M., & Macklin, H. B. (1963). *Psychiatric disorder among the Yoroba.* Ithaca, NY: Cornell University Press.

Low, B. S. (1988). Measures of polygyny in humans. *Current Anthropology, 29*(1), 189–194.

Makanjuola, R. O. A. (1987). The Nigerian psychiatric patient and his family. *International Journal of Family Psychiatry, 8*(1), 363–373.

Marks, E. (1974). *The Bedouin society of the Negev.* Tel Aviv: Reshafim Press. [In Hebrew.]

Marsella, A., Sartorius, N., Jablensky, A., & Fenton, R. (1985). Cross-cultural studies of depressive disorders: An overview. In A. Kleinamn & B. Good (Eds.), *Culture and depression: Studies in the anthropology and cross-cultural psychiatry of affect and disorder* (pp. 299–324). Berkeley: University of California Press.

Mass, M., & Al-Krenawi, A. (1994). When a man encounters a woman, Satan is also present: Clinical relationships in Bedouin society. *American Journal of Orthopsychiatry, 64*(3), 357–367.

Racy, J. (1985). Commentary on psychotherapy of Arab-Israeli patients. *The Journal of Psychoanalysis and Anthropology, 8*(4), 231–233.

Rosenberg, M. (1979). *Conceiving the self.* Melbourne, FL: Krieger.

Rosenberg, M., Schooler, C., Schoenbach, C., & Rosenberg, F. (1995). Global self-esteem and specific self-esteem: Different concepts, different outcomes. *American Sociological Review, 60,* 141–156.

Shalhoub-Kevorkian, N. (1997). Wife abuse: A method of social control. *Israel Social Science Research, 12*(1), 59–72.

Sinha, D., & Bharat, S. (1985). Three types of family structure and psychological differentiation: A study among the Jaunsar-Bawar society. *International Journal of Psychology, 20,* 693–708.

Topouzis, D. (1985). The men with many wives. *New Society, 74,* 13–15.

Valsiner, J. (1989). Organization of children's social development in polygamic families. In J. Valsiner (Ed.), *Child development in cultural context* (pp. 67–86). Toronto: Hogrefe and Huber.

Ware, H. (1979). Polygyny: Women's views in a transitional society, Nigeria 1975. *Journal of Marriage and the Family, 41*(1), 185–195.

White, D. R. (1988). Rethinking polygyny: Co-wives, codes, and cultural systems. *Current Anthropology, 29*(4), 529–572.

■ ■ ■ ■ ▨ ▨ ■ ■ ■ ■

52   "THE WORST HASSLE IS YOU CAN'T PLAY RUGBY": HAEMOPHILIA AND MASCULINITY IN NEW ZEALAND

Julie Park

Hemophilia is a disease with a straightforward genetic explanation, but each person's experience is shaped by a unique interaction between human biology and sociocultural forces. The disease appears with different degrees of severity, and cultural interventions such as prophylactic treatment with clotting factors modulate the degree to which it restricts activities that otherwise would be too dangerous. This means that many people with hemophilia are able to pursue sports, with benefits to their psychosocial well-being.

This selection shows how the anthropology of sport can contribute to medical anthropology, a teaming up that should be fostered in light of the importance of physical activity for health promotion and disease prevention and treatment. The selection explains that in New Zealand, one's ability to play rugby is a central idiom for men with hemophilia, representing either normality for those able to play the sport or deep distress for those unable to play. Playing, following, and being passionate about rugby demonstrates national pride together with commitment to hegemonic constructions of masculinity and, by exclusion, femininity. These constructions are reinforced through play in diffuse settings, from backyards to stadiums, which sets apart and penalizes boys and men who do not participate. The sport has particular importance for father–son relationships.

This selection traces the history and politics of rugby in New Zealand to elucidate the components of male gender identity that the sport has expressed and encouraged over the decades and to explain the

Source: Park, Julie 2000. "'The Worst Hassle Is You Can't Play Rugby': Haemophilia and Masculinity in New Zealand." *Current Anthropology* 41(3):443–453. ©2000 by The Wenner-Gren Foundation for Anthropological Research. With permission from the University of Chicago Press.

passion it evokes in New Zealanders. The analysis shows how recent feminist and antiracist criticisms may be helping to open the way to variant expressions of masculinity and to safer forms of the sport. It examines the ways in which rugby values can be at odds with those favored by contemporary society and with those that coincide with optimal surveillance and treatment of hemophiliac boys and men.

The expression and outcome of hemophilia are affected by both sex and gender (see selection 49). As hemophilia is sex linked, only males get the disease, although some females show similar yet relatively mild symptoms. Females are known as carriers. Males carry and pass on the disease to the same degree, but cultural beliefs including gender constructions obscure their role to the extent that many people believe that men do not pass on the disease and family planning efforts tend to focus on women only. Park points out that this cultural blindness may increase the number of cases of the disease, raising difficult ethical and practical questions.

Questions to keep in mind

What values and attributes did the colonial elite in New Zealand promote through the spread of rugby in the late 1800s?

What is unique about rugby in New Zealand, and how does this relate to the country's history?

In what ways has the sport changed in recent years?

What do you think about the ethics of preventing the disease through counseling or other methods?

A New Zealand farm woman, mother of two and a carrier of haemophilia, reports:

> When [my second son] was born with haemophilia [it] was pretty hard. 'Cause my husband is just the typical, kiwi, farming male—like the rugby playing. It sounds flippant but it's actually quite relevant. . . . There was a bit of a wedge there that took a long time to sort out. . . . He was very stand-offish.

This birth drove a wedge between husband and wife and between the father and his new baby that took many months to overcome. The mother chose to typify the grief, loss, and disappointment that her husband felt at having another son with haemophilia by the short-hand phrase "like the rugby playing": He would not be able to play rugby with his son or watch him play or coach him and his team.

Haemophilia narratives are replete with rugby stories. Not being able to play a particular sport may seem a rather trivial restriction compared with the other problems which people with haemophilia confront, but it is not. In this paper I examine the place of rugby as an idiom of distress or normality in the lives of men with haemophilia and as a symbol for and a practice of a hegemonic form of masculinity in New Zealand. I argue that this historically produced gender order creates particular difficulties for some men with haemophilia in several areas of life: sport and recreation, development of a respected masculine identity, acceptance of haemophilia treatment in line with best practice, and recognition that men, too, carry haemophilia. The erasure of men's roles as carriers has important implications for the haemophilia community and for society at large.

HAEMOPHILIA

Haemophilia is a coagulation disorder. People with haemophilia have much less clotting factor than normal in their blood; therefore they bleed more easily and bleeding is very slow to stop. As an X-chromosome-linked, recessive hereditary disorder, haemophilia is closely associated with men. Men are the "people with haemophilia"; women are the "carriers." Despite the genetic control of haemophilia, social, cultural, and economic forces interact with one another and with the biology of haemophilia to create each person's experience. Internationally, major differences exist in the care and treatment of haemophilia, the organization and funding of health services, the degree of associated risks, such as blood-borne infections or mobility problems, and life expectancy. Such things can be counted, measured, and tabulated;

they are key measures of how it might be different having haemophilia for a member of the urban poor in India and a member of the middle class in northern Europe. But there are also less visible, cultural influences at work which interact with these more obvious factors. Gender is one.

In its mildest forms, haemophilia may cause few problems in daily life and may become an issue only if an accident occurs or if surgery is contemplated. In its moderate or severe forms it can cause major disruptions to daily living, health problems, and difficulties in education and employment. Bleeding may start at any time or as a result of even minor knocks or twists. Bleeds into joints and muscles can cause long-term damage, intense pain, and mobility problems, while bleeds into organs and especially into the central nervous system may be life-threatening. Severe haemophilia affects mainly males (Roberts and Jones 1990). However, about one-third of women who have the haemophilia mutation also experience bleeding problems, although these are less severe than men's (Paper 1993). Many women are aware that they are carrying the disorder and may pass it on to the next generation.

Treatment is available in the form of transfusions of clotting factors that are derived from plasma or synthetically manufactured (Rosendaal, Smit, and Briët 1991). For most New Zealand boys and young men with severe haemophilia, prophylactic treatment is available to increase clotting-factor levels. People with haemophilia are advised to avoid high-impact physical activity. However, because general fitness is protective against bleeding, low-impact sports and exercise are recommended (Friedman 1997). In cultural contexts where sports are important, participation may also enhance psychosocial well-being. For example, Super and Block (1992) found in a small U.S. study that disabled men's involvement in sports was related to more favourable self-concepts and higher need for achievement.

RESEARCH BACKGROUND

This examination of masculinity, rugby, and haemophilia is based on research carried out in New Zealand in 1994–96 with a national sample of people with haemophilia (see Park et al. 1995). As haemophilia is a random mutation that occurs in a population regardless of ethnicity, class, or other characteristics, families with haemophilia represent a small "random sample" of New Zealand families. The research design included qualitative and quantitative methods to document and analyse the social characteristics of people living with haemophilia, their experiences of living with this disorder and its treatment, and the services available. After a series of focus groups and key-person interviews, a postal questionnaire was completed by 193 people with haemophilia, who constituted over half of the total population invited to participate. The questionnaire covered the condition, its treatment and complications, living situation, family life, education, employment, and leisure activities. Participants were similar to the national haemophiliac population except that they included more people with severe or moderate haemophilia. Subsequently, 80 people were selected nationwide for face-to-face interviews to provide a cross-section of people with haemophilia in terms of region, age, occupation, living situation, severity, and complications. The interviews focused on the participants' experiences, particularly of the more delicate issues, such as HIV and hepatitis C, having children, and bringing up children with haemophilia. During the research period, members of the research team were participant observers in activities of the New Zealand Haemophilia Society. Society members and other participants were extensively consulted when recommendations based on the research findings were prepared.

This study differed from most published social research on haemophilia in that it adopted an anthropological rather than a psychological approach (cf. Triemstra et al. 1998). Although it included the blood-borne infections of HIV and hepatitis C, the focus of much research since the mid-1980s (cf. Miller and Telfer 1996), it attempted a comprehensive understanding of haemophilia in the particular sociocultural context of New Zealand. This approach allowed us to see the salience of leisure activities for people with haemophilia. One hundred and fifteen of the 187 people (62%) who answered the questionnaire section on "Leisure" named sports and related activities in which they could not actively participate. These included high-risk, high-impact sports, especially contact and team sports, which had 46 specific mentions, most relating to rugby football. However, because such sports had been "out of the question" for many men for years, in many cases they were not mentioned specifically but covered by a general comment such as "stopped high-risk pursuits." One-quarter of respondents reported that haemophilia did not hinder their recreational pursuits, and a similar number reported that they were not greatly restricted. As expected, the majority of these had mild haemophilia, but they included some (15) with severe haemophilia. A large proportion of people with haemophilia (78%) reported exercising to keep fit. Ninety percent of respondents also added marginal comments, particularly about their strategies, their philosophies, and the difficulties and restrictions they faced in their leisure activities. This was a high level of spontaneous comment in comparison with other sections of the questionnaire. The strong engagement with sports was also borne out by our observations and interviews. The emphasis on rugby, then, is part of a more general pattern of interest in fitness, sports, and recreation.

RUGBY AND HAEMOPHILIA

The opening quotation was not an isolated example of rugby's role in families with haemophilia. A solo mother pointed to disappointment over not being able to carry on the family tradition of rugby playing as the main reason for her former husband's having left her and her two boys: "He's a sporty sort of a man and was brought up in the tradition of wanting to play rugby and representing the family, and he couldn't cope with having two boys who couldn't do it." In this case, rugby was not just a typical example of a restriction that comes with haemophilia; it was identified as the chief problem in the family relationships.

While the mothers might suggest that other physical activities and team sports were adequate substitutes for rugby, the fathers and sons did not agree. An urban mother of an 11-year-old with severe haemophilia told us that he was much more settled now that he was playing tennis, mountain-biking, and shooting. But the boy himself volunteered, privately and plaintively, "I would love to

play rugby!" A rural mother of a slightly older boy with moderate haemophilia commented during a family discussion that "touch rugby," a safer version of the game, was "a good compromise," but the father added that "the worst hassle" about haemophilia "is you can't play rugby," and his son agreed that this was "stink."

Fathers with haemophilia also regretted their inability to participate in their sons' rugby as the boys got older, heavier, and faster. A tradesman in a provincial city who had some damage to his knees found it hard to keep up with his 5-year-old and had to be very careful kicking the rugby ball around with him. He could see, he said, that by the time the boy was 10 or 11, "I won't be able to do those sorts of things with him. But, OK, we've got other things, but it does have an effect, you know." Infection with hepatitis C and the treatment for it (both of which can cause extreme fatigue and flu-like symptoms) on top of their haemophilia further restricted some fathers' ability to interact in physical games with their children.

Many of the men with mild haemophilia impressed on us that it had made little difference in their everyday lives. Rugby playing was the common idiom of normality: "I have done most things that normal people do. I played rugby in my youth." At the other end of the spectrum, when a high school boy with the invisible disability of severe haemophilia did not play rugby and was hassled by his mates, he said to his mother, "I'd rather have my legs cut off so people could see it." He wanted it to be obvious that he could not, rather than would not, play rugby. Stories from a generation back indicate that rugby was compulsory in some schools even for boys with severe haemophilia, so strong was this normative practice. One such boy's team position was described as the "drawback." A middle-aged professional with a mordant sense of humour wrote, "The impact of haemophilia has certainly controlled my life because without it I would have been playing for the All Blacks [the national rugby team]." He was a severely disabled man whose whole life had to be arranged to cope with haemophilia. He added, "I'd have to say that's the only regret that I've really had." The grandparents of a newborn boy were thrilled at his bonny appearance, and the granddad predicted that he would be a front-row prop for the All Blacks, a position where a solid build is an advantage. Then came the diagnosis of haemophilia. Granddad got very upset: [Baby] "was never going to play rugby and never going to be a front-row prop and never going to do this and never going to do that." The mother sympathized, "because our family has always been real sports-minded and to think that he'd never do things competitively was hard." After hearing these families talk about rugby it was impossible to dismiss the restriction as trivial. The inability to play rugby was the single most pervasive idiom of distress for men with haemophilia. However, reference to this idiom was not confined to people with haemophilia and their immediate families. Medical personnel also used it, as in this remembered diagnosis and prognosis: "Your son has haemophilia and will never play rugby."

RUGBY, SPORT, AND MASCULINITY

Rugby is part of and stands for a dominant, if not hegemonic, New Zealand masculinity, and this gender practice patterns the lives of people with haemophilia and influences the incidence of this disorder. While this analysis applies only to hegemonic pakeha (New Zealanders of "European" descent) masculinity, a similar argument would probably apply to Maori, as rugby has a special place in Maori culture also.

Rugby Union football is a team game in which 15 boys or men per side engage in intense physical contact with each other, the ball, and the field. Scrums, rucks, tackles, long, high kicks of the ball, the amount of running involved, the collisions, the dives, and the relative lack of protective clothing make it dangerous for people with haemophilia. Even perfectly fit men end up with severe damage to their joints, bone, muscles, and tendons, and accidents often occur to eyes, noses, ears, and genitals. Indeed, if one wanted to design a sport to inflict maximum damage on people with haemophilia, rugby would be a strong contender. One of the reasons rugby looms so large, then, is that it is definitely proscribed for people with bleeding problems. Unlike other New Zealand men, men with moderate or severe haemophilia and many of those with mild haemophilia cannot play rugby and cannot even choose to not play

rugby. As rugby is a ubiquitous game in New Zealand, being played in backyards, playgrounds, and paddocks at any time of year, it is a constant reminder of one's limitations or a temptation to ignore them. This helps to account for the frequency of the discussions about rugby, but it does not account for the passion.

The passion can best be accounted for by an understanding of the place rugby holds in New Zealand and, more generally, by reference to work in the anthropology and sociology of sport (see Blanchard 1995). Identity theories provide an initial set of understandings. National, regional, ethnic, class, gender, sexual, colonial, and postcolonial identities may all be expressed, manufactured, modified, and studied through the medium of sports (Connell 1983, 1987, 1990, 1995; MacClancy 1996; Messner 1992). All of these aspects are relevant to rugby in New Zealand. For example, the popular equation of the national rugby team, the All Blacks, with the nation was accomplished as early as 1905 (Sinclair 1986), along with the equation of rugby-playing with "the kiwi bloke": heterosexual, aggressive, stoic, physically strong and skilled, and a good (homosocial) mate. This version of masculinity was one of several, but it became hegemonic.

Connell defines hegemonic masculinity as "the configuration of gender practice which embodies the currently accepted answer to the problem of the legitimacy of patriarchy, which guarantees (or is taken to guarantee) the dominant position of men and the subordination of women" (1995:77). Hegemonic masculinity is part of an ordering of social practice, a gender order, which consists of relations of alliance, subordination, and dominance between masculinities and femininities. Connell's research on gender has been influential in recent social analyses of sport (e.g., Messner and Sabo 1990) and in the study of Western masculinities in general (e.g., Mac an Ghaill 1996). In company with other social scientists, such as Blaxter (1995), Messner (1992), and Phillips (1987), Connell (1995:37), argues that in England, the United States, Canada, Australia, and New Zealand sportsmen are exemplars of currently hegemonic masculinity and even those males who reject both this form of masculinity and the sports associated with it cannot ignore it. Connell (p. 29) refers to Phillips's study of the pakeha male as the "most remarkable historical study of masculinity that has yet appeared." In it Phillips construes organized sport, especially rugby football, as the "device for bridging the contradictions around masculine violence and social control." Connell is at pains to point out that the status of sport as a test of masculinity in New Zealand was produced historically, as a deliberate political strategy, and although the specifics of this history are local the general approach is broadly relevant to other histories. Connell's insistence on the centrality of embodiment to gender studies, his attention to power, production, and emotional attachment, and his emphasis on gender as a complex, contradictory order of social practice intimately connected with social processes such as race and class, as in the New Zealand case, encourage a comprehensive understanding of the social practice of sport. His analysis implies that attempts to change the gender order will be similarly complex. He calls for alliance politics and work on "degendering" and "re-embodiment." By these he means attempts to dismantle the nexus of hegemonic masculinity and to find "different ways of using, feeling and showing male bodies" (pp. 232–33).

As the gender order is always contested and always interacts with other social processes and institutions, work on sport and masculinities connects to studies of the economics and politics of sport, which draw mainly from theories of political economy and from Foucauldian-inspired theories of disciplinary societies and governmentality (e.g., Brohm 1978, Foucault 1991). Much of this work also takes a critical perspective on sport, which is analysed as an instrument of hegemonic domination by the state or an elite. These analyses have illuminated aspects of rugby in New Zealand such as the link between producing good rugby players and providing good troops for the empire and the role of rugby in Maori-pakeha relations. Representations of sports and sports people in literature, the popular media, sponsorship, and advertising are also part of the discursive field of sport relevant here (Perry 1994; Parker 1996:131).

Sport as a means of enculturation and socialization has been investigated for insights into the moral values which colonizers, parents, or educators seek to inculcate in players and how these may make them "fit" members of society (Messner 1992; Blanchard 1995). But players are by no means passive recipients. Sports are a mode of negotiation of multiple identities and complex networks of social relations as an individual moves through his or her life span and between social groups or as a particular group—for example, gay men (Pronger 1990), women (Bryson 1990), or disabled men (Connell 1995:54–55)—seeks to create new spaces for itself in society (MacClancy 1996).

RUGBY IN NEW ZEALAND

Rugby was introduced into New Zealand in 1870 by men of the colonial elite who had learned it in England and were determined to introduce it to that outpost of the empire. Rugby's rapid spread within New Zealand has been partially attributed to the ability of this elite to organize a network of competing and cooperating clubs (Phillips 1987:89; Fougere 1989:114; Macdonald 1996: 5–10). Rugby displaced the various existing forms of football played especially in the remote rural districts, gum- and goldfields, and logging and military camps, where males greatly outnumbered females and men relied on their mates for company, support, and entertainment. To these relatively unorganized districts rugby brought the possibility of playing games away and hosting teams which more or less adhered to an agreed-upon set of rules. However, it is important not to overstress the degree of order in the early games of rugby. Indeed, the roughness of the game, noted by contemporary observers, may have particularly appealed to pre-existing masculine values and helped it achieve its dominance (Phillips 1987:92). That strength and courage rather than skill and tactics were the main components of the early game has also been suggested as a reason for its popularity, as many of the early players were extremely strong as a result of their daily work but had little time to practise or to develop the finer points of the game.

Although in England rugby was an elite sport (Mangan 1981; White and Vagi 1990) and much of the early organization of clubs was carried out by the middle classes in New Zealand, the players and club members were extremely varied in terms of ethnicity and class. Maori made names for themselves from the very earliest days and visited Britain as part of overseas touring sides. Contemporary commentary from British observers indicates that Maori players were received with a mixture of indulgent contempt and surprised respect (Ryan 1997). Players were drawn from all classes, from labourers to landowners to university men (Phillips 1987:99). The egalitarian practices of rugby accorded well with the values of mateship and with the ideal of an egalitarian society, a hallmark of national ideology then and for many decades thereafter. Rugby players and supporters from all strata of society could be counted on to help one another in times of need (de Jong 1987:42–43)—a typical expression of the code of conduct of mateship. Combining the values of strength, courage, and mateship with the discipline of rules, rugby embodied much of the ideal New Zealand male character.

Between 1870 and 1900, English Rugby Union rules were progressively introduced in response to public outcries about the violent, dangerous, and unregulated nature of play, to say nothing of the swearing on the field and the drinking off it (Phillips 1987:95–97). This increasing codification of sport was paralleled in other English-speaking nations, such as Australia (Bryson 1990) and the United States (Kimmel 1990). By the turn of the century there was increasing emphasis on skill and tactics, and a referee with a whistle became a fixture in every rugby match. Rugby was championed as necessary training for the manly New Zealand gentleman. By this time the country had a balanced gender ratio and was rapidly becoming urbanized. Sport historians have pointed out that by the 1900s those most involved in playing rugby were not mainly manual labourers but led more sedentary lives and lived in towns. Worries about the fitness of these urbanized sons of empire were felt in New Zealand as elsewhere; the muscular masculinity embodied by rugby players was a great antidote to such anxieties in New Zealand, as were other sports elsewhere (Whitson 1990), providing a reassuring response to the late-19th-century "crisis of masculinity." Schools took up the sport with enthusiasm in their efforts to produce fit citizens for war and peace. For New Zealand boys, rugby became a compulsory part of the curriculum from around 1900 on. As Vincent and Harfield (1997) demonstrate, rugby's imperial

touring networks were important components of both empire and manliness and a site of struggle between imperialists and nationalists.

The colonial heritage of rugby has often been noted (Mangan 1981; Phillips 1987). Although the game is played in many countries, it is particularly important in parts of Britain and in the former settler colonies of South Africa, New Zealand, Australia, and, increasingly, such Pacific islands as Fiji, Tonga, and Samoa. Sinclair (1986) argued that New Zealand's experience of participation in the Boer, First, and Second World Wars as well as in countless games of rugby with other empire and later Commonwealth nations was an important component of that country's view of itself as a mature Commonwealth citizen.

As the 20th century wore on the game changed, particularly through the differentiation of positions: there was a place for huge, strong men, for tall men, for wiry fleet-of-foot men, and for men of great tactical intelligence. Rugby values, clearly articulated as boys learned lessons for life on the rugby fields or in the changing room, were about competing and cooperating, about not passing the ball just to save yourself, about generosity in getting the ball out to a teammate who could use it to advantage, about mateship and teamship and giving everything you've got to win but being stoic in defeat (Zavos in King 1988). In a culture that offered little opportunity for physical or emotional intimacy for men, rugby provided one, but one which was homophobic and frequently misogynist. But rugby was also about suppressing emotions, overcoming pain, taking terrible risks and taking them like a man (Phillips 1997). Despite the multiple discourses discernible in rugby, ultimately they reinforce a hegemonic masculinity (Star 1993:74).

In its social structure, rugby was a grassroots organization in which local clubs and schools competed with each other, then joined together to compete against outsiders and, eventually, against other nations—a neat example of segmentary opposition. Indeed, it is the bottom-up nature of rugby organization which Fougere (1989) singled out as a major feature of its popularity: the kind of social organization which New Zealanders valued most highly. It was also a way of structuring relationships with women, especially mothers, wives, and girlfriends, in which they appeared in a supporting role if at all. More often, their support was invisible: endless laundry services, home nursing, food and transport provision. In this regard rugby is a typical male sport (Whitson 1990), producing a gendered relationship of dominance and subordination. Nonetheless, many New Zealand women have an expert knowledge of and keen interest in rugby, becoming complicit in this power relation (Connell 1995:80) through their love of the game and its players.

In the late 20th century a rugby connection can still be the "open sesame" to the fellowship of strangers for men, even for visiting anthropologists (Fairweather and Campbell 1990:90). *One of the Boys* (King 1988), a collection of autobiographical essays by 15 prominent New Zealand men, demonstrates the power of rugby in their lives. These accounts parallel those of men with haemophilia, demonstrating that the love and anguish inspired by rugby are shared more generally by New Zealand men and not just an artefact of "forbidden fruit." Shelf-metres of rugby writing, particularly biography and autobiography, make the same points.

In this collection, the noted educator Jack Shallcrass (b. 1922) reported that one of the few times his father had raged at him was when he discovered that Jack had been watching a soccer game. Thereafter he played rugby and became engrossed in the game with his father as guide. He recalled that when he was grieving over the 1936 defeat of the All Blacks by the Springboks his mother told him for the first time about her loss of her beloved brother in the First World War—an unusual moment of intimacy. At high school, he reported, those who could not play rugby were allowed to play hockey and pitied; soccer was forbidden. A World War II veteran, husband, and father, Shallcrass resumed his rugby after the war as a player and later as a coach. With the wisdom of hindsight he noted that rugby could be a barrier to intimacy in marriage. (Opposed to the exclusion of Maoris from All Black sides touring South Africa and the racial selection of all Springbok Tour teams, he cut his ties with the game after having witnessed the "sour violence" of the 1956 tour and the overt racism of the South African rugby boss towards black Africans [Shallcrass, in King 1988:29].)

While Shallcrass's account is more detailed than many in the collection, in nearly all of the sto-

ries rugby is a fact of life—to be embraced or circumvented, part of "normal" boyhood. Maori and pakeha, local-born and immigrant, straight and gay, these 12 men attest to the power of rugby. As for the former athletes in Messner's (1992:25) U.S. study, for these men the sport was as natural as brushing their teeth, unavoidable.

One aspect of rugby evident in these narratives, as in the haemophilia stories, but not so widely discussed in the social science of sports literature is rugby's role as a mediator of intergenerational kinship relationships with boys (fathers, a grandfather, and a mother in the King volume). Messner (1992:27) writes: "Athletic skills and competition for status may often be learned from older brothers, but it is in boys' relationships with fathers that we find many of the keys to the emotional salience of sport in the development of masculine identity." In the King volume, in each case a moment of intimacy or, indeed, a long-term close relationship was provided through the shared medium of rugby. While fathers predominated, other kinship relationships also figured. Otherwise the familiar themes of gender and sexuality definition (male and heterosexual if you played rugby but questionable if you played other sports, especially soccer), nationalism, racism, morality, normality, attracting girls but otherwise rendering them invisible, mateship, compulsion, and conformity are all there.

Fougere (1989:114–15) argued that the work of the physical but controlled competition between men's rugby teams was of two kinds: work on relationships between men and work on visions of character and nationhood. Comradeship in the face of competition and segmentary opposition ultimately creating community out of difference characterized the relationships, while provincialism and rurality, the antithesis of the corrupt metropolis driven by economic gain, characterized the identity work. Rugby told the largely urban-dwelling New Zealand population a story about the golden age of rural cooperation, as did baseball in the United States (Kimmel 1990). It has also played a key role in the domestication of the "wild colonial boy." Weekends and evenings at the rugby club are part of an arrangement whereby a man can have a family and still maintain his relationships with his mates and his links to his rural or pioneering heritage (Phillips 1987).

The decades covered by the essays in King's book extend from the 1920s until the 1980s, a time of rapid urbanization in New Zealand and of very rapid and major changes in its international relationships and internal structures. Towards the end of this period, rugby and New Zealand's image of itself were dealt a severe blow by the passionate division of opinion in the country, including violent clashes between opposing factions and police, on issues of racism and politics in sport raised by the 1981 Springbok Tour (Fougere 1989). The fracture in the taken-for-granted acceptance of rugby allowed feminist and Maori critiques of rugby and the hegemonic masculinity it stood for to reach a wider audience. The egalitarian ideology conveyed by rugby was not matched by life experience. Included on the rugby field, Maori were disadvantaged in nearly every other sphere of national life. For women, a national identity based on a man's sport both excluded them and glorified violence and repression.

By the time rugby had recovered, the situation had changed markedly. Although juniors still turn out for their games all over the country and are coached by volunteers, rugby is now also a commodity, to be delivered to diverse TV audiences as a means of selling advertising or enhancing the sponsor's image and profits (Star 1992). Top players may earn executive-level dollars and may be poached by rival sports or play for rival countries for periods. Soccer and other kinds of football no longer have pariah status and are keen rivals for players, supporters, and dollars. Great players of Pacific Islands backgrounds have joined Maori and pakeha players at all levels, including the All Blacks. Touch rugby, women's rugby, and, most recently, gay men's rugby (*New Zealand Herald,* February 11, 1998) challenge both hegemonic masculinity and the link between it and rugby.

Despite all these changes and increased competition from other sports for the hearts and minds of young New Zealanders, rugby has not been displaced as the national sport or rugby greats supplanted as boys' heroes. An analysis of 700 entries in a recent art competition for children in which they depicted the person they most admired showed that after family members, the most chosen type of person for boys was an All Black, contrasting with girls' choice of a friend (*New Zealand Herald,* January 9, 1998). And in 1998, when the

All Blacks performed badly, a commonly heard joke was that New Zealand was the only country where the entire population sank into clinical depression when its rugby team lost.

Playing rugby is a part of a "normal" boyhood to the point where masculinity and citizenship may be suspect if a boy does not play. Hence the compulsion to play for an earlier generation of men (with or without haemophilia) and the wish for some visible disability as an obvious reason for not playing in the current one. This is why rugby may be used synecdochically to stand for the whole of "normal" masculinity, as in the diagnosis of the baby with haemophilia. But rugby is not just a figure of speech. It is a set of powerful gendered practices and social organization deeply embedded in families and in the larger society. Some fathers were genuinely at a loss to know what to do with their sons if they could not play rugby with them. As boys with haemophilia always inherit it from the mother's side, the fathers of these boys were relative newcomers to haemophilia. For a very few men, the disappointment was so severe that it also disrupted their marital relationship. Most men, however, managed to live with it, but the other physical activities they pursued with their sons or encouraged them in often seemed like substitutes.

The emphasis on rugby as a symbol of a compelling but constricting construction of masculinity is contested. In a discussion in a national weekly magazine about why girls are doing well and boys poorly at school (Stirling 1998), most of the researchers, teachers, and successful girls interviewed laid the blame at the door of narrow gender stereotypes for boys, which frustrate and create feelings of inadequacy in boys who try to fit them. A headmaster commented, "We expect them to be dominant, independent, aggressive, fearless and unemotional"—all part of rugby values and, he pointed out, at odds with what is required in school. A young female achiever expressed concern about her brother, who like most boys cared about "just sport, just rugby." Several noted that doing anything that was in the least bit "feminine," like trying hard or excelling in English, was just too risky for most boys. Even with high-achieving boys, a drama teacher introducing himself to his new class found it necessary to say, "We're not all queers and poofters. . . . I like rugby as much as anybody." The headmaster's message for fathers was for role-modeling which was more than "just throwing a rugby ball around." Playing rugby indicates that a boy is definitely not a girl, definitely not a "queer or a poofter," and rugby stands for a hegemonic masculinity which is recognized by educators as having negative effects on many New Zealand boys. Nonetheless, its hegemony continues.

Some of our research participants expressed similar ideas. One young pakeha man found a role in rugby as a supporter and went round with the rugby crowd. He maintained that it was good for his friends "to be exposed to people like me who can't play sport. It sort of kicks them out of that mind-set they tend to get into." He saw himself as widening the definition of "normal" masculinity. Similar responses have been reported from other studies of men with physical disabilities, despite the disabilities' (e.g., sudden-onset paraplegia) having some important differences from haemophilia. Gerschick and Miller (1994), on the basis of research with ten U.S. men with physical disabilities, suggest that such rejection of hegemonic masculinity is part of a successful mode of responding to disability but that it requires structural support. Young Maori parents of boys with haemophilia in a small rural town voiced a similar critique:

> I'm against rugby anyway cos I feel it fosters an image that men have to live up to and keep to. Like [this] is a rugby-oriented town. I can't see the point of going to training and just getting drunk afterwards. . . . It's too rough and too many people get hurt, even without haemophilia. Overall, society has to change how they are bringing up their men, their boys [mother speaking].
>
> Yes, that was a big hurdle for us to get over, the whole macho scene around here [father speaking].

Although these people are opposed to the narrow definition of masculinity that rugby typifies, their discussion also underlines the importance of rugby to boys and men in New Zealand. The last speaker also indicates that the emphasis on rugby creates a particular context for haemophilia in which there are specific difficulties for boys and men in fitting in, establishing friendship networks, and generally being accepted by their peers. Rugby creates an immediate basis for sociality, and it also acts as an "old boys' network"—a mutual support and infor-

mation network, a source of mateship, long after a person's playing days are over.

IMPLICATIONS AND CONCLUSION

A commonplace of medical anthropology is the insistence that "disease" is a combination of multiple factors (Anderson 1996:42). Even a genetic disorder such as haemophilia is never pure biology. In New Zealand, the hegemonic masculinity so intimately linked with the national sport of rugby sets up a series of everyday challenges for men and boys with haemophilia, for their families, and for the wider community which has echoes elsewhere but is not exactly duplicated (*Echo* 1994).

Recreational Strategies

Individual boys and men developed their own strategies for recreational pursuits. Some found friends who were not keen on rugby or took on administrative roles at rugby clubs which playing members valued. Others played team sports, such as soccer, which was marginally safer than rugby at least until boys started getting heavy, or cricket, where protective clothing could be worn, especially by wicket-keepers. Becoming very knowledgeable about rugby and other sports, taking up more individual sports, or developing non-sporting interests also featured. Certain recent changes to sporting codes have made things easier and safer for people with haemophilia, among them the introduction of children's versions of many sports into schools, the development of rugby without tackling (touch rugby), and the insistence on wearing protective clothing (Benseman and Park 1988).

Adolescent Development

The attraction of rugby is strongest just at the time when boys with haemophilia need to avoid contact sports. Small boys having adequate prophylactic treatment for their haemophilia may be able to play contact sports for a few years, but as they grow the combination of their own and their opponents' increased body weight and capacity for speed makes it too dangerous. As Whitson (1990:23) points out, during adolescence, when other sources of recognized masculine status are still some way off, sports assume prime importance in the task of learning to be a man—of learning to embody force and competence, as Connell (1987) puts it. As a result, shepherding haemophilic boys through late childhood and adolescence without cosseting them while protecting them from permanent damage to joints and muscles is a great challenge to their parents, health professionals, and older peers, many of whom are wise after the fact. Boys find it hard to resist the immediate pleasures of rugby in favour of a distant, disability-free future.

Stoicism

The risk-taking, pain-suppressing values of hegemonic masculinity also run counter to haemophilia treatment best practice, which includes being extremely attentive to any signs of bleeding and treating the bleed immediately and adequately (Szucs et al. 1996:211). Even when treatment was readily available, many men took a "wait and see" approach and had damaged limbs as a result. Others confessed to playing rugby and concealing it from mother or wife, again usually with rather damaging consequences (Park et al. 1995:203). Haemophilia health care givers reported that educating men to look after themselves and submit to regular haemophilia reviews was not always an easy task (Park, Scott, and Benseman 1999).

Male Carriers

A striking outcome of the emphasis on the active male is the erasure of the father's role in passing on haemophilia. Men and women who have the gene mutations which result in haemophilia transmit it to roughly half their offspring. All the daughters of men with haemophilia are carriers and none of the sons; half the sons and half the daughters of women who carry haemophilia will inherit the gene (Haemophilia Foundation Australia 1993). If the frequency of the mutations for haemophilia in the population is considered, men and women pass haemophilia on to the same extent. The difference is that haemophilia from men is hidden for a generation, whereas only half the haemophilia from women is hidden. To reduce

the incidence of haemophilia in the population, logic would suggest that both men and women should be seen as carriers and have attention focused on their fertility. Instead, only women are referred to as carriers, and with few exceptions only women carriers are the focus of family planning efforts. One man in his middle years, for example, had been told that "a haemophiliac could never have a haemophiliac child." Until a daughter was born, he did not know that all his girls would be carriers, as he believed that only women passed it on. A few men, almost all in the oldest age-group, had been advised by their doctors not to have children, but not many had taken the advice. Men's bleeding problems have almost completely eclipsed their more passive and hidden fertility issues, raising questions about folk theories of physiological paternity (Park et al. 1995:147; Park and Strookappe 1996).

Increased Incidence

This lack of emphasis on men's fertility has the potential to increase the incidence of haemophilia in the population. With welcome improvements in treatment, including increased safety of clotting factors, virtually all men with haemophilia can expect to live well beyond reproductive maturity. The almost exclusive focus on women rather than men carriers has personal consequences for families as well as social consequences for the community at large. At the time of the study, 45% of men with severe haemophilia A and 34% of men with moderate haemophilia A or severe and moderate haemophilia B were under 20, indicating a very large youthful cohort (Park 1998). It is likely that the numbers of young women carriers are increasing in proportion, haemophilia has negative health consequences for individuals. Men with haemophilia suffer a range of health and psycho-social problems; carrier women, whether symptomatic or not, face a range of problems (Paper 1996); haemophilia creates difficulties for families (Berger 1989) and is often difficult and always very expensive to treat. The increase in the number of people with haemophilia is therefore both a sensitive and a challenging issue for families, the health service, and the wider community.

Understanding Rugby, Masculinity, and Haemophilia

Analysing the links between rugby and a hegemonic masculinity as part of a gender order detaches this sport and hegemonic masculinity from being facts of nature (Connell 1990:83) and allows conceptual space for other forms of respected masculinity. It helps prevent facile "solutions" such as "Let them play golf" to the challenges which boys and young men face in achieving a respected masculinity in the New Zealand context. The sense of loss felt by some of those men who have not been able to play rugby becomes more explicable as rugby is shown to be part of the social practice of a hegemonic masculinity and a medium of male sociality. One can understand why other sports are seen as poor substitutes. Nonetheless, some changes in the configurations of sports are helpful, and not just to boys with haemophilia. The changes assist all young people as they challenge the prevailing gender order while offering more physical protection and choice to players (Bryson 1990:183; Benseman and Park 1998).

However, rugby-playing is unlikely to lose its status in the short term. Ultimately, work on de-gendering and reembodiment is likely to bring more lasting and satisfactory resolutions. Thus, in a new gender order, respected masculinity might be achieved as much by devotion to caring for small children as by pursuing an oval ball over a line. The achievement of such a utopian vision depends on alliances that go beyond gender politics (Connell 1995:232). Such an alliance was achieved in New Zealand in 1981, when indigenous, antiracist, and feminist groups forced recognition that rugby was not "just a game" but a political and ideological practice (Fougere 1989). In the current climate, educators, health workers, people with disabilities and chronic illnesses, gay men, feminists, women rugby players, and some male rugby enthusiasts have common interests in de-gendering rugby in Connell's sense. This analysis also alerts us to what is at stake: a historically produced gender order of social practices deeply embedded in New Zealand social institutions in which many men and women have strong investments—a gender order which is sustained by those who benefit, including globalizing corporate institutions (Connell 1995:241; Perry 1994). In the meantime, resourceful men with haemophilia experiment with strategies for achieving full masculine status and fulfilling lives.

REFERENCES

Anderson, Robert. 1996. *Magic, science, and health.* Fort Worth: Harcourt and Brace.

Benseman, J., and J. Park. 1998. A bleeding nuisance: The educational implications of haemophilia. *Australasian Journal of Special Education* 21:81–97.

Berger, Marie. 1989. *Understanding haemophilia.* Bath: Ashgrove Press.

Blanchard, K. 1995. Revised edition. *The anthropology of sport: An introduction.* Westport, Conn.: Bergin and Garvey.

Blaxter, M. 1995. "What is health?" in *Health and disease: A reader.* Edited by B. Davey, A. Gray, and C. Seale, pp. 26–32. Buckingham: Open University Press.

Brohm, J-M. 1978. *Sport: A prison of measured time.* [London]: Pluto Press.

Bryson, L. 1990. "Challenges to male hegemony in sport," in *Sport, men, and the gender order.* Edited by M. Messner and D. Sabo, pp. 173–84. Champaign, Ill.: Human Kinetics Books.

Connell, R. W. 1983. *Which way is up? Essays on class, sex, and culture.* Sydney: Allen and Unwin.

———. 1987. *Gender and power: Society, the person, and sexual politics.* Stanford: Stanford University Press.

———. 1990. "An Iron Man: The body and some contradictions of hegemonic masculinity," in *Sport, men, and the gender order.* Edited by M. Messner and D. Sabo, pp. 83–96. Champaign, Ill.: Human Kinetics Books.

———. 1995. *Masculinities.* St. Leonards, N.S.W.: Allen and Unwin.

De Jong, Piet. 1987. "The old rugby grows on you": The making of a game in a small New Zealand town. *SITES* 14: 35–56.

Echo. 1994. I want to play ball with the other guys. 15:4–6.

Fairweather, J., and H. Campbell. 1990. *Public drinking and social organisation in Methven and Mt. Somers.* Lincoln, Canterbury: Lincoln College A&ERU Research Report 207.

Foucault, Michel. 1991. "Governmentality," in *The Foucault effect: Studies in governmentality.* Edited by G. Burchell, C. Gordon, and P. Miller, pp. 87–104. London: Harvester Wheatsheaf.

Fougere, Geoff. 1989. "Sport, culture, and identity: The case of rugby football," in *Culture and identity in*

New Zealand. Edited by D. Novitz and B. Willmott, pp. 110–12. Wellington: GP Books.

Friedman, S. 1997. Play ball or play it safe. *New Zealand Haemophilia Society Newsletter* 25(4):7–8.

Gerschick, Thomas J., and Adam S. Miller. 1994. Gender identities at the crossroads of masculinity and physical disability. *Masculinities* 2:34–55.

Haemophilia Foundation Australia, Inc. 1993. *Meeting haemophilia for the first time.* Hartwell, Victoria.

Kimmel, M. 1990. "Baseball and the reconstitution of American masculinity, 1880–1920," in *Sport, men, and the gender order.* Edited by M. Messner and D. Sabo, pp. 55–66. Champaign, Ill.: Human Kinetics Books.

King, Michael. Editor. 1988. *One of the boys: Changing view of masculinity in New Zealand.* Auckland: Heinemann.

Mac an Ghaill, Máirtín. Editor. 1996. *Understanding masculinities: Social relations and cultural arenas.* Buckingham: Open University Press.

Mac Clancy, J. Editor. 1996. *Sport, identity, and ethnicity.* Oxford: Berg.

Macdonald, Findlay. 1996. *The game of our lives: The story of rugby and New Zealand—and how they've shaped each other.* Auckland: Viking.

Mangan, J. A. 1981. *Athleticism in the Victorian and Edwardian public schools.* Cambridge: Cambridge University Press.

Messner, Michael. 1992. *Power at play: Sports and the problem of masculinity.* Boston: Beacon Press.

Messner, M., and D. Sabo. Editors. 1990. *Sport, men, and the gender order: Critical feminist perspectives.* Champaign, Ill.: Human Kinetics Books.

Miller, R., and P. Telfer. 1996. HCV counselling in haemophilia care. *Haemophilia* 2:1–4.

Paper, Renée. 1993. Females bleed too! *HANDI Quarterly* 3:1–9.

———. 1996. Gynecological complications in women with bleeding disorders. *The Treatment of Haemophilia* 5:1–7.

Park, J. 1998. Technologies for prenatal testing: Consequences for women and families with an inherited condition. *Pacific Science Association Information Bulletin* 49 (3–4):33–37.

Park, J., K. Scott, and J. Benseman. 1999. Dealing with a bleeding nuisance: A study of haemophilia care in New Zealand. *New Zealand Medical Journal* 112:155–58.

Park, J., K. Scott, J. Benseman, and E. Berry. 1995. *A bleeding nuisance: Living with haemophilia in Aotearoa/New Zealand.* Auckland: Department of Anthropology, University of Auckland.

Park, J., and B. Strookappe. 1996. Deciding about having children in families with haemophilia. *New Zealand Journal of Disability Studies* 3:51–67.

Parker, A. 1996. "Sporting masculinities: Gender relations and the body," in *Understanding masculinities: Social relations and cultural arenas.* Edited by M. Mac an Ghaill, pp. 126–38. Buckingham: Open University Press.

Perry, Nick. 1994. *The dominion of signs.* Auckland: Auckland University Press.

Phillips, J. O. C. 1987. *A man's country? The image of the pakeha male, a history.* Auckland: Penguin Books.

Pronger, B. 1990. "Gay jocks: A phenomenology of gay men in athletics," in *Sport, men, and the gender order.* Edited by M. Messner and D. Sabo, pp. 141–52. Champaign, Ill.: Human Kinetics Books.

Roberts, H., and M. Jones. 1990. "Disorders of hemostasis: Congenital disorders of blood coagulation factors. Hemophilia and related conditions," in *Hematology,* 4th edition. Edited by W. Williams, E. Beutler, A. Erslev, and M. Lichtman, pp. 1453–753. New York: McGraw-Hill.

Rosendaal, R., C. Smit, and E. Briët. 1991. Haemophilia treatment in historical perspective: A review of medical and social developments. *Annals of Haematology* 62:5–15.

Ryan, G. 1997. "Handsome physiognomy and blameless physique": Indigenous colonial sporting tours and British racial consciousness, 1868–1888. *International Journal of the History of Sport* 14:67–81.

Sinclair, Keith. 1986. *A destiny apart: New Zealand's search for national identity.* Wellington: Unwin Paperbacks and Port Nicholson Press.

Star, Lynne. 1992. "Undying love, resisting pleasures: Women watch telerugby," in *Feminist voices.* Edited by R. Du Plessis, pp. 124–40. Auckland: Oxford University Press.

———. 1993. Macho and his brothers: Passion and resistance in sports discourse. *SITES* 26:54–78.

Stirling, P. 1998. Girls on top. *New Zealand Listener* 162:8–21.

Super, J. T., and J. R. Block. 1992. Self-concept and need for achievement of men with physical disabilities. *Journal of General Psychology* 119:73–80.

Szucs, T., A. Öffner, B. Kroner, P. Giangrande, E. Berntorp, and W. Schramm. 1998. Resource utilisation in haemophiliacs treated in Europe: Results from the European study on socioeconomic aspects of haemophilia care. *Haemophilia* 4:498–501.

Triemstra, A., H. Van Der Ploeg, C. Smit, E. Briët, H. Adèr, and R. Rosendaal. 1998. Well-being of haemophilia patients: A model for direct and indirect effects of medical parameters on physical and psychological functioning. *Social Science and Medicine* 47:581–93.

Vincent, G., and T. Harfield. 1997. Repression and reform: Responses within New Zealand rugby to the arrival of the "Northern Game," 1907–8. *New Zealand Journal of History* 31:234–50.

White, P., and A. Vagi. 1990. "Rugby in the 19th-century British boarding-school system," in *Sport, men, and the gender order.* Edited by M. Messner and D. Sabo, pp. 67–78. Champaign, Ill.: Human Kinetics Books.

Whitson, D. 1990. "Sport and the social construction of masculinity," in *Sport, men, and the gender order.* Edited by M. Messner and D. Sabo, pp. 19–30. Champaign, Ill.: Human Kinetics Books.

■ ■ ■ ■ ■ ■ ■ ■ ■

53 DOING GENDER, DOING SURGERY: WOMEN SURGEONS IN A MAN'S PROFESSION

Joan Cassell

The last selection explained how the construction of masculinity in sports such as rugby implies notions about femininity. Women perform various supporting functions of both practical and emotional type, but also serve as an excluded group, a category against which men define and measure themselves. This selection analyzes an analogous system of gender constructions in the traditionally male field of surgery (see also Cassell 1998). Cassell argues that the exclusion of women in surgery and medicine in general, as in firefighting and the military, is linked to myths about males giving or taking life at will. Consequently, the presence of women in these fields is seen as highly threatening and destabilizing. As in the case of rugby analyzed in the last selection, participants in the sphere of surgery, including nurses, actively enforce what they consider to be gender-appropriate behaviors, policing the boundaries between masculinity and femininity.

Cassell focuses on the performance aspect of gender, rather than gender as an attribute. This is to counter a tendency to think in terms of gender as an essence rather than a cultural product. Indeed, even ideas about gender essences are cultural products. For example, the production and activities of male gametes are described in terms of accomplishment, industriousness, and decisiveness, whereas the production and activities of female gametes are depicted in terms of wastefulness, aimlessness, and passivity. Sperm and egg are often given personalities even in scientific literature, with the former cast as directed, relentless lovers/warriors and the latter as coy, immobile targets. The reality of their nature and interaction is quite different, but this does not prevent gendered interpretations from serving to reinforce cultural beliefs about men and women's "nature" (Martin 1991).

Rather than seeking to determine whether men and women "really are" different in their behavior, Cassell analyzes what happens when either acts in ways that are culturally constructed as appropriate to the other. For example, female nurses indulge tantrum behavior in male surgeons but condemn and resist it in female surgeons. Far more than professional status, gender seems to be an overriding trait that takes precedence over other characteristics in shaping expectations about workplace behavior. This is a matter of gender constructions rather than sex-linked biology that impacts both men and women and can have real impacts on patient care (see selection 49).

Questions to keep in mind

To what extent do the people in this selection behave in the ways predicted by American gender constructions?

What are some examples of the same behavior being interpreted in different ways because of the gender of the surgeon?

How does the enforcement of behavior considered gender appropriate among surgeons and nurses recall the discussion in selection 52 about rugby and masculinity?

Do you think that the changing proportions of men and women in the fields of surgery, medicine, and nursing will affect how hospitals are run and patients are treated?

When I began studying surgeons more than a decade ago, I was struck by the martial, masculine ambience of surgery. The surgical temperament or ethos (Bateson 1936; Cassell 1987a, 1991) involves characteristics that are traditionally ascribed to men: arrogance, aggressiveness, courage, and the ability to make split-second decisions in the face of life-threatening risks. Surgeons take the metaphor of the war on disease literally: from "the front lines" or "trenches," they carry out "blind maneuvers," attack "invading tumors," and conduct "search and destroy" missions. I found a certain distrust and exclusion of women. In the 1980s, surgery was a "men's club"—it still is, in many ways, although the number of women in surgery has increased almost tenfold from 1970 to 1993 and is still growing.[1] Similar distrust and exclusion of women is found in all the "adrenalized vocations:" (Dorothy J. Douglas, personal communication) firefighting (Kaprow 1991), waging war (New York Times 1994), test piloting (Wolfe 1979). Such masculine thinking is familiar to anthropologists: the sacred flutes, trumpets, bullroarers, will lose their potency if women learn their mysteries (Murphy and Murphy 1974:85–100; Gillison 1993:265–276), and in fact, Kaprow (1990) compares the all-male firehouse to an Amazonian men's house.

During thirty-three months of research in the 1980s. I met only seven senior female general surgeons.[2] When I finished my study of general surgeons (Cassell 1986, 1987a, 1987b, 1989, 1991), I resolved to study women in surgery. I wanted to learn whether the women were different from the men, and what went on when women gained entrance to the men's house.

GENDER DIFFERENCES

In the last fifteen years, the study of gender (or gender-related) differences has grown exponentially (see Haraway 1991). A central issue, under debate by scholars, scientists, and philosophers, is whether women and men are fundamentally different or essentially the same. The "difference theorists" (Gilligan 1982; Chodorow 1978; Ruddick 1989) contend that women are, or tend to be, more nurturant, caring, and cooperative as opposed to men, who are more independent, detached, and hierarchical. "An ethic built on caring is, I think, characteristically and essentially feminine," says Noddings (1984:8), adding a cautionary, "which is not to say, of course, that it cannot be shared by men." (Noddings attributes the ethic of caring to "our experiences as women, just as the traditional logical approach to ethical problems arises more obviously from masculine experience.") In a similar vein, Gilligan and Wiggans (1988:112) assert that "stereotypes of males as aggressive and females as nuturant, however distorting and limited, have some empirical basis."

Observations by women surgeons echo the arguments of the difference theorists. "The surgeon is seen as a John Wayne type," notes a woman surgeon, who criticizes this macho, martial approach; she suggests that "qualities that women in general bring quite unselfconsciously to patient care and resident and student teaching," such as sensitivity, warmth, and compassion, might improve the way surgery is taught, learned, and practiced (Kinder 1985:103). A number of her female colleagues agree. One contrasts the "female" with the "male" operating room: the atmosphere "of peace, tranquillity, and contentment" when a woman surgeon is in charge, is opposed to the "tense, hostile, and even explosive" atmosphere generated by a "typical male surgeon" (Anon. 1986). Another woman, discussing her relationship with patients, says: "I spend more time [than male surgeons] in empathy, talking, explaining, teaching, and it's a much more equal power relationship"; she noted that she holds the patient's hand before that person is anesthetized, while "the boys scrub, then come in when the patient's asleep" (Klass 1988).

Kessler and McKenna (1978) point to a significant weakness of such binary comparisons: one cannot talk about differences without classifying the members of the two categories being compared. Thus, in order to compare "women" and "men," *one must already know what women and men are, and who belongs to each category.* They note that among biological, social, and behavioral scientists alike, classification precedes comparison, the basis for classification being the "incorrigible proposition" that humans are "naturally" divided into two genders.

In contrast to such dichotomies, some sociologists examine the effects of structural issues, such as opportunity, power, and relative numbers, upon the way men and women behave at work. Kanter (1977a, 1977b) challenges the view that "women are different," showing how apparent differences in attitudes or behavior can be explained by situation. She describes the effects of relative numbers on "tokens" (people whose type is represented in very small proportion in a particular role): their heightened visibility increases pressures to perform well; they feel isolated from informal social and professional networks; and they are encapsulated into gender-stereotyped roles. Kanter's interesting and insightful work, however, is placed firmly within the positivist sociological tradition; she tends to reify "structural factors" and organizes findings in terms of ranked, testable hypotheses. Such an approach flattens the give and take of human interaction, as though "variables" are interacting in a magisterial relatively predictable pattern. The liveliness, interest, and suspense of human interaction is transformed into a "parsimonious" over-determined and essentially unreal construction. The more "scientific" such work attempts to be, the more distant it becomes from the "booming buzzing confusion" of human reality, human motivations, and in the end, human behavior. Other sociologists, such as Lorber (1994), who argue that gender and even sex differences are wholly social constructions, focus on the economic, social, political, and emotional advantages to men of the current systems of gender inequality.

GENDER DIFFERENCES AMONG SURGEONS

When I designed a pilot study of women surgeons in the early 1990s, I thought in terms of *difference.* Although I planned to explore the structural constraints discussed by Kanter, my primary focus

was on contrasting women's perspectives, values, and behavior with those of men. My research inquired whether women surgeons differed from their male colleagues, if so, how, and whether such differences might affect patient care. I envisioned the possibility of two overlapping bell-shaped curves, with the female central tendency more in the direction of caring, cooperation, and compassion.

For my pilot study of women surgeons, carried out in a medium-sized city in the United States, I used the medical grapevine to list every senior woman surgeon and chief resident (excluding ophthalmology and ob-gyn, which were treated as separate populations[3]). I managed to study 18 of the 24 I located, spending five working days, from dawn to dark, with each. Subsequently, I conducted research in four additional geographic areas within eastern and midwestern North America (three in the U.S. and one in Canada). In these sites, I made a lessened effort to recruit all the women surgeons, and concentrated upon finding women who appeared to be significantly different: if I learned of a surgeon who was African American or Orthodox Jewish, or one in a specialty I had not yet observed, or in a particularly interesting personal or professional situation, I tried to study her. In addition, I spent time observing 3 (of the 7) women surgeons whom I had met and spent time with ten years ago when studying general surgeons (Cassell 1991). I spent two to five days with each woman, depending upon her schedule and my own. I then conducted a tape-recorded open-ended interview with each,[4] inquiring about her surgical education and training, having a mentor, being a mentor, ideas about differences between men and women surgeons, and relationships with superiors, colleagues, and subordinates.

My findings were more complex, ambiguous, and interesting than "difference theory" would have predicted. I observed women surgeons who acted nurturant and caring, as did some men; others appeared as detached and hierarchical as many of their male colleagues. When questioned, some women asserted that women surgeons were more compassionate and caring; others denied any difference between the behavior of female and male surgeons: admitting that some surgeons were more caring than others, these women rejected any relation of caring to gender. Although I observed the phenomena described by Kanter, I was unable to correlate the presence or absence of "gender differ-ences" with the structural features she implicates. At the same time, I observed exchanges between women surgeons and patients, nurses, chiefs of surgery, colleagues, and residents, where *expressions of difference* were elicited and rewarded, while agonistic "masculine" displays were sanctioned.

GENDER AS INTERACTIONAL PROCESS

While struggling with the relation of my findings to the concepts of the difference theorists, I en-countered a small body of recent theory and re-search that focuses on gender as a negotiated and constructed category (West and Zimmerman 1987; Coltrane 1989; Ginsburg and Tsing 1990; DeVault 1991; Unger 1989). Gender, in this view, is not a *ding an sich,* a thing in itself; instead, it is *produced.* Discussing West and Zimmerman's for-mulation, DeVault explains:

> Doing gender, in this approach, is not just an indi-vidual performance, but an interactional process, a process of collective production and recognition of "adequate" women and men through concerted ac-tivity (DeVault 1991:118).

Without negating the path-breaking research, in-sights, and theories of the difference theorists, or those of Kanter, this research alters the emphasis. Rather than examining differences *per se,* these scholars explore the *social construction* of such dif-ferences. Unlike Kanter's positivist search for law-like generalizations, which simplifies complexity into "variables," this processual approach to gen-der does not attempt to prune the richness and di-versity of human interaction. As Ginsberg and Tsing (1991:2) explain their approach:

> By "gender" we mean the ways a society organizes people into male and female categories and the ways meanings are produced around these categories. . . gender is not seen as fixed or "natural" but rather as a category subject to change and specifically to *nego-tiation.* As ethnographers, we pay attention to the ways in which people learn, accept, negotiate and re-sist the categories of "difference" that define and constrain them in everyday life.

Focusing on process and interaction rather than searching for "deep structure" makes profound

sense when conducting ethnographic research. Al-though the question of whether women and men are fundamentally similar or basically different has profound epistemic and political import, observed behavior provides inconsistent evidence for either contention. Gender is a slippery and on occasion contradictory category (Unger 1989:15). The more one reflects on its complexities, the more ambigu-ous it becomes. Unlike sex, which is a relatively fixed classification based on perceived morpho-logical criteria—defining an individual as male, female, or hermaphrodite—gender is a socio-cultural construction, which is not necessarily bi-nary (Kessler and McKenna 1978; Herdt 1994), or even tripartite (Jacobs and Cromwell 1992). Based on beliefs, behavior, and interaction, gender may be done, or enacted most successfully by someone of the opposite sex (Garfinkel 1967). The notion of "gender difference," even when softened as "gen-der-associated difference" has a certain circular quality: differences that members of various cul-tures believe exist and therefore focus on. Biologi-cal determinism (Wilson 1975, 1978; Moir 1991) cuts through such Gordian knots; in this view, a binary sexual division, based on physiological and anatomical differences, underlies gender assign-ment, making gender differences both natural and necessary; anatomy, in short, is destiny. A social scientist who refuses to be tempted by the simplic-ity, parsimony (and perhaps mythology) of such genetic exegeses, however, may wonder whether the term "gender difference" is not more a descrip-tion of behavior than an explanation for it (Unger 1989:15). Even the *comparison* of gender differ-ences may be epistemologically suspect. As Kessler and McKenna (1978) indicate, investiga-tors begin with the "incorrigible proposition" that humans are divided into two and only two gen-ders, then describe and classify the behavior of those whom they have placed in these dichoto-mous categories.

The notion of *doing* gender helped make sense of my otherwise ambiguous and confusing data. I observed the unspoken "rules" of the surgical gen-der game in action and noted what happened to those who violated these rules. Exempted from having to speculate about whether a particular woman surgeon was different from or similar to her male colleagues (which colleagues? when? in what ways?), absolved from generalizations on "deep structure" or conjectures about what some-one was "really like," I was free to focus on observ-able phenomena. They were not only observable, they were important: I could investigate the elici-tation, encouragement, and enforcement of gen-der-appropriate behavior among women in surgery. I found that patients, chiefs of surgery, colleagues, and subordinates all had notions of ap-propriate female conduct; all had techniques for invoking their categories of difference. Naturally, the women themselves possessed categories and behaviors that emerged in response to such defini-tions and constraints.

Otherwise puzzling incidents and remarks ob-served during research make sense when viewed through the lens of "doing gender." For example, a chief resident described how all her male col-leagues confide in her about their romantic diffi-culties. "I don't know why they're telling me this," she protested. Here, we see the gender-appropriate characteristics of sympathy and empathy being elicited. Whether or not she was particularly inter-ested, as the only woman in the training program, she was expected to be the repository of emotional confidences. A plastic surgeon complained that in the operating room (OR), she can only ask for one instrument at a time or the nurses label her as "de-manding." "The guys ask for three or four at once and no one bats an eye," she complained. The nurses are encouraging, perhaps enforcing, the gender-appropriate trait of "thoughtfulness." Op-erating room (OR) nurses invariably inquire about surgeons' partners, spouses, children; they do such "sentimental work" (Strauss *et al.* 1985) with both male and female surgeons. But the female surgeon who does not remember and inquire about the *nurses'* partners, spouses, children is labeled "cold," "snobby," and "standoffish." This per-sonal interest is not expected from the men, nor is its absence apparently resented.

The *enforcement* of gender appropriate behavior is even more visible. A transplant surgeon de-scribed how, during an emergency when she was a chief resident, a hospital operator was obtuse and obstructive; the surgeon finally said, "Goddamit, someone's dying, get me Dr. so-and-so!" The op-erator reported her to the chief of surgery. Male surgeons do this all the time; there is no way a man would be sanctioned for (merely) swearing. Every woman studied agreed that women surgeons are

not allowed to throw (what the male mentor of one woman called) "doctor fits." A male surgeon who has tantrums in the OR is characterized as "tem-peramental" or "high strung" (Cassell 1991: 128–152). Nurses may joke and complain behind his back, but in the OR they pay scrupulous atten-tion to his wants and needs, acting as though he were a volatile substance that might ignite if they make the wrong move. A woman surgeon who throws a "fit" is described as a "bitch"—the woman I studied were unanimous about this. Rather than being more attentive, nurses become slow and sulky in the face of female tantrums; a slow operation is more dangerous to the patient, who is kept under anesthesia for a longer period of time.

Interested in female styles of leadership, I ex-tended my observations from senior attending sur-geons to chief residents, whose tasks include teaching and supervising the junior residents. I learned that, whether or not they wished to do so, women are not permitted to employ a common surgical teaching style, which I think of as "teach-ing by humiliation." This ranges from displays of rage, to ferocious teasing, including brutal nick-names, to commemorate less-than optimum per-formance; although the "victim" may not relish such treatment, he (and it usually is he) is in no position to complain.

> After watching an intern close a breast biopsy very very slowly, as the surgeon stood above him, slowly shaking her head, as she instructed him, I later com-mented to her about the ugliness of the closing. She agreed, but said that making him feel bad, wouldn't improve his performance; he'd just get sullen and conclude he couldn't work with her. "I know what I wanted to say, though," she told me: "What's the matter, first day with a new hand?" I suspect that's what novices were told in the prestigious, brutal pro-gram where she, herself, was trained.

Even firmness from female chief residents ran-kled. "You had a leadership choice," explained one woman: "You could be a pushover or a bitch." (The male equivalent of a "bitch" would be a "strong" chief resident.) Another described how the male residents gave her a "whip lady" award, with one remarking that doing rounds with her was like making stations of the cross. Her chief of surgery asked why she was so "castrating" to the residents under her.

Many of the women I observed had devised alternate, "feminine" ways of teaching juniors, relating to nurses, and running an operating room. One described how, when she was a chief resident leading rounds on hospitalized patients (when chief residents query juniors on correct procedures, medications, and treatment plans), she would send an intern to buy a bag of candies. Each correct response to her questions was rewarded by a candy. The same young surgeon had a sure-fire way to obtain a missing instrument in the OR: she would plaintively say, "I'll give ten cents to anyone who'll find me a bipolar Bovie [or whatever else she needed]; amid laughter, someone would run and get it."

When questioned about differences between a "female" and a "male" operating room, a neurosurgeon responded:[5]

> I do think that a woman surgeon's leadership qualities have to be Captain of the Team as opposed to King of the Hill. And so women surgeons, I think, recognize that they will not get the cooper..[she interrupts herself, and says]—they'll have more trouble than men will trying to exert their authority through force. And therefore have learned, one way or another, have learned in order to get the results they need they have to be the captain of a team and encourage each player to feel their part is important to the workings of the team.

Discussing her relationship with nurses, a high-ranking woman said:[6]

> I think that the nurses, especially in the operating room, and perhaps in the intensive care units, are probably nurses that are at a very high level of achievement, often. And, uh, frankly would rather be doctors than nurses. I suspect that's the underlying difficulty. And they are very resentful of women who make demands on them. (JC: Which means that you have to make demands in a different way?) I think so. I think quite differently. I think that it's important to be firm with the nurses, but not to be at all petty with them. And even being firm is often not a successful tactic. But certainly resorting to, "oh, why did you do this to me again" sort of behavior is simply not a successful tactic. (JC: And you can't have what someone I knew called a "doctor fit"?) No, you really can't. And I learned that probably the hard way. (JC: By having them.) (She laughs) By having them and having them totally unsuccessful!

Are these women fundamentally different from their male colleagues? It is impossible to determine. But it is clear that they cannot afford not to *act* differently. Moreover, someone who has been socialized all her life to produce gender-appropriate behavior, who finds that tantrums and shows of force invoke rebellion rather than compliance, already possesses a rich repertoire of "feminine" stratagems she can employ to ease her way.

Nurses act as "enforcers" of gender-appropriate behavior. The husband of a woman surgeon, also a surgeon, wrote:

> . . .women surgeons who happen to have "male surgeon"—type personalities are not accepted as quickly by the nursing staff (predominantly female). This is in sharp contrast to women surgeons who have a more traditional "female surgeon"-type personality. It is expected that male surgeons throw tantrums, whine, and complain. However, when this behavior comes from a woman and is directed at women nurses, tension escalates much more rapidly (personal communication).

Kanter (1977:204) notes that powerless women resent a boss's advantage, particularly if they think they could just as easily be the boss. True, so far as it goes, but why do powerless nurses resent women surgeons and not men? Because only when women become surgeons does the nurses' lack of mobility become apparent to them? Because, as "tokens," women are more vulnerable than the men? Then why do nurses resent those who do *not* produce gender appropriate behavior more than those who do? Is gender-appropriate behavior rather like Nora's "squirrel dance" in Ibsen's *The Doll's House:* does it demonstrate that a woman, even a woman surgeon in a superordinate position, "knows her place"—which is *with* the other women, not above them? Same-sex policing is a particularly effective way of maintaining gender categories. Who has a better knowledge of the refinements of the "natural" behavior that defines and creates a gender category, and the "unnatural" behavior that challenges it, than those who have a lifetime's exposure to the same distinctions, values, and constraints?

Before examining doing masculine gender, let's think about Nora's squirrel dance in *The Doll's House.* Nora uses this "adorable" performance to beguile and manipulate her husband: enacting smallness, cuteness, and harmlessness emphasizes (or, more correctly, generates) a complementary expansiveness, assertiveness and power in her husband, who then benevolently does what she wishes. It is a common reciprocal form of gender interaction. The woman's diminishment of self amplifies the man's consciousness and enactment of grandeur. Is it possible that similar diminution is enacted by OR nurses? Is the surgeon "pumped up"—the way body builders pump up their muscles before competitions—by the nurses' self-constriction? Are the women (West and Zimmerman 1987:146) "doing deference" so that the men can "do dominance?" Although sterility has its demands, it is conceivable that interactions between nurses and surgeons, in the OR, are more impelled by the requisites of doing gender than the exigencies of sterility. For example, why do nurses scrub, dry their hands, don their own sterile gowns and gloves, give surgeons towels to dry their hands, and then gown and glove the surgeons (see Felker 1983:354–355)? It's a balletic ritual: each step is precisely choreographed as the subordinate nurses wait upon the super-ordinate surgeons. On occasion, I've seen hard-pressed women surgeons dress themselves, but I have never observed a male surgeon gown or glove himself. If the nurses' "sterile dance" is seen as a way of amplifying the surgeon's greatness, instrumentality, power—in short, his "masculininity"—it becomes clearer why nurses might resent "pumping up" other women. In return for nurses' enactments of gender subservience, women surgeons may also be required to do gender, portraying cooperation and a kind of egalitarianism as opposed to the dominance and hierarchy acted out by the men: Captain of the Team, not King of the Hill.

Men surgeons are particularly adept at producing agonistic gender displays (Cassell 1991). Surgeons whom I interviewed in the 1980s compared themselves to test pilots (Wolfe 1979; Cassell 1987a), and indeed, the legendary Chuck Yeager, who walked away from demolished planes to become the first man to fly faster than the speed of sound, might well exemplify the western warrior masculine gender ideal: taking risks, defying death, coming close to the edge, and carrying it off. "The right stuff" (Wolfe 1979) can be decoded as the quintessential masculine performative elements—no wonder there's no word for this ineffable assemblage, a name might destroy its quasi-magical power.

The surgeons I observed in the 1980s characterized colleagues who produced inadequate gender performances as "wimps" (Cassell 1986). A wimp is the symbolic inversion of the heroic masculine exemplar; he does *not* portray nerve, daring, self-confidence, flair, machismo. A "wimp," like a "bitch," exhibits behaviors associated with the opposing category. In surgery (as in the other "adrenalized vocations," I suspect) super-ordinate men as opposed to subordinate women in the case of nurses, police the performances of other men.

Although gender is a binary classification defined through its "opposite," the relation of male gender to its opposing category is not isomorphic. The extreme "adrenalized" enactments of masculine gender have need of women, not only as wives, sexual conquests, and servitors—but perhaps most importantly *as a category to be excluded*. This renders displays of "the right stuff" somewhat fragile: the participation of women is perceived as radically destructive to the entire enterprise. This does not seem to be true of all-female gender displays (Kaprow 1990). If we think of the "adrenalized vocations" as a kind of essential or archetypal western male gender display, it seems logical that there should be similar archetypal female vocations, with associated gender enactments. And yet, so far as I can tell there is only one: motherhood (Ruddick 1989). All others—sex goddess, seductress, beauty queen, *et al.*—seem to be invented by, or primarily reacted to by men. Psychoanalytically inclined commentators have suggested that the institution, idea, and reality of motherhood is so overwhelming to the male child that the entire complex of masculine gender elaborations have been developed to cope with its power and terror.

Anthropologists have noted the myths and fantasies of "male parthogenesis" associated with ritualized male development in societies where warlike males are needed and highly valued: Adams (1993) discerns a similar theme, of monosexual male procreation, in the rituals of a Southern all-male military college; and Kaprow (1991:102) observes that firefighters think of their heroic activities in terms of "giving life." Would the very presence of women in such all-male groups invalidate the "mythic scenario" (Herdt 1981:277) of men giving birth? Objections to the participation of women in the western "adrenalized vocations" are always vague; there are no words for the devastation that the presence of women would inevitably wreak; they would destroy "morale," "efficiency," "unit cohesion"—or as the senior cadet president of the all-male military college declared: "The very thing that women are seeking would no longer be there" (Adams 1993:3).

If such speculations have validity, what can they tell us about a phallic vocation where women have managed to gain entrance? Perhaps, they suggest that the very thing (the men believed) that the women were seeking in surgery *is* no longer there: that women have gained entry into the "men's house" because economic and political factors were already in the process of transforming the hypermasculine surgeon–warrior into an endangered and, even, extinct species.[7]

FINAL REFLECTIONS

I have described how my exploration into differences between women surgeons and their male colleagues challenged dichotomous categorizations. The more I attempted to grasp and apply notions of "gender difference," the more evanescent they became. Concepts of "doing" or "negotiating" gender were more effective in helping to illuminate my findings. But although I am convinced that gender is indeed "negotiated" and "done," there is more to gender than social structure, process, and interaction. Something else is going on, something deeper, less easily altered or eradicated. I now believe that gender exists not only "in the head," although it surely is a social and conceptual phenomenon, but also "in the body." In other words, gender is not only *performed,* it is *embodied* (Cassell 1996).

NOTES

1. The number of women surgeons grew from 485 in 1970 to 4754 in 1993 (Rogers 1995). The proportion of women in surgery increased more slowly, from less than 1% in 1970 to 5% in 1993.
2. By "senior," I mean above the rank of house officer. Of these, 3 had finished their surgical training within the past two years.
3. These specialties have separate training programs and (I believe) somewhat different temperaments. Every surgeon I discussed the issue with agreed that they

were a separate population. (Interestingly, the ob-gyns I talked to were offended by this exclusion; they claimed they were "just like" the surgeons.)
4. With the exception of one woman, who refused to be interviewed.
5. This is from a tape-recorded interview, where a surgeon was asked to respond to the following quotation by an anonymous woman surgeon:

"The atmosphere in an operating room in which there is a woman surgeon in charge is generally one of peace, tranquility, and contentment; when a typical male surgeon is in charge, the atmosphere tends to be tense, hostile, and even explosive at times."

6. This, too, comes from a tape-recorded interview, in response to a question about what she did, when she walked into an operating room, and found the instruments she had requested for the procedure were not there. Before the passage quoted, she responded: "I probably reacted in ineffective ways. I became angry, resentful, critical, and that usually reinforced the behavior of the nurses. And so, uh, I don't think that's an effective behavior for women surgeons. It's clearly what men do all the time, but the women should not do that with their nursing colleagues." The quote cited followed, when I asked her if she would elaborate on that. ("JC" indicates my questions and remarks.)
7. A similar politically and economically-induced "proletarianization" or "routinization of charisma" seems to be occuring in firefighting, at a time when women are beginning to gain entry (Kaprow n.d.).

REFERENCES

Adams, Abigail E. 1993. Dyke to Dyke: Ritual Reproduction at a U.S. Men's Military College. *Anthropology Today* 9(5):3–6.

Anonymous. 1986. Why Would a Girl Go Into Surgery? *Journal of the American Medical Women's Association* 41(2):59–61.

Bateson, Gregory. 1951. *Naven: A Study of the Problems Suggested by a Composite Picture of the Culture of a New Guinea Tribe Drawn from Three Points of View.* Stanford, CA.: Stanford University Press. (Originally published in 1936.)

Cassell, Joan. 1986. Dismembering the Image of God: Surgeons, Wimps, Heroes and Miracles. *Anthropology Today* 2(2):13–16.

———. 1987a. Of Control, Certitude and the "Paranoia" of Surgeons. *Culture, Medicine and Psychiatry* 11(2):229–249.

———. 1987b. The Good Surgeon. *International Journal of Moral and Social Studies* 2(2):155–171.

———. 1989. The Fellowship of Surgeons. *International Journal of Moral and Social Studies* 4(3):195–212.

———. 1991. *Expected Miracles: Surgeons at Work.* Philadelphia: Temple University Press.

————. 1996. The Woman in the Surgeon's Body: Understanding Difference. *American Anthropologist* 98(1): 41–53.

Chodorow, Nancy. 1978. *The Reproduction of Mothering: Psychoanalysis and the Sociology of Gender.* Berkeley: University of California Press.

Coltrane, Scott. 1989. Household Labor and the Routine Production of Gender. *Social Problems* 36(5):473–490.

DeVault, Marjorie L. 1991. *Feeding the Family: the Social Organization of Caring as Gendered Work.* Chicago: The University of Chicago Press.

Felker, Marcie Eliott. 1983. Ideology and Order in the Operating Room. In *The Anthropology of Medicine: From Culture to Method.* Lola Romanucci-Ross, Daniel E. Moerman, Laurence R. Tancredi, M.D. and Contributors. South Hadley, MA.: J.F. Bergin, Publishers.

Fine, Michelle. 1992. *Disruptive Voices: The Possibilities of Feminist Research,* Ann Arbor, MI.: University of Michigan Press.

Garfinkel, Harold. 1967. *Studies in Ethnomethodology.* Englewood Cliffs, N.J.: Prentice-Hall.

Gilligan, Carol. 1982. *In a Different Voice: Psychological Theory and Women's Development.* Cambridge, MA: Harvard University Press.

Gilligan, Carol, and Grant Wiggans. 1988. The Origins of Morality in Early Childhood Relationships. In *Mapping the Moral Domain: a Contribution of Women's Thinking to Psychological Theory and Education.* Carol Gilligan, Janie Victoria Ward, Jill McLean Taylor, with Betty Bardige, eds. Pp. 111–137. Cambridge, Massachusetts: Harvard University Press.

Gillison, Gillian. 1993. *Between Culture and Fantasy: A New Guinea Highlands Mythology.* Chicago: University of Chicago Press.

Ginsburg, Faye, and Anna Lowenhaupt Tsing. 1990. In *Uncertain Terms: Negotiating Gender in American Culture.* F. Ginsburg and A. L. Tsing, eds. Pp.1–16. Boston: Beacon Press.

Haraway, Donna J. 1991. "Gender" for a Marxist Dictonary: The Sexual Politics of a Word. In *Simians, Cyborgs, and Women: The Reinvention of Nature.* Pp.127–148, New York: Routledge, Chapman and Hall, Inc.

Herdt, Gilbert H. 1981. *Guardians of the Flutes: Idioms of Masculinity.* New York: Columbia University Press.

————. 1994. *Third Sex, Third Gender: Beyond Sexual Dimorphism in Culture and History.* Cambridge, MA.: Zone Books/MIT Press.

Horney, Karen. 1932. The Dread of Women, *International Journal of Psycho-Analysis* 13:348–360.

Jacobs, Sue-Ellen and Jason Cromwell. 1992. Visions and Revisions of Reality: Reflections on Sex, Sexuality, Gender, and Gender Variance. *Journal of Homosexuality* 23(4):43–69.

Kanter, Rosabeth Moss. 1977a. *Men and Women of the Corporation.* New York: Basic Books.

————. 1977b. Some Effects of Proportions on Group Life: Skewed Sex Ratios and Responses to Token Women. *American Journal of Sociology* 82:985–990.

Kaprow, Miriam Lee. 1990. *Men's Studies, Male Firefighters,* Paper presented at the V° Congreso de Antropologia, Granada (Spain).

————. 1991. Magical Work: Firefighters in New York. *Human Organization* 50(1):97–103.

————. n.d. Genteel Proletarianization: Regulating Leisure, Domesticating the Citizenry. Unpublished Manuscript.

Kessler, Suzanne J. and Wendy McKenna. 1978. *Gender: An Ethnomethodological Approach.* New York: John Wiley & Sons.

Kinder, Barbara K. 1985. Women and Men as Surgeons: Are the Problems Really Different? *Current Surgery* 42:101–103.

Klass, Perri. 1988. Are Women Better Doctors? *New York Times Magazine* (April 10).

Lorber, Judith. 1994. *Paradoxes of Gender.* New Haven and London: Yale Univ. Press.

Moir, Anne. 1991. *Brain Sex: The Real Difference Between Men and Women.* New York: Carol Publishing Group.

Murphy, Yolanda and Robert F. Murphy. 1974. *Women of the Forest.* New York: Columbia Univ. Press.

New York Times. 1994. *Generals Oppose Combat By Women* (June 17).

Noddings, Nell. 1984. *Caring: A Feminine Approach to Ethics and Moral Education.* Berkeley: University of California Press.

Rogers, Carolyn M., ed. 1995. *Socio-Economic Fact Book for Surgery 1995.* Chicago: American College of Surgeons.

Ruddick, Sarah. 1989. *Maternal Thinking: Toward a Politics of Peace.* Boston: Beacon Press.

Strauss, Anselm, Shizuko Fagerhaugh, Barbara Suczek, and Carolyn Weiner. 1985. *Social Organization of Medical Work.* Chicago: University of Chicago Press.

Unger, Rhoda K. 1989. *Representations: Social Constructions of Gender.* Amityville, New York: Baywood Publishing Company, Inc.

West, Candace, and Don H. Zimmerman. 1987. Doing Gender. *Gender and Society* 1(2):125–151.

Wilson, Edward O. 1975. Human Decency is Animal. *The New York Times Magazine,* (October 12).

————. 1978. *On Human Nature.* Cambridge, MA: Harvard University Press.

Wolfe, Tom. 1979. *The Right Stuff.* New York: Random House.

■ ■ ■ ■ ■ ■ ■ ■ ■

54   THE COW TIPPING POINT

David Ehrenfeld

This selection explores the effect of choosing a level of analysis on the information that may be obtained through research (see also selection 7). This is a valuable lesson for any kind of research and is directly relevant to studies on health and medical care. The selection ties together topics from the begining of Part IV concerning food and agriculture, with topics raised in the following selections about the social uses and ethical implications of technological innovations (see also selection 50).

Although any number of examples would serve the purpose, Ehrenfeld focuses on the use of recombinant bovine growth hormone (rBGH) to increase milk yields in dairy cows. He argues that by limiting debate to the lowest-level questions about potential harm to cows or humans, the drug's producers are able to delimit a small area of concern and maintain it in a cloud of scientific uncertainty. Restricting the debate to these questions deflects attention away from the significant added financial and labor inputs required by the technology and from the larger context in which it is embedded.

Step-by-step, the selection takes us outward from the narrow questions to indicate how the use of the technology leads to potential far-reaching health problems associated with antibiotic resistance and diseases spread by feed produced from dead animal carcasses. The technology raises questions about the rights of cows to a normal life span and the desirability of favoring industrial-scale farming. The latter is associated with reduced job satisfaction, increased injuries and accidents, reduced personal attention to individual animals, and reduced technological diversity and, therefore, long-term biological viability. By contrast, small farms bring social benefits through resident owners and environmental benefits through maintenance of threatened ecosystems. Yet, small farms lack the financial and organizational resources to counter large agribusiness's ability to persuade politicians and government officials to approve the drug. That other countries and international health and food institutes have not done so indicates a need to ask questions at every level from that of basic biology to politico-economic systems.

Questions to keep in mind

What impacts on the health and general well-being of people and cows become apparent by asking questions at the various levels outlined in this selection?

What does the bog turtle or the fen buck moth have to do with the use of rBGH in dairy cows?

How might you use Ehrenfeld's framework to ask questions about the suitability of other advances in biotechnology and to analyze the public debate and official (industry/government) discourse surrounding them?

Our exploding technology and the resulting worldview that we can manage and tinker with everything on the planet have made these times the most complex in human history. Arriving at practical and ethical decisions about controlling technology has become difficult, especially for laymen, who often find themselves looking on, bewildered, while opposing scientists hurl incomprehensible jargon at one another. But in most of these controversies it is wrong to confine the debate to narrow technical subjects; the right context is usually much broader and far more accessible to the public. Widening the scope of inquiry lets us see truths that cannot be derived from scientific

Source: Ehrenfeld, D. 2002. "The Cow Tipping Point." *Harper's Magazine* 305(1829):13–20. With permission from the author.

analysis alone. As the physicist and Nobel laureate Philip Anderson wrote in 1972, the more we learn "about the nature of the fundamental laws, the less relevance they seem to have to the very real problems of the rest of science, much less to those of society."

If we confine ourselves to the narrowest scientific contexts while trying to decide the critical issues of the moment, we are very likely to go astray. This is not a problem for everybody, however. There are those who, for one reason or another—usually for short-term profit—do not care to approach the truth too closely. For them, complexity is a godsend. Like a squid escaping its pursuers in a cloud of ink, they use complexity to obscure their movements, to hide the significance of what they are doing. By selecting the narrowest from the many available contexts in which to evaluate their own actions, and by cloaking those actions in a haze of technological intricacy, they can get away with behavior that society would not countenance if it were thinking clearly. Biotechnology, including genetic engineering, provides many examples of this kind of activity, from genetically modified food to cloning. Perhaps the most egregious is the story of rBGH.

Recombinant bovine growth hormone, rBGH for short, sometimes called recombinant bovine somatotropin, or rBST, is a growth hormone for cattle produced by taking the growth-hormone gene from cows, modifying it very slightly, and inserting it into bacteria, using the techniques of genetic engineering. The altered *E. coli* bacteria can be grown in vats, producing large quantities of rBGH, vastly more than could be obtained economically by extracting the unmodified growth hormone directly from cows. This rBGH, like its parent gene, is very slightly different from the natural product, having a substitution of just one amino acid for another at the end of the large molecule. In the United States, rBGH is marketed by Monsanto under the name of Posilac. When injected into lactating cows, it increases overall milk yields by approximately 10–15 percent, although greater increases are occasionally observed.

This is a dramatic kind of biotechnology, albeit dependent on a relatively rare phenomenon: a single gene coding for a product that is directly or indirectly commercially valuable. Not surprisingly, the marketing of rBGH has engendered a great deal of controversy, as is the case with all new technologies that cause radical changes in production systems, economics, and cultural systems.

From the beginning, the controversy swirled around two questions: Is the milk of cows injected with rBGH different from the milk of untreated cows; and, if so, is it harmful to the humans who drink it? Second: Does the injection of rBGH into lactating cows harm the animals in any way? Monsanto has not been able to provide an unequivocal no to either of these questions, and this may be part of the reason why Posilac has by many accounts proved to be something less than a cash cow for the company. Yet I imagine that Monsanto would prefer to keep the rBGH controversy confined to these issues, because the context of the questions is pleasingly narrow—in other words, most of the ethical concerns generated by the use of rBGH do not come up at all. Moreover, the two questions, because of their nature, can be drawn into a mire of complex and often contradictory technical and scientific details that make clear judgments difficult to achieve. This confusion works well for Monsanto, because the company wants sales, not judgments.

Is rBGH milk different from other milk? Yes and no. According to a paper published by Samuel Epstein in the International Journal of Health Services in 1996, and earlier reports summarized by T. B. Mepham in the *Journal of the Royal Society of Medicine* in 1992, rBGH milk contains elevated levels of Insulin-like Growth Factor-1 (IGF-1), a suspected cause of human breast and gastrointestinal cancers. Supporters of rBGH are quick to point out that IGF-1 also occurs in milk from untreated cows, and that its carcinogenic effect is not conclusively proved. Opponents respond that there is at least a three- to fourfold increase of IGF-1 in rBGH milk, and that more of it may be in an unbound, free form, which might be biologically more active. It also should be noted that rBGH itself is present in the milk of treated cows, perhaps in elevated levels over the natural hormone, and it is possible that this unnatural protein could cause allergic reactions or, after partial digestion in the human gut, mimic the metabolic effects of human growth hormone. Lots of "mights" and "maybes," credible suspicion but no proof, no smoking gun. The ink is swirling in clouds. Let's look at the second question: Does rBGH injection harm cows?

At first glance, rBGH does not come off so well. According to the manufacturer's label, use of Posilac causes "feed intake increases over several weeks" after starting injections. No surprise there; the laws of thermodynamics hold for cows. The animals are producing more milk, so they must eat more food. Use of Posilac also "may result in reduced pregnancy rates," "increases in cystic ovaries and disorders of the uterus," "small decreases in gestation length and birth weight of calves," "reductions in hemoglobin and hematocrit values," "periods of increased body temperature unrelated to illness," "indigestion, bloat, and diarrhea," "increased numbers of enlarged hocks and lesions [of the knee]," and "disorders of the foot region." But the biggest health problem for rBGH-injected cows is "an increased risk for clinical mastitis (visibly abnormal milk)." The label says that there is also an increased risk of "subclinical mastitis (milk not visibly abnormal)." "Visibly abnormal milk" means there is pus in the milk.

The label's recommendations for how to cope with this constellation of problems seem quite sensible. Be sure you are ready to deal with increased veterinary problems, presumably by keeping more veterinarians on staff or on call; be ready to differentiate between fevers caused by rBGH and fevers caused by disease; and for cows running a fever, control heat stress, I suppose by means of air-conditioning, and implement a "comprehensive and ongoing herd reproductive health program," whatever that means.

It is worth noting that none of the ailments listed as being associated with rBGH injection are unique to this treatment; cows can get mastitis, bloat, and sore knees even if they are raised under strict conditions of organic husbandry. And Monsanto has pointed out that the increase in mastitis may be a result of increased milk production itself, and thus only indirectly caused by rBGH injection. The clouds of ink thicken. Again, we are left with legitimate worries that have not been properly addressed by the Food and Drug Administration, but also left without an absolutely clear-cut mandate to condemn the technology.

In a situation of this kind, what usually happens is a continuation of the status quo. The results of peer-reviewed research produced by independent scientists are contradicted by the results of peer-reviewed research sponsored by the company.

Each study, regardless of authorship, is run in a different way under different conditions, making comparisons problematic. Some necessary analyses, such as distinguishing between natural BGH and rBGH in milk, prove difficult or impossible. The federal regulators, some of whom were formerly executives in the regulated industry, feel justified in keeping the product on the market. And the worries persist.

This is the time to widen the context of the inquiry, to reject efforts to keep questions confined to a narrow space where visibility can always be obscured by more convenient ink. I propose to widen the context gradually so that we always know the vantage point from which we are viewing the bioethical landscape. Eventually, the basic truths of the matter should be fairly clear, if they aren't already; and the conclusions we ought to reach about the technology will be obvious.

The first small step to take is to see what happens when we merge questions one and two. The most solid finding from the inquiry into the effects of rBGH on the health of cows is that treated cows get significantly more mastitis than untreated ones. This is a finding admitted by Monsanto and confirmed by the FDA. Mastitis in cows, like breast infections in humans, is usually treated with antibiotics, and these antibiotics may well find their way into the milk. In an ideal world, milk containing antibiotics is kept off the market. This is not an ideal world. Government agencies test milk for only a small number of antibiotics, and they do not test every batch; there are many antibiotics that can slip through into supermarket milk. Careless or unscrupulous milk producers may sell milk containing antibiotics, and some may be willing to deliberately treat their cows with antibiotics that they know are not going to be screened in government tests. When antibiotics get into the milk, antibiotic resistance can be transferred from the bacteria normally in the milk to the bacteria that normally live in the intestinal tract of humans, and this resistance can be transferred again during illness to the bacteria causing the disease. The result is that when antibiotics are given to sick people they do not work.

Let's widen the context a little more. I mentioned earlier that rBGH injection increases the food intake of cattle; they need more calories, particularly in the form of protein. One of the best and cheapest sources of high-grade protein is the carcasses of dead farm animals, including sheep, horses, cows, and others. For at least 100 years, the rendering industry has been converting dead animals into food supplements for livestock, but the advent of high-milk-yielding-cattle, and rBGH has increased the demand for this animal protein in cow fodder. Cows have been turned into carnivores, even cannibals. In recent years, we have become aware, however, that a terrible neurological disease, worse than Alzheimer's, called spongiform encephalopathy, is transmitted from individual to individual and even from species to species by eating brain, nerve, and other tissue from infected animals. In cattle, we call this mad cow disease; in deer and elk, chronic-wasting disease; in humans it is Creutzfeldt-Jakob disease; and there is little doubt that it has been spread in England and the Continent by the practice of feeding rendered, processed carcasses of other ruminants to cattle. Here, then, is another serious worry caused by the use of rBGH: will it increase the incidence of spongiform encephalopathy in the United States, where this constellation of diseases already exists?

As we move further and further from the original narrow context, we gradually leave the realm of science and medicine and we enter the territory of ethics, economics, and social well-being. Our next consideration in this widening inquiry takes us to the rights of cattle. Apart from the ethical implications of increased disease caused by rBGH, there are other important questions. Do we have the right to treat cows as if they were mere machines for producing milk, with all the suffering and lack of respect that this implies? Do we have the right to burn them out, to shorten their useful and productive lives, which is what rBGH appears to do? According to the farmer and agricultural writer Gene Logsdon, dairy farmers used to be able to keep their cows on the milking line for twelve to fifteen years; now, with many cows being treated with rBGH, they frequently last only two or three years. Accordingly, the price of replacement heifers has risen sharply, reflecting the increased demand.

Now we can widen the context again and look at the welfare and rights of dairy farmers, and, beyond that, at the welfare of the communities and larger society in which they live. Matthew Shul-man, owner of a small farm in Lansing, New York, and former director of information for the New York State Grange, was one of the first to write on this subject, in 1987. He questioned the claim of proponents of rBGH that this technology is farm-neutral, that if used properly it will work as well on small farms as on large ones. He was concerned with the prohibitive cost of high-tech feed-management systems and high-protein rations, which would price rBGH right out of the market for small farmers. He also noted that the hormone was marketed primarily to large farms anyway.

Four years later, Charles Geisler and Thomas Lyson, professors of rural sociology at Cornell, confirmed Shulman's fears in an article on the social and environmental costs of dairy-farm industrialization. As Geisler and Lyson pointed out, large dairy farms have lower technological diversity, a higher rate of accidents, worse environmental impact, more labor strikes, decreased personal knowledge of individual animals, and, finally, greater centralized control and more nonresident owners, with a consequent breakdown in "economic vitality and social cohesion in rural communities." A big part of the problem, they wrote, is debt; farm debt as a percentage of a farm's value increases dramatically as the size of its dairy herd increases. And as the debt-to-asset ratio increases, partly to pay for the additional, expensive veterinary care, climate control for feverish cows, and high-priced feed supplements that go along with the use of rBGH, control of dairy farming shifts away from the farmer and the farm community to distant banks.

Once the small dairy farms are gone, the industrialized farms that remain will become completely dependent on the new milk-production technologies because they cannot produce milk any other way. This will lead to the same kind of corporate vertical integration that has placed a few oil, chemical, and pharmaceutical companies in control of much of the world's agricultural seed production, resulting in the rapid, irreversible loss of thousands of agricultural food varieties of great and irreplaceable value, and putting the world's food supply in jeopardy.

There is one more context in which I want to evaluate rBGH. In the eastern states from North Carolina to Massachusetts and beyond, small dairy farms have long given a particular look and character to the rural countryside. Typically, such a farm comprises 80–95 percent upland pasture and 5–20 percent wet grazing areas. The whole is divided into small fields through which the cattle are rotated. It has become clear in recent years that the cows on these small dairy farms accomplish much more than just milk production. They have serendipitously replaced, in the wetland areas, other large eastern grazing mammals, the mastodons, elk, and bison, which have been progressively eliminated by waves of human settlers, starting eleven or twelve thousand years ago. Like these former native grazers, cows eat and therefore control the invasive, often exotic species that are modifying and eliminating wetland species and plant communities. They eat red maples and alders, phragmites, reed canary grass, purple loosestrife, and similar invasives that otherwise choke out wetland vegetation all over these eastern states. Thus, if you want to find the tiny bog turtle, the fen buck moth, the showy lady's-slipper orchid, or the spreading globeflower—all of them rare and endangered—you will have to go to a small dairy farm, or land that was a small dairy farm until recently; you probably will not find them anywhere else. So here is yet another effect of rBGH: the big, industrialized dairy farms that rBGH promotes, with cows being fed high-protein food supplements in temperature-controlled buildings, do not serve the smaller farms' unexpected function of maintaining the flora and fauna of wetlands.

Given this disturbing roster of direct and indirect problems stemming from the milk-hormone injections, and considering that prior to the introduction of rBGH billions of taxpayers' dollars were spent to buy surplus milk and slaughter surplus dairy cows, why has the government been pushing rBGH so hard? And how have they gotten away with it? The first question is easy to answer: Monsanto has been a major contributor to both the Republican and the Democratic parties. The second question is easy to answer, too. The government has gotten away with it because it has confined the ethical debate to the narrowest possible context, where the waters were muddy and the larger issues lay hidden.

Yet in spite of its conveniently narrow context, the government's case for rBGH is so weak that only the most skillful political damage control has kept it on the American market. Canada and the European Union have both declined to approve rBGH, primarily because of animal health. And in 1999 the Codex Alimentarius, the food safety standards organization of the Food and Agricultural Organization and the World Health Organization of the United Nations, refused to certify rBGH as safe. It effectively tabled the rBGH issue as a way of saving face for the United States, which would have lost a formal vote.

In summary, we must look at the entire picture of the effects of rBGH: not only IGF-1 in the milk and animal health but antibiotic resistance, spongiform encephalopathy, animal rights, the welfare of farmers and farm communities, the well-being of agriculture, and the maintenance of whole ecosystems. Is it legitimate to widen the context so broadly when evaluating a new technology? Yes, it is more than legitimate. It is practically and ethically essential if the truth is to emerge, for the message produced by these overlapping and widened contexts is really quite simple to understand: rBGH is a very bad technology indeed.

With so many ethical stalemates occurring in agricultural and medical biotechnology, why do we fail to widen the context when we debate these critical issues affecting society? It is not just because we are being kept to a narrow, controllable venue of debate by vested interests, though that is usually the case. Nor is it just that much of the public, dumbed and numbed by television and advertising, is incapable of digesting anything more complicated than a sound bite. I think the deeper problem is that more than two hundred years of potent scientific discoveries and technological inventions—from the steam engine to the laser scalpel—have taught us to believe that science and technology, the fruits of our own reason, constitute the highest power we need consult in our daily lives. In our euphoria we forget that technology is unable, both in theory and in practice, to resolve most of the practical problems that it itself creates. We also forget that science and the exercise of reason cannot by themselves provide the moral framework we need to judge our own inventions. If we restrict the context of our ethical inquiries to a narrow review of selected scientific facts, if we respect only technical information, we will never reach the sources of wisdom best suited to guide us on a just and sustainable path.

■ ■ ■ ■ ▦ ▦ ■ ■ ■

55   KEEPING AN EYE ON THE GLOBAL TRAFFIC IN HUMAN ORGANS

Nancy Scheper-Hughes

This selection concerns "international transplant tourism," in which people in wealthy countries receive kidneys from live donors abroad. The issue draws attention to the intersection between technology and ethics (see also selections 34, 50, 56) and raises level-of-analysis issues as discussed in the previous selection. To illustrate, the analysis might be allowed to settle on the question of whether kidney donation harms the giver during the operation and immediately afterward. If so, the analysis could be moored to technical questions about which sufficient scientific uncertainty can be generated to challenge the evidence that in fact living with one kidney is not the same as living with two, especially in settings of poverty and all they imply about living conditions and access to medical care. This is aside from the negative social, economic, and psychological impacts on donors and their families.

Another level-of-analysis problem concerns the application of the "four principles" of biomedical ethics to non-Western or international contexts or even to the complex situations encountered by biomedicine itself (see Grinnell et al. 2002). The principles of autonomy, beneficence, nonmalfeasance, and justice are considered universal, but they strongly reflect Western and especially American values surrounding individualism and market thinking. For example, the idea that each individual is a decision-making unit may not make sense in cultures where collective values prevail (see selections 26 and 27). How a healer should act to further the best interest of the patient also varies across cultures, as the selections in Parts I and III demonstrate. Non-malfeasance, or "do no harm," is not straightforward for issues such as euthanasia or where healers may be required to inflict harm, as seen in selection 9 on shamans/sorcerers. Justice depends on notions of fairness, a clearly value-laden, culturally specific concept.

Scheper-Hughes finds that where ethical considerations are voiced concerning the kidney trade, they tend to be resolved through the notion of individual autonomy and choice. However, free choice is an illusory concept for people who are pressured by others or forced by poverty to take the extreme measure of selling an organ. That prices for kidneys vary widely across countries, and that kidneys flow in predictable directions determined by geography, gender, economic status, and skin color is evidence of a practice that takes advantage of steep gradients of socioeconomic inequality (see selection 34). It is a practice that expresses consumer-oriented values and notions of the commodified body. These considerations suggest that a different framework is needed to assess the technology in terms of its full impact on individuals, families, societies, and humanity itself.

Questions to keep in mind

In which directions do kidneys flow, and what does this say about politico-economic relations within and across countries?

Are there ethical rules that apply in all cultural contexts? If so, what are they?

What does Scheper-Hughes mean when she describes kidneys, and life itself, as commodity fetishes?

Source: Scheper-Hughes, N. "Keeping an Eye on the Global Traffic in Human Organs." Reprinted with permission from Elsevier (The Lancet, 2003, Vol. 361 No. 9369, pages 1645–1648).

How does commodity fetishism conflict with humanistic discussion of morals and ethics?

What are some alternative ways of meeting or reducing the demand for live kidneys among patients in wealthy countries?

If a living donor can do without an organ, why shouldn't the donor profit and medical science benefit?

Radcliffe-Richards J, et al.
Lancet 1998; 351: 1951.

From its origins transplant surgery presented itself as a complicated problem in gift relations and gift theory, a domain to which anthropologists have contributed a great deal. Today the celebrated gift of life is under assault by the emergence of new markets in bodies and body parts to supply the needs of transplant patients. Global capitalism has distributed to all corners of the world, not only advanced medical technologies, medications, and procedures, but also new desires and expectations. These needs have spawned in their wake strange markets and occult economies.

The ideal conditions of economic globalisation have put into circulation mortally sick bodies travelling in one direction and healthy organs (encased in their human packages) in another, creating a bizarre kula ring of international trade in bodies. The emergence of the organs markets, excess capital, renegade surgeons, and local kidney hunters with links to organised crime, have stimulated the growth of a spectacularly lucrative international transplant tourism, much of it illegal and clandestine. In all, these new transplant transactions are a blend of altruism and commerce; of consent and coercion; of gifts and theft; of care and invisible sacrifice.

On the one hand, the spread of transplant technologies has given the possibility of new, extended, or improved quality of life to a select population of mobile and affluent kidney patients, from the deserts of Oman to the high rises of Toronto and Tokyo. On the other hand, these technologies have exacerbated older divisions between North and South and between haves and have-nots, spawning a new form of commodity fetishism in the increasing demands by medical consumers for a new quality product—fresh and healthy kidneys purchased from living bodies. To a great many knowledgeable transplant patients morgue organs are regarded as passé and relegated to the dustbins of medical history. In these radical exchanges of body parts, life-saving for the one demands self-mutilation on the part of the other. One person's biosociality is another person's biopiracy, dependent on whether one is speaking from a private hospital room in Quezon City, or Istanbul, or from a sewage-infested banguay (slum) in Manila or a hillside favela (shantytown) in Rio de Janeiro.

The kidney as a commodity has emerged as the gold standard in the new body trade, representing the poor person's ultimate collateral against hunger, debt, and penury. Thus, I refer to the bartered kidney as the organ of last resort. Meanwhile, transplant tourism has become a vital asset to the medical economies of poorer countries from Peru, South Africa, India, the Philippines, Iraq, China, and Russia to Turkey. In general, the circulation of kidneys follows established routes of capital from South to North, from East to West, from poorer to more affluent bodies, from black and brown bodies to white ones, and from female to male or from poor, low status men to more affluent men. Women are rarely the recipients of purchased organs anywhere in the world.

In the face of this postmodern dilemma, my colleague Lawrence Cohen and I—both medical anthropologists with wide experience and understanding of poverty and sickness in the third world—founded Organs Watch in 1999 as an independent research and medical human rights project at the University of California, Berkeley, as a stop-gap measure in the presence of an unrecognised global medical emergency, and in the absence of any other organisation of its kind. We have since undertaken original fieldwork on the changing economic and cultural context of organ transplant in 12 countries across the globe.

With the help of our postgraduate and medical student research assistants we have followed desperate kidney buyers and their equally desperate kidney sellers, their surgeons, and their brokers and intermediaries. We have gone to all the places where the economically and politically dispossessed—the homeless, refugees, undocumented workers, prisoners, soldiers who are absent without leave, ageing prostitutes, cigarette smugglers, petty thieves, and other marginalised people—are lured (and sometimes tricked) into selling their organs. We have followed patients from dialysis clinics to meetings with organ brokers in shopping malls, tea shops, and coffee houses, to illicit surgeries in operating rooms of hospitals—some resembling five-star hotels, others reminiscent of clandestine back alley abortion clinics. We have observed and interviewed hundreds of transplant surgeons who practise or facilitate, or who simply condone illicit surgeries with purchased organs; we have met with organ brokers and their criminal links; and we have communicated some of our findings to medical ethics and licensing boards and to Ministries of Health as well as to US congressional hearings and to special meetings of the Council of Europe.

In all, we have begun to map the routes and the international medical and financial connections that make possible the new traffic in human beings, a veritable slave trade that can bring together parties from three or more countries. In one well travelled route, small groups of Israeli transplant patients go by charter plane to Turkey where they are matched with kidney sellers from rural Moldova and Romania and are transplanted by a team of surgeons—one Israeli and one Turkish. Another network unites European and North American patients with Philippine kidney sellers in a private episcopal hospital in Manila, arranged through an independent internet broker who advertises via the web site Liver4You. Brokers in Brooklyn, New York, posing as a non-profit organisation, traffic in Russian immigrants to service foreign patients from Israel who are transplanted in some of the best medical facilities on the east coast of the USA. Wealthy Palestinians travel to Iraq where they can buy a kidney from poor Arabs coming from Jordan. The kidney sellers are housed in a special ward of the hospital that has all the appearances of a kidney motel. A Nigerian doctor/broker facilitates foreign transplants in South Africa or Boston, USA (patient's/buyer's choice), with a ready supply of poor Nigerian kidney sellers, most of them single women. The purchase agreement is notarised by a distinguished law firm in Lagos, Nigeria.

Despite widespread knowledge about these new practices and official reports made to various governing bodies, few surgeons have been investigated and none have lost their credentials. The procurement of poor people's body parts, although illegal in almost every country of the world, is not recognised as a problem about which something must be done—even less is it viewed as a medical human rights abuse. There is empathy, of course, for the many transplant patients whose needs are being partly met in this way, but there is little concern for the organ sellers who are usually transient, socially invisible, and generally assumed to be making free, informed, and self-interested choices.

From an exclusively market oriented supply and demand perspective—one that is obviously dominant today—the problem of black-markets in human organs can best be solved by regulation rather than by prohibition. The profoundly human and ethical dilemmas are thereby reduced to a simple problem in medical management. In the rational choice language of contemporary medical ethics, the conflict between non-malfeasance (do no harm) and beneficence (the moral duty to do good acts) is increasingly resolved in favour of the libertarian and consumer-oriented principle that those able to broker or buy a human organ should not be prevented from doing so. Paying for a kidney donation is viewed as a potential win–win situation that can benefit both parties. Individual decision making and patient autonomy have become the final arbiters of medical and bioethical values. Social justice and notions of the good society hardly figure at all in these discussions.

Rational arguments for regulation are, however, out of touch with the social and medical realities pertaining in many parts of the world where kidney selling is most common. In poorer countries the medical institutions created to monitor organ harvesting and distribution are often underfunded, dysfunctional, or readily compromised by the power of organ markets, the protection supplied by criminal networks, and by the impunity of outlaw surgeons who are willing to run donor for dollars programmes, or who are merely uninterested in where the transplant organ originates.

Surgeons who themselves (or whose patients) take part in transplant tourism have denied the risks of kidney removal in the absence of any published, longitudinal studies of the effects of nephrectomy on the urban poor living in dangerous work and health conditions. Even in the best social and medical circumstances living kidney and part liver donors do sometimes die after the surgical procedure, or are themselves in need of a kidney or liver transplant at a later date. The usual risks multiply when the buyers and sellers are unrelated because the sellers are likely to be extremely poor, often in poor health, and trapped in environments in which the everyday risks to their survival are legion. Kidney sellers face exposure to urban violence, transportation and work related accidents, and infectious diseases that can compromise their remaining kidney. If and when that spare part fails, most kidney sellers we have interviewed would have no access to dialysis let alone to transplantation.

The few published studies of the social, psychological, and medical effects of nephrectomy on kidney sellers in India, Iran, the Philippines, and Moldova are unambiguous. Kidney sellers subsequently experience (for complicated medical, social, economic, and psychological reasons) chronic pain, ill health, unemployment, reduced incomes, serious depression and sense of worthlessness, family problems, and social isolation (related to the sale).

Even with such attempts as in Iran to regulate and control an official system of kidney selling, the outcomes are troubling. One of our Organs Watch researchers has reported directly from Iran that kidney sellers there are recruited from the slums by wealthy kidney activists. They are paid a pittance for their body part. After the sale (which is legal there) the sellers feel profound shame, resentment, and family stigma. In our studies of kidney sellers in India, Turkey, the Philippines, and Eastern Europe, the feelings toward the doctors who removed their kidney can only be described as hostile and, in some cases, even murderous. The disappointment, anger, resentment, and hatred for the surgeons and even for the recipients of their organs—as reported by 100 paid kidney donors in Iran—strongly suggests that kidney selling is a serious social pathology.

Kidney sellers in the Philippines and in Eastern Europe frequently face medical problems, including hypertension, and even kidney insufficiency, without having access to necessary medical care. On returning to their villages or urban shanty-towns, kidney sellers are often unemployed because they are unable to sustain the demands of heavy agricultural or construction work, the only labour available to men of their skills and backgrounds. Several kidney sellers in Moldova reported spending their kidney earnings (about US$2700) to hire labourers to compensate for the heavy agricultural work they could no longer do.

Moldovan sellers are frequently alienated from their families and co-workers, excommunicated from their local Orthodox churches, and, if single, they are excluded from marriage. "No young woman in this village will marry a man with the tell-tale scar of a kidney seller," the father of a kidney seller in Mingir (Moldova) told me. Sergei, a young kidney seller from Chisinau (Moldova) said that only his mother knew the real reason for the large, sabrelike scar on his abdomen. Sergei's young wife believed his story that he had been injured in a work-related accident in Turkey. Some kidney sellers have disappeared from their families and loved ones, and one is reported to have committed suicide. "They call us prostitutes," Niculae Bardan, a 27-year-old kidney seller from the village of Mingir told me sadly. Then he added: "Actually, we are worse than prostitutes because we have sold something we can never get back. We are disgrace to our families and to our country." Their families often suffer from the stigma of association with a kidney seller. In Turkey, the children of kidney sellers are ridiculed in village schools as one-kidneys.

Despite frequent complaints of pain and weakness, none of the recent kidney sellers we interviewed in Brazil, Turkey, Moldova, and Manila had seen a doctor or been treated in the first year after their operations. Some who looked for medical attention had been turned away from the very same hospitals where their operations were done. One kidney seller from Bagon Lupa shantytown in Manila was given a consultation at the hospital where he had sold his organ, and he was given a prescription for antibiotics and painkillers that he could not afford. Because of the shame associated with their act, I had to coax young kidney sellers in Manila and Moldova to submit to a basic clinical examination and sonogram at the expense of Organs Watch. Some were ashamed to appear in a public clinic because they had tried to keep the sale (and their ruined bodies) a secret. Others were fearful of receiving a bad report because they would be unable to pay for the treatments or medications. Above all, the kidney sellers I interviewed avoided getting medical attention for fear of being seen and labelled as weak or disabled by their potential employers, their families, and their co-workers, or (for single men) by potential girl friends.

If regulation, rather than more effective prohibition, is to be the norm, how can a government set a fair price on the body parts of its poorer citizens without compromising national pride, democratic values, or ethical principles? The circulation of kidneys transcends national borders, and international markets will coexist with any national, regulated systems. National regulatory programmes—such as the Kid-Net programme (modelled after commercial blood banks), which is currently being considered in the Philippines—would still have to compete with international black markets, which adjust the local value of kidneys according to consumer prejudices. In today's global market an Indian or an African kidney fetches as little as $1000, a Filipino kidney can get $1300, a Moldovan or Romanian kidney yields $2700, whereas a Turkish or an urban Peruvian kidney can command up to $10 000 or more. Sellers in the USA can receive up to $30 000.

Putting a market price on body parts—even a fair one—exploits the desperation of the poor, the mentally weak, and dependent classes. Servants, agricultural workers, illegal workers, and prisoners are pressured by their employers and guardians to enter the kidney market. In Argentina, Organs Watch visited a large asylum for the mentally deficient that had provided blood, cornea, and kidneys to local hospitals and eye bank, until the corrupt hospital director was caught in a web of criminal intrigue that brought him to jail and the institution put under government receivership. In Tel Aviv, Israel, I encountered a mentally deficient prisoner, a common thief, who had sold one of his kidneys to his own lawyer and then tried to sue him in small claims court because he was paid half what he was promised. In Canada a businessman recently received a kidney from his domestic worker, a Philippine woman, who argued that Filipinos are a people "who are anxious to please their bosses." Finally, surgeons, whose primary responsibility is to protect and care for vulnerable bodies, should

not be advocates of paid mutilation even in the interest of saving lives at the expense of others.

Bioethical arguments about the right to buy or sell an organ or other body part are based on Euro-American notions of contract and individual choice. But these create the semblance of ethical choice in an intrinsically unethical context. The choice to sell a kidney in an urban slum of Calcutta or in a Brazilian favela or a Philippine shantytown is often anything but a free and autonomous one. Consent is problematic, with the executioner—whether on death row or at the door of the slum resident—looking over one's shoulder, and when a seller has no other option left but to sell a part of himself. Asking the law to negotiate a fair price for a live human kidney goes against everything that contract theory stands for.

Although many individuals have benefited from the ability to purchase the organs they need, the social harm produced to the donors, their families, and their communities gives sufficient reason for pause. Does the life that is teased out of the body of the one and transferred into the body of the other bear any resemblance to the ethical life of the free citizen? But neither Aristotle not Aquinas is with us. Instead, we are asked to take counsel from the new discipline of bioethics that has been finely calibrated to meet the needs of advanced biomedical technologies and the desires of postmodern medical consumers.

What goes by the wayside in these illicit transactions are not only laws and longstanding medical regulations but also the very bedrock supporting medical ethics—humanist ideas of bodily holism, integrity, and human dignity. Amidst the tensions between organ givers and organ recipients, between North and South, between the illegal and the so-called merely unethical, clarity is needed about whose values and whose notions of the body are represented. Deeply held beliefs in human dignity and bodily integrity are not solely the legacy of Western Enlightenment.

The demand side of the organ scarcity problem also needs to be confronted. Part of the shortfall in organs derives from the expansions of organ waiting lists to include the medical margins—infants, patients aged over 70 years, and the immunologically sensitive—especially those who have rejected transplanted organs after four or more attempts. Liver and kidney failure often originate in public health problems that could be preventively treated more aggressively. Ethical solutions to the chronic scarcity of human organs are not always palatable to the public, but also need to be considered. Informed presumed consent whereby all citizens are organs donors at (brain) death unless they have stipulated their refusal beforehand is a practice that preserves the value of transplantation as a social good in which no one is included or excluded on the basis of ability to pay.

Finally, in the context of an increasingly consumer-oriented world the ancient prescriptions for virtue in suffering and grace in dying appear patently absurd. But the transformation of a person into a life that must be prolonged or saved at any cost has made life itself into the ultimate commodity fetish. An insistence on the absolute value of a single life saved, enhanced, or prolonged at any cost ends all ethical inquiry and erases any possibility of a global social ethic. Meanwhile, the traffic in kidneys reduces the human content of all the lives it touches.

In his 1970 classic, *The gift relationship*, Richard Titmuss anticipated many of the dilemmas now raised by the global human organs market. His assessment of the negative social effects of commercialised blood markets in the USA could also be applied to the global markets in human organs and tissues: "The commercialism of blood and donor relationships represses the expression of altruism, erodes the sense of community, lowers scientific standards, limits both personal and professional freedoms, sanctions the making of profits in hospitals and clinical laboratories, legalises hostility between doctor and patient, subjects critical areas of medicine to the laws of the marketplace, places immense social costs on those least able to bear them—the poor, the sick, and the inept—increases the danger of unethical behaviour in various sectors of medical science and practice, and results in situations in which proportionately more and more blood is supplied by the poor, the unskilled and the unemployed, Blacks and other low income groups."

The division of the world into organ buyers and organ sellers is a medical, social, and moral tragedy of immense and not yet fully recognised proportions.

■ ■ ■ ■ ■ ■ ■ ■ ■

56 THERAPEUTIC AND REPRODUCTIVE CLONING: A CRITIQUE

Finn Bowring

This selection concludes the volume with a topic that unites themes from throughout the four parts and provides an example of the construction of ethical arguments through a merging of humanistic and scientific knowledge. The selection provides a history of developments in technology and bioethics relative to cloning and embryonic stem cells as a backdrop for an analysis that reaches past low-level questions about clinical risk to broader social and ethical concerns (see selection 54).

Bowring explains that the distinction between therapeutic and reproductive cloning is weak and would be difficult to police. In an era of medicalization, it would be a simple step to define childlessness as a condition treatable by the new technology. Moreover, the history of in vitro fertilization, with its

Source: Reprinted from *Social Science and Medicine*, Vol. 58, Bowring, F., "Therapeutic and Reproductive Cloning: A Critique," Pages 401–409, Copyright (2004), with permission from Elsevier.

enormous failure rate, indicates that any technological shortcomings not resolved by efforts to improve therapeutic cloning would not deter people from using reproductive cloning.

While parents already exercise the right to shape the conditions of their children's upbringing, Bowring argues that to allow them to clone or genetically enhance their children represents a form of deliberate determination that is qualitatively different and of a much greater magnitude. Rather than actually being able to produce the product parents expect, genetic manipulation feeds into a misguided but common form of extreme genetic determinism. In reality, each individual's development depends on the interaction of the genotype with environmental conditions and chance events from the moment of conception on. Hence, the danger lies not in an unrealizable plan to make human beings to order, but in parents' expectations that they will obtain the product they have designed. This would violate the child's right to be a unique, unpredictable surprise with an indeterminate future. It could also lead to recriminations against parents who do not use the technology, for they could be held responsible for any perceived defects in their children (see selection 28).

To illustrate, Bowring argues that parents who predetermine their child's sex are those who are also most likely to believe that biological sex determines gender-based behaviors and aptitudes. Such parents are the least likely to accept any gender transgressions by their child. Similarly, parents who used cloning or genetic enhancement would expect their children to make proper use of their predetermined biological attributes. They would exercise a tyrannical, lifelong effect over their children, robbing them of the freedom to choose their own path and to create an identity out of an unknowable origin. Genetic manipulation on the part of parents and communities would only make differences between people seem more solid and irreconcilable and eliminate the basis of mutual sympathy and understanding that is rooted in our common biological inheritance.

Questions to keep in mind

Why are cultural beliefs about genetic determinism a greater problem than genetic manipulation itself?

Is there a difference between sex selection in Western societies and the same practice in Asian societies as described by Miller?

Do you think many people would use cloning or genetic enhancement if given the chance?

How might one argue against Bowring's position concerning therapeutic and reproductive cloning?

THE ORIGINS OF CLONING

In 1891 the science of embryology was shaken by the work of the cosmopolitan German biologist and vitalist philosopher, Hans Driesch. Experimenting with sea urchin embryos in the Adriatic, Driesch discovered that by isolating one of the two cells formed with the first cleavage of a fertilised egg, he could enable the separated cell to grow into a whole organism (Sander, 1992). His findings, which were later corroborated by other embryologists working on frogs and salamanders, proved that the cells of an embryo do not, as they divide, lose the genetic resources necessary for them to develop into a whole and independent animal.

By the early 1950s, the discovery of a more sophisticated method for the non-sexual reproduction of animals raised the possibility that the differentiated cells of an adult could also be used to generate a living clone. Robert Briggs and Thomas King, embryologists funded by the US National Institutes of Health, called this new technique "nuclear transplantation." By extracting the nuclei from frogs eggs and then injecting into each genetically evacuated egg a replacement nucleus taken from a tadpole embryo cell of the same species, they created tadpoles that were healthy copies of their nuclear donors (Briggs & King, 1952).

The next major breakthrough in the area of animal cloning did not occur until the early 1980s, by which time a new economic climate had emerged favouring commercially oriented research in the agricultural sciences. Funded by the multinational W.R. Grace and Co., and charged with the task of producing multiple copies of the embryonic off-spring of prize cattle, Neal First and colleagues at the University of Wisconsin pioneered the use of an electronic current to stimulate the fusion of an embryonic cell with an enucleated egg. Months before the Wisconsin team celebrated the birth of the world's first cloned cow (see Prather et al., 1987), the Danish scientist, Steen Willadsen, an-nounced that he too had produced a cloned mam-mal—in this case a sheep—using the nucleus of a cell taken a relatively mature eight-cell embryo (Willadsen, 1986). Unlike most embryologists, Willadsen was convinced that he could take this process a stage further, and produce clones from cells that were visibly differentiated. Although this work was never published, he claims to have achieved precisely that, using cells from the differ-entiated outer and inner structures of week-old cow embryos to produce live cloned calves (see Kolata, 1997).

In contrast to the agricultural focus of the Wis-consin team, the work of Ian Wilmut and his col-leagues at the Roslin Institute in Scotland was driven by medical science. The challenge was to genetically engineer animals capable of producing in their milk (or their urine, blood, or semen), pharmaceutically valuable proteins too complex to be synthesised in genetically modified bacteria.

The standard method for the genetic alteration of mammals at this time involved injecting foreign DNA into the nuclei of fertilised eggs. By 1989, Wilmut and his colleagues had achieved some suc-cesses with this technique, producing sheep that expressed in their milk human clotting factor IX (Clark et al., 1989), and 2 years later they were able to manipulate the genomes of other sheep so as to cause them to synthesise in their milk alpha-1-antitrypsin (Wright et al., 1991).

Yet the microinjection of single-cell embryos was, and still is, an extremely inefficient proce-dure, with success rates currently ranging from 0.7 per cent of injected cattle embryos to 4.4 per cent of injected rat embryos (Rutovitz & Mayer, 2002, p. 18). Having been convinced personally by Willadsen that cloning the cells of later-stage em-bryos was indeed a feasible project, Wilmut de-cided that nuclear transplantation could bring an unprecedented leap in productivity in the produc-tion of these living "bioreactors," since it could be used to multiply those few embryos, or indeed adult animals, that had been successfully geneti-cally engineered.

Wilmut's breakthrough came with the help of a cell biologist, Keith Campbell. Campbell's expert understanding of cell-cycle rhythms paved the way for the birth in 1995 of two fit lambs cloned from differentiated foetal skin cells which had been grown in the laboratory from sheep embryo cells (Campbell, McWhir, Ritchie, & Wilmut, 1996). The birth of Dolly in July 1996 was an even more important milestone, because the lamb was the first mammal to be cloned from the cells of an adult (Wilmut, Schnieke, McWhir, Kind, & Campbell, 1996).

THE STEM CELL REVOLUTION AND 'THERAPEUTIC' CLONING

Philosophers, theologians, and some biologists, had, by the mid-1960s, already begun reflecting on the ethical dilemmas raised by the prospect of human cloning. Their concerns were initially pre-cipitated by the frog experiments of Briggs and King, and the later cloning work of Oxford biolo-gist Gurdon (1962). Whilst public confidence in the progressive role of science seemed relatively solid at this time, scandals in the domain of med-ical research—such as the 1972 exposure of the Tuskegee experiment, in which hundreds of black men in rural Alabama suffering from syphilis were over a 40 year period studied without treatment—were provoking support in the US medical and scientific communities for a new bioethics move-ment.

Willard Gaylin, co-founder of the Hastings Centre, thought that a public debate on cloning, initiated in the pages of the *New York Times Maga-zine,* could win bioethics the social prominence it deserved (Gaylin, 1972). After all, in 1971 James Watson had, in his testimony to a committee of the House of Representatives, warned that human cloning was within the reach of modern science, and Edwards and Steptoe had in the same year begun implanting IVF embryos in women in the UK. Equally unsettled by these trends, Leon

Kass, a trained biochemist who joined the Hastings Centre and turned to moral philosophy (and who in August 2001 was appointed head of the President's advisory panel on stem cell research), outlined the dehumanising ramifications of the new reproductive technologies in a seminal article in *The Public Interest* in 1972 (republished as Kass, 1985).

By the end of the 1970s the cloning controversy had largely died away, with most biologists agreeing that the reproduction of human beings without the unification of gametes was a fantasy beyond the world of serious science. The arrival of Dolly dispelled two decades of complacency, reviving the belief that nuclear transplantation was a technology that could revolutionise the biological foundations of human relationships. Yet while media attention was soon drawn to the declared cloning intentions of publicity-seeking eccentrics like Richard Seed, members of the Raelian cult, and the maverick fertility expert Severino Antinori,[1] more pressing ethical concerns were being raised by the growth of research into the therapeutic potential of human embryonic stem cells.

As the term implies, stem cells are cells which are the origin or precursor of more specialised cells. Stem cells exist at every stage of the mammalian lifecycle, although the younger the organism the greater the plasticity of these cells. An embryonic stem cell, which is the precursor to all the specialised cell types that make up an adult organism, has the greatest versatility of all stem cells. In 1998, a Wisconsin University scientist, funded by the ambitious biotech company Geron Corporation, achieved "prolonged undifferentiated proliferation" of embryonic stem cells derived from human blastocysts (Thomson et al., 1998). His breakthrough involved the use of a blocking factor which, when removed, allowed the multiplying cells to revert to specific developmental pathways. With this discovery science appeared, in many people's eyes, to have conquered the limits of human mortality. Once the precise chemical and genetic signals which direct the differentiation of embryonic stem cells have been deduced, the cells may be grown and cultivated to produce an endlessly renewable supply of human tissue, cells, and potentially whole organs, to replace or regenerate those of diseased or ageing patients. From heart disease to diabetes, from cancer and Alzheimer's to spinal cord injuries, stem cell therapy signalled the birth of a new therapeutic paradigm: the future lay with "regenerative medicine."

Research into embryonic stem cells of course requires embryos. If embryonic stem cell research is to lead to viable forms of regenerative medicine, *cloned* human embryos will almost certainly be required for this enterprise. The main reason for this is that replacement cell therapy, like organ transplants, must overcome the obstacles posed by immune-system incompatibility. Cloning by nuclear transfer offers an attractive solution to this problem. Scientists would take the nucleus of a cell from the patient, insert it into the enucleated egg of an anonymous female donor, nurture the resulting embryo to the blastocyst stage, then harvest the embryonic stem cells from the inner cell mass. Each such cell would then be almost identical in genetic terms to the cells of the patient who would be treated with them.[2]

It is because treatments derived from embryonic stem cells are likely to require the production of human embryos by cloning, that scientists and politicians have popularised the distinction between "therapeutic" and "reproductive" cloning, and made strong moral and legal cases for prohibiting the latter (defined as implanting a cloned embryo in a woman's womb). Much of the current ethical debate on the rights and wrongs of human cloning has focused, for good reason, on the moral and semantic legitimacy of this distinction. Aside from the argument, which is strongest in theological doctrines, that cloning embryos for research purposes violates the sanctity of human life (and is far from "therapeutic" for the embryo), it is the belief that therapeutic cloning will place society on a slippery slope to reproductive cloning which is the most compelling critique of this distinction.

THE SLIPPERY SLOPE

At the purely semantic level, if we take the supposedly "therapeutic" function of cloning as the main criterion for its moral legitimacy, then consistency demands that reproductive cloning should also be considered as a legitimate medical treatment for adults afflicted with non-viable gametes who want to have a genetically related child. This is indeed the argument of fertility experts like

Antinori, and it is close to the position, articulated in the language of reproductive rights, which has been adopted by bioethicist Harris (1999) as well as the esteemed British philosopher Grayling (2002). Whether you or I believe that childlessness is a disease entitling the victim to corrective medical treatment is of course not the issue here. The point is that, in an over-medicalised society, where few deviations from convention escape the therapeutic gaze, almost any product, procedure or technology can find a condition to demonstrate its "therapeutic" benefit. Medical value is thus a weak criterion with which to distinguish acceptable and unacceptable forms of human cloning.

The moral boundary separating therapeutic from reproductive cloning is endangered practically as well as logically. In response to the Raelian cloning claim made in December 2002, the most vocal criticisms of human reproductive cloning came from medical scientists aware of the high risks involved. Surveys of the literature show that, on average, the percentage of cloned animals reaching adulthood per manipulated egg is as low as 0.3 per cent for cows and less than 1 per cent for sheep (Solter, 2000). Though the majority of cloned embryos are lost before birth, a small but significant percentage of the failed clones is accounted for by animals born with serious abnormalities, including deformed limbs, organs and blood vessels.

For many embryologists these findings indicate that there are formative processes, vital to the creation of healthy animals, which are unique to the developmental sequences initiated by the fertilisation of the egg. As scientists studying the effects of cloning in mice discovered, at least 4 per cent of the genes of cloned mice embryos exhibit abnormal expression patterns in the placenta, with less pronounced gene dysfunction observed in the mice's livers (Humpherys et al., 2002). All the evidence therefore suggests that human cloning would be extremely wasteful of embryos and foetuses, that it would be an abuse of the women who supplied the eggs and miscarried the foetuses, and that any humans born live from such an experiment would more than likely suffer impaired health and development.

Though these arguments certainly seem persuasive today, if scientists are allowed to create cloned embryos for therapeutic purposes, we can be sure that, in the long term, this will lead to a progressive improvement in the success rates for human cloning, and the perfecting of the techniques involved. If genetic instability is the cause of the multiple defects observed in the clones of non-human animals, for example, then solving this problem will also be the primary concern of stem cell researchers, since no regulatory agency would allow them to transplant unstable cell lines into living humans.

We should also recognise that, as long as reproductive cloning is seen as a potential medical treatment for infertility, the complete elimination of risk and wastage will not be a required precondition for its public acceptance. "No matter how you look at the numbers," Lee Silver writes of the success ratio involved in the cloning of Dolly, "they are better than those obtained during the initial development of IVF" (Silver, 1999, p. 122). Even today, few IVF clinics can boast birth-per-cycle-of-treatment ratios greater than 1:5, while research now shows that children born via assisted conception face greater health risks than those conceived naturally (Hansen, Kurinczuk, Bower, Webb, 2002; Moll et al., 2003). If the existing methods of assisted conception form the baseline against which the risks of reproductive cloning will be assessed, it will be difficult to sustain moral opposition to cloning as a reproductive right in the long run.

Courting the danger that research into therapeutic cloning will make reproductive cloning more likely is also controversial when scientists have made significant strides in investigating the therapeutic potential of *adult* stem cells (e.g. Körbling et al., 2002; Jiang et al., 2002). Adult stem cells can in principle be extracted from patients themselves (thus avoiding immune rejection), they have much cheaper resource implications (not only will cloning be unnecessary, but adult stem cells are unlikely to be covered by costly patents), and, because their growth and differentiation is less flexible and more stable, adult stem cells have far better safety implications, being unlikely to cause the kind of uncontrollable cell growth observed in the brains of Parkinson's patients given transplants of foetal brain tissue (Freed, Greene, & Breeze, 2001). Given the obvious advantages of adult stem cells, it is small wonder that many observers believe that the dominant interests driving research into so-called therapeutic cloning are economic, the ultimate prize being the removal of the technical and moral impediments to the full cloning, and genetic engineering, of human beings.

THE RIGHT TO AN OPEN FUTURE

If the legalisation of therapeutic cloning does indeed place us on a slippery slope to the creation of living human clones, then there is an urgent need—before cloning for embryonic stem cells gains widespread public acceptance—to clarify the social and ethical ramifications of human cloning, and to move beyond naïve and revocable concerns about clinical risk.

One of the more compelling arguments against human cloning—and one which also applies to the positive selection of embryos and their genetic modification for the purposes of "enhancement"—is that it removes a primordial barrier to the deliberate determination, or "predetermination," of human beings. This barrier is the *contingency* of human life—what Hilary Putnam refers to as "the 'right' of each newborn to be a complete surprise to its parents" (Putnam, 1999, p. 13), and what in legal debates contesting the absolute freedom of parents to shape the preferences, values and talents of their offspring, has been called "the child's right to an open future" (Feinberg, 1980). As senior molecular biologist and member of the French National Consultative Ethics Committee, Axel Kahn, wrote in the wake of Dolly's arrival: "part of the individuality and dignity of a person probably lies in the uniqueness and unpredictability of his or her development. As a result, the uncertainty of the great lottery of heredity constitutes the principal protection against biological predetermination imposed by third parties, including parents" (Kahn, 1997a, p. 119).

"One of the components of human dignity is undoubtedly autonomy, the indeterminability of the individual with respect to external human will," Kahn (1997b, p. 320) later added. Yet his words were not without ambiguity. Did he mean that the genetic uniqueness and unpredictability of children created by natural fertilisation is the reason why such children *should* be treated with re- spect and dignity, or the reason why they *are* treated so? In other words, is the cloned child, reduced to an artefact of human design, *undeserving* of love and respect, an inappropriate object of dignity and moral consideration in Kahn's eyes, or rather is such a child *unlikely to receive* this consideration in a society which has permitted his or her creation?

Many commentators who have reflected on this issue see the arguments of Kahn and other ethicists as flawed because they pander to an extreme form of genetic reductionism. A cloned child would only be undeserving of human respect and kindness *if* one subscribed to the kind of genetic determinism—whereby the genetically predetermined person is immune to the competing influences of chance, environment and volition—which makes intelligent sociologists and scientists see red. As both advocates and opponents of cloning have frequently pointed out, different uterine environments, random cellular processes, interaction with diverse post-natal personal and social environments, and of course the spontaneous choices and projects of cloned individuals themselves, mean that in the real world any resemblance between cloned people and those with whom they share a genetic identity is not likely to be overwhelming. As Leon Eisenberg elaborated:

> To produce another Wolfgang Amadeus Mozart, we would need not only Wolfgang's genome but his mother's uterus, his father's music lessons, his parents' friends and his own, the state of music in 18th-century Austria, Haydn's patronage, and on and on, in ever-widening circles. . . If a particular strain of wheat yields different harvests under different conditions of climate, soil, and cultivation, how can we assume that so much more complex a genome as that of a human being would yield its desired crop of operas, symphonies, and chamber music under different circumstances of nurture. (Eisenberg, 1999, p. 474)

It is the second interpretation of Kahn's argument—namely, that cloning fosters an unwarranted disrespect for human life—which therefore makes most sense. The effects of eugenic technologies like human cloning are mediated by a cultural attachment to genetic determinism which both underpins and is consolidated by those same technologies. The problem is not that the autonomy and uniqueness of individuals will be lost, and hence they will be undeserving of the respect and dignity normally accorded to human beings. It is, rather, that the respect, love and recognition ideally expressed by adults towards the child will be subverted by their *expectation* that they have ordered a predetermined product, and this expectation will in turn promote the misrecognition or repression of the child's attempts to assert its autonomy and uniqueness. The issue, as Lewontin put it with characteristic candour, "is not whether genetic identity per se destroys individuality, but whether the erroneous state of public understanding of biology will undermine an individual's own sense of uniqueness and autonomy" (Lewontin, 1997, p. 20).

SEX SELECTION

We can better illustrate what is a stake in this discussion by considering a form of biological predetermination which is increasingly defended by liberal champions of "reproductive autonomy": namely, sex selection. Apparently free of the patriarchal pressures that have led millions of women to terminate female foetuses in Asia, some Western populations are now being consulted over whether they have a right to sex selection as a means of ensuring a "balanced" family. Studies of the attitudes of medical professionals on this matter show a growing sympathy for greater reproductive rights, and "a clear trend in most of the world toward greater willingness to perform or refer for sex selection" (Wertz & Fletcher, 1998, p. 270). The authors of this 1998 report found that a third of geneticists and genetic counsellors practising in the US would perform pre-natal sex identification if requested by a hypothetical couple with four girls who want a son and would abort a female foetus, and that 40 per cent of the US public support unrestricted access to sex selection at the preconception stage.

Sex selection for non-medical reasons is legal in the US and Canada (though in the latter there is a badly observed moratorium on the practice), and prohibited in most EU countries, including France and the UK. There is no reliable record of the number of pregnant women who have used foetal testing for the purpose of sex selection, nor of those who have terminated their pregnancies as a result (though in the study mentioned above, nearly half of all respondents reported that they had received outright requests for prenatal diagnosis solely to select the parents' preferred sex). What is more certain, however, is that both sexual inequality (which diminishes the cultural value and material life-chances of women) and the stark differentiation of gender roles (which leads to the fetishisation of the "other" sex and makes families feel "unbalanced" without their fair share of both sexes), together create significant incentives for the selective abortion of foetuses when they are the less favoured sex. These incentives are strengthened by society's rightful endeavour to restrain scientific paternalism and defend the reproductive rights of women, as well as by the development of new, safer and less invasive selection methods, such as the pre-fertilisation sorting of sperm into separate X and Y chromosome-containing gametes.

Because the medical risks involved in sex selection are declining, and because the dominant reason for seeking sex selection in the wealthy world—the desire for a balanced family—is not seen as a threat to the population's sex ratio, some medical ethicists have openly argued that the option to choose the sex of one's child should be legally available in a liberal democracy (McCarthy, 2001). Yet, as with human cloning, the trouble with sex selection in this context is not that it involves the deliberate creation of an irresistible biological identity. The problem, rather, is that sex selection nourishes adults' belief that the physiological and anatomical characteristics of a particular sex determine the social behaviour, temperament, attitudes and values of *gender*. As Rothman (1998, pp. 199–206) points out, parents who choose the sex of their child are unlikely to tolerate the "unbalancing" of their family by a boy who wants to learn ballet, or a girl who plays football, eschews the conventional trappings of femininity, and curses like her brothers. Legitimising sex selection on the grounds of family balancing thus panders to the worst forms of biological reductionism and gender stereotyping, giving scientific legitimacy to our habitual intolerance of the wide spectrum of temperaments and behaviours which do not conform to the binary definition of sex.

DESIGNER BABIES

What is true of sex selection is even more applicable to human genetic enhancement or cloning. Though both these practices will almost certainly be introduced to us in forms susceptible to medical justification and the compassionate perception of need, the line between necessary treatment and willful enhancement is another fragile boundary that will be difficult to police. Eventually a child will, one imagines, be designed for increased physical attractiveness and, like the problems that face the sex-selected child who fails to fulfil his or her gender role, such a child is likely to be a source of considerable parental displeasure if it finds intimacy difficult, is acutely shy or shows no interest in sexual relationships. A child selected or manipulated to grow to a generous height may be deeply flawed in the eyes of its parents if it fails to corroborate the well-known link between tallness and economic success, preferring to work with the homeless or hang around on the dole.

The point is that the desire for genetically enhanced babies is unlikely to be a simple wish to bestow one's children with advantageous biological attributes. It is more likely, given the self-evident costs and risks of scientifically mediated human reproduction, that adults who invest in these technologies will aim to produce offspring who will follow a specific life-plan—children who will exploit their chosen biological assets in an acceptable manner, and live out the future that is expected of them. Despite the claims of some sociobiologists, there is no possibility of delivering this degree of social control and predictability by simply altering the human genome.

Of course one may conclude from this that the experimental cloning and genetic manipulation of humans will, through its practical results, finally put paid to the ideology of genetic determinism. But this assumes that the protagonists of these experiments are disinterested observers rather than people with deep economic and emotional investments. The real danger is that by gratifying people's desire to predetermine the genetic inheritance of their children, reproductive science will legitimise and dignify the prejudices of biological determinism without which such desires would be fleeting and inconsequential.[3] By stamping the instinct for parental despotism with the ratifying mark of scientific neutrality, these biotechnologies will, when the product falls short of expectations, inevitably result in attempts *to programme and control those variables which genetics leaves untouched.* As Hans Jonas wrote, in one of the first major philosophical reflections on the ethical dangers of human cloning:

> Note that it does not matter one jot whether the genotype is really, by its own force, a person's fate: it is *made* his fate by the very assumptions in cloning him, which by their imposition on all concerned become a force themselves. It does not matter whether replication of genotype really entails repetition of life performance: the donor has been chosen with some such idea, and that idea is tyrannical in effect. It does not matter what the real relation of "nature and nurture", of genetic premise and contingent environment is in forming a person and his possibilities: their interplay has been falsified by both the subject and the environment having been "primed" . . . [E]xistentially significant is what the cloned individual *thinks*—is compelled to think—of himself, not what he "is" in the substance-sense of being. In brief, he is antecedently robbed of the *freedom* which only under the protection of ignorance can thrive; and to rob a human-to-be of that freedom deliberately is an inexpiable crime that must not be committed even once. (Jonas 1974, pp. 161–2, his emphasis)

GENETIC CHOICE AS PARENTAL DESPOTISM

Jonas rightly enjoins us here to consider the effects of cloning on the child itself. Liberal theorists who believe we should defend adults' right to exercise freedom of choice over their children's genetic inheritance, invariably refer their opponents to the freedom which capitalist democracies grant to all parents to mould the character and enhance the aptitudes of their offspring by selecting the particular domestic, educational, social and dietary conditions under which they are raised (Harris, 1999; Silver, 1999; Stock, 2002). Much can be said about the legitimate breadth of these parental rights, and whether the mediation of science, in the case of the new reproductive technologies, establishes a stamp of approval which is withheld to formally comparable rights which may legally tolerated but morally reprehended. But the genetic programming of unborn lives does not just represent an incremental increase in the capacity for parental domination. It is also implies a whole new order of power, a recasting of the relationship between parent and offspring, and indeed a potential convulsion in relations between adult individuals themselves.

In the normal circumstances of upbringing, the socialising efforts and ambitions of parents, though exercised on a dependent and unequal subject, are always in principle contestable, for parents must win some degree of consent from their children to the actions and values they impose on them. By critically reevaluating the interpersonal and communicative processes which brought about the adaptation and consent of the child to its parents' demands, the reflective adolescent can reappraise and break free from the restrictive expectations of those parents, and from a socialisation process which necessarily *comes to an end*. This end is marked by the accession of the youth to the world of autonomous and equal adults.

With the cloned or genetically enhanced child, however, the parents' intentions are fixed in a past which predates the offspring's experience and memory, as well as projected into a future from which the genetically engineered adult will never be free. The modified genetic programme, in the eyes of the zealous programmers, does not fall silent when the child reaches physical maturity, and the latter's adult life will be as much the intended object of the parents' instrumental (and experimental) intervention and curiosity as his or her childhood. As Habermas describes the distinctive character of this form of parental power:

> The programme designer carries out a one-sided act for which there can be no well-founded assumption of consent, disposing of the genetic factors of another in the paternalistic intention of setting the course, in relevant respects, of the life history of the dependent person. The latter may interpret, but not revise or undo this intention. The consequences are irreversible because the paternalistic intention is laid down in a disarming genetic programme instead of being mediated by a socialising practice which can be subjected to reappraisal by the person "raised". (Habermas, 2001, p. 111)

The problem is not only that the intentions of the programming parents are fixed in a mute and unanswerable form that cannot be addressed and challenged, but also that the authors of these intentions do not appear as opponents inhabiting a shared world. The struggle to be and be recognised as an autonomous subject is originally a struggle to transcend the dependent state of childhood. It is the mutual recognition by parent and offspring that the latter's dependency has come to an end, which gives personal substance to the moral-political belief in the fundamental rights of all individuals. With genetic programming, however, a permanent asymmetry prevails which precludes the genetically designed being from exchanging roles with its designer, from inhabiting a symmetrical relationship of reciprocity and mutual recognition.

THE DISSOLUTION OF THE SUBJECT

Habermas also argues that the development of identity and autonomy—of a sense of being a coherent and stable centre of initiative and originator of meaning—requires more than participation in a world of reciprocity and generalised norms. It presupposes a continuity of self, a sense of selfhood to which one can "be true," which is jeopardised by genetic intervention, the logic of which leads imperiously to the dissolution of the boundary between the natural and the made. Following Hannah Arendt, Habermas suggests that the capacity to see oneself as the irreducible origin of one's own actions and judgements requires the opportunity to locate this origin in a beginning which eludes human disposal, which reaches back beyond the vagaries and contingencies of culture and socialisation.

> It is only by referring to this difference between nature and culture, between beginnings which we cannot dispose of and the plasticity of historical practices, that the acting subject may proceed to the self-ascriptions without which he could not perceive himself as the initiator of his actions and aspirations. For a person to be himself, a point of reference is required which goes back beyond the lines of tradition

and the contexts of interaction which constitute the process of formation through which personal identity is moulded in the course of a life history. . . We can achieve continuity in the vicissitudes of a life history only because we may refer, for establishing the difference between what we are and what happens to us, to a bodily existence which is itself the continuation of a natural fate going back beyond the socialisation process. The fact that this natural fate, this past before our past, so to speak, eludes human disposal seems to be essential for our awareness of freedom. (Habermas, 2001, pp. 103–104)

By dissolving the boundary between nature and nurture, and by preventing the genetically engineered person from facing his or her progenitors as an equal, the cloning, selecting and enhancement of human genomes is likely to obstruct the self-understanding of persons as autonomous and responsible selves. More than this, human genetic engineering threatens to destroy the anthropological self-understanding of the species which, elaborated in our world religions and in our metaphysical and humanistic traditions, portrays all humans, whatever their cultural situation, to be heirs to the biological inheritance of "man," and thus born equal in dignity and freedom.

THE SELF-UNDERSTANDING OF THE SPECIES

One reason for this, as Fukuyama (2002, p. 157) has pointed out, is that by replacing the lottery of natural heredity with deliberately enhanced genetic endowments, the parents of genetically designed children will deprive their offspring of the sense of good fortune which normally enables those dealt a strong hand to feel sympathy for the less fortunate. Instead of attributing their advantageous start in life to the favourable accidents of birth and upbringing, they may identify their talents and opportunities as benefits merited by the superior choices and planning of their parents. And the aristocratic mentality nurtured in such people may be all the more imperious if their sense of superiority can be justified by reference to their superior genes.

In the form of "genetic communitarianism" considered by Allen Buchanan and his colleagues, on the other hand, parents would be free to trans-

mit to their children by means of genetic engineering the models of human virtue and the good life shared by the social and moral communities to which those adults belong. Assuming such traits were perceived to be amenable to genetic manipulation, the members of one benevolently minded community may choose to enhance their offsprings' capacity for self-sacrifice, empathy and generosity, while another community may pursue the perceived virtues of physical strength, competitiveness and individualism. Where the transmission of a particular way of life were an overriding goal, adults might even seek to *limit* their offspring's capacities—an option already exercised by members of the deaf community—in order to create the biological conditions which best prime the child to internalise the parents' culture.

One foreseeable result of this scenario, as Buchanan and his colleagues point out, would be a declining commitment to the liberal principle of mutual tolerance and respect, based as it is on the conviction "that we are all 'reasonable people' who have come, for complex reasons having to do with the limits of human judgement and facts of history, to believe different things." Instead culture would be transfigured into biology, and open political communities, based on reason rather than birth, would be discredited as an unnatural ideal. As these authors summarise the dangers of this version of liberal-communitarian eugenics:

> Genetic communitarianism might result in different communities coming to view their differences as no longer the result of commitment and persuasion, but of their different "natures" with the result that these differences come to be regarded as irreconcilable. Under these conditions any suggestion of compromise with the values of another community might be regarded as literally a threat to the identity and hence the survival of one's group. . .

> The threat of locking-in is thus not just a threat to the individual and his or her rights to an open future. It is a threat to the basis for political cooperation in a liberal society that involves a respect for individual liberties and toleration for those who are different. The threat is that people will come to think of themselves as different in ways even more fundamental than they do today. (Buchanan, Brock, Daniels, & Wikler, 2000, p. 178)

If human genetic engineering becomes practicable, conception and childbirth will cease to be in any sense an act of reproducing the human species, realised in the creation of a unique individual, and will instead become a means of duplicating those who best represent a culture's prevailing preferences and values. Permitting human cloning will set us on a course whose ultimate destination is the destruction of modern humanism, if not the obsolescence of humanity itself. We should think very hard before we make this course our own.

NOTES

1. Richard Seed is a physicist from Chicago whose declared intention to set up a human cloning business was given extensive media coverage in the US in early 1998. The Raelians are a Canadian-based cult whose members believe human beings were created by the genetic experiments of alien scientists. In 1997 they announced the establishment of a biotech company called Clonaid, whose first paying clients were a US couple hoping to clone their 10-month-old daughter who died due to a medical error. Embryos were reported by the company to have been implanted in several host mothers in early 2001. Antinori, along with US fertility specialist Panayiotis Zavos and Israeli–American biotechnologist Avi Ben Abraham, established an international cloning consortium in 2001, the aim of which is to develop cloning as a service for adults with fertility problems. Antinori is a millionaire gynaecologist and fertility expert who pioneered the technique that became intracytoplasmic sperm injection, and who famously enabled a postmenopausal 63-year-old Italian woman to become a mother in 1994. In March 1999 he also announced at a conference in Venice that he had enabled four sub-fertile men to father children by maturing their sperm for 3 months in the testes of rats. Recent claims by Antinori that he already has several women who are pregnant with cloned embryos have not been taken seriously by the scientific community, and have apparently prompted the other members of the cloning consortium to sever their links with him.

2. "Almost," because a small number of genes, carried in circular strips called mitochondria, inhabit the cytoplasm of cells, which is the jelly-like substance that envelops the nucleus. When an egg is enucleated—when its nucleus is removed—it still retains its mitochondrial DNA, which is inherited from the female line of the egg donor. (The cytoplasm of sperm cells degenerates during fertilisation of the egg, hence mitochondria can be used to trace female lineage in the same way that the Y chromosome is used to identify male genealogy.) This of course means that, unless the egg is donated by the patient's mother (or grandmother, etc.), nuclear transfer does not produce exact genetic copies.

3. This is also why the jumbling up of kinship ties by cloning—a child cloned from her mother would have a

father who is the lover of her sister, siblings who are her offspring, and so on—*matters*, because the decision to resort to cloning (instead of adoption or donor gametes) must be made by adults for whom meaningful bonds of kinship and parental responsibility can only be conceived of (by them) as an elaboration of linear and unambiguous genetic ties.

REFERENCES

Briggs, R., & King, T. J. (1952). Transplantation of living nuclei from blastula cells into enucleated frogs' eggs. *Proceedings of the National Academy of Sciences USA, 38*(5), 455–463.

Buchanan, A., Brock, D. W., Daniels, N., & Wikler, D. (2000). *From chance to choice: Genetics and justice.* Cambridge: Cambridge University Press.

Campbell, K. H. S., McWhir, J., Ritchie, W. A., & Wilmut, I. (1996). Sheep cloned by nuclear transfer from a cultured cell line. *Nature, 380*(6569), 64–66.

Clark, A. J., Bessos, H., Bishop, J. O., Brown, P., Harris, S., & Lathe, R., et al. (1989). Expression of human anti-hemophilic factor IX in the milk of transgenic sheep. *Bio/Technology, 7*(5), 1450–1454.

Eisenberg, L. (1999). Would cloned humans really be like sheep. *New England Journal of Medicine, 340*(6), 471–475.

Feinberg, J. (1980). The child's right to an open future. In W. Aiken, & H. LaFollette (Eds.), *Whose child? Children's rights, parental authority, and state power* (pp. 124–153). Totowa, NJ: Rowman & Littlefield.

Freed, C. R., Greene, P. E., & Breeze, R. E. (2001). Transplantation of embryonic dopamine neurons for severe Parkinson's disease. *New England Journal of Medicine, 344*(10), 710–719.

Fukuyama, F. (2002). *Our posthuman future: Consequences of the biotechnology revolution.* Straus and Giroux: New York: Farrar.

Gaylin, W. (1972). The Frankenstein myth becomes a reality—we have the awful knowledge to make exact copies of human beings. *New York Times Magazine,* 5 March.

Grayling, A. C. (2002). We should not let baby eve tempt us away from progress. *Independent on Sunday,* 29 December.

Gurdon, J. B. (1962). Adult frogs derived from the nuclei of single somatic cells. *Developmental Biology, 4,* 256–273.

Habermas, J. (2001). *Die zukunft der menschlichen natur.* Frankfurt/Main: Suhrkamp Verlag.

Hansen, M., Kurinczuk, J. J., Bower, C., & Webb, S. (2002). The risk of major birth defects after intracytoplasmic sperm injection and in vitro fertilization. *New England Journal of Medicine, 346*(10), 725–730.

Harris, J. (1999). Clones, genes, and human rights. In J. Burley (Ed.), *The genetic revolution and human rights* (pp. 61–94). Oxford: Oxford University Press.

Humpherys, D., Eggan, K., Akutsu, H., Friedman, A., Hochedlinger, K., & Yanagimachi, R., et al. (2002). Abnormal gene expression in cloned mice derived from embryonic stem cell and cumulus cell nuclei. *Proceedings of the National Academy of Sciences USA, 99*(20), 12889–12894.

Jiang, Y., Jahagirdar, B. N., Reinhardts, R. L., Schwartz, R. E., Keene, C. D., & Ortiz-Gonzalez, X. R., et al. (2002). Pluripotency of mesenchymal stem cells derived from adult marrow. *Nature, 418*(6893), 41–49.

Jonas, H. (1974). Biological engineering—a preview. In H. Jonas (Ed.), *Philosophical essays: From ancient creed to technological man* (pp. 141–167). Englewood Cliffs, NJ: Prentice-Hall.

Kahn, A. (1997a). Clone mammals. . .clone man? *Nature, 386*(6621), 119.

Kahn, A. (1997b). Cloning, dignity and ethical revisionism. *Nature, 388*(6640), 320.

Kass, L. R. (1985). Making babies. In L. Kass (Ed.), *Towards a more natural science: Biology and human affairs* (pp. 43–79). New York: Free Press.

Kolata, G. (1997). *Clone: The road to dolly and the path ahead.* London: Penguin.

Körbling, M., Katz, R. L., Khanna, A., Ruifrok, A. C., Rondon, G., & Albitar, M., et al. (2002). Hepatocytes and epithelial cells of donor origin in recipients of peripheral-blood cells. *New England Journal of Medicine, 346*(10), 738–746.

Lewontin, R. (1997). The confusion over cloning. *New York Review of Books, 44*(16), 18–23.

McCarthy, D. (2001). Why sex selection should be legal. *Journal of Medical Ethics, 27*(5), 302–307.

Moll, A. C., Imhof, S. M., Cruysberg, J. R. M., Schouten-van Meeteren, A. Y. N., Boers, M., & van Leeuwen, F. E. (2003). Incidence of retinoblastoma in children born after in-vitro fertilisation. *The Lancet, 361*(9354), 309–310.

Prather, R. S., Barnes, F. L., Sims, M. M., Robl, J. M., Eyestone, W. H., & First, N. L. (1987). Nuclear transplantation in the bovine embryo: Assessment of donor nuclei and recipient oocyte. *Biology of Reproduction, 37*(4), 859–866.

Putnam, H. (1999). Cloning people. In J. Burley (Ed.), *The genetic revolution and human rights* (pp. 1–13). Oxford: Oxford University Press.

Rothman, B. K. (1998). *Genetic maps and human imaginations: The limits of science in understanding who we are.* New York: W.W. Norton.

Rutovitz, J., & Mayer, S. (2002). Genetically modified and cloned animals. All in a good cause? GeneWatch UK <www.genewatch.org>.

Sander, K. (1992). Shaking a concept: Hans Driesch and the varied fates of sea urchin blastomeres. *Roux's Archives of Developmental Biology, 201*(5), 265–267.

Silver, L. M. (1999). *Remaking Eden: Cloning, genetic engineering and the future of humankind?* London: Phoenix.

Solter, D. (2000). Mammalian cloning: Advances and limitations. *Nature Reviews Genetics, 1*(3), 199–207.

Stock, G. (2002). *Redesigning humans: Our inevitable genetic future.* Boston, MA: Houghton Mifflin.

Thomson, J. A., Itskovitz-Eldor, J., Shapiro, S. S., Waknitz, M. A., Swiergiel, J. J., Marshall, V. S., & Jones, J. M. (1998). Embryonic stem cell lines derived from human blastocysts. *Science, 282*(5391), 1145–1147.

Wertz, D. C., & Fletcher, J. C. (1998). Ethical and social issues in prenatal sex selection: A survey of geneticists in 37 countries. *Social Science & Medicine, 46*(2), 255–273.

Willadsen, S. M. (1986). Nuclear transplantation in sheep embryos. *Nature, 320*(6057), 63–65.

Wilmut, I., Schnieke, A. E., McWhir, J., Kind, A. J., & Campbell, K. H. S. (1997). Viable offspring derived from fetal and adult mammalian cells. *Nature, 385*(6619), 810–813.

Wright, G., Carver, A., Cottom, D., Reeves, D., Scott, A., & Simons, P., et al. (1991). High level expression of active human alpha-l-antitrypsin in the milk of transgenic sheep. *Bio/Technology, 9*(9), 830–834.

REFERENCES

Aijmer, Göran and Jon Abbink, eds. 2000. *Meanings of Violence: A Cross Cultural Perspective.* New York: New York University Press.

Amoss, Pamela T. and Stevan Harrell, eds. 1981. *Other Ways of Growing Old: Anthropological Perspectives.* Stanford: Stanford University Press.

Aylward, Bruce, Karent A. Hennessey, Nevio Zagaria, Jean-Marc Olivé, and Stephen Cochi. 2000. When Is a Disease Eradicable? 100 Years of Lessons Learned. *American Journal of Public Health* 90(10):1515–1520.

Baer, Hans A. 2001. *Biomedicine and Alternative Healing Systems in America: Issues of Class, Race, Ethnicity, and Gender.* Madison: University of Wisconsin Press.

Baer, Hans A., Merrill Singer, and Ida Susser. 1997. *Medical Anthropology and the World System: A Critical Perspective.* Westport, CT: Bergin and Garvey.

Barsky, A.J. and J.F. Borus. 1999. Functional Somatic Syndromes. *Annals of Internal Medicine 130* (11):910–921.

Beall, Cynthia M. 2000. Tibetan and Andean Patterns of Adaptation to High-Altitude Hypoxia. *Human Biology 72*:201–228.

Becker, Gaylene. 2000. *The Elusive Embryo: How Women and Men Approach New Reproductive Technologies.* Berkeley: University of California Press.

Beja-Pereira, Albano, Gordon Luikart, Phillip R. England, Daniel G. Bradley, et al. 2003. Gene-Culture Coevolution between Cattle Milk Protein Genes and Human Lactase Genes. *Nature Genetics 35*(4):311–313.

Benjamins, Maureen Reindl and Carolyn Brown. 2004. Religion and Preventative Health Care Utilization among the Elderly. *Social Science and Medicine 58*(1):109–118.

Bledsoe, Caroline, Susana Lerner, and Jane I. Guyer, eds. 2000. *Fertility and the Male Life Cycle in the Era of Fertility Decline.* Oxford: Oxford University Press.

Braun, Lundy. 2002. Race, Ethnicity, and Health. *Perspectives in Biology and Medicine 45*(2):159–175.

Brody, Howard. 1983. Does Disease Have a Natural History? *Medical Anthropology Quarterly 14*(4):3, 19–22.

Browdin, Paul, ed. 2000. *Biotechnology and Culture: Bodies, Anxieties, Ethics.* Bloomington: Indiana University Press.

Caldwell, John C., I. O. Orubuloye, and Pat Caldwell. 1997. Male and Female Circumcision in Africa from a Regional to a Specific Nigerian Examination. *Social Science and Medicine 44*(8):1181–1193.

Campbell, Catherine. 1995. Male Gender Roles and Sexuality: Implications for Women's AIDS Risk and Prevention. *Social Science and Medicine 41*(2):191–210.

Cassell, Joan. 1998. *The Woman in the Surgeon's Body.* Cambridge: Harvard University Press.

Commoner, Barry. 2002. Unraveling the DNA Myth. *Harper's Magazine.* February. Pp. 39–47.

Connor, Linda H. and Geoffrey Samuel, eds. 2001. *Healing Powers and Modernity: Traditional Medicine, Shamanism, and Science in Asian Societies.* Westport, CT: Bergin and Garvey.

Cooke, Graham S. and Adrian V. S. Hill. 2001. Genetics of Susceptibility to Human Infectious Disease. *Nature Reviews Genetics. 2*(12):967–977.

Cordain, Loren, S. Boyd Eaton, Jennie Brand Miller, Staffan Lindeberg and Clark Jensen. 2002a. An Evolutionary Analysis of the Aetiology and Pathogenesis of Juvenile-Onset Myopia. *Acta Opthalmologica Scandinavica 80*:125–135.

Counihan, Carole M. 1999. *The Anthropology of Food and Body: Gender, Meaning, and Power.* New York: Routledge.

Counihan, Carole M. and Penny Van Esterik, eds. 1997. *Food and Culture: A Reader.* New York: Routledge.

Couzin, Jennifer. 2003. The Great Estrogen Conundrum. *Science 302*(5648): 1136–1138.

Crosby, Alfred W. 2004[1986]. *Ecological Imperialism: The Biological Expansion of Europe, 900–1900.* 2nd edition. Cambridge: Cambridge University Press.

Csordas, Thomas J. 1999. Ritual Healing and the Politics of Identity in Contemporary Navajo Society. *American Ethnologist 26*(1):3–23.

Das, Veena, Arthur Kleinman, Margaret Lock, Mamphela Ramphele, and Pamela Reynolds, eds. 2001. *Remaking a World: Violence, Social Suffering, and Recovery.* Berkeley: University of California Press.

Davis-Floyd, Robbie and Joseph Dumit, eds. 1998. *Cyborg Babies: From Techno-Sex to Techno-Tots.* New York: Routledge.

Davis-Floyd, Robbie and Carolyn F. Sargent, eds. 1997. *Childbirth and Authoritative Knowledge: Cross-Cultural Perspectives.* Berkeley: University of California Press.

DeGusta, David. 2003. Aubesier 11 Is Not Evidence of Neanderthal Conspecific Care. *Journal of Human Evolution 45*(1):91–94.

Desjarlais, Robert, Leon Eisenberg, Byron Good, and Arthur Kleinman. 1995. *World Mental Health. Problems and Priorities in Low-Income Countries.* New York: Oxford University Press.

DeVries, Raymond, Cecilia Benoit, Edwin R. van Teijlingen, and Sirpa Wrede. 2001. *Birth by Design: Pregnancy, Maternity Care, and Midwifery in North America and Europe.* New York: Routledge.

Diamond, Jared M. 1999. Dirty Eating for Healthy Living. *Nature 400*(6740):120–121.

Douglas, Mary. 1992. *Risk and Blame: Essays in Culture Theory.* London: Routledge.

Doyal, Lesley. 1995. *What Makes Women Sick: Gender and the Political Economy of Health.* New Brunswick, NJ: Rutgers University Press.

Dressler, William W. 1999. Modernization, Stress, and Blood Pressure: New Directions in Research. *Human Biology 71*(4):583–605.

Dressler, William W. and James R. Bindon. 2000. The Health Consequences of Cultural Consonance: Cultural Dimensions of Lifestyle, Social Support, and Arterial Blood Pressure in an African American Community. *American Anthropologist 102*(2):244–260.

Dressler, William W., Gerald A. C. Grell, and Fernando E. Viteri. 1995. Intracultural Diversity and the Sociocultural Correlates of Blood Pressure: A Jamaican Example. *Medical Anthropology Quarterly* 9(3):291–313.

Ehrlich, Paul. 2000. *Human Natures: Genes, Cultures, and the Human Prospect.* Washington, D.C.: Island Press.

Ellison, Peter T. 2001. *On Fertile Ground: A Natural History of Human Reproduction.* Cambridge: Harvard University Press.

Ember, Carol R. and Melvin Ember. 2001. *Cross-Cultural Research Methods.* Walnut Creek, CA: AltaMira Press.

Ewald, Paul. 1994. *Evolution of Infectious Disease.* New York: Oxford University Press.

Fábrega, Horacio Jr. 1997. *Evolution of Sickness and Healing.* Berkeley: University of California Press.

Fábrega, Horacio Jr. 2002. Medical Validity in Eastern and Western Traditions. *Perspectives in Biology and Medicine* 459(3):395–416.

Farmer, Paul. 1999. *Infections and Inequalities: The Modern Plagues.* Berkeley: University of California Press.

Farmer, Paul. 2003. *Pathologies of Power: Health, Human Rights, and the New War on the Poor.* Berkeley: University of California Press.

Featherstone, Mike and Mike Hepworth. 2001[1991]. The Mask of Ageing and the Postmodern Life Course. In *The Body: Social Process and Cultural Theory.* Mike Featherstone and Mike Hepworth, eds. Pp. 371–389. Thousand Oaks, CA: Sage Publications.

Finkler, Kaja. 1994. Sacred Healing and Biomedicine Compared. *Medical Anthropology Quarterly* 8(2):178–197.

Finkler, Kaja. 2003. Illusions of Controlling the Future: Risk and Genetic Inheritance. *Anthropology and Medicine* 10(1):51–71.

Førde, Olav Helge. 1998. Is Imposing Risk Awareness Cultural Imperialism? *Social Science and Medicine* 47(9):1155–1159.

Foster, George. 1976. Disease Etiologies in Non-Western Medical Systems. *American Anthropologist* 78(4):773–782.

Foster, George M. 1994. *Hippocrates' Latin American Legacy.* Berkeley: University of California Press.

Foucault, Michel. 1973. *Birth of the Clinic: An Archaeology of Medical Perception.* New York: Pantheon Books.

Frank, Steven A. 2002. *Immunology and Evolution of Infectious Disease.* Princeton: Princeton University Press.

Fratkin, Elliot M., Eric Abella Roth, and Martha N. Nathan. 1999. When Nomads Settle: The Effects of Commodization, Nutritional Change, and Formal Education on Ariaal and Rendille Pastoralists. *Current Anthropology* 40(5):729–735.

Ginsburg, Faye D. and Rayna Rapp, eds. 1995. *Conceiving the New World Order: The Global Politics of Reproduction.* Berkeley: University of California Press.

Goode, David. 1994. *A World Without Words: The Social Construction of Children Born Deaf and Blind.* Philadelphia: Temple University Press.

Goodman, Alan H. and Thomas L. Leatherman. 1998. *Building a New Biocultural Synthesis: Political-Economic Perspectives on Human Biology*. Ann Arbor: University of Michigan Press.

Graves, Joseph L, Jr. 2001. *The Emperor's New Clothes: Biological Theories of Race at the Millennium*. New Brunswick, NJ: Rutgers University Press.

Greenhalgh, Susan, ed. 1995. *Situating Fertility: Anthropology and Demographic Inquiry*. New York: Cambridge University Press.

Grinnell, Frederick, Jeffrey P. Bishop, and Laurence B. McCullough. 2002. Bioethical Pluralism and Complementarity. *Perspectives in Biology and Medicine 45*(3):338–349.

Gruenbaum, Ellen. 2001. *The Female Circumcision Controversy: An Anthropological Perspective*. Philadelphia: University of Pennsylvania Press.

Haggett, Peter. 2000. *The Geographical Structure of Epidemics*. Oxford: Oxford University Press.

Hahn, Beatrice H., George M. Shaw, Kevin M. De Cock, and Paul M. Sharp. 2000. AIDS as a Zoonosis: Scientific and Public Health Implications. *Science 287*(5453): 607–614.

Hahn, Robert. 1995. *Sickness and Healing: an Anthropological Perspective*. New Haven: Yale University Press.

Hahn, Robert. 1997. The Nocebo Phenomenon: Concept, Evidence, and Implications for Public Health. *Preventive Medicine 26*(5):607–611.

Harmsworth, K. and G.T. Lewith. 2001. Attitudes to Traditional Chinese Medicine amongst Western Trained Doctors in the People's Republic of China. *Social Science and Medicine 52*(1):149–153.

Hassel, Craig A., Christopher J. Hafner, Renne Soberg, Jeff Adelman, and Rose Haywood. 2002. Using Chinese Medicine to Understand Medicinal Herb Quality: An Alternative to Biomedical Approaches? *Agriculture and Human Values 19*(4):337–347.

Hoffmaster, Barry, ed. 2001. *Bioethics in Social Context*. Philadelphia: Temple University Press.

Høg, Erling and Elisabeth Hsu. 2002. Introduction. *Anthropology and Medicine 9*(3):205–221.

Hsu, Elizabeth. 1999. *The Transmission of Chinese Medicine*. Cambridge: Cambridge University Press.

Hutchinson, Janis Faye. 2001. The Biology and Evolution of HIV. *Annual Review of Anthropology 30*:85–108.

Ingstad, Benedicte and Susan Reynolds Whyte. 1995. *Disability and Culture*. Berkeley: University of California Press.

Inhorn, Marcia C. and Peter J. Brown, eds. 1997. *The Anthropology of Infectious Disease: International Health Perspectives*. Amsterdam: Gordon and Breach.

Inhorn, Marcia C. and Frank van Balen, eds. 2002. *Infertility around the Globe: New Thinking on Childlessness, Gender, and Reproductive Technologies*. Berkeley: University of California Press.

Jankowiak, William and Dan Bradburd, eds. 2004. *Drugs, Labor, and Colonial Expansion*. Tucson: University of Arizona Press.

Jonas, Wayne B., Ted J. Kaptchuk, and Klaus Linde. 2003. A Critical Overview of Homeopathy. *Annals of Internal Medicine* 138(5):393–400.

Joralemon, Donald. 1995. Organ Wars: The Battle for Body Parts. *Medical Anthropology Quarterly* 9(3):335–356.

Kaptchuk, Ted J. and David M. Eisenberg. 2001a. Varieties of Healing. 1: Medical Pluralism in the United States. *Annals of Internal Medicine* 135(3):189–195.

Kaptchuk, Ted J. and David M. Eisenberg. 2001b. Varieties of Healing. 2: A Taxonomy of Unconventional Healing Practices. *Annals of Internal Medicine* 135(3):196–204.

Katz, Pearl. 1999. *The Scalpel's Edge: The Culture of Surgeons.* Needham Heights, MA: Allyn & Bacon.

Kaufman, Sharon R. 2000. In the Shadow of "Death with Dignity": Medicine and Cultural Quandaries of the Vegetative State. *American Anthropologist* 102(1):69–83.

Kitson, Alison L. 2003. A Comparative Analysis of Lay-Caring and Professional (Nursing) Caring Relationships. *International Journal of Nursing Studies* 40(5):503–510.

Kleinman, Arthur. 1980. *Patients and Healers in the Context of Culture: an Exploration of the Borderland between Anthropology, Medicine, and Psychiatry.* Berkeley: University of California Press.

Kleinman, Arthur. 1988. *The Illness Narratives: Suffering, Healing, and the Human Condition.* New York: Basic Books.

Kleinman, Arthur, Veena Das, and Margaret Lock, eds. 1997. *Social Suffering.* Berkeley: University of California Press.

Koch, Thomas. 2002. *Scarce Goods: Justice, Fairness, and Organ Transplantation.* Westport, CT: Praeger.

Koplow, David A. 2003. *Smallpox: the Fight to Eradicate a Global Scourge.* Berkeley: University of California Press.

Kretchmer, Norman. 1978. Genetic Variability and Lactose Tolerance. *Progress in Human Nutrition* 8:197–205.

Kunitz, Stephen J. 2002. Holism and the Idea of General Susceptibility to Disease. *International Journal of Epidemiology* 31(4):722–729.

Kusserow, Adrie Suzanne. 1999. Crossing the Great Divide: Anthropological Theories of the Western Self. *Journal of Anthropological Research* 55(4):541–562.

Lamb, Sarah. 2000. *White Saris and Sweet Mangoes: Aging, Gender, and the Body in North India.* Berkeley: University of California Press.

Lebel, Serge and Erik Trinkaus. 2002. Middle Pleistocene Human Remains from the Bau de l'Aubesier. *Journal of Human Evolution* 43(5):659–685.

Lentz, Carola, ed. 1999. *Changing Food Habits: Case Studies from Africa, South America, and Europe.* Newark, NJ: Gordon and Breach Publishing.

Leslie, Charles 1997. *Asian Medical Systems: A Comparative Study.* Berkeley: University of California Press.

Levy, Stuart B. 2001. Antibacterial Household Products: Cause for Concern. *Emerging Infectious Diseases* 7(3):512–515.

Lindenbaum, Shirley and Margaret Lock, eds. 1993. *Knowledge, Power, and Practice: The Anthropology of Medicine and Everyday Life.* Berkeley: University of California Press.

Littlewood, Roland 2002. *Pathologies of the West: An Anthropology of Mental Illness in Europe and America.* Ithaca, NY: Cornell University Press.

Livingstone, Frank B. 1958. Anthropological Implications of an Advantageous Gene: The Sickle Cell Gene in West Africa. *American Anthropologist* 60(3):533–562.

Lloyd, Geoffrey and Nathan Silvin. 2002. *The Way and the Word: Science and Medicine in Early China and Greece.* New Haven: Yale University Press.

Lock, Margaret. 1993. *Encounters with Aging: Mythologies of Menopause in Japan and North America.* Berkeley: University of California Press.

Lock, Margaret. 2002. *Twice Dead: Organ Transplants and the Reinvention of Death.* Berkeley: University of California Press.

Lock, Margaret, Allan Young, and Alberto Cambrosio, eds. 2000. *Living and Working with New Medical Technologies: Intersections of Inquiry.* Cambridge: Cambridge University Press.

Loewe, Ronald, John Schwartzman, Joshua Freeman, Laurie Quinn, and Steve Zuckerman. 1998. Doctor Talk and Diabetes: Towards an Analysis of the Clinical Construction of Chronic Illness. *Social Science and Medicine* 47:1267–1276.

Lomas, Jonathan. 1998. Social Capital and Health: Implications for Public Health and Epidemiology. *Social Science and Medicine* 47(9):1181–1188.

Mackenbach, Johan and Philippa Howden-Chapman. 2003. New Perspectives on Socioeconomic Inequalities in Health. *Perspectives in Biology and Medicine* 46(3):428–444.

Martin, Emily. 1991. The Egg and the Sperm: How Science has Constructed a Romance Based on Stereotypical Male-Female Roles. *Signs: Journal of Women in Culture and Society* 16(3):485–501.

Martin, Emily. 1994. *Flexible Bodies: Tracking Immunity in American Culture from the Days of Polio to the Age of AIDS.* Boston: Beacon Press.

Martorell, Reynaldo. 1989. Body Size, Adaptation, and Function. *Human Organization* 48(1):15–20.

Mascie Taylor, C. G. N. and Barry Bogin, eds. 1995. *Variability and Plasticity.* Cambridge: Cambridge University Press.

Mattingly, Cheryl. 1998. *Healing Dramas and Clinical Plots.* Cambridge: Cambridge University Press.

Mattingly, Cheryl and Linda C. Garro, eds. 2001. *Narrative and the Cultural Construction of Illness and Healing.* Berkeley: University of California Press.

McGuire, Michael T. and Alfonzo Troisi. 1998. *Darwinian Psychiatry.* New York: Oxford University Press.

McKeown, Thomas. 1979. *The Role of Medicine: Dream, Mirage, or Nemesis?* 2nd Edition. Princeton: Princeton University Press.

McKeown, Thomas. 1988. *The Origins of Human Disease.* New York: Basil Blackwell.

McNeill, William H. 1999[1976]. *Plagues and Peoples.* Garden City, NY: Anchor Press/Doubleday.

Mintz, Sidney W. 1985. *Sweetness and Power: the Place of Sugar in Modern History.* New York: Penguin Books.

Mintz, Sidney W. and Christine M. Du Bois. 2002. The Anthropology of Food and Eating. *Annual Review of Anthropology 31*:99–119.

Moerman, Daniel. 2002. *Meaning, Medicine, and the "Placebo Effect."* New York: Cambridge University Press.

Nestle, Marion. 2002. *Food Politics: How the Food Industry Influences Nutrition and Health.* Berkeley: University of California Press.

Nestle, Marion. 2003. *Safe Food: Bacteria, Biotechnology, and Bioterrorism.* Berkeley: University of California Press.

Nichter, Mark and Mimi Nichter. 1996. *Anthropology and International Health: Asian Case Studies.* Buffalo, NY: Gordon and Breach.

Panter-Brick, C. and C.M. Worthman, eds. 1999. *Hormones, Health, and Behavior: A Socio-Ecological and Lifespan Approach.* New York: Cambridge University Press.

Parens, Erik and Adrienne Asch, eds. 2000. *Prenatal Testing and Disability Rights.* Washington, DC: Georgetown University Press.

Parker, Richard. 2001. Sexuality, Culture, and Power in HIV/AIDS Research. *Annual Review of Anthropology 30*:163–179.

Payer, Lynn. 1996[1988]. *Medicine and Culture: Varieties of Treatment in the United States, England, West Germany, and France.* New York: Henry Holt and Company.

Pelto, Gretel H. and Pertti J. Pelto. 1983. Diet and Delocalization: Dietary Changes since 1750. *Journal of Interdisciplinary History 19*:507–528.

Prendergrast, H.D.V., N.L. Etkin, D.R. Harris, and P.J. Houghton, eds. 1998. *Plants for Food and Medicine: Proceedings of the Joint Conference of the Society for Economic Botany and the International Society for Ethnopharmacology.* London: Royal Botanic Gardens.

Rapp, Rayna. 1999. *Testing Women, Testing the Fetus: The Social Impact of Amniocentesis in America.* New York: Routledge.

Reilly, David. 2001 Comments on Complementary and Alternative Medicine in Europe. *Journal of Alternative and Complementary Medicine 7*(1):S23–S31.

Rekdal, Ole Bjørn. 1999. Cross-Cultural Healing in East African Ethnography. *Medical Anthropology Quarterly 13*(4):458–482.

Romanucci-Ross, Lola, Daniel E. Moerman, and Laurence R. Tancredi, eds. 1997[1983]. *The Anthropology of Medicine: From Culture to Method.* 3rd edition. Westport, CT: Bergin and Garvey.

Ruff, Christopher. 2002. Variation in Human Body Size and Shape. *Annual Review of Anthropology 31*:211–232.

Russell, Andrew, Elisa J. Sobo, and Mary S. Thompson, eds. 2000. *Contraception across Cultures: Technologies, Choices, Constraints.* New York: Berg.

Scheper-Hughes, Nancy. 1992. *Death without Weeping: the Violence of Everyday Life in Brazil.* Berkeley: University of California Press.

Scheper-Hughes, Nancy, and Carolyn Sargent, eds. 1999. *Small Wars: The Cultural Politics of Childhood.* Berkeley: University of California Press.

Schmidt, Bettina and Ingo Schröder. 2001. *The Anthropology of Violence and Conflict.* London: Routledge.

Schofield, Penelope, David Ball, Jennifer G. Smith, Ron Borland, et al. 2004. Optimism and Survival in Lung Cancer Patients. *Cancer 100*(6):1276–1282.

Schwartz, Lisa M., Steven Woloshin, Floyd J. Fowler, and Gilbert H. Welch. 2004. Enthusiasm for Cancer Screening in the United States. *JAMA 291*(1):71–78.

Schoenberg, Nancy E. and Elaine M. Drew. 2002. Articulating Silences: Experiential and Biomedical Constructions of Hypertension Symptomatology. *Medical Anthropology Quarterly 16*(4):458–475.

Sears, Barry. 2001. Afterward. *In* Upton Sinclair, *The Jungle.* New York: Penguin Putnam Inc.

Silla, Eric. 1998. *People Are Not the Same: Leprosy and Identity in Twentieth-Century Mali.* Portsmouth, NH: Heineman.

Sluka, Jeffrey A., ed. 2000. *Death Squad: The Anthropology of State Terror.* Philadelphia: University of Pennsylvania Press.

Smith, Patrick K., Barry Bogin, M. Inês Varela-Silva, Bibiana Orden, and James Loucky. 2002. Does Immigration Help or Harm Children's Health? The Mayan Case. *Social Science Quarterly 83*(4):994–1002.

Solomon, Gregg E. and Nicholas L. Cassimatis. 1999. On Facts and Conceptual Systems: Young Children's Integration of their Understandings of Germs and Contagion. *Developmental Psychology 35*(1):113–126.

Spiegel, Herbert. 1997. Nocebo: the Power of Suggestibility. *Preventive Medicine 26*(5):616–621.

Starr, Paul. 1982. *The Social Transformation of American Medicine.* New York: Basic Books.

Stinson, Sara, Barry Bogin, Rebecca Huss-Ashmore, and Dennis O'Rourke, eds. 2000. *Human Biology: An Evolutionary and Biocultural Perspective.* New York: Wiley-Liss.

Swedlund, Alan C., and George J. Armelagos, eds. 1990. *Disease in Populations in Transition: Anthropological and Epidemiological Perspectives.* New York: Bergin and Garvey.

Terry, Jennifer. 1999. *An American Obsession: Science, Medicine, and Homosexuality in Modern Society.* Chicago: University of Chicago Press.

Trevathan, Wenda R., James J. McKenna, and E.O. Smith, eds. 1999. *Evolutionary Medicine.* New York: Oxford University Press.

Trevathan, Wenda and Karen Rosenberg. 2000. The Shoulders Follow the Head: Postcranial Constraints on Human Childbirth. *Journal of Human Evolution 39*(6):583–586.

Ungar, Peter S. and Mark F. Teaford, eds. 2002. *Human Diet: Its Origin and Evolution.* Westport, CT: Bergin and Garvey.

Wakeford, Tom. 2001. *Liaisons of Life: From Hornworts to Hippos. How the Unassuming Microbe has Driven Evolution.* New York: John Wiley and Sons, Inc.

Watts, Sheldon. 1998. *Epidemics and History: Disease, Power, and Imperialism.* New Haven: Yale University Press.

Wayland, Coral. 2001. Gendering Local Knowledge: Medicinal Plant Use and Primary Health Care in the Amazon. *Medical Anthropology Quarterly 15*(2):171–188.

Webby, Richard J. and Robert G. Webster. 2003. Are We Ready for Pandemic Influenza? *Science 302*(5650):1519–1522.

Weiss, Kenneth M. 1998. Coming to Terms with Human Variation. *Annual Review of Anthropology 27*:273–300.

Whitaker, Elizabeth. 2000. *Measuring Mamma's Milk: Fascism and the Medicalization of Maternity in Italy.* Ann Arbor: University of Michigan Press.

Whiteford, Linda M. and Lenore Manderson, eds. 2000. *Global Health Policy, Local Realities: The Fallacy of the Level Playing Field.* Boulder: Lynne Rienner Publishers.

Wiesenfeld, Stephen L. 1967. Sickle-Cell Trait in Human Biological and Cultural Evolution. *Science 157*(3793):1134–1140.

Wills, Christopher. 1996. *Yellow Fever, Black Goddess: the Coevolution of People and Plagues.* Reading, MA: Addison-Wesley.

Young, Allan. 1995. *The Harmony of Illusions: Inventing Post-Traumatic Stress Disorder.* Princeton: Princeton University Press.